SWIFT
The Man, his Works, and the Age
VOLUME III

SWIFT

THE MAN, HIS WORKS, AND THE AGE

VOLUME THREE

Dean Swift

Irvin Ehrenpreis

HARVARD UNIVERSITY PRESS

CAMBRIDGE, MASSACHUSETTS

1983

Library of Congress Cataloging in Publication Data
(Rev. for volume 3)

Ehrenpreis, Irvin, 1920–
Swift: the man, his works, and the age.

Bibliography: v. 1, p.
CONTENTS: v. 1. Mr. Swift and his contem-
poraries.—   —v. 3. Dean Swift.
1. Swift, Jonathan, 1667–1745.
PR37226.E37   828.5   62-51793
ISBN 0-674-85835-2

An index to the complete work appears
at the end of this volume

To Polly and Donald Hirsch

ἐσλῶν γὰρ ὑπὸ χαρμάτων πῆμα θνάσκει παλίγκοτον δαμασθέν

CONTENTS

[vii]

CONTENTS

CONTENTS

[x]

CONTENTS

[xi]

CONTENTS

PREFACE

In this volume I have tried to show that, so far from avoiding society, Swift enjoyed companionship and conversation more than any other employment of his time. This pleasure did not fade as he aged but remained intense until the disabilities of his final three or four years made it hard for him to talk at all. I have insisted that while Swift allowed himself notable eccentricities of behaviour, he was fundamentally rational and self-possessed. In my examination of his public career, I have argued that Swift worked closely with Archbishop King, and that political partisanship did not dominate his view of the Irish nation. I have suggested that in his social philosophy he lost his confidence in the gentry and became peculiarly sympathetic with the common people. In tracing Swift's literary career, I have documented the vitality of genius during the dozen years following the completion of *Gulliver's Travels*.

As guides I have leaned heavily on two books: Louis A. Landa, *Swift and the Church of Ireland*, and Oliver W. Ferguson, *Swift and Ireland*. But I have added much material from later scholarship and from unpublished sources—mainly the correspondence of Archbishop King, but also the letters of John Evans, William Nicolson, and others. I have striven to provide fresh judgments and interpretations of Swift's works along with historical and biographical data often derived from newspapers that earlier scholars did not consult.

In addition to the friends and colleagues whose help I recorded in earlier volumes, I must name two meticulous scholars who have the same surname but no other kinship apart from a patient and unfailing readiness to share the treasures of their Swiftian learning with me: David Woolley and James A. Woolley. I have acknowledged other obligations in the appropriate notes to my text.

[xiii]

For financial aid in support of my researches I am indebted to the corporate Maecenas of modern universities and philanthropic foundations: Indiana University, the University of Virginia, the J. S. Guggenheim Memorial Foundation, the American Council of Learned Societies, the National Endowment for the Humanities. To these I must add with affection two magnificent institutions that were gracious enough to award me visiting fellowships: Merton College and All Souls College, Oxford. Only somebody fortunate enough to have enjoyed such hospitality will realize how necessary the amenities and resources of these colleges were to the accomplishment of my labours.

I am constantly grateful to those research libraries that have made scholarship a privilege as well as an eager pursuit: the libraries of Trinity College, Dublin, and Christ Church, Oxford; the National Library of Ireland and the British Library; the Houghton Library of Harvard University, the Huntington Library, and that house of light and truth, the Bodleian Library, Oxford.

The one who would have felt the strongest pleasure in the completion of this book is dead. But readers who follow my account of Swift's response to the loss of Esther Johnson may wish to know that I could not help thinking of Anne, my wife, as I wrote.

I. E.
June 1982

A NOTE ON QUOTATIONS

With rare exceptions, I have freely altered the texts that I quote, in spelling, punctuation, use of capitals and of italics. I do not indicate omissions except within a quotation. But I never change the language.

Part One

THE EXILE 1714–20

Chapter One

HOMECOMING

Over the years, Swift's idea of integrity changed subtly but deeply. In his early twenties he had come straight from Trinity College, Dublin, to live in England with Sir William Temple, who was then a retired statesman of great distinction and a confidant of the new king, William III. Employed as Temple's secretary, Swift had hoped that his master's connections with the royal court might fix even a penniless provincial in a secular career; and he weighed this hope against another inclination, to be an Anglican priest.

Temple disappointed Swift, and never provided him with a place. After ten years, on and off, in the great man's household, Swift found himself with few backers and no advancement. By this time he was an ordained and experienced clergyman in the Church of Ireland; and when Temple died, it was to his native country that Swift returned. There at least he could find a niche in the church.

During the decade that followed Temple's death, integrity, for Swift, meant balancing private ambitions against obstinate idealism. It also meant reconciling service to religion with Swift's more worldly yearnings. Not only did he try to make fidelity to the Established Church harmonize with a devotion to his own interests. He also strove to succeed in his career by means that would strengthen the church.

Then, during the Tories' tenure of power (1710–14), integrity took the form of loyalty to a couple of political leaders, especially the devious Robert Harley, who was soon ennobled as Earl of Oxford. Now Swift wished to be of use to the church and to himself precisely by obliging Harley and his impulsive young

[3]

colleague, Henry St John, who received and immortalized the title of Viscount Bolingbroke.

Only after Queen Anne died was Swift able to relax this attachment to particular men. Gradually then, as Dean of St Patrick's Cathedral, he came to devote himself to the good of a nation. During the years when he wrote *The Drapier's Letters*, his dedication grew deeper until the object of Swift's finest allegiance became humble, productive humanity (1724–5).

It is a mark of Swift's nobility that so little selfishness entered into his despair on the Queen's death in August 1714. His great friends fell from power as George I began ruling Britain with their enemies; and Swift had to withdraw from the brilliance of England to the obscurity of Ireland. There his political allies were disgraced, and he had to pick up the burden of his old, love–hate relation to William King, the domineering Archbishop of Dublin. If his own condition made Swift sigh bitterly, the danger to his English friends now frightened him. A glimpse of the truth also preserved him—sadly—from some illusions that other men enjoyed. The hopes of Lord Oxford, the schemes of Lord Bolingbroke, the complacency of Archbishop King, disagreed with Swift's character. While our own hindsight may now dissolve bits of his truth, it also shows his errors to be agreeably free from self-service.

Gloom was, after all, a decent response to the collapse of so many hopes. Not only had he failed—after twenty years of trying—to establish himself in the England he loved. Not only had forces he could not resist thrown him back on a people he pitied but despised. Soon he also found himself rejected even by this wretched nation, which his highest motives drove him to defend.

Resettled in Dublin, Swift lived for a while almost as though under house arrest, like an exile in his own country, cut off from those he admired, and avoided even by those who needed him. As a literary genius he suffered a kind of temporary suffocation. What he wished to write he could not publish, and what he nevertheless wrote he had to hide. Since the healthiest parts of his ego were his conscience and his art, he felt sick with mortification and lassitude. No wonder he spoke of 'anneantissement'.[1]

Although Swift came home to Ireland that summer, he could hardly free himself from English obsessions. He felt tragically burdened. His powers seemed obstructed by the thought that his disgraced friends were enduring an atrocious injustice. For all their wrangles and blunders, he still thought they were the proper leaders of their nation, and that the Whigs ought to be excluded from every important office. Without the lessons of the next five years, without the softening, deepening effects of changing a way of life that he loved for one he resented, Swift would have remained a brilliant pamphleteer, satirist, and poet. But he would never have risen to the power of *The Drapier's Letters*, *Gulliver's Travels*, and *A Modest Proposal*.

Speaking for Ireland was a challenge that speaking for England could never be. In the history of Europe and the world, England occupied a central position. To do battle for her welfare was obviously to engage a man in meaningful action. As one fought the corruptions blamed on Whig finance and intrigue, one could in imagination emulate Cicero trying to revive Roman virtue. Such a scene invited a genius to act himself.

But Ireland was a theatre in a barn, notable only as it reflected the aims of a Louis or a George. 'The truth is', said Dr Delany, 'he considered Ireland as a scene too little for his genius.'[2] To dignify Irish politics, one had to see them not as directing a nation but as testing mankind. After Swift dropped his hope of settling in England, after he fully understood that the Tories he admired could not retake the government of Britain, he let his natural roots in Ireland feed his conscience and support his art. He could then come to identify his own being with that of a community of miserable people.

This was the rôle proper to his genius. In Dryden's most powerful satire, what remains distasteful is a complacent attachment to the winning side. What establishes Pope's moral depth in the last, splendid poems is his revulsion from men in the highest places. What weakens the lasting appeal of Swift's *Conduct*

---

[1] Letter of Aug. 1714, to Charles Ford; Williams II. 126. [2] Delany, p. 218.

of the Allies is a sneer at people and virtues that should have stirred the author's admiration. Swift triumphant is seldom noble. In defeat he can be heroic.

Defeat is precisely what met him on his return to Ireland. Not only had his friends fallen and he himself gone into exile. Not only was his voice silenced. The causes he had striven for—whether grand or mean—were lost as well. He had set his heart on the not very magnificent office of Historiographer Royal. It went not to Swift but to the hardworking, genuine scholar Thomas Madox, a protégé of Lord Somers, the mentor of the Whigs. Three Irish bishoprics that Swift had passionately desired to see filled with proper Tories stood vacant until King George gave them to bona-fide Whigs. Swift could not even finish writing a pamphlet he had begun to compose in England.

He would have loved to speak out. But naturally a cautious man, Swift was brave in conscience and timid by instinct. The daring of his political essays was matched by his discretion in publishing them. Besides, his mood was wrong. Swift rarely permitted a concern about public affairs or personal danger to dampen the joy he found in good company. But his hours of serious reflection exposed him to nagging anxiety and despondence. He had enough uneasy hours in the years following Queen Anne's death.

II. IRELAND UNDER THE WHIGS

Swift reached Dublin on 24 August 1714. He was nearly forty-seven years old. On political accounts he felt ready to give himself up to the feelings of helplessness and failure that had dogged him for a year. The Irish autumn disagreed with his health. He was plagued with colds and 'twenty ailments'.[1] Letters kept coming from his sweet-tempered, high-church friend, Dr Arbuthnot, who was still prosperous but no longer a royal physician and no longer welcome at court. Letters came from the magnificent but malleable Duke of Ormonde, grandest

---

[1] Williams II. 138–9.

of Irish peers, but now vilified by the Whigs in power because he had displaced Marlborough and had co-operated with Boling-broke (in unsavoury ways) to end the War of the Spanish Succession. As tidings and salutations arrived from these and other friends he left behind, Swift was bitterly reminded of his distance from the society he admired. Although now the dean of the premier cathedral of the kingdom, he seemed isolated, old, dependent on enemies.

A poem written under the pressure of disease and loneliness reveals how hard it was for Swift to keep *la bagatelle* in the centre of his view. Forced to accept the event of his leaders' collapse, he wrote,

> 'Tis true,—then why should I repine,
> To see my life so fast decline?
> But, why obscurely here alone?
> Where I am neither lov'd nor known.[1]

The triumph of the Whigs rose as high in Ireland as in England. Yet the death of the Queen did not at once mean to Swift the end of all political hopes. He must have remembered the troubles King William had endured in managing his British subjects. When Anne succeeded her brother-in-law, Swift had watched the gradual transformation of Godolphin's ministry and the deliberate stages by which Harley ousted Godolphin. For the juggernaut rapidity of the new men cherished by George I, he was ill prepared; and he thought at first that the elections to the first Hanoverian Parliament would be decisive:

> I shall judge of what will happen by the great or little pains to manage by the court against next elections; without much pains and pence the Whigs cannot have a majority; and without a majority, I think they cannot prudently take any large steps.[2]

Swift's tone reflects the company he was keeping; for he had too many conversations with the outgoing Chancellor of Ireland, Constantine Phipps, an English Jacobite whose Tory optimism had survived an unbroken record of defeats by the Whigs. Swift

---

[1] 'In Sickness'; *Poems* I. 203.   [2] Aug. 1714, to Charles Ford; Williams II. 127.

also passed too many hours with Phipps's jackal, Richard Nutley (called 'Nutbrain' by his enemies[1]), another English Jacobite—though long settled in Ireland—who had become a justice of the Queen's Bench there with the help of the Duke of Ormonde.[2] In this milieu Swift's attitude would not seem unnatural; but it was hardly prescient.

It did not take long for the shadow of the future to grow black. Soon after Swift landed in Ireland, he heard that Bolingbroke had been dismissed from his post as Secretary of State. Yet he tried to console himself with the thought that the Regents and not the new King had ordered the removal. Later he found the command had come directly from Hanover.

In September, Swift witnessed an overhaul of the senior judiciary of Ireland. Among the Lords Justices, Primate Lindsay and Chancellor Phipps—both very high churchmen—were replaced by veteran Whigs, one of whom was Swift's suzerain, Archbishop King. In the middle of the month, King George arrived at Greenwich, and the wheels turned faster. Alan Brodrick, an Irish Sunderland, became Lord Chancellor in the place of Phipps; and the three top judges were changed. Among lesser judges, the first to be dropped was Nutley. Since his original promotion was due to singleminded Toryism, his fall was natural. But other judges followed as the autumn wore on. The Privy Council of Ireland was of course reconstituted. A new Attorney-General and Solicitor-General were named. The military establishment underwent a sea change.

Seeing Tory gentlemen systematically excluded from the new regime, Swift lost heart. 'Everything is as bad as possible,' he said; 'and I think if the Pretender ever comes over, the present men in power have traced him the way.'[3] There was at least one touch of comic relief in the fate of Constantine Phipps. For Abel Boyer, the Huguenot, Whig journalist, reported that Phipps was almost mobbed the day he stepped down as Lord

---

[1] Ball, *Judges* II. 39. [2] *Ibid.*, pp. 38–40, 49, 72.
[3] 6 Oct. 1714, to Knightley Chetwode; Williams II. 135–6.

Justice, and that he had to find sanctuary in the Castle.[1] His departure for England became a flight. But when he landed, he proceeded to Oxford, where the University showed their opinion of the Whigs by conferring an honorary D.C.L. upon Phipps and choosing for the ceremony a day when loyal Hanoverians swarmed to London to celebrate the coronation.[2]

By now the machinery of readjustment had turned itself upon the Church of Ireland, where the three vacant bishoprics were filled by supporters of the King's friends. One of these was the same Edward Synge whom Swift had opposed for John Stearne's sake in the contest for the deanship of St Patrick's ten years before. Synge now became Bishop of Raphoe, a watering place along his route to an archbishopric. No Whig had to be told how the lower clergy of both kingdoms would respond as their world trembled to such earthquakes. To intimidate them, King George sent out directions that preachers should not 'intermeddle in any affairs of state' except as required by special feasts.[3] Swift said, 'I saw in a print that the [King] has taken care to limit the clergy what they shall preach; and that has given me an inclination to preach what is forbid.'[4]

That Swift yielded to this naughty impulse we know from his sermon on 'False Witness'. But by the time he preached on that subject, new storms had precipitated more alarming disasters than his coldest fears had expected. Eager to back up their denunciations of the old ministry and to terrify any trimmers, the English Whigs began working the engines of impeachment. Their own propaganda drove them to prosecute the Tory chiefs for high treason. Erasmus Lewis, Swift's English friend from Harley's circle, wrote warning him to hide his personal papers;[5] and the dean told an Italian acquaintance that the Whigs were determined to behead half a dozen of the best men in England.[6] As it happened, the only evidence of genuine treason—the efforts of Oxford and Bolingbroke to help the Pretender—were

---

[1] Boyer VIII. 246–7, 340. [2] *Ibid.*, p. 369, from the *Post Boy*, 23 Oct. 1714.
[3] 11 Dec. 1714; *ibid.*, p. 538. [4] 3 Jan. 1715, to Chetwode; Williams II. 155.
[5] *Ibid.*, p. 156. [6] *Ibid.*, p. 157.

buried in secret French archives. So the Whigs' case had to focus itself on the diplomacy used to end the War of the Spanish Succession. Lord Oxford was thus to play the part that he himself had assigned, at the turn of the century, to the ministers who arranged the Second Partition Treaty.

In the highly charged atmosphere of the new reign, it was simple enough to build a prosecution on such fragile foundations. But too many peers had winked at these or similar negotiations for them now to condemn the Tory peacemakers. Unluckily, Bolingbroke had no faith in the power of moderate men. He suspected that Oxford might supply his Whig enemies with evidence to convict him of Jacobitism. When the new government ordered the papers of Matthew Prior to be seized in Paris, Bolingbroke panicked. Inevitably, the ministers of the King soon asked him to give up his own papers; and he then arranged to leave England. Prior, returning at last from France, reached London on Friday, 25 March 1715. On Saturday, Bolingbroke made a well-planned appearance at the Drury Lane theatre. The next day, he disguised himself as a servant to a French courier and embarked for Calais, just in time to avoid arrest.[1]

III. ARCHBISHOP KING AND THE TORIES

To frame Archbishop King's view of these events, one need only invert Swift's view. 'I observed', King said placidly of the Queen's death, 'that all persons testified as much joy as was decent.'[2] With his usual jaundiced optimism he hoped the clergy would prove 'hearty' in their allegiance and not provoke the new King as they had provoked William III.[3] Where Swift desponded over the vacant Irish bishoprics, the archbishop rejoiced. ' 'Tis a providence that the church preferments are yet to be filled,' he told one of his own candidates for elevation;[4] and he looked forward benignly to the promotion of another, his

[1] Harry T. Dickinson, *Bolingbroke* (London, 1970), pp. 134–5; Boyer IX (Jan.–Jun. 1715). 226–8.
[2] 10 Aug. 1714, to Fitzwilliam.   [3] 10 Aug. 1714, to Foley.
[4] 14 Aug. 1714, to Godwin.

beloved Edward Synge. He looked further as well, and said, 'If any removes be thought on, I think the Bishop of Dromore [i.e., his old protégé and friend, John Stearne], who was made a bishop of no merit of his own, but to make room for Dr Swift, might yet deserve for his merit a removal.'[1] Some of the Dublin clergy took the first opportunity of preaching fiercely against consubstantiation, a doctrine attributed to the Lutherans, and thus they vented some truly sincere feelings about their Lutheran monarch. The archbishop was not amused.

Politically the archbishop saw only good in the abrupt reversal of the government's motions. He delighted to contemplate the doom of those who had been trying to 'brow-beat and turn out of all business honest men that had any regard to their country'.[2] Such opinions were appreciated by the advisers of King George; and when the first Lords Justices of the new reign were appointed, his grace became one of the three governors of Ireland. If the duties soon grew onerous, the manipulation of power remained an agreeable exercise. The archbishop sounded cautiously content when the Earl of Sunderland was made Lord Lieutenant, but he regretted losing the sympathetic Shrewsbury. Soon after, he heard that two of the three new bishops were to be his special favourites, and he told the Archbishop of Canterbury that he had a high opinion of Sunderland.

The foolish hopes of Swift's party did not charm Archbishop King, who thoroughly understood the programme the dean himself approved of:

> They pretend the danger of the Church is so great that they must stand in her defence ... and make such a party, that being the majority, the King may be obliged to turn out the Whigs and take them again into the ministry.[3]

Unlike Swift he expected the elections for the Irish Parliament to produce a vast majority of Whigs. But he also believed that in England Lord Oxford and his colleagues would go unpunished. In a spirit of curiously misguided scepticism he prophesied that the English House of Commons would fail to make a proper job

[1] *Ibid.*   [2] 26 Aug. 1714, to Coningsby.   [3] 20 Nov. 1714, to Mountjoy.

[11]

of exposing the old ministry.[1] While Swift resented the royal edict against preaching on public affairs, the archbishop liked nothing better. 'I wish clergymen would content themselves with preaching obedience to superiors,' he said.[2]

When the English House of Commons did begin prying into the diplomacy that produced the Treaty of Utrecht, the archbishop yearned for a rough prosecution of the villains. He regretted that his beloved Duke of Shrewsbury would not support a charge of treason against Lord Oxford and the others.[3] After Bolingbroke fled, the archbishop looked for the ugliest possible sequel—'There wants yet one thing to make Lord Bolingbroke's flight perfectly significant, which is his going to the Pretender'—and the prayer was soon answered.[4] The papers that English Tories circulated among their Irish friends naturally disgusted his grace,[5] and the contempt he already felt for Primate Lindsay took a furious turn when he discovered that Lindsay's secretary was involved in reprinting a treasonable pamphlet.[6]

While Swift kept wishing the government would conciliate the anxious parsons with some reassuring gesture, the archbishop condemned the clergy for disobliging the government:

> Many of the clergy . . . prepare the people to expect nothing less than the subversion of our constitution, the destruction of the hierarchy, the abolishing the liturgy, and setting up Presbytery. They have given themselves strange airs on these topics in tragical complaints, mournful representations and pathetical exhortations to the people to prepare themselves for sufferings.[7]

But he also had the wisdom to observe what Swift did not like to admit, that as a religious body the church reached more people when it did not enjoy official encouragement than when it did: 'The diligence, piety, humility, and prudent management of the clergy, when they had nothing else to trust to, [proved] much stronger motives to gain people, than the favour

[1] 14 Dec. 1714, to Molyneux.   [2] 14 Dec. 1714, to Annesley.
[3] 5 Apr. 1715, to Molyneux.   [4] 7 Apr. 1715, to Foley.
[5] 7 May 1715, to Nicolson.   [6] 26 Apr. 1715, to Ashe.   [7] 20 Apr. 1715.

of the government.'[1] An archbishop who talked like this could not see much of a dean like Swift without hard feelings on both sides. It took less than a year for their cold war to turn hot.

IV. SWIFT IN THE WORST OF TIMES

Like most defeated parties, the Tories busied themselves during retirement with the divisions that had brought on their ruin. Loss of power only complicates the quarrels started by ambition, and a contest to place the blame superseded the contest for political leadership. One ugly token of the mutual resentments was a series of foolish pamphlets meant either to defend the actions of a coterie or else to rally the veterans of the lost cause. Among these anonymous futilities was a group produced by Defoe for Lord Oxford and called *The Secret History of the White Staff*. Archbishop King, whose simplicity often thwarted his shrewdness, thought the earliest of them was a 'libel' on his lordship. He said it showed Swift's hero to be 'the worst and weakest of men'.[2] Arbuthnot said the same pamphlet seemed 'either contrived by an enemy or by himself, to bring down vengeance'.[3]

A more dangerous piece was *English Advice to the Freeholders of England*, by Francis Atterbury, the most aggressive Tory among the English bishops. Writing anonymously and using veiled but not cryptic language, Atterbury exhorted the Tories to rescue King George from the Whigs.[4] The pamphlet was found seditious by the government, and a reward was offered for the discovery of the author.[5] John Barber—the printer whom Swift had helped to enrich—wrote from London to the dean, 'We have twenty frightful accounts of your being sent for up, and your papers seized, for you are the reputed author of every good thing that comes out on our side.'[6] But Swift lifted the skirts

---

[1] 20 Apr. 1715, to Charlett.   [2] 25 Nov. 1714, to Southwell.   [3] Williams II. 136.
[4] Gareth V. Bennett, *The Tory Crisis in Church and State* (Oxford, 1975), pp. 192–3.
[5] 11 Jan. 1715.   [6] Williams II. 168.

of his coat high above such muddy squabbles, and the Duke of Ormonde correctly surmised that he had no wish to receive from English friends such news bulletins as would put them and himself in danger.[1]

Yet Ormonde was foolish enough to send Swift, by a private agent, messages and pamphlets that would embarrass if not incriminate him.[2] Among these unsolicited gifts was an ill-conceived apology for the Duke's captain-generalship, *The Conduct of the Duke of Ormonde in the Campagne of 1712*. But the dangerous bundle was never delivered; and the reasons appear in an account (one of many such reports) sent to Sir William Trumbull—who had been Secretary of State for a couple of years under William III—by an ecclesiastical nephew:

> They have published the Duke of Ormonde's Conduct, which is said to be drawn up by Dr John Freind. It has been printed above a month since and was not intended to have been published till after the Secret Committee had made their report. But some of the Duke's friends having thought fit to send over a copy to the famous Dr Jonathan Swift now in Ireland, a private gentleman carried over this and several other letters with abundance of libels upon the present administration, which the government having had advice of, seized the gentleman at his landing in Ireland; and so got a copy of this book etc.[3]

When the inept messenger reached Dublin, his goods were searched by a customs officer who discovered two packets addressed to the Dean of St Patrick's.[4] It is a mark of Swift's notoriety that the address alone was enough to make the officer turn the packets over to his superiors, who delivered them at once to the Lords Justices.[5] Of course, the fact was reported to

[1] *Ibid.*, p. 167.

[2] I assume that the Duchess's chaplain would never have sent these if the Duke had not told him to do so.

[3] Letter of 31 May 1715 to Trumbull from the Rev. Ralph Bridges, among the Downshire MSS. in the Berkshire County Record Office. I have changed the spelling and punctuation. I owe this reference to the benevolence of the late George Sherburn—one of his innumerable acts of paternal kindness to me.

[4] *Whalley's News-Letter*, Dublin, 21 May, reported that the customs officer at first thought the 'large packet' addressed to Swift was a trick to conceal smuggled lace.

[5] Williams V. 230.

the arch-Whig Sunderland as Lord Lieutenant; and his secretary gave some hint of the government's attitude toward Dr Swift when he said, 'His excellency ... hopes that if there appears enough against the doctor to justify it he is kept in confinement.'[1]

But nothing at all appeared; and Archbishop King declared, for Sunderland's benefit, that the letters to Swift 'seemed to acquit the dean by complaining of his not writing, which they interpreted as forbidding them to write'.[2] Although several accounts of the episode that got out exaggerated the danger Swift faced, there is no sign that he felt much disturbed. Boyer, his journalist enemy in London, published a story that when the packets were seized, 'the famous libeller Swift, having notice ... thought fit to abscond.'[3] In fact, Swift had a defiant conversation with his archbishop and went about his own affairs untouched.

As a Lord Justice, Archbishop King wrote to members of the English government in a style clearly designed to shield the dean. But to Swift's old friend Bishop Ashe he said the confiscated letters contained 'very bad matter'.[4] I suppose he expected Ashe, who had the same political colour as King, to scold Swift for clinging to such treacherous allies. He also tried himself to tame the wayward dean. A month after the packets were seized, Swift told a friend what emerged from this confrontation:

> I was this morning with the Archbishop who told me how kind he had been in preventing my being sent to &c. I said I had been a firm friend of the last ministry, but thought it beneath me to trouble myself in little parties without doing good, that I therefore expected the protection of the government, and that if I had been called before them, I would not have answered one syllable or named one person. He said that would have reflected on me. I answered I did not value that, and that I would sooner suffer more than let anybody else suffer by me, as some people did. The letter which was sent was one from the great lady you know and enclosed in one from her chaplain. My friends got it, and very wisely burned it after great deliberation, for fear of being called to swear; for which I wish them

[1] *Ibid.*, p. 232. [2] *Ibid.*, p. 233.
[3] Boyer IX (May 1715). 430–1. [4] Williams V. 231.

[15]

half hanged.... I said a good deal more to the Archbishop not worth telling at this distance.[1]

It was like the archbishop to claim credit for keeping Swift out of gaol when nobody could have put him anywhere else if the government had unearthed the evidence needed to damn him. But it was also like Swift to give the archbishop no credit for benevolence when good will was genuinely if not conspicuously at work. Neither bachelor admitted how thoroughly the other shared his instinctive devotion to Ireland and the church. Yet these were the links that would finally join them.

To avoid any look of fearfulness, Swift put in an appearance at the Four Courts, as public a place as one could visit with dignity. While he spoke to some friends there, one of them warned him against a man standing nearby, supposed to be a paid informer. 'It seems', said Swift in writing about the episode, 'there is a trade going of carrying stories to the government.'[2] He had already, as he told Archbishop King, hidden some papers that might get him in trouble,[3] and years later he said he was still going over them one sheet at a time—'lest the humour of searching and seizing papers should revive'.[4]

When Swift decided to preach on matters forbidden by King George, it was natural for him to select the topic of political informers. In a sermon on 'false witness' he referred pointedly to his own experience, and excoriated men who linger in public places in order to 'catch up an accidental word'.[5] A hint of the tone he used with Archbishop King vibrates in some climactic sentences:

And, I do not in the least doubt, that when those in power begin to observe the falsehood, the prevarication, the aggravating manner,

---

[1] 21 Jun. 1715, to Chetwode; *ibid.*, II. 173. The great lady was the Duchess of Ormonde. Her chaplain was Arthur Charleton. The reading 'beneath me' is an emendation of 'brought me' (which is the reading of the transcription of Swift's letters to Chetwode from which the text is printed, the originals having been lost by damp). I gratefully accept the emendation as proposed by Professor James Woolley, to whose meticulous scholarship I am indebted for many other favours.

[2] 28 Jun. 1715, to Chetwode; *ibid.*, pp. 174-5.

[3] *Ibid.*, p. 173.   [4] *Ibid.*, p. 367.

[5] Davis IX. 183. His anger died slowly. Gulliver's savage fulminations against informers (*ibid.*, XI. 291) are matched by Swift's language in a sermon of 1724 (*ibid.*, IX. 236). For the role of the Atterbury case in reviving these feelings, see Rosenheim, pp. 174-204.

the treachery and seducing, the malice and revenge, the love of lucre; and lastly, the trifling accusations in too many wicked people, they will be as ready to discourage every sort of those whom I have numbered among false witnesses, as they will be to countenance honest men, who, out of a true zeal to their prince and country, do, in the innocence of their hearts, freely discover whatever they may apprehend to be dangerous to either. A good Christian will think it sufficient to reprove his brother for a rash unguarded word, where there is neither danger nor evil example to be apprehended; or, if he will not amend by reproof, avoid his conversation.[1]

Swift devotes half the sermon to a denunciation of Whig activists, whom he represents as different sorts of false witness. But the second half carries his real purpose, which is to counsel those on his own side. This part becomes in effect a warning that turncoats who betray their friends for the sake of personal advancement are criminal. Having first lumped the Whigs with the persecutors of the early Christians, Swift more briefly warns the Tories not to drop to the level of apostasy. He also advises them to act with caution and keep from giving offence. His own practice shows itself distinctly in one sentence that he might have addressed to the archbishop:

But, where our prince and country can possibly receive no damage or disgrace; where no scandal or ill example is given; and our neighbour, it may be, provoked by us, happeneth privately to drop a rash or indiscreet word, which in strictness of law might bring him under trouble, perhaps to his utter undoing; there we are obliged, we ought, to proceed no further than warning and reproof.[2]

When one considers how many of Swift's companions flirted with Jacobitism, one realizes that he continually practised what he preached.

The bitterness of Swift's language, in this sermon, shows how pent up he felt. He was prepared to take great risks to show that he stood fast in a time of many changes. Vicarious indignation is perhaps Swift's finest passion—the voicing of anguish over the oppression of people weaker than himself. Speaking from the pulpit in subtle defiance of a royal edict, he exposed himself to dangerous reprisals from the powers ruling Ireland. But his need

[1] Davis IX. 184. [2] *Ibid.*, p. 188.

to lament publicly the humiliation of the vanquished by the victors would not let him be still.[1]

V. THE WHIGS AND THE DEAN

In the British House of Commons the Whigs formed a much-touted 'Committee of Secrecy' chaired by Robert Walpole, to look into—or, rather, to produce evidence of—the Tory leaders' treason. The report of the committee was published in June 1715, and excited in Swift a mixture of disbelief and contempt.[2] But when the original report was read in Parliament (9–10 June), the Whig spokesmen received it as solid enough to support the impeachment of Bolingbroke, Oxford, Strafford, and Ormonde. In the middle of the next month Oxford was delivered to the Tower.

If Swift felt battered by the news of Bolingbroke's ill-advised flight, or crushed by the frightening skill with which Walpole went about sending Oxford to the very place that Oxford had sent Walpole to (three-and-a-half years before), he was devastated when the great Duke of Ormonde, who seemed as invulnerable as the King, followed Bolingbroke to France (20 July). Swift told a friend, 'Though it be unworthy of a philosopher to admire at anything ... yet I am every day admiring at a thousand things.'[3] He could not yet credit what soon became irrefutable, that Ormonde, like Bolingbroke, had entered the service of the Pretender.

As the outlook for the Tories went dark, Swift's loyalty to his own past deepened. His characteristic impulse was to identify himself with a fallen hero. One of his earliest poems was a panegyric on the deprived Archbishop Sancroft, who, 'in the exaltation of retreat', shone with a brightness that the throne of Canterbury had obscured.[4] Now, watching the new court

---

[1] On the date of this sermon see Daw, pp. 87–8. Thomas Birch said that John Lyon dated it 1715 (B.L. Add. MS. 35397, fol. 266ᵛ). Compare the language of the last paragraph of Swift's letter to Chetwode, 17 Dec. 1715 (Williams II. 191) with that of the sermon (Davis IX. 183).

[2] Williams II. 175.

[3] *Ibid.*, p. 183; for an echo of the phrase see Davis VIII. 133.   [4] *Poems* I. 41.

trample on the honour of his patrons, Swift rushed to declare his allegiance. As soon as the news of Bolingbroke's dismissal as Secretary of State reached Ireland, Swift wrote to him. In his usual style of praise through blame he congratulated the Viscount on his 'new station of retirement, which was the only honourable post that those who gave it you were capable of conferring'.[1] Soon the same rhetoric had to be refurbished for Prior: 'You have the honor to be used ill with the best men of the kingdom.'[2] By the end of March 1715 Bolingbroke was gone. Next Swift learned of Oxford's ordeal and Ormonde's disappearance. Now he abandoned the mode of irony and composed a meticulous piece of complimentary prose, assuring Oxford that his virtues would be known to posterity through the portrait Swift had composed. Referring to Guiscard's attempt to murder Oxford, Swift said,

> Your life has been already attempted by private malice, as it is now by public resentment. Nothing else remained: you were destined to both trials; and the same power which delivered you out of the paws of the lion and the bear, will I trust, deliver you out of the hands of the uncircumcised.[3]

The bottom of the abyss still lay below. During the summer there were Jacobite uprisings in Scotland and England, led by Tories whom the new regime made desperate. The Earl of Mar, who had served as Secretary of State for Scotland near the end of Oxford's ministry, published a declaration supporting the Pretender.[4] Ireland remained so calm that regiments of soldiers were withdrawn and sent to help put down the rebels in Britain. But the threat of an invasion immensely fortified the Irish Whigs during the elections for a new Parliament. Someone asked Swift why he thought there were so many Jacobites in England. He replied (according to Dr Delany) that the government might thank themselves: 'When I find myself in pain, as I lie upon my right side, I naturally turn to my left; though

---

[1] Williams II. 128—a draft, not the final copy.   [2] *Ibid.*, p. 158.
[3] *Ibid.*, p. 182.   [4] 6 Sept. 1715.

I have no prospect of being better there; but perhaps worse.'[1]
In a private memorandum he wrote,

> If the king of a free people will choose to govern by a faction inferior
> in numbers and property to the rest and suspected of principles
> destructive to the religious or civil part of the constitution, I do not
> see how a civil war can be avoided because the bulk of the people
> and of the landed interest, who profess the established principles,
> will never endure to see themselves entirely cut out and rendered
> incapable of all employments of trust or profit, and the whole power
> most unnaturally vested in the hands of a minority, whose interest
> it must of necessity be to alter the constitution, and oppress their
> fellow subjects.[2]

It was during the epidemic of panic and mistrust that the first
Irish Parliament of King George met.[3] To prepare for the
session, which Sunderland, though Lord Lieutenant, would not
attend, the government was changed. Archbishop King and his
colleagues found themselves dismissed as Lords Justices. In their
place appeared two men peculiarly disgusting to Swift: the
Duke of Grafton, whom he called 'almost a slobberer without
one good quality', and the Huguenot general Lord Galway—
whom he called 'a damnable hypocrite of no religion'.[4]

After dutifully electing William Conolly as their Speaker, the
Irish Members of Parliament busied themselves not with law-
making but with revenge, intimidation, and blackmail. To
paralyse the Tories, the Whigs chose as their point of attack a
performance by which their clumsy enemies had tried to control
them during the last Parliament under Queen Anne. At that
time the Whigs had forced through the Irish House of Commons
an address to the Queen requesting the dismissal of Phipps
as Lord Chancellor; and the Tories had done battle by sending
off counter-addresses supporting Phipps. Now the new Whig
majority resolved it was a breach of privilege to 'misrepresent'
an address of the House of Commons.

Those present members or former members who had signed
the Tory addresses were rudely summoned to apologize for their

---

[1] Delany, p. 215.   [2] Davis VIII. 218.
[3] Dublin, Saturday, 12 Nov. 1715.   [4] Davis v. 258, 261.

turpitude or else to risk being taken into custody by the Serjeant at Arms. Sheriffs who had signed with the Tories were put under the same discipline. Most of those subjected to these spiteful menaces gave in to the order and recanted. Among them were Swift's friends Robert Cope and Peter Ludlow, both former M.P.s. A few months later, when it looked as if the Pretender might invade Ireland, a number of suspected Jacobites were seized and shut up in Dublin Castle. One was Swift's silly admirer, Judge Nutley.[1]

Swift detested the chest-beating and public paranoia that blighted the political landscape. He might be cautious, but like his friends, he could not escape suffering some of the ugliness in his own person, as one grotesque incident will testify. Swift's favourite exercise was of course riding. He would go out with two mounted servants, the groom ahead of him and the footman behind; and the ground he generally preferred in the cold months was the strand between Dublin and Howth, a popular course for recreational riders. During the winter of 1715–16 Swift was returning one day from Howth when a chaise carrying two men and drawn by a pair of high-spirited horses raced up to him from behind. Instead of keeping out of Swift's way and passing quietly, the men chased after the dean, who rode left and right across the road to clear their path. Finally, he got over to the side of a ditch, where the chaise could not follow, and from this undignified podium he reproached his pursuers.

One of the men in the chaise was Lord Blayney, an Irish peer in his early twenties. Blayney had married a relation of the Duke of Shrewsbury, and Archbishop King praised him for serving the King by hunting down the 'robbers and rappareers that almost everywhere infest us'.[2] Swift claimed that he introduced the young peer to Addison.

According to Swift's report, Blayney answered the dean's mild expostulations with a threat. 'Damn you,' said his lordship, 'is not the road as free for us as for you?' He called to his own servant, who rode behind, 'Is the pistol loaden with ball?' The

---

[1] Boyer X. 553, 568; XI. 48.   [2] 1 Mar. 1714, to Shrewsbury.

servant said it was, and gave him the weapon. So Swift said, 'Pray, sir, do not shoot, for my horse is apt to start, by which I shall endanger my life.' Blayney's idiocy gave out at this point, and his party went forward, leaving Swift in peace.[1] To feel so vulnerable to casual brutality infuriated Swift more than it scared him, but Blayney did not have to trouble himself about consequences. The men in power would hardly have touched him if he had carried his infantile exercise a stage further.[2]

VI. THE DEAN AND THE ARCHBISHOP

The new regime had perhaps secured the Protestant Succession. It certainly reduced the Tories to near-impotence. Yet among Irish Whigs the few real patriots soon observed that they would rarely be allowed to employ their illusory strength for the good of the people or the advancement of the Established Church. One might have expected this insight to free a bit of ground on which Swift and his archbishop could stand together. But their mutual distrust blocked a rapprochement.

Meanwhile, the Whigs in the Irish House of Commons were too busy establishing their own supremacy to find time for drafting bills that might relieve the suffering of the kingdom. What they did propose on such lines received no backing from the government; for an English ministry could hardly conceive of Ireland as deserving any consideration that failed to increase the riches or power of England. Instead of a sound economic policy, Sunderland offered immense but ineffectual pressure to repeal the Sacramental Test. At the same time the prostrate Tories saw new dangers in an Act giving the Irish executive authority to imprison suspected conspirators without a trial. 'I expect to be among the first of those upon whom this law will be executed,' said Swift.[3]

While the parliamentary session lasted, he made visits, prudently extended, to friends in the country. 'The Parliament

---

[1] Davis v. 199–200.

[2] Swift may nevertheless have appealed for protection to the Irish House of Lords. See *ibid.*

[3] 18 Apr. 1716, to Atterbury; Williams II. 198.

here are as mad as you could desire them,' he told a friend; 'all of different parties are used like Jacobites and dogs.'[1] As it happened, the archbishop disliked the law for the gaoling of malcontents,[2] and he fought stubbornly to preserve the Sacramental Test. But in Swift's eyes he still belonged to the gang of the oppressors; and so far from making up to his grace, the dean actually scolded him for fostering the thorny relationship that held between them. 'It is thought a matter of accusation [i.e., by the archbishop] for any one to cultivate my acquaintance,' Swift wrote to King, who had taken his gouty body to Bath.[3] In a tranquillizing reply to Swift, his grace tried to evade the complaint, and lingered on cooler topics.

But a new spark soon fired Swift up again. The long visit to England furnished the archbishop with the sort of rumours that nourished his own fear of the Jacobites and the Pretender. While Swift was 'under a thousand uneasinesses' about the fate of Bolingbroke, the archbishop lay awake anticipating a French invasion. Political antipathies still veiled the deep agreement of the two priests on Ireland and the church. Swift kept assuring the archbishop that he himself had never plotted against the constitution, and that he thought the same of his old ministerial friends. 'I had no ill designs', he said, 'nor ever knew any in them.'[4]

As if to refute Swift and to humble him after his recent defiance, King wrote from London,

> We have a strong report that my Lord Bolingbroke will return here and be pardoned, certainly it must not be for nothing. I hope he can tell no ill story of you.[5]

Accustomed to the give and take of both ecclesiastical and political administration, the archbishop was too much in the habit of power for him to mind the scratches and bruises that went with it. He was so thoroughly used to commanding and seeing parsons obey that he could easily tolerate other men's doubts about his motives. But Swift, who had never ruled over

---

[1] 17 Dec. 1715, to Chetwode; *ibid.*, p. 191.   [2] 24 Mar. 1716, to Annesley.
[3] Williams II. 206.   [4] *Ibid.*, p. 206.   [5] *Ibid.*, pp. 227–8.

many inferiors, made a prize of his own integrity. The vanity of highmindedness drove him to resent the smallest insinuation against his moral character. Since the connection with Archbishop King was the determining framework of his ecclesiastic career, it was also the place where he could least tolerate any moral blame. The archbishop's innuendoes against Bolingbroke as a venal informer and the dean as a crypto-Jacobite show that he appreciated Swift's character as little as Swift did his. 'He plainly let me know', Swift told a friend, 'that he believes all I have said of my self and the last ministry with relation to the Pretender to be court lies.' [1]

The dean delivered a response to the archbishop that marks the lowest point in thirty years of reluctant collaboration. But while this letter reads magnificently today, its striking feature is that it neither altered the archbishop's opinion nor gave him the least pain. Yet these were Swift's aims—to persuade and to wound:

> I should be sorry to see my Lord Bolingbroke following the trade of an informer, because he is a person for whom I always had and still continue a very great love and esteem. For I think as the rest of mankind do, that informers are a detestable race of people, though they may be sometimes necessary.... But I am surprised to think your grace could talk or act or correspond with me for some years past, while you must needs believe me a most false and vile man, declaring to you on all occasions my abhorrence of the Pretender, and yet privately engaged with a ministry to bring him in, and therefore warning me to look to my self and prepare my defence against a false brother coming over to discover such secrets as would hang me. Had there been ever the least overture or intent of bringing in the Pretender during my acquaintance with the ministry, I think I must have been very stupid not to have picked out some discoveries or suspicions; and though I am not sure I should have turned informer, yet I am sure I should have dropped some general cautions, and immediately have retired. When people say things were not ripe at the Queen's death [i.e., for Jacobite ministers to proclaim the Pretender as King], they say they know not what [.] Things were rotten, and had the ministers any such thoughts they should have begun three years before, and they who say otherwise

[1] 19 Dec. 1716, to Thomas Walls; *ibid.*, p. 235.

understand nothing of the state of the kingdom at that time. But whether I am mistaken or no in other men, I beg your grace to believe, that I am not mistaken in my self; I always professed to be against the Pretender, and am so still; and this is not to make my court, (which I know is vain) for I own my self full of doubts, fears and dissatisfactions [viz., concerning the new government], which I think of seldom as I can; yet, if I were of any value, the public may safely rely on my loyalty, because I look upon the coming of the Pretender as a greater evil than any we are like to suffer under the worst Whig ministry that can be found. I have not spoke nor thought much of party these two years; nor could any thing have tempted me to it now, but the grief I have for standing so ill in your grace's opinion.[1]

Unluckily, one of Swift's expressions radically weakened his argument. He said he would have retired from court if he had suspected the ministry of making overtures to the Pretender. Yet he had in fact withdrawn from court in the fatal spring of 1714, because he had lost all hope of reconciling Oxford and Bolingbroke.[2] Under all his protestations he must (I think) have wondered whether more had not gone on, between the Tory ministers, than they had let him see. If he would indeed have been stupid not to pick out some discoveries, we may assume that he picked a few out. Unless Swift's nerve-endings were dead, the impact of Bolingbroke's and Ormonde's flights to the Pretender's court must have started or confirmed doubts that he would breathe to nobody. The archbishop, for all his stolidity, was not a man to overlook a clue; and he replied to Swift, 'I never believed you for the Pretender, but remember that when the surmises of that matter run high, you retired, which agrees with what you say you ought to have done in that case.'[3] Swift had the prudence not to follow this argument further.

VII. THE IRISH INTEREST

From this nadir the mutual respect of Swift and his archbishop started climbing almost at once, as the mischief and blunders of the English united the friends of Ireland. Although the two men

[1] *Ibid.*, pp. 237-9. [2] Davis VIII. 132. [3] 12 Jan. 1717; Williams II. 248.

never stopped blocking each other in church preferments, they began to co-operate elsewhere in support of Irish interests. By the spring of 1717 Swift could address King with a warmth of filial feeling that suited their community of purpose: 'I pray God preserve your grace for . . . the happiness of those whom you are pleased to honour with your friendship, favour, or protection.'[1] It is true that the same month Swift wrote this compliment, he also confided to a friend that he was going to oppose a clergyman's preferment precisely because the archbishop desired it: 'Nothing could put me more against him than the A.B.'s declaring, and I am resolved to oppose it, as long as I can.'[2] But he was then trying to keep himself strong in the cathedral chapter, and this man's promotion would have increased King's power to thwart him. It is more revealing that in 1719 Swift called the archbishop 'half a Tory',[3] and that a year later someone who knew them both said, 'The [Archbishop] and the Dean are now joined in great amity.'[4]

If it took three years of Irish Whiggery to make their sympathies bloom, it was not for want of vernal tokens on the archbishop's part. From the moment he heard of Queen Anne's death, though he smiled to see the Tories ejected, he also hoped the government would not be vengeful or provoke the clergy. Too knowledgeable to suppose a British Parliament might wish to help Ireland, he still yearned for some willingness to let the Irish help themselves. The archbishop had modest desires: to improve the kingdom's trade and to strengthen his own church. Conciliatory but not weak government, firmness without re-crimination, were what he recommended to the deaf adders of Dublin and London. One of his complaints against the defeated Tories was that they had dismissed from office everyone 'that would not swear and bawl and mob and coffee-house [i.e., spread rumours] and preach and inform against his honest quiet neighbours'.[5] He had no wish to see his own side use the same

---

[1] *Ibid.*, p. 267. [2] *Ibid.*, p. 268. [3] *Ibid.*, p. 331.
[4] Timothy Godwin to Archbishop Wake, 28 Dec. 1720, in Wake MSS., Christ Church, Oxford, quoted by Landa, p. 172.
[5] 18 Sept. 1714, to Southwell.

methods. Unlike Swift, King did not believe that in an ideal state the interest of the church would be identical with that of the secular powers.[1] But he was so much an optimist that he thought King George would give the Dissenters only the token support required by law and nothing further.[2]

A thoroughly partisan administration of any sort did not appeal to the archbishop. If the great courtiers disagreed among themselves, he was not troubled: 'It might be worse for the public if all drew one way.'[3] He was even attracted by the old chimera of government above party, and had enough naïveté to imagine the King might select his ministers and officers without regard to their connections: 'If nothing be expected [in Parliament] but what is for the common good, opposing the court will make no body popular,' he said.[4] After only four months of Whig sunshine, he was ready to admit, 'I am so blind that I see no great regard had to the public; for persons seem not put in stations to secure the public good, but places are made without necessity to gratify friends and dependents.'[5] Like Swift, he abominated the habit, more common under Whigs than Tories, of turning Irish public offices into sinecures for English favourites,[6] and of passing over native churchmen in order to promote opportunists from England:

> Our chief governors are changed commonly once in three years, and they commonly bring their chaplains with them [i.e., from England], who succeed to bishoprics if they fall, or to the best preferments . . . and hence your lordship may guess what encouragement there is for the clergy educated here.[7]

During the Irish parliamentary session of 1715–16 the archbishop showed more and more what might be called 'Swift's' principles. He wrote a treatise, circulated in manuscript, to demonstrate how unfairly the English were handling the Irish economy.[8] The Irish House of Commons wished to reverse the old trend of sacrificing agriculture to cattle-growing. So they

[1] 2 May 1715, to St George Ashe.   [2] 28 Sept. 1714, to Molyneux.
[3] 24 Nov. 1714, to Merion.   [4] 8 Jun. 1715, to Mountjoy.
[5] 14 Dec. 1714, to Molesworth.   [6] 23 Apr. 1715, to Southwell.
[7] 11 Dec. 1714, to Trimnell.   [8] Ferguson, pp. 187–8.

drew up a bill requiring the cultivation of five acres out of every hundred. But the English Privy Council thought a few years of such a policy might find Irish farmers competing with English in the export of corn, and it might correspondingly reduce the supply of raw wool for the English cloth trade. Therefore, they altered the bill in a way that made the Irish Parliament throw it out.[1] The archbishop, like Swift, groaned over this determination of the government to stifle the healthiest direction of Irish industry.

The archbishop hurled all his great strength against the campaign to repeal the Test and complained (to the Archbishop of Canterbury), 'Those enemies who claim the King is subverting the Established Church will now have so-called ground to press their claim.'[2] When a second round of bishops were to be selected for Ireland, he prayed anxiously that the choice might fall on Irish names; already the two English appointees had made shambles of their dioceses.[3]

Still the archbishop clung to his nonpartisan idealism, declaring, 'An honest man ... will come into no parties, he will keep steady to justice and to the interest of his country.'[4] Consequently, he was unhappy over the move in England to repeal the Triennial Act; and he bemoaned the tendency of Irish Whigs to push their victory to the limit of insolence:

I could name perhaps half a dozen ... steps taken here that have made more heart burnings and screw faces than can well be imagined nor can I see any reason for them except people have a mind to try their friends' patience.[5]

Six months after the Irish Parliament rose, the appointment of yet another Lord Lieutenant seemed imminent; and the comic realism that underlay the archbishop's hopefulness came out with a sound like desperation: 'If he be not a good one, we may be the more easy, because if he be like his *predecessor* [i.e., short-lived in office] he will be no lasting evil.'[6]

[1] *Ibid.*, pp. 47–8. Even if the bill had been enacted, it would have been ineffective. But more useful regulations might have followed.
[2] 24 Mar. 1716.   [3] 2 May 1716, to Molyneux.   [4] 24 Mar. 1716, to Annesley.
[5] 16 Apr. 1716, to Molyneux.   [6] 12 Jan. 1717, to Coghill.

A recurrent centre of King's fears for Ireland was the jurisdiction of the British House of Lords in Irish lawsuits. Early in
the new reign he complained that anyone who could afford to
carry an appeal to England might hope to escape prosecution.
The reason this constitutional issue heated his resentment was
double. His own endless litigation with the dean and chapter
of Christ Church Cathedral had been carried to England at
great expense (though with some satisfaction) to himself. But
more fundamental was his national spirit, much inflated by the
notorious Annesley Case.

In 1709 and 1710 the Court of the Exchequer of Ireland
had decided a suit between Maurice Annesley and Hester
Sherlock in favour of Annesley. In 1716 Mrs Sherlock
belatedly appealed this decree to the Irish House of Lords.
Their lordships debated the propriety of receiving such an
appeal six years after the original decree; and the Whig
Lord Chancellor Brodrick implored them not to limit their
own power to hear the case. Part of the original decree was
then reversed, with Brodrick arguing skilfully in favour of
Mrs Sherlock. But in 1717 Annesley appealed to the British
House of Lords; and Mrs Sherlock was summoned to plead
her case there.

When the Irish Lords met later that year, Mrs Sherlock
petitioned them to assert their appellate and final jurisdiction.
They debated the question frantically, in many words and
across party lines. Brodrick, now elevated to the peerage as
Viscount Midleton but still Lord Chancellor, stood off and
delivered gingerly cautions against considering Mrs Sherlock's
new request. He made it clear that he sympathized with the
consensus of the House but dreaded the reaction in England to
an Irish display of parliamentary hubris. Archbishop King, on
the contrary, spoke as a hot advocate of the petition even though
he was again, like Midleton, a Lord Justice. As the debate
stormed along, the archbishop collided head on with the Lord
Chancellor and found himself uncharacteristically aligned with
the Tory Primate Lindsay. Finally, the members of the House
voted to support their own jurisdiction and privileges by giving

Mrs Sherlock relief, while Lord Chancellor Midleton abstained from voting.[1]

At the time, the contest could not have given Swift much grief. He was taken up with reflections on the ordeal of Lord Oxford, who had just been released from the Tower. In a highly political sermon preached near the end of the parliamentary session, Swift never alluded to the Annesley Case; and in a pamphlet published two-and-a-half years later, he sneered at the energy their lordships had wasted on it.[2] But in 1725 Swift was to devote a furious thrust of sarcasm to an Irishman's having to 'travel five hundred miles by sea and land, to *another kingdom*, for justice'.[3] During the autumn of 1717 the archbishop's sentiments were at least as violent; and it is worth recording that in this season it was Swift whose views seemed to approach those of Sunderland's protégé Midleton.

The archbishop had been relieved of his duties as Lord Justice in the autumn of 1715, when Sunderland had it in mind to force the repeal of the Test through the Irish Parliament. But in March 1717 he was reappointed. When this second term was renewed the following year, he said it meant an 'ungrateful drudgery which amongst many other disgusting views gives a nearer and most afflicting knowledge of a miserable country that every day falls under new misfortunes'.[4] The opinion might have been dictated by Swift. King's aversion to the post deepened as he saw his powers circumscribed, his recommendations overridden, and his instructions confused by the feuds then erupting within the British ministry and the royal family. The endless promotion of Englishmen not only to bishoprics but to good church livings in Ireland wore down his discretion; and he told an intimate,

We have reason to fear that there will never want a rapacious covetous English or Welsh bishop who merely for filthy lucre's sake, though he quits his honour and seat in the British Parliament and can never expect too much good in Ireland, will cast his eye on our

---

[1] William Caulfeild, 1 Oct. 1717, in P.R.O., S.P.I., 1717, bundle 375, item 475A.
[2] Ferguson, p. 50; Davis IX. 16.   [3] *Drapier*, p. 159.
[4] 1 Feb. 1718, to Bladen.

fat bishoprics, and leave his lean one to provide for his church locusts, that eat up every green thing, that belongs to our church.[1]

Like Swift, the archbishop seldom looked behind the probity of his own rhetoric to observe that he was delivering a judgment on all English immigration into Ireland, and that his own family would have stayed in Britain if not driven by the same kind of greed.

[1] 12 Jul. 1718, to Molyneux.

Chapter Two

THE DEANSHIP

I. LIFE IN A DEANERY

If most of Swift's readjustments in 1714 were the kind that saddened him, a few brought reasons to be cheerful. Setting up house in the deanery he inherited from John Stearne meant a number of chores. But while Swift complained about some, he clearly enjoyed many. An improver by nature, he loved to advise friends about laying out their grounds and building their mansions. At his rural parish of Laracor, the willows he planted and the canal he cut gave him seasonal pastimes. Now in Dublin he grumblingly took pleasure in ordering shelves for his books and getting a new chimney-piece made. He expelled Stearne's cat and searched endlessly for a good horse at a price he liked. Though Swift kept the deanery sparsely furnished, he could hardly run so large an establishment with the few servants he was used to. As housekeeper, he installed Mrs Brent, his Presbyterian standby. The newer servants took unusual trials and errors before he could feel even moderately content. There were a steward, a footman, and a cook-maid indoors; a groom and helper in the stable, where he kept three horses.[1] For some tasks he drew on the cathedral staff.

These domestic alterations betokened the change in his public place. Swift no longer sank into an undistinguished mass of beneficed clergy. He could lift up his head as the handsomely paid dean of an ancient cathedral in the capital city. Privileges and powers, status and security belonged to him for life. This was far from the eminence he had prayed for. All its amenities

---

[1] Williams II. 135, 177; Delany, p. 6. Delany is wrong to say Swift had no helper for the groom, for Swift himself says he had one—see Williams II. 177.

never freed him from those unnerving embarrassments that his own health and the rigours of Irish civilization imposed on his fastidiousness. Its advantages carried penalties with them, because the violence of the Whigs soared with the weakness of the Tories; and the dean met with insults that the vicar had not known. But it was visible success, begrudged him by many and envied by more. In a time of many trials here was a singular comfort.

The servant class being even more degraded and yet more necessary in Ireland than in England, Swift's standards were hard to satisfy. Dr Delany tells how the dean went about hiring servants:

> Humility was always the test by which he tried them. Among other questions, he always asked, whether they understood the cleaning of shoes. Whether they answered, that they did, or did not, he always added, 'My kitchen-wench [a deliberately misleading term for the dignified office of cook] hath a scullion, that does her drudgery; one constant business of my groom, and footman, is to clean her shoes by turns.'
> If they stomached [i.e., resented] this, he instantly turned them off; but if they humbly submitted he gave them farther hearing.[1]

Swift paid high wages, with extra money for special duties; and he treated servants with so much real consideration (under his scolding and teasing) that he rarely saw one leave him voluntarily.[2] They got four shillings a week for their board (top wages) even though Swift normally supplied them with meals. Mrs Brent as housekeeper was much better paid than the rest, and she took her dinner or supper with Swift himself if he had no guests. 'Nor did he ever deprive his household', says Dr Lyon, 'of any of those comforts, that he thought them intitled to receive from an indulgent master.'[3]

For his cook-maid Swift soon chose a large, pock-marked woman named Mary, who kept the kitchen, made his bed, and mended his stockings. She endeared herself to Swift and was

---

[1] Delany, pp. 213–14; my punctuation.
[2] *Ibid.*, pp. 185–6. [3] Lyon, pp. 16–22.

[33]

old and plain enough for him to call her 'sweetheart'.[1] An even happier but later discovery was Alexander McGee, or 'Saunders', a footman whom Swift described as 'the best servant in the world'—a model of diligence, discretion, and fidelity.[2] But Sweetheart and Saunders were not the rule. A new groom stacked the hay on a rainy day, and Swift could not easily dismiss an unwelcome old woman who had secured her humble office in the deanery before his own administration.[3]

Swift's passion for riding produced an almost symbolic episode; and this will suggest how thoroughly he experienced the frustrations of existence in an underdeveloped country. One day during his first Christmas season back in Ireland, the dean was on his way to Belcamp, five miles north of Dublin. Finding he had forgotten something, he decided to return to the deanery alone. So he asked the usual pair of servants to take the horses over a bridge and wait for him with his riding cloak at a ferry station that he himself would use to gain time. Later in the day, when he rejoined the men, they were standing unpromisingly outside a shop where brandy was sold. They helped him on with his cloak but turned it wrong side out. Swift observed that Will, the groom, was drunk, but decided to ride on anyhow. Next, Tom, the footman (Saunders' predecessor), failed to come along. Swift waited till he galloped up and then scolded him. Tom, so drunk he could hardly sit in his saddle, answered foolishly.

Their way was Swift's common riding ground, the strand toward Howth. Now tottering on his horse, Tom rode sometimes into the sea and sometimes back to Swift; yet he swore he wasn't drunk. Swift tried to whip him and ordered him to go ahead. Soon Tom changed his language, said he was drunk indeed, and began coming back every moment to Swift, who still commanded him to keep on. At last the galloping and

[1] Delany, pp. 186–7; *Poems* III. 985–7; Williams II. 177. She was evidently hired in October 1714; see *Poems* III. 985.
[2] Delany, pp. 194–6; Williams II. 422 and n. 5.
[3] Williams II. 135.

turning back and forth made Tom's horse so wild that he threw the footman down. Swift called a boy and a man who happened to be nearby and asked them to help get the horse away from Tom. But the footman was so far gone that he fought off all three of them. After a struggle, they tore the bridle from him, forcing him to release the horse. Swift told the boy to mount. Then Swift, Will, and the boy rode away with Tom reeling after until they lost him. As if it were all a fable, the horse—brought over from England—was named Bolingbroke.

Swift still had to worry that Tom might stagger back to the deanery and rob him. So he sent the boy to Archdeacon Walls with a letter begging Walls to stop in at the deanery and make sure the footman was not allowed to stay there. 'I would have his great coat, boots and whip taken from him; let him have a crown in part of his wages, and the rest he shall have when I come, and his account is given up.'[1]

But nothing could stop Swift from riding. When he said he absolutely had to ride for his health, he did not exaggerate. The compulsion to exercise and the belief that no exercise did more good than riding were among the most rigid of his fixed ideas. But he also loved walking; and when bad weather or a tolerable illness kept him indoors, he would run up and down the deanery stairs. Dr Delany, who disapproved of Swift's addiction to 'incessant and intemperate exercise', reports that he walked erect,[2] and says,

> He had a fixed persuasion, that a certain degree of exercise was absolutely necessary, not only to health, but also to cleanliness, to keep those pores of the skin free and clear, by which the great and important discharges of our frame, by insensible perspiration, are performed. . . . Upon this principle, no question oftener recurred to his acquaintance of the other sex, than this: Why do not you exercise?[3]

[1] *Ibid.*, pp. 152–3.   [2] Delany, p. 147.
[3] *Ibid.*, pp. 174–5; my punctuation. Although Swift's devotion to physical exercise was remarkably intense, the medicinal value of exercise, and of riding in particular, was a commonplace of the age. When Pope as a youth had poor health, his doctor recommended daily riding.

Swift constantly prescribed riding as a panacea; and while Mary Vanhomrigh—sister of Swift's devoted 'Vanessa'—was daily weakening from the illness that would soon kill her, he still recommended riding as her best medicine.

How much he benefited from his own prescription is less certain. During the first few years after Queen Anne's death Swift suffered extraordinary attacks of the deafness and vertigo symptomatic of Ménière's syndrome. For long periods he could hardly pass a month without a deaf spell that might last for weeks, depressing him until he could not bear to leave the house or see anyone but his intimate friends. One day when he expected guests for dinner, his giddiness chose to descend and forced him to lie miserably in bed while a friend deputized as host. 'This is the most mortal impediment to all thoughts of travelling,' Swift said, 'and I should die with spleen to be in such a condition in strange places.'[1] To the tribulations contrived by his servants and the insolence of the party in power, he had to add the humbler, more tenacious pains of his mysterious disease.

II. THE DEAN AND HIS CHAPTER

Swift could have immersed himself cheerfully in the business of managing the cathedral; and this would have given him some relief from the illness and indignities that beset him elsewhere. His wishes were busy enough. He meant to strengthen the finances of the cathedral, to improve the music, dignify the fabric, and elevate the service. More than all these, he meant to promote the welfare of his friends and other good men. 'My notion', he said, 'is, that if a man cannot mend the public he should mend old shoes if he can do no better; and therefore I endeavour in the little sphere I am placed [?in] to do all the good it is capable of.'[2] Lord Orrery, who knew Swift in his old age, says the chapter of the cathedral at first thwarted Swift 'in every point he proposed' but that the dean soon reduced them to

[1] 4 Apr. 1720, to Ford; Williams II. 342.
[2] 3 Jan. 1715, to Chetwode; *ibid.*, p. 154.

[36]

'reason and obedience'.[1] Dr Delany, who met Swift around 1717, confuted Orrery and said he himself was assured 'by persons who knew it well'—presumably, himself among them—that the reception Swift met with was 'as kind, and honourable as he could wish'.[2] However, Delany also admits that Archbishop King and his protégés in the chapter 'gave some check to that plenitude of power, which they saw plainly [the dean] intended to assert, and exert there'.[3] Dr Johnson observed that Delany's description referred to the summer of 1713, when the Tories still prospered, but that Orrery had in mind the bleak autumn of 1714.[4]

Yet party conflicts were only the surface of the whirlpool. Maybe if Swift had stayed in Ireland during the year before Queen Anne died, he could have dug himself in while his friends at court backed his power with their own. More likely not; for no matter who governed the kingdom, so long as Archbishop King governed the province, Swift could not hope for easy sovereignty in the cathedral. It was this connection that made his deanship one more spring of frustration.

Orrery said Swift's spirit was 'ever intractable':

> The motions of his genius were often irregular. He assumed more the air of a patron, than of a friend. He affected rather to dictate than advise.[5]

This may not be how Swift struck Addison, but it is how he struck his juniors in the church. Delany did not choose to contradict Orrery on this point. The role of Nestor, which Swift assumed in irony with those he admired, he acted seriously with those he thought needed his guidance.

Unfortunately, the archbishop had the same confidence as Swift in his own judgment, the same tenacity in his prejudices, the same zeal to advance his friends, and rather more power than Swift to accomplish his aims. Of him one might say what Dr Delany said of Swift, that 'his spirit was formed with a strong reluctance to submission of any kind.'[6] If the two men were

---

[1] Orrery, p. 51.   [2] Delany, p. 87.   [3] *Ibid.*, p. 88.
[4] *Life of Swift*, para. 63.   [5] P. 47.   [6] Delany, p. 146.

finally able to collaborate in public affairs, and if they did come to appreciate each other's virtues, they never could take the same view of ecclesiastical patronage. Quite apart from their characters, they simply had different sets of protégés competing for the same jobs.

What provided the arena for their quarrels was a state of overlapping jurisdictions. When he acted together with his chapter, Swift was lord of the manor over the inhabitants of the liberty of St Patrick's, a territory of five or six acres surrounding the cathedral. The dean and chapter as a legal body stood beyond the jurisdiction of most secular magistrates; and they were quite untouched by the authority of the archbishop, who felt 'cramped' by their exemption.[1] But geographically Swift's empire lay inside the archbishop's own liberty of St Sepulchre, making contact between the two powers impossible to avoid and opening the way for collisions of the most palpable sort. More important than this physical contact was the abrasive fact that the archbishop possessed the right of appointing prebendaries to the cathedral chapter,[2] while the dean and chapter could present clergymen to livings that the archbishop wanted for his clients.

The more one reflects on these points of friction, the less one inclines to accept the old account of Swift's decanal tribulations. Scholars have supposed that a political opposition started the wrangling between the archbishop and his dean. Yet there is no record of a serious clash that one could attribute to national politics. Their predecessors had sometimes fought over temporal rights. Swift and King did not. In 1713, when Swift wished to keep the vicars choral from leasing land without his consent, the archbishop let him proceed.[3] Yet the would-be lessee was a Whig lord who had quarrelled with Swift.[4] In 1723 a clergyman wished to lease some land from the vicars choral, and Archbishop King agreed to the terms. Swift refused to let the lease be fixed until the tithes involved were clearly defined. King

[1] See the letter of 12 Feb. 1703 from King to Weymouth.
[2] Lawlor, p. 30.   [3] Landa, pp. 75–6.   [4] *Journal* II. 592–3, 607.

did not oppose him.[1] From the time of Queen Elizabeth, the prebendaries of St Patrick's had taken their turns preaching in Christ Church Cathedral. Swift decided to end this practice. The outraged Dean of Christ Church complained that 'the new Dean of St Patrick's is bringing a new broil upon us';[2] but the archbishop did not interfere.

Of course, Swift and King had very different political opinions; and King was willing to turn Swift's Tory reputation against him when it suited the archbishop to enlist Whig officialdom on his own side. The Tories had been in power when Stearne, the archbishop's favourite, became Bishop of Dromore; and the archbishop said, 'I find it whispered that my friendship did him hurt.'[3] On Swift's promotion, King told an acquaintance, 'The deanery has taken a turn, which I could not foresee.'[4] He rejoiced that Swift rose no higher in the church, because 'a dean could do less mischief than a bishop.'[5]

At the same time, of course, the narrowest Tory churchmen distrusted Swift for his old Whig tie. When he received the deanship, Robert Molesworth reported that the appointment 'vexed the godly party'. An English high-flyer wrote to a friend,

> You are not a stranger to the character of ... Dr Swift, and I am persuaded that Hoadly would have been a more acceptable man to the clergy of Ireland, because he is in point of episcopacy more orthodox than the other. The clergy of that kingdom detest Dr Swift because they think him an enemy to the order. When he lived among them he was a vehement Whig. Even in bad times a Whig clergyman was there thought a monstrous composition, and abhorred by the rest of the body, and even the station Dr Swift is now preferred to, will gain him very little respect from them.[6]

The compound of ignorance and prejudice in this statement tells us less about Swift than about the coteries of the church party.

---

[1] See letter of 11 Jun. 1723 from Archbishop King to Bishop Godwin.
[2] Landa, p. 72.   [3] 16 May 1713, to Southwell.
[4] He insinuated that he would have preferred Thomas, 6th Viscount Ikerrin; see Ball II. 29, n. 2.
[5] 8 May 1716, to Wake; Gilbert Collection (Dublin), MS. 8.
[6] Ezekiel Hamilton to Arthur Charlett, 30 Apr. 1713; Bodl. MS. Ballard 36, fol. 111; quoted by Landa, p. 73. I have altered the spelling, capitalization, and punctuation.

But it does suggest how little difference the extremists could see between the archbishop and his dean.

Yet in the day-to-day running of the cathedral, so long as no preferment or right of appointment was under discussion, neither Whig nor Tory, neither prebendary nor archbishop, gave the dean trouble. King was not trying to save a ministry; he was trying to secure his own power. At the same time, it was precisely the business and power of awarding church livings that absorbed the ecclesiastical energies of both Swift and King. So it became natural for the dean to complain that the archbishop 'upon all occasions' made him uneasy in his station.[1] Besides, Swift regularly complained that party differences were the grounds of his persecution, and scholars have accepted his view—but only at the cost of misrepresenting the archbishop as a blind Whig.

As soon as Swift became dean, his own vacated prebend had to be filled, and this of course was in the gift of the archbishop. Swift wrote to King at once, urging him to name Thomas Parnell to the place. Not very presciently, Swift commented, 'I flatter myself that his being agreeable to me, will be no disadvantage to him in your grace's opinion.'[2] The archbishop, who had been Parnell's guardian, might have been expected to feel predisposed in his favour. But he did not. Instead, he countered with the name of Joseph Espin, to whom he had already promised the prebend (or so he said).[3] Even though Swift's ministerial friends were in office at the time, it was Espin and not Parnell who succeeded to the prebend of Dunlavin.

A month after Swift was installed as dean, and while he was still in Ireland, another prebendary died. This time, Swift begged the place for Thomas Warburton, his curate at Laracor. 'It will be a great use to me', he misguidedly told the archbishop, 'to have a vicar in one of my rectories, and upon my deanery, in whom I can confide.'[4] The prebend went to Dr Drury, master of the cathedral school.

At the beginning of 1714, Thomas Lindsay became the Arch-

---

[1] Williams II. 206.   [2] *Ibid.*, I. 344, 353.   [3] *Ibid.*, p. 356.   [4] *Ibid.*, p. 377.

bishop of Armagh (and Primate of all Ireland). Swift had supported him for that eminence, and Lindsay immediately began working with Swift to strengthen the Tory side in the Church of Ireland. About the same time, another prebend, Rathmichael, was vacated in St Patrick's Cathedral. Archbishop King recommended Philip Chamberlain—whom Swift considered an anticlerical Whig—for this opening. Months later, King told Addison that Chamberlain was a good man and an excellent preacher who had been treated badly by the Tory government.[1] Years afterward, Swift was to describe Chamberlain as 'a man of very low parts and understanding, with a very high conceit of himself, and party-mad into the bargain'.[2] But Chamberlain became the Prebendary of Rathmichael in February 1714.

If this was the treatment the dean could expect while Queen Anne lived and his influence with the government was at its peak, he should not have been surprised by events after her death. When Lindsay became Primate, he left the see of Raphoe open. Since the Tories failed to fill this, the Whigs had the pleasure of promoting Edward Synge (son and namesake of the prudent Archbishop of Tuam), who had been Chancellor of St Patrick's. So the chancellorship was ready for bids. Archbishop King wrote promptly to Sunderland, the Lord Lieutenant, recommending Theophilus Bolton, who was a prebendary of the cathedral. After praising Bolton's piety and so forth, the archbishop said,

> Besides, I believe your excellency knows Dr Swift the Dean of my cathedral and what I am to expect from him, and except I have such a person as Dr Bolton in a station in the chapter, I am afraid my affairs there will not go very well.[3]

King also wrote to Addison (then secretary to the Lords Justices) on the same business.[4]

It was only five years since Swift, in a desperate push for

---

[1] Letter of 18 Dec. 1714.
[2] 18 Jun. 1716; Williams II. 208.
[3] Letter of 29 Oct. 1714, quoted by Landa, p. 78.   [4] 16 Nov. 1714.

preferment, had published a description of Sunderland as 'that most learned and excellent lord',[1] but the Earl had known Swift in the household of Sir William Temple and had dealt with him over the business of the First Fruits. Sunderland could only have shared the attitude of his mother-in-law, the Duchess of Marlborough, toward a Tory churchman who supported the Test Act and admired Lord Oxford. It is ironical that Addison (himself the son of a clergyman), who once had served Lord Wharton in opposition to Swift's aims, now had to help Lord Sunderland weaken Swift's power as dean.

Bolton easily secured the chancellorship. Being an accomplished canon lawyer, he gave vital strength to the archbishop's coterie in the cathedral chapter. So well did he fulfil his patron's hopes that Swift said, after two-and-a-half years, 'He has taken every opportunity of opposing me, in the most unkind and unnecessary manner.'[2]

To replace Bolton in his old prebend, the archbishop selected John Wynne. Swift had expected 'difficulties with the chapter' about a successor to Bolton,[3] but we know nothing more of the circumstances of the promotion. (Fifteen years later, Wynne was to join with two other prebendaries in a small rebellion against Swift's authority.)[4]

Less darkness surrounds the proceedings the following year, when Robert Dougatt became one of the dignitaries of the chapter as Archdeacon of Dublin. Swift had liked his predecessor, Thomas Hawley; and in 1713, when Hawley seemed at death's door, Swift had picked Theophilus Bolton as his own private choice out of a list of four possible successors.[5] But in October 1715, after Hawley at last saw fit to die, the promotion went to Robert Dougatt, Prebendary of Swords. Since Dougatt's uncle was Archbishop King, the machinery of his advancement is visible, and one cannot feel startled by Swift's judgment: 'It is impossible for Dougatt to keep his honesty in the way and company he is.'[6]

[1] Davis I. 268.   [2] 9 Jul. 1717, to Robert Cope; Williams II. 275.
[3] Ibid., p. 146.   [4] Landa, p. 93.   [5] Williams I. 391.
[6] 18 Jun. 1716, to Thomas Walls; ibid., II. 208.

In the wake of Dougatt's rise, other adjustments had to be made, giving yet more strength to the archbishop's hand. But his grace still did not feel invincible. During the spring of 1716, therefore, he decided to revive a dormant prebend, which no one had held since the reign of James I. This preferment he now bestowed on William Gore, much to Swift's annoyance.[1] Meanwhile, another prebendary died conveniently, and Swift's friend Thomas Walls pined for the place. But the archbishop looked elsewhere and bestowed it on Charles Whittingham.

Now Swift decided that four years of courteous evasion were enough. So he wrote a letter of honest expostulation to the archbishop:

I confess, every friend I have discovered long before myself that I had wholly lost your grace's favour, and this to a degree that all whom I was disposed to serve were sure to thrive the worse for my friendship to them; particularly, I have been assured that Mr Walls would not have failed of the prebend of Malahidert, if he had not been thought too much attached to me; for it is alleged, that according to your grace's own scheme of uniting the prebends to the vicarages it would almost have fallen to him of course; and I remember the poor gentleman had always a remote hope of that prebend whenever Dr Moore should quit it. Mr Walls came lately down to me to Trim upon that disappointment, and I was so free as to ask him, whether he thought my friendship had done him hurt; but he was either so meek, or so fearful of offending, that he would by no means impute his misfortune to any thing beside his want of merit, and some misrepresentations; which latter I must confess to have found with grief, to have more than once influenced you against some, who by their conduct to your grace have deserved a quite different treatment. With respect to myself, I can assure your grace, that those who are most in your confidence make it no manner of secret, that several clergymen have lost your grace's favour by their civilities to me. I do not say any thing of this by way of complaint, which I look upon to be an office too mean for any man of spirit and integrity, but merely to know whether it be possible for me to be upon any better terms with your grace, without which I shall be able to do very little good in the small station I am placed.[2]

[1] *Ibid.*, p. 206 and n. 2. [2] 17 Jun. 1716; *ibid.*, pp. 205–6.

Instead of replying squarely to Swift's points, the archbishop, with more wisdom than candour, dodged them in a vague message of reconciliation.[1]

On the dean's side the best weapon to use for counter-attack was the power the dean and chapter had of appointing clergymen to a number of churches. Although his enemies in the cathedral might outvote him, Swift claimed the right to propose candidates for these livings, and he also claimed a power of veto over the votes of the rest of the chapter.[2] The archbishop constantly wished to retain his own followers by obliging them with livings in the gift of the dean and chapter. In the city of Dublin only two parishes were directly under his own patronage.[3] Yet city churches were in the greatest demand. So the foundation was laid for a series of mutual favours.

But as long as the archbishop could himself bestow further patronage through other channels, as long as he could effectually recommend priests to bishoprics, ambitious prebendaries were ill-advised to neglect his desires. Even in the dean's own province, therefore, Swift found himself on a short tether. He liked to compare himself (Delany says) to 'a poor Duke of Lorraine, unhappily situated too near the King of France, whose tyranny bore him down'.[4]

Early in his deanship Swift had discovered how little he might accomplish by the most stubborn exercise of his prerogatives. Theophilus Bolton, when he became Chancellor of St Patrick's, also received the living of St Werburgh's Church, which was normally joined to that dignity. Bolton therefore gave up the living of St Nicholas Without, which he had held since the spring of 1713. This living could hardly have been handier for a prebendary of the cathedral, since the congregation used a transept of St Patrick's for its church. Swift had once hankered after it himself, and never forgave his longtime friend John Stearne for denying it to him. Now Swift determined to see St Nicholas Without bestowed on his modest, long-suffering

[1] *Ibid.*, p. 210.   [2] *Ibid.*, pp. 376–7; Landa, pp. 85–6, 93.
[3] Letter of 12 Feb. 1703, to Lord Weymouth.
[4] Delany, p. 89; my punctuation.

comrade Thomas Walls. The memory of the incidents that followed lay behind the letter of expostulation finally written to King.

If ever Swift might have expected to get his own way, this was the time, inasmuch as the archbishop approved of Walls too. Describing him as one of those who had 'suffered' for refusing to ally themselves with the Tories, King recommended Walls to the government.[1] But at once another issue opened. If the incumbent of certain livings was promoted by the Crown, the government claimed the right to name his successor. When the archbishop was Dean of St Patrick's, he resisted this claim. With Swift in the deanship, his grace discovered new merits on the other side, and urged the political authorities to insist on their rights. I suppose he thought the Lord Lieutenant would be more tractable than the cathedral clergy. Knowing the dean and chapter would have to contest the claim, he urged the Lord Lieutenant to name a person acceptable to them; for he supposed the period of litigation would then be brief. If a person they disliked was nominated, they would of course protract the lawsuit. So he wrote to Addison, the Lord Lieutenant's secretary,

> There is one Dr Wall [*sic*] beneficed in this diocese, a grave and good man. He is agreeable to the Dean and Chapter and I understand by them if the Crown present him they will be content that the cause immediately come to a trial on the mere right.[2]

All might have gone well, and Swift might have been able to serve his friend if the archbishop had not learned how very intimate Walls was with the dean; for he then spun around and decided the proper man for the place was Philip Chamberlain.[3] Whatever the true merits of the candidates may have been, Chamberlain at least had the advantage of being a full member of the chapter; for the curates of St Nicholas Without had usually been prebendaries of the cathedral.[4] Since Chamberlain was a Whig, and King at this time was a Lord Justice of Ireland,

---

[1] Letter of 16 Nov. 1714, to Addison.   [2] 18 Dec. 1714; cf. Landa, p. 80.

[3] Although the evidence is not quite conclusive, it is strong enough for me to accept Swift's explanation.

[4] Lawlor, p. 272.

the archbishop's man would obviously have served the government better than a protégé of the Tory dean.

With King acting as puppeteer to the prebendaries, Swift
could do nothing for Walls. But with Swift asserting his powers
of proposal and veto, King could do nothing for Chamberlain.[1]
While months passed and other plums ripened on other trees,
Swift and Walls changed their programme. At one point Walls
thought that by doing a good turn for John Wynne, Swift might
persuade the archbishop to let Walls have St Nicholas.[2] A year
later, Swift was hoping that if he let Chamberlain have St Luke's
Church, Dublin, the archbishop would let Anthony Dopping
have St Nicholas and give Walls a small rectory lately vacated in
co. Cork.[3] (Dopping's elder brother, an old friend of Swift, was
a rich Tory M. P. whose good will would have been acceptable
to the archbishop.) But Chamberlain insisted on clinging to
St Nicholas, and King told Swift he would compel no clergyman
to 'go further than was consistent with his inclination and
interest'.[4] The upshot of the tug-of-war was that in the summer
of 1716, after a year-and-a-half of degrading intrigues, the
election of Chamberlain to the cure of St Nicholas Without
passed, as Swift wrote to King, 'quietly while I was in the
country'; and Walls made do with the small rectory of
Castlehaven.[5] Although Swift might reflect that he had snatched
something out of the grab-bag for his crony, he could hardly feel
triumphant.

Before this episode ended, another, just as ignominious,
began. The desirable church of St Bride's, Dublin, was in the gift
of the dean and chapter of St Patrick's. James Duncan, the
minister for more than twenty years, started aspirations in
several breasts when he fell off a horse early in the year 1717. But
he inconsiderately recovered and lasted a few months longer. 'I
think his life is entirely to be ascribed to providence,' said the
archbishop, 'for I am assured none else is, or would be, concerned to preserve it.'[6] When Duncan finally died, Swift

---

[1] Williams II. 169–70, 194, 196, 198, 202, 203–4.   [2] *Ibid.*, p. 169.
[3] *Ibid.*, p. 203 and n. 5.   [4] *Ibid.*, p. 210.   [5] *Ibid.*, p. 221; Lawlor, p. 272.
[6] Williams II. 261–2.

remarked on 'a great encrease of disinterested correspondents' and owned to the archbishop that in choosing a successor to Duncan, he would be glad to proceed with the approbation of his grace—'which is less a compliment, because I believe my chapter are of opinion, I can hardly proceed without it'.[1] By this time, according to one calculation, nearly two-thirds of the prebendaries were 'friends' of the archbishop;[2] and Swift complained, 'To oppose me in everything relating to my station is made a merit in my chapter.'[3]

The most audible claimant to St Bride's was Robert Howard, whose father, an old acquaintance of Swift, had been Regius Professor of Physic in the University of Dublin. Howard was already a prebendary of the cathedral and the vicar of St Anne's, Dublin. A couple of years before, when Howard was preparing to travel abroad, Swift had signalized his good opinion of the young man by writing letters of introduction for him.[4] Howard summed up their connection—for the archbishop's benefit—by saying, 'Though I was never a favourite [viz., of Swift's], I have always been on good terms with him.' One reason Swift would have liked to promote him was that Howard had the right to name his own successor at St Anne's, and Swift believed, rather innocently, that in return for help in reaching St Bride's, Howard would appoint Swift's nominee to St Anne's.[5]

The dean told the archbishop that he would like to place Anthony Dopping in St Bride's.[6] The archbishop, who was then in England, described himself as highly inclined to 'take care of Mr. Dopping'.[7] But Howard had been ardently wooing the archbishop. In several letters he declared his devotion to Whig principles, his fidelity to the archbishop—and his willingness to present King's candidate to the living of St Anne's. King now wrote to his nephew Robert Dougatt, Archdeacon of Dublin, and advised him to back Howard in the chapter. At the same

---

[1] *Ibid.*, p. 266. [2] Landa, p. 91.
[3] 18 Jul. 1717, to Atterbury; Williams II. 279. [4] *Ibid.*, pp. 156–9.
[5] Howard's letter of 4 Jun. 1717, quoted by Landa, p. 88; and Landa's comment.
[6] Williams II. 258. [7] *Ibid.*, p. 262.

time, Howard won over the elder Edward Synge, Archbishop of
Tuam, whose son (also Edward Synge) was a prebendary of St
Patrick's. Howard had hinted to Archbishop King that the
younger Synge might follow him at St Anne's. 'The Archbishop
of Tuam has very kindly assisted me to the utmost in my
application to the chapter,' Howard told King.[1]

Swift had no idea of Howard's manœuvring, but stepped
more cautiously than when he was a fire-new dean. Although he
first recommended Dopping, he later took a different stand and
declared he would try to fit in with the archbishop's wishes: 'I
desire only two things: first, that those who call themselves my
friends may have no reason to reproach me; and, the second,
that, in the course of this matter, I may have something to
dispose of to some one I wish well to.'[2]

Of course, the archbishop's general policy was to avoid disposing of anything good to someone Swift wished well to. When
Howard told Swift that the archbishop had 'declared' for him
and that the prebendary now hoped the dean would consent,
Swift told a friend, 'Nothing could put me more against him
than the A.B.'s declaring, and I am resolved to oppose it, as long
as I can.'[3] One wonders how thoroughly he understood that the
archbishop gave precisely the same response to the dean's recommendations. It was almost a year since Swift had complained to King himself, 'that all whom I was disposed to serve
were sure to thrive the worse for my friendship to them'.[4] Only
when Swift offered hard bargains could he hope to influence
King's decisions. But when Swift told Howard that, in return for
his own support, he wished to name the successor to St Anne's,
that sensible prebendary failed to reply.[5] Evidently, both the
archbishop and the dean ended up doing what Howard wished;
for not only did none of Swift's several candidates[6] receive St
Anne's, but Howard kept it for three years after he succeeded to
St Bride's![7]

If one asks how the thread of politics entered into the tangle of

[1] Landa, p. 89.   [2] 19 May 1717, to Walls; Williams ii. 266.
[3] *Ibid.*, p. 268.   [4] *Ibid.*, p. 205.   [5] Landa, p. 89.
[6] Dopping, one of the Grattans, Sam Holt, Forbes.   [7] Landa, p. 90.

such negotiations, the answer is, not as primary motive. Clearly, the archbishop, at least between 1714 and 1720, was inclined to promote Whigs. Clearly, he used their political affiliations as an argument to keep the government on his side. Yet it was hardly the Whig colour that recommended them to him. It was their accommodation to his grace. When King wrote to friends during this period, he made it clear how profoundly he distrusted the Whig administration of Ireland and Whig policy in the Church of Ireland. He was one of those who inspired a man in the English interest to say, 'There is not one [bishop of Irish background] that can justly be called a Whig.'[1] In 1713, when he was rejecting the men whom Swift desired as prebendaries, King supported a Tory candidate for Parliament in these terms:

> I believe him an honest man and well affected to the constitution of church and state. I am informed that he approved himself so last Parliament and did not give one vote to the Whigs. If therefore you design to have such as will not vote for them now, I am of opinion a tried Member is preferable to others.[2]

In 1714, when he did not yet appreciate how firmly Walls had tied himself to Swift, the archbishop said, 'I am now contriving to get Mr Walls into St Nicholas.'[3] He did not wish to appoint Swift's Tory friends, not because they were Tories but because they were aligned with the dean. I wonder whether he would have advanced any Whig clergyman patronized by Swift.

III. IRISH DEAN AND BRITISH BISHOP

Swift's gift for sympathetic anger marked both his conduct and his literary works. When he exercised the power of feeling indignant on behalf of others, those others did not have to be persons he liked or respected. But they were usually the victims of unfair treatment, especially of institutional tyranny or political oppression. The whole kingdom of Ireland excited this rage as Swift saw it trodden under heel by the British. The Church of

---

[1] Froude I. 428–9.   [2] Letter of 26 Oct. 1713, to Billon.
[3] Letter of 7 Dec. 1714, to Stearne.

Ireland drew the same response, for suffering under the greed of Anglican landlords. Within the church Swift, even as a highly privileged dean, identified himself with the lower clergy against the arrogance of many bishops.

Swift's bishop-baiting often found reinforcement in his principles. Among churchmen, for example, the lower clergy were less likely than the bishops to be Whigs or to feel tolerant of Latitudinarian doctrines. In the Church of Ireland the bishops were more likely to be born and educated in England, and launched on ecclesiastical careers there before they accepted a see in Ireland—where episcopal stipends often rose higher than in England, and where the cost of living was less. Consequently, they represented a bundle of connections opposed to the interest of Ireland. The Whigs might have triumphed in the accession of George I, but they had as much trouble infusing their beliefs into the clergy as the Protestants had in converting their Irish Catholic tenants.[1]

When Swift flared up at a bishop, these ideas warmed his anger. John Evans[2] was a proper person to make him blaze. After taking his B.A. degree at Oxford, Evans was ordained and became the rector of a parish. But in 1678, when he was approaching the age of thirty, he went to India as one of the Company's chaplains, remaining for twenty years. There he took such extraordinary advantage of commercial opportunities that he offended the officers of the Company. 'Mr Evans busies himself too much in trade and merchandise, for a man of his coat!' one of them complained.[3] When at last he returned to Britain, he served a parish in Wales for a few years, and then became Bishop of Bangor. In 1716 he was translated to a

---

[1] How deeply they wished to convert them is another question.

[2] Born 1650. His father died about 1658, but his mother sent him to Jesus College, Oxford, where he matriculated 1667 and took the B.A. degree 1671. (In his letter of 12 Feb. 1720 to Archbishop Wake, Evans says he is seventy; in his letter of 16 Sept. 1721 to Wake, he mentions his father's death and his mother's sending him to Oxford. See the Wake Letters in the library of Christ Church, Oxford. I agree with the *DNB* that he is the John Evans who graduated from Jesus College in 1671.) Unless I give other indications, my quotations from the letters of Bishop Evans come from the manuscripts in Christ Church.

[3] *Diary of William Hedges* (Publications of the Hakluyt Society, vol. 74), p. 148.

valuable Irish bishopric and proceeded to work for the English interest in his new country as singlemindedly as Archbishop King worked on the other side. Even his English friend Bishop Godwin of Kilmore said Evans was 'as national [i.e., nationalistic] almost as his grace of Dublin; that is in my mind to some extreme.'[1]

Yet Evans never tired of condemning the nationalism of the Irish. He never tired of delivering confidential reports of their scandalous misdeeds. He rattled away about their hypocrisy and self-service, their disregard for law, and the inability of Englishmen to appreciate their depth of abomination. 'It is hard to conceive', he said, 'there should be so much deceit, hypocrisy, and lying as we daily find.'[2] But paranoia can lead to genuine insights. So Evans only told the truth when he said, 'Among the common people (Protestants I mean) from the least upwards, hardly one of them but looks upon England to be their worst enemy, putting all hardships upon them in respect of trade, etc.'[3]

Swift had ample grounds for disliking Evans. To begin with, the man had been imported from Britain. He was not even English but Welsh, and had shown himself to be Latitudinarian enough for William III to make him a bishop. In the House of Lords he had sided with the Whigs, dutifully opposing the Peace of Utrecht. Under George I he was rewarded with his Irish elevation and the profitable diocese of Meath, in which Swift's country parishes lay.

In spite of their political antipathy, Swift may be trusted when he writes to Evans and recalls,

I had been more than ordinary officious in my respects to you from your first coming over. I waited on you as soon as I knew of your landing. I attended on you in your first journey to Trim. I lent you a useful book relating to your diocese; and repeated my visits, till I saw you never intended to return them.[4]

[1] Wake papers, 12/119b.
[2] Letter of 18 Nov. 1719, to Wake.
[3] 16 Oct. 1717, to Wake.
[4] Williams II. 327.

It was Swift's custom to put men in the wrong if he might be forced to quarrel with them; and in a private letter it would have been absurd for Swift to remind Evans of deeds that were never performed.

From the start, Evans coupled Swift and Archbishop King as twin agents of evil, and never even hinted that they might differ in their politics. Evans believed in maintaining the dignity of the cloth, and was scandalized by a clergyman (not Swift) who published a doggerel ballad—'a pretty employment for a D.D.!'[1] One can imagine what he thought of Swift's efforts. When the great agitation erupted over Irish independency, Evans said,

> Dublin[2] and his dean have (I am told) a great hand in these sad managements. The last invented this new health, viz. 'To the immortal memory of Queen Anne, *who* never hurt Ireland'.[3]

Years afterward, when anglophobia was rising to a new pitch, Evans again invoked the Satanic pair: 'No one has a greater hand in these heats than Dublin and his worthy Dean. Both equally hate every thing called English.'[4]

When Evans wrote to the Archbishop of Canterbury, he exuded the spite of a jealous child. So he sneered at Swift's claim to have moved the remission of the First Fruits.[5] It is always hard for a narrow character to imagine the motives that drive a subtle one. Ignorant of the effort that Swift poured into his mission, ignorant of the satisfaction Swift felt over the service he thought he had performed for his church, Evans saw only vanity in the dean's yearning for recognition.

The bishop complained about the many parsons in Ireland who did not reside on their livings—'under the pretence', he said, 'of want of glebes and a Protestant flock'[6] (i.e., the want of land attached to the living, with a house for the priest's use, and of a congregation that required the service of a Protestant pastor). The complaint against non-residence was well-founded; and Evans was at pains to build a house in which he

---

[1] Wake Letters 12/447. [2] I.e., Archbishop King. [3] 20 Apr. 1720, to Wake.
[4] 28 May 1723, to Wake. [5] Landa, p. 65, n. 2. [6] 10 Jul. 1717; *ibid.*, p. 119.

himself could reside as bishop. He also worked hard supervising his clergy. But it hardly occurred to Evans that he might (like Archbishop King) exemplify the good will and self-sacrifice that he expected of the Irish-born clergy. Instead, he gave his most concentrated attention to the improvement of the episcopal revenues.

When Evans's successor at Bangor, the egregious Benjamin Hoadly, preached his notorious sermon against the right of the church to define doctrine or enforce discipline, the clergy in England and Ireland were horrified; and even the convocation of the English clergy had to be suspended. In Ireland, bishops of the English interest correctly dreaded the effect of a convocation at this time; and Evans warned the Archbishop of Canterbury that Swift might be made prolocutor if a session were held.[1] Soon he was telling Canterbury how Swift and his associates all over Ireland were rallying their party: 'I hear Dr Swift with other dignitaries etc. in several parts of this kingdom endeavour to keep up the spirits of their party by assuring them that the Whigs will soon be down and that their friends will sway.'[2] Half a year later, his political sensibility was set trembling by 'a strange sermon' that Swift preached before the chief officers of the government. 'It was somewhat like one of Montaigne's essays,' he wrote to Canterbury, 'making very free with all orders and degrees of men amongst us—lords, bishops, &c. men in power. The pretended subjects were pride and humiliation.'[3]

The day before Evans wrote this letter, Swift's dear but Whiggish friend, St George Ashe, died, and left the well-paying see of Derry vacant. Evans wished to secure the prize for his English Whig friend Nicolson, and naturally intrigued against Archbishop King's choice, John Stearne. In a flat half-truth he wrote to Canterbury, 'I am told Swift made him [i.e., Stearne] bishop to come into the deanery and is very great with him....

[1] 13, 16, 19 Jul. 1717—Swift mentioned 19 Jul.; *ibid.*, p. 182.
[2] 23 Sept. 1717; *ibid.*
[3] 28 Feb. 1718; *ibid.* I have, as usual, altered the spelling and punctuation. Carl P. Daw has argued persuasively that the sermon in question was *Mutual Subjection* (Davis IX. 141-9); see his article, 'Swift's "Strange Sermon"', *HLQ* 38 (1975), 225-36.

The most knowing and honest among our friends assure me that his bias is toward the disaffected [i.e., the Tories].'[1] As Archbishop King shoved on the other side, the rumour of Stearne's translation lingered, and Evans turned frantic: 'Jonathan Swift, and that tribe are his particular friends and correspondents ...,' he wrote misleadingly; 'in short, he is thought to be Tory ... all over, which (here) is reckon'd by every honest man Jacobite.'[2] He lamented the fact that Theophilus Bolton, Chancellor of St Patrick's Cathedral, was 'entirely govern'd by Swift'—an observation probably meaning only that Bolton, Archbishop King, and Swift were now (in 1719) in substantial agreement as to public policy.[3]

With two such antagonists in the same diocese, a collision easily followed. In the middle of June 1718, Evans as Bishop of Meath held a visitation—or inspection of the clergy of Meath—at Trim. Swift attended as vicar of Laracor. Evans seized the occasion to deliver a public censure of three clergymen who shared the dean's principles. Naturally, Swift was outraged. The next day there was a synod at which the lower clergy had a right to be heard. Swift rose up to speak in a scene recorded (with less than absolute objectivity) but not witnessed by Dr Delany:

> The dean took notice of the treatment which his lordship had given to [his brethren] the day before; and rebuked the bishop, apparently, in the most gentle and respectful manner, and with great coolness of temper; but at the same time, with as much severity, and fine satire, and in one of the finest speeches that ever was uttered.[4]

Swift also promised never again to attend the bishop's visitation if he could lawfully escape the duty.

Evans was not soothed by Swift's eloquence, and conveyed some of his exacerbated emotions to the Archbishop of Canterbury:

[1] 18, 21 Jan. 1718; Landa, p. 182, n. 5.   [2] 22 Apr. 1718; *ibid.*, p. 182.
[3] 5 Feb. 1719; *ibid.*, pp. 182–3. The 'chancellor' must be Bolton because Meath had no chancellor.
[4] Delany, p. 217; cf. the unconvincing version in Deane Swift, pp. 274–5.

I could entertain your grace with the insolent rudeness of Dr Swift at my visitation last week, where he had never appeared before. He endeavoured to arraign me before my clergy for my unkind carriage towards three of them, who were all of them very criminal, as plainly appeared when I stated the several cases—so that I hope he has gained nothing by this vile attempt.[1]

Another visitation of the diocese was scheduled for August, this time by the Primate of all Ireland, Lindsay, who appointed Bishop Stearne of Clogher to assume his function. Pyrotechnics were awaited by those who knew about the June outburst, because a complaint had been registered with the Primate. Bishop Nicolson, newly arrived and warm in his British sympathies, wrote to Canterbury that the Bishop of Clogher would probably

have the rehearing of a late dialogue betwixt the Bishop of Meath and Dean Swift, whereof your grace has already had an account. I have (as desired) given notice of this to my friend [i.e., Bishop Evans]: though my informer knows not whether his lordship or the dean is the complainant.[2]

Since Primate Lindsay held even higher views on church and state than Swift did, and since Stearne was not only an old friend of Swift but also a protégé of Archbishop King (and a former aspirant to the bishopric which Evans had helped Nicolson to get), the Bishop of Meath must have realized that he would only comfort his enemies by carrying the affair further. Anyhow, the scandal seems to have halted here.

But the following year, Swift named a man not yet in holy orders to be his curate, and asked Evans to ordain him. The bishop was furious because an earlier curate of Swift, imbued with sound Tory doctrine, had received a living from the Primate and was therefore sowing the dragon's teeth in a new parish. A man could not properly be ordained until he had the promise of some sort of church living; and Swift was obviously employing his various resources to bring into the church men

[1] 10 Jun. 1718; Landa, 'The Insolent Rudeness of Dr Swift', *MLN* 68 (1953), 223–6; my spelling and punctuation.
[2] 8 Jul. 1718; Landa, *MLN*, p. 225; my spelling and punctuation.

who shared his own principles. He had tried to have his way with Evans a year earlier, before their public duel; but the bishop had refused loftily and rehearsed his triumph for the Archbishop of Canterbury:

> Dr Swift has two rectories here[1] (without dispensation). One of his curates was lately preferred by the Primate, and he would put upon me a curate[2] to be licenced who has a great living in the diocese of Clogher, which I have absolutely refused to do. I hope law, reason, and practice will support me in it. This man is a free liver, and assisting to the dean in keeping up the spirit of the faction[3] among the neighbouring clergy.[4]

By the time Swift asked Evans to ordain a second curate for him, the abyss between them was too deep for simple courtesy; and Evans again refused, even though he knew Swift would merely get a sympathetic bishop to perform the ceremony. Another visitation was approaching, and Swift refused to appear—'not', he said, 'from any contempt of your lordship's jurisdictions, but that I would not put you under the temptation of giving me injurious treatment, which no wise man, if he can avoid it, will receive above once from the same person'.[5] Evans predictably refused to admit Swift's proxy, fruitlessly indulging his spleen at the cost of his reputation.

Two years later, the position was the same. Swift did not attend the bishop's visitation and sent a proxy whom Evans did not admit. Now Swift wrote him a letter reviewing the case in a style that joined the coolness admired by Delany to the astringency habitual with Swift. He concluded as follows:

> I am only sorry that you, who are of a country famed for good-nature, have found a way to unite the hasty passion of your own countrymen, with the long, sedate resentment of a Spaniard: But I have an honourable hope, that this proceeding has been more owing to party than complexion.[6]

---

[1] I.e., in the diocese of Meath.
[2] Probably Mr Warren, mentioned in Williams II. 266.
[3] I.e., Tories.
[4] 24 Jun. 1717; Landa, p. 182.
[5] 22 May 1719; Williams II. 327.
[6] 5 Jun. 1721; *ibid.*, pp. 389–90.

One might be surprised that Swift contented himself with so mild a chastisement if a mysterious paragraph had not appeared, a few months afterward, in a London newspaper. It was a false announcement of Evans's death, slyly insinuating that his family was mean, that he himself was avaricious, and that he had finally changed from Whig to Tory in his political allegiance:

he was promoted to the see of Bangor, worth about five or six hundred pounds per annum; and from thence in the present reign, translated to the rich see and diocese of Meath in this kingdom, which he farmed out at two thousand three hundred pounds per annum. He was a man at his first coming over esteemed entirely zealous for the present government, but he was justly suspected afterwards of favouring some contrary principles, and has not in the general opinion of people here, died much lamented.[1]

This delicious hoax infuriated Evans, who assigned it at once to the hand of Swift and emitted the usual bleats to Canterbury:

I verily believe Jonathan Swift is the inditer of the letter, which is so full of falsities in fact that I was not much moved when I read the prints; only it grieved me that the villain said I changed my principles.

He went on to refute the hints of the hasty necrologist,[2] and gave two reasons for the malice shown against him by Swift and other aborigines:

One is, because [the bishop] was thought to be (in our last session)[3] the most zealous stickler against their claims of independency etc. and to have influenced all his English brethren to be of the same opinion with himself in those matters .... The other is (besides the innate malice of the man) that he and others lately fearing the Archbishop of Dublin would soon drop off, and that the Bishop of Meath (in their opinion) was to succeed him, they betook themselves [to] the wretched methods of lying, slandering etc. which they thought the best way to prevent such a succession.[4]

---

[1] Davis XIV. 41; my spelling. Although Williams (II. 390, n. 1) dismisses the attribution, I accept it, partly because of the skilfulness of the hoax and partly because Swift had played such tricks before. Apart from the Bickerstaff papers, there is the allusion to Lambert's principles in the *Letter concerning the Sacramental Test* (Davis II. 284).
[2] Davis XIV. xiv.   [3] I.e., of Parliament.   [4] Davis XIV. xiv.

These clues are attractive guides to speculation, but history does not disclose what success the bishop had in clearing his character.

Happily enough, when Evans died in fact, two-and-a-half years later, he performed a deed that not only softened Swift but associated the bishop in a most acceptable way with the lower clergy; for he left his entire estate for 'the benefit of the poorer clergy' of England, Wales, and Ireland.[1]

[1] Williams III. 11 and n. 5.

Chapter Three

THE EXILE'S FRIENDS

I. CHETWODE

A disturbing appeal of Swift's work is his refusal to stratify virtue. He rarely associates poverty with high moral character, except as it eliminates some temptations to evil. He rarely associates greatness with goodness except when he compliments patrons or heroes on their lineage. The wide range of Swift's friendships, from a Duke of Ormonde to the curate at Laracor, taught him how little a man's piety or good will depends on his money or his name. Of course, youthful anglophilia sometimes disarmed Swift; and *A Tale of a Tub* shows how early he framed an ideal figure combining high social class, moral integrity, and intellectual distinction. But at home in Ireland, he was too close to the gentry and the aristocracy to be misled. If he liked some of them, it was not because he revered their status.

It is therefore a pathetic mark of Swift's solitude that he let a man so graceless as Knightley Chetwode establish himself as a good friend of the dean. Chetwode searched Swift out when he felt friendless, and courted him when he felt slighted. The attacks on Swift that appeared in print suggest how vulnerable he was to what Johnson has called the 'mutilation of a compliment'.[1] One pamphleteer, in a clever parody of Swift's diary letters, attacked the dean as irreligious and time-serving.[2] In another pamphlet Swift appeared as Jonathan Wormwood, the Tories' amanuensis, 'a companion and hanger on' to Lord Oxford, and an evil, lying scribbler against the Whigs.[3] In yet

---

[1] Johnson, review of S. Jenyns, in *Works*, ed. F. P. Walesby (Oxford, 1825), VI, 55.
[2] *An Hue and Cry after Dr S——t*, 1714.
[3] *A Farther Continuation of the History of the Crown-Inn*, Part III, 1714.

another he is named 'Smut', and is described as an infidel and as a toady to Lord Oxford.[1]

With such labels pinned on him and no one to disprove the charges, Swift had to guard himself against random acquaintanceships. To avoid acute embarrassments in conversation, he had to avoid the company of those who might wish to humiliate him. Pride and caution turned him toward men whose opinions were at least as strong on the Tory side as his own. Rising clergymen who held other political doctrines must have been eager to escape any appearance of friendship with Swift; and since clergymen were his ordinary source of new companions, his social horizons had to shrink. Even the blameless George Berkeley suffered from Swift's patronage; and an ambitious young parson competing with Berkeley for a Dublin church described him as an abject Tory and Jacobite who 'has been and is still a creature of Dean Swift'.[2] Though the Prince of Wales recommended Berkeley for this living, the Lords Justices opposed him as politically unreliable, and he lost it.[3]

At Dublin Castle, of course, the dean could not have been less welcome. In social terms he had lost the whole of officialdom—the viceregal court, the Parliament men, the bureaucracy. What he said many years later about this situation is hyperbolic but not essentially false, i.e., that when he came to Ireland in 1714, he 'hardly knew two faces in the nation'.[4]

It was in the summer of 1714 that Chetwode, a nosy, abrasive squire, fastened himself on the dean. Chetwode was much younger than Swift. His grandfather, moneyless but descended from the well-known family in Buckinghamshire, had come over to Ireland, like Swift's family, at the Restoration. Like Godwin Swift, this grandfather had rebuilt his family's fortune with

---

[1] *The Enigmatical Court*, 1714.

[2] Letter of 14 Mar. 1716, from Mr Duke Tyrrell to Robert Molesworth, forwarded by Molesworth to Stanhope, P.R.O., S.P. 63/374.

[3] Luce, p. 75.

[4] Letter to Lord Castle-Durrow, 24 Dec. 1736; Williams IV. 556. Cf. the acute and persuasive analysis by James Woolley supporting Swift's claim, in later years, that he 'was not acquainted with' (i.e., did not exchange visits with) Irish peers or bishops: 'Autobiography in Swift's Verses on His Death', *Contemporary Studies in Swift's Poetry*, ed. J.I. Fischer *et al.* (Newark, Del., 1981), pp. 118–20.

the help of the first Duke of Ormonde. The grandson and only surviving heir married in 1700 the heiress of a Devonshire family that had also emigrated to Ireland.[1] Swift liked her mother, Mrs Stopford, and of course her half-brother, James Stopford, a young priest who was destined to become one of Swift's confidants.

Although he often lived in Dublin, Chetwode owned two country seats, Woodbrook and Martry. But instead of taking up his position as a responsible and influential landlord, he ran after titled aristocrats, indulged himself in extravagant building programmes, and joined in the visionary manœuvres of the Pretenders' partisans. He lacked not intelligence but direction. Yet he possessed attractions: he was eager to be Swift's host, and he talked engagingly.

The most disgusting of Chetwode's faults was his morbid suspiciousness. Less than a year after they met, Swift had to assure him that he had not (as somebody declared) made malicious remarks against Chetwode.[2] The self-indulgent squire confused a quick temper with courage and mistook vindictiveness for honour. He loved notoriety and bored listeners with the names of grandees whom he claimed to know. Swift once said he wished Chetwode would swear 'never to mention a prince or princess, a foreign or domestic lord, an intrigue of state or of love'.[3] It was Chetwode's passion for involvement in great public affairs and for intimacy (real or imagined) with magnificoes that drove him to pursue the Dean of St Patrick's. Clinging but prickly, he was a burr in Swift's life for over seventeen years.

Although Swift had known Mrs Chetwode as a child,[4] he cooled toward her husband after a rash and almost ruinous visit that Chetwode made to Ormonde and the Jacobite exiles in France. Not his silly politics but his tiresome chatter was what alienated the dean. Swift called him Ventoso;[5] and after four years of Chetwode's aggressive amiability Swift told Charles Ford,

[1] Swift, *Unpublished Letters*, ed. G. B. Hill (London, 1899), p. xxiv.
[2] Williams II. 191.   [3] *Ibid.*, V. 251.
[4] *Ibid.*, III. 339.   [5] *Ibid.*, V. 250.

I desire I may never hear more from you of the person you reproach me with. Since his coming from abroad I have had twenty letters from him, teazing me to death to write to him about an information he apprehends against him, and about his family.... He came to know me in spite of my teeth, and writes to me in spite of my teeth, and there's an end.[1]

When Chetwode quarrelled with his wife and decided on a separation from her, Swift's coolness sank to frigidity; and though Chetwode kept after him, the last six years of their connection were absurdly one-sided. Finally, Swift told him, 'Your whole scheme of thinking, conversing, and living, differs in every point from mine.'[2]

II. SHERIDAN

For the comforts of real friendship, Swift had to go outside Chetwode's social scene, to a man with no advantage of rank and no guile. About the middle of 1717, the dean got to know Thomas Sheridan, a brilliant schoolmaster whose charm and learning made him an irresistible companion.[3] Sheridan was twenty years his junior; but once Swift was introduced to him, the middle-aged dean was wholly fascinated, and the two remained on terms that seem more like boyish affection than mature friendship. The slender little man's audacity exasperated Swift as Sheridan's blending of Feste with Parson Adams delighted him.

---

[1] *Ibid.*, II. 306.

[2] *Ibid.*, III. 462. Since the letters to Chetwode contain some of Swift's strongest representations of his bad health, a warning is appropriate. Chetwode belonged eminently to the class of men whom one avoids; and Swift regularly found it convenient to play up his ailments as a screen against the squire's possessiveness; e.g. *ibid.*, II. 306.

[3] In his accounts under the date 11 Dec. 1717 Swift records giving 5s 5d 'at the Greek play', which I take to mean a play put on by Sheridan's pupils (*Accounts 1717–18*, fol. 12ᵛ); Sheridan was celebrated for producing such plays. (In Nicolson's *Letters*, under the date 10 Dec. 1724, Sheridan's students are mentioned as giving a Greek play [II. 590].) The productions may well have been annual events, but the work chosen was not always Greek. It was *Julius Caesar* in 1718 and 1732, and the *Adelphi* on at least two other occasions (as James Woolley has generously informed me). Swift dined with Sheridan and others ca. 17 May 1718, also 30 Aug. and ca. 27 Sept. (*Accounts*, fols. 6ᵛ, 9, 9ᵛ). On 25 Dec. 1734 Sheridan wrote to Swift that it was 'above sixteen years' since Swift had met him (Williams IV. 281). Swift's poem *Ad amicum eruditum Thomam Sheridan* is dated October 1717 in Faulkner's edition; see *Poems* I. 211.

For all the fame of his descendants, Sheridan's origins remain obscure.[1] He was born in county Cavan (1687), and his father's name was Patrick. After schooling in Dublin, he went to Trinity College at the curiously late age of twenty. But he did so well there that in his third year he was elected to one of the 'native' scholarships. He took his B.A. degree in 1711. Marriage quickly followed, to the heiress of a Cavan landlord named McFadden. But the estate his wife brought him could not support their family, and Sheridan opened a boys' school in Capel Street, Dublin. Domesticity easily exhausted any fund of affection the couple may have started with; and Mrs Sheridan was seldom named by her husband or by Swift without a train of pejoratives. In his will Sheridan would call his wife 'unkind' and cut her off with five shillings.[2] Yet she gave him all the children he could wish for; and in 1719 Swift was able to stand godfather to their third and most distinguished son, the father of the playwright.[3]

Sheridan shared some of the defects that spoiled Chetwode. He was extravagant and over-hospitable; he held high Tory principles and quarrelled with his wife. But so far from being suspicious or vindictive, he was much too trustful. Swift found his absent-mindedness maddening, and did not sympathize with his addiction to mathematics and music—he was a violinist. It was Sheridan's learning that Swift bowed to; it was his humour and ebullience that Swift loved. The two men amused each other with learned games; they praised and insulted each other, fought and made up like schoolmates. Swift's admiration for Sheridan's skill as a teacher appears in a charming (if unclassical) Latin eulogy:

> Aureus at ramus venerandae dona Sibyllae,
> Aeneae sedes tantum patefecit Avernas:
> Saepe puer, tua quem tetigit semel aurea virga,
> Coelumque terrasque videt, noctemque profundam.[4]

[1] For accurate information about Dr Sheridan I am indebted to information supplied by James Woolley, both in person and in his excellent essay, 'Thomas Sheridan and Swift', in *Studies in Eighteenth-Century Culture*, ed. R. Runte, 9 (1979), 93–114.

[2] Esther K. Sheldon, *Thomas Sheridan of Smock-Alley* (Princeton, 1967), p. 19, n. 86.

[3] Sheridan, pp. 373–5.   [4] *Poems* I. 214.

(The golden bough, gift of the reverend sibyl, laid open to Aeneas only the regions of Hell: often a boy whom your gold wand has once touched, sees heaven and earth and the deep night.)

A sign of how deeply Swift attached himself to Sheridan is his handling of an early quarrel between them, for here Swift chose to act as he acted with others to whom he felt ambivalently close. For instance, when Vanessa once worried Swift by her indiscreet behaviour, he wrote a letter to a common friend with a passage analysing the girl's character. Then he sent the letter to Vanessa, unsealed, for her to deliver to the friend. She was of course intended to read it and discover her faults.[1] Swift had used the same indirection when he was furious with Steele. He had written a letter on the subject to Addison, suggesting that he go between them.[2]

The difference with Sheridan began in an elaborate literary contest which the two men carried on. One used to send the other a riddle or a message in rhyme. The recipient had to answer as fast as he could with a rhyming solution or challenge. The verses tended to become mock-panegyrics or low insults, and the level of the humour quickly sank. Swift's private wit of this sort often sounded close to contempt. He expected younger or humbler comrades to accept these familiarities without resentment and to imitate them without his asperity—as adults tease children but do not want mockery from them. Swift implied that for him to play in verse with men so much his junior showed a certain benevolence of attention. The others, being in no position to confer favours, must keep their ridicule within the pale of respect. The relation, though hard to define, is obviously like that between teacher and pupil or parent and child.

But Sheridan was too mercurial for rules like this to hold him. The vivacity that charmed Swift with a cascade of witticisms could also madden him by an act of disrespect. 'His thoughts are sudden,' said Swift, 'and the most unreasonable always comes uppermost.'[3] In their rhyming contests Sheridan's coarseness

---

[1] Williams I. 275–9.   [2] *Ibid*., pp. 347–8.   [3] Davis V. 223.

outran Swift's, and his belligerence mortified the touchy dean. In one poem Swift affectionately warned Sheridan that what seemed funny to him was disgusting to Swift:

> My offers of peace you ill understood.
> Friend Sheridan, when will you know your own good?
> 'Twas to teach you in modester language your duty;
> For, were you a dog, I could not be rude t'ye.[1]

Swift uneasily expected him to commit an outrage and unmistakably warned him to be cautious. But Sheridan was too headstrong for the most explicit hints and plunged ahead, heavily campaigning for the doggerel laureateship:

> Thy rhymes, which whilom made thy pride swell,
> Now jingle like a rusty bridle:
> Thy verse, which ran both smooth and sweet,
> Now limp upon their gouty feet.[2]

Soon, working on the theme of the death of Swift's muse, Sheridan went so far as to write a long poem describing the muse's funeral, complete with asses and owls; and he liked this production enough to circulate it among their friends.[3]

Swift fumed. He could not trust himself to discuss the affair with Sheridan and could not bear to give up seeing him. A beautiful letter from Addison, blowing freshly upon the coals of their old friendship, arrived about this time and may have reminded Swift of the awkwardness with Steele.[4] He certainly let himself indulge again in the manœuvre that in Steele's case had failed so unpleasantly.

To begin with, Swift wrote a verse essay on wit. This he addressed not to Sheridan himself but to their friend, Patrick Delany. The poem opens with praise of Delany, goes on to an examination of 'humor, raillery, and wit', and closes with a warning that Sheridan had been abusive when he meant to be witty. The lines are not only better polished and more interesting than the childish couplets Swift had been matching with

---

[1] *Poems* III. 968.   [2] *Ibid.*, p. 970.   [3] Davis V. 222.
[4] Williams II. 298-9.

Sheridan. They are also a good example of Swift's literary criticism:

> Voiture in various lights displays
> That irony which turns to praise,
> His genius first found out the rule
> For an obliging ridicule:
> He flatters with peculiar air
> The brave, the witty, and the fair;
> And fools would fancy he intends
> A satyr where he most commends.[1]

In the poem Swift gives a neat characterization of Sheridan—

> Who full of humor, fire and wit,
> Not allways judges what is fit;
> But loves to take prodigious rounds,
> And sometimes walks beyond his bounds.[2]

But he reveals his own psychology when he asks Delany to set their friend right.

Even this degree of indirection was not enough for Swift. He shied away from talking openly with Delany about his uneasiness. His hesitancies are visible, since he held on to the poem for a month (10 October to 10 November). He must have been wondering whether or not to give it to Sheridan. Meanwhile, he went ahead duelling in verse with him, but dropped new hints of his vexation. When Swift went so far as to call the schoolmaster a goose, Sheridan in turn felt aggrieved. Halfway through a teasing epistle, Swift tried to mollify him:

> You're my goose, and no other man's;
> And you know all my geese are swans.[3]

Yet he also closed the poem with a caution against jokes about Swift's death. Sheridan missed the point and ridiculed the warning, in language that tells us why Swift, who loved him, rebuked him:

> Though you call me a goose, you pitiful slave,
> I'll feed on the grass that grows on your grave.[4]

---

[1] *Poems* I. 216.   [2] *Ibid.*, p. 218.   [3] *Ibid.*, III. 983.   [4] *Ibid.*, p. 984.

To control and employ his irritation, Swift now withdrew behind a mask; for he came back at Sheridan with *Mary the Cook-Maid's Letter*, a cunningly rhymed poem in the style of *Mrs Harris's Petition*. In these seesawing couplets, the dean takes on his cook-maid's voice in order to repeat the warning against rude jokes. Mary speaks:

> You say you will eat grass on his grave: a Christian eat grass!
> Whereby you now confess your self to be a goose or an ass.[1]

Thus even while he was about to let Delany convey the dean's views as his own, Swift impersonated yet another speaker delivering the same message. It is one more instance of his most notorious literary device showing itself in his private conduct. The poem also happens to have seductive humour, giving us, in Mary the cook-maid, the sense of a lovable character, strongly individual, whose speech abounds in aromatic turns of phrase. The mask of his lowly 'sweetheart' clearly enriched Swift's imagination.

Compared with *Mrs Harris's Petition*, the later poem has striking features. The author's delight in impersonating a woman suggests a triumph over deep uneasiness. Mrs Harris was ridiculed, and one reason was that she set her eyes on the chaplain whom she had offended. *Mary the Cook-Maid* is not satirical. The speaker in fact performs one of Swift's favourite roles, the defence of a man unfairly maligned; and her fondness for the dean is reciprocated by him. Yet the earlier poem has stronger elements of drama and narrative, a larger setting, and a variety of amusing portraits. It remains the more interesting work.

When the month was up, the uneasy dean at last took action. He sent the verse essay on wit to Delany along with a letter begging him to keep Swift's appeal a secret. In the letter he said that a number of Sheridan's compositions, especially *The Funerall*, broke the rules of friendly teasing. 'If you think the same,' he went on, 'you ought to tell him so in the manner you

---

[1] *Ibid.*, p. 986.

like best, without bringing me into the question, else I may be thought a man who will not take a jest.'[1]

Delany was a sedate though genial character who did think the same. So he passed a copy of the poem on to Sheridan. The transaction was full of risks from beginning to end. But Swift had judged his man correctly, and the event was near enough to what he wanted. Sheridan felt so contrite that he burned his copy of Swift's poem.[2] With this misery past, the volatile rhymesters could return to their contests in doggerel; and the new effusions were noticeably less provocative than the old.

There are morals to the tale. Swift had subjected Sheridan to the sort of test he liked to give candidates for friendship. The egregious Chetwode was spared the challenge. But Oxford and Bolingbroke had faced their tests when Swift forced quarrels on them. A passing mark did not mean intimacy was guaranteed. It did mean Swift hoped for intimacy—hoped so hard, he had to mask the desire with a show of reluctance. That a schoolmaster twenty years his junior could now mean so much to Swift is a token of the change in his spirit. It is a question whether he would have made himself available to Sheridan if he had not endured the privations of Ireland under George I. The heart-aches that gave life to Gulliver also let Swift set a proper value on the charms of his new friend.

[1] Williams II. 301.

[2] Delany, pp. 17–18. By 'the person they were addressed to', Delany means Sheridan, not himself.

Chapter Four

THE DEAN AS PRIEST

I. FAITH AND WORKS

In a mind as subtle as Swift's one does not expect to find a simple form of religious faith. Swift himself supports this view by such remarks as, 'I am not answerable to God for the doubts that arise in my own breast, since they are the consequence of that reason which he hath planted in me,'[1] or his comment on the Nicene Creed: 'confessio fidei barbaris digna'.[2] Swift's frivolous treatment of several Christian doctrines violates one's idea of an orthodox priest. A man who writes a comic rhapsody on the number of the Trinity,[3] or who handles the Reformation in terms of Big-Endians and Little-Endians, hardly sounds pious.

Yet in his private notes and marginalia, and the intimate records of his behaviour, Swift bears out the character of 'hypocrite renversé' given him by Bolingbroke. The best evidence we have of his performance as a parish priest comes from two prebendaries of his cathedral, Patrick Delany and John Lyon. Their observations range back and forth over a twenty-year period. They knew Swift's acquaintances as well as the dean himself; and Lyon, who saw him most when he was declining, had access to Swift's personal papers and made a start on writing a biography.

---

[1] Davis IX. 262.

[2] 'A creed suitable for barbarians' (*ibid.*, XIV. 35). The tone is ironic. Swift means it is foolish for a missionary to expect uninformed barbarians to grasp and be attracted to the creed. He is not commenting on the creed itself.

[3] See the 'Introduction' to *A Tale of a Tub* (*ibid.*, I. 35). The satire is directed against the polemical writers who produced a great controversy over the doctrine of the Trinity during the years around the turn of the eighteenth century. It is not directed against the doctrine.

[69]

Dr Delany gives an illuminating account of Swift's management of family prayers:

> [Delany] resided with him for more than six months, before he knew, or so much as suspected that ever he read prayers to his family [i.e., household]. Which nevertheless he constantly did, at a fixed hour every night, in his own bed-chamber. To which the servants regularly and silently resorted, at the time appointed: without any notice from a bell, or audible call of any kind; except the striking of a clock.[1]

Dr Lyon has an equally penetrating story:

> [When] his deafness increased, his friends retired about ten o'clock after which he spent some time in his private devotion, and made use of the liturgy of the church as his pattern for prayer, turning such parts thereof to his own private occasions as he thought proper— His prayer book (which I have) being fouled with the snuff of his fingers shews the parts thereof he most approved of.[2]

These descriptions suggest a traditional piety screened by an unconventional character. They suggest the faith of a man who could write, 'The Scripture-system of man's creation, is what Christians are bound to believe, and seems most agreeable of all others to probability and reason. Adam was formed from a piece of clay, and Eve from one of his ribs.'[3] It was in fact precisely Swift's desire for simplicity in religious principles that produced his appearance of frivolity. Of the Athanasian Creed, he said to a congregation, 'Although it is useful for edification to those who understand it; yet, since it contains some nice and philosophical points which few people can comprehend, the bulk of mankind is obliged to believe no more than the Scripture-doctrine [of the Trinity], as I have delivered it.'[4]

An eagerness to keep the principles of Christianity simple and rational marked the thinking of most Anglican divines at the time. This branch of Hooker's great argument flourished in the forest of apologetics. Swift's contemporary, Archbishop Synge, wrote, 'All the duties of religion, which God requires of any man, must needs be easy enough for him to understand, how-

---

[1] Delany, p. 44.   [2] Lyon, p. 31.
[3] Davis IX. 264.   [4] *Ibid.*, p. 160.

ever hard they may be to be practised.' Nearly all religious controversies, Synge declared, proceeded not from the difficulty of determining the 'things necessary in religion' but from humbler causes:

> *partly from the pride of some learned men*, who have loved to start new and difficult questions, and to impose their private sentiments upon the world, that they might be admired for their wit and subtlety; *partly from the covetousness and ambition of some*, whether learned or unlearned, who have found that their worldly interest will be better served by some doctrines (no matter how false and precarious) than by others; *and partly from the prejudice of most men*, who are apt with great zeal and eagerness, to contend for all those things which, from their childhood, they have been taught to have a reverence for.[1]

Rejecting the obscure, the complex, and the passionate, Synge races toward clarity, simplicity, and rationality as signs of true doctrine. So does the author of *A Tale of a Tub* and *Gulliver's Travels*. Like the coats of Martin and his brothers, Christianity for Swift had to be a seamless garment, 'fitted to all times, places, and circumstances'.[2] Like Gulliver among the Houyhnhnms, Swift ridiculed the stiff-neckedness of those who fought over differences in opinions—'whether *flesh* be *bread*, or *bread* be *flesh*: whether the juice of a certain *berry* be *blood* or *wine*', and so forth.[3] How commonplace such views were, I may suggest by quoting the words not of a learned theologian but of Swift's master, Sir William Temple: 'For Christianity, it came into the world, and so continued in the first age, without the least pretence of learning and knowledge, with the greatest simplicity of thought and language.'[4]

If a doctrine was essential to salvation, Swift thought, it must be demonstrable from Scripture, reason, and authority.[5] If it

---

[1] Edward Synge, *A Gentleman's Religion*, 6th ed. (London, 1737), pp. 4–5.
[2] *Tale*, p. 73, n.†.　　[3] Davis XI. 246.　　[4] *Miscellanea* III. 266.
[5] 'God hath placed conscience in us to be our director only in those actions which Scripture and reason plainly tell us to be good or evil. But in cases too difficult or doubtful for us to comprehend or determine, there conscience is not concerned; because it cannot advise in what it doth not understand, nor decide where it is itself in doubt: But, by God's great mercy, those difficult points are never of absolute necessity to our salvation' (Davis IX. 150–1).

was not essential, the individual should conform to the practice of his nation. What then could be left to quarrel about? 'Violent zeal for truth hath an hundred to one odds to be either petulancy, ambition, or pride,' said Swift.[1] Consequently, he aimed his satire against the trouble-makers. God could hardly mind whether or not we thought bread was flesh; and only petulant, ambitious, or proud men would compel others to say it was. Peace is difficult enough to maintain in a state or an institution without the efforts of fools and knaves to assert their dangerous opinions. As Tillotson said, 'All truth is good, and all error bad; but there are many truths so inconsiderable, and which have so small an influence upon practice, that they do not deserve our zeal and earnest contention about them.'[2]

Swift's view was that the Established Church, with all its faults, was the best one available. His simply duty was to strengthen it every way he could, and to preach its plain word. 'I look upon myself, in the capacity of a clergyman, to be one appointed by Providence for defending a post assigned me, and for gaining over as many enemies as I can.'[3] One reason he marched so willingly to defend the church was precisely that it looked frail. Like his other heroes, Irish Episcopal Christianity faced defeat.

By fortifying that limb of the church which belonged to him alone, Swift could most conveniently infuse some strength into the whole body. From the time the government preferred him to Laracor, Swift laboured to improve the living. He worked up the original acre of glebe with a canal bordered by willows and a walk alongside it. He built a 'neat cabin' valued at sixty pounds, to make a manse. He kept the church in excellent repair.[4] There were yet two elements of the living that he wished above all to enhance: the glebe and the stipend.

In the summer of 1716 Swift opened negotiations with his land-hungry parishioner, John Percival. Swift wished to buy

---

[1] *Ibid.*, p. 261.
[2] On Rom. x. 2, 'Danger of Zeal' (Tillotson II. 177).
[3] Davis IX. 262.   [4] Landa, p. 39.

twenty acres outright from Percival by drawing on the First Fruits fund of the Church of Ireland, and to lease an additional twenty acres at a fine (or immediate payment) of fifty-five pounds and a fixed annual rent of fourteen pounds. He planned to beautify the property until his successors should come into 'forty acres of good glebe, with house, gardens, etc.' for only fourteen pounds a year. The scheme would cost him, he estimated, two hundred and fifty pounds.[1]

As it turned out, Percival was hard to handle, and other blocks arose until finally Swift was satisfied to have the twenty acres and no more. Although Percival got two hundred pounds for this property, it was not Swift but the trustees of the First Fruits who supplied the money.[2]

It was now that Swift gave voice once more to his old, pathetic wish that some public notice be taken of his role in the remission of the First Fruits. When he applied to the trustees, he asked them to add a clause to the deeds stating that he had been instrumental in procuring the First Fruits for the Church of Ireland. The Board met in June 1716 and approved the transfer of Percival's land.[3] They met in October and ordered Swift's deeds to be engrossed. But at no time and in no place did they record any allusion to his special request.[4] At a meeting of the Board two years later, Swift's friends moved that he be thanked for his good services to the church. But one of the trustees was Welbore Ellis, Bishop of Kildare and Dean of Christ Church, Dublin. Swift had deliberately offended this bishop by ending the custom that prebendaries of St Patrick's should preach in turn at the other cathedral. Archbishop King was still in litigation with the bishop over the question of his own enthronement. Ellis opposed the motion, and it was lost.[5] Swift's old ache was to remain unsolaced.

---

[1] Williams II. 235–6, correcting Ball and Landa; my spelling and punctuation.

[2] Landa, pp. 40–1; Registry of Deeds, Dublin, memorial no. 8629. The map of the property mentioned in Swift's letter of 13 Dec. 1716 to Archdeacon Walls is in the collection of the late Sir Harold Williams, now in the Cambridge University Library.

[3] Williams II. 218, n. 2. [4] Ball II. 336 and n. 3.

[5] Landa, p. 65, n. 2. My assumption that the motion was made in Convocation in 1711 is wrong; see above II. 403.

The other gift which the vicar made to his vicarage was more straightforward. To raise the stipend of Laracor, Swift decided to buy for himself and his successors the impropriate tithes of a small rectory called Effernock in the neighbouring parish of Trim. These tithes belonged to Swift's friend Anthony Raymond, rector of Trim; the trustees were Bishop Ashe and his bibulous brother Tom; so the negotiation made little trouble for the philanthropist. Yet though the first deed was signed in June 1718, the last was not done till April 1722. Swift says in his will that he paid two hundred and sixty pounds for these tithes.[1]

II. PREACHING

Such material, forthright actions on behalf of the church testify that Swift took personal responsibility for the institution, whatever faults he might find with the priests and congregations. He cared for it as instinctively as he contributed to his mother's support. His attitude toward preaching was straightforward too. He never doubted its importance, though he often bemoaned its inefficacy. Dr Lyon reports Swift as saying that while he strove to preach well, he lacked the talents for it. This is why he would not publish any sermons when his friends pressed him to do so.[2] Delany says Swift would complain that his involvement in public affairs diverted him from early ambitions to shine in the pulpit. (His ordinary conversation ran more to politics than religion.)[3] As a young man Swift had hoped—said Delany—that by study and practice he might become so well known for his sermons that people would ask the sexton on Sunday morning, 'Pray, does the Doctor preach today?' But Swift felt he had given too much of his mind to politics and that when he did exert himself, 'he could never rise higher than *preaching pamphlets*.'[4]

If these remarks encourage anyone to think Swift took his

[1] Landa, p. 41; Davis XIII. 152–3; Registry of Deeds, Dublin, memorials no. 15200, 18573, 20445.
[2] Lyon, p. 75.   [3] Orrery, p. 5; Delany, p. 38.
[4] Delany, pp. 41–2; Pilkington I. 52; Lyon, p. 75.

preaching lightly, they are misleading. Lyon says the dean used to hear the choir sing the anthem on Sunday evening although he had no taste for music. He would sit with the score before him; and while he could not read the notes, he would follow the words to make sure the choir left none out.[1] With preachers Swift went further. Delany says,

> As soon as any one got up into the pulpit, he pulled out his pencil, and a piece of paper, and carefully noted every wrong pronunci- ation, or expression, that fell from him. Whether too hard, or scholastic (and of consequence, not sufficiently intelligible to a vulgar hearer) or such as he deemed, in any degree, improper, indecent, slovenly, or mean; and those, he never failed to admonish the preacher of, as soon as he came into the chapter-house.[2]

With his short, plump figure and prominent blue eyes Swift must have been less striking in public devotions than in private. His eyebrows were heavy; his complexion lacked colour.[3] His voice, when he read prayers, was not graceful and harmonious but strong and sharp.[4] Yet he could move listeners by his manner. When he said grace, he employed few words, lifted up his clasped hands, no higher than his breast, and spoke 'with an emphasis and fervor which everyone around him saw, and felt'.[5]

Swift may have run down his sermons; but when it came his turn to preach at the cathedral, he was 'well attended by a crowded audience'.[6] It is hard to think he did not enjoy the opportunity of broadcasting his opinions every fifth Sunday. Arbuthnot congratulated Swift on the privilege: 'I can never imagine any man can be uneasy, that has the opportunity of venting himself to a whole congregation once a week.'[7] That Swift laboured on his sermons and followed his own advice to young parsons, is easy to establish.

The one sermon preserved in manuscript was begun a week before Swift delivered it and finished five days later. He wrote

---

[1] Lyon, p. 75.   [2] Delany, pp. 206–7.
[3] So I interpret the expressions in 'Lady A—s—n Weary of the Dean': 'His tallow face and wainscot paws,/His beetle-brows and eyes of wall' (*Poems* III. 861).
[4] Orrery, p. 5; Delany, p. 42.   [5] Delany, p. 43.   [6] Lyon, p. 75.
[7] Williams II. 144.

the entire work out in a large round hand on twenty numbered pages with margins and indented paragraphs. Naturally, he made changes as he wrote, and many pages may be fair copies of drafts that grew illegible. To get his intonation right, Swift put a broad, sloping stroke above words he meant to emphasize in irony. Since all these details agree with his own description of a good preacher's habits, I suppose the rest of that description also applies to Swift, i.e., that he read the sermon aloud once or twice for a few days, and then

> on Sunday morning, he took care to run it over five or six times, which he could do in an hour; and when he delivered it, by pretending to turn his face from one side to the other, he would (in his own expression) pick up the lines, and cheat his people, by making them believe he had it all by heart.[1]

Intelligibility is what Swift put first in his prescription for good preaching. He wished the congregation to hear distinctly and to understand each word he uttered. The fuss he made over diction has this great purpose. When Swift criticized a preacher's vocabulary, he paid little attention to literary decorum. He condemned slang drawn from common pastimes like card-games, and he condemned coarse words. Otherwise he barely noticed whether the language of a sermon was refined or elevated enough for the occasion. If he warned young parsons against clichés and unnecessary epithets, he was only stating an axiom of all good style. The peculiar desideratum of a sermon is to avoid hard words, obscure words, highly literary expressions: 'For a divine hath nothing to say to the wisest congregation of any parish in this kingdom, which he may not express in a manner to be understood by the meanest among them.'[2]

More fundamental than any issue of diction or phrasing are Swift's views on pathos, or the emotional appeal proper to sermons. Here is his principle of decorum. It is easy to say he disliked deeply impassioned speech because it was the mark of

[1] Davis IX. 71. My paragraph is derived from Herbert Davis, 'The Manuscript of Swift's Sermon on Brotherly Love', in *Pope and His Contemporaries: Essays Presented to George Sherburn* (Oxford, 1949), pp. 147–58.
[2] Davis IX. 66.

the old Puritans and the new Methodists. But in fact Puritans often delivered rational, coolly analytical sermons; and if Anglicans had never produced 'enthusiastic' sermons, there would have been no point in Swift's warning the clergy of his own church against the danger. It would be more illuminating to say that Swift's character gave rise to both his obsession with clarity and his disgust with enthusiasm. Reason, for Swift, was an element of human nature that needed all the strengthening it could get against the inroads of fantasy and feeling. A style intended to convey proper thoughts must almost by definition appeal to the rational part of humanity. In terms of decorum, reason calls for simplicity and clarity.

In his letters Swift rarely mentions preaching except as a job to be done. If he refers to his sermons, it is normally to speak ill of them. When he was thirty years old, he wrote to a parson friend who had found and transcribed some,

> Those sermons you have thought fit to transcribe will utterly dis-grace you, unless you have so much credit that whatever comes from you will pass; they were what I was firmly resolved to burn and especially some of them the idlest trifling stuff that ever was writ, calculated for a church without a company or a roof.[1]

Yet the common habit of taking Swift's word for the quality of these efforts seems wrong. The eleven that happen to be pre-served are (nearly all of them) written with enough elegance and force to raise them above the work of all but the finest preachers of Swift's day.

If he spoke of his sermons as pamphlets, the reason may not have been simply to fault them. Lord Orrery, discussing three of them, decided that two belonged to another genre, the moral or political essay.[2] We have heard John Evans, Bishop of Meath, say of a sermon by Swift that it was like an essay by Montaigne.[3] In fact, if one judges by the specimens extant, Swift rarely

---

[1] I.e., Kilroot; Williams I. 31.
[2] Orrery, pp. 289–96; Carl Daw points out the implications of Orrery's remarks (Daw, p. 2).
[3] Landa, p. 182; cf. above, p. 53.

worked as an exegete, interpreting a piece of Scripture or expounding a theological doctrine. He said himself, 'The two principal branches of preaching, are first to tell the people what is their duty; and then to convince them that it is so.'[1] The expounding of texts and mysteries is only incidental to these purposes.

It looks as if normally Swift decided to preach on a topic (moral, social, or political) and then chose a suitable text embedded somewhere in the readings and liturgy prescribed for the week preceding his performance.[2] But after selecting this, he pursued it with less than single-minded attention. Often he even neglects the primary text and cultivates instead a secondary one that harmonizes with his theme.[3] So also he uses Biblical quotations in a way that is not particularly homiletic. They serve less for demonstration than for rhetoric. He does not quote a passage to show there is divine authority for his position but to supply sentences that resonate happily with his own expression.[4]

If this is Swift's habit of composition, it reflects his tendency to skirt the traditional territory of homiletic literature. Although he does not produce anti-sermons, he repeatedly implies that exegesis and doctrinal controversy darken more minds than they illuminate. The impulse of his preaching is to separate the distinctively religious principle in religion from the discussable matter, and to leave that principle sacred and untouched, as if it were dangerous to put forth one's hand to the ark of God. Speaking of the Trinity, Swift says, 'This union and distinction are a mystery utterly unknown to mankind. This is enough for any good Christian to believe on this great article, without ever inquiring any farther.'[5]

Doctrines that do not bear on action did not feed Swift's imagination but troubled it. The mysteries of the Trinity and the Incarnation excited ambivalent responses from him. He preferred not to stand on such holy ground. In some notes published posthumously, Swift wrote,

---

[1] Davis IX. 70.   [2] Daw, pp. 3–4.   [3] *Ibid.*, pp. 7–8.   [4] *Ibid.*, p. 5.
[5] Davis IX. 162.

The Christian religion, in the most early times, was proposed to the Jews and Heathens, without the article of Christ's divinity; which, I remember, Erasmus accounts for, by it's being too strong a meat for babes. Perhaps, if it were now softened by the Chinese missionaries, the conversion of those infidels would be less difficult: and we find by the Alcoran, it is the great stumbling-block of the Mahometans. But, in a country already Christian, to bring so fundamental a point of faith into debate, can have no consequences that are not pernicious to morals and public peace.[1]

In an essay conceived when he was in his late thirties, he said, 'I leave it among *divines* to dilate upon the danger of *schism*, as a spiritual evil; but I would consider it only as a temporal one.'[2] Although he wrote this essay in the character of a layman, the gist of the remark fits Swift as a preacher: he would leave it to *other* divines, not because the spiritual evil dwindles before the temporal one, but because rhetorically, dealing with the audience he faces, temporal arguments carry more weight.

Swift not only believed that the expounding of disputed articles of faith was useless. He thought the experience of all the years since the Restoration proved the futility of dropping such exotic seed upon the dry earth of British congregations. Preaching to men in whom natural religion burned with the dimmest of flames, he could better arouse them to right conduct by arguments that did not rest on revelation. This is why he not only liked to deal with public and moral issues but why he appealed so often to the rational self-interest of his hearers. In this attitude he went beyond the traditional stress of Anglican divines on 'operative' rather than speculative truths.

The connection between Swift's gingerly handling of doctrinal thorns and his taste for simplicity is natural. He once wrote to a clergyman about the style of sermons and said that preachers should 'recover that simplicity which in every thing of value ought chiefly to be followed'.[3] It is notable that his standard for style is so near his standard for faith. Before the complexity there had been plain clarity. By striving to recover

---

[1] *Ibid.*, IX. 262.   [2] *Ibid.*, II. 11.
[3] 12 Dec. 1734, to Henry Clarke; Williams IV. 274.

something easily corrupted and painfully brought back to its original state, we may restore the purity of our church and our language. Hard doctrines, like obscure words, are the stigmata of error. The good preacher strips away the enveloping folds to arrive at the true reality.

Finally, one must observe that the simplicity of the sermons is itself part of Swift's characteristic, subtle rhetoric. The surface of the prose is a brilliant contrast to the ambiguity of his tone and allusiveness. It was Swift's felicity that the common rhetoric of parsons encouraged him to create just those figures that blossomed naturally from his own speech. In all homiletic literature the priest talks for the order of God but addresses men caught in the order of mortality. Things that decorate our earthly life, says the priest, defile our heavenly aspirations. The demands of his office drive him to argue in ironies. For him what seems like death is life; what seems like life is death. By their nature the preacher's ironic contrasts hinge on the opposing of material to spiritual pleasures. Just as he learns to make the visible world emblematic of the world to come, so he depreciates the palpabilities of this world by comparison with the in-tangibles of the heavenly city. Carnal passion must yield to divine love; palaces are hovels beside our father's house.

Now Swift lisped in irony, and he liked no metaphors better than those which set physical against spiritual attributes. The satiric mode of *A Tale of a Tub* required him to treat the Puritans' inspiration as wind in their bowels. In *The Conduct of the Allies* he reduced the glory of Marlborough's triumphs to a few tattered flags hanging from the roof of Westminster Abbey. Even the exegetical preachers' habit of explaining the sense of words in Scripture lent itself to Swift's natural manner; for his obsession with correctness of language led him to practise definition and redefinition as part of his rhetoric.

When Swift produces his ambiguities and subtleties in the sermons, his pose of simple candour doubles their strength. Part of the sermon on *The Testimony of Conscience* deals with the Dissenters. Because Swift wishes to cut down rather than enlarge the scope of their activities, he puts forward the narrowest definition of 'liberty of conscience' and then complains that the Dissenters, under the colour of another, false definition, wish not only to propagate their misguided beliefs but to destroy the Established Church. On the foundation of his own, partisan definition, Swift then builds a structure of ironies involving the relation of spiritual doctrine to worldly politics; for he assumes that all Presbyterians are intolerant Whigs:

> Those very persons, who under a pretence of a public spirit and tenderness toward their Christian brethren, are so jealous for such a liberty of conscience as this, are of all others the least tender to those who differ from them in the smallest point relating to government; and I wish I could not say, that the majesty of the living God may be offended with more security than the memory of a dead prince. But the wisdom of the world at present seems to agree with that of the heathen emperor, who said, If the gods were offended, it was their own concern, and they were able to vindicate themselves.[1]

If *persons*, here, are Presbyterians, if *those who differ* are Tories, if the *dead prince* is William III, and if the *world* is the government of Ireland, the sarcasm becomes open. Swift is saying that the Whig ministers of King George would sooner punish those who speak ill of William III than enforce the laws against conventicles. He treats the toleration of Dissent as equivalent to the toleration of blasphemy, and implies that the present regime is modelled on that of a heathen tyrant. Yet Swift crowds all this savagery of innuendo into the room of a few sentences made of the plainest words. His air of simplicity, frankness, common sense, and spontaneity disarms the listener, who can hardly be prepared for the whiplash of 'government' at the end of one sentence, or of 'prince' at the end of another. Language more literary, allusions more concretely historical, a more philosophical approach to political theory, would be more decorous, more in keeping with thrust of the speech. They would also weaken the power of the passage to disturb an audience.[2]

[1] Davis IX. 151.   [2] Cf. Price, pp. 16–22.

III. 'A LETTER TO A YOUNG GENTLEMAN'

Besides speaking directly to men who preached from St Patrick's pulpit, Swift threw his general observations together in the form of an essay called *A Letter to a Young Gentleman*.[1] Here he made no sustained effort to arrange his paragraphs in a systematic order but seems to have inserted thoughts as they occurred, expatiating on themes that excited him. What he brought out is a lively, sprawling miscellany of hints on preaching.

If the essay still attracts readers, it is mainly for Swift's views on prose style. Among the varieties of advice he delivers, Swift only glances at the subjects on which ministers ought positively to preach. He gives more space to reflecting on those they should avoid, such as the depreciation of ancient philosophy or the refuting of atheism. But the topic to which he surrenders himself is literary style, with special attention to diction. It is obvious which chapter he thought himself equipped to contribute to the Irish parson's vademecum.

Still the essay does not belong to the tradition of secular rhetorics but to that, also ancient, of manuals of preaching. What separates Swift's work from its many forerunners is the framework of impersonation. Instead of writing as a priest sharing his experience with other priests, Swift disguises himself as a layman, 'a person of quality', delivering caveats to a young man who has just been ordained. In this device Swift carries on his habit of taking a worldly point of view on ecclesiastic subjects. He had followed the same method in *The Sentiments of a Church-of-England Man*. The germ of *A Letter to a Young Gentleman* is a passage in a *Tatler* which Swift wrote ten years before, masked as an anonymous layman.[2]

Besides echoing his own *Tatler*, he echoes the style and themes of John Eachard's celebrated *Grounds and Occasions of the Contempt*

---

[1] The received text is dated 9 Jan. 1720, which is presumably when Swift finished writing it. The first Dublin edition is dated 1720, and is entitled *A Letter from a Lay-Patron to a Gentleman, Designing for Holy Orders*. The title-page has a motto from Lactantius, 'Quid igitur profuit vidisse te veritatem quam nec defensurus esses nec secuturus.' I suppose Swift was responsible for both the title and the motto. The first English edition is dated 1721 and was published 3 Jan. 1721. See Teerink.

[2] Davis II. 177.

of the Clergy (1670). Eachard had exhorted preachers to study and practise English speech. He ridiculed the addicts of hard words, pedantic quotations, false wit, and scholastic terms. For all Eachard's popularity, he was only one in a tribe of reformers of preaching.

Swift's judgments agree generally with those of Restoration churchmen, whether high churchmen like Eachard and the eloquent Dr South, or Latitudinarians like Bishop Wilkins and Archbishop Tillotson. The need for rational rather than emotional appeal was central to Restoration Anglicanism, if only to counter the Puritans and Roman Catholics. The eagerness to turn preachers away from controversy derived from a normal reaction against the polemics of the Civil War. A clear, unaffected style went naturally with the commonly prescribed clarity of doctrine and argument.

Wilkins wrote a best-selling manual for preachers, *Ecclesiastes* (1646). Here he defended the universities and called for a learned ministry. He recommended 'plain and natural' language, although his idea of plainness was barer than Swift's. He condemned the use of scholastic terms, and discouraged preachers from expounding speculative doctrines. If Swift departs from Wilkins, it is when that even-tempered guide teaches 'meekness and lenity in differences not fundamental'.

South is closer in character to Swift. In his famous sermon *The Scribe Instructed* (1660) he foreshadows most of Swift's opinions. South dwells on the need for 'bestowing a competent and sufficient time in universities', and he urges the preacher to deliver his sermon by heart rather than to read it. These are themes that Swift also lingers on. South attacks false wit but goes out of his way to praise suitable eloquence and ornament. In another sermon, on Luke xx. 15 ('For I will give you a mouth', 1668), South again foreshadows Swift, not only by recommending clarity and plainness but also by sneering at 'latitude' and praising the apostles' vigour in fighting those who opposed them. Here South also recommends a 'suitable zeal and fervour', which he carefully distinguishes from the wild enthusiasm ascribed to the Puritans.

[83]

Since Swift, in the passage most often quoted from the *Letter to a Young Gentleman*, condemns preachers who move the passions, one might suppose he would repudiate South's 'fervour'. Yet that well-known passage ends with a little-known qualification. What Swift rejects is not a moving manner but an irrational indulgence in pathos: 'If your arguments be strong, in God's name offer them in as moving a manner as the nature of the subject will properly admit.... But beware of letting the pathetick part swallow up the rational.'[1]

Swift's whole essay represents one more simple, rational service to the Church of Ireland. Swift hoped by its means to raise the quality of her servants. Anglicans giving instruction to preachers often welcomed the opportunity of drawing invidious comparisons with the Dissenters. Swift's paragraphs on pathos would have led easily to such a satire. Yet Swift, who rarely passed up such openings, hardly alludes to the Dissenters anywhere in the *Letter to a Young Gentleman*. The reason is that he is not addressing ministers in general or an audience of laymen. He has in mind the Episcopal clergy of 'this kingdom' at the time he is writing.[2] Although Swift liked to publish his works in London, this *Letter* appeared first in Dublin. When he regrets that the young parson has not studied English, he laments the barbarisms 'peculiar to the nation' of the Irish.[3] When he declaims against those corruptions of manners that he links with the growth of impiety, he lashes specifically Irish country gentlemen for 'oppressing their tenants ... talking nonsense, and getting drunk at the sessions'.[4]

It is to be more useful to his own church that Swift wears the periwig of 'a person of quality'. Times are bad for the clergy, he says, not because of irreligious books but because the men of property have sacrificed their principles to greed and ambition, because political ties rather than moral character have become the standard by which men are chosen for advancement, because Irish landlords are equally lacking in 'learning, manners, temperance, probity, good-nature, and politics'.[5] For a priest to

---

[1] *Ibid.*, IX. 70.   [2] *Ibid.*, p. 65.   [3] *Ibid.*   [4] *Ibid.*, p. 78.   [5] *Ibid.*

utter such denunciations would be fatuous. The judge here must belong to the class he condemns.

The mask also liberates Swift rhetorically. When he defends the natural religion of the ancient philosophers, he is not afraid of being denounced as a false shepherd. He can without embarrassment dismiss the narrow prejudices of the church fathers. The mask establishes the writer's authority. He need not report at second hand the boredom of a congregation; he can speak as a participant. When he pleads for sermons to be delivered without notes or text, he explicitly opposes himself as layman to the reader as priest, and urges the value of his own experience. When he ridicules pathos, the reason is that he himself feels unpersuaded by it, not that a parishioner has said he is not. Finally, Swift always tends to assume that morality from a professional moralist is heavily discounted, and that the amateur teaching of a man of the world is heard more eagerly. The parson mouths his lessons; the man of quality speaks of what he has observed.

Chapter Five

THE DEAN IN SOCIETY

I. DELANY AND OTHERS

S wift hated to give in to gloom, or 'the spleen'. If it loured, he escaped by pursuing *la bagatelle*—any harmless pastime that kept him busy and cheerful. When he could not have the dignified company of minds like Addison's, he made do with the fun of young men who were willing to be frivolous. He found a severely reduced facsimile of the Addisonian character in the Rev. Patrick Delany, whom Swift had asked to serve as diplomat between himself and Sheridan.

Only a few years older than the playful schoolmaster, Delany was far more prudent and self-seeking. But he too supported the old, high Tory principles. Apart from his eagerness to climb toward wealth and high place, Delany has little colour for us. Lord Carteret once said he was 'cheerful in himself, and agreeable to all that know him'.[1]

Although Delany's family lacked money and connections, he was clever enough to sparkle as an undergraduate at Trinity College. There his ambitions won the backing of Swift's old classmate Peter Browne, who served as Provost at the time. Delany was made a scholar in his third year and became a junior fellow of the College when he was twenty-five, during a period when the odour of high Toryism permeated the institution. Besides accepting the status of Browne's protégé, Delany really admired the Provost's style of preaching, which he set out to imitate. His success received an accolade that he must have prayed for, when Constantine Phipps became the Lord Chancellor of Ireland. Phipps made Delany one of his chaplains,

[1] Williams IV. 233.

an act that carried with it the promise of early advancement. To please this patron, Delany and a friend of his wrote an anonymous pamphlet defending Phipps's schemes to defy the Irish Parliament of 1713. In the pamphlet Nonconformity is lumped with atheism. The authors declare that Dissenters prefer faction and schism to loyalty and Christian communion. The whole work is seasoned with disparagements of the Whigs' moral character.[1]

By 1718 Delany was thirty-four years old, a fellow of Trinity College, with a fine name as a teacher and preacher.[2] It was probably Sheridan who introduced him to Swift; and since the dean warmed to clever young men who shared his own principles, their friendship grew rapidly. I suppose Swift felt delighted to meet a clergyman so learned, right-minded, and obliging. His pleasure shines through the soaring compliment he paid Delany in the dedication of a poem:

> To you, whose virtues I must own
> With shame, I have too lately known;
> To you, by art and nature taught
> To be the man I long have sought.[3]

For compatible but less dignified company the dean found a set of gentlemen and young parsons who gave him a chance to play master and jester at once. In these often mindless pastimes Delany was willing to join, and Sheridan was a ringleader. Others on the team included several sons of Patrick Grattan—a senior fellow of Trinity College and prebendary of St Patrick's (now deceased)—and two sons of Robert Rochfort, the rich lawyer who had sat as presiding judge, or Lord Chief Baron, in one of Ireland's highest courts. Rochfort's younger son, John, was Swift's 'particular favourite'[4]—a bachelor in his mid-twenties, well-educated and sweet-tempered.[5] The elder son,

---

[1] Delany and Richard Helsham, *A Long History of a Short Session of a Certain Parliament in a Certain Kingdom* (Dublin, 1713).

[2] Swift met Delany no later than October 1718, when he addressed 'To Mr. Delany' to him; see *Poems* I. 214.

[3] *Ibid.*, p. 215.   [4] Davis IX. 85.   [5] *Ibid.*, p. 89.

George, was a good-humoured family man, a Member of Parliament in his mid-thirties.

When Swift wrote to his great friends in England, he liked to restore his dignity by ridiculing his games; so he told Bolingbroke,

> I have gone the round of all my stories three or four times with the younger people, and begin them again. I give hints how significant a person I have been, and no body believes me: I pretend to pity them, but am inwardly angry. I lay traps for people to desire I would show them some things I have written [i.e., and not yet published], but cannot succeed. . . . The worst of it is, that lying is of no use; for the people here will not believe one half of what is true. If I can prevail on any one to personate a hearer and admirer, you would wonder what a favourite he grows.[1]

But as Delany said, Swift seemed to keep every friend (at least, every Irish friend) 'in some degree of awe';[2] and one reason is that he secured friends who let themselves be awed or entertained as he desired. During a five-month visit to the Rochforts, he was able to institute regular readings of Lucretius before breakfast with George and John.[3]

In a sour and hyperbolic mood Swift wrote to Charles Ford, 'I am very confident, that in the whole year I do not speak to above a dozen persons, and make choice onely of such with whom it is of no manner of consequence what I say to them, or what they say to me.'[4] But the amusements usually enjoyed by the select gathering of Swift and his young partners give little support to the myth of the dean as a brooding misanthrope. One example will illustrate the tone. George Rochfort's wife, Lady Betty, cut out a silhouette of Daniel Jackson, a big-nosed young parson (and cousin of the Grattans) in the Swift–Sheridan (etc.) circle. To celebrate the lady's accomplishment, Swift, Sheridan, and Delany wrote verses ridiculing Jackson's nose and some other features; and the victim retaliated ponderously in kind.[5]

---

[1] Williams II. 333–4.   [2] Delany, p. 18.
[3] Cf. 'The Journal', *Poems* I. 278.
[4] 8 Dec. 1719; Williams II. 330.
[5] *Poems* III. 990–1012. Since Swift alludes to the incident in 'To Mr Delany' (I. 102), which is dated Oct. 1718, I assume it occurred not long before he wrote that poem.

An attack by Jackson on Sheridan in Anglo-Latin hexameters is still funny; so I give a distich:

> Cur me bespateras, blaterans furiosè Poeta
> Cum foulo moutho, putridae cum flaminae breathae.[1]

Swift yielded gladly to the currents of prankfulness and made up scurrilities in Jackson's name as well as a mock-confession by Sheridan of his supposed defeat in the contest. Jackson or somebody wrote a 'Last Speech and Dying Words of Daniel Jackson' in verse and prose; and so the laborious fun dragged on.[2] Too many of these squibs are preserved, for they can amuse few readers today. But they do suggest how far Swift travelled in his quest for *la bagatelle*. We may wonder whether the flow of disagreeable public events did not push him even further than usual into these private circuses, and we may remember the less clumsy rhymes of the Scriblerians during the grim months of 1713–14. But of course Swift never was averse to such games.

II. ESSAYS ON MANNERS

Swift thought much about the rules of social decorum, and regarded his own views as authoritative. If the essays[3] on the subject are largely of biographical interest, the reason is not that he was frivolous in dealing with it but that he was too rational. Although Swift knew perfectly how to charm both men and women, he did not have the habit of elegant manners; and the observations he made were seldom precise, witty, or refined. When he spied on servants, he produced more serviceable and

---

[1] *Ibid.*, p. 996—perhaps by Swift.   [2] *Ibid.*, pp. 1008–10.
[3] 'Hints towards an Essay on Conversation', 'On Good Manners and Good Breeding', 'Hints on Good Manners', 'Of the Education of Ladies'—all in Davis IV. The poem 'To Mr Delany' deals with conversation and raillery. C. P. Daw has shown that Swift probably composed 'Hints towards an Essay on Conversation' in 1708 (possibly earlier), and that the piece first appeared in vol. 10 of Faulkner's 18mo edition of Swift's works—a volume published in 1762. For further information, including corrections of Davis IV, see Carl P. Daw, 'The Date of Swift's Hints towards an Essay on Conversation', *The Scriblerian* 8 (Spring 1976), 119–21. From the parallels between 'To Mr Delany' and 'Hints towards an Essay on Conversation' one may infer the stability of Swift's views on the subject.

pleasant information than when he mixed with their masters.

Swift considered the society he knew—whether English or Irish—as continually in need of reformation. Northern decorum seemed less the work of instinct than of art, and always ready to lapse into rudeness.[1] 'We are naturally not very polite,' said Swift.[2] He insisted that reason without experience was a sufficient teacher of good manners.[3] 'Ignorance of forms cannot properly be stiled ill-manners; because forms are subject to frequent changes; and consequently, being not founded upon reason, are beneath a wise man's regard.'[4] So he ignored a crucial fact: that just those cases in which reason cannot possibly serve one, have the points to embarrass both the blunderer and the company. What Swift really does is to condemn any social conventions that appear irrational to him; and this attitude will account for much of his own eccentricity. Remarks on the rules of good breeding become, therefore, not so much an exposition as a critique; so his anecdotes illustrate the weakness of common forms: 'I have seen a dutchess fairly knock'd down by the precipitancy of an officious coxcomb, running to save her the trouble of opening a door.'[5] One suspects that the Irish parson did not like to admit he had ever fairly embarrassed himself or others by his individuality.

The greatest social pleasure, for Swift, was conversation. He did not refuse to play card-games, but he blamed them for stifling convivial talk.[6] According to his own accounts and those of others, he really set up for his pattern the sort of conversation that Gulliver describes among the Houyhnhnms, a style of decency without ceremony—'where there was no interruption, tediousness, heat, or difference of sentiments', and a short silence from time to time improved the talk.[7] Delany says Swift tried to speak briefly and then wait for others to take up the thread; if they did not (and one assumes they learned to hesitate), he felt

---

[1] Davis IV. 92.   [2] *Ibid.*, p. 12.   [3] *Ibid.*, p. 213.   [4] *Ibid.*, p. 218.
[5] *Ibid.*, p. 215.
[6] *Ibid.*, pp. 115–16. The passage is part of a comic impersonation, but this point is serious as well as ironical.
[7] *Ibid.*, XI. 277.

he had the right to start again.[1] Another witness says, 'He told a story in an admirable manner: his sentences were short and perspicuous, his observations were piercing.'[2] How far he could occasionally submit himself to the dominion of a particular and privileged guest, one may infer from his behaviour during a Sunday evening at the deanery (around 1732) when Charles Ford joined the company. Ford, according to another guest,

> took upon him not only to dictate to the company, but to contradict whatever any other person advanced, right or wrong, till he had entirely silenced them all: And then having the whole talk to himself, (for, to my great surprise the dean neither interrupted nor showed any dislike of him) he told us a whole string of improbabilities.[3]

Conversation was Swift's real measure of manners. It is significant that he associated the reign of Charles I with both the greatest improvement of the English language and the 'highest period of politeness'.[4] Again, just as he recommended the presence of women to purify manners, so he recommended their speech as an element to polish language.[5] It is striking how much of his advice to young ladies is to enable them to join in the conversation of men, especially that of their husbands. If he thought the best part of marriage was talk, it is no wonder that he remained single.

---

[1] Delany, p. 203. [2] Orrery, p. 226. [3] Pilkington I. 65–6.
[4] Davis IV. 9, 94. [5] *Ibid.*, p. 13.

Chapter Six

THE DEAN IN PRIVATE

I. CADENUS AND VANESSA

Behind the difficulties of his outer existence Swift found his inner ways complicated by a dangerous liaison. This was his intimacy with Esther Vanhomrigh, the clever, moody woman, more than twenty years his junior, for whom he invented the name Vanessa. A melodrama that began as comedy was now evolving through pathos to tragedy.

For those who cannot judge Vanessa's character by her actions, she herself described it in words addressed to Swift: 'I was born with violent passions which terminate all in one, that inexpressible passion I have for you.'[1] When Swift left England in August 1714, he hoped the separation would end her attachment. In fact, I believe one reason he indulged himself in the rash pleasures of their friendship was the assumption that it could not last long. Yet in his amazing need to entice through discouragement, he sent Vanessa (before he went to Dublin) an adieu that pointed to a reunion:

> If you are in Ireland while I am there I shall see you very seldom. It is not a place for any freedom, but where every thing is known in a week, and magnified a hundred degrees. These are rigorous laws that must be passed through: but it is possible we may meet in London in winter, or if not, leave all to Fate, that seldom cares to humour our inclinations.[2]

With her immense attraction to this unattainable object, Vanessa could hardly linger in London. Her father, mother, and younger brother were all dead. She did not feel close to the

---

[1] Williams II. 364 (a draft); date uncertain; my punctuation.
[2] *Ibid.*, p. 123.

surviving brother, Bartholomew. Her mother's debts and her own shortage of money would be easier to manage in Ireland. Surrendering as usual to the 'inexpressible passion', she took her pliable sister Mary and hurried after Swift.

At Celbridge in the country eleven miles west of Dublin, Vanessa owned an imposing house and a handsome estate left by her father.[1] In town she rented lodgings in Turnstile Alley (now Parliament Row), beside the Houses of Parliament. Next, she sent a messenger to Swift, then in Trim, asking him to stop at Celbridge—which would not have been far out of his way— when he returned to Dublin. But Swift had already started riding another way, to Chetwode's house near Portarlington, where he was to keep an old engagement. When Vanessa's messenger caught up with him, Swift replied at once with a quick negative. But he followed this with a letter in which he made a scolding promise, characteristically vague, to see her in Dublin. At the end of the letter there rose an emotion which he perhaps would have called pity, but which was compounded with his determination not to lose this woman; it drove Swift to remind her seductively of their common past: 'Is Kildrohod [i.e., Celbridge] as beautiful as Windsor, and as agreeable to you as the prebends lodging there; is there any walk about you as pleasant as the Avenue and the Marlborough Lodge.'[2]

In a matter of weeks they arrived again at their old, exciting cross-purposes. Vanessa owned solid social resources if she wished to use them; Archbishop King and Swift's crony, Dr Pratt (the Provost of Trinity College), were among her callers. But she preferred to keep to herself. Avoiding company, she brooded on her deprivations and legal entanglements; and by reiterated complaints she fed Swift's sense of guilt. Resisting the independence of her nature, she harped on the need for his guidance. Swift said he disliked 'anything that looks like a secret'.[3] Possibly, he never saw her in Celbridge until 1720; certainly, he made the visits to her in Dublin as discreet as he could. For a while at least, he seems to have taken a boy along—

[1] See *ibid.*, p. 142, n. 2.   [2] *Ibid.*, p. 142.   [3] *Ibid.*, p. 239.

probably a charity child whom Stella was supporting.[1] But as he had expected, the outcome did not make for serenity; and he felt driven to send her warnings that only refined the tensions between them:

> This morning a woman who does business for me, told me she heard I was in—with one—naming you, and twenty particulars, that little master and I visited you, and that the A—B [i.e., Archbishop King] did so; and that you had abundance of wit &c. I ever feared the tattle of this nasty town; and I told you so; and that was the reason why I said to you long ago that I would see you seldom when you were in Ireland and I must beg you to be easy if for some time I visit you seldomer.[2]

Except by small inference and large guess, there is no way to tell what went on at their meetings. Mary Vanhomrigh seems to have been an easy, docile sister to live with; Swift was genuinely fond of her, and she sat through many (if not all) of his visits to her sister. I suppose that their grand debate continued—that he wished to limit their conversation to her financial problems, to his suggestions for her self-improvement, and to other edifying or innocent topics; and that Vanessa recklessly dipped into forbidden and personal depths. If he would not yet join in the consummation she always yearned for, she would at least hope to revive the milder thrills of their London days. But this was hardly Swift's idea of a compromise. He helped her borrow money and sympathized deeply with her material worries—lightened though these were by the death of Bartholomew, her 'wretch of a brother', in the summer of 1715.[3] But Swift did not disguise his anger when she became too demanding. As early as 1714 she writes, 'I could have bore the rack much better than those killing, killing, words of yours.'[4]

Having concentrated her desires on the middle-aged priest, Vanessa could not bear the threat of his disengagement. Drawing on a well-stocked arsenal of emotional blackmail, she enjoyed the thrill of humiliating herself before the father–lover who remained deliciously out of reach.

---

[1] Like the girl mentioned in her will; see also Ball III. 461.
[2] Williams II. 150.   [3] *Ibid.*, p. 148.   [4] *Ibid.*, p. 150.

Sometimes I have resolved to die without seeing you more, but those resolves, to your misfortune, did not last long, for there is something in human nature that prompts one so to find relief in this world, I must give way to it, and beg you'd see me and speak kindly to me, for I am sure you'd not condemn any one to suffer what I have done. Could you but know it, the reason I write to you, is because I cannot tell it you, should I see you, for when I begin to complain, then you are angry, and there is something in your look so awful, that it strikes me dumb. Oh that you may but have so much regard for me left that this complaint may touch your soul with pity.[1]

Only misery could dispose an intelligent person to give way to such language. But it was more than misery that directed a wealthy, charming woman away from the plainly eligible men surrounding her, and toward a self-imposed emotional exile. The more she grieved, the more she could touch Swift with her grief. To emerge and join in the conventional routines of a society they both belittled would mean abandoning the strongest hold she had on him.[2]

Swift could only have felt pleased, in a manner he dared not confess, by the sight of so desirable a woman sacrificing other opportunities for masculine companionship in order to wait mournfully for him to put in his fleeting appearances. (How different she was from that mother of his who had been willing to live without her child, or from that sister who had married against his will!) As his conscious motives, guilt and pity may have predominated. But when he assured Vanessa of his support and cheered her gloom, he operated with compliments that expressed the buried longing he felt to be with her. If Swift deliberately avoided visits in order to smother scandal, he thereby pained himself as well as Vanessa. The comfort he could administer not only consoled but also enchained her. Sometimes he resorted to bad French for sentiments he would not risk in good English:

vous qui estes incapable d'aucune sottise si ce n'est l'estime qu'il vous plaist d'avoir pour moy, car il n'y a point de merite, ni aucune

[1] *Ibid.*, p. 150.
[2] Against my interpretation is the fact that Vanessa thought of moving to England in 1718; see Ball III. 34, n. 2.

preuve de mon bon goût de trouver en vous tout ce que la nature a donnée à un mortel, je veux dire l'honneur, la vertue, le bon sens, l'esprit, la douceur, l'agrement, et la firmitè d'ame, mais en vous cachant commes vous faites, le monde ne vous connoit pas, et vous perdez l'eloge des millions de gens. Depuis que j'avois l'honneur de vous connoitre j'ay toujours remarquè que ni en conversation particuliere, ni general aucun mot a echappè de votre bouche, qui pouvoit etre mieux exprimè; et je vous jure qu'en faisant souvent la plus severe critique, je ne pouvois jamais trouver aucun defaut ni en vos actions ni en vos parolles. La coquetrie, l'affectation, la pruderie, sont des imperfections que vous n'avois jamais connu. Et avec tout cela, croyez vous qu'il est possible de ne vous estimer au dessus du reste du genre humain. Quelles bestes en juppes sont les plus excellentes de celles que je vois semeès dans le monde au prix de vous; en les voyant, en les entendant je dis cent fois le jour—[i.e., Vanessa] ne parle, ne regarde, ne pense, ne fait rien comme ces miserables, sont ce du meme sexe—du meme espece de creatures?[1]

If these hyperboles were translated into English, the Dean of St Patrick's is the last man that a knowledgeable reader would attribute them to. Swift wanted a powerful incentive to make him disguise his character so completely, and the consolation of the lonely was not a sufficient cause.

Vanessa saved many though not all of Swift's letters, and over two dozen of them are still extant. He saved none of hers, but she kept drafts of some; and we can tell from those to which we have replies that the drafts are reasonably close to the letters she sent. In the fragmentary correspondence as we know it, a number of letters cannot be dated; and only during one or two periods have we anything like a coherent series of datable messages with replies.

The summer of 1720 is a moment when the affair 'surfaces' in this way. Vanessa has gone to Celbridge with her sister, who is ill of the disease that will soon end her life. Swift writes from Dublin to cheer up the two women, enclosing a 'love-letter' to Mary and some verses for Vanessa. She replies complaining that he has kept her waiting an extra week for his letter, and that she has been ill. He writes pointing out that it is hard to send letters to

[1] Williams II. 325–6.

her. He scolds her humorously and announces that Charles Ford
has arrived in Ireland.

He also shows once more how he can entice Vanessa when he
means to brighten her mood: 'Yesterday I was half way towards
you; where I dined, and returned weary enough. I asked where
that road to the left led, and they named the place—[i.e.,
Celbridge].'[1] Responding to the enticement, Vanessa gives way
to sexual innuendo: 'We have had a vast deal of thunder and
lightning. Where do you think I wished to be then, and do you
think that was the only time I wished so?'[2] Swift now grows
more provocative, saying that he may stop off at Celbridge with
Charles Ford ('Glass Heel') on their way to Wood Park. Then
he goes so far as to propose writing a new poem like *Cadenus and
Vanessa*:

> What would you give to have the History of [Cadenus and Vanessa]
> exactly written through all its steps from the beginning to this time. I
> believe it would do well in verse, and be as long as the other. I hope it
> will be done. It ought to be an exact chronicle of twelve years.[3]

—and he lists two dozen clues, only half of which can be guessed
at today. Vanessa found them all exhilarating, and Swift's near
promise to visit Celbridge sent her into an ecstasy:

> Is it possible that you will come and see me, I beg for God sake you
> will. I would give the world to see you here (and Molkin[4] would be
> extremely happy). Do you think the time long since I saw you? I did
> design seeing you this week but will not stir in hopes of your coming
> here.[5] I beg you'll write two or three words by the bearer to let me
> know if you think you'll come this week. I shall have the note to
> night. You make me happy beyond expression by your goodness.[6]

There is a break in our knowledge at this point; so we remain
ignorant whether or not Swift and Ford did visit Celbridge. I

---

[1] *Ibid.*, p. 353.   [2] *Ibid.*, p. 354.

[3] *Ibid.*, p. 356. I suspect that when Swift told Vanessa that he had shown Ford both her
own last letter and his present one, he was teasing her with a hoax; but if he was serious,
his conscious innocence is so much the more obvious.

[4] Vanessa's sister, Mary.

[5] Evidently, she made special trips to Dublin for the purpose of seeing him there.

[6] Williams II. 357.

simply assume they did; he seldom made such half-promises without fulfilling them. But other information that has come down about Swift's dealings with Vanessa at the time adds darker complexities to the ambivalent partnership.

II. SWIFT AND STELLA

Swift's deepest gain from settling once more in Ireland was the restored presence of Esther Johnson, whom he had induced to move there from England at the turn of the century, and whose abiding affection, in sickness and in health, was the solace of his life. Thanks to the leap in his income, he could now guarantee her dignity and comfort as never before. She and her older, simpler companion, Mrs Dingley, still lodged near St Mary's Church, in easy reach of the deanery. Although Swift spent as much time as possible in the country, they were free to join him at Trim with the Raymonds, or at the homes of other friends. In Dublin they saw much of Archdeacon Walls and 'Gossip Doll' his wife. Christmas 1716 they passed with their old friend John Stearne, now Bishop of Clogher, while Swift, detained by business and a lack of horses, could not leave Trim.[1]

In Dublin under George I the number of families that mattered was not so great that Mrs Johnson could avoid hearing about Mrs Vanhomrigh. For long periods over a span of nine years they were living in town at the same time. Given the small area that persons of quality frequented, at least a few chance meetings seem likely. Yet if we are to judge by Swift's rigidity in similar corners, we must suppose that he discussed neither woman with the other. 'The common forms of manners', he once wrote, 'were intended for regulating the conduct of those who have weak understandings.'[2] How he reconciled his two devotions was a process to be adjusted within his own breast. But to accomplish it, he must have drained his considerable powers of self-deceit.

A couple of months before Swift assured Vanessa (in French)

[1] *Ibid.*, pp. 235, 248–9. [2] Davis IV. 214.

that she possessed honour, good sense, wit, grace, and firmness of spirit—before he said that compared to her all other women were beasts in skirts[1]—he assured Stella (in verse) that no two women combined could supply her charms:

> Oh, would it please the gods to split
> Thy beauty, size, and years, and wit,
> No age could furnish out a pair
> Of nymphs so gracefull, wise and fair
> With half the lustre of your eyes,
> With half thy wit, thy years and size.[2]

Of course, the gods had long since heard his prayer and punished Swift by granting it.

In the autumn of the following year he declared to Mrs Vanhomrigh that she still excited his fixed admiration: 'I have the same respect, esteem and kindness for you I ever professed to have and shall ever preserve, because you always merit the utmost that can be given you.'[3] About the same time he paid another versified tribute to the excellence of Mrs Johnson:

> Pallas observing Stella's wit
> Was more than for her sex was fit;
> And that her beauty, soon or late,
> Might breed confusion in the state,
> In high concern for human kind,
> Fixt *honour* in her infant mind.
>
> .   .   .
>
> Her hearers are amaz'd from whence
> Proceeds that fund of wit and sense;
> Which though her modesty would shroud,
> Breaks like the sun behind a cloud,
> While gracefulness its art conceals,
> And yet through ev'ry motion steals.[4]

The monotony of the sentiments reveals not the cousinhood of the subjects or the duplicity of the admirer but the identity of the

---

[1] Williams II. 325–6.
[2] *Poems* II. 722. The joke about Stella's weight introduces a touch of irony that makes these compliments sound less hollow than those to Vanessa.
[3] Williams II. 360; my comma after *respect*.   [4] *Poems* II. 723, 726.

model he set before them. The two women's real differences are
historically visible. Mrs Johnson had humble parents and a little
fortune. Fixed routines, the steadiness of her domestic life, and
her public acceptance by Swift's circle assigned her to the part of
the motherly wife. When Swift reproached her, it was not for
imprudence but for stubborn anger:

> Your spirits kindle to a flame,
> Mov'd with the lightest touch of blame,
> And when a friend in kindness tries
> To shew you where your error lies,
> Conviction does but more incense;
> Perverseness is your whole defence....
> And what is worse, your passion bends
> Its force against your nearest friends;
> Which manners, decency, and pride
> Have taught you from the world to hide.[1]

I suspect that he would nag her ill-advisedly on subjects like her
health or social behaviour, and that she would finally flare up.

Esther Vanhomrigh was not only younger and more exciting
than her rival; she was rich and came from a family with a high,
secure place in polite society. When Swift scolded Vanessa, it
was for her melancholy, her seclusion, her failures to be secretive. He visited her as privately as possible, giving her the role of
daughter–mistress. When the mother became too oppressive, he
could flee, in fact or fantasy, to the daughter; and when
Vanessa's passions frightened him, he found safety in Stella's
uniformity. When both women excited more guilt than he could
endure, he had substitute families to visit in the country, or
dependent men to soothe him in town.

III. POEMS TO STELLA

So far as we know, Swift first used the name 'Stella' for Esther
Johnson in the poems he began writing for her birthday when
she was thirty-eight. Serving as her volunteer laureate, he im-

---

[1] *Ibid.*, p. 730.

plicitly condemned the anniversary odes that Lawrence Eusden had just begun supplying to the royal court. Yet one can also discern, behind the style of the poems for Stella, three stages of literary tradition: the conceited gallantry of Waller or Cowley, the burlesque of gallantry by Butler, and the sexual naturalism of Rochester or Prior. From these Swift derives a plain manner that takes account of the others but proves its own veracity by consciously opposing them. If we recall Waller's fantastic flattery of Sacharissa, we shall know what elements Swift is inverting: the irrationality and earnestness of conventional eulogies of a mistress, the paradoxical union of immaterialism with a delight in physical beauty:

> Sacharissa's beauty's wine,
> Which to madness doth incline:
> Such a liquor, as no brain
> That is mortal can sustain.
> Scarce can I to heav'n excuse
> The devotion, which I use
> Unto that adored dame.[1]

Waller means not that his speech is true but that the ingenuity of his figures reflects the depth of his love. Swift hears the figures as absurd exaggeration. When Butler takes up the theme of courtship, he anticipates Swift's exposé of romantic passion but not his tender feeling for Mrs Johnson. In *Hudibras* the widow challenges the knight to admit that he desires her money more than herself. He determines to woo her in her own fashion and replies,

> I do confess, with *goods* and *land*,
> I'd have a wife, at second hand;
> And such you are: Nor is't your person,
> My stomach's set so *sharp*, and *fierce* on,
> But 'tis (your better part) your *riches*,
> That my enamour'd heart bewitches;
> Let me your *fortune* but possess,
> And settle your person how you please.[2]

This would hit the reductive note of Swift's address if Butler were not running down all affection. Swift's view is that most

---

[1] 'To Amoret'.   [2] Part II, Canto I, ll. 471–8.

modern love grows out of deceit but that the mutual affection of
Stella and himself is rooted on a union of decorum with honesty.
Prior supplies a salacious model in a poem dealing with false
vows. Here, after Celia and Celadon have exchanged long lies
about their adoration of each other, the swain must leave:

> He thank'd her on his bended knee;
> Then drank a quart of milk and tea;
> And leaving her ador'd embrace,
> Hasten'd to court, to beg a place.
> While she, his absence to bemoan,
> The very moment he was gone,
> Call'd Thyrsis from beneath the bed;
> Where all this time he had been hid.[1]

Swift cannot match the versification. But he drops the prurience
and keeps the frankness. The affectation and ambivalence of the
poems he wrote for Vanessa never tinge the lines to Stella. We
meet Prior's comedy and Butler's rhythms. We also find something attributable to Waller—what Swift described elsewhere
when he said that 'a little grain of the romance is no ill ingredient
to preserve and exalt the dignity of human nature, without
which it is apt to degenerate into every thing that is sordid,
vicious and low'.[2]

> Stella this day is thirty-four,
> (We won't dispute a year or more).
> However Stella, be not troubled,
> Although thy size and years are doubled,
> Since first I saw thee at sixteen
> The brightest virgin of the green,
> So little is thy form declin'd
> Made up so largely in thy mind.[3]

Herbert Davis suggested that in choosing the name 'Stella' Swift
was marking the difference between his own expressions of
tenderness and those of Sidney in *Astrophel and Stella*.[4] Here Swift

---

[1] 'To a Young Gentleman in Love'.
[2] Davis IV. 95.   [3] *Poems* II. 721–2; my spelling and punctuation.
[4] *Stella: A Gentlewoman of the Eighteenth Century* (New York, 1942), p. 12.

characteristically celebrates the lady by dwelling on what common love songs would hide: her bulk and her age. Petrarchan solemnity gives way to humour; pulchritude becomes avoirdupois; enthusiasm evaporates into smiles at incongruities but leaves a true appreciation of real virtue; and if hyperboles survive, their matter is humble—they cannot be mistaken for anything but ingenious tokens of honest affection. While the elaborate, central conceit is derived from the hackneyed polarity of flesh and spirit, Swift's comic art characteristically inverts the usual design and makes the heaviness of her body harmonize with the purity of his beloved's soul.

IV. THE COMEDY OF SEXUAL PROSTHESIS

In March 1719 Prior published the high-rise folio edition of his *Poems*,[1] and Swift worked as his agent for distributing copies to Irish subscribers. Among the epigrams in the collection were half a dozen on what might be called the comedy of sexual prosthesis.[2] This is the ridicule of women who use artificial replacements for eyes, teeth, and other features of seductive

[1] Dated 1718.

[2] The comedy of sexual prosthesis is well-known in folklore; see 'Deceived Lover' in Stith Thompson's *Motif Index*. It also appears in many poems, ancient and modern, as well as essays and plays: the *Palatine Anthology* (e.g., XI. 310); Ovid, *Ars amatoria* II. 217–34, *Remedia amoris* 341–56, 437–8; Martial (e.g., IX. xxxvii. 118–20, XII. xxiii); Lyly, 'A Cooling Carde for Philautus' (a selective paraphrase of Ovid, *Remedia amoris*), in *Euphues* (*Complete Works*, ed. R. W. Bond [Oxford, 1902], I. 254–5); Jonson (*Epicene* I. i. 116–21, IV. ii. 91–5 *passim*); 'Newes from Hide-Park' (*ca.* 1640–3; Wing N970); Thomas Killigrew, *The Parson's Wedding* (IV. 1, speeches by Wanton and Captain) and *Thomaso, or, The Wanderer*, Part One (I. ii, Paulina's 4th speech); John Evelyn, *Mundus Muliebris: or, The Ladies Dressing-Room* (1690: gently humorous satire, in octosyllabic couplets, of female extravagance in clothes, jewels, and toilet articles); Richard Ames (?), *The Folly of Love* (1691; Wing A1970; ll. 124–37); Ned Ward, *Female Policy Detected* (1695: only a brief paraphrase of Ovid in the opening chapter); Prior, 'Phyllis's Age' and other poems (*Literary Works*, ed. H. Bunker Wright and Monroe Spears [Oxford, 1959], I. 456–8); the anonymous, burlesque English version of Quevedo's *Visions* (1702, p. 142); see also *PQ* 51, 775. In prose fiction the motif is a staple of American humour: see Poe, 'The Man That Was Used Up', Hawthorne, 'Mrs Bullfrog', Twain, 'Aurelia's Unfortunate Young Man', Nathanael West, 'A Cool Million'. See also Le Sage, *Le Diable boiteux*, Ch. 3; Comtesse d'Aulnoy, *Gracieuse et Percenet* (Duchesse Grognon). For a bitterly serious treatment, see Sylvia Plath's poem, 'The Applicant'. I am indebted to Professor James Turner for generous assistance with this note.

beauty. It has a literary genealogy that goes back at least as far as Ovid. Prior's poems in the genre involve less anger than amusement, and their language is decorous:

> Helen was just slipt into bed:
>   Her eye-brows on the toilet lay:
> Away the kitten with them fled,
>   As fees belonging to her prey.[1]

—and so forth. About the same time as Prior's book appeared, Swift began writing similar but longer poems, of a kind he is notorious for:

> So Celia went entire to bed,
>   All her complexions safe and sound,
> But when she rose, white, black, and red
>   Though still in sight, had chang'd their ground
>
>   .   .   .
>
> The paint by perspiration cracks,
>   And falls in rivulets of sweat,
> On either side you see the tracks,
>   While at her chin the conflu'ents met.
>
>   .   .   .
>
> Two balls of glass may serve for eyes,
>   White lead can plaister up a cleft,
> But these alas, are poor supplyes
>   If neither cheeks, nor lips be left.[2]

The non-moralizing humour of Prior has vanished. Swift's language is repeatedly coarse; his burlesque is savage. Again he seems to be dividing himself from his predecessors. Just as the poem to Stella suggests a sympathy with the lady he smiles at, so the description of Celia sounds not only comic but bitter as well. In the shock of the last line quoted above (which so neatly but surprisingly outdoes the shock of the lines before), the reader seems an object of hostility along with the lady.

Earlier satirists like Martial and Prior have two attitudes toward women who hide deformities with mechanical devices:

---

[1] *Literary Works* I. 457.   [2] 'The Progress of Beauty', *Poems* I. 226–9.

either smiling tolerance, or disgust; and if disgust, the onus falls on the crime of deceiving a man who desires a healthy, handsome woman for voluptuous recreation. Swift refuses to distinguish between healthy and harmless vice, and he builds all his satire on physical equivalents of moral evil. Therefore, whoever is unchaste must appear deformed and infectious in Swift's poetry—as if fornication invariably produced syphilis.

The obsession with women—rather than with men—who disguise their blemishes, makes one suspect that in these poems Swift was not simply condemning lust but defending spinsters like Vanessa and Stella. 'Time', he once said, 'takes off from the lustre of virgins in all other eyes but mine.'[1] It was unusual in Swift's day to treat women as not necessarily marriage-fodder. Yet he himself felt satisfied, in opposition to Puritan doctrine (and in keeping with his own preferences), to remain a celibate priest. And since he delighted in the company of young ladies, it was natural for him to think they required no special justification for remaining single. In fact, he sometimes invoked a pessimistic paradox: that if a woman did rise to proper standards of virtue and culture, no eligible man would appreciate her, and she would find no husband; so also if a man was the sort Swift admired, he would hardly meet a suitable bride.[2] 'Half the number of well-educated nobility and gentry must either continue in a single life, or be forced to couple themselves with women for whom they can possibly have no esteem.'[3]

The ugliness of the matter is essential to the quality of poems like *The Progress of Beauty*. Their incongruities are clever and funny; but unlike those in the verses to Stella, they cut the reader off from the object and render the vicious women as belonging to a different species from his own. Unlike Baudelaire, Swift never distils beauty from horror. His versification often adds the grotesque to the disgusting. The heavily regular beat, the frequently thumping rhymes, and the coolly systematic parallels or analogies, make a sardonic vehicle for the sharp observations.

[1] Williams I. 46.
[2] Cf. *Cadenus and Vanessa* and 'To Lord Harley'. [3] Davis IV. 228.

When the poet succeeds, the effect is distaste and hilarity at once.

The logic of the poems supports decent concealment, not full exposure. In none of these satires does the reader find that he is wrong to feel repelled by the sight, smell, and sound of defecation. This is one reason the poems were funny and why they confuse some modern readers. To simple post-Freudians, the author's assumption that farting smells bad seems doubly wrong; for they believe a preoccupation with bowels and wrinkles is the mark of a sick mind, and they also believe that natural functions or the body's decay should not disgust a wise man.

Swift's comedy of sexual prosthesis depends on the principle that few bodies are perfectly inviting. In order for friends and lovers to remain attractive to one another, they must cover up, in manner and in clothing. If at the same time they are not to be deceitful, they must underneath be as clean and healthy as they can; and if they are not to invite deceit, they must found their mutual affection on moral qualities, not visible ones.

The man taken in by Celia is looking for ageless perfection in the body, which can never provide such excellence. He invites not modesty but trickery, and gets a body and mind as corrupt as his own. The poem demands that we laugh frigidly at the physical consequences of vice. But many readers hesitate to respond appropriately because the author's tone seems wrong. The poems are too detailed, too sharply focused, too emphatic. One feels uneasily that Celia is only the immediate target, and that through her surfaces the poet attacks a larger group including the reader. Whores exist because of a conspiracy of women and men. If conventional courtship and sexuality did not share the false ideals of women like Celia, such characters could not exist. They are as much victims as seducers.

This principle connects Swift's filthy poems with his political and economic arguments. When he came to write his *Letter to a Young Lady*, Swift included a paragraph asking the new bride to spend no money on fine clothes:

> For, the satirical part of mankind will needs believe, that it is not impossible, to be very fine and very filthy; and that the capacities of a lady are sometimes apt to fall short in cultivating cleanliness and

finery together. I shall only add, upon so tender a subject, what a pleasant gentleman said concerning a silly woman of quality; that nothing could make her supportable but cutting off her head; for his ears were offended by her tongue, and his nose by her hair and teeth.[1]

About the time he wrote *The Progress of Beauty*, Swift also wrote a pamphlet on the Irish economy in which he urged Parliament to forbid women to wear expensive, imported materials.[2] The fine ladies of Ireland, he implied, waste the wealth of their nation on brocades that merely distract men's eyes from the ladies' ignorance and frivolity. One might call the clothing prosthetic.[3]

---

[1] *Ibid.*, IX. 87. [2] *Ibid.*, p. 16.
[3] For a discussion of other filthy verse satires on women, by Swift, see below, pp. 688–95. I am much indebted to Professor James Turner for help with these discussions.

Chapter Seven

MEDDLING IN POLITICS

I. DEFENDING THE FALLEN

It seems a fair question to ask why the retrospective essays Swift wrote on English politics after Queen Anne died were so much weaker than those that followed, on Irish affairs. At first the matter of England filled his mind like the memory of a great storm in which one's comrades were lost and one only escaped alone to tell the tale. Swift's impulse was to leap ashore and make a pamphlet on 'the consequences hoped and feared from the death of the Queen'.[1] Even before leaving England, he began to write this, and hoped to incorporate into it pieces of *Some Free Thoughts*, which he realized could not now be published. The new pamphlet was meant, I think, to rally the party behind Oxford. But it soon looked as if Oxford might be abandoning the party and striking a bargain with the Whigs.[2] Instead of completing the pamphlet, Swift dropped it when he reached Ireland.

Now, I believe, he felt in no position to write propaganda for the Tories. Cut off from direct information about the startling changes in London, edgy about his own safety in Dublin, he stopped trying to influence public events. But during his first autumn in Ireland, while the political landscape suffered its enormous upheavals, he put his hand to what he had often desired from other possessors of state secrets, a record of the events in which he had a share.

One probably learns something about Swift's state of mind from the fact that these autobiographical pages survive in a copy

---

[1] Davis VIII. 101. [2] Williams II. 118, 124, 127.

made from dictation.[1] Swift was used to have his correspondence inspected at the post office; and when he wished to send a
message to Bolingbroke, he had it delivered by hand.[2] In
January 1715, as we have seen, Erasmus Lewis warned him to
hide his papers.[3] Swift had kept many memoranda of the years
1710–14; and he once said he had been 'digesting' them into
order one sheet at a time, 'for I dare not venture any further, lest
the humour of searching papers should revive'.[4] I suppose he
was afraid that if his house were searched, the *Memoirs* would be
a dangerous discovery.

Unfortunately, these *Memoirs* provide first-hand accounts of
only a few episodes of Swift's life. Otherwise they rely on the
information that Lady Masham, Lord Oxford, and the rest saw
fit to share with him. Besides, it becomes quickly apparent even
to a casual reader that Swift could not let himself be full and
frank in the *Memoirs*. The material he had, however limited in
range, was too damaging to those whom he wished to bolster.
One finds names, details, reasons omitted or evaded when they
might hurt Oxford or Bolingbroke; one finds dubious suspicions
erected into established facts when they might hurt the enemy.
Thus Swift refuses to admit that Guiscard's death wounds were
really due to the courtiers' swords,[5] but he blandly asserts that
the Duchess of Marlborough was Godolphin's mistress.[6] The
Memoirs were never completed—I suppose, because Swift's
loyalties got in the way of his original design—and their limited
value is mainly biographical.

When the *Report from the Committee of Secrecy* appeared
(obviously a step toward the impeachment of his chiefs), Swift
began all over again. Using some of the old materials, he wrote
an essay that he seemed to think might be published soon.[7]

---

[1] See Davis VIII. 210–14. The misspellings could only be due to dictation, but I assume
that Swift read aloud from an earlier copy.
[2] Williams II. 218, n. 4.   [3] *Ibid.*, p. 156; cf. above, p. 9.
[4] 10 Jan. 1722, to Pope; Williams II. 367. (I accept the date given by Ball; see *ibid.*,
p. 365 n. 2.)
[5] Davis VIII. 127.   [6] *Ibid.*, p. 111.
[7] *An Enquiry into the Behaviour of the Queen's Last Ministry, ibid.*, pp. 129–80.

Whatever he may have lacked for this project, he certainly had the leisure, the inclination, and (as he believed) the facts needed to create a rational and indeed honest justification of the fallen leaders. He worked on the essay during the summer of 1715, stunned by the attainder of the Duke of Ormonde. In Chapter One, addressed implicitly to Tories, he lays out the internal reasons for the decline of Oxford's ministry. We remember that various injudicious authors had—in a series of hasty pamphlets —tried to defend one or another of the Tory leaders by maligning the rest.[1] Swift apparently wished to rectify their accounts. After a review of the clashing ambitions of Oxford and Bolingbroke, Swift blamed the ministry's failures on the wilfulness of the Queen. Precisely when he finished this first chapter, we do not know.

But he began a second and final part in 1717, probably when Oxford was released from the Tower. Here Swift tried to show that the Earl's ministry had not plotted to bring in the Pretender. Although he may have completed the new chapter in a year or so, he kept polishing the whole essay and making small changes.[2]

So meticulous a process of composition should have brought forth a prose treatise that deserved to stand beside the brilliant journalism of the ministerial years. But it did nothing of the sort. Having little privileged information, Swift was forced to sound moderate and sensible in his arguments. He wished to conciliate, not to antagonize or play games with his reader. Here was no scope for his reckless rhetoric, teasing humour, or impersonations. Consequently, his most dazzling effects are missing.

Abundant leisure was not what Swift needed to write well. Defence and apology were not his happiest manners. Even the tone of shrewdness, fundamental to his strategy, was badly spoiled by the innocence of many remarks. When Swift described Lady Masham as 'a most excellent lady, upon whose veracity I entirely depend',[3] he gave his game away. It was bad

---

[1] See above, p. 13.

[2] See the introduction to my edition of Swift, *An Enquiry into the Behavior of the Queen's Last Ministry* (Bloomington, Indiana, 1956).

[3] Davis VIII. 149.

enough to believe such a statement oneself; it was worse to
suppose readers would trust one for believing it. Swift was
demonstrating his loyalty to old friends who were out of favour;
this is not the best way to persuade strangers of one's own
sagacity.

He also spoke with more frankness than discretion. In order to
answer the complaints brought against his friends by other Tory
critics, Swift blamed the Queen because she kept Oxford from
rooting his ministry in thoroughly Tory doctrines (which of
course Oxford never wished to do). Then to clear the ministry of
the charge of Jacobitism—brought mainly by the Whigs—he
could supply no fresh evidence but founded his case on a rational
analysis of probable motives. The combination of the two approaches misses fire. Hostile readers would get little indication of
the author's expertise; and while they might accept his claim to
candour, that in turn would only leave him looking too simple
for the task he had set himself.

Ideally, Swift should have been able to handle the Queen as a
villain and to represent Oxford as a victimized hero. The Lord
Treasurer would then seem to have sacrificed himself to serve
the nation—putting up with the vilification of the Whigs, the
misunderstandings of his colleagues, and the obstinacy of the
Queen in order to bring peace and financial stability to a sinking
people. Oxford would seem to have sacrificed his own reputation magnificently for the sake of the Queen's. But Swift's own
constitutional argument and the historical evidence required
him to present the political changes as due to a co-operation of
monarch with minister. The Queen's errors therefore had to
appear due to caprice, not calculation; and this analysis laid her
approved policies open to the same charge of blind impulse.
Swift himself said her resentment of the Whigs' behaviour was
due less to principles than personalities. He could not avoid
suggesting that her acceptance of Harley and Mrs Masham
had the same origin. Swift's habit of reducing political history to psychology always has this weakness of eliminating
moral aspects from the very issues he feels most passionate
about.

Swift gave his long essay the title, *An Enquiry into the Behavior of the Queen's Last Ministry*, which has the right overtones for a fairly systematic, reasonable account of a complicated state of affairs. The work is well planned and coherent. The style is correct. But the only section with vitality enough to bear reading by non-specialists is a set of paragraphs devoted to the characters of Ormonde, Bolingbroke, and Oxford. Here it is not the argument or wit that holds us, not any irony or fantasy, but the pathetic strength of the author's devotion to three men in disgrace.

One feature of the *Enquiry* suggests that by 1717 Swift was recovering a bit of his old confidence, perhaps because the widespread discontent which George I's government was producing in England and Ireland could no longer be concealed. The Septennial Act had distressed many admirers of the British constitution. Walpole, Townshend, and their powerful associates were battling in the loyal opposition. The Prince of Wales was openly defying his father. In Ireland economic conditions were such that Archbishop King (then a Lord Justice) told a friend,

> I take this kingdom to be more miserable as to the generality, than ever you knew it, things being doubled nay trebled in their rates since you were here, the poor squeezed to death by excessive rents to maintain the luxury of a few; the consequence is like to be that all the English farmers and tradesmen [i.e., those of Protestant English extraction] will be driven out of the kingdom.[1]

With such symptoms in mind one may return to Swift's *Enquiry* and observe that in Chapter Two he shifts his point of view. Instead of using present circumstances to explain past events, he makes the old into a solid ground for attacking the new. The comparisons are increasingly invidious and one-sided. In this rhetoric the goodness of the policies from 1710 to 1714 shows up the badness of 1715 and following—a badness which Swift takes for granted. So he says that when the Queen died, there were not five hundred English Protestants who supported

[1] 7 Nov. 1717, to Tollet.

the Pretender, but 'how it hath come to pass, that severall millions are said to have since changed their sentiments, it shall not be my part to enquire.'[1] He mentions the 'prodigious disaffection at present'.[2] He insults King George by saying that it would have been hard under the Oxford ministry to render the Elector odious and the Pretender amiable, 'neither of which is to be soon compassed towards absent princes, unless by comparing them with those of whom we have had experience, which was not *then* the case'.[3]

It looks as though, in this short series of essays on English affairs, Swift started out defensively and apologetically but ended on the attack. He also changed in those years from a concentration on English issues to an involvement in Ireland's needs. At first he said, 'But I hope I shall keep my resolution of never medling with Irish politicks.'[4] Five years and three Irish parliamentary sessions later, he said, 'No cloyster is retired enough to keep politicks out.'[5] The fecklessness of the Lords and Commons, and the deepening wretchedness of the Irish people combined to tease Swift out of his reflections on the Oxford ministry and beyond the caution of his sermon on brotherly love.

II. THE CONDITION OF IRELAND

Looking back now, one sees Ireland as a case of an accepted economic theory gone mad. In the early eighteenth century most European governments believed a favourable balance of trade, with a surplus of specie coming into the country, was the mark of prosperity. They treated colonies mainly as a device to enrich the mother country in this sense. But the sufferers from the practice were normally the doomed aborigines, whose freedom and health were an easy sacrifice to the greed of their conquerors. In Ireland the ruling minority themselves were threatened with economic oppression, barely distinguished from

---

[1] Davis VIII. 165; I follow the original version, given in my edition, pp. 66–7.
[2] Davis VIII. 168. [3] *Ibid.*, p. 173.
[4] Letter to Ford, Aug. 1714; Williams II. 127.
[5] Letter of 8 Dec. 1719, to Ford; *ibid.*, p. 330.

the lesser breed without the law. Behind our sympathy with Swift's rage over the fate of his country must always remain the knowledge that if Ireland had enjoyed the advantages of the American colonists, Swift (who once wished to be made Bishop of Virginia) might have troubled himself about the native Roman Catholics little more than a high-minded American did about the red Indians.

But his rage is not to be cheapened. Justice and charity are imperial virtues, and nobody in Ireland exhibited more of them than Swift. And even if one could set the moral standards aside, his practical economic case remains. It would be hard to show that England benefited from the degradation of Ireland.[1] But one could persuasively argue that Ireland was ruined by a policy which added the burdens of a kingdom to the disabilities of a colony. The coastline of Ireland was provided with numberless good harbours, several of them beautifully suited to transatlantic trade. But the English were a seafaring people, and after the Restoration they narrowly controlled the shipment of Irish goods to America.[2] The soil and climate of Ireland were in general excellent for pasture and tillage. Arthur Young said, 'Natural fertility, acre for acre, over the two kingdoms is certainly in favour of Ireland.'[3] But the English were a farming people; they would not let the Irish export livestock to England, and even discouraged them from growing their own wheat. The sheepfarmers and weavers of Ireland could together produce fine cloth. Young said, 'Their sheep are on an average better than those in England,'[4] and he said a friend of his who wore a suit of Irish poplin during a tour of France and Spain found 'it was more admired and envied than any thing he carried with him'.[5] But the English were a manufacturing people, who thought the textile trade was the keystone of their prosperity; and after the turn of the eighteenth century they denied the Irish

---

[1] See the excellent argument by Arthur Young on this subject (II. 217–20).
[2] The restrictions were less harmful than has been thought, partly because in manufactured goods the Irish could not compete with the English anyhow; see Cullen, pp. 64–5 and (on the Navigation Acts) 12, 37–8.
[3] II. 5. [4] *Ibid.*, p. 106. [5] *Ibid.*, p. 220.

the right to export finished woollens to any country.[1] The unworked wool could legally be exported only to England.

The landlords of Ireland (who were now overwhelmingly of Protestant English extraction) responded to such destructive colonialism with their own style of foolishness. If they kept land under cultivation, they let it to middlemen who divided and subdivided it into sections too small to be farmed properly. They rackrented the tenants, and they often lived abroad—especially in London. Many landlords got rid of their penniless tenants altogether and turned the land into pasture, which was far simpler to keep up. The raw wool could be smuggled to France for claret and silks. The cattle could be sold outside England in the provisioning trade. Archbishop King once told this story:

> A gentleman gave me a visit tother day and entertained me with dis-
> course, how he had improved his estate. He told me he had a farm
> on which there lived about an hundred families that paid him rent
> very ill and he lost much every year, that he had turned them off,
> and set it dearer to one man who stocked it [i.e., with cattle], lived
> well upon it, and paid his rent punctually. I asked him what came of
> the hundred families he turned off it. He answered that he did not
> know.[2]

To weaken the economy still further, the English used the Irish establishment to soak up pensioners, office-seekers, and military personnel who would would have been found incon-venient on the English establishment. So the crumbling Irish structure had to carry royal mistresses, retired secretaries, and British half-pay officers, all of whose money went out of the kingdom and never came back. For elaborately political reasons the bulk of the deaneries, bishoprics, and valuable public places had to go to recipients imported from Britain. Consequently, those Irish gentlemen with energy enough to desire a public career were discouraged from the outset.

When Swift's friend St George Ashe died, Archbishop King

---

[1] The Irish could not have competed with English manufacturers in the quality and cheapness of their goods. But they might have striven to improve their methods of production if knowledge of the law had not inhibited them.

[2] Letter of 20 Dec. 1712, to Nicolson.

chose John Stearne (born and educated in Ireland) as the clergyman who most deserved the vacated bishopric of Derry. With an income of twenty-four hundred pounds a year, Derry was one of the biggest plums on the ecclesiastical tree. King himself had laboured immensely, decades earlier, to build up the congregations, churches, and benefices of the diocese. He had watched sadly while his two successors let the improvements decay. Now he hoped to see Derry thrive under the active guidance of an active resident bishop.

But the English Whigs were tired of being obstructed by Irish bishops, and they decided that the place must go to an Englishman. The Archbishop of Canterbury, William Wake, whom King had long considered an ally, picked out William Nicolson, Bishop of Carlisle, as the best candidate. Nicolson, afflicted with three sons and four daughters, was very willing to give up an English diocese for one in Ireland that would triple his income. So the appointment was made.

If the gentry and merchants of Ireland had united in their policies, they could still have maintained a viable economy within the British strait-jacket. But religious and racial hatreds drove them apart. Presbyterians and Anglicans squabbled for profit and power while native Catholics endured too many agonies to mind what became of their tormentors. Of course, the least care of the English Whigs under George I was to improve the condition of Ireland. They accelerated the programme of settling carpet-baggers on the Irish establishment. They refused to encourage agriculture, and blocked Irish efforts to do so. As a replacement for the woollen manufacture, they offered to build up the linen industry. But this flourished mainly in the north and was not on a scale to meet the need. Meanwhile, landlords who were eager to trade money-losing cornfields for efficient cattle pasture continued to evict unhappy families. Merchants who could not sell cloth dismissed thousands of weavers. The smuggling of wool to France was not an industry that could support thriving domesticity. Although emigration to the American colonies or enlistment in European armies might give relief to those who were strong or prosperous enough to travel, the poorest and weakest had to starve in their homeland.

Because St Patrick's Cathedral stood in a neighbourhood populated by weavers, Swift had daily experience of their distress, which became acute after the South Sea Bubble collapsed. 'The return of those [families] who are starving for want of work', he said bitterly, 'amounts to above 1600, which is pretty fair for this town, and one trade, after such numbers as have gone to other countries to seek a livelihood.'[1] We do not have to rely on his words of outrage. In Dublin, Archbishop King found the outcries of the wretched weavers unbearable.[2] As for rural poverty, Bishop Nicolson, on his autumnal journey to Londonderry, said he had

> never beheld (even in Picardy, Westphalia or Scotland) such dismal marks of hunger and want as appeared in the countenances of most of the poor creatures that I met with on the road. The wretches live in reeky sod-hovels; and have generally no more than a rag of coarse blanket to cover a small part of their nakedness. Upon the strictest inquiry, I could not find that they are better clad, or lodged, in the winter season. These sorry slaves plough the ground, to the very tops of their mountains, for the service of their lords; who spend the (truly rack-) rents . . . at London. A ridge or two of potatoes is all the poor tenant has for the support of himself, a wife, and (commonly) ten or twelve bare-legged children. To complete their misery, these animals are bigotted Papists; and we frequently met them trudging to some ruined church or chapel, either to mass, a funeral or a wedding, with a priest in the same habit with themselves.[3]

Three years later, after the South Sea Bubble, he was more graphic and less restrained:

> What lies most heavy on my spirits is the inexpressible (and daily increasing) poverty whereinto most parts of this kingdom are fallen, and falling; and most especially the starving inhabitants of Ulster. The hard winter killed most of their cattle; which died after the poor owners had bestowed (not only all their small stocks of forage, in hay and straw, but) most of their corn in endeavouring to keep them alive. The demands lately made from abroad (by the men of Manchester chiefly) for our yarn, and by others for our linen-cloth, is at a full stop . . . . One of my coach-horses, by accident, was killed in a field within view of my house. Before the skin could be taken off,

---

[1] 15 Apr. 1721; Williams II. 380.   [2] 8 Apr. 1721, to Col. Flower.
[3] Letter of 24 Jun. 1718, to Wake; Wake Letters XII, fol. 275.

my servants were surrounded with fifty or sixty of the neighbouring cottagers, who brought axes and cleavers, and immediately divided the carcase, every man carrying home his proper dividend, for food to their respective families.[1]

The Irish Parliament could have striven to improve the national economy. But both the Commons and the Lords attempted little and accomplished less. During the session of 1719, the Lord Lieutenant was the Duke of Bolton, a Junto Whig whom Swift rightly considered 'a great booby'.[2] Britain was now engaged in a little war with Spain, and the government expected the Duke of Ormonde to land in Ireland. Worried about native support for the enemy, they desired a tightening of restrictions on the Roman Catholics, whose priests travelled back and forth to the continent. In the normal Whig style, Bolton at the same time pressed hard for an easing of restrictions on the Dissenters, who had naturally done all they could to support the government during the Jacobite troubles of 1715.

The House of Commons cheerfully passed a savage new penal bill against the Roman Catholics, with a clause decreeing that unregistered priests should be branded on the cheek. This punishment seemed mild to the Irish Privy Council, who improved it to castration. But Westminster preferred the original clause. Yet when the amended bill came back from England, it met defeat in the House of Lords, to the consternation of the witty Bishop Nicolson, who was stunned to see the whole tribe of Irish bishops join to throw it out.[3] Archbishop King wrote, 'I think, we should execute some of those acts we have already made against Popery, before we call for more.'[4]

All the forces of the church united could not prevail to stop the passage of a Toleration Act for the Dissenters, although it emerged from its trial far weaker than the relief wanted by the government. Every assault on the Test Act, however, was turned back. Archbishop King and his friends were indefatigable,

---

[1] 2 Jun. 1721, to Wake; Wake Letters XIII, no. 249; spelling and punctuation altered.
[2] Davis v. 258.   [3] Letter of 30 Nov. 1719, to Wake; Wake Letters XIII, no. 131.
[4] Letter of 12 Nov. 1719, to Southwell.

Bolton complained, 'in perverting as many as they [could]';[1] and Primate Lindsay, a highest-flying Tory, ended his contribution to the debate by 'assuring their lordships that schism was a damnable sin'.[2]

The battle over the Toleration Act was furious, but the government interest in the Commons and the English-bred bishops in the Lords produced the needed artillery. We have already noticed how little Archbishop King supported the Lord Lieutenant's programme during the parliamentary session of 1715–16.[3] Now too in his resistance to the Toleration Act he was not alone. 'We fought our ground inch by inch', his grace wrote to London; 'if our brethren that came from your side the water had not deserted us, we had thrown out the bill.'[4] The law finally enacted relaxed earlier regulations of church attendance and allowed Dissenting clergymen to administer the eucharist. The archbishop spoke for many Anglicans when he declared furiously to Canterbury that the Act allowed 'every man that pleases to set up for a teacher, to make proselytes and parties, and vent what doctrines he pleases'.[5]

It was also during this session of Parliament that sane men tried again to reverse the mischievous agricultural regimen prescribed by the English for Ireland. Absurd laws had been established to prohibit tenant farmers from changing pasture into cultivated soil. By the time of George I the Irish were importing most of their grain from England. In 1716 the Commons had at last produced the heads of a bill that repealed the statutes against tillage and, instead, mildly required that at least five out of every hundred acres should be cultivated. We have seen that instead of strengthening this weak plank, the English Privy Council mutilated it so that the Irish Parliament could no longer accept it.[6] In the summer of 1719 the heads of a Tillage Bill were passed again, and the M.P.s even asked Bolton to recommend it 'in the most effectual manner to his majesty'.[7]

[1] Letter of 15 Oct. 1719, to Craggs.
[2] Letter of 22 Oct. 1719, from Webster to Delafaye.
[3] Cf. above, pp. 27–8.   [4] 10 Nov. 1719, to Annesley.   [5] 5 Mar. 1720, to Wake.
[6] Cf. above, pp. 27–8.   [7] Ferguson, p. 48.

Bolton's secretary wrote to Westminster that it was 'very much desired by the gentlemen of this kingdom'.[1] The bill never came back from England.

The cause that really thrilled Parliament—or at least the peers—and that was again continued from the session of 1715–16, was also one that inflamed Archbishop King. This was not a matter of religion or agriculture but of the Lords' own power, embodied in the litigation between Maurice Annesley and Hester Sherlock which came to be known as the Annesley Case. It will be remembered that the Irish House of Lords had reversed the original decree (in favour of Annesley), and that Annesley had infuriated them by taking the case to England and appealing to the House of Lords there. The Irish Lords had then asserted their own appellate and final jurisdiction.[2]

Nevertheless, the British Lords received Annesley's appeal; and they upheld the original decree of the Irish Court of the Exchequer in his favour, whereupon the judges of that court gratefully accepted and obeyed the order in favour of the plaintiff, early in 1718. When the Parliament of Ireland met in the summer of 1719, the Lords, worked up and led by Archbishop King, denounced the Exchequer judges and finally committed them (for the three-month duration of the parliamentary session) to the expensive custody of the black rod.

What made the case a landmark in constitutional law was its implications. If a decision of the Irish peers could be appealed to the British, no Irish law or property was secure. Any litigant who could afford to take his case across St George's Channel might defy the united government of the kingdom. The old issue of Ireland's dependence on England, never really closed, gaped wide. In the loud arguments that thundered on for months, the spokesmen for the Irish interest employed a line of reasoning that they hoped would prove their fundamental loyalty even while they opposed the will of the British legislators. This was the principle that the King alone stood constitutionally above

[1] Webster to Delafaye, 10 Sept. 1719.
[2] Cf. above, pp. 29–30.

the Irish Parliament, and that the British House of Lords were infringing on the royal prerogative.

Nobody in England seemed to be enchanted by the analysis. But the defiant language and conduct of the Irish peers made their impression. Lord Cowper pointed out to his brothers in Westminster that among the Irish proceedings was an article implying national independence of Britain. A bill was therefore ordered 'for better securing the dependency of Ireland on the crown of Great Britain'.[1] Theoretically, the Irish peers may have had the same jurisdiction as the British. But Parliament had been sitting very irregularly in Dublin since 1640; its authority had shallow roots; and in recent years a few cases had been appealed from the Court of Chancery in Ireland to the British House of Lords.

The driving force behind the new bill was naturally not justice but love of power; for the British peers were humanly glad to increase their own authority. As the bill moved through its readings, Irish exasperation swelled audibly. 'It must make Ireland the most miserable people in Europe', said Archbishop King. 'It will separate them from the common interest and God knows what desperation may make a people do.'[2] In the long debate on the second reading, Molesworth and others spoke against the bill, but they were defeated (140 to 88).[3] On 26 March 1720 the Declaratory Act[4] was finally passed, and two weeks later it received the royal assent.[5]

This event annihilated any Irish pretensions to genuine self-government. According to the Act, the kingdom was 'subordinate unto and dependent upon the imperial crown of Great Britain'; and the King, Lords and Commons of Great Britain had 'full power and authority to make laws ... to bind the kingdom and people of Ireland'.[6] Such a statute inevitably shrank the difference between native Irish families and the

---

[1] *Dublin Courant*, 22 Feb. 1720.
[2] Letter of 13 Feb. 1720, to Molesworth.
[3] *Parliamentary History; Dublin Post-Man*, 11 Mar. 1720.
[4] Often called the Dependency Act.
[5] *Dublin Courant*, 12 Apr. 1720.   [6] 6 Geo. I, c. 5.

descendants of English settlers, even while it deepened the gulf between the Irish interest as a whole and the English interest. It attached Dissenters to Anglicans in the face of a menace to all landlords, merchants, and tradesmen. Nobody whose livelihood or property lay in Ireland could think of the new law without anxiety. The sequel, said Archbishop King, was a 'universal disaffection of all people':

> They vent their anger with such speeches as perhaps may not be very safe, but above all the Whigs seem most provoked; they say they will do every thing, but forfeit their estates and others say they know not whether they have any estates or no after this enslaving act.[1]

The qualms of the Protestants of Ireland were not soothed by another stroke of the British Parliament, where a bill was brought in 'to improve' the English woollen and silk industry.[2] This involved a protectionist programme that, as every informed person foresaw, would undo the calico industry in all parts of the British Isles but with a uniquely crushing impact on Ireland, where the export of finished woollens was already illegal. The spring of 1720 aggravated the spreading gloom by giving Dublin an epidemic of fever that killed many and ruined others. 'The poor people are like to be undone,' said Archbishop King, 'for they are not able to earn any thing by their labour, and can't so much as sow their potatoes which is in a manner the one support is left to them.'[3]

Charles Ford, in a letter to Swift, would not sympathize with Irish resentment of the Declaratory Act. Swift replied,

> I believe myself not guilty of too much veneration for the Irish House of Lords, but I differ from you in politics; the question is whether people ought to be slaves or no.... I do assure you I never saw so universal a discontent as there is among the highest most virulent and anti-church Whigs against that bill and every author or abetter of it without exception. They say publickly that having been the most loyal submissive complying subjects that ever prince had, no subjects were ever so ill treated.[4]

[1] Letter of 10 May 1720, to Molesworth.
[2] Introduced 1719, passed 1721.
[3] Letter of 12 May 1720, to Stearne.
[4] 4 Apr. 1720; Williams II. 342–3.

By now Swift was on excellent speaking terms with Archbishop King, whose proceedings in the House of Lords must have tickled him; and it was now that he called his grace 'half a Tory'.[1] I suppose that in the political atmosphere created by the Declaratory Act, and with the encouragement of the archbishop, Swift felt ready once more to mount the stage of public debate. Toward the end of May, the sick and troubled Dubliners were entertained with a pamphlet called *A Proposal for the Universal Use of Irish Manufacture*.[2]

III. 'IRISH MANUFACTURE'

The reasoning Swift followed in this dazzling performance went back humbly enough to the early years of Queen Anne's reign, when a few thoughtful Irish leaders conceived of a safe way to reply to the disastrous Woollen Act passed by the English Parliament in 1699.[3] They proposed simply that the Irish should wear only goods manufactured in their own country. In several sessions, the Irish Parliament voted resolutions against the importing of foreign cloth, and the public prints often recommended the scheme. While Parliament was sitting in the autumn of 1719, a Dublin newspaper published 'Proposals for the Encouragement of Trade' that included the rejection of foreign 'silks, calicoes, printed and striped linens'.[4] Bishop Nicolson complained that the Irish bishops refused to distribute (among Presbyterians) any Bibles printed in London, because they were 'English manufactures'.[5]

What Swift did was to combine the straightforward economic principle with the manic nationalism generated by the Declaratory Act. In Westminster a few months earlier the Peerage Bill had gone down to a tempestuous defeat in the British Commons. Glancing at the arguments brought forth against

---

[1] 8 Dec. 1719, to Ford; *ibid.*, p. 331. Cf. above, p. 26.

[2] Probably between 24 and 28 May; Ferguson, p. 54, n. 82. It was presented by the grand jury on 30 May.

[3] I realize that the immediate commercial effect of the Act may not have been serious, but I think the discouragement to the Irish textile industry was indeed disastrous.

[4] *Dublin Courant*, 25 Nov. 1719.

[5] Nicolson, 9 Feb. 1719, to Wake; Wake Letters XIII, no. 40.

that bill, Archbishop King echoed Locke and Molyneux in saying,

> It was urged that whatever people were governed by laws, in the making of which they had no interest were slaves and not subjects, which will concern Ireland very much, and will infer either that we are slaves or that we ought not to be bound by laws in the making of which we have no part.[1]

King's rhetoric underlies Swift's indignation. The *Proposal for the Universal Use of Irish Manufacture* deals with two relationships: that of Ireland to England and that of individual to nation. Swift shows no more fury against the English for their bestiality to a sister race than he shows against the Irish for conniving at their own destruction. He is as deeply outraged by the landlords' oppression of their tenants, or the merchants' indifference to standards of workmanship, as he is by the people's bending of their necks to the British yoke. The dramatic heat of Swift's pamphlets on Ireland rises from the grinding together of two sorts of despair. one over Britain's treatment of Ireland, the other over the Irish people's treatment of one another.

So he attacks the landholders for turning ploughland into pasture, and letting agriculture decay. He scolds the Irish Parliament for ignoring the plight of the country and busying themselves with political and ecclesiastical shadows—the Annesley Case and the Toleration Act. He damns the British for treating Ireland as a colony and for delivering every office of any value to men of English birth and education. He blames all the inhabitants of Ireland, but especially the women, for flinging away their country's small supply of gold and silver on imported luxuries. He denounces Irish landlords for crushing the tenantry with exorbitant fines and for sacrificing long-term prosperity to immediate profit. He ridicules—in the wake of the South Sea Bubble—the possibility of a national bank.

In elaborating his doctrines, Swift charges the whole essay with delicious irony by setting the spontaneity of his manner

---

[1] Letter of 28 Dec. 1719, to Southwell.

against the deliberation of his moral judgment. The syntax and the general disposition of paragraphs seem to lack premeditation. By avoiding obvious balance, antithesis, and the common resources of formal rhetoric, he gives himself a naïve tone, as if he were scribbling down unguarded thoughts. Yet the reader quickly realizes that the author is self-conscious and artful, calculating his effects.

From this opposition between outward style and inner meaning Swift starts the dramatic irony that keeps his reader from staying passively outside the argument. One cannot refuse the invitation to work—and it is easy, pleasant work—at righting the author's inversions. Even if Swift avoided figures, images, examples, analogies, and weighted language, this division between the casualness of his style and the subtlety of his character would establish an ironic structure for all his satire.

Of course, he employs the restricted techniques as well. So the elegant carelessness with which Swift orders his paragraphs leads the reader to sort out the relative values himself: he decides which are the central ideas and which peripheral, and the task is agreeable. Swift makes the effort worth his while by enticing him with immediate diversions. Among these are the reductive fables or anecdotes that Swift uses to enliven his meaning. The *Proposal* has the myth of Arachne and Athene, incongruously expounded as Ireland and England. This kind of conceit can also be shrunk into a brief analogy, as Swift, with an air of picking only the handiest comparison, will produce one peculiarly damning to his victim. Thus the laws passed by the Irish Parliament over thirty years would 'fill a volume as large as the *History of the Wise Men of Goatham*'. Similes and other concise figures are equally tendentious; and the nouns and verbs are often selected to be ironically honorific, like the 'felicity and prudence of the people in this kingdom'. Sometimes a fable generates a pun; sometimes a pun generates a fable. But the reader's mind is teased to see always the same moral dichotomies, terrifying and explosive, behind the wit.

For direct rhetorical power, this pamphlet stands among Swift's most accomplished works. Some of the phrases created or used in it are now common sayings.[1] It climbs to no elevation above the understanding of the invited audience; yet it displays remarkable syntactic polish and wit. As a specimen of composition it is like Samuel Johnson's prose in disproving a common notion that good essays open themselves to systematic outline or proceed by orderly logic. Swift often applied that principle backwards, in the mock-argumentative or mock-oratorical manner of several pamphlets, in *An Argument against Abolishing Christianity*, and parts of *A Tale of a Tub*. But his normal method of composition was to list topics associated with his theme, to produce separate sentences or paragraphs around the hints, and then to cluster these into a complete work with no more order than Montaigne's essays.

The opening is more likely to be careful than the close, and the irregularity throughout seems to strengthen the tough weave of the writing. Swift relies on short rhythmic units, asymmetrical balance, and a magnificently idiomatic phraseology. His language, while colloquial, is far-ranging; and he has the great author's genius for introducing an unusual word to brighten the texture of an otherwise plain-spoken passage. Swift is the only author that Pope considered an authority for diction in prose, burlesque verse, and serious verse, all together.[2] Addison is hardly read today, while Swift and Johnson survive.[3] One reason is that Addison sacrificed flavour and force to a conventional idea of structure and polish.

For all its power, the *Proposal* has an element of absurdity that illuminates Swift's genius. The Irish could not in fact have replaced English goods with their own. While labour was cheaper in Ireland, the organization, experience, and skill of English manufacturers made it easy for them often to undersell and generally to outclass the Irish except in coarse materials.[4] If

---

[1] In July 1947 when I was reading in the National Library, Dublin, a stack-boy asked me what I was studying. 'Jonathan Swift,' I said. 'Oh yes,' said the page, '"Burn everything English but their coal"'.

[2] Joseph Spence, *Anecdotes*, ed. James Osborn (Oxford, 1966), I. 170-1.

[3] See my discussion in *Literary Meaning and Augustan Values* (Charlottesville, 1974), pp. 43-4, 94-8.

[4] Cf. Cullen, pp. 64-5.

Ireland could have instituted a protectionist policy of her own, she might have built up the home industries. But the law prohibited duties on goods imported from England. Besides, the quality of Irish workmanship was so uneven that careful buyers were often discouraged. Swift in a mood of desperation once said, 'They would rather gain a shilling by cheating you, than twenty in the honest way of dealing, although they were sure to lose your custom.'[1] General standards were not established or followed, and *caveat emptor* was the rule. Swift himself complained that the weavers should stop trying to thrive by 'imposing bad ware at high prices'.[2]

The elementary unreasonableness only enriches the appeal of Swift's pamphlet. He implies that he is concerned not with probabilities but with rights and wrongs. The boycott of England itself comes to represent only a rallying point and not a final goal. What the author desires is to whip up national sentiment, to drive the Irish to help themselves, to start a racial metamorphosis.

In its rhetorical indifference to consequences the pamphlet exhibits one of the strongest marks of Swift's literary character. It also looks forward to the *Drapier's Letters*. For example, in one quick innuendo Swift says the King would be delighted to know that his loyal subjects celebrated his birthday dressed in cloth of their own manufacture. Although the suggestion is fantastic, it implies a serious argument—that in claiming to make laws for Ireland, the British Parliament was infringing on the royal prerogative; so also it implies a distinction between the King as tender father of his faithful people, and the British ministry as enemies of Ireland. This is a polarity that we shall see Swift develop with dazzling skill when he comes to write the *Drapier's Letters*.

The *Proposal* joins not only the *Drapier's Letters* but all Swift's tracts on Ireland in its paradoxical view of human misery. The

---

[1] Davis XIII. 90.
[2] *Ibid.*, p. 91. Swift delivered himself of similar judgments in other tracts during the decade 1720–30.

sufferers whom he wishes to help are people for whom he has a degree of contempt. There is an element of justice, or even of punishment, in his charity. 'Drown the world, I am not content with despising it, but I would anger it if I could with safety.'[1] His attitude is unlike that of some modern humanitarians, who try to find moral elevation in the victims of injustice, and who are often, therefore, tempted to falsify the character of those who need their care. The modern liberal social conscience would like to identify misery with merit. Swift had no such illusions, and is therefore still cogent. He believed that starving families need food because they are starving, not because they are virtuous. He believed that poverty, ignorance, and dependence are likely to reduce, not enlarge, the human spirit. In a way his attitude suggests the Christian account of God's relation to humanity: there is no good in us, and yet He wishes to save us. In this moral vision resides perhaps the deepest claim that Swift's work makes on men.

It is hard to estimate the popularity of the *Proposal*. Swift said it was widely read. Persons in high places certainly felt troubled by it. Bishop Nicolson identified the style as 'the Dean of St Patrick's witty and bantering strain', and made the obvious connection with the rage over the Declaratory Act. He sent a caustic account of the tract to the Archbishop of Canterbury, quoting the passages he found most offensive.[2] Bishop Evans said the 'vile pamphlet' openly called for armed rebellion. The author was Swift, he said, 'but the imprison'd printer will not discover him'.[3]

The government took direct action. The ambitious Lord Chancellor Midleton and his rival Whitshed, Chief Justice of the King's Bench—who was intriguing to get Midleton's place— vied with each other to impress the British ministers with their zeal to stifle disloyalty. The carefully biased grand juries of the city and county of Dublin were cajoled into presenting the

---

[1] Letter of 26 Nov. 1725, to Pope; Williams III. 117.
[2] 9 Jun. 1720; Wake Letters XIII, no. 178.
[3] Letter of 19 Jun. 1720, to Wake.

pamphlet as 'false, scandalous, and seditious'; and the printer
Edward Waters was brought before the King's Bench. Accord-
ing to Swift, when the trial jury found the printer not guilty,
Whitshed

> sent them back nine times, and kept them eleven hours, until being
> perfectly tired out, they were forced to leave the matter to the mercy
> of the judge, by what they call a special verdict. During the trial, the
> Chief Justice, among other singularities, laid his hand on his breast,
> and protested solemnly that the author's design was to bring in the
> Pretender.[1]

This angry story might sound improbable. But Bishop Evans
wrote, 'Waters the printer's jury, after being sent back eight
times, brought in a special verdict, though he owned the printing and publishing *the vile pamphlet*.'[2]

Swift was now driven down into the same kind of intrigue that
he despised in Whig politicians. Waters was no skilled and
conscientious craftsman printing serious or elegant books.
He was a crude and careless workman who took advantage of
passing sensations to bring out shoddy pamphlets and
ephemera. But Swift had got him in trouble and was determined
to rescue him.[3] To keep the printer from being ruined for the
dean's sins, he sought out powerful men of both parties and
asked them to intervene. In June, Swift visited Lord Molesworth, whom he had attacked seven years earlier for his anticlerical Whiggism.[4] Molesworth, who agreed with Swift and
Archbishop King in Irish policy, though not in church affairs,
readily promised to help. He thought so well of the *Proposal* that
for a time he considered reprinting it in England; he had spoken
on the Irish side in the debate of the British Lords on the
Declaratory Act; and his deistic protégé Toland—much maligned by Swift—had published an excellent pamphlet against
that bill. Molesworth wrote to Toland, 'You may believe it [i.e.,
the *Proposal*] to be S——'s; for he was here to get me to use my

---

[1] Davis IX. 27; cf. Williams II. 358; Ball, *Judges* II. 96–7; and Coghill's account of
Whitshed's handling of the case of the *Fourth Drapier's Letter*, in *Drapier*, pp. 268–9.
[2] Letter of 7 Jul. 1720, to Wake.   [3] Cf. Williams II. 380.
[4] Davis IV. xxiv–xxviii.

interest that no hardship be put upon the printer, and did in a manner own it.'[1]

Sir Thomas Hanmer, chief of the Hanoverian Tories, whom Swift had worked with in the Oxford ministry, was the step-father of the new Lord Lieutenant of Ireland, the Duke of Grafton. Swift wrote to him and to Lord Arran, the Jacobite brother of the Duke of Ormonde. They both agreed to support the printer. Swift hovered more than a year for the outcome, putting off a visit to England, waiting around Dublin, and fuming over Hanmer's fecklessness. Finally, Grafton himself, in spite of his responsibilities as Walpole's errand boy, gave in to the pressures put on him. And so Waters came forth at last unharmed, freed by the Lord Lieutenant's *nolle prosequi*. The whole spectrum of British politics, from Jacobite peer to Whig republican, had joined to rescue an Irish printer for the sake of an Anglican dean.

---

[1] Williams II. 359, 365; Molesworth to Toland, 25 Jun. 1720, in H.M.C. *Various Collections* VIII. 291, quoted by Ferguson, p. 58. My two paragraphs follow Ferguson closely.

Part Two

THE HIBERNIAN PATRIOT
1720–6

Chapter One

ENGLISH PACKETS

As the years passed, England remained for Swift the arena of memorable deeds. To be forgotten there was to be lost to greatness. In his imagination he clung to England. It embodied his ideals and illusions. It meant society, civilization—above all, language. For a man with literary ambitions, Ireland meant a double exile. One might as well be dead as be unknown to English readers. Swift avoided Irishisms in his own speech and condemned their use by others.[1] The purity of his expression was to some extent the purity of an alien fastidiousness seeking the most idiomatic strains of the speech he admired.

But Ireland also embodied reality. Swift's moral energy, his deepest patriotism, sprang from the condition of his own country. For all their cultivation, the English were savages when they dealt with the Irish. England was the oppressor, the enemy; Ireland was the victim. In defending his people, Swift was defending humanity. An ambivalence underlay his wavering between the two nations, and found expression in his style: the English vocabulary, the Irish mockery; English restraint, Irish exuberance; English scepticism, Irish fantasy.

Swift carefully preserved letters he received from English peers or poets, and begged the great men who had known him under Queen Anne to send portraits of themselves. He implored Pope to commemorate him, and sent his Irish protégés to meet the eminences of his season of glory. Swift yearned to visit England and renew his friendships there in person. During the first years of the new reign the journey was unthinkable: too

---

[1] See Davis IV. 277–9 for collections of Irishisms. See also Swift, *A Dialogue in Hybernian Stile...*, ed. A. Bliss (Dublin, 1977).

many of his friends were facing prosecution, and the Whigs were acting so vindictive that it would have been imprudent for Swift to show his head where he had no need to appear. For the time being, his safest course was to bolster up the position of dean and to establish some kind of community for himself in Dublin.

But soon he saw the resentments against the new regime begin to accumulate—not only Tory but Whig complaints, not only Irish but English. Gradually, Swift came to feel less isolated and more secure. The quarrels among the Whig leaders, the divisions within the royal family, the fury of the Irish over the Annesley Case and the Declaratory Act all gave him a sense of living again in a comfortable environment.

Meanwhile, letters from England begged him to come over. 'You will pardon me for being a little peevish', said the consumptive poet and diplomat, Matthew Prior, 'when I received [your letter] ... which told me I must not expect to see you here.'[1] In an open-hearted gesture the amiable John Gay started a correspondence with Swift and said, 'I think of you very often, no body ... longs more to see you.'[2] Pope followed his comrade Gay's charming lead, and said, 'Whatever you seem to think of your withdrawn and separate state, at this distance, and in this absence, Dr Swift lives still in England, in every place and company where he would chuse to live.'[3]

As early as the summer of 1717 Swift asked the ageing Lord Oxford to invite him to visit the Harley seat in Herefordshire. But that was a peculiar wish for a special purpose, and his lordship easily put off the dean.[4] Soon after, Swift wrote seriously to Charles Ford (as intimate a friend as he had) about coming over: 'I have as great a desire as my nonchalance will permit me to pass some months in England.'[5] Lassitude and local occupations weakened this desire. Summer passed; and in midwinter he promised, 'I will try next spring what can be done.'[6] Over the five years that followed, he regularly uttered

[1] 5 May 1719; Williams II. 323.   [2] 22 Dec. 1722; *ibid*., p. 439.
[3] Aug. 1723; *ibid*., p. 458.
[4] 9, 16 Jul. 1717; 17 May, 20 Dec. 1718; *ibid*., pp. 276, 278, 289–90, 308.
[5] 6 Jan. 1719; *ibid*., pp. 309–10.   [6] 8 Dec. 1719; *ibid*., p. 330.

the wish to friends whom he trusted, and as regularly produced reasons to keep him at home. 'I cannot think of a journey to England till I get more health and spirits.'[1] While the dean waited, Prior wasted away and died;[2] and Swift said, 'I pray God deliver me from any such trials. I am neither old nor philosopher enough to be indifferent at so great a loss.'[3]

The backward–forwardness of Swift's attitude toward England reveals itself in the turnabouts of his travel plans. He certainly worried about illness. In Ireland he could afford to be sick, both financially and socially. There he was a giant among pigmies, and did not terribly mind people's observing how often he felt indisposed, hard of hearing, too dizzy to stand. He could afford to be comfortable, to ride out with his servants mounted. He could also afford to let friends down, to miss engagements and to deny himself to callers. Mrs Johnson could watch over the sick-bed. In England his best foot always had to be forward. He loathed the expense of English servants, English horses, London lodgings. Giddiness and deafness were not the features he wished the peers and statesmen to identify him with.

Not only England but the continent attracted Swift. He thought the hot sulphur springs of Aix-la-Chapelle might relieve his disorders. 'I should not scruple going abroad to mend [my health]', he told Ford,

> if it were not for a foolish importunate ailment that quite dispirits me; I am hardly a month free from a deafness which continues another month on me, and dejects me so, that I can not bear the thoughts of stirring out, or suffering any one to see me, and this is the most mortal impediment to all thoughts of travelling, and I should die with spleen to be in such a condition in strange places.[4]

When Swift thought about England, he had one fear born almost inevitably of his career as an anonymous writer. Other men's effusions were blamed on him; and Swift did not like his English friends to suppose he really had fathered pages of rubbish. Even today a few scholars still believe that Swift wrote *A*

[1] *Ibid.*   [2] 18 Sept. 1721.   [3] 28 Sept. 1721; Williams II. 406–7.
[4] 4 Apr. 1720; *ibid.*, p. 342.

Letter of Advice to a Young Poet, published as his at the end of 1720.[1]
A particular humiliation was a pamphlet called *A Dedication to a Great Man*, which came out in 1718. Readers attributed this to Swift at once. It was even translated into French as 'du fameux M. Swift'. The real author—probably a Whig journalist—eulogized King George and condemned the Anglican clergy for failing to honour his majesty.[2] In a reply to this pamphlet, some unknown writer taunted Swift for turning his coat:

> Some have wondered how Doctor Swift, whose affection to the church was never doubted, though his Christianity was ever questioned, should think the worse of some of the clergy for their trampling upon loyalty and oaths; and, for all his reverence for the late Q—and her counsellors, should make such honourable mention of King George and his ministers [i.e., in *A Dedication to a Great Man*]; but as it is well known you never were a slave to constancy and principle, we can easily account for this your behaviour, and in defence of it say, That in this instance, you have put off prejudice, and resumed your understanding.[3]

Doubly mortified—by the bad writing and by the Whiggish sentiments of *A Dedication to a Great Man*—Swift felt driven to defend himself. He drew up an account of his literary activity and of his political doctrines, addressed this as a letter to Pope, and then decided after all not to release it.[4] One easily understands why he kept the copy in his desk, for it was dangerously indiscreet (especially concerning the pamphlet on *Irish Manufacture*)

---

[1] See Davis IX. xxiv–xxv; also Herbert Davis, 'The Conciseness of Swift', in *Essays on the Eighteenth Century Presented to David Nichol Smith* (Oxford, 1945), p. 27. Although the pamphlet was dated 1721 on the title-page, a London edition published by W. Boreham was advertised in the *Post Boy*, Dec. 29–31, 1720. For a distressing aberration of taste and scholarship, see John Holloway, 'The Well-Filled Dish', *Hudson Review* IX (1956), 20–37.

[2] See Davis IX. xii, n. 1; Teerink, p. 408, no. 894.

[3] *A Letter to the Reverend Mr Dean Swift*; text dated 30 Jan. 1718–19; title-page dated 1719. See Davis IX. xiii, n. 2.

[4] Williams II. 365–74; Davis IX. 25–34. The history of the composition of the letter is in doubt. For earlier discussions, see Craik II. 60, n. 2; Ball III. 113, n. 5; Davis IX. xii, n. 1; Williams II. 366, n. 2 to p. 365. I believe Swift began writing the letter on 10 Jan. 1722 but completed it much later. The reference to the Duke of Grafton must have been made after 28 Aug. 1721; the 'plot discovered', involving paid informers, is probably Layer's Plot, which became public in Apr. 1722; the reference to a law suspended (p. 373) must be to the suspension of the Habeas Corpus Act in Oct. 1722; the suspension in 1715 seems too remote for this reference. Cf. below, p. 445, n. 4.

to be circulated at the time. The account of his philosophy of government disclosed nothing that does not appear elsewhere, although some of the expressions are uniquely exquisite—'I shall never lose a thought [upon present times or persons] while there is a cat or a spaniel in the house.'[1] But the anger that rattles the leaves of this public epistle tells us how fiercely Swift minded his London reputation. He says,

> All I can reasonably hope for by this letter, is to convince my friends and others who are pleased to wish me well, that I have neither been so ill a subject nor so stupid an author, as I have been represented by the virulence of libellers, whose malice hath taken the same train in both, by fathering dangerous principles in government upon me which I never maintained, and insipid productions which I am not capable of writing.[2]

Here one tastes the bitterness that nourished other suppressed essays in self-justification—like the *Memoirs* and the *Enquiry*—and that would find sublimated expression in Part One of *Gulliver's Travels*.

Meanwhile, the devotion of Swift's English friends illuminated their respect for his genius. Not only literary figures but titled grandees like Bolingbroke, the Duchess of Queensberry, and the second Earl of Oxford delivered their praise in agreeably strong language when they wrote to him. The old Earl of Oxford indulged himself in his congenital procrastination: after he emerged from the Tower, he never replied directly to Swift's letters. When he died, in the spring of 1724, Swift felt it as the loss of a fund of memory but not of a living limb. Yet he still insisted on fitting the Earl into the image of a humanist statesman cheerfully retired; Swift praised him for his scholarship, friendship, and conversation.[3] Oxford's example contributed to the character of Lord Munodi in *Gulliver's Travels*; for the ideal of such a figure stayed with Swift long after the Earl's death.

While the first Lord Oxford was sinking into his decline,

---

[1] Williams II. 367.
[2] *Ibid.*, p. 374; cf. the letter to Atterbury when Swift wished to clear his name in 1716 (*ibid.*, pp. 278–80).
[3] *Ibid.*, p. 369; III. 18.

another friend of Swift's in England had to suffer the same ordeal that his lordship had undergone. One of the devices Walpole used to keep himself in power was the claim that constitutional government in Britain might be overthrown by a conspiracy of Jacobites. Since the exiled Prince of Wales and his supporters at home were always manufacturing new dreams of rebellion, it was easy enough for Walpole to find evidence of their activity. King George may be said to have helped by maintaining a level of unpopularity conducive to uprisings. Historians sometimes measure the quality of Walpole's administration by its longevity. It might also be measured by the persistence of the Jacobites.

In England the most brilliant supporter of the Pretender had become Francis Atterbury, now Bishop of Rochester. For ten weeks in 1711, Swift had been his neighbour in Chelsea.[1] Although I think Atterbury's violence in church doctrine offended Swift, and the bishop's support for the Pretender certainly went against Swift's grain, they had both been protégés of Harley, and they had charmed one another during the Chelsea period. Even while their careers drew them apart, their friendship survived, and the tightening lines of politics united them in the same camp. When Swift was gloomiest about his affairs in the cathedral, he wrote confidentially to Atterbury for advice; and it was Atterbury who defended him when a false rumour went around of a change in his principles.[2]

Years after that episode, the bishop's notoriety reached a zenith when the government accused him of plotting its destruction. The scandal began as Walpole received intelligence of a new Jacobite conspiracy centred on an attorney named Christopher Layer.[3] This dreamer had talked with the Pretender in Rome, and he tried to recruit soldiers for an insurrection. It was easy enough for government agents to intercept letters in which the conspirators mixed code words with domestic trifles; and it was not difficult for cryptographers to show that the letter-writers hoped to seize the Tower of London and other key

[1] See above, I. 448-9.   [2] Williams II. 193-9, 278-80.   [3] Apr. 1722.

places. According to Walpole's agents, the letters also revealed that Atterbury was a leader of the plot.

Yet the investigation produced no incriminating document in the bishop's hand, no deposition as to words spoken by him, and not a single conspiratorial message that named him. So Walpole could not hope to convict him of treason by strictly legal procedures. Instead, he had a bill offered to Parliament that would send Atterbury into exile for his part in the conspiracy; and the Lords who sat in judgment did not therefore have to feel bound by the ordinary rules of evidence. Among the materials used to identify the bishop as a chief conspirator were a lame spaniel named Harlequin, which the Pretender had sent to Atterbury, and some letters found in the episcopal privy.

The affair stank of improbabilities. One of the crucial depositions came from a man who happened to be drowned before the hearings. The intercepted letters had been in code and had been sent on to their destination; consequently, only copies of the decoded versions could be produced for examination. The letters in the privy and the spaniel Harlequin were offensively bizarre. The prosecutors themselves confessed that according to the 'ordinary course of justice', the evidence was 'not all of it strictly legal'.[1] Although irrefutable proof of the bishop's guilt emerged a century and a quarter later, friends of Atterbury's at the time could easily suppose the whole case was fabricated in order to strengthen a shaky government.

It was June 1722 when the details of Layer's Plot began to leak out; but Atterbury was only sent to the Tower in August. The published report of the House of Commons committee followed in March 1723. Swift could easily put himself in Atterbury's place as victim of false witnesses, misreadings of intercepted letters, and Whig vengefulness; and he watched the case closely. Writing to a confidential friend, he bristled with satirical reactions against the discoverers of the plot, but without

[1] See Rosenheim, p. 178 and n. 2. My discussion of Swift's interest in the Atterbury case is immensely indebted to this essay. I have also profited from the concise, masterly, and dramatic account by G. V. Bennett, *The Tory Crisis in Church and State* (Oxford, 1975), pp. 256–73.

denying that there was one:

> I escaped hanging very narrowly a month ago; for a letter from Preston, directed to me, was opened in the post-office, and sealed again in a very slovenly manner, when Manley [the postmaster] found it only contained a request from a poor curate.[1]

When Gay urged him to visit England, Swift replied, 'What a figure should I make in London while my friends are in poverty, exile, distress, or imprisonment, and my enemies with rods of iron.'[2] In May 1723 Parliament passed the bill condemning Atterbury to exile, and soon afterward the King set sail for Hanover. With sarcastic ambiguity Swift wrote to his friend, 'The next packet will bring us word of the King and Bishop of Rochester's leaving England; a good journey and speedy return to one and the other is an honest Whig wish.'[3]

For the amusement of the Tories, Swift wrote but did not publish a careless poem on Harlequin, which I suppose he circulated in manuscript among his friends. Here again, while he ridiculed and denigrated the prosecution witnesses, he did not deny that Atterbury was involved in a plot.[4] One may suppose that Swift's real judgment appeared in the epistolary essay addressed to Pope, where he declares that the mere exposure of a plot strengthens a government better than any 'diligent inquiries into remote and problematical guilt, with a new power of enforcing them by chains and dungeons to every person whose face a minister thinks fit to dislike'.[5] More remarkable than this reflection is the final shape Swift's response to Atterbury's case took, in the account of plot discoveries and conspirators' codes in Part Three of *Gulliver's Travels*,[6] which he wrote the year after the bishop went into exile.[7]

Precisely because this is among the less subtle passages of Swift's masterpiece, it can be used to show how complicated are the biographical and historical origins of his satire; and I shall digress briefly for that purpose. When Swift came to write this

---

[1] 9 Oct. 1722, to Robert Cope; Williams II. 435.
[2] 8 Jan. 1723; *ibid.*, p. 442.   [3] 1 Jun. 1723, to Cope; *ibid.*, p. 456.
[4] 'Upon the Horrid Plot Discovered by Harlequin', *Poems* I. 297–301.
[5] Williams II. 373.   [6] Ch. vi, par. 10–13.   [7] See Rosenheim.

section of *Gulliver's Travels*, the immediate occasion was of course the prosecution of Atterbury. With this in his mind, I believe he naturally remembered the impeachment of the Tory ministers in 1715. Blending the two dramas in his reveries, he also responded deeply to them because his own experience had brought him close (at least in fantasy) to the same threats. Such indignation on behalf of others and the transfer of their experience to his own seem to me fundamental aspects of Swift's imagination. Those innate impulses were nourished—as he planned and wrote *Gulliver* (during the years 1720-5)—by that desire to justify himself which had found powerless expression in the series of unpublished essays.

But if these were the forces behind the satire on plots and codes in Part Three of *Gulliver* (Chapter Six), Swift's playful method of ridicule—for all its likeness to the evidence of Layer's plot—was derived from other aspects of Swift's character, especially his addiction to word-games, his obsession with filth, and his habit of building narrative designs on analogies and literalized metaphors: in Gulliver's burlesque of codes, a sink is a court, a sieve is a court lady, a codpiece is a king. Finally, the detachment of the satire from its external occasion and private associations is profoundly true to Swift's genius. Both the comedy and the moral implications of the passage in Part Three belong to human nature and not to the history of Walpole's administration. Ignorant children and jaded politicians recognize the universal instincts on which Swift established his fantasy, though they may want some guidance before they grasp its pertinence to the history of their own times and the consequences of the doctrine that the state has a right to preserve and strengthen itself even at the sacrifice of legality. In denouncing such a doctrine, Swift speaks for the Enlightenment and against the mock-rationality by which the Whigs veiled their yearnings for a one-party state.[1]

To close this digression, let me finally suggest that some critics

---

[1] Alas, Swift had disclosed the same yearnings in *Some Free Thoughts* and other pieces written while his own party was in power.

may have failed to grasp the positive meaning of Swift's vicarious fury because they were preoccupied with the techniques of satire and therefore paid less attention to what Swift defended than to what he opposed. Studies of satirical method often amount to little besides the analysis of methods of attack. In his treatment of plots and codes Swift does not defend the purposes of the Jacobite plotters. He defends a Lockean view of the limits of good government. When his friends stood on top, he forgot this view. One benign effect of defeat, for Swift, was that it recalled him to humanity.

Few of Swift's works illustrate his peculiar nobility so well as the correspondence he kept up with Bolingbroke and Pope during these years.[1] In the letters of these two friends, the insistent motifs are false contempt of the world and false equanimity. Not only do the Viscount and the poet boast of their withdrawal from the struggles of ambition; not only do they celebrate their delight in retirement; they also ridicule the notion of sacrificing one's peace of mind to improve the condition of mankind. According to them, such attempts are doomed, and only a dreamer would engage in active, public benevolence. Their view of common humanity represents the least admirable tradition of the Enlightenment, i.e., the doctrine that humble, ignorant, irrational men are not worth one's anxiety—Voltaire's wish that farmhands should remain illiterate.

For *Gulliver's Travels*, which Swift was writing at the same time as this correspondence, the opposite attitude is fundamental. The author wished to vex the world if he could not mend it. The humour and comedy that colour the fantasy give way, in the last part, to bitter sermons. Swift himself summed up the implicit attitude once when he told Arbuthnot, 'I could not live with my Lord Bo— or Mr Pope; they are both too temperate and too wise for me, and too profound, and too poor.'[2]

---

[1] Charles Ford visited Ireland in the summer of 1716 and received from Swift a letter to Pope and one to Bolingbroke. He delivered both. Pope replied on 30 Aug. 1716; Bolingbroke replied 23 Oct. 1716, N.S. See Ford, pp. xvi–xvii and 64, n. 5; Williams II. 213 and n. 2, 218 and n. 4.

[2] Nov. 1734; Williams IV. 268. 'Poor' is an ironical epithet; he was tired of their boasts about low diet, etc.

When Swift told Bolingbroke about his troubles with the pamphlet on *Irish Manufactures*, the reply was that Swift would deserve to be tossed in a blanket (viz., like the visionary Don Quixote) 'the next time you offend by going about to talk sense or to do good to the rabble'; and his lordship exclaimed, 'Is it possible that one of your age and profession should be ignorant that this monstrous beast has passions to be mov'd, but no reason to be appeal'd to?' He invited Swift to share his own moral philosophy: 'Leave off instructing the citizens of Dublin. Believe me, there is more pleasure, and more merit too, in cultivating friendship, than in taking care of the state.'[1]

In Part Three of *Gulliver's Travels*, Swift was to exalt Cato the Younger for dying, sooner than yield to tyranny, and for sacrificing his life to his country's freedom.[2] But when Swift praised this hero to Bolingbroke, the reply was that Cato used to make tiresome speeches, and that as a political physician he prescribed the wrong medicine (i.e., Stoic severity): 'Like a true quack, he gave the remedy, because it was his only one, though it was too late. He hastened the patient's death; he not only hastened it, he made it more convulsive and painful.'[3]

Bolingbroke said his own favourite philosopher was Aristippus (who believed one could remain a virtuous man while freely indulging in sensual pleasure and while accepting money for teaching wisdom).[4] 'Reflection and habit', he claimed,

> have rendered the world so indifferent to me, that I am neither afflicted nor rejoiced, angry nor pleased at what happens in it, any farther than personal friendships interest me in the affairs of it, and this principle extends my cares but a little way: perfect tranquillity is the general tenor of my life.[5]

Writing to Charles Ford (who sided with him in the quarrel about Cato), Bolingbroke ridiculed Swift as a romantic vi-

[1] 28 Jul. 1721; *ibid.*, II. 395; my punctuation. I assume that 'tossed' is a reference to *Don Quixote*.
[2] Ch. vii, penultimate paragraph.
[3] Williams II. 397; cf. *ibid.*, p. 413. Cf. Bolingbroke's savage dismissal of Cato in his letter to Ford, 1 Jan. 1722, N.S. (Ford, p. 235).
[4] Williams II. 414; to Ford, 1 Jan. 1722, N.S.
[5] Williams II. 462; to Ford, Aug. 1723.

sionary, and suggested ironically that the dean was preparing himself for 'some apostolical mission among savage Indians, or the barbarous people of Africa'.[1]

When Bolingbroke returned to England, he drew Pope into a correspondence with Swift that was to last as long as the dean could write letters. The warmth and sincerity of Pope's opening message lose some of their force when one observes that the most striking sentence in it is repeated from a farewell letter that Pope had recently sent to Atterbury.[2] The themes of exile and friendship were in all their minds, with Swift in Ireland, Bolingbroke just returned to England, and Atterbury banished to France. It is no wonder that Swift makes so much of this theme in *Gulliver's Travels*. Pope said, 'Surely [England] is a nation that is cursedly afraid of being overrun with too much politeness, and cannot regain one great genius but at the expense of another.'[3]

Pope's moral reflexions—and these letters abound in them—sound oppressively like those of Bolingbroke: 'I have acquired a quietness of mind which by fits improves into a certain degree of cheerfulness, enough to make me just so good-humoured as to wish [the] world well.'[4] This is hardly Swift's vein. When Pope said, 'My friendships are increased by new ones, yet no part of the warmth I felt for the old is diminished,'[5] Swift, in a spontaneous but beautifully composed letter, replied,

> Your notions of friendship are new to me; I believe every man is born with his quantum, and he cannot give to one without robbing another.... I have often endeavoured to establish a friendship among all men of genius, and would fain have it done. They are seldom above three or four cotemporaries and if they could be united would drive the world before them.[6]

The definition of friendship meant more in the days of George I —when there were so few *carrières ouvertes aux talents* without a comrade or patron to open the door—than it does now, especially to frail and middle-aged bachelors.

---

[1] Aug. 1723; Ford, p. 237; cf. *ibid.*, pp. 238-40.
[2] Cf. Williams II. 458, 11. 9-14, and Sherburn II. 167.
[3] Williams II. 458-9.   [4] *Ibid.*, p. 459.   [5] *Ibid.*   [6] *Ibid.*, p. 465.

The contrast between Pope and Gay should not perhaps surprise anyone familiar with both. The greatest poets must often drain off from their friendships and blood ties the energy they need for their poems. A less ardent poet, like Gay, could afford to be candid: 'You find I talk to you of myself, I wish you would reply in the same manner.'[1]

Candour evoked candour. When Swift replied, he affirmed his addiction to English culture with an elegiac eloquence that makes me wonder what would have become of his literary character if he had remained in the land of his choice. Surely he would have been a narrower, more comfortable personality, satirizing his friends' enemies, ridiculing the vices of the highest society, but never producing *Gulliver's Travels* or *A Modest Proposal*. Here is his outburst to Gay:

> The best and greatest part of my life till these last eight years, I spent in England, there I made my friendships and there I left my desires; I am condemned for ever to another country, what is in prudence to be done? I think to be *oblitusque meorum obliviscendus et illis*; what can be the design of your letter but malice, to wake me out of a scurvy sleep, which however is better than none, I am towards nine years older since I left you. Yet that is the least of my alterations: My business, my diversions, my conversations are all entirely changed for the worse, and so are my studies and my amusements in writing; yet after all, this humdrum way of life might be passable enough if you would let me alone. I shall not be able to relish my wine, my parsons, my horses nor my garden for three months, till the spirit you have raised shall be dispossessed.[2]

The sombre brilliance of this passage is no sign that Swift wrote worse to Pope or Bolingbroke. Their elevation as historic and literary figures, along with his desire to be memorialized as their friend, called out his gifts as an epistolary stylist. When they delivered effusions on the bliss of retirement, Swift almost replied that his own genius fed on the difficulties of thinking and writing in an unhappy country. From irony he advanced through eulogy to triumphant mock-despair; here he speaks

[1] *Ibid.*, p. 439.   [2] *Ibid.*, pp. 441-2.

to Pope:

> I have no very strong faith in you pretenders to retirement; you are
> not of an age for it, nor have you gone through either good or bad
> fortune enough to go into a corner and form conclusions *de contemptu
> mundi et fuga seculi*, unless a poet grows weary of too much applause as
> ministers do with too much weight of business.—Your happiness is
> greater than your merit, in choosing your favourites so indifferently
> among either party; this you owe partly to your education and
> partly to your genius, employing you in an art where faction has
> nothing to do. For I suppose Virgil and Horace are equally read by
> Whigs and Tories. You have not more to do with the constitution of
> church and state than a Christian at Constantinople, and you are so
> much the wiser, and the happier because both parties will approve
> your poetry as long as you are known to be of neither. But I who am
> sunk under the prejudices of another education, and am every day
> persuading my self that a dagger is at my throat, a halter about my
> neck, or chains at my feet, all prepared by those in power, can never
> arrive at the security of mind you possess.[1]

In corresponding with his friends, Swift acted like a touch-
stone, exciting them to display the special marks of their character. Arbuthnot's humour and benevolence shine through the
letter in which he joined the procession of British friends renewing their claims on the dean. 'I know you wish us all at the devil
for robbing a moment from your vapours and vertigo. It's no
matter for that, you shall have a sheet of paper every post, till
you come to yourself.' He implored Swift to try visiting the
original Belgian Spa for his dizziness, and assured him that
he need not let the imaginary menace of a legal prosecution
frighten him away from England: 'I my self have been at a great
man's table and have heard out of the mouths of violent Irish
Whigs, the whole table talk turn upon your commendation.'[2]
By the time Swift wrote Part Four of *Gulliver's Travels* (which he
completed before what is now Part Three), he was regularly in
touch with all those who meant most to him in England, only
excepting the unresponsive Earl of Oxford.

---

[1] *Ibid.*, pp. 464–5; my punctuation, etc.
[2] 7 Nov. 1723; *ibid.*, p. 469. I have freely modernized the spelling, punctuation, and
division into sentences.

Between Swift on one side, and Pope and Bolingbroke on the other, something like an intellectual duel went on behind the screen of genuine friendship—a duel with paradoxical implications that may (I think) surface in *Gulliver's Travels*. Although Ford was his supreme epistolary confidant,[1] sooner or later Swift told his entire circle, in varying degrees of detail, about the book he was producing. But it was with Bolingbroke in particular that he fenced over the great moral theme on which the satire turns.

Swift on guard took up his usual position of savage critic of human nature. Pope and Bolingbroke belonged like Steele to a later age, in reaction against the sceptical morality of the Restoration. They assumed the pose of easy benevolence, and declared themselves unwilling to believe that true men had to be coerced into virtuous conduct. From these initial standpoints the opponents moved to places that were just the opposite of what one might expect. Since Swift wished to advance right morality, he chose to tease, vex, and lure men into it. Since the other two declared it was seductive in itself, they devoted themselves to friends who ostensibly found it seductive. While claiming to sympathize with La Rochefoucauld's reduction of all motives to self-love, Swift carried the burden of charity in every form, from alms-giving to dangerous political action. By claiming to trust in human nature, Bolingbroke relieved himself of the need to care for men who fell beneath his standard. 'As you describe your public spirit,' he told Swift, 'it seems to me to be a disease.'[2]

In these feints and coupes, the language easily misleads one. For example, Swift said that exile was the greatest punishment to a virtuous man, because virtue consists in loving one's country.[3] As if he were making himself the example in an inverted argument *ad hominem*, he used to bemoan his own isolation in Dublin. It might seem that what the dean needed was a recipe for stoicism. Bolingbroke had written an essay on exile, which he paraphrased when he wrote to Swift. His lord-

[1] See Ford, pp. xxxviii–xlii.
[2] Williams II. 474.   [3] *Ibid.*, III. 29.

ship insisted that banishment was no hardship for a virtuous character. 'A man of sense and virtue may be unfortunate but can never be unhappy,' the rich Viscount informed the Christian priest.[1] One might assume that Bolingbroke possessed and could administer the austere doctrine that Swift required.

But the truth was hardly so plain. Swift of course believed one should make the best of one's lot, and accept misfortune as part of the mysterious dispensation of Providence. Whatever he might write about Dublin, he set about improving the condition of the community as soon as he was free to do so; and he brightened his own days by the pleasantest society and pastimes that he could get. He simply never pretended that misfortunes were unreal; and he believed that the power of human nature to rise above moral and physical evil was small at best. On the other side, Bolingbroke attributed to himself and his circle a devotion to rational morality that would have done credit to Socrates.

Bolingbroke described the common people as a 'monstrous beast', with passions to be stirred but 'no reason to be appealed to'.[2] He condemned the enemies of religion for taking 'at least one curb out of the mouth of that wild beast man when it would be well if he was check'd by half a score others'.[3] One might easily infer that he shared Swift's misgivings about the weakness of human nature and the need of a church to strengthen it. But of course it was merely the vulgar, irrational horde that Bolingbroke thought to be in need of such controls. Revealed religion, Christianity, was essential for them, because they could not appreciate the superiority of natural religion.

But this contemptible mass did not represent true human nature any more than a blind cripple represents the true human body.[4] People like Pope and himself did so. When Bolingbroke wrote cautiously, he described himself as labouring to be 'a man who makes a free use of his reason, who searches after truth without passion, or prejudice, and adheres inviolably to it'[5]; and so

---

[1] *Ibid.*, II. 414. [2] *Ibid.*, p. 395. [3] *Ibid.*, III. 27.
[4] My own analogy, not Bolingbroke's. But cf. Locke, *Essay concerning Human Understanding*, IV. iv. 13–16.
[5] Williams III. 28.

he wrote to Swift, who was then composing Part Three of *Gulliver's Travels*—the last in order of composition. But more commonly Bolingbroke wrote as if he and the real human beings whom he accepted as worthy friends had already achieved that desirable state of rationality.

Swift's view of course was that the defects of human nature were universal, and that even the striving toward Christian morality or rational conduct was a tragically rare phenomenon. Bolingbroke, like Voltaire, took Locke's observation that reason governs very few men,[1] and debased it to the view that poor, humble labouring men must always exist, that they must always be ruled by passion and superstition, and that the few real men governed by reason would always be found among those of his own quality. It was Swift's judgment that Yahoos flourish in the governing class, and that if one were to separate real men from beasts in human shape, the standard would have to be strictly moral. This truth alarms minds that in one age deny humanity to the poor and in another to the rich. Few social evils cannot be traced to the principle that one group of people is more truly human than another, and that the class which is not, deserves to be treated as cattle for slaughter.

Swift was halfway through the composition of *Gulliver's Travels* when Bolingbroke at last received a pardon that let him visit England without fear of arrest.[2] At Calais, in a scene of life-turned-allegory, he arrived just before Atterbury (going the other way), who said, 'Then I am exchanged'—as if they had both been hostages; but the two did not meet.[3] Although Bolingbroke later settled himself at Dawley, near Pope's house at Twickenham, he left for the continent soon after this first arrival in England. Only in 1725 did an Act of Parliament (sped by a colossal bribe to the most powerful of the royal mistresses) restore him to his title and estates. But even then he was excluded from the House of Lords—lest, as he said, so corrupt a

---

[1] Cf. *Essay concerning H.U.*, IV. xviii–xx.
[2] May 1723.
[3] G.V. Bennett, p. 276.

member might, with his base leaven, 'sour that sweet untainted mass'.[1]

Meanwhile, Swift was finishing his *Travels*, and Pope was provoking him into writing the most celebrated of all his letters. When Pope said he would translate no more, Swift congratulated him and begged him to turn satirist:

> But since you will now be so much better employed, when you think of the world, give it one lash the more at my request. I have ever hated all nations, professions, and communities, and all my love is towards individuals. For instance, I hate the tribe of lawyers, but I love Counsellor such a one, Judge such a one. For so with physicians (I will not speak of my own trade), soldiers, English, Scotch, French; and the rest. But principally I hate and detest that animal called man, although I heartily love John, Peter, Thomas and so forth. This is the system upon which I have governed myself many years (but do not tell) and so I shall go on till I have done with them. I have got materials towards a treatise proving the falsity of that definition *animal rationale*; and to show it should be only *rationis capax*. Upon this great foundation of misanthropy (though not Timon's manner) the whole building of my travels is erected.[2]

I suppose Swift was rallying Pope with this declaration that individuals had to transcend the limits of common human nature before they became worthy of affection. But Pope merely stood the doctrine on its head by observing that the way to have a public spirit was 'first to have a private one'. He spoke of opposing La Rochefoucauld's principles, and challenged Swift with the maxim, 'No ill-humoured man can ever be a patriot, any more than a friend.'[3] He also looked forward once again to a tranquil reunion of Swift with his comrades.

Swift came back with the meaning behind his ironies:

> I tell you after all that I do not hate mankind, it is *vous autres* who hate them because you would have them reasonable animals, and are angry for being disappointed. I have always rejected that de-

[1] Williams III. 82. Cf. H.T. Dickinson, *Bolingbroke* (London, 1970), pp. 174–7.
[2] 29 Sept. 1725; *ibid.*, p. 103. Cf. the important discussion of this passage by Ronald S. Crane, 'The Houhynhnms, the Yahoos, and the History of Ideas', in *The Idea of the Humanities and Other Essays* (Chicago, 1967), II. 272–82. See below, p. 452.
[3] 15 Oct. 1725; *ibid.*, p. 108.

finition and made another of my own. I am no more angry with [Walpole] then I was with the kite that last week flew away with one of my chickens and yet I was pleased when one of my servants shot him two days after. This I say, because you are so hardy as to tell me of your intentions to write maxims in opposition to Rochfoucault who is my favourite because I found my whole character in him.[1]

As a *hypocrite renversé*, Swift was imitating the *apatheia* of Pope and Bolingbroke and turning it against them. His own impulse to serve humanity emerges as simply a congenital, self-pleasing instinct—no more admirable than Walpole's equally natural impulse to oppress mankind is blameable. The virtue lies in the action; and Walpole is to be destroyed because of what he does, not what he intends to do. To excuse villainy on the basis of motive becomes impossible in this rhetorical strategy; so we must remember that the strategy is only a temporary, ironical method of dealing with Pope's declared position. As we see again and again, when Swift dealt soberly with the good and evil of human behaviour, he put extraordinary, if not definitive, stress on motive.

[1] 26 Nov. 1725; *ibid.*, p. 118. See below, p. 449.

Chapter Two

THE CONDITION OF IRELAND

If England seemed to Swift the home of civilization, she also seemed the enemy of his own people. The depth of the enmity is easy to document, for some of the worst sufferings of the Irish were due to the presence of the English. No class of British people except a few families with property in Ireland felt any concern over the misfortunes of their subject neighbours. The Irish represented most of all a threat, and less often a resource, but never a nation to be sympathized with. In times of war or unrest, invaders and trouble-makers might come from Ireland; so the country had to be kept under strict military surveillance. If Ireland grew prosperous, she might provide enough royal revenue for the King to make himself independent of Parliament; so she must be kept poor. If the Irish made a success of any industry that was already established in England, their lower wages and costs might give their products a competitive edge; so manufacturing had to be discouraged unless it was in some sense non-competitive.

At the same time, certain natural resources, like Irish raw wool, were valuable to English industry; and the Irish establishment was a useful shelter for British pointers sniffing after sinecures, offices, and pensions. Handled as a colony, Ireland might be serviceable. When the Duke of Grafton became Lord Lieutenant, Archbishop King summed up a common opinion:

> The better he is beloved here and more popular, the more ill he must do; for you are well apprised that he must not act according as he would do if left to his own judgment but according to the directions of those that have procured him to be sent here shall give him, and consider with yourself what and how great favours we are to expect from them.[1]

---

[1] 30 Sept. 1720, to Lt. Gen. Richard Gorges. I have freely altered the spelling, punctuation, etc.

From the Glorious Revolution to the passage of the Declaratory Act, the British Protestants of Ireland had forty years in which to learn that the fate they were imposing on the native Roman Catholics was to be their own. Just as they excluded the great bulk of the people from the government and arrogated to themselves the responsibility for the whole population, so the English assumed an authority over them. Just as they denied to the natives any source of wealth that they wished to possess themselves, so the English denied to them any property that could be exported.

Since most other forms of investment might be seized or destroyed by their deaf, remote rulers, the safest repository of capital remained the land. But the land itself had been appropriated from the natives, and British power was needed to guarantee its security. Archbishop King wrote,

> The Protestants of Ireland are sensible that they have no other security for their estates, religion, liberty or lives but their union to England and their dependence on the Crown thereof, and therefore in all events that have happened since the Reformation, they have ever stuck close to it, and ever will and must whilst there are six or seven Papists for one Protestant in it.[1]

So the cycle renewed itself. Without British backing, Swift's class could not survive. With British backing they could only survive.

It was with such feelings in their bellies that the Irish heard, during the summer after the Declaratory Act, a warning of what might yet be inflicted on them. For the scandalous South Sea Bubble then extended its malign influence from England to her frail neighbour. At the beginning of the year 1720, the British government had agreed to assign the entire national debt to the South Sea Company. The Company's directors agreed in return to pay the government over seven million pounds and also to accept a declining rate of interest on the value of the debt they would then hold. The Company would make up its profit by investing the vast credit of the debt in its monopoly of British trade with Spanish America. Those myriads who had taken government annuities in return for loans to the state could

[1] 5 Mar. 1720, to Archbishop Wake.

exchange these for stock in the Company on bargain terms. The directors of the Company rightly assumed that the capital value of the stock would rise sharply as investors scrambled for it, while the value of the annuities would necessarily remain fixed. Every week fewer shares of stock would be needed in exchange for the same amount in annuities. The Company would therefore be able to keep much of its capital even while retiring the debt of £51,000,000.

The venture was so successful that the shares were worth seven times as much in August as in January. In May 1720, Archbishop King wrote to England,

> I have enquired of some that have come from London, what is the religion there? they tell me it is South Sea Stock; what is the policy of England? the answer is the same; what is the trade? South Sea still; and what is the business? nothing but South Sea.[1]

Many rival schemes were invented to absorb the capital that was flushed out of hiding; and thousands of investors devoted their fortunes to perilous speculations. Soon, however, the sales of shareholders who wished to realize their gains weakened the foundation of the structure, and it began to fall in.

By the end of September 1720, the shares had tumbled below a fifth of their peak value; the mob who came late into the game and bought expensive shares on credit were ruined. Now, therefore, directors were quite correctly denounced for abusing the public, manipulating the market, and bribing Members of Parliament and courtiers. A financial panic followed at once, and quickly became an explosion of rage against the directors of the Company, the government, and the court. Because the King was in Hanover, Parliament could not assemble until December. By then Walpole had come forward, elaborating the scheme suggested to him by his own financial agent, and this proposal (along with the sacrifice of a number of directors and politicians during the tumultuous parliamentary investigations), calmed the storm before spring arrived.

During the Christmas recess of the British Parliament, a poem

---

[1] 10 May 1720, to Lord Molesworth.

by Swift called 'The Bubble' was published in London.[1]
Dubliners had not escaped the fallout of the South Sea disaster.
Archbishop King wrote,

> It is hardly credible what sums of money have been sent out of the
> kingdom and drowned in [the South Sea Company]. Men mort-
> gaged their estates, gave bonds and judgments and carried their
> ready money there, and if we believe some, in money and debts and
> contracts Ireland is engaged a full million, which I believe is near
> double the current cash of the kingdom.[2]

According to a London newspaper, the gentlemen of Ireland

> went late into the stocks, bought dear, extracted all the foreign gold
> out of Ireland, which was the best part of their current-coin, to make
> those purchases, so that money is become extreme scarce, the want
> of which makes the country people backward to bring their corn to
> market, in hopes the times will mend; whereby provisions are near as
> dear again as hath been known in that city for many years.[3]

In his new poem, as in most of his satires against social evils,
Swift wasted no pity on the victims. So far from sympathizing
with the bankrupts of the Bubble, he jeered at them for leaping
to their own doom. The directors of the Company appear in the
poem not as erring entrepreneurs but as knaves cheating fools;
and the poet looks forward to their hanging. As usual, Swift
based his design on a set of analogies, and incorporated proverbs, familiar quotations, and myths into the language. The
image of the salt sea became unnaturally fertile in this scheme,
and the poem grew to fifty-seven stanzas.

If he had kept the manuscript a while longer before publishing it, Swift would have added still more stanzas to convey the
devastation made by the Bubble in Ireland. The English enjoyed a flourishing economy in which trade regularly expanded.
The real force of their Bubble worked to redistribute capital, not
to destroy it. Many misguided families lost their savings. A few

---

[1] The manuscript is dated 15 Dec. 1720. The title 'The Bubble' may have been Ford's
choice. The poem was advertised in the London *Daily Courant* and *Post Boy* 3 Jan. 1721.
For an account of its printing history see Ball, *Swift's Verse*, pp. 160–1; Ford, pp. 182–5;
Poems I. 248–59.
[2] 24 Dec. 1720, to Annesley.
[3] London *Mercury*, 29 Apr. 1721, quoted by Ball, *Swift's Verse*, pp. 175–6, n. 43.

lucky, cunning, or thieving individuals came into huge gains. But the nation as a whole remained strong. The Irish, however, existed so precariously that a tremor was dangerous. A landslide like the Bubble meant a shock to the entire economy. As early as October 1720 Swift wrote to Vanessa, 'Conversation is full of nothing but South-Sea, and the ruin of the kingdom, and scarcity of money.'[1]

Other weaknesses, like those in the production of textiles, aggravated the crisis. Weaving remained a principal industry of the city of Dublin. But it was vulnerable to many ills. In Ireland, unlike England, the manufacture of woollen goods was based in towns, while the linen industry was rural. The capital had become the main centre for weaving and finishing certain kinds of woollens that required unusual skill. But the urban location weakened the industry because the high cost of living meant that the weavers had to be paid more than villagers, and they could join in combinations that put up the employers' costs. The English woollen industry lay in the countryside; its relatively low costs were one reason it could outsell Irish goods. Besides, the English workers were more specialized and therefore more expert. It was an over-simplification for Swift and others like him to think that merely by urging people to buy Irish manufactures, they could give a broad, strong foundation to a home industry.[2]

During the heyday of the Bubble, moreover, the fever or ague already mentioned[3] spread among the poor working people of Dublin. 'The ague rages most violently here, and many die of it,' Archbishop King wrote.[4] During the summer, reports of the plague in France—the same reports that inspired Defoe to write his *Journal of the Plague Year*—produced a quarantine. The archbishop observed correctly that the quarantine would be a clog on Irish trade, which depended on foreign markets. If the danger reached the point where all shipping from France was stopped, he said, 'that will in a manner knock our trade on the

---

[1] Williams II. 361.   [2] Cullen, p. 64.   [3] See above, p. 122.
[4] 12 May 1720, to Stearne.

[156]

head for the time.'[1] The plague did its damage and passed over; but there was still a shortage of money. The cattle market went badly, and during the winter of 1720–1 the number of street and house robberies became alarming.

Before the warm weather came, as credit followed money out of sight, the condition of the humblest Dubliners sank to the level of a famine. Weavers were said to be dying of hunger. In the middle of Lent, the archbishop found the misery of the town unspeakable. Thirteen hundred weavers were listed as unemployed, with starving families. The number rose steadily:

> I used to say that one third of Dublin needs charity, but this and other inquiries have assured me that at least one half are in those necessitous circumstances. The misery is partly due to the South Sea but more to the griping landlords who grind the faces of the poor, and most of them living in England, with the officers civil and military and pensioners, have drained us of our money and contribute nothing to the burthens of the kingdom or the employment of the poor or their relief, so that we that live here are forced to maintain the beggars they make, or let them starve, which has been the case of many and is like to be of great numbers more.[2]

On Holy Saturday his account was sadder. The outcry of the weavers had become unbearable. 'They pawned and sold all they had for bread—household stuff, cloths, looms, and tools. There remained nothing behind but to starve.' The number of families wanting food had climbed to 1700. The churchmen appealed for charity. The playhouse gave a benefit performance of *Hamlet* (bringing in seventy-three pounds); and a total of fifteen hundred pounds was collected, of which a thrifty government supplied no more than a hundred. 'But what will this be among so many?' asked the archbishop. 'The gentlemen and ladies did their part by clothing themselves in the manufactures of the country—I mean, many of them—which has been a great help but still short of necessity.'[3]

For the benefit production of *Hamlet*, Sheridan wrote a prologue and Swift wrote an epilogue. Swift's piece was in careful

---

[1] 10 Sept. 1720, to Molesworth.   [2] 23 Mar. 1721, to Francis Annesley.
[3] 8 Apr. 1721, to Colonel Flower.

couplets. Here he returned to the argument of *Irish Manufacture*. In an ingenious passage he contrasted the courtiers in the drama with those of reality. The Dublin actors, he promised, would use native cloth for their costumes:

> We'll rig in Meath Street, Egypt's haughty queen,
> And Anthony shall court her in ratteen.
> In blue shalloon shall Hannibal be clad,
> And Scipio trail an Irish purple plaid.
> In drugget dressed of thirteen pence a yard,
> See Philip's son amidst his Persian guard;
> And proud Roxana fir'd with jealous rage,
> With fifty yards of crape, shall sweep the stage.[1]

For literary allusions, in these few lines, there are two plays by Lee to one by Dryden; but the humorous gravity of the style is all Dryden's.

In the midst of the distress not all observers took the line of the archbishop and the dean. It was hardly in the English interest to dwell on the wretchedness of Ireland. While Swift and King added their voices to the howls of the poor, Bishop Evans gave a different turn to the catastrophe:

> What [Archbishop King] wrote about the present state of this town has some truth in it, though he may (possibly) much exceed in his account of the poor. The idlest race of men (the weavers) have long wanted employments, which I presume may be chiefly occasioned by the present decay of the French trade, whither (against law) these people were used to send great quantities of woollen cloth, as well as wool; and provisions becoming much dearer, the manufacturers still keep their workmen to the old low rates for weaving etc. Shopkeepers complain heavily that they receive little ready [i.e., ready money] for their goods; and book debts [i.e., credit] are more in fashion here than in any other part of the world. They who are really able, pay very often at their own leisure, and in their own short way too, as tradesmen tell me.—The late collections (here) have been very considerable towards the relief of the poor, but our two archbishops and Lord Mayor are at a loss how to distribute profitably these charities, which had been much greater if the

---

[1] The play was produced on 1 Apr. 1721. For the printing history of the epilogue, see *Poems* I. 273–6. I have modernized the spelling and punctuation.

Archbishop of Dublin had permitted the ministers and church wardens to collect from house to house, which he thinks even the government can't appoint without an Act of Parliament.[1]

The misdeeds of Irish nationalists bothered Evans more than the troubles of the poor, and he worried about Popish conspiracies. But the native spokesmen do not mislead us. According to historians, the whole decade 1720–30 was one of economic crisis. The linen industry alone seemed to thrive; agriculture and the woollen manufacture stagnated.[2] Swift may have misunderstood the causes and the cure of the morbidity; he did not exaggerate its effects.

Meanwhile, a small group of ill-advised projectors had chosen this of all times to commit the kingdom of Ireland to a new and menacing financial institution. The purpose of the scheme was to relieve the tightness of the Irish money supply and to provide large-scale credit for merchants, landlords, and entrepreneurs. It would take the shape of a national bank, chartered by the King and backed by the Irish Parliament.[3] As planned, it would issue up to half a million pounds in notes and would lend money at a maximum rate of five per cent.

During the speculatory fever of the years 1719–20 the plan might have looked feasible and even attractive, especially to those who would manage the fund. In its early stages the idea of a bank got strong support. Before a charter was granted, the Lord Lieutenant was assured that the project represented the wish of the kingdom.[4] But when Ireland lay gasping from the effects of the Bubble in England and the plague in France, and when the long reaction to the Declaratory Act had just begun, no important class of people was ready to try a financial experi-

---

[1] 8 Apr. 1721, to Wake; my spelling and punctuation.
[2] Cullen, pp. 44–50.
[3] Early in 1719 the idea of a national bank was being discussed in Dublin; on 8 Sept. a petition for a charter was presented to the King by Lord Abercorn, Lord Boyne, Sir Ralph Gore, Bart., Oliver St George, and Michael Ward. Bishop Evans wrote to Wake, 9 Jan. 1721, that St George, Gore, and Ward were going to England 'as plenipos to establish a bank here'. The King approved the charter on 29 Jul. 1721. Henry Maxwell was a leading propagandist in favour of the bank; his uncle, Hercules Rowley, wrote excellently on the other side. See Mason, pp. 325–6, notes s and t; Ferguson, p. 64.
[4] 8 Jun. 1721, King to Annesley.

ment. As it happened, six decades had to pass before a national bank finally came to birth in Ireland; and then it hardly influenced the economy, because its early activity was seldom more than rediscounting the bills of other financial houses.[1]

The controversy over the bank was to show how far the leaders of Ireland had moved from the positions they held while Swift's friends were in power. Here was a crisis that brought together Whigs and Tories, clergy and laity, bishops and parsons, Nonconformists and churchmen—even the English interest and the Irish. Although the first impulse of the attack on the bank did not seem anti-British, it proved that a national union might be established quickly, without English guidance, and for the common weal. To the extent, therefore, that Westminster's direction of Irish affairs relied on disunion, an organization of forces became conceivable that might turn against England.

Spokesmen for the scheme went to England in the summer of 1721, and in July the King granted a charter, subject to Irish parliamentary approval. When the proposal first came before the Parliament of Ireland (in September 1721), the Commons sounded eager to back it. But as the opposing arguments were heard, this support shrank. In December, both houses threw the bill out, and the Lords voted that any peer who tried to get a charter for a bank would be 'a betrayer of the liberty of his country'. Theoretical arguments for and against the bill had less effect than a radical suspicion of England and a paucity of distinguished names among the subscribers. One enemy of the bank pointed out,

As Ireland is a dependent kingdom, and can neither make laws, nor repeal them, when it pleases, without the consent of other people, not so much interested in the welfare of this country, as I could wish; we ought, in my humble opinion, to be very cautious how we pin any thing down upon ourselves, the consequences whereof are at least very doubtful; for if in process of time we should find it ever so disadvantageous and ruinous; yet if it either increases the power, or tends to the profit of those who have the negative on us, we must

[1] Cullen, p. 95.

bear the burthen, and perhaps with an additional weight which we never consented to.[1]

Archbishop King's immediate response to the scheme could have surprised no one. 'It will only put it in the power of a few to cheat the whole kingdom, and bring in a villainous trade of stock jobbing and paper credit to the ruin of the unwary.'[2] During the parliamentary debate, he told his confidant Bishop Stearne, 'We need no South Sea to drown us, for a little water will do it.... all the speaking men in the House of Commons are for it, being concerned as subscribers, many are against it but can't speak their minds.'[3] His pessimism was misguided. Bishop Evans detested the bank as much as Archbishop King; and the day Parliament met, he wrote to the Archbishop of Canterbury, 'I hear the bank you have granted us will be universally opposed by all the trading people as well as by country gentlemen.'[4] While the wretched bill was being debated in committee, Evans reported a crucial vote:

> The question was, whether a bank in Ireland on a solid etc. foundation was for the interest of this kingdom, which passed in the negative, to the wonderment of such as were warmly concerned in the scheme. A member yesterday told me (who was on the other side) that if they had further considered the bill, he believed there would not have been ten persons in the House for it, besides those who had reason to believe they would have been chosen directors, or such who are immediately under their influence. The people (without doors) are said to be unanimous against it, both gentle and simple, all which (put together) might justly occasion some wonder that the gentleman (from hence) who managed this important scheme on your side, should possess you with an opinion that the generality of these people were for a bank, than which nothing now appears to be more untrue.... If it had passed (under our present constitution) I can't help thinking but that our fourteen directors would (soon) have had a greater interest in the nation than his majesty's chief governor, and also his Privy Council here, though of very extensive authority—nay, the very House of Commons in a short time must have truckled to them, who would have the nation's money in their hands.[5]

[1] Mason, pp. 325–6, notes s and t; Ferguson, p. 64.
[2] 30 Sept. 1720, King to Gorges.   [3] 5 Oct. 1721, King to Stearne.
[4] 12 Sept. 1721.   [5] 16 Oct. 1721, to Wake.

One could easily surmise Swift's opinion from his inborn distrust of the moneyed interest (so-called). In the *Proposal for Irish Manufacture* he found room for an afterthought damning the 'thing they call a bank'.[1] During the early discussions of the bill in Parliament he believed his fellow countrymen would as usual co-operate with their own destroyers, and he wrote bitterly to Archbishop King,

> I hear you are likely to be the sole opposer of the bank, and you will certainly miscarry, because it would prove a most perfidious thing. Bankrupts are always for setting up banks: how then can you think a bank will fail of a majority in both houses?[2]

Archbishop King told Stearne a week later, 'Dean Swift offered to lay me five guineas this morning the bill would pass, for a good natural reason to be sure, which was no other than that it was for private advantage and public mischief.'[3]

When the bill finally failed, Swift produced an exultant poem celebrating the vote. Here as usual he reduced the financial issue to a fight between money and land.[4] Even though great landlords like Abercorn promoted the bank project, Swift conferred the glory of its defeat on the landowning gentry.[5] Money was always a key that unlocked his imagination, and he easily assembled the images his satiric mode required.[6] The design that put them together was yet once more a set of analogies, the best of which is a conceit linking rags to riches through the idea of paper credit:

> Oh! then but to see how the beggars will vapour,
> For beggars have rags and rags will make paper,
> And paper makes money, and what can be cheaper?[7]

---

[1] Davis IX. 22. I suppose he had just heard of the bank, because the paragraph sounds tagged on to the end of the pamphlet.

[2] Williams II. 405.   [3] 5 Oct. 1721.

[4] Cf. Davis IX. 290: 'N.B.' and 'Quaere'. In 1783, when a Bank of Ireland was finally established, the bulk of the Protestant subscribers were landowners; see L. M. Cullen, *Anglo-Irish Trade*, pp. 23–4.

[5] See the last stanza of *The Bank Thrown Down*.

[6] He had probably already written *The Run upon the Bankers*, which I take to be a satire on English bankers, not Irish.

[7] *Poems* I. 287. The rags-and-paper conceit had already appeared in a letter to Ford, 15 Apr. 1721; Williams II. 380–1.

Swift was wrong to declare that any single group had saved the nation. Lord Midleton himself moved quickly over to the anti-bankers. Bishop Nicolson shared Bishop Evans's instincts. Francis Annesley, a rich English friend of Archbishop King, warned him that the bank would 'do more mischief with your legislature than any one thing that can be invented'.[1] There was nothing of party in such fellow feeling.

Although Parliament would not support the bank, the bankers still possessed their charter, and they tried for a while to draw in subscribers who would make up the capital needed in return for shares of stock. Their persistence did not pay off, and the scheme collapsed. To speed its burial, Swift made a number of pamphlets, of which two were riddling papers based on conceits. In one he compared the bank to the rectum, following the common analogy between gold and faeces. This work took the shape of a mountebank's advertisement, and it makes its scabrous way from pun to pun: 'He has the reputation to be a close, griping, squeezing fellow; and that when his bags are full, he is often needy; yet, when the fit takes him, as fast as he gets, he lets it fly.'[2] The combination of money and bowels over-excited Swift, and he clung to his motif obsessionally: 'He [i.e., the bank as arse] peruses pamphlets on both sides with great impartiality, although seldom till every body else hath done with them.'[3]

In another pamphlet Swift advertised a mountebank who performed incredibly dangerous feats upon the spectators: 'He heats a bar of iron red hot, and thrusts it into a barrel of gunpowder before all the company, and it shall not take fire.'[4] The implication is that only a suicidal idiot would risk exposing himself to such entertainments. The paper ends with a promise that this same famous 'artist' will take everyone's ready cash and

[1] Ferguson, pp. 66–7.
[2] Davis IX. 281–2. Sondra Armer has suggested that the piece is an elaborate form of the old joke called selling a bargain; see Armer, pp. 69–70. If so, Sheridan's *Blunderful Blunder* is a solution of the riddle.
[3] *The Wonderful Wonder of Wonders*, Davis IX. 283.
[4] Davis IX. 285. The implication is clear from another use of the same idea in Swift's *Thoughts* (*ibid.*, IV. 249): 'A man would have but few spectators, if he offered to shew for three-pence how he could thrust a red-hot iron, etc.' But see also the illuminating analysis by Ferguson, pp. 72–5.

keep it for his own use—'and this he as certainly performs to their satisfaction, as any of his indubitable operations before-mentioned.'[1] The interesting feature of these squibs is that by implication they blame the Irish themselves for any disastrous consequences of the bank project; and this attitude is of course simply one more example of Swift's normal view.

The best of the pamphlets is very good.[2] Here Swift pretends that a Dublin lady has been instructed by a friend in the country to buy her some shares in the bank. She reports her own conversations with spokesmen on both sides and explains why she has chosen not to invest the friend's money in the scheme. Apart from exhibiting Swift's talent for impersonation, the piece has plenty of restrained humour. Swift's problem (I think) was that he could not run down Lord Abercorn, the proposed governor of the bank, because that lord was an old friend of his and a leader of the church party. Putting the arguments in the mouth of a woman who gets them from a banking gentleman and a critical lord, Swift keeps the references to Abercorn respectful and indirect.

The general constraint refines Swift's satire, which does not get out of hand. No one could have read *A Letter from a Lady in Town* as a true experience. But the dramatic effect of a debate at second hand, between a foolish promoter and a wise analyst, has its charm and affords the author many subtle ironies.[3] The whole framework implies that even a frivolous woman would not be taken in by the fraud.

For its rational arguments, Swift's *Letter from a Lady in Town* draws not on anglophobia but on the obscurity of the subscribers and the danger of lodging great power in a few uncontrolled hands. Besides invoking the supposed polarity of money and land, Swift insinuates that French refugees abound among the subscribers. The most careful statement in the piece rests on his mercantilism, and his characteristic view that

[1] Davis IX. xviii.
[2] *A Letter from a Lady in Town ... concerning the Bank.*
[3] Much of *Gulliver's Travels* takes the same form.

Ireland was a crazy exception to the normal principles of economics:

> He could not well understand how a country wholly cramped in every branch of its trade, of large extent, ill peopled, and abounding in commodities, which they had neither liberty to export, nor encouragement to manufacture, could be benefited by a bank, which by all he had read, or heard, or observed in his travels, was only useful in free countries where the territory was small, and the trade general and unlimited, and consequently where the profit consisted in the buying and selling of goods imported from other nations, and wholly accrued to the public.[1]

Surely the imaginary lord who said this was an ancestor of the King of Brobdingnag, whom Swift was inventing about this time.

[1] Davis IX. 302.

Chapter Three

THE BENCH OF BISHOPS

In the years following the Declaratory Act, the cycle that corrupted the Church of Ireland never wound itself down. The bishops of Irish birth drew together in resentment against English greed for Irish preferments. To discourage further invasions of their hierarchy, some of them openly challenged the immigrants, who often felt excluded from what should have been a familiar society. In the Irish House of Lords the native bishops resisted measures in the English interest. Reacting to these irritations, the English government could only try to strengthen their own hand by making fresh appointments from the ranks of the English clergy. With each nomination a wave of Irish anger broke out. The Erastian church was suffering martyrdom at the hand of its secular arm.

Swift never thought of transforming the social order. He considered Irish frailty, English arrogance, and the general decay of human nature as elements of permanent reality. It was against these that the moral conscience had to define itself. If he sided with the lower clergy against the bishops or with the Irish nation against the English, it was never because he attributed innocence or virtue to them. It was because he saw that with all their sinfulness these were indeed downtrodden and needed succour. So it was that in 1716, when Archbishop King opposed the assembling of the Convocation of the Church of Ireland— where he feared the clergy would defeat their own cause by baiting the government in power—Swift supported the holding of a convocation. I suppose he thought the clergy deserved at least a vent for their spleen.[1]

---

[1] Evans to Wake, 9 Jun. 1716. Cf. Swift's defence of convocations in his letter of 4 Apr. 1720 to Ford; Williams II. 342.

Archbishop King took a simpler view. He believed the Irish Protestants of English descent could indeed be led to stand fast against the enormities of their rulers; and he also thought they might govern themselves reasonably well without English interference. According to Evans, the Archbishop became so furious with the English for their intrusions that he repudiated the usual practice of wise episcopal landlords. When a bishop renewed a tenant's lease on lands attached to the see, he could easily accept a modest 'fine' (or fee for the new lease) and raise the rent for the benefit of his successors; or else he could demand a large fine for his own benefit and set a long lease for a low rent. Swift, as Dean of St Patrick's, invariably raised the rent and lowered the fine.

But Archbishop King realized that Irish bishoprics attracted English priests because of their high incomes. The archbishop believed the episcopal stipends were high in Ireland because the bishops had conserved them by sound financial policies. If Evans may be trusted, King now began to stand prudence on its head. In 1723 Evans said King had talked 'for many years against bishops' increasing their yearly rents (choosing to take larger fines instead of them)', and that his aim was 'to keep Englishmen from being sent over to be bishops by keeping the churches' revenue (yearly) at a stay'.[1]

Evans was scandalized: he, like Swift, clung to the old principle; and both of them furiously opposed a bill to give bishops more freedom in setting leases. Obviously, Swift wished to raise the prosperity of the church whether or not its bishops were native; obviously, he did not believe the danger from immigrants was worse than the danger of undermining the whole institution.

The number of English-born bishops grew alarmingly, while their quality hardly improved. Between the time Evans came over and the time Primate Lindsay died (1716-24), about half the new bishops were outsiders. This is when one of Swift's better-known stories began to circulate. Here is a version handed down by his acquaintance, Lord Egmont:

[1] 5 Dec. 1723, to Wake.

King George ... having made several odd and illiterate English clergymen bishops in Ireland, when they came over, the kingdom were surprised at his choice, and were very free to condemn it. Upon which Swift said with a grave face, 'Ye are in the wrong to blame his Majesty before you know the truth. He sent us over very good and great men, but they were murdered by a parcel of highwaymen between Chester and London, who slipping on their gowns and cassocks here pretend to pass for bishops.'[1]

When the Bishop of Derry died in 1717, the government followed Archbishop King's recommendations, which involved five distinct translations or promotions, all of Irish-born clergymen. The chief move was of Swift's old friend St George Ashe to the valuable bishopric of Derry. I suppose this would have palliated the recent appointment of Evans to the great responsibility of Meath. When Ashe himself died, a year after his translation, King again listed a set of recommendations: three names, of which two were Irish-born and one was an Englishman already holding the poor bishopric of Killala. At the head of this class stood his darling John Stearne, whom King had once described to Canterbury as

unblemished and untainted in the whole course of his life. His heart is set on doing good; excellently skilled in the discipline of the church; thoroughly acquainted with our constitution and the business of the kingdom; of great learning, piety, prudence and courage, universally loved and esteemed.[2]

Evans had never liked the appointment of Ashe to Derry. He predicted correctly that Ashe would not spend much time in his diocese and that he would serve first his own and then the Irish interest. Evans wished to see Bishop Nicolson brought over from Carlisle; and the moment he heard that providence had removed Ashe, he wrote to Canterbury, 'If Carlisle does not succeed, I am sure the government will lose by it.'[3]

I have already glanced at Nicolson's response,[4] and will now step back in time to provide some graphic details. A year earlier,

[1] See above, II. 771.
[2] 8 May 1716; cf. 3 Mar. 1718.
[3] 16 Feb. 1718.
[4] See above, p. 116.

when Ashe's predecessor lay dying, Nicolson had written to
Canterbury about Bishop Evans's pressure on him:

> My Lord of Meath . . . rightly argues that if it was worth his while to
> waft over the sea from Bangor to Meath, it will be much more
> convenient for me to ferry it from Carlisle to Londonderry, where,
> he assures me, I shall have a rental of £2400 beside fines. The very
> dreaming of such a land of Havilah[1] must be pleasant to a man with
> a cargo of seven children. But where's that gracious hand that will
> reach out to us these apples of gold? However happy I may be in
> being uppermost in my good Lord of Meath's thoughts, I have cause
> to doubt of my making so good a figure in the opinion of the Lord
> Lieutenant. And (to be plain with your Grace) I am not very fond of
> being transplanted, at the age of sixty-two years, into the kingdom of
> Ireland. The circumstances of my poor family do indeed call (loudly
> enough) for a better support than I can afford them. I have four
> daughters unmarried, the youngest whereof is in her sixteenth year;
> and I am sometimes troubled (God forgive me!) that I cannot
> furnish out portions proper for their respective settlements in the
> world.[2]

This plea was remembered when Bishop Ashe died, and
Stearne's claim was quietly disallowed. When Archbishop King
realized that he had failed to bestow the prize of Derry on his
favourite, or indeed on any other native, he composed a letter
that was all sarcastic bite, very different from the sort the Archbishop of Canterbury expected to receive from clergymen of any
rank; here is a piece of his anger:

> I do consider that a man may govern a country diocese in Ireland as
> well if he lives in London as in Dublin; that he may live as cheap
> there as here, and houses are cheaper; that he will have so many and
> strong precedents to justify him in the practice that he need not fear
> any condemnation from the world for his absence, most of his
> brethren being examples to justify him in it.

Nicolson, he said, could get an Act of Parliament for taking the
oaths (as Bishop of Derry) in England rather than Ireland,

> and so without any trouble, or giving himself the pain of visiting a
> miserable country, he may get above two thousand pounds per

---

[1] I.e., of gold: Gen. ii. 11.
[2] 31 Jan. 1717; Wake Letters xx, fols. 317–17ᵛ; spelling and punctuation altered.

annum instead of eight or nine hundred ... a precedent of commendable frugality, and very grateful to his family as well as to your grace.

As for the diocese of Derry, said King, 'I see no reason why it may not do as well without a resident bishop for fifteen years to come, as it did for the fifteen years last past.'[1]

When Archbishop Wake protested that this was an extraordinary letter, King shot back new reproaches, and accused him of sacrificing the welfare of the church to the interest of a private family. He warned him that the Irish were sickened by the choice and predicted that the authority of men in his own position (King was then a Lord Justice) would be shaken by the precedent:

> I pray God your grace may have interest enough to fill the places made void in Britain by such removals with as good men as you send away; and that in time it do not come to that pass, that every obnoxious bishop or worse, who is disliked or troublesome in England, be not sent into Ireland to our best bishoprics to be rid of him.[2]

In consequence of the Irish protests, King George particularly commanded Nicolson to reside in his new diocese. Nicolson was 'much stunned' to be reminded in such mortifying style of what was to him a normal duty; and he hastened to Ireland, only to be dismayed on the eve of departure by warnings from Evans of the unpleasantness that faced him. 'Had I known', said Nicolson, 'a fortieth part of what I now hear and see, I would not have gone into that kingdom for the primacy.'[3]

This contretemps did not persuade the Archbishop of Canterbury to alter his principles. When the Bishop of Elphin died, his successor was an Englishman who had been Bishop of Killala. That diocese in turn went to Charles Cobbe, an Englishman whom Evans himself had thought unsuitable even for a fashionable parish church in Dublin: 'I could wish', said Evans, '[the Lord Lieutenant] had pitched upon one who could discharge

---

[1] 25 Mar. 1718; Gilbert MSS. 28, pp. 273-4. Cf. above, pp. 53, 115-16.
[2] 10 May 1718.   [3] 10 May 1718, to Wake; Wake Letters XII, fol. 265.

the duty of that troublesome station with advantage and order.'[1]

On the death of the Bishop of Down, a Derbyshire man, Francis Hutchinson, was brought in to succeed him. 'He is honest and well affected,' said Evans,

> but very narrow-souled, imprudent, and almost incapable of brotherly advice.... In short (my Lord) he shames us all. The Lord Lieutenant disowns him, telling me he is Norwich's etc.[2] 'Bishop, what!' says Dublin[3] to the Lord Chief Justice Levinge. 'Have you sent us the flower of Derby to be an ornament to Ireland?'[4]

Evans said Hutchinson had paid two visits to Down, 'and his conduct there was such, that he is (to our great sorrow) in much contempt among them all.'[5]

When the Bishop of Ferns died, the nomination went to Hort, an Englishman who had been educated in a Nonconformist academy and had never taken a university degree. Evans gave him up and wrote to Canterbury that if this man must be preferred, he would make a better dean than bishop.[6] Hort became a bishop. He had originally come to Ireland as chaplain to Lord Wharton, and was disliked by Swift *a priori*. To commemorate Hort's elevation, Swift wrote a clever, savage libel in couplets, called *The Storm*.[7] The poem circulated in manuscript and got back to the victim himself, who complained to Archbishop King—I suppose as being Swift's friend. The archbishop spoke to Swift, who apparently found a formula for dissembling, and his grace was able to offer Hort a fatuously detailed assurance:

> I have not read that scandalous libel, your Lordship mentions, but have heard of it. My neighbour [i.e., Swift] complains grievously of one Curll, who printed vile end abominable papers in his name. As for this he most solemnly protests, that he has no concern in it and I verily believe him. He says it is true that sometimes he passes a jest or an irony on his friend or any obnoxious person, but for black calumny as this is represented to be, he detests it. He discoursed me

[1] 11 Mar. 1718.   [2] I.e., a protégé of the Bishop of Norwich.
[3] I.e., Archbishop King.   [4] 12 Jan. 1722.   [5] *Ibid.*   [6] *Ibid.*
[7] *Poems* I. 301–6.

frankly on this subject, and told me, that perhaps he would not have been forward to give his vote to make you a bishop; but now you are one, he thinks it a wicked thing and a mischievous office to the church and public to say or do anything may make you less serviceable in your station, and that none but an enemy to the church and religion would be guilty of such a practice.[1]

It would be false to say that all the English-born bishops were unfit for their duties, or that all the Irish were excellent. But the tendency of the appointments was hardly calculated to explode Swift's fable about bishops and highwaymen. As early as 1716, I believe, Swift tried his hand at blocking a bad appointment. This was when the clergy of Dublin heard that Charles Carr had been nominated to the see of Killaloe. Archbishop King, still furious over the importation of Evans ('All on this side joined in the recommendation for Meath, and yet it had no effect'),[2] recommended two sound clergymen educated in Trinity College, Dublin, and tested in burdensome parishes.[3] But Carr was, among other things, chaplain to the House of Commons of Ireland, and the government saw fit to give him this promotion. (He never rose further.)

Carr was indeed Irish, son of a Kildare landowner and a graduate of Trinity College. He married a daughter of the rich Joshua Dawson, who had for years been Under-Secretary at Dublin Castle. As chaplain, he had preached a sermon before the House of Commons denouncing the Tories. Swift mentioned him to Atterbury once: 'We . . . recommended to a bishopric one whom you would not allow a curate in the smallest of your parishes.'[4]

About the same time as this remark, the Archbishop of Canterbury received an anonymous letter that I think Swift wrote. In it he warned his grace against Carr:

I have heard no objection to his morals, and he is reckoned a good natured man; but as to other qualifications, there could hardly in the whole kingdom be picked out another clergyman, so distinguished for weakness of understanding, and want of literature, and

[1] 16 Feb. 1723, to Hort.   [2] 5 May 1716, to Howard.
[3] 2 May 1716, to Molyneux.   [4] Williams II. 198; 18 Apr. 1716.

this to so great a degree, that when any of those who are called Tories had a mind to say a reflecting thing on the designs of the other party, they would charge them in a jeering way, that they designed to make Charles Carr a bishop, which was always resented as an injury and slander.

My Lord, the writer of this letter is of the party out of credit, yet what he says may perhaps have not less weight, since his humble request is only that your grace would give yourself the trouble of ordering some enquiry to be made among the gentlemen of Ireland now in London, with relation to that part of Mr Carr's character which I have above mentioned. The party in power do not want much abler men to place in so important a station, and there can be no imaginable design in raising that poor gentleman, so far above all the hopes, wishes, or dreams of himself and his friends, unless it be to bring the sacred order into contempt, and if your grace had any knowledge of the persons who chiefly contribute their credit toward his promotion you would be of the same opinion. His only plausible title is being chaplain to the House of Commons.[1]

Swift's reputation for cynicism is perhaps belied by this letter. Archbishop Wake, to whom he addressed it, had of course opposed Atterbury in the voluminous debate over Convocation. He was a Whig and a low enough churchman to be raised to the primacy by King George. Yet Swift hoped to move him with an anonymous appeal to his ecclesiastical conscience. Inevitably, the letter had no effect. Carr got the bishopric, and any leanings Swift felt toward cynicism were reinforced.

If Swift's first loyalties had been political or national, one might have expected him to disregard all causes that might ally him to bishops of English extraction. But the letter about Carr implies another attitude. When a choice faced him between promoting a fellow countryman and strengthening the institution of Christianity, he easily sacrificed the national element. This choice appeared in a starker shape when a bill came before the Parliament of Ireland that would weaken the economy of the Established Church.

The logic that brought together the Anglican landlord and his priest was always paradoxical. Religion gave the Irish gentry

---

[1] 17 Apr. 1716, among Wake Letters.

their ultimate claim to rule the affairs of the kingdom. But religion also bridled them (however lightly) in their bottomless greed. The tithes the landlords had to pay the church always irritated them; and when they held leases on properties which formed the endowments of the bishoprics, they begrudged every quarterly payment to the spiritual lord.

In such a climate it was hard for bishops to enforce their rights before a court of law. Therefore, they normally accepted far less than a fair payment. Bishop Evans calculated that if the lands of the average diocese should be honestly worth three thousand pounds a year,

> our tenants, or lessors, pay us no more (by a very fair computation), as the lands are set to them by the present leases, than poor five hundred pounds per annum. The rest they (the lessors) have in their pockets. And yet all these things can't satisfy this generation of men, who deal not so by their lessors and tenants, who are screwed by them infinitely beyond any thing practised in France or in any other country more arbitrary than it, if any such be.[1]

Evans's point is that the landowners did not cultivate the soil themselves but merely rented it out again to subtenants at the highest possible rate. So the actual tiller of the earth—and, in turn, the consumer of the produce—gained nothing from the cheapness of episcopal rents.

Since the Irish church, even more than the English, lacked the wealth to afford a decent supply of ministers or missionaries to its people, friends of the church made sporadic efforts to build up its resources. But the landowners normally bristled, swarmed together, and defeated them. According to Archbishop Synge, many Members of Parliament thought their clergy had too much wealth.[2] In 1720 a bill to provide glebes for poorly endowed livings was lost in the House. A year later, when another church bill failed, Bishop Godwin said, '[The] House of Commons will not suffer any bill to pass that may do us good.'[3]

Soon the squirearchy pushed harder. One solid bulwark of

---

[1] 5 Dec. 1723, to Canterbury. Cf. Swift's language in his *Proposal for Irish Manufacture*, Davis IX. 21.

[2] 15 Aug. 1720, to Canterbury.   [3] Landa, p. 98.

episcopal revenues in Ireland was an Act of Charles I. The law provided that no lease of episcopal lands would be valid if it ran for more than twenty-one years or if the rent fell below half the true value. These provisions kept selfish bishops from taking large fees (or 'fines') to renew leases at low rents for long terms. Thus the church as a landlord would always reap the advantage of any rise in the market price of its property.

For any country the danger of divorcing rent rates from true land values was obvious. In Ireland, where the land settlement had changed crazily for several generations, the danger to the church was catastrophic. Archbishop King said,

> I have a farm set 160 years ago, worth between three and four hundred per annum. The leases will expire within sixteen years, and the present rent is £7 10s. 0d. Another in the same circumstances set for thirteen pounds per annum, worth an 150. My archbishopric is at £2200 per annum, and about £300 of this are fee farm rents, which can never rise or yield fines.[1]

In the autumn of 1723 the tension between the bishops and the gentry grew sharper. Many people blamed the economic decline of those years on absentee landlords and English policies. But the landlords themselves suffered from the effects of the Bubble, and those living in London were hurt by a worsening of the exchange. At the same time, rents were rising. Much land had been leased on 21- or 31-year leases at low rates just after the Williamite campaigns. As these leases fell in, landlords eagerly put the rents up.[2] Naturally, the churchmen wished to share in this return to normal. Naturally, their great tenants wished to prolong the old leases. Parliament became the arena of the contest that followed.

In 1723 a bill 'for the preservation of the inheritance, rights, and profits' of ecclesiastical lands was introduced into the House of Commons of Ireland. The bishops smiled weakly at the fantasy of the title. It would allow bishops to accept a rent as high (i.e., as low) as any paid in the preceding two decades, and

[1] 5 Dec. 1723, to Francis Annesley.   [2] Cullen, pp. 44–5.
[3] 5 Dec. 1723, to Francis Annesley.

would let them make leases for lives or at fee farm (i.e., for a perpetual fixed rent). Clearly, the bill, if passed into law, would enable unscrupulous bishops to make money for themselves at the expense of their successors and the church. Evans, Nicolson, Godwin, Hort, and Henry Downes—all of them British-born—complained to Canterbury against the measure,[1] and two of the chief judges of Ireland undertook to explain their objections to the highest law officers of England.[2]

The original stimulus to which this bill became a reaction was a suit brought by Bishop Evans. When he first came over to take possession of his temporalities, he found that the market in land had risen 'double to what it was thirty years ago'; and yet that bishops were 'kept down to the old rent'.[3] His own predecessor had made a lease of 13,000 acres at two hundred pounds a year to the powerful Mr Henry St George of county Roscommon, a relation of Swift's old mentor and friend, Bishop Ashe.[4] But the true value of the property was at least three times that amount.[5]

When Evans tried to re-negotiate the lease, Mr St George told him bluntly that 'he would never advance a penny rent.' Instead of retreating or seeking a compromise, Evans located an agreeable Whig who would pay five hundred pounds a year for the land, as well as a large fine—if he could evict St George. Of course, St George quite simply refused to surrender; and Evans, with his peculiar mixture of reluctance and indignation, took the case to court. Justice and truth may have accompanied his grace; but a sheriff in the St George interest was also foisted on him, with perfectly Irish consequences:

> He packed up a jury of my tenant's relations, friends, dependents, and such who had profitable church leases of their own—who notwithstanding the known and notorious perjuries of the tenant's witnesses (whose proofs still made for me) ... brought in a verdict (as one of the judges owned) contrary to evidence.[6]

[1] Landa, pp. 101–2.
[2] Nicolson to Wake, ca. Dec. 1723; Wake Letters XIV, fol. 143.
[3] 23 May 1718, to Wake.
[4] Henry Downes (then Bishop of Killala) jokes about the litigation between Evans and St George in letters to Nicolson, 20 Feb. and 22 Mar. 1720 (Nicolson II. 508–9, 512).
[5] 23 May 1718 and 15 Jun. 1720, to Wake.   [6] 15 Jun. 1720, to Wake.

As a Britisher, Evans got no sympathy from Archbishop King:

His grace said he had foretold what would become of my cause—the
jury having given it against me contrary to the plainest evidence in
the world, my witnesses (substantial men, ten or twelve in number)
proving the lands to be worth near £800 per annum, and even their
own (perjured wretches as they are) making them to be £470—
which is £70 more than the half-value per statute. But this is
nothing at all with these people—who (as his grace was pleased to
say) will never advance the revenue of bishoprics here to invite
Englishmen over to enjoy them. He laid it to my conscience whether
I did a right thing to leave my station on the other side to come
thither.

I could have said a great deal to him on the subject, but only
replied that I was very well pleased his majesty commanded me
hither without my seeking, and hoped neither church or country
would be the worse for it.

The archbishop flaunted his own policy, which went the
opposite way from Evans's; and this declaration long antedates
the report I have already quoted on the subject:[1]

He added (among many other hard sayings) that he might have
increased the yearly revenues of Derry and Dublin, but that he
would not do it, lest Englishmen should be his successors—or words
to that purpose—and that he had agreed with some of his brethren
not to advance the revenues of the sees for the aforegoing reason, but
to be contented with fines, etc., which is directly contrary to my
present scheme, which has been £1500 out of my way, as knowing
men tell me . . . . He did as good as tell me that if he had been of the
jury, he would have given it against me for the aforesaid reason,
notwithstanding plain law, reason, and Acts of Parliament.

Evans on his side went on to illustrate how property rights
and nationalism intersected in Ireland, for he declared to the
Archbishop of Canterbury, 'I am resolved to pursue my cause to
your House of Lords, where I doubt not to meet with justice.'[2] If
King cheerfully gave up equity to patriotism, Evans set property
rights before national self-government. No wonder the Declaratory Act would be hailed by the British bishops and loathed by
the natives!

[1] See above, p. 167.   [2] 1 Jul. 1718, to Wake.

Archbishop King's declaration to Evans may have been savagely ironical; it was certainly misleading. Evans tells a story about King that confuses his methods with his motives:

He was renewing his lease with a tenant who offered to raise his rent, which he rejected, appointing him to pay a year and a half's fine instead of an increase of rent. And when the leases were to be signed, his grace made a speech to the company to this purpose, that it was unfortunate for Ireland that the English ever knew the value of Irish church preferments, to induce them to flock hither to fill all beneficial vacancies to the great hurt of the kingdom.[1]

This anecdote complicates the evidence of a series of letters in which Archbishop King opened his mind to his trusted correspondents; for in them he denounced the bill supposed to 'preserve' the profits of ecclesiastical lands.[2] 'We see the effect of this liberty in England,' he told Edward Southwell—

and by it the bishoprics there are so reduced that they can't maintain the bishops, but they are forced to transplant them into Ireland, or give them commendams, and so make them parish ministers instead of pastors of their dioceses.[3]

I suppose King thought that if a bishop used his fines not to enrich himself but for the good of the church, he had a right to grant long leases at low rents.

By this time Evans had blown a good deal of fire in the direction of Mr St George. It was a prop to the bishop's faith in Providence that seven out of eight of his enemy's perjured witnesses died soon after they gave their testimony—three of them, he reported, 'in a strange manner'.[4] Furthermore, the St George interest, for all its tentacular extension, fell short of the judges in the case. They could not accept the jury's rather imaginative view of the evidence, and granted Evans a 'special verdict'.[5] This in turn had to be tested before the Lord Chief Baron of the Exchequer, who happened to be Jeffrey Gilbert, an English friend of Evans. Gilbert had been chastised by the

---

[1] 28 Mar. 1720, to Wake.
[2] 1, 25 Nov., 5 Dec. 1723, to F. Annesley; 2, 26 Dec. 1723, to E. Southwell.
[3] 26 Dec. 1723.   [4] 15 Jun. 1720, to Wake.
[5] 15 Jun. 1720, to Wake.

Irish House of Lords for his part in the Annesley Case; and he aspired to a seat on the English bench;[1] so he was immune to native sympathies. But he was inconveniently lingering in Westminster, where he had his own dynastic interests to promote. When he returned to Ireland, he finally granted Evans the much-longed-for decree:

> I at least obtained a decree in the Exchequer. This cost me already above £1,000. My adversaries have brought in their writ of error, for no other purpose (as I am told) but to create delays. They already owe me for rent above £1,000.[2]

Meanwhile, the slow-moving litigation applied its peculiar stimulus to Irish politics, for it inspired the Irish gentry in the House of Commons to draw up their bill easing the restrictions on episcopal leases. 'All this bustle', Nicolson observed to Wake, 'has been raised by an unlucky (but very just) suit commenced by the Bishop of Meath.'[3] The Irish bishops in the House of Lords felt queasy about opposing the Commons outright in this crisis. They did not wish to endanger those measures which they themselves sponsored for the good of the church. Even while working against the gentry, therefore, some bishops—at least, King, Synge, and their aides—brought forward a bill in the Lords that seemed to ease the restrictions on leases without harming the church.

But the English bishops distrusted the device. They anxiously suspected that the natives on their bench were indeed willing to reduce episcopal incomes if that would discourage carpetbaggers. Bishop Godwin of Kilmore thought so, and he gave the same report of Archbishop King that Evans gave: 'The great man at St Sepulchre has been heard to say that *he would not increase his rents because he expected an Englishman would probably succeed him.*' Hort said this was a national policy among the 'Irish prelates of the first rank'.[4] Evans reported that only the coterie of the two 'arches' (Archbishop King and Archbishop Synge) backed the substitute bill:

---

[1] Coxe II. 175–8.   [2] 1 May 1722, to Wake.   [3] 2 Nov. 1723.
[4] Landa, p. 109.

It is the opinion of most of us bishops (Irish as well as English), baiting the two arches and their—,[1] framers and contrivers of this scheme, that if it become law, the church will be in a much worse case than now it is.[2]

Though King's own language shows him systematically opposing the Commons' bill,[3] he fought hard for the substitute. But the House of Commons passed their own bill anyhow. King, however, could outreach them in the Privy Council of Ireland, where he had collaborators. On that level he could make sure the Commons' bill was dropped while the so-called 'Bishops' Bill' went to England for approval; and of course he wrote recommending it to the powers there. They, in turn, also met a barrage of counter-arguments from Evans and his platoon. So like most legislation originating in Dublin, the 'Bishops' Bill' sank to an obscure death in the English Privy Council.[4]

The divisions over the bishops' leases involved the darkest polarities in Swift's feelings toward church and state. He had grown up during a period when titles to estates were altered suddenly and unpredictably. He had seen enormous fluctuations in the market value of land. Money had undergone repeated changes of shape, intrinsic value, and rate of exchange. He had identified himself with a victimized motherland that he could not respect. He had undertaken to serve a church that was failing in every way. Every aspect of the controversy touched him.

By the autumn of 1723 the dependence of Ireland on England was assuming a new and explosive form in the rage over an Englishman, William Wood's patent to make copper coins for the Irish people. With this element superimposed, the issue of the leases stood framed for Swift in distinct, familiar alternatives: Irish people or English, church or gentry, land or money. If he sided with the Irish bishops, he gave up his economic principles. If he sided with the English bishops, he weakened his

[1] ?Creatures.
[2] 17 Dec. 1723, to Wake. This and the letter of 5 Dec. are pointedly informative.
[3] 2 Dec. 1723, to E. Southwell; 1, 29 Nov., 5 Dec. 1723, to F. Annesley.
[4] Landa, pp. 108–9 and p. 108, n. 3.

national loyalties. In fact, Swift seldom made a more revealing decision than when he chose to write his pamphlet on the subject: *Some Arguments against Enlarging the Power of Bishops, in Letting of Leases*.[1]

With an independence that tells us where his noblest sympathies carried him, Swift put on a mask of Whiggery, detached himself from Archbishop King's bloc, and played Greek warrior with Bishop Evans against the Persians of the House of Commons. Dissolving the apparent antagonism between priesthood and laity, he rationally identified the welfare of the church with that of the productive classes of the nation.

In the pamphlet Swift defended the old limitations on leases and used language like that of the English bishops. Rejecting Archbishop King's logic, he pointed out that if the bishoprics of Ireland should indeed sink in value, they would still go to Englishmen. Only, since the competition would be weaker, they would become easier to dispose of to undeserving men.

> And besides, when bishoprics here grow too small to invite over men of credit and consequence, they will be left more fully to the disposal of a chief governor, who can never fail of a chaplain, fond of a title and precedence. Thus will that whole bench, in an age or two, be composed of mean, ignorant, fawning gown-men, humble suppliants and dependents upon the *court* for a morsel of bread, and ready to serve every turn that shall be demanded from them, in hopes of getting some *commendam* tacked to their sees; which must then be the trade, as it is now too much in England.[2]

Swift traced the history of the impoverishment of the Irish church, celebrating those endowments of James I and that law of Charles I which revived her strength. He showed how unfair it was to fix ecclesiastical income in terms of money, seeing that the purchasing power of gold and silver fell unceasingly. He also

---

[1] Swift dated it at the end, 21 Oct. 1723, which I suppose is the day he completed it. Nicolson, writing to Wake on 26 Oct., says it is 'this day publish'd'. See Ferguson, p. 81, n. 80. The history of gross misinterpretation of this pamphlet by Walter Scott, W. Monck Mason, Temple Scott, and Ricardo Quintana deserves the tearful attention of historians of scholarship. It was Louis Landa whose intelligence and learning at last made Swift's meaning clear. The pamphlet should be read in the text of the first edition.

[2] Davis IX. 53; I follow the reading of 1723; see *ibid.*, p. 371.

recalled how seldom the law on episcopal leases was enforced, how systematically juries sided with lay landlords against churchmen.

Swift compared ecclesiastical titles to hereditary lay titles, observing that they all rested on the same foundation, and hinting that whoever disturbed the one sort was inviting a disturbance of the other. He suggested as well that the bishops managed their tenants and employed their money more beneficially for Ireland than the gentry did.

The Commons' bill would effectually have repealed the law of Charles I. In attacking it, Swift made an angry comment on the economy of his country.[1] Here the textile industries (or 'manufactures'), commerce with other nations ('trade'), and agriculture become the focuses of his attention. He explicitly separates the gentry from these vocations and treats them as mere titular holders of resources that other men work and improve—in fact, as impediments to the improvers, as absentees who screw their farming tenants 'up to the utmost penny' and then spend their income outside the kingdom. He almost goes so far as to oppose the good of the people to that of the landlords. Certainly he lines up himself—and his church—with the truly productive classes:

> To say the truth, it is a great misfortune as well to the public as to the bishops themselves, that their lands are generally let to lords and great 'squires, who, in reason, were never designed to be tenants; and therefore may naturally murmur at the payment of rent, as a subserviency they were not born to. If the tenants to the church were honest farmers, they would pay their fines and rents with cheerfulness, improve their lands, and thank God they were to give but a moderate half value for what they held.[2]

Behind this outburst lay the shift in his loyalties that followed his final settlement in Ireland. Here, where he had no illusions about the culture or moral character of the landed gentry, Swift did not take up their burden even though they were the natural allies of the church.[3] The lustre was gone from great peers like

---

[1] *Ibid.*, pp. 47–8.   [2] *Ibid.*, pp. 55–6.
[3] See Landa, p. 107, and J. C. Beckett, 'The Government and the Church of Ireland under William III and Anne', *Irish Historical Studies* II (1941), 280–302.

Ormonde, or hereditary proprietors like Chetwode. Instead of attaching himself to them (as he had done in England under Queen Anne), he now took sides with the humbler, industrious farmers, manufacturers, and merchants. These men did not lack corruptions, but their welfare bore a direct relation to their productivity.

In his *Proposal for Irish Manufacture* Swift had blamed the gentry for much of the wretchedness of the kingdom:

> I would now expostulate a little with our country landlords; who, by unmeasurable *screwing* and *racking* their tenants all over the kingdom, have already reduced the miserable *people* to a *worse condition* than the *peasants* in *France*, or the vassals in *Germany* and *Poland*; so that the whole *species* of what we call substantial *farmers*, will, in a very few years, be utterly at an end.

In the pamphlet he already denounced them for undermining the bishops' leases; already he saw in them the ruin of their people:

> Whoever travels this country, and observes the *face* of nature, or the *faces*, and habits, and dwellings of the *natives*, will hardly think himself in a land where either *law*, *religion*, or *common humanity* is professed.[1]

Exceptional men could be found, like Robert Cope of Loughgall. But they hardly sufficed to leaven the mass. Swift never completed the 'character of an Irish squire' that he once tried to write. But the fragment affords us some eloquent hints of his contempt for the class:

> Every squire, almost to a man, is an oppressor of the clergy, a racker of his tenants, a jobber of all public works, very proud, and generally illiterate.... The detestable tyranny and oppression of landlords are visible in every part of the kingdom.[2]

Swift, like the bishops, saw the subterranean flaw in the argument of those landlords who supported the new bill. They spoke as if the rent paid the bishops were a load on the producer of crops, and consequently as if a lowering of the rent must mean

[1] Davis IX. 21.   [2] T. Scott XI. 193–4.

a benefit to agriculture. So they identified the prosperity of the landowner with the good of the nation, opposing these to the avarice of the non-productive priests. But as Swift declared, the landowners rarely bothered to engage in agriculture directly. Rather, they rented their property to tenants who sublet them. The difference between the bishop's rent and the tenants' rent fell uselessly into the hands of the gentry.

The extraordinary rhetoric of Swift's pamphlet reflects the strains in his view of the church and gentry. The amazing feature is the definition of the audience. Although readers guessed the authorship of the work the day it appeared, it was of course anonymous.[1] Swift tried to disguise himself as a Whig appealing to Whigs. So one not only finds passages referring to 'our party' and 'our good cause'.[2] One also meets bows in the direction of the 'late excellent' Bishop Burnet and that 'most wise and faithful counsellour' Archbishop King, along with a thoroughly sympathetic mention of 'the present Bishop of Meath's case' and a compliment to Lord Molesworth.[3] Swift even defends Evans and Nicolson for moving from England to Ireland![4]

Swift does not try to reach all Whigs—merely those who were faithful members of the Established Church and not over-tolerant of Dissent. So also he goes curiously out of his way to exclude from his audience those Tories who injure the clergy:

> neither will [this discourse] suit the talk or sentiments of those persons who, with the denomination of churchmen [i.e., Tories], are oppressors of the inferior clergy, and perpetually quarrelling at the great incomes of the bishops.[5]

As for the bad practices of bishops who enrich themselves at the expense of the church, Swift traces them not to modern Whigs but to Roman Catholics of the Middle Ages, whom Whigs above all would repudiate.

> About the time of the Reformation, many Popish bishops of this kingdom, knowing they must have been soon ejected, if they would

---

[1] Cf. Nicolson to Wake, 26 Oct. 1723. [2] Davis IX. 45, 50, 56.
[3] *Ibid.*, pp. 58–9. [4] *Ibid.*, p. 52. [5] *Ibid.*, p. 45; cf. *ibid.*, II. 8.

not change their religion, made long leases and fee-farms of great part of their lands, reserving very inconsiderable rents.[1]

On the contrary, he identifies the present bench of bishops not with Tories but with Whigs, and urges his readers not to be 'determined upon the ruin of our *friends*':

> For is not the present set of bishops almost entirely of that number, as well as a great majority of the principal clergy? And a short time will reduce the whole, by vacancies upon death.[2]

The informed modern reader can please himself with the many ironical hindsights that a familiarity with the true author will impart. He can also observe how Swift peeled off some of the Whiggisms when he republished the essay twelve years later. Then Burnet became merely the 'late' bishop; and the type of Englishman that the author foresees filling the depressed bishoprics became not merely 'a chaplain' but 'some worthless illiterate chaplain'.[3]

The mask of a Whig did not fit comfortably on the face of a Tory dean. Although some readers may have been misled, the disguise kept Swift from developing, as fully as his nature yearned to do, the collapse of old dichotomies and the building of new ones. To some degree the idea of the church in this essay is only a scaffolding. One may remove it and leave the central design strong and clear. If the merit of the church is that it improves the condition of productive men, and if the fault of hereditary landlords is that they clog the industry of their inferiors, the terms of opposition are no longer priest and layman but industry and idleness.

The landlords blamed the church for parasitism. Swift turns the same charge against them. If there is no divine right of tithes, Swift suggests, there is by the same argument none of hereditary property. If the fees of the church depend upon its service to the nation, so do those of the gentry. Swift had not yet been drawn into the volcanic controversy over Wood's copper coins, and he does not mention it here. But the revolutionary rhetoric of his

---

[1] *Ibid.*, IX. 45.   [2] *Ibid.*, p. 57.   [3] *Ibid.*, pp. 52, 53, 371.

defence of the true people was ready to be used. We should not be surprised that when he addressed a public letter to his fellow countrymen, he described them as 'the shopkeepers, tradesmen, farmers, and common-people of Ireland'.

Chapter Four

WOOD'S PATENT

W e think of Swift as a solitary hero, finding out dragons and running them through with his single spear. This idea fits many of his labours for the public. He produced *Some Free Thoughts* without consulting his friends. He worked alone when he wrote the *Proposal for Irish Manufacture* and when he condemned the bill to weaken bishops' leases. By the time he was fifty-five, I suspect, he liked to imagine he was emulating Cato or Thomas More, and devoting his life to preserve a people on the edge of ruin.

But in the most triumphant accomplishment of his whole career, Swift began as a follower. The initiative and the programme belonged to others; and if Swift did come to serve as champion, it was because those in the van invited him to join them. Yet without Swift the cause would have remained narrow and insular. He raised it from the bleakness of one more chapter of British mistreatment of Ireland to be an illustration of our concept of liberty. Still, the first materials for his brilliant design were supplied to him by simpler minds.

The crisis that eventually called Swift into action probably sprang from a venal transaction between a greedy mistress and an ambitious statesman. It looks as if the Duchess of Kendal, George I's favourite, was approached in 1718 by a speculative ironmaster named William Wood.[1] This entrepreneur thought he could make a fortune for himself if he got a patent to manufacture copper coins for Ireland.

---

[1] Ferguson, p. 84. For biographical information concerning Wood, and for evidence that Swift gave a fair representation of his character, see J. M. Treadwell, 'William Wood and the Company of Ironmasters of Great Britain', *Business History* 16 (1974), 97–112.

The Irish were indeed short of small change and could have used a good supply of farthings and halfpence. But silver was what they mainly wanted. Yet the Crown had the prerogative of issuing money, and earlier kings had established the policy of licensing private persons to make coins for Ireland. Most of these operations were carelessly supervised. Consequently, the Irish had suffered painfully from the effects of Gresham's Law.[1] To deepen the crisis, the government had set the value of gold coins too high; so bankers and merchants tried always to export silver and import gold (which, unfortunately, could not be used in the ordinary commerce of shillings and pence).

Copper coinage was a stepchild of monetary policy in England as well as Ireland—'uncherished by the Mint and unprotected by the law'. In England, too, it had become a 'lucrative monopoly for favoured individuals'. The issue of copper coins was separated from the normal activities of the royal mint, and laws against counterfeits were poorly enforced; 'throughout the eighteenth century, coins in base metal were not thought of as proper currency at all', and shortages were common.[2] The situation in the American colonies was comparable.[3] So the Irish crisis was only a local instance of a general grievance. In the whole course of the controversy over Wood's patent I don't believe the Irish ever recognized this truth, which would of course have weakened their case. But the darkness enveloping Wood's intrigue with the royal court was exceptionally sinister.

On the evidence that survives, it seems that the Earl of Sunderland, who was struggling to hold his place as chief minister, wished to oblige King George by obliging his mistress. The Duchess received a colossal bribe from William Wood, and Sunderland committed himself to her benefactor's scheme. But Westminster's relations with Dublin were cool enough, thanks to the Annesley Case and the birth pangs of the Declaratory Act.

[1] See above, I. 15–16; for gruesome details, see Joseph Johnston, 'Irish Currency in the Eighteenth Century', *Hermathena* 52 (Nov. 1938), pp. 1–26.

[2] Peter Mathias, 'The People's Money in the Eighteenth Century', in *The Transformation of England* (London, 1979), pp. 190–208, especially 191–7.

[3] See Roger W. Weiss, 'The Colonial Monetary Standard of Massachusetts', *Economic History Review* 27 (1974), 577–92.

Sunderland probably hid the negotiations with Wood as darkly as possible while putting off the consummation of the patent.[1]

Then Sunderland—that 'declared and mortal enemy'[2] to Ireland—died; and Walpole emerged as the most likely successor. The new chief and his comrade Townshend wanted the backing of the Duchess themselves. So when Sir Robert discovered the commitment to William Wood, he could not repudiate it. At least, this is the history that transpires from the hints of the best early source. Certainly, Walpole did authorize the passage of Wood's patent, which was dated 12 July 1722.

Even before the patent was passed, the effort to keep it secret failed. Archbishop King learned of the scheme from newspapers.[3] Touchier than ever on the old sore of Ireland's independence, and remembering very well the earlier misfortunes of Irish money, he let fly at once. In a letter of 10 July he wrote to the Duke of Grafton, who was then Lord Lieutenant, 'I hear there is a design to coin brass money for Ireland.... If it be not managed with the utmost caution, it will drain the kingdom of the little gold and silver that is left in it':

> I hear an hundred thousand pounds is to be coined; if the grant be to some favourite or courtier, as has been formerly, the consequence will be that double that sum will be coined, and the patentee will gain one half at least and that will be carried in gold or silver out of the kingdom, which is a fourth part of all the current cash in it when richest. In time we shall have little but brass passing in it, and whoever gets silver or gold will hoard it up or send it away.
>
> I hope therefore your grace will consider well of this before you let it pass; and I am humbly of opinion that if it be resolved such a design should be prosecuted, the people here should be consulted before this be imposed on them, and that the mint should be set up by his majesty, and only he have the benefit of the coinage.[4]

Accustomed as he was to the deafness of lord lieutenants, the archbishop had the wisdom to write again, more pointedly and in the most audible detail, to Grafton's secretary. He now

---

[1] In this and in the following paragraph I am relying on Coxe I. 218.
[2] Archbishop King to Archbishop Wake, 15 May 1722.
[3] Archbishop King to E. Hopkins, 21 Jul. 1722.
[4] 10 Jul. 1722, to Grafton.

reported that the leaders of Ireland believed a thing 'so monstrous' could not be 'attempted at all'. To force the facts on the unwilling attention of his correspondent, the archbishop went systematically through the objections to the scheme. There was, he declared, no real need for the coins, and there was no way to control the amount the patentee would produce. The novelty and bad composition of the coins would make them easy to counterfeit. Anyhow, the chief officers of Ireland should be consulted in a decision so momentous for the kingdom.[1]

We know that all these topics were to be endlessly canvassed as the controversy ramified and burgeoned. ''Tis certain', the archbishop reminded the forgetful secretary,

> the Protestants of Ireland were most zealously attached to his majesty and government. I believe you are sensible how much they were soured of late by the treatment with which they have met. I am afraid this patent, if it pass, will complete their ruin, for so they reckon; so it may put an end to their good affections. And in as much as it is supposed that the patent is granted to gratify some private persons—sure it ought to be considered whether it be good policy to sacrifice a whole kingdom to their particular profit.[2]

There is an element of absurdity in this passage; for it shows the archbishop did not yet know the patent had already been passed, and did not know that Grafton himself had promoted it. But there is also an element of tragedy which Swift was to incorporate into his own rhetoric.

The Irish Commissioners of the Revenue (responsible, of course, for tax collections) were mainly Englishmen; four of them generally lived in England. They worked at this time under the domination of the immensely rich and powerful William Conolly.[3] But though Conolly was born and bred in Ireland, he acted as an agent for the English interest. A self-made man whose rise offended the older families, he had to keep the confidence of the ministry. If one holds these conditions in mind, the commissioners' response to the rumours of Wood's

---

[1] 21 Jul. 1722, to Hopkins.　[2] *Ibid.*

[3] Henry Downes in 1724 said that Conolly's estate was 'reckoned worth £15,000 per annum clear and of his own raising' (letter to Archbishop Wake, 4 Feb. 1724).

patent comes to seem less docile than one might expect. I think they honestly feared the effect of Wood's coins on their collections.

In England the commissioners had an agent of their own, Humphrey French.[1] He took alarm at the earliest inkling of Wood's patent and handed in a protesting memorial to the Lords of the Treasury. In this statement, so early as the summer of 1722, French expounded several of the main arguments later to be heard from Swift's lips when he finally entered the debate. French composed the memorial in the name of the Irish commissioners, and he must have got lucid instructions from Ireland. I suspect that the chief instructor was ultimately Archbishop King. Meanwhile, all our evidence suggests that Swift had no opinions on the subject until the winter of 1723–4.[2]

The commissioners also appealed directly to the Lord Lieutenant. They wrote two letters to Edward Hopkins, his secretary, adding a couple of arguments to those of the memorial. Of course, persons speaking officially could hardly touch on the theme that was to become Swift's loudest cry—the independence of Ireland, or the meaning of freedom. Neither did they challenge Grafton with the crucial fact that the coins would not be legal tender, and consequently that the people would not have to accept them.[3] But the commissioners did insist—with imperfect honesty—that Ireland lacked neither halfpence nor farthings—'there being at present not the least want of such small species of coins'.[4]

It is true that the country needed silver more than copper. There was no Irish mint; the law prohibited the export of specie from England; so Ireland depended on her intake of gold and

[1] I assume that 'Mr. French' was Humphrey French, who seemed to accept such commissions at this time; see Williams III. 338 and n. 2. See also *Cal. Tr. P.* 1720–8, p. 161.

[2] He never mentions it in his extant letters before producing the first of the *Drapier's Letters* (probably composed in February 1724). It would be unlike him to omit the topic from *Some Arguments against Enlarging the Power of Bishops* (Oct. 1723) if he had it on his mind.

[3] In the words of the patent the coins would be used only by persons willing to receive them; but this fact was not yet commonly known.

[4] 9 Jun. 1724, to Southwell.

silver money from the kingdoms she traded with and on English coins brought in surreptitiously but steadily. Meanwhile the East India Company quarried Ireland for foreign coins to use in its own business, paying a premium for them and leaving few for inland trade. I have already noticed that the value of gold coins was fixed at a higher rate in Ireland than in England, and Irish merchants therefore liked to remit payments to English correspondents in silver (receiving gold whenever possible). This habit again shrank the ridiculously small supply in their own country.[1]

Yet a shortage of silver does not argue an abundance of copper. And in fact, whatever polemicists might say, the kingdom could well have used ten or twenty thousand pounds in copper coins. What terrified the Irish was that Wood was entitled to ship them more than a hundred thousand pounds' worth, with no effective regulation of the quality or even of their number. The commissioners recalled that earlier patentees had debased their coins.

Wood's coppers might easily have been made at the royal mint in London. They might have been inspected by a royal comptroller. They might have been backed by an obligation for the patentee to redeem his coins with gold and silver. The grant might have run for a term of years checked by government officers.

Instead of these controls, the patent laid down only that the intrinsic value of the coins should be thirty pence to a pound's weight of copper. Not only was this ratio far cheaper than the English, which had to be twenty-three to the pound. But Wood might easily cheapen it further, because he was authorized to do the work in Bristol and had charge of the comptroller himself. He did not have to offer specie in exchange for the coins. Neither did the time limit count. The patent was stipulated to last fourteen years; but since no penalty or safeguard would be

---

[1] See Joseph Johnston; also Boulter's many excellent letters on the subject, especially those of 21 Apr. 1731 to Dorset, 25 May 1736 to Walpole, 27 May 1736 to Anglesea, 10 Jun. 1736 to Dorset, 3 Aug. 1736 to Dorset, and 11 Nov. 1736 to Cary.

applied at that period, nobody could stop Wood from putting coins into circulation as long as he liked.

When the Irish Commissioners of the Revenue wrote to Hopkins, they did not of course go so far as to reflect on the royal prerogative. But they observed that it was 'inconvenient' to bestow so valuable a licence on any private subject. They also ventured to comment delicately on the darkness in which the grant was made, with a faint insinuation that the Irish people had been treated with contempt:

> We humbly hope that the importance of the occasion will excuse our making this representation of a matter that has not been referred to us, and of which we should have had no knowledge but from the public newspapers, if our agent had not sent us an account of it.[1]

One detail that the commissioners did not neglect is trifling but humorous—that when an earlier patentee deluged the kingdom with bad money, the collectors of the revenue had trouble storing it, and finally put the coins in casks. A more disturbing remark was that the debased coppers of that issue found their way into circulation among the sellers of 'beer, ale, brandy and other liquors, tobacco and such like commodities'.[2] For these little retailers of goods that might be consumed before they were paid for, were the most vulnerable to bad money. Yet their ignorance and illiteracy would make it hard for wiser heads to warn them against the danger.

Swift was eventually to inherit the whole set of those arguments. But he would give them very different weights and would superimpose his own ringing slogans. The problem of storage, for instance, would become a source of extended fantasy, while the possibility of the King's minting the coins himself would be slighted. Swift's rhetoric would of course reach peaks of outrage that other men never tried.

Meanwhile, the supreme legal defence against Wood's money found lucid expression. Although the Commissioners of the Revenue sent in their agent's memorial and two urgent letters,

---

[1] *Drapier*, p. xiv; spelling and punctuation altered.   [2] *Drapier*, p. xiii.

they got no reply. Like the archbishop they had innocently referred to the patent as 'about to be passed.' An English clerk (I suppose) drily endorsed their second letter, 'The patent hath been long since passed.' But the commissioners were not told.[1] It was about the time the second letter went out, that Archbishop King set forth the principle on which the campaign against Wood's coins finally had to rest. Now familiar with the language of the patent, he said—if the grant should be confirmed—'We have only one remedy, and that is not to receive these [coins] in payments; the patent obliges none but such as are willing.'[2]

By law there could be no legal tender except gold and silver; copper was no more than a convenience. Regardless of the royal prerogative, therefore, no subject might be legally forced to take Wood's money. But the patent itself went further and specified that the coins were to pass between those persons who would 'voluntarily and willingly and not otherwise pay and receive the same'.[3] Consequently, if the people could be made to refuse the money, they would defeat the whole scheme.

The summer passed with no further motion. Autumn and winter brought little but official silence. On New Year's Day, 1723, Edward Southwell wrote to Archbishop King that Wood had sunk to mortgaging the patent to buy materials for his evil work:

> For the new copper coin intended, it is some time ago that I was not displeased to hear that the patentee, having employed his current cash in procuring [it], was hawking about his patent at a mortgage to raise supplies to go on.[4]

Was the ministry in Whitehall deliberately encouraging the Irish to imagine the grant was dead?[5]

Behind scenes, Wood was busier than ever. He had Walpole on his side, and Walpole made sure of Grafton, who remained as Lord Lieutenant. The Irish Parliament was to meet in August 1723, and Grafton would then go over. Wood probably planned

---

[1] *Cal. Tr. P.* 1720–8, p. 161.   [2] 3 Sept. 1722, to Annesley.
[3] *Drapier*, p. 191.   [4] 1 Jan. 1723.
[5] Cf. Archbishop King's charge, *Drapier*, p. 230.

to launch his coinage about the same time, so as to get the advantage of the Duke's personal support. Certainly he had no doubt of Grafton's co-operation. Six months after the patent was passed, English newspapers reported that Wood had hired a house in London for manufacturing the coins. Soon they also announced that production had begun.[1]

In a few more weeks Wood felt cocky anough to tell his Irish brother-in-law, John Molyneux, that he was empowered to coin two hundred tons of copper (over fifty thousand pounds' worth of coins) as soon as he wished. In order to draw various persons into the scheme, Molyneux was so indiscreet as to show them Wood's message. Letters from others were also passed about, disclosing that Wood and his agents expected to make enormous profits.[2]

The following June, while Swift was starting on a long southern journey in Ireland and Grafton began to think of leaving London, Wood perfected the arrangements for shipping his coppers over. As Archbishop King wrote sourly to Grafton's secretary, 'Hogsheads [of Wood's farthings and halfpence] are come into our ports, but none of them yet vented. Everybody looks on these as the greatest cheat can be put on a nation, and it is resented with universal dislike and indignation.'[3] The secretary returned neither denials nor affirmations. But Wood's operations continued. In a letter of 1 August 1723, two London brokers offered to supply John Molyneux in Dublin with £580 of Wood's coins for £500—'which is after the rate of £116 copper money for £100 sterling'.[4]

So far as we know, Walpole at this time gave Grafton no clear instructions for dealing with the patent. But a little before the Duke went to Ireland, Wood saw both him and Sir Robert. At the patentee's suggestion, the Comptroller of the Royal Mint now ordered an assay to be made of the new coins. The specimens to be tested were chosen and submitted by Wood himself,

[1] *St James's Evening Post*, 10 Jan. 1723 and later; *Whitehall Evening Post*, 17 Jan. 1723 and later.
[2] *Drapier*, p. xv; Coxe II. 370.   [3] 2 Jun. 1723, to Hopkins.
[4] *Drapier*, p. xv.

and the comptroller inevitably delivered a report finding them highly satisfactory. Wood armed Grafton with a copy of the report.[1] Another copy was sent to Ireland.[2] To his brother-in-law, Wood now wrote, 'I have such interest as not to fear any ill consequences and if your kingdom refuseth the coin it will easily be disposed of elsewhere.'[3] He was not bluffing.

Yet Wood did know his project was threatened, and so did Grafton. But neither foresaw how ugly the reaction to it would be. A Dubliner named James Maculla prepared the battlefield by bringing out a pamphlet just before Parliament sat. It had a title like a tocsin: *Ireland's Consternation in the Loosing* [*sic*] *of Two Hundred Thousand Pounds of Their Gold and Silver for Brass Money*, etc. In four folio pages and fifteen queries and replies, Maculla made several fresh points, though the feature of his work was its frantic tone. Mainly he denounced the poor quality of the coins. But he also complained that the profit would go to England and that Ireland would lose her specie. He warned readers that the coins had already been smuggled into circulation; and like Archbishop King, he declared that the people of Ireland must not accept them.[4]

Maculla reported that part of Wood's issue was lighter than the rest; he found the workmanship contemptible and grossly uneven: the edges not milled but 'snagled and bulged', the composition of the metal uncertain. Like the archbishop, he warned that the pieces would be easy to counterfeit. In an honest but improbable computation he foreshadowed the mathematical hysteria that was to mark Swift's rhetoric; for he estimated that Ireland would lose two hundred thousand pounds from coins worth one hundred thousand. Maculla's prose also had an Elizabethan (or Swiftian) fecundity that must have held its audience: 'All the clippers and counterfeit coiners in this kingdom are or will be at work making the money ... in bogs and mountains, dens and caves.'[5]

Thus the arguments and tone of the resistance to Wood's

---

[1] *Ibid.*, p. xvii.   [2] *Cal. Tr. P.* 1720–8, p.221.   [3] *Drapier*, p. xvi.
[4] *Drapier*, pp. xviii–xix, 352–3.   [5] *Ibid.*, p. xix.

patent were established before the Irish Parliament went to work. The grand moral and political principles, the subtle rhetoric of Swift lay still in the future. Meanwhile, Grafton was hardly the man to compete with even humble rivals in language or logic. He was the illiterate son of a bastard of Charles II. Among his favourite pursuits, hunting stood second only to adultery.[1] Archbishop King was struck by Grafton's politeness, 'which is to be expected from a man bred from his childhood at court, and who hath well learned all the arts used there'.[2] But Swift—many years later—called him 'almost a slobberer, without one good quality'.[3] In politics he seldom arrived at a decision that was not forced on him.[4] Though he had been Lord Lieutenant of Ireland since 1720, his solitary distinction in office was a sedulous devotion to the new Whig interest. For once, Lord Hervey's judgment sounds accurate as well as feline: 'The natural cloud of his understanding, thickened by the artificial cloud of his mistaken court policy, made his meaning always as unintelligible as his conversations were uninteresting.'[5]

---

[1] *Complete Peerage.*   [2] 23 Aug. 1723, to S. Molyneux.   [3] Davis v. 258.
[4] Waldegrave, *Memoirs*, p. 114.   [5] *Memoirs* I. 266.

Chapter Five

ENGLISH STATESMANSHIP

O n 13 August 1723 Grafton found himself once more
in Dublin, manœuvring among local cliques, selecting
and drawing together those men who he thought would
be most use to him when the parliamentary session began. If
anybody imagined that the government's mistakes could not be
compounded, Grafton soon proved him wrong. But certain
features of British politics in Dublin, London, and Hanover
aggravated the effects of the Duke's autonomous bungling. The
most insidious of these elements was an intrigue reaching from
Hanover to Ireland, which we must quickly review.

The two English secretaries of state, Lord Townshend and
Lord Carteret, had gone with the King to Hanover, where they
worked hard to destroy each other. Townshend was Walpole's
solid ally; but Carteret wished to eliminate Sir Robert and make
room for himself. So he tried to involve the prime minister in
crises that would make him look disloyal to the King or incompetent. Therefore, Carteret represented the affair of Wood's
coins as purely a test of royal prerogative; and he laboured in
secret to force Walpole to abandon the patent; for he hoped this
failure would weaken the King's faith in him. Outwardly, Carteret supported Wood in Hanover and London, while covertly
striving to ruin him in Dublin.

Carteret's chief Irish aides were the great Brodrick family—
Thomas, his brother Alan (Viscount Midleton), and Alan's two
sons, St John and young Alan. Sunderland had quarrelled with
them in 1719 over the Peerage Bill; and thereafter, during his
period of ascendancy, he had excluded them from power. But
when he died, in 1722, they regained their authority and acted,

in politics, with great independence.[1] Although the Brodricks had a consistent record as eager Hanoverians and aggressive Whigs, they honestly disliked Wood's coins. The first grounds of their foreboding were rational and economic; and they found themselves combining with very different men who shared and elaborated their own fears.

For instance, an old-fashioned Whig like Archbishop King felt angry about Ireland's dependence on a parasitic England, and resented not simply the patent but also the style of its passage. This constitutional objection, by which Wood's patent became a large shadow of the Annesley Case, appealed more generally to Tories, parsons, and others whose interests suffered from English callousness. The great mass of people in Ireland had naturally the same leaning. But beyond them the collaboration was even international. The Irish Tories, with their constitutional arguments, and the Irish Whigs, with their economic anxieties, could join forces with those British Tories and Whigs who wished to see Walpole toppled.

The tribe of Brodricks might take the initiative because Lord Midleton was one of the two or three strongest men in his country. His brother, his son, and he himself held seats in the British Parliament; and Midleton was Speaker of the Irish House of Lords. He had long been accepted as leader of the Whigs in Ireland. Since the accession of King George, he had been Lord Chancellor of Ireland; and when the Earl of Sunderland died, he chose to back not Walpole but Carteret.[2] Midleton was a stubborn, independent man; yet he wanted allies. Walpole's complete disregard for the welfare of Ireland was an incentive for the Brodricks to give Carteret their preference; but his lordship gave them back as much strength as he received.

Grafton misguidedly thought he could overwhelm the Brodrick clan with those Irish Whigs who followed William Conolly,

---

[1] See the invaluable biographical sketches of Alan, St John, and Thomas Brodrick in Romney Sedgwick, ed., *History of Parliament: The House of Commons 1715–1754*, I (London, 1970), 489–92.
[2] Coxe I. 220.

Midleton's rival. But Conolly, though Speaker of the House of Commons, was to see himself isolated at last; and even his Whigs had to repudiate the patent. In England, meanwhile, Walpole was less than helpful. He had misinterpreted the first reports from Dublin, thinking the discontent was blown up and narrowly political.[1] With his usual shortsightedness in popular crises, he said, ''Tis rather a popular run without consideration, than any real solid mischiefs that occasion this clamour.'[2] Walpole knew all about Carteret's intrigue, and thought the resistance to Wood's coins was a mere ramification of a plot against himself.

So Grafton felt his way. He had no useful advice from England, no trustworthy counsellors in Ireland, and no insights or wisdom of his own to direct him. Conforming to the easy pattern of his inertia, he did nothing except to complain that he could do nothing. 'Even those who are most forward to enter into measures agreeable to our side of the water in all other instances [i.e., Conolly's Whigs]', he told Walpole (before Parliament met), 'dare not undertake the defense of this patent.'[3] Since the Irish Privy Council and most members of both houses of the Irish Parliament detested Wood's coins, there was in fact not much he could do, by this time.

We are told that Grafton had secretly committed himself to Wood's job when he was first made Lord Lieutenant.[4] But officially he pretended to have no knowledge of it. In his speech opening Parliament,[5] he asked for 'necessary supplies' and saw no need for new taxes. His other themes were equally mild or non-committal, and he did not even mention the topic on everyone's mind. If he thought evasions would shield him, he was mistaken.

The Irish House of Commons immediately went into committee to debate Wood's patent. They asked the Lord Lieutenant for a copy of it and for papers relating to the grant. Grafton tried

---

[1] *Ibid.*, II. 348–9; 31 Aug. 1723.   [2] *Ibid.*, p. 348.   [3] *Ibid.*, p. 347.
[4] *Ibid.*, I. 218. Cf. Archbishop King's suspicion of Grafton in his letter to E. Southwell, 7 Apr. 1724.
[5] 5 Sept. 1723.

to put them off, and declared that he had nothing to show them. But they proceeded to examine tradesmen who seemed active in the importation of the coins.

Suddenly, Grafton did produce a copy of the patent, saying that he had just received it. No one believed him. An Irish chemist now (upon order) made an assay of the coin, with very different results from those of the royal mint. The floundering Lord Lieutenant felt brushed aside; but when Walpole heard what was going on, he blamed Grafton squarely: 'The Parliament under your administration is attacking a patent already passed in favour of whom and for whose sake alone you know very well. Will it be for that service to suffer an indignity in that vein?' Walpole defended the legitimacy of Wood's grant—'I never knew more care taken upon any occasion than in passing this patent'—and misguidedly assumed that if the grant was technically sound, the whole purpose of the opposition must be to embarrass himself: 'It was passed under the peculiar care and direction of one upon whom the first reflection must fall.'[1]

The Irish leaders, believing quite correctly that Grafton had connived at their humiliation, did not trouble themselves over his. In two brisk weeks the House of Commons managed to adopt a report on the affair, which they proceeded to convey, in the form of a Humble Address, to the King himself, over the heads of Grafton and Walpole. Here they accused Wood of fraud, and begged for action to stop the 'fatal effects' of his coins.[2] The House of Lords, spirited up by Archbishop King and the Earl of Abercorn, did the same.

Wrestling with his runaway Parliament, Grafton exploded impotently to Walpole: 'I am labouring from morning to night under the greatest difficulties and uneasiness, and fear at last that the event will be very far from ... agreeable either to you or myself.'[3] He got, in return, more contempt than consolation: 'There are some people', Walpole said, 'that think they are ever to fatten at the expense of other men's labours and characters,

---

[1] 24 Sept. 1724, to Grafton, in S.P.I. 1723–4, 381/808, fol. 46.
[2] *Drapier*, pp. 193–4. [3] Ballantyne, p. 106.

and be themselves the most righteous fine gentlemen. It is a species of mankind that I own I detest.'[1]

The day after the Humble Addresses passed, Grafton wrôte in despair to Townshend, whimpering with feckless fury against Midleton:

> I think myself most unfortunate, that such an affair happened in my time; however, I beg that you will depend upon my truth in this case, that the whole earth could not have got through this affair without its being laid before the King. You see how the Chancellor [i.e., Midleton] acts. If he has liberty to go on in the way he does, it is every way possible that something may happen that will be disagreeable in the progress of the King's business.[2]

In other words (if we penetrate what Hervey called the 'natural cloud' of Grafton's mind), Parliament might refuse to pass the Appropriations Bill if the King ignored the addresses. Tenderness, Grafton discovered, was not to be had; in October he received another piece of icy insolence from Walpole: 'Pray', said the prime minister, 'don't do in this, as you have in every other step, stay till all is over and then speak.'[3]

Meanwhile, the egregious William Wood rashly supposed that because the Irish memorials impugned his honesty, they required a public contradiction from him. So he placed an enormous though evasive statement in some London papers. *The Evening Post* for 5 October filled two double-columned pages with his point-by-point answer to the resolutions against the patent; and the complete *Flying Post* for 8 October was devoted to the same 'observations', somewhat expanded.

The very conception of a public reply to a parliamentary complaint seems reckless. But Wood's language was as arrogant as his policy. He denied that he had hurt Irish trade, or misrepresented the state of Ireland to the King, or broken the terms of his patent. He denied that his own gain or the cost to the Irish nation was abnormal, and he declared that his modest profit arose from the use of his own supply of copper. He denied that his coinage was a fraud and protested that it was only reasonable

---

[1] *Ibid.*, pp. 108–9.   [2] Coxe II. 349.   [3] Ballantyne, p. 107.

to expect payment for the labour of making metal into money. He defended the purity and workmanship of the coins. He also invoked the royal prerogative, appealed to the terms of earlier patents, and quoted the closing sections of his own patent, with an implicit threat that if the coins were not accepted voluntarily, coarser pressures might be used.

When the most cautious restraint would have sounded bold, Wood used inflammatory figures—for example, speaking of the Irish people's rejection of his coins, 'This is like to a hungry man, who will rather choose to starve, than eat of a dish of wholesome meat, because it is not cooked exactly to his mind.' In the *Flying-Post* he was imprudent enough to add five amazing paragraphs suggesting that if there were any faults in his coinage, they would more likely be due to the carelessness of his employees and of the royal comptroller—perhaps in fraudulent combination! —than to himself.

Two-and-a-half weeks later, Matthew Barton, the comptroller, published a statement that the insinuation against his integrity was 'notoriously false and scandalous'.[1] On the same day a full refutation of Wood appeared in the London *Weekly Journal*, published by Nathaniel Mist, a Tory journalist with Jacobite sympathies.[2]

Meanwhile, a royal *Answer* to the Irish Parliament had become unavoidable. What Walpole least desired had taken place: his enemies had succeeded in rising above the ministry and going directly to the monarch. Walpole must have overseen the composition of this *Answer*, which though short was meticulously worded to avoid offence and to evince no sign of guilt. It expressed his majesty's concern over the response to the patent and his eagerness to punish 'any abuses committed by the patentee' —if indeed he found any existed. The propriety of the original patent was explicitly stated, as being 'agreeable to the practice of his royal predecessors'.[3]

---

[1] *Drapier*, p. 196.

[2] 26 Oct. 1723. Mist had special sources of information in Ireland. The refutation, signed J.G., covers two double-columned sides of a folio leaf. Since it was printed so long after Wood's challenge, I suppose it was sent over from Dublin.

[3] *Drapier*, p. xxii. The *Answer* was received on 16 Nov.

While performing nothing, the *Answer* seemed to promise everything. As a public act it also joined together Mr Wood, Sir Robert, King George, and indeed the government of Great Britain, in a covenant against the will of the Irish people. What might have been a contest between William Wood and the Parliament of Ireland had become a struggle between two nations.

When Parliament reassembled in Dublin after a long recess, the members had the mitigated pleasure of hearing this *Answer* read to them (12 Dec.). But the Commons were irrepressible. While both House returned votes of thanks, that of the Commons closed with a particular request that his majesty would direct his revenue officers not to receive the coins. The danger they correctly envisaged was that Wood's coppers might slip into common use while the government in Westminster procrastinated.[1]

Lord Percival, an Irish peer, was in England at this time. A self-important viscount with ties to the church, he had a large English estate and was much at court. To his brother in Ireland, Percival wrote that he expected the patent to be recalled, 'for which there may be private as well as public reasons, the former for fear of the effect it may have on the great pensions on our establishment, the other to satisfy the united desires of the kingdom'.[2]

Percival was a bad prophet, but he does indicate the common opinion; for his brother replied from Dublin, in the wake of the royal *Answer*, that people were obviously satisfied with 'the account we have that the brass project is like to be laid aside'.[3] Yet all that happened was that around the beginning of March, Walpole finally set up a committee of inquiry, chosen from the British Privy Councillors. Nevertheless, by this time a new phase of the controversy had begun, the phase that gave to Wood's copper halfpence and farthings a meaning as rich and as enduring, for Irish history, as any event since the Revolution. The

---

[1] *Ibid.*, p. xxiii.   [2] 8 Dec. 1723; B.L. Add. MS. 47030, pp. 88–9.
[3] 30 Jan. 1724; *ibid.*, p. 111.

opponents of the patent in Dublin had decided to call in the Dean of St Patrick's.

I don't think Swift possessed any early knowledge of Wood's patent. Charles Ford spent over a year in Ireland from the middle of 1722 till late in 1723; and Swift was much taken up with him in Dublin and at Wood Park. The late spring, the summer, and early autumn of 1722, Swift passed in a series of long country visits. In February 1723 he was drafting his *Letter to a Young Lady*. Vanessa suffered a long, fatal illness in the spring of that year, when Swift must have been glad to avoid public occasions; and as soon as he learned she was dead, he left Dublin—'on account of health', he told Pope—for a four-month tour of southern Ireland.[1]

Although Swift was home in time for the opening of Parliament, the question that troubled him then was not Wood's patent but the bill to let bishops make long, cheap leases. It is remarkable that in the pamphlet attacking this bill, while he dwelt on the 'perpetual decrease' in the value of money,[2] he in no way alluded to the omens of a storm over Wood's coins. Yet he had a concise passage on Ireland's economic ills;[3] and Swift usually managed to bring his peripheral (sometimes irrelevant) complaints into the discussion of any limited topic. All through the winter of 1723–4, the egregious Chetwode's affairs were in a critical state; and Swift was halfheartedly assisting the fool—talking much with Bishop Stearne, Dr Marmaduke Coghill (an ecclesiastical judge), Archbishop King (not to mention others), and enduring the attentions of Chetwode himself.

Even if Swift had not been exposed to these shifting winds, he enjoyed one occupation that was taking up his literary energy, the writing of *Gulliver's Travels*. In a letter of January 1724 to Charles Ford, he observed that he was done with the 'country of horses' and was writing about the 'flying island'—for he composed the voyage to the Houyhnhnms before the voyage to Laputa.[4] In Part Four, on Houyhnhnmland, he mentioned

[1] 20 Sept. 1723, Sherburn II. 198.   [2] Davis IX. 47–51.   [3] *Ibid.*, pp. 47–8.
[4] Williams III. 5 (19 Jan. 1724).

Irish parliamentary affairs but not the halfpence, which in fact got into Part Three of *Gulliver*, the last part written.

In February 1724 Swift did say something about Wood's coins, remarking cheerfully that they might drive absentee landlords back to Ireland by reducing their income. He wrote to Ford,

> I cannot tell whether I shall see you in the spring, for I am afraid our farthings will not pass in and we are daily threatened with them. If they pass, they will bring you Englishmen with Irish estates [i.e., absentees], hither with a vengeance. Aliquisque malo fuit usus in illo.[1]

By now it was beginning to look as if Walpole's government would never withdraw the patent. Irish leaders became more than ever afraid the coins would be foisted on them through the compliance of Conolly's Commissioners of the Revenue, who might pay the army with Wood's coppers. So the scheme of resistance suggested by Archbishop King was adopted: to organize a universal rejection of the dangerous coins. Whoever originated the plan of a boycott would have realized that it could not succeed without intense publicity. If Archbishop King, Lord Abercorn, and Lord Midleton were responsible for leading the campaign, they were probably responsible for involving Swift.

Few of Swift's political wheels came so full a circle as the curve of his acquaintance with Lord Midleton. In 1708 Swift had attacked him, largely for his opposition to the Sacramental Test. 'An honest bellwether of our House' (i.e., the Irish House of Commons), Swift sarcastically labelled him in one pamphlet, while in another Swift's whole aim was to prevent Brodrick's election as Speaker of the Irish House of Commons.[2] But their united loathing of Wood's project brought them so close together that Swift was finally to address one of his masterpieces to Midleton, revealing 'after many years' intermission' their new familiarity.[3]

---

[1] 13 Feb. 1724; *ibid.*   [2] Davis II. 117, 129–35.   [3] *Drapier*, p. 123.

Chapter Six

MARCUS BRUTUS, DRAPIER

All the leaders of the kingdom, with the wavering exception of Conolly, now stood like a Roman square against Wood's patent. The weakness lay not in the gentry, merchants, or bankers but in humbler classes. These had to be terrified into resisting every trick or pressure that Wood and his backers might employ to lure them into taking the coins. I think it was for this particular purpose that the other leaders summoned Swift. He loved to write for a sub-literary audience, and was celebrated for his mastery of the appeals that moved such minds. Probably he accepted the invitation—which I assume he welcomed—in February 1724, and went to work at once.

Among Swift's early decisions was the choice of a pseudonym. In general, when Swift wished to assume a mask, he would disguise himself as a superior member of the class he addressed. So when he decided to produce an essay attacking the patent, he pretended to be a shopkeeper. The industry that meant the most to Swift (besides agriculture) was the manufacture of textiles: that was the subject of his essay on *Irish Manufacture*. The streets near his cathedral were crowded with weavers and drapers. Swift had already championed the weavers, and they were coming to accept him as an arbiter.[1] He therefore made his mask that of a dealer in cloth, a draper.

He also chose to identify himself with a pair of initials, M.B. Thus he not only made his character more concrete. By placing the letters under his title, he also set himself apart from the bulk of mankind and connected himself with a tyrannicide who had

---

[1] *Drapier*, p. 186; Ferguson, pp. 58-9.

put futile patriotism above self-preservation. Swift had once said in a poem,

> 'How shall I act?' is not the case.
> But 'How would Brutus in my place?'[1]

About the time he wrote that poem, he also described Brutus as one of the two most virtuous men in ancient Rome, a hero who thought it base to 'stand neuter' when the liberties of his country were at stake, and who undertook to preserve the laws and constitution against the usurpations of a tyrant.[2] In the part of *Gulliver's Travels* that busied him during the spring of 1724, Swift picked out Brutus for the highest praise: when Gulliver told of seeing the spirits of ancient heroes, he said,

> I was struck with a profound veneration at the sight of Brutus; and could easily discover the most consummate virtue, the greatest intrepidity and firmness of mind, the truest love of his country, and general benevolence for mankind in every lineament of his countenance.[3]

This was precisely the character Swift claimed when writing against Wood's coins; and consequently (I believe) he called himself 'M.B. *Drapier*'.[4]

For the Drapier's address, Swift chose St Francis Street, which lies near St Patrick's deanery and has a religious resonance.[5] I think he thereby pointed at himself as a clergyman. Swift's identity as a Christian preacher shows through his writing as M.B., in audible contrast to the voice of Lemuel Gulliver. Certainly he wished to add evangelical ardour to the urgent tone already established by pamphleteers like Maculla. But I also suspect that he wished his listeners to know they were being rescued by a clergyman; and I think this desire sprang from his policy of tying the Established Church to the welfare of Ireland. Swift may have belittled his own pulpit oratory and said he never rose higher than 'preaching pamphlets';[6] but he

---

[1] *Poems* II. 724.   [2] Davis VI. 134.   [3] *Ibid.*, XI. 196.
[4] I was first persuaded to adopt this view by Jack Gilbert, 'The Drapier's Initials', *N. & Q.* 208 (Jun. 1963), 217–18.
[5] *Drapier*, p. 289.   [6] Davis IX. 97–8.

might also have said that his best pamphlets work like sermons.

In dealing with a narrowly economic theme, a sharp debater meets the risk of appearing materialistic. The more strident one sounds in quarrels about money, the more one seems to make it the root of all good. Swift's case in *The Conduct of the Allies* has lost its hold on modern readers by being too hard-headed. His attack on Wood's coins remains exhilarating for its idealism. Instead of describing his programme as leading to prosperity pure and simple, Swift bathes it in a radiance of magnanimous patriotism and religious salvation. In the grounds of its ultimate appeal— as in its rhetoric—the new essay echoes the highmindedness of the essay on *Irish Manufacture*.[1]

Swift called it 'A Letter' to shopkeepers, farmers, and 'common-people'. Thus he gave it a confidential nature and ingratiated himself with the humble listener by evincing a particular concern with his welfare. At the beginning and end of this *Letter to Shopkeepers*, etc., Swift brings in God, salvation, and Christianity yoked with love of country. The penultimate paragraph has a loud allusion to Scripture. All through, the style crackles with the language of desperate bravery:

> Therefore, my friends, stand to it one and all: Refuse this *filthy trash*. It is no treason to rebel against Mr Wood.[2]

What a pleasure for the shopkeeper or farmer to feel that heroism pays, and that he will gain ready cash by serving God and country!

In the *Proposal for Irish Manufacture*, where Swift had recommended another kind of boycott as if it were a renunciation of sin, he had closed his central paragraph with a Biblical exhortation: '*and let all the people say*, AMEN'.[3] The *Letter to Shopkeepers* has some of the drama and kinesthetic language of an evange-

---

[1] The idea of a boycott is carried over from the *Proposal for Irish Manufacture*; Swift explicitly connects the two pamphlets at the start of the *Letter to Shopkeepers*; and in that essay he implicitly identifies the Drapier as the author of the earlier tract when he says, 'I cannot but warn you once more' (*Drapier*, p. 4).

[2] *Drapier*, p. 14.

[3] Davis IX. 16; Psalm cvi. 48. (Professor James Woolley kindly called this to my attention.)

list's call to repentance. It opens with the urgency of a prophet's descent. There is the headlong impetus of Christian, *Pilgrim's Progress*, shouting, 'What shall I do? Our city will be burned with fire.'[1] The panic of a soul facing damnation is one source of M.B.'s anxious undertone.

The vocabulary remains simple enough for rustics to grasp. It is heavily monosyllabic. History, law, and morality are reduced to their humblest terms. Where Swift is forced to deal with legal principles or precedents, he apologizes for their obscurity, translates the Latin, rewrites archaic prose, and summarizes the whole in the plainest expressions.

But emotions stream from every phrase. They are unmixed emotions, with anger the most pervasive. The Drapier feels indignant with his listeners for neglecting their country, with Wood for his greed and insolence, with the absentees for their selfishness. He feels pity for Ireland, for Mr Harding (who was jailed for printing *Irish Manufacture*), for the farmers, tradesmen, artisans who would be ruined by Wood's coins.

Yet the attitude that startles and captivates a reader is the Drapier's recklessness. He has the confidence to name and characterize any person who belongs to his argument. On the loathsome Mr Wood and his works he dumps a vigorous fecundity of elementary insolence: Wood is a mean, ordinary man; an ordinary fellow; a bloodsucker;[2] his patent is a wicked cheat, an abominable project; his money is cursed coin, filthy trash, 'like the accursed thing which . . . the children of Israel were forbidden to touch'. At the other extreme the Drapier makes free with the name of the King, which he treats with ostensibly respectful epithets only to undercut them by the boldness of the reference:

His MAJESTY in his patent obliges nobody to take these halfpence, our GRACIOUS PRINCE hath no so ill advisers about him; or if he had,

---

[1] *Pilgrim's Progress*, opening, condensed.
[2] Archbishop King uses 'bloodsucker' as a term of abuse for Irish office-holders who live in England and spend their salaries and fees there; cf. his letter of 10 Nov. 1722, to S. Molyneux.

yet you see the laws have not left it in the KING's power, to force us to take any coin but what is lawful, of right standard *gold* and *silver*.[1]

This kind of violence is, as usual with Swift, framed in rational self-possession; for Swift always acts the part of a cool man who has, against his nature, been provoked to heat. So the essay falls into orderly sections: an opening exhortation and a closing plea that men should refuse the coins; between these sections, a historical survey, a reckoning of the financial implications of Wood's scheme, a deduction of its socio-economic consequences, and an account of the laws that apply to the case.

Here is the machinery of logic without the rigour. Swift backs up his alarums with specious facts and apparent demonstrations. The reasoning, the linkages of cause to effect, are sometimes valid, but mostly exaggerated, and the elaborations run into fantasy. Nothing in the Drapier's logic is so effective as his disorderly tone and lurid illustration.

Swift's genuine debating points had been made before. He declares that Wood's money will ruin Ireland. It is so debased that trademen will have to raise their prices if they take it; forgers will easily copy it; and honest men will hoard their gold and silver. Yet the patent is so loosely worded that Wood may go on coining indefinitely. Happily, says the Drapier, the law requires no one to accept the coins. Therefore, everyone must spurn them.

These arguments are drowned in their own magnification. The Drapier claims that the true value of Wood's coins comes to a tenth of their face value. He then gives colourful, humble examples of their effect on shopkeepers, customers, bankers, and landlords, not excluding beggars:

> For example, if a *hatter* sells a dozen of *hats* for *five shillings* apiece, which amounts to *three pounds*, and receives the payment in Mr WOODS's coin, he really receives only the value of *five shillings*.[2]

Since gold and silver will disappear, all payment must be made in bad money, and the transfer of funds becomes a nightmare.

[1] *Drapier*, p. 14.   [2] *Drapier*, p. 5.

Having destroyed the value of Wood's coins, Swift proceeds to inflate their bulk:[1]

> They say 'SQUIRE C[ONOLL]Y has *sixteen thousand pounds a year*. Now if he sends for his *rent* to town, *as it is likely he does*, he must have *two hundred and forty horses* to bring up his *half year's rent*, and two or three great *cellars* in his house for stowage.[2]

All Ireland's money will at last be replaced by Wood's change: then disaster must follow, but it is the lower classes (to whom, of course, this letter is addressed) that will suffer most.

> When once the *kingdom* is reduced to such a condition, I will tell you what must be the end: The *gentlemen of estates* will all turn off their *tenants* for want of payment ... run *all* into *sheep* where they can, keeping only such other *cattle* as are necessary. Then they will be their own *merchants* and send their *wool* and *butter* and *hides* and *linen* beyond sea for ready *money* and *wine* and *spices* and *silks*. They will keep only a few miserable *cottiers*. The *farmers* must *rob* or *beg*, or leave their *country*. The *shop-keepers* in this and every other town, must *break* and *starve*.[3]

Along the way, Swift produces some of his favourite economic doctrines, such as blaming absentees for wasting their country's wealth, and describing agriculture as the foundation of a nation's welfare. But he is also outrageously provocative, uttering sentiments that do not advance his case and yet must infuriate the government:

> We are at a great distance from the *King's court*, and have nobody there to solicit for us, although a great number of *lords* and *squires*, whose estates are here, and are our countrymen, spend all their *lives* and *fortunes* there. But this same Mr WOODS was able to attend constantly for his own interest; he is an ENGLISH MAN and had GREAT FRIENDS, and it seems knew very well *where to give money*, to those that would speak to OTHERS that could speak to the KING and could tell A FAIR STORY. And HIS MAJESTY, and perhaps the great lord or lords who advised him, might think it was for our *country's good*. ... And I am sure if his MAJESTY knew that such a patent, if it should take

---

[1] Here I not only follow but echo Ferguson, p. 100.
[2] *Drapier*, p. 8.   [3] *Ibid.*, p. 9; spelling and punctuation altered.

effect according to the desire of Mr WOODS, would utterly ruin this kingdom, which hath given such great proofs of its *loyalty*, he would immediately recall it, and perhaps shew his displeasure to SOME BODY OR OTHER, *but a word to the wise is enough*.[1]

Swift had enough experience of censorship—both as victim and as agent—to know how inflammatory such expressions would sound. He knew the government could hardly avoid prosecuting the author and the printer. In ordinary times few people would have denied that such passages deserved the wrath of the powers that be. Yet Swift's gains were enormous. If the government refrained from prosecution, it would invite wilder combustions, leading maybe to riots. If it did prosecute, the effect might be the same as with the pamphlet on *Irish Manufacture*. The country would unite behind the Drapier; trimmers would have to take sides; Parliament might be drawn in; and the vote on supplies might be lost. The King, who hated bother, would be troubled again; and turmoil of any sort would hurt Walpole's standing with his majesty.

At the same time, Swift is strengthening his rhetoric of confidentiality. By appearing to expose his rawest emotions, he implies that he trusts the listener to understand his candour. He seems to hide nothing. Besides, there are the heavy, mock-subtle allusions to Walpole and company. By thus appealing to the shrewdness and insight of the listeners, he pretends to take them behind the scenes of government and pays a compliment to their political sagacity.

Whether or not Swift planned at this moment to add sequels to his *Letter to Shopkeepers*, we cannot say. But long experience must have deepened his intuition that sequels were normal for his kind of propaganda—even as this *Letter* itself was a sequel to the *Proposal for Irish Manufacture*. Certainly he established in the *Letter* a number of rhetorical principles that he was to develop in later work.

The great mainstay of his edifice is a set of dramatic conflicts.

---

[1] *Ibid.*, pp. 5–6.

These may rise at last to high abstractions, but they start from particular personalities. The first need of a propagandist is to supply his audience with a human focus for their feelings. Swift's need was urgent because the natural targets of the Drapier were King George and his majesty's prime minister. To attack either of them openly would have meant something like lese-majesty or scandalum magnatum, and would have alienated many of the Drapier's sympathizers. So Swift descended to William Wood, though knowing too little about him even to spell the name right.

The *Letter to Shopkeepers* drives almost as much against Wood's character as his coins. We are roused more quickly to hate a man than an idea. The Drapier can rant as ferociously as he likes against the villainy of Wood's own aims without directly affronting the Crown or the government.

Not only does Swift give Wood a deceitful, treacherous nature, a mercenary cunning, and a mean origin. Not only does he represent him as arrogant, underhanded, and supremely avaricious. But he also treats Wood as an isolated figure, a name with no friends except those venal courtiers who got the patent for him, or those collaborators who will find their criminal profit in vending his brass.

In opposition to Wood, Swift sets up M.B., a selfless patriot, well-informed, reasonable and public-spirited. There are hints enough that Ireland lies behind M.B. and England behind Wood, or that one means freedom and the other oppression. An earlier pamphleteer had already described the contest as one fought between the kingdom of Ireland and William Wood.[1] Wood may become large, mysteriously powerful, faintly comic. M.B. may seem unarmed and vulnerable. But pure evil sides with one, and the armies of the living God support the other. For all his power Wood remains a contemptible opponent, and the Irish (we infer) will be contemptible if they let him defeat them. By rousing the decent pride of his listeners while he demeans their enemy, the Drapier teases them into joining him. By

[1] *The True State of the Case*; see *Drapier*, p. 355.

harping on the need for men to declare their hatred of the patent and by condemning the treachery of those who hold back, Swift intimidates any undecided minds into joining his party. The use of Conolly's name may well be malicious.

In order to give his argument the widest possible circulation, Swift himself paid for printing the pamphlet, which was published in March 1724 in an edition of 2000 copies selling for two or three pence apiece. Early in April, Swift said that 'about 2000' had been 'dispersed by gentlemen in several parts of the country'. In May, a Dublin newspaper announced a new price of three dozen pamphlets for two shillings, and this probably signalized a new edition.[1]

---

[1] In the letter itself Swift declares that he has paid for the printing, and he indicates the price by saying twelve persons may read the pamphlet for less than a farthing apiece. He mentions the distribution of 2000 copies in a letter to Ford, 2 Apr. 1724. See also *Drapier*, pp. lxxxi and 186; also Davis x. 207–8. The *Dublin Journal* for 11 May 1724 announced the new cheap price and urged tradesmen, gentlemen, and farmers to read and distribute the *Letter*.

Chapter Seven

WALPOLE'S WISDOM

I. WAITING FOR CARTERET

While the *Letter to Shopkeepers* was finding its audience, the Lord Lieutenant was covering himself with ignominy. Before February 1724, Dubliners heard that he would soon be removed;[1] and early in March came reports that some of his horses and furniture were being embarked for England.[2] Grafton himself remained less fortunate. He had prorogued the Irish Parliament in December, but then he went on fumbling with his difficulties week after week while waiting for relief.

In Westminster, Walpole moved on several fronts. He made a great show of wishing to get ahead with the inquiry promised long ago in response to the addresses of the Irish Parliament. So Carteret as Secretary of State wrote to Grafton,[3] asking him to send over witnesses and evidence. This simple and obvious request, the Lord Lieutenant could never meet. Parliament had risen. Consequently, it could not appoint official witnesses or deliver up the documents in its keeping.

Meanwhile, Archbishop King was furious. About this time, it looked as if Primate Lindsay were at last going to fulfil the many expectations of his dying; and all persons in the Irish interest wished the archbishop to succeed him. King knew better than anyone else how heavily the court frowned on him, and he might have been expected to talk prudently for the sake of the final and supreme preferment. Yet he held back little of his rage when he

---

[1] Coxe II. 380.   [2] London *Weekly Journal*, 7 Mar. 1724.
[3] 10 Mar. See *Drapier*, p. xxiii.

wrote to Edward Southwell:

> My Lord Lieutenant sent for several lords and commoners of the
> Privy Council, and communicated to them a letter from my Lord
> Carteret, writ by his majesty's command, in which ... his grace is
> required to send over the witnesses and evidences against the paten-
> tee or patent. This has surprised most people, because we were borne
> in hand that the affair was dead, and that we should never hear any
> more of it.
>
> His grace's design was to be advised by what means and methods
> he might effectually comply with his majesty's commands, and by
> what I could perceive it was the sense of all that it was not possible in
> the present situation of affairs to answer his majesty's expectations or
> those of the kingdom.

The archbishop pointed out that 'this is a controversy between
the Parliament of Ireland and William Wood,' and that no Irish
subject could possibly speak for Parliament without permission.
He observed that there was no way to prove abuses of the patent,
because Wood could claim that any defective coins were the
work of forgers. The archbishop insisted that the opposition to
the patent did not depend on the charges which the English
government was investigating but on the mischief the coins
would bring and on the falsity of the information produced to
secure the patent; for the Irish people did not need copper coins.
After an important review of other arguments we have already
heard (several of which Swift was to employ), the archbishop
closed with a warning to the ministry and an insinuation against
Grafton:

> I farther observe that I do not remember any thing ever so univer-
> sally disgusted the people of Ireland as this patent, insomuch that I
> never met or heard of any one person that was not in a kind of fury
> when it was talked of, and if any one should now seem to encourage
> the execution of it, he would have an ill time of it, and must
> incapacitate himself from doing any real service to his majesty or the
> country by his losing all credit here. And let me discover a sort of
> secret to you. The people entertained (at least a great many) a
> jealousy [i.e., suspicion] that my Lord Lieutenant had some hand in
> it, or had not opposed it with that vigour they expected from him,

and nothing but this has done his grace any harm in the opinion of the people of Ireland.[1]

What the Irish Parliament would not do for itself, nobody might do in its stead. Anyone rash enough to speak for Parliament would risk very unpleasant handling when the members met again. Neither could original documents be removed from the authorities to whom they were entrusted. Officially, Grafton could not even secure the names of those men who had testified before the committees of Parliament.[2] Archbishop King wrote to Edward Southwell, .

> Those who are most calm and moderate (a part which very few act) look on it as a jest to expect anybody from hence to object or witness against Wood's patent, after the Parliament both Lords and Commons have given their judgment and testimony against it, and declared the mischievousness of it to the kingdom. 'Pray', say they, 'who should send over witnesses? Who should bear their charges? Who should fee lawyers or manage such a cause or who dare undertake it without an appointment and commission from the Parliament who is the party against Woods?'[3]

Other dangers swarmed outside Parliament. Any witness who went over from Ireland, any officer who gave evidence, would expose himself to sinister rumours if the government then failed to reverse its policy. His own countrymen would suspect him of assisting in their destruction. Besides, so few examples existed of the Crown's rescinding a bad order as a result of rational argument, that only the least experienced citizens would have turned to fact and logic as their resource. Irish leaders quietly agreed that group complaints and non-cooperation were their strongest weapons. If the councillors in Westminster reached a judgment without hearing any evidence from Ireland, it would appear ex parte and of doubtful validity.

Grafton was far too inept to accomplish Walpole's ends through tact and persuasion. He reported accurately that

---

[1] 23 Mar. 1723–4, to E. Southwell. The impossibility of proving abuses is analysed again, very ably, in a letter of 7 Apr. 1724 to Southwell.
[2] King to Southwell, 23 Mar. 1723–4; *Drapier*, pp. 229–31.
[3] 19 Apr. 1724.

witnesses and evidence were out of the question. Walpole could not help getting the impression, quite apart from Grafton's breathtaking incompetence, that the Irish had arrogantly refused to follow the procedures of British justice; for he disregarded the unscrupulous use he wished to make of those procedures.

By the end of March Walpole had found a replacement for Grafton; politics imitated art in a splendidly ironical turn of court intrigue. The deaths of Stanhope and Sunderland had long deprived Carteret of his best support against the trio—Walpole, Townshend, and Newcastle—now managing King George's business. These three gradually manœuvred the King into displaying a lack of confidence in Carteret that drove him to resign as Secretary of State.[1] Yet he retained so much of royal favour that the ministry had still to find a respectable place for him; and they chose the nest he had helped to make so uncomfortable for Grafton—Dublin Castle. The crisis that Carteret had hoped would disgrace Walpole was now to become his own charge. A lapidary sentence conveyed the bright idea to Grafton, in a message from Townshend with the suitable date of 1 April:

> I am persuaded, that your grace is so well convinced of the necessity there was of removing Lord Carteret from the employment he was in, and of the impossibility there was of doing it without giving some considerable equivalent, that you are sensible his having the government of Ireland, was in a manner unavoidable.[2]

Walpole, with less amplitude but more light, told Newcastle, 'I should not be for sending [Carteret] over now if I did not think it would end in totally recalling him. We shall at least get rid of him here.'[3]

Walpole did not have to be informed that Midleton, as Lord Chancellor of Ireland and Privy Councillor, was blocking the chief minister's policy in the matter of Wood's patent. But he meant for a while to act pacific. So he named Midleton, as well as the more reliable Conolly (Speaker of the House of

---

[1] Basil Williams, *Carteret and Newcastle*, p. 60.   [2] Coxe II. 296.
[3] Ballantyne, p. 70.

Commons) to be among the Lords Justices appointed to govern the kingdom between the departure of Grafton and the arrival of his successor. This lamblike gesture, Walpole balanced with a lupine menace; for he named among the Commissioners of the Revenue in Ireland three Englishmen who lived entirely in his camp, and he saw to it that they were sworn in, in England and dispensed from taking the oaths in Ireland.[1] If the Commissioners of the Revenue accepted Wood's coins and paid them out again, the country would of course be flooded with the money.

Not surprisingly, Archbishop King's crony the Archbishop of Tuam now wrote to Canterbury and pleaded that King George should 'give no direction to the officers of his revenue here to take that copper coin';[2] and the Irish Privy Council sent over an address (never promulgated) particularly asking his majesty to tell the Commissioners of the Revenue to 'do what in them lies for the allaying and quieting' the fear of the coins.[3] Grafton was by now in England; but all three Lords Justices (Midleton, Conolly, and Lord Shannon) signed this address on the very day they were sworn in, making it clear that no one in Irish public life could separate himself from the opposition to Wood's patent.[4]

The temperature of Irish emotions soared as a committee of the English Privy Council proceeded with its own investigation of the miserable patent.[5] Unable to fetch oral or written testimony from Ireland, the members willingly fell back upon what England could provide. Wood disinterred four witnesses, of whom two were involved in distributing the coins and two had been indicted for serious crimes.[6] They testified to a shortage of small change in Ireland; and Wood buttressed their declarations with letters to the same effect. The Crown also ordered an assay of Wood's coppers to be made at the royal mint. Toward the end of April, Sir Isaac Newton and his assis-

---

[1] Dodington, Edgecombe, and Viscount Falmouth.
[2] Synge to Wake, 25 Apr. 1724, in Wake Letters.   [3] *Drapier*, pp. xxx, 209–11.
[4] 20 May 1724.   [5] The committee began sitting on 9 Apr. 1724.
[6] *Drapier*, pp. 226–9.

tants reported that the coins were excellent in every respect.[1]

When accounts of the earliest meetings of the English committee got to Ireland, the *Dublin News Letter* reprinted a bland paragraph from a London paper, stating that no evidence had appeared 'to prove the mischiefs complain'd of', that Wood was heard in his own defence, and that an assay of his coppers had been ordered.[2] I think it was Swift who had the paragraph reprinted, for the Dublin paper belonged to John Harding, printer of the *Letter to Shopkeepers*. Swift certainly wrote a marvellous, anonymous commentary that the *News Letter* added to the matter. Here he pretended to think that Wood himself had composed the original London account. This seems unlikely: even if Wood did place the brief statement in the press, it was pretty colourless and factual. But in order to keep up the drama of a quarrel between the kingdom of Ireland and the patentee, Swift detached the incident from King George or his government, and fixed it entirely on Wood.

So it is Wood whom Swift (in the *News Letter*) blames, furiously and utterly, for requiring evidence of an Irish Parliament's assertions. He blames Wood for supposing the assay will be reliable. He opposes Wood to the 'gracious' King. Swift also reminds his readers of the *Letter to Shopkeepers* and warns them that no man is bound to take the worthless coins. Then he closes with an eruptive, Swiftian howl:

> But after all, is it possible without some indignation to conceive a whole kingdom kept in fright for so many months by one *obscure, inconsiderable, insignificant, ill-designing mechanick*?[3]

Even in this small episode we see features of Swift's method: to dwell on ambiguous polarities, to make one person the screen through which he attacks another (and higher) person, to whet his indignation on any materials that come to hand. Archbishop King had said the quarrel lay between the Parliament of Ireland

---

[1] The report was dated 17 Apr. 1724 (*ibid.*, pp. 205–7).

[2] *Ibid.*, pp. xxv–xxvii.

[3] *Ibid.*, p. xxvi. Of course, the paragraph is not signed. The date of the newspaper is 21 Apr. 1724.

and William Wood;[1] but Swift seizes on the lopsided antinomy and works out its satirical implications. At this moment his game depends on the visible gap between Wood's true powers and the deeds attributed to him. It was of course not Wood but Walpole who required evidence of the Irish Parliament's assertions. It was not the patentee but His Royal Majesty who had ordered the new assay. The contrast between the venom of Swift's comment and the insipidity of the paragraph it deals with is a subtle parallel to his misrepresentation of the chain of command. The reader has only to recognize the true objects of the writer's fury for that emotion to become intelligible.[2]

We get a hint of Swift's effectiveness from the way his rhetoric was echoed, two weeks later, by Lord Percival, writing from England:

> 'Tis now given out that care will be taken whereby we shall not suffer so as we apprehended, although the patent should not be totally recalled. This, time must show: however 'tis a strange thing that the interest of such an obscure fellow as the patentee is, should be put in competition with that of a whole kingdom and the honour of our Parliament who have opposed it.[3]

His brother replied from Dublin as if coached by the Drapier:

> You seem to give us some little hopes that we shall not be quite undone by the halfpence, though the patent should not be totally suppressed; but I believe it must [be] total or not at all, for while he has the power to utter £16,000 publicly, he will or certainly may utter six times as many privately, and no possibility of being detected: and as to the trial at the pyx, there's no doubt he had the proof made on his best sort.[4]

Walpole was trying to argue from a position of overwhelming strength. He and his partners threw out hints that they could easily crush Ireland if resistance to the patent went too far.[5] But he avoided blatant provocations. Against him the organizers of

---

[1] 23 Mar. 1724, to E. Southwell.
[2] I am following the analysis made by Price (pp. 52–5) and Ferguson (pp. 106–7).
[3] 6 May 1724; B.L. Add. MS. 47030, p. 128.
[4] 26 May 1724; *ibid.*, p. 130.
[5] Cf. Newcastle's remark to Conolly, quoted in *Drapier*, p. xxxii.

the boycott reacted with two distinct strategies, one for their own people and one for the government in Westminster. If the boycott was to succeed, it must be universal. Everyone had to be persuaded or intimidated into refusing the coins. Representative groups were therefore led or coerced into publishing their abhorrence of Wood's money. Ultimately, citizens were encouraged to spy on one another and to expose any man who compromised with evil. (Swift—unlike Archbishop King—was willing to use the procedures of a police state to advance a cause that he considered of fundamental value.)

It was also crucial that the ministry should believe Wood's cause did not deserve the trouble it must bring on them. Petitions and addresses had to bombard Whitehall, and the danger of a breakdown in the whole administration of Ireland must be made palpable.

Swift devoted himself to both strategies. It looks to me as if the petition of the Grand Jury of Dublin, sent to England along with the address of the Privy Council, was at least partly composed by him; for it mixes hyperbolic asseverations of loyalty to the Crown with the sharpest repudiation of Wood's patent. The signers 'beg leave to return your most sacred majesty our unfeigned thanks for the enjoyment of our civil rights and liberties under your most auspicious reign': even for the ear of a German prince the adulation sounds loud. But at the same time they protest that the new coins will lower the royal revenue, destroy Irish trade, and 'tend to the ruin and impoverishing your majesty's most dutiful dubjects'.[1] One easily observes that some of these sentiments are less candid than others.

Carteret, as the new Lord Lieutenant, digested this petition and the address of the Irish Privy Council only a month before he became a figure in the comic underplot of Swift's drama. Just as King George and the Drapier were enemies disguised as allies, so Carteret and Swift were to take up the rôles of allies disguised as enemies. During the years when his lordship presided over the destiny of Ireland, the dean was to be one of his social pleasures

[1] *Ibid.*, pp. 286–7.

while remaining a political liability. Both men's insight into the limits and ironies of their connection were to raise it to the plane of a comedy of manners. We can judge how much this linkage meant to Swift from the fact that he saved not only Carteret's letters to him but copies of his own to Carteret.[1]

Swift was familiar with Carteret's family and had been on friendly terms with his lordship in London. He had known and liked the young Whig peer when Carteret was taking his first steps in public life. Ten years had passed since their last meeting. Carteret had made his way as a member of Sunderland's coterie. Equipped with courtly manners, an excellent classical education, and a command of modern languages, he distinguished himself as a diplomat and became an effective ambassador to Sweden before he was thirty. His tact and his fluency in German endeared him to King George; but of course he had lost out in the competition with Walpole at the moment he accepted the lord lieutenancy. In Carteret, Swift was to find, I think, one of the truest embodiments of the ideal statesman that he first envisaged in the shape of Sir William Temple; and it is no wonder that his praise of the Lord Lieutenant sometimes echoes Gulliver's remarks on the King of the Giants.[2]

Swift was in the habit of establishing a special friendship with accessible viceroys. When he heard of Carteret's appointment, he wrote to his excellency in a style that hid real courtliness under real candour. With much dignity and no irony he revived their old acquaintanceship and then told his amply informed listener about Wood's patent—how dangerous it was, how united the people felt against it, and how gracious the Lord Lieutenant would be if he helped to rescue them from 'the most ruinous project that was ever contrived against any nation'.[3]

For Carteret to reply to the point would have been awkward unless he wished to embarrass himself in Ireland or England.

---

[1] I assume that the five letters to Carteret printed by Deane Swift were from drafts, there being no sign that Deane Swift retrieved the final copies. To see the kind of change Swift would make between the draft and the fair copy, the reader may compare the two texts of Swift's letter of 4 Sept. 1724 in Williams III. 30–3 and v. 245–7.

[2] Cf. Davis XI. 133, second paragraph, and XII. 155—not a deliberate echo.

[3] 28 Apr. 1724; Williams III. 12.

Maybe this is why he failed to reply at all. After waiting almost six weeks with no word, Swift wrote again, even more elegantly. He produced an exquisitely charming letter of reproach from a clergyman of an older generation to a great lord of a younger:

> I have long been out of the world, but have not forgotten what used to pass among those I lived with, while I was in it: And I can say, that during the experience of many years, and many changes in affairs, your excellency, and one more, who is not worthy to be compared to you, are the only great persons that ever refused to answer a letter from me, without regard to business, party, or greatness; and, if I had not a particular esteem for your personal qualities, I should think myself to be acting a very inferior part in making this complaint.
>
> . . .
>
> I often told a great minister, whom you well know, that I valued him for being the same man through all the progress of power and place. I expected the like in your lordship; and still hope that I shall be the only person who will ever find it otherwise.[1]

Carteret rose to the challenge like a dancer in a pas de deux. Swift had long practice in ironic modesty, and he chose this victim well. The courtier almost surpassed the churchman at his own game; for he gracefully apologized for the appearance of negligence while evading the main issue with a plea of ignorance:

> The principal affair you mention is under examination, and till that is over, I am not informed sufficiently to make any other judgment of the matter, than that which I am naturally led to make, by the general aversion which appears to it in the whole nation.[2]

Swift might now have let his lordship off, and allowed the correspondence to lapse until there was business between them; but I think he imagined he might now bowl Carteret over with a letter of pure though self-possessed compliment.[3] Carteret's appetite for this kind of duel was, however, equal to his own; and the great man came back with a eulogy that gives some indication of his powers as a diplomat:

> Methinks I see you throw this letter upon your table in the height of spleen because it may have interrupted some of your more agreeable

[1] *Ibid.*, pp. 13–14.   [2] *Ibid.*, p. 17.   [3] *Ibid.*, pp. 17–18.

thoughts, but then in return you may have the comfort of not answering it, and so convince my Lord Lieutenant that you value him less now than you did ten years ago. I don't know but this might become a free speaker and a philosopher. Whatever you may think of it, I shall not be testy, but endeavour to show that I am not altogether insensible of the genius, which has outshone most of this age, and when you display it again can convince us that its lustre and strength are still the same.[1]

By this time Swift had other things to write besides courtly flourishes. In July 1724 the committee of the English Privy Council received the official account of Newton's assay and heard Wood make new proposals in response to the outcries of his victims. The patentee's witnesses had agreed that Ireland needed the coppers, and the assay seemed to demonstrate the high quality of the coins. Wood now offered to meet the objection to their quantity. In place of the original amount of £100,800 he would scale the total value down to £40,000; and he would take Irish goods for his money, obliging no one to accept more than five pence halfpenny in a single transaction. Wood was also prepared to sell his coins in Bristol for 2s. 1d. a pound, or else to sell his bulk copper for 1s. 8d. a pound.[2]

Newspapers in London and Dublin printed a short account of the committee's meeting, which may have been planted by the irrepressible Mr Wood.[3] This article included several ugly turns of phrase, the least fortunate appearing in the last sentence: 'N.B. No evidence appear'd from Ireland or elsewhere, to prove the mischiefs complain'd of, or any abuses whatsoever committed in the execution of the said grant.'[4] Harding reprinted the article in his *Weekly News-Letter* with a pointed comment, added I suppose by Swift—

> if we once suffer this same Wood's half-pence and farthings to pass among us, the consequences will be the utter ruin and destruction of this country, which is fully prov'd in a pamphlet lately publish'd, entitul'd *A Letter to the Shopkeepers* etc. Rate—Two English shillings three dozen.[5]

[1] *Ibid.*, pp. 25–6.   [2] *Drapier*, p. 203.
[3] Swift thought so; see *A Letter to Mr Harding*, first paragraph.
[4] *Drapier*, p. 203.   [5] 1 Aug. 1724; *ibid.*, pp. xxxii–xxxiii, 202–3.

A few days later, Harding advertised a second pamphlet by
M.B., and this, *A Letter to Mr Harding*, came out on 6 August.[1]

Nobody identified with the Irish interest could feel sanguine
about the direction being followed by the kingdom's establishment. Swift's old enemy, Bishop Evans of Meath, had died
suddenly in March. But his successor was an Englishman, Henry
Downes, educated at New College, Oxford. Downes had been in
Ireland for seven years, as Bishop of Killala and then of Elphin.
So his translation was not the shock that a newcomer's would
have been. The effect of Downes's preferment was also softened
by the translation of the native-born Theophilus Bolton to
the vacated bishopric of Elphin. Nevertheless, Swift could not
have wished Meath, a dignity that ranked after the four arch-
bishoprics, to be filled by an Englishman.

When Primate Lindsay died in July, much worse news came.
No ecclesiastical preferment—hardly any civil preferment—
was more important from any point of view. Not only the
families in the Irish interest but Nicolson himself would have
been glad to see Archbishop King recognized as the unrivalled
candidate for the elevation. Letters from a dazzling spectrum
of political opinions are extant, recommending him. But the
English ministers had determined on the narrowest programme
of English appointments.

Marmaduke Coghill, ecclesiastical judge and a friend of Swift
and King, wrote to Southwell,

> Our Lord Primate died yesterday about one a clock, and the wishes
> generally of the whole kingdom are for the Archbishop of Dublin to
> succeed him, and indeed no man in the kingdom can so justly claim
> it as himself.[2]

When Coghill learned that Hugh Boulter, Bishop of Bristol, was
to be sent over, he wrote a lament to Southwell against 'putting
any body over the head of our Archbishop':

[1] *A Letter to Mr Harding the Printer, upon Occasion of a Paragraph in His News-Paper*, signed
4 Aug. 1724, advertised 4 Aug. to appear 6 Aug., when it did. A second Dublin edition
appeared the same month; another edition was printed in Limerick, and included a
declaration of Dublin bankers dated 15 Aug.
[2] 14 Jul. 1724, in B.L. Add. MS. 21, 122, fol. 11.

His personal merit is as great as any Christian bishop in the world, but when his steadiness and sufferings at the time of the Revolution, and his zeal for the cause here in the worst of time ... are considered, it is amazing that any body should be thought of for this station but himself.[1]

Coghill's quivering emotions will represent those of thousands, including Swift.

On top of these disappointments had fallen the disgraceful report of the committee of the British Privy Council concerning Wood's patent. This, in pretty rough language, put great and repeated weight upon the failure of the Irish to submit evidence of their charges; it found that Wood had proved his case—i.e., that Ireland did indeed need copper coins and the patent had not been abused. It accepted Wood's new proposals, particularly the reduction of the value of the coins to a maximum of £40,000. And it recommended that the King should order his officers in Ireland to revoke any directions they might have given against the passing of the coins, which were to circulate without any obstruction. Yet the words of the recommendation still limited the use of the coins to 'such as shall be willing to receive the same'.[2]

Coghill told Southwell that, from the proceedings of the committee about the coins,

> we apprehend it is intended they should be forced upon us, and what the consequence of that will be, God knows, for there is so general an aversion to them through the whole kingdom that it will be impossible (without some particular order to the Treasury to take them there) to make them pass; and if such orders should come, I do not see how the officers dare execute them. Some of them I am sure will give up their employments rather [?than] comply with such directions; and I am sure whenever a Parliament meets, it will be impossible to keep either Lords or Commons in any temper, for they will highly resent the indignity offered to them by [the] despising their addresses and applications about these halfpence, which they have so unanimously represented to be so pernicious to his majesty's revenue and the public welfare of this unhappy country.[3]

[1] 1 Aug. 1724, *ibid.*, fol. 13^v.
[2] The *Report* is dated 24 Jul. 1724; it was presented to the whole Privy Council of Great Britain on 6 Aug. See *Drapier*, pp. 213–25.
[3] 1 Aug. 1724, in B.L. Add. MS. 21, 122, fol. 13.

It is a withering comment on the history of Ireland's relation to England that although Coghill's account was supported by every respectable authority, it was a year before the ministry in Whitehall responded to the fact with any decency. We can now imagine with what feelings the Dean of St Patrick's sat down to compose M.B.'s second letter, *A Letter to Mr Harding*.

II. THE DRAPIER'S SECOND LETTER

To begin with, Swift redefined his audience. Throughout the new pamphlet M.B. addresses Harding the printer and considers with him the implications of the paragraph—on the Privy Council's report—reprinted in his newspaper. But Swift obviously intended the arguments to be heard by a wide range of men, above the humblest class. The leading figures of the nation had already fixed their judgment and hardly feared a break in their own ranks. Yet King George might issue a proclamation declaring Wood's coins to be legal tender, or else he might direct the Commissioners of the Revenue to accept them. Either order would intimidate the middle classes and the common people. To infuse boldness into them, Swift now called upon the landed gentlemen of Ireland to sign and circulate declarations that they would refuse the coins themselves and would instruct their tenants to refuse them—a programme Archbishop King had already advocated. To stop sneaks from helping Wood, M.B. asked the public to act as informers, publishing the names, trades, and abodes of any such 'betrayers of their country'.[1] Thus while seeming to narrow his audience to a single man, Swift has broadened it to include all but the most exalted persons.

As before, Swift is careful to impose a façade of reasonableness upon his rhetoric. So he focuses M.B.'s preliminary attention on several points raised in the newspaper article: the need for copper coins in Ireland, the quality of Wood's product, the offer to reduce the amount, and the other proposals—for selling the coins or the copper, for accepting merchandise, and for limiting the amount of Wood's coppers accepted in any transaction.

[1] *Drapier*, pp. 29–31.

On each point M.B. rejects the published assertions. The need for the coins, he says, is small and should be met by a mint in Ireland; Wood's witnesses were a few treacherous confederates of the man himself; the assay was made on an unrepresentative sampling. As for the reduction in quantity, since the coins are debased, M.B. says, it would be a fatal error for the Irish to accept any of them, or to think of buying them at any rate. Wood's pledge to exchange the coins for merchandise and to limit the amount in any transaction is received as monstrous insolence, or even treason.

At last, M.B. arrives at the assertion that 'no evidence' was produced to discredit Wood. In reply, M.B. invokes the Parliament and Privy Council of Ireland, because their statements suffice at once to condemn a patent whose only justification must be the wants of the Irish people. So in the closing third of his pamphlet, M.B. reproaches his fellow countrymen for their own timidity and inaction; and then he puts forth his plans for exposing delinquents and for declarations by landlords.

All M.B.'s arguments had already been detailed by Archbishop King in letters to Edward Southwell.[1] The archbishop was particularly eloquent in calling for an Irish mint.[2] But as before, M.B.'s rational argument is only the scaffolding of his real structure. It makes far less of an impression than his tone, which rises to nearly hysterical rage when he ponders the fivepence-halfpenny limit that Wood said he would place on the share of his coins in any transaction. M.B. declares that by the offer (to 'oblige' no one to accept more), Wood really means to 'oblige' people to accept that amount—a demand that goes beyond the law and the royal prerogative:

> So that here Mr Wood takes upon him the *entire legislature*, and an absolute dominion over the properties of the whole nation.
>
> GOOD GOD! Who are this wretch's *advisers*? Who are his *supporters*, *abettors*, *encouragers*, or *sharers*? Mr Wood will OBLIGE me to take fivepence halfpenny of his brass in every payment. And I will shoot Mr Woods and his deputies through the head, like *highwaymen* or

[1] See his letters of 7, 19, 30 Apr., 9 Jun., and 4 Jul.
[2] See his letters of 9 Jun. and 4 Jul.

housebreakers, if they dare to force one farthing of their coin upon me in the payment of an hundred pounds.

M.B. then goes through one of Swift's wild but dazzling calculations and reckons that a shopkeeper who accepted the proposal would lose 'at least' £140 a year. So he concludes,

> If the famous Mr Hambden [i.e., John Hampden] rather chose to go to prison, than pay a few shillings to King Charles 1st. without authority of Parliament, I will rather choose to be *hanged* than have all my substance taxed at seventeen shillings in the pound, at the arbitrary will and pleasure of the venerable Mr Woods.[1]

The tone of inflammatory violence runs through the pamphlet and works as before to rouse up the Irish listeners and to menace the English government. Declarations like this could not be made by the Dean of St Patrick's in his own person; the incandescence of the emotion requires him to put on the mask of M.B. even though the fiction is palpable. The style of the second letter, as of the first, is simple or coarse, with Swift kicking out in every paragraph. The language shakes with hatred hardly kept back, and infuses its energy into the reader.

A stress on M.B.'s singlehandedness also persists through the pamphlet, and reflects Swift's sense of his own superiority to the other participants in the quarrel. Corresponding with the Lord Lieutenant, Swift wrote as if he and Carteret were isolated, in their authority, from the many planted around them, like the tallest oaks in a forest. So also, in M.B.'s rhetoric of polarities, the isolation of the Drapier matches that of Wood; and the contest is between them. At the same time, Swift enlarges the reference of M.B. so that he speaks not for a single shopkeeper but for the nation, making Wood's claim appear insanely arrogant at the same time that it is fatally weak. *How dare he oppose a nation?* is also, *How can he hope to oppose a nation?*

Swift not only loads Wood with fresh contempt and insult; he also dwells on the contrast between his insignificance and the magnitude of his accomplishment. As Ferguson has said, the reader feels driven to find a more adequate cause of these

---

[1] *Drapier*, pp. 25–6.

enormities; and consequently he must seek out the true criminals in Walpole and King George, who are themselves reduced to serving as tools of the contemptible ironmaster.[1]

This innuendo against the King seems the feature of Swift's climactic figure of speech. As if he were heaping wood on a blaze, Swift loads his text with conceits. There are half a dozen of these in the pamphlet, all applied to Wood. Several are medical and ferocious. When M.B. admits the kingdom does need some copper coins, he says, 'What then? If a physician prescribes to a patient a *dram* of physick, shall a rascal apothecary cram him with a *pound*, and mix it up with *poison*?'[2] In other figures M.B. compares Wood to a robber, a confidence man, an invader, a madman.

But there are as well the hints that Wood has pre-empted the place of a king and assumed the royal prerogative. When M.B. aligns himself with Hampden, he implies that Wood is acting like Charles I. Newton, Master of the Mint, is described as if he worked not for the Crown but for Mr Wood. M.B. represents Wood as 'daring to prescribe what no King of England ever attempted', and calls him a 'little arbitrary *mock-monarch*'. In the course of a stream of sarcasm halfway through the pamphlet, M.B. brings out his climactic metaphor:

> It is no loss of honour to submit to the *lion*, but who, with the figure of a *man*, can think with patience of being devoured alive by a *rat*?[3]

Swift thus implies that King George has abnegated his responsibilities as father of his people and has allowed Wood not only to seize the royal privilege of minting money but also to act as an oppressive tyrant. The lion has in fact become a rat. To underline the irony, M.B. himself handles the King with apparent circumspection if not with reverence.

As Martin Price has observed, Swift in some poems developed the theme of the King's displacement by an ironmonger. In one poem Wood becomes a false Prometheus, stealing Jove's gold chain of authority (to make coins of it) and substituting a slack

---

[1] Ferguson, pp. 106–7. [2] *Drapier*, p. 19. [3] *Ibid.*, p. 25.

string of brass. In another Wood, like the ancient Salmoneus, drives brass-shod horses before a chariot of brass in the hope that the Irish will mistake the specious glitter and noise for the true lightning and thunder of Jove.[1]

Once more, the elements of reasonable persuasion cannot be taken as Swift's real contribution to the debate. His union of ferocity with clarity is what counts, along with the high, patriotic, religious note. The number of Biblical allusions in this second letter rises to half a dozen—not to mention homiletic turns of phrase. The delicious identification of self-sacrifice with self-preservation, in the programme of the boycott, appears here as in the first letter. In the plan of the landowners' declaration, Swift has adopted a device to embody the unity of Ireland behind the Drapier; and he thus evokes a patriotic nationalism that revives the furore over the Annesley Case.

But style and rhetoric are not all. The great political doctrines touched on in the first letter also make themselves heard. While implying that Wood has changed places with the King, M.B. complains of the secrecy in which the patent was passed, and the failure to consult any representatives of the people directly concerned; he complains of the lack of a national mint; and so he suggests that Ireland is no self-governing nation but an enslaved people. The King thus becomes a savage despot, though only by subtle implication. Ultimately, the doctrine invoked is that a king, or indeed a government, deserves obedience not so long as it acts according to statute law or customary procedures but so long as it serves the good of the people:

> To what end did the King give his patent for coining of halfpence in Ireland? Was it not, because it was represented to his sacred majesty, that such a coinage would be of advantage to the good of this kingdom, and of all his subjects here?[2]

[1] *Poems* I. 343–7, 352–3; Price, p. 53.
[2] *Drapier*, p. 26. The sentiment is echoed in Letter VII, para. 17 (*ibid.*, p. 153).

Chapter Eight

THE REPORT OF THE
PRIVY COUNCIL

I. THE REPORT COMES OUT

In opposing the patent, Swift was, after all, performing the deeds of a mythical hero. It is true that he inherited many of his arguments and facts. It is true that he belonged to a troop of men who fought together against Wood's coins. But Swift was not doing what he had done in 1711. He was not taking his line from a coterie, or confusing partisan aims with human needs. He responded to his own convictions, taught his own truths, wrote as a master, not a servant.

Swift held no public office that drew him into the battle. He had no position of power that the campaign enlarged. No one could accuse him of promoting his selfish interests in this struggle, for he would gain as little if he won as if he lost. Few of the other labourers on his side were so disinterested.

Meanwhile, his rhetoric produced action. In the Drapier's second letter, *To Mr Harding*, Swift had called for resolutions to be circulated against the new coins. The appeal was heard. Among the first to respond was a group of Dublin bankers who signed a declaration (15 August) that they would never receive the coppers. Irish newspapers reported that the merchants and leading tradesmen of the city were also preparing a statement; and they predicted correctly that the example would be followed all over the kingdom.[1]

Lord Percival's brother wrote to him about Wood's coins,

The landlords have forbade their tenants from receiving them, and my Lord Abercorn told me yesterday, that at Strabane and Lurgan,

[1] Ferguson, p. 107.

[234]

two considerable trading towns in the north, the people are so incensed, that whoever offers to pass one of those halfpence will be torn limb from limb, and that murders will be the first effect of Woods his project.[1]

But across these motions cut those of the English ministry. The report of their committee, minutely supervised by Walpole, came before the full Privy Council of Great Britain on 6 August and was of course approved. The Commissioners of the Treasury in England were then ordered to limit the amount of Wood's coins to £40,000. The Commissioners of the Revenue in Ireland were instructed to revoke any commands they had given to hinder the movement of the coins. Wood's new proposals were to be sent to the Lords Justices of Ireland.

But the ritual of authority was empty. The English ministers might transmit all the instructions they pleased. What they could not send was the energy to carry them out. When the Lords Justices received their packet from Westminster,[2] they discussed the issues raised but could agree on no action and returned no advice to their taskmasters. By now the situation in Ireland was too tense: nobody dared to move in a way that might be construed as supporting Wood's patent; and there was no other way of acting that would seem respectful to the English Privy Council. Lord Shannon, commander of the armed forces in Ireland, could not risk the blame for the army's circulating the money. Midleton, Speaker of the House of Lords, and Conolly, Speaker of the House of Commons, could not risk opposing the express resolutions of Parliament. These men were the Lords Justices; and all three of them, patriotism aside, were compelled to ignore the orders from England. The Commissioners of the Revenue, obliged to accept only legal tender, were afraid to accept the coins without a positive order from the King.[3]

[1] 15 Aug. 1724; B.L. Add. MS. 47030, p. 162.
[2] On Friday, 14 Aug. 1724, according to Marmaduke Coghill (writing to Southwell, 18 Aug.; B.L. Add. MS. 21, 122, fol. 15).
[3] For a detailed and powerful exposition of the motives of the Lords Justices, see Archbishop King's letter of 10 Sept. 1724 to E. Southwell. Coghill also covers the ground in his letter just cited.

Marmaduke Coghill wrote to Southwell that in Dublin the report and the accompanying orders produced 'such a general consternation and dejection through this whole town as is not to be expressed'—the King's order being taken as a command to the officers of the revenue to receive the coins:

> And if the officers of the revenue receive them, they must go from them to the soldiers, and the soldiers must pass them. The general aversion of all people here to these halfpence is such, that I think nothing but force can make them pass, and that is what will never be used. And to prevent their passing, the city concerted such measures as they think will be more effectual. And the bankers began with an advertisement which I have enclosed sent you, and also that of the brewers and merchants, whose proceedings I have also sent you. And all the corporations of the city are doing the same, and you will have all the gentlemen through the whole kingdom do the like.[1]

When Conolly told the Duke of Newcastle (as Secretary of State) about the Lords Justices' passivity, his grace frigidly observed that it meant a challenge not to the King or any individual but to the whole of England. Dropping the mask of legality for the face of terror, he said the affair was 'plainly a national concern':

> it is a renewal of attempts, ill-founded in themselves, very ill-timed (for I am sure it shows no skill to choose to attack a government and a nation in full prosperity and vigour), attempts that every man in England of however different principles in other things will unite to oppose, and which should they succeed must end in the ruin of Ireland.[2]

With these words the royal ministers upheld the claim of a foreign whore to an English bribe against the protests of a subject nation. In Newcastle's open threat we hear Swift's rhetoric of polarities produced as a monumental drama.

Now the full report of Walpole's committee got into print, not quite accurately; and copies quickly reached Dublin. Swift had one by 18 August. Long excerpts came out in a Dublin news-

---

[1] 18 Aug. 1724; B.L. Add. MS. 21, 122, fol. 15–15ᵛ.
[2] *Drapier*, p. xxxii.

paper the next day.[1] But the menacing tone of the report back-fired. Instead of submission, the public response was only more turbulence. Swift, who never became more playful than when he felt angry, started a number of games with his propaganda. He put his neighbours up to one of these; and so on 20 August those persons living within the 'liberty' of the cathedral—the small area of Dublin under his jurisdiction as dean—waited formally on Dr Swift. Led by their grand jury, they presented him with a declaration against Wood's coins, in a style curiously like the dean's own.[2] Other Irish declarations kept coming out—made by individuals and by groups—several of them looking like Swift's solemn or comical brainchildren. Coopers and brewers, bricklayers and smiths, braziers and pin-makers showed off their patriotic fervour. And so did the 'flying stationers . . . commonly called news-boys'.[3]

The weavers and butchers of Dublin, traditionally feuding enemies, found themselves publicly united against bad money. Harding's *News Letter* published a declaration of the beggars—'lame and blind, halt and maimed, both male and female . . . with all their children legitimate and merry-begotten'.[4] The church wardens of Dublin (or somebody else, in their name) put an advertisement in Harding's paper: 'Whereas some persons indiscreetly put some of Wood's *counters* into the poor-boxes last Sunday, this is to caution those who made this mistake, not to do it again, the POOR of every parish refusing to except [*sic*] of any of them.' Even Wood's Dublin brothers-in-law advertised that they had no connection with the patent apart from a couple of coins sent in a letter and handed over to the Lords Justices.[5]

II. THE DRAPIER'S THIRD LETTER

For a systematic demolition of the report of the English Privy Council, Swift hastily provided M.B. with a third letter, *Some*

---

[1] Swift says he had a copy 'sent' to him on 18 Aug.; I suppose this means received on that day, since the excerpts were published in the newspaper the next day; and Swift's information would have been at least as good as the printer's. See *ibid.*, pp. xxxiii, 35.

[2] *Ibid.*, p. xxxiii. [3] *Ibid.*, p. xxxix. [4] Ferguson, pp. 111–12.

[5] *Drapier*, p. xxxvii.

Observations upon ... the Report of the ... Privy-Council, etc., and addressed it to the 'nobility and gentry' of Ireland.[1] Although this is twice as long as its predecessor, Swift probably completed it in a week, and may have added matter to the text while it was in the press. Modern readers will be offended by the disorder of the essay. It is digressive and repetitious, with sudden shifts in tone. Not only was Swift in a hurry when he wrote; he was also moving in a track that cramped him—i.e., the point-by-point rebuttal of another man's case. Because M.B.'s main job is to answer the *Report*, he must go over much of the ground he surveyed in his second letter. Nevertheless, the separate sections remain masterly, and give us remarkable examples of high art propelled by moral energy.

There are ten lively paragraphs of introduction and as many bold, forceful paragraphs of conclusion and recapitulation. The rest of the essay makes a vigorous, assured argument, diversified by two sorts of byplay. One of these is a pattern of mocking innuendo running under the layer of sober persuasion. With laborious sarcasm M.B. denies (and therefore asserts) that the patent was 'a JOBB for the interest of a particular person' (i.e., the Duchess of Kendal);[2] or he asserts (and therefore denies) that Grafton told the truth when he said the patent was a secret to him.[3]

In a more important pattern of iteration Swift invokes the theme of liberty. This mixes easily with his juxtaposition of England and Ireland: 'Were not the people of Ireland born as *free* as those of England?'[4] or, 'Therefore whatever justice a FREE PEOPLE can claim we have at least an *equal* title to it with our brethren in England.'[5] But the implications of liberty took Swift dangerously far from the immediate crisis, and

---

[1] *Some Observations upon a Paper, Call'd, The Report of the Committee of the Most Honourable the Privy-Council in England, Relating to Wood's Half-Pence*. Swift had received a copy of the *Report* on 18 Aug., and he signed this letter with the date 25 Aug. Davis observes that the letter-press changes to smaller type from p. 27 to p. 29, and suggests that additions may have been made while the pamphlet was being printed. Harding announced it in his *News Letter* on 29 Aug. and advertised it on 5 Sept. as published that day. Coghill also said it was published that day, in a letter to Southwell, 7 Sept.; B.L. Add. MS. 21,122, fol. 18. See *Drapier*, pp. lxxxiv–lxxxv and 33.

[2] *Ibid.*, p. 44. [3] *Ibid.*, p. 47. [4] *Ibid.*, p. 40. [5] *Ibid.*, p. 45.

reached toward the principle of complete independence for Ireland. Such boldness in no way suited the Irish political leaders, whose strength never rested on the common people of Ireland but derived entirely from British power. The estates and authority of men like the Lords Justices would have crumbled in a 'free' Ireland.

This *Letter to the Nobility and Gentry* (or *Some Observations*), with all its disorder, left smaller room for Swift's high spirits than the earlier letters. The audience was now more responsible and better informed; for it comprised those ruling families that might feel intimidated by the ministry's open support of the patent. M.B. had to appear more learned, even though he represented his learning as second-hand; and while the new letter hardly sounds dispassionate, the tone is more restrained than before. The pleasure of the changed approach lies in the availability of Socratic irony. As an humble tradesman instructing his social superiors, M.B. could make much of his own simplicity; and he invited contrasts with learned advocates on the other side—e.g., 'How shall I, a poor ignorant shop keeper, utterly unskilled in law, be able to answer so weighty an objection?'[1]

The tone may be controlled, but it remains provocative. When M.B. does bring out his reasoned arguments, he seldom stops at expounding them, but makes them—as before—the occasion for inflammatory outbursts and execrations against English tyranny. What looks like a digression is usually an irruption of high moral principles of the sort that the English *Report* ignored. Responding to Whitehall's support for Wood, Swift elevated each point of his rebuttals into a fanfare of Irish resistance.

So when he takes up the finding that Ireland needs copper coins, M.B. not only denies that there is a critical shortage but he also denounces the obvious prejudices of the English Privy Council against the Irish people. The *Report* had included a proof that—contrary to Irish claims—there was no unusual secrecy about the passage of the patent, because it had gone

[1] *Ibid.*, pp. 46–7.

through all the customary forms in England. M.B. smothers this sophistry with a blanket of artless innuendo:

> When the two houses represented to his majesty, that this *patent* to
> WOOD *was obtained in a clandestine manner*, surely the committee could
> not think the Parliament would insinuate that it had not passed in
> the common forms, and run through every office where fees and
> perquisites were due. They knew very well that persons in places
> were no enemies to grants, and that the officers of the Crown could
> not be kept in the dark. But the late *Lord Lieutenant of Ireland* affirmed
> it was a secret to him (and who will doubt of his VERACITY . . .). It
> was a *secret* to the people of Ireland, who were to be the *only sufferers*,
> and those who best knew the state of the kingdom and were most
> able to advise in such an affair, were wholly strangers to it.[1]

After this display of syntactic skill,[2] M.B. goes on to show that by hiding the matter from Irish statesmen, the English ministry had in effect negated the rights of a free people. Similarly, the *Report* had relied on the royal prerogative to coin money. M.B. ridicules this narrow legal defence and opposes to the prerogative the higher doctrine of *salus populi suprema lex*.

The *Report* contained a misleading account of precedents for Wood's patent. M.B. examines these in detail to show how they actually weaken the patentee's claims. Then he turns on the very principle of arguing from precedents, and appeals from blind judicial process to nature and reason, in a magnificent passage that was echoed by Lemuel Gulliver, and that would still serve to explode the pretensions of oppressive governments.[3]

When M.B. proceeds to his remedies, he falls back on the fundamental—and by now familiar—truth that nobody is legally required to accept the coins; and he points out that even if the Commissioners of the Revenue were directed to do so, they could only obey by violating statute law. Once again he exhorts his readers to reject the coins, and yet once more he calls for the declaration signed by landowners and conveyed to their tenants.

---

[1] *Ibid.*

[2] The force of the passage depends a good deal on the periodic character of the clauses or sentences, in which the essential meanings and turns are exquisitely delayed.

[3] *Drapier*, p. 52; Davis XI. 249.

Among the springs of the pamphlet's vitality there is a brilliant effect, to be seen in the framing paragraphs at the beginning and the end. Here M.B. blames the language of the *Report* not on Walpole or the Privy Council but on William Wood himself. Swift pretends to believe that the *Report* may be a new contrivance of the patentee to terrorize his victims. Although he drops this pose in the body of his argument, he takes it up again as he bows out.

By thus separating the *Report* from its real artificers and assigning it to Wood, Swift freed M.B. from the rules hedging an ordinary citizen's public remarks on matters emanating from the supreme magistrate. It would have been one thing to blame the Privy Council of Great Britain for 'the most false impudent and fraudulent representations'; it is quite another to blame them upon 'Wood and his accomplices'.[1]

The same ironic procedure winds another way when M.B. simply denies propositions, essential to the controversy, that everyone knows to be true, or when he affirms one that is plainly false. And often, like most propagandists of the time, Swift employs typography to emphasize these elementary effects—as when the Drapier says, 'Surely his majesty, when he consented to the passing of this patent, *conceived* he was doing an act of grace to his most loyal subjects of Ireland, without any regard to Mr Wood, farther than as an *instrument*.'[2] The very coarseness of the device transforms sarcasm into humour.

Irony aside, the rhetorical structure of the *Letter to the Nobility and Gentry* departs from that of the earlier letters; for Swift now detaches Ireland from her Drapier defender. M.B. still figuratively weighs the private profit of a single adventurer against the welfare of a nation; and the old duel continues, between M.B. singly and William Wood. But these private contestants are now seconds to a fresh pair of principals, Ireland against England herself—in the struggle foreseen by the Duke of Newcastle. Over the familiar contrasts Swift now hovers with a fresh illumination, by putting the stronger nation in the place of

---

[1] *Drapier*, p. 62.   [2] *Ibid.*, p. 45.

the weaker and imagining the scene if England had to suffer Irish mortifications:

> Put the case, that the two Houses of *Lords and Commons* of England, and the PRIVY COUNCIL there should address his majesty to recall a patent, from whence they apprehend the most ruinous consequences to the whole kingdom: and to make it stronger if possible, that the whole nation, almost to a man, should thereupon discover the *most dismal apprehensions* ... would his majesty debate half an hour what he had to do?[1]

This kind of similitude, if not a logical demonstration, is even today quite unanswerable. Swift sharpens it by dwelling on Ireland's record of unbroken loyalty since the Revolution.[2] In 1715 it had been England, not Ireland, that lent herself to a Jacobite invasion.

So Swift's characteristic, all-pervasive rhetoric of polarities climbs to a higher pitch. While Ireland battles with England, M.B. comes near challenging the King himself, and Swift's hand no longer falls so lightly upon George I: from 'his sacred majesty'[3] the monarch shrinks in style to a 'limited prince'.[4] Once, M.B. had opposed the King to the burglar, Wood. Now they appear in the same crew, with the burglar as chief. Not only does Swift use Wood as surrogate for the Privy Council; he also uses the Council as surrogate for Walpole and George. Up and down, each of the figures on either side of the affair becomes an equivalent for any or all of his comrades, and the entire Privy Council is reduced to Wood's 'counsel'.[5]

In this more dignified essay, Swift employs few conceits. But he keeps up the Biblical allusions; and the climactic figure, near the end, is splendidly derived from the story of David. Swift uses his favourite device, of a systematic but bizarre analogy, and applies it to Wood as Goliath. Humour and indignation join, as so often when Swift, with the energy of his rage, draws out absurd parallels:

---

[1] *Ibid.*, pp. 39–40. Archbishop King had harped on this theme in his letters (and, no doubt, in his conversation).

[2] *Ibid.*, p. 45.   [3] *Ibid.*, p. 26.   [4] *Ibid.*, p. 36.

[5] *Ibid.*, p. 41, 'Wood and his COUNCIL'.

And I may say for Wood's honour as well as my own, that he resembles Goliah in many circumstances, very applicable to the present purpose: for Goliah had *a helmet of brass upon his head, and he was armed with a coat of mail, and the weight of the coat was five thousand sheakles of brass, and he had greaves of brass upon his legs, and a target of brass between his shoulders.* In short he was like Mr Wood, all over brass; and *he defied the armies of the living God.*[1]

The association of 'David' with 'Jonathan'—later brought out by one of the Drapier's admirers—does not hurt the idea.

The strongest and most enduring effect of the third letter is hardly rhetorical. It is the dismissal of the legal brief of the Privy Council and the substitution of those final sanctions on which the concept of justice has to rest. This transcendent motion makes explicit what Swift had implied in the earlier letters, that national law must be validated by a larger authority. The motion might perhaps have been a kind of response to the Declaratory Act. By that law the British had encouraged the Irish to go beyond their own legislature to the Lords in West-minster. Swift might unconsciously be pushing the process one stage further, leaping beyond the English government to nature and reason as the voice of God. Where the Privy Councillors had agreed that the royal prerogative empowered King George to dispose of the privilege of minting coins, Swift wonders whether the prerogative was not meant to be exercised for the nation's benefit; and setting the Parliament of Ireland against the King of England, he asks which of them speaks for the nation. With his eye on Irish manufactures, trade, finance, he asks what sort of handling will nourish them best.

One beauty of these issues is that Walpole's party lived by them. These are Whig slogans, not Tory. Swift has in effect accepted his new rulers, the Hanoverian Whigs, and seems to urge them to judge their Irish conduct by their English ideals. For Swift openly followed the advice he once gave Knightley Chetwode:

I do not see any law of God or man forbidding us to give security to

---

[1] *Ibid.*, p. 63.

the powers that be; and private men are not [to] trouble themselves about titles to crowns, whatever may be their opinions. . . . For the word lawful, means according to present law in force; and let the law change ever so often, I am obliged to act according to law, provided it neither offends faith nor morality.[1]

It is within this frame and from the declared point of view of Whigs like Sunderland that Swift draws a parallel between King George and James II.[2]

Against this largest of backgrounds M.B. can fairly throw up at the British their other oppressions of Ireland, in complaints not directly tied to the controversy over Wood's patent. All these burdens had reflected the same indifference to the rights and needs of productive classes and to the instincts of humanity: the Navigation Acts, the Declaratory Act, the weight of pensions and taxation unfairly imposed on the Irish establishment. The new patent was merely one more in a train of brutalities.

Swift's approach to these questions remains valid today. It requires no privileged information and is independent of all parties. It served the American colonists; it will serve any people suffering under terror and theft disguised as law. Heard against such afternotes, Swift's expert modulations of tone, from reasonable to furious, from sober to sarcastic, are found to be not oratory but the natural movement of the soul responding to evil.

[1] 29 Apr. 1721; Williams II. 384.   [2] *Drapier*, p. 51.

Chapter Nine

THE GOVERNOR AND THE DRAPIER

Meanwhile, the patent was abused, ridiculed, and denounced in other pamphlets, in poems, broadsides, and public declarations. The commotion fed on itself, and the Irish government did not interfere with much rigour. They arrested a printer or two, blocked a parade, saved a ship in Cork harbour, and stopped a few of the pamphlets.[1] But the Lords Justices also joined in a humble representation to the King, setting forth their reasons for not complying with the orders they had received. Coghill said that if they were absolutely commanded to act against their conscience, the three Justices would ask to be superseded.

Now the English Lords of the Treasury sent an order to the Irish Commissioners of the Revenue to instruct their inferiors not to take more than fivepence halfpenny of Wood's coins in one payment. But the Commissioners replied with a letter of protest, declaring that such an order would make the coins current. Even Conolly signed this letter.

Coghill wrote to Southwell,

The whole kingdom have universally associated under their hands not to take these half pence, and you will have as soon as possible petitions from every corporation and county in Ireland to his majesty setting forth the mischiefs that must attend the uttering these half pence. This day we had a mob up ... who carried about a wooden man representing the patentee with a rope about his neck, and I suppose this night they have burned or hanged him in effigy. We had an account this day that a ship arrived at Cork with some tobacco and seven casks of these halfpence from Bristol. As soon as

---

[1] Letter of 17 Oct. 1724 from Archbishop King to Gorges.

notice thereof came to the town, the whole country took all the boats and lighters they could get, and went with a resolution to burn the ship and its cargo. But the prudent, sober people prevailed so far, as to let the tobacco be landed, provided the ship would immediately go back again and carry their halfpence with them.

Coghill sent Southwell a copy of the Drapier's new letter and attributed it to Swift. He was troubled by the rashness: 'Though there are many observations that are very proper, yet I think, besides the mistakes, there are some things in it, that may give offence and so hurt us.'[1]

A petition from the city of Dublin came out on 8 September, soon followed by others—Drogheda, Wexford, Galway, and so forth.[2] These symptoms did not mean that people felt confident; and certainly Irish affairs were not prospering. Trade became difficult as people hoarded their good money; and Coghill said,

> The bankers are pressed hard by demands on them. Our fairs and markets are entirely spoiled by the fear and apprehension all people are under, nobody being willing to part with their money at this time, and our public credit begins to fail.[3]

About this time Swift gave another push to his engine of destruction when he preached a sermon on 'Doing Good'.[4] Here he supplied a religious foundation for the moral doctrine of the *Drapier's Letters*, arguing that even humble individuals could serve as instruments either to help or to hurt the commonwealth. He denounced men who would ruin their country for the sake of a temporary advantage to themselves; he denounced informers and the spreaders of false rumours; he denounced those wicked enough to support a scheme so destructive as Wood's coins. He said the welfare of nations was under the care of God's pro-

[1] 7 Sept. 1724; B.L. Add. MS. 21, 122, fols. 15, 17–18.
[2] *Drapier*, pp. xxxv–xxxvi.   [3] *Ibid.*
[4] In the *Letter to Midleton*, dated 26 Oct., Swift says he preached such a sermon 'very lately', which I interpret as during the same month but before the *Letter to the Whole People* (number four) came out. For discussions of the date of the sermon see Landa in Davis IX. 134–6, and Daw, pp. 160–1, 164, 179. It is hard for me to believe that Swift would have preached such a sermon on the heels of the fourth letter, as Daw suggests, especially when he seems to have been too ill to venture out (Williams III. 34–7). But 'very lately' seems to imply a date within a few weeks of 26 October. I am inclined to early October, perhaps 4 October.

vidence and therefore in God's eyes no crime against an individual was so heinous as one against the public:

> All government is from God, who is the God of order, and therefore whoever attempts to breed confusion or disturbance among a people, doth his utmost to take the government of the world out of God's hands, and to put it into the hands of the Devil, who is the author of confusion.[1]

Swift thus produced the doctrine normally used to condemn agitators like himself, and turned it against the government in power.

Meanwhile, Archbishop King was delivering similar opinions in private. He wrote a splendid letter to Southwell, whom he berated for putting his name to Newton's account of the assay. Quite on his own, the archbishop went over arguments that M.B. had used, pressing them almost as far, and drawing out the unpleasant implications. He rejected systematically the case made by the Privy Council; and although he disparaged the many 'scurrilous papers' that were going round (including—I assume—Swift's), he refused to separate himself from the authors' work:

> The generality here are of opinion that the insisting on honour or prerogative is but a pretence, and the true occasion of all the zeal and art used to put this copper on Ireland proceeds from another motive.[2] Mr Wood, as I am assured by a person who was with me the other night, offered him ten thousand pounds to be his agent to procure such a patent for him. If it came for less, all the surplus should be his own; but he refused to be concerned in it. This is no secret, and the conclusion is that the like or perhaps a greater sum was placed somewhere. The receiver to be sure is not willing to refund; and if the affair do not succeed, Wood will squeak, and that may not be for the honour of somebody. I think I durst swear his majesty had none of the money; and therefore all this zeal and bustle to force the resolution, judgement, and inclination and interest of a whole nation is to secure the honour and profit of some other persons.
>
> I confess there are some methods taken to obstruct the currency of these halfpence which I can by no means approve, such as mobs,

---

[1] Davis IX. 238; cf. 1 Cor. xiv. 33.   [2] I.e., bribery.

and scurrilous papers, which were as little necessary as proper. But who can stop the madness of an enraged multitude?—who reckon themselves not only undone if this copper take place, but that they are treated with the utmost contempt and scorn, which is more intolerable to a free people than oppression and robbery in their fortunes. And to say truth, could a greater contempt be put on a nation than to see such a little fellow as Wood favoured and supported against them.[1]

In Londonderry, Bishop Nicolson, as usual, turned Archbishop King's judgments upside down. But he agreed that the political weather was inclement: 'I am not surprised at your grace's wondering at our unaccountable warmth about *Wood's halfpence*,' he wrote to the Archbishop of Canterbury:

The matter seemed as strange to me, and I freely expressed my thoughts as long as I durst. By degrees we are now come into a general conflagration. All our pedlars and petit merchants are confederating into solemn leagues and covenants against the currency of them. In one of the little borough towns of this diocese, the shopkeepers and ale-drapers have subscribed a formal engagement, wherein they *abhor*, *detest*, and *abjure* Master Wood and his copper in the same words wherein their ringleaders have bid defiance to the Pretender and his false money. This frenzy (which is indeed epidemical throughout the whole kingdom) had seized several of my neighbours in this town.... I am told that some hotspurs among our justices of the peace have drawn up a declaration, in the fashionable way.... I hope to suppress that also.[2]

Rumours and commotion were now ordinary. Certain London newspapers gave out the sinister report that in Ireland the Roman Catholics had 'entered into an association to refuse Mr Wood's copper money'.[3] This gossip may have been a Walpolian contrivance to besmirch the enemies of the patent. From a more sympathetic paper came the report that many shops had signs up. 'No goods for Wood's raps'.[4] In October, the

---

[1] 10 Sept. 1724.

[2] 2 Oct. 1724; Wake Letters XIV, no. 295 (out of order); spelling and punctuation altered.

[3] *Flying Post* and *St James's Evening Post*, 19 Sept. 1724. These papers generally supported the government.

[4] Mist's *Weekly Journal*, 26 Sept. 1724. Mist generally opposed the ministry, and he seems to have had special sources of information in Ireland.

Dublin Intelligence published an amazing paragraph which is itself an index of the universal irritability:

> We have an account also, that a certain noble man of England, My L——— W—————e, who was the chief in gaining Wood his patent, hearing of the joint declarations of the people of Ireland against the brass coin, has sworn that since he gain'd the patent, if the people of Ireland still persisted in their refusal of the brass coin, he would make them swallow it in fireballs![1]

When a scream is loud enough, it will carry even across the Irish Sea. Walpole had already reconsidered his position. As early as 1 September he wrote to Newcastle,

> The popular frenzy and aversion to the taking this money, I am afraid, is now carried to such a degree, that it will scarce be prudent to attempt forcing their inclinations, especially when they are supported and countenanced in their obstinacy by their governors.[2]

For all his deafness to public opinion, Walpole understood how dangerous it would be either to remove or to retain the Lords Justices. So he naturally wished to take the chaotic action out of their motionless hands, and therefore despatched Carteret to the battlefield.

In mid-September, London newspapers reported that Carteret would go over very suddenly—'about the middle of the next month'—and that the Irish Parliament would be called sooner than people expected.[3] Swift had the news by 22 September if not earlier.[4] The announcement alarmed Irish leaders, who thought Carteret would try to compel them to bow to the government's policy. Newcastle also alarmed them by warning the Lords Justices to take positive action and not to risk a charge of conniving at sedition.[5] He asked them to issue a proclamation

---

[1] 10 Oct. 1724; *Drapier*, pp. xxxvi, xli.

[2] Goodwin, p. 664, n.1; spelling and punctuation altered.

[3] *Evening Post*, 17 Sept.; other newspapers, 19 Sept. The *Flying Post* and other papers of later dates report that Carteret will leave on 12 Oct. The *Post Man*, 13 Oct., and other papers report that he left the day before.

[4] Williams III. 35.

[5] For evidence that Newcastle wished to intimidate the Irish Privy Council and to screen Carteret, see Archbishop King's discussion of Newcastle's letter of early October—discussed in a letter from King to Gorges, 17 Oct., and in another from King to Southwell the same day.

and enclosed a fresh and (as usual) ill-timed offer by Wood to hold back his coins until the government should agree on regulations to 'prevent my exceeding the quantity now agreed to'.[1]

The Irish Lords Justices replied to Newcastle with a large defence of their inertia. However, they also called a meeting of the Lord Mayor, the sheriffs, and the magistrates of Dublin to consider measures for maintaining public order. Nothing brave was accomplished there—only recommendations that these officers should suppress tumults and prosecute dangerous libels; but it was a few days afterwards that some printers were jailed for producing seditious pamphlets.[2] Then the Lords Justices turned to their other selves, the Privy Council of Ireland. Yet the Council too showed no zeal to satisfy Newcastle, and only agreed that no advice could be tendered to the government in England.[3] By now anyone could see that the Lords Justices were relying upon passive resistance to block Walpole's coercion, and that even when Carteret did arrive, he would meet an obstacle in them.[4]

The approach of the Lord Lieutenant a year ahead of his proper time was bound to worry people in Ireland, because many of them assumed that he came in order to dissolve the great union against Wood's patent. Their fearfulness grew deep enough, in turn, to alarm Swift. Here, he decided, was one more mission for M.B.; and he timed it with particular care. By 3 October, Dubliners knew the exact date of Carteret's departure from London; and this may have been the impulse that started Swift writing.[5] He began to compose the essay then, and finished on 13 October, but chose to put off publication to a dramatic moment.

Meanwhile, Carteret at last stepped out of his house in highly fashionable Arlington Street (where he lived near Walpole and Pulteney), gave five guineas to the poor standing at his door, and set off, with his wife and two daughters, in a splendid

---

[1] Goodwin, p. 664.

[2] The meeting was held 12 Oct.; see *The London Evening Post*, 29 Oct., and other newspapers of the same and later dates.

[3] Goodwin, p. 665.   [4] *Ibid.*, p. 666.   [5] *Drapier*, pp. 251–2.

equipage.[1] At Coventry, two days later, he was greeted by the scarlet-gowned mayor and aldermen, flanked by companies of the corporation with their banners and insignia.[2] Embarking at Holyhead, he landed in Dublin at noon on Thursday, 22 October. As he came ashore, the three Lords Justices deferentially met him, with a train of nobles and gentlemen. Carteret himself climbed into Midleton's coach, his wife into Lord Shannon's, his daughters into Conolly's; and the whole crowd drove off to the Castle, where he took the oaths at once.[3] Some observers must have commented on the irony of Carteret's riding with his old ally during a crisis in which they would have to act as adversaries.

But it was a deeper irony that a great lord, descended from Norman ancestors, should make such a ceremonious journey when his humble purpose was a rendezvous with an imaginary Irish shopkeeper. For the whole parade amounted to a gorgeous curtain-raiser for the debut of Swift's new effort, *A Letter to the Whole People of Ireland*.[4] This pamphlet, held back for the Lord Lieutenant's arrival, had itself come out the day before, and was being 'cried about by the hawkers' even within the walls of the Castle as the Lord Lieutenant made his entry.[5]

Although Walpole had defeated Carteret in their duel over the chief ministry, his lordship easily surpassed Sir Robert as a judge of popular feeling. Walpole's career is a 'record of ineptitude'[6] in gauging the strength of public distaste for certain policies; and Wood's patent was the earliest of his great miscalculations. Yet even if Carteret's first inference had been that the government must withdraw the patent, he dared not say so. To give in easily would have meant weakening his position in Dublin as Lord Lieutenant and his strength in Westminster as a political strategist.

Walpole hoped that if Carteret resisted the Irish interest, he

---

[1] *St James's Evening Post*, 13 Oct., and other papers. Carteret left London on 12 Oct.
[2] *St James's Evening Post*, 22 Oct., and other papers.
[3] *Whitehall Evening Post*, 24 Nov., and other papers.
[4] Published 21 Oct. 1724; see *Drapier*, p. lxxxvi and correction in Ferguson, p. 115, n. 111.
[5] Coxe II. 396.   [6] Plumb I. xiii.

would ruin himself as Grafton had done; if he agreed with the Irish, he would seem to jettison a part of the royal prerogative and would therefore undermine his place near the King. Evidently, Carteret understood that a show of firmness and decision was essential to restore the directing authority of the Castle. He might at last yield, but slowly and as if persuaded by experience, not driven by fear.

On Tuesday, five days after his landing, Carteret assembled the Privy Councillors of Ireland. The sole business he wished to take up with them was the response they should make to *A Letter to the Whole People*. Carteret had seen a copy on Friday and discussed it with Midleton (as Lord Chancellor) on Saturday; and Midleton reported,

> His excellency shewed it to me, and told me, it struck at the dependency of Ireland on the crown of Great Britain. I had not read it over, but had bought one of them from Mr Tighe in the Council chamber, who told me, he bought two in the Castle from an hawker.

The other high legal authorities—Chief Justice Whitshed, Chief Baron Hale, and Attorney-General Rogerson (the first and last being Irish by birth and education)—had all agreed with Carteret that it was 'a seditious and vile libel, and fit to be prosecuted'. Midleton reports he himself 'freely told' Carteret that he 'thought the pamphlet was highly seditious' and the author and printer deserved to be punished.[1]

These attitudes were no simple effect of Carteret's pressure: the pamphlet had scared leaders in the Drapier's camp. With his fourth letter Swift transformed himself from an aide into a manipulator of those who were fighting the patent. He climbed back into the independent, threatening position which he had momentarily established for himself in England ten years before, when he wrote *Some Free Thoughts*, and which he enlarged when he wrote the *Proposal for Irish Manufacture*. The *Letter to the Whole People* represents his separate policy, not his service to another man's party.

---

[1] Coxe II. 396–7; letter of 31 Oct. 1724, from Midleton.

Chapter Ten

THE DRAPIER'S FOURTH LETTER

S wift may have begun writing the new pamphlet to neu-
tralize the effect of Carteret's coming. But I think he soon
added other reasons, some of them subtle enough. Supporters of the ministry were inventing quite false grounds to
revile the alliance against the patent, and Swift wished to expose
these lies. He hoped as well to hamstring any leader who advised
that the English government would recall the patent without
further pressure. Still other motives will soon appear.

Because of his mixture of intentions the important and
abiding passages of the essay are encumbered with weaker
members. Thus Swift gives space, near the beginning, to a
charge that the Roman Catholics were behind the anti-Wood
campaign. This absurdity M.B. efficiently explodes. Near the
end of the essay, at much greater length, he refutes a dull English
pamphlet. This fatuous work had blandly asserted that the Irish
were satisfied with Wood's money until evil propagandists per-
verted them; it also revealed that the coins were excellent and
that Wood's profit was too small. Swift answers the points with
fairly plain arguments but with unusually caustic vigour.

It is the remaining two-thirds of the essay that display Swift's
brilliant powers. Here he considers in sequence the relevance of
the King's prerogative, the purpose of Carteret's approaching
visit, and the nature of political freedom. Though he explicitly
broadens his audience to include the entire population, Swift in
fact shifts from one class to another as he proceeds. So he relies
on a simple style at the start and climbs to intricate fireworks as
he closes.

Taking up the complaint that the Irish are disputing the
prerogative, M.B. opens with a rational, fatherly tone and

humble language. He shows how narrowly the King's independent authority is limited; and instead of being gingerly, goes on to sound almost insolent when he explains that no British king may compel his subjects to take coin other than sterling or gold. In effect, M.B. defines the royal prerogative so strictly that any officer of the government would have to disagree with him:

> But we are so far from disputing the King's *prerogative* in coining, that we own he has power to give a patent to any man for setting his royal image and superscription upon whatever materials he pleases, and liberty to the patentee to offer them in any country from England to Japan, only attended with one small limitation, that *nobody alive is obliged to take them.*[1]

As if to distinguish the new Lord Lieutenant from his master, M.B. treats Carteret with peculiar respect. Among bitter reflections on other viceroys (and on English office-holders in general), M.B. praises Carteret in superlatives which his excellency must have found embarrassing. Writing before Carteret's arrival, Swift pretends that the whole idea of a viceregal visit is in doubt. The ingenuous Drapier cannot believe (he says) that so elevated a figure as the Lord Lieutenant himself will stoop to visit Ireland as the tool of an obscure ironmaster. Yet if Carteret should indeed come over, and should try to weaken Parliament, he would find the members incorruptibly opposed to the patent. And even if they were not, the government has by now exhausted its supply of bribes (in the form of sinecures and pensions) upon the crowd of Englishmen who already possess Irish offices. Besides, no stipends in Wood's money could be worth the losses the M.P.s would suffer from accepting the coins.

One example is picked out with exquisite malice, for it is the new Primate, who sat on the high eminence that should have been Archbishop King's. The income of Primate Boulter would be reduced by seven-eighths, says M.B., if the bad coppers were to pass:

> The *gentleman they* have lately made *Primate* would never quit his seat in an English House of Lords, and his preferments at Oxford and

[1] *Drapier*, p. 70.

Bristol, worth twelve hundred pounds a year, for four times the denomination here, but not half the value.[1]

Halfway through his essay, M.B. produces the tremendous question of Irish freedom. In three paragraphs of crescendo he rejects the ordinary sense of 'depending kingdom' and declares that the people of Ireland possess by right every kind of liberty that belongs to those of England. Then he brings out a theme that will attract dangerous harmonies in his finale; for he dissolves the idea of law as a pretext for English despotism and leaves force alone as the foundation of Ireland's 'depending' state:

> 'Tis true indeed, that within the memory of man, the Parliaments of England have *sometimes* assumed the power of binding this kingdom by laws enacted there, wherein they were at first openly opposed (as far as *truth, reason* and *justice* are capable of *opposing*) by the famous Mr Molyneux, an English gentleman born here, as well as by several of the greatest patriots, and *best Whigs* in England; but the *love and torrent* of power prevailed. Indeed the arguments on both sides were invincible; for in *reason*, all *government* without the consent of the *governed* is the *very definition of slavery*: but in *fact, eleven men well armed will certainly subdue one single man in his shirt*. But I have done. For those who have used *power* to cramp *liberty* have gone so far as to resent even the *liberty* of *complaining*, although a man upon the rack was never known to be refused the liberty of *roaring* as loud as he thought fit.[2]

Locke himself had said that even when a nation was conquered in a just war, the people might not fairly be deprived of their property; and some such reference seems the point of Swift's 'eleven men armed'. Locke had also, notoriously, said that the people had the right to resist their government when it invaded property rights; so it is no wonder if Walpole (for I assume it was he), in the report of the English Privy Council, denied that Wood's patent was 'derogatory, or invasive, of any liberties or privileges of [the King's] subjects of Ireland'.[3] Swift, of course—like Archbishop King—held precisely the opposite view.

Swift's great readjustment in this essay follows from his view of force as the solitary sanction of an oppressive regime. Regard-

---

[1] *Ibid.*, p. 77.   [2] *Ibid.*, p. 79.   [3] *Ibid.*, p. 220.

less of law or custom, if a government ignores the needs and wishes of its subjects, it deserves, according to his reasoning, no loyalty. This is the sustaining and spinal column of the *Fourth Letter*; and with this support, M.B. changes the alignment of his polarities. Instead of confronting Wood, Walpole, and King George, he now reduces all of them to the level of agents of England herself.

It is worth observing that constitutional history supports Swift. Poyning's Law, the Act on which the English rested their claim to make laws for Ireland, had nothing to do with the people or Parliament of England. Henry VII had been troubled by the wilfulness of his officers in Ireland. To curb the independence of his chief governors there, he called for a law under which all Irish bills must be approved by the King and the Privy Council in England. Designed to shield the Irish people from the excesses of their rulers, this Act was later misunderstood by English statesmen to mean that their Parliament might legislate for Ireland. From the reign of Charles I, Irish constitutional lawyers had objected to the original law and to the claim of the English Parliament to rule Ireland directly. When William Molyneux demonstrated that Ireland was no depending kingdom, he only added his friend Locke's political philosophy to a gathering of earlier proofs; and Archbishop King (another friend of Molyneux) had echoed them years before Swift took them up. The Drapier was perfectly correct to insist that there was no way to comprehend the Declaratory Act within the theory of government universally accepted by English statesmen.

Once, Swift had identified himself with England, her culture, her government, her foreign policy. He had justified England against her enemies and her false allies. He had seen in English leaders the most approximate realization of civilized Christian statesmen. He had disregarded English imperialism, taken the slave trade for granted, and suppressed his sympathy with Ireland.

But now his illusions were burned away, and he spoke as the disinterested moral conscience of humanity—'the whole people'. This was the spirit of Swift that was to gain new life in American revolutionary propaganda, in Irish nationalism, in the genius of Yeats and Joyce. A double experience of exile had purified Swift's mind. His years in England had taught him to see Ireland dwindled, feckless, and vulnerable; his identification with Ireland had taught him to see the hollowness of English pretensions.

If Swift's own decayed people lacked the virtues that strengthened their masters, they at least owned the merit of being victims. One day Swift would declare (in *A Modest Proposal*) what he already knew, that the Irish too could be oppressors. But for the time being, they represented the upper side of our human ambivalence. As a poor, dependent, fatherless boy, Swift had undergone enough humiliation to leave him most at ease when he defended the weak.

M.B.'s fury against the nation of England is not only moral but also rhetorical. Wise men were saying that the government in Westminster had received the message trumpeted by the dozens of pamphlets, songs, broadsides, and demonstrations. They were saying the work of the boycott was accomplished, and the Irish could now let the English ministers settle their account with Wood. But Swift (I think) had no such confidence, and believed that to abandon the campaign before the patent was formally withdrawn would be to sacrifice the gains made so far and to relax a unity that might be turned to larger purposes. He suspected (I think) the counsellors who gave such advice of collaborating with the ministry. Unlike these blinkered guides, Swift no longer aimed to satisfy the interests of particular classes, institutions, or men. He invoked the idea of a community prior to any government; he appealed to the rights and liberties of men as such.

For somebody like Swift, who felt so close to periods of political chaos—the Irish uprising of 1641, the Civil War in England, the Glorious Revolution, the Irish Troubles of 1688–90—it was natural to conceive of society as distinct from government— indeed, as embodying a morality that government ought to serve. It was instinct for him to heal the breach between community and sovereignty that Hobbes and the absolutist princes had insisted upon. Living in a narrow social order descended from English, episcopal immigrants—an order that excluded peasants and servants—it was easy for Swift to return to the postulates of Molyneux, Locke, Hooker, and St Thomas, and to assume that mere government was no synonym for true order.

But for Walpole and the new Whig supremacy, with their need to pull country gentlemen, London merchants, and German courtiers together, it was just as natural to take the opposite line and make the revised political constitution and parliamentary law the definition of a free nation. Swift and the Whigs had changed sides from the time when the Junto talked so fearfully of the Peace and the Pretender. When Steele attacked Swift in 1713 and 1714, he rested on precisely the high ground that M.B. now occupied when he attacked the people of England. Life without liberty and property—they agreed—was hardly worth preserving. Swift therefore was seething Walpole's Whigs in their ancestral broth; he was relying on the Lockean principles that had justified the Glorious Revolution.

The flaw in Swift's case glares at modern readers: he never so much as hinted that the native Roman Catholics must 'consent' to the laws of their Irish government. This difficulty Swift handled in two ways. First, although he spoke of government by consent, he defined consent as the agreement of those who hold the property in land. The axiom that power follows property derives from Harrington; and the priority of property rights both to society (in a state of nature) and to political government, was taught by Locke. Swift addressed his 'letter' primarily to the Anglican gentry and bourgeoisie; and since they indeed controlled the land, Swift did not have to face the fallacy that we today cannot ignore. So while *five hundred thousand hands* [1] might indeed subscribe to a declaration of Wood's perjury, it was only (for M.B.) those whose ancestors 'reduced this kingdom to the obedience of England' [2] who ought to govern the country.

But Swift also had a better way to take care of the native Roman Catholics. In the scheme of polarities that he established

---

[1] *Ibid.*, p. 82.   [2] *Ibid.*, p. 70.

between those who opposed the patent and those who supported it, Swift linked not only justice but productivity with the opposition. In fact, he tended, during his discussion of political freedom, to leave the immediate controversy behind, and to make the patent simply an entry into the larger subject of Ireland's economic welfare. In that very great matter he implicitly set the productive landowners, farmers, manufacturers, and tradesmen against the parasites and drones: i.e., the absentee landlords, the idle pensioners, the government officers—the tribe of mercenary English opportunists who not only failed to perform their jobs but even stepped out of their way to injure the country they lived on. Eventually, Swift would be tempted to exclude the resident landlords themselves from the productive group because of their irresponsibility, oppressiveness, and greed; but that was a turn he was not yet ready to take.

The 'people' therefore had two senses in *A Letter to the Whole People*. It could mean either the 'true English' minority, or else the nobility, farmers, artisans, and so forth, who lived in the kingdom and contributed to its wealth. Certainly those whom M.B. tried to unite against the patent included Presbyterians and Roman Catholics.

The ministers in Whitehall had no doubt which meaning was primary. Their ability to control Ireland hinged on the disunion of the people. By playing Whig against Tory, Anglican against Dissenter, Protestant against Roman Catholic, landlord against priest, they could block actions that did not suit the English whim. If the parties should congregate in an 'Irish interest' solidified against the English, the ministers would face challenges they had no wish to meet. But such a union was precisely what M.B. and his programme fostered. Hugh Boulter, the new Primate, warned Newcastle of the danger:

> People of every religion, country, and party here, are alike set against Wood's halfpence, and . . . their agreement in this has had a very unhappy influence on the state of this nation, by bringing on intimacies between Papists and Jacobites, and the Whigs, who before had no correspondence with them.[1]

---

[1] 19 Jan. 1725; Boulter I. 8 (Dublin, p. 7).

Swift's lack of obvious method, in *A Letter to the Whole People*, makes me place it (like the pamphlet on *Irish Manufacture*) in a different class from works like *A Discourse of the Contests and Dissensions*, or *The Conduct of the Allies*—and indeed in a different category from the report of the English Privy Council. All those works either follow a systematic method of going about their business, or else pretend to do so. In the *Discourse* Swift makes a great show of starting from postulates and arriving by inference and evidence at his conclusions. This design is in the tradition of seventeenth-century philosophy, which replaced the syllogism by quasi-mathematical demonstrations. Hobbes and Descartes had given their works a winning appearance of rigour by seeming to move carefully from one small step to the next.

Rejecting their methods, Swift rejects the anti-libertarian and mechanistic views that might be associated with them. He employs instead the agglomerative manner of Locke. This may be one reason for M.B.'s mathematical fantasies. Hobbes had made so much of the mathematical model that in both *The Drapier's Letters* and *Gulliver's Travels*, Swift may (in part) have been ridiculing that whole approach to social and political problems when he made such a display of numerical nonsense.

Not that the separate paragraphs and sections of the *Letter* are without a harmony of themes and devices. Reworking his old polarities, Swift deepens the effect of Wood's relation to his betters. For all the insults heaped on his head, Wood has shrunk to the size of a tarbrush. On the one hand he is again a surrogate for Walpole and King George. So M.B. blames the ironmaster for lies told against the Irish people. He blames Wood for declaring that the Irish are rebellious, managed by Papists, disloyal to their king. On the other hand, Wood's own meanness disgraces his allies. The reader knows that the chief minister and the King's Councillors have published these lies, and he must therefore humble those grandees to the level of their patron, Mr Wood.

The metonymy by which any element on either side of the quarrel stands for any of its companions receives new power. The English gang looks miscellaneous. Spreading beyond

Wood, Walpole, the King, and the pamphleteers, it now encompasses the whole English people. But the Irish seem represented by M.B. alone, who is correspondingly more inflammatory than ever. By excluding Lord Carteret from the polarities, the Drapier gives him an ambiguous quality, as if Swift understood his earlier collaboration with Midleton and were cajoling him into renewing that benevolence. His excellency has remained unsullied and may keep his integrity if he will void the contamination of the English gang. So the real Swift may be appealing to the real Carteret across the barriers of nation and party.

Yet what M.B. seeks is no compromise but an outright defiance of England. Swift wished not simply to defeat but to humiliate the government in Westminster. To set this defiance on a height, Swift approaches it by elaborate modulations of feeling. From the restrained, fatherly opening we plunge into his usual alternations of calm reasoning and outbursts of anger and irony. Discussing England's ignorance of the Ireland which she pretends to command, M.B. employs the coolest sarcasm. Elsewhere, his irony becomes lusciously humorous. I admire a paragraph in which M.B., after praising Carteret, contrasts the enlightened rule of the present regime with the sinister practices of earlier governors. As he surveys those practices, it becomes clear that all of them have just been used by the Duke of Grafton and will probably be used again by Carteret.[1] So M.B. here is alerting his audience to the temptations that will be put before their susceptible leaders. I suppose Swift by now felt pretty certain that the patent would be defeated, for throughout the essay he infused a new degree of humour into his irony.

The game of polarities takes us into a topsy-turvy landscape where a forger gives orders to a great minister, a viceroy is praised at the expense of his monarch, and a nation is sacrificed to the greed of a concubine. These inversions are so handled as to enrich the humour of the style. At the same time, as if the priest were making room for the clown, the Biblical tags fade.[2] But the

---

[1] *Drapier*, pp. 75–6.
[2] Gen. xxv. 29–34, in *Drapier*, p. 67; Mark xii. 16, *ibid.*, p. 70; Acts i. 25, *ibid.*, p. 84.

essay opens with a telling allusion to the story of Jacob tricking Esau out of his birthright, a tale of injustice which was also a traditional explanation for the ascendancy of one nation over another—the Hebrews over the Edomites.

M.B.'s conceits, divided between medical and animal analogies, are no longer concentrated on Wood. Some illustrate the sickly, subhuman condition to which the English have reduced their neighbours, and others suggest the bestiality and insignificance of the patentee. One vivid figure anticipates the despair Swift was to express about helping his fellow countrymen when he said, years later, 'I would not prescribe a dose to the dead.'[1] Similarly, in the fourth *Letter*, he dismisses the rumours spread by Wood as 'no more than the last howls of a dog dissected alive'. But he also prophesies that if the nation should let Wood's coins in, it could no more regain its well being 'than a dead carcass can be recovered to life by a cordial'.[2] Doubtless without realizing it, Swift thus touches on the parallels between the bestialized Irish people and their beastly English oppressors; and he evokes his usual impatience with a people who can hardly be kept from leaping on their own funeral pyre.

In the conceit that dominates the final paragraphs of the essay, Swift mixes humour and fantasy, violence and death, by way of a set piece that matches the passage on liberty. In that declaration of Ireland's independence (midway through the essay) he had suggested that the English tried to murder the Irish commonweal by their economic and legislative policies. Since force was their sole justification, Swift indicated that the Irish could not survive unless they resisted with as much force as the English used to enslave them:

> The remedy is wholly in your own hands, and therefore I have digressed a little in order to refresh and continue that *spirit* so seasonably raised amongst you, and to let you see that by the laws of GOD, of NATURE, of NATIONS, and of your own country, you ARE and OUGHT to be as FREE a people as your brethren in England.[3]

[1] 26 Oct. 1731; Williams III. 501.
[2] *Drapier*, pp. 68, 77.   [3] *Ibid.*, p. 80.

The joyous conceit that matches this battle cry and ends the essay is the working out of a rumour. Walpole was—we have seen[1]—supposed to have said that if the Irish did not accept the money voluntarily, he would make them '*swallow his coin in fire-balls*'.[2] M.B. with mock-logic sardonically doubts the rumour, just as he had doubted that Carteret was coming over. To disprove it, he calculates how many 'operators' would be needed—i.e., how large an army England would have to send if she compelled the Irish to accept Wood's coins:[3]

> Now the metal [Wood] hath prepared, and already coined will amount to at least fifty millions of halfpence to be *swallowed* by a million and a half of people; so that allowing two halfpence to each *ball*, there will be about seventeen *balls* of *wild-fire* apiece to be swallowed by every person in this kingdom, and to administer this dose, there cannot be conveniently fewer than fifty thousand *operators*, allowing one *operator* to every thirty, which, considering the *squeamishness* of some stomachs and the *peevishness* of *young children*, is but reasonable.[4]

In other words, the trouble of the experiment would hardly be worth the profit. And this moral is of course the very lesson which the whole essay is intended to drive home.

[1] Cf. above, p. 249.   [2] *Drapier*, p. 85.
[3] I think the figure he reaches is roughly the size of the English force in Ireland at the time of the Battle of the Boyne.
[4] *Drapier*, p. 86.

Chapter Eleven

THE DEAN AND THE DRAPIER

I. A PROCLAMATION AGAINST THE AUTHOR

The *Letter to the Whole People* frightened the leaders of Swift's side, for obvious reasons. The doctrines M.B. taught, if truly applied, would have undone the property settlement of Ireland. Even their expression would anger the British government to the point of unpredictable retaliation. The Drapier's scorching ridicule of English office-holders in Ireland might please the Domviles, Percivals, and Boltons who, like Swift's relations, could conveniently disregard the recent origin of their own power. But families that had suppressed the civil provisions of the Treaty of Limerick had no wish to wrestle with the rights of man, or to shake a stability only twenty years old.[1]

As the Drapier himself was to express it, the cloth he wove displeased the mighty of the land:

> some *great folks* complain ... that when they had it on, they felt a *shuddering in their limbs,* and have thrown it off in a rage, cursing to Hell the poor *drapier* who invented it, so that I am determined never to *work for persons of quality* again.[2]

To the uninitiate, Archbishop King might sound like one of those 'great folks'. Writing to trusted friends about the four *Drapier's Letters* that had appeared, he said they were 'in a ludicrous and satirical style' and that he did 'by no means approve of several things' in the fourth, which he also described as 'very unnecessary' because the kingdom was resolved 'to a man' to have nothing to do with the halfpence.[3] To infer from

---

[1] See above, I. 11–15. [2] *Drapier*, p. 103.
[3] 24 Nov. 1724, to S. Molyneux; 12 Dec. 1724, to Gorges; 3 Nov. 1724, to Annesley.

such epithets that the archbishop disagreed with the Drapier's teachings would be an error of naïveté.

Many years before, the archbishop had seen a lawsuit of the deepest consequence, which he brought against a society of English land speculators, decided by the Irish House of Lords in his favour but then had seen that judgment reversed on an appeal to the English House of Lords.[1] About the same time, the Woollen Act (prohibiting the Irish from exporting their woollen textiles) had gone through the English Parliament.[2] It was the constitutional implications of such events that drove the archbishop's friend William Molyneux to compose his *Case of Ireland*, demonstrating that the English Parliament had no rightful power to make laws for their neighbours; and in the archbishop's judgment at that time, Molyneux did not go far enough in denying any such authority to England.[3]

So early as those years, and in letter after letter, the archbishop had put forward doctrines and recommendations that the Drapier was to adopt. He had argued that the King was a safer guardian of Ireland than the English Parliament, that the English Commons were destroying Irish trade while the Lords were destroying the Irish constitution.[4] He had complained that the Irish Protestants were over-timid and unwilling to take action to preserve themselves: 'nobody', he had said, 'can be prevailed upon to do anything towards their own freedom'.[5] He had urged the Irish grand juries to address the Lords Justices of England (during King William's absence) against the Woollen Bill.[6] In a characteristic remark to Bishop Lindsay (later Primate) he had declared,

> For my part I value nothing [that] can be taken from me without my consent, or that I hold by the arbitrary pleasure of another; and therefore if I shall be taxed and bound by laws to which I am no party, I shall reckon myself as much a slave, as one of the Grand Signior's mutes.[7]

---

[1] C. S. King, pp. 35–6.
[2] L. M. Cullen carefully analyses the difference between the probable causes or effects of the Act and the fears or accusations of the Irish (*Economic History of Ireland*, pp. 30–7).
[3] 16 Apr. 1698, to Annesley.   [4] 8 Feb. 1698, to Bishop Hough.
[5] 12 Mar. 1697, to Bishop Lindsay.   [6] 2 Apr. 1698, to Annesley.
[7] 13 May 1698, to Bishop Lindsay.

To another friend he had said the issue was not 'whether Ireland be subject to England' but 'whether the people of Ireland be slaves or freemen, whether they be more the subjects of England than the people of England are the King's subjects'.[1]

During the more recent storm over the Annesley Case and the Declaratory Act, the archbishop had revived and elaborated his old principles. Anticipating the Drapier, he denounced the advantage given to rich men by the removal to England of cases on appeal; this, he said, seemed 'an imposition on mankind'.[2] When the Peerage Bill of 1719 menaced the Scottish interest in the British House of Lords, the archbishop observed, 'It was urged that whatever people were governed by laws, in the making of which they had no interest, were slaves'; and consequently, he said, the Irish might infer 'either that we are slaves or that we ought not to be bound by laws in the making of which we have no part'.[3] When the Declaratory Act was passing through the British Parliament, the archbishop repeated what he had said twenty years before: 'nor do I value anything that I hold at the mere will and pleasure of another; that is the title of slaves.'[4] Pondering the indifference of the English to the merits of Ireland's case, he burst out, 'I do not find that there is any doubt of our right but those on your side have the power; and as the principles of many men stand at present, that is the only right.'[5]

It is manifest that a quarter-century's experience and more lay behind the archbishop's determined stand against Wood's patent and his choice of the methods to be employed in defeating it. He may have thought the Drapier's rhetoric would embarrass his cause; but so far from disagreeing with the doctrines, he must have taught many of them to the author.[6] No wonder he could retort to a friend who disliked the *Letter to the Whole People*,

---

[1] 19 May 1698, to Annesley.
[2] 1 Dec. 1719, to Annesley; 23 Feb. 1720, to Molesworth.
[3] 18 Dec. 1719, to Lord Southwell.
[4] 13 Feb. 1720, to Lord Southwell.
[5] 23 Feb. 1720, to Percival; cf. *Drapier*, p. 79.
[6] For another opinion see Goodwin, p. 671.

You commend the spirit that this poor kingdom has showed, and own that it has hitherto prevented the currence of [the halfpence]. But you should consider that spirit was due, and has been kept up by the pamphlets published on this occasion, particularly that condemned in the proclamation.[1]

At the opposite pole from the archbishop stood as usual Bishop Nicolson, who had already made savage comments on earlier *Drapier's Letters* (which he credited to Swift), and who had reported angrily and sarcastically the forming of associations to refuse Wood's coins.[2] From Londonderry, Nicolson sent to Canterbury a tirade against the new pamphlet:

> To complete our security, our spiritual *Draper* wrote a fourth letter on this fruitful subject, directed to the whole people of Ireland, wherein he exhorts the kingdom most steadfastly to adhere to that glorious combination whereunto they have bound themselves. This alone he thinks necessary at this juncture, because of a report spread abroad, that *The Lord Lieutenant is coming over to settle Wood's halfpence.* In a sneering manner he represents this as a groundless falsehood; and proves it to be so by a sneering panegyric on his excellency and Mr Walpole etc. Care was taken to publish this satire the very day before the Lord Lieutenant landed; and within two days after, it had a second edition. This gallant patriot asserts, in words at length, that *Ireland no more depends on England, than England does upon Ireland; that they who assert the contrary, talk without any ground of law, reason or common sense; that the parliaments of England have sometimes assumed a power of binding this kingdom by laws enacted there, but this has been opposed by invincible arguments from truth, justice and reason etc.* Thus, my Lord, are we come to the highest round in our ladder; and if no mark be set on this insolent writer, little safety will be expected (but in your prayers) by ... W. Derry.[3]

Between these extremes Lord Midleton set up his own platform. Midleton's devotion to the Irish interest was narrowly qualified by a warmer devotion to his own; and although he opposed the patent for economic reasons, he could hardly challenge the English ministers on constitutional grounds, having benefited so variously from English sponsorship in recent years.

---

[1] 12 Dec. 1724, to Gorges.   [2] 21 Aug. 1724, to Wake.
[3] 30 Oct. 1724, to Wake. The signature is of course normal for William, Bishop of Derry.

Like his brother and son, he held a seat in the British House of Commons; and in spite of his headstrong arrogance he had been Lord Chancellor of Ireland for ten years. During the first session of the Irish Parliament under the new King, he had boldly asserted the dependence of Ireland upon England even while proclaiming the right of Irishmen to receive preferment in their own church and state. Like Carteret, he had aligned himself with Sunderland rather than Walpole.[1]

In the Annesley Case, Midleton had refused to support the jurisdiction of the Irish House of Lords. When Swift's *Proposal for Irish Manufacture* came out, he voted to prosecute Harding the printer. Midleton was simply too prudent to defy the English government in order to break Wood's patent. His son had carefully briefed the Lord Lieutenant on the patent; and it seems clear that Carteret too would have liked to see it revoked but had to protect himself by striving with all his powers to soften the opposition.[2] Among the other intrigues that wound themselves into the affair was a rivalry between Midleton and Lord Chief Justice Whitshed; for the Chief Justice hoped to displace Midleton as Lord Chancellor, and Archbishop King was one of those who thought he deserved the office.

To Carteret in private the *Letter to the Whole People* must have seemed interesting for several reasons—his enmity to Walpole, his friendship with the secret author, his discomfort (which I have assumed) over the eulogy on himself. He could best appreciate the comedy of his asking Midleton, who had worked so well with Carteret against Walpole, to crawl under his own gate and help defeat the resistance he had connived at.

But the Irish Privy Council felt no whiff of their governor's amusement. When they met on 27 October, Carteret opened the programme by concisely damning the pamphlet. Midleton then criticized it in detail and asked for a prosecution. This motion passed speedily, and only Archbishop King (among the twenty-one Councillors present)[3] refused to sign. Midleton had

---

[1] Ball, *Judges* II. 69–70, 78, 90.   [2] *Drapier*, pp. 256–7, 305–6.
[3] Not counting Carteret.

hoped to weaken the archbishop without fortifying Conolly. Earlier, and behind scenes, he had blamed the archbishop for infusing the notions of William Molyneux into the Dean of St Patrick's; and he had also blamed Conolly's faction for trying to ingratiate themselves with Grafton by veiling their disapproval of the patent until popular indignation threatened to burst out in violence. No wonder the Chancellor so ably seconded the Lord Lieutenant at the meeting![1]

When Carteret went further and asked the Council to offer a reward for discovering the author (whose identity was of course known to them all), he embarrassed his audience. Many felt that the people would read such a proclamation as repudiating the Drapier's attack on the halfpence. Several Councillors had signed a declaration against the patent, and none wished to appear on the other side. They all agreed to reword the proclamation and focus it not on the pamphlet as such but on its seditious or scandalous paragraphs; any reference to Wood's coins was carefully omitted. The enormous value of the reward, three hundred pounds—enough to keep four modest families for a year—also troubled some Councillors. It was far greater than the usual sum for such purposes and might terrify the people into imagining dark intentions. But I suppose Carteret and Midleton wished to blazon to the English ministers their condemnation of the Drapier.

Coghill, one of the Councillors who would not sign this proclamation, told Edward Southwell that the critical passages in the Drapier's new letter were those on royal precedents and on Irish independence.[2] These, he said, were singled out as so provocative that 'the people of England would so highly resent it, as to force the halfpence upon us, to shew us that we were dependent'—and therefore

the enclosed proclamation was agreed on, but some of our friends apprehending this to be a step to bring the halfpence upon us, would not sign the proclamation, but there are a great number of hands to it. The people here on the coming out of this proclamation have the

[1] Coxe II. 395–9.   [2] *Drapier*, pp. 70–1, 78–9.

same notion of it, and are under great uneasiness about it, and think the reward so high, that some further mischief is intended by such an unusual offer for the discovery of the author. But still they keep up their spirits, and are determined never to take any of these half-pence; and it will be impossible for my Lord Carteret to gain them a currency if he should attempt it. And I think he will have a most uneasy government if he goes into any measures to make them current amongst us.[1]

Carteret wrote to Newcastle regretting that he had to take so unpopular an action but justifying it ostentatiously. In Dublin Castle he carefully refrained from speaking about the patent and concentrated instead on the problem of sedition. All the judges and officers of state in Dublin who wanted English backing for their personal ambitions strove to act rigorously against rioters or libellers, with the hope that such zeal would be rewarded in Westminster. Yet no steps were actually taken to introduce Wood's coins.

The poet Thomas Tickell (Addison's loving friend and Swift's old acquaintance) had come over as secretary to Carteret. He enjoyed the paradoxical farce of the scene before him, and reported it in a letter to England. The hawkers, he said, were afraid to peddle the Drapier's fourth letter; and yet 'great endeavours are using to get Dr Swift the freedom of the city in a gold box'.[2]

While the government waited for an informer to claim the three-hundred-pound reward, a verse from 1 Samuel began to appear 'fixed up in publick places'. We may take this text as marking how deeply the popular unrest was weakening the machinery of the law, or how easily Swift might mobilize the citizens of Dublin against their rulers; for it told of Saul's wishing to kill his son for an innocent trespass that had aided a great victory, and of the Israelites' rescuing their hero:

And the people said unto Saul, Shall Jonathan die, who hath wrought this great salvation in Israel? God forbid: as the Lord liveth, there shall not one hair of his head fall to the ground; for he hath wrought with God this day. So the people rescued Jonathan, that he died not. (1 Sam. 14: 45)

[1] 31 Oct. 1724; B.L. Add. MS. 21122.   [2] *Drapier*, p. xlv.

As this symbolic pledge went around the city, Swift could rejoice. He had driven the government into a position which it
could hardly maintain and from which it could withdraw only
after a painful loss of dignity. And Wood's chances for success
dwindled daily.[1]

Yet Swift decided that the moment had come for the Drapier
to produce one more letter. A prolonged spell of deafness and
vertigo was keeping him at home for months—except for some
easy visits; but if he could not attend his old friend Lord Carteret, he could still write against his lordship's government.
Soon after the day of the proclamation he was at work.[2]

II. LETTER 6/5

Maybe Swift began writing the Drapier's new letter as soon as
he read the proclamation—to which it sounds like an immediate reply. But he waited eleven years to publish it, for
reasons that will soon transpire. The essay received the title, *A
Letter to the Lord Chancellor Midleton*, and although fifth in order of
composition is usually counted sixth. So I shall mark it '6/5'. In
this essay the seriousness and even the moderation of Swift's
feelings are demonstrable. It almost hums with pained sincerity;
and anybody looking at it today will regret that Dubliners had
no chance to read the argument during the crisis that provoked
it.

Here for once Swift decided not to hide the identity of the
author. Consequently, he employed a method and a style appropriate to his character as dean of a great cathedral. With
orderly care he laid down propositions, supported them with
evidence, and inferred conclusions. At the same time he chose to
address the letter to Lord Midleton; for besides rebutting the
statements made in the proclamation, Swift wished, I think, to

---

[1] Cf. Ferguson, p. 123.

[2] Davis suggests that the date Swift set on the new pamphlet (addressed to Midleton),
26 Oct., might be correct even though Swift pays much attention to the proclamation
issued 27 Oct.—for Midleton might have warned Swift of the Council meeting. But
Swift, in this *Letter to Midleton*, quotes the exact language of the proclamation, and we
know the text was revised during the meeting on 27 Oct. Swift also refers to Midleton's
name appearing first among the signatures, a fact one could hardly have foreseen. See
Drapier, p. 137; Ferguson, p. 124, n. 141.

turn tables on the guardians of the law, to identify the defence of the Drapier with resistance to the patent, and to establish the Lord Chancellor of Ireland at the centre of that resistance even though Midleton had been the first to sign the proclamation against M.B. In addressing a person so eminently legal, it would obviously be appropriate to use a dignified manner.

Yet the defiance remained. Without confessing that he wrote the earlier letters, Swift defended them so unyieldingly that he invited prosecution. I believe he wished to precipitate a great public hearing in the form of a trial. The purpose would have been to debate the principles of government on which British legislators pretended to rule Ireland. Perhaps Swift thought of the Sacheverell Case. Not only did he invite such a trial; he outlined, in this essay, the course of the pleadings. In prosecuting the pamphleteer, the government would have had to face the constitutional issues he raised.

In this essay, therefore, Swift does not merely survey the old topics and retrace the old reasonings. He lifts the theme of Wood's patent into an image of all that was wrong in the connection of two kingdoms. Starting from the fact that the coins are an overwhelming threat to the Irish people, he infers that it is every subject's duty to warn his countrymen against them. Next he pretends to show that the Irish are loyal to the King, are supposed to be free, and could not be taught otherwise by the Drapier. According to the proclamation of 27 October, the *Letter to the Whole People* tended to alienate the affections of the Irish and English people from each other. Swift soberly reveals how little the English concern themselves with the Irish at all, how powerless the native Irish Roman Catholics are, and how closely the Protestants of the two countries must be tied together—not without a flick of his irony on the subject of job-hunters: 'And yet, I will appeal to you, whether those from England have reason to complain when they come hither in pursuit of their fortunes?' (a theme on which Midleton and Swift sang in unison).[1]

---

[1] *Drapier*, p. 129.

Taking up the matters of liberty and the prerogative, he reduces them to the plainest terms of Lockean philosophy and common law, which of course amply support the Drapier's case. Where it suits him, Swift gladly follows specious logic; but this is a mode of satire, not misrepresentation: thus he says in mock-innocence that because Letters One to Three were not noticed by the government, 'I look upon them to be without exception.'[1] As for the provocative language of the fourth letter, he defends that by the goodness of the writer's motives.

In the remaining half of the essay the most important section deals with the matters that ought to be clarified in a public trial of the Drapier: the claim of a private individual to speak out on public affairs, the limits of the royal prerogative, especially in determining the coinage; the true meaning of Ireland's status as a 'depending kingdom', and the difference as to civil rights between the Irish and the English. Commenting on these matters in the pages that follow, he particularly dwells on the hateful advantages of England over Ireland and on the danger of the new coins—pointedly illustrating his remarks by references to Midleton's own conduct.

Swift gathers up the charges made against the Drapier and replies to them in the most eloquent and least flamboyant plain style—Swift at his most imitable. His tone, that of a tired schoolmaster, magisterial and apologetic by turns, sounds like Addison with trumpets. There is enough irony to keep one smiling, but it is relaxed compared to the tense sarcasm of the *Letter to Shopkeepers*.

But the *Letter to Midleton* is also peculiar in implicitly revealing the name of its author. Having already separated his fictitious self from the rest of his party, Swift now brings his true self into play along with its shadowy twin. So his beloved game of impersonations replaces the fireworks of the earlier letters. As the real Dean of St Patrick's he can involve the real Lord Chancellor—perhaps the strongest figure in the national government—in his machinery.

---

[1] *Ibid.*, p. 132.

I suppose Swift wished to intimidate, if not to incriminate, Midleton and his colleagues, so they would withstand the blandishments of the Lord Lieutenant. At the same time, by associating Midleton with the campaign against Wood, and then unfolding his own propositions as consequences of that campaign, Swift yoked the government to his wagon: to condemn him would be to condemn Midleton. Yet because the act of discreet self-revelation had its own purpose, Swift took care not to say that he and the Drapier were one and the same; he merely acknowledged writing the new pamphlet, and he defended the Drapier.

This defence brought out the purest rhetoric that Swift commanded, equal in lucidity and ease, idiomatic flavour, and grace to the best of his *Examiners*. In keeping with his practice in familiar letters and, I believe, conversation, he set aside Biblical allusions and flamboyant conceits in favour of courtly anecdote and literary tags. Known to be a clergyman, he sounds like a cultivated gentleman.[1]

One of the games with the two identities is that Swift tenaciously marks himself off from the Drapier without ever diverging from the latter's pronouncements: 'I do think it my duty, since the Drapier will probably be no more heard of, so far to supply his place as not to incur his fortune'—so far but no further.[2] As usual, he would like to feed the flames without scorching himself. And the polarity within by no means eliminates the polarities without. Instead, Swift has extended the old division. Although Midleton opposed the patent, he had built up his estate in England, as Swift mordantly observes. Midleton therefore represents the overlap between the anti-Wood party and the English interest. Irish absentee landlords—and Midleton had been publicly reprimanded for abandoning his responsibilities as Lord Chancellor in order to linger in Surrey[3]— might detest the bad money without loving their own country.

---

[1] Cf. the allusions to Lucan (*Drapier*, p. 130), Leti (p. 136), and Cervantes (p. 141).
[2] *Drapier*, p. 124.   [3] Ball, *Judges* II. 99–100.

Thus Swift has begun to shrink the community that he will at last define as the true Irish interest.

Why did Swift wait eleven years to publish this essay? A note of explanation, when Letter 6/5 came out, gave the reasons as the success of the Drapier and Swift's unwillingness to antagonize 'the people in power'.[1] But he usually made such determinations under advice. I suspect he took his lead from those who had already guided him—Archbishop King and Robert Lindsay (who was legal counsel to St Patrick's Cathedral). Holding his place as archbishop for life, and knowing he would never climb higher, King, of all the Irish leaders, could best afford to alienate the English ministry.

On 30 October (I suppose, while Swift was writing the *Letter to Midleton*), the archbishop went to see Carteret. He said the Drapier was contemplating an open declaration of authorship, with a readiness to stand his trial. Carteret replied, according to his own account, that 'no man in the kingdom, how great and considerable soever he might think himself, was of weight enough to stand a matter of this nature.' The next day, Carteret wrote meticulously to Newcastle and announced that as far as he was concerned, any such declaration would be followed by the author's arrest.

Carteret had heard rumours that Swift was considering such a scheme, but his lordship would not trust them until the archbishop's visit. Then he realized that 'the author' might have to be held under a military guard until King George's pleasure should be known. So he consulted the two chief judges, Hale and Whitshed, both of whom recommended vigour without regard to popular reactions.

'The event of this is uncertain,' Carteret told Newcastle,

> but I must acquaint your grace, and beg you will lay it before the King, that if the boldness of this author should be so great as the Archbishop intimates, I am fully determined to summon him before the Council; and though I should not be supported by them as I

[1] *Drapier*, p. 121.

could wish, yet I shall think it my duty to order his being taken into custody and to detain him if I can by law till his Majesty's pleasure shall be further signified to me; for if his offer of bail should be immediately accepted and he forthwith set at liberty, after so daring an insult upon his Majesty's government, it is to be apprehended that riots and tumults will ensue, and that ill-disposed persons will run after this author and represent him to be the defender of their liberties, which the people are falsely made to believe are attacked in this affair of the halfpence.... Tis the general opinion here that Doctor Swift is author of the pamphlet, and yet nobody thinks it can be proved upon him, though many believe he will be spirited up to own it. Your grace by this may see what opinion the Archbishop of Dublin and Swift have of the humour of the people whose affections they have exceedingly gained of late by inveighing against the halfpence.[1]

Swift stood primed for heroics. The seven bishops under James II, Sancroft under William III, perhaps even the despised Sacheverell, had all reached this brink and stepped from the stage into the roaring crowd.[2] They had made the final gesture. If Swift wished to live up to his grandfather's part and be turned out of his church preferments sooner than stifle 'superior zeal',[3] the world was ready. His few dependants were secure; he had no family; his powers (he thought) sank daily; and his illnesses gained. Atterbury had just marched into exile after a state trial which the dean had never looked on as other than a dumb show.[4] In his own life there were precedents like his resignation of Kilroot[5] and his refusal to work for the Junto.[6]

But Swift's rashness was bound up with prudence. Like his friend Pope he desired the crown of martyrdom without the agony. And he habitually let cool heads guide him. The archbishop's account of how Carteret had answered his question would by itself, no doubt, have deterred Swift from an exercise in self-immolation. His own bent turned him against violent resistance except to the most aggravated tyranny. If he hesitated

---

[1] *Ibid.*, pp. xlvi–xlvii.
[2] Sancroft's crowd is in Swift's imagination: see his ode to Sancroft, stanza xi.
[3] Davis V. 190.
[4] Archbishop King shared some of Swift's reservations concerning Atterbury's trial; see his letters at the time.
[5] See above, I. 171.   [6] See above, II. 220–5.

a week, he met a conclusive reason to end his indecision; for Harding the printer, along with his wife, was arrested on 7 November.

III. 'SEASONABLE ADVICE'

If the government had been driven to prosecute Swift himself, the Lord Lieutenant might have made the action an affair of state, and taken the case up on levels where the Irish interest would find no purchase. But a Dublin printer could not aspire to treatment so ceremonious. By helping the humble tradesman, therefore, those who abided with Jonathan could still rally the Israelites and exercise in a Dublin court all the strategies they might have been denied if their dean had submitted to trial. So I think that when Swift discarded the *Letter to Midleton*, it was not to retreat but for the sake of a more cunning enterprise.

Harding the printer was no stranger to brushes with authority. Five years before, a report had described him as hiding from arrest for issuing a Jacobite document. In 1721 he had gone to jail for publishing the Lord Lieutenant's speech without permission—the speech announcing the commission for a national bank. By that time, Harding had also published several pieces by Swift. I suppose a printer took such risks at least partly in return for solid payment, and I am sure Harding knew enough to recognize a dangerous manuscript when he saw one.[1]

The charge brought against him was that he had printed a seditious pamphlet. Before he could be prosecuted for this offence, the grand jury had to find a 'true bill'. But this was hardly feasible unless witnesses appeared to testify that Harding had indeed known what he was about when he set his press to work. So long as the members of the jury were disposed to take the printer's word for his ignorance of the authorship and evil tendency of *A Letter to the Whole People*, the government could not proceed.

Harding showed his bravery as he and his wife sat in prison

---

[1] These paragraphs are derived from *Drapier*, p. xlviii; Ferguson, p. 125.

awaiting the action of the grand jury. He swore that he could not identify the Drapier, that all the *Letters* had reached him by an unknown hand, and that he had found nothing objectionable in them. Carteret believed the printer had been 'spirited up to stand the prosecution and persist in concealing the author'; and I believe so too.[1]

Carteret reported to the Duke of Newcastle that some of his advisers did not expect the grand jury to find a bill against the printer.[2] Swift evidently decided that this possibility should be the engine to pry Harding loose from his captors. So he gave the affair a new and farcical turn. Before the teeth of the law could begin to close on the accused, Swift brought out a clever squib that completely diverted the attention of the government. In three or four days he wrote and saw printed (most likely on Harding's press) a broadside which was then distributed through the post.[3] He called it *Seasonable Advice*, dated it 11 November, and addressed it to the panel of grand jurors.

While the government's proclamation had been worded to touch the purely seditious ingredients of the *Letter to the Whole People*, and had nicely evaded any expression indirectly sheltering Wood's patent, the nine paragraphs of *Seasonable Advice* rushed in exactly the opposite direction. Swift insisted that to damn the printer was to rescue Wood, that the Drapier, whose first three letters had found a unanimously cordial reception, deserved the benefit of any trivial doubt which might attach itself to the language of his fourth letter. 'Which will be of the worst consequence,' he asked, 'to let pass one or two expressions, at the worst only *unwary*, in a book written for the public service; or to leave a free open passage for Wood's brass to overrun us, by which we shall be undone for ever.'[4]

This argument made the edge of his weapon, though he also warned the prospective jurymen to pity the innocent printer; and he showed that those who refused the government's bill (against Harding) would seem far more impressive as lovers of

---

[1] *Ibid.* [2] 8 Nov.; *Drapier*, p. 267. [3] *Drapier*, pp. lxxxvii and 267.
[4] *Ibid.*, p. 91.

their country than the place-hunters and place-holders who might approve it. Among the old themes of his rhetoric a new one sounds clear and cutting—the one that sets Swift apart from many Irish patriots who shared his background. This is the conflict between productive and non-productive classes; for he not only sneers at place-holding opportunists. He also praises 'merchants, and principal shopkeepers' as being identified by nature with the best interests of their country.[1]

Carteret, perhaps less innocently than one used to think, let himself be turned aside from his first trajectory. Instead of pressing on with the prosecution of Harding, he asked the Attorney-General and the Solicitor-General to deal with *Seasonable Advice*, which did of course represent an unlawful attempt to influence the jury. Archbishop King called the broadside 'a very foolish, unseasonable, and, I may justly say, a wicked paper'.[2] Midleton thought it amounted to 'a most impudent and illegal practice', and considered that he himself was 'directly libelled by it'.[3] Yet he and others felt surprised (at least, afterwards) that Carteret did not now go ahead with the charges against the printer.[4]

As O. W. Ferguson says, Carteret's decision gave Swift a test case that involved the least possible danger to Harding or himself, for *Seasonable Advice* carried no imprint or author's name. To present the paper successfully would injure no one.[5] A week after the Lord Lieutenant received his copy of *Seasonable Advice*, the grand jury met. *Seasonable Advice* was read to them; its villainy was expounded; they were urged to present the paper as seditious. The Attorney-General, the Solicitor-General, and three judges (with Lord Chief Justice Whitshed the most persistent) exhorted, questioned, and persuaded them.

But the twenty-three jurymen behaved themselves with rare obstructiveness, and refused to make a presentment. Whitshed sent them back to 'consider further'. Still only eleven admitted to being convinced, and no indictment followed. Marmaduke

---

[1] *Ibid.*   [2] 24 Nov. 1724, to Molyneux.   [3] *Drapier*, p. 270.
[4] Coxe, II. 405.   [5] Ferguson, pp. 126–7.

Coghill, a friend of Swift and Archbishop King, was in the court
and wrote a dramatic account of the scene:

> My Lord Chief Justice ordered them to be called by their names
> respectively. Beginning with the youngest, he asked him his reasons
> why he did not present the paper as the court expected. His answer
> was that he thought he had done his duty, and discharged his oath
> and his conscience honestly and justly. Others of them said they
> thought the presenting that paper might be a step towards bringing
> in the halfpence amongst us; others of them said they thought the
> fifth paragraph [declaring that those who desired Harding's indict-
> ment really wished to keep or improve their income from govern-
> ment offices] was liable to censure, and that they were willing to
> present that, but their brethren would not come into it. My Lord
> Chief Justice ordered them to return and consider of it again, but the
> foreman told him it was to no purpose, for they would not alter their
> opinion.[1]

Until the nationalist movement seized Ireland, there were few
such instances of public and united resistance to coercion.

For a judge to cross-examine and intimidate a grand jury was
hardly lawful. But Whitshed's zeal carried him still further, for
he now dismissed the jury altogether and ordered the sheriffs to
impanel another. There were precedents for considering this
action a violation of his oath; yet the Lord Lieutenant had every
reason to support it. So the farce dragged on. 'I cannot sufficiently commend the zeal, prudence, and integrity of my Lord
Chief Justice,' Carteret wrote next day to Newcastle—perhaps
choosing his terms with more concern for his correspondent's
sensibility than for his own. Whitshed's conduct had in fact only
a single precedent in Ireland. 'Some people', wrote Carteret—
did he smile ironically as he wrote?—'pretend to find fault with
my Lord Chief Justice, but he is a person of too much courage
and sense to regard what they say.'[2] In other words, Whitshed
was reviving his performance of 1720 in the Waters case.

At the same time Coghill was saying, 'This procedure of dis-
charging the jury has exasperated the city and all others to a
great degree, most censuring it as an illegal act, others as a very

---

[1] 24 Nov. 1724, quoted in *Drapier*, p. 268.   [2] *Ibid.*, pp. l–li.

imprudent one at least, and all people apprehending that these violent measures may be used for passing these halfpence as well as they have been for presenting this paper.'[1] Meanwhile, one of the jurors who had wished to present *Seasonable Advice*—a banker—had so violent a run on his funds that he almost stopped payments.[2]

In order to improve Whitshed's blunder, Swift produced a fresh comic turn. He got hold of a resolution passed by the House of Commons of England in 1680: to wit, that dissolving a grand jury before the end of their term 'is arbitrary, illegal, destructive to public justice, [and] . . . a means to subvert the fundamental laws of this kingdom.'[3] Then he had the resolution printed up as a circular which went around Dublin a day or two after the dissolution of the jury.[4] This paper not only helped to destroy the reputation of Swift's old enemy; it also built up the contrast that the Drapier had established between liberty in England and oppression in Ireland.

By the time the sheriffs assembled a new jury, the noise against Whitshed rose to a pitch of riot. Carteret felt as insecure with the new men as the old: fourteen, he said, were 'reputed Jacobites'.[5] Even so, Whitshed tried haranguing them on the dangers of independency. But then he himself saw that the new jury would be yet more rock-ribbed than the old, and hardly willing to present Swift's *Seasonable Advice*. He did not dare to set the broadside before them; neither did he dare to dismiss them. Instead he waited till the end of the week, which would be the day before the end of the law term and therefore of the jury's life. Meanwhile, no other seditious libels could be prosecuted, although several were more than ready to be brought up.[6]

Swift too had his eye on the end of the term, which was Saturday, 28 November. He planned an audacity so bizarre that nobody in the government of England or Ireland could have looked for it. This piece of bravado was to drop the curtain on his farce just after he intended to leave town for a salubrious

[1] B.L. Add. MS. 21, 122, fol. 23.   [2] *Drapier*, p. lv.   [3] *Ibid.*, p. 93.
[4] *Ibid.*, pp. lii, lxxxvii, 93.   [5] *Ibid.*, p. liii.   [6] *Ibid.*, pp. liii–liv.

visit to the country. What Swift did was to concoct one more paper, in the form of a grand jury's true bill. But instead of presenting Harding or *Seasonable Advice*, it presented all those who might attempt to impose Wood's coins upon the Irish people. To strengthen the challenge, Swift joined with it a vibrant expression of devotion to King George:

> So do we . . . declare our abhorrence and detestation of all reflections on his majesty, and his government, and that we are ready with our lives and fortunes to defend his most sacred majesty against the Pretender and all his majesty's open and secret enemies both at home and abroad.[1]

Through these rattling hyperboles Swift juggled his rhetorical oppositions into a familiar design pitting the Irish people, their government, and their king, all together, against Wood's coin— and thus brushing Whitshed aside as the mere legality which corrupts true justice.

Swift arranged to have his mock-presentment copied out in form[2] and delivered very secretly to the new jurymen. On Friday, 27 November he wrote to Charles Ford, 'The grand jury has been dissolved for refusing to present a paper against Wood; a second was called who are more stubborn. The government and judges are all at their wits' end.'[3] The next day he left Dublin.

While Swift went on his way, Whitshed in all innocence assembled the jurors. In a scene radiating dramatic irony he told them they now had an opportunity of doing their country the justice that the former grand jury had refused to do. One of the jurymen then solemnly consulted the others and so proceeded to answer Whitshed. He said they had all spent two days in drawing up the paper which he now offered to the Lord Chief Justice, and they were 'of opinion, that nothing could be added to it'![4]

---

[1] *Ibid.*, pp. liv–lv, 96.
[2] Davis says it was printed for the grand jury (*ibid.*, p. lxxxviii). But Carteret's language on 1 December—'The presentment is just printed'—implies that the jury produced a manuscript. If Swift had printed it, he would have risked losing the element of surprise.
[3] Williams III. 43.   [4] *Drapier*, p. lv.

We are not told how Whitshed's face looked as he studied the mock-presentment; but we know that in his judicial capacity he refused to accept it because it was 'informal',[1] and we also know the gist of what he said when he gave the Lord Lieutenant a copy of the paper. As Carteret told the Duke of Newcastle, 'Lord Chief Justice Whitshed ... thinks it of so extraordinary a nature, that it may serve to give your grace a truer notion of the madness of the people, than any account I can possibly transmit to you.' As for the document itself, Carteret naturally doubted that the jury had composed it unaided: 'there is great reason to believe the paper came from a hand that has been employed before now with too much success in disturbing the peace of this kingdom.'[2]

We also know how Swift felt. He had been turning out verses that besmirched Wood and celebrated Archbishop King. Now he produced a savage flurry of rhymed invectives against Whitshed.[3] But at the same time he wrote victoriously to a friend, '[I] hardly thought such a spirit could ever rise over this whole kingdom.'[4]

---

[1] *Ibid.*, p. 284.   [2] *Ibid.*, p. lv.   [3] *Poems* I. 347–50.
[4] 19 Dec. 1724, to Chetwode; Williams III. 44.

Chapter Twelve

MOLESWORTH AND WHIGGERY

W ith Michaelmas law term over and Christmas approaching, it grew harder to keep up the noise about Wood's coins.[1] Belligerent pamphlets still came out; but as Bishop Nicolson lamented,[2] they could not be prosecuted—and therefore made little stir. All possible declarations had been signed. The Lord Lieutenant turned his public attention elsewhere and ostentatiously busied himself—to general applause—in reforming the management of the treasury and the army.

Yet offstage there was enough activity. Carteret sent his reports to England, and Newcastle at last asked him to recommend a course of action. Carteret then advised the ministry to cancel the patent and find another means of paying Wood back. Newcastle retorted that King George was surprised to hear such a proposal.[3] I think Walpole had by now come to accept Carteret's view[4] but saw no need to act on it till the Irish Parliament had to meet. Meanwhile, I suppose, he hoped delay would harm Carteret.

Certainly the man whom Walpole trusted most in Ireland gave him the same advice as the Lord Lieutenant. This was the new Archbishop of Armagh, Hugh Boulter. Unassailable merit had raised Boulter to his eminence. He clung to low-church principles, devoted himself to George I, complied blindly with the ministerial Whigs, and was determined to wipe out any smudge of independence in his new country. Boulter had fixed his loyalty on Lord Townshend, Walpole's brother-in-law, and had found his reward first as Dean of Christ Church, Oxford,

---

[1] Cf. *Drapier*, p. lvi.   [2] 1 Jan. 1725, to Wake.   [3] *Drapier*, p. lvi.
[4] He had pretty much done so in his letter of 1 Sept. 1724 to Newcastle; Coxe II. 364.

and then as Bishop of Bristol. Lord Percival, who considered him a 'heavy but honest' man, recorded a partisan impression of Boulter when he was made Primate of Ireland. Percival was then at Richmond with the Prince and Princess of Wales:

> I met the Bishop of Bristol there, who came to kiss hands on his promotion to the primacy of Ireland. He told me he wished he might be able to do his majesty service there, which was an odd speech. He thought, I suppose, the service of God might go on as well there, if any other were Primate, and in that he was not mistaken; but his chief business, it seems, is to serve the King. Sure you must allow him to be superlatively modest, when Count Staremberg and other foreign ministers attacked our religion, being led into it by something the Princess said; for he answered never a word. But perhaps he don't understand French.[1]

In Boulter's adopted country, Anglicans of the Irish interest, like Percival, felt more than ready to dislike the new Primate. He did little to appease them. One of his first acts was to bestow a church living on an utterly disreputable Englishman.[2] Archbishop King soon quarrelled with the ambitious English prelate. More than a year after Boulter moved to Ireland, his conduct was described by Percival's brother:

> As to the Primate, he is looked upon as a dull-headed man who in the House of Lords engrosses all the talk to himself, which they say was one reason he was sent over, they being tired out with him in England.[3]

Taking up his residence shortly after Carteret came over, Boulter soon warned Newcastle that the ranks of those set against Wood's coins included every class ('all sorts') of Irishmen—in Archbishop King's words, everyone 'from the herb women to the nobles'.[4] The force of this truth was at last coming

---

[1] B.L. Add. MS. 47025, p. 209; letter from Lord Percival to Daniel Dering, 7 Aug. 1724, in Add. MS. 47030, p. 146.

[2] In fact, while serving as his father's curate at Easthampstead, this scandalous parson had been an *agent provocateur* for Walpole. See the startling account given by E. P. Thompson, *Whigs and Hunters* (London, 1975), pp. 68–72, 221. See also below, pp. 356–7.

[3] Philip Percival to Lord Percival, 1 Feb. 1726; Add. MS. 47031, p. 183.

[4] Boulter I. 3 (Dublin, also I. 3); Goodwin, p. 674; letter from Archbishop King to Southwell, 9 Jun. 1724.

home to the British government. On 29 December, the very day Newcastle rejected Carteret's advice, London newspapers began to report that the affair of Wood's patent was 'as good as accommodated, to the satisfaction of all parties': the minting of coins had come to a halt, and Wood had been ordered to give an account of his expenses.[1] If Swift heard any advance rumours of such a settlement, he did not trust them. Until the start of the Christmas season he was with his friends the Grattans at Belcamp, a few miles from town.[2] But when he returned to Dublin, he brought with him the manuscript of another letter from the Drapier, dated 14 December. It looks as if Swift kept the pamphlet back from publication until New Year's Eve.[3] Maybe he spent the interval getting his dedicatee's permission to address the pamphlet to him; for no one could have foreseen the person Swift chose: it was old Viscount Molesworth.

Robert Molesworth (who died a few months later) had made himself conspicuous for two principles which the government could have wished at this time to be mutually exclusive: a concern for the welfare of Ireland and a loyalty to Whig traditions and the House of Hanover. Although in matters of religion Swift had set Molesworth among the damned, in political economy he found his lordship's zeal angelic. Molesworth's *Considerations for Promoting Agriculture* (1723) offered doctrine of the same tendency as the programme of Swift and Archbishop King. Since King George had ennobled him, his good name was inviolate to a party which now (unlike him) stood for strengthening the royal prerogative.

The association of Molesworth with the line of radical Whigs went back to the Glorious Revolution, when he boldly supported William III. In a book he wrote soon afterwards (about Denmark), Molesworth sounded violently anticlerical; here he attacked the Tory doctrines of passive obedience and divine right, aligning himself with Locke and Sidney. He became a member of both the Irish and the British parliaments, sitting of

---

[1] *St James's Evening Post*, 29 Dec. 1724.
[2] Ball III. 225. I accept Ball's inference.   [3] Williams III. 46.

course with the Whigs in both. For years Molesworth belonged to the Privy Council of Ireland, where he spoke out against the clergy of the Established Church.

In 1712 Swift sneered at him as a deist.[1] The following year, he condemned Molesworth as 'the worst' of the Irish Councillors; and Swift's friend Lord Oxford removed Molesworth from the Council.[2] Contrariwise, George I appreciated his Hanoverian ardour: he was ennobled in the new reign, finally becoming Viscount Molesworth.

All this does not make him look like one of Swift's chosen few. But by 1724 Swift himself had changed. His connection with the Tories lost any ideological force apart from the deep attachment to the church. His intimates included a startling number of would-be Jacobites; yet in politics he was now more libertarian and anti-monarchical than the ruling party. Meanwhile, during the controversy over the Annesley Case, Molesworth had joined forces with Archbishop King. Bishop Nicolson described him as 'a brisk assertor of the independent rights of this kingdom'.[3] In England Molesworth's protégé Toland wrote a pamphlet against the Declaratory Bill. In Ireland his lordship denounced the bill with Swiftian eloquence: 'I do not think myself one jot more a freeman, if an illegal and tyrannical power hangs over me to be exerted at will and pleasure.'[4] In letters to Molesworth, Archbishop King had canvassed the same topics that the Drapier was to deal with in his fifth *Letter*.[5]

During Swift's difficulties with the government over the *Proposal for the Universal Use of Irish Manufacture*, he turned to Molesworth for help in rescuing the printer from prosecution.[6] The relations between the two became so friendly that at the end of 1720 Molesworth wrote from London to his wife,

Pray take the first good opportunity of sending my compliments to Mr Dean of St Patrick's. I have received [a] very kind and civil letter from him to which I design to return an answer speedily, but I would

[1] Davis IV. 70.   [2] *DNB*.; *Drapier*, p. 288.
[3] 2 Oct. 1719; Wake Letters XIII, no. 113.
[4] Ferguson, pp. 52–3.   [5] 23 Feb., 3 and 5 Mar., 16 Apr. 1720.
[6] Williams II. 359.

have some notice taken of his civility by you, that he may be convinced I am pleased with it.[1]

Swift's desire to improve the economy of Ireland kept him at the side of Molesworth, whose *Considerations for Promoting Agriculture* (1723) the dean had praised as 'an excellent discourse, full of most useful hints'.[2]

The importance of their strange bedfellowship will be obvious to anyone who compares Dean Swift's judgment with that of other churchmen. In 1720 the Whig Bishop Nicolson, champion of the English interest, had complained acidly to Archbishop Wake about Molesworth's sympathy with Roman Catholics and his anti-British vigour in the Irish House of Lords: 'None more violent', he said, 'in fomenting the warmth of our zeal against foreign oppressors and encroachments'.[3] But Swift, a few years later, declared, 'I am not a stranger to his lordship; and, excepting in what relates to the church, there are few persons with whose opinions I am better pleased to agree.'[4]

By this time (1722–3) Archbishop King's intimacy with the Viscount was attracting the critical attention of bishops who were in the English interest. In December 1722, Henry Downes told his close friend Nicolson that the archbishop 'spent some time last week at Lord Molesworth's, where, I dare say, there was not a word spoken in favour of the King's ministry'.[5] The following spring, Bishop Godwin of Kilmore murmured to Wake that 'his grace spends two or three days in a week with good Lord Molesworth whom your grace knows and have had experience of his friendship to churchmen'.[6] Yet King's crony, the cautious Edward Synge, steered clear of Molesworth and, although lacking the irony of his brethren, protested, 'I have very little acquaintance with the *noble patriot* . . . and am perfectly a stranger to his religious principles.'[7] Thus the rapprochement of Swift, King, and Molesworth set them apart from the usual alliance of Whig, Tory, church, or English interest, and joined them in a union for the economic improvement of Ireland.

---

[1] Ferguson, p. 58, n. 96.   [2] Davis IX. 58–9.   [3] 23 Feb. 1720.   [4] Davis IX. 59.
[5] 8 Dec. 1722; Nicolson, *Letters* II. 556.   [6] 23 Mar. 1723.
[7] 4 Nov. 1723, to Wake.

Nicolson found Molesworth's essay on agriculture so offensive that he sent extracts from it to England, to scandalize Archbishop Wake.[1] His friend Evans heaped contempt on it.[2] But the dedication of that essay could only have completed the reversal of Swift's attitude toward Molesworth; for it was inscribed to the Irish House of Commons in recognition of their brave stand against Wood's patent; and in it Molesworth eulogized the Commons' votes as

> an eminent instance of your wisdom and love to your country, in your just censure and vigorous resolutions against a patent calculated to destroy your trade, rob you of your money; and which calls you slaves and fools to your faces.[3]

By tracing his own allegedly wicked expressions to a man whom the King delighted to honour, Swift once more confounded the royal ministers and instilled confidence into their opponents. Unlike the printer Harding and Lord Chancellor Midleton, Molesworth was a deeply significant addressee for a letter from the Drapier. His true opinions, selectively summarized, agreed with Swift's own and made an unflattering looking-glass for the Drapier's foes. Rhetorically, Swift thus turned the English policy of divide-and-rule against the government. Cutting across the outworn distinction between Tory and Whig, his arguments brought all the productive and public-spirited men of Ireland together in a bloc defying the oppressors of their country. The framework of the *Fifth Letter* therefore became a dramatic situation in which Swift imagined M. B. Drapier conversing with Molesworth and anticipating his lordship's sympathy: a partnership of plebian and peer, merchant and agriculturalist, priest and defamer of priests.

To support the drama, Swift filled most of his title-page with three epigraphs, two from Scripture and one from Virgil. The first of these refers to the persecution the Drapier had suffered on account of his patriotic conduct. The others suggest Whitshed's sacrifice of integrity to greed, or his unsuccessful effort to supersede Midleton as Lord Chancellor—for it was to this ambition

---

[1] *Drapier*, p. 288.   [2] 19 Oct. 1723, to Wake.   [3] Ferguson, p. 81.

that Swift (I think correctly) attributed Whitshed's venom against Waters and Harding.[1] Taking these epigraphs for our cues, we may hear in the new letter a supposedly Tory ecclesiastic talking confidentially to an anticlerical Whig peer about the crimes of a Whig judge.

In such a scheme the Whig–Tory polarity fades. We are left with a pair of patriots—representing between them the nobility, t⁻e church, agriculture, and trade—who condemn the injustice of a corrupt placeman. As an episode of the drama it is no accident that Swift should give away the secret of his authorship; and he does so twice: once when the Drapier mentions the '*secular* hands of the rabble', which is a pointless allusion if the speaker is no priest; and again in the next sentence when he says he has signed a declaration against Wood's coins, as Swift in fact had done.[2]

The author's identity becomes central to Swift's meaning in this essay because M.B. no longer stands for Ireland as a whole. Instead, he is now called upon to slough off the disloyal elements at the top; and he comes to embody not a person, a principle, or a party, but a selection of classes above politics and the law. Swift's distrust of human nature was such that he would not idealize public spirit but saw it always as dependent on self-interest. He had once supposed that the landed gentry, being the possessors of the soil, would naturally try to improve agriculture and thus to raise the condition of the labouring farmer and ultimately of the church (dependent on agricultural tithes) and the state. In Ireland he painfully discovered that the landlords as a class felt small responsibility for the soil they owned, or the men who tilled it, or indeed the nation that relied on it. He found that an alien jurisdiction, not merely indifferent but actually hostile to the interests of the nation, controlled its institutions of law and government with the connivance of the landlords.

He now took it upon himself to speak for the healthy elements, those who would benefit from the improvements he desired in the economy of Ireland: 'The little *virtue* left in the world', he

---

[1] Ball, *Judges* II. 96–100.   [2] *Drapier*, p. 110.

said, 'is chiefly to be found among the *middle* rank of mankind, who are neither *allured* out of her paths by *ambition*, nor *driven* by *poverty*.'[1] And by 'virtue' we know he meant love of one's country.[2] As shopkeeper, priest, friend to the common people, and ally of agricultural reform, he stands against the absentee landlords, the judges, and the highest officers of the law. Not only does the Drapier now oppose justice to legality and freedom to government; he also opposes prosperity to unproductive riches, and he turns to Lord Molesworth not for his wealth or power but for his devotion to liberty and the cultivation of the soil.

Swift pretends, in this pamphlet, that the Drapier wishes to clear himself of the charges brought against him. But by going over them, he aggravates them, seizing this opportunity to shout the slogans he had advanced in earlier letters. To give them new life, he now makes Whitshed a prime object of his polemic while ostensibly designing the essay as an orator's self-justification. Following traditional rhetoric, therefore, he opens by establishing the integrity of his character.

So in the first quarter of the essay the Drapier gives an autobiographical account of his good intentions, his education, and his accomplishments. He humbles himself before the judicious listener and asseverates his innocence. In the next quarter he takes up the three charges against himself: that he reflected upon the King's majesty, that he declared Ireland was independent of England, and that he offered to rebel against a pretender to the throne. He shows that none of the passages cited will bear the malicious interpretation given them by the government's lawyers.

He examines the meaning of 'dependency' as the relation of Ireland to England, and concludes again that this thing signifies no more than the acceptance by Ireland of the same king as England. The chief complaint in the proclamation had been against the passage in which Swift swore to die before accepting a pretender as king, even if the English should enthrone him. On this charge Swift performs an elated jig which involves the ideas

---

[1] *Ibid.*, p. 112. [2] Davis IX. 233.

of Locke, Molyneux, Sidney, and Molesworth. 'Liberty' and 'property', the most ordinary Whig counters, slip in and out of the climactic paragraph, and Swift writes, 'Freedom consists in a people being governed by laws made with their own consent, and slavery in the contrary.' After sarcastically regretting this outburst, Swift goes on to declare, 'Your lordship hath said and writ fifty times worse.'[1]

In the third quarter of the essay Swift wanders from self-justification. Here M.B. bestows several virulent paragraphs upon the malice of William Wood, and also declares that the Drapier will not again tempt the vengeance of the Lord Chief Justice. Then he reverts to mock-apologia, jeering at the allegations brought by people like Whitshed against *Seasonable Advice* and the 'extract' concerning grand juries. In the last quarter of the essay, like a good defensive orator, the Drapier softens the heart of his noble listener by accepting the latter's beliefs. So he praises liberty in its various forms; he ridicules the government's suppression of freedom of the press, contrasts Irish liberty with English, and wittily identifies the sentiments of M.B. with those of Molesworth.

Swift's violent slogans might be the theoretical development of constitutional issues implicit in the campaign against the patent. But they might more simply be a means of embarrassing the ministry into withdrawing the patent. Probably Swift himself could not have said whether he was following public opinion or leading it. I should like to think that he employed the coins as a jumping-off point for the exposition of his political philosophy. But he may rather have been implicitly warning the government that if they supported the patent, they would risk hearing a more inflammatory propaganda than they were equipped to counteract. Or else he may only have been exercising a colossal *ad hominem* rhetoric which would rip open the self-contradictions of Hanoverian Whig policy in Ireland. Addressing Molesworth, M.B. certainly says that his slogans are an expendable instrument in the campaign: 'Let me have but *good city security* against

[1] *Drapier*, p. 108.

this pestilent coinage, and I shall be ready ... to *renounce* every syllable in all my four letters.'[1]

In the *Letter to Molesworth*, as Ferguson says, Swift gloats over his defeat of Whitshed.[2] The Drapier's tone is mock-despair. Pretending that he must give up the struggle, he really flaunts his insouciance in the face of the law. By seeming to regret the boldness of his principles, he affords himself occasions (in the old rhetoric, *occupationes*) for reviewing them, one by one.

The form Swift's glee takes is a display of impudent virtuosity in the use of pseudonyms. The Lord Chief Justice would have liked to apprehend the man who broke his laws. Swift offered him half a dozen men. As the Drapier defends the various papers which have been held up as seditious, he gets into a lively game of distinguishing the several authors without really denying what everyone knew—that Swift himself stood behind them all. So M.B.'s little autobiography becomes an allegory of Swift's own career as a political propagandist for Ireland. Again, when the Drapier says 'my own' name appeared on one of the declarations, he invites us (as we have noticed) to recognize the true author. Then he moves on to paraphrase the advice of 'a certain Dean', who of course is Swift again. The dean in turn refers to the author of the *Proposal for the Use of Irish Manufacture* ('a writer as innocent, as disinterested and as well meaning as my self'), who yet once more is Swift. Next he defends *Seasonable Advice* as the work of another person, 'a more artful hand than that of a common *drapier*'. And finally there remains the 'publisher' of the extract concerning grand juries.[3]

It would be imprudent to treat these half-dozen characters as self-contained or deceptive 'personae'. If they were not seen through at once, they would lose their point. What they have in common reveals (as the author intended) more than what each possesses separately; and that is the parcel of attributes itemized by Swift: they are all disinterested, well-meaning, and innocent; and they naturally agree in these virtues because Swift not only

[1] *Ibid.*, p. 109.   [2] Ferguson, pp. 128–31.
[3] *Drapier*, pp. 102–4, 107–9, 111–14.

thought of himself as one who at bottom was blessed with them but also believed them to constitute a useful rhetorical pose.

Maybe it is because he was flaunting his identity that Swift loaded his style with so many allusions to texts both sacred and secular. Besides the Biblical allusions in his epigraphs, he has half a dozen in the body of the essay. The boldest is a parallel between the betrayal of the Drapier and the betrayal of Christ.[1] But these are mingled with Virgil, Lucretius, and Herodotus, and with anecdotes—ancient and modern—that verge on irreligion.[2] The effect is of that peculiar character of pious worldliness which Swift had made his own. It implied that he had ample learning, ample experience of frivolous society, but still preserved his religion and his morals. Unlike the selfish landlords, he could not be seduced from the paths of virtue by a lust for the life of fashion.

There are few bold conceits in the essay. But the allegory of the Drapier's career and his games with identity have the joyous effect of many conceits. Besides, Swift sounds so sure of himself; he uses so many witty parallels; he changes his tone so freely, from anger to sarcasm, from direct speech to Socratic irony, from humour to invective; he makes such an exhilarating contrast between the pretence of despair and the style of triumph, that one must agree with the judgment of Herbert Davis: 'It is in some ways the best written of all the *Letters*.'[3]

---

[1] *Ibid.*, p. 110.

[2] *Ibid.*: Virgil, p. 97; shirt of Nessus, p. 103; Matt. v. 25–6, p. 104; 2 Kgs xvii. 33–4, p. 105; Sedley's renouncing, p. 109; Matt. xx. 1–16, p. 110; Matt. xviii. 7, *ibid.*; Luke xix. 40, *ibid.*; Scipio's 'great victory', p. 111; 1 Sam. i. 10, *ibid.*; dumb boy, *ibid.*; Lucretius II. 1–2 (on watching in comfort the agony of others), p. 112; story of Moyese, *ibid.*; Herodotus on Cambyses, pp. 114–15.

[3] *Ibid.*, p. lvii.

Chapter Thirteen

THE DEFEAT OF THE PATENT

I. BLACKOUT

For three seasons now a cloud of ignorance lay over Dublin. The Irish leaders kept all their antennae out, trying to pick up the signals of English policy. But only faint and confusing noises came through. Carteret distracted the people in the best possible way, by his close attention to the government. He strove to be fair-minded and energetic, courteous and accessible, committing himself to no party. Above all, he looked into the accounts of the Irish treasury, with sensational results. Archbishop King said, 'No Lord Lieutenant that I remember since Lord Essex seems to have laid to his heart the business of the kingdom so much as he doth or to have been more equal to it.'[1] Bishop Nicolson, in rare agreement, praised him as warmly.[2]

About Wood's patent, the Lord Lieutenant remained prudently evasive but never dishonest. He urged the Irish leaders to trust their king, yet admitted that he had got no direct orders. In January 1725, the rumour ran that the danger was over. 'This day's news-letter', said the new Bishop of Meath, 'tells us we shall (through his majesty's goodness) get rid of Wood's halfpence';[3] and Archbishop King said several informants assured him that orders were sent. Yet Carteret made no declaration about the patent.[4] Meanwhile, Boulter sent the Duke of Newcastle a report on the coinage crisis which was long, accurate, and objective enough to be called a work of scholarly research. While his definitive version of the case matches, in all

[1] 7 Aug. 1725, to E. Southwell.   [2] 1 Jan. 1725, to Wake.
[3] Letter of 7 Jan. 1725, from Henry Downes to William Nicolson, in Nicolson, *Letters* II. 593.
[4] 28 Jan. 1725, to Southwell.

essentials, the picture given by Carteret and others, he also reveals plainly where the fears of the ministry lay. The peculiar threat was the unity of the nation, because if that held and was cleverly directed, no English government could force its measures on Ireland.[1] He proposed that the government should rescind the patent and grant Wood a pension—in the name of an agent—sufficient to compensate him for his losses; and this was indeed to be the action that Walpole finally took. The leaders of the Irish Parliament, said Boulter, 'do not doubt being able ... to provide for such payment'.[2]

Although as far back as 1 September 1724 Walpole admitted that it was 'impracticable to hope to change the minds of the people',[3] he had reasons for a leisurely wait before relieving the anxiety he had created. He would gain nothing by haste. The Irish Parliament generally met every second year and voted supplies for the establishment. When that necessary evil came, the government might suffer painful embarrassments if the patent still survived; for the Members already felt the ministry had cheated them in 1723, when they accepted vague assurances and granted the sums requested.

But until the new session, Walpole could ignore the hullabaloo. He had two advantages to gain by waiting. First, he wished the Irish protestors to supply Wood with compensation, and a menacing delay would encourage them to be generous. Secondly, the person who had to bear the immediate complaints and questions was Carteret; and any annoyance to his excellency pleased Walpole. Besides, some agreeable chance might allow the government to enforce Wood's patent after all.

The patent, Archbishop King decided at the end of January, 'is to hang over our heads till an opportunity offer either to put it in execution, or to screw money out of us to buy it off':

> We have been treated in this whole affair, and in every step of it with the utmost contempt endeavoured to be imposed upon us, fools and

[1] 19 Jan. 1725; Boulter I. 8 (Dublin, p. 7).
[2] *Ibid.*, p. 13 (Dublin, p. 11). Cf. Walpole's decision in his letter of 12–21 Oct. 1725, to Townshend; Coxe II. 367.
[3] Coxe II. 364. Cf. above, p. 249.

children, as if we had not common understanding, or understood [not] when we are abused.[1]

Carteret's popularity was hardly calculated to delight the government in Westminster. But in Ireland the praise was universal. Nicolson uneasily reported threats that the Lord Lieutenant would be recalled: 'This continues to be the harsh tale that comes from all our friends on your side', he told Wake; 'and I freely own to your grace, it affects me much more, than the late tinkling of our brass-farthings.'[2]

As the spring approached, Irish defiance did not let up. The boycott of the coins went on. Carteret, having no instructions, prorogued Parliament from 24 March to 6 August 1725. Primate Boulter repeated his observations to the Duke of Newcastle.

Possibly, the Primate had promised more than he could deliver when he assured Newcastle that the Irish Parliament was willing to pay Wood off. Boulter may have hearkened too much to Speaker Conolly and not enough to Lord Chancellor Midleton. 'Nobody', the Lord Chancellor wrote in March 1725, 'would go into the giving anything to Wood in the nature of a compensation for giving up the patent.' Midleton assumed that the reason for the prorogation was to bully the Irish into accepting the coins. Carteret, he thought, had determined to push the session through without mentioning the patent, and would be glad to see the Lord Chancellor removed as a hindrance. But Midleton said he would not quit his opposition, and was ready to resign.[3]

Meanwhile, Archbishop King kept warning everyone not to trust the English court: 'We have no positive promise from his majesty that these halfpence shall not be pressed upon us.' The Irish, he said, now wanted legal security—'and nothing can give us that but voiding the patent.' He believed Carteret would stay and hold the Parliament, but he foresaw no productive session so long as the patent remained in force. The archbishop

[1] 28 Jan. 1725, to Gorges. [2] 30 Mar. 1725, to Wake.
[3] 15 Mar. 1725; Coxe II. 413–17.

wondered whether the ministry would go so far as to let their own business in Parliament miscarry simply in order to make Carteret look 'useless'.[1]

Tremendous defalcations were being revealed in the treasury, thanks to Carteret's penetration; and these findings heightened the sense of crisis. Then in mid-April came a Swiftian diversion. A feature of public life was the honouring of chief governors or of persons in very high office by bestowing the freedom of the city upon them, in a ceremony usually performed by the mayor and aldermen. During the manœuvres and intrigues of the campaign against Wood's patent, some leading citizens decided to rally the patriots by conferring the freedom of Dublin on the Dean of St Patrick's.

When they first tried to pass the motion, the Recorder of Dublin was present. This was John Rogerson, who, in another robe, served as Attorney-General of Ireland. He had of course presented the indictment of the author of *Seasonable Advice* to the grand jury, and could hardly participate contritely in the Drapier's exaltation. Rogerson therefore opposed the motion, and it was lost. But at an adjournment of the Dublin City sessions, the patriots tried again. This time Rogerson was absent, and the motion passed. Bishop Nicolson drily reported the event to illustrate the feverish state of Dublin passions:

> We have some that are as busy as ever in keeping up the jealousies of our populace about their approaching ruin by Wood's brass-money: and these warm patriots declare, that they will never cease their clamours, till his majesty's letters patent are formally recalled and annulled.[2]

Swift was now installed as a father of his country; and the health, opinions, and activities of the dean began to receive public comment as matters of general interest. For weeks Swift's old deafness and dizziness had afflicted him; and he hoped to fight them with country air and exercise. I think he believed the same medicine might halt the alarming decline of his beloved friend. So he got Mrs Johnson and Mrs Dingley to join him in a

[1] 2 Mar. 1725, to Gorges.   [2] 24 Apr. 1725, to Wake.

long visit (described below)[1] to Sheridan's estate at Quilca, in county Cavan. To Nicolson's surprise and disgust, the fact appeared duly published in a newspaper. Writing to Wake about Swift, he said,

> One of the prints of this day gives the following remarkable account of the gentleman: 'This week the Reverend Dean Swift regrettedly left this city, and is not expected home till towards the first of August.'[2]

While Swift was away, the double pressure on Carteret never relaxed. The English government refused to give him instructions, and the Irish leaders badgered him for definite statements about the patent. He asked them to trust the word of King George. They replied, 'We have it not.' At least, so reported Archbishop King, according to whom they also asked, 'Will his excellency from the throne assure us that no brass money shall be sent us into Ireland?' To which they heard no answer.[3]

Unpromising auguries followed. Midleton did finally resign. But his successor was not the eager Whitshed—who for all his zeal to please Westminster at least belonged to an eminent Irish family—but Richard West, son of a London merchant. West was a learned lawyer and a Member of Parliament, distinguished enough to serve in the state trial of Lord Macclesfield. But he was English, and in Ireland could only represent the English interest. Bishop Nicolson predictably felt heartened—'very cheerful', he said, 'upon the hopes given us of the great abilities and good temper of our new Lord Chancellor West'.[4] Archbishop King was less sanguine. At the same time another Englishman was made Lord Chief Baron, one of the three highest judges.

Yet at the end of May, Edward Southwell wrote from London encouraging Archbishop King to believe the patent had been rescinded. His grace remained sceptical: 'I see you fancy Wood's patent is taken up,' he replied, 'but it must be more than fancy before this kingdom will be satisfied.'[5] A month later, people in

---

[1] See below, pp. 375–9. [2] See Williams III. 57, n. 2.
[3] 12 May 1725, to Gorges. [4] 6 June 1725, to Wake.
[5] 5 Jun. 1725, to Southwell.

Dublin still felt that the coins could not 'obtain a currency here'.[1] Midleton, like the archbishop, was saying that Carteret neither had any orders concerning the patent nor admitted that he wanted any to manage the Parliament. He also felt sure the Lord Lieutenant had warned the ministry that 'it's not to be expected things will do in Parliament here, without giving the people satisfaction in the matter of Wood's patent.'[2]

Like the archbishop again, Midleton easily expressed what it was that enraged him in the curve of policy since the death of Queen Anne. He complained to his brother that the patent was of a piece with the project of a bank, and that the Irish Parliament had begun to rear and swerve when they saw that 'their money was going into private pockets (I mean the projectors of the bank and Mr Wood and his partners).'[3]

Carteret hoped that when the new Chancellor West came, he would carry secret instructions about the way the Lord Lieutenant should handle the patent in Parliament. But West brought no sparkle of light, and Carteret wrote at once to the Duke of Newcastle. He warned the Duke that Parliament might become the scene of an unpleasant disturbance and asked, 'in case of any attempt of this nature', how he was to behave himself: 'If you have thought of any expedient, that may be proper to put an entire end to this unhappy affair, I hope you will be so good as to acquaint me with it.'[4]

Parliament had to be prorogued until September. Yet at the beginning of August, Archbishop King could say he still did not find that Carteret had received the much-discussed orders. Advisers in England warned the archbishop that the Irish leaders would be wise not to bring up the matter in Parliament—'by which', he said, 'I guess that they there resolve not to demolish the patent; and if my Lord Lieutenant can't assure us that it is cancelled I very much apprehend that it will not be possible to prevail with the Parliament *sub silentio*.' Once more he gave vent to Ireland's over-fed sense of outrage: 'And in

[1] Coxe II. 420.   [2] *Ibid.*, p. 423.   [3] *Ibid.*, p. 426.
[4] 27 Jul. 1725; *Drapier*, p. lx.

truth we were so barbarously used, with such contempt and injustice, after our easy acquiescence last time [i.e., in the Parliament of 1723], that it burns yet in the heart of every Member.'[1]

The opposite complaint could as usual be heard from Bishop Nicolson, far north in Londonderry and remote from the currents of news in Dublin or Westminster. As he prepared to go up for the session of Parliament, Nicolson said, with his customary sarcasm,

> 'Tis still believed that the greatest part of our heat [i.e., in Parliament] will arise from our raking in the dross and embers of Mr Wood's copper money. Some of the zealous patriots of poor Ireland will not be persuaded that the dread of that plague can be laid aside till his majesty is pleased (by solemn proclamation) formally to void and make null his letters patents granted to the said gentleman on that occasion. Others are for giving the thanks of both houses to Master Drapier, for the late great deliverance that he wrought for us; and to secure his person against all future attempts of ambitious judges and corrupt juries. Some little efforts of this kind will probably be made; but in the main I am confident that we shall behave with a good tolerable stock of duty to the King and respect to his Lieutenant.[2]

Well into August the ministers in London received flares of warning not only from the suspect Carteret but also from their own men, Boulter and the newly arrived West.[3] Carteret had too much finesse to oblige his enemies by making elementary mistakes. Before the Irish he kept up every appearance of meaning to slip the coppers down their throats; to the ministry he sent a bold series of storm signals. At the beginning of July, Boulter had reminded Newcastle that Carteret must be empowered, in his speech opening Parliament, to 'rid this nation of their fear' of the patent.[4] Since no proper assurance was forthcoming, Boulter wrote again in mid-August, and said that without relief from the patent, Parliament would suffer a 'heat' too great to 'keep

[1] 7 Aug. 1725, to E. Southwell.
[2] 27 Aug. 1725, to Wake. It looks as if Swift in Quilca had not got the news of Wood's surrender by this time; so I suppose Nicolson in Londonderry had not heard.
[3] *Drapier*, p. lx.   [4] Boulter I. 35 (Dublin, p. 29).

within any bounds of decency'.[1] To such alarms the new Lord Chancellor West added his echo. The triple pressure released the stuck mechanism in England, and the long-awaited turn-around began at last.

Luckily, it was now too late to stop Swift's hand: he had another *Letter* ready to be published when Parliament assembled. But once he heard the patent was cancelled, he recalled the copy from the press, and Irish readers waited ten years before they could see it.[2]

II. 'AN HUMBLE ADDRESS'

Pessimistic about the government's course, Swift completed his pamphlet in June or before, while he stayed at Quilca. Nobody had to egg him on. With so much kindling lying about, Swift could hardly help making a fire. Yet some patriot sent him an anonymous note to say he must have 'got a sop to hold [his] tongue'.[3]

Living in the country, Swift had plenty of leisure for the job; but he lacked the excitement of Dublin news and conversation, and did not labour enough to sharpen the style of this seventh *Letter*. In it, he makes little use of the Drapier's character and is casual about his own identity.[4] He offers some perfunctory echoes of the Bible and commonplace fables, some tags of ancient history, but no brilliant conceits; and only at a few points does he infuse into this essay the audacious element that holds us in the best parts of the *Letters*.

Yet he still emits a mood of provocative menace that lours over Englishman and Irishman alike. On the one hand he solicits Parliament to heap public shame on any Irish leader who does not condemn the patent. On the other hand he incites

---

[1] *Ibid.*, p. 36 (Dublin, p. 30).

[2] I believe that when Swift released the manuscript for Faulkner to publish, he restored the deletions made by his friends.

[3] Williams III. 91.

[4] Cf. *Drapier*, p. 147, 'my own degree of a shopkeeper'; p. 149, 'in great security'; p. 150, 'than a good clergyman' (suggesting Swift); p. 151, 'my reading'; and p. 164, 'set us an example'.

them to actions that would mortify the English ministers, such as an inquiry into the origins of the patent. The principal wish of the people, the Drapier tells Parliament, is 'that your *first* proceeding would be to examine into the pernicious fraud of William Wood'.[1] By such words I think he warns the government, here as in the *Fourth Letter*, that if the patent is not recalled, they may expect hideous embarrassments.

Judging from the nature of his argument, I think Swift wished to lead the Irish Parliament toward unity in a programme to strengthen the nation's economy. Opposition to Wood's patent was to serve as the barbed point of his goad; it would be a pretext for organizing the Irish to labour in harmony for their own self-interest. Swift therefore divided his pamphlet between a rallying cry against the patent and a set of proposals to help agriculture, forestry, and the textile industries.

Here the specific reforms are less important than the idea of such reforms. Supposing the nation had adopted them and they had not in fact produced a decisive improvement, so long as the idea of self-help was deeply implanted, more effective schemes might have superseded the failures, and there would have been a powerful impulse toward material progress. Without this impulse, the Irish could sink into despair; they could turn their backs frivolously on the national crisis; or they could blame England and fulminate. But they could hardly lift the kingdom out of her slough. Swift strove to instil into his countrymen the principle that while the English were fundamentally responsible for the wretched condition of Ireland, the people of the country still had resources that would secure them against misery. It is this moral impulse that drove him to write his pamphlet and that he wished to convey to its readers.

Fourteen years earlier, when he published the *Conduct of the Allies* on the eve of a British parliamentary session, Swift had got his starting power from provocative attacks on individuals like Marlborough and Godolphin, whom he blamed for prolonging the war and sacrificing the nation to their own greed; by inciting

[1] *Ibid.*, p. 150.

Parliament to punish the Queen's evil counsellors, Swift had drawn the peacelovers together as representing the real people of England.

In the Drapier's new *Letter*, which Swift called *An Humble Address to Both Houses of Parliament*, he used the same strategy. Two-fifths of this long essay deals with the enormities of Wood and his satanic allies. Swift virulently analyses the motives of those who would in any way tolerate the patent; he denounces Whitshed with fresh energy, and implores the Members of Parliament to stigmatize 'by public *censure*' anyone who has violated the privileges of juries. In his inflammatory manner he reviews the process by which the patent was honestly condemned in Ireland and fraudulently investigated in England.

This preliminary fling has few obvious links with the remaining three-fifths of the pamphlet. After it, Swift sets out the table of his proposals for the economic salvation of Ireland. Opening with the desire for a national mint, he digresses to enumerate the loss of revenues taken by England. This is mainly through rents paid to absentees, but Swift also dwells on salaries from the Irish establishment going to place-holders who rarely live in the country, and on the unnecessary importation of English goods, food, and fuel. He arrives at the stunning total of seven hundred thousand pounds a year, all counted as profit received by England.[1] He proceeds, in five paragraphs, to detail the harm inflicted by absentee landlords. Next, Swift mentions the offices in Ireland granted to Englishmen, with the consequent exclusion of Irish candidates. This tale of England's mistreatment of her sister kingdom serves the same rhetorical purpose as the opening section of the pamphlet: to fan the flame of resistance by reminding the Irish of their wrongs.

He then digresses and allows himself a political analysis which is at best recklessly cheerful. He argues that there is no longer a basis for factions of any sort, and that the resulting concord (though due to the lack of anything worth quarrelling over) should promote a rapid solution of those difficulties which rest

[1] I suspect that Swift got this entire calculation from Archbishop King.

within the power of the people. A pathetic footnote of 1735 confesses that 'the author was much mistaken in his conjectures.'[1]

Swift now calls upon Parliament to assume the leadership of a united nation. He magnifies the dignity of the legislators, dwelling upon their power and their service to the community. Not only does he address this pamphlet to them as a humble petition. He even suggests that if they passed resolutions clearly in the public interest and with near-unanimity, they might govern Ireland by their votes without the assistance of King George.[2] This respectful note is not (like the tributes to Midleton and Molesworth in earlier letters) a way of shielding Swift's doctrines under another man's prestige. It is an older use of flattery; for by attributing his own views to the legislators' voices, Swift hopes to lure them into following his lead. So he carefully sets them apart from the King while opposing them to Wood.

Implicit in the praise of Parliament, of course, is a reproach to the King. Swift therefore echoes his *Second Letter* and provides a thunderous piece of oratory elaborating a motif which has become familiar. This is a dramatization of the *salus populi* principle. Appealing beyond the legal or constitutional merits of his case, Swift asks what must be the last justification of a patent such as Wood's. Is it not, he says, the good of the people? Then— he goes on, in two dazzling paragraphs of forensic display—can any logic prevail against the unanimous fears of the kingdom that this thing will be their destruction?

> But, in the name of *God*, and of all *justice* and *piety*; when the King's majesty was pleased that this patent should pass; is it not to be understood, that he *conceived*, *believed*, and *intended* it as a gracious act, for the good and benefit of his subjects, for the advantage of a great and fruitful kingdom.... Can it be denied, or doubted, that his

---

[1] *Drapier*, p. 163.
[2] Unlike Ferguson (p. 132) I take Swift seriously when he urges the inquiry and other actions on the Parliament. Cf. Williams III. 61: 'I hope the Parliament will do as they ought, in that matter, which is the only public thing I have in my mind'—'that matter' being Wood's patent (27 May 1725, to Chetwode).

majesty's ministers understood and proposed the same end, *the good of this nation*, when they advised the passing of this patent? Can the *person* of Wood be otherwise regarded, than as the *instrument*, the *mechanic*, the *head-workman*, to prepare his furnace, his fuel, his metal, and his stamps?[1]

In this way, yet again, while the ministry justified their misdeeds by their laws, Swift appealed from legality to the purpose of law. The distinction was like one to be made by another Irishman half a century later, in Burke's speech on conciliation with the American colonies: that what is lawful for the King's ministers to do may not always be right.[2]

Swift's way of embodying this appeal is irony through literalization. He pretends to take seriously what he knows to be figurative or perfunctory. The patent had included some ceremonial phrases about the King's concern for his people. In answering the addresses of the Irish Parliament, the King had promised to do 'everything that is in his power for the satisfaction of his people'. When Swift treats these stony formulae as the language of the heart, he turns them into explosive weapons.

Contrariwise, it becomes the duty as well as the prerogative of the Drapier's listeners in Parliament to examine into 'the detestable fraud of one William Wood'[3] and to censure those who (like Whitshed) have broken the law relating to juries.[4] Anyone in sympathy with the crime is thus associated with royal injustice and opposed to Parliament. Swift has squared off his sides once more. Seeking the broadest political base, he no longer separates the productive gentry from the unproductive. The M.B. who in his first letter stood with the King against Wood, now unites with a Parliament embattled against both.

Returning to economic issues, Swift pleads for several improvements in the manufacture and sale of woollens and silks. Above all he urges the Irish to wear their own goods. But at the

---

[1] *Drapier*, p. 153; cf. *ibid.*, p. 26.
[2] Burke says the question is 'not whether you have a right to render your people miserable; but whether it is not your interest to make them happy. It is not, what a lawyer tells me I *may* do; but, what humanity, reason, and justice, tell me I ought to do.'; *Writings and Speeches*, World's Classics edition (Oxford, 1906), II. 202.
[3] *Drapier*, p. 145.   [4] *Ibid.*, p. 149.

same time he calls on the weavers and drapers to establish guaranteed standards of quality for their products. Digressing yet once more, he condemns those who set up the royal prerogative against all proposals to advance the national welfare; and so he brings in Whitshed and Wood for new lashings.

At last, Swift summarily reviews a set of six desiderata, half of which he has already considered at length. The remainder include the deliverance of the native Irish from their barbarous condition by 'civilizing' them—i.e., persuading them to accept 'our language and customs'; the encouragement of tillage as against pasture; and the reforestation of Ireland. To these Swift tacks on the conservation of turf, which was freely and destructively cut for fuel.

Obviously, Swift has not bothered, in this essay, to work out the connection of his chief themes, viz., the fight against Wood's patent, the reorientation of Irish politics, and the strengthening of Ireland's economy. His style sounds most dramatic when it meets familiar topics like Wood's coins, Whitshed's crimes, and England's oppressions. It sounds flat in the passages proposing reforms. The case Swift makes for the dwindling of parties has little force, and his economic programme unfolds itself mechanically.

Yet the political and economic doctrines reveal fascinating developments. I do not suggest that Swift reasoned acutely on these issues. That he of all men should have thought cliques and coteries might lose their influence on Irish public life only shows how ebulliently his hopes quarrelled with his experience.[1] As for the schemes to improve agriculture, forestry, and trade, historians have demonstrated that the sickness of Ireland's economy was immune to such palliatives.[2]

The interest of Swift's programme is less economic than moral. The impracticality of his scheme is beside the point. Swift was giving the idea of national independence a new and exalted

---

[1] We know he meant the observation about the decline of parties seriously, because he told Stopford, during the parliamentary session, that 'all party but that of court and country seems to be laid asleep'—26 Nov. 1725; Williams III. 114.

[2] Cf. L. M. Cullen, pp. 36–49.

meaning that identified political unity with material blessings. Various articles in his programme might have to be moulded to fit particular circumstances. Some might be dropped and replaced by others. But when he taught that virtue had patriotism as its essence, that patriotism meant not military courage but the submission of personal and class privileges to the common weal, that the common weal signified above all a thriving economy, that it required legislative independence, that it was separate from loyalty to a king or a church, and that it must direct and not wait on statute law—when he taught these lessons, Swift brought out the true principles of modern nationalism and supplied a language to the revolutionary leaders of Ireland and America.

III. STOPPING THE PRESS

Harding, poor man, had died in jail the week Swift left for Quilca, but his wife carried on the printing business. When Swift finished writing *An Humble Address*, he left it to his friends to pick a printer,[1] and they chose the widow. Meanwhile, Swift called into motion the machinery he had used before.

In a preface to the *Letter to Molesworth*, he had outlined his methods. There he said he used to dictate (i.e., from his own draft) to an apprentice who could write in a 'feigned hand' and to send the manuscript to the printer by a 'blackguard boy'. I take this account as essential truth, for it fits what we know of his methods elsewhere.[2] But I suppose the apprentice was a young clergyman whom Swift trusted, and I suppose the blackguard was a street urchin who could be watched as he went on his errand. While Swift lived at Quilca, he had to write some instructions; since the recipients saved the messages, we possess first-hand evidence of the transaction.

A circle that included Sheridan, Delany, Worrall, and John

---

[1] Williams III. 91.
[2] Cf. Swift dictating to John Barber (*Journal*, 4 Sept. 1711) and Sir Harold Williams's account of the publication of *Gulliver's Travels* in *The Text of Gulliver's Travels*.

Grattan worked along with Swift.[1] Sheridan went down to Quilca while Swift was there, collected the manuscript essay, and carried it back to Dublin in June.[2] At the end of the month Swift wrote to him,

> Pray remember to leave the pamphlet with Worrall, and give him directions, unless you have settled it already some other way. You know it must come out just when the Parliament meets.[3]

Even as Swift liked his books to appear in London while he himself was in Ireland, so he now proposed to stay at Quilca till the beginning of October while his friends worked as his literary agents. This, I suppose, is what Swift meant when he told Ford he had 'some reasons not to be in Dublin till the Parliament here has sate a good while'.[4] I also believe his understrappers decided some passages in the essay were too bold, because it looks as if John Grattan visited Swift at Quilca and got his permission to make alterations. Late in August, Swift wrote to Worrall,

> I gave Jack Grattan the papers corrected and I think half spoiled, by the cowardly caution of him and others. He promised to transcribe them time enough, and my desire is that they may be ready to be published upon the first day the Parliament meets. I hope you will contrive it among you, that it may be sent unknown (as usual) to some printer, with proper directions.[5]

By this time Walpole had come about. Wood had agreed to surrender his patent in return for an immense compensation, arranged according to Boulter's original prescription.[6] Wood was to receive £24,000 in pensions over a period of eight years. To smother all suspicion, Walpole had the warrants made out in the name of Thomas Uvedale. Since any rumour of this piece of statesmanship would open it to the howling rage of the Irish Lords and Commons, Walpole kept the warrant in his own hands, 'not to be given out till all difficulties in the Parliament of

---

[1] Swift asks for the agreement of Worrall, Grattan, and Sheridan when he decides to cancel the seventh *Drapier's Letter*. See Williams III. 93.

[2] So I infer from Swift's letters of 25, 26, 28, and 29 June.

[3] Williams III. 69.   [4] 16 August 1725, to Ford; *ibid.*, p. 89.

[5] *Ibid.*, p. 91. Notice how cautiously Swift refers to the patent.

[6] See above, p. 296.

Ireland are over'.[1] In spite of the mutterings of Archbishop King and his comrades, the money was indeed to be squeezed out of the bowels of Wood's victim; for Walpole put the pension on the Irish establishment.

We may infer the depth of Walpole's discretion and the degree to which he assumed management of the affair by his manner of delivering the legal copy of Wood's resignation. Instead of trusting it to the ordinary correspondence between the Secretary of State and the Lord Lieutenant, he sent an English M.P. This was Richard Edgcumbe, later Lord Mount-Edgcumbe (a Commissioner of the Revenue of Ireland), one of Walpole's most trusted subordinates, and an intimate of the Walpole family. Even so, the secret trickled out sufficiently for Midleton to know (about the surrender but not the pension) by a private letter dated 14 August.[2] Not till five days later did the Lords Justices of Great Britain despatch their message to Carteret, declaring that Wood had given up the patent.[3]

Edgcumbe arrived in Dublin on 25 August. The next day, the Privy Council of Ireland met and proclaimed the news.[4] It speedily reached Quilca, and Swift decided to recall his pamphlet: 'Since Wood's patent is cancelled', he wrote to Worrall,

> it will by no means be convenient to have the paper printed, as I suppose you, and Jack Grattan, and Sheridan will agree; therefore, if it be with the printer, I would have it taken back, and the press broke, and let her [i.e., Mrs Harding] be satisfied.
>
> The work is done, and there is no more need of the Drapier.[5]

In dismissing the Drapier, Swift was bowing out of his highest public drama. When one reads over the *Drapier's Letters* with the hindsight of two-and-a-half centuries, they still keep the radiance of disinterested virtue trampling on radical corruption. Whoever wishes to define patriotism may use them to illustrate his meaning. Yet if one narrows the frame to the remaining years of Swift's career, *An Humble Address* can seem one of the sombrest of Swift's works. The supposed misanthropist, nearly sixty years

---

[1] Coxe II. 367.   [2] *Ibid.*, p. 430.   [3] *Drapier*, p. lx.   [4] *Ibid.*, p. lxi.
[5] Williams III. 93.

old, with the frustrations of his deanship and his early efforts for Ireland behind him, tries to consolidate the good forces which he thinks a common threat has at last aroused, and to turn them in permanently useful directions. After a brilliant triumph he must watch the forces decline and dissipate themselves. He must see the British government easily dispose of his allies, while the corrupt absentees, feckless landlords, and irresponsible tradesmen return to their ancient habits.

It was to take another four years to persuade Swift that prescribing for Ireland was administering a dose to the dead. Anybody who today might hesitate to believe that the anguish of *A Modest Proposal* was more than a spark of the ageing dean's rancour, should review the energy and weight of thought which underlay his tracts on Irish wretchedness.

Swift's years of practice on the larger stage of England had closed with the enthronement of everything he battled against. He contracted his purposes to the narrow arena of Ireland but was to fail outwardly again. The final period of his life he would devote to the church within the kingdom. But he was at last to feel the Anglican establishment decaying, like the surface of the countryside, from a shallow greensward into a deep bog.

The *Humble Address to Parliament* represents a false dawn before the real dusk. Swift had hopes, not too sanguine, that a spirit had been born which could be moulded into the regular breath of a common weal. What followed after the splendour of 1725 was the expiration of public conscience in three years of famine, an age of 'undertakers', a reduction of the Irish bishops to the function of weathercocks for ministerial winds, and of the Church of Ireland at its best to a thin-muscled social agency ineffectually ameliorating the catastrophe of English rule.

IV. WISDOM'S DEFEAT

Swift was still at Quilca when the Irish Parliament finally met, on 21 September 1725. The chambers that had fostered so many absurdities were now to provide a farce for the epilogue of the Drapier's career. In his opening speech Carteret made the most

[311]

of the King's revocation of Wood's patent and asked fulsomely for such acknowledgements as might 'convince the world, that you are truly sensible of the happiness you have enjoyed under his majesty's most mild and gracious government'.[1]

Members who recalled the fraud of another Lord Lieutenant's speech exactly two years before might have heard Carteret's suavity as insolence. Those like Conolly, who had tried to ingratiate themselves with the government by exertions on Wood's side, displayed the most audible joy over the cancellation, and described King George's action as an 'extraordinary instance of favour and indulgence from the crown'.[2] Those like Archbishop King, who had most savagely fought the patent, were less lyrical, and called the cancellation 'a piece of justice done by his majesty to this kingdom'.[3] Midleton, though loathing Conolly, represented himself as standing between the extremes, and said that while it was an act due in justice, it was also one of voluntary goodness.[4]

To Edward Southwell, the archbishop wrote with Swiftian disgust,

> The exemplification of [the] resignation of Wood's patent was produced with great pomp, and the favour magnified, and we must do everything in requital. For my own part I put the case thus: a man throws me into a pit, where I am throughly [*sic*] wet, and ready to be drowned, and then upon much importunity and many prayers, and finding it to his interest that I should not perish, he helps me out. Am I not infinitely obliged to him?[5]

The factions showed themselves in the House of Lords during a bizarre debate over the proper language for replying to the Lord Lieutenant's speech. An address of thanks had sprung dutifully from the Commons; and the Lords' committee had begun their work with a motion decorously celebrating his majesty's 'royal favour and condescension'. But a diversion followed which was recorded at second hand by Marmaduke Coghill. According to him, Archbishop King moved in commit-

---

[1] *Drapier*, p. lxiv.   [2] *Ibid.*, p. lxi.   [3] Coxe II. 431.   [4] *Ibid.*
[5] 3 Oct. 1725, to E. Southwell.

tee to amend the motion by making the expression 'his majesty's great wisdom, royal favour, and condescension'. We know the archbishop had already written pointedly to a friend that King George 'wisely' removed the parliamentary stumbling block of Wood's patent.[1] We also know that in 1723 he had played a similar game when he moved in a committee of Lords that the word 'happy' should be deleted from the phrase 'our happy constitution' in the address to the King.[2] His new motion was certainly not innocent, but Midleton and the Archbishop of Tuam[3] seconded him; and it carried.

As soon as the vote was passed—according to Coghill—the archbishop allowed himself a surprising indiscretion; for we are told that he

> could not contain himself, but out of the fullness of his heart, he said to the Primate [i.e., Boulter], who sat next him, that he had clinched the matter, for if it was wisdom to get the patent surrendered, it must have been the contrary to have granted it.

Coghill says the archbishop's blunder gave the alarm to Boulter and his bloc.[4] But the Primate claimed he saw at once that the motion was intended as a 'reflection on what is past'.[5] Certainly he led the unheroic battle against it. Nicolson naturally marched with Boulter, observing biliously, on the day of the first round, 'The meaning of that word, on this occasion, was plainly discernible.' Nicolson then hoped that either the committee or the whole House would throw 'wisdom' out.[6] But *dis aliter visum*, for his hope was not realized. The Irish bishops stuck together, and enough lay peers went along to defeat Boulter's bloc.

The Primate was no Achilles. He carried the quarrel outside the House and appealed to the Olympian powers of the Lord

[1] 18 Sept. 1725, to Colonel Foley.
[2] Letter from the Bishop of Ferns to Archbishop Wake, 26 Sept. 1723. The reflection was on the Declaratory Act. The motion failed.
[3] Archbishop King's crony, the elder Edward Synge.
[4] *Drapier*, p. lxv.
[5] Boulter I. 42 (Dublin, p. 35). Though of course an eye-witness, he would naturally have preferred to exhibit his own acumen rather than attribute his awakening to a whisper from his rival. But one assumes that if he had at once detected the innuendo, he would have fought sooner against it.
[6] 21 Sept. 1725.

Lieutenant. Carteret promptly called in several of the lay peers, flourished their pensions before their noble eyes, and laboured virtuously to bring them to a 'proper temper'.[1] He succeeded, especially with the young Lord Roscommon. The debate still kept its bloom for two days. After it was brought before the whole House, says Coghill, the government spokesmen solemnly declared that 'wisdom' had been added as an insult 'either to his majesty or his ministers',

> and therefore [it] would be improper and indecent to use it in an address of thanks for the greatest act of favour that could be done us. On the other side it was urged that nobody could deny his majesty's wisdom in all his actions, that the word was inserted by order of the House and could not be struck out, and that nothing could be a greater affront than putting a negative on that word.[2]

Swift's friend, Lord Forbes, held out—he could afford to, having recently added four hundred pounds a year to an already large income[3]—with Midleton and of course Archbishop King, as well as nine more stalwarts. But Roscommon and the other deserters were quite enough to prevail over the patriots. In the last division, after three days' debate, the vote went against them.[4] 'Archbishop of Dublin and Lord Midleton were those who most strongly insisted for that word [i.e., 'wisdom'],' Coghill reported, 'and the Archbishop went so far as to enter his protest, but in this he was single.'[5]

This mighty action was quickly told to Swift, who managed in very few days to compose and have Mrs Harding publish a little poem, of a size commensurate with their lordships' accomplishments: 'On Wisdom's Defeat in a Learned Debate'—

> Minerva has vow'd since the bishops do slight her,
> Should the reverend peers, by chance e're invite her,
> She's resolv'd never more to be known by the MITRE.

> The temporal lords, who voted against her,
> She frankly forgives, as not having incensed her,
> For securing their pensions is best proof of their sense Sir.

[1] Boulter I. 43. [2] *Drapier*, p. lxv. [3] Williams III. 11, n. 4. [4] *Drapier*, p. lxv.
[5] 9 Oct. 1725; *ibid.*

At first putting the question, their lordships were for't,
And his grace's wise motion did bravely support,
Till positive orders was whisper'd from court.

So this they allege in their justification,
They vote for their bread in undoing the nation,
And the first law of nature is self-preservation.

Rose Common,
Shameless Woman.[1]

The closing lines sound like a version of the Drapier's remark, in *A Letter to Parliament*, that some people would consent to the 'ruin ... of a nation' sooner than sacrifice their private 'avarice and ambition'.[2] In general, the verses have Swift's emphatic rhythms, tricky rhymes, and crowding of the sense. Like many of Swift's poems, this is built on a mythological conceit: that Minerva renounces the bishops for standing against Archbishop King's amendment, but forgives the temporal lords; for the churchmen cannot lose their sees, but the peers (who have therefore shown prudence) can lose their pensions.

Though effective enough, the poem is one of Swift's inferior squibs. Yet it does illustrate another face of his irony-in-reverse. Just as the comedy of the coin-swallowing conceit (in the *Letter to the Whole People*) depends on taking metaphorical language literally, so this witticism depends on taking plain words figuratively. Swift treats 'great wisdom' as a personification of the goddess, and so the rejection of the words becomes a rebuff to Minerva.

The broadside came out on 30 September and was sold publicly for two days. But the Irish peers united to retrieve their dignity. Nicolson called the poem an '*infamous and seditious libel*', and thought the allusion to Roscommon 'a most villainous

---

[1] *Poems* III. 1118. The reference to Roscommon implies that he has sold himself and that he is pusillanimous. The attribution of the poem to Swift is not certain, but I accept it. He used similar, four-beat triplets in 'An Elegy on Dicky and Dolly' (*Poems* II. 429–31). He used similar rhymes in 'The Storm', ll. 8–9: spite her/mitre; 'On Censure', ll. 5–6: support/court (also found in 'Horace, *Epistles* I. vii', ll. 1–2; 'The Author upon Himself', ll. 27–8; 'On Poetry', ll. 185–6; and 'Death and Daphne', ll. 11–12); 'Helter Skelter', ll. 17–18: big, Sir/wigs, Sir; 'Dan Jackson's Reply', ll. 36, 40: hold Sir/bold Sir.
[2] *Drapier*, pp. 146–7.

reflection on a sober young lord'.[1] Archbishop King merely said it was a 'short lampoon' that had given 'great offense' to the House of Lords.[2] Meanwhile, their lordships acted with uncharacteristic speed and harmony. They condemned the dangerous composition, had the sheriff burn it, stopped the sale, and ordered the wretched widow Harding to be hauled before them. A committee of lords gravely proceeded to examine that much abused female. Nicolson was still sanguine enough to believe some evidence might materialize, but he knew no action could be taken:

> 'Tis expected that, in the course of their enquiries, they'll discover the true author of the *Drapier's Letters*. I do very much question whether such a discovery will be of any sort of use in our present circumstances. That writer is, at present, in great repute, the darling of the populace, his image and superscription on a great many signposts in this city and other great towns.[3]

Learning nothing as usual from Mrs Harding or any other source, the Lords went on to propose that a reward be offered for the discovery of the author of 'Wisdom's Defeat'; and they earnestly addressed the Lord Lieutenant for that purpose. Carteret cheerfully agreed to this clownish piece of spite; he carried through the dumbshow of a solemn proclamation, and offered the reward of a hundred pounds as requested. Of course, nobody came forward to claim it,[4] a fact which seems a smaller token of Swift's popularity than of the noble lords' indifference to shame.

V. DEAN AND DRAPIER

A charming aspect of the Drapier's performance is the way it fed one of Swift's deep yearnings. His hunger for anonymous fame was served by the exquisite mingling of M.B.'s notoriety with the suppression of the true author's name. All his literary games of impersonation worked to connect the inner character of the

---

[1] 2 Oct. 1725.   [2] 2 Oct. 1725, to Annesley.   [3] *Poems* III. 1117; 12 Oct. 1725.
[4] *Ibid.*

much-discussed dean with the course of public affairs. Dramatic irony became an instrument of politics when the government were forced to pretend ignorance of what everybody knew, and to obey a man they could not name.

For Swift the strongest flavours of the delicious compound were success and recognition. Though he had often tasted fame, and several of his projects had reached fulfilment, he was seldom known widely to have fathered the work. His responsibility for *Queen Anne's Bounty* lay buried. The popularity of *A Tale of a Tub* became a disaster for his career in the church. While *The Conduct of the Allies* was political triumph (since the peace was made), it took the side of a party; and the fame of Swift's authorship, known to many who read the book, had nothing like the universal reach of the Drapier's reputation. Swift had at last managed to gratify his ambition without overstepping the strange barriers he set for himself: that his authorship should be ostensibly a secret but covertly told to the world. No enemy could prove he was the Drapier, and no friend would deny it.

To increase his satisfaction, Swift found a fresh tribute waiting when he returned from Quilca. On 2 October 1725, as if to welcome the dean home, the first collected edition of *The Drapier's Letters* appeared. This was called *Fraud Detected: or, The Hibernian Patriot*,[1] and included the five letters already printed, Swift's poem *Prometheus*, and several songs and pieces of verse associated with the Drapier. I suspect that Swift helped to prepare the volume, and had a hand in the printer's preface. Certainly the printer pleased him with it: in the preface are several flatteries of the author, with an appreciation of his style and rhetoric. Now Swift showed tangibly how his secretiveness played with his love of fame; for he gave to the Bodleian Library a copy of *Fraud Detected* richly bound and endorsed unmistakably in his own handwriting, 'Humbly presented ... by M. B. Drapier'.[2]

George Faulkner, the printer and publisher of the book, was

---

[1] *Drapier*, p. lxxxix.
[2] *Ibid.*, p. xc. The title stamped on the spine is *The Drapiers Letters*.

then an earnest young man of about twenty-five, who had worked for the fine English printer, William Bowyer. He had recently set up his own shop in Dublin and had launched a newspaper, the *Dublin Journal*, in which he naturally advertised *Fraud Detected*. After the retirement or death (or remarriage) of Sarah Harding (about 1730), Faulkner was to give Swift so much satisfaction that by 1732 he would become something like the dean's official (if unacknowledged) publisher. There is evidence that he produced work for Swift as early as the beginning of the year 1730.[1]

---

[1] James Woolley, 'Arbuckle's "Panegyric"', p. 202. (The whole essay is a model of rigorous but imaginative scholarship.)

Chapter Fourteen

THE PATRIOT AT HOME

While the Drapier throve in glory, Swift humbly contended with bodily afflictions and managed his domestic economy. There was not much tempering of prudence with rashness, or preaching with clowning, in this aspect of his life. Dealing with his health, Swift was all sermons and sobriety. Once when he fell ill in the country, he wrote to a friend who was anxious in Dublin, 'Do you not believe, that if I had any sickness of consequence, I should have got a coach to come to town, or sent there for a doctor. I assure you I have been very careful of myself.'[1] And so he was; and consequently, for all his talk of sickness, Swift, with one exception, had remarkably good health in an age of valetudinarians.

The exception was Ménière's syndrome, or Swift's familiar attacks of giddiness and deafness. Apart from that, he suffered in his fifties only from such illnesses, accidents, or frailties as did not threaten one's life. So he used to bruise his shins badly. He caught his share of colds, and agues and fevers that sound like influenza. But he would stay in for a week or two, and be nursed until the trouble passed.[2] His ancient discomfort of piles flared up in a hideous form during the spring of 1724, when the haemorrhoids were strangulated—

> a cruel disorder that kept me in torture for a week, and confined me two more to my chamber ... which with the attendance of strangury, loss of blood, water-gruel and no sleep require more of the stoic than I am master of, to support it.[3]

He recovered of course. But he rarely felt safe from the eruptions of vertigo, or from a deafening sound like rushing waters—

---

[1] Williams II. 218. [2] *Ibid.*, pp. 390, 391; III. 112, 116. [3] *Ibid.*, p. 9.

'seven water-mills'[1]—in his ears, that blotted out normal human voices. Doctors told Swift that these were symptoms of the same disorder—'united in their causes'; but he believed they were 'not always so';[2] and he never learned that they were unrelated to diet and uncontrollable by the remedies he knew. The deafness seemed to yield at last when Swift was fifty-four to a cure he learned from his tailor, viz., 'a clove of garlic steeped in honey, and put into his ear'.[3] But after a couple of years' relief the misery returned, pursuing him week after week till he left Dublin for Quilca.[4] In the summer of 1725 he said he seldom went a whole month without a fit of deafness.[5] By this time, incidentally, he was such a public figure that his illness was reported in the *Dublin Weekly Journal*.[6]

These attacks not only gave Swift discomfort. They mortified and frightened him. He could not bear to lose his dignity before strangers or men of rank. Only intimate or humble friends, the two ladies or his servants, were tolerable when he had to strain to hear a word—he whose pleasure of pleasures was conversation. I am inclined to think that he suffered fewer and lighter fits of deafness or vertigo while living in the country or travelling through rural parts, and that the strain of prolonged self-control and self-consciousness in the more demanding society of the capital exacerbated the physical causes of Swift's disability. So it does not seem odd that he should have been ill in the midst of the excitement over Wood's patent, or that he should have left Dublin in order to cure himself.

Once he invited several gentlemen to dine with him in the deanery.[7] After they arrived, a fit of giddiness took hold of him. In spite of his need to preside as host, the humiliated dean had to give up. Ironically enough, it was All Fools' Day, his favourite festival. He turned at last to one of the Grattans who was present, left him to 'do the honors of the house', and went to spend a miserable five hours in bed.[8] Such disasters worried him sufficiently in Dublin. In London they would have undone him. 'While I am thus incommoded', he said of his deafness, 'I must

---

[1] *Ibid.*, p. 36.   [2] Letter of 20 Nov. 1733, to Ford; Williams IV. 210.
[3] *Ibid.*, II. 421.   [4] *Ibid.*, III. 24, 36, 40, 46, 49, 57.   [5] *Ibid.*, p. 86.
[6] 24 Jul. and 9 Oct. 1725.   [7] 1 Apr. 1720.   [8] Williams II. 342.

be content to live among those whom I can govern, and make them comply with my infirmities.'[1]

Inevitably, he looked for methods of prevention; and his chief medicine remained physical exercise. The old fear of fresh fruit—which of course he loved and kept eating—stayed with him. But he had few other shibboleths. Typically, he thought of his regimen as a moral system: 'If you knew how I struggle for a little health, what uneasyness I am at in riding and walking, and refraining from every thing agreeable to my taste.'[2] It sounds as if backsliding were not merely perilous but sinful.

The exercise he always preferred was riding. When he could not ride, he walked, climbed (stairs, if nothing else), or even rowed. Staying with the Rochforts at Gaulstown, he boasted, 'I row or ride every day, in spite of the rain, in spite of a broken shin, or falling into the lakes'—the lakes being large, ornamental ponds that the Lord Chief Baron had made on his property.[3]

But riding suited him best, and he strove to be properly mounted. So the purchase of a suitable horse became Swift's equivalent of a quest for the holy grail. He worried about price and hated to be cheated. In a land where trading in horseflesh was a national pastime, Dean Swift met many temptations and disappointments. From the time he returned to Ireland after Queen Anne's death, he troubled his friends, his agents, and above all himself with this compulsion to secure the best mount possible. He did come upon an excellent creature not yet four years old, and bought him for twenty-six pounds. Then the prudent dean trained the horse carefully for eighteen months. Finally, the steed was ready for service. Alas, the groom handled him badly, and Swift lamented, 'When he grew fit to ride, behold my groom gave him a strain in the shoulders, he is roweled, and gone to grass. Show me a misfortune greater in its kind.'[4]

The medicine he took himself he was more than willing to prescribe to others; and now as in earlier decades, he urged his friends to exert themselves. When Chetwode first knew Swift

[1] *Ibid.*, III. 84. [2] *Ibid.*, II. 392. [3] *Ibid.*, p. 403. [4] *Ibid.*, p. 348.

and was zealous to ingratiate himself, he declared that he followed the dean's advice: 'Your recipes guide me. I drink wine more, small beer less, eat no salads, walk so much that Sub[1] pronounces me distracted.'[2] Swift believed in walking or exercising till he perspired, on the theory that perspiration cleansed the body.[3]

At Quilca with Mrs Johnson and Mrs Dingley, in the spring and summer of 1725, Swift found splendid opportunities for muscular development. The weather was often too wet for riding. So Swift marched about in a greatcoat, supervising Sheridan's servants and workmen as they improved the place under his direction.[4] He got Mrs Johnson, whose bad health frightened him, to walk as well, and thought she grew better —though with worrying relapses.[5] In August he said she was walking 'three or four Irish miles a day over bogs and mountains'.[6]

Here his deafness troubled him only sporadically.[7] When his modest friend John Worrall visited Quilca, Swift decided he too would benefit from vigorous ambulation, and took him on a hike of eight or nine miles. At one point Worrall jumped down a ditch and wrenched his foot. Instead of dwindling as it ought, the hurt persisted and finally embarrassed the great dispenser of exercise by turning into what was diagnosed as a case of gout.[8]

To a man in uncertain health few blessings mean more than a supply of good servants; and Swift during his fifties saw the deanery in efficient hands. Mrs Brent, his Presbyterian housekeeper, was intelligent, honest, and dependable. Robert, the valet, was well trained. But Archy, the groom, turned out badly and was at last dismissed.[9] There were also an old man and woman for miscellaneous chores.[10]

---

[1] Probably Warburton, Swift's former curate and now Chetwode's parson.

[2] Williams II. 178. Cf. Pulteney's remark twenty years later, that he would 'follow your rules of rising early, eating little, drinking less, and riding daily' (*Ibid.*, IV. 552).

[3] Cf. above, pp. 34–6.   [4] *Ibid.*, III. 60.   [5] *Ibid.*, pp. 72, 75, 86.

[6] *Ibid.*, p. 89.   [7] *Ibid.*, p. 86.   [8] *Ibid.*, p. 90.   [9] *Ibid.*, p. 139.

[10] *Ibid.*, II. 440. The younger Thomas Sheridan, in his life of Swift, mentions a butler named Robert Blakely as employed by Swift at the time of the *Drapier's Letters* (Sheridan, p. 244).

Yet Swift's ideal of servants, Saunders McGee, died in the spring of 1722. During McGee's last days, Swift wrote to Chetwode, 'I have the best servant in the world dying in the house, which quite disconcerts me. He was the first good one I have had, and I am sure will be the last. I know few greater losses in life.'[1] On a modern sensibility such words start no deep vibration, but Swift behaved himself remarkably. He bestowed a gentleman's funeral on McGee's body;[2] and in his own cathedral he put up a tablet which he intended to bear the following inscription:

> Here lieth the body of Alexander McGee, servant to Dr Swift, Dean of St Patrick's. His grateful friend and master caused this monument to be erected in memory of his discretion, fidelity and diligence in that humble station.[3]

But according to Delany, Swift was persuaded, by 'a gentleman more distinguished for vanity than widsom'[4] to omit the words 'friend and'. That the sentiment remained fixed in his breast we know from a lamentation to a man Swift trusted: 'Poor Saunders dyed on Saturday last[5] and was buryed on Easter Sunday, and in him I have lost one of my best friends as well as the best servant in the kingdom.'[6]

If Swift found himself well served, it was partly because he treated his people with consideration and paid them well. But it was also because he observed them sharply and insisted on good work. Swift's *Directions to Servants* make a monument to his acuteness. He would pay his staff board wages so they might get their own food; yet he commonly provided them with all their meals at the deanery. During his own meals he scrutinized those who were waiting at table. For example, he made it a point of cleanliness and safety that the footman should rest the back of his plate on the hollow of his hand and not under his armpit.[7] Once when Swift stayed with the Rochforts, their man Tom tucked his plate under an armpit, and Swift became so cross that

[1] Williams II. 422.   [2] *Ibid.*, V. 216.   [3] *Ibid.*, II. 422–3.
[4] Probably Dr Sheridan.
[5] 24 Mar. 1722.   [6] Williams II. 423.
[7] Davis XIII. 34–5.

he 'pulled Tom's locks the wrong way'.[1] At Quilca the fecklessness of Sheridan's easygoing servants ground Swift between
anger and laughter. Sheridan and his wife were scandalously
incompetent managers of their domestic affairs.[2] Swift complained that every one of the local people stole food. Their
barbaric manners, he said, corrupted his own servants: Robert,
Swift's valet, turned lazy and forgetful; William, the groom
(Archy's successor) became a 'pragmatical, ignorant and conceited puppy'.[3]

Swift felt responsible for his servants' spiritual health, and
took care to read prayers to the whole household every evening.
Instead of assembling them by a special signal which might
attract the notice of guests or visitors, he relied on the chiming
of the clock.[4] He went himself to nine o'clock prayers in the
cathedral every morning (when it was convenient), and often at
three in the afternoon as well.[5] If his deafness troubled him, he
would have his friends leave about ten at night and then spend
some time in private prayer. For this he used the liturgy as his
pattern; and a man who looked after him in his old age writes,
'His prayer book (which I have), being fouled with the snuff of
his fingers, shews the parts thereof he most approved of.'[6]

Good domestic economy, for Swift, depended above all upon
the care of one's money. Advancing years only strengthened his
devotion to gold and silver, although his charities kept pace.
Besides the income from his benefices—the deanship, the prebend of Dunlavin, the livings at Laracor—Swift loaned money
at interest, bought and sold land, and invested in stocks and
bonds.[7] Whatever his emotions were, Swift's deliberate remarks
about money were more subtle than they have often been represented. On the one hand he admired neither wealth nor the
wealthy. Speaking of the rich printer John Barber, he said, 'If
heaven had looked upon riches to be a valuable thing, it would
not have given them to such a scoundrel.'[8] On the other hand,

---

[1] Williams II. 181.　　[2] Davis v. 222–6.　　[3] *Ibid.*, pp. 220–1.　　[4] Delany, p. 44.
[5] Lyon, p. 76.　　[6] *Ibid.*, p. 31.
[7] Notice Gay buying East India or South Sea stock for Swift—Williams III. 460.
[8] *Ibid.*, II. 356.

he knew how hard it was to do good for others or to be virtuous oneself without an ample provision of filthy lucre. This is what he meant when he told Vanessa, 'Riches are nine parts in ten of all that is good in life, and health is the tenth.'[1]

By the time we reach Swift's fifties, we are familiar with the irony that for all his setting of 'landed men' above and against 'moneyed men', he belonged himself to the moneyed class. Though he loved gardening and encouraged his tenants to improve their land, Swift's typical investments were loans against security. The security he preferred was of course land. But when he received a great sum of money from an agent who had almost lost it, Swift's question was 'where the money may be safely put out at six pound *per cent.*'[2]

For all his economies and investments, Swift continued to give away a large fraction of his income, besides reserving the accumulated capital for a public benefaction. Even his money-lending was often charity in disguise. In 1721, when the weavers suffered their terrible distress, the dean set aside a fund out of which he made small loans, at very low interest, to needy, honest tradesmen. As the loans were repaid, money was put out to new sufferers. Mrs Brent, Swift's housekeeper, looked after the accounts; and the little interest served to repay her for her labour.[3]

So also when Swift appeared to be speculating in real estate, an examination of the documents shows that whatever he might gain for himself, he was also doing a favour for a friend. Thus he sold a property called Talbot's Castle for £223. But it had been acquired some months earlier by Esther Johnson for £65; and she had sold it to Swift for two hundred pounds. I suspect that the whole transaction was a device for putting gold in Mrs Johnson's pocket.[4]

In 1722 Swift bought back the impropriate tithes of Efferknock (a rectory that belonged to Swift's living of Laracor) from the Rector of Trim—who was then his old friend Dr Raymond. Swift paid £260 for this addition to his income.[5]

[1] *Ibid.*, p. 427.   [2] *Ibid.*, III. 74.   [3] *Ibid.*, p. 403 and n. 3.
[4] See deeds in Registry of Deeds, Dublin.
[5] See Swift's will, Davis XIII. 147–58.

But the effect was not so much to give Swift the modest stipend as to bestow it on his successors as Vicar of Laracor.[1]

In a more complicated series of transfers, Dr and Mrs Raymond borrowed money from Mrs Johnson, using some leases of property as security. Mrs Johnson then sold her interest to Swift; and eventually, after Raymond himself died, Swift and Mrs Johnson joined with Mrs Raymond to sell the leases to a fourth party. The outcome was that while Swift may have got something for himself, both Mrs Johnson and Mrs Raymond came out with surprisingly solid sums.[2]

Swift's minute economies, his fascination with moneymaking, his zeal to keep track of income and expense, all suggest a neurotic obsession, related to his obsession with dirt. Even in his own day, the dean's acquaintances regarded his outspoken attention to thrift and accumulation as eccentric. Yet he directed his obsession into the channels of benevolence and imaginative creation. The value of his money lay not in its power to aggrandize the Dean of St Patrick's but in the opportunities it gave him to ease the lives of weak, humble, dependent people. In its literary aspect the same neurosis produced the arithmetical fantasies of the Examiner, the Drapier, and Gulliver.

One sign of Swift's attitude toward wealth is what he did with it. Another is his response to the threat of losing it. He had placed an enormous sum in the hands of Captain John Pratt, Deputy Vice-Treasurer of Ireland. Pratt was Swift's old friend and financial adviser, as well as brother to Swift's crony the former Provost of Trinity College; and he was accustomed to getting large returns from the public funds that passed through his hands, by investing them shrewdly. This was a well-established, lawful method for officers of the government to enrich themselves; and Pratt invested money for other persons as well. When Lord Carteret began poking into the finances of Ireland, it quickly appeared that Pratt had been, at the least, irresponsible in his keeping of the public accounts. Incredible sums seemed to be missing, and Pratt was imprisoned.

---

[1] Landa, p. 41. [2] See deeds in Registry of Deeds, Dublin.

Swift meanwhile had gone to Quilca with Stella and Dingley, leaving Thomas Staunton and John Worrall in charge of his business affairs in Dublin and Laracor. He heard about Pratt's imprisonment and asked Staunton and Worrall to rescue what they could of the debt to himself. Since that sum came to more than a year's income—Swift estimated it as £1200 (easily enough for a dozen families to live on)—one might expect to hear sharp language from him. But he did not return to Dublin in the crisis; and in his comments to several friends, Swift sounded invariably reconciled to the prospect of the loss.

When he told Sheridan to ask Staunton and Worrall to keep up their efforts to get his money back, Swift's language was low-keyed; and he ended, 'but let it succeed or not, I hope I shall be easy.'[1] When he found, two weeks later, that he would not lose much, his first response was to boast of his equanimity:

> I have witnesses enough, that I behaved myself with sufficient temper in that matter, neither was I in raptures, to find I had saved something out of that shipwreck, by which the public would have been greater losers than I.[2]

Out of context this remark sounds sanctimonious if not homiletic. But I am ready to accept it as true. Swift had shown the same attitude in 1712, when he nearly lost four hundred pounds through the bankruptcy of his friend Stratford.[3] If he lost money on objects for his own benefit, like a horse, or a garden wall, Swift had no shame about lamenting the disaster. It was precisely because he designed his fortune for a public charity that he felt unthreatened by its loss. So he could heartily praise and congratulate Worrall for saving all but a hundred pounds of the money; he could tease him with affectionate gratitude; and he could ask him (like Horace's moneylender) how the money might safely be put out again.[4]

Swift could feel so comfortable about his supply of cash because his pleasures were cheap. He liked to rise early, and expensive vices never seduced him. He played cards only to

---

[1] Williams III. 64.   [2] *Ibid.*, p. 73.   [3] *Journal* II. 463.
[4] Williams III. 74.

oblige his friends—'I know you do not like cards,' said Vanessa.[1] *Haute cuisine* rarely delighted him. Sometimes he would dine alone, quickly, on a beef steak, with a pint of wine to 'encourage cheerfulness'.[2] Sometimes he would invite himself to the house of an obliging friend, supplying or paying for his share of the food. He spent little on clothes. Even respectable hobbies like building, or the lavish style of hospitality affected by Irish gentlemen, failed to stir Swift's blood, although he once devoted an extraordinary amount of time and cash to putting a high wall around a piece of land. Good French wine was an indulgence he required—'you may be said to water your flock with French wine,' said Lord Bathurst.[3] He took snuff and liked to have elegant snuff boxes; and he owned a large service of silver, such as would be expected of the dean of the premier cathedral of Ireland. Otherwise, Swift seems to have spent as little money as was consistent with a determination to maintain the dignity of his station. So he kept no coach until he was past seventy.[4]

Even more than social conversation and the exercise of riding and walking, Swift loved to read. Some books, like the Bible, Rabelais, or Clarendon's *History of the Rebellion*, he never stopped reading. He valued humanistic learning and clung to friends like Ford and Sheridan who possessed it.[5] In his fifties he reviewed a fair amount of classical literature, probably with Sheridan's help.[6] An intimate of his later years reports that Swift used to say his weakness in Greek 'obliged him sometimes [I should say more often than not] to cast his eye on the left side of the leaf, where the Latin translation is generally printed'.[7]

Apart from the books normally gone through at school and university we find in *Gulliver's Travels* traces of Lucian, Philostratus, Lucretius, and Dionysius of Halicarnassus; in the *Drapier's Letters* are traces of Plutarch and others. When Swift wrote to friends who affected classical culture, his allusions burgeoned: we meet Ovid, Juvenal, and Virgil in a single letter to Ford. We

---

[1] *Ibid.*, II. 428. [2] *Ibid.*, p. 308. [3] *Ibid.*, III. 454.

[4] That is, until he set one up to celebrate Walpole's fall.

[5] Cf. the number of classical allusions in Swift's letter of 13 Feb. 1724 to Ford; Williams III. 5–7.

[6] Lyon, p. 77. [7] *Ibid.*

know Swift read his old favourite Lucretius with the young Rochforts.[1] He knew Pliny and Galen well, and quoted from Euripides.[2] He re-read Herodotus in 1720.[3] We still have his notes, from this period, on Aristophanes and Suetonius,[4] and we have poems he wrote in imitation of Petronius and Callimachus.[5]

In his letters, although Swift seldom mentions particular titles, he shows his old fondness for travels, memoirs, and history.[6] So he told Vanessa that he was reading 'I don't know how many diverting books of history and travels'.[7] In this taste Swift agreed with the age. Few books were more widely read, during the early eighteenth century, than travels and geographical compilations.[8] *Gulliver's Travels* shows traces, among others, of Hakluyt's and Purchas's collections, Samuel Sturmy's *Mariner's Magazine* (1661), *Dampier's New Voyage round the World* (1697), and 'William Symson's' *New Voyage to the East-Indies* (1715).[9] Swift read Thomas Herbert's travels (1634) in 1720.[10]

The *Drapier's Letters* show a wide familiarity with political theory, from Bodin to Algernon Sidney.[11] Although Swift sometimes pretended to ignore newspapers and pamphlets dealing with public affairs, they belonged to his daily diet. Of course, he also found time for *Don Quixote* (that universal favourite),[12] as also for French belles lettres[13] and English poetry or essays, especially by his friends. One of the sharpest responses Swift

---

[1] *Poems* I. 278.   [2] See letter to Bolingbroke, 1719.
[3] Davis V. 243.   [4] See 'Swiftiana in Rylands MS.'
[5] *Poems* II. 303–4, 381–8. Of course, I pass over the poems and passages in imitation of Horace, Ovid, Virgil, Juvenal, Martial, etc., and Swift's reading of those authors or of Homer, Livy, Tacitus, Cicero, etc. For marginalia on Philostratus and Aulus Gellius, see Scott, *Memoirs*, pp. 260–1.
[6] On Philippe de Commines and Swift, see Davis V. xviii.
[7] Williams II. 430.
[8] Edward Arber, quoted by P. G. Adams in his introduction to Dampier.
[9] Ray Frantz, 'Gulliver's "Cousin Sympson"', *HLQ* I. 329–34.
[10] Davis V. 243.
[11] In the *Drapier's Letters* are references, among others, to Bodin (cf. Swift's marginalia, 1725, in Davis V. 244–7), Coke, Bacon, Hobbes, Filmer, Algernon Sidney, Locke, Molyneux.
[12] He alludes to *Don Quixote* in the sixth *Drapier's Letter* (dated 26 Oct. 1724; *Drapier*, p. 141) and in a letter to Dr Sheridan (11 Sept. 1725; Williams III. 94).
[13] E.g., Rabelais, Voiture, Cyrano de Bergerac, La Rochefoucauld, Molière, Bussy Rabutin, Anthony Hamilton. Rabelais and Cyrano are among the most important sources of *Gulliver's Travels*.

made to his reading in this period was the poem he wrote on Edward Young's *Universal Passion*.[1] But the best evidence of the compulsiveness of the reading habit is found at Quilca. When Swift ran out of new books to read there, he re-read old ones. When he ran out of old books, he called on Sheridan (in Dublin) to send down some of his pupils' work: 'Pray send me a large bundle of exercises, bad as well as good, for I want something to read.'[2]

Much of Swift's conversation dealt with literature. But when he named his pleasures in a letter to John Gay, he failed to include something so obvious as books, and only listed 'my wine, my parsons, my horses, [and] my garden'.[3] For any approach to intellectual conversation he could not stray far from the walks of the church. A doctor like Helsham, a lawyer like Lindsay, a placeman like Tickell, a cultivated gentleman like Ford might add colour to the dark gowns. But Swift's staple of social intercourse had to be clergymen.

As the dean he entertained the whole chapter of the cathedral once every quarter;[4] and at the annual feast on St Patrick's Day he was 'overloaded with his chapter but without any expense'.[5] As a private gentleman he was regularly at home to his friends on Sundays;[6] and although he would rather spend money on good wine than good food, he liked to give small dinner parties. When he could please himself—an intimate of Swift's says—'a couple of plain dressed dishes or meat, chiefly roasted, were his choice; and in drinking he rarely exceeded a pint of claret, which he sweetened in every glass either with some luscious wine or with sugar.'[7] In fine summer weather he enjoyed dining in a garden house.[8] Once when he was trying to lure Pope to Ireland, Swift offered him (among other things) 'small dinners of what you [like], and good wine ... six or eight gentlemen of sense, learning, good humour and taste'.[9]

---

[1] *Poems* II. 390–2; discussed below, pp. 772–3.
[2] Williams III. 69.   [3] *Ibid.*, II. 442.   [4] Lyon, p. 111.
[5] Williams V. 180.   [6] *Ibid.*, IV. 367.
[7] Lyon, p. 157.
[8] Williams II. 171. I suppose a machine for dining *sub dio* is a garden house.
[9] *Ibid.*, IV. 170 (8 Jul. 1733).

Swift also offered Pope more garden than the poet had at Twickenham: a deanery garden, which Swift said was as large as Pope's 'plot that fronts the Thames' (i.e., the piece of land that was divided from Pope's main property by the London road) and another only two hundred yards south of the deanery, larger than Pope's main ground 'and with more air; but without any beauty'.[1] This detached field of Swift's, which compensated him for having so little time among the willows and cherries at Laracor, lay near St Kevin's Port. He acquired it around 1722 and named it Naboth's Vineyard. 'I am as busy in my little spot of a town garden', he told a friend, 'as ever I was in the grand monde.'[2] The Vineyard occupied about three acres.[3] Characteristically, Swift arranged for it to become a perquisite of his successors as dean.[4] He planted elms,[5] fruit trees, and grape vines; made a paddock and laid out walks. The fruit he grew certainly included apples, peaches, nectarines, pears, and grapes. I suppose he also had cherries, as at Laracor, and I doubt that he ever stopped improving the place. 'I know nothing I should more desire', he said, 'than some spot upon which I could spend the rest of my life in improving.'[6] He prided himself on his connoisseurship in fruit and liked to show off the produce of Naboth's Vineyard. Celebrating his apples, he said, 'I pretend to have the finest paradise stocks of their age in Ireland.'[7]

Swift could grow soft or 'wall' fruit (like pears) in the Irish climate because he determined in 1724 to surround the Vineyard with the best wall in Ireland.[8] Discovering that he could not trust a groom to exercise the horses properly, he decided to supply them with a secure paddock.[9] So he hired masons to build a stone wall eight or nine feet high[10] all around the field! It was an immense project that fixed Swift in Dublin through the spring and summer, keeping him from the pleasure of his warm-

---

[1] *Ibid.*   [2] *Ibid.*, II. 449; winter of 1722–3.   [3] Davis XIII. 156.
[4] *Ibid.*   [5] Williams II. 436.   [6] *Ibid.*, III. 199.
[7] *Ibid.*, 'Paradise stocks' are for dwarfing apple trees.
[8] Pilkington I. 77–9.   [9] Williams III. 373; cf. IV. 154.
[10] Davis XIII. 156.

weather rambles.[1] Besides the enormous expense, he involved himself with careless workmen whom he watched like a drill sergeant. 'I am over head and ears in mortar', he said, 'and with a number of the greatest rogues in Ireland, which is a proud word.'[2] Swift would examine the rising courses for rotten stones or poor workmanship; and where he found either, he would have the servants pull down the offending sections.[3] It cost at last nearly six hundred pounds—well over half his year's income.[4] But the delight that gardening (and fruit) gave him, and the health of his horses, made it worth his while.

[1] Williams III. 14–15, 43.
[2] I.e., a boast, there being so many rogues in Ireland (*ibid.*, p. 21; 14 Jul. 1724).
[3] *Ibid.*, p. 383.   [4] *Ibid.*, IV. 154.

Chapter Fifteen

EASIEST FRIENDS

S wift understood the injunction, 'He that hath friends must show himself friendly.' For someone traditionally identified with misanthropy, he kept a startling variety of loyal intimates. If the dean plumed himself on his familiarity with magnates like Carteret, he never scrupled to pass his leisure hours with humbler companions, so long as they were intelligent, polite, honest, and in some way serviceable. The nearest and most obliging people he saw were of course parsons, especially those connected with the cathedral; for he dealt with them constantly in the routines of his work, and they had reason to think he might speed their careers. Though Swift could be playful and commanding by turns, he seldom expected too much of those he liked; and he repaid their good nature with hospitality, wit, and strenuous efforts to win them preferment.

Swift trusted nobody more than John Worrall, who was master of the choirs of both St Patrick's and Christ Church cathedrals. In every kind of important or personal responsibility, Worrall served him: the affairs of the chapter, his own private finances, Stella's health (Mrs Worrall sometimes looked after her), the printing of the *Drapier's Letters*. Worrall was about Swift's age[1] and had been at Trinity College with him. There he took the B.A. and B.D. degrees but no doctorate. Long before Swift, he had come into the cathedral chapter, being made Dean's Vicar, or director of music, in 1695; and he was probably responsible for the excellence of the organ and the choir in St Patrick's.

[1] He was born around 1666, was admitted to Trinity College, Dublin, in 1684, took the B.A. degree 1689; M.A. 1692; B.D. 1702. He died in 1751; there was an obituary in the *London Magazine*, vol. 20, under the date of 13 July.

From the clues that remain, I think Swift always felt well disposed toward Worrall but that the real intimacy grew up several years after Swift became dean. The choirmaster was a kind of inheritance from the earlier dean, Stearne, who, on his own elevation, asked Swift to help the self-effacing vicar to rise. 'I am very glad it lies in my way to do any service to Mr Worrall,' Swift replied, 'and that his merits and my inclination agree so well.'[1] Writing to Worrall soon after, about an issue dividing the vicars choral from their new dean, Swift addressed him as 'Sir' and sounded formal.[2] Eight years later, Swift sent him an intimate, chatty letter, saluting him as 'Dear Jack' and teasing him affectionately.[3]

Worrall had lost his parents early and was then sent to the Blue Coats School. So he owned no rich or well-placed relations to promote his interests. But he possessed so much discretion and conscience that he won the backing of his superiors. Delany described him as 'a man of sense, and a great deal of humour'.[4] We know that he did not drink much and loved to walk.[5]

Though Worrall was married, he had no children. His wife, Mary, was vivacious and had the virtues Swift prized in a woman: cheerfulness, cleanliness, and great benevolence. Delany says she was 'remarkably cleanly, and elegant in her person, in her house, and at her table, where she entertained her friends with singular cheerfulness, hospitality, and good humour'.[6]

As master of the cathedral music, Worrall would have had business with Swift whenever the dean came to St Patrick's, especially a dean so eager as Swift was to improve the musical service. He would walk after Swift. The two would stroll together. The strolls ended with dinner (then of course a midday meal) either at the Worralls' or in the deanery.

---

[1] Williams I. 418.
[2] *Ibid.*, p. 247. Perhaps the formal tone was wanted because the letter would be read to the offenders.
[3] *Ibid.*, p. 402.   [4] Delany, p. 91.   [5] Williams III. 90.
[6] Delany, p. 91. Her character and hospitality may have been essential to Swift's friendship with Worrall, which seems to have dwindled after her death.

But as the dean was a single man, the former happened more frequently: and this intercourse at last ended in the dean's dining with them, as often as he pleased, at a certain rate; and inviting as many friends as he pleased, upon the same terms.[1]

When Captain Pratt almost lost the whole of Swift's savings entrusted to him, it was, we have seen, chiefly Worrall who saw to rescuing the money; and Swift told him, 'I know not anybody, except yourself, who would have been at so much trouble to assist me.'[2]

If Worrall represents middle-aged humility, James Stopford stands for youthful promise—the well-endowed filial character that supplied an element of hopefulness to Swift's view of the future. Stopford was Swift's junior by thirty years. He belonged to a prominent family and had a modest fortune. Knightley Chetwode's wife was his half-sister; the Earl of Courtown was his cousin; and Stopford eventually married (in 1727) the Earl's own sister. At Trinity College, Stopford had been a first-rate student and acquired enough classical learning to be elected a fellow. But he remained a modest, steady young man who avoided controversy and loved to travel on the continent.

By the time of the excitement over Wood's coins, I suppose that aspiring young parsons had stopped looking for much in the way of solid benefit from patrons in the English interest, and that Swift's fame and his active good will made up for the blemishes on his political reputation. Men like Stopford were no longer afraid to appear as his friends. At the same time, Swift's isolation, his reverence for classical erudition, and the high value he set on modesty in young men would have made Stopford magnetically attractive to him.

In letters, Swift saluted Stopford as 'Dear Jim', a form he rarely used—suggesting avuncular intimacy and affection. He exposed some of his most private emotions to Stopford, showed the deepest concern for his welfare, and once sounded a note of panic when he thought his young friend was neglecting his health: the College porter had told Swift that Stopford

[1] *Ibid.*, p. 92.   [2] Williams III. 74.

was suffering from 'an ague' and had no one to take care of him. 'For God sake', Swift wrote to him, 'have some understanding body about you and do not rely on a College bedmaker.'[1] When the dean used to describe Stopford or recommend him, the praise had few limits. After Stopford came home from his first round of foreign touring (in the summer of 1724), Swift said, 'He is in all regards the most valuable young man of this kingdom.'[2]

One trip around Europe only made Stopford yearn for another; and in 1725 he arranged with a very rich, very foolish youth to go abroad as his governor, on terms that would pay off the debts Stopford had already accumulated through travel.[3] An amusing duel followed between Stopford's diffidence and the dean's patronage. Swift contrived to have Stopford introduced to Lord Carteret by way of his excellency's secretary. But Stopford never followed up the opening, and left his patron to explain the anticlimax to the willing go-between.[4] Swift also wrote a beautiful letter to Pope, celebrating the protégé's merits and asking Pope not only to entertain him at Twickenham but also to introduce him to Arbuthnot, Gay, 'and others whom you will think fit'.[5] Instead of presenting the letter early in his London visit and awaiting the blessings Swift intended, Stopford only delivered it to Pope on the verge of departing for France, too late for any favours. I doubt that the poet felt hurt by the disappointment, but he teased Swift drily: 'Perhaps it is with poets as with prophets, they are so much better liked in another country than their own, that your gentleman, upon arriving in England, lost his curiosity concerning me.'[6] Swift was left to stammer out an apology for his friend's bashfulness— a trait in which, he said, Stopford was 'excessive to a fault'—and also to observe flatteringly, 'He treated you just as he did Lord Carteret.'[7]

For common, easy entertainment Swift could rely on a cluster

---

[1] *Ibid.*, p. 56. [2] *Ibid.*, p. 22. [3] *Ibid.*, p. 61.
[4] *Ibid.*, p. 102. I take the clever reasoning in the dean's letter to Tickell, that Stopford 'desires the honor' and 'foresees', etc. (*ibid.*, p. 77) to be an invention of Swift's.
[5] *Ibid.*, p. 78. [6] *Ibid.*, p. 95. [7] *Ibid.*, p. 102.

of landed families distinctly superior to Worrall but not quite so well connected as Stopford. These were the Rochforts, Grattans, and Jacksons. Gaulstown House, the family seat of the Rochforts, lay in Westmeath, near Trim; and although the former Lord Chief Baron had amassed a great fortune and dispensed lavish hospitality, it was easier for Swift to visit his second son John—a favourite of the dean—who took over the estate that his father had at New Park, about six miles north of Dublin. It was to John's young bride that Swift addressed his 'Letter to a Very Young Lady on Her Marriage' (1723). Adjoining the village of New Park was the parish of Finglas, where successive vicars were friends of Swift—from Dillon Ashe and Thomas Parnell to James Stopford.

Still easier for Swift to visit were the Grattans, whose seat on the north side of Dublin Bay was only five miles from town. While Chief Baron Rochfort's father had been an army officer, and his own lucrative career had been in the law, the Grattans (good friends of the Rochforts) were mainly parsons, and two of them belonged to Swift's chapter. Belcamp, the Grattans' house, lay in the parish next to Santry, where their cousins Dan and John Jackson lived. The Jackson brothers had been, in turn, vicars of Santry, like their father; and Swift found them to be thoroughly agreeable companions.

But the family that meant the most to him was the Grattans. The father, now dead, had been chaplain to the first Duke of Ormonde and Prebendary of Howth in the chapter of St Patrick's. The seven sons all distinguished themselves, the eldest (Henry) being the ancestor of the great patriot. James was one of the leading physicians of Dublin. Richard, a merchant, became Lord Mayor. The youngest, Charles, was master of Portora School, a royal foundation in the north. Three were priests, and of these, two were favourites of Swift: Robert, the fourth son, and John, the fifth. Both were eventually among the executors of Swift's will.

The dean worked hard to win preferment for the Grattans; and in a letter to a Lord Lieutenant he once drew a loving portrait of the tribe. The Grattans, he said, were the 'governors of all Ireland' in the absence of the viceroy, 'and your vice-gerents when you are here':

> They consist of an alderman whom you are to find Lord Mayor at Michaelmas next; of a doctor kills or cures half the city, of two parsons my subjects as prebendaries, who rule the other half, and of a vagrant brother who governs the north. They are all brethren, and your army of twelve thousand soldiers are not able to stand against them.[1]

Belcamp, the family seat, being close to Howth, was quick and pleasant to ride to by a route Swift liked, especially since he might shorten it by taking a ferry after sending his men around with the horses. Swift could meet the Jacksons there or at Gaulstown, where he spent the summer of 1721.[2]

We know reasonably well how he entertained himself during this Gaulstown summer and can guess from those pastimes what in general he liked to do on his many country visits. In the early part of June 1721 Swift was ill with an ague, 'as miserable as a man can possibly be' with sweating and vomits and quinine.[3] Toward the end of the month he set off for the Rochforts'. After an uncomfortable journey in a primitive stagecoach, Swift settled down with the senior Rochfort, his sons George and John, and Daniel Jackson. Quickly he involved himself in schemes of planting and draining, labouring alongside the workmen.[4] The weather was so bad that he did not take several side trips he had planned.[5] But he exercised himself daily out of doors. 'I row after health like a waterman, and ride after it like a post boy,' he told Archbishop King.[6] It is obvious that Swift's visit pleased his host, for when he decided to return home, he had to go secretly, only warning Jackson, whose company he particularly enjoyed. But Swift felt out of touch with the younger people,

> who I confess had reason enough to be weary of a man who entered into none of their tastes, nor pleasures, nor fancies, nor opinions, nor talk.[7]

---

[1] 15 Apr. 1735, to the Duke of Dorset.
[2] He arrived at the end of June, certainly after 19 June; and he left about 3 Oct. See Williams II. 391, 392, 401, 402, 404, 405–9.
[3] *Ibid.*, p. 390.   [4] *Ibid.*, p. 393.   [5] *Ibid.*, p. 401.
[6] *Ibid.*, p. 406.   [7] *Ibid.*, p. 408.

From Swift's poem 'The Journal' we learn what his own tastes and pleasures were. On a typical day at Gaulstown, the dean rose at seven and woke up the young Rochforts and Jackson. Before breakfast he read Lucretius for an hour with George and John. After breakfast (which began at ten) Swift and the young Rochforts rowed. Dinner followed at two; then some wine and backgammon. From four until sundown, there was more rowing. Then came prayers, more backgammon, and an hour of drink and talk before bedtime.[1]

Such occasions also lent themselves to literary diversions. Besides commemorating house parties with poems like 'The Journal', Swift liked to trade verse epistles and riddles with his friends. Their variety is as striking as their ingenuity. Some are easy to recognize as Swift's by their style or subject. The mock-conceits of an octosyllabic invitation to Sheridan remind us that Swift wrote it.[2] Verses on a privy, or the following ones on the backside reveal their author in the way he plays off elegant language and smooth meters against coarse themes:

> My *words* are few, but spoke with *sense*:
> And yet my *speaking* gives offence:
> Or, if to *whisper* I presume,
> The company will fly the room.
> By all the world I am oppress't
> And my *oppression* gives them *rest*.[3]

So also those from a louse to her host:

> Ah, Strephon, how can you despise
> Her, who, without thy pity, dies?
> To Strephon I have still been true,
> And of as noble blood as you;
> Fair issue of the genial bed,
> A virgin in thy bosom bred;
> Embrac'd thee closer than a wife;
> When thee I leave, I leave my life.[4]

But few readers would connect Swift with the charming lines on the vowels, or these on snow:

[1] *Poems* I. 276–83. [2] *Ibid.*, III. 1020–2.
[3] *Ibid.*, pp. 917–18, ll. 5–10; for the privy, see *ibid.*, pp. 921–4.
[4] *Ibid.*, pp. 924–5, ll. 1–8.

From heav'n I fall, though from earth I begin,
No lady alive can shew such a skin.
I am bright as an angel, and light as a feather,
But heavy and dark, when you squeeze me together.[1]

The mixture of fun with eloquence is not only Swiftian but Irish;
and it seems more than a coincidence that the names attached to
the *jeux d'esprit* of Belcamp and Gaulstown also belong to works
like *Gulliver's Travels*, *The Rivals*, and the speeches of Henry
Grattan.

[1] *Ibid.*, pp. 928–9, ll. 1–4.

Chapter Sixteen

THE CHURCH

I. M'CARTHY'S BRIEF

Swift mixed so freely with younger clerics because it was easy and convenient for him to do so. They were near at hand and adaptable. But his instinctive sympathy with the underdog also led him to promote their interests as a class. Swift possessed more friends among the bishops than he liked to admit. Yet in issues of church and state he thought of himself as working for the lower clergy—young or old—against their overseers.

The case of Charles M'Carthy shows how tender the dean felt about the rights of parsons. In August 1723 M'Carthy's house in College Green was burned. Some people believed that he himself had set the fire in order to make capital of it.[1] The advantage would have been realized by means of what was called a 'church brief', a form of benevolence no longer known.

For centuries a common practice in the Established Church (as in the Roman Catholic Church earlier) had been to single out specially worthy objects of charity in 'briefs'—or letters patent by the Crown—printed up for wide distribution and instructing the clergy to recommend the objects from their pulpit. The device had often been abused; and we hear Pepys complaining (in June 1661) that he would give no more to such appeals.

When the need seemed extraordinary, a 'walking brief' might be issued. And this, we are told, brought in the most money; for under its terms 'the church wardens in the country and the churchwardens and beadles (in the city), with their gold-laced

---

[1] Davis v. 88, n.

hats, gold-headed canes, and all the paraphernalia of their office, went round and "teased" the inhabitants out of their money.'[1] The fees charged by persons authorized to produce, print, stamp, and distribute briefs were absurdly high: 'for an ordinary fire or for the rebuilding of a church the net profit was but little, and indeed sometimes the collection resulted in a loss.'[2] But the 'undertaking' of briefs became a trade, and 'undertakers' would therefore encourage victims of disaster to petition for one.[3]

The loss of a house by fire was a common reason for securing the privilege; and M'Carthy evidently received a 'walking' brief through the good offices of somebody on correct terms with the Lord Chancellor.[4] So a missive went out to the Archbishop of Dublin, instructing him to recommend M'Carthy's case to the clergy of the diocese, who were in turn to transmit the appeal from their pulpits on the first Sunday or other opportunity after receiving the notice.

For years Archbishop King had detested such procedures. In 1720 he complained to Bishop Nicolson about a peremptory order concerning some houses burned in Castle Dermot: 'We have had three or four such briefs [sc.] before, and I would not suffer my clergy to obey them.'[5] When one of the Lords Justices wrote to him about the case, the archbishop replied, summarizing the absurd requirements laid down by the brief and commenting, 'We are slaves enough already; but to subject ourselves to such commands, which we conceive we are no ways obliged to obey, would make us much more so; and we know not where it may end.'[6]

Both Swift and the archbishop must have considered the M'Carthy affair a gross imposition by an irresponsible government upon the limited energies of underpaid and oppressed parsons. Swift decided to attack the whole institution of fund-

[1] Wyndham Anstis Bewes, *Church Briefs* (London, 1896), p. 1.
[2] *Ibid.*, p. 34.   [3] *Ibid.*, p. 39.
[4] The sufferer petitioned the King for a brief; but from the time of the Restoration briefs were relegated to the discretion of the Lord Chancellor or the Lord Keeper.
[5] 23 May 1720, in Mant II. 360.
[6] 26 May 1720, *ibid.*, p. 361.

raising briefs by exposing the absurdities of M'Carthy's case. The respectful language he employed toward the archbishop in his comments on the affair, and his remark that the archbishop had 'desired us to consider of the said brief, and give our opinions thereof' suggest collusion between them.[1] I suspect that King gave Swift a copy of the order he himself had once delivered on the subject to his clergy. Certainly Swift addressed to the archbishop the paper which he drew up on M'Carthy's case, entitled 'The Humble Representation of the Clergy of the City of Dublin'.[2] This was never published in Swift's lifetime; so I presume the manuscript was to be passed around by his grace.

Not only was M'Carthy's a 'walking brief'. It also used the style of imperious instructions resented by Archbishop King— asking the whole body of the clergy to contribute money of their own, and telling ministers of parishes to be peculiarly quick and systematic in making and delivering their collections. Swift's 'representation' includes a warning about the number of briefs that must follow if this one should succeed.[3]

Although he voices resentment on behalf of the entire Church of Ireland, Swift refers very lightly to the involvement of bishops, and reserves the weight of his sarcasm for the defence of parsons. Here his implications are serious, though the expressions are witty. The drift of the argument is that the brief-makers were singling out priests to bear arbitrary and unreasonable burdens through decisions in which they played no part, for purposes that did not relate to their proper duties, and under obligations weighing at least as heavily on the rest of mankind as on themselves.

The most entertaining objection he raises takes the form of an arithmetical fantasy. Because, according to the brief, the ministers were to 'persuade and exhort' their parishioners on the first Sunday 'or opportunity' after receiving the brief, Swift makes believe that the clergy were expected to preach a sermon on the subject, and to do so in private homes if such opportunities came sooner than a Sunday in church!

[1] Davis v. 87.　[2] *Ibid.*, pp. 87–92.　[3] *Ibid.*, pp. 91–2.

Neither is it possible for the strongest constitution among us to obey this command (which includes no less than a whole sermon) upon any other opportunity than when our people are met together in the church; and to perform this work in every house where the parishes are very populous, consisting sometimes here in town of 900 or 1000 houses, would take up the space of a year, although we should preach in two families every day; and almost as much time in the country, where the parishes are of large extent, the roads bad, and the people too poor to receive us, and give charity at once.[1]

But the genuine sense of outrage that underpins the document emerges when Swift compares the position of the clergy with that of other professions, and the language of the Irish brief with that of English briefs. Thus he points out that in England, under the law, ministers are required to do no more than barely to read the briefs in their churches; and he hopes the clergy of Ireland will not 'be put to greater hardships in this case than their brethren in England'.[2] More bitterly, he delivers the following remark, which conveys the same sense of indignation that inspired M. B. Drapier:

We observe in the said brief, that the Provost and fellows of the university, judges, officers of the courts, and professors of laws common and civil, are neither willed, required, nor commanded to make their contributions; but that so good a work is only recommended to them. Whereas we conceive, that all his majesty's subjects are equally obliged, with or without his majesty's commands, to promote works of charity according to their power; and that the clergy, in their ecclesiastical capacity, are only liable to such commands as the rubric, or any other law shall enjoin, being born to the same privileges of freedom with the rest of his majesty's subjects.[3]

This is much like the principle he had laid down a few months earlier, when he rejected the common argument that landlords who wished to improve agriculture would be helped by a reduction in certain tithes. Swift had said he could not see why, if the 'industrious farmer' deserved a reward, it should be at the expense of the clergy alone.[4]

I assume that Swift was acting in collusion with Archbishop

[1] *Ibid.*, p. 88. [2] *Ibid.*, p. 91. [3] *Ibid.*, p. 91.
[4] *Some Arguments against Enlarging the Power of the Bishops*, in *ibid.*, IX. 59.

King, because during the months that followed the writing of the *Representation*, King tried to have other bishops back him in a petition against the issuing of church briefs. Downes, the new Bishop of Meath, wrote to his much-loved friend Bishop Nicolson,

> I wish you were in town, that you might join with some of your brethren in advising the Archbishop of Dublin about a petition, or memorial, which his grace is disposed to present to the government against his majesty's letters patent for a brief; in which, he says, very arbitrary impositions are laid upon the bishops and the clergy.[1]

Although the English bloc on the episcopal bench remained cool to the plan, the archbishop characteristically held to it, as we know from a feline comment made by the English-born Bishop Godwin of Kilmore when King went to England in the spring of 1726:

> My Lord Archbishop of Dublin is going to the Bath.... He has forbidden his clergy to read briefs in the city and the churchwardens to gather them and will not suffer anything to be read in the church but by his direction. Which the lawyers say is an open denial of the King's supremacy.[2]

If his grace was resisting a legalistic view of the royal prerogative, it was from the same spirit that informed M. B. Drapier. We must not suppose that political partisanship or blinkered nationalism drove them on. They saw themselves as standing against tyranny and as improving the condition of the whole people of Ireland.

II. THE IRISH INTEREST

So also when Swift promoted the careers of clergymen born and educated in Ireland, he hardly meant to narrow his sympathies. What might look like a zeal to find jobs for Tories and protégés was more nearly an effort to entrench the healthiest stock in the

---

[1] 13 Jun. 1724, in Nicolson, *Letters* II. 577. Cf. Nicolson's own report of Archbishop King's attitude, in his letter of 9 Jun. 1720 to Wake.

[2] To Archbishop Wake, 31 Mar. 1726, in Wake Letters XIV, no. 333.

livings that needed them. Swift did not simply hope to keep the church 'Irish'; he wished to keep it strong and serviceable to the people. The competent parsons normally came from the families of the native gentry. These landed proprietors directed the most important industry, viz., agriculture; and they kept their political strength—under the Test Act and the Penal Laws—as members of the Established Church. Not only did their cadets often chose the priesthood as a vocation; but the Church of Ireland also depended on the gentry for its tithes and its privileges.

There is a revealing letter from Swift to Robert Cope, showing concentrated energy on behalf of a young client of Cope's named Barclay. Here Swift involves Judge Nutley, Sir William Fownes (Cope's father-in-law), Primate Lindsay, the Primate's chaplain, and others in a scheme to get Barclay a living in the county of Armagh. All the people named are Tories if not Jacobites; and the dean might seem to be doing a job for a comrade at arms.[1]

But we know Swift deeply admired Cope and considered him an excellent landlord. He also admired Mrs Cope as a model gentlewoman and Fownes as a public-spirited statesman. By advancing a man they approved of, Swift would be helping not the Tories but the church and country together. In the wake of the Annesley Case and the Declaratory Act the efficiency of the British government in filling Irish offices with English job-hunters aroused such resentment that the division between Tory and Whig soon meant less than the division between Irish and English interests. Swift only put the truth hyperbolically when he said, 'The Whigs are grown such disaffected people that I dare not converse with them.'[2] Among clergymen the effect was peculiarly intense. Each lord lieutenant brought a train of chaplains to be placed in superior livings. Each bishop who came over trailed a cloud of sons and relations wanting careers in the Church of Ireland.

As a satirist and political journalist Swift gave his most luminous energy to the exposing of cracks that other men papered

[1] Williams II. 348–9.
[2] 22 Mar. 1722; *ibid.*, p. 422.

over. But as a moralist and public benefactor he tried to heal dangerous divisions between classes that ought to work together. So he often vilified Irish squires for undermining the church to satisfy their avarice. But he also tried to build up the mutual dependence of priests and gentry. Throughout Christian history, the two classes have rarely agreed as to the proportion of income from land that each ought to possess. In Ireland, by the reign of George I, it was instinct for landlords to assume that rents would rise if tithes declined; and they encouraged their tenants to fret about the 'sacred tenth'. Swift spoke for the common wisdom of parsons when he observed that to eliminate tithes would not help the tenant but would merely give the landlord a higher income.

He could not persuade the landlords that they would be richer if they faithfully paid their tithes. But he could insist that the parson performed indispensable services very cheaply, and that the life of the gentry would be bleak without the environment of a strong church. Especially after 1720 he tried to bring the two sides together for their common good. The more livings were filled with immigrants, the less sympathy the Irish landlords—including those who sat in Parliament—would feel with the needs of the Anglican establishment. Consequently, as the British government pursued the implications of the Declaratory Act and shipped strangers over to absorb bishoprics and deaneries, several old splits deepened. The lower clergy remained more in touch with the Tory remnant; they felt less tolerant of Dissent; and they grew more hostile to the English interest. The 'foreign' bishops felt isolated; they and their clients imported still more connections so as to enlarge the party of the right-minded; and as these newcomers tended to be men who could not find advancement in England, they rarely belonged to the highest grade of churchmen.

Swift and Archbishop King not only saw alike. The archbishop probably gave the dean some of the arguments he used to buttress their position. In 1720 Bishop Godwin of Kilmore told Archbishop Wake, 'The Archbishop [*sc.* of Dublin] and the Dean [*sc.* of St Patrick's] are now joined in great amity. But how they will do to stop this inundation of English bishops I know not.'[1] When Swift recommended several clergymen to Lord Carteret as deserving promotion, he did not limit the list to his own tribe but included the younger Edward Synge, who was far from intimate with him.[2] Later, Swift also prepared a dignified declaration of broad, non-partisan principles that had their effect on his lordship. Hardly a gentleman in the nation, Swift said, had not a 'near alliance' with some of the clergy—

> and most of them who have sons, usually breed one to the church; although they have been of late years much discouraged and discontented, by seeing strangers to the country almost perpetually taken into the greatest ecclesiastical preferments, and too often, under governors very different from your excellency, the choice of persons was not be accounted for either to prudence or justice.
>
> The misfortune of having bishops perpetually from England, as it must needs quench the spirit of emulation among us to excel in learning and the study of divinity, so it produces another great discouragement, that those prelates usually draw after them colonies of sons, nephews, cousins, or old college-companions, to whom they bestow the best preferments in their gift; and thus the young men sent into the church from the university here, have no better prospect than to be curates, or small country-vicars for life.[3]

Of course the flow in the other direction ran pitifully thin, for not only did English bishoprics almost never fall to priests of the Church of Ireland; but even the small livings of England were practically all reserved for natives. Swift did not say this, I suppose, because it was so patent and elementary.

Neither did he expatiate on the irony which always strikes his modern admirers and which the immigrant clergy did not overlook, viz., that Swift's own generation in the Church of Ireland would not have existed if their fathers had never done precisely what the sons objected to. It is sourly amusing to watch the process at work with the newcomers as well; for as they rooted themselves in Irish soil, they too could be dismayed to find the great men in Westminster subjecting them to the high-

---

[1] 28 Dec. 1720; in Wake Letters. [2] Landa, pp. 89, 180.
[3] 3 Jun. 1725; in Williams III. 70.

handedness that the Irish-born loathed. Thus we meet Archbishop Boulter himself fretting because a new list of Irish Privy
Councillors was made up without his being consulted; upon
which he complained, in terms his enemies might have used,
that his own power must dwindle 'if it appears that things of the
greatest consequence are fixed on the other side of the water
without our privity'.[1]

III. LARACOR AND DUBLIN

If Swift believed that for an established church, natives worked
better than foreigners, he had a chance to exemplify the principle in his own conduct. At Laracor, as a country vicar, he
belonged himself to the lower clergy. Rarely in residence, he
should above all have supplied the living with a good curate.
Fortunately, we know he took care to do so and to pay the man
well.[2] In 1722 he chose Stafford Lightburne, five years his senior
and a native of Trim.[3] Lightburne had taken the B.A. degree at
Trinity College in 1684 and married a daughter of Swift's cousin
Willoughby. He was in line for a substantial estate unluckily tied
up in litigation.[4] When Swift's earlier curate Warburton left in
1717, Lightburne applied for the post. But Swift had other plans
then and thought his letter foolish.[5] Yet Swift already intended
to help him; and five years later, when a new curate was again
wanted, he employed Lightburne, who stayed for eleven years.[6]
Swift also persuaded the Duke of Grafton, as Lord Lieutenant,
to do something for Lightburne even against the opposition of
Archbishop King.[7]

A good opinion of Lightburne is evident in the care Swift
devoted to the curate's legal miseries. 'He has had a long suit
about the fortune,' Swift told Ford, 'and has been used like a

---

[1] 19 May 1726, to Newcastle; Boulter I. 73 (Dublin, pp. 59–60).
[2] Landa, pp. 38–9; cf. above, II. 94–7.
[3] I don't know who was Swift's curate 1717–22.   [4] Williams II. 445.
[5] 3 Feb. 1717; *ibid.*, p. 254.
[6] In May 1721 Swift told Thomas Wallis he was getting him a 'companion to cure
your spleen', by which I think he meant a new curate at Laracor (*ibid.*, p. 388).
[7] *Ibid.*, pp. 444–5.

dog: I was referee for him, but by some accidents the reference would not stand.'[1] Swift rallied members of the English House of Lords to Lightburne's support in the final appeal, and told him, when he won, 'I always believed you had justice on your side.'[2]

During these years Swift was also at pains to keep up the little house and the grounds at Laracor. For improvements he consulted a friendly and hospitable neighbour, Thomas Wallis, vicar of Athboy, which lies seven or eight miles beyond Laracor. Wallis was prepared to supervise projects like the building of a walk down to Swift's modest canal, and getting the place ready for spring.[3] We may judge the quality of Swift's attention from the report of a 1723 visitation, praising the condition of the church, the glebe, and the small vicarage.[4]

As a country vicar Swift might have been faulted for his unpleasant relations with the Bishop of Meath. While Evans filled the post, it was a question whether Swift went out of his way to exasperate a British Whig, or vented his anger on behalf of the oppressed parsons of the diocese. But when Henry Downes succeeded Evans, one saw that the old quarrel had been a collision of personalities, and that if anybody was subject to paranoid nationalism, it was not Swift.[5]

Although Downes was an Englishman, not only did Swift not quarrel with him; Swift courted him. A few weeks after becoming the Bishop of Meath, Downes set out to hold his first triennial visitation at Trim. As vicar of Laracor, Swift attended both the visitation and the synod that followed next day. On each occasion he treated Downes with conspicuous courtesy. On the third day he visited the episcopal residence with the new bishop and helped him plan a house and gardens. He offered as well to lend his small house at Laracor to the bishop. Touched by so much good will, Downes wrote to Nicolson,

> I spent all last week in or near Trim. On Wednesday I held my visitation, and on Thursday a synod there; and, through the un-

[1] *Ibid.*, III. 45.   [2] *Ibid.*, p. 59.   [3] *Ibid.*, II. 409, 449–50.
[4] Landa, p. 39; cf. above, II. 94.   [5] Cf. above, p. 227.

expected goodness of the Dean of St Patrick's, was made perfectly easy on both days, as if he had a mind to atone (by his uncommon civilities to me) for the uncommon trouble he had given to my predecessor. The dean went with me on Friday to visit Ardbracken, and to lay out the ground for my new house and gardens; but we returned *re infectâ*, not having allowed time for so necessary a work.[1]

I suppose the dean did not simply admire the bishop so much that he wished to make him happy in a new home. Such affability, like Swift's overtures to Carteret, suited his policy of coming to terms with individual members of the ruling party regardless of his distaste for their principles, and of co-operating with them to promote any action that would benefit the country. In a quiet way Swift was practising the doctrine he overstated to Sheridan: 'Frequent those on the right side, friends to the present powers.'[2]

If we reverse the scene and watch Swift as, in effect, one of the upper clergy, the implications change slightly. A dean of St Patrick's had a dignity and privileges comparable to those of many bishops;[3] and Swift could (in the long run) dominate the economy and clergy of the cathedral almost as a strong bishop might manage the affairs of a see. In everything we learn about the middle years of Swift's deanship, he keeps up the attention to the cathedral's welfare that he displayed at the start. If one ignored his willingness, year after year, to spend as much as two of the four seasons outside Dublin, one might make him sound too good to be true.

But Swift's style as dean was of course patriarchal; and he hardly encouraged in the prebendaries the sort of independence he valued in himself. 'It is an infallible maxim that not one thing is done here without the dean's consent,' Swift declared in 1721.[4] Yet we know that in a weakened form there continued to be the resistance to his leadership that had bothered him in the early years; and if Archbishop King joined with Swift in eco-

---

[1] Nicolson II. 572, 574; the Wednesday was 29 May. Sheridan wrote a jocular poem on Swift's kindness to Downes; see *Poems* III. 1044–5.
[2] 11 Sept. 1725; Williams III. 95.
[3] Cf. Swift's description of his responsibilities in a letter to Bishop Evans; *ibid.*, II. 387.
[4] *Ibid.*, p. 377.

nomic and ecclesiastic policy, he did not therefore relax his efforts to control the membership or the decisions of the chapter.

We must also go back to Delany's memories of Swift's strictness about the finances and the fabric of the cathedral. The dean, said Delany, would not allow a shilling of the endowed revenues to go to anything but the rightful purpose narrowly defined—not excepting unauthorized charity. Whenever he had the chance to increase the value of the deanship to his successors, even at the expense of his own income, Swift 'never failed' to make the sacrifice.[1] As for the repair and improvement of the building, Delany thought more money was devoted to its 'support, preservation and ornament' under Swift than under any earlier dean.[2] Out of doors we know he beautified the churchyard (and the deanery garden) with plantations of elms, even shifting tombstones, and angering parishioners, to make room for them.[3]

No feature of Swift's care for the cathedral is more touching than his preoccupation with the music. 'I understand music like a Muscovite,' he said; but because the choir had deteriorated under his predecessors, he strove to build it up. 'If you had recommended a person for a church living in my gift,' he said to an acquaintance who told him about a singer, 'I would be less curious; because an indifferent parson may do well enough, if he be honest, but singers like their brother poets must be very good, or they are good for nothing.'[4]

Happily, St Patrick's owned a superb, if hot-tempered, organist in Daniel Roseingrave, who held the joint appointment at Christ Church—for the two cathedrals pooled their musicians. Roseingrave had started in London as one of the children of the Chapel Royal, and was said to have studied under Blow and Purcell. After serving as organist of three English cathedrals in succession, he came in 1698 to Dublin, where he remained till his death (1727). An excellent performer and conductor, Roseingrave was also a prolific composer of church music, praised by

---

[1] Delany, p. 207. [2] *Ibid.*, pp. 200–1. [3] Williams II. 412, 436.
[4] 9 Feb. 1720, to Edward Harley; *ibid.*, p. 339. The reference to indifferent poets is from Horace, *Ars poet.* 372.

Dr Burney; and Swift prudently relied on his judgment in the selection of singers. A son, Ralph, trained at home, became a vicar-choral of St Patrick's in 1719 and probably did duty for his father from that time. Ralph too was a first-class musician and a composer, though less quarrelsome than his father.[1]

Swift kept up a lively correspondence on the choice of choristers. He did not lack for friends eager to place their candidates among his vicars. But Swift's resistance to solicitation was steady. Unless a good judge praised a voice, and—whenever possible—unless Roseingrave also approved, Swift gave no encouragement. To an early testimonial from a close friend, on behalf of a vocal candidate, he replied that merit alone mattered; and 'if we want a singer, and I can get a better, that better one shall be preferred, although my father were competitor.'[2] The scrupulosity with which a connoisseur like Dr Arbuthnot advised Swift suggests the quality of the dean's ambition.[3] When Lord Oxford himself sent a recommendation in a letter from his brother to the dean, Swift replied that he was indeed the captain of a band of nineteen musicians (including boys), but that

> my choir is so degenerate under the reigns of former deans of famous memory, that the race of people called gentlemen lovers of music, tell me I must be very careful in supplying two vacancies, which I have been two years endeavouring to do. For you are to understand that in disposing of these musical employments I determine to act directly contrary to ministers of state, by giving them to those who best deserve.... I wish my Lord Oxford had writ to me on this subject that I might have had the pleasure of refusing him in direct terms.[4]

For the sake of the cathedral music Swift could not only deny a supreme friend like Oxford. He could also make common cause with an enemy like Welbore Ellis, who was Dean of Christ Church when Swift became Dean of St Patrick's. Swift's pains in raising the musical standard of both cathedrals won him an accolade from Ellis even when they were on the verge of a quarrel.[5] Delany expatiates on Swift's devotion to the cathedral

---

[1] See Grove and Lawlor. [2] Williams I. 392. [3] See *ibid.*, II, 186, 304–5.
[4] 9 Feb. 1720, to Edward Harley; *ibid.*, p. 339. [5] *Ibid.*, I. 392–3.

music, and produces one story that brings out the comedy of a tuneless man's cultivating sacred harmony. Daniel Rosein-grave's eldest son Tom had played a magnificent voluntary on the organ of St Patrick's, and Swift's crony Dr Pratt had heard him. When Pratt rhapsodized on the beauty of the performance, at a Sunday evening party, several of the guests wished they had heard it. 'Swift cried out,' according to Delany, 'you shall hear it this minute; I'll sing it for you. And immediately sung out as ridiculous, and as lively an imitation of it as ever was heard.'[1]

In non-musical preferments the case was different. Swift never lost his old disposition to help friends on their way. When all other things seemed roughly equal, he naturally leaned toward those who shared his opinions. Even while aiming at the good of the whole people, he might perhaps hear St Paul's warning that if any provide not for those of his own house, 'he is worse than an infidel.'[2] At least, Swift knew that other patrons were filling places with men from other houses, and that he could only begin to correct the imbalance.

The details of the rise of Theophilus Bolton will suggest how hard it is to tell prejudice from principle. We know that Bolton was Archbishop King's man and gave Swift disagreeable hours. As a master of ecclesiastic law and chancellor of the cathedral, he became a tenacious opponent to Swift in chapter disputes. King wished to make a bishop of Bolton and praised him highly to Archbishop Wake. The virtues singled out were not such as would weaken a proud dean's partisanship. Apart from his legal erudition, said King, Bolton was 'not only well affected to the present government, but zealous for his majesty's interest, and I know none more able to defend our constitution'.[3] Failing with one bishopric, King tried again six months later, adding fresh qualifications: 'He has a great reputation for prudence and piety, as well as learning.'[4] The new effort succeeded with the government, and Bolton became Bishop of Clonfert. In

---

[1] Delany, pp. 190–1.
[2] 1 Tim. v. 8. Actually, this doctrine troubled Swift; see Davis IV. 251–2.
[3] 13 Jan. 1722.
[4] Jul. 1722; Mant II. 381.

St Patrick's Cathedral he was replaced as chancellor by another trouble-maker, Robert Howard.

Swift hoped that during the removals to follow, he might satisfy an old yearning to help Sam Holt and (more important) Robert Grattan.[1] Ultimately Howard's vicarage of St Bride's did go to Grattan, and Howard's prebend of Maynooth fell to Holt.[2] But Swift had to use the same sort of rhetoric as King; and a sign of the struggle that led up to the happy resolution is the tale in the chapter minutes that six of Archbishop King's men dissented from Grattan's appointment and both Robert Dougatt (King's nephew) and Charles Whittingham protested formally against the dean's right to nominate in all elections.[3]

One might have expected an era of bitterness to follow, between the dean and the new bishop. But instead, the very summer after his consecration, Bolton invited Swift to visit him in the west;[4] and we discover Swift writing cheerfully to Sheridan from Clonfert about Bolton's improvements to the episcopal lands—'in four months, twelve miles of ditches'.[5] Soon Bolton rose to a higher-paid bishopric and was sworn of the Privy Council. Yet he then joined Archbishop King in opposing the proclamation against the Drapier;[6] and the next year, when Swift was trying to get a piece of preferment for Sheridan, Bolton obliged him by offering a formal recommendation to the Lord Lieutenant.[7] I think both men knew enough to keep chapter disputes apart from the deepest claims of conscience, and that the friendship they preserved as Bolton continued to climb betokens a mutual respect and affection founded partly on character and partly on a common striving for the welfare of their church and nation.

When Primate Lindsay died, all good churchmen sacrificed any shallower differences to a deep recognition of Archbishop King's merit.[8] Only the strain between English and Irish interests told against him. It is a tribute to Swift's moral growth that ten years after he supported the feckless Lindsay on wholly

---

[1] See Williams II. 268, 449.   [2] Landa, p. 92.   [3] *Ibid.*
[4] Williams II. 453, 455–6.   [5] *Ibid.*, p. 463.   [6] *Drapier*, pp. xliv–xlv.
[7] Williams III. 58, 97.   [8] Cf. above, pp. 227–8.

partisan grounds, he should have joined with almost the whole community of his church to pray for King's succession. In all honesty but quite uncharacteristically, he told King himself, 'I should never be at an end if I were to number up the reasons why I would have your grace in the highest station the crown can give you.'[1]

It is also a mark of the 'English' bishops' destructive narrowness that they saw the issue only in Swift's discarded terms. Bishop Godwin of Kilmore apprehensively told Archbishop Wake, 'My brother Derry [i.e., Nicolson] writes that of late they talk on both sides of the water of a certain Archbishop [i.e., King] to succeed [sc. Lindsay, who was then failing fast]. If so, new English comers will have but a cold welcome.'[2] Of course, Godwin's side won, and Boulter came in, with a programme that put the crudest sort of politics above the humanity and charity which also belonged to his nature.[3]

There is an anecdote about ecclesiastic preferment that may set off Boulter's patronage from that of Swift and King. This is the case of the 'Waltham Black'. Before Boulter left England, and solely to oblige his Whig patrons, he had promised Lord Townshend to confer a good living on Thomas Power, an Englishman whom he did not otherwise know. In Ireland he handed the creature a benefice worth £150 a year.[4] Lord Percival's brother said that 'his providing for the Waltham Black by turning a worthy man out of a living on purpose to make room for him will never be forgiven.'[5] The Irish were correct in charging that Power was rewarded for betraying a gang of deer-stealers (whom he had pretended to join); but Boulter evinced no anxiety about the man's character or training. Whatever Power's poaching skills may have been, he certainly showed himself unsuitable for a priest's vocation; and one can only feel Hibernian satisfaction to learn that he retained enough vices for Boulter to have his secretary write to the

---

[1] Williams III. 20.   [2] 13 Jul. 1723.   [3] Cf. Ferguson's characterization, p. 137.
[4] Boulter, letter to Townshend, 4 Sept. 1725; Boulter I. 37–8 (Dublin, p. 32); cf. above, p. 285.
[5] Philip Percival to Lord Percival, 1 Feb. 1726; B.L. Add. MS. 47031, p. 183.

dissolute cleric in this furious style:

> What I write to you now is by the express orders of my Lord
> Primate, to inform you that his grace hears from persons of credit
> such things of you as are highly displeasing to him. You are re-
> presented as a person who have neither discretion in your words and
> conversation, nor proper decency in your actions and conduct, nor a
> due regard to the offices of your function; and that the result of your
> whole behaviour has given such offence to the generality of your
> parishioners that your congregation falls off daily from you. I am
> ordered to acquaint you, that my Lord is very much troubled to
> have so indifferent a character of a clergyman, whom he has pro-
> moted; and that he will not rest satisfied with such a behaviour as
> brings a scandal on religion, and a disrepute on himself.[1]

Swift willingly handed the story on as he received it from
Archbishop King, who attacked Boulter in Dublin Castle for
the misdeed. 'This fellow was leader of a gang [i.e., of deer-
stealers],' Swift told Stopford, then on his travels, 'and had the
honour of hanging half a dozen of his fellows in quality of
informer, which was his merit. If you cannot match me that in
Italy, step to Muscovy, and from thence to the Hottentots.'[2] It is
against this shady background that we must place Swift's own
obsession with the advancement of parsons he approved of.

---

[1] Philips to Power, 24 Feb. 1726; Boulter I. 65 (Dublin, p. 53).
[2] 26 Nov. 1725; Williams III. 116; Swift does not exaggerate.

Chapter Seventeen

THE SCHOOLMASTER AND
THE DEAN

I. RINCURRAN

It was inevitable that Swift should have wished to raise up Thomas Sheridan.[1] On the deepest level of emotion the schoolmaster's mixture of fun and learning must have given the dean (twenty years his senior) distinctly parental pleasures.

[1] For a meticulous account of Sheridan's career, see James Woolley, 'Thomas Sheridan and Swift', *Studies in Eighteenth-Century Culture* 9 (1979), 93–114. Sheridan's son, in his *Life of Swift* (1784) provides many details of his father's friendship with the dean (pp. 369–405, 443–74). Much of this material is directed against the account given in Orrery pp. 81–5. Since the valid information in Orrery's book comes mainly from Swift's own letters and memoirs, which are more accurately preserved in published editions, and since the rest of Orrery's information is often dubious or malicious, the younger Sheridan's attack is well-founded.

But his own work is also unreliable. A number of his statements and stories about Swift can be disproved. Often when they cannot, Sheridan himself traces them to questionable sources. Though he made a general claim to receive anecdotes from his father (p. 396), he attributes few of them explicitly to him, and few seem derived from his own recollection. He was no more than nineteen, and perhaps only sixteen, when Dr Sheridan died; and he had spent the five preceding years living in Westminster School or in Trinity College, Dublin. (*Alumni Dublinenses* gives his age as sixteen on admission, 26 May 1735; but *Record of Old Westminsters*, ed. G. F. R. Barker and A. H. Stenning, gives his age as eleven on admission to Westminster School in February 1733.) During those years he would have talked little with a father who did not give his leisure to domestic conversation.

Dr Sheridan moved to Cavan in 1735; and after that change, the son had few opportunities to observe the friendship of his father and the dean except when Swift, at the age of sixty-eight, visited Cavan (Williams IV. 416–18). The language of Swift's references to the younger Sheridan in his own memoir of the father (written in 1738) suggests to me that the dean, though interested in the lad, was not then in touch with him (Davis v. 217). Finally, the younger Sheridan wrote his life of Swift about forty-five years after his father died, and I am struck by the thinness of the few anecdotes which he specifically traces to his own encounters with the dean.

Therefore, and because much of the material strikes me as prima-facie improbable, I distrust his concrete details. Nevertheless, he was Swift's godson and did receive first-hand impressions. He must also have heard enough to know how other people responded to Swift. I am therefore inclined to accept his broad view of the friendship between his father and the dean.

[358]

His youth, poor health, and need for advice would have excited Swift's paternal anxiety. Sheridan's informality, amounting at times to rudeness, undercut his fundamental respect for Swift rather as a boy's defiance of a strict, loving father undercuts his obedience. The eager hospitality and willingness to fit in with Swift's whims easily outweighed the thriftlessness and want of direction.

Mrs Johnson cemented the friendship by acting a maternal part. Swift once told Sheridan, '[A] great share of the little merit I have with you, is owing to her solicitations,'[1] by which I suppose he meant that she urged him to put up with the indiscretions of his favourite. Certainly Sheridan was as indiscreet with the lady as with the dean. Mrs Johnson entertained him, Swift said, 'as she would a brother'. But when she gave him some tactful hints about his hated wife, Sheridan broke into rudeness and drew coarse analogies between the two women.[2]

Stella was not invariably tactful. The form her motherliness could take may be imagined from some examples given by Swift. Once when Sheridan wished to 'sell a bargain' at a party, he announced that he had made a very good pun. When somebody asked what it was, Sheridan said, 'My arse.' The victim took offence, but Stella eased the strain by insisting that Sheridan was in the right, because everyone knew that punning was his 'blind side'.[3] Another time, Sheridan was sitting near the fire, took out his purse, and found the coins were hot. Stella said the reason was that his money burned in his pocket.[4]

Only a person ignorant of the range and number of Swift's friends would suppose that Sheridan was a *sine qua non* for him. I am struck by the dean's care in choosing his epithets when he defended Sheridan against malicious gossip. Absentmindedness, naïveté, studiousness, poverty, and addiction to mathematics are the traits singled out by the apologist:

> [As] he is a creature without cunning, so he hath not overmuch advertency. His books, his mathematics, the pressures of his fortunes, his laborious calling and some natural disposition or indisposition give him an égarement d'esprit as you cannot but observe.

[1] Williams II. 147. [2] Davis v. 222. [3] *Ibid.*, p. 238. [4] *Ibid.*, p. 237.

But he hath other good qualities enough, to make up that defect, truth, candour, good nature, pleasantness of humour, and very good learning.[1]

The analysis makes Swift sound not infatuated with Sheridan but deeply appreciative—tender and critical at once. The style of his offhand letters to Sheridan—telegraphic and inquisitive— suggests the strength of the attachment, along with Swift's fatherliness and the festive associations of Sheridan's company.[2] They revive the spirit of the happiest letters to Vanessa, and it seems right that he should describe himself in one as stealing away from a card party to write to Sheridan 'like a lover writing to his mistress'.[3]

Yet for all the dean's devotion to the schoolmaster, he had far too many other hosts and guests to feel desolate without him. He admired Sheridan's skill as a teacher, respected his honesty, sympathized with his politics, shared his religious principles, and felt protective in response to his poor health and feckless-ness. He was godfather to Sheridan's third and favourite son; he was a debtor to Sheridan's vivacity, wit, and readiness to join Swift in the pursuit of trifles. If the dean had been more isolated, these attitudes could have led to dependence; but they did not.[4]

No wonder Swift included the schoolmaster among the men he named to Lord Carteret as deserving promotion in the church. After preparing the way carefully—getting Sheridan to be made one of the viceregal chaplains,[5] and having Carteret attend a tragedy of Sophocles produced in Greek by Sheridan's pupils[6]—Swift wrote a free-speaking letter to the Lord Lieu-tenant, apologizing for an illness that kept him from speaking in person, and recommending Sheridan in frank, courtly terms:

---

[1] Letter of 18 Sept. 1725, to Tickell; Williams III. 98.

[2] *Ibid.*, II. 440–1, 463–4. [3] *Ibid.*, p. 441.

[4] I think the tradition of Swift's over-dependence on Sheridan may be traced to Orrery's report (p. 83) of Swift's possessiveness, which is contradicted by documentary evidence: 'Swift fastened upon him, as upon a prey with which he intended to regale himself, whenever his appetite should prompt him. Sheridan therefore was kept con-stantly within his reach.'

[5] I assume Swift and Tickell arranged this between them; see Davis V. 223.

[6] Sheridan, p. 379; Davis XII. 162–3.

I have only one humble request to make to your excellency which I
had in my heart ever since you were nominated Lord Lieutenant,
and it is in favour of Mr Sheridan. I beg you will take your time for
bestowing him some church-preferment to the value of £140 a year.
He is agreed on all hands to have done more public service by many
degrees in the education of youth than any five of his vocation, and
hath much more learning than usually falls to the share of those who
profess to teaching, being perfectly skilled in the Greek as well as the
Latin tongue, and well acquainted with all the ancient writers in
poetry, philosophy and history. His greatest fault is a wife and seven
children, for which there is no excuse but that a wife is thought
necessary to a schoolmaster. His constitution is so weak, that in a few
years he must give up his business, and probably must starve without some preferment, for which he is an ill solicitor.[1]

The specifying of the income suggests that Swift had in mind a
particular preferment, such as the living of Rincurran in the
county of Cork, which was then vacant.[2] Not only Bolton but
two other spotlessly Whig bishops joined Swift in his request.[3]
At the end of May 1725, Carteret named one of his English
chaplains to be Bishop of Limerick; and among the rearrangements which followed this translation, Sheridan secured
Rincurran, valued at two hundred pounds a year.[4] What the
English party thought about the deed we may judge from the
comment of John Pocklington, an English lawyer and former
M.P. now on the Irish Exchequer bench; he wrote to his friend
Archbishop Wake, 'Mr Sheridan (a schoolmaster in town and
second to Swift in the battle about the halfpence) has got a
living, which last is surprising to all here.'[5]

Swift heard the marvellous news while he was living in
Sheridan's country house in county Cavan. He replied to the
happy man with a fusillade of advice, urging him to flatter his
bishop (Swift's old college acquaintance Peter Browne), to
introduce himself formally to the nearby clergy, and make a
careful estimate of the value of the living. Sheridan was to seek
advice from reliable and trustworthy fellow-parsons, to in-

[1] 17 Apr. 1725; Williams III. 57–8.   [2] *Ibid.*, p. 66, n. 3.
[3] *Ibid.*, pp. 58, 97.
[4] His letters of presentation are dated 2 July; he was instituted 19 July.
[5] July 1725.

gratiate himself with the local gentry, and be sure of going regularly through the legal forms of oaths and inductions:

> You must learn the extent of your parish, the general quantity of arable land and pasture in your parish, the common rate of tithes for an acre of the several sorts of corn, and of fleeces and lambs, and to see whether you have any glebe; pray act like a man of this world.[1]

The weight put on financial details in the letter not only reflects Swift's deep preoccupation with money, his frankness about the link between a minister's dignity and his income. It also evinces his sympathy with the lower clergy in their battle for tithes against the landlords' greed.

Not satisfied with the scope of one letter, Swift sent another, the next day, pressing fresh instructions on Sheridan, imploring him to be thrifty and to maintain a grave and pious character: 'Keep very regular hours for the sake of your health, and credit, and wherever you lie a night within twenty miles of your living, be sure call the family that evening to prayers.'[2]

Swift was careful to return his thanks to Lord Carteret in good style with a touch of flattery. Following the rule that gratitude is a lively expectation of favours yet to be received, he made a general plea for the advancement of home-grown parsons. To the five he had named in conversation (besides Sheridan) he now added three more, all of them fellows of the College.[3]

Meanwhile, Sheridan went down to take possession of his living and was courteously invited to deliver a sermon in a church in Cork. The Sunday fell on 1 August, anniversary of the King's accession. But Sheridan acted true to Swift's description of him as one '[whose] thoughts are sudden, and the most unreasonable always come uppermost'; for of all the texts in Holy Writ he chose to preach on 'Sufficient unto the day is the evil thereof.'[4] Richard Tighe, a short, dull man, was in the congregation. Being a Whig M.P. and a Privy Councillor, Tighe saw to it that a virulent account of Sheridan's blunder

---

[1] Williams III. 67. [2] *Ibid.*, p. 69, corrected by Ball III. 247.
[3] Williams III. 71. [4] Davis v. 223.

reached Dublin, to the embarrassment of the Lord Lieutenant. In the whole sermon there was no syllable of politics of any sort. But Sheridan at once saw his name removed from the list of chaplains[1] and was warned to keep away from Dublin Castle.[2] Swift tells the story:

> [Sheridan] in the height of his felicity and gratitude, going down to take possession of his parish, and furnished with a few led-sermons, whereof, as it is to be supposed, the number was very small, having never served a cure in the church; he stopped at Cork, to attend on his bishop; and going to church on the Sunday following, was, according to the usual civility of country clergymen, invited by the minister of the parish to supply the pulpit. It *happened* to be the first of August; and the first of August *happened* that year to light upon a Sunday: And it *happened* that the Doctor's text was in these words; sufficient unto the day is the evil thereof; and lastly, it *happened* that some one person of the congregation, whose loyalty made him watchful upon every appearance of danger to his majesty's person and government, when service was over, gave the alarm. Notice was immediately sent up to town; and by the zeal of one man *of no large dimensions of body or mind*, such a clamour was raised, that we in Dublin could apprehend no less than an invasion by the Pretender, who must be landed in the south.[3]

The gates of further preferment were now shut against Sheridan, and one might have expected that the dean would abandon all hope of advancing any such blunderer. But Swift's loyalty prevailed, as it normally did with the lowly and the fallen. Sheridan sent him a characteristic apology, protesting his blamelessness. He declared that it was absurd to suppose he would at such a time have intended an aspersion on those in power; that he did not value his temporal interest but wished to preserve his reputation; that he would spend less time in Dublin

---

[1] Williams III. 106.

[2] I cannot accept the younger Sheridan's story of Archdeacon Russel's gift of Drumlane (Sheridan, pp. 383-4). Nevertheless, Professor James Woolley has pointed out to me that Sheridan did own lands in the manor of Drumlane, and there are documents in the Registry of Deeds, Dublin, concerning these lands and involving Sheridan, Russel, and his wife.

[3] Davis XII. 163-4. The words in italics allude to Tighe's small size. I am assuming (perhaps wrongly) that he was the 'person' in the congregation.

and more at Quilca; that he might publish the sermon to demonstrate his innocence.[1]

Instead of berating him, Swift tried to buoy him up, and teased him humorously, dismissing his protests and resolutions: 'Too much advertency is not your talent,' Swift wrote, 'or else you had fled from that text, as from a rock. For as Don Quixote said to Sancho, what business had you to speak of a halter, in a family where one of it was hanged?'[2] The flavour of his spiritual consolation will seem cynical or profound as the reader is reclusive or worldly. But the crux of the matter is that the man who uttered such sentiments clung so unprofitably to a weak, needy friend:

> [Contract] your friendships, and expect no more from man than such an animal is capable of, and you will every day find my description of Yahoes more resembling. You should think and deal with every man as a villain, without calling him so, or flying from him, or valuing him less.[3]

The letter in which these injunctions appear is superbly written, carrying one into the heart of Swift's moral doctrine and showing yet again that for him, as later, for Samuel Johnson, charity was to serve want, not merit.

A week after bolstering Sheridan, Swift approached Tickell, defending the schoolmaster nobly and requesting that Carteret would signify to the unhappy outcast that the Lord Lieutenant did not privately believe Tighe's charges. 'For I know too well', said Swift, 'how often princes themselves are obliged to act against their judgment amidst the rage of factions.'[4] Then he returned to bestow fresh advice and reassurance on the bleating lamb; and he sent Sheridan the letter to Tickell for him to approve, seal, and send on.[5] While waiting for the scandal to fade and for Carteret to mellow, Sheridan and Swift agreed to punish Tighe (whom Swift had always disliked)[6] for his treachery. So a number of lampoons soon appeared, of uncertain

---

[1] Williams III. 94–5.   [2] *Ibid.*   [3] 11 Sept. 1725; *ibid.*, p. 94.
[4] *Ibid.*, p. 98.   [5] *Ibid.*, p. 100.   [6] Cf. *Journal* I. 71 and n. 24.

quality and authorship; and for years Swift managed to insert poisonous allusions to Tighe into his writings on Irish politics.

II. QUILCA

One easily sees how mutual usefulness entered into the friendship of the two men. While Sheridan could not be a patron to Swift, he could take his generous turn as host. A room was kept for him at the deanery, but Swift was constantly welcome at the schoolhouse in Capel Street; and Sheridan further induced him to visit his small country house, thereby serving the dean's passion for rural retreat.

What the schoolmaster could afford in town we may guess from Sheridan's comic exaggerations. He described the amenities of his back parlour in a versified burlesque of Swift's visits. Here we are told that the house had no bootscraper at the entrance; the stair carpet was torn 'by boys and ball', and the floor was flecked with lime. The door of the little parlour itself was smeared with chalk and nicked with knives; it stuck so that Swift and Sheridan took turns prying it open:

> How oft by turns have you and I
> Said thus—'Let me—no—let me try—
> This turn will open it, I'll engage—'
> You push me from it in a rage,
> Turning, twisting, forcing, fumbling,
> Stamping, staring, fuming, grumbling,
> At length it opens—in we go—

When they get in, the parlour chairs are all too weak to hold the distinguished caller. The fire smokes, but no poker or tongs can be found. Swift tries the nose of the bellows; but when he begins to rake, the grate collapses. A flame springs up, needing air, but the decayed bellows cannot puff the smoke away.

> And is your reverence vext at that?
> Get up in God's name, take your hat.
> Hang them, say I, that have no shift.
> Come, blow the fire, good Dr Swift.

[365]

Sheridan offers meat and wine with a compliment, but Swift quarrels with the compliment, fusses because there is no water, declares the butter is rancid, and complains that Mrs Sheridan has provided too much meat: all he wants is a slice. At last the pair are brought a plate of sliced beef from the common dining room, where the twenty-odd boarders eat. I quote a passage with Swift speaking and Sheridan replying:

> 'For water I must keep a clutter,
> Or chide your wife for stinking butter,
> Or getting such a deal of meat,
> As if you'd half the town to eat.
> That wife of yours, the devil's in her.
> I've told her of this way of dinner
> Five hundred times, but all in vain—
> Here comes a rump of beef again.
> Oh that that wife of yours would burst—
> Get out, and serve the boarders first.
> Pox take 'em all for me—I fret
> So much, I shall not eat my meat—
> You know I'd rather have a slice.'
> 'I know, dear Sir, you are not nice.
> You'll have your dinner in a minute.
> Here comes the plate and slices in it—
> Therefore no more, but take your place—
> Do you fall to, and I'll say grace.'

One doubts that King's Mint House was quite so disreputable as Sheridan makes it, but Swift's scolding sounds as authentic as Sheridan's tolerance; and the rage against Mrs Sheridan echoes both men's letters.[1]

Although Swift once said that Sheridan lost money by his marriage,[2] Mrs Sheridan, an only child, was in fact heiress to her father's estate, part of which was the property of Quilca House in county Cavan, about fifty miles northwest of Dublin.[3] The property had become Sheridan's when his father-in-law died. In

---

[1] Sheridan, pp. 444–74. I prefer his text to that used by Williams in the *Poems* III. 1045–8.

[2] Davis V. 217.

[3] For some impressions of the place in 1852 see R. S. Brooke, 'A Pilgrimage to Quilca in the Year 1852', *Dublin University Magazine*, 40 (1852), 509–26.

that wooded and watered, rolling and rocky terrain Swift visited him during a summer's tour of northern Ireland in 1722. When the dean later recalled the pleasures of the visit, he wrote to Sheridan, who was spending Christmas there,

> You will find Quilca not the thing it was last August; nobody to relish the lake; nobody to ride over the downs; no trout to be caught; no dining over a well; no night heroics, no morning epics; no stolen hour when the wife is gone; no creature to call you names. Poor miserable Master Sheridan! No blind harpers! no journeys to Rantavan![1]

The tone of boyish frolic makes one understand why Swift wished to return a year later, when he was making a southern tour. Then he came to Quilca from Clonfert, over 'rivers, bogs, and mountains'.[2] The following winter he was confident enough to take the ailing Mrs Johnson and Mrs Dingley with him for a Christmas visit, which Swift described as providing 'good fare, warm rooms, and mirth: all of us well in going, residing and returning, without any accident or other offence than abundance of dirt and wit'.[3]

Sheridan was inspired to produce couplets enumerating the dean's rustic pastimes in a Swiftian poem:

> To see him now a mountaineer!
> O what a mighty fall is here!
> From settling governments and thrones
> To splitting rocks and piling stones;
> Instead of Bolingbroke and Anna
> Shane Tunelly and Bryan Granna;
> Oxford and Ormonde he supplies
> In ev'ry Irish Teague he spies,
> So far forgetting his old station,
> He seems to like their conversation.
> Conforming to the tatter'd rabble
> He learns their Irish tongue to gabble,
> And what our anger more provokes,
> He's pleased with their insipid jokes,
> Then turns and asks them who does lack a
> Good plug, or pipe full of tobacca.

---

[1] Williams II. 441.　　[2] *Ibid.*, p. 463.　　[3] *Ibid.*, III. 3.

All cry they want; to ev'ry man
He gives, extravagant, a span.

. . .

At night, right loath to quit the park,
His work just ended by the dark,
With all his pioneers he comes
To make more work for whisks and brooms.
Then seated in an elbow-chair,
To take a nap he does prepare.[1]

Such were the joys that would finally inspire a living mock-pastoral—that is, a withdrawal to Quilca, by Swift and the ladies, that would last whole seasons without Sheridan's presence. But before that semi-pathetic migration, other friends and other travels were to intervene.

[1] *Poems* III. 1039–41.

Chapter Eighteen

DON CARLOS, WOOD PARK, AND QUILCA

I f Swift had been inhumanly consistent, he would have limited his friendships among the gentry to men who stayed at home, improved their land, and resisted English wickedness. He would have clung to those who shared his addiction to the country life and supported the cause of his church. He would have rejected the men of fashion who preferred a coffee-house in St James's to the hall of their family seat.

But of course he was far too tolerant, far too catholic in his appreciation of human natures, to grant himself so little range. As Swift notoriously said, it was communities he hated; his love was toward individuals.[1] His attachments included English carpet-baggers and Irish expatriates. He detested Presbyterianism and ridiculed the new generation of Whiggery. But he delighted in a Presbyterian housekeeper and his guests were often Whigs. So he cultivated Tickell's society, and so also he remained the uncensorious intimate of Charles Ford.

In Ford Swift had a confidant who had known him as well in England as in Ireland, who could visit Vanessa and entertain Stella, whose worldliness overlay ripe, classical learning, and who always admired Swift's genius. With the discreet 'Don Carlos' Swift did not have to be dignified, tactful, or cautious. Most great writers need a close-mouthed, sympathetic critic whose intelligence and taste they may consult regularly without having to accept any advice. Ford could do this kind of work for Swift on top of the offices of fraternity. 'My greatest want here', Swift told him, 'is of somebody qualified to censure and correct what I write.'[2]

---

[1] Letter of 29 Sept. 1725; Williams III. 103.   [2] 19 Jan. 1724; *ibid.*, p. 5.

Ford also remained close to Swift's English friends. He knew the Mashams, Dr Arbuthnot, and the Duchess of Ormonde. He visited Bolingbroke in France and Pope at Twickenham.[1] Gay named him 'joyous Ford' in the poem 'Mr Pope's Welcome from Greece'.[2] He was ferried back and forth between England and Ireland, spending as long a time as he could in London but returning home in order to cut his expenses, visit his mother (who lived in town), and look after the family seat, which lay conveniently for Swift halfway between Dublin and Laracor.

Ford arrived in midsummer 1720 and stayed till mid-November.[3] It looks as if he took Swift with him to see Vanessa and her ailing sister in Celbridge. At least, Swift said he would do so; and I assume Swift prompted him, employing Ford as in the old days he had used Sir Andrew Fountaine, to screen a risky visit he wished to make himself.[4] I suspect that for the Dean of St Patrick's this visit to Celbridge was the most dramatic hour of the season.

But if Ford was cheerful, compliant, and communicative, he was no Addison. Most Irish gentlemen bored him. Few wished to join in his style of public sociability. There was a limit to strolls around St Stephen's Green and playing chess in the coffee-house for threepence a game. When the painter Jervas was in Dublin, Ford could see him (perhaps at the deanery) and challenge his talkative self-aggrandizement, or he could visit Stella and Dingley over a game of cards.[5] But these elementary pleasures were no substitute for the round of fashion in London: Hyde Park, the coffee-house, and the anterooms of Parliament; the opera, the company of duchesses, the conversation of genius.[6] He fell back on the deanery, and the dean tired in his turn. Ford,

---

[1] For the report that Ford gave Swift of his visit to Twickenham, see *ibid.*, p. 103.

[2] Line 131.

[3] Writing to Vanessa on 4 Aug. 1720, Swift says Ford 'is come over' (Williams II. 353). Writing to Ford on 15 Dec. 1720, he says, 'We were for some days in a good deal of pain about [you], but at last were assured you were safe in London' (*ibid.*, p. 364)—evidently referring to the storms of 19–20 Nov., which must have occurred about the time Ford crossed to England.

[4] *Ibid.*, pp. 353, 355.   [5] *Ibid.*, p. 431.

[6] Cf. Swift's list, *ibid.*, p. 466.

he admitted to Vanessa, 'takes up abundance of my time in spite of my teeth.'[1]

Two summers later, when Ford returned to stay for more than a year,[2] Swift left him and went to the country on one of his own long visits. While the ramifications of Layer's Plot revealed themselves, Ford preferred not to be highly visible in London.[3] But he became a lonely tourist in his motherland; for he did not ride; he depended upon companionship, and yet he was choosy about acquaintances.[4] He made his ennui known; and Swift told Vanessa that according to Ford there was 'not a conversable creature in Ireland' apart from Swift.[5] Such compliments were not worth the fatigue of winning them, and the dean complained to his energetic friend Robert Cope about Ford's passivity:

> Mr Ford is heartily weary of us, for want of company. He is a tavern-man, and few here go to taverns, except such as will not pass with him; and what is worse, as much as he has travelled, he cannot ride. He will be undone when I am gone away; yet he does not think it convenient to be in London during these hopeful times.[6]

[1] *Ibid.*, p. 361.

[2] The chronology of Ford's visits to Ireland needs clarification. He may have come over in 1721. Swift wrote 30 Sept. expecting him (*ibid.*, p. 407); and Bolingbroke addressed him in Dublin, 1 Jan. 1722, mentioning a letter of 19 Oct. 1721 that he had received from Ford in Ireland and saying as well, 'You pass the winter where you are' (Ford, pp. 235–6). Yet it is hard to believe he would have returned to England early in 1722 and then come back to Ireland in June of the same year. Perhaps he simply stayed on.

In 1722, if he had not remained from the preceding summer, he must have arrived before 1 Jul., because Swift wrote to him 22 Jul., after three weeks at Loughgall, implying that he had seen Ford before leaving Dublin at the end of April (Williams II. 431). Writing to Gay, 8 Jan. 1723, Swift sent Ford's service and said, 'We keep him here as long as we can' (*ibid.*, p. 444). I assume that Ford had not gone to England in the meantime. At the end of Jan. 1723, we have a birthday poem from Swift to Ford (*Poems* I. 309–15); and from April to 3 Oct. we know that Stella and Dingley were at Wood Park with Ford. In Aug. 1723 Bolingbroke addressed Ford in Ireland; in Dec. 1723 he said he had received a message from Ford in a letter from Swift (Ford, pp. 237–9); presumably, Ford was still in Ireland not long before the latter date.

I think Ford returned to England in Nov. 1723, because when Swift wrote to him there in Jan. 1724, he referred to the composition of poems for his own birthday, 30 Nov., as an affair Ford had missed (*ibid.*, p. 3); and in Aug. 1725, when Ford was due to return by the beginning of winter (Williams III. 83), Swift congratulated him on having made his money hold out 'almost two years' (*ibid.*, p. 88), which implies that Ford had left Ireland shortly before the beginning of winter in 1723.

[3] Swift indicates the effects of the discovery of the plot upon his circle in the autumn of 1722, *ibid.*, pp. 434–6; he mentions Ford's caution *ibid.*, p. 454.

[4] *Ibid.*, II. 454.　　[5] *Ibid.*, p. 433.　　[6] *Ibid.*, p. 454.

I have been separating the threads of Swift's complex life during the early 1720s, re-examining the same period from different points of view: the *Drapier's Letters*, the church, the friendship with Sheridan, and so forth. Ford's importance is hard to establish because although he appears again and again, he was a confidant rather than a vivid actor in the drama. It seems almost symbolic that he was to entertain the ladies without Swift shortly before Swift and the ladies were to go to Quilca without Sheridan. Meanwhile, purposefulness was no part of his routine.

To the dean's disgust, Ford established himself in Dublin as he would have done in St James's. Scolding him afterwards, Swift said,

> No men in Dublin go to taverns who are worth sitting with, and to ask others, is just to desire them to throw away half a crown for bad wine, (which they can ill spare,) when they know where to get good, for nothing, and among company where they can amuse themselves with play or trifling.[1]

Swift had Ford for Christmas,[2] and for much of the winter in town. At the end of January he presented him with a fine, strong poem for his birthday. It is in Swift's usual couplets; and one can learn something about the two friends' conversation from the themes of the poem, because the underpinning is the case for Ford to live in Ireland. To persuade him to linger, Swift produced one of his characteristic analogies, this time between praiseworthy Dublin and faulty London. On the one hand he shows London to be corrupt and not deserving of Ford's residence; on the other hand he shows Dublin to have in fact the amenities of her rival. As usual, Swift's peculiar tone appears in the unexpected violence of the satire and, by contrast, in the easy restraint of the compliments to his own town. Denouncing the South Sea Bubble and the supposed fraudulence of Layer's Plot (which was a cause of Ford's tolerating Ireland as long as he did), Swift anticipates the sculpturesque opening of *The Dunciad*, Book IV:

[1] Williams III. 89.   [2] *Ibid.*, II. 444.

> To see a scoundrel strut and hector,
> A foot-boy to some rogue director?
> To look on Vice triumphant round,
> And Virtue trampled on the ground:
> Observe where bloody Townshend stands
> With informations in his hands,
> Hear him blaspheme, and swear and rail,
> Threat'ning the pillory and jail.[1]

Balancing the furious blame is the ingenious, analogical praise:

> If you have London still at heart,
> We'll make a small one here by art:
> The diff'rence is not much between
> St James's Park and Stephen's Green;
> And Dawson Street will serve as well
> To lead you thither, as Pell-Mell.
>
> .   .   .
>
> When to your friends you would enhance
> The praise of Italy or France
> For grandeur, elegance and wit,
> We gladly hear you, and submit:
> But then, to come and keep a clutter
> For this, or that side of a gutter,
> To live in this or t'other isle,
> We cannot think it worth your while.[2]

The neatness of the couplets subtly accentuates the weakness of the reasoning; and the underlying sympathy with Ford's preference gives the whole poem a humorous implication. It is as though the poet were turning a supposed quarrel with his friend into a real quarrel with himself. Soon Swift would be planning his own trip to London.

Then Stella's birthday came round; and Swift planned a deanery party—Ford, Sheridan, a Rochfort, some Grattans, and so on. Poetical tributes were in order, and Swift gave Stella one.[3] If this seems less attractive than his offering to Ford, the reason is that the tone sounds more constrained. It is hard to

---

[1] 'Director' of South Sea Company; Townshend as manufacturer of the plot; 'informations', meaning denunciations by paid informers.
[2] 'To Mr Ford', *Poems* I. 312–15.   [3] *Ibid.*, II. 740–3.

celebrate joyously the advancing age of a failing invalid. Swift's tenderness had not yet been exercised to the point where he could praise the dearly beloved in wit that reconciled her to mortality. As in his early odes, so here he transfers his attention from the subject of the poem to the problems of composition, as if to shield Mrs Johnson from over-nice scrutiny.

Meanwhile, as spring drew near, the dean's mind fixed itself on country visits. Stella was already showing the frightening signs that would send him with her to Quilca for the long stay that I have foreshadowed. He had a better plan at this earlier time. If Ford must remain through the summer and he disliked being alone, Swift could provide him with society and also give Mrs Johnson a season of healthful air and exercise, by getting Ford to invite her to Wood Park with Mrs Dingley. They could go from 'Liffey's stinking tide' to 'purling streams and fountains bubbling'.[1] And he could then go off himself on a southern ramble to match the difficult northern tour he had accomplished the summer before. Swift deposited the two ladies at Wood Park,[2] and made an April excursion from that stop to the Copes at Loughgall, with sidetrips to Laracor and Quilca.[3] After revisiting Wood Park and the pair of vacationers, he had a breathing spell in Dublin. Then at the beginning of June[4] he took off for his travels through strange parts of Munster and Connaught while Ford found his enlarged household so agreeable that in four months he never went to Dublin.[5] Stella luxuriated in the comforts and attentions provided by 'Don Carlos', as we know from Swift's exaggeration of her pleasures recounted in a set of comic couplets:

> She look'd on partridges with scorn
> Except they tasted of the corn;
> A haunch of ven'son made her sweat

[1] 'Stella at Wood Park', ll. 27–8.

[2] Writing to Cope, 1 Jun. 1723, Swift says that Ford 'passes the summer at his country house with two sober ladies'—which to my ears suggests that Stella and Dingley had been with him for some time (Williams II. 456).

[3] He was at a chapter meeting of St Patrick's on 18 Mar. and was back in Dublin several days before 11 May (*ibid.*, pp. 452–3 and 453, n. 1).

[4] *Ibid.*, p. 453.   [5] *Ibid.*, p. 466.

Unless it had the right fumette:
Don Carlos earnestly would beg,
'Dear Madam, try this pigeon's leg,'
Was happy when he could prevail
To make her only touch a quail:
Through candlelight she view'd the wine
To see that ev'ry glass was fine.[1]

In September Swift was home again. In October, the ladies
droopingly followed; and soon Ford took ship for London.
Although Swift purposely made too much fun of Stella's come-
down, it is obvious that she kept invidiously clear memories of
her days in Wood Park, and sighed more than once to be
reduced to 'small beer, a herring, and the Dean'.[2] Hired lodgings in Ormond Key barely warmed the heart after Ford's
spacious house, gardens, orchard, woods, and hundred acres.
The following summer, Swift told Ford, the exiles were still
pining for Wood Park 'like the fleshpots of Egypt'.[3]

When Ford reappeared two years later, his friends were sum-
mering in Quilca. He arrived in mid-August;[4] and although
Swift warned him not to fall into his old habits, I suspect that is
just what he did.[5] He must have leaped on the deanery trio as
soon as they reached town at the start of October; and we may
be sure there was one new topic of conversation, because Swift
was now ready to go to London himself when spring came.
Otherwise, we know little about the reunion. It is possible that
in due course Swift and Ford sailed for England together.[6]

But as if to provide the most dramatic contrast to the urbanity
which was to follow, Swift had, for months, been giving the

---

[1] *Poems* II. 750.
[2] 'Stella at Wood Park', l. 72. They left Wood Park on 3 Oct. 1723. See *Poems* II. 744.
[3] Williams III. 16.
[4] On 14 Aug. 1725 Swift wrote assuming Ford was still in London (*ibid.*, p. 86). Almost
at once he received a letter from him in Dublin (*ibid.*, p. 88).
[5] *Ibid.*, pp. 88–9.
[6] On 26 Nov. Swift writes to Pope that Ford has just explained a passage in a letter
(*ibid.*, p. 117). On 14 Dec. Pope asks, 'What is become of Mr Ford' (*ibid.*, p. 121),
implying that Swift sees him in Dublin. The lack of any letters from Swift to Ford during
the three months that followed would suggest that Ford did not go to England before
Swift: it would have been normal for them to exchange messages as soon as he got there
(although they may have disappeared). We know that Swift crossed in Mar. 1726 and
found lodgings near Ford (*ibid.*, p. 127, n. 2).

ladies the rural experience that I have already anticipated. It had begun in the spring of 1725, when I think Swift wished to replace his usual summer journeys by a vacation in which Stella could join him; for he was more than usually worried about her failing health, and had urged her to try the effect of Bath, Tunbridge, or Montpellier.[1] Besides, he would probably have been glad to be out of Dublin while the affair of Wood's patent was reaching its climax and resolution. Above all, his own fits of deafness and vertigo were making the limitations of Dublin less and less acceptable.[2]

Getting ready for the expedition, Swift wrote an extraordinary poem about Stella's loss of weight, comparing her to a cow that dwindles in winter and fattens in summer; for Quilca was to restore her bulk and well-being:

> Why, Stella, should you knit your brow,
> If I compare you to the cow?
> 'Tis just the case: for you have fasted
> So long till all your flesh is wasted,
> And must against the warmer days
> Be sent to Quilca down to graze.[3]

The play of tender feeling against low imagery makes for Swiftian pathos, as characteristic as his satire but largely limited to his verse.

The party of Stella, Dingley, Swift, and their servants set off from Dublin around 20 April 1725.[4] When they reached Quilca, they found that a long stay multiplied its discomforts. The 'country house in no very good repair'[5] became less Arcadian when the weather kept them crowded together indoors; and Swift complained of a 'rotten cabin, dropping rain', smoking

---

[1] Williams III. 147.

[2] On the *Drapier's Letters* and Swift's deafness cf. his comments to Ford, 16 Aug. 1725, especially the reference to 'some reasons' (Williams III. 89).

[3] *Poems* II. 759.

[4] Williams once inferred from the 1725 birthday poem that Stella and Dingley left before Swift (*ibid.*, p. 758). But in his edition of the correspondence he assumes (as I do) that they all travelled together (Williams III. 57, n. 2).

[5] *Poems* III. 1034.

fireplaces and broken chairs, rickety tables and beds, too little food and lazy servants.[1] The nearest town was Kells, seven difficult miles away,[2] from which much of their food and all their post were carried once a week. When Swift wished to discourage Chetwode from visiting him, he wrote,

> I live in a cabin and in a very wild country; yet there are some agreeablenesses in it, or at least I fancy so, and am levelling mountains and raising stones, and fencing against inconveniencies of a scanty lodging, want of victuals, and a thievish race of people.[3]

Yet Stella seemed to improve. Tickell had presented her with a small pickaxe, and she enjoyed assisting Swift in his work on the estate. After two months of Irish weather, he told Sheridan,

> Mrs Johnson swears it will rain till Michaelmas. She is so pleased with her pick-ax, that she wears it fastened to her girdle on her left side, in balance with her watch. The lake is strangely overflown, and we are desperate about turf, being forced to buy it three miles off.[4]

Sheridan's servants evidently acted like characters out of *Castle Rackrent* or *Some Experiences of an Irish R.M.*; and although Swift had long experience of below stairs in Dublin, he enlarged his imagination in Cavan:

> The ladies' room smokes; the rain drops from the skies into the kitchen; our servants eat and drink like the devil, and pray for rain, which entertains them at cards and sleep, which are much lighter than spades, sledges, and crows [i.e., crowbars].[5]

Nevertheless, the prescription still worked on the patients; and Swift after two-and-a-half months could tell Archdeacon Walls,

> Mrs Johnson is generally much better, and I after a short return of deafness recovered in ten days, and in spite of the weather which is worse than ever was heard of, we make a shift to walk, and use exercise.[6]

[1] *Ibid.*, p. 1035. [2] Williams III. 59. [3] *Ibid.*, p. 60.
[4] *Ibid.*, p. 64. For anecdotes about Swift's accomplishments as Sheridan's landscape architect, see Sheridan, pp. 400–1. I don't know how reliable they are. Swift makes so many other references to the doings at Quilca, I am inclined to think he would have mentioned these if they had really occurred.
[5] Williams III. 64. [6] *Ibid.*, p. 72.

When Chetwode again threatened a visit, Swift brought out his hyperboles but also revealed his occupations:

> The weather is so bad and continues so beyond any example in memory, that I cannot have the benefit of riding and am forced to walk perpetually in a great-coat to preserve me from cold and wet, while I amuse myself with employing and inspecting labourers digging up and breaking stones, building dry walls, and cutting through bogs, and when I cannot stir out, reading some easy trash merely to divert me.[1]

After four months he reported that he still had periods of deafness but that Mrs Johnson was 'better in strength though often in her old disorders'.[2] He declared that Stella was walking three or four Irish miles (about five English miles[3]) a day; and he complained,

> We live here among a million of wants, and where everybody is a thief. I am amusing myself in the quality of bailiff to Sheridan, among bogs and rocks, overseeing and ranting at Irish labourers, reading books twice over for want of fresh ones, and fairly correcting and transcribing my Travels [i.e., *Gulliver*], for the public. Any thing rather than the complaint of being deaf in Dublin.[4]

They had visitors, certainly Worrall and John Grattan,[5] besides rural neighbours. And finally, at the beginning of October, they made the two-days' journey back to town.[6] The attitude that coloured his progress home can easily be inferred from the contemptuous mock-heroics of his report to Pope:

> I am now returning to the noble scene of Dublin in to the Grande Monde, for fear of burying my parts, to signalise myself among curates and vicars, and correct all corruption crept in relating to the weight of bread and butter through those dominions where I govern [i.e., the 'liberties' of the cathedral].[7]

The whole long episode of the seasons in Quilca betokens the mutual confidence and easy relations of three persons. Swift

---

[1] *Ibid.*, p. 76. [2] *Ibid.*, p. 86.
[3] Eleven Irish miles make fourteen English miles. [4] Williams III. 89.
[5] *Ibid.*, p. 90, n. 4.
[6] The plan was to leave Quilca on 4 October and reach Dublin the next day. In the absence of other evidence I assume this was followed.
[7] 29 Sept. 1725; Williams III. 102.

tended to 'adopt' his protégés; and the lower clergy of Dublin sometimes operated for him as a family. Sheridan was playing the protective rôle for a change, as a son might shelter his parents. Swift's willingness to endure the privations of Quilca for Mrs Johnson's sake suggests the uxorial side of her friendship with him. Although he was trying to restore his own health too, a neglected feature of his sensibility appears in his choosing to do so by hiding himself in rustic isolation for practically half a year. The man who required Naboth's Vineyard to support life in town was no cosmopolite. When Swift pined for England, it was people and conversation he missed, not courts, exchanges, and shops. We should also observe that when the Drapier secluded himself in Cavan, he passed many of his hours with the humblest farmhands, as if to show his sympathy with the whole people of Ireland in their productive functions.

Chapter Nineteen

VANESSA

―――――◆―――――

I. DIDO AND AENEAS

Once again I shall violate chronology and move back in time to the early years of the decade 1720–30, when Swift gave up the habit of retirement. Having dealt with public affairs and visible friendships, I turn to his most secret attachment, Esther Vanhomrigh. If Ford ever went to see Vanessa after 1720, we have no evidence of the fact.[1] I doubt that Swift encouraged him to do so. Swift's tone to her begins to sound at times like his tone to Chetwode. The difference is that she could, if she pleased, cause him scandalous embarrassment. He delighted in the *frissons* of her company, spent hours with her at a time, and kept her in touch with the travels of Gulliver (which he carefully hid from strangers). He wrote poems for her and sent her extravagant compliments.

Yet it was she who laboured to maintain their unequal partnership; and if Vanessa had not persisted, Swift would surely have thrown off the yoke. What she could do in the way of persistence we hear in the two most piercing messages of all the letters that passed between them. I think she wrote these during the months before her sister's death. I assume that Swift was avoiding the sickroom and hoping that if he kept away, the infatuation would wither for lack of nourishment. Instead, Vanessa cried in the language of Dido:

'Tis now ten long weeks since I saw you and in all that time I have never received but one letter from you and a little note with an

―――――――――――――――

[1] I think Vanessa would have left Ford money for a ring if he had kept in touch. But she does not mention him in her will. I also think that somewhere in the extant letters between Swift and Vanessa there would have been a reference to such visits.

excuse. O————[1] how have you forgot me. You endeavour by severities to force me from you, nor can I blame you, for with the utmost distress and confusion I behold myself the cause of uneasy reflections to you. Yet I cannot comfort you but here declare that 'tis not in the power of art, time, or accident to lessen the unexpressible passion which I have for————. Put my passion under the utmost restraint. Send me as distant from you as the earth will allow, yet you can not banish those charming ideas which will ever stick by me whilst I have the use of memory. Nor is the love I bear you only seated in my soul, for there is not a single atom of my frame that is not blended with it. Therefore don't flatter yourself that separation will ever change my sentiments, for I find myself unquiet in the midst of silence, and my heart is at once pierced with sorrow and love.[2]

These amazing flights do not mark the limit of her self-indulgence. She could reach a higher pitch:

I firmly believe, could I know your thoughts (which no human creature is capable of guessing at, because never any one living thought like you), I should find you have often in a rage wished me religious,[3] hoping then I should have paid my devotions to heaven. But that would not spare you, for was I an enthusiast, still you'd be the deity I should worship. What marks are there of a deity but what you are known by? You are present every where; your dear image is before my eyes; some times you strike me with that prodigious awe, I tremble with fear; at other times a charming compassion shines through your countenance, which revives my soul. Is it not more reasonable to adore a radiant form one has seen than one only described?[4]

Swift may well have been intimidated by the fear of what such a temper could do to bring scandal on his head.

To keep him attached, Vanessa advanced beyond emotional extortion and a rise in epistolary heat; for she also exacted tribute in kind. While Swift might have withstood mere seductiveness, he yielded to her combination of weapons. He knew the dangers as well as the uses of written documents; he rationed his

---

[1] The dashes stand for endearments.
[2] *Ibid.*, p. 363; my spelling and punctuation. When I say Vanessa sounds like Dido, it is the Dido of the *Heroides*, not the *Aeneid*, that I have in mind.
[3] Perhaps meaning a nun.
[4] Vanessa may be echoing *Eloisa to Abelard*; see especially ll. 277–84.

visits medicinally; and yet he supplied Vanessa with letters in which the ciphers sound more incriminating than open language would have been. Vanessa said she would pester him with letters if he failed to visit her:

> Did I not know you very well, I should think you knew little of the world, to imagine that a woman would not keep her word when she promised anything that was malicious. Had you not better a thousand times, throw away one hour, at some time or other of the day, than to be interrupted in your business at this rate? For I know 'tis as impossible for you to burn my letters without reading them as 'tis for me to avoid reproving you when you behave yourself so wrong.[1]

Swift was the first one to appreciate such wit, and threatened to pay fewer visits in order to get more of her prose. The illness of her sister Mary probably drove Vanessa from Dublin to the country at Celbridge, where it would have been harder for Swift to call without being noticed. But visits, correspondence, and much tantalizing continued: 'I wish I were to walk with you fifty times about your garden,' wrote the dean, 'and then—drink your coffee.'[2]

He did not approach the shade of tenderness she required. Although he kept playing upon her recollection of experiences they had shared, he added little to her list of such pleasures. He ran over the old histories willingly enough, but for the immediacy which she wanted he substituted thudding hyperboles, sometimes in semi-literate French:

> Car il n'y a point de merite, ni aucun preuve de mon bon goût, de trouver en vous tout ce que la nature a donné à un mortel, je veux dire l'honneur, la vertue, le bon sens, l'esprit, la douceur, l'agrément et la fermeté d'âme.[3]

As Berkeley said, where Vanessa offered passion, Swift countered with compliments.[4]

He asked her to use dashes and symbols for the names and

---

[1] Williams II. 335.   [2] 18 Oct. 1720; *ibid.*, p. 361.
[3] 12 May 1719; *ibid.*, p. 325. My spelling, punctuation, etc.; also quoted above, pp. 95–6.
[4] Delany, p. 123, gives us Berkeley's opinion, which is not otherwise known.

endearments of her rhapsodic style.[1] His own title had shrunk from 'Cadenus' to 'Cad—'. From 'Vanessa' or 'Miss Hessy' she had become 'Misheskinage' and then 'Skinage', etc. But while she could use language like Pope's *Eloisa*, he often sounded less like Abelard than St Jerome (writing to Eustochium). If only Swift had been consistent in this, Vanessa might have learned to tolerate a decade without him. But he could not repress the instinct to lead her on, as when he rode out to dine with some friends not far from Celbridge and then reported to her how he had asked them where a road went, which in fact went to Celbridge.[1]

It is always a question whether the moody, dissatisfied woman charmed others as she charmed the dean, or how much of his care sprang from pity. Along with the suggestion of Dido and Aeneas in their relationship, one thinks of archetypal possibilities, or symbolic parallels like Swift's tale of the 'Unfortunate Lady'. In public affairs as in private life, weak and downtrodden characters fixed his benevolence. Swift's hate-love devotion to Ireland, his loyalty to the fallen Earl of Oxford, have something in common with the submission to Vanessa. But so has his tolerance of Chetwode.

II. TURNSTILE ALLEY AND CELBRIDGE

Although the friendship was static in essence, there were subtle changes. Socially, Swift grew independent as the Whig-Tory antitheses of public life in Ireland gave way to the division between the English interest and the Irish. By 1720 he no longer had to rely upon Jacobite sympathizers and Tories for secure conversation; and churchmen of all levels were glad to know him. The social superiority that Vanessa would have enjoyed when she was sixteen had been levelled by Swift's rise. At the same time the call to public service that fostered the *Proposal for Irish Manufacture* and *Some Arguments against Enlarging the Power of Bishops*—the impulse that was to produce *The Drapier's Letters*—brought Swift out of retirement and sent him back into the

[1] Williams II. 353.   [2] *Ibid.*

marketplace of national politics. When he passed an afternoon with Vanessa, the Dean of St Patrick's could feel more and more that he was conferring, not receiving, a favour, while her explicit admiration enhanced the mood.

Vanessa remained desirable. The death of her brother in 1715 had given her fresh legal difficulties but also a promise of added wealth. The decline of her sister Mary, hideous though the ordeal was, would leave her sole heiress to the family fortune. In her early thirties she was a blown rose but still over twenty years younger than the man she desired. The hoard of shared and secret memories which Swift kept polishing in his letters obviously gave their conversations a resonance that nobody's else could match. Vanessa's air of helplessness appealed to the deepest elements in his character. In her own yearning for a surrogate father who would prefer the daughter to her rival brothers, I think she responded magically to Swift's effort to enjoy sexual excitement while transcending sexuality. So she naturally provoked and satisfied emotions that Swift could indulge in few other relationships.

Yet the dangers and fatigues of the friendship grew more quickly than the rewards. Vanessa's stubborn irrationality, her depressions and self-pity were less charming in a mature spinster than in an adolescent girl. Her dependence was onerous as well as flattering. The position of a rich, unmarried heiress not only subjected all her comings and goings to the scrutiny of Mrs Grundy; it put her in a painfully vulnerable position during an era when male guardians were thought essential to the solvency of the weak-minded sex. Lady Mary Wortley Montagu once described the perils of a young and wealthy widow in terms that reflect a wide experience of English and continental mating habits: 'She appears to me walking blindfold upon stilts, amidst precipices.'[1] Simply the rigidity of Vanessa's character would have cooled the ardour of an instructor who had been trying for half her life to mend her faults.

An outward and disturbing sign of their widening difference

---

[1] *Letters*, ed. R. Halsband (Oxford, 1965–7), III. 47.

was the contrast between Swift's mobility and Vanessa's imprisonment. As he rode off on summer rambles or to country-house parties, Vanessa remained in Celbridge or Turnstile Alley, either because most society gave her the spleen, or because she had to linger over the legal processes on which her fortune rested, or else because she was nursing a consumptive sister.[1] One must always remember that the confinement was at least partly self-imposed. Archbishop King, Bishop Bolton, and Robert Lindsay were some of the men who advised her. She had cousins to visit in town. Even walking in the garden (when Swift was absent) was a pleasure she rarely allowed herself.[2]

We know Swift kept visiting Vanessa, although in 1721 and 1722, when (on top of his crowded schedule) he was away from Dublin for half the year, he would have had trouble fitting her in. During his northern tour he wrote to her complaining of the discomforts of travel but also cheering her with gallant recollections of their Dublin meetings in the house of a discreet acquaintance. The length of time they could pass together goes well beyond what one would have thought possible in their cramped circumstances: up to four hours ending before dinner (a midday meal) or five hours beginning with dinner:

> It would have been infinitely better to have met Kendall, and so forth, where one might pass three or four hours in drinking coffee in the morning, or dining tête à tête, and drinking coffee again till seven.[3]

III. THE END OF VANESSA

I think the death of Mary Vanhomrigh (February 1721) narrowed the arena for both of them. Swift had included 'Molkin' in his attentions to Celbridge, sending her a 'love letter' and making her a curtain for the drama with Vanessa.[4] In the

---

[1] I assume the illness was consumption.

[2] Cf. Swift's sarcasm about her ignorance of the weather; Williams II. 432 (7 Aug. 1722).

[3] 1 Jun. 1722; *ibid.*, II. 426–7. Elsewhere he gives three and five hours as the respective limits.

[4] *Ibid.*, pp. 349–56.

autumn of 1720, when Vanessa's anxieties were properly acute, Swift wrote offering his normal recipe of physical exercise and cheerful books:

> I am in much concern for poor Molkin, and the more because I am sure you are so too. You ought to be as cheerful as you can for both your sakes, and read pleasant things that will make you laugh, and not sit moping with your elbows on your knees on a little stool by the fire.[1]

The prospect of Mary's dying seems to have frightened Swift, who always disliked seeing friends in painful situations.[2] Having failed to write, he explained illogically, 'I was in great apprehension that poor Molkin was worse [i.e., dead?], and till I could be satisfied in that particular, I would not write again.'[3] With this panic added to his ordinary scruples—to the hardships of winter journeys, his own bad health, and the cathedral administration—he pulled back (I think) from Vanessa's enticements. During the winter of 1720–1, he was busily worried about suppressing the prosecution of Waters (for printing the *Proposal for Irish Manufacture*); and he endured a long spell of illness.

Mary's final hours were passed in February 1721. Swift had seen her a few days before; but as usual he lacked the emotional resilience to offer help to Vanessa in person. Neither was the message he sent the sort one would have anticipated from a professional frequenter of deathbeds, nor did it sound as if Vanessa's new ordeal would supply the ground for a more perfect union:

> I am surprised and grieved beyond what I can express. I read your letter twice before I knew what it meant nor can I yet well believe my eyes. Is that poor good creature dead? I observed she looked a little ghastly on Saturday but it is against the usual way for one in her case to die so sudden. For God's sake get your friends about you to advise and to order everything in the formes. It is all you have to do. I want comfort myself in this case, and I can give little. Time alone must give it to you, nothing now is your part but decency. I

[1] 15 Oct. 1720; *ibid.*, p. 360.
[2] Cf. his unwillingness to see Captain Pratt under arrest (*ibid.*, III. 89).
[3] 4 Aug. 1720; *ibid.*, II. 353.

was wholly unprepared against so sudden an event, and pity you most of all creatures at present Monday.[1]

I assume that for a while the effect of Mary's loss was to soften Swift's resistance to the lonely mourner. Yet he would not consciously feed her reveries. 'Cad—assures me', he wrote the following summer, 'he continues to esteem and love and value you above all things, and so will do to the end of his life, but at the same time entreats that you would not make your self or him unhappy by imaginations.'[2] Even as he tried to hold his distance, he could still respond to the need for consolation; and Vanessa had still to endure her genuine trials of grief, law, and finance.

Meeting fresh problems created by Mary's will, Vanessa made inevitable demands on Swift's unique knowledge of her affairs. Along with other advisers like the young lawyer Robert Marshall, he counselled her; and he also dispensed doses of wisdom on the conquest of melancholy. He reminded her of the wish she had had in 1718 to return to England (a plan which Archbishop King had discouraged).[3] Was it without selfish motives that he now urged her to settle her affairs and leave Ireland?[4]

Vanessa was now thirty-three, and Swift was fifty-four; but the seesaw of their eager reluctance never faltered. Certainly the clandestine visits did not halt. While Vanessa lodged in Dublin, they could meet (weekly, perhaps!) at the home of a close-mouthed sympathizer, as they had done at Barber's house in London, years before. Writing to her from the country in the summer of 1722, Swift said,

> I see you this moment as you are visible at ten in the morning. And now you are asking your questions round and I am answering them with a great deal of affected delays, and the same scene has passed forty times as well as the other from two till seven; longer than the first by two hours, yet each has ses agremens particuliers.[5]

---

[1] ?27 Feb. 1721; *ibid.*, pp. 377–8. Mary Vanhomrigh was baptized 7 Sept. 1694 (Ball III. 456); she probably died 27 Feb. 1721 (Williams II. 377, n. 4); and she was buried on Friday, 3 Mar. 1721 in the churchyard of St Andrew's, Dublin (Ball III. 73, n. 1). In her will she bequeathed all her property to her sister (*ibid.*).

[2] 5 Jul. 1721; Williams II. 392.   [3] Ball III. 34, n. 2.

[4] 5 Jul. 1721; Williams II. 393.   [5] 7–8 Aug. 1722; *ibid.*, p. 433.

He sent her frayed compliments, reminded her of their harmless, long-past escapades, warned her against expecting more of them, and ordered books and riding as preventives of spleen:

> Remember, I still enjoin you reading and exercise for the improvement of your mind and health of your body, and grow less romantic, and talk and act like a man of this world.[1]

Although, to give herself recreation, Vanessa went to call on more ladies than before, she found society no relief from dreariness. She supervised her litigations and delivered to Swift the immemorial laments of righteousness under the afflictions of the blind goddess. Above all else, she reproached him for neglecting her.[2] Swift replied from the country, 'When you are melancholy, read diverting or amusing books: it is my receipt, and seldom fails.'[3]

He came back to Dublin about the beginning of October. Vanessa probably moved into town near the same time. Yet the awkwardness of visiting a spinster with no companion would have been more troublesome than seeing her with poor Mary. Besides, by the time Swift returned from his northern tour, it would have been manifest that Vanessa's feet were now set on the same terrible path her sister had followed. The winter would then have weakened her health as it had hurt Mary's. Being the first-born (and having therefore the best constitution), she was the last of her family to fail.

Swift, I am sure, could tolerate the closing pathos of Vanessa's life as little as he could that of any person dear to him. The fear of presiding over her death would have given the last thrust to his wish to stand outside the turbulence. I am inclined to speculate that he foresaw the end, curtailed his visits, and waited for release. He spent the Christmas season 1722 in the country (where I think he also went, on 19 January, to the wedding of John Rochfort); and the following March he gave Stella a mock-heroic poem for her birthday. At the end of that month he left

---

[1] 1 Jun. 1722; *ibid.*, p. 427. Cf. the advice to Sheridan to 'act like a man of this world' (*ibid.*, III. 67).
[2] Probably Jun. 1722; Williams II. 428.   [3] 7 Aug. 1722; *ibid.*, II. 432.

town again, for a country visit of five or six weeks; and by then, with his talent for expecting disaster, he must have thought Vanessa's death was imminent. Before he returned, she had enough foreboding to make a will (1 May 1723). If Swift is not named in it, I believe one reason is that he preferred to be omitted; but thoughtful scholars have inferred that the two quarrelled.[1]

Vanessa died on 2 June 1723. Swift had long planned to make a great southern tour this summer, matching his northern tour. Maybe he tried to time it so he would be gone from Dublin when the news of the death got around. But considering how regularly he made long expeditions in the warm seasons, I hesitate to say so. Certainly he left town shortly after the event;[2] and meanwhile, thanks to Ford's kindness, Stella and Dingley were able to stay on at Wood Park.

At the same time the scandal was spreading. Vanessa's will was proved on 6 June, and must have excited heavy currents of gossip. The intentions behind it seem dark. There are seventeen recipients of small legacies (twenty-five pounds or less), including old friends, relations, servants, and advisers. Among these are Archbishop King, Bishop Bolton, Erasmus Lewis, and Robert Lindsay.[3] I suspect that Bolton and Lindsay were recommended to Vanessa by Swift for their extraordinary knowledge of the law; and since they, like King and Lewis, were on excellent terms with him, their names suggest no revulsion against his influence.

To everyone's astonishment, the bulk of the still substantial estate (it finally came to five thousand pounds) was left to the two executors: Robert Marshall, the lawyer who was probably Vanessa's chief legal adviser, and George Berkeley, of whom Swift spoke as he did of Addison and Stopford—with tenderness and admiration. As the two legatees were talented and young, it

---

[1] See Ball and Williams on Swift's last letter to her, 7–8 Aug. 1723; I disagree with them.

[2] Williams II. 457.

[3] An Irish country gentleman and lawyer, graduate of Trinity College, who was well known to Swift as counsel to the proctor of the cathedral, which he became in 1722, probably at Swift's recommendation.

looks as if Vanessa wished to enrich two gentlemen who needed only money to make their careers secure. It was not a will Swift would have approved of—the lack of any large bequest to a public charity would have angered him—but otherwise I doubt that it reveals a sudden turn away from Swift.

When Berkeley learned of his fortune, he gave no sign of having expected it. 'Mrs Hester Van Omry,' he wrote (4 June 1723),

> a lady to whom I was a perfect stranger, having never in the whole course of my life, to my knowledge, exchanged one single word with her, died on Sunday night [2 June]. Yesterday her will was opened, by which it appears that I am constituted executor, the advantage whereof is computed ... to be worth three thousand pounds.[1]

As an executor Berkeley had to go through the letters Vanessa had saved, but he pronounced Swift immaculate. Delany says Berkeley 'found, upon examination, (as he frequently assured me) that they contained nothing, which would either do honour to her character, or bring the least reflection upon Cadenus. ... not the least hint of a criminal correspondence between them'.[2] Marshall, years later, gave the same assurance to the younger Sheridan.[3] Swift's enemy Bishop Evans had other news; and he told the Archbishop of Canterbury,

> 'Tis generally believed she lived without God in the world. When Dean Price (the minister of her parish) offered her his services in her last minutes: she sent him word no Price no prayers with a scrap out of the Tale of a Tub ... and so she died.[4]

Between these end points we may assume the other rumours of the time could be graphed.

IV. EPILOGUE

The paradoxes of this dismal entente call for some resolution. Swift, I suppose, wanted a rational friend who would appear to

---

[1] Luce, p. 130.   [2] Delany, p. 123.   [3] Sheridan, p. 339.   [4] 27 Jul. 1723.

respect conventions, a junior Stella with money and social rank added. But the docility he asked for could never have worn well on a mistress who felt independent of him; and yet he preached independence, just as he told her that 'common forms were not designed/Directors to a noble mind'.[1] His addiction to first-born, fatherless girls in poor health and much younger than himself, I have already connected with his own child-hood.[2]

The wish to escape from sexuality without losing its thrills, can be seen in his effort to endow Vanessa with masculine attributes. In the poem about their friendship he was careful to include the following lines—after a passage in which Venus and the graces have blessed the girl with female charms, Athene is tricked into thinking the babe is male—

> Then sows within her tender mind
> Seeds long unknown to womankind,
> For manly bosoms chiefly fit,
> The seeds of knowledge, judgment, wit.
> Her soul was suddenly endu'd
> With justice, truth and fortitude;
> With honour, which no breath can stain,
> Which malice must attack in vain;
> With open heart and bounteous hand.[3]

Sexuality and marriage were not elements in Swift's scheme. So long as Vanessa put up with his caprices, showered him with affection, copied his ideas, and took his advice seriously, he could indulge himself in the titillations of her seductiveness. Her bad health had a charm beyond that of a mirror-image; for it meant that death might cut their tie before it grew intolerable. 'I never knew a very deserving person of that sex [i.e., the female sex]', he once told Bolingbroke, 'who had not too much reason to complain of ill health.'[4]

---

[1] *Cadenus and Vanessa*, ll. 612–13. Cf. Williams II. 148–9.
[2] See above, II. 70.
[3] *Cadenus and Vanessa*, ll. 692–3.
[4] 5 Apr. 1729; Sherburn III. 28.

That Vanessa could not bring herself to give up Swift is less puzzling. His scoldings and aloofness added power to his fundamentally attractive union of father and lover. Secure in the sense that he would never give her physical satisfactions, she could let her quasi-incestuous fantasies expand. In her growing loneliness, as she lost each member of her family and her English roots as well, she needed such a figure more.

But here at least Swift does not bear the guilt of his dealings with Stella. It would be fatuous to charge him with misleading a rich woman who at the age of twenty-six tracked him against his express cautions from London to Dublin and who pursued him nine years more. Since, during that slow-paced finale, their relationship was basically static, and since Vanessa, though the eldest of the four Vanhomrigh children, was the longest-lived, he can hardly be blamed for her death.

Was it unnatural for Swift to suppose that a young lady who had accepted so many conditions could be brought to accept all? I think not; but it was certainly naïve. If Swift was not always a myopic reader of men, his incompetence to handle those who engaged his most subterranean feelings is glaringly exposed in this case.

We must also remember that Esther Vanhomrigh did not exist uniquely for the Dean of St Patrick's. Apart from the men he knew—Ford, Lindsay, Dr Pratt, Bishop Bolton, Archbishop King—she had an independent range of acquaintances, and other employments besides watering her couch with tears. Indeed, she herself once said, 'You know, I love law-business.'[1] The letters which she saved, she had written while beating herself into agonies that might move Swift. She did have resources of her own—a bright, curious mind, a home furnished and maintained in great comfort, an assured position in society. Without him she was in misery often but not continually. Nobody could make groans her meat day and night for nine uninterrupted years.

---

[1] June 1713; Williams I. 372.

V. HEROIC EPISTLES

As for the letters,[1] which did not begin to appear in print for over forty years, they deserve to be treated as something more than biographical documents. The best of Swift's represent one kind of rhetoric; Vanessa's represent another. For coherence of structure, intensity of expression, and modernity of style Vanessa's letters are superior to those which Swift wrote to her or to Stella.

The mark that distinguishes and dominates them is passion. Maybe the letters actually sent were more reserved than the drafts the lonely spinster kept. But these drafts maintain a directness and single-mindedness typical of love letters. Like Boswell, Vanessa had two subjects: her listener and herself. External events could only frame this relationship. Anecdotes are rare and vague in her letters; she gives few characterizations of interesting persons; she rehearses little news or gossip, gives no account of recent books. In other words, she lacks the substantive quality of typically good letters of the eighteenth century— say those of Lady Mary Wortley Montagu or of Horace Walpole.

But the immediacy and impetuosity of her style are hardly ever relaxed; the confessional exposure of the heights and depths of feeling is continual but varied, and may reflect the influence of the *Lettres portugaises*. Besides these prehensile gifts Vanessa has wit, and uses it in ways that her particular correspondent will appreciate. In doing so, she illustrates a critical principle, that the form of a letter is dictated by the relation between the writer and the recipient. Thus, complaining as usual of Swift's failure to write to her, she once wrote,

> you must needs be extremely happy where you are to forget your absent friends and I believe you have formed a new system and think

---

[1] Twenty-eight of Swift's letters are preserved, seventeen of Vanessa's drafts. Of all these, Hawkesworth published all or part of eighteen (and referred to another) in his edition, 1766; Scott published forty-four (all from a transcript and some incomplete) in 1814; A. Martin Freeman published forty-five (all but one from holograph MSS.) accurately in 1921; and Sir Harold Williams corrected that text in his own edition, 1963–5.

there is no more of this world passing your sensible horizon. If this be your notion I must excuse you; if not you can plead no other excuse, and if it be so I must reckon myself of another world. But I shall have much ado to be persuaded till you send me some convincing arguments of it. Don't dally in a thing of this consequence but demonstrate that 'tis possible to keep up a correspondence between friends though in different worlds.[1]

The wit in this early letter is good enough for Dorothy Osborne writing to William Temple. But it is cut to suit a quite different correspondent. When Vanessa mocks at philosophical systems, she consciously mirrors Swift's own attitudes; and the spontaneity with which she gives her conceit a series of graceful turns suggests his own manner of gallantry. When she explicitly considers the foundation of their friendship, she (oddly enough) sees it as rational—as he would have wished; yet the rational element is just what her style ignores. In fact, her accomplishment as an epistolary author depends on the fixity of her passion, which gives, over the years, a lyric pathos to her yearning for an inactive, absentee lover.

Swift's replies to his suffering satellite reveal other qualities. He could be *galant* and *sympathique* and *précieux*. But he could also achieve bathos with his incongruous appeals to reason—as in this response to her single-minded ardour,

> We differ prodigiously in one point, I fly from the spleen to the world's end; you run out of your way to meet it. I doubt the bad weather has hindered you much from the diversions of your country house; and put you upon thinking in your chamber. The use I have made of it was to read I know not how many diverting books of history and travels. I wish you would get yourself a horse, and have always two servants to attend you, and visit your neighbours, the worse the better.[2]

In other words, Do as I do.

Many of Swift's letters to Vanessa are unusually coherent. He concentrates on the themes of her own character and its relation

---

[1] 1 Sept. 1712; Williams I. 309. I suppose there is an allusion to Berkeley's immaterialism.

[2] *Ibid.*, II. 429–30; 13 Jul. 1722.

to his. But he also brings in a miscellany of names and events. Often he reports on his recent trips or pastimes; he tells what people are doing around him; he gives advice about her health and gloom. Into the closeted air of her own letters Swift brings fresh scenes of the great and petty world.

Yet his are seldom excellent letters. The finest passages often deal with facts he could tell anyone. The most conventional, threadbare phrases are usually found in the passages devoted to the merits of his panting admirer, and suggest the tradition of *lettres galantes*. Often it would be hard to decide from the language what sort of connection there was between the recipient and himself: it might be addressed to a father, a brother, or an old friend not seen for years.

I pass over the many piquant or touching sentences from Swift's letters to Vanessa because they would misrepresent the general effect of a man straining to transform a romantic obsession into a placid, playful intimacy. In his best prose it is normal for Swift to turn style against meaning, to sound casual when he means something shocking. It is normal for Vanessa to make style and meaning congruent, as Swift often does in verse. Her prose suggests the manner we think of as Romantic: she exerts herself to sound pathetic and sincere.

But Swift leans another way. As his relation to the person addressed grows more emotional, his manner turns formal, whimsical, or hollowly conventional. He will impose the distance the other person wishes to bridge. He will convey love through teasing humour; or he will mechanically echo the rhetoric of compliment. Too often with Vanessa he is mechanical, or else he gives up the enterprise altogether and turns didactic. The truly irrational spring of the partnership between the uneasy dean and his quasi-mistress drives him not only to use private codes and a foreign language but also to express himself with a reserve that compensates for her extravagance. He remains Swift, and cannot write badly. But the more she resists the part of a cheerful spinster—fond of books, normal society, and improving conversation—the more evasive he must become.

VI. ADVICE TO A WIFE

At the very time when Swift was absorbing the fact that Vanessa would soon die, he was also composing an essay of instruction for a young bride. I think the dean may have attended the marriage (19 January 1723), because of his involvement with the two families. Deborah was the daughter of Thomas Staunton, a master in chancery, who gave Swift legal and financial counsel; he was soon to receive an honorary LL.D. from Trinity College.[1] John Rochfort, second son of the former Chief Baron, was one of Swift's favourite young men, and described by him as 'of good education and learning, of an excellent understanding, and an exact taste ... great modesty, a most amiable sweetness of temper, and an unusual disposition to sobriety and virtue'.[2] And of course Swift spent long holidays at Gaulstown, the Rochfort family seat, with John among the others.

As if he wished to give the young couple a wedding present, Swift wrote the essay a few weeks after the ceremony, and called it 'A Letter to a Very Young Lady, on Her Marriage'.[3] It fascinates me as showing how Swift—at a time when his anxious asexualism was heightened by the crisis of Vanessa's passion— could reach down into his deep, centrifugal fear of sexuality and relate its eccentric patterns to an object and an ideal in the social order, making the connection through an acceptable literary form, the letter of advice. Where a common neurotic would have suffered panic, Swift converted the incipient emotion into rhetorical energy.

As usual, the anonymous or pseudonymous letter had the advantage for Swift of releasing him from the constraints of his public dignity while affording the candour and intimacy of a private message. Like Samuel Johnson, Swift could evade the onus of his self-criticism by using a disguise; he could also enjoy the pleasures of impersonation that meant so much to his ego;

[1] He died 20 Mar. 1732; cf. *Gentleman's Magazine*, 1732, p. 678.
[2] Davis IX. 89.
[3] The holograph manuscript, in the Huntington Library, is dated 11 Feb. 1722-3. The essay was first published in 1727, in the first volume of the Pope–Swift *Miscellanies*. See Davis IX. xxvii–xxx and 373–5.

and simultaneously, by hiding his bachelorhood, he gave his case more force.

An exemplary passage will reveal what is most important in Swift's doctrine. Starting, I suppose, with an unconscious wish to eliminate sexual differences, he achieves not an embodiment of eccentric prejudice but a sane moral principle, that virtue itself has no gender. A woman's conduct, therefore, should be based not on the theoretical limitations of her sexual nature but on what is proper for male and female alike. Unlike the Puritans, Swift would not conceive of women as quintessentially mothers. Neither would he treat spinsters as freaks. One might of course blame him for implying a contempt for the womanly features of women. But one might also praise him for elevating them to the status of intellectual creatures.

His attitude fits into the main tradition of Anglican thought. It can be derived from St Paul's saying that in Christ 'there is neither male nor female, but all are one',[1] and it was embodied in Richard Allestree's *The Ladies Calling* (1673), which achieved an eleventh impression in 1720.[2] In the 'sublimest part' of human nature, Allestree said, women were the equals of men: 'they have souls of as divine an original, as endless a duration, and as capable of infinite beatitude. That spiritual essence, that ray of divinity, owns no distinction of sexes.'[3] But where Allestree contrasted the retired existence of women with the active life of men, Swift refused to allow any moral distinction, and declared—I think, nobly—

I am ignorant of any one quality that is amiable in a man, which is not equally so in a woman: I do not except even modesty, and gentleness of nature.[4] Nor do I know one vice or folly, which is not equally detestable in both. There is, indeed, one infirmity which is generally allowed you, I mean that of cowardice. Yet there should seem to be something very capricious, that when women profess

---

[1] Gal. iii. 28.
[2] I assume it was by Allestree, although some excellent scholars doubt the attribution.
[3] Fol. b3ᵛ.
[4] Possibly a response to Allestree's dwelling upon modesty, pp. 1–30 and throughout the book.

their admiration for a colonel or a captain, on account of his valour, they should fancy it a very graceful becoming quality in themselves, to be afraid of their own shadows; to scream in a barge, when the weather is calmest, or in a coach at the ring; to run from a cow at an hundred yards distance; to fall into fits at the sight of a spider, an ear-wig, or a frog. At least, if cowardice be a sign of cruelty (as it is generally granted) I can hardly think it an accomplishment so desirable, as to be thought worthy of improving by affectation.[1]

The moral similarity in turn upholds an intellectual similarity. Again Swift was drawing on a strong tradition, not only Christian but humanistic. Halifax, in his *Advice to a Daughter* (1688), took the more common line that women were born with less understanding than men; for, he said, 'the men, who were to be the lawgivers, had the larger share of reason bestowed upon them'.[2] Halifax thus accepted the old consensus that women are, as Castiglione said, imperfect creatures, incapable of the same virtues as their husbands.[3]

But Swift sided with a powerful minority. The education of Queen Elizabeth and other learned princesses on the continent had produced an exemplary effect, all the stronger for resting on a bottom of careful theory. Even before Elizabeth's birth, Thomas More had delivered a famous statement on the intellectual powers of women; and More stood among Swift's heroes as Elizabeth stood among his heroines:

> Nor do I think it affects the harvest, that a man or a woman has sown the seed. If they are worthy of being ranked with the human race, if they are distinguished by reason from beasts; that learning, by which the reason is cultivated, is equally suitable to both. . . . But if the female soil be in its nature stubborn, and more productive of weeds than fruits, it ought, in my opinion, to be more diligently cultivated with learning and good instruction.[4]

More's admiring contemporary, the learned Luis Vives, had taught the same principle, rejecting the notion that scholarly studies inclined women toward evil manners; a mind set upon

---

[1] Davis IX. 92–3.   [2] P. 8.

[3] *The Courtier*, trans. T. Hoby, Everyman's Library (London, 1928), p. 196.

[4] *Correspondence*, ed. E. F. Rogers (Princeton, 1947), no. 63, as quoted by Ruth Kelso, *Doctrine for the Lady of the Renaissance* (Urbana, Ill., 1956), p. 62.

learning, said Vives, will abhor lust and light pleasures.[1] Thomas Elyot and Roger Ascham followed the same pro- gramme,[2] and the great educator Richard Mulcaster said that God would never have given women 'their own towardness' if it was to be left idle.[3]

The Puritans undermined such ideals with their picture of women as, at best, obedient wives, sober mothers, and efficient housekeepers. By insisting on one standard of morality for both sexes, the Puritans did strengthen the integrity of the family.[4] But they also hurt the dignity of spinsters and bachelors. The normal Protestant identification of ideal ladies with chaste matrons tightened the chains on females; and the Puritans made the chains heavier.

Puritan ministers felt driven to exhibit their detestation of Popish error by embracing matrimony as a holy rule. A tiny remnant might be supposed to enjoy the gift of continence; but otherwise none might escape the duties of the marriage bed. One scholar says, 'This dedication of the Puritan clerical caste to conjugal life was hardly less important in its effect than that of courtly poets to the worship of feminine beauty.'[5] Inevitably, women found their place defined by such teachings. 'Who can be ignorant', cried Milton, 'that woman was created for man, and not man for woman?'[6]

Allestree, who had fought against the Puritans in the Civil Wars, disliked such reductive simplifications. Like Ascham, he found the agricultural metaphor expressive: speaking of women's 'principal endowment of the rational nature, I mean their understanding', he said,

> it will be a little hard to pronounce, that they are naturally inferior to men; when 'tis considered how much of extrinsic weight is put in

---

[1] *De institutione feminae Christianae* I. iv, as quoted by Kelso, *ibid.*

[2] Kelso, p. 74; Carroll Camden, *The Elizabethan Woman* (Houston, Texas, 1952), pp. 47–8.

[3] *Positions . . . for the Training Up of Children* (1581), pp. 166–74, as quoted by Camden, p. 47.

[4] Louis B. Wright, *Middle-Class Culture in Elizabethan England* (Chapel Hill, N.C., 1935), p. 218.

[5] W. R. and M. Haller, 'The Puritan Art of Love', *HLQ* v (1942), 238.

[6] *Doctrine and Discipline of Divorce* II. xv.

the balance to turn it on the men's side. Men have their parts cultivated and improved by education, refined by learning and the arts, are like an inclosed piece of a common, which by industry and husbandry, becomes a different thing from the rest, though the natural turf owned no such inequality. And truly had women the same advantage, I dare not say but they would make as good returns of it.[1]

Yet even Allestree said almost nothing about the choice of books or intellectual pursuits for young women, except that they ought not to read romances, and that 'writing' and 'languages' belonged in the list of their worthwhile employments.[2] As for spinsters, he paid tribute to women who renounced marriage to devote themselves to God; and he even had a good, non-Puritan word to say for nunneries properly rectified and regulated.[3] But spinsters in general tempted this generally sober moralist to turn satirical.[4]

Swift had a different tendency. Hating the Puritans as venomously as he did, it is no wonder that he felt satisfied to remain a celibate priest. He may remind us of Tertullian and Jerome when he extols the crown of virginity. He may be a self-deceiver or a hypocrite when he laments the advantage, to a woman like Esther Johnson, of becoming a wife—'since it is held so necessary and convenient a thing for ladies to marry; and that time takes off from the lustre of virgins in all other eyes but mine'.[5] But he deserves some credit for respecting the character of independent, single females.[6]

Although Swift's essay is short, and limited to a few themes, it is not orderly; for the same topics are discussed in widely separated paragraphs, and some important topics receive less attention than insignificant ones. For all Swift's dwelling on the common qualities of both sexes, his language grows sharp when he handles what he calls women's faults. Some of these are the vices dealt with by most 'advisors' of ladies: e.g., the desire for expensive clothes, the enjoyment of trifling conversation, over-

---

[1] 11th impression, 1720, fols. b2^v–c1.   [2] Pp. 163–5.   [3] Pp. 156–8.
[4] Pp. 157–60.   [5] Williams I. 45–6.
[6] Cf. my discussion in 'Letters of Advice to Young Spinsters', in Earl Miner, ed., *Stuart and Georgian Moments* (Berkeley, 1972), pp. 246–51.

indulgence in visits, intimacy with a favourite servant. But others are Swiftian: showing fondness for one's husband before strangers, over-anxiety for an absent husband. So also the virtues Swift recommends are sometimes commonplace, such as modesty and reserve. But some are surprising, like the advice to prefer the society of men to that of women: 'I never yet knew a tolerable woman to be fond of her own sex.'[1]

Obviously, he is not trying to survey all the duties of a wife, only those that interest him and that have point for the addressee. Mrs Rochfort is very young, and while of excellent character, has had little education; yet she is married to a highly cultivated gentleman. With these facts in mind one remains startled to see Swift ignoring the duties of motherhood, barely mentioning domestic economy, and dwelling on the obligations of a good hostess. I am struck to realize how much of the essay would be suitable for a spinster who wished to enjoy intellectual male society without losing her reputation.

Furthermore, Swift never suggests that equality of virtue and understanding should imply equal authority. Rather he dwells on the need for the wife to gain her husband's respect; and he insists that the way to do so is by improving her mind. She is to entertain male acquaintances (chosen by her husband), to attend to the conversation of learned men, and to read books chosen by Swift:

> You must improve your mind, by closely pursuing such a method of study, as I shall direct or approve of. You must get a collection of history and travels, which I will recommend to you; and spend some hours every day in reading them, and making extracts from them, if your memory be weak. You must invite persons of knowledge and understanding to an acquaintance with you, by whose conversation you may learn to correct your taste and judgment: And when you can bring yourself to comprehend and relish the good sense of others, you will arrive, in time, to think rightly yourself, and to become a reasonable and agreeable companion. This must produce in your husband a true rational love and esteem for you, which old age will not diminish.[2]

---

[1] Davis IX. 88.   [2] *Ibid.*, 90.

The restrained though imperative tone of this prescription echoes the advice to Vanessa and tells us how Swift must have trained Stella (who had a poor memory). It also provides the reasonable alternative to the very different tone Swift brings to his picture of a false marriage, reliant upon affectation and 'romantic' emotion. When he erupts in contempt for the bride who shows 'the least degree of fondness to [her] husband before any witnesses whatsoever', he is perhaps over-reacting against his own fear of womanly caresses. But he is also ridiculing the hypocrisy of many marriages he knew only too well.

A trouble with the essay is that these intensities so regularly rise with Swift's attention to female faults. It is a normal source of his power that, as in the paragraph I have quoted about the amiable qualities of men and women, a style of moderation should give way to anger; that abstract virtues should yield to a descending order of concrete unpleasantness—a colonel, a barge or coach, a cow, a spider; that a languid affirmation should open the paragraph and a biting aphorism should close it. In effect we have that sense of imprisonment giving way to free feeling which marks both the style of Swift's sentences and the rhythm of *Gulliver's Travels* as a narrative. But we cannot feel easy to notice that the strengths of women receive such brief approval and their weakness such extended blame.

That Swift was capable of another style we know from a charming poem 'The First of April',[1] written about the time Vanessa was composing her will. Swift stayed with Robert Cope at Loughgall in the spring of 1723, probably arriving at the end of March and leaving at the beginning of May.[2] He wrote a letter of gratitude, unusually vigorous and direct, when he got back:

> I will put the greatest compliment on you that ever I made; which is, to profess sincerely that I never found anything wrong in your house; and that you alone of all my Irish acquaintance have found out the secret of loving your lady and children, with some reserve of

---

[1] *Poems* I. 320–2. I agree with Williams's guess about the date of composition.
[2] Williams II. 453.

love for your friends, and, which is more, without being troublesome; and Mrs Cope, I think, excels even you, at least you have
made me think so, and I beg you will deceive me as long as I live.[1]

The contrast between Celbridge and Loughgall must have
reassured a man who had no personal memories of a stable,
cheerful, coherent (and prosperous) family, and whose own
failure as a parental figure must have troubled him bitterly at
this moment.

I suppose he wrote the poem as an April Fool tribute to the
Copes. It is a successful eulogy in octosyllabic couplets. As usual
Swift needed a *donnée*—a humorous analogy, riddle, hoax,
transformation; a burlesque of mythology (especially for a compliment), or a simple farcical drama—to organize it; and he
chose the idea of a practical joke played by Apollo on 1 April.
The god sends the muses to the Copes' house to bestow blessings
on the children. But when the emissaries arrive, they find they
have been tricked, because the children already possess everything that heaven could intend as a blessing. The peculiar
feature of the poem is that its most memorable couplets are
devoted to motherhood, a rare theme for Swift:

> They peep'd, and saw a lady there
> Pinning on coifs and combing hair;
> Soft'ning with songs to son or daughter,
> The persecution of cold water;
> Still pleas'd with the good-natur'd noise,
> And harmless frolics of her boys;
> Equal to all in care and love,
> Which all deserve and all improve;
> To kitchen, parlour, nurs'ry flies,
> And seems all feet, and hands, and eyes.
> No thought of hers does ever roam,
> But for her 'squire when he's from home;
> And scarce a day, can spare a minute
> From husband, children, wheel, or spinet.[2]

The poem is also neat and symmetrical, in three sections, with
the lines of eulogy in the middle, between the setting-up of the

---

[1] *Ibid.*, p. 453.   [2] *Poems* I. 321–2.

joke at the beginning and the éclaircissement at the end. The tight design may spring from the conventionality of the doctrine. In 'A Letter to a Very Young Lady' the looseness of design suggests that Swift was asserting his own principles against a conventional opposition. Of course, the 'Letter' was planned for a particular girl marrying a man whose special requirements were in the author's mind. But that husband is close to an ideal for Swift; and if we reflect on the emphases of the essay (without mistaking it for Swift's considered statement on all the responsibilities of a wife), we may guess at the deep source of its peremptory, tutorial manner—more appropriate for a child than for a married woman however young. By ignoring motherhood, by concentrating on the intellectual education of the young bride, on her responsibilities as a hostess and as a rational companion for a well-read man of taste, Swift is starting Mrs Rochfort on the same programme he had offered Esther Johnson and Esther Vanhomrigh. He is in effect acquiring a new pupil to replace one who is dying; and unlike her predecessor this candidate will be unable to propose marriage to him.[1]

[1] I do not accept as genuine the poems supposed to be by Vanessa (*Poems* II. 717–20).

Chapter Twenty

STELLA

C learly, Swift had a single mould into which he tried to press the character of any young lady who attracted him, and that mould was constructed from his own experience as a child. He evaded marriage[1] in order to escape his father's fate: an untimely death, with the abandonment of a pregnant wife to the dependence of poverty. So also his way of showing love was to offer the most valuable gift he knew, the rôle of the father he never possessed. He had to educate the woman in such a way as to eradicate the sexual difference that excited and troubled him; he had to depreciate the physical basis of her seductive power and to elevate the moral and intellectual qualities. Yet he kept the prerogatives of male hegemony in an enlarged form and even added those of a female; for he required women to make the first advances to him rather than he to them.[2] He chose frail women and separated them from their mothers to increase their dependence; but he attentively guarded their interests and urged them to learn independence; because as surrogates for his younger self they had to be cherished and respected as he had not been. In caring for them, he was

---

[1] I do not believe that Swift ever went through a marriage ceremony with Esther Johnson, any more than that he ever had sexual relations with her. There is no way to prove either of these negatives, however. But neither have we any document recording such a marriage. Besides, an unwitnessed ceremony would have been invalid. In documents sworn to by Esther Johnson, she described herself as a spinster; and of course she had nothing to gain from an unacknowledged, invalid marriage that left both of them living as celibate friends. I put great weight on the language of Swift's letters to Sheridan and Stopford on Stella's approaching death, and on the language of the prayers he wrote for her. In all of these he could have avoided the issue but chose words that specified their connection as merely one of friendship.

[2] Davis v. 197; Williams III. 196 (Mrs Howard has made 'the first advance'). He reserved to himself the privilege of not seeing the Princess except when she sent for him (*ibid.*, III. 230, IV. 98).

both repeating and mending the wrongs he had once suffered.

When Swift felt secure with the woman, he left her for long periods of time and went to visit other friends, even as his mother had left him. But he liked the beloved to have a female companion, as his sister had had his mother. He supplied the beloved with the money he had lacked as a child, and did so in such a way that she would not feel humiliated by the gift: so both Stella and Vanessa were assisted from his purse.

For such a personality the most enduring intimacy would have to be one that could evolve and deepen even more than the marital tie—one with a woman who had an instinct for suiting her conduct to his needs: a woman who could act maternal while letting Swift keep his sense of fatherly dominion, who could tolerate his absences as a mother tolerates those of a successful son, who could be self-contained and decisive as a man, accept Swift's tutoring like a daughter, but preside at his table like a wife. Stella must have had this adaptability; and unlike the liaison with Vanessa, Swift's friendship with her changed and grew.

But it is hard to discover the details of her character except from Swift's biased descriptions. Delany, who could have given a full account of Stella, was respectfully brief and vague. He said she had 'a great fund of natural cheerfulness', and that her wit, elegance, and humour 'set off [Swift's] slightest entertainments'.[1] Delany also mentioned the soothing effect, upon Swift, of her 'sweet temper and lenitive advice'.[2]

Swift endows her with a happy conjunction of 'civility, freedom, easiness and sincerity'.[3] Even more than Delany, he dwelt on her humour and wit, good sense and sound judgment.[4] He tells us that she had a poor memory[5] but was remarkably attentive in conversation:

> She never had the least absence of mind in conversation, nor given to interruption, or appeared eager to put in her word by waiting impatiently until another had done. She spoke in a most agreeable

---

[1] Delany, p. 62. [2] *Ibid.*, p. 144. [3] Davis v. 230.
[4] Williams III. 46; Davis v. 228-9,236. [5] Davis v. 228.

voice, in the plainest words, never hesitating, except out of modesty before new faces, where she was somewhat more reserved; nor, among her nearest friends, ever spoke much at a time. She was but little versed in the common topics of female chat; scandal, censure, and detraction never came out of her mouth. Yet among a few friends, in private conversation, she made little ceremony in discovering her contempt of a coxcomb, and describing her contempt of a coxcomb, and describing all his follies to the life; but the follies of her own sex she was rather inclined to extenuate or to pity.[1]

Like many people who do not talk freely, Mrs Johnson could be sharp-tongued when she spoke at all; and like most people who have been strictly brought up, she judged moral failings severely.[2] This tinge of manly rectitude matched her unfeminine bravery. 'With all the softness that became a lady', Swift said, 'she had the personal courage of a hero.'[3] Once when she was about twenty-four, and living in William Street,[4] an isolated quarter of Dublin, a gang of burglars tried to break into the house. There was a boy among the servants but no man. While the other females and he withdrew in terror, Stella tiptoed to her dining-room window, carrying a pistol. She wore a black hood to prevent her from being seen in the darkness. Quietly raising the sash, she aimed straight at one of the thieves and shot him so neatly that he died the next day.[5] When Swift described her courage in a poem about fifteen years later, he used language anticipating that of 'A Letter to a Very Young Lady'[6] and continued,

> Say, Stella, was Prometheus blind,
> And forming you, mistook your kind?
> No: 'Twas for you alone he stole
> The fire that forms a manly soul.[7]

One is not surprised that her visitors were more often men than women, particularly clergymen. When Swift wished to give examples of Mrs Johnson's friends, he named half a dozen

[1] *Ibid.*, p. 230.   [2] *Ibid.*, pp. 234–5.   [3] *Ibid.*, p. 229.
[4] I accept Ball's identification of the street and his suggesting 1703–5 as the approximate date (IV. 453).
[5] Davis V. 229–30.   [6] 'To Stella, Visiting Me', ll. 65–78.
[7] *Ibid.*, ll. 85–8.

bishops.[1] One reason for the preference was that she enjoyed reading and discussing books which women seldom read: history, especially that of Greece and Rome, though also that of France and England; books of travel; the higher levels of recent poetry and essays. She read French; and Swift claimed that she understood Platonic and Epicurean philosophy (by which I suspect he meant the versions of those doctrines summarized in a handbook like Thomas Stanley's *History of Philosophy*), that she could point out the errors in Hobbes's materialism (I suppose, as expounded by Swift), and showed good taste in literature generally. An author, Swift said, might rely on her advice 'if he intended to send a thing into the world, provided it was on a subject that came within the compass of her knowledge'—from which I infer that he sometimes asked her to criticize his own productions, though he obviously preferred the taste of Charles Ford.[2]

Stella, in other words, had gone through the curriculum laid down in 'A Letter to a Very Young Lady' and had emerged with first-class honours. The congruence of her attributes with the ideals of the instructor must be due in part to the fact that we get most of our information from his record. Yet the difference from Vanessa glares at one. Supremely important was the maternal care that Vanessa, like most secret mistresses, could seldom display. Even in the years when her own health was failing, Stella would make little of her pains and fatigues if Swift wanted attention. She nursed him through his illnesses, heard out his daily complaints, and threw a motherly screen between his irritable nature and the haze of annoyances that beset it. In the couplets he wrote praising her solicitude, Swift marks his own lack of manliness, suggesting a filial attitude toward the nurse:

> When on my sickly couch I lay,
> Impatient both of night and day,
> Lamenting in unmanly strains,
> Call'd ev'ry pow'r to ease my pains,
> Then Stella ran to my relief
> With cheerful face, and inward grief;

[1] Davis v. 233–5.   [2] *Ibid.*, p. 231.

> And, though by Heaven's severe decree
> She suffers hourly more than me,
> No cruel master could require
> From slaves employ'd for daily hire
> What Stella by her friendship warm'd,
> With vigour and delight perform'd.[1]

The lines sound weak, because Swift's verses rarely succeed when he tries to match a positive emotion with a simple, appropriate style.

Swift also shows Stella re-enacting the old scene of the mama who tastes the medicine herself in order to persuade the child to down it:

> My sinking spirits now[2] supplies
> With cordials in her hands, and eyes.
> Now, with a soft and silent tread,
> Unheard she moves about my bed.
> I see her taste each nauseous draught,
> And so obligingly am caught;
> I bless the hand from whence they came,
> Nor dare distort my face for shame.[3]

The boyishness of the difficult patient shows one more aspect of Swift's character that we could never have guessed. Here the dean who prizes his dignity exposes his weakest self to the woman who will never betray him. In another poem, Swift puts yet more sharply the contrast between Stella's maturity and his unreasonableness:

> She tends me, like an humble slave;
> And when indecently I rave,
> When out my brutish passions break,
> With gall in ev'ry word I speak,
> She, with soft speech, my anguish cheers,
> Or melts my passions down with tears;
> Although 'tis easy to descry
> She wants assistance more than I,
> Yet seems to feel my pains alone,
> And is a Stoic in her own.[4]

---

[1] 'To Stella, Visiting Me', ll. 97–108. [2] 'She', understood.
[3] 'To Stella, Visiting Me', ll. 109–16. [4] 'To Stella', 1724, ll. 9–18.

I think I detect a still higher level of moral authority in a prose sentence of Swift's about Stella's indifference to the violence of others in argument. She was 'never positive', he said; and when people were foolishly stubborn, she generally drew them out—to their own disadvantage—rather than to resist them. In this, Swift says, she was like Addison:

> when she saw any of the company very warm in a wrong opinion, she was more inclined to confirm them in it, than oppose them. The excuse she commonly gave when her friends asked the reason, was, That it prevented noise, and saved time.[1]

Then Swift goes on to use a turn of phrase by which he could refer to himself: still speaking of the 'infirmity' of positiveness in argument, he says he has known her to be 'very angry with some whom she much esteemed for sometimes falling into that infirmity'.[2] I think of his picture of her quizzically surprised by one of his outrageous remarks, turning up her forehead and striking the table with her hand.[3] Stella knew, it seems, when she could properly open Swift to her displeasure; and he acknowledged her justice, although he refused to tolerate Vanessa's complaints.

Stella was conspicuous for virtues that we miss in Vanessa even if Swift recommended them. He enlarges on Stella's thrift in a style that might make a modern hedonist uncomfortable. Until the girl was in her early twenties, he says, she was careless in her expenses, finally running deeply into debt with shop-keepers. But when she reformed 'and continued all her life a most prudent economist'—living neatly and even elegantly, but well within her income; avoiding expense in clothes so she might have enough for decent hospitality and for charity. She and Mrs Dingley always lived in lodgings, and had three servants: two maids and a man.[4] When Swift vacated the deanery to go on his travels, the ladies often moved in, to save money.

Unlike Vanessa, Stella enjoyed society and conversation; she only wished she could entertain her friends more often and more

---

[1] Davis v. 235. [2] *Ibid.* [3] Williams II. 145.
[4] Davis v. 231–3.

generously than her income allowed.[1] Swift of course helped out
by including her in his own parties and by quietly supplying
food and drink when he expected her to entertain guests like
himself. One of the most appealing letters he ever wrote was a
mock-invitation. He wished Stella to share a dinner with Swift
and some friends. So he sent an ingenious message pretending
that she had already invited herself to the deanery. Actually, she
was to bring the food, and he would provide the wine. In his
mock-protestations he tells her who the other guests will be—
viz., Sheridan, John Grattan, and, after dinner, Delany; and he
specifies the wine as Margaux:

> Jack Grattan said nothing to me of it till last night; 'tis none of my
> fault: how did I know but you were to dine abroad? You should have
> sent your messenger sooner; yes, I think the dinner you provided for
> yourselves may do well enough here, but pray send it soon. I wish
> you would give a body more early warning; but you must blame
> yourselves. Delany says he will come in the evening; and for aught I
> know Sheridan may be here at dinner: which of you [i.e., Dingley or
> Stella] was it that undertook this frolic? Your letter hardly ex-
> plained your meaning, but at last I found it. Pray don't serve me
> these tricks often. You may be sure, if there is a good bottle you shall
> have it. I am sure I never refused you, and therefore that reflection
> might have been spared. Pray be more positive in your answer to
> this.
>   . . .
> [Postscript.] *Margoose*, not *Mergoose*; it is spelt with an *a*, simpleton.[2]

Swift's hours with Vanessa were spent in private. Other persons had to be excluded. So also Vanessa seemed to feel that she
showed more affection for Swift, the more she withdrew from
general society. Such possessiveness, along with a lack of economy, suggests a nature more melancholy than charitable. So
one is hardly surprised that in her will, Vanessa left only five
pounds to the poor of the parish and nothing else to charity.
Swift may have exaggerated Stella's benevolence; but her soci-

[1] *Ibid.*, p. 232.
[2] Williams II. 385; 30 Apr. 1721. Stella endorsed it, 'An answer to no letter'. This is one
of the two surviving letters from Swift to Stella outside the so-called *Journal to Stella*.

ability confirms it. One expects a person who enjoys offering food and presents to friends to enjoy as well giving help to the needy. Swift described her as kind to servants but strict with them.[1] He praised her for sacrificing fine clothes to the demands of charity:

> She bought clothes as seldom as possible, and those as plain and cheap as consisted with the situation she was in; and wore no lace for many years. Either her judgment or fortune was extraordinary, in the choice of those on whom she bestowed her charity; for it went further in doing good, than double the sum from any other hand. And I have heard her say, she always met with gratitude from the poor: which must be owing to her skill in distinguishing proper objects, as well as her gracious manner in relieving them.[2]

In a prayer for her he once begged God to restore Stella's health 'for the sake of those poor, who by losing her will be desolate, and those sick, who will not only want her bounty, but her care and tending'.[3] We know from her will that she had a 'charity child' whom she looked after; and in that will, of course, she left the bulk of her estate to a public charity, Steevens' Hospital in Dublin.

The giving of presents, Swift describes as a 'pleasure she could not resist'. But her delicacy appears in his details; for he says she defined a present as 'a gift to a friend of something he wanted or was fond of, and which could not be easily gotten for money'. As one might expect, she discouraged presents to herself.[4]

Stella's charity blends with her religion. Vanessa deliberately trod on the margin of blasphemy when she wrote of her love for Swift, and she nowhere expressed a serious concern with religion. Among all the advantages bestowed on her by the divinities of *Cadenus and Vanessa*, piety is not mentioned. I think this is partly because Swift always feared suggesting hypocrisy by religion. But he observed that Stella could point out Hobbes's errors in religion;[5] and in a prayer for her he once begged God to continue to her 'that contempt of worldly things and vanities,

[1] Davis v. 229. [2] *Ibid.*, p. 233. [3] *Ibid.*, IX. 254.
[4] *Ibid.*, v. 233. [5] *Ibid.*, p. 231.

that she hath shewn in the whole conduct of her life'[1]—which I suppose is the closest he could come to specifying her piety. We also know that the bequest of a thousand pounds to Steevens' Hospital was for the support of a chaplain.

With all her merits, Stella had her faults. Yet the one Swift singled out distinguishes her from Vanessa. When he frowned on the younger woman, she responded with depressed anxiety over the possibility of losing him. When he irritated Stella with his fault-finding, she responded far more maturely, with quick anger, which I am confident he deserved.

> Your spirits kindle to a flame,
> Mov'd with the lightest touch of blame.[2]

Clearly, she could give advice as well as take it; she could also reject it; and even an advice-factory like Swift would at times submit to her control. Stella's readiness to stand up to her governor implies a confidence that must have made Swift dread the prospect of losing her.

Yet the greatest change in their relationship, after she passed forty, was also the saddest and the most provocative of anxiety. Her health began to fail badly. The symptoms Swift kept noticing were pain and lack of appetite. In February 1723 Swift told a good friend, 'Mrs Johnson eats an ounce a week, which frights me from dining with her.'[3] In 'To Stella, Visiting Me'[4] Swift dwells on her suffering, and fears that the strain of nursing him may complete the ruin of her health.[5] In poems of 1723 he worries about her lack of appetite; and speaking of their both being ill, he says, 'She wants assistance more than I.'[6] He made pathetic efforts to discover reassuring signs. After they all had Christmas 1723 at Quilca, Swift told Ford, 'Mrs J———— was

[1] *Ibid.*, IX. 253.
[2] 'To Stella, Who Collected ... His Poems', ll. 87–8. Cf. above, p. 100.
[3] 12 Feb. 1723, to Wallis.
[4] Williams dates this 1720. I suggest 1723. The development of the theme of courage is like that of 'A Letter to a Very Young Lady', the same year; the attack on kings and ministers of state (ll. 61–4) sounds like a passage in the poem for Ford's birthday 1723 (ll. 35–50): see *Poems* I. 312.
[5] *Ibid.*, II. 726–7, ll. 93–124.   [6] 'To Stella' 1724, l. 16.

much better in the country, and is at present not so ill as usual.'[1] But a few weeks later, he admitted, 'Mrs J——— returns to her old rate [i.e., of illness] for want of steel, walking, country air, Don Carlos, and Pontack.'[2] One mark of Swift's tenderness and concern was the trouble he took to repair a favourite snuffbox for her.[3] But the bad omens went on. In December 1724 Swift told Ford, '[Those] who see Mrs Johnson seldom, say she grows leaner, she eats about two ounces a week, and even drinks less than she did.'[4]

If she had not continued to decline, I doubt that Swift would have arranged the long visit to Quilca. In March 1725 he told Ford, 'Our friend with the weak stomach eats less than ever, and I am in pain about her, and would fain persuade her to go for England, but she will not.'[5] While they lived in Quilca, his accounts of her health were doggedly hopeful but sadly uneven. The rigours she survived in Sheridan's house do not suggest a body *in extremis*; but riding became difficult for her[6] and it is clear that she remained chronically ill. Here are notes from April 1725:

> Not a bit of turf this cold weather, and Mrs Johnson and the dean in person, with all their servants forced to assist at the bog . . . .

> The grate in the ladies' bed-chamber broke, and forced to be removed, by which they were compelled to be without a fire, the chimney smoking intolerably; and the dean's great coat was employed to stop the wind from coming down the chimney . . . .

> Mrs Dingley full of cares for herself, and blunders and negligence for her friends. Mrs Johnson sick and helpless: the dean deaf and fretting . . . .

> Two holes in the wall of the ladies' bed-chamber, just at the back of the bed, and one of them directly behind Mrs Johnson's pillow.[7]

---

[1] 19 Jan. 1724; Williams III. 3.

[2] Steel could be any chalybeate medicine derived from infusions of iron, steel, iron chloride, etc. Pontack's was a London tavern celebrated for luxurious food and wine; see *Journal* I. 334, n. 13.

[3] Williams III. 9.   [4] 31 Dec. 1724; *ibid.*, 47.

[5] 11 Mar. 1725; *ibid.*, p. 53.   [6] *Ibid.*, p. 79.

[7] Davis V. 219–21, dated 20 and 28 Apr. 1724, in error for 1725.

In July he claimed Stella was 'generally much better'.[1] But then he admitted that 'Mrs Johnson, after a fortnight's great amendment, had yesterday a very bad day'.[2] In August he said she was 'better in strength though often in her old disorders',[3] yet declared that she could walk long distances.[4] She survived the test, in other words, but did not win good health. When Swift thought a visit to England might help, perhaps he felt it could be her last chance. She never did see England again.

Against this setting, the loss of Vanessa in 1723 meant mischief along with good. I assume that Stella knew about the liaison, that Swift did not discuss it with her, and that she felt relief when it ended. Delany, writing thirty years after the event, is explicit for once. He confuses the time of publication of *Cadenus and Vanessa* (1726) with the time of Vanessa's death; but we know that manuscript copies got out. Delany says a friend of his, whom I take to be Sheridan, visited and comforted Stella at Ford's house while the scandal of the poem was spreading; and the friend told him this story:

> As [Ford] was an hospitable, open-hearted man, well beloved, and largely acquainted, it happened one day, that some gentlemen dropt in, to dinner, who were strangers to Stella's situation. And as the poem of *Cadenus and Vanessa* was then the general topic of conversation, one of them said, surely that Vanessa must be an extraordinary woman that could inspire the Dean to write so finely upon her. Mrs [Johnson] smiled, and answered, that she thought that point not quite so clear; for it was well known, the Dean could write finely upon a broomstick.[5]

The story is second-hand, but the examples of Stella's wit preserved by Swift have the same style; and I more than half believe it.

---

[1] 9 Jul. 1725; Williams III. 72.   [2] 9 Jul. 1725; *ibid.*, p. 75.
[3] *Ibid.*, p. 86.   [4] 16 Aug. 1725; *ibid.*, p. 89.
[5] I am almost willing to believe this story; but Delany also says that because of the publication of *Cadenus and Vanessa*, Swift made a southern tour, and Stella went to stay with Ford. However, Stella began her visit to Ford before Swift left on his tour; both those moves were planned in detail before Vanessa died; even the manuscript of the poem only circulated after Vanessa's death (and the departure of Stella and Swift); and publication followed only three years later. So I don't see how the causal connection can be maintained.

Much of my discussion of Stella and Vanessa is speculation based on Freudian psychology or on inferences drawn from a few data. I still have one far-fetched theory to expound. For Stella's birthday in 1723 Swift wrote a charmless poem based on a grotesque image.[1] In it he says that when he tried to praise Stella, his invention failed him; he did not know what to write; and he appealed to Apollo, the god he claimed as patron. Apollo replied to the prayer, and told Swift to have an old bottle of wine, buried in the cellar, dug up. If Swift would drink the decanted wine, he would be able to write a new poem praising the lady.

I assume the anecdote is based on an event in Swift's domestic life—the discovery of a long-lost bottle of wine when somebody was scraping the earthen floor of the cellar. But the poem is thin, slow, and bathetic. Swift seems to be writing in spite of himself. Some aspects of the poem disturb me, especially the treatment of the central image and the fact that the poet, while briefly reviving old praises of Stella, produces no new ones. He is really telling us about a poem that never got written.

The bottle has a 'neck elated tow'rds the skies', and it contains a 'strong inspiring juice'. As one raises the neck from 'its tomb', says Swift, 'It drags behind a spacious womb.' The bottle neck pointing upward, with its inspiring juice ready to emerge, looks phallic to me. The *womb*-and-*tomb* rhyme sounds like buried femininity. I wonder whether Swift is not exorcizing the spirit of Vanessa, who is soon to die; whether he is not, as so often, cancelling the danger of female sexuality by joining it with masculinity and, in a symbolic resurrection, hoping that the death of Vanessa will give life to Stella. However unpersuasive such an interpretation may be, I assume that vague thoughts like these were hovering just below the level of Swift's consciousness in the spring of 1723.

If his attachment to Stella was so profound and complicated, his repeated desertions of her must represent an effort to prove his independence, more to himself than to Stella. Once when he

[1] *Poems* II. 740–3.

[416]

expected to lose her any day, Swift wrote to Stopford, 'I think there is not a greater folly than that of entering into too strict and particular a friendship, with the loss of which a man must be absolutely miserable.'[1] For his own sake he was probably acting out such a loss repeatedly in order (without of course realizing it) to toughen himself for the event.

But their difference in age was so great that Swift, more consciously, must have expected to die first, abandoning Stella as his father had deserted him. He may even have rationalized his long absences as training her for quasi-orphanhood; and there may be a shadow of his conscious attitude in the scorn he cast (in 'A Letter to a Very Young Lady') on wives who affect to be anxious when their husbands are away.[2]

Not that the demands he made on her could be justified in reason. Until he became dean, he might feel he must go out into the world to seek preferment. But when he was in his mid-fifties, and still left her for a month, a season, or half a year, he could no longer tell himself that he was advancing his career in London. Having removed Stella from her family when she was twenty, having isolated her in a strange city and then failed to stay at her side, he seemed to be testing Stella's devotion by the standard of his mother's. She must remain loyal to him and reject all suitors; she must not follow him or expect marriage; and he must be free to enjoy a secret friendship with a young heiress. No wonder Orrery compared her to Penelope![3]

Swift's notion of the relationship was explicitly anti-romantic. Herbert Davis has suggested persuasively that when Swift called Mrs Johnson 'Stella', he was ridiculing the attitude of Astrophel to Stella in Sidney's poems.[4] Since Swift was familiar with Temple's praise of Sidney as 'the greatest poet and the noblest genius of any that have left writings behind them'[5] and since we know Swift had admired the love poetry of Cowley when he was young, the allusion is plausible. Certainly he always ridiculed

---

[1] Williams III. 145.
[2] Davis IX. 87. Cf. below, p. 549.   [3] Orrery, p. 23.
[4] Davis, *Stella: A Gentlewoman of the Eighteenth Century*, pp. 12–16.
[5] 'Of Poetry', in Spingarn III. 91.

the *grandes passions* of romance and the Petrarchan tradition; and in 'A Letter to a Very Young Lady', he congratulated the new Mrs Rochfort for not having foolish fantasies:

> I hope, you do not still dream of charms and raptures; which marriage ever did, and ever will put a sudden end to. Besides, yours was a match of prudence, and common good-liking, without any mixture of that ridiculous passion which hath no being, but in play-books and romances.[1]

Swift's poems to Stella invariably embody this attitude. His problem was to find fresh language and imagery to give it enough life to compete with the vigour of the other tradition. By and large it is the phrases or separate couplets that charm us in Swift's poems. The best passages seldom last more than six lines, and Swift was often not dainty about the syntax, the transitions, the gradations of feeling, or the order of the parts. But he had a genius for discovering flavoursome words that would fit neatly into his strong rhythms; and when his conceits are right—either undercutting a positive emotion or overstating a violent one—the effect is memorable. Sometimes he troubles himself with a careful scheme of development, often laying the second half of an analogy beside the first, or first elaborating a hoax and then exposing it; and so a whole poem can have an effect larger than the sum of its parts.

Yet to imply that technique is what gives Swift's poetry its strength would be wrong. He packs his lines with things freshly seen, speech truly heard, emotions deeply felt. It is our impression of crowded, crackling reality that makes his verse a living substance.

In the poems to Stella he had to convey tenderness through a jocular medium, and not overstate the emotion for fear it would sound literary. But he could indicate the value he set on pleasing her by the startling inventiveness of his similes. This is why he turned poetic decorum around, why he chose precisely the motifs that traditional love poetry avoids, and made them seem appropriate to tenderness; this is why he so variously redeems

---

[1] Davis IX. 89.

the decay of the body by the persistence of friendship. Dwelling on the passage of time, he inverts the *carpe diem* theme by depreciating voluptuous pleasure and urging the superiority of moral and intellectual sympathy, of mutual assistance and frank conversation.

Yet for his eulogistic purposes, Swift does not discard the familiar superlatives, as one might expect. Instead, he mingles them with the opposing motifs. The effect is to retain the pleasing associations of the old flatteries while associating them with spiritual graces. For the language of sober compliment he follows the tradition of didactic and religious verse. Without meaning to suggest influence or deliberate echo, I shall give some examples to show what styles he could draw on. Here are the closing lines of Henry King's elegy on his wife:

> But heark! My pulse, like a soft drum,
> Beats my approach, tells *Thee* I come;
> And slow howe'er my marches be,
> I shall at last sit down by *Thee*.
>
> The thought of this bids me go on,
> And wait my dissolution
> With hope and comfort. *Dear* (forgive
> The crime), I am content to live
> Divided, with but half a heart,
> Till we shall meet and never part.

This kind of poetry is of course beyond Swift's reach. But it has two qualities he inherited. First is the explicitness, the willingness to forewarn the reader of the meaning of the images rather than leave it to be inferred.[1] The second is the validating of a serious emotion by touching its expression with wit.[2] So Swift says that Stella's 'size and years are doubled' since he first saw her, at sixteen 'the brightest virgin of the green'—a superlative suggesting Waller's style of flattery. He goes on in Waller's manner but developing his image as a comic version of Petrarchan conceit. The truth of his love still appears in the

---

[1] Cf. Rosamund Tuve, *Elizabethan and Metaphysical Imagery*, pp. 175–9.
[2] Cf. George Williamson, *The Proper Wit of Poetry*, p. 7; cf. pp. 4–6, 14, 22, 56–7.

energy he has devoted to finding and working the image. The meaning is not left in doubt:

> Oh, would it please the gods to split
> Thy beauty, size, and years, and wit,
> No age could furnish out a pair
> Of nymphs so graceful, wise and fair,
> With half the lustre of your eyes,
> With half thy wit, thy years and size.

In the vein of ironic gallantry Swift also recalls Carew's manner, as when that poet laments his mistress's physical perfections and wishes she were more like him, because similarity creates love. Carew then turns on his own conceit and says,

> Yet I confess I cannot spare
> From her just shape the smallest hair;
> Nor need I beg from all the store
> Of heaven, for her one beauty more:
> She hath too much divinity for me,
> You gods teach her some more humanity.[1]

The meaning is the opposite of Swift's; the manner is close to his. So also Carew mourns the death of Lady Mary Villiers by saying her soul was too great for her body:

> The purest soul that e're was sent
> Into a clayey tenement
> Inform'd this dust, but the weak mold
> Could the great guest no longer hold ....
> So the fair model broke, for want
> Of room to lodge th'inhabitant.[2]

Swift describes honour as Stella's chief attribute and defines it as the worldly equivalent of religious faith:

> As nat'ral life the body warms,
> And, scholars teach, the soul informs;
> So honour animates the whole,
> And is the spirit of the soul.[3]

---

[1] 'A Divine Mistress', ll. 11–16.
[2] 'An Other', in *Poems*, ed. R. Dunlap (Oxford, 1949), p. 54.
[3] 'To Stella, Visiting Me', ll. 11–14.

This device of topping a familiar conceit with a new one based on it is a mark of Swiftian wit in prose and verse. So is the device of going through a quick series of riddling conceits to show how vigorously the poet is inspired by the idea of the person he loves (or hates). Henry King (or Francis Beaumont) gives an elegant and touching example:

> Like to the falling of a star;
> Or as the flights of eagles are;
> Or like the fresh spring's gaudy hue;
> Or silver drop of morning dew;
> Or like a wind that chafes the flood;
> Or bubbles which on water stood;
> Even such is man, whose borrow'd light
> Is straight call'd in, and paid to night.
> *The wind blows out; the bubble dies;*
> *The spring entomb'd in autumn lies;*
> *The dew dries up; the star is shot;*
> *The flight is past; and man forgot.*[1]

Swift liked the effect of cumulated images,[2] but his are more likely to be coarse or grotesque than refined, and more likely to seem freshly observed. Here is a heavy-handed example from 'Stella's Distress':

> From purling streams and fountains bubbling,
> To Liffey's filthy side in Dublin:
> From wholesome exercise and air
> To sossing in an elbow chair;
> From stomach sharp, and hearty feeding
> To piddle like a lady breeding.[3]

These images are not more concrete or better turned or more suggestive than King's; but one feels that a unique sensibility has perceived them and that they come out of genuine, recent experience.

We may sum up the tendencies I have been sketching as

---

[1] 'Sic Vita'. For ten imitations, see George Saintsbury, ed. *Minor Poets of the Caroline Period* (Oxford, 1905–21), III. 236–7.
[2] The most brilliant is the passage about wisdom in *A Tale of a Tub*, 'Introduction'; Davis I. 40.
[3] *Poems* II. 744–5.

Swift's lowering of high literary traditions. But he worked almost as hard to elevate the sub-literary. The best-known instance is the remarkably varied employment he gave to Butler's Hudibrastics. In the political satires, lampoons, mock-eulogies and epitaphs of the Restoration we find Swift skilfully anticipated. One specimen among hundreds is an imaginary Oxford barber's verses on the death of Queen Mary:

> Soon as the dismal news came down
> And spread itself about the town,
> I, in a trice, with heavy soul,
> As snails their horns, drew in my pole;
> Shut shop and, in a passion, swore
> I'd never use my scissors more,
> Since Lachesis so rash had been
> To cut the thread of gracious Queen.
> But I, designing more
> Than ever barber did before,
> Resolved on this too sad occasion
> To exercise a strange vocation—
> Rhyme, the great business of the nation.
> I thought it arrant shame to fetter
> Free English sense in foreign metre;[1]
> For none do bury, I conjecture,
> Folks in outlandish manufacture.[2]

This has so many 'Swiftian' marks—octosyllabics, double rhymes, low conceits, impersonation—it could pass as his if it were more concise, concrete, and acerbic.

The best of the poems Swift wrote for Stella are not technically more refined than those I have used for comparison; but they have more going on. The poet sounds as if he were responding immediately and directly to the idea in his mind. He is weakest when he merely enumerates praises, strongest when he makes the visible decay of her body into the groundwork of his affection. So he compares Stella to the fading sign of an excellent inn which he calls 'The Angel':

---

[1] I.e., Greek, Latin, Hebrew, in which Oxford poetical lamentation used to abound.
[2] *Poems on Affairs of State*, v, ed. W. J. Cameron (New Haven, 1971), pp. 441–3, ll. 1–17.

And though the painting grows decayed
The house will never lose its trade;
Nay, though the treach'rous rascal Thomas[1]
Hangs a new angel two doors from us
As fine as daubers' hands can make it
In hopes that strangers will mistake it . . . .
   Now, this is Stella's case in fact;
An angel's face, a little crack't.[2]

Instead of brilliance it is the unexpected degradation of the conceit that conveys the tenderness of the poet. Only a loyal admirer would dare to join the coarse image to the delicate sentiment.

Among the poems Swift addressed to Stella, the superiority of conceited designs—verse planned around an undercut analogy—to unmediated statement is seen in the difference between 'To Stella' (1724) and 'Stella's Birthday' (1725). The earlier poem—praising her selflessness as she tends his sick-bed—rests on biography. It amounts to a rhymed appreciation of Stella's solicitude, with no design but the paradox that the nurse is more painfully ill than the patient. If we could not name them both, the effect would be pedestrian.

The later poem plays with the language of Waller but fits it into a scheme of reversing common forms and then topping the reversal with a new invention. Here, in his preoccupation with eyes, Swift recalls Metaphysical conceits of lenses, fluids, looking glasses ('through a glass darkly'), hour glasses—as, for example, Henry King's lines in 'The Exequy';

               For thee (lov'd clay)
      I languish out, not live, the day,
      Using no other exercise
      But what I practise with mine eyes:
      By which wet glasses,[3] I find out
      How lazily time creeps about
      To one that mourns . . . .
      [After Judgment—] then we shall rise

[1] Presumably a waiter who becomes the rival of his master.
[2] 'Stella's Birthday', 1721; *Poems* II. 734.
[3] Hour glasses, slow because wet.

> And view ourselves with clearer eyes
> In that calm region, where no night
> Can hide us from each other's sight.

'Stella's Birthday' also deals with the relation between time and sight, framed within a self-conscious, conventional setting of stale mythology, and the old association of youth with love and poetry:

> Beauty and wit, too sad a truth,
> Have always been confin'd to youth:
> The god of wit, and beauty's queen,
> He twenty-one, and she fifteen.
> No poet ever sweetly sung,
> Unless he were like Phoebus, young;
> Nor ever nymph inspir'd to rhyme,
> Unless, like Venus, in her prime.
> At fifty-six, if this be true,
> Am I a poet fit for you?
> Or at the age of forty-three,
> Are you a subject fit for me?
>
>   .   .   .
>
> 'Tis true, but let it not be known,
> My eyes are somewhat dimmish grown;
> For nature, always in the right,
> To your decays adapts my sight,
> And wrinkles undistinguish'd pass,
> For I'm asham'd to use a glass;
> And till I see them with these eyes,
> Whoever says you have them, lies.[1]

Both poets contrast spiritual and fleshly vision. King, by turning inward and reflecting on his intellectual associations, conveys the feeling of loss with delicate sincerity. We have no sense that he is thinking of particular 'glasses', days, or nights. Swift refers to actual ages, his own peculiar eyes, Stella's grey locks. He does not render them concretely, but asks us to identify them. In King's lines the purity of the emotion derives from its being drawn through the filter of the deliberately literary con-

---

[1] *Poems* II. 757–8. Swift in fact refused to wear glasses.

ceits. In Swift's lines the pathos emerges from the opposition of the old, literary figures and present reality.

In Swift's poem the physical bodies of the two friends do not become insignificant beside the transcendent importance of unchanging spirit. Swift refuses to bring the truths of religion into his design. On the contrary, he ridicules his own premise with this very song composed by an elderly Apollo for a middle-aged Venus. It is sublunary comfort that he offers; and for it to take effect, he must employ it on sublunary bodies.

Chapter Twenty-one

GENTRY AND JOURNEYS

I. QUESTIONS OF TRAVEL

By an irony of conduct, when Swift deserted Stella for long holidays, his normal destination was the world in which he first met her, that of the country gentry. It would be absurd to suggest that he deliberately wished to get away from Mrs Johnson. He preferred the country to the town on most accounts; and he disliked the provinciality of Dublin, along with its urban discomforts, and the irritants that the seat of government must foster in a man of his tastes and politics. 'I keep much in the country,' he once told Ford, 'because it is more unlike Dublin than anything I can find on this side the water.'[1] And once he told Robert Cope that he had stayed at Trim for three weeks 'out of perfect hatred to [Dublin], where at length business dragged me against my will'.[2] He could get the exercise he desired more easily out of town than in. He believed that rural air and diet improved his health.

Swift obviously loved travel for its own sake. The record of his trips to England shows how glad he was to have business that drew him there. During the decade after Queen Anne's death, when he kept wondering whether or not to visit his old friends in the world that mattered, some of Swift's travels over Ireland were a sublimation of that nostalgic yearning. There was also the immense pleasure of changing rôles, letting one's inner self peep out. In the country he could more easily play games with his identity. In Dublin he was too well known, too easily distinguished, always on show—spied on. There he had to keep up the public dignity of his office. In the country he could throw off

---

[1] 20 Aug. 1718; Williams II. 292. [2] 9 Jul. 1717; *ibid.*, p. 274.

the gown of deanship and by putting on the character of the rich squires he visited, he could (half-consciously) enjoy the fantasy of being one of them.[1]

Sometimes it was simply business that carried Swift out of town. During his mid-forties and early fifties he spent time at Laracor and Trim to serve the cure or to work out the endless details of acquiring additional glebeland from Mr Percival. He visited Kildare to look into the management of deanery lands there. But he also liked to be out of the way of troublesome parliamentary sessions. He rarely seemed to lack an excuse for escaping when he could.

A connection with the voyages of Gulliver suggests itself. Themes of exile and return, imprisonment and freedom, stasis and mobility, underlie the design of the book and are reflected in its author's restlessness. They are different expressions of the same primitive impulse, the desire to be at home in the world, to reach out and explore the strangeness just beyond the crib, nursery, schoolroom, and college chamber.

In Swift's nature the most elementary kind of sightseeing curiosity was deeply rooted. When he travelled, he instructed his servants to 'enquire in every town if there be anything worth seeing. Observe the country seats, and ask who they belong to; and enter them [*sc.* in a pocket book], and the counties where they are.'[2] As a child he had been willy-nilly picked up, shifted about, and put down, even more than most children. As an adult he never tired of the pleasure of determining his own goings and comings.

During his mid-fifties, therefore, Swift found the hospitality of the squirearchs delightful for many reasons. After years of accepting more than he should have done from Chetwode, he quietly gave him up.[3] But their common friend Robert Rochfort—either directly or through his sons—afforded better satisfaction. The former Lord Chief Baron had given Gaulstown

[1] 'As deep employed in other folks' plantations and ditchings as if they were my own concern'—*ibid.*, p. 393.
[2] Davis XIII. 165.
[3] Cf. the letter to Ford, 20 Dec. 1718; Williams II. 306.

House, the family seat, to the eldest son, George, when he was married in 1704; and the dean took many holidays there.

Not to mention shorter stays, Swift was at Gaulstown for at least four weeks in the summer of 1718, after three or four with Peter Ludlow at Ardsallagh.[1] While the old judge was in England, Swift visited George Rochfort at the great house during the summer of 1719,[2] and he must have spent other days there in cooler seasons. In 1721, he arrived at Gaulstown about 21 June and did not leave for over three months. Now he was joined by a series of fellow guests, some congenial enough, including the senior Rochfort—back from England—and the younger son, Swift's favourite. What hints we have of their pastimes suggest that Swift tried to uphold his humanist ideals but only half succeeded.[3]

After he left, he wrote to another guest, who had stayed on, 'You [i.e., plural] are now happy, and have nobody to tease you to the oar or the saddle [i.e., rowing or riding]. You can sit in your nightgown till noon without any reproaches.'[4] In other words, Swift's regime of exercise, regular hours, and good books was not to everyone's taste.

In 1722 old Robert Rochfort seems to have suffered something like a stroke, for Swift said he had 'got a dead palsy'.[5] This change may be connected with the decline in Swift's visits—although our information is radically incomplete, and a comfortable intimacy with the family lasted till his own death. In 1723 Swift's spring holiday certainly included Gaulstown, along with Wood Park and other stops.[6] Among Swift's cronies of this period the Rochforts were probably the wealthiest—Swift called the father 'old Lombard Street'[7]—and they dispensed the most lavish hospitality.

---

[1] *Ibid.*, p. 292, n. 2.

[2] I assume he made good his intention of 3 May 1719; *ibid.*, p. 322.

[3] *Poems* I. 276–83.

[4] Williams II. 407–8. Cf. my discussion above, pp. 338–9.

[5] Williams II. 436.

[6] *Ibid.*, p. 453, n. 1. I assume that Williams and Ball (from whom the note derives) are correct in their inferences.

[7] I.e., money-lender.

Meanwhile, the friendship with the Copes expanded.[1] Swift loved staying in their northern house; and his attachment to them may serve as a counterweight to the notions, fed by *Gulliver's Travels* and other satires, of a Swiftian prejudice against the family as an institution. He probably went to Loughgall (which stood about four miles north-east of the city of Armagh) during the summer of 1720.[2] When Cope invited him, Swift replied with a superbly candid appreciation of the couple's 'good-nature and generosity'.[3]

Two years later, having gone back for a long visit, Swift relayed his impressions to Ford and illustrated his idea of a good marriage; for here the celibate dean made made clear how much store he set by the correct rearing of children and the management of a household:

> I have been here three weeks[4] with your old friend Mr Cope, who is the most domestic man you ever saw, with a wife whom he is so silly as to love, and who deserves it as well as a wife can; and with nine children, with whom he troubles himself as much and his friends as little as possible. . . . My comfort [in bad weather] is, that the people, the churches and the plantations make me think I am in England. I mean only the scene of a few miles about me, for I have passed through miserable regions to get to it.[5]

Yet another year later, Swift's style rose to rhapsody as he contemplated an invitation from Cope:

> The neighbours you mention may be valuable, but I never want them at your house; and I love the very spleen of you and Mrs Cope, better than the mirth of any others you can help me to.[6]

One cause of Swift's indifference to the neighbours was that they included his old friend and Stella's suitor Tisdall, whom advancing years had endowed with more vanity and abrasiveness than the dean could excuse.[7]

---

[1] Cope had been imprisoned by the Irish House of Commons in 1715, an ordeal that probably contributed to Swift's fondness for him. See above, p. 21.
[2] Williams II. 347–8 and p. 347, n. 6.   [3] *Ibid.*, p. 347.
[4] He remained from about 1 Jul. to 7 Aug.; *ibid.*, p. 430, n. 2.
[5] *Ibid.*, pp. 430–1. Cf. my discussion above, pp. 402–3.
[6] Williams II. 453–4.   [7] *Ibid.*, p. 454.

Swift built his four-month northern tour around the Copes, leaving Dublin at the end of May,[1] going to visit Stearne at Clogher, and stopping off elsewhere before reaching Loughgall. He moved on from the Copes' early in August,[2] visited Quilca, and only returned to Dublin around 9 October.[3]

The southern journey (summer, 1723) is harder to map; but we know he went so far afield as to the parish of Skull in the wild south-west corner of county Cork; for he wrote a set of indifferent Latin verses on the view from the Carbery Rocks.[4] (Delany praises the poem for its 'true and conspicuous sublimity'.)[5] We also know that he rode on to the west of Ireland and county Galway, where he stayed, at the beginning of August, with his old friendly enemy Bolton at Clonfert, south of Ballinasloe.[6] There he said he had covered four hundred miles and hoped to visit Quilca on the way to Dublin; he wished to be in town before September;[7] during the next few weeks, he probably called at Loughgall as well.[8] When at last Swift did reach town, it was nearly 20 September, and he had been gone almost four months.[9]

Swift never had to go far for hospitality. Close to home he found eager hosts like his favourite Grattans. Their house at Belcamp was a haven he could easily visit for short stays. In 1724, when he sacrificed a summer ramble in order to invigilate the men building his wall around Naboth's Vineyard, Swift was able to compensate himself with three weeks among the Grattans, before Christmas,[10] and I do not doubt there were other visits as well.[11]

Some of this activity may have been a sublimation of Swift's

---

[1] *Ibid.*, pp. 426, 428.   [2] 7 Aug; *ibid.*, p. 432.

[3] *Ibid.*, p. 434 and n. 1.   [4] *Poems* I. 315–19.   [5] Delany, p. 135.

[6] Swift writes 3 Aug. from Clonfert but does not say when he arrived or when he will leave; Williams II. 463.

[7] *Ibid.*, p. 463.

[8] He more or less promised Cope a visit (*ibid.*, pp. 453, 456), and I assume he included it in the 'one or two short visits' mentioned 3 Aug. to Sheridan (*ibid.*, p. 463).

[9] Swift himself says 'four months' on 20 Sept. (*ibid.* p. 464); but he had not left Dublin before 3 Jun. (*ibid.*, p. 457).

[10] *Ibid.*, III. 44.

[11] He had probably visited Belcamp in Sept.; see *ibid.*, III. 33–4 and 34, n. 1.

homesickness for England. But his half-year at Quilca in 1725 I take as a mark of his worries about Mrs Johnson. While there, Swift must have determined to satisfy himself at last, and see once more the friends of Queen Anne's last years. At Quilca he made a fair copy of *Gulliver's Travels*; and close to the date of his fifty-eighth birthday he told Pope he felt he was 'pretty near seeing you'.[1] This time, he was a good prophet.

II. DUTIES OF SERVANTS

We know a bit about the style in which Swift travelled. When he rode any distance, he liked to have two servants mounted, one ahead and one behind. They were to be ready before he left, to ride out before him, and to keep within forty yards on the road. When the party stopped at noon, Swift wanted the horses well looked after. Among the rules he laid down for servants, he said,

> Leave your master to the servants of the inn; go you with the horses into the stable; choose a place farthest from the stable-door; see the standing be dry; send immediately for fresh straw; see all the old hay out of the rack, and get fresh put in; see your horses' girths be loosed and stuffed; take not off the bridle till they be cool, nor saddles in an hour; see their hoofs be well picked; try if the heads of the nails be fast, and whether they be well clinched; if not, send presently for a smith; always stand by while the smith is employed.

The second servant was to watch over his master:

> bestir yourself to get a convenient room for your master [i.e., to dine in]; bring all his things into his room, full in his sight; enquire what [*sc.* food] is in the house, see it yourself, and tell your master how you like it. Step yourself now and then into the kitchen to hasten dinner or supper, and observe whether they be cleanly. Taste the ale, and tell your master whether it be good or bad. If he wants[2] wine, go you with the drawer and choose a bottle well filled and stopped: If the wine be in hogsheads, desire to taste and smell it.... See the salt be dry and powdered, the bread new and clean, the knives sharp.
>
> At night observe the same rules: But first choose him a warm

---

[1] *Ibid.*, III. 116.

[2] 'Wanteth' in Faulkner's text and in Davis—which I take to be the publisher's emendation.

room, with a lock and key in order; then call immediately for the
sheets, see them well aired, and at a large fire; feel the blankets, bed,
bolster, and pillow, whether they be dry, and whether the floor
under the bed be damp. Let the chamber [i.e., bedroom] be that
which hath been last lain in:[1] enquire about it. If the bed be damp,
let it be brought before a large fire, and air it on both sides.[2]

Although Swift could not expect all his requirements to be met
everywhere, such rules tell us what pleased him best. They also
suggest a sharp-eyed, if appreciative (and generous) master, and
a man more likely to be pleased at home than abroad. In
connection with *Gulliver's Travels* they indicate that the delight
in horses and the acute observation of them which appear in
Houyhnhnmland are derived from an immense firsthand knowledge, and that the contrast with humans was drawn in part from
Swift's trials with grooms and footmen.

[1] So it will be dry and aired.
[2] *The Duty of Servants at Inns*, Davis XIII. 163–5. First published by Faulkner, vol. VIII,
1746.

Chapter Twenty-two

CARTERET

Of all the acquaintances Swift saw during his late fifties, the one who came nearest to his anglophile ideal of statesman and humanist was no squire, however rich and kind, but the Lord Lieutenant himself. In Carteret was realized again the heroic figure Swift once believed he had found in Temple: greatness and goodness united, or a virtuous man benevolently wielding political power. Carteret in private was a faithful husband and a loving father; in public he was an energetic, just, and tactful governor. He combined talents that were simply opposed in most politicians: the manners of a courtier, the candour of a man of good will, the learning of a scholar, the penetration of a manager of men. For Swift he had even the advantage of losing in the match with Walpole. Ireland for Carteret (during his limited stays there) was a kind of exile, even as it was for Swift, and as Moor Park had been for Temple. The myth of justice defeated after a brief triumph seemed embodied in the viceroy.

We know there was nothing eccentric about Swift's judgment. Archbishop King, who thought Carteret had 'exerted himself wonderfully',[1] represented the consensus. King wrote to a trusted friend,

> Our Lord Lieutenant is a person of very great parts, learning and experience, and indefatigable in his inquiries into all offices and matters relating to the public, and does not pass over more private affairs, apprising himself of the estates, conditions and circumstances of both the nobility, gentry and clergy.[2]

---

[1] 18 Sept. 1725, to Samuel Foley. Cf. above, pp. 223–4, 295.
[2] 3 Oct. 1725, to Samuel Molyneux.

The testimony of bishops in the English interest is as strong. Nicolson called Carteret 'a Daniel come to judgment'.[1] Bishop Downes reported on a dinner with Carteret, Midleton, Archbishop King, and others at Whitshed's:

> It was a dismal day without-doors, but we made it as bright as we could within. We had no politics; as not being all of one mind in any thing, unless in our public respect to our Lord Lieutenant, who amazes me every day more and more. On Thursday night he took me with him to hear a Greek play at Mr Sheridan's school; his excellency being disposed to encourage learning, from the school to the college.[2]

Swift found himself unable to meet Carteret until January 1725. Meanwhile, he took care to make friends with Tickell, the Lord Lieutenant's secretary and Addison's protégé. Tickell had arrived in Dublin at the beginning of June 1724.[3] Swift and he cottoned on to each other and began almost at once to exchange hospitality. Tickell was a cheerful bachelor, modest and scholarly, with some reputation as a poet. He had been a fellow of Queen's College, Oxford, and an intimate of Addison's, who had made Tickell his literary executor. He had also served as an under-secretary of state. Though Swift called him a 'bird of passage',[4] Tickell was to marry an Irish heiress in the spring of 1726. With so many tastes and associations to share, the two men easily became genial comrades. By the autumn of 1725, Swift could ask Tickell to make himself 'a guest when you please' at the deanery.[5]

Carteret only followed Tickell to Ireland toward the end of October 1724, when the dean's deafness and vertigo forced him to substitute a message of apology for a call in person.[6] Swift told Ford that Carteret had sent him 'one cold compliment'—I suppose, in return for the apology.[7] We may be sure the lack of viceregal attention bruised Swift, for he mentioned it in three letters to other correspondents.[8] But he also told Ford, 'I intend

---

[1] Quoted by Basil Williams, *Carteret and Newcastle* (1943), p. 73.
[2] 12 Dec. 1724; Nicolson II. 590.
[3] Williams III. 15, n. 2.   [4] *Ibid.*, p. 77.   [5] 12 Nov. 1725; *ibid.*, p. 113.
[6] *Ibid.*, p. 37.   [7] *Ibid.*, p. 42.   [8] *Ibid.*, pp. 40, 42, 46.

to see him when I can. He has shewn more abilities than anyone I ever knew in his station.'[1]

At last, in the middle of January 1725 the dean had an audience at the Castle. 'I was the other day well enough to see the Lord Lieutenant', he told Chetwode, 'and the town has a thousand foolish stories of what passed between us; which indeed was nothing but old friendship without a word of politics.'[2] The report is not ingenuous, for Swift could hardly have kept himself from uttering a few sarcasms on public affairs; and we know he urged Carteret to offer preferments to a list of Irish clergymen not distinguished for their Whiggery.[3]

One of the best of the 'foolish stories' is that when the dean went to the Castle, he could not at once be admitted to the viceregal presence, and that while he waited, he wrote a couplet on a card which he left in a window:

> My very good Lord, 'tis a very hard task,
> For a man to wait here, who has nothing to ask.[4]

The lines were soon in general circulation, and Sir William Fownes supplied an answer:

> My very good Dean, there's few come here
> But have something to ask or something to fear.[5]

Few details are preserved of the courtesies exchanged between Carteret and Swift at this time. Her ladyship had known and teased Swift in London when she was a girl of fifteen or sixteen—before and after her marriage.[6] In Dublin we know he saw something of her during the early months of 1725;[7] and he wrote to the second Earl of Oxford, 'I sometimes see my old friend Lord Carteret, who uses me with his old kindness.'[8] In April, on the verge of departing for Quilca, he thanked Carteret for 'great civilities' from him and his wife. I take it for granted

[1] 31 Dec. 1724; *ibid.*, p. 46.   [2] *Ibid.*, p. 49.   [3] *Ibid.*, p. 71.
[4] *Poems* II. 368. The rhythm and diction of Nichols's version sound to me more like Swift than the version given by J. Molesworth.
[5] *Ibid.*   [6] *Journal* I. 217, 287; *Poems* I. 123 and n.
[7] Williams III. 56; 18 Mar. 1725. Swift sounds as if he has seen her more than once.
[8] Ball III. 263; 14 Aug. 1725. (Williams, III. 85–6, omits 'his'.) As Swift had not been in Dublin since mid-April, the reference must be to the period January to April 1725.

that these included more than one visit.[1] When Swift returned from Quilca, Lady Carteret invited him to dinner; and Swift persuaded her in turn to stroll around Naboth's Vineyard, to taste his fruit (in a year when fruit was scarce)[2] and admire his roses.[3]

The poem Swift wrote about these occasions—'An Apology to the Lady Carteret'—tells how comfortable he felt with the viceregal couple.[4] According to its story, her ladyship was out when Swift arrived at the Castle; and he decided too quickly that he had misunderstood the message. So he left for the deanery. The next morning, he was invited again, returned, and apologized. The lady consented to pardon him and to look at Naboth's Vineyard if he would promise to write up the whole incident in a poem. Then she paid her visit and praised his offerings. But the walk and the changeable weather fatigued her. Swift pretended to draw a moral, viz., that just as the unusual exposure to wind and sun oppressed her, so the unusual exposure to courtly ceremony troubled him.

Apart from illustrating Swift's biography, the poem is a good example of his talent for fitting dramatic, idiomatic speech into octosyllabics. What produces humour is the surprising fit of two modes that ought to collide: the strong rhythmic pattern and the notably spontaneous language. So when the lady tells her equerry to fetch the dean again, Swift finds these couplets:

> My Lady could not choose but wonder:
> 'Captain, I fear you've made some blunder;
> But pray, to morrow go at ten,
> I'll try his manners once again;
> If rudeness be th'effect of knowledge,
> My son shall never see a college.'
>
> (ll.65–70)

---

[1] I agree with Ball III. 234, n. 2; but Williams disagrees (III. 57, n. 3).
[2] Williams III. 76.   [3] *Poems* II. 378–9.

[4] *Ibid.*, pp. 374–80. Unlike Williams, I do not believe 'The Birth of Manly Virtue' is by Swift. It is neither sharp, concrete, nor flavoursome enough. The history of its publication makes me wonder why it should have been excluded from the various Swiftian miscellanies that appeared in the late 1720s, and from Faulkner's edition. I wonder whether Delany could not have written it on a hint from Swift and with Swift's help. See *ibid.*, pp. 381–8.

The point about 'seeing a college' is that Carteret himself had enjoyed academic studies; and in Dublin he sought out those who could provide him with literary and learned conversation. Writing about this time to the second Earl of Oxford, Swift drew a eulogistic comparison:

> I am glad to hear of your lordship's manner of life, spent in study, in domestic entertainment, in conversation with men of wit, virtue and learning, and in encouraging their studies.... [My] Lord Carteret seems to imitate you here as far as party will suffer him.[1]

When Oxford had a son, Swift went to the Castle to share the news with the Carterets.[2] Writing to Stopford a month later, Swift complained that Carteret was too good for his job: 'He could govern a wiser nation better, but fools are fit to deal with fools; and he seems to mistake our calibre.'[2]

While Carteret was providing one of the models for the King of Brobdingnag, and his secretary was reviving Addisonian pleasures for Swift, the prospect of England, which had beckoned so many years, became definite. Swift had completed the transcription of *Gulliver's Travels*; he had apprised his friends of his plans. The session of the Irish Parliament was ending. The Lord Lieutenant would soon be going over. In keeping with old habits, Swift thought of crossing in the spring.

Meanwhile, some bizarre contrasts to Carteret and Tickell reminded him of earlier times in England. One was a quarrel with Lord Palmerston. The other was the fate of Ambrose Philips. In the years when he consorted with Addison and Steele, Swift had for a while been an eager friend of Philips, but at last turned against him after deciding Philips was 'more of a puppy than ever'.[3] While Swift was resettling himself in Georgian Ireland, Pope had moved out of Addison's circle and cemented the enmity of Philips by ironic criticisms of his pastorals.[4] Since then, much scraping for preferment had brought Philips a bathetic transformation, and he now appeared in Dublin (November 1724) as secretary to Primate Boulter.

---

[1] 1 Oct. 1725; Williams III. 105. [2] 26 Nov. 1725; *ibid.*, p. 115.
[3] *Journal*, 30 Jun. 1711. [4] Sherburn, *Early Career*, pp. 115–21.

Searching for better employment, the unfortunate Philips wrote poems to Carteret's nine-year-old daughter and even thought of turning clergyman. But quite unlike Tickell, he avoided Swift, who told Pope,

> I have not seen Philips, though formerly we were so intimate. He has got nothing, and by what I can find out will get nothing.... Philips is a complainer, and on this occasion I told Lord Carteret that complainers never succeed at court though railers do.[1]

Though the secretary and the dean might not meet, Swift heard enough about Philips to confirm his dislike. He told Pope,

> Mr Philips is fort chancellant [i.e., wavering much] whether he shall turn parson or no.... [We] think it a severe judgment that a fine gentleman, and so much the finer for hating ecclesiastics should be a domestic humble retainer to an Irish prelate. He is neither secretary nor gentleman usher, yet serves in both capacities. He hath published [i.e., made public] several reasons why he never came to see me, but the best is that I have not waited on his lord.[2]

The sour note is all the more audible when one reflects that Tickell, who enjoyed the same sponsorship as Philips, should have grown close to Swift. Yet once more we see how little the labels of Whig or Tory, English or Irish, counted now in Swift's private affections.

The Palmerston story is more dramatic and almost as revealing. The winter before he left for England, Swift was drawn into the affairs of a young clergyman named William Curtis, who had paid for the use of a room in Trinity College, Dublin. The right to dispose of the chamber belonged to a nephew of Sir William Temple: Henry, first Viscount Palmerston, ancestor of the great statesman.

Palmerston, though living in England, had property in Ireland and held the lucrative office of Chief Remembrancer of the Exchequer there. Swift had known him and his younger brother, John, at Moor Park, which John now possessed. In 1711 Swift had gone to much trouble to recommend Thomas Staunton to Henry Temple—as he was then—for an office

---

[1] 29 Sept. 1725; Williams III. 117.   [2] 26 Nov. 1725.

which they all expected to become vacant soon.¹ Palmerston did place Swift's friend in the office but did not keep him because Staunton wanted a higher salary than Palmerston would pay. Swift chose to believe that his lordship had turned against Swift for political reasons and then against Staunton for being Swift's protégé.

Now came the turn of the Reverend Mr Curtis. Palmerston had never assigned the room to the gentleman directly. But in 1706, partly at Swift's request, he had granted its use to John Elwood, a fellow of the college.² On becoming a senior fellow, Elwood had moved into a better apartment and had then turned the old room over to Curtis—either directly or through an intermediate tenant. Poor Curtis now found his claim contested by coarse and vigorous rivals, and he appealed to Swift for help.³

Instead of writing in a tactful, courtly style, such as he used with Carteret, Swift produced an insolent, careless letter which reflected the rage he felt over Staunton's dismissal. I presume that he disliked going through the motions of requesting a favour from a man who stood for so many divisions in his own nature. Palmerston replied with admirable restraint, justified himself, but unfortunately reproached Swift with ingratitude to the Temple family. Swift came back with more details and deeper fury. He defined very exactly the degree of his indebtedness to Sir William Temple, and rose to a fresh height of insolence.

Over the years, Swift's uneasy attitude toward the Temple family had shown itself several times. He had responded in an affectionate tone to an invitation from John Temple to visit Moor Park in 1706.⁴ But both Henry and John Temple had—necessarily—sided with their aunt, Lady Giffard, when she protested against Swift's publication of her brother's final volume of memoirs in 1709.⁵ Yet Swift was willing to visit Henry Temple little more than a year afterward, in order to help

---

¹ *Ibid.*, I. 209–10.   ² *Ibid.*, p. 54.   ³ *Ibid.*, III. 124–5.
⁴ *Ibid.*, I. 54–6.   ⁵ *Ibid.*, p. 156.

Staunton, to whom he wrote,

> It is the first time I have done so since I came to England, [i.e., in
> September 1710] as indeed the first visit I ever made him in my life,
> though we were very well acquainted before he was married.[1]

Twice, in the autumn of 1710, he mentioned John Temple as
somebody he preferred to avoid, and even said, 'I am glad I
have wholly shaken off that family.'[2]

I suspect that Swift did not feel pleased with the humble
posture in which the Temple boys would have been used to see
him. I also suspect that he had received distasteful information
about the Staunton affair. The Temples, however, were a bridge
between England and Ireland, as well as a reminder of Swift's
obscure beginnings. Furthermore, Henry, Lord Palmerston was
a government hack in the British House of Commons, voting
with the ministry in power.[3] He had been rewarded with his
Irish peerage in 1723, not a distinction to exalt him in the view of
the Dean of St Patrick's.

It is against this difficult background that I read not only
Swift's angry expressions but his definition of the part Sir
William Temple had played in the formation of his character;
for he told Palmerston,

> I own myself indebted to Sir William Temple, for recommending
> me to the late king, although without success, and for his choice of
> me to take care of his posthumous writings. But, I hope you will not
> charge my living in his family as an obligation, for I was educated to
> little purpose, if I retired to his house, on any other motives than the
> benefit of his conversation and advice, and the opportunity of
> pursuing my studies. For, being born to no fortune, I was at his
> death as far to seek as ever, and perhaps you will allow that I was of
> some use to him. This I will venture to say, that in the time when I
> had some little credit I did fifty times more for fifty people, from
> whom I never received the least service or assistance. Yet I should
> not be pleased to hear a relation of mine reproaching them for
> ingratitude, although many of them well deserve it; for, thanks to
> party, I have met in both kingdoms with ingratitude enough.[4]

---

[1] 10 Feb. 1711; *ibid.*, p. 209.   [2] *Journal*, pp. 9, 113.
[3] Romney Sedgwick, ed., *The History of Parliament: The House of Commons 1715–1754*, II
(London, 1970), 464–5.   [4] 29 Jan. 1726; Williams III. 125–6.

If we consider how high Swift stood in Ireland by this time, and how little he cared to be linked to defeated English aspirations, we may conceive one reason for his anger. That he came to regret the episode in a cooler season, we may also conclude from a letter written many years later to John Temple, to whom Swift had sent a portrait of Lady Giffard. The style is unusually polite, dignified, and careful. Here Swift apparently tries to paper over the old division, for he says,

> I know nothing more of your brother, than that he hath an Irish title (I should be sorry to see you with such a feather) and that some reason or other drew us into a correspondence, which was very rough. But I have forgot what was the quarrel.[1]

I don't think Swift expected to see Lord Palmerston when he went to England in 1726.

---

[1] *Ibid.*, v. 6.

Chapter Twenty-three

'GULLIVER'S TRAVELS'

I. COMPOSITION

The first reference we have to the composition of *Gulliver's Travels* turns up in a letter from Swift. On 15 April 1721 he told Ford, 'I am now writing a history of my travels, which will be a large volume, and gives account of countries hitherto unknown; but they go on slowly for want of health and humor.'[1] Swift must have given a general hint to Bolingbroke as well, for in a letter of 1 January 1722 his lordship said, 'I long to see your travels.'[2]

Six months later we meet our earliest mention of a detail of the actual narrative. This is in June 1722, when Vanessa alludes to Chapter Five of the voyage to Brobdingnag. Writing to Swift, she describes how a large company of men and women offended her when she went to visit a great lady. After comparing the guests to baboons and monkeys, she says that one of them snatched her fan and 'was so pleased with me ... that I apprehended nothing less than being carried up to the top of the house and served as a friend of yours was.'[3]

The next month, while visiting the Copes, Swift told Ford, 'The bad weather has made me read through abundance of trash, and this hath made me almost forget how to hold a pen, which I must therefore keep for Dublin, winter and sickness.'[4] The pen, I assume, would otherwise have been employed on *Gulliver's Travels*. After this we have no reference to the book until Christmas Day 1723. Then Bolingbroke, writing to Ford, says that Stella has preserved Swift from losing himself in fan-

[1] Williams II. 381.
[2] *Ibid.*, p. 415. This is a reply to a letter from Swift that has disappeared.
[3] *Ibid.*, p. 428.   [4] 22 Jul. 1722; *ibid.*, p. 431.

tasies or acting like a horse 'in that country which he discovered not long ago, where horses and mules are the reasonable creatures, and men the beasts of burden.'[1] Swift read this letter by mistake, and reproached Ford for telling Swift's secrets to Bolingbroke:

> you are a traitor ... else how should [Bolingbroke] know any thing of Stella or of horses.... I would have him and you know that I hate Yahoos of both sexes, and that Stella and Madame de Villette [Bolingbroke's second wife] are only tolerable at best, for want of Houyhnhnms.... I have left the country of horses, and am in the flying island, where I shall not stay long, and my two last journeys will be soon over.[2]

The next month, he wrote again, and replied to Ford's efforts to excuse himself: '[Bolingbroke] talks of the Houyhnhnms as if he were acquainted with [them], and in that shows you as a most finished traitor.'[3] One doubts that Swift felt genuinely distressed.

In April 1724 the end was in sight, and he told Ford, 'I shall have finished my travels very soon if I have health, leisure, and humour.'[4] But the *Drapier's Letters* came between; and it was not till 14 August 1725 that Swift at last wrote to Ford, 'I have finished my travels, and I am now transcribing them; they are admirable things, and will wonderfully mend the world.'[5] Two days later, writing again, he said he was 'reading books twice over for want of fresh ones, and fairly correcting and transcribing my travels, for the public'.[6] Meanwhile, Bolingbroke, writing directly to Swift, had mentioned the latter's promise 'to come to London loaden with [his] travels',[7] and had described those travels as being 'into ... countries of giants and pygmies'.[8]

The circle of knowledgeable friends naturally included Sheridan. Writing to him in September 1725, Swift alluded to Part Four of *Gulliver*, saying Sheridan should 'expect no more from man than such an animal is capable of, and you will every

---

[1] Ford, p. 238. [2] 19 Jan. 1724; Williams III. 4–5.
[3] 13 Feb. 1724; *ibid.*, p. 6. [4] 2 Apr. 1724; *ibid.*, p. 11. [5] *Ibid.*, p. 87.
[6] 16 Aug. 1725; *ibid.*, p. 89. [7] 12 Sept. 1724; *ibid.*, p. 29.
[8] 24 Jul. 1725; *ibid.*, p. 82.

day find my description of Yahoos more resembling'.[1] A few days later, Pope wrote to Swift, 'Your travels I hear much of.'[2] At the end of the month, writing to Pope from Quilca, Swift said,

> I have employed my time (besides ditching) in finishing, correcting, amending, and transcribing my travels, in four parts complete, newly augmented, and intended for the press when the world shall deserve them, or rather when a printer shall be found brave enough to venture his ears.[3]

Apart from such external references to the composition of *Gulliver's Travels*, the story itself often alludes to recent public affairs. The latest of these that one can date refers to the withdrawal of Wood's patent,[4] which became known around 1 September 1725, after Swift told Ford he had 'finished' the book. So we may assume that the process of composition continued during the labour of transcription and later. This in fact may be the meaning of Swift's expression, 'newly augmented', in the letter to Pope from Quilca. We had better think of the process as lasting until the copy went to the printer.

Yet the book which Swift began early in 1721 was substantially complete by August 1725. He had written Chapter Five of Part Two no later than June 1722. He had completed Part Four by the end of 1723. He was approaching the end of Part Three in April 1724, but then joined the controversy over Wood's patent, which slowed down the work on *Gulliver*.

Swift's allusive but secretive style of dealing with the progress of his masterpiece suggests what one would assume from reading it with attention—i.e., that he wished it to surprise his readers and yet wanted a chosen few to be prepared for the hoaxes and ironies. When he decided to place Part Four at the end, although written before Part Three, he also indicated a desire for the sequence of parts to have its own power.

---

[1] 11 Sept. 1725; *ibid.*, p. 94. [2] 14 Sept. 1725; *ibid.*, p. 96.
[3] 29 Sept. 1725; *ibid.*, III. 102.
[4] Davis XI. 309–10. Cf. Firth, p. 258. I assume that this passage was written before the publication of the first edition, because it appears in Ford's interleaved copy. But it could have been added later. See Davis's note in his edition, XI. 310. Firth suggested that the passage on coloured threads in Part One, Chapter Three (p. 39) refers in part to Walpole's receiving the Garter in May 1726 (Firth, p. 245).

We know now, contrary to what once was thought, that Swift produced *Gulliver's Travels* not when he had little else to occupy his genius but after the lure of Irish politics drew him back into the business of pamphleteering. There is only a grain of truth in the old view that the book had its origins in the Scriblerus Club.[1] Before launching *Gulliver*, Swift published his *Proposal for the Universal Use of Irish Manufacture* and suffered the consequences of its prosecution. More than four months after Swift's first known reference to his new book, the Duke of Grafton at last brought over a *noli prosequi* to relieve Waters.

From the time of his retirement to Letcombe Bassett in the spring of 1714, Swift had been trying to produce memoirs or reflections on his experience of politics.[2] One after another, they had remained incomplete or unpublishable. 'There are few things he ever wrote', said Delany, 'that he did not wish to be published.'[3] Yet of these pieces the earliest to appear (*Some Free Thoughts*) only emerged in 1741. Swift transferred his energy to Irish affairs; but the *Proposal* raised maddening difficulties for him. He tried to compress his anger and insight into the so-called 'Letter to Pope' (January 1722) but decided very wisely to leave that in manuscript until 1741.[4]

I believe, therefore, that when Swift embarked on *Gulliver's Travels*, it was to convert these repressed impulses into the shape

[1] See John Arbuthnot *et al.*, *Memoirs of Scriblerus*, ed. C. Kerby-Miller (New Haven, 1950), pp. 315–20.

[2] See above, pp. 108–13.

[3] *A Letter to Deane Swift* (London, 1755), p. 17.

[4] I think Swift wrote the 'Letter to Pope' after he began composing *Gulliver's Travels*. The pamphlet is headed 'January 10, 1721'. Herbert Davis thought its proper date was Jan. 1721 by the modern calendar, rather than 1722, as Craik and Ball had argued. Williams agreed with Davis. (See Craik II. 60; Ball III. 113, n. 5; Davis IX. xii, n. 1; Williams II. 365, n. 2.) Craik had observed that Swift's reference to Grafton's relief of Waters (Williams V. 27) must have been written after the event, which occurred in August 1721. Davis said this sentence of Swift's seemed an awkward, later insertion into a text which otherwise referred to events preceding Jan. 1721. I do not find the sentence awkward or a break in the train of thought. The reference to 'man' in the next paragraph is awkward, but not remarkably so; similar breaks will be found often enough in Swift's prose and verse. Besides, the form of the date is significant. Swift normally used double dates for the period 1 Jan. to 25 Mar.; and when he used single dates, they carried on the old year. (Cf. Williams II. 9, 340, 341; V. 6.) So Swift's 'Jan. 10, 1721' would be our '1722'. Cf. above, p. 136, n. 4.

of a fantasy. He would thus generalize his response to the public events he had known and deliver his confirmed views on human nature as it was exhibited in English society, especially in the conduct of government. But rather than speak out directly, he would speak both ironically and simply in turns, through the mouths of various spokesmen, including an eponymous narrator. By employing fictitious persons and places in a pseudo-memoir, he would escape the frustrations that had smothered his less covert speech. Thus the self-transforming energy of the unprintable essays found a new vehicle, bold enough to satisfy Swift's anger, expressive enough to convey his doctrine, but so disguised that it could be sold in London.

The literary form belongs to the tradition of narrative satire which Swift had drawn on for *A Tale of a Tub* and *The Battle of the Books*, and which the members of the Scriblerus Club had talked about. Their figure of Martin Scriblerus had contained enough of Pantagruel to make its Rabelaisian ancestry clear. On this character Swift and his friends had set the humours of an obsessed virtuoso who was to go on Quixotic and Hudibrastic travels.

What Swift now did was to turn the idea inside out. He kept the biographical framework of Rabelais. But instead of having Martin (like Don Quixote) follow his mad vocations among normal people, he sent a sane Gulliver to be educated among oddities.[1] So he combined the pattern of *Gargantua* with that of More's *Utopia*—the most profound English (at least, in authorship) influence upon *Gulliver*. Arbuthnot had dramatized the politics of the War of the Spanish Succession in an animal fable with John Bull as the innocent hero. Gulliver's voyage to Lilliput is an analogous treatment of the same and later events, with pigmies instead of animals.[2]

One point where the machinery of sublimation grows visible is in Gulliver's defence of himself against the charge of treason.

---

[1] Cf. the analysis by C. Kerby-Miller in Arbuthnot, *Memoirs of Scriblerus*, p. 317.

[2] For some comparisons of Arbuthnot with Swift, see John Arbuthnot, *The History of John Bull*, ed. A.W. Bower and R.A. Erickson (Oxford, 1976), pp. xix–xxii, lxxxiv–xcvii.

Two high ministers, he says, had represented his acquaintance with the ambassadors from Blefuscu (i.e., France) as treasonable—'a mark of disaffection, *from which I am sure my heart was wholly free*'.[1] We must recall how Archbishop King, in 1716, had warned Swift that the exiled Bolingbroke might turn informer, receive a pardon, come home from France, and tell some 'ill story' about Swift.[2] In reply, the archbishop had got a furious defence of the exile. After reviewing Bolingbroke's relations with the French court and identifying himself with his friend's destiny, Swift had said, 'But whether I am mistaken or no in other men, I beg your grace to believe, that I am not mistaken in myself; I always professed to be against the Pretender, and am so still.'[3] In this whole passage Swift echoed a section of the pamphlet he had begun writing eighteen months earlier, defending the ministry of Oxford and Bolingbroke. There he had introduced the character of Bolingbroke with the words, '*As my own heart was free from all treasonable thoughts*, so I did little imagine myself to be perpetually in the company of traitors.'[4] The parallels of thought and phrase suggest how deeply the story of Gulliver reflected the experience of the author.[5]

Swift's wish to hide what he was doing from the profane while revealing it to the initiate fits his scheme. It would have been pointless to produce a book that no one understood. He relied on a core of enlightened readers to pick up clues which *hoi polloi* would miss—a chosen few who might join him in laughing at the rest. The friends whom he entrusted with his secret stood for that select audience. They would know without being told that the author was only clowning when he made a parody of seaman's language (p. 84), but that he was denouncing the impeachment of Oxford and Bolingbroke when he recorded the charges against Quinbus Flestrin (pp. 68–9).

[1] Davis XI. 54. My italics.   [2] Williams II. 228; cf. above, pp. 23–5.
[3] 22 Dec. 1716; *ibid.*, p. 238.
[4] Davis VIII. 134. My italics.
[5] For a fuller discussion, see my essay on *Gulliver* in *The Personality of Jonathan Swift* (London, 1958), pp. 83–116. I no longer hold the views expounded in section iv of that essay, or in the last paragraph of section v.

II. COMEDY

The comic basis of the fantasy was Swift's ambiguous relation to the doctrine he might have preached; for whenever he tried seriously to win men over, he had to smile to himself at the hopelessness of the project. Ten years after *Gulliver* came out, Swift wrote to an English statesman about his own rules for preserving health,

> I desire that my prescription for living may be published, which you design to follow, for the benefit of mankind, which however I do not value a rush, nor the animal itself as it now acts, neither will I ever value my self as a philanthropus, because it [i.e., mankind] is now a creature (taking a vast majority) that I hate more than a toad, a viper, a wasp, a stock, a fox, or any other that you will please to add.[1]

There are two paradoxes in this sentence, both of which inform *Gulliver's Travels*. One is that the writer wishes to serve mankind while professing to hate the species. The other is that although he condemns human nature as essentially corrupt, he congratulates the very statesman to whom he addresses these remarks, for being uncorrupted—for having 'public and private virtues' and for defending the liberties of his country 'with more than an old Roman spirit'.[2] While Swift tries faintly to resolve these paradoxes by applying his condemnation only to the 'vast majority' of men, he makes no sustained effort to bring his two attitudes together.

So also the King of Brobdingnag applies his famous denunciation to only the bulk of Englishmen: 'I cannot but conclude the bulk of your natives to be the most pernicious race of little odious vermin that nature ever suffered to crawl upon the surface of the earth' (p. 132). But the ferocity of the language obscures the restraint of the qualifier. Is Gulliver himself the only exception? We remember the emotion better than the limitation.

Here is the spring of the humour and comedy of *Gulliver's Travels*. Behind each ironic proposition, Swift recognizes a point of view from which it will seem an expression of despair. Behind each serious proposition is a point of view from which it will seem

[1] 7 Mar. 1737, to Pulteney; Williams v. 7.   [2] *Ibid.*, p. 7.

absurd. In a kind of infinite regress, alternating comic tone with bitter tone, Swift keeps surprising us with shifts in point of view. So it is that he leaps from a mode of simple speech to irony; and so also he represents human nature as utterly vicious and at once produces men or women who are admirable.

Outside *Gulliver's Travels* Swift often sounded contemptuous of mankind and yet offered to help people at considerable self-sacrifice. We could impose a transcendent synthesis on such dilemmas by invoking a few conventional pieties. But this is not Swift's way. To suggest the relation between creature and creator, we may notice an echo of a famous letter of Swift's in Part Four of *Gulliver's Travels*. Writing to Pope, he says,

> I tell you after all that I do not hate mankind, it is vous autres who hate them because you would have them reasonable animals, and are angry for being disappointed. I have always rejected that definition and made another of my own. I am no more angry with [Walpole] than I was with the kite that last week flew away with one of my chickens and yet I was pleased when one of my servants shot him two days after.[1]

In the same way Gulliver's master among the Houyhnhnms says,

> That, although he hated the Yahoos of this country, yet he no more blamed them for their odious qualities, than he did a *gnnayh* (a bird of prey) for its cruelty, or a sharp stone for cutting his hoof.[2]

The striking facts are that Swift had said, in an earlier letter to Pope, that he 'ever hated mankind',[3] and that in *Gulliver's Travels* he had described the Houyhnhnms as free from vices and unreasonable passions. One hardly expects Swift suddenly to reverse himself and say he does *not* hate men. Nor does one expect a Houyhnhnm to say that although he does not blame the Yahoos, he does hate them.

To ask which attitude is valid would be a step in the wrong direction. Rather we should observe how casually Swift makes the kind of shift that his characters make. For each attitude there are alternatives that undercut it. On this principle and on the

---

[1] 26 Nov. 1725; *ibid.*, III. 118.   [2] Davis XI. 248.   [3] Williams III. 103.

casualness with which Swift moves from one to the other, the comedy of the book depends.

Thus it is that anger suddenly becomes separable from the pleasure one feels in seeing a hateful object destroyed; thus also hating a repulsive creature is suddenly opposed to blaming it. Gulliver is disillusioned in one speech and credulous in the next. The Houyhnhnms are serious embodiments of moral ideals until they become, for a moment, the butt of a little farce. If the satirist embodies himself in his work, he also keeps withdrawing from it, smiling at the naïveté of his own ideals. The harmony of Swift's book lies in comic themes—confrontations of mind and body—connected by an ironic tone which is focused in turn on the ambiguous relation of the author to his project. This comic, ironic self-awareness, flickering on and off without warning, is the true, animating spirit that bathes Swift's masterpiece. In the jurisprudence of this sensibility there is always an appeal from the sublime to the ridiculous.

The reflex by which Swift passed from sober preaching to self-mockery is hard to illustrate conclusively in *Gulliver's Travels* because he is not himself the narrator; and the constant puzzle of interpretation is whether or not, at this or that point, the author is indeed ridiculing the protagonist. But in Swift's letters we hear the reflex constantly. Writing to Bolingbroke about the relation between wealth and virtue, Swift soberly denounces the view that all ages of the world are equally virtuous or vicious; and he alludes to a serious scheme of his own to make virtue the central principle of government. But after some quite earnest sentences he suddenly catches himself and reverses his tone:

> I have a scheme in spite of your notions, to govern England upon the principles of virtue, and when the nation is ripe for it, I desire you will send for me. I have learned this by living like a hermit, by which I am got backwards about nineteen hundred years in the aera of the world, and begin to wonder at the wickedness of men. I dine alone upon half a dish of meat, mix water with my wine walk ten miles a day, and read Baronius. *Hic explicit epistola ad Dom. Bolingbroke.*[1]

[1] 5 Apr. 1729; Sherburn III. 29.

From a straightforward, serious recommendation of his proposal, Swift has slipped into ridicule of himself for pressing it on
the reader. This reversal of tone is the same as what we hear in
Gulliver's Travels.

The exclusiveness of the various points of view—the failure to
reconcile them—counts heavily. The more self-contained each
side of the ethical drama appears, the more comical and horrify-
ing the dialectic can be. While Swift was writing *Gulliver*, he
delivered the memorable advice to Sheridan that I have quoted
above:

> expect no more from man than such an animal is capable of, and you
> will every day find my description of Yahoos more resembling. You
> should think and deal with every man as a villain, without calling
> him so, or flying from him, or valuing him less.[1]

Johnson, whose antipathy to Swift was partly a reaction against
early admiration and partly the effect of their deep similarity,
once spoke much like this:

> Lady M'Leod asked, if no man was naturally good?—*Johnson*. 'No,
> madam, no more than a wolf.'—*Boswell*. 'Nor no woman, sir?'
> *Johnson*. 'No, sir.'—Lady M'Leod started at this, saying, in a low
> voice, 'This is worse than Swift.'[2]

The judgment was not eccentric. It was a common Christian
view of unredeemed humanity. Yet Christian charity has always
been urged to exercise itself on such unpromising material.
Shortly before writing his advice to Sheridan, Swift risked his
security by writing the *Drapier's Letters* for the benefit of the Irish
people. So also Gulliver returns from the utter disillusionment
of his last voyage and yet publishes his memoirs in the hope
of serving his fellows. There is something clownish in this
behaviour, though Swift, like many moralists and prophets,
soberly persisted in it.

But Swift departs from the pulpit view of unredeemed humanity, because that prospect includes always the mysterious

---

[1] Williams III. 94; cf. above, p. 364.   [2] Boswell v. 211.

possibility of redemption; and the rhetoric of Swift's satires does not. Whatever he may have taught in his sermons, Swift in his greatest work seems to disallow the idea of a sinner's being converted to virtue. Driven by his congenital reflex, he turned on himself in his own mind, mocking his benevolent didacticism. So when he expounds the meaning of *Gulliver* in a letter to Pope, after a calm opening which rises to a bitter outburst against men in general (with a reservation of beloved individuals), Swift makes a characteristic transition to a third and then a fourth stage of his satirical dialectic, viz., self-consciousness and self-ridicule:

> Upon this great foundation of misanthropy (though not Timon's manner) the whole building of my travels is erected: And I never will have peace of mind till all honest men are of my opinion: by consequence you are to embrace it immediately and procure that all who deserve my esteem may do so too. The matter is so clear that it will admit little dispute. Nay I will hold a hundred pounds that you and I agree in the point.[1]

The shift from impersonal rhetoric to self-parody is a process audible throughout the *Journal to Stella*. It is rooted in Swift's consciousness and can be observed guiding the syntax of his best prose. It is the true internal structure of *Gulliver's Travels*.

When I thus associate the character of Swift with the design or argument of his great book, I do not imply that one must familiarize oneself with his life order to appreciate the work. Quite the contrary. Read by itself, *Gulliver* will yield up something like the meanings I have expounded. But the reader who cannot accept them must square his rejection with the biographical data.

III. INTERPRETATION

Unlike most of Swift's works *Gulliver's Travels* does not finally stand within a specific context of public events. It refers to many external facts; we can identify many allusions to persons. But the

---

[1] 29 Sept. 1725; Williams III. 103. See above, p. 150.

stories do not require us to notice these historical matters; they do not invite us to keep in mind the particularities of the author's ambience.

Normally, it is in such a framework that we interpret Swift's satire. By connecting his attacks with their objects in the life of his time, we often infer the doctrines he is advocating; and he normally encourages us to proceed along such tracks.

In the *Drapier's Letters* we arrive at specific principles of politics and economics by listening to the speaker's explicit statements and by comparing his sarcasms with the doctrines of the person they ridicule. If Mr Wood wishes to manufacture coins for Ireland in Bristol, and the Drapier denounces Mr Wood, we may suspect that Swift believes Ireland should have her own mint. Since the Drapier himself asserts this doctrine openly, and Swift lays it down elsewhere, we can be sure of our interpretation.[1]

Gulliver's Travels is less simple. The teaching of doctrine abounds in the book. When the King of Brobdingnag denounces standing armies (p. 131), we may suspect that the author agrees with him, because the statement is so bold and unqualified. We find support for our suspicion in the sympathy with which Swift represents the giant monarch. But we also verify our inference by going outside the fantasy and learning that in Britain at the time, the coterie with which Swift grouped himself regularly exhibited a distrust of standing armies.[2]

So also in Part One of *Gulliver's Travels*, Chapter Seven, when Gulliver reports the praise heaped on the Emperor of Lilliput for his merciful disposition, we notice that some crucial words are in italics, a feature inviting us to scrutinize them. Research discloses that the words echo the language of Suetonius on Domitian and Tiberius. They also echo the language used by and about George I in connection with the suppression of the 1715 rebellion and again with the trial of Atterbury. We may suspect therefore that the passage refers specifically to the King and asks us to regard him as a bloodthirsty hypocrite in the

---

[1] *Drapier*, pp. 20, 44, 155, 169.   [2] Cf. Davis XI. 131 and Williams II. 372.

fashion of the sadistic emperors of Rome. When we go outside the book, our suspicion is confirmed by a letter in which Swift mentions the topic and also by some of his marginalia.[1]

Thus in *Gulliver's Travels* as in other works by Swift we may of course meet doctrines conveyed by allusions operating within a historical context. Yet the spirit of the book as a whole hardly blows this way. Rather the direction is toward a challenging of both reader and author by the situations represented. The most profound and essential ingredients of the fantasy detach themselves from time and place, and point at the various definitions of our nature which men of various cultures have accepted. In this fundamental realm the book becomes a machine designed not to advance a set of doctrines but to start readers on the way to reflection, self-doubt, and fresh thought.

For example, in Part Four, when the traveller describes the social institutions of the Houyhnhnms, his language does not direct us toward external references. It is flat and unemphatic, with no obvious sarcasm or irony:

> When the matron Houyhnhnms have produced one of each sex, they no longer accompany with their consorts, except they lose one of their issue by some casualty, which very seldom happens: But in such a case they meet again; or when the like accident befalls a person, whose wife is past bearing, some other couple bestows on him one of their own colts, and then go together a second time, until the mother be pregnant. (Davis XI. 268)

Gulliver surely sounds as if he approves of such institutions. Yet Swift cannot expect the reader to agree intuitively with Gulliver's judgment. Neither does any simple alternative exist which one might appeal to after rejecting Gulliver's position. Marriage and domestic habits take too many forms in too many cultures. Historical context will not carry us far toward an interpretation of such passages.

It remains clear that the institutions of the Houyhnhnms are at odds with those of humans, and that Swift calls attention to the differences. But if he does not expect us to adopt the insti-

---

[1] Cf. Williams II. 436; Davis V. 254.

tutions of the Houyhnhnms, and he condemns those we maintain, he throws us back upon the most general considerations. In
effect, he appeals to intuitive reason or morality.

Now in rational terms it would be harder to defend human
practices than those of the Houyhnhnms. Consequently, we
may presume that Swift is urging us to bring our institutions
closer in line with reason, or defensible principles. So whatever
our marital customs may be, we must see ourselves hard put to
tolerate the policy of leaving them unchanged.

This then is the most general impression left by the book: that
we feel drawn into a radical, comical criticism of human nature
which leaves us unsure of our axioms, offers no clear set of rules
to replace them, and challenges us to reconsider our instinctive
patterns of life.

IV. STRUCTURE AND EXPLICIT THEMES

The shape of *Gulliver's Travels* derives naturally from the main
argument. If one is to examine human nature as such, without
regard to differences of time and place, one must take specimens
from many countries and periods. Geographically, by planning
four voyages, Swift suggests the four directions, or a survey of the
whole world. Historically, he probably refers to the four great
empires of antiquity (Assyria, Persia, Greece, and Rome). At
many points he dips into history, in order to set the past beside
the present; and in Glubbdubdrib he even revives several ancients so that we may compare their character with our own.

Swift also had the example of Sir William Temple's essay 'Of
Heroick Virtue'. Here Temple set himself the problem of defin-
ing human nature by its noblest powers—those which enable
truly great men to serve their race, sometimes by patriotic
leadership and self-sacrifice, sometimes by fundamental inventions that improve the conditions of life, but above all by in-
stituting wise and just governments. Temple tried to enlarge the
common idea of heroism by going outside European tradition.
Instead of examining the four great empires of antiquity, he
surveyed four that represented the extremes of east, west, north,

[455]

and south: i.e., China, Peru, Scythia, and Arabia. His essay is among the very few literary works of which one hears verbal echoes in *Gulliver's Travels*.[1] It may be significant that Gulliver went to Temple's college, Emmanuel, and that his story begins in the year of Temple's death. At points we might even think of him as a humorous reincarnation of Sir William.

In the friendliest way Swift may have been replying to his old master. He went about his work like Temple, by recommending good examples in strange places. Both men dwell on virtue and reason as the essential marks of a good life.[2] But Temple tried to stir his contemporaries to noble acts by encouraging them to believe that virtue was possible. Swift argued that men cannot be improved, yet tried to change his readers by holding up many pictures of their corruptions along with a few specimens of virtue.

In effect, Temple defined human nature by its heroic representatives, not by its defects. The spirit of his essay is positive and hopeful. He devoted his strongest rhetoric to the virtues of the nations and heroes which he discussed. To the failings of men he gave fleeting attention and small emotion.

So in concluding a survey of the Arab empire, Temple lists the most admirable Mohammedan princes, then the names of great ancients, Goths, and moderns, concluding,

> Whoever has a mind to trace the paths of heroic virtue, which lead to the temple of true honour and fame, need seek no further than in the stories and examples of those illustrious persons here assembled; and so I leave this crown of never-fading laurel, in full view of such great and noble spirits as shall deserve it in this or succeeding ages. Let them win and wear it.[3]

Temple treats his heroes as rare and exceptional, but he does not debase the rest of mankind in order to exalt the exceptions. The

---

[1] *Gulliver* Pt I, Ch. iv, par. 2, and Temple (ed. Monk), p. 111, ll. 32–6; *Gulliver* Pt I, Ch. vi, par. 2, and Temple, p. 116, ll. 13–16; *Gulliver* Pt I, Ch. vi, par. 6, and Temple, p. 120, ll. 30–2.

[2] Temple interprets Confucius (one of his heroes) as teaching that 'every man ought to study and endeavour the improving and perfecting of his own natural reason' (p. 114), and he attributes similar doctrines to Mango Copac of Peru (p. 132).

[3] Ed. Monk, p. 166. For Swift's matching passage, see Pt III, Ch. vii, par. 10.

hero and his people are mutually responsive; his virtues do not serve to show up their vices; for Temple interpreted 'heroic virtue' as equivalent to 'deserving well of mankind'.[1] But for all the refinement and charm of his language, Temple writes with little humour, wit, or irony. In his style the comic element hardly exists. It was when Swift composed his early odes that he came nearest to this lack of humour; and it was at this time that he lived most under the influence of Temple's example. We may therefore think of *Gulliver* as replying both to Swift's younger self and to Sir William.

The rhythm of the four parts of *Gulliver* suggests stages in Swift's memories. In its historical allusions, Part One points mainly to the public events of the years 1708–15. The dispelling of Gulliver's illusions as he learns more and more about the imperial court evokes the enlightenment Swift suffered during the years 1711–14. Part Two, I suspect, reverts to the private events of the years 1688–99. The giant king and his wife have touches of Temple and Dorothy Osborne. Glumdalclitch—who leaves her family to join Gulliver, and whom he then deserts— has touches of Esther Johnson; and so has the queen (whose 'weak stomach' is like Stella's).[1] Part Three, the least coherent, alludes to the public events of the years 1715–25. The material is not yet digested; the narrative is fragmentary. Part Four, I speculate, alludes quite unconsciously to Swift's childhood and youth, suggesting an early lack of self-respect, of hostility toward adults, and fear of sexuality. So Swift assigns the Houyhnhnms to a remarkably primitive culture, lacking metals and the wheel. They exist in the pastoral, Saturnian myth of an innocence preceding civilization and associated with childhood.

The design of *Gulliver* also shows the effects of Swift's travels and of his fondness for travel books. The ease and regularity with which Gulliver leaves his wife and children correspond to Swift's habit of abandoning Stella. Swift's voyages between England and Ireland were, for him, like shuttlings between civilization and barbarism. When he travelled within Ireland, he seemed

[1] Temple, ed. Monk, p. 106.

often to navigate seas of bestiality in order to reach islets of human culture;[1] and the sharpness of the contrasts gave him a point of view for his comic, ironic survey of mankind.

V. RELIGION AND MORALITY

The books Swift read and remembered while composing *Gulliver* only added to his store of real travels. The hints supplied by more or less true accounts, such as Dampier's, are numberless.[2] But their significance for *Gulliver* is clarified by the implications of the fantasies.

Travel books as a group sometimes provoked English readers to humorous reflections on the faults of European society or of human nature as such. More often they fed the European and Christian sense of easy superiority to the outlanders. A few writers of imaginary voyages used that form to shame Europeans out of their vices by exalting the merits of remote pagans. And several, especially in the seventeenth and eighteenth centuries, used it to show how virtue could thrive without the help (or weakening effect!) of Christianity. These, then, are the usual implications of the books Swift knew.

Lucian's *True History* underlay Swift's parodies of historians and writers of travels, providing a tone of genial, easygoing ridicule of all mankind. Rabelais inspired much of the satire on learning or science, as well as the farce of some giant–pigmy incidents. He had the idea of drowning a city in the urine of a giant. Rabelais' preoccupation with the functions of the body showed Swift how to use them to ridicule spiritual aspirations. Rabelais' oscillations between benevolence toward mankind and contempt for them foreshadowed Swift's comedy.[3] More's *Utopia* gave Swift the most impressive model for shaming Europeans with the moral accomplishments of pagans. The still

---

[1] Cf. his comments on Cope's neighbourhood (Williams II. 431).

[2] R. W. Frantz, 'Swift's Yahoos and the Voyagers', *Modern Philology* 29 (Aug. 1931), 49–57.

[3] Cf. Huntington Brown, *Rabelais in English Literature* (Cambridge, Mass., 1933), pp. 161–71.

broader satire of comparing humans with animals (though common in antiquity and natural to Swift) was most pertinently
embodied in the travesties of travel literature composed by
Cyrano de Bergerac.[1]

The tendency of such literature was ambiguous, as I have
suggested. It could enforce reason and religion. It could also
undermine Christianity by implying that the highest virtue was
available to men who never knew Christian revelation.[2] Swift, I
believe, had his own reservations about Christian creeds, but
not to the extent of supposing that men without religion might
be superior to those who possessed it. In *Gulliver's Travels* the
remote peoples serve as both positive and negative depreciators
of the European. If these new nations seem admirable, their
effect is to expose European corruptions. If they are evil, their
vices are identified with those of Christian Europe.

The implications for religion could only be troubling. I think
Swift recognized the fact and tried to build his case on moral
grounds that gave decisive importance to the physical aspect of
human existence. But not only does religion keep entering into
the story. Swift's morality also keeps clashing with Swift's history; i.e., his general principles are often undermined by his
particular judgments.

There are methods by which a diligent critic might transcend
these contradictions between history and morality. But I think
we might be wiser to let them stand and to admit that like many
a genius, Swift gave himself up to a topic when it excited him,
and that he would not weaken the intensity, drama, or humour
of a particular passage by a regard for the applications that
readers might make to other topics. Absorbed in the depiction of
the moral life, the life of reason, he represented the Houyhnhnms
as dignified or awesome. Absorbed in the historical drama of his
narrative, he let them appear limited and fallible.

The importance of religion for the author becomes obvious
from his many discussions of the subject. But some of the refer-

[1] Cf. W. A. Eddy, *Gulliver's Travels: A Critical Study* (Princeton, 1923), pp. 61–4.
[2] Cf. Kathleen Williams, *Swift and the Age of Compromise* (Lawrence, Kansas, 1958),
pp. 179–83.

ences are treacherous. The Lilliputians bury their dead standing on their heads because they imagine the earth will be upside down at the resurrection.[1] No doubt Swift means to ridicule an over-literal idea of the resurrection of the body. But it would be hard for most readers to take the joke as advancing Christianity. The Lilliputians also quarrel about which end of an egg to break when they eat one.[2] Here is a shrunken version of the argument behind *A Tale of a Tub*; and one assumes that Swift is condemning schism. But the Church of England is not obviously strengthened by the tale.

Gulliver's own attitude toward Christianity appears at the beginning of Part Three, when his sloop is boarded by pirates. One of the pirate leaders is a Dutchman whom Gulliver begs, 'in consideration of our being Christians and Protestants, of neighbouring countries, in strict alliance', that he would ask the chief of the pirates to show mercy. The Dutchman grows furious, but a Japanese captain promises that Gulliver and his men will live. So the pagan is morally superior to a Dutch Protestant.[3]

In case we have ignored the implication, Swift goes further. At the end of Part Three, Gulliver pretends himself to be a Dutchman, and asks the Emperor of Japan to excuse him from performing the ceremony of trampling on the crucifix. The Emperor is surprised because no Dutchman had ever before requested such a privilege. Gulliver says his majesty began to doubt 'whether I were a real Hollander or no; but rather suspected I must be a Christian'.[4] A little historical research into the differences between religious toleration in the Netherlands and in England, along with a little knowledge of Swift's own attitude toward the Dutch, will persuade most readers that the implications are clear enough. We are being asked to regard the tolerant Dutch as not truly Christian. It is no accident that the benevolent seamen of Part Four are Portuguese Roman Catholics.

But Swift can be more worrying. He confuses the issue in Part Three, Chapter Seven, when the spirits of the dead are called up

[1] Pp. 57-8.   [2] Pp. 48-50.   [3] Pp. 154-5.   [4] P. 216.

for Gulliver's edification. A Christian priest of Swift's generation normally held that revealed religion is essential to keep
men morally upright, and we know that in his sermons Swift
preached this doctrine. Admittedly, there were virtuous pagans,
but these were rare exceptions with extraordinary gifts.
Humanity as a whole could not expect to resist vice without the
threat of damnation and the promise of heavenly bliss.

Yet when Gulliver visits Glubbdubdrib, and thinks of men
who were truly great, he does not illustrate the doctrine.
Although Gulliver lists six heroes of public virtue, only one of
them is a Christian and he is no Protestant. Nevertheless,
Gulliver says that 'all the ages of the world cannot add a seventh'
to these.[1] Grace works in mysterious ways if Gulliver is right.

One could handle the crux by remembering St Paul's declaration in Romans ii.14, 'For when the Gentiles, which have not the
law, do by nature the things contained in the law, these, having
not the law, are a law unto themselves.'[2] Just as St Paul
reproached the Jews for being outdone in virtue by the Gentiles,
so Christians have often reproached their fellow-believers for
sinking below the moral standard of eminent pagans. St Paul
even matches Swift's disregard for the applications that might
be made from one passage to another, because—as commentators point out—he had delivered an unqualified denunciation
of Gentile morals in the first chapter of the epistle.

But elsewhere Swift goes still further. In Part Four, Chapter
Five, when Gulliver is holding forth on the causes of war in
Europe, we meet the following paragraph:

> Difference in opinions hath cost many millions of lives; for instance,
> whether *flesh* be *bread*, or *bread* be *flesh*; whether the juice of a certain
> *berry* be *blood* or *wine*; whether whistling be a vice or a virtue; whether
> it be better to *kiss a post*, or throw it into the fire.[3]

The expression, 'difference in opinions', is a euphemism for
religious differences. The controversy over flesh and bread is of
course over the doctrine of transubstantiation, which divides

---

[1] Pt III, Ch. vii, penultimate paragraph.   [2] Cf. Rom. ii. 26.
[3] Pt IV, Ch. v, par. 3.

Protestants from Roman Catholics. So also is the controversy over blood and wine. Whistling is a reference to the use of instrumental music in church, which the Church of England favoured and certain Dissenting sects opposed. The post is the cross, and the controversy here is over its veneration or its destruction as a misleading symbol.

Surely the common reader of the passage infers that the author believes such differences are insignificant. So also in Lilliput, when we learn about the Big-Endians and Little-Endians, we are not inclined to think the author takes seriously the divisions between Protestants and Roman Catholics. The Lilliputian notions concerning death and resurrection must leave many readers doubting that the author held serious views on those subjects.

Yet we know that Swift had the strongest convictions on transubstantiation and the use of music in church, on the veneration of the cross and the Roman Catholics (not to mention death and resurrection). We also know how bitterly he attacked those who disagreed with him, in *A Tale of a Tub* and in his writings on the church. From our knowledge of Swift's self-consciousness, our sense that he realized the implications of his language, we draw an assurance that he must have understood the probable effect of the inconsistencies.

If we seek a harmony of doctrine, we may force a synthesis on the apparent disagreements. But I am not inclined to do so. Of course, it is monstrous that Christians should be more vicious than pagans, that they should murder one another for religious differences, that they should corrupt the most valuable of institutions. This was Swift's general, moral outlook. In particular instances, however—in historical cases—he normally took sides and felt intolerant of other positions. Speaking to his Houyhnhnm master, Gulliver deplores religious dissension leading to war; and Swift simply does not care that from such a statement the reader may draw secondary inferences undermining the historical positions which the author held.

This, I believe, is Swift's usual practice. He ridicules political differences in a similar way, even though he had strong prejudices in politics and denounced those of the other party. It is the way Swift naturally works. He inculcates his opinions one by one, and does not try to erect a synthesis that will encompass all of them. Not merely in *Gulliver's Travels* but in his writings generally, he pushes separate arguments to extremes without regarding the inferences that persistent and learned readers might elicit from them. For those who attend closely to his writing this feature becomes an aspect of his literary self, and they come to look for it. But as a result, although *Gulliver's Travels* abounds in challenging doctrines and intense rhetoric, it would be an unrewarding task to bring them all happily together.

VI. BODY AND SOUL

In Swift's story, following a common moral tradition, the physical is opposed to the spiritual as disappointing reality is opposed to ideal conduct. Swift was instinctively fascinated and repelled by the relation of bodily processes to filth. Unpleasant smells, perspiration, body oils, urine, faeces excited his imagination. But he could self-consciously turn these deep preoccupations to moral and aesthetic use. By dwelling on them, he could correct men's habit of regarding the body as easily subordinate to their higher faculties. In Christian tradition it is normal to link such imagery to the idea of sin,[1] and Swift could therefore hope that his representation of the Yahoos would remind the reader of old descriptions of fallen humanity—as when John Bradford said, 'What a charnel-house of stinking carrion is this body and life of wicked man.'[2]

It was not, however, to the peculiarly Christian tradition that Swift mainly appealed. Rather it was to the comic and moral association of flesh with filth—associations that children share with adults, and that Christians share with pagans. These are associations the Lilliputians, Brobdingnagians, and Englishmen

---

[1] Cf. Roland M. Frye, 'Swift's Yahoos and the Christian Symbols for Sin', *JHI* 15 (1954), 201–17.

[2] Smithfield martyr, quoted by Frye, p. 207.

have in common. On the one hand, the body is the spirit's tragedy; on the other, it is the spirit's farce. *Gulliver's Travels* is designed to keep both these attitudes in sight at once, and to destroy the dignity of man in all his shapes by their constant juxtaposition.

This is why Swift delights in the quarrel between physical needs and human ambition, between the tangible world and the ways of men. It is why he builds his work on the physical contrasts of size and shape, why he draws attention to Gulliver's bowels and bladder, to his genitals, to the freckles of Lilliputian ladies,[1] to the breast of the giant wet nurse,[2] the stinks of the maids of honour,[3] the cancer of the giant beggar-woman.[4] It is one reason that Part Three, which is not based on such contrasts, is the weakest section of the book.

From the physical point of view, farce and horror coincide. What is loathsome in the beggar is absurd in the maids of honour. Looking into a Brobdingnagian mirror, Gulliver feels ridiculous (p. 107). Looking at his reflection in Houyhnhnm-land, he is horrified (p. 278). Each response implies the other.

These materials are managed most deftly in the Voyage to Lilliput, and with growing clumsiness in the later voyages— Part Four being heavy-handed in its didacticism and Part Three using filth and body functions in the most elementary manner.

We must look at Lilliput to see Swift's finest talent for comedy. Here, when Gulliver wakes up, he suffers pains of several kinds. His body is immobilized and tied down. At the same time, the cause of his pain and imprisonment appears as a race of contemptibly small, doll-like creatures. Their spokes-man, who addresses Gulliver, acts like a dignified court orator. Yet he is measured, in the hero's view, beside a young page 'somewhat longer than my middle finger' (p. 23). Gulliver's pain is due to the condition of his body; and it blends with the absurdity of another tiny, pretentious body wasting a grand manner on a giant who cannot understand the language. Both the intellectual and the physical collisions seem ultimately

[1] P. 92. [2] P. 91. [3] P. 118. [4] Pp. 112–13.

harmless, and therefore comic, to the reader who knows the author survived to write the book.

Swift's syntax runs parallel to the comic process, in a line of suspenseful containment followed by an absurd release: e.g., the sentence introducing the orator, which starts with a leisurely clutter of verbal phrases to reveal the construction of a tiny stage, then goes through a faster, continuous clause that brings forth the orator; and at last drops to a short, bathetic clause in which the final word makes the joke. I quote the latter elements:

> From whence one of them, who seemed to be a person of quality, made me a long speech, whereof I understood not one syllable. (p. 23)

In keeping with Swift's stylistic instincts, the early part of the sentence not only kept us in suspense but quietly misled us into expecting a far more serious action than we were finally offered.

The undercutting of Lilliputian grandeur by Gulliverian physique goes on in phrase after phrase, as when 'a person of high rank from his imperial majesty' must speak to Gulliver, and we are told, 'His excellency having mounted on the small of my right leg, advanced afterwards up to my face' (p. 25). But the doll-like comedy soon gives way to something less refined, when Gulliver pisses:

> I was able ... to ease myself with making water; which I very plentifully did, to the great astonishment of the people, who conjecturing by my motions what I was going to do, immediately opened to the right and left on that side, to avoid the torrent which fell with noise and violence from me. (p. 25)

Insensibly, we had been led to connect Gulliver's mere size with a kind of moral dignity. His pain, his imprisonment, his literally superior point of view, and of course his Englishness excited our respectful sympathy. The vivid, unexpected picture of his urinating suddenly ties us to him on a level we had buried. Embarrassment at the author's indelicacy matches a humbler embarrassment over the exposure of our own coarseness (we too would have had to piss), producing Swift's comedy of shameful truth.

[465]

It would be a mistake to base Swift's satirical comedy on literary allusion. Mainly the comedy revives those experiences of childhood, shared by us all, in which a natural shame mysteriously attaches itself to a normal process. A simpler example from the Voyage to Brobdingnag will clarify this analysis. At the end of Chapter Five, Gulliver recalls an attempt he made to display muscular agility:

> There was a cow-dung in the path, and I must needs try my activity by attempting to leap over it. I took a run, but unfortunately jumped short, and found myself just in the middle up to my knees. I waded through with some difficulty, and one of the footmen wiped me as clean as he could with his handkerchief; for I was filthily bemired, and my nurse confined me to my box until we returned home; where the Queen was soon informed of what had passed, and the footmen spread it about the court; so that all the mirth, for some days, was at my expense. (p. 124)

The comedy here sets Gulliver's exhibitionist vanity against the coarseness of his humiliation. Pride goeth before a fall. If he had not foolishly aspired to show his vigour, there would be little humour in the accident. If he had been physically harmed, there would be still less. But the body is insulted and the spirit suffers.

One might recall celebrated parallels in ancient epic: Ajax with dung in his mouth during the funeral games for Patroclus (*Iliad* 23. 773-7), Nisus prone in filthy manure during the funeral games for Anchises (*Aeneid* 5. 327-33). But Gulliver is not like Ajax, whose ambition seemed admirable to Homer, and whose fall is funny but not ironical.[1] And Gulliver is even less like Nisus, whose ambition is yet more worthy and whose fall is pathetic.

Swift's farce gets its edge not from literary precedent but from the turn of his prose. In this passage the language does not underline the sense but cuts across it. A distinct opposition appears between the colourless tone of the plain narrative and the grossness of the material. It is a contrast supporting the moral opposition between false heroism and unheroic bathos;

[1] Cf. James A. K. Thomson, *Irony: An Historical Introduction* (Cambridge, Mass., 1927), pp. 114-15.

and it irradiates the honest, physical body imposing its truth on a self-deceiving imagination. Swift's ability to call up the child's ambivalence toward filth and to make it work for subtleties of style, marks him off from lesser satirists.

So also the suffering of the body matters. When Gulliver, in Part One, receives an account of the Lilliputian court's plan to do away with him, Swift endows the friendly reporter with an amazing style, in which the sympathy of the speaker is undercut by the coolness with which he tells of the murderous proposals. Through all the sinister assumptions of the informative but accomplished courtier, a physical reality looms—that Gulliver is to be first blinded and then starved to death. The tangible, carnal facts—

> five or six thousand of his majesty's subjects might, in two or three days, cut your flesh from your bones, take it away by cartloads, and bury it in distant parts to prevent infection; leaving the skeleton as a monument of admiration to posterity (Davis XI. 71)

—these details overpower the ethical fallacies of the speaker. It is gruesome but hilarious that the good-natured courtier should assign the virtue of lenity or mercy to either of the two sides (in the division among the councillors) when the issue is whether Gulliver should be burned, poisoned, or blinded.

The reader may if he wishes think of the Marian martyrs, of Samson, or of Hercules as parallel cases. We know that the description of Gulliver tied down by the Lilliputians echoes the description by Philostratus of Hercules tied down by pygmies;[1] and when Flimnap and Bolgolam want Gulliver's servants to 'strew poisonous juice on your shirts and sheets, which would soon make you tear your own flesh and die' (p. 69), we think of the shirt of Nessus. Yet these possibilities again must remain barely audible. Swift's syntax, irony, and humour give the passage its brilliance. Any references to history or literature are secondary. Only because Gulliver did in the end escape without harm can the comic tone be maintained and the series of gruesome possibilities become merely a prologue to the farce of the

---

[1] Philostratus, *Imagines* II. 22.

recommendation made by Reldresal, a kind-hearted minister of state who tries to defend Gulliver—

> That if his majesty, in consideration of your services, and pursuant to his own merciful disposition, would please to spare your life and give order to put out your eyes; he humbly conceived, that by this expedient, justice might in some measure be satisfied, and all the world would applaud the *lenity* of the emperor. (p. 70)

In the whole of *Gulliver's Travels* there are few stretches of sustained, comic, ironic brilliance to equal the paragraphs from which I have chosen these specimens.[1] It is such manipulations of tone, it is such thematic patterns, that give the book its deepest harmony.

VII. THE ATTACK ON THE READER

Few readers of *Gulliver's Travels* come away from it feeling that the author has strengthened their devotion to Christianity. So it is fortunate that Swift's real argument lies elsewhere. By locating it not in the soul but in the body, Swift can simply compare the account of human nature generally accepted with the data of experience. He can set our theory of morals beside our visible practice. If religion has failed to touch the hearts of men, perhaps they may be moved by elementary shame, by the sight of the abyss between the principles they themselves preach and the corruption of their lives. Merely on the grounds of enlightened self-interest they may then turn away from their deformities.

This is why Swift chose a repetitive, narrative fantasy. In his story, the inventive form, the imaginative incidents, and not the doctrine, are what touch us first and draw us in. The social or political institutions we hear about come before us first as phenomena to be examined, not as teachings we must accept. They belong to a comic fantasy that may refer to us but that seems initially self-contained and no attack on our character. We begin as external spectators, privileged to criticize not only these remote and freakish people but the narrator himself.

---

[1] Davis XI. 69, l. 24, to p. 72, l. 6 (Pt I, Ch. vii).

Inevitably, we go beyond acceptance and rejection; for soon, half-consciously, we set up our own ideals beside theirs. We are lured into competition with Gulliver, whose judgments often put us off.

When the éclaircissements come, therefore, we are caught with our guard down; for then we realize that the author is judging us as we judge his creatures; and treacherously we are tempted to share his point of view. At these moments we dimly realize that it does not matter whether we accept the Lilliputians' high principles of law, government, and education (pp. 58–63), or the doctrines of the King of Brobdingnag, or those of the Houyhnhnms; for they do not represent eccentric novelties but ultimate possibilities, rational morality pressed all the way. In Swift's design they stand for what the reader, rather than the middle-aged Dean of St Patrick's, might accept as irreproachable (if unreachable) ideals. If we could re-cast them to shape the view of human possibility bequeathed to us by Goethe or Tolstoy, Swift's final argument would still obtain: viz., that judged by whatever reasonable standard we may affect to approve, our lives must appear vile betrayals of our principles.

VIII. EXILE, IMPRISONMENT, AND SLAVERY

Relations of servant to master are omnipresent in *Gulliver's Travels*. The word 'master' runs through the opening paragraphs of the book, blending with words like 'commander' and 'captain' as Gulliver progresses from apprentice to surgeon, and then ship's captain. This contractual bond gives way to that of captive to captor when Gulliver wakes up in Lilliput. After he arrives in Lorbrulgrud, the capital, he becomes a prisoner chained by the leg. The first words he learns in the Lilliputian language are 'to express my desire that [the emperor] would please to give me my liberty' (p. 33). At last he is freed.

The theme of slavery joins that of imprisonment when Gulliver, after capturing the war fleet of Blefuscu, refuses to bring the rest of the enemy's ships into the ports of Lilliput: 'And

I plainly protested, that I would never be an instrument of bringing a free and brave people into slavery' (p. 53). This refusal becomes the spring of the emperor's determination to blind and starve him; but Gulliver gets away in time.

In Brobdingnag, once Gulliver is caught by a reaper, he always remains a prisoner of one sort or another. First, the farmer becomes his 'master' and the farmer's wife his 'mistress' (p. 90). Then Gulliver goes to court and finds himself to be the queen's 'most humble creature and vassal' (p. 102). He lives in a box and is kept as a kind of royal pet while pining for liberty. 'I was the favourite of a great king and queen, and the delight of the whole court; but it was upon such a foot as ill became the dignity of human kind' (p. 139). (The comic note of 'dignity of human kind' places Gulliver exactly where Swift wants us to see him.) At last the box itself is carried off by a Brobdingnagian eagle, and Gulliver makes his way home.

In Part Three, he rises to be master of a sloop with fourteen men under him. But pirates capture them; they are tied up; and Gulliver is then set adrift, isolated in a canoe. Rescued by the Laputans, he soon tires of the flying island and thinks of it as a place to escape from. It is easy to do so, and the themes of servitude and imprisonment fade from the voyage.

In Part Four, Swift inverts the motifs. Now Gulliver starts as a captain with fifty hands serving under him. The men mutiny, and Gulliver becomes a prisoner in his cabin, bound hand and foot. The mutineers set him ashore in a strange land. The captive has become an exile once more. Meeting the Houyhnhnms, Gulliver is converted to the life of reason and radically changes his attitude. His clothes veil his shape and keep him from being treated as a Yahoo. Soon Gulliver calls the Houyhnhnm with whom he lives his master (p. 234); and in an early conversation the two discuss the whole problem of authority; for the master is disturbed to learn that European horses are the slaves of Yahoos (pp. 241–2). The master then declares that if, in Europe, Yahoos alone are endowed with reason, they must certainly be 'the governing animal' (p. 242). As Gulliver stays with the Houyhnhnms, he comes to detest his own kind, flinching to see his own face in a lake (p. 288). When at last he must leave, he feels he is going into exile (pp. 280, 282). But of course he is now taken back to Europe and eventually returns to his family. Life in England seems exile indeed. Here, reason, which should unite men, keeps them apart. Gulliver thinks now of living as a recluse, i.e., like an isolated prisoner, cut off from mankind (p. 289). But finally he does not.

If we think of *Gulliver's Travels* as having a thread of allegory, one reference of these themes is from microcosm to macrocosm. They reflect in a single person that yearning for freedom and that lust for power which are ineradicable from human nature and which also mark the condition of nations. The obsession with liberty as a political idea in *The Drapier's Letters* is matched by the character of Gulliver.

But another implication also exists. A peculiarity of the shifting relations of master and slave in *Gulliver's Travels* is that they so often depend on shape. This is why the motifs dwindle in Laputa, where the natives, for all their eccentricities, look like ordinary men. Elsewhere, slave and master, exile and slave, captive and captor are distinguishable by their appearance. It is the size or shape of the body which tells them apart; and I suspect that Swift is drawing on an old, symbolic paradox, that the body is regrettably the master (or warden, or conqueror) of the rational soul which should be its lord.

On the level of morality Gulliver echoes the claim of St Paul in Swift's favourite epistle: 'But I keep under my body, and bring it into subjection.'[1] The motif of liberty and slavery has the same resonance, e.g., in the epistles of Peter: 'While they promise them liberty, they themselves are servants of corruption: for of whom a man is overcome, of the same is he brought in bondage' (2 Pet. ii. 19). Ultimately, all men are jailed not only on their islands of racial culture but in the sensuality and corruption of their flesh. Nature itself is foreign territory for mankind. The Houyhnhnms may live at home in the world. Men are aliens.

Not only are such themes integral to the design of Swift's book. They also suggest the themes of Swift's correspondence with English friends during the years when he was working on

---

[1] 1 Cor. ix. 27. The whole epistle abounds in imagery of the body.

Gulliver. Exile and banishment are perennial topics there.[1] Especially in writing to Bolingbroke and Pope, Swift returned continually to his isolation, his sense of living in exile,[2] his desire to rejoin ancient comrades, his contempt for the people and affairs of Dublin.[3] Of course, he complained of the slavery imposed on the Irish by the English and discussed the fears which some friends voiced, that Swift might be imprisoned if he went to England.

In two celebrated letters to Pope, Swift expounded the meaning of *Gulliver's Travels*.[4] The moral implications of *Gulliver* came out in these letters and were debated by Pope and Bolingbroke. Both men urged Swift to detach himself from passions and from public affairs;[5] they recommended notions of friendship that Swift rejected, while he compared his life in Ireland to a life in jail.[6] It is significant that Swift saved drafts of several of his letters to Bolingbroke. Did he wish to refresh his mind with their contents? Swift wrote that exile was the worst punishment of a virtuous man, because love of one's country is the definition of virtue. Bolingbroke, who composed an essay in praise of exile, disagreed.[7] Swift made Cato the Younger one of his great heroes;[8] Bolingbroke vilified him.[9] Bolingbroke claimed that living in exile did not trouble him, and that 'tranquillity' was the tenor of his life.[10] He insisted that reason alone sufficed to guide the operations of the mind.[11] He quarrelled with Swift's definition of man.[12]

At last it was the completion of *Gulliver* that turned these epistolary duels into conversation face to face. When the book was ready, Swift wished to arrange for its publication himself. This motion, added to the accumulated yearnings of a dozen years, was strong enough to defeat the scruples Swift had so often bowed to; and yet once more he left for England.

---

[1] Williams III. 117, 122.   [2] Cf. Pope on exile, *ibid.*, II. 458.   [3] *Ibid.*, III. 102.
[4] 29 Sept. and 26 Nov. 1725.   [5] Williams II. 397, 461.   [6] *Ibid.*, pp. 464–5.
[7] *Ibid.*, p. 414; III. 29.   [8] Davis XI. 196.   [9] Williams II. 397, 413.
[10] *Ibid.*, pp. 315–16, 462.   [11] *Ibid.*, III. 27–8.
[12] *Ibid.*, pp. 121–2. Cf. my discussion on *Gulliver* in *The Personality of Jonathan Swift* (London, 1958), pp. 104–7.

Part Three

FIRST CITIZEN 1726–30

Chapter One

A VOYAGE TO LANGDEN

L eaving Dublin on Sunday, 6 March, Swift arrived in London toward the middle of the month, carrying a manuscript of *Gulliver's Travels*.[1] I suspect that he travelled with Charles Ford, who went over about the same time.[2] Certainly, Swift took lodgings near Ford, in Bury Street ('next door to the Royal Chair').[3]

Pope described his friend's arrival in a letter to the second Earl of Oxford, the cultivated, easygoing son of Swift's hero. The poet said guardedly—with an eye, no doubt, to post-office readers—that he had been sitting down (in Twickenham) to write to his lordship when he received notice that 'a person' had come to London who 'demanded my immediate repair thither'; and the letter went on to give a first impression of the visitor:

> He is in perfect health and spirits, the joy of all here who know him, as he was eleven years ago, and I never received a more sensible satisfaction than in having been now two days with him.[4]

Four days later, Pope told Lord Oxford that Swift had just gone to stay for 'some days' at Dawley, Bolingbroke's new seat near Uxbridge, only four miles from Twickenham. Dawley was a mock-farm of 245 acres with radiating avenues and grand, formal gardens in the French style. Pope expected Swift to

---

[1] For the date of Swift's departure, see the *Dublin Weekly Journal*, 12 Mar. 1726. We have two indications of the day he reached London. On 16 Apr. he told Tickell he had been there for a month (Williams III. 128). And Pope, writing on 22 Mar. from Twickenham, replying to a letter of 10 Mar. from Essex, tells Lord Oxford that he would have written sooner if Swift had not arrived just as Pope was about to begin a reply (Sherburn II. 371–2). We know Swift carried a manuscript of *Gulliver's Travels* because he says so—'I brought away a copy'—to Sheridan (letter of 8 Jul. 1726; Williams III. 139; cf. pp. 137–8).

[2] See above, p. 375.

[3] Sherburn II. 372–3.   [4] 22 Mar. 1726; *ibid.*, pp. 371–2.

return to London in about a week. Again on 2 April, Pope wrote
to his Whig lawyer friend Fortescue,

> Dr Swift is come into England, who is now with me, and with whom
> I am to ramble again to Lord Oxford's and Lord Bathurst's, and
> other places. Dr Arbuthnot has led him a course through the town,
> with Lord Chesterfield, Mr Pulteney, &c. Lord Peterborough and
> Lord Harcourt propose to carry him to Sir R. Walpole, and I to Mrs
> Howard, &c. I wish you were here to know him.[1]

As Fortescue was an intimate of Walpole's and had been his
private secretary, we may suppose that the poet expected the
information to be passed on. The prime minister was no longer
in the condition of easy power that he had enjoyed during the
early months of 1725. William Pulteney—a brilliantly persuasive speaker with shrewd political judgment—had turned
against his one-time leader, after receiving no ministerial post;
and as a dissident he had lost the profitable place of Cofferer of
the Household. Proud and ambitious, Pulteney had joined with
Bolingbroke and Wyndham to head a troublesome union of
Tories and opposition Whigs known as the 'Patriots'. Although
he was a gifted writer, and a very rich, greedy man, Pulteney
finally lacked resolution.

Chesterfield, a much younger man, had given up a seat in
Parliament to accept an office under the Crown; and he had only
just inherited a peerage. But he failed to co-operate systematically with Walpole; and as he had no independent power, he
was dismissed (in May 1725) from his post of Captain of the
Yeomen of the Guard. Chesterfield belonged to the coterie of the
Prince of Wales, whose mistress, Mrs Howard, he cultivated.

Among Swift's old acquaintance, Peterborough had survived
his alliance with the Tories and was in touch with the court.
Harcourt had done even better, rising a step in the peerage and
serving as a Lord Justice of the realm during the King's absence.
He had doubled his pension without abandoning his old friends.
Arbuthnot, though his health was poor and he held no office,

---

[1] Sherburn II. 373.

was welcome at Leicester House, the London residence of the Prince of Wales.

Through these avenues Swift could try to exert some influence on behalf of Ireland and his comrades. As usual, he combined energy with scepticism. While he knew how unlikely it was that Walpole should waste favours on anyone who failed to contribute to the great man's power, Swift determined to speak as strongly as he could. I'm not sure he also understood that Walpole in turn might use their meetings to discredit Swift and impugn his loyalty to his own side.

Meanwhile, Pope tried again to bring Swift and the new Earl of Oxford together. On 3 April he gave his lordship fresh details of the dean's visit, and reported that Swift had been waiting to hear from him since Pope's last letter:

> He has been at Twitenham, in expectation of hearing further of your lordship's movements, and we were not without hopes you might call at Dover Street [i.e., Oxford's town house], before your further summer journeys to Wimpole &c. I find the Dean had nothing in his view, in coming to England for a few months, but the seeing his friends, and principally to wait on you in relation to Lord Oxford's [i.e. the first Earl's] papers.

But Lord Oxford was delayed at Wimpole, his Cambridgeshire seat, which young Charles Bridgeman was improving. The death of Bridgeman's father, he said, prevented him from enjoying 'the great pleasure of waiting upon the Dean which I much long to do'.[1]

By now there were even grander claims on Swift's leisure. Arbuthnot, who was one of the physicians of the Princess of Wales, wrote that she wished to meet him. 'Her Royal Highness begs the honour of a visit from you on Thursday night next at seven a clock.'[2] The Princess, Caroline of Ansbach, was not deeply intellectual. But she enjoyed playing the bluestocking, and had corresponded with Leibniz. Yet her real strength lay in judging character and in political wisdom. She dominated her

---

[1] *Ibid.*, p. 377.   [2] Tuesday, 5 Apr. 1726; Williams III. 127.

husband and received the most careful attention from Walpole, who steadily avoided the Prince's mistress, Mrs Howard.

That lady was building a Palladian villa at Twickenham—or, rather, the Prince of Wales was building it for her, on a site flanking the Thames and conveniently no more than a mile upstream from Richmond Lodge, the country house of the Prince himself. Pope helped Bridgeman plan the handsome gardens that Mrs Howard ordered for Marble Hill—as her property was called.

The lady herself was more elegant than beautiful. Fair, witty, and cool, she had grown slightly deaf without losing the regular attendance of her royal lover. Besides serving as mistress to his highness, she was a woman of the bedchamber to his wife. But she had no influence over either, as her Scriblerian admirers and the 'Patriots' were to discover when George I died.

The Prince himself had long since made up the savage quarrel with his father. Yet the reconciliation was only a façade; and he allowed his residence in Leicester Fields to be the unofficial headquarters of the anti-ministerial party. When Swift arrived, the Prince was living in Leicester House while Parliament was in session, but he had no visible rôle in public affairs.

Swift's account of his visits to the shadow court is preserved. Years later, irritated by disagreements with Lady Betty Germaine over the character of Mrs Howard, he wrote to her about his relations with that lady (now the Countess of Suffolk) and the Princess:

> It is but six years last spring [Swift was writing in January 1733] since I first went to visit my friends in England, after the Queen's death. Her present majesty [then Princess of Wales] heard of my arrival, and sent at least nine times to command my attendance before I would obey her, for several reasons not hard to guess [i.e., reasons for Swift to delay]; and, among others, because I had heard her character from those who knew her well. At last I went, and she received me very graciously. I told her the first time that I was informed she loved to see odd persons; and that, having sent for a wild boy from Germany, she had a curiosity to see a wild dean from Ireland. I was not much struck with the honour of being sent for because I knew the same distinction had been offered to others, with

whom it would not give me much pride to be compared. I never went once but upon command; and Mrs Howard, now Lady Suffolk, was usually the person who sent for me, both at Leicester House and Richmond. Mr Pope (with whom I lived) and Mr Gay were then great favourites of Mrs Howard, especially the latter, who was then one of her led-captains.[1]

Swift met the Princess on Thursday, 7 April, and wrote the following week to Tickell,

> I am here now a month, picking up the remnant of my old acquaintance, and descending to take new ones. Your people [i.e., the Whigs in power] are very civil to me, and I meet a thousand times better usage from them than from that denomination in Ireland. This night I saw the wild boy, whose arrival here hath been the subject of half our talk this fortnight. He is in keeping of Dr Arbuthnot, but the King and court were so entertained with him, that the Princess could not get him till now. I can hardly think him wild in the sense they report him.[2]

Soon a more consequential audience than that of the Princess was made available. The Prime Minister invited the Dean of St Patrick's to dinner. It was an occasion unquietly anticipated by the Dublin establishment. Two months earlier, Archbishop Boulter had warned the Duke of Newcastle about Swift's impending visit to England:

> The general report is, that Dean Swift designs for England in a little time; and we do not question his endeavours to misrepresent his majesty's friends here [i.e., in Ireland], wherever he finds an opportunity: but he is so well known, as well as the disturbances he has been the fomenter of in this kingdom, that we are under no fear of his being able to disserve any of his majesty's faithful servants, by anything that is known to come from him: but we could wish some eye were had to what he shall be attempting on your side of the water.[3]

The warning was of course hardly necessary, but reflects Boulter's wish to keep the reins of affairs in his own hands. Swift would of course spread information discrediting the conduct of the ministry in Ireland. He would hope to strengthen the oppo-

---

[1] 8 Jan. 1733; *ibid.*, IV. 98.
[2] 16 Apr. 1726; *ibid.*, III. 128.
[3] 10 Feb. 1726; Boulter I. 62 (Dublin, p. 51).

sition and would probably write papers and verses ridiculing the men in power. To weaken his effectiveness, the ministerial claque would plan to make his own friends doubt Swift's fidelity.

Walpole, I assume, decided to seize the opportunity to hurt the Drapier's reputation. Service to one's country was not a motive he looked for or acknowledged in men who opposed him. He asked the dean and some of his friends to dine at Chelsea a few weeks after Swift reached London.[1] Swift had Gay on his mind, and believed Walpole had been turned against the modest poet by a report that Gay had written a libel on the Prime Minister. Years later, Swift said that

> although Mr Walpole owned he was convinced that it was not written by Gay, yet he would never pardon him, but did him a hundred ill offices to the Princess. . . . After dinner I took an occasion to say, what I had observed of princes and great ministers, that, if they heard an ill thing of a private person, who expected some favour, although they were afterward convinced that the person was innocent, yet they would never be reconciled. Mr Walpole knew well enough that I meant Mr Gay. . . . But [he] gave it another turn: for he said to some of his friends . . . that I had dined with him, and had been making apologies for myself.[2]

Swift's belief that Walpole maliciously represented him as a self-seeking turncoat was (I think) justified. But in spite of his suspicions, he determined to see Walpole again in the thin hope of doing some good for Ireland. So he asked Lord Peterborough to make an appointment. On 23 April Peterborough reported that Walpole would be glad to see Swift at the Prime Minister's London house 'any morning except Tuesday and Thursday, which are his public days, about nine in the morning'.[3] The two met on the morning of 28 April. Swift arrived at eight and had 'somewhat more than an hour's conversation' with his host. Next day, he sent Peterborough an account of the meeting. Swift's purpose was certainly (as he said) to ask nothing for himself but to bring the real situation of Ireland to the attention

---

[1] Williams IV. 98. The date had to be after the 7 Apr. meeting with the Princess and before 16 Apr.; see *ibid.*, III. 128, n. 2.
[2] *Ibid.*, IV. 98.   [3] *Ibid.*, III. 131.

of those who determined her fate.[1] Walpole may have hoped to defame Swift by twisting their conversation to suit his policy, but he had to hear the suppliant out. As O. W. Ferguson has shown, Swift co-ordinated his own campaign with that of Archbishop King, who was in Ireland about the same time and had supplied Swift with elaborate data to support his arguments.[2]

Swift wrote to Peterborough,

> I failed very much in my design; for, I saw, he had conceived opinions from the examples and practices of the present and some former governors, which I could not reconcile to the notions I had of liberty.... Sir Robert Walpole was pleased to enlarge very much upon the subject of Ireland, in a manner so alien from what I conceived to be [the] rights and privileges of a subject of England, that I did not think proper to debate the matter with him so much as I otherwise might, because I found it would be in vain.[3]

Although the interview was a failure, Swift persisted in putting the case of Ireland before the Prime Minister, for he filled most of the letter to Peterborough with a memorandum on the subject, which he begged his lordship to give to Walpole.

The contents of Swift's memorandum were the usual arguments that Archbishop King, Molyneux, and other spokesmen had been rehearsing: that the Irish descendants of English settlers should have the same rights as if they lived in England; that Irish trade and manufacture should not be fettered by English restrictions; and above all, that places in the church and offices in the state should not be filled by persons sent over from England, to the exclusion of the native-born gentry. It was, as we know, an oft-told tale.

In an illuminating, if unpersuasive, analysis Swift connected this shutting of career doors with the wretchedness of Irish peasants:

> the whole body of the gentry feel the effects [of these hardships] in a very sensible part, being utterly destitute of all means to make provision for their younger sons, either in the church, the law, the

---

[1] For another view, see Murry, pp. 403–4, and Plumb II. 104, 175.
[2] Ferguson, pp. 141, 189–90.   [3] Williams III. 131–2.

revenue, or, of late, in the army: and, in the desperate condition of
trade, it is equally vain to talk of making them merchants. All they
have left is, at the expiration of leases, to rack their tenants; which
they have done to such a degree, that there is not one farmer in a
hundred through the kingdom who can afford shoes or stockings to
his children, or to eat flesh, or drink anything better than sour milk
or water, twice in a year; so that the whole country, except the
Scotch plantation in the north, is a scene of misery and desolation,
hardly to be matched on this side Lapland.

Swift insisted that contrary to the usual talk of the King's
advisers, Ireland gave an immense financial return to his
majesty. He itemized the value of Irish rents spent by absentees
in England and argued in Archbishop King's manner that in
proportion to its population and wealth, Ireland rendered more
than her just share unto Caesar.

Swift's summary statement is in his best plain style, its cumu-
lative power rising from a series of verbal phrases, each opening
with a parallel participle but then going its own way as to length
and shape, so that one gets the impression of variety in oppressive similarity, to suggest how many sources there could be for
the same wretchedness:

> I think it manifest, that whatever circumstances can possibly con-
> tribute to make a country poor and despicable, are all united with
> respect to Ireland. The nation controlled [i.e., restrained] by laws to
> laws to which they do not consent, disowned by their brethren and
> countrymen [i.e., in England], refused the liberty not only of
> trading with their own manufactures but even their native com-
> modities, forced to seek for justice many hundred miles by sea and
> land, rendered in a manner incapable of serving their king and
> country in any employment of honour, trust, or profit; and all this
> without the least demerit: while the governors sent over thither can
> possibly have no affection to the people, further than what is instilled
> into them by their own justice and love of mankind (which do not
> always operate).[1]

Besides giving splendid utterance to cries that Irish nationalists and American colonists were to imitate, these words echo
those which Archbishop King was delivering about the same

---

[1] *Ibid.*, p. 134.

time to his namesake, the Lord Chancellor of England. The archbishop was at Bath for his health, and could not visit Lord King in London. After complaining about the exclusion of the Irish gentry from the offices of their own establishment, he said, 'I am not so ignorant as to expect any government should be perfect, but there is I conceive a difference between tolerable and intolerable oppressions.'[1] Swift and the archbishop were of course deliberately concerting their information service. How intimate the friendly enemies had now grown, may be guessed from what the archbishop wrote to his friend Francis Annesley in London:

> As to our Irish copper farthen Dean, he has behaved himself very well in his station, very agreeable to me, and been useful to the public both by his charity and his labours. All that I wish in his behalf [is] that you would not spoil him in London.[2]

In putting Ireland's case before Walpole, Swift not only wished to exert what slight pressure might be in his grasp. He also made it impossible for the ministry to declare that they lacked knowledge of the Irish situation. But Swift was hardly a person to whom Walpole would look for instruction, and Walpole was hardly the man to give where he did not receive. The great man had another use for their encounters. Pope later told Swift that when he saw Walpole after Swift returned to Ireland, the Prime Minister

> expressed his desire of having seen you again before you left us. He said he observed a willingness in you to live among us; which I did not deny; but at the same time told him, you had no such design in your coming this time, which was merely to see a few of those you loved.[3]

Walpole could easily repeat Pope's qualified assent as proof of Swift's venality. To defend himself, Swift had to do battle with rumours floating back to him from both sides of the Irish Channel. The younger Thomas Sheridan has some penetrating

---

[1] 2 Jul. 1726, to Lord Chancellor King.
[2] 30 May 1726.
[3] 3 Sept. 1726; Sherburn II. 395.

observations on the affair. Speaking of Swift's second interview with the Prime Minister, he says,

> [In] consequence of this interview, all the Walpolians, and the whole party of the Whigs, gave out, that Swift at that time made a tender of his pen to Sir Robert, by whom the offer was rejected; and even to this day I am well informed that some of that family, and their connections, assert it as a fact.

Sheridan points out that Swift only met Walpole twice, that witnesses heard what passed at the dinner, and that Swift gave a distinct account of the interview in his letter to Peterborough. Sheridan goes on,

> If Walpole afterwards represented any thing in a different light, whose testimony is to be credited? That of a man of long tried integrity, and undoubted veracity, giving an account of a transaction, wherein he sustained a part exactly suitable to his whole character and conduct in life: or that of a wily statesman, who stuck at nothing to answer his ends, charging Swift with a fact utterly incompatible with his well known wisdom and grandeur of mind, and which must have shown him in the light of a perfect changeling.

Sheridan also observes that Walpole himself never made the allegations which Swift's enemies repeated, because the work would be better done by underlings. To illustrate the point, he quotes from his own college tutor Henry Clarke,[1] who gave Sheridan the following anecdote:

> When Lord Chesterfield was Lord Lieutenant of Ireland, I was present at his giving an account of Swift, which, from a less creditable author would be utterly disbelieved. He said, that to his knowledge Swift made an offer of his pen to Sir Robert Walpole: that the terms were, his getting a preferment in England, equal to what he had in Ireland; and that Sir Robert rejected the offer.[2]

Swift was capable of deceiving his friends, but not repeatedly, blatantly, and on such a topic.[3] From Swift's own letters we learn that he did indeed toy with the possibility of moving to England, though only through a private exchange or commuta-

---

[1] B.A., Trinity College, Dublin, 1720; Fellow, 1724.
[2] Sheridan, pp. 253–8.
[3] Craik offers a sane analysis of the affair, II. 114–17.

tion of livings.[1] On this subject the most fascinating reflections
were addressed to Dr Sheridan:

> This is the first time I was ever weary of England, and longed to be in
> Ireland, but it is because go I must; for I do not love Ireland better,
> nor England, as England, worse; in short, you all live in a wretched,
> dirty doghole and prison, but it is a place good enough to die in. I
> can tell you one thing, that I have had the fairest offer made me of a
> settlement here that one can imagine, which if I were ten years
> younger I would gladly accept, within twelve miles of London, and
> in the midst of my friends. But I am too old for new schemes, and
> especially such as would bridle me in my freedoms and liberalities.[2]

We have no further account of this 'fairest offer'. Besides involving a painful drop in income, it would probably have obli-
gated Swift in a way that he preferred to avoid. Meanwhile,
Ireland produced a silly episode that spurred on the gossip-
mongers.

On 26 June, Charles Crow, Bishop of Cloyne, died. We know
in detail the range of candidates considered for this vacancy.
Merely as a polite gesture, Boulter recommended his own chaplain, Dr Skirret. But if this name did not please the ministry, he
proposed his true choice, Henry Maule, who was already the
Dean of Cloyne: 'He is counted one well affected to his majesty,
and is very diligent in the discharge of the cures he has at
present, and has the honour of being known to several bishops in
England.'[3]

Lord Carteret had another candidate, Robert Howard, who
was still Chancellor of St Patrick's and Rector of St Werburgh's.
Inevitably, the ministry preferred Boulter's man. The Primate's
letters on the appointment reached Westminster while Carteret
was in the country.[4] As Swift learned from Jervas, an eye-witness

---

[1] Cf. Sheridan, pp. 255–6.   [2] 8 Jul. 1726; Williams III. 140.
[3] 28 Jun. 1726; Boulter I. 85 (Dublin, p. 69).
[4] When the Lords Justices of Ireland drew up an official recommendation on 30 Jun.,
they named Maule, Howard, and Dean Gore of Down, with a clear preference for Maule
(*ibid.*, I. 70–1). Hence Swift's annoyance with them for not agreeing on 'some one
person' (letter of 11 Jul. 1726 to Delany, full text in Paul V. Thompson, 'An
Unpublished Letter from Swift', *The Library*, 5th ser., 22 (1967), 57–66; Thompson's
note 12 is mistaken).

of the scene, the ministers settled the issue on 8 July; and Jervas's own support for Howard (who seems to have been Swift's choice as well) had no effect.

Archbishop King, now at Bath, must have got word of the vacancy late; for it was not till 12 July that he wrote to Carteret about it. After acknowledging Maule's claims—'promises from some great men in the ministry'—he said he understood that Howard would be picked, and remarked, '[To] be sure I have no objection against him.'[1] Actually, the archbishop assumed that Westminster no longer paid attention to his judgment.[2] But Carteret's word hardly counted either. The Lord Lieutenant was supposed to transmit the nomination to Ireland; yet he held it for a while in the hope of altering the decision. The publisher of Boulter's letters comments, 'His excellency perhaps was not in haste to give an account of a transaction he did not like.'[3] At last, of course, he had to accept the decision of the court.

Naturally, Swift's name never appeared in any part of the proceedings; nor did he dream of such a thing. So he hardly felt amused when people asked him about the bishopric. Delany evidently went further than most. His eyes were always clouded by the smoke of preferment; and I suppose he could not help attributing his own greed to others. When he suggested that the Dean of St Patrick's might hope to become the Bishop of Cloyne, Swift replied at once; I think he hoped to stifle the gossip:

> if you knew me better, and I did not know you so well, I should have thought you in jest as far as your letter relates to me. I never set out [i.e., for England] on the foot of promotion. I have writ too many ludicrous things, have been suspected with some grounds to have writ more, and have been charged with hundreds I never writ. Judge if this be a character to expect or aim at what you speak of.... The part I have played since I came here hath been in perfect opposition to the premier [ministre]. I never saw him but twice, and the second time we differed in every point.... I refused to be presented to [the King]. And the person I have visited [i.e., the Princess of Wales] was by the force of frequent messages to me, and

---

[1] Letter of 12 Jul. 1726. [2] Cf. letter of 13 Jul. 1726 to Dr Trotter.
[3] Boulter (Dublin edn), I. 78, n.

what made me consent was only because that family is known to be out of all favour—Judge whether I have gone the proper steps to make my court. I will tell you further that unless I were offered promotion with a public declaration that I should not be the least hinted at to change one opinion, or so much as be quiet, I would not accept it; because it is too late at fifty-eight to lose honour and hazard one's soul. Before I came over, at the earnest entreaty of a certain friend of ours whom I much value [i.e., Stella], I did solemnly promise never to accept of anything from those in power: though at the same time I knew it was an idle thing, and that they would prefer the Devil much sooner than me. On Saturday the ninth Jarvis [i.e., Charles Jervas] met me in the Park, and said the thing was given the day before, while he was by, to one Mall [i.e., Henry Maule], whom I have seen, and who by ten years' solicitation, sanctification, and party zeal found friends here (Lord Townshend and others) while the Lord Lieutenant was forty miles off, to finish the matter.... I know further that the Lord Lieutenant is on no good terms with [Walpole] and my knowledge is good because the latter told me to that effect, and I am sure he would not tell me a secret.[1]

How common such rumours had become, we may judge from what Swift told Worrall; for even Worrall thought the bishopric might be in Swift's mind:

As to what you say about promotion you will find it was given immediately to Maule (as I am told) and I assure you I had no offers, nor would accept them, my behaviour to those in power hath been directly contrary [since] I came here.[2]

It looks as if Swift repeated his story to a number of correspondents, for wide circulation. The version sent to Stopford is extant:

I was latterly twice with the chief minister; the first time by invitation, and the second at my desire for an hour, wherein we differed in every point. But all this made a great noise, and soon got to Ireland, from whence upon the late death of the Bishop of Cloyne, it was said I was offered to succeed, and I received many letters upon it, but there was nothing of truth, for I was neither offered, nor would have received, except upon conditions which would never be

---

[1] Letter of 11 Jul. 1726; in Thompson, 'An Unpublished Letter from Swift'.
[2] 15 Jul. 1726; Williams III. 142.

granted. For I absolutely broke with the first minister, and have never seen him since.[1]

Apart from quarrelling with the government and instructing the Princess, Swift had the social pleasures of England to occupy him. But these are hard to specify because in May and June, when he was busiest with visits, Swift naturally had little time to write about them. We do know that he stayed mainly at Twickenham, where Pope kept a kind of open house for Swift's friends. We know that while there, he encouraged Pope to work on the poem that eventually became the *Dunciad*.[2] The two also went to stay in other houses; and Gay was often with them. We know they visited Lord Cobham at Stowe, Lord Bathurst at Oakley Park near Cirencester, and the village of Bibury in the same neighbourhood.[3] At this inconvenient time Pope suffered from piles. He told Broome, his Homeric collaborator,

> I have had a long and troublesome disorder upon me of the piles, which has put me more out of humour than out of health. And, as if it were fatal to me to be sedentary to no purpose, I had a hundred impertinent people continually coming to me, that were as troublesome as gnats in this season.[4]

Swift worried about Pope's chronically delicate health. But the two friends made the most of their opportunities. A hint of what they could do is preserved in a reminiscence of Lord Bathurst's, retailed by a common friend writing to Swift years later:

> My Lord Bathurst talked with great delight of the pleasure you once gave him by surprising him in his wood, and shewed me the house where you lodged . . . which you may remember but a cottage, not a bit better than an Irish *cabin*.[5]

There is another hint in a letter from Swift to the Earl of Oxford, in July 1726, about plans for Gay, Pope, and Swift to join his lordship:

---

[1] 20 Jul. 1726; *ibid.*, p. 144.
[2] See the conjectures of Sherburn and Sutherland in Pope, *Poems* v. xiv.
[3] Williams III. 156.   [4] 4 Jun. 1726; Sherburn II. 378.
[5] Letter of 24 Oct. 1733 from Mrs Pendarves (later Mrs Delany) to Swift; Williams IV. 199.

[Mr Pope] prescribes all our visits without our knowledge, and Mr Gay and I find ourselves often engaged for three or four days to come, and we neither of us dare dispute his pleasure. Accordingly this morning we go to Lord Bathurst,[1] on Tuesday company is to dine here; however I will certainly attend your lordship towards the end of the week.[2]

Writing to Tickell a few days later, Swift said he was leading 'so restless, and visiting, and travelling, and vexatious a life' that he had not time to congratulate Tickell on his marriage:

I have lived these two months past for the most part in the country, either at Twitenham with Mr Pope, or rambling with him and Mr Gay for a fortnight together. Yesterday my Lord Bolingbroke and Mr Congreve made up five at dinner at Twitenham.[3]

(One can hardly keep from reflecting how much like a costume drama such a scene was: Gay, Congreve, Bolingbroke, Pope, and Swift!)

By this time Swift was planning to wind up his English occupations and come back in the spring.[4] After three or four days in London 'upon some business'—which I take to be arranging the publication of *Gulliver*—he would return to Pope's at Twickenham and remain there until the end of July. Then he would go up to London and stay with Gay before leaving for Ireland in mid-August.[5]

Over all his comings and goings loured the bleakness of Stella's illness. Bulletins from Ireland kept Swift in touch with her sinking vitality. The ladies had moved into the deanery while Swift was away.[6] Tickell called twice at one o'clock but was told that Stella 'was not stirring'.[7] Swift sounded cool and rational:

I have been told that Mrs Johnson's health has given her friends bad apprehensions and I have heard but twice from them; but their

---

[1] Not now at Oakley Park but at Richings Park, near Colnbrook.
[2] Sunday, 3 Jul. 1726; Williams III. 136.
[3] Thursday, 7 Jul. 1726; *ibid.*, p. 137.
[4] Cf. Pulteney's remark, *ibid.*, p. 162.
[5] 8 Jul. 1726; *ibid.*, p. 139.
[6] *Ibid.*, pp. 136, 138.   [7] *Ibid.*, p. 136.

secretary Dr Sheridan just tells me she is much better, to my great satisfaction.[1]

Yet his voice was less calm the next day, when he wrote to Sheridan:

> I had two months of great uneasiness at the ill account of Mrs Johnson's health, and, as it is usual feared the worst that was possible, and doubted all the good accounts that were sent me.... I had a letter two days ago from Archdeacon Walls, dated six days before yours, wherein he giveth me a better account than you do, and therefore I apprehend she hath not mended since; and yet he says he *can honestly tell me she is now much better*.[2]

Then came a letter from Worrall which frightened him again. I assume that the ladies had moved to the country in the hope of doing some good for Stella, and that Mrs Worrall helped care for her. I also assume that Swift had made Worrall promise to send him perfectly accurate reports of her condition. In one of the most astonishing documents of his biography, Swift replied,

> What you tell me of Mrs [Johnson] I have long expected with great oppression and heaviness of heart. We have been perfect friends these thirty-five years. Upon my advice they both came to Ireland and have been ever since my constant companions, and the remainder of my life will be a very melancholy scene when one of them is gone whom I most esteemed upon the score of every good quality that can possibly recommend a human creature. I have these two months seen through Mrs [Dingley's] disguises, and indeed ever since I left you my heart hath been so sunk that I have not been the same man, nor ever shall be again, but drag on a wretched life till it shall please God to call me away. I must tell you as a friend, that if you have reason to believe Mrs [Johnson] cannot hold out till my return, I would not think of coming to Ireland, and in that case, I would expect of you on the beginning of September to renew my licence for another half year, with time I will spend in some retirement far from London till I can be in a disposition of appearing after an accident that must be so fatal to my quiet.

He suggested that Stella should make her will, and mentioned the chief points it should cover, then went on,

---

[1] 7 Jul. 1726; *ibid.*, p. 138.   [2] *Ibid.*, p. 139; Swift's emphasis.

I would not for the world be present at such a trial of seeing her depart. She will be among friends that upon her own account and great worth will tend her with all possible care, where I should be a trouble to her and the greatest torment to my self. In case the matter should be desperate I would have you advise if they come to town, that they should be lodged in some airy healthy part, and not in the deanery, which besides you know cannot but be a very improper thing for that house to breathe her last in.

He asked Worral to burn the letter, then went on,

Pray write to me every week, that I may know what steps to take, for I am determined not to go to Ireland to find her just dead or dying— Nothing but extremity could make me familiar with those terrible words applied to such a dear friend. Let her know I have bought her a repeating gold watch for her ease in winter nights. I designed to have surprised her with it, but now I would have her know it, that she may see how my thoughts were always to make her easy—I am of opinion that there is not a greater folly than to contract too great and intimate a friendship, which must always leave the survivor miserable.[1]

Again he asked Worrall to burn the letter. But of all the letters he ever wrote, if only one were to be preserved, this would be my choice; and I suppose Worrall had the same feeling. Yet Swift could not help telling the story over again to Stopford:

I never was in so great a dejection of spirits. For I lately received a letter from Mr Worrall, that one of the two oldest and dearest friends I have in the world is in so desperate a condition of health, as makes me expect every post to hear of her death. It is the younger of the two, with whom I have lived in the greatest friendship for thirty-three years. I know you will share in my trouble, because there were few persons whom I believe you more esteemed. For my part, as I value life very little, so the poor casual remains of it, after such a loss, would be a burden that I must heartily beg God Almighty to enable me to bear.

He repeated the despairing statement about intimate friendships:

I think there is not a greater folly than that of entering into too strict and particular a friendship, with the loss of which a man must be

[1] 15 Jul. 1726; *ibid.*, pp. 141–2.

absolutely miserable; but especially at an age when it is too late to engage in a new friendship. Besides, this was a person of my own rearing and instructing, from childhood, who excelled in every good quality that can possibly accomplish a human creature.—They have hitherto writ me deceiving letters, but Mr Worrall has been so just and prudent as to tell me the truth; which, however racking, is better than to be struck on the sudden.

Then with one of those veil-rending strokes which seem in his satires like the height of art, he rises to a pitch heard nowhere else in all his writings:

Dear Jim, pardon me, I know not what I am saying; but believe me that violent friendship is much more lasting, and as much engaging, as violent love. Adieu.[1]

The shift to a past tense—'there *were* few persons' and 'this *was* a person'—suggests the mingling of guilt with grief. Swift could not help writing as if death had already taken his beloved friend. His own responsibility for Stella's situation troubled him so keenly that he would have liked (unconsciously, of course) to end it soon. When Sheridan sent him even bleaker news, Swift tried to relieve himself by wishing Stella had gone to Montpellier, Bath, or Tunbridge, as he had begged her to do. But he also admitted that the symptoms had moved beyond that kind of palliation. 'I look upon this', he said, 'to be the greatest event that can ever happen to me, but all my preparations will not suffice to make me bear it like a philosopher, nor altogether like a Christian.' At last his expressive power gave way under the force of irresistible feelings and the need for self-punishment; and he used language flattened by banality:

—Nay if I were now near her, I would not see her; I could not behave my self tolerably, and should redouble her sorrow.—Judge in what a temper of mind I write this.—The very moment I am writing, I conclude the fairest soul in the world hath left its body.

Interrupted by a visitor, Swift soon returned to close the elegy:

I have long been weary of the world, and shall for my small remainder of years be weary of life, having for ever lost that conver-

[1] 20 Jul. 1726; *ibid.*, p. 145.

sation, which could only make it tolerable.—I fear while you are reading this, you will be shedding tears at her funeral.[1]

This ultimate anxiety blended with Swift's fear for his host at Twickenham. The alarms over Pope's valetudinarianism complicated the gratitude for his splendid hospitality. Lord Peterborough arranged a dinner in Swift's honour at the beginning of August. But Pope was not well enough to come. By now Swift was staying with Gay in London;[2] and from this staging area he wrote beseeching Pope to look after himself better; as so often, he fell back—not very subtly—on his common device of berating an excellent friend for his kindness:

> I am gathering up my luggage, and preparing for my journey: I will endeavour to think of you as little as I can, and when I write to you, I will strive not to think of you; this I intend in return to your kindness; and further, I know nobody has dealt with me so cruelly as you, the consequence of which usage I fear will last as long as my life.[3]

But before his departure, Swift faced the complicated task of getting the manuscript of *Gulliver's Travels* to a responsible publisher.[4] This was the most dramatic episode in the long comedy of his games with the press. Swift determined to arrange the business even more cautiously than usual, because he had passed through so many ordeals with his recent works. To his own gifts for impersonation and deceit were added the subtleties and the financial cunning of Pope. By the time the whole operation came to its triumphant end, other members of Swift's circle had been enlisted as cheerful aides: Ford, Gay, and Erasmus Lewis.

Characteristically, Swift planned to see the book published after he left the country. But against his old habits, he decided to make money out of Gulliver, following the wisdom of Pope. It was essential for Swift to deal with a knowledgeable, discreet

---

[1] 27 Jul. 1726; *ibid.*, p. 147.
[2] At Gay's lodgings in Whitehall, in the gatehouse to the royal garden (Gay I. 11).
[3] 4 May 1726; Sherburn II. 384.
[4] Cf. H. Teerink, 'The Publication of *Gulliver's Travels*', *Dublin Magazine*, Jan. 1948, pp. 14–27; Harold Williams, *The Text of Gulliver's Travels* (Cambridge, 1952), pp. 4–19. My account is based on their scholarship.

bookseller who could be trusted to keep promises and to say no more than he must. He chose Benjamin Motte, who had succeeded to the publishing establishment of Swift's old friend Benjamin Tooke.

It was also essential for the author to cover his traces so the bookseller might swear (if necessary) that he did not know him.[1] Nor could Swift complete the negotiations without some resort to written messages and documents; these might be kept for the record and yet must reveal nothing dangerous.

To begin with, Swift may perhaps have arranged for a copy to be made of the manuscript he had brought over (if that was actually in his hand).[2] I am inclined to think not. For if he had wanted one in an unknown hand, it could have been prepared more quietly in Ireland; and he would not have been sure how much time he might find for such operations during the visit to England. However, he certainly showed the work to his cronies—once he arrived—and altered it to fit some of their suggestions. After coming up to town and establishing himself in Gay's lodgings,[3] he composed a letter of efficient mystification, addressed to Motte and copied out for Swift by Gay.

In this letter, signed 'Richard Sympson' (supposed to be Gulliver's cousin), Swift said that he was submitting about a quarter of the whole manuscript of the *Travels* to Motte, that friends had advised him the work would sell well, and that the publisher must judge for himself whether or not the satirical passages would give too much offence for the book to be acceptable. 'Sympson' gave Motte three days in which to make up his mind. If he agreed, he would have to pay two hundred pounds at once for the copy. This pseudonymous letter, along with the chunk of manuscript, was delivered by a messenger—

---

[1] Unlike the late Sir Harold Williams, I believe Swift did not worry about Motte's guessing his identity but rather expected he would know it. Cf. Williams, *The Text of Gulliver's Travels*, pp. 18–19.

[2] I suppose the copy finally used by the printer was later destroyed for security's sake.

[3] Judging from Swift's letters of 1 and 4 Aug. 1726 to Pope, I should say Swift came up to London around 1 Aug. (Williams III. 148–9). If one compares headings, dates, and references to hospitality in the following letters, it will be clear that Swift stayed with Gay from early August till he left England: *ibid.*, pp. 147, 149, 164–5, 208–9, 273.

presumably someone who would not be recognized in the shop; and the reply was to be collected by the same hand at a specified hour.

For all the staginess of these manœuvres, they succeeded as the conspirators wished. I wonder whether Motte did not receive cues beforehand to prepare him for some of the tricks. He certainly had no warning about the money; for he said he could not put his hands on so much so quickly. He offered to publish the book within a month after receiving the complete copy and to pay the sum within six months. 'Sympson' accepted the offer and said he wished the book to come out before Christmas.[1]

At last Swift could go home. He wrote at once to Worrall, saying he would travel by way of Chester and Holyhead, and asking for a letter to be sent to Chester—no doubt so he would know (depending on Stella's health) whether to cross the Irish Sea or to remain in England.[2]

Leaving London on 15 August, Swift took seven days to reach his deanery.[3] He travelled by stagecoach to Chester, where he stayed once more with Mrs Greenfield. The trip displeased him, what with hot weather, bad inns, the crowding of an uncomfortable coach, and the rough roads.[4] In Dublin, the anxious man, loaded with his fears for Stella, met one last irony. For while his inner spirit was darkened by the misery of his friend, he found his public character acclaimed by the town. Swift's return, like his departure, was a matter of public notice; and on 23 August the *Dublin Gazette* reported, 'Last night the Reverend Dean Swift, arriv'd here from England, and was receiv'd with much joy.' The younger Thomas Sheridan gives an elaborate account of Swift's reception. I presume that something of the sort happened, but I don't know how far to trust the details:

In his return to Dublin, upon notice that the ship in which he sailed was in the bay, several heads of different corporations, and principal citizens of Dublin, went out to meet him in a great number of

---

[1] The correspondence opened on 8 Aug. and closed on 13 Aug. 1726 (*ibid.*, pp. 152–5).
[2] 13 Aug. 1726; *ibid.*, p. 156.   [3] *Ibid.*, pp. 157–8.
[4] For details of the trip see Pope's comments, in Sherburn II. 388. For Mrs Greenfield, see Williams III. 186.

wherries engaged for that purpose, in order to welcome him back. He had the pleasure to find his friend Dr Sheridan, in company with a number of his intimates, at the side of his ship, ready to receive him into their boat, with the agreeable tidings, that Mrs Johnson was past all danger. The boats, adorned with streamers, and colours, in which were many emblematical devices, made a fine appearance; and thus was the Drapier brought to his landing-place in a kind of triumph, where he was received and welcomed on shore by a multitude of his grateful countrymen, by whom he was conducted to his house amid repeated acclamations, of *Long live the Drapier*. The bells were all set a ringing, and bonfires lit in every street.[1]

This report, written long after the event, sounds hyperbolic; and yet a contemporary newspaper supplied equally striking details:

On this occasion the bells of St Patrick's, and other adjacent churches were rung, and bonfires made in the neighbouring streets, there was a very particular one made with a good number of flaming torches on the top of the steeple of his cathedral, which illuminated the whole town. And so grateful a sense do the people preserve of the merits of the author of the Drapier's books against Wood's brass coin, that there's scarce a street in town without a representation of him for a sign.[2]

[1] Sheridan, p. 261.
[2] Mist's *Weekly Journal*, 3 Sept. 1726, under the date of 25 Aug.

Chapter Two

'GULLIVER' IN PRINT

Motte may have been in a hurry to publish *Gulliver's Travels*, but the political and social satire evidently nagged him; and he delayed long enough to have somebody—Swift said it was Andrew Tooke,[1] a learned schoolmaster and F.R.S., soon to become Master of Charterhouse—castrate the text. This editor softened the attack on lawyers, reversed some of the sense of the attack on prime ministers, and excised the allegory of Wood's patent in *Laputa*, Chapter Three. He made many further changes calculated to enrage Swift, who sometimes did not mind simple deletions[2] but always resented insertions.

In order to get the book out quickly, Motte gave each of the four parts to a different printer; so they have independent pagination and signatures.[3] On 28 October 1726, or soon after, *Gulliver's Travels* was at last published, in two octavo volumes. The price, surprisingly high, was eight shillings and sixpence. A few copies were printed on large paper.[4] When Swift went through the book, the alterations made in his text infuriated him. 'The style is debased,' he said of the corrupt passages, 'the

---

[1] Williams IV. 198. Andrew Tooke was the brother of Swift's erstwhile bookseller, Benjamin Tooke, the younger (as David Woolley points out, p. 176, n. 67).

[2] The language of 'Richard Sympson' to Motte—'you must judge for your self'—almost invites some excision (*ibid.*, III. 153). Certainly, Swift did not forbid Motte to alter the text.

[3] Initials and ornaments differ as well. See Herbert Davis, 'Bowyer's Paper Stock Ledger'.

[4] *The Monthly Catalogue*, Oct. 1726; Teerink, pp. 192–8. The normal size was 19.5 cm. Most large paper copies measure from 22.5 to 23 cm. The Rothschild (formerly Ham House) copy in boards measures 25.1 cm (Teerink, p. 194). For measurements, see also Lucius Hubbard, *Contributions toward a Bibliography of Gulliver's Travels* (Chicago, 1922), pp. 127–8; *Gulliver's Travels*, ed. Harold Williams (London, 1926), p. lix.

humour quite lost, and matter insipid.'[1] He corrected a copy of the first London edition in his own hand but without systematic reference to a manuscript; and he saw to it that the publisher of a Dublin edition, John Hyde (who had a long connection with Swift), made many of the revisions.[2]

Gay and Pope said, perhaps with the exaggeration of friendship, that 'the whole impression sold in a week'.[3] A contemporary pamphleteer wrote, 'Several thousands sold in a week.'[4] A French translator claimed to have information that ten thousand went in three weeks.[5] Samuel Johnson recalled the sale as being so quick that the price of the first edition was raised before the second could be brought out.[6] But these reports are imperfectly reliable.[7] Certainly, Motte put an octavo reprint of the first edition on sale in November, probably around the middle of the month.[8]

A third, octavo edition, of 2500 copies, was ready by 1 December. William Bowyer, who printed Part Four of this, delivered his share in amounts of 500 on 1 December, 500 on 9 December, 1000 on 18 December, and 500 in January 1727.[9] The text was taken from the second edition.

Soon prints of scenes from *Gulliver* went on sale. Swift bought one of Gulliver being taken out of the bowl of cream in Brobdingnag.[10] But it was more than a year after the first edition that Motte raised the question of illustrations. (In the hurry of the early editions there would have been no time for such ornaments.) Swift then felt diffident because pictures would put the price up, but he made shrewd suggestions. On Gulliver in

---

[1] Williams IV. 197–8, 211–12. Cf. the textual notes in Davis XI, especially pp. 309–22. The allegory of the resistance to Wood's patent was not published as part of *Gulliver's Travels* until the edition by G. R. Dennis appeared (London, 1899).

[2] See David Woolley, pp. 136, 142–8. Woolley gives an invaluable account of the career of John Hyde and his relations with Swift (pp. 142–3).

[3] Sherburn II. 413.   [4] *Gulliver Decypher'd*, p. 44.

[5] Pierre-François Guyot Desfontaines, translator, *Voyages de Gulliver* (Paris, 1727), p. xxxii.

[6] *Lives of the Poets*, ed. G. B. Hill (Oxford, 1905), III. 38.

[7] My paragraph is based on Harold Williams's introduction to Davis XI. 22–4.

[8] Williams, introduction to *Gulliver's Travels* (London, 1926), p. lxix.

[9] Davis, 'Bowyer's Paper Stock Ledger', pp. 82–3.   [10] Williams III. 257.

Brobdingnag, Swift wrote,

> He would appear best, wedged in the marrow bone up to the
> middle, or in the monkey's arms upon the roof, or left upon the ridge
> and the footman on the ladder going to relieve him of fighting with
> the rats on the farmer's bed, or in the spaniel's mouth, which being
> described as a small dog, he might look as large as a duck in ours; one
> of the best would I think be to see his chest just falling into the sea
> while three eagles are quarrelling with one another. Or the monkey
> hauling him out of his box.[1]

Around January 1728 Motte brought out a duodecimo with
poor illustrations and an inferior text based on the third octavo.[2]
But a new element may have kept it off the market for a long
time. This was the correction of the text of *Gulliver*, a business
that calls for detailed, even digressive analysis, beginning with
the author's manuscript. After considering the evidence, I believe that Swift saved the foul copy of his book when he made a
fair copy for the printer. Before leaving Ireland in March 1726,
Swift really did, I think, essentially what he said he had done
when Tickell asked him about the manuscript; for in London
Swift received a charming inquiry from that newly married
placeman:

> If it be true that an account of imaginary travels is left in some
> friend's hands in Dublin, I should think it a great distinction to be
> allowed a sight of them, before I should have a right, which the
> author could not prevent, of reading them in print.[3]

Swift replied,

> As to what you mention of an imaginary treatise, I can only answer
> that I have a great quantity [of] paper somewhere or other of which
> none would please you, partly because they are very uncorrect, but
> chiefly because they wholly disagree with your notions of persons
> and things. Neither do I believe it would be possible for you to find
> out my treasures of waste papers without searching nine houses and
> then sending to me for the key.[4]

---

[1] *Ibid.* [2] Teerink, p. 192.
[3] 10 May 1726; Williams III. 135–6.
[4] 7 Jul. 1726; *ibid.*, p. 138.

Swift also wrote to Sheridan,

> Our friend at the Castle writ to me two months ago, to have a sight of
> those papers, etc. of which I brought away a copy. I have answered
> him, that whatever papers I have are conveyed from one place to
> another through nine or ten hands, and that I have the key. If he
> should mention anything of papers in general, either to you or the
> ladies, and that you can bring it in, I would have you and them to
> confirm the same story, and laugh at my humour in it, etc.[1]

Although Swift calls his account a 'story', I take it to be near the
truth; and I suppose that the foul copy of *Gulliver's Travels* was
left in Ireland with people (or a person) whom he trusted. We do
not know that the copy carried by him to England was in his
own hand.

I turn now to the process of correction, beginning with the
labours that Charles Ford undertook soon after the book came
out. In January 1727, when Ford was in Dublin, he sent Motte a
letter which included a list of verbal corrections of the first
edition, along with descriptions of long passages that had been
tampered with. It seems clear that, in doing his work, Ford must
have relied on material given him by the author, and that most
(if not all) of the remarks made in his letter were originally
composed by Swift himself.[2] Furthermore, although the comments were made without reference to a manuscript, Ford also,
but separately, copied out long passages in correct form; and
these transcriptions must have derived from an authorial copy.
Since he did not send the transcriptions to Motte, I infer that
Ford prepared them after the letter went off. Swift may have
assumed that Motte still had the manuscript copy used by the
printer, and could refer to it. Swift and Ford would also have
been in a hurry to deliver the corrections while the book was still
being reprinted, and the foul copy may not have been in a
convenient place. Anyhow, Ford not only transcribed the long
passages, but he also entered the whole body of corrections, long
and short, in two copies of the first London edition which are still
extant.[3]

[1] 8 Jul. 1726; *ibid.*, pp. 139–40.   [2] David Woolley, pp. 161–5.
[3] One is in the Forster Collection, Victoria and Albert Museum, South Kensington;
the other is in the Pierpont Morgan Library, New York.

I return now to Motte. When the publisher received the account of his errors, he decided to produce an improved text; and the first copies of this were delivered to him on 3 May 1727.[1] They went on sale immediately.[2] In this so-called 'Second-Edition, Corrected' (really the fourth of the octavo editions), Motte followed nearly all the minor improvements submitted by Ford, but he ignored the large restorations of whole passages. He also added still further typographical blunders to those of the first edition, which was his copy text. The result had 'The Second Edition' blazoned on the title-page of Volume One and 'The Second Edition, Corrected' on the title-page of Volume Two.

Motte did not publish the scolding letter Swift composed 'from Capt. Gulliver, to His Cousin Sympson', which now commonly appears at the beginning of the book. Either Swift decided not to give it to him, or—as is more likely—the publisher chose not to spoil his own reputation by using it.[3] Instead, Motte accepted the superb burlesque poems which Pope wrote around various characters in *Gulliver*; and these the binder incorporated as best he could into the new edition after it went through the press. The edition was advertised for sale on 4 May 1727; but Bowyer, the printer, delivered four of Pope's Gulliverian productions to Motte on 11 May, and they were prefixed to many copies of the book in a quarter-sheet. The verses (a fifth poem was added in a reissue) were sold separately as well, at sixpence a copy, from 6 May; and they were added at the end of the second volume of the Swift–Pope *Miscellanies*.[4]

Serial editions of *Gulliver* came out in at least two newspapers.[5] In 1726 there were two Dublin editions, one of them appearing

---

[1] Davis, 'Bowyer's Paper Stock Ledger', pp. 82–3.

[2] See the advertisements in the newspapers of the time.

[3] It is possible that Swift only wrote this letter much later, for Faulkner's edition (dated 1735), in which it first appeared. But see below, p. 516, n. 3.

[4] Bowyer entered the quarter-sheet in his ledger on 11 May; see Davis, 'Bowyer's Paper Stock Ledger', p. 83. On Pope's poems and the so-called Second Edition in general, see *ibid.* and Pope, *Poems* VI. 266–81; Teerink, pp. 194–5, 200–1, 245–6 (no. 1224).

[5] Teerink, p. 205.

around 2 December.[1] Dutch, French, and German translations came out in the course of the following year.[2] Spurious continuations also appeared.[3] But there was a limit to the triumph.

'The world glutted itself with that book at first,' said Swift (in December 1727), 'and now it will go off but soberly, but I suppose will not be soon worn out.'[4] He was right. Only two thousand of the 'Second Edition, Corrected' were printed; yet it was not exhausted for many months. Motte received a first shipment of a mere twenty-five copies on 3 May and 450 more before the end of the month; but it was not till February 1728 that the last shipment arrived, and it amounted to as many as 1450 copies.[5] It seems possible (since there are no extant advertisements for the duodecimo in 1727 or 1728) that he held back the duodecimo until the so-called 'Second Edition' was gone, and then released the smaller, illustrated volumes in 1731.

Motte's original eight shillings and sixpence was a high price to set on *Gulliver*, and he threatened immediate prosecutions against pirates. To cash in on the demand without legal embarrassments, other literary entrepreneurs used simple evasions. Abel Boyer summarized the book—with long stretches of direct quotation—in his monthly *Political State of Great Britain*.[6] Sympathizing with Swift's moral and political satire but disliking his 'filthy images',[7] Boyer gave an essentially favourable account of the book. He noticed that the author (whom he identified correctly) 'spares the *ecclesiastical*' while criticizing the other institutions of contemporary civilization.[8] Through quotations, italics, and capitals, Boyer brought out the satirical implications wherever he could; but in general he briefly summarized those episodes which seemed to him no more than

---

[1] David Woolley, p. 143; Teerink, p. 205. The edition that can be dated is not Hyde's.

[2] *Ibid.*, pp. 222–3, 225–6, 236–7. *Le Catalogue général des livres imprimés de la Bibliothèque Nationale* lists five Paris editions dated 1727 and one at The Hague ('plus exacte et plus fidèle que celle de Paris'). On the anticipations, the translations, and the reception of *Gulliver's Travels* in France, see the detailed account by Sybil Goulding, *Swift en France* (Paris, 1924), pp. 56–8.

[3] Teerink, p. 199, no. 292, and *passim*.

[4] Williams III. 257. [5] Davis, 'Bowyer's Paper Stock Ledger', p. 82.

[6] Nov., Dec., and Jan. 1726–7. [7] Boyer, Nov. 1726, p. 486.

[8] *Ibid.*, Nov. 1726, p. 461.

facetious adventures. When he presented the coarse sections of the narrative, such as the description of beggars and maids of honour in Brobdingnag, Boyer made a satirical show of doubting Swift's authorship—the dean being a man of 'the nicest breeding'.[1] His response to the Academy of Lagado is so similar to the comments of more recent scholars and critics that his language is worth reproducing:

> This is intended to expose and ridicule the *follies* and *whimsies* of . . . *crack brained experimental philosophers*: But, in my opinion, his satyr is so be daub'd and clogg'd with *filthy*, and *loathsome* images, that it cannot but be *fastidious* and *fulsome*, to persons of a delicate taste, and nice breeding.[2]

The last part of Boyer's summary[3] closes with a headlong but justified attack upon two pretended keys to *Gulliver*. He also offered the suggestion that in *Laputa* the flying island stands for the royal prerogative; and he provided a recapitulatory critique which again anticipates later comments:

> *Gulliver's Travels*, are an ingenious romantick satyr, in imitation of Plato's *Commonwealth*, Moor's *Utopia*, Bacon's *New Atlantis*, Rabelais, and *The History of the Severambi*: But it were to be wish'd the author had not follow'd Rabelais so close, in some filthy, and obscene descriptions; nor dwelt so long as he has done, on some mean, minute, and trivial subjects, unworthy the dignity of a *grand satyrist*, as, in many places we must in justice, allow him to be. As to his *allusions*, and *allegories* they are, for the most part so strong, so glaring and so obvious, that a man must be a great stranger to the world, in general, and to *courtiers, statesmen, corrupt senators, rakes of quality, lawyers, physicians, virtuosi, soldiers, sharpers*, and *women*, in particular to have need of a *key*.[4]

Boyer shows himself to be knowledgeable, and he may be correct in claiming that the last paragraph of *Laputa*, Chapter Three, is 'a late interpolation, not to be found in the original manuscript'.[5] This is the law that neither the King nor his two eldest sons may leave Laputa, nor the Queen until she is past child-bearing. The law is a brazen allusion to King George's sojourns

---

[1] *Ibid.*, p. 485. [2] Boyer, 32, pp. 525–6. [3] Dated 31 January 1727.
[4] Boyer, 33 (Jan. 1727), 27. [5] *Ibid.*, 32, p. 523.

in Hanover, and Swift may have added it after he got to London.

Edmund Curll got around Motte's prohibition by publishing the earlier of the two keys mentioned by Boyer. Beginning to appear less than a month after *Gulliver* itself, it was completed in four parts and addressed to Swift by name. The first part, signed 'Corolini, *di Marco*' and dated 18 November 1726, from St James's Place, probably went on sale around 24 November.[1] The whole collection, '*Lemuel Gulliver's Travels . . . Compendiously Methodized . . .*', at two shillings and sixpence a copy, was no bargain.

Among puffs of Curll's other wares, and among masses of summary, misinterpretation, and irrelevance, the author drops a few suggestions that might be worth entertaining; these are mainly for Lilliput: that the South Sea locale refers to the Bubble; the temple of Mildendo is the Banqueting House at Whitehall, where Charles I was beheaded; the search of Gulliver refers to the futile search for weapons during the 1715 uprising; the lucky fall of Flimnap refers to the Walpole–Townshend rivalry; Gulliver's imprisonment and release refer to Oxford's imprisonment and release; the articles of Gulliver's impeachment refer to the articles of Oxford's impeachment. In the commentary on Laputa, the annotator plausibly supposes that the satire opening the second chapter refers to William Whiston, John Desaguliers, John 'Orator' Henley, and 'other displayers of the abstruse *arcana* of nature'.[2]

The other 'key', *Gulliver Decypher'd*, was published by J. Roberts in the first few days of December 1726.[3] It is really an attack on Swift's character, with generous sideswipes at Arbuthnot, Pope, and Gay, all composed in a fumbling imitation of *A Tale of a Tub*. The most curious feature is an insistence that *Gulliver's Travels* derives from the Scriblerus material. The

---

[1] See advance notice in *Whitehall Evening Post*, 10 Nov. 1726; then 'This Day is Published', *ibid.*, and in *The Evening Post*, 24 Nov.

[2] P. 7.

[3] 'This Day is publish'd', in *Post Boy* and *Whitehall Evening Post*, 3 Dec.; a second edition is advertised as published 'this day' in Mist's *Weekly Journal*, 24 Dec. 1726.

writer blames Pope for the 'obscene' touches in *Brobdingnag*.[1] He also says that several thousand copies of *Gulliver* were sold in a week.[2]

A similar pamphlet, *A Letter from a Clergyman ... with an Account of the Travels of ... Gulliver ...*, closes over the date of 7 December 1726. This is a crude attack on Swift for being irreligious, obscene, and malicious. It describes him as time-serving, misanthropic, and envious, and finds him guilty of sedition and slander, for which he should be prosecuted. Much of the pamphlet is really a fatuous panegyric on Walpole.

The author finds the first three parts of Gulliver to be agreeably diverting, apart from the gross language and lewd descriptions. These parts, we are told, have wit and invention, though also some 'unnatural' incidents and some inconsistencies; but the last voyage, says the critic, shows a loss of vivacity:

> In this long tedious part the reader loses all that might have been engaging to him in the three former; the capacity and character given there of brutes, are so unnatural; and especially the great preeminence asserted of them, to the most virtuous and noble of humane nature, is so monstrously absurd and unjust, that 'tis with the utmost pain a generous mind must indure the recital; a man grows sick at the shocking things inserted there; his gorge rises; he is not able to conceal his resentment; and closes the book with detestation and disappointment.[3]

From the wide range of responses to Swift's masterpiece by Boyer and the pamphleteers, we may see how deeply the success of the book was mixed misunderstanding and distaste. We may see how early those issues of morality and meaning arose which still are provoked by the imagery and the ambiguous satire. Characteristically, the man who invited such controversy objected to it; and yet even readers who shared many of Swift's opinions were troubled by his work. In Gulliver's letter to Sympson, first published in the 1735 edition of *Gulliver*, I think we hear the author's own voice complaining of 'libels, and keys, and reflections, and memoirs ... wherein I see myself accused of reflecting upon great states-folk; of degrading human nature ...

[1] P. 32 n.   [2] P. 44.   [3] P. 7.

and of abusing the female sex'.[1] The complaint is ironic in its references to statesmen, human nature, and women; but the tone derives from genuine irritation. Even Lord Foley—who was brother-in-law to the first Earl of Oxford—felt such distaste for *Gulliver's Travels* that his family avoided mentioning the book in front of him.[2] Swift must have been aware of such judgments.

Yet he could console himself not only with the sale figures but also with the reports of his friends, who assured him that everyone enjoyed the book, and for the most part as acceptable satire and comic entertainment. The fault they mentioned was the comparative flatness of Part Three. From Arbuthnot, Pope, and Gay came judgments and anecdotes that keep being repeated today. Arbuthnot visited the Princess of Wales soon after *Gulliver* came out and found her reading it. She had, he said, 'just come to the passage of the hobbling prince, which she laughed at'. He himself thought the 'least brilliant' section of the book was 'the part of the projectors'. Whether by this he meant all of Part Three (probably so) or merely the chapters dealing with the Academy of Lagado (to which he contributed), is not clear. He also said that Erasmus Lewis grumbled a little, wanted a key, and would not stop 'refining'—or reading meanings into the text. As for the popular success, Arbuthnot said,

> I will make over all my profits to you, for the property of Gulliver's Travels, which I believe, will have as great a run as John Bunian. Gulliver is a happy man that at his age can write such a merry book.

Arbuthnot told some anecdotes that vividly suggest the range of the book's readers:

> Gulliver is in everybody's hands. Lord Scarborow, who is no inventor of stories told me that he fell in company with the master of a ship, who told him that he was very well acquainted with Gulliver, but that the printer had mistaken, that he lived in Wapping, and not in Rotherhithe. I lent the book to an old gentleman, who went immediately to his map to search for Lilly putt.[3]

[1] Davis XI. 7.

[2] This is the report of William Stratford, in H.M.C. *Portland* VII. 445–6. Stratford says (20 Dec. 1726) that he himself has read *Gulliver's Travels* 'with pleasure', and that Foley's wife 'was wonderfully delighted with them' (*ibid.*).

[3] 5 Nov. 1726; Williams III. 179–80.

Pope's account was both weaker in its details and sharper in its implications than Arbuthnot's:

> I congratulate you first upon what you call your cousin's wonderful book, which is *publica trita manu*[1] at present, and I prophecy will be in future the admiration of all men. That countenance with which it is received by some statesmen, is delightful; I wish I could tell you how every single man looks upon it, to observe which has been my whole diversion this fortnight....
>
> I find no considerable man very angry at the book: some indeed think it rather too bold, and too general a satire: but none that I hear of accuse it of particular reflections (I mean no persons of consequence, or good judgment; the mob of critics, you know, always are desirous to apply satire to those that they envy for being above them) so that you needed not to have been so secret upon this head.[2]

But Gay's story is the most straightforward and genial, and the best told:

> About ten days ago a book was published here of the travels of one Gulliver, which hath been the conversation of the whole town ever since: The whole impression sold in a week; and nothing is more diverting than to hear the different opinions people give of it, though all agree in liking it extremely. 'Tis generally said that you are the author, but I am told, the bookseller declares he knows not from what hand it came. From the highest to the lowest it is universally read, from the cabinet-council to the nursery. The politicians to a man agree, that it is free from particular reflections, but that the satire on general societies of men is too severe. Not but we now and then meet with people of greater perspicuity, who are in search for particular applications in every leaf; and 'tis highly probable we shall have keys published to give light into Gulliver's design. Your Lord [Bolingbroke] is the person who least approves it, blaming it as a design of evil consequence to depreciate human nature, at which it cannot be wondered that he takes most offence, being himself the most accomplished of his species, and so losing more than any other of that praise which is due both to the dignity and virtue of a man. Your friend, my Lord Harcourt, commends it very much, though he thinks in some places the matter too far carried. The Duchess Dowager of Marlborough is in raptures at it; she says she can dream of nothing else since she read it: she declares, that she hath now found out, that her whole life hath been lost in caressing the worst part of mankind, and treating the best as her foes; and that if she

---

[1] Worn away by the public hand.   [2] 16 Nov. 1726; Sherburn II. 412.

knew Gulliver, though he had been the worst enemy she ever had, she would give up all her present acquaintance for his friendship. . . . Among lady-critics, some have found out that Mr Gulliver had a particular malice to maids of honour. Those of them who frequent the church, say, his design is impious, and that it is an insult on Providence, by depreciating the works of the Creator. Notwithstanding I am told the Princess[1] hath read it with great pleasure. As to other critics, they think the flying island is the least entertaining; and so great an opinion the town have of the impossibility of Gulliver's writing at all below himself, that 'tis agreed that part was not writ by the same hand, though this hath its defenders too. It hath passed Lords and Commons, *nemine contradicente*; and the whole town, men, women, and children are quite full of it.[2]

---

[1] I.e., the Princess of Wales.   [2] Sherburn II. 413-14.

Chapter Three

COLD SEASONS

S wift could not have felt easy in the Ireland of the years
1726–7. Unlike the early 1720s, the second half of the
decade was a time of droughts and harvest failure.[1]
Instead of selling grain abroad, the nation had to import it.
Consequently, agricultural prices rose, encouraging landlords
to set higher rents. At the same time, leases made at low rents
during the unstable 1690s were falling in, and the renewals were
naturally made with augmentations and fines. Unfavourable
rates of exchange punished absentees like Charles Ford. But the
misery of the poor also deepened. Tenants, resident landlords,
and absentees all felt dissatisfied. When Ford joined Swift in
Dublin during the autumn of 1726, I suspect he was waiting for
his pocketbook to fill up.[2].

The money shipped to absentees amounted to something
between a sixth and a quarter of the total rent roll of Ireland. As
rents in general went up, the amount of this drain rose and
alarmed many observers. Meanwhile, the agricultural surplus
shrank, and the importation of grain hurt the balance of trade.
To make things worse, Irish economic activity still suffered from
the disastrous speculations fostered by the South Sea Company
and the Mississippi Company; and the outbreak of plague in
southern France had disrupted a lively trade with that region.

Normally, beef, butter, hides and wool were exported openly
and profitably, in a trade improved by cattle diseases on the
continent. But agricultural products needed more elaborate
planning than dairy or pasture produce; they brought slower

---

[1] My opening remarks on economic affairs are based on L. M. Cullen, *An Economic
History of Ireland since 1660* (London, 1972), pp. 26–50.

[2] Williams III. 173.

returns and sometimes could not be legally sold abroad. The export provision trade worked to the advantage of landlords and merchants, who spent much of their gains on inessential imports, thereby further weakening the native economy.

A decline in agriculture made bread and ordinary food less available to the common people, especially when supplies had to be imported. Since pasture needs less supervision than tillage, the trend meant agricultural unemployment; and the feeling, common among landlords, that tithes on pasture were illegitimate, helped to embarrass the clergy financially even while it embittered the relations between church and gentry. The painful implications of the cycle become vivid in Thomas Prior's remark, made in 1729, when the suffering of the Irish—for want of food—was beyond description: 'There is no country in Europe which produces and exports so great a quantity of beef, butter, tallow, hides and wool as Ireland does.'[1]

In 1726 the crop failures were so terrible that imports climbed to the highest level of the decade. Between the summers of 1726 and 1727, the rates of exchange (for Irish money against English) sank lower than they had been since the 1690s. Speaking of the consequent rise in the value of English money against Irish, Archbishop King complained, 'The exchange . . . rises to the great grievance of this country.'[2]

Rightly or wrongly, Irish leaders—churchmen, in particular —often blamed the nation's difficulties on trends in the use of land, as they saw pasture replacing tillage. Archbishop King was in England from May to September 1726, mainly at Bath. He went to London and—along with Swift—tried to plead Ireland's case at court but came away frustrated as usual by the ignorance and callous indifference of the English.[3]

At home in October, he traced Ireland's economic crisis to the decline of agriculture:

The laying down the plough everywhere in my diocese has had a very ill effect on the kingdom by obliging us to send abroad even as

[1] *Observations on the Present State and Condition of Ireland* (1729), p. 32.
[2] 7 Jan. 1727, to Richard Hart.   [3] Jun. 1726, to Lord King; cf. above, pp. 480–2.

far as the West Indies and Italy for grain to the value of some hundred thousand pounds, but though we all suffer by it, the clergy and impropriators are the greatest losers, for I know some parishes reduced in their annual income nine parts in ten.[1]

In a survey of the nation's plight six weeks later, the archbishop lamented the loss of gold and silver coin (due to the difference in English and Irish values and to the poor balance of trade); he bemoaned the high rate of exchange; and he said the hard times were driving humble Protestant families to the West Indies.

Ireland, of course, had no mint of her own. For gold and silver she had to rely on English and foreign coin. But as we have seen, the law set such a difference between Irish and English values that it profited Irish merchants to send silver abroad, and to import gold coins—which were legally overvalued. For similar reasons, English bankers preferred specie to bills of exchange, especially when the balance of trade was running against Ireland. Some impression of the chaos that resulted can be got from Archbishop King's outburst (the 'moidore' that he mentions was a Portuguese coin, overvalued and therefore much in use):

As to coin we have hardly any silver left, for the proportion between gold and silver being wrong stated, and the advantage given to the former, it is worth the bankers' while to carry away the silver and exchange it for gold; but the case is yet much worse, for we have no return at all for what silver is sent out of the kingdom, for the balance of trade is so much against us, that there is no species of gold passes here but if one carry it to England he will gain three or four per cent more than if he took a bill of exchange, for exchange is at between thirteen and fourteen per cent; whereas if one carries moidores, the worst species, he will lose but ten. If he carry an hundred guineas, which here make an 115 pound, he loses but ten pounds in that same, and so proportionably in all other species of gold current here.... In a little time we must have no money at all.[2]

The author of the *Drapier's Letters* shared the archbishop's views on agriculture, money and trade; and he must have felt

[1] 22 Oct. 1726, to William Moore.
[2] 6 Dec. 1726, to Lord King; cf. similar remarks, 7 May 1727, to Francis Annesley. I have normalized the spelling, punctuation, etc., of the passage quoted, here, as in general.

uneasy about the illnesses which sent the old man to Bath. Quite apart from his attachment to King, Swift knew what kind of successor the government would appoint. The cure at Bath was no cure for the archbishop, and in the spring of 1727 he told a friend about the physical suffering which a Dublin winter inflicted on him:

> I had first a cough, which grew by degrees upon me till it degenerated into a chincough[1] which took away my breath and endangered my senses. After, I was seized with the gout in both my hands, in both my feet and knees. After this I fell into a fever, and after that into a pleurisy. I am still very weak and the worse for a pain in my back and a sciatica.[2]

When the crisis of these ailments was over, Swift hinted his own relief in his drily ironical manner: 'The Archbishop of Dublin is just recovered after having been despaired of, and by that means hath disappointed some hopers.'[3]

But he was also waiting for another death: Stella's sickness never left his mind. She remained ill throughout the year 1727. In the twelve months, Swift wrote, 'she never had a day's health.'[4] Yet there were ups as well as downs; and in mid-October 1726, he told Stopford, 'Mrs Johnson is much recovered since I saw her first, but still very lean and low.'[5] He arranged for her and Mrs Dingley to live in the deanery during the late spring and summer when he would be away.[6] But a few weeks before he left Ireland, Swift composed the last of her birthday verses, dated 13 March 1727.

This poem suggests a link between the private and public aspects of Swift's character. For Swift, like Pope, it was convenient by now to associate virtue with the middle or humble life and vice with the high. Edward Young, in his satires, had committed the blunder of singling out courtiers as examples of merit even while, in general terms, he contrasted low-born

---

[1] I.e., whooping cough.
[2] 6 May 1727, to Francis Annesley.
[3] 14 Feb. 1727, to Chetwode, whom Swift was systematically avoiding; Williams III. 199.
[4] Davis V. 228.   [5] Williams III. 170.   [6] *Ibid.*, p. 205.

benevolence with aristocratic frivolity.[1] Swift ridiculed him savagely:

> If ev'ry *peer* whom you commend
> To worth and learning is a friend,
> If this be truth, as you attest,
> What *land* was ever *half so blest?*[2]

Unlike Young in his praise of Queen Caroline,[3] Swift dwelt on Stella's exemplary deeds, her private charities and her integrity. The argument of the birthday poem will carry little conviction to a worldly modern: Swift declares that his friend's record of good works ought to cheer her in her last ordeal. But doctrine aside, the opening lines still charm us with their open-eyed, humorous earthiness:

> This day then, let us not be told,
> That you are sick, and I grown old,
> Nor think on our approaching ills,
> And talk of spectacles and pills;
> To morrow will be time enough
> To hear such mortifying stuff.

The comic tone undercuts the grimness of the facts. Swift quietly identifies his own defects of age with Stella's very different symptoms, and thereby softens the truth about her imminent death.

The end of the poem opens suddenly into uncomfortable autobiography:

> O then, whatever Heav'n intends,
> Take pity on your pitying friends;
> Nor let your ills affect your mind,
> To fancy they can be unkind.
> Me, surely me, you ought to spare,
> Who gladly would your suff'rings share;
> Or give my scrap of life to you,
> And think it far below your due.[4]

---

[1] *Love of Fame* I. 139–46.
[2] 'On Reading Dr Young's Satires', *Poems* II. 391; written in 1726.
[3] *Love of Fame* VI. 569–80—written after Swift's poem to Stella.
[4] *Poems* II. 763, 766.

He was to leave Ireland less than a month after the date of this poem; and they both knew he might never see her again. Such a prospect would have produced a terrible strain between his guilt and her suffering; and I suppose the disheartened woman must at times have spoken harshly.

The dean's public reputation was small comfort in the face of his friend's agony. Even so, Swift had to mingle quiet pleasure with a show of contempt in his response to the celebrity he now enjoyed in Ireland. However much he might sneer at the Irish people, their acclaim touched and pleased him. To mark his birthday (30 November), a procession of gentlemen went to the cathedral for prayers and an anthem. Afterwards, they regaled themselves 'with a splendid entertainment being prepar'd, accompanied with a curious set of vocal and instrumental musick; bells ringing, bonfires and other illuminations in many parts of the city'.[1] These tributes were a form of protest against the leadership which the English imposed upon the nation. But they also signalized Swift's right to the place he had won in his countrymen's affections.

Meanwhile, from September to March, memories of England made a disturbing contrast to conditions in Ireland. Responding to a tender message from Pope, Swift wrote about his reveries: 'I can every night distinctly see Twitenham, and the grotto, and Dawley, and Mrs B. [i.e., Martha Blount] and many other et cetera's.'[2] He had sent Pope a pair of silver cups inscribed to the poet with the motto, 'Pignus amicitiae exiguum ingentis' (a slight token of a great friendship), for which the poet had gently scolded him.[3]

While waiting for spring and his promised return to London (with the first swallow),[4] Swift kept wittily in touch with the Scriblerians, as well as Mrs Howard and some leaders of the opposition to Walpole. In September came news that Pope had

---

[1] *Dublin Journal*, 3 Dec. 1726; see also the *Dublin Intelligence* for the same day.
[2] August 1726; Sherburn II. 393.
[3] Williams III. 157 and note.
[4] 'Cum hirundine prima'; Sherburn II. 414.

cut his hand badly and nearly lost his life when the coach he travelled in was overturned while fording a river. Swift received distinct and alarming accounts from the victim and other friends.[1] He also had a cordial message from Pulteney, breathing ambitious good will in reply to a complimentary letter from himself.[2] I suspect that Swift's interest was mainly to support Bolingbroke's schemes; he did not need Pope to warn him that Pulteney's highmindedness derived from his being out of power while wishing to be in.[3] On the other side, Pulteney must have hoped that Swift would be a help with *The Craftsman*, a new periodical that he was launching with Bolingbroke.[4]

Not only did Swift exchange witty letters with Mrs Howard.[5] Having received the gift of a ring which he had demanded from her, he made that token the excuse for a new advance. In October 1726 he sent the lady a beautiful piece of Irish plaid (i.e., poplin made of silk and wool), hoping to capture the attention of the Princess, who might then advertise Irish manufactures by dressing herself in the material.[6] Her highness did see the plaid, rose to the bait, and not only took it but ordered dresses made of the cloth for her daughters and herself.[7] Swift was delighted to supply the additional goods. He cheerfully wrote to Mrs Howard in the character of Lemuel Gulliver and presented her with the tiny crown of Lilliput, rescued from the flaming palace.[8]

It is clear that Swift was eagerly cultivating the courtiers of Leicester House and Richmond Hill. At the same time he was afraid of being taken in. So he guarded himself against private disappointment and public gossip by ironical depreciations of Mrs Howard.

Swift wished to visit England once more not merely for its social amenities. He hoped to finish some tasks which he had left

[1] *Ibid.*, pp. 399–403. [2] Williams III. 162–3.
[3] Sherburn II. 395. Cf. Swift's comment on Pope's warning, *ibid.*, p. 419.
[4] This may be the reference, in Pulteney's letter, to 'something which I would willingly have communicated' (Williams III. 162).
[5] *Ibid.*, pp. 187–8. [6] *Ibid.*, p. 177. [7] *Ibid.*, pp. 179, 184–5.
[8] *Ibid.*, pp. 190–1.

undone in the summer. Yet Stella's danger was not the only argument against his going. His own disabilities were another. He could just tolerate his periods of deafness or vertigo when he was in the harbour of the deanery, comforted by homely friends and habitual servants. Such incapacities among an élite like Pope, Bolingbroke, Peterborough, Arbuthnot, and Gay—not to mention the court of the Prince and Princess—were an intolerable humiliation. The expense of the visits troubled him as well; and Swift expected this crossing to be his last.[1]

In February his young and much-loved friend James Stopford returned from England, bringing messages, pamphlets, and presents from Gay, Pope, and the Bolingbrokes.[2] Besides rejoining those old friends, Swift still hoped to get from the second Lord Oxford some materials for an account of his father's ministry; and he wanted him to read over Swift's *History of the Four Last Years of the Queen*. The repair of the text of *Gulliver* was another desideratum; and Swift wrote 'A Letter from Capt. Gulliver, to His Cousin Sympson', which he intended to have Motte place at the head of his next edition.[3] In this he complained both seriously and jokingly about the errors of the first edition, and he characteristically signed it the day after All Fools' Day.[4] Swift also wanted a new financial understanding with Motte about the book; and there were fresh publications to be arranged with Pope, for a volume of *Miscellanies*. During the summer of 1727 Swift hoped to spend two months in France and Aix-la-Chapelle (i.e., Aachen),

---

[1] *Ibid.*, pp. 198, 205.

[2] *Ibid.*, pp. 199, 200, 202.

[3] I am not persuaded by the argument that Swift wrote this for Faulkner's edition (Dublin, 1735). Had he done so, there was no need for him to date it 1727 or to suggest that it might be used for a second edition, if there should ever be one; nor would Swift have failed to allude to public events since 1727. Motte might well have boggled at publishing an attack on his own workmanship. Besides, the language of Gulliver's complaints is close to the language of Ford's letter to Motte, 3 Jan. 1727, which Swift surely composed (*ibid.*, pp. 194–5); and that in turn is probably the letter which 'Gulliver' mentions in his opening paragraph. The rhetoric of Gulliver's third paragraph is curiously close to that of the fourth paragraph of the 'Letter to the Writer of the Occasional Paper', which was written before 18 May 1727—probably in the early part of that month (Davis v. 94–5).

[4] Davis XI. 5, 8.

where he was advised a long stay would improve his health.[1]
Finally, there was a faint chance of doing some good for Ireland
and his comrade parsons.[2]

[1] In requesting his licence of absence, Swift said he might go to Aix-la-Chapelle
(Williams III. 204–5), a city which he could have visited with the Bolingbrokes (cf. the
heading of Bolingbroke's letter, *ibid.*, p. 347).
[2] *Ibid.*, p. 211.

Chapter Four

GOODBYE TO LONDON

I t looks as if Swift left Dublin on 9 April 1727. As soon as he landed in England, he struck the elegaic note which was to cling to his travels this year. From Chester he went to Herefordshire, where he visited the old family house in Goodrich and his grandfather's church.[1] Here he presented to the church a chalice used by the Rev. Thomas Swift, with inscriptions dated 1726; these identified himself as the donor and described his grandfather as 'notus in historiis ob ea quae fecit et passus est pro Carolo Primo'.[2]

During his stay in England, Swift also sketched a design for a simple tablet commemorating his grandfather, which he sent to Mrs Howard and which inspired Pope to write some exellent comic verses on Swift's connection with Goodrich. This monument was duly erected under the altar of the church.[3] The pilgrimage and the memorials suggest the valedictory spirit which pervaded the months Swift now spent in familiar places.

On 18 April he turned up in Oxford, surprising Canon Stratford, an old connection of the Harleys, in Christ Church. 'He sat chattering with me till twelve o'clock,' Stratford wrote. Next day, Swift dined with him, along with a son of Dr Arbuthnot and a nephew of Lord Oxford. 'He is as little altered, I think,' said Stratford, 'of any man I ever saw, in so many years'

---

[1] Williams III. 205–6, and notes.

[2] N. & Q., 2nd ser., 1858, no. 6, p. 138; Ball III. 426, n. 4. A draft of the inscription, dated 1725, appears among the papers of Thomas Tickell, who, I suppose, scrutinized the inelegant Latin ('known in history on account of the things he did and suffered for Charles I'). See R. E. Tickell, *Thomas Tickell* (London, 1931), pp. 112–13.

[3] The authority for this episode is Scott, who had documentary evidence now lost. See Scott I, 5–6, n.*; Pope, *Poems* VI. 251–2. As Ball suggests, the many references to Goodrich in the correspondence of Swift, Pope, and Gay during the year 1727 persuade one that this year (and not 1726) is the date of the presentation (Ball III. 386, n. 2).

time.' Much of their conversation ran on Carteret, and points to the cause of Swift's quarrel with his lordship:

He opened with great freedom against him to me [wrote Stratford]. There was a very ingenious man [i.e., Delany], who had been introduced to Carteret at Carteret's own desire [i.e., on Swift's recommendation]. Carteret had seemingly entered into great friendships with him, and had invited himself often to his house, and lived very freely on him. He had frankly promised him any preferment in his gift.[1] When the preferment fell which the man most desired, being very convenient for him, though of no great value, Carteret told him he could not give it to him, though he esteemed him much, because he was suspected to be somewhat of a Tory, and gave the preferment to a Frenchman recommended to him by the Duchess of Kendal.[2]

From Oxford, Swift went by way of Tetsworth to London and Twickenham.[3] He proceeded to live mainly with Pope but to make forays into town, where he stayed again at Gay's lodgings in Whitehall (in the gatehouse to the royal garden).[4] Soon enough, they were receiving invitations from Lord Oxford;[5] but we now begin to hear the undertone of frustration that was to accompany the long farewell. For the attempt to see his lordship became a comedy of false starts as the illness of Pope, Swift or Pope's mother got in the way. The dean and his poetic host almost had the long-sought meeting with the Earl in London the week after Swift arrived.[6] But a reunion had to be postponed until after Oxford left for Wimpole,[7] where Swift finally succeeded in visiting him with Pope near the end of July;[8] and the

---

[1] Of course, Carteret never could have committed such an imprudence.

[2] H.M.C. *Portland* VII. 446–7. We may doubt the turn that Swift and Stratford gave the story; but Delany's link with the party of Phipps would indeed have made him a risky candidate for preferment.

[3] Stratford mentions Tetsworth (*ibid.*). On 22 Apr. Pope writes as if Swift had arrived earlier; Sherburn II. 430–1.

[4] Gay I. 11. Pope exaggerates when he says that Swift 'made my retirement his own for near four months' (5 Oct. 1727; Sherburn II. 448).

[5] Sherburn II. 430–1.   [6] *Ibid.*

[7] 6 May 1727, Canon Stratford writes to Lord Oxford that he assumes Swift saw the Earl 'before you went to Wimpole'; but on 17 Jun. he writes, 'I was misinformed as to Swift's being with you'; H.M.C. *Portland* VII. 447, 448.

[8] Ball III. 387, n. 3.

three then returned to London together.[1] Not only illness but literary occupations made other meetings impossible, even though Swift had planned carefully to spend time with Oxford.

Apparently, Swift had brought over a manuscript of his *Four Last Years*, which Bolingbroke and Pope were to read before sending it on to the Earl. One of the subjects Swift must have gone over with his lordship was the revision and publication of that troublesome book. We may be sure that both Bolingbroke and Oxford ultimately discouraged the tired author, and that their judgment did not please him.[2]

The business of *Gulliver* also kept the lord and the dean apart. Evidently, Motte still owed Swift money, or else contracted to pay him more than the original amount. To keep up the style of anonymity, Swift brought Erasmus Lewis into the negotiations, and wrote a letter in a clumsily disguised hand, making his old comrade the agent to receive money for 'Richard Sympson' on account of *Gulliver's Travels*.[3] Then the so-called 'Second Edition, Corrected' came out,[4] lacking the letter to Sympson, and in a form that must have irritated Swift.[5]

Meanwhile, Pope, in giving Lord Oxford an excuse for putting off an engagement to visit him, blamed the delay on 'the idle Dean's great businesses'.[6] But I think it was not only *Gulliver* that caused the delay. Pope was probably veiling his own wish for time to work out, with Swift, the details of a strange collaboration. This was taking shape as some volumes of *Miscellanies*, probably inspired by an unauthorized pair of *Miscellanea* which Curll had published the summer before (to Pope's annoyance), and which included letters and poems by both Pope and Swift.[7] Although the Twickenham scheme was ostensibly to mingle the

---

[1] On 2 Aug. See Sherburn II. 441; Williams III. 228.

[2] Cf. the following references: Pope to Oxford, 15 Aug. 1726 (Sherburn II. 387); 17 May 1728, Book I sent by Pope to Oxford (*ibid.*, p. 493); 25 Jun. 1728, Book II sent (*ibid.*, p. 502); 17 May 1739 (*ibid.*, IV. 177). See also Williams's introduction to Davis VII. xii.

[3] Williams III. 206 and n. 1.

[4] 3 May 1727.

[5] See above, p. 501.   [6] 23 Apr. 1727; Sherburn II. 431.

[7] See E. L. Steeves and R. H. Griffith, 'Bibliographical Notes on "The Last Volume" of Motte's *Miscellanies*, 1727', in Pope, *The Art of Sinking in Poetry*, ed. E. L. Steeves (New York, 1952), p. 197.

works of the two authors under their joint supervision, it grew
into something very different. The collections that emerged had
little in them by Pope, a great deal by Swift, and several pieces
by their friends.

We do not know much about the planning of the first two
volumes, but they were printed before Swift arrived—by the
middle of February 1727;[1] and a third, to be called *The Last
Volume*, was also well under way; for he had sent contributions
from Ireland. Volumes One and Two were not actually published until June 1727, when they carried a remarkable preface
which both authors signed, and which is dated at Twickenham,
27 May 1727. I think Pope mainly responsible for the oddly
worded statement. Its language seems far more concerned to
disown certain works which are not in the volumes than to claim
any that are. I find it hard to believe Swift felt perfectly happy
with Pope's editorial arrangements, though he certainly was a
willing collaborator.[2]

Another sour note was struck by the Parisian translator of
Gulliver's Travels,[3] Desfontaines. I think he heard that Swift
would be visiting France, and wished to avoid embarrassment.
In the first edition[4] of his translation, he had devoted a section of
the preface to the coarseness and obscurity of the original book;
and in the body of his version he ruthlessly abridged, enlarged,
and distorted Swift's narrative in order to fit it to what he
regarded as the French taste.[5] Here is his richly compulsive
survey of Swift's defects:

> je ne puis . . . dissimuler ici que j'ai trouvé dans l'ouvrage de M. Swift
> des endroits foibles et même très mauvais; des allégories impéné-
> trables, des allusions insipides, des détails puérils, des réflexions
> triviales, des pensées basses, des redites ennuieuses, des poliçonneries

---

[1] Sherburn II. 426.

[2] For a general account of the Swift–Pope *Miscellanies* see below, pp. 736–51.

[3] There was an earlier French translation published at The Hague; see Teerink,
pp. 225–32.

[4] The *Journal des Savants* for April 1727 announced the forthcoming appearance of the
translation, which probably came out in the second or third week of April; see Sybil
Goulding, *Swift en France* (Paris, 1924), p. 60.

[5] For a systematic account of Desfontaines' enormities see Goulding, pp. 60–71.

grossières, des plaisanteries fades, en un mot, des choses qui, renduës littéralement en françois ... auroient révolté le bon goût qui règne en France, m'auroient moi-même couvert de confusion, et m'auroient infailliblement attiré de justes reproches, si j'avois été assés foible et assés imprudent, pour les exposer aux yeux du public.[1]

Writing to Swift, Desfontaines tried at one and the same time to praise the masterpiece and to account for the insults which he had prudently deleted from the second edition of the Paris text: 'Je ferois volontiers encore davantage', he told Swift, 'pour effacer jusqu'au souvenir de cet endroit de la preface.' He then went on, in Gallic hyperbole, to welcome Swift to France: 'On ne parle ici que de votre arrivée, et tout Paris souhaitte de vous voir.'[2]

Swift blew aside the smoke of Desfontaines' incense and pounced on the cold facts. The significance of his reply lies in the confidence he displays in his own accomplishment; and his language echoes the strong words he had used sixteen years earlier to establish the excellence of *A Tale of a Tub*:

[Vous] n'avez pas craint, de donner au public la traduction d'un ouvrage, que vous assurez etre plein de pollisoneries, de sottises, de puerilites &c. Nous convenons icy que le gout des nations n'est pas toujours le meme. Mais nous sommes portes a croire que le bon gout est le meme par tout ou il y a des gens d'esprit, de judgement et de scavoir. Si donc les livres du Sieur Gulliver ne sont calcules que pour les Isles Britanniques, ce voyageur doit passer pour un tres pitoyable ecrivain. Les memes vices, et les memes follies regnent partout, du moins, dans tous les pays civilises de l'Europe, et l'auteur qui n'ecrit que pour une ville, une province, un royaume, ou meme un siecle, merite si peu d'etre traduit qu'il ne merits pas d'etre lu.

Les partisans de ce Gulliver, qui ne laissent pas d'etre en fort grand nombre chez nous, soutiennent, que son livre durera autant que notre langage, parce qu'il ne tire pas son merite de certaines modes ou manieres de penser et de parler, mais d'une suite d'observations sur les imperfections, les folies, et les vices de l'homme.[3]

---

[1] *Voyages de Gulliver* (Paris: V. Coustelier, chés J. Gerin, 1727), I. xv–xvi.

[2] Williams III. 217.

[3] *Ibid.*, p. 226. The roughness of Swift's French is due in part to our possessing only a draft of the letter, and not the final copy. Notice the echo (no doubt unconscious) of the 'Apology' for *A Tale of a Tub*—'[The] book seems calculated to live at least as long as our language, and our taste admit no great alteration'; Davis I. 1.

By the time Swift finished scolding Desfontaines, the sudden death of George I had utterly transformed the political scene. In the new state of affairs Swift played a serious part. But I'm not sure he quite realized the impression he made. Whatever Swift said or wished to believe about himself, he was not a man to stand by coolly while his friends marched off to war. He must have known much about Pulteney's and Bolingbroke's partnership. He must have read the early numbers of their brilliantly written organ, *The Craftsman*. He had not flattered Mrs Howard with epistolary wit and Irish plaids only to receive payment in kind. Briefly now, to establish Swift's attitudes once he was settled in the neighbourhood of London, I shall review some aspects of his behaviour during May and June of 1727, just before and just after the King died.

In his most candid letters Swift had revealed the split in his character; for he almost boasted of his proximity to greatness:

> I have at last seen the [Princess—as she still was] twice this week by her own commands; she retains her old civility, and I my old freedom; she charges me without ceremony, to be the author of a bad book, though I told her how angry the ministry were; but she assures me that both she and the [Prince] were very well pleased with every particular; but I disowned the whole affair, as you know I very well might, only gave her leave, since she liked the book, to suppose what author she pleased.[1]

It was Mrs Howard who delivered the invitation of the Princess to Swift. His notion that the ministry objected to *Gulliver's Travels* is not borne out by other accounts, although we may assume that Walpole resented Swift's satire as much as he normally resented such attacks.[2] But Swift's air of consequence, in the letter, hardly supports a tone of indifference to the court.

Neither does a poem Swift wrote (a month or so later) to compliment Mrs Howard and celebrate the intimacy of Pope, Gay, and Swift with the royal *ménage à trois*. It was called 'A Pastoral Dialogue between Richmond-Lodge and Marble-Hill'. This imaginary dialogue between the country house of the

---

[1] 13 May 1727; Williams III. 207–8.
[2] See Plumb II. 131, 175.

Prince of Wales and that of Mrs Howard was not printed till 1735. But the publisher declared—and the information must have come from Swift—that the poem was written in June 1727, soon after the death of George I, and that it was taken to court and read to the new King and Queen.

In themselves the couplets are neither the best nor the worst of Swift's compositions, but the substance suggests that the poet misunderstood the relation between Caroline and her bed-chamber woman as well as his own relation to both. The opening line—'In spight of Pope, in spight of Gay'—is a hint that his friends tried and failed to set the dean right.

'A Pastoral Dialogue between Richmond-Lodge and Marble-Hill' represents the country houses of George II and Mrs Howard as conversing sadly and foreseeing they will suffer from the succession of the Prince to the throne. Both houses, it transpires, will be neglected and left empty. In the course of the poem Swift implies that Mrs Howard is an incorruptible servant who has only lost money through her connection with the court. Swift also depicts Pope as a loyal and selfless devotee of his king and country.

But the most prominent figure in the poem is that of Swift, as the poet dramatizes his own supposed familiarity with both houses; this characterization emerges when the two speakers mourn his absence. Their nostalgia suggests that the weighty preoccupations of kingship will end the old style of casual, princely hospitality:

> *Marble-Hill.* No more the Dean, that grave divine,
> Shall keep the key of my (no) wine;
> My ice-house rob as heretofore,
> And steal my artichokes no more....
> *Richmond-Lodge.* Here wont the Dean when he's to seek,
> To sponge a breakfast once a week;
> To cry the bread was stale, and mutter
> Complaints against the royal butter.
> But, now I fear it will be said,
> No butter sticks upon his bread.
> We soon shall find him full of spleen,
> For want of tattling to the Queen;

Stunning her royal ears with talking;
His reverence and her highness walking.[1]

There was in fact less intimacy here than meets the eye; and
Swift should have realized, first, that he was inviting the reader
to see him as a courtier in the common sense and, secondly, that
no wife, let alone a queen, would wish a poet to presume she was
on excellent terms with her husband's mistress. The poem belongs to a genre which Swift cultivated, the versified account of
the dean's playfulness with grandees who are used to solemnity.
But the success of the genre depends on the reader's confidence
in the poet's lack of affectation, and that confidence is hard for
one to feel here.

A similar ambiguity is evident in a report Swift had written in
May, while George I still reigned. Swift certainly wished to
appear above the battle, cunningly sceptical of the effectiveness
of political intrigue. At the same time he could scarcely enjoy
access to the court of the Prince without trying to direct it
toward some tangible benefit for his friends, his nation, or
indeed himself. A letter to Sheridan, bristling with political
gossip, shows us a Swift immersed in the drama to which he
claimed to feel indifferent:

We are here in a strange situation; a firm, settled resolution to
assault the present administration, and break it if possible. It is
certain that [Walpole] is peevish and disconcerted, stoops to the
vilest offices of hiring scoundrels to write billingsgate of the lowest
and most prostitute kind, and has none but beasts and blockheads
for his pen-men, whom he pays in ready guineas very liberally. I am
in high displeasure with him and his partisans; a great man, who was
very kind to me last year, doth not take the least notice of me at the
[Prince's] court, and there hath not been one of them to see me. I am
advised by all my friends not to go to France, (as I intended for two
months) for fear of their vengefulness in a manner which they cannot
execute here.—I reckon there will be a warm winter, wherein my
comfort is, I shall have no concern.[2]

---

[1] *Poems* II. 409–10.
[2] 13 May 1727; Williams III. 207; I have emended the corrupt text.

Parliament had met in January, months before Swift's arrival; and then for the first time Walpole had faced a session of the Commons with a strong opposition united against him. *The Craftsman* of 27 January had published 'The Vision of Camelick', a heavy-handed, transparent allegory of the Prime Minister's corruption, which maddened Walpole. In March, he and Pulteney had attacked each other mercilessly in Parliament. Meanwhile, Bolingbroke had managed to win over the Duchess of Kendal and secured an audience with the King, which his majesty promptly revealed to Walpole, but only in the vaguest terms.

The striking mark of Swift's indulgence in politics was his willingness to contribute a pamphlet to the Pulteney–Bolingbroke campaign. Some time before 18 May,[1] he had begun composing an essay in the form of a letter to the writer of the *Occasional Paper* (which was a cadet of the *Craftsman*). The not very persuasive doctrine of the piece was that a ministry supported by illiterate apologists could not be sound. But Swift's focal image almost convinces us: 'I always thought the lion was hard set, when he chose the ass for his trumpeter.'[2] Swift worked closely with Bolingbroke, who made suggestions which Swift incorporated into the text.[3] As usual in the propaganda of Walpole's opponents, the great theme was 'corruption', or the use of bribery to keep men in line. A related theme is Walpole's secretive mishandling of the nation's finances; another, the condemnation of the government's appeasement of France and Spain. But Swift harped upon the bad writing of those who supported the ministry: 'scurrility, slander, and billingsgate'.[4] It is thin material, lacking freshness of insight or expression; and one does not regret that Swift failed to complete the essay. Bolingbroke may have seen its essential weakness and discouraged him. It is also possible that events overtook the

---

[1] The date is set by Bolingbroke's letter, *ibid.*, p. 211. Notice the echo of the words 'billingsgate' and 'guineas', used in the letter of 13 May to Sheridan.

[2] Davis v. 97.

[3] See Bolingbroke's letters of 18 May and 6 Jun. 1727 to Swift; Williams III. 211, 212–13.

[4] Davis v. 94.

essayist, and that he was advised not to attack those in power. For now at last the change of changes took place.

Parliament having risen on 15 May, King George left for Hanover on 3 June. Eight days later, he died of apoplexy. A messenger who rode post-haste from Germany gave the news to Walpole. The Prime Minister's coach took him at once to Richmond, where the new king lay in bed with Caroline. A lady-in-waiting had to call the sleeper. He came ill-tempered and half-dressed. Walpole sank to his knees, addressed him as 'majesty', and asked from whom the minister himself should take his orders. George II, who had long hated Walpole, said, 'From Sir Spencer Compton at Chiswick,' and returned to the bedroom while a dispirited Walpole rode back to London. It looked as if the Speaker of the House of Commons was to be the head of the government.[1]

The news flew across England. Swift's friends raised their crests, preened themselves, and fluttered their wings. Behind the voluble philosophy of men like Bolingbroke was suddenly revealed, as Pope said, 'the strange spirit and life, with which men broken and disappointed resume their hopes, their solicitations, their ambitions'.[2] His lordship wrote to Swift (for whom the royal death must have foreshadowed Stella's),

> There would not be common sense in your going into France at this juncture.... Much less ought you to think of such an unmeaning journey, when the opportunity of quitting Ireland for England is I believe fairly before you. To hanker after a court is fit for men with blue ribbands, pompous titles, gorgeous estates. It is below either you or me, one of whom never made his fortune, and the other's turned rotten at the very moment it grew ripe. But without hankering, without assuming a suppliant dependent air, you may spend in England all the time you can be absent from Ireland, and faire la guerre a l'orgeuil.[3]

Swift's emotions were certainly drawn into such hopes and schemes. He wrote to Sheridan,

[1] Plumb II. 154–64.   [2] 24 Jun. 1727; Sherburn II. 437.
[3] 17 Jun. 1727; Williams III. 215–16. The French words mean, 'make war on arrogance'—i.e., on Walpole, a man with a blue ribbon, pompous titles and gorgeous estate.

The talk now is for a moderating scheme, wherein nobody shall be used the worse or better for being called Whig or Tory, and the King hath received both with great equality; showing civilities to several who are openly known to be the latter. I prevailed with a dozen that we should go in a line to kiss the [King's] and [Queen's] hands. We have now done with repining, if we shall be used well, and not baited as formerly; we all agree in it, and if things do not mend it is not our faults: We have made our offers: If otherwise, we are as we were. It is agreed the ministry will be changed, but the others will have a soft fall; although the [King] must be excessive generous if he forgives the treatment of some people.[1]

The details of the scene, when Swift kissed his new rulers' hands, came out in a Dublin newspaper:

The Reverend Dr Jonathan Swift, Dean of St Patrick's in Dublin, having been to make his compliments to their majesties, express'd the utmost loyalty and affection for their majesties persons and government, with an address peculiar to himself, representing at the same time the strict adherence of his majesty's faithful subjects of Ireland to his royal person and family, with their most grateful acknowledgements for favours granted to that kingdom; the continuation whereof they will endeavour to preserve by a distinguish'd loyalty, as they have hitherto been remarkable for in the worst of times, hoping the participation of the benign influence of his majesty's shining vertues &c: Which declaration, their majesties received with the utmost satisfaction, shewing a particular regard to the welfare of the kingdom of Ireland, as well as to the merit of that truly great man, and he had the honour to kiss their majesties hands.[2]

The unction and irony of the account point to Swift as the ultimate source and suggest the strength of his will to help Ireland as well as his desire to co-operate with Pulteney and Bolingbroke. But the court went another way. Caroline, who dominated her husband, was determined to keep Walpole in power. Compton was effective as a Speaker of the House of Commons, but he was weak and unsure as a chief minister. The King quickly discovered that Walpole could supply pleasures that were more solid than vengeance. On 15 June he had a long

---

[1] 24 Jun. 1727; Williams III. 219.
[2] *Dublin Journal*, 8 Jul. 1727.

talk with Sir Robert about the civil list and realized that his income might be larger with that servant's help than without. The next day, the French ambassador told his government that the old ministry would continue; and Swift proved to be out of touch, to a degree that meant more than one mischance for him.

This may be the time when he began writing two pieces on English affairs which he never completed: 'An Account of the Court and Empire of Japan' and 'A Proposal for Virtue'.[1] They reflect similar preoccupations and seem closely related. The account of Japan is a thinly disguised analysis of English politics at the accession of George II. The proposal for virtue sounds like the writer's notion of a way out of the impasse described in the 'Account'.

Swift obviously hoped to publish 'An Account of ... Japan' while the new king and his Parliament were still undecided about policies and leadership. Swift does not address the Whigs; for he stigmatizes them as furious intriguers. He also heaps contempt on George I and represents the Tories as favoured by a great majority of the people.[2] Walpole receives the usual vituperation; his power, according to Swift, derives only from his mastery of parliamentary procedure and a limitless use of bribery. 'The whole system of his ministry was corruption,' Swift says.[3]

But he praises George II and Sir Thomas Hanmer, the Hanoverian churchman who had attached himself to the Prince of Wales, but who faded out of public affairs after 1727. Swift also avoids singling out Pulteney or Bolingbroke. I suspect that he did not wish to weaken his case by sounding like one of their spokesmen. He was offering advice directly to the King.

The fragment closes with a speech in which Walpole explains why the nation must be governed by various forms of bribery: by

---

[1] Davis v. 99–107; XIV. 14–15. Both were probably written in 1727. The 'Account' ends with an imaginary scene based on rumours of the interview between George II and Walpole on 15 Jun. 1727; and it breaks off as if the speedy re-establishment of Walpole in the days that followed left Swift unable to carry out his plan. For the date of the 'Proposal', see George Mayhew, 'Swift's First Will', *HLQ* 21 (1958), 306, and his review of Davis XIV in *PQ* 48 (1969), 399.

[2] Davis v. 99, 101, 105.   [3] *Ibid.*, p. 102.

pensions, sinecures, and simple gifts of money. The argument runs that since the people are naturally Tory in sympathy, and since the Tories wish to bring in the Pretender, consequently the electors and Members of Parliament must be paid to support the House of Hanover. Walpole also promises that if the King will leave the government to him, his majesty will never be troubled by the ennui of administration and will also receive an income greater than that of his predecessors.[1]

At the end of the fragmentary 'Account', the King gives an order that some other counsellor should speak either to confirm or to oppose the principles of the chief minister. Although we do not then learn what the response might be, we may infer the gist of it from a set of rhetorical questions put to the chief minister by his sovereign. The tendency of the questions is to imply that the officers chosen through bribery will only want further payments to keep them steady. Yet a rational foreign policy should not depend on gifts to the ministers of other courts but on prudence and real strength. Above all, if the Members of Parliament consisted of men with substantial property in land, they would naturally follow policies that were good for the kingdom.[2]

That these are the truths which Swift would have recommended in response to Walpole's cynicism, we may gather from the notes for 'A Proposal for Virtue'.[3] Here Swift reflects on the loss of national wealth to pensioners, mercenary voters, placemen, etc. He declares that if the King called a free Parliament chosen from landed gentlemen, he would save the nation great sums of money, he would establish a government naturally inclined toward wise policies, and he would be able to rule his people with less labour and no art. 'What can a King reasonably ask that a Parliament will refuse him?' Swift demands.[4]

The conception of the 'Proposal' is not ironical. But Swift realized that it might sound too hopeful; and he could smile at himself for advancing it. In a letter to Bolingbroke, he made a mock-solemn reference to the scheme, which suggests his ambiguous point of view. On the one hand, he believes that if it

---

[1] *Ibid.*, p. 106.   [2] *Ibid.*, pp. 103–4.   [3] *Ibid.*, XIV. 14–15.   [4] *Ibid.*, p. 14.

were honestly tried, it could work; on the other hand, he knows it is most unlikely to be tried. So he turns the whole project into a joke. Yet even while doing so, he seriously objects to the notion that 'human creatures' are not more virtuous in one era than in another. The present age, he implies, is abnormally vicious, to the point where men are not afraid to acknowledge their corruption.[1]

The 'Account' and the 'Proposal' are fascinating as proof of that faith in rational self-interest which was the upper side of Swift's ambivalence toward common human nature. Depravity, for him, was neither easier nor more comfortable than reasonable virtue; and yet it was the choice of men who had nothing to lose and all to gain from self-reform. When he asked, 'What can a King reasonably ask that a Parliament will refuse him?' he may have been complimenting George II. He was certainly brushing aside his own experience of courts and princes, and was showing how vulnerable he remained to the temptation of influencing the sources of power.

Yet Swift would not admit his temptation openly, and asked Sheridan to say in Dublin that the dean never went to court.[2] This is odd enough when he also said that after staying a week in Twickenham, he would go to London again 'just to see the [Queen], and so come back hither'.[3] And yet he professed to feel detached from the bustle: 'Here are a thousand schemes wherein they would have me engaged, which I embrace but coldly, because I like none of them.'[4] In August, when deafness and vertigo seized him at Twickenham, Swift told Sheridan,

The [King] and [Queen] come in two days to our neighbourhood, and there I shall be expected, and cannot go; which however, is none of my grievances, for I had rather be absent, and have now got too good an excuse.[5]

But a month later, on the eve of his departure from England, while Swift was still disabled by illness, he composed a proper

[1] 5 Apr. 1729; Sherburn III. 29. See my discussion above, pp. 450–1.
[2] 1 Jul. 1727; Williams III. 222.   [3] *Ibid.*, p. 221.
[4] *Ibid.*   [5] 12 Aug. 1727; *ibid.*, p. 229.

courtier's letter to Mrs Howard, even resorting to formulae:

> I hope you will favour me so far as to present my most humble duty
> to the Queen and to tell her majesty my sorrow that my disorder was
> of such a nature as to make me incapable of attending her, as she was
> pleased to permit me. I shall pass the remainder of my life with the
> utmost gratitude for her majesty's favours.[1]

Yet along with this farewell bow went a different and more
sincere disappointment. For Swift's prospect of a summer in
France had now faded into the haze of political vapour. Swift
might have made Pope's comment on the solicitations and
ambitions of broken men.[2] But the effects of the old king's death
not only involved him in futile scheming; they also had frustrated elaborate plans. In mid-June Swift had been about to
embark for the continent. Bolingbroke stood ready to provide
introductions.[3] Voltaire, who was in England, supplied him
with letters to Frenchmen of great distinction, who would have
taken him into a brilliant society.[4] Arbuthnot's brother in Paris
waited to entertain him.[5] On 15 June Swift came up from
Twickenham to prepare for the voyage which should have commenced six days later.[6] But the forces he relied on conspired
to baffle him. Once George I was known to be dead, all human
pressures turned the prudent adventurer away from his modest
escapade:

> I came to town in order to begin my journey. But I was desired to
> delay it, and I then determined it a second time: when upon some
> new incidents, I was with great vehemence dissuaded from it by
> certain persons whom I could not disobey.[7]

His regrets haunted him over the weeks, the months, the years.
'If the [King] had lived but ten days longer, I should be now at

---

[1] ?14 Sept. 1727; *ibid.*, pp. 238–9.
[2] Sherburn II. 437; see above, p. 527.   [3] Williams III. 213.
[4] 16 Jun. 1727; *ibid.*, pp. 214–15. In view of Voltaire's letter to Swift, it is hard not to
assume that the two men met during Swift's stay in England. But we have no proof that
they did so. The letter of 14 Dec. 1727 from Voltaire to Swift sounds as if they had not
met (*ibid.*, p. 256).
[5] *Ibid.*, p. 253.
[6] I.e., ten days after George I died; see *ibid.*, p. 222.
[7] 24 Jun. 1727, to Sheridan; *ibid.*, pp. 218–19.

Paris,' he wrote mournfully on 1 July.[1] 'Plusieurs accidens, qui sont arrivé m'empêcheront de faire le voyage de la France presentement,' he lamented bitterly to Desfontaines,

> et je ne suis plus assez jeune pour me flatter de retrouver un autre occasion. Je scais, que j'y perds beaucoup, et je suis tres sensible a cette perte. L'unique consolation que me reste, c'est de songer, que j'en supporteray mieux le pais, au quel la fortune m'a condamné.[2]

Considering the long, difficult, uncomfortable journeys that Swift was to undertake within Ireland, one cannot easily understand why he closed the French door so sharply. He seems not merely to have accepted defeat but to have embraced it. There was certainly a part of his character that found merit in self-denial disguised as loss of opportunity.

Meanwhile, as if to make Ireland yet more disgusting to its ambivalent first citizen, a quarrel arose between Swift and Archbishop King. Although the two men were firm allies, and respected each other's extraordinary services to church and state, they were also jockeying each other for what might be called moral pre-eminence. The archbishop liked to signalize his authority over the dean. Swift liked to demonstrate his independence of his superior. Behind their hate–love lay decades in which Swift had looked to a paternal figure for blessings which his grace had reserved for compliant protégés and blood kin.

The new quarrel sprang from Swift's failure to supply a proxy for the archbishop's visitation of St Patrick's Cathedral, which took place while the dean was in England. King's attitude of schoolmasterly approval toward a man who disliked seeming his pupil shows in the terms he used praising Swift the year before: 'he has behaved himself very well in his station.'[3] Although the visitation was mainly a ceremonious occasion, King was not one to surrender a tittle of what he believed to be his due; and when no document was produced in Swift's name, he adjourned the whole visitation while 'a rule [was] entered that a proxy be exhibited within a month'.[4]

---

[1] *Ibid.*, p. 222.　　[2] *Ibid.*, pp. 226–7.
[3] 30 May 1726, to Annesley; see above, p. 483.　　[4] Williams III. 210.

Swift duly received word of the débâcle, and responded with the bitterness of a child denied his birthright: suddenly the underside of the ambivalence is uppermost, and a quarter-century's accumulation of resentment bursts out. That history, precedent, or justice lay on Swift's side is doubtful; but the rhetoric of the passion is splendid: he exalts a private squabble to the level of a dispute between nations, and one may infer the source of his energy when he did write about national politics:

If your grace can find, in any of your old records or of ours, that a proxy was ever demanded for a Dean of St Patrick's, you will have some reason to insist upon it: But, as it is a thing wholly new and unheard of, let the consequences be what they will, I shall never comply with it.... My proceeding shall be only upon one maxim: never to yield to an oppression, to justify which no precedent can be produced. I see very well how personal all this proceeding is; and how, from the very moment of the Queen's death, your grace hath thought fit to take every opportunity of giving me all sorts of uneasiness, without ever giving me, in my whole life, one single mark of your favour, beyond common civilities. And, if it were not below a man of spirits to make complaints, I could date them from six and twenty years past. This hath something in it the more extraordinary, because during some years when I was thought to have credit with those in power, I employed it to the utmost for your service, with great success, where it could be most useful against many violent enemies you then had, however unjustly, by which I got more ill-will than by any other action in my life, I mean from my friends. My Lord, I have lived, and by the grace of God will die, an enemy to servitude and slavery of all kinds: And I believe, at the same time, that persons of such a disposition will be the most ready to pay obedience wherever it is due. Your grace hath often said, you would never infringe any of our liberties. I will call back nothing of what is past: I will forget, if I can, that you mentioned to me a licence to be absent. Neither my age, health, humour, or fortune, qualify me for little brangles.... It is a little hard, that, the occasion of my journey hither, being partly for the advantage of that kingdom, partly on account of my health, partly on business of importance to me, and partly to see my friends, I cannot enjoy the quiet of a few months, without your grace interposing to disturb it. But, I thank God, the civilities of those in power here, who allow themselves to be my

[534]

professed adversaries, make some atonement for the unkindness of others, who have so many reasons to be my friends.[1]

And so forth. The posthumous son, the disappointed protégé of Temple, and the champion rejected by Queen Anne speak here along with the Dean of St Patrick's. One suspects that Swift was struggling to convince himself. Certainly the archbishop found his eloquence easy to resist: 'I had yours without date time or place,' he replied drily. 'For answer to it I am advised that it is necessary you should appear either in person or by proxy. If a proxy come any time this month it will do.' He apologized rationally for the shortness of his message and left it at that.[2]

Luckily, Swift's friends did not encourage his self-indulgence. He told Sheridan that if the archbishop carried the affair to the stage of litigation, the dean would have an appeal made. 'I will spend a hundred or two hundred pounds', he said, 'rather than be enslaved, or betray a right which I do not value three-pence, but my successors may.' Yet at the same time he also stated the case to his chancellor, Edward Synge, and instructed him to 'proceed as he shall be advised'.[3] In the last we hear of the case, it dwindles to a compromise. The chancellor, son of King's friend the Archbishop of Tuam—and a man indebted to King for his own preferment—was not likely to recommend defiance. He wrote a long letter to Swift which could not have been inflammatory. 'Pray, tell [Mr Synge] that I return him great thanks,' Swift wrote to Sheridan, 'and will leave the visiting affair to his discretion.'[4] I assume that Synge was discreet.

Although Swift declared that true enemies in England were kinder to him than false friends at home, the sweetest honey of friendship that he tasted during the spring and summer of 1727 flowed from Twickenham. Pope's hospitality and good nature grew more impressive as the illnesses of the poet, his mother, and their guest kept calling for attention.

---

[1] 18 May 1727; Williams III. 210–11; almost certainly printed from a dated draft and therefore differing in unknown ways from what the archbishop saw. King, below, says Swift's letter was undated.
[2] 3 Jun. 1727; *ibid.*, p. 212.   [3] 24 Jun. 1727; *ibid.*, p. 219.   [4] *Ibid.*, p. 222.

A frequent occasion for anxiety and care was the peculiar ills Swift's flesh was heir to. Physical frailty blended itself with the elegiac mood of these months in England. Not only did Swift believe he would never come back. He also envisaged himself as an old man with a short span of stricken years remaining. When sickness fell, it seemed to verify an intuition, to give substance to the mood of disappointment. Deafness descended about 5 August; vertigo followed in less than a week:

> I was so very ill, that yesterday I took a hearty vomit, and though I now totter, yet I think I am a thought better; but what will be the event I know not.... Since my dinner my giddiness is much better, and my deafness a hair's breadth not so bad. 'Tis just as usual, worst in the morning and at evening. I will be very temperate; and in the midst of peaches, figs, nectarines, and mulberries, I touch not a bit.[1]

Unable to converse with Swift, Pope worked on the *Dunciad*, warmly encouraged by his guest. Gay spent time with them and worked on *The Beggar's Opera*. But the deafness continued. Instead of the simple embarrassment which others might have felt, Swift underwent acute humiliation and said he would not stay in Pope's house if the attacks went on. He could not bear to think of hanging about in Twickenham, avoiding the friends who came to see him, and adding the work of a nurse to the duties of his host. 'I want to be at home', he told Sheridan, 'where I can turn you out, or let you in, as I think best.'[2] Pope told Lord Oxford, 'The dean is so much out of order, and withal so deaf, that he has conversed with no body, and fled all company.'[3] Ten days later, the report was no better:

> [The] person whose health you enquire after, is not at all on the mending hand. He was for two days only, better, and ever since very bad: and the attendance I owe him will keep me here till I see some alteration.[4]

Dr Arbuthnot examined the patient and reported that he would soon be well.[5] But the sick man could not prolong his dependence. He considered various alternatives if the illness

---

[1] 12 Aug. 1727, to Sheridan; *ibid.*, p. 229. [2] *Ibid.*
[3] 15 Aug. 1727; Sherburn II. 443. [4] *Ibid.*, p. 444. [5] *Ibid.*, p. 445.

continued. His favourite plan was to ask his cousin Patty Rolt—now Mrs Lancelot—to take care of him at her house in New Bond Street or somewhere else near London;[1] and this is the scheme he finally adopted. Slipping away from Twickenham at the end of August, he moved first to London and then to Hammersmith.[2] Pope came to see him regularly, and Swift soon felt well enough to think of returning to Ireland.

The separation produced strong expressions of attachment from Pope. The poet's language became womanly in its affection as he reproached Swift for creeping away under camouflage to avoid burdening his host:

> I can't tell what to say to you; I only feel that I wish you well in every circumstance of life: that 'tis almost as good to be hated, as to be loved, considering the pain it is to minds of any tender turn, to find themselves so utterly impotent to do any good, or give any ease to those who deserve most from us.... I was sorry to find you could think yourself easier in any house than in mine, though at the same time I can allow for a tenderness in your way of thinking, even when it seemed to want that tenderness. I can't explain my meaning; perhaps you know it.[3]

We know that Pope liked to sound virtuous in his letters, and we know he may have tampered with this one to dignify its style.[4] But a comparison of his language to Swift with his language to other correspondents deepens one's impression of his attachment. In a letter which Pope did not edit, he told Sheridan, after Swift left Twickenham,

> Upon pretence of some very unavoidable occasions, he went to London four days since, where I see him as often as he will let me. I was extremely concerned at his opiniatrety[5] in leaving me; but he shall not get rid of the friend, though he may of his house.[6]

We must not simplify Pope's character. He was perfectly capable of feeling so tender without missing opportunities of em-

<hr>

[1] Williams III. 229.

[2] Sherburn II. 448 and n. 2. He left Twickenham on 31 Aug. On 29 Aug. he writes from Twickenham, on 2 Sept. from London (Williams III. 234–5).

[3] 2 Oct. 1727; Sherburn II. 447.   [4] Cf. *ibid.*, I. xiv–xv.

[5] Stubbornness.   [6] 6 Sept. 1727; Sherburn II. 445.

ploying Swift's friendship to advance schemes of his own. For
Pope, usefulness, conscious or unconscious, was a natural part of
amiability—as perhaps it is for most of us.

For Swift, meanwhile, plan succeeded plan. If the illness
turned manageable, he might stay the winter in England, or go
to France after all, especially if Stella died before he could
travel.[1] Yet he was hoping to begin a homeward journey in mid-
September.[2] I suspect that the symptoms of his own illness, like
the confusion of his travel plans, had much to do with the
hideous emotional strain which I have hardly mentioned but
which troubled Swift during every day of the long visit to
England.

The darkness of Stella's pain and failing strength had stood
before him from the moment he arrived in England. Through
the spring and summer he had received the terrifying bulletins
from Sheridan and Worrall. His anxiety rose to the point where
Sheridan, alarmed by the frantic tone, asked Pope for advice.[3] If
Swift could hope to have time with Stella, living and speaking,
he wished to go to Dublin when his disabilities let him travel. If
she were to die before he could reach her, he wished to
strengthen himself in England or France. His responses to the
warnings expose his deepest nature and show yet again that the
irony and harshness we think of as Swiftian were casings for a
soft vulnerability.

Early in September, while he was still at Twickenham, he had
written to Sheridan,

> I have had your letter of the nineteenth, and expect, before you read
> this, to receive another from you with the most fatal news that can
> ever come to me, unless I should be put to death for some ignomini-
> ous crime. I continue very ill with my giddiness and deafness, of
> which I had two days' intermission, but since worse, and I shall be
> perfectly content if God shall please to call me away at this time.
> Here is a triple cord of friendship broke, which hath lasted thirty
> years, twenty-four of which in Ireland. I beg if you have not writ to
> me before you get this, to tell me no particulars, but the event in

[1] Williams III. 234.   [2] *Ibid.*, p. 229.
[3] Sherburn II. 445.

general: my weakness, my age, my friendship[1] will bear no more. . . .
I will tell you sincerely, that if I were younger, and in health, or in
hopes of it, I would endeavour to divert my mind by all methods in
order to pass my life in quiet; but I now want only three months of
sixty. I am strongly visited with a disease that will at last cut me off, if
I should this time escape, if not, I have but a poor remainder, that is
below any wise man's valuing. I do not intend to return to Ireland so
soon as I proposed; I would not be there in the very midst of grief.[2]

The surprising thought of an ignominious crime suggests the
guilt Swift felt for his treatment of Esther Johnson. Another
account from Sheridan produced a still more bitter outburst.
Swift had fallen back on his custom of delaying the reading of
letters that might tell him what he most dreaded, and thereby he
characteristically extended his torment. He thought of repeating what he had done when Vanessa died—making a journey to
'forget myself'.

If I had any tolerable health, I would go this moment to Ireland; yet
I think I would not, considering the news I daily expect to hear from
you. I have just received yours of August 24; I kept it an hour in my
pocket, with all the suspense of a man who expected to hear the
worst news that fortune could give him; and at the same time was
not able to hold up my head. These are the perquisites of living long:
The last act of life is always a tragedy at best; but it is a bitter
aggravation to have one's best friend go before one. . . . I long knew
that our dear friend had not the *stamina vitae*; but my friendship
could not arm me against this accident although I foresaw it. . . .
I know not whether it be an addition to my grief or no, that I am
now extremely ill; for it would have been a reproach to me to be in
perfect health, when such a friend is desperate. I do profess, upon my
salvation, that the distressed and desperate condition of our friend,
makes life indifferent to me, who by course of nature have so little
left, that I do not think it worth the time to struggle; yet I should
think, according to what hath been formerly, that I may happen to
overcome this present disorder; and to what advantage? Why, to see
the loss of that person for whose sake life was only worth preserving.
I brought both those friends over, that we might be happy together
as long as God should please; the knot is broken, and the remaining
person you know, has ill answered the end; and the other who is now
to be lost, was all that is valuable.[3]

[1] I.e., love for Stella. [2] 29 Aug. 1727; Williams III. 234.
[3] 2 Sept. 1727, to Sheridan; *ibid.*, p. 236.

The turn of phrase, 'it would have been a reproach', in the reference to his own illness strengthens one's suspicion that the vertigo and deafness were in part acts of self-punishment. (The aetiology of Ménière's disease is mysterious.) But the most remarkable of all Swift's expressions broke forth in a letter to Worrall. It suddenly occurred to the Dean of St Patrick's that the death of an unmarried woman in his house, even while he was away, could only blacken his reputation. He had cautioned his housekeeper to make other arrangements. He now went so far as to deliver a further instruction to Worrall, shifting into Latin for secrecy and also, I think, as a half-conscious mark of embarrassment:

> I desire to know where my two friends lodge. I gave a caution to Mrs Brent, that it might not be in domi decanus, quoniam hoc minime decet, uti manifestum est, habeo enim malignos, qui sinistrè hoc interpretabuntur, si eveniet (quod deus avertat) ut illic moriatur.[1]

He said he was still unfit to travel. But soon there was an intermission of health, and he decided to take advantage of it. On Monday, 18 September 1727, Swift, along with his servant Watt, boarded the Chester coach from an inn in Aldergate Street, and started for Dublin by way of Coventry, where they stopped the next day. His deafness faded; and when they reached Chester, Swift was fortunate enough to meet Captain Lawson, who commanded the government yacht sailing between the nearby port of Parkgate and Dublin. Lawson offered the Dean of St Patrick's a place in the yacht; but Swift thought he might have to wait too long until it sailed. So he preferred to hire a guide, ride to Holyhead, and hope to catch the packetboat there.[2]

The dénouement was more outrageous than Swift would have thought bearable, a grimly appropriate close to the ordeal of his stay in England. Friday morning, 22 September, they left

---

[1] 12 Sept. 1727; *ibid.*, p. 237. The carelessness of the Latin (*decanus* for *decani*) reflects his agitation. Translation: 'in the deanery, since that would be most improper, as is evident, for I have enemies who will give it an evil meaning if it happens (which God forbid) that she should die there'.

[2] Sherburn II. 454–5.

Chester on horseback for Holyhead, staying at Ridland that night and near Bangor the next. Sunday morning at 4:00 Swift started on the remaining twenty-two miles. But he felt the burden of his six decades and had to stop for a couple of hours' rest.

Then Watt's horse lost both foreshoes. Next, Swift's horse lost a shoe, and the dean went on foot for more than two rough miles. It being Sunday, a smith was not easy to find. At last they discovered one, left the horses, and walked on to an inn three miles from Holyhead. 'There I stayed an hour, with no ale to be drunk.' He found a boat that could take him to Holyhead, and went on it with Watt. Arriving finally at the port, they were told the maddening news that the packetboat had sailed the day before.[1]

By the Monday, Swift had enough fatigue, anxiety and frustration to unstring a healthy boy. In this worn plight he felt almost frantic. But so he was forced to remain, becalmed at Holyhead, day after day, for just over a week, as he waited until the weather and a sufficient number of passengers might entice the captain of a ship now at anchor to sail to Dublin.

For a while, there was only a single prospective passenger besides himself; and the captain waited:

> Not a soul is yet come to Holyhead, except a young fellow who smiles when he meets me, and would fain be my companion; but it is not come to that yet.[2]

On Tuesday the captain still waited:

> I reckon my self fixed here: and have a mind like Marechall Tallard[3] to take a house and garden.[4]

He had a blank book with him which he had got from Dodington (a tool of Walpole and one of the Lords of the Treasury). To occupy himself during these days of acute anxiety, he made journal entries in this book, recording places he

---

[1] Davis v. 201–3.   [2] *Ibid.*, p. 203.
[3] French general, prisoner of war in England during the War of the Spanish Succession.
[4] Davis v. 204.

[541]

saw, people he talked to, and inns he stayed at. Unconsciously, he began addressing his remarks to friends in Ireland:

> I dare not send my linen to be washed, for fear of being called away at half an hour's warning, and then I must leave them behind me, which is a serious point; in the mean time I am in danger of being lousy, which is a ticklish point. I live at great expense without one comfortable bit or sup. I am afraid of joining with the other passengers for fear of getting acquaintance with Irish. The days are short, and I have five hours at night to spend by myself before I go to bed. I should be glad to converse with farmers or shopkeepers, but none of them speak English. A dog is better company than the vicar, for I remember him of old. What can I do but write everything that comes into my head.[1]

The worst reflection was that he could have avoided the misery by accepting Lawson's offer: 'As it happened, if I had gone straight from Chester to Parkgate, eight miles, I should have been in Dublin on Sunday last.'[2]

Watt provided the stuff of farce. Having been caught in a shower while out walking, Swift drenched his clothes before finding shelter in a Welshwoman's hovel:

> [When] we were in the Welsh cabin, I ordered Watt to take a cloth and wipe my wet gown and cassock—it happened to be a meal bag, and as my gown dried, it was all daubed with flour well cemented with the rain. What do I, but see the gown and cassock well dried in my room, and while Watt was at dinner, I was an hour rubbing the meal out of them, and did it exactly; he is just come up, and I have gravely bid him take them down to rub them, and I wait whether he will find out what I have been doing. The rogue is come up in six minutes with my gown, and says there were but few spots (though he saw a thousand at first).[3]

Here speaks the compiler of *Directions to Servants*.

Swift walked and climbed among the rocks. He was caught in the rain. He kept his journal. He wrote verses:

> I never was in haste before
> To reach that slavish hateful shore. . . .
> But now, the danger of a friend

[1] *Ibid.*   [2] *Ibid.*, p. 206. Swift was writing on Wednesday.
[3] *Ibid.*, pp. 206–7.

On whom my fears and hopes depend
Absent from whom all climes are curst
With whom I'm happy in the worst,
With rage impatient makes me wait
A passage to a land I hate.[1]

More passengers appeared. But on Wednesday the captain still waited. The rain grew heavier and stopped Swift from walking:

I am in the worst part of Wales under the very worst circumstances; afraid of a relapse; in utmost solitude; impatient for the condition of our friend; not a soul to converse with, hindered from exercise by rain, cooped up in a room not half so large as one of the deanery closets. My room smokes into the bargain.[2]

Yet in the smoky room, ironically enough, Swift lost what remained of the labyrinthine vertigo; perhaps he had enough external discomfort to feel on a par with his dying friend. He now toyed with venturing to make a friend of the young man.

On Thursday they seemed to sail. Half an hour out, they met a wind rising against them, but the captain persisted. The wind also persisted. So the boat turned back, docking again at eight o'clock on this black, wet night. Swift would not risk the accidents of returning to his room in the dark. Alone of all the passengers, he spent the night on board. In the morning he went back to the inn. 'I must stay, and get in a new stock of patience.'

On Sunday or Monday (1 or 2 October) they sailed again, and this time made it safely to Ireland. But the port was Carlingford, co. Louth, sixty miles from Dublin. Swift and Watt had to ride through a region of poverty and desolation, on lazy, dull post horses, over a road that offered bad inns or none. The relief came some distance from Dublin, when Sheridan appeared before them, riding out to meet the dean. Swift's last letter, posted at Chester, had made it clear that he would be sailing from Holyhead;[3] and I suppose Sheridan had early information of the boat's landing at Carlingford. Swift probably got to Dublin on 4 October.[4]

---

[1] *Poems* II. 420.   [2] Davis V. 207; omissions not indicated.
[3] *Ibid.*, p. 208; Sherburn II. 454–5, 460.
[4] There is a pamphlet with a speech dated 4 Oct. 1727, congratulating Swift on his safe arrival; see Trinity College, Dublin, Irish Pamphlets 1725–7 (A. 7. 5), p. 195.

Chapter Five

THE DEATH OF A FRIEND

I. STELLA

The return to Dublin meant a return to vistas of desolation. So large a number of the Irish people existed chronically near starvation that any failure of crops—especially of potatoes—brought down disaster.[1] Near-famine was a common state. Many landlords wanted their land to be free for pasture, and discouraged tenants from using the plough. The Parliament of Ireland had enacted laws forbidding the conversion of pasture into tillage. In 1716 and 1719 the members tried to invalidate such laws and encourage agriculture, but the English Privy Council blocked these efforts.[2] An Act requiring the tillage of five out of every hundred acres was finally passed in 1727, but could not be enforced.[3] Most of the leases in the counties of Dublin, Wicklow, Kildare, Carlow, Meath, and Kilkenny had articles restricting cultivation; so the amount of grain produced in the country declined while the price rose.[4] In Dublin, grain could at times fetch a higher price than in London.[5]

The first acute famine of the century struck the poor of Ireland in 1727. Primate Boulter, detested by Swift, would sooner have hidden the truth than exposed it, for he had no reason to weaken the government's claim to be helping the kingdom. Yet he was a man of the deepest charity, and his

---

[1] George O'Brien, *The Economic History of Ireland in the Eighteenth Century* (Dublin and London, 1918), p. 102.

[2] Ferguson, pp. 47–8.

[3] Alice E. Murray, *A History of the Commercial and Financial Relations between England and Ireland* (London, 1903), p. 143.

[4] *Ibid.*, p. 142–3.

[5] Cf. the letter from Archbishop King to Archbishop Wake, 15 Nov. 1725.

description of what happened is lurid. He lamented

> the great damage to this kingdom by landlords tying up their
> tenants from ploughing, the throwing so many families out of work
> that might be employed by tillage, and the terrible scarcity next to a
> famine that a great part of the kingdom now labours under by the
> corn not yielding well last year, and to which we are liable upon any
> the least accident in our harvest.[1]

Boulter reported the reduction of hardworking families to
starving beggary:

> [Last] year the dearness of corn was such that thousands of families
> quitted their habitations to seek bread elsewhere, and many hun-
> dreds perished; this year the poor had consumed their potatoes,
> which is their winter subsistence, near two months sooner than
> ordinary, and are already through the dearness of corn, in that
> want, that in some places they begin already to quit their
> habitations.[2]

This was in the spring. In the cold season at the end of the year,
the scene darkened. When grain was bought in the well-
supplied south, to be sent for relief to the suffering north, worried
mobs stopped its removal.[3] Swift and Archbishop King were to
bear vivid witness to the accuracy of Boulter's impressions.

Meanwhile, Swift's ailments had not abandoned him. After
nine weeks of deafness and vertigo in England, he passed a
tolerable autumn in Dublin. But the cold weather revived his
twin afflictions, and they lingered with him from December to
March. Although he had periods of remission, he declared in
February that he had been 'these ten weeks confined by my old
disorders of deafness and giddiness'.[4]

It was this cheerless winter that ended Stella's ordeal. Swift
got home from England in time to look wanly for almost four
months on the wasting face of his beloved friend. To avoid
malicious gossip, the ladies had been moved into lodgings near

---

[1] Boulter I. 187–8; 20 Jul. 1727. Cf. pp. 221–2. (Or, in the Dublin edition, pp. 151 and
181.)
[2] 7 Mar. 1728 (dated 1727); *ibid.*, p. 226 (Dublin, p. 181).
[3] *Ibid.*, pp. 285, 287 (Dublin, pp. 228, 230).
[4] Williams III. 263.

the deanery, where Mrs Worrall and other intimates helped Mrs Dingley to nurse the pained, weakening invalid.

While she was failing, Swift visited her not only as an inconsolable lover but also as a priest. He prayed with her and copied out the words he used on some of these familiar occasions. In them, besides teaching Christian resignation and Christian hope, he made appeals which, spoken in his own person, sound weighted for himself as well as miserable for Stella. About a fortnight after his return Swift composed an eloquent prayer which gave voice to his bleak anxiety. He mentions Stella's 'long, constant weakly state of health' and the firmness of mind with which she endured bodily pains—pains which he beseeched God to soften. But the focus of the prayer shifts easily from the sufferer to her desperate lover; the cry for mercy is as much for himself as for the woman to whom mortality had become so harsh:

> O all-powerful being, the least motion of whose will can create or destroy a world; pity us the mournful friends of thy distressed servant, who sink under the weight of her present condition, and the fear of losing the most valuable of our friends: restore her to us, O Lord, if it be thy gracious will, or inspire us with constancy and resignation, to support ourselves under so heavy an affliction.... And if thou wilt soon take her to thyself, turn our thoughts rather upon that felicity which we hope she shall enjoy, than upon that unspeakable loss we shall endure.[1]

It was not God alone to whom Swift addressed these words. Stella herself was to hear them and to be assured by them of his abiding attachment. Soon he wrote another prayer. The pain of the illness sharpened. Stella's composure was not always unruffled; and Swift's fears for his own security were almost as piercing as his desire for hers:

> Give her strength, O Lord, to support her weakness; and patience to endure her pains without repining at thy correction. Forgive every rash and inconsiderate expression, which her anguish may at any time force from her tongue.

---

[1] Davis v. 253–4.

Again the speaker becomes the subject:

> Let not our grief afflict her mind, and thereby have an ill effect on her present distempers. Forgive the sorrow and weakness of those among us, who sink under the grief and terror of losing so dear and useful a friend.

Yet once more he wrote another prayer:

> We beseech thee also, O Lord, of thy infinite goodness to remember the good actions of this thy servant; that the naked she hath clothed, the hungry she hath fed, the sick and fatherless whom she hath relieved, may be reckoned according to thy gracious promise, as if they had been done unto thee.[1]

Swift's duty and affection probably separated him from Stella on the day (Saturday, 30 December) when she made a new and final will; for although this was modelled on his own, he would have feared the unseemliness of his witnessing or executing the document. Her body was to be set (where his could lie beside it) under the great aisle of the cathedral. Her fortune, after the death of her mother and sister, was to provide the stipend for a chaplain for Dr Steevens' Hospital, then under construction. We may assume that Swift drew up the will. He was one of the trustees of the charitable fund for building the hospital, and most of the other trustees were his friends. The most active of them, the distinguished surgeon Thomas Proby, was—with his wife—among Stella's intimates. Her executors again were near to Swift: Thomas Sheridan, John Grattan, Francis Corbet, John Rochfort.[2]

A month later, 28 January 1728, Swift was as usual entertaining Sunday evening guests at the deanery when a servant brought him a note, about eight o'clock, stating that Mrs Johnson (who had probably passed many hours in a coma) had died at six. Swift must have remembered the Wednesday even-

---

[1] *Ibid.*, IX. 254–6. I suspect that the third prayer, which is the least anguished, was written first.

[2] The will is printed in William R. Wilde, *The Closing Years of Dean Swift's Life*, 2nd ed. (Dublin, 1849), pp. 97–101. I have also drawn on T.P.C. Kirkpatrick, *The History of Doctor Steevens' Hospital, Dublin 1720–1920* (Dublin, 1924).

ing in May 1710, when guests were with him, about eight
o'clock, and a letter came to say that his mother's long sickness
('being ill all winter, and lame, and extremely ill a month or six
weeks before her death') had ended.[1]

Late that night, when the company were gone, he sat alone,
sick in his room, and put down memoirs of her life and character.
About midnight he stopped and went to bed. The second night
he went on, but his head ached so that he could not add much.
The third night was the funeral, which his illness mercifully
would not permit him to attend. But the windows of his bedroom looked out on the cathedral. Therefore, he moved into
'another apartment', where he might not face the 'light in the
church'. As the holy office proceeded, he continued to mem-
orialize his beloved. But he felt too much to be contained in the
spare hours of three single nights; and he added paragraph on
paragraph later, as he found time:

> She had a gracefulness, somewhat more than human, in every
> motion, word, and action. Never was so happy a conjunction of
> civility, freedom, easiness and sincerity. There seemed to be a com-
> bination among all that knew her, to treat her with a dignity much
> beyond her rank.
>
> . . .
>
> She spoke in a most agreeable voice, in the plainest words, never
> hesitating, except out of modesty before new faces, where she was
> somewhat reserved; nor, among her nearest friends, ever spoke
> much at a time.
>
> . . .
>
> Honour, truth, liberality, good-nature, and modesty, were the vir-
> tues she chiefly possessed, and most valued in her acquaintance; and
> where she found them, would be ready to allow for some defects, nor
> valued them less, although they did not shine in learning or in
> wit. . . .
>
> . . .
>
> She had . . . the esteem and friendship of all who knew her, and the
> universal good report of all who ever heard of her, without one

[1] Davis v. 196.

exception, if I am told the truth by those who keep general conversation. Which character is the more extraordinary in falling to a person of so much knowledge, wit and vivacity, qualities that are used to create envy, and consequently censure; and must be rather imputed to her great modesty, gentle behaviour, and inoffensiveness, than to her superior virtues.[1]

The tone is valedictory, of course, and the sentiment properly overstated. But under the elegy of praise, a darker grief is heard, like that which Swift revealed when his mother died: 'I have now lost my barrier between me and death.'[2] He felt—I think—that his real life was over.

Having lost his father before he was born, Swift grew up with a sense that he had been abandoned. One reason he was attracted to girls much younger than himself was that he might expect them to outlive him. If anyone was to be deserted, it would not be he. When he left Stella for his long visits to England or to his friends in the country, he was enacting a ritual of abandonment. But now he found the reverse of what he might unconsciously have planned. With all her fourteen years of junior age, she had gone ahead of him.[3]

It would be a mistake to suppose that religion went far to console Swift for his loss. Whatever the immortality of the soul meant to the Dean of St Patrick's, it did not guarantee a reunion with those whom one desperately missed. Writing to Pope while Stella lay suffering, Swift hardly dared to utter his wistful desire:

> I have often wished that God almighty would be so easy to the weakness of mankind, as to let old friends be acquainted in another state; and if I were to write an utopia for heaven, that would be one of my schemes. This wildness you must allow for, because I am giddy and deaf.[4]

Less than eight weeks before the end, Swift had to write a letter of condolence to a good friend whose favourite child had died. His restraint seems notable, as is the obvious unwillingness to speak a word that he could not soberly justify. Since he also

---

[1] *Ibid.*, pp. 227–36. [2] *Ibid.*, p. 196. [3] Cf. above, pp. 406, 416–17.
[4] 27 Oct. 1727; Sherburn II. 452.

delivered the same reflections in other letters, and applied them to himself, we may believe that he employed similar principles to support him in the face of his loneliness. Such sorrows, he wrote,

> are the necessary consequences of too strong attachments, by which we are grieving ourselves with the death of those we love, as we must one day grieve those who love us, with the death of ourselves. For life is a tragedy, wherein we sit as spectators awhile, and then act our own part in it. Self-love, as it is the motive to all our actions, so it is the sole cause of our grief. The dear person you lament, is by no means an object of pity, either in a moral or a religious sense. Philosophy always taught men to despise life, as a most contemptible thing in itself, and religion regards it only as a preparation for a better; which you are taught, to be certain that so innocent a person is now in possession of.... [You have other children;] religion will tell you, that the truest way to preserve them, is not to fix any of them too deep in your heart; which is a weakness God seldom leaves long unpunished: common observation shewing us, that such favourite children are either spoiled by their parents' indulgence, or soon taken out of the world; which last is, generally speaking, the lighter punishment of the two.[1]

Few modern readers would turn their minds this way for a defence against misery. But when Congreve died, a year after Stella, Swift replied in terms we still use, and which had surely helped him to bear her loss. 'Upon his own account', Swift wrote of Congreve (to Pope), 'I could not much desire the continuance of his life, under so much pain, and so many infirmities.'[2] Yet if the end came as a release for her it meant only vacancy for him. When a friend's wife died, ten months after Stella, Swift came near to expressing the effect of his mournful isolation: 'I am truly grieved at your great loss,' he said. 'Such misfortunes seem to break the whole scheme of a man's life: and although time may lessen sorrow, yet it cannot hinder a man from feeling the want of so near a companion, nor hardly supply it with another.'[3]

II. GIDDY AND DEAF

It did not lighten Swift's grief that he was coping with physical ailments at the same time as his emotions were being drained. As

---

[1] Williams III. 254. [2] Sherburn III. 16. [3] Williams III. 304.

usual, he might exaggerate symptoms in order to screen himself from undesirables like Chetwode. To 'people of quality', he said, he was deaf a week or two after he was well.[1] But even allowing for hyperbole, one must acknowledge that he suffered extraordinary attacks. To Chetwode he wrote that he had endured nine weeks of giddiness and deafness in the last months of the visit to England, although 'by a hard journey' he was able to throw off both.[2] By Christmas he had to admit new defeats, and told a correspondent,

> My head is so confused with the returns of my deafness to a very great degree, (which left me after a fortnight and then returned with more violence), that I am in an ill way to answer a letter which requires some thinking.[3]

We have seen that he could not go to Stella's funeral. It was in the following month that he said he had been kept in for ten weeks by his chronic disorders.[4] Only at the end of March could he describe himself as tolerably well.[5] That summer, he embarked on a tremendous visit to the Achesons', in the north of Ireland. Here, he told Pope, all the attentions of his friends could not save him:

> If I am not a good correspondent, I have bad health, and that is as good. I passed eight months in the country, with Sir Arthur and my Lady Acheson, and had at least half a dozen returns of my giddiness and deafness, which lasted me about three weeks a piece.... This disorder neither hinders my sleeping, nor much my walking, yet is the most mortifying malady I can suffer. I have been just a month in town, and have just got rid of it in a fortnight: and, when it is on me, I have neither spirits to write, or read, or think, or eat.[6]

Pope urged Swift to visit Aix-la-Chapelle, to which he might travel with Lady Bolingbroke. But Swift could not bear to contemplate the double affliction of being deaf and hearing a foreign language.[7]

---

[1] Sherburn III. 22. [2] Williams III. 248.
[3] 28 Dec. 1727, to Motte; *ibid.*, p. 257. Cf. *ibid.*, p. 255.
[4] Feb. 1728, to Motte; *ibid.*, p. 263.
[5] 28 Mar. 1728, to Gay; Sherburn II. 481.
[6] 6 Mar. 1729; *ibid.*, III. 20–1. Cf. Williams III. 317.
[7] Sherburn III. 21.

We might suppose that Swift was misleading Chetwode when he told him that he hardly spent a month without an attack.[1] But he also wrote to Pope, a few months later, that his head was never perfectly free from giddiness, and especially towards night. So far from desiring pity, he became witty on the subject: 'Yet my disorder is very moderate, and I have been without a fit of deafness this half year; so I am like a horse which though off his mettle, can trot on tolerably.'[2]

Among the consequences of his frailty, of course, was Swift's old obsession with temperance, which he urged on his friends as if he had discovered it. He implored Gay to be thrifty[3] and informed Pope that temperance was 'a necessary virtue for great men'.[4] He advised Charles Ford to 'walk more, and drink and eat less'.[5] He even tried to persuade Bolingbroke to be careful with his money: 'I am not the only friend you have who hath chid you in his heart for the neglect of [economy], though not with his mouth, as I have done.'[6] In fact, the preoccupation with money grows obtrusive; and when Swift says that 'a wise man ought to have money in his head, but not in his heart,'[7] one is tempted to add, 'nor on his tongue'.

III. ABSENCE FROM FELICITY

Another consequence of poor health was Swift's failure to see England again. It is true that he had described the 1727 visit as to be his last. But he certainly expected to return, and gave his friends hints that he was on his way. Bolingbroke tried to arrange for a suitable benefice in the hope that Swift might give up the deanery for an English residence. But nothing emerged with an income that could keep Swift in the style he required.[8] Meanwhile, he told Motte that, health permitting, he would come over at the end of the summer of 1728;[9] and Gay heard the news from Mr Lancelot, the husband of Swift's cousin.[10] Then

---

[1] Williams III. 317.   [2] 11 Aug. 1729; Sherburn III. 42.   [3] *Ibid.*, II. 460.
[4] *Ibid.*, p. 498; cf. p. 505.   [5] Williams III. 322.   [6] Sherburn III. 28.
[7] *Ibid.*   [8] *Ibid.*, II. 503.   [9] Williams II. 263.   [10] *Ibid.*, p. 291.

Lord Oxford told Swift of 'some kind of whisper as if the Dean of St Patrick's would be in England this winter'.[1] But Swift replied that he had been forced to give up the scheme on account of his giddiness and deafness.[2] We may assume that the expense bothered him too, because he would have liked to live comfortably. When he explained the decision to Pope (in the spring of 1729), he implied as much:

> No: I intended to pass last winter in England, but my health said No: and I did design to live as a gentleman, and, as Sancho's wife said, to go in my coach to court.[3]

All this did not mean that his antennae were withdrawn. Swift volleyed questions to and about his friends[4] and exchanged elegant epistles with them. The letters on both sides leave us in no doubt of a mutual admiration that stretched itself across St George's Channel. If Swift leaned on his elbow when he wrote to the people he admired, they returned the compliment. Even the self-indulgent Bolingbroke was capable of producing something like fifteen hundred quasi-philosophical words for Swift's perusal while travelling from Aix-la-Chapelle to Dawley Farm by way of Brussels.[5] The sincerity of Arbuthnot's affection is as obvious as his wit.[6]

In contrast to these warm attachments there lingered Swift's resentment against Queen Caroline and Lady Suffolk (as Mrs Howard became in 1731). In spite of his knowledge that royalty could seldom afford to be generous to persons who performed no material service, he had tried what charm would do. He had stooped to play the courtier, had sent expensive pieces of plaid, and had written seductive verses. Caroline was not so innocent as to mistake his intentions. The serious claims on her patronage left small room for the cronies of her capricious husband's clever mistress. But Swift had invested too much thought and emotion in his stratagem to take defeat lightly. He wrote to Ford (in

[1] 27 Jul. 1728; *ibid.*, p. 507. Cf. Pope's regret, Sherburn II. 522.
[2] 21 Sept. 1728; Williams III. 299. Cf. Pope to Motte, Sherburn II. 526.
[3] 6 Mar. 1729; *ibid.*, III. 21.   [4] E.g., *ibid.*, II. 475.
[5] *Ibid.*, III. 47–50.   [6] Williams III. 252–3.

the spring of 1729) that her majesty had 'neither memory nor manners', and that she owed him some mark in return for his gift.[1] Besides the indifference to himself and Ireland, he could not ignore the neglect of Gay; and he wrote angrily to Pope about the 'perfidiousness of some people' in forgetting their promises.[2]

IV. SCRIBLERIANS TOGETHER

The sense of coterie was something Swift rejoiced in; and the achievements of his English confrères pleased him as much as his own. With Gay and Pope in particular he felt a camaraderie of genius. The dispatches they sent about the success of *Gulliver's Travels* illustrate their share in such emotions, and Swift's exultation over *The Beggar's Opera* and *The Dunciad* suggests boyish glee.

Swift helped to shape both works. It is not easy to define the Scriblerian spirit, but at its humblest level it starts from the comic hoax. In October 1727 when Swift left Carlingford, on his travels from London, and met Sheridan on the road to Dublin, he did not suspect that his friend would gather all the information Swift gave him about the nerve-wracking journey, and post it at once to Pope, asking him to return the details to Swift as if they had come by magic. Pope and Gay followed the instructions, and baffled the dean completely. Swift wrote that he had received their letter with 'a very exact account of my journey from London to this place, wherever you got it, or whatever familiar you dealt with'. After commenting on their accuracy, he said that 'nothing but the devil could have informed you, for I kept no company but travelled alone. Or else it must be poetical conjuring.'[3]

The trick was highly Scriblerian, but in a different sense from *The Beggar's Opera*. How great a part Swift had in Gay's master-

[1] Sherburn III. 23. The letter is finally to Pope, but Swift thought at first that he was writing to Ford.
[2] *Ibid.*, p. 28.
[3] *Ibid.*, II. 460; cf. *ibid.*, pp. 454–5 and Ball III. 425–6 and notes.

piece, we cannot be sure. He was always supplying his friends with hints, and he certainly mentioned a Newgate pastoral to Gay as early as 1716.[1] The poet himself says that Swift advised him to visit Newgate in order to finish his scenes 'more correctly'.[2] Pope told Joseph Spence that the hint of a Newgate pastoral was the germ of the play, but that Swift did not at first encourage the idea of a comedy. Pope said that Swift and he 'now and then gave a correction or a word or two of advice', but that was all[3]—even though Gay wrote much of the play while Swift and he were staying with Pope at Twickenham.[4] In all his many references to *The Beggar's Opera*, Swift took no credit for any part of it.[5]

The satisfaction which Swift felt in his friend's triumph was blended with anger at Gay's lack of preferment. Swift could not get over the belief that a nation owed its poets a living. The doctrine is ancient and ubiquitous, receiving classic expression from Horace and Pope.[6] Addison and Prior were incarnations of its recent viability. But Swift had enough experience to know it was moribund; and he was hardly reasonable to expect that a government should honour talents bent on ridiculing those in power. George II and Walpole had few virtues that Swift admired; and taste (he well knew) was not among them.

Yet the Prime Minister had been willing to indulge the Queen's Scriblerian leanings so far as to offer Gay a place valued at £200 a year when the poet already held one (as a commissioner of lotteries) giving him £150 a year, as well as the lodgings in Whitehall. Two families could have lived decently on the total income, not to mention the advantage of a free residence in the centre of town.

But the new post was not honorific, and Walpole may even have designed it to humiliate Gay; for the appointment was as gentleman usher to an infant girl, one of the daughters of the Queen; and Gay's duty would have been to walk before the child

[1] Sherburn I. 360.   [2] 22 Oct. 1727; *ibid.*, II. 455.
[3] Spence, I. 107, no. 244.   [4] *Ibid.*, p. 57, no. 137.
[5] Cf. Gay, *The Beggar's Opera*, ed. W. E. Schultz (New Haven, 1923), pp. 122–7.
[6] Horace, *Epistles* II. i, and Pope's imitation.

on ceremonial occasions. He had just completed *The Beggar's Opera*, and perhaps reflected that the theatrical production would have seemed an odd response to regal bounty—for the post was in the gift of the Queen herself. Certainly an usher's place did not strike him as what he had been working toward in the years of attendance at Leicester House, or when he dedicated his gracefully turned fables to Prince William.

After due reflection and consultation, he wrote acknowledging the favour but declining the place on account of his age. To Swift he said that he had 'endeavoured, in the best manner I could, to make my excuses by a letter to her majesty'.[1] Both Pope and Swift congratulated him.[2] Swift blamed Gay's failure on Walpole; but unlike Pope, he advised him still to seek preferment:

> I entirely approve your refusal of that employment, and your writing to the [Queen]. I am perfectly confident you have a firm enemy in the [minister].[3] God forgive him, but not till he puts himself in a state to be forgiven. Upon reasoning with myself, I should hope they are gone too far to discard you quite, and that they will give you something, which although much less than they ought will be as far as it is worth, better circumstantiated.[4]

It is a mark of Swift's fundamental hopefulness—perhaps even of naïveté—that he should have thought it worth Gay's while to linger on the verges of majesty after failing to meet the courtly standard of obsequiousness. In the tone of over-righteous indignation which he reserved for injustices suffered by his friends (a tone probably sharpened by the knowledge that Stella was dying), Swift wrote to Lord Carteret,

> Your friend[5] Walpole hath lately done one of the cruellest actions I ever knew, even in a minister of state, these thirty years past; which, if the Queen hath not intelligence of, may my right hand forget its cunning.[6]

Gay's ballad opera opened in London the day after Stella died. It was Scriblerian in being a parody of serious forms of art—Italian opera and pastoral romance. The relation between

---

[1] Sherburn II. 455.   [2] *Ibid.*, pp. 453–4, 460.   [3] The text reads 'ministry'.
[4] Sherburn II. 460.   [5] Heavy irony.
[6] Williams III. 260, probably from a draft.

parody and hoax is easy to trace, for both of them offer a comic yet satisfying defeat of the expectations of the audience. Like *Gulliver's Travels* and *The Dunciad*, Gay's work is also a bitter satire on the leaders of society and government, whom it equates with whores, pimps, and thieves. Like them, moreover, its significance reaches beyond the author's time and place through allusions to traditional embodiments of heroism like Alexander and Brutus.

The amplitude of Gay's report of his success (in a letter to Swift) shows the poet's confidence in the dean's sympathy. Two and a half weeks after the opening of *The Beggar's Opera*, he wrote dwelling on the financial returns, which he knew would delight Swift. The emphasis on his lack of patronage is another bow in the dean's direction. To appreciate Gay's exultation, one must remember that six nights was the normal run for a play:

> I have deferred writing to you from time to time till I could give you an account of the Beggar's Opera. It is acted at the playhouse in Lincoln Inn's Fields, with such success that the playhouse hath been crowded every night; tonight is the fifteenth time of acting, and 'tis thought it will run a fortnight longer. I have ordered Motte to send the play to you the first opportunity. I made no interest either for approbation or money nor hath anybody been pressed to take tickets for my benefit, notwithstanding which, I think I shall make an addition to my fortune of between six and seven hundred pounds. I know this account will give you pleasure, as I have pushed through this precarious affair without servility or flattery. As to any favours from great men I am in the same state you left me, but I am a great deal happier as I have no expectations.[1]

Five weeks later the flood of spectators was unabated, and Gay could send an account which, for all its exuberance, was only a station in an unprecedented progress. There is something filial in his eagerness to share the information:

> The Beggar's Opera hath now been acted thirty-six times, and was as full the last night, as the first, and as yet there is not the least probability of a thin audience.... I have got by all this success between seven and eight hundred pounds.

[1] Sherburn II. 473–4.

The special relation between the poet and the dean appears in a modest reflection:

> I would not have talked so much upon this subject, or upon anything that regards myself but to you; but as I know you interest yourself so sincerely in everything that concerns me, I believe you would have blamed me if I had said less.

Gay closes with a peculiarly endearing promise of hospitality, offering Swift more than his fair share of windows in the gate house at Whitehall:

> I really miss you every day, and I would be content that you should have one whole window to yourself, and half another to have you again.[1]

In its first season *The Beggar's Opera* finally established a record for the London stage, with sixty-two performances and greater receipts than had ever been known before.[2] It was extraordinary as well in receiving a Dublin production during the first season. In March 1728 a Dublin newspaper reported, 'The new opera which is again to be play'd to night was on Thursday more crowded with spectators than ever.'[3] Now Swift could mirror Gay's satisfaction:

> We have your opera [i.e., in print] for 6d and we are as full of it pro modulo nostro as London can be—continual acting, and house crammed, and the Lord Lieutenant several times there, laughing his heart out.[4]

Characteristically, he offered some hints to sharpen the satire, and he worried paternally about the investment of Gay's money—expressing himself in an unclerical figure drawn from the play itself:

> Ever preserve some spice of the alderman and prepare against old age and dullness[5] and sickness—and coldness or death of friends.[6] A whore has a resource left that she can turn bawd: but an old decayed poet is a creature at mercy when he can find none.[7]

---

[1] *Ibid.*, pp. 478–9; cf. Pope's account, *ibid.*, p. 480.   [2] Schultz, p. 10.
[3] *Dublin Intelligence*, 23 Mar.; quoted by Ball IV. 20, n. 2.
[4] Dash added.   [5] I.e., loss of creative power.   [6] Dash added.
[7] 28 Mar. 1728; Sherburn II. 482.

In May he told Pope, 'Mr Gay's opera hath been acted here twenty times, and my Lord Lieutenant tells me it is very well performed; he hath seen it often, and approves it much.'[1] There may be an allusion here to Carteret's pleasure in the thrusts against Walpole.

At last Swift took it on himself—in one of his rare essays of literary criticism—to defend *The Beggar's Opera* against religious and political objections. Swift had launched a weekly paper, *The Intelligencer*; and in the third number (25 May 1728) he replied to those who found Gay's work mean, immoral, or politically subversive. The Rev. Thomas Herring, a royal chaplain and a noisy Whig, who finally became Archbishop of Canterbury, had delivered a sermon condemning *The Beggar's Opera* for making heroes of vicious characters and thereby encouraging robbers, drunkards, and other criminals.[2] Soon afterwards, a London newspaper sponsored a parallel attack in a letter signed 'Philopropos' which Swift could have seen.[3] (A Dublin paper reprinted it, but only a year later.)[4] The indignant writer denounced Gay for bringing on the stage the lives of 'robbers and night-walkers' represented so seductively as to make them seem 'agreeable, and full of mirth and jollity'. The writer complained that Gay had chosen, as a 'proper subject for laughter and merriment',

> a gang of highwaymen and pick pockets, triumphing in their successful villainies, and braving the ignominious death they so justly deserve, with the undaunted resolution of a Stoical philosopher.[5]

Years later, Hazlitt was to give a direct reply to the charge in a brilliant essay: 'The moral of the piece is to show the *vulgarity* of vice.'[6]

---

[1] 10 May 1728; *ibid.*, p. 492.

[2] Sunday, 24 Mar. 1728, according to the *London Evening-Post*, 28 Mar.; see also Schultz, pp. 226–8.

[3] *London Journal*, 30 Mar. 1728. The writer of the letter (composed, apparently before the sermon was preached) was William Duncombe; see Schultz, p. 376.

[4] Thomas Hume's *Dublin Gazette: or, Weekly Courant*, 18 Mar. 1729; copy in the library of Trinity College, Dublin, shelfmark A. 7. 5, fol. 54ᵛ. This is not the publication usually referred to as the *Dublin Gazette*.

[5] Schultz, pp. 230–1.

[6] 'On the Beggar's Opera', in *Works*, ed. P. P. Howe (London, 1930–4), IV. 65–6.

Swift handled the problem differently. Not only would he speak up for Gay; but also, by praising *The Beggar's Opera*, he would condemn the courtly and fashionable society aped by the poet's characters. Anyone who reads the text with understanding (Swift suggests) will find it a blunt exposure of the savagery of criminal careers. The element of idealization is only the attribution to whores and bandits of a rhetoric associated with the polite world. A fine language used by gentlemen to veil their lust and greed becomes the medium in which murderers candidly disclose bestial motives. (In 1732 Swift was to describe *The Beggar's Opera* as a 'very severe satyr upon the most pernicious villainies of mankind'.)[1]

As literary criticism the essay takes off from the famous passage in which Swift's mentor Temple had praised what he declared to be a uniquely English gift for humour—i.e., for sympathetic comedy derived from eccentricity of character.[2] Swift refuses to make Temple's connection between literary genre and social or political institutions. Instead, he sees the taste for humour as rooted not in national character but in common human nature. He also invokes what had become the usual polarity between humour and wit, but unlike Dryden prefers the former.[3] Swift is traditional in regarding comedy as morally didactic through its satirical aspects. He is traditional again in preferring Horatian (or laughing) satire to Juvenalian (or tragic), as the more useful—even though his own practice was hardly Horatian.

Yet Swift rejects Shaftesbury's trust in unlimited ridicule,[4] and allows some things to be too serious or sacred for mockery. It is the corruptions of valuable institutions that make proper topics for comic satire.[5] Here Swift echoes his own 'Apology' for *A Tale of a Tub*. In a more remarkable passage he ventures to

---

[1] Williams IV. 53.

[2] 'Of Poetry', near the end (in *Five Miscellaneous Essays*, ed. S. H. Monk (Ann Arbor, 1963), pp. 198–200). Temple is probably following Dryden, in the *Essay of Dramatick Poesy*, who of course followed Jonson. See Dryden, *Works*, California Edition, XVII. 59–61 and notes.

[3] Davis XII. 32. Cf. Spingarn I. lviii-lxiii.

[4] *Letter concerning Enthusiasm*, sect. II.   [5] Davis XII. 33.

defend the practice of writing satire in order to give oneself pleasure, and asks,

> whether I have not as good a title to laugh, as men have to be ridiculous; and to expose vice, as another hath to be vicious. If I ridicule the follies and corruptions of a *court*, a *ministry*, or a *senate*, are they not amply paid by *pensions*, *titles*, and *power*; while I expect, and desire no other reward, than that of laughing with a few friends in a corner? Yet, if those who take offence, think me in the wrong, I am ready to change the scene with them, whenever they please.[1]

At this point Swift shifts into political argument, blaming the government for neglect of Gay and defending *The Beggar's Opera* by a device which was typical of the age. This is to pretend that a piece of satire has no application to present persons even while making such an application ironically:

> And although it is highly probable, he meant only the courtiers of former times, yet he acted unwarily, by not considering that the malignity of some people might misinterpret what he said, to the disadvantage of present *persons* and affairs.

Finally, Swift resorts to the ancient formula of *dulce et utile*, asserting the moral effect of the play and supporting any well-behaved clergyman who might go to see it. The closing paragraphs add little to the points already made. But they strike a reverberating blow against the anti-theatrical campaign derived from bigots like Jeremy Collier:

> But when the *Lords Chancellors*, who are keepers of the King's conscience; when the *judges* of the land, whose title is *reverend*; when *ladies*, who are bound by the rules of their sex to the strictest decency, appear in the *theatre* without censure; I cannot understand, why a young *clergyman*, who comes concealed,[2] out of curiosity to see an innocent and moral play, should be ... condemned.[3]

---

[1] Cf. the very different defence of personal satire in *An Answer to ... A Memorial*, in *ibid.*, pp. 23–5, written about the same time. For two instances, at this time, of Swift writing personal satire for his own enjoyment, see 'Dean Smedley Gone to Seek His Fortune' and 'On Paddy's Character of the Intelligencer', in *Poems* II. 454–8.

[2] I.e., in layman's clothing.

[3] Davis XII. 34–6.

V. ORNA ME

Pope's friendship with Swift was a more complex operation than Gay's. Each of these two was proud to be intimate with the other, and each wished to enhance his fame through the connection. Neither one could keep from making the other an instrument to serve his private ends. Given the physical and emotional deprivations which Pope endured, it was natural for him to go further than Swift in such manœuvres; and he certainly pushed his evasions—in the long run—beyond the limits of hypocrisy into the realm of slander. Yet if Swift's deceits were essentially harmless, they were not altruistic.

So we must remember that strong, genuine friendship and active, mutual benevolence were the fundamental links between them. When Swift begged Pope to visit him, it was not only to balance the accounts of hospitality or to display a captive lion to admiring Dubliners. It was also to enjoy the pleasure of Pope's conversation, to bathe in his affection, and to cherish him.

Swift's apology to Pope for leaving Twickenham in the summer of 1727 is tender and spontaneous.[1] When he told Martha Blount of the satisfaction it would give him to see her and Pope nearby, he rose to his most natural, charming language:

> I will give you eight dinners a week and a whole half dozen of pint bottles of good French wine at your lodgings, a thing you could never expect to arrive at, and every year a suit of fourteen penny stuff, that should not be worn out at the right side;[2] and a chair costs but sixpence a job, and you shall have catholicity as much as you please, and the catholic Dean of St Patrick's, as old again as I, to your confessor.[3]

To Pope himself, Swift delivered assurances of Ireland's amenities and promises of comfort in travel and housing; he would even send escorts:

---

[1] Sherburn II. 477.
[2] Perhaps an allusion to the condition of her clothes when he saw her in England.
[3] Sherburn II. 477.

As to Ireland, the air of this house is good, and of the kingdom very good, but the best fruits fall short a little. All things to eat and drink, except very few, better than in London, except you have £4000 a year. The ridings and coachings a hundred times better in winter. You may find about six rational, good, civil learned easy companions of the males; fewer of the females; but many civil, hospitable, and ready to admire and adore.... No Paulteneys nor Dawleys[1] nor Arbuthnots. A very good apartment, good French wine, and port, and among the extravagant, hoch, burgundy, rackpunch &c but too dear for me.... The sea, the towngates, and the door of this house are open. You can have an eighteenpenny chicken for seven pence. I will send Dr Delany and Mr Stopfort as far as Chester to conduct you.[2]

Pope, on his side, tantalized Swift by promising to visit Dublin. Some of his expressions do not convince me.[3] But at times he does sound ready to go. He told Sheridan, 'Were I my own master ... I would infallibly see Ireland before I die.'[4] In October 1729, replying to Swift's report of poor health, Pope wrote, 'But if we are not to see you here, I believe I shall once in my life see you there. You think more for me, and about me, than any friend I have, and you think better for me.'[5]

Other friends, like Bolingbroke and Arbuthnot, wrote less often but as warmly, reinforcing any nostalgia Swift might have felt.[6] Even among themselves they made plans to have Swift with them. After Stella died, when Mrs Pope was failing, and her son heard that Gay was ill, he wrote anxiously to him,

If, as I believe, the air of a better clime as the southern part of France may be thought useful for your recovery, thither I would go with you infallibly; and it is very probable we might get the Dean with us, who is now in that abandoned state already in which I shall shortly be, as to other cares and duties.[7]

This free suggestion, made without Swift's knowledge, is one more token of the feelings that bound together the three

[1] I.e., Pulteneys or Bolingbrokes.
[2] Sherburn II. 461–2. Cf. *ibid.*, p. 492, and III. 21.
[3] Cf. *ibid.*, II. 447–8, 468.
[4] *Ibid.*, p. 524. He means, if he were not looking after his ailing mother.
[5] *Ibid.*, III. 57.
[6] Cf. especially Bolingbroke's letter of 30 Aug. 1729; Williams III. 347–50.
[7] Sherburn III. 1. Stella has died, and Mrs Pope will die soon.

Scriblerian bachelors. The part played by mutual admiration in the wish of Swift and Pope for poetic immortality becomes starkly visible in their attitudes toward *The Dunciad*. Swift had said, 'Orna me'—celebrate me—to Pope; and when Pope made a similar request, Swift replied, 'I most heartily thank you for your desire that I would record our friendship in verse, which if I can succeed in, I will never desire to write one more line in poetry while I live.'[1] The flatness of the language suggests the over-familiarity of the sentiment.

Swift said once that it was he who 'put Mr Pope on writing the poem called the *Dunciad*'.[2] Pope called it Swift's poem.[3] To Sheridan he wrote that Swift was 'properly the author of the Dunciad: It had never been writ but at his request, and for his deafness: For had he been able to converse with me, do you think I had amus'd my time so ill?'[4] In a note to the text the poet recalled that when he threw the first sketch of the *Dunciad* into the fire, Swift snatched it out and 'persuaded his friend to proceed in it'.[5] In a polished set of quatrains Swift described the days when he was staying at Twickenham and Pope was composing the *Dunciad*; the ironic point is that if Swift's deafness had not made conversation impossible, Pope would never have written his couplets:

> Yet to the Dean his share allot;
> He claims it by a canon;
> *That without which a thing is not*
> Is *causa sine quâ non*.[6]

But Swift's eagerness to see the poem in print sprang only in small part from his share in its paternity. He loved to think of the Scriblerians as taking turns capturing the literary imagination of England. 'The Beggar's Opera hath knocked down Gulliver,' he wrote to Gay, 'I hope to see Pope's Dulness knock down

---

[1] *Ibid.*, p. 30.
[2] Williams IV. 53; cf. Sutherland's doubt, in Pope, *Poems* V. xiii.
[3] Sherburn II. 522; but see Sherburn's objection, *ibid.*, n. 4.
[4] *Ibid.*, p. 523.   [5] Pope, *Poems* V. 201, note a.
[6] *Ibid.*, II. 406. The refinement of the versification makes me suspect that Pope, who edited the poem, also corrected it.

the Beggar's Opera.'[1] However, Pope's multiplex scheme for launching his *magnum opus* involved much advance publicity, concealment of authorship, and evasion of legal responsibility. Although the mystifications were Scriblerian, they tantalized Swift, who regretted the long sequence of promises and delays. 'Why does not Mr Pope publish his *Dulness*?' Swift broke out to Gay. 'The rogues he mauls will die of themselves in peace, and so will his friends, and so there will be neither punishment nor reward.'[2]

Pope was waiting to consummate the clever arrangements for justifying and publicizing his poem before it came out.[3] But Swift wished to keep the Scriblerian banner afloat. 'You talk of this Dunciad,' he told Pope, 'but I am impatient to have it *volare per ora*[4]—there is now a vacancy for fame: the Beggar's Opera hath done its task, *discedat uti conviva satur.*'[5] Although the *Dunciad* was to appear on 18 May 1728, Pope would not risk sending Swift a copy for fear of losing his legal anonymity. 'My poem (which it grieves me that I dare not send you a copy of . . . .) will shew you what a distinguishing age we lived in.'[6]

When Swift at last got hold of a copy, many of the allusions baffled him. He wanted longer, more explicit notes. He wanted names and accounts of the dunces. He wanted parodies identified and linked to their originals. Twenty miles from London, he said, 'nobody understands hints, initial letters, or town-facts and passages.' Then he discovered that Pope was shortly to satisfy all his demands in the apparatus of the *Dunciad Variorum*; and he offered hints for Pope's mock-scholarship—a Scriblerian attack on pedantry:

> I would be glad to know whether the quarto edition is to come out anonymously, as published by the commentator, with all his pomp of prefaces &c. and among the complaints of spurious editions?—I am thinking whether the editor should not follow the old style of,

---

[1] Sherburn II. 484.   [2] 26 Feb. 1728; *ibid.*, p. 475.

[3] Pope, *Poems* v. xvi–xvii.

[4] Fly on men's lips: *virum volitare per ora* (Virgil, *Georgics* III. 9).

[5] Sherburn II. 492–3; the Latin means, 'Let it depart like a well-fed guest' (Horace, *Sermones* I. i. 119).

[6] Sherburn II. 455–6.

This excellent author, &c. and refine in many places when you mean no refinement? and into the bargain take all the load of naming the dunces, their qualities, histories and performances.[1]

Whether or not he got the programme from Swift, Pope cheerfully adopted these practices of giving imaginary commentators responsibility for the misleading information supplied by his apparatus. But the *Variorum* could not be allowed to emerge until the fantastic joke of its delivery at court was acted out. Somehow, the poet persuaded three noble lords to serve as accoucheurs and take responsibility for issuing the work. Then at last, on 12 March 1729, Sir Robert Walpole, of all people in the world, presented a copy of the enlarged *Dunciad* to the King and Queen in St James's Palace.[2] Life imitated art as his majesty (Dunce the Second), flanked by an avatar of Dulness, declared (according to Arbuthnot) that Mr Pope was 'a very honest man'.[3] And so the court became a theatre for Book Four of the poem.

Swift's satisfaction in these events was not unprejudiced. The inscription with which Pope had promised to celebrate him had not seen print. After exciting Swift by sending him drafts,[4] Pope withdrew the passage from the poem rather than show his hand too openly. Swift did not pretend to be pleased when Delany reported from Pope that the inscription would only appear in the *Variorum* edition: 'The Doctor told me your secret about the Dunciad,' Swift wrote, 'which does not please me, because it defers gratifying my vanity in the most tender point and perhaps may wholly disappoint it.'[5]

Only when the *Variorum* was in the press did Pope tell him,

The inscription to the Dunciad is now printed and inserted in the poem. Do you care I should say any thing farther how much that poem is yours? since certainly without you it had never been.[6]

---

[1] *Ibid.*, pp. 504–5. To 'refine' is to give subtle interpretations. Swift is preaching what he had practised in *The Battle of the Books*, in which the term 'modern' signifies very much what Pope meant by 'dullness'.

[2] *Ibid.*, p. 502 and n. 3; III. 26 and n. 1; Pope, *Poems* V (3rd ed., 1963), 461–2.

[3] Williams III. 326.   [4] Sherburn II. 455–6, 468–9.

[5] *Ibid.*, p. 498.   [6] 12 Oct. 1728; *ibid.*, p. 522.

In its final form the inscription was easily worth waiting for; and Swift must have been touched not only by the lavishness of the praise but also by his sense of the emotional energy that underlay the rich versification:

> O thou! whatever title please thine ear,
> Dean, Drapier, Bickerstaff, or Gulliver!
> Whether thou chuse Cervantes' serious air,
> Or laugh and shake in Rab'lais easy chair,
> Or praise the court, or magnify mankind,
> Or thy griev'd country's copper chains unbind.[1]

The imitation of Swift's irony is as much a tribute as the trick of naming the masked author by his impersonations. But the sweetest flattery was probably the ranking of Swift with two writers whom he particularly admired.

'It was my principal aim in the entire work', Pope told Swift, 'to perpetuate the friendship between us.'[2] This was pardonable exaggeration. Swift replied that, like everybody else, he approved all parts of the book, 'but am one abstracted from everybody, in the happiness of being recorded your friend, while wit, and humour, and politeness shall have any memorial among us'.[3] They both sound a little tired.

VI. HOME THOUGHTS

Secure against the pull of anglophile nostalgia there remained, as always, Swift's rootedness in his impoverished homeland. His devotion to Ireland took forms that his English friends never heard about. Among its ramifications was one that suddenly flourished and faded during these difficult months. It was Swift's concern with Trinity College, Dublin. After the government of Ireland had changed in 1714, Swift's friend Pratt could not long remain as provost. Some tortuous negotiations left Pratt at last as Dean of Down while the arch-Whig Richard Baldwin was installed as his successor in the College. Baldwin, in opposing the bent of the senior fellows, became the Richard Bentley of

---

[1] *Dunciad* I. 19–24.   [2] Sherburn III. 57.   [3] *Ibid.*, p. 64.

Dublin, and strove to weaken the element represented by Swift's friends Delany and Helsham. When Boulter came over to be Primate (1724), he strengthened Baldwin's hand in reconstituting what Boulter described as a 'seminary of Jacobitism';[1] and the ambitious provost felt strong enough to set aside a junior fellowship candidate preferred by a majority of the senior fellows, in order to install a proper young Whig of his own (or Boulter's) choosing.

It seems that Baldwin acted with the law barely on his side. But of course he infuriated the hostile senior fellows. All five of them entered a protest in the College register; and Delany, among them, sent a copy of the censure to Swift, while he was in England, in May or June of 1727, before George I died. The dean composed a full statement of the case and had Mrs Howard present it to the Prince of Wales, who served as Chancellor of the University of Dublin. But then followed the death of the King, leaving his son far too busy to concern himself with a remote academic fracas; and Molyneux, his majesty's secretary, was advised that Baldwin had acted within his rights.

Not long before these events, Swift had thought of leaving some of his fortune to establish a new fellowship in Trinity College. He consulted Delany and made notes for a will under which land would be bought to provide income for a generous stipend. Next, however, came word of Baldwin's high-handedness, and Swift changed his mind abruptly. I am persuaded that a pamphlet dealing with the controversy tells us very nearly what happened:

> a certain person, who had applied great part of his fortune towards founding a fellowship in this University, with a more ample income than usual; did, upon notice he received of the Provost's demeanour, in this flagrant case, immediately tear all the papers relating to that settlement, with a resolution never to dispose of one farthing in favour of the Society.[2]

Baldwin was to some extent aiding Boulter in the campaign to

---

[1] Boulter I. 180 (Dublin ed., p. 145).
[2] I have taken the entire story of Swift's plan for a fellowship from Mayhew, pp. 94–114. See also Williams III. 221.

give Irish offices to English invaders, and Swift's support of Delany's side might seem therefore part of his nationalism. But Swift did not confuse patriotism with provinciality. During the winter of 1727–8 the Lord Lieutenant asked the fellows of the College to advise him about the tenure of professorships in the University of Dublin. In their answer they recommended that all professors be chosen from among the fellows, and that they should hold professorships only so long as they remained fellows. Swift saw the tendency of such principles and wrote to Carteret denouncing them:

> I need not inform your excellency, how contrary such a practice is to that of all the universities of Europe. Your excellency well knows how many learned men of the last two ages, have been invited by princes to be professors in some art or science, for which they were renowned; and that the like rule hath been followed in Oxford and Cambridge. I hope your excellency will shew no regard to so narrow and partial an opinion, which can only tend to mend fellowships and spoil professorships.[1]

If fat pigs were to be greased, Swift thought it was just as well that they should be Irish pigs; and if Irish scholars were equal in ability to foreign rivals, he would have wished them to be preferred. But just as he invited the best singers of England to join the choir of his cathedral, so also he hoped that the College of Dublin would put learning before nationality.

The tone Swift used in addressing Carteret was that of the first citizen of Ireland; and from his treatment by others one might easily conclude that he was justified in his self-confidence. A man whom he had vilified for misconduct in the affair of Wood's patent pleaded with Swift to reconsider his judgment because 'that fatal genius of yours in an instant ruined my character'; and he begged Swift to help him recover his good name.[2] When a projector thought he had found a way of establishing the longitude of a ship at sea, he asked Swift to give the invention his support. Swift sent a mildly ironic, discouraging reply; and a Dublin newspaper thought the not very amusing exchange was

[1] Williams III. 259.   [2] *Ibid.*, pp. 280–3.

worth publishing.[1] When Swift wrote to Pope and Gay about the satisfaction of living in Dublin, he sounded as if the human resources of the kingdom were at his disposal. The cathedral chapter did not always bow to his authority, and Swift complained, 'There might be a Lutrin[2] writ upon the tricks used by my chapter to tease me.'[3] But after the *Drapier* years no evidence of painful friction is forthcoming.[4]

In 1728 and 1729 Swift was reading and annotating the *Annales ecclesiasticae* of Baronius, making bitter but shallow remarks on the superstition and poor Latinity of the author, with special attention to the doctrine of papal infallibility.[5] When he ridiculed the miracles recorded, did he think of his own modest wish for a reunion of friends after death?

VII. THE CONDITION OF IRELAND

As always, the ineluctable sign of Swift's identification with Ireland was his serious writing on the condition of the kingdom. The concept of nationhood established by the Drapier now made the principle from which his reflections began. One king, one church, one language, one state—this was not a formula that excited Swift. During these years he thought in terms of a productive community united by rational self-interest. Two visits to England had taught him how little the British government would do to advance such a community. So this reflex of indignation turned as usual on the victims who co-operated in their own ruin. On the way back to Ireland in the autumn of 1727 Swift raged against the people whom he laboured to preserve, and he wrote furious verses on their suicidal proclivities:

> Remove me from this land of slaves
> Where all are fools, and all are knaves,
> Where every knave and fool is bought,
> Yet kindly sells himself for nought,

[1] *Ibid.*, pp. 239–40.
[2] Mock-epic by Boileau, on dissension in a cathedral chapter.
[3] Sherburn II. 498.   [4] Landa, p. 93.   [5] Davis XIV. 16–35.

Where Whig and Tory fiercely fight
Who's in the wrong, who in the right,
And when their country lies at stake
They only fight for fighting's sake,
While English sharpers take the pay,
And then stand by to see fair play.
Meantime the Whig[1] is always winner
And for his courage gets—a dinner.
His excellency[2] too perhaps
Spits in his mouth and strokes his chaps.[3]

Archbishop King, housebound by illness in the winter of
1727–8, amplified the chorus of Swift's despair and added
terrible details to the reports of his enemy Boulter:

The condition of Dublin and in truth of all Ireland is most miserable, all necessaries of life being excessive dear and no money
stirring, insomuch that many of the poor have already starved and
many more are like to perish, nor do I see any possibility to help
them. I do my part to the utmost of my power, but that goes but a
little way.[4]

The prospect of his oncoming death lost itself in the spectacle of
wretchedness surrounding him:

Besides my want of health, the great misery of this town is a most
sensible affliction to me. The cry of the poor for bread is a stab to my
heart, to [find] them dying every day for want and being unable to
relieve them.

Like Swift, he acknowledged that their own brethren were
crucifying the sufferers for pieces of silver:

The landlords, the unmerciful landlords, are the chief cause of this,
partly by hindering the tenants to plough, partly by keeping their
land in their own hands and stocking them with black cattle, and
partly by selling them [i.e., the cattle] in great parcels to tenants that
do the same and lastly by screwing up their fines to such a price that
the poor people are not able to raise their rents and then the
landlord seizes all that the poor men have and turn them out to
beg. There is no work or employment for the poor except the linen

---

[1] I.e., Irish Whig.   [2] I.e., Carteret.
[3] *Poems* II. 421–3; punctuation added, some spellings altered. The whole poem deserves quotation as a concise expression of Swift's contempt for Irish self-destructiveness.
[4] 10 Apr. 1728, to the dowager Lady Southwell.

manufactory in the north and they are so hardly dealt with that they are getting out of the kingdom as fast as they can.[1]

If the archbishop's irony lacked Swift's edge, it still turned in the same direction: one of his maxims, he said, was that 'if you intend to do people good, it must be against their will.'[2]

In the summer of 1728 the archbishop thought there was enough cheap food to supply the poor. 'We have hope of a good harvest,' he told Lady Carteret. 'Your ladyship know that the poverty of the people will allow the generality ... no other food but buttermilk and potatoes and we have a reasonable plenty of both and tolerably good.'[3]

The winter brought a different report: 'As to the kingdom it is in a most wretched condition. We generally want bread and in Dublin fire, whereof many perish.' The Irish government issued the proclamation against the export of grain—except to England. But its legality was doubtful; and besides, if the grain could not be spared, any exportation at all seemed, to the archbishop, 'plain murther, it being to starve a great many for a profit to a few'.[4] Seeking funds from a charitable lady, he said, 'I design the money for some relief for the numerous poor that are starving, and it will lie on your ladyship if they perish for want of it.'[5] He had already given all he could from his own pocket.

It was against this background that Swift dealt with economic issues. The large political framework offered few opportunities to his rhetoric, partly because Carteret and Boulter between them managed the Irish Parliament cleverly enough to keep political crisis from burgeoning, and partly because Swift realized that the constitutional impasse was hopeless. In the spring of 1728 he produced a cutting, comprehensive analysis called *A Short View of Ireland*.[6] In England, *Mist's Weekly Journal* noticed it with the comment that everyone could identify the author by 'the bold strokes in it'.[7]

---

[1] 23 Apr. 1728, to Edward Southwell.
[2] 9 Jul. 1728, to Robert Howard, Bishop of Killala.   [3] 14 Aug. 1728.
[4] 30 Jan. 1729, to Edward Southwell.
[5] 4 Feb. 1729, to the Dowager Lady Southwell.
[6] Published 19 Mar. 1728; see Ferguson, p. 144.   [7] 30 Mar. 1728.

As we have seen, Boulter himself was warning the English ministry of the horrors which lay ahead;[1] 'this summer', he said, 'must be more fatal to us than the last.'[2] Yet superficial English visitors and Irish time-servers (misled perhaps by the abundance of food at the tables of gentlemen) were declaring that Ireland was in a 'flourishing condition'.[3] There had even appeared a pamphlet called *Seasonable Remarks on Trade* (1728) in which the author emphasized the potential wealth of the kingdom, in such a way as to overshadow his admission of her present poverty.[4]

In *A Short View of the State of Ireland*, Swift replied with a long list of the causes of true prosperity; but under each head he showed how Ireland violated the principle implied. This approach is a standard device for lending an air of impartial science to Swift's tendentious discourse. He appears to start from general principles and then to apply these to particular instances. But he has in fact chosen generalizations that uniquely suit the applications he has in mind.[5]

It will be noticed that although Swift might speak theoretically of the supreme importance of agriculture, he gave at least equal attention, in his practical advice, to trade—i.e., the manufacture of cloth, the sale of produce, raw materials, and goods to other countries, etc. During the 1720s Swift devoted himself to two sets of economic ills: first, the Irish neglect of agriculture and forestry, the absenteeism of landlords, etc.; secondly, the bad state of native manufactures, the oppressive limitations on trade, and the importation of luxuries.

In *A Short View*, Swift renews his furious complaints about the kingdom's lack of self-government and the denial of public offices to qualified natives. But some of Swift's burden falls on what the people could accomplish even under such oppressions. He harps of course on the narrow tyranny of the English. Yet he also dwells on Irish neglect of Irish opportunities.

---

[1] See above, pp. 544–5.   [2] Boulter I. 222 (Dublin ed., p. 178).
[3] Ferguson, pp. 145–6.
[4] John Browne, 1728. This was the man denounced by Swift for testifying on behalf of Wood's patent. See Ferguson, p. 146.
[5] Cf. *A Discourse of the Contests and Dissensions* and *The Conduct of the Allies*.

Of all the indispensable prerequisites to a flourishing economy—Swift says—only two exist in Ireland: a fertile soil and an abundance of good harbours:

> The conveniency of ports and havens which nature hath bestowed so liberally on this kingdom, is of no more use to us, than a beautiful prospect to a man shut up in a dungeon.

. . .

> As to improvement of land; those few who attempt that, or planting through covetousness, or want of skill, generally leave things worse than they were; neither succeeding in trees nor hedges; and by running into the fancy of grazing,[1] after the manner of the Scythians, are every day depopulating the country.[2]

A vivid summary statement gives body to an idea which keeps appearing in Swift's discussions of Ireland, and which shades into another recurrent theme. It is the idea of the uniqueness of the kingdom, and it blends with the theme of Ireland's crazy inversion of the normal axioms of economics.

> If we do flourish, it must be against every law of nature and reason; like the thorn at Glassenbury,[3] that blossoms in the midst of winter.[4]

After a passage of ironic fantasy on a tourist's misguided impression of prosperity, Swift, in a beautiful modulation, drops his pitch; and pathetic truth breaks through bitter irony:

> But my heart is too heavy to continue this irony longer; for it is manifest, that whatever stranger took such a journey, would be apt to think himself travelling in Lapland, or Ysland,[5] rather than in a country so favoured by nature as ours, both in fruitfulness of soil, and temperature of climate. The miserable dress, and diet, and dwelling of the people. The general desolation in most parts of the kingdom. The old seats of the nobility and gentry all in ruins, and no new ones in their stead. The families of farmers, who pay great rents, living in filth and nastiness upon butter-milk and potatoes, without a shoe or stocking to their feet; or a house so convenient as an English hog-sty to receive them.[6]

---

[1] I.e., turning tillage into pasture.   [2] Davis XII. 8.
[3] Glastonbury.   [4] Davis XII. 10.   [5] Iceland.
[6] Davis XII. 10.

Carrying through the motif of Ireland's uniqueness—her violation of the true laws of economics—Swift sketched (but never completed) another essay, 'Maxims Controlled in Ireland'.[1] Again he offered a set of rules which a nation must follow to be prosperous, and showed that they do not operate in Ireland. The implication is not that the rules are defective, but only that Ireland is ruinously singular. From his paradox Swift draws the inference that normal remedies cannot apply to this doomed country. Both in the notes for 'Maxims Controlled' and in the essay itself, Swift produces the maxim that 'people are the riches of a nation', and comments, 'Not so among us till we can sell them as the Africans do'[2]—a donnée which he was to refine memorably.

The last paragraph of the fragmentary sketch is a savage outburst of irony which again foreshadows a memorable development in a more famous essay. In this outburst Swift echoes (perhaps unknowingly) Archbishop King's denunciation of Irish landlords, especially the absentees, and delivers one mocking falsehood after another:

> I must vindicate myself to the reader so far, as to declare solemnly that what I shall say of those lords and squires, doth not arise from the least[3] regard I have for their understandings, their virtues, or their persons. For, although I have not the honour of the least acquaintance with any one among them (my ambition not soaring so high) yet I am too good a witness of the situation they have been in for thirty years past, the veneration paid them by the people, the high esteem they are in among the prime nobility and gentry, the peculiar marks of favour and distinction they receive from the court: The weight and consequence of their interest, added to their great zeal and application for preventing any hardships their country

[1] 'Controlled' here means 'opposed' or 'contradicted'. For evidence of 1729 as the date of composition, see Ferguson, p. 148, n. 29. An additional scrap of evidence is the fact that Swift uses the same Latin maxim in his notes for this essay and in a letter of 5 Apr. 1729 to Bolingbroke (Davis XII. 309; Williams III. 329). Herbert Davis pointed out similarities between 'Maxims Controlled' and works written in 1729: see Davis XII. xxiii, 66, 124. We know that the passage on p. 66 was written in Apr. 1729; see Davis XII. xvi. 'Maxims Controlled' was not published until 1765.

[2] Davis XII. 135–6, 309. I quote from the notes, but the same principle is expressed in the essay.

[3] I.e., very small.

might suffer from England, wisely considering that their own fortunes and honours were embarked in the same bottom.[1]

It is obvious that Swift here is not dividing the criminally
irresponsible 'lords and squires' from the 'prime nobility and
gentry' on the basis of religious faith, political party, social class,
or source of wealth. The families in both groups are Anglican
landed gentry or peers, and indifferently Whig or Tory. Swift's
division between them starts from their rôle in the economy. The
'lords and squires' are essentially unproductive, careless of the
welfare of their people, unconcerned to improve the arable land
or the forests, and preoccupied only with social pleasures and
the effortless distillation of money from property.

'I write pamphlets and follies merely for amusement,' Swift
once told Pope, 'and when they are finished, [or] I grow weary
in the middle, I cast them into the fire, partly out of dislike, and
chiefly because I know they will signify nothing.'[2] Except for the
burning of manuscripts (which I think seldom occurred), it
looks as if Swift spent much of his leisure this way in the years
1728 and 1729.

A few days after *A Short View* came out, a small pamphlet
appeared called *The Memorial of the Poor Inhabitants ... of Ireland*.[3]
The author addressed it to the Dean of St Patrick's and asked
him to speak on behalf of a scheme for importing a hundred
thousand barrels of wheat in order to relieve the scarcity in
Ireland. To quicken the scheme, the author recommended imposing taxes on imported luxuries. He wished the money so
derived to go as a premium of ten thousand pounds given to
merchants and others who brought the grain over. Absurdly
enough, he never dealt with the cost of the grain itself.

Swift's *Answer to a Paper, Called A Memorial*[4] has a wider scope
than the tract which provoked it; and the central section has
peculiar value as expounding Swift's idea of the 'Irish interest'.
Referring modestly to his own earlier warnings against the

---

[1] Davis XII. 137.   [2] 15 Jan. 1731; Sherburn III. 161.
[3] On the date and the authorship see Davis XII. xii, 324; Ferguson, pp. 151, 189–90.
[4] Dated 25 Mar. 1728; noticed in *Mist's Weekly Journal*, 23 Apr.; abstracted, *ibid.*, 23
Apr. See Ferguson, pp. 151–2 and n. 42. Swift sent a copy to Pope; see Sherburn II. 493.

dangers threatening the nation, Swift complains that some
gentlemen had ignored their responsibilities as landlords in
order to seek government employments; others were equally
reckless while striving to defeat their political opponents; and
the country, in the mean time, came to ruin:

> A fair issue of things, begun upon party rage, while some sacrificed
> the public to fury, and others to ambition! While a spirit of faction
> and oppression reigned in every part of the country; where gentle-
> men, instead of consulting the ease of their tenants, or cultivating
> their lands, were worrying one another, upon points of *Whig* and
> *Tory*, of *high church* and *low church*; which no more concerned them,
> than the long and famous controversy of *strops for razors*: while
> *agriculture* was wholly discouraged, and consequently half the
> farmers, and labourers, and poorer tradesmen, forced to beggary or
> banishment.[1]

Once again Swift excludes considerations of religion or
politics from his idea of a healthy community. The first section of
the *Answer to ... A Memorial* runs over the history of Irish
agriculture. Swift admits that to begin with, the landlords did
indeed have to limit ploughing because the tenants exhausted
the land with indiscriminate, repeated sowing of the same crops.
But he of course denounces the opposite excess of replacing
tillage with pasture: 'Ajax was mad when he mistook a flock of
sheep for his enemies: But we shall never be sober, until we have
the same way of thinking.'[2]

Swift easily disposed of the plan to import wheat, by showing
that the nation possessed neither the money nor the time.
Instead, he recommended providing potatoes and buttermilk
for the poor until a new harvest came in.[3] More interestingly, he
appealed to the maxim, which he himself accepted, that wealth
and populousness marched hand in hand; for Swift believed, like
his contemporaries, that emigration was a national misfortune:

> But, why all this concern for the poor? We want them not, as the
> country is now managed; they may follow thousands of their leaders,
> and seek their bread abroad. Where the plough has no work, one
> family can do the business of fifty, and you may send away the other

---

[1] I.e., emigration. Davis XII. 23.   [2] *Ibid.*, p. 19.   [3] *Ibid.*, p. 22.

forty-nine. An admirable piece of husbandry, never known or practised by the wisest nations; who erroneously thought people to be the
riches of a country.[1]

Finally, in a brilliant digression, he answered those who had
blamed him for an unkind allusion to the late Judge Whitshed,[2]
in *A Short View of the State of Ireland*. There, Swift had sarcastically
observed that although the Irish were governed by laws to
which they had never consented, he dared not describe their
condition as slavery, for fear of Whitshed's ghost, 'with his
Libertas & natale solum,[3] written as a motto on his coach, as it
stood at the door of the court, while he was perjuring himself to
betray both'.[4]

In a diatribe no way related to feeding the poor, and with a
ferocity remarkable even for him, Swift defends his practice of
personal satire, arguing that notorious villainy has a claim to be
remembered as much as superlative virtue. In replying to the
objection that Whitshed was dead, Swift says,

> He was armed with power, guilt, and will to do mischief, even where
> he was not provoked; as appears by his prosecuting two *printers*, one
> to death and both to ruin, who had neither offended God, nor the
> King, nor him, nor the public.

Then in a crescendo of vituperation, he broadens the argument
to encompass villains and satirists in all ages, with a defence that
fits Juvenal and Bulgakov as well as Swift:

> What an encouragement to vice is this? If an ill man be alive, and in
> power, we dare not attack him; and if he be weary of the world, or of
> his own villainies, he has nothing to do but die, and then his
> reputation is safe. For, these excellent casuists know Latin enough,
> to have heard a most foolish precept, that *de mortuis nil nisi bonum*;[5] so
> that if Socrates, and Anytus his accuser, had happened to die
> together, the charity of survivors must either have obliged them to
> hold their peace, or to fix the same character on both.

At last the displaced indignation attaches itself to statesmen and
office-holders who give no thought to the good of others:

[1] *Ibid.*   [2] He had died 26 Aug. 1727.   [3] Liberty and my native land.
[4] Davis XII. 8.   [5] (One should say) nothing but good of the dead.

I have now present before me the idea of some persons, (I know not in what part of the world) who spend every moment of their lives, and every turn of their thoughts while they are awake, (and probably of their dreams while they sleep) in the most detestable actions and designs; who delight in *mischief*, *scandal*, and *obloquy*, with the *hatred* and *contempt* of all mankind against them; but chiefly of those among their own party, and their own family; such, whose *odious qualities* rival each other for perfection: *avarice, brutality, faction, pride, malice, treachery, noise, impudence, dulness, ignorance, vanity*, and *revenge*, contending every moment for superiority in their breasts. Such creatures are not to be reformed; neither is it prudence, or safety to attempt a reformation. Yet, although their memories will *rot*, there may be some benefit for their survivors, to smell it while it is *rotting*.[1]

The 'idea' or picture that Swift has in mind is of Richard Tighe.[2] It was Tighe who had complained to the authorities about Sheridan's unfortunate sermon. The unbridled violence of Swift's rage against this Irish M.P. was due to Tighe's narrow partisanship, his reluctance to see any employment fall to someone without Walpolian Whig connections, his opposition to Carteret, and his indifference to the welfare of the people. In a series of poems that bubble with cheerful contempt, Swift ridiculed Tighe under the name of 'Timothy' or 'Dick'.[3]

Although these poems hardly mention Tighe's failure to benefit Ireland, they dramatize Swift's conception of the anti-patriot, the man who desires a public career in order to injure his enemies and improve his private fortune. As usual, Swift associates his victim with filth—garbage, farts, turds. He also puts oaths and curses in Tighe's mouth, suggesting that these were his habitual forms of speech. But the marked feature of Swift's attack is the treatment of Tighe as an exhibitionist, eager to catch anyone's attention: to make noise, to stink, to insult, to intimidate. When the public office is unsanctified by social conscience, it becomes an excuse for evil self-indulgence.

---

[1] Davis XII. 23–5.

[2] Compare the last paragraph quoted above with the descriptions of Tighe as Tim in *Poems* III. 772–89 and as Pistorides in Davis XII. 156–7. The comment on the hopelessness of reformation is echoed in *The Legion Club*, l. 57. The reference to dreams may be a link with Swift's poem 'On Dreams' (*Poems* II. 363–4), which may perhaps belong to this period rather than 1724; it was published in 1727.

[3] *Poems* III. 772–89.

The form of the longest poem is of special interest for two reasons; it is a dramatic dialogue, and the second speaker is a madman. The dramatic form, which influenced Yeats,[1] produces a brilliant dialectic as the speakers, who start out opposed, end up together. The rich, powerful M.P., isolated by his belligerence and stupidity, at first disagrees with 'Mullinex', the beggarly madman (whose name was in fact Molyneux). Gradually, however, Mullinex convinces him that he is not feared but laughed at, and that the only way for him to remain conspicuous is to adopt the clothes, manners, and friends of the beggar.

The theme of madness which runs through Swift's work normally carries the motif of power without responsibility. In Irish affairs it grows into the concept of a nation gone mad: Parliament as a bedlam populated by lunatics who think themselves statesmen, the kingdom as a land of absurdities, where the rules for prospering are reversed.[2] When Swift compares Tighe to Punch in the puppet show, he implies that the machinery of government in Ireland has for its true function that of a farcical entertainment, diverting the people from their real problems.

The short lines, the outbreaks of stichomythia, the powerful rhythms, sudden enjambments, and absurd rhymes generate a propulsive motion which suggests contempt and laughter at once:

> Thy peevish, and perpetual teasing
> With plots and Jacobites and treason;
> Thy busy never-meaning face,
> Thy screwed up front, thy state grimace;
> Thy formal nods, important sneers,
> Thy whisp'rings foisted in all ears
> (Which are, whatever you may think,
> But nonsense wrapt up in a stink)
> Have made thy presence in a true sense,
> To thy own side so damned a nuisance,
> That when they have you in their eye,
> As if the devil drove, they fly.[3]

---

[1] Cf. the series of poems about Crazy Jane and the Bishop.
[2] Davis XII. 131, 309.   [3] *Poems* III. 775.

This poem came out in *The Intelligencer*, a weekly paper which began appearing in May 1728,[1] after the Irish Parliament rose. Swift and Sheridan were the main contributors, and Swift described the scheme to Pope:

> Two or three of us had a fancy . . . to write a weekly paper, and call it an Intelligencer. But it continued not long; for the whole volume . . . was the work of only two, myself and Dr Sheridan. If we could have got some ingenious young man to have been the manager, who should have published all that might be sent to him, it might have continued longer, for there were hints enough. But the printer could not afford such a man one farthing for his trouble, the sale being so small, and the price one halfpenny; and so it dropped.[2]

Besides the inconsequential introductory number and the essay on *The Beggar's Opera*, Swift contributed generously to the *Intelligencer*.[3] The introduction is less impressive as prediction than aspiration; for in it Swift promises to give news of the town and to celebrate acts of virtue as they are performed in Dublin. In a limited sense, perhaps, he does so.[4] But neither of those themes really finds much space in his papers, which deal with more general topics than the affairs of the capital.

In two essays Swift shows his disgust with the selection of candidates for ecclesiastical dignity. These reflections on the fates of clergymen embody Swift's form of the eighteenth-century ambivalence toward the virtue of prudence. They look back to his own distinction between magnanimity and regu-

---

[1] The first number is dated 11 May 1728. The others are undated on their title pages. But the last regular number produces a letter dated 2 Dec. 1728; and an extraordinary number, which appeared separately, includes a notice dated 7 May 1729. From the numbering of Swift's contributions, I infer that he and Sheridan were supposed to take turns providing a weekly essay. See Teerink, pp. 330–3; Davis XII. xiv–xv, 29–61, 306, 325–9. Parliament rose on 6 May 1728. (For this note I am largely indebted to Professor James Woolley, whose superb edition of *The Intelligencer* will soon appear.)

[2] Sherburn III. 292.

[3] Altogether, he contributed nos. 1, 3, 5, 7, 8, 9, 10, and 20. Swift designed his poem, *The Journal of a Modern Lady*, for the *Intelligencer*, but at last it appeared separately (*Poems* II. 443).

[4] No. 3, on *The Beggar's Opera*, nos. 8 and 10 (on Tighe's politics and the coffeehouse response to no. 8) might qualify as news of the town. Sheridan's numbers, especially 2, 4, and 6, are more topical. The reference to acts of virtue is in part ironical (there being so few); but Sheridan's essay on Swift (no. 18) handles the subject. (This note is thankfully derived from Professor James Woolley.)

larity in advice once offered to Bolingbroke.[1] They also look forward to Fielding's habit of recommending prudence but bestowing it on knaves who reduce the principle to low cunning.[2]

When Swift ridicules methodical, cautious men who make their way straight up by offending nobody and gratifying persons in power, he seems to compliment himself. He even quotes his own observation that 'when a great genius arises in the world, the dunces are all in confederacy against him.'[3] Yet Swift urged friends like Sheridan, Gay, and Bolingbroke to 'preserve a spice of the alderman'. Such a mixture of attitudes is not Swiftian or Aristotelian. It is Christian: 'The children of this world are in their generation wiser than the children of light.... Make to yourselves friends of the mammon of unrighteousness.'[4]

In the church as in the state Swift condemned the judgment of those who distrust any exhibition of shining talents. At the same time he reproached shining talents which failed to employ common prudence to advance themselves. The two essays, which contrast the success of a nonentity with the failure of a gifted fellow, represent only the upper side of Swift's moral vision; and the irony is no more than moderately effective. As one might expect, the strongest passages deal with the happy career of Corusodes,[5] the example of self-promoting caution.

An essay on education has more flavour. But this is a subject on which reflection without special information rarely sheds new light. Swift's argument is that the quality of a man's learning is inversely related to the social status of his family, and that a nobleman is the least likely to gain a sound classical education. Consequently—Swift complains—the very persons set to govern the nation lack the wisdom which their responsibilities call for.

---

[1] Davis VIII. 138–9; Williams II. 332–3.

[2] Cf. H. K. Miller, *Essays on Fielding's Miscellanies* (Princeton, 1961), pp. 227–8; also Fielding's essay 'On the Knowledge of the Characters of Men', in his *Miscellanies*, ed. H. K. Miller (*Works*, ed. W. B. Coley *et al.*, II, Oxford, 1972), pp. 153–78, especially 157–8.

[3] Davis XII. 39; cf. *ibid.*, I. 242.   [4] Luke xvi. 8–9.

[5] Drip-nose: one who suffers from catarrh (Greek)—probably suggesting the nasal drone that Swift associated with Dissenting preachers.

Not until we reach No. 19 of the *Intelligencer* do we find a theme that powerfully engages Swift's rhetoric.[1] Once again the subject is Ireland's economic crisis. But the aspects examined now are the shortage of silver money and the loss of people to America. Except for debased copper coins, the currency of the nation was made up of English or foreign gold and silver. As we have already noticed, the fixed rate of silver to gold in Ireland was unluckily too low; the English gold guinea was set at threepence more in Ireland than in England. So the bankers and tradesmen of the kingdom paid their English debts in silver rather than gold. Besides, the balance of trade ran against Ireland, and English bankers offered a premium for specie over bills of exchange. Small change in silver therefore became a painfully scarce commodity. Landlords had trouble getting in their rents. Employers could not pay men until the earnings mounted to a considerable sum. Moneychangers made inordinate profits.[2]

Money was one of the themes that always excited Swift's imagination. Here, the use he makes of his excitement is to reflect in new ways on the mindless tyranny of the English. It would of course have been simple and effortless for the government in Westminster to reduce the coinage crisis by revaluing the money used in Ireland. The failure to do so was yet another sign of Westminster's perfect unconcern for Irish welfare. Swift's positive recommendation is undramatic, merely that great employers and landlords should pay for goods and services in small promissory notes, ranging in value from twopence to a pound. These could then pass current among the shops, markets, and public houses in a neighbourhood.

But the absorbing parts of the essay are spun off from this centre. There is a double protest, one against the oppressions of the English, the other against the legal dangers of complaining about these oppressions. Swift brilliantly transforms economic injustice into a problem in rhetoric.

The ground-bass of the piece is the speaker's sympathy with

[1] I do not count No. 3, on *The Beggar's Opera*, or No. 15, which is a reprint of 'A Short View of the State of Ireland'; and I set aside the poems.

[2] I follow closely the account given by Ferguson, p. 158; cf. above, p. 511.

the poor. Swift pretends to be a landowner with over two hundred tenants, a man deeply troubled by the wretchedness surrounding him. In this rôle he can play back and forth between the superior knowledge and wealth of the speaker, and the vulnerable innocence of his dependants. The latter, he says, bemoan their genuine hardships, but 'their weak reasonings never carry them to the hatred and contempt born us by our neighbours and brethren [i.e., the English], without the least grounds of provocation; who rejoice at our sufferings, although sometimes to their own disadvantage.'[1]

Speaking as a grandee, the author can sound personally untouched by the difficulties which common people endure. His consequent air of objectivity is ironically undercut by the fierceness of his imagery:

> It is true indeed that under our circumstances in general this complaint for the want of *silver* may appear as ridiculous as for a man to be impatient about a *cut-finger*, when he is struck with the *plague*: and yet a poor fellow going to the gallows, may be allowed to feel the smart of *wasps* while he is upon *Tyburn-Road*.[2]

The weight of Swift's argument falls not upon the hardships (severe though they are) caused by the shortage of silver but on the speed with which they could be relieved if only the English would condescend to utter a word. He points out that the difference in the value of gold between England and Ireland makes bankers send their silver to London and change it for gold, thereby gaining threepence Irish for every guinea. Then he observes,

> To a common thinker, it should seem, that nothing would be more easy, than for the government to redress this evil, at any time they shall please. When the value of guineas was lowered in England from 21s. and 6d. to only 21s. The consequences to this kingdom were obvious and manifest to us all: and a sober man may be allowed at least to wonder, although he dare not complain, why a new regulation of *coin* among us, was not then made; much more, why it hath never been since. It would surely require no very profound skill in *algebra* to reduce the difference of . . . *three pence* in a *guinea* to less

[1] Davis XII. 55.   [2] *Ibid.*

than a farthing; and so small a fraction could be no temptation, either to *bankers* to hazard their *silver* at sea, or tradesmen to load themselves with it, in their journeys to England. In my humble opinion it would be no unseasonable condescension, if the *government* would graciously please to signify to the *poor loyal Protestant* subjects of Ireland either that this miserable want of silver is not possible to be remedied in any degree by the nicest skill in arithmetic; or else that it doth not stand with the good pleasure of England to suffer any *silver* at all amongst us. In the former case it would be madness to expect impossibilities; and in the other we must submit: for lives and fortunes are always at the mercy of the *conqueror*.[1]

Swift raises the issue of a public mint in Ireland, and he connects the shortage of coin with the emigration of Protestants to America, which he treats as a calamity both for Ireland and for the departing families; for he believes they have been ill-informed about the perils and vexations they will face. But the power of the pamphlet comes from the reflex by which Swift comments on the danger threatening his own dissident voice. It is lawful, he says, to submit petitions in England,

But what is lawful for a subject of Ireland, I cannot determine: nor will undertake that your *printer* shall not be prosecuted in a *court* of *justice* for publishing my *wishes* that a poor shopkeeper might be able to change a *guinea* or a *moidore* when a customer comes for a *crown's* worth of goods. I have known less crimes punished with the utmost severity under the title of *disaffection*. And I cannot but approve the wisdom of the *ancients*, who, after Astraea had fled from the earth, at least took care to provide *three upright judges for Hell*.[2]

The sinuous turns and reversals of the paragraph, flicking itself from cool generalization to hot particularity, is typical of Swift's best prose. The syntax is as well, combining an appearance of casual spontaneity with a skilful delay of resolution and a rise in emotion till one meets the whip-cracking close of the last sentence quoted. So also the theme of injustice, which comes up continually in Swift's writings at this time, unites the speaker with his nation.

Swift performs the same feat with the image of the gout in the

[1] *Ibid.*, p. 56.
[2] I.e., Ireland has not got three upright judges; *ibid.*, p. 57.

following paragraph, all the more bitter for being an illness associated with luxury but applied to a people on the verge of famine:

> You may observe, that I have very superficially touched the subject I began with, and with the utmost caution: for I know how criminal the least complaint hath been thought, however seasonable, or just, or honestly intended; which hath forced me to offer up my daily prayers that it may never, at least in my time, be interpreted by innuendo's as a false, scandalous, seditious, and disaffected action, for a man to roar under an acute fit of the *gout*, which, beside [*sic*] the loss and danger, would be very inconvenient to one of my age, so severely afflicted with that distemper.[1]

Here the problem of literary style—i.e., the very manner in which Swift is writing—ties itself to the already complicated theme of national and personal injustice. Swift as an author, in the self-conscious turns of his apparently unpremeditated prose, is joined with the Irish community as an inarticulate people forbidden to voice their terrible grievances.

[1] *Ibid.*, p. 61.

Chapter Six

HENRIETTA HOWARD

Among the bitterest of Swift's preoccupations in this season was Henrietta Howard, whom he had met in 1726 and whom he was to mention for the last time we know of in 1737. Their friendship could hardly have been avoided. Not only did she have qualities which always excited his interest, but she also belonged to the circle of his most eminent friends: Arbuthnot, Gay, Pope, Peterborough, Bolingbroke, Lady Betty Germaine, and the Duchess of Queensberry. Peterborough is said to have composed the well-known verses, 'I said to my heart', for Mrs Howard. Pope described her in 'On a Certain Lady at Court'. Her second husband was to be George Berkeley, whom Swift had known as a child in the family of his father the Earl of Berkeley. With this marriage she would become Lady Betty's sister-in-law.

To bring out the importance of Swift's angry fascination with this subtle woman, I must review certain events of the years 1725 to 1727; for the connection began while he was still in Ireland, completing *Gulliver's Travels*. Before Swift met Mrs Howard, he heard of her through Pope:

> I can also help you to a lady who is as deaf, though not so old as yourself; you'll be pleased with one another, I'll engage, though you don't hear one another: you'll converse like spirits by intuition. What you'll most wonder at is, she is considerable at court, yet no party-woman, lives in court, yet would be easy and make you easy.[1]

Swift took the description as allegory and interpreted it to mean

[1] 14 Sept. 1725; Sherburn II. 322. For details of the poems by Pope and Peterborough, see Pope, *Poems* V. 250–1 and III, Pt. ii, p. 63, note to ll. 157–80. The character of Cloe in Pope's *Moral Essays* II, ll. 157–80, is drawn from Mrs Howard, and should be compared with that written by Swift.

Riches.[1] When Pope said he was mistaken, Swift suggested the Duchess of Queensberry.[2] The riddle held out[3] almost until Swift came to England in 1726 and met the lady herself. By then his curiosity had been raised in just the way to make him anticipate liking her.

The introduction took place, as we have seen, when Swift met the Princess of Wales at Leicester House, the London residence of the Prince. Arbuthnot presented him to her highness, and Mrs Howard, in attendance as a woman of the bedchamber, met Swift on the same occasion. The lady possessed enough charms to have captured the Prince at Hanover, shortly before his father's accession. Born in 1688, she was Vanessa's age and seemed to have only a younger brother surviving from a large family. Her own father had died while she was an infant, and her mother when the daughter was still a very young girl.

Mrs Howard shared Swift's deafness but added to it headaches (probably migraine[4]), eye troubles, and other illnesses of her own; and Swift took an immediate interest in both her age and her diseases.[5] To all these attractions she joined traits and manners which must have delighted him. She always behaved herself with propriety and decency; her manner was 'grave and mild'; she seemed discreet but not reserved; her memory was accurate; she prided herself on being sincere and honest.[6]

Horace Walpole (her neighbour for many years) described Mrs Howard as 'of a just height, well made, extremely fair, with the finest light-brown hair'. He says her face was 'regular and agreeable' rather than beautiful, but that she dressed with 'taste and simplicity' and seemed 'remarkably genteel'. Walpole confessed to no great admiration for her intelligence. Yet he found the deepest pleasure in her conversation; and when she died, he wrote that he had lost the only 'rational acquaintance' in his neighbourhood.[7]

---

[1] *Ibid.*, p. 326.

[2] *Ibid.*, pp. 332, 343. I agree with Ball (against Sherburn) that 'Gay's steward' would be the Duchess of Queensberry. Cf. Pope's comment on Ford's explanation, *ibid.*, p. 350.

[3] *Ibid.*

[4] Arbuthnot mentions her having a headache on one side; Williams III. 166.

[5] *Ibid.*, pp. 232–3.   [6] Suffolk, *Letters* (1824), introduction, *passim*.

[7] *Reminiscences*, pp. 65–6; *Correspondence*, ed. W. S. Lewis, 10 (New Haven, 1941), 247.

Lord Hervey, who, as vice-chamberlain, constantly saw Mrs Howard at the court of George II, neither loved nor respected her. But he says, 'Good sense, good breeding, and good nature were qualities which even her enemies could not deny her.... She was civil to everybody, friendly to many, and unjust to none.'[1]

Swift's letters to Henrietta Howard make misleading guides to his attitude. In her own right, she obviously delighted him; but he would have treated her with less consideration if he had not mistakenly thought of her as a way to reach the Queen. I think, too, that he always doubted her motives, and that by his own manner he wished to expose his friends' credulity. He was in effect allowing them to have their way, and playing up to the court to accommodate them but insisting that neither the favourite nor her princess would ever really oblige them. Yet for all his attempt to sound sceptical, he in fact developed hopes of his own even while cultivating disillusionment.

Decades after their first meeting, the lady, who was then the elderly Countess of Suffolk, gave her account to Horace Walpole:

> I had introduced Swift to the Queen, then Princess;[2] she had asked him a thousand questions, particularly about ... his changing his principles, and she made him write to me, that she might see the letters. He had writ me on this subject; she ordered me to answer it, and in a style of joke. I would fain have been excused, but she insisted and said she would see my letter.[3]

The Countess told Walpole that Caroline saved copies of both the lady's letters and the Dean's replies. 'These and any other curious papers she could get, the Queen pasted into a book.'[4]

Mrs Howard certainly valued Swift's acquaintance. During the spring and summer of 1726, she freely invited him to Marble Hill, and often arranged for him to see the Princess (whom Swift—with one exception—would only visit when sum-

[1] *Memoirs*, ed. R. Sedgwick (1931), I. 42.

[2] The language in which Arbuthnot relayed Caroline's invitation to Swift makes it almost certain that he presented the Dean to the Princess. See Williams III. 127.

[3] Horace Walpole, *Reminiscences*, ed. Paget Toynbee (Oxford, 1924), pp. 119–20.

[4] *Ibid.*, p. 116. I assume the reference is to the time when Caroline was still Princess, and that the actual mounting of the letters was done by the lady-in-waiting.

moned). He would have realized that Her Highness read what
he wrote to the lady, and we know that Mrs Howard kept his
letters.

In Ireland during the autumn and winter of 1726–7, Swift
worked to strengthen her friendship with him; and his letters to
her could not have been more gracious without sounding ful-
some. The gifts of a ring, the plaids, and the tiny crown were
exchanged.[1] But Swift plainly warned her that he would expect
the worst upon the death of the old King: 'When the princess
grows a crowned head, you shall have no more such compliments; and it is a hundred to one whether you will deserve
them.'[2] Thus he tried unsuccessfully to forestall his own
disappointment.

Returning to England in the spring of 1727, Swift wrote a
character of Mrs Howard, dated 12 June. This is a transparent
attack on her sincerity. He says she has 'long affected to desire'
that her being the chief favourite at the court of the Prince of
Wales 'might not be believed'; she always fits her opinions to the
policies of the court; she gets enormous credit for infinitesimal
favours:

> She abounds in good words and expressions of good wishes, and will
> concert a hundred schemes for the service of those whom she would
> be thought to favour: Schemes that sometimes arise from them, and
> sometimes from herself; although, at the same time, she very well
> knows them to be without the least probability of succeeding. But, to
> do her justice, she never feeds or deceives any person with promises,
> where she doth not at the same time intend a degree of sincerity.[3]

Swift ends the character by foreseeing that when the Prince
succeeds to the throne, Mrs Howard will sacrifice her benevolence to her talents as a courtier. By delivering to the lady herself
a slightly softened version of this elaborate insult, Swift challenged her to disprove it through her actions.[4]

---

[1] See above, p. 515. [2] Williams III. 196. [3] Davis V. 215.

[4] Compare the text in *ibid.*, pp. 213–15 with that in Scott XI. 145–50. Although the
character is dated 12 June, or two days before the fact of the King's death became known
in England, it is barely possible that Swift delivered it after 14 June in order to dramatize
his challenge.

As we have seen, George II succeeded to the throne less than two months after Swift came back to England in 1727. The dean now waited grimly for Mrs Howard either to fulfil some of the hopes which his friends insisted on having, or else to verify the most severe insinuations of his 'character'. Partly on account of her advice, he cancelled his trip to France and joined in the various political manœuvres of his friends.

Pope and others, it seems, grossly overestimated Mrs Howard's influence on either Caroline or her spouse; for Swift claimed to have learned from them that she, in 1725, had been responsible for the understanding that kept Walpole at the head of the government under the new reign.[1] Certainly, Pope had said that Gay put 'his whole trust at court' in Mrs Howard.[2] As Gay obtained nothing substantial and Swift received none of the promised acknowledgements for his plaids—in fact, as all things rumbled along in their ancient tracks—the dean exploded two months after leaving England. In a letter to Pope he broke into scorching reflections on courts: the maxim that a minister never forgives those he has injured (meaning Walpole and Gay); the insincerity of persons who 'would be thought best friends'; the court habit of sacrificing those whom we 'really wish well' to a 'point of interest or intrigue'; the principle of keeping everything worth taking for those who 'can do service or disservice':

> with all the partiality of my inclination, I cannot acquit this charac-
> terized person [i.e., Mrs Howard] ... Neither will your mutato
> nomine, etc. [i.e., blaming Caroline rather than Mrs Howard]
> satisfy me unless things are monstrously changed from what you
> taught me. For I was led to believe that the present unexpected
> situation or confirmation of things [i.e., Walpole's continuance in
> office] was brought about above two years ago by the intervention of
> that person whose character was drawn.[3]

Of course, things were indeed 'monstrously changed', or, rather, Bolingbroke and Pope had given Swift a false measure of Mrs Howard's weight; and she herself had never succeeded in disabusing him. For Swift, moreover, Mrs Howard probably

[1] Sherburn II. 461.   [2] *Ibid.*, p. 332.   [3] 23 Nov. 1727; *ibid.*, p. 461.

recalled another 'lady of the bedchamber to a great queen'[1]—
Mrs Masham. The two women were both associated with men
like Bolingbroke, Arbuthnot, and Peterborough; and in the
courtly intrigues of national politics, both women served as
hope-giving omens to the party of Swift's friends. In Queen
Anne's favourite too, he had found 'a plain sound understanding', 'great truth and sincerity', 'an honest boldness and
courage', and a 'firm and disinterested' style of friendship.[2] I
think this parallel was a hidden reason for his disappointment
with Mrs Howard and for his certainty that all their friends,
from Pope to Lady Betty Germaine, had misunderstood her.
Swift could not believe that a royal favourite might have so little
power as Mrs Howard in fact possessed. At the same time, since
he had enjoyed a far deeper intimacy with Mrs *Masham* than
Pope, Gay, or Lady Betty, he felt no qualms about preferring his
own judgment of Mrs *Howard* to theirs. Furthermore, although
Mrs Howard must have reminded Swift of Vanessa, she did not
treat him as Vanessa had done. He sent Mrs Howard the sort of
'character' that he had sent Esther Vanhomrigh. Leaving
England in 1727, he wrote letters to her like those he had written
to her predecessor. But she neither chased him nor pleaded with
him; and like Lady Masham she did nothing for his career. It is
remarkable that he (like so many others!) should have thought
Queen Caroline would be influenced by a woman who was her
husband's mistress.

Yet it would be shallow for one to blame Swift's faulty judgment. We know that Caroline's husband entertained Swift's
friends and hated Walpole until George I died. Mrs Howard
could not have foreseen the transformation in the sentiments of
the Prince that greed and other pressures would effect. She was
cautious. Yet she did enjoy the Scriblerians' charms, and must
have received signals from her royal mistress that led her to feel
hopeful on Swift's and Gay's accounts. In August 1727, when
everyone knew that Walpole would remain the chief minister,

[1] Davis V. 215: description of Mrs Howard; cf. discussion of Mrs Masham and the
Duchess of Somerset, II. 518.
[2] *Ibid.*, VIII. 153: description of Lady Masham.

she still wrote to Swift in language that could only encourage him to expect benefits for his cronies and himself.[1] I believe Swift when he says that to his friends Mrs Howard 'enlarged upon the good intentions of the [new] court to me'.[2] So she too must have been misled; and indeed the lady said as much when she told Swift, in 1731,

> If I cannot justify the advice I gave you by the success of it; yet you know I gave you my reasons for it; and it was your business to have judged of my capacity by the solidity of my arguments; if the principle was false you ought not to have acted upon it; so you have only been the dupe of your own ill judgment and not to my falsehood.[3]

During the time when he dealt kindly with Mrs Howard, Swift apparently found in her language encouragements which she never intended to give him. I think that he added the interested overtones of 1710–14 to the more social friendship of 1726–7. Either he assumed that Mrs Howard did have the power of finding places for him and his friends, or he believed that she pretended to have that power. When the years brought no fulfilment of his private, half-suppressed expectations; and when besides losing Stella, he observed the frustration of Gay's shy search for a place, Swift probably revived his mortification of 1713 ('neither can I feel joy at passing my days in Ireland: and I confess I thought the ministry would not let me go'[4]). He had not mastered the situation as he had thought he would do; he had not outsmarted the woman; he had not proved wiser than his friends. He had given without receiving; he felt mortified and charged the mood on Mrs Howard.[5]

---

[1] Williams III. 231.   [2] *Ibid.*, IV. 99.   [3] *Ibid.*, III. 499.
[4] *Journal*, 18 Apr. 1713.
[5] In my analysis of the relation between Mrs Howard and Swift, I have been deeply influenced by the learned and penetrating essay of James Woolley, 'Friends and Enemies in *Verses on the Death of Dr Swift*'.

Chapter Seven

A DOSE FOR THE DEAD

I. BEEF, MUTTON, AND PARTRIDGES

S wift's complaints of poor health, like the fury of his figures of speech, might lead one to imagine him as a bitter, isolated Timon. But he did not believe in letting spleen dictate his social habits. Sometimes, of course, he pretended to live in gloomy isolation. Yet he could also admit the truth—that Ireland was more than tolerable for him. Apart from the lack of English friends and the anger over political or economic mischief, Hibernia offered many comforts to the first citizen of his country. Urging Pope to visit him, Swift went over the amenities he enjoyed:

> [Both] summers and winters are milder here than with you; all things for life in general better for a middling fortune; you will have an absolute command of your company, with whatever obsequiousness or freedom you may expect or allow. . . . I have said enough, yet not half. Except absence from friends, I confess freely that I have no discontent at living here; besides what arises from a silly spirit of liberty, which as it neither sours my drink, nor hurts my meat, nor spoils my stomach farther than in imagination, so I resolve to throw it off.[1]

The dean's ailments did not divorce him from society. They only directed his choice of companions. Pope, who suffered worse limitations, went the opposite way and attached himself to grandees. But Swift wrote to him,

> I reckon that a man subject like us to bodily infirmities, should only occasionally converse with great people, not withstanding all their good qualities, easinesses, and kindnesses. There is another race

---

[1] Sherburn II. 492.

which I prefer before them, as beef and mutton for constant diet before partridges: I mean a middle kind both for understanding and fortune, who are perfectly easy, never impertinent, complying in everything, ready to do a hundred little offices that you and I may often want, who dine and sit with me five times for once that I go to them, and whom I can tell without offence, that I am otherwise engaged at present. This you cannot expect from any of those that either you or I or both are acquainted with on your side; who are only fit for our healthy seasons, and have much business of their own.[1]

He admitted that his old evasion, of exaggerating honest diseases as a defence against unwanted callers, came into play with the high but not with the low.[2]

There were obnoxious people in Ireland, and some of them were burrs. Chetwode haunted Swift by letter, with demands for advice about his wife, his son, his property. He affected an intimacy which rasped on Swift, who returned dusty answers, discouraging any replies.[3] It is a tribute to Chetwode's insensibility that he should have persisted in spite of the dean's language. 'I am vexed whenever I hear a knocking at the door, especially the raps of quality,' said Swift, 'and I see none but those who come on foot.'[4]

So he kept clear of Chetwode, clung to old friends, and gathered some new ones. He enjoyed the hospitality of Delany, repaying him with aids to preferment. He depended on John Worrall in the usual way, but took none of his goodness for granted. '[I] should never have done', Swift told him, 'if I returned you thanks so often as I ought for your care and kindness.'[5]

Other friends belonged to Swift through the circles of his cathedral chapter. A good satire on lawyers called 'The Answer' testifies to his appreciation of Robert Lindsay, the legal adviser (or seneschal) of St Patrick's. Swift scolds him, in ironic couplets, for stooping to be a Member of Parliament; but he also praises

[1] *Ibid.*, p. 492.
[2] 6 Mar. 1729; *ibid.*, III. 22.
[3] Williams III. 248–9, 255–6, 317–18, 333–4, 339–40, 344–7.
[4] *Ibid.*, p. 249.   [5] *Ibid.*, pp. 301–2, 307–8.

Lindsay for nearly preserving his integrity among a tribe of rogues:

> But, shift him to a better scene,
> Got from his crew of [rogues] in grain;
> Surrounded with companions, fit
> To taste his humour, and his wit;
> You'd swear, he never took a fee,
> Nor knew in law his *A, B, C.*
>
> 'Tis hard, where dulness over-rules,
> To keep good sense in crowds of fools;
> And we admire the man, who saves
> His honesty in crowds of knaves;
> Nor yields up virtue, at discretion,
> To villains of his own profession.
> [Lindsay,] you know what pains you take
> In both, yet hardly save your stake.[1]

The geniality of these lines, in a poem bristling with coarse satire, suggests the easy pleasure Swift could take in the company of men barely remembered now except as his acquaintants. 'I want only to be rich,' he wrote to Pope in a passage of self-ridicule,

> for I am hard to be pleased; and, for want of riches, people grow every day less solicitous to please me. Therefore I keep humble company, who are happy to come where they can get a bottle of wine without paying for it. I give my vicar a supper, and his wife a shilling,[2] to play with me an hour at backgammon once a fortnight .... But, on Sunday evenings, it costs me six bottles of wine to people whom I cannot keep out.[3]

Nobody gave more comfort to Swift, or took more punishment from him, than Sheridan. The schoolmaster's good nature and affection made up for his irresponsibility. But his vanity and forgetfulness opened him to Swift's sarcasm. Not everyone shared the dean's tolerance of his protégé's fecklessness. In the summer of 1728, on holiday from his school, Sheridan was

---

[1] *Poems* II. 435–6.   [2] Probably for the supper she wasn't getting.
[3] I.e., he has regular entertainments for his friends on Sunday evenings (6 Mar. 1729; Sherburn III. 22).

rambling around the south of Ireland while Swift visited friends of his own in the north. Sheridan aspired to a good church living, and the Dean of St Patrick's tried to help by recommending him to the Bishop of Cork. So the southern ramble had point. But nothing came of the effort, and Swift meanwhile missed his chum's company. At the same time, Sheridan, partaking of southern hospitality, overlooked a number of duties. As a schoolmaster, he was supposed to appear before the ecclesiastical registrar in Dublin by a specified date. The moment went by, and he never showed up. Archbishop King rebuked him:

> I spake to the Registrar in your behalf, and he told me you never yet appeared on the proper day when schoolmasters were summoned; that it is expected that clergymen who know the rules and canons of the church, should give the most exact obedience to them, and be an example to other people, and when they fail [they] deserve most to be made examples; he intimated further that the pretenders to be the highest churchmen are commonly the most negligent and refractory, by which they encourage such as profess less regard to religion to contemn the ecclesiastical jurisdiction. I did not know what to answer to this, but the court being adjourned . . . , I will take care to have an *expectator* put upon you, and do hope when you come to Dublin you will take care to make yourself *rectus in curia*.[1]

For the dean, unlike the archbishop, paternal authority was only an element in his attitude toward Sheridan. It was as a crony that he chiefly relied on him. Swift exchanged verse lampoons with Sheridan[2] and made friends of his hospitable friends the M'Gwyres of Ormond's Key.[3] While Swift now lingered in the north, he hankered for a visit from Sheridan. Hoping they might both travel back to Dublin together, he put off his own departure.[4]

During the period of delay, Swift thought of a Scriblerian hoax, to tease the wanderer and perhaps punish him for desertion. It was in the tradition of their rhyming contests. Sheridan had written and printed a ballad on the Irish spa of Ballyspellan (near Kilkenny), which he visited with a lady. He was proud of

[1] Ball IV. 41, n. 2.   [2] *Poems* II. 424–9.   [3] Ball V. 463.
[4] Williams III. 296.

finding all possible rhymes on the place name. 'But we have found fifteen more,' Swift announced to Worrall, 'and employed them in abusing his ballad, and Ballyspelling too.' Swift asked Worrall to have his verses printed and published without any notice to the victim.[1]

The trick succeeded too well, for it hurt Sheridan's fragile self-esteem, and he resented Swift's parody as 'an affront on [the lady] and himself'.[2] How far he was justified, one may perhaps determine from a specimen stanza:

> But, Tom[3] will prate
> At any rate,
> All other nymphs expelling
> Because he gets
> A few grisettes
> At lousy Ballyspelling.[4]

In any case, the incident suggests pointedly what Swift expected from the beef and mutton of friendship, and what he could provide as sauce. At the same time one must remember that this was when Swift wrote to Bishop Browne on Sheridan's behalf, that Swift got Pope to read the manuscript of his friend's translation of Persius, and that the greatest poet of the age wrote kindly to Sheridan for Swift's sake.[5]

One of the dean's least trustworthy habits, when he implied that he had withdrawn from society, was to sound alienated from his family and contemptuous of his relations. In fact, he not only kept in touch with several cousins but worked hard to help them. A remarkable case is his readiness to present the considerable sum of five pounds to a woman he had never met, merely 'on account of her mother and grandmother, whom my mother used to call cousin'.[6]

A stronger case is Swift's dealings with Stafford Lightburne, the clergyman who married Hannah, daughter of Swift's cousin Willoughby. It was he whom Swift had made his curate at Laracor. The fortune of Lightburne's wife was in danger from

---

[1] *Ibid.*, p. 302; *Poems* II. 437–43.
[2] Davis v. 225.   [3] I.e., Sheridan.   [4] *Poems* II. 440–3 (ll. 49–54).
[5] Williams III. 296, 220–1; Sherburn II. 445.   [6] Williams III. 309.

her father's creditors, and he needed cash on hand. Swift said he was prepared to lend him eight hundred pounds because 'he married the daughter of my near relation, for whom I had great kindness, and to whom I owe some obligations.'[1]

Almost like a relation, and certainly a bridge between England and Ireland, there was Charles Ford. Swift had hoped to pass the winter of 1728–9 in London, but the usual disabilities worried him: 'I am forced to prefer a scurvy home where I can command people to speak as loud as I please, before the vexation of making a silly figure and tearing the lungs of my friends,' he told Lord Oxford.[2] So it was a peculiar pleasure for him to be able to expect his old friend's return from London in the summer of 1729. He knew it was a shortage of money that brought Ford back, but he gave him the sort of advice about friends which suggests how carefully Swift chose his own companions, and how much he took regular society for granted, as a necessity:

> I could wish you would cotton more with the valuable people while you are here. I do suppose nobody hates and despises this kingdom more than myself, and yet when I am well I can be easy among a set of honest people who neither shine in titles nor wit: but I do not recommend my text to you. The time may come when you will have a less relish for variety.[3]

The truth is that those who credit Swift's language of contempt for Ireland, and who believe that he wore out the last thirty years of his existence rancorously burning for the English scene, have failed to see that his reflections on Irish absentees are exactly applicable to himself:

> I used to wonder, how a man of birth and spirit, could endure to be wholly insignificant and obscure in a *foreign* country, when he might live with lustre in *his own*; and even at less than half the expense, which he *strains* himself to make, without obtaining any one end; except that which happened to the *frog* when he would needs contend for size with the *ox*.[4]

---

[1] *Ibid.*, p. 306.   [2] 21 Sept. 1728; *ibid.*, p. 299.
[3] *Ibid.*, p. 322.
[4] *Drapier*, p. 158. Of course, Swift can also make the opposite judgment about his life in Ireland: cf. Williams III. 3.

II. MARKET HILL

Instead of a visit to England, an easier prospect had opened itself
to Swift's uncertain health. He had got to know the Achesons,
a northern family long settled in the county of Armagh. Sir
Arthur, a forty-year-old baronet, came from Scottish ancestors
who had secured his estate early in the seventeenth century.
Swift estimated his income at fifteen hundred pounds a year.[1]
Acheson had married Anne Savage, heiress of Swift's acquaintance Philip Savage, Chancellor of the Exchequer of Ireland. She
was a slender, intelligent woman who liked to dress well but
enjoyed conversation and appreciated Swift's company.[2] One of
her friends was Deborah Rochfort, to whom Swift had addressed
his *Letter to a Very Young Lady*.[3] Although the Achesons had seven
children, three died young. The survivors included two boys,
one about ten years old and the other about seven.[4]

Sir Arthur had entered the Irish House of Commons the year
before, and may have become familiar with the Dean of
St Patrick's through the connections that followed. I think
he came near to Swift's ideal of a cultivated gentleman who
advances the prosperity of the common weal. He was well-born,
being fifth in the line of baronets, and had been educated at
Trinity College, Dublin. He was naturally studious, fond of the
classics; and Swift considered him a 'man of taste'. But he did not
talk easily.[5] Although Sir Arthur owned a house in Dublin
(Capel Street), he resided at the ancestral seat near Newry. The
capital was not agreeable, he said, 'when it wants a Lord
Lieutenant and Parliament'.[6] Lady Acheson liked the town
better. She played cards there, lost money, and stayed up late.[7]

[1] 'The Revolution at Market-Hill', l. 38 (*Poems* III. 884).

[2] She was separated from her husband about 1732. Swift seems to juxtapose Lady
Acheson and his new friend Orrery in that year (Williams IV. 91–2); and Orrery seems to
say she was separated about the time he met her (*Poems* III. 902). She died about 1 Nov.
1737; see *Complete Baronetage* II. 334–5, and Mayhew, p. 51.

[3] Mayhew, p. 51.

[4] John Lodge, *The Peerage of Ireland* (Dublin, 1789), VI. 82–3. For the sons, Archibald
and Arthur, see *Alumni Dublinenses*.

[5] Swift, 'The Dean's Reasons', ll. 22, 41–4 (*Poems* III. 899–900); also Williams's
headnote, *Poems* III. 847.

[6] H.M.C. *Various Collections* VI. 68.   [7] Williams IV. 92.

Sir Arthur was an Anglican churchman and, though no Tory, stood for the Irish interest while collaborating with Walpolian flunkeys like Dodington. He visited England but was no absentee. Instead of indulging himself in the dissipations of London, like Charles Ford, he felt proud of his heritage and his Scottish ancestry. 'We are', he said,

> in the best improved part of Ireland; not inferior to many parts of England; and the fullest of people, and yet a hundred and thirty years ago there was not one British man in all these northern counties.... Never surely was any country so much altered in so short a time. We have few or none of the old Irish amongst us; we have indeed plenty of everything but money,[1] which is very much wanted. However, we can live comfortably enough if we are satisfied with our obscurity.[2]

When a 'family so agreable'[3] asked Swift to pay them a long visit, he felt happy to accept the invitation; and in June 1728 he made his first arrival at their home, Market Hill (now Gosford Castle), which lay between Newry and Armagh. So far from seeming disappointed by his reception, he was soon urging Sheridan to join him.[4] Every four or six weeks his deafness and giddiness kept returning, in spells which lasted about three weeks apiece.[5] But the Achesons put their voices up, and communication survived.[6] Her ladyship combined charity with candour. She had modest good manners and made no promises which she failed to keep.[7] At Market Hill, Swift assumed his old prerogative of assisting in the departments of agriculture, landscape gardening, and the design of out-houses. 'I am a very busy man,' he smilingly told Sheridan.[8]

Indoors he undertook the education of the lady, correcting her orthography and prescribing Milton and mythology to

---

[1] I.e., silver and copper coins.   [2] H.M.C. *Various Collections* VI. 68.
[3] Williams III. 299.
[4] 2 Aug. 1728; *ibid.*, p. 296. There is a tradition that Sheridan introduced Swift to the Achesons.
[5] 6 Mar. 1729; Sherburn III. 21.
[6] 13 Jan. 1729; Williams III. 307.
[7] Swift, 'Epistle to a Lady', ll. 65–80; *Poems* II. 631–2.
[8] 2 Aug. 1728; Williams III. 296.

supply her defective resources of literature:

> No book for delight
> Must come in [her] sight;
> But instead of new plays
> Dull Bacon's essays.[1]

Inevitably, he led her on long walks, corrected her diet, and criticized her clothes. It was Moor Park and Hetty Johnson all over again, with Temple's character divided between the dean and Sir Arthur. Although Lady Acheson was good-natured and hospitable, she was also in poor health; for she coughed, was underweight, and short of breath;[2] so she easily fitted the old stereotype.

When Pope heard about her ladyship, he wrote presciently that he was glad to know Swift was planting and building—

> two things I envy you for, besides a third, which is the society of a valuable lady: I conclude ... that you quarrel with her, and abuse her every day, if she is so. I wonder I hear of no lampoons upon her, either made by yourself, or by others because you esteem her.[3]

Evidently, Sheridan had quietly written to Pope about their friend's attachment to 'Skinnybonia'.[4]

We have few details of Swift's experiences during his long stays with the Achesons. But I assume that one of the attractions for him was the sense of recreating the hours he had passed at Esther Johnson's side. As for his host and hostess, anyone living in a big country house with plenty of servants and leisure would have welcomed an amusing and immensely distinguished guest. Swift spent much time alone at Market Hill (especially when he was ill) or with the gardeners and workmen, and he visited Henry Leslie nearby. The dignified and laconic Sir Arthur must have felt grateful for the dean's attention to his vivacious lady. When Swift later summed up a visit which finally lasted two and

---

[1] Swift, 'My Lady's Lamentation', ll. 145–8; *Poems* III. 855.

[2] Williams IV. 12, 375. She may have been consumptive, for she died young.

[3] 28 Oct. 1712; Sherburn II. 522.

[4] Information generously supplied by Professor James Woolley. Cf. *Poems* III. 861, textual note to l. 42.

a half seasons, he told Pope,

> I lived very easily in the country: Sir [Arthur] is a man of sense, and
> a scholar, has a good voice, and my Lady a better; she is perfectly
> well bred, and desirous to improve her understanding, which is very
> good, but cultivated too much like a fine lady. She was my pupil
> there, and severely chid when she read wrong; with that, and
> walking and making twenty little amusing improvements, and writ-
> ing family verses of mirth by way of libels on my Lady, my time
> passed very well and in very great order; infinitely better than here
> [i.e., in the deanery], where I see no creature but my servants and
> my old Presbyterian house-keeper, denying myself to every body till
> I shall recover my ears.[1]

In August 1728 Swift told Sheridan he was well off at Market
Hill and hoped to hang on till they could both return to Dublin
together. He would have liked Sheridan to settle at Hamilton's
Bawn, a property belonging to Acheson. I suppose he thought
Sheridan could set up a school there. 'Sir [Arthur]', Swift wrote,
'on hearing your letter, pressed me to stay longer.' Swift also
wished to remain for the fun of planting and pruning. 'I hate
Dublin,' he said, 'and love the retirement here, and the civility
of my hosts.'[2]

Seven weeks later he wrote to Ford that he had been bothered
by the usual illnesses, 'but with a family so agreeable, that joined
to the happiness of being absent from Dublin, I do not much pity
myself.'[3] In November he was planning to stay till Christmas.[4]
In January he was waiting for the weather to thaw and for 'that
beast Sheridan' to come.[5] But he did not finally get home until
6 February 1729.[6]

III. FAMILY VERSES

Besides gifts to the Achesons and vails to the servants, Swift
balanced the large account of hospitality with verses very different from those he had written about the Temples. The central

---

[1] 13 Feb. 1729; *ibid.*, III. 15.   [2] 2 Aug. 1728; Williams III. 296.
[3] 20 Sept. 1728; *ibid.*, p. 299.   [4] 16 Nov. 1728; *ibid.*, p. 304.
[5] 4 Jan. 1729; *ibid.*, p. 307.   [6] Sherburn III. 21.

figure now was Lady Acheson. Swift told Pope that she teased him to write about her and kept all the copies of the poems.[1] But he clearly delighted in the exercise, liked the subject, and produced some remarkable compositions.

As usual, the poems are humorous in tone and burlesque in style. Swift pays special attention to the lady's appearance. Concrete particularity, for him, signifies lack of respect, but in these poems the disrespect is an ironic means of showing fondness. So also the design usually involves mimicry and impersonation. Swift mocks the lady's speech or speaks in her person, making her ridiculous either way. But the ridicule is an ironic revelation of tender feelings. The forms of the poems set the writer difficult problems of versification and rhyme; and his mastery suggests a challenge met to honour a lady love. The burlesque of high styles and genres, of eulogy and epic, implies a preference for reality over fantasy, and the lady's virtues are part of that reality.

In the earliest poem, 'My Lady's Lamentation',[2] Swift takes dimeter couplets for his form. They run like regularized Skeltonics, although I don't know that Swift ever read Skelton's works. The jocularity, like Swift's self-mockery, sweetens the moral didacticism in passages like this:

> But sense gives a grace
> To the homeliest face:
> Wise books and reflection
> Will mend the complexion.[3]

In the poem Swift pretends to be Lady Acheson complaining about the dean's attempts to improve her character—which means, for us, recasting her in Stella's mould. But the difficult verse pattern is not only a task which the poet performs for his lady's sake. It also recalls her appearance. The short lines are as thin as their subject, and the pitching rhythm gives us her angular movements, especially when the dean corrects her posture; here the tick-tock beat and the image of collapsing clock-

---

[1] 6 Mar. 1729; *ibid.*, p. 22.
[2] Dated 28 Jul. 1728; *Poems* III. 851–8.   [3] Ll. 99–102.

work go together:

> When my elbows he sees
> Held up by my knees,
> My arms, like two props,
> Supporting my chops,
> And just as I handle 'em
> Moving all like a pendulum;
> He trips up my props,
> And down my chin drops,
> From my head to my heels,
> Like a clock without wheels;
> I sink in the spleen,
> An useless machine.[1]

There are also the two common attractions of Swift's verse—the neat accommodation of colloquial syntax to a demanding metre and the vitality of the poet's inventive energy:

> And then he grows mild;
> Come, be a good child:
> If you are inclin'd
> To polish your mind,
> Be ador'd by the men
> 'Till threescore and ten,
> And kill with the spleen
> The jades of sixteen,
> I'll shew you the way:
> Read six hours aday.
> The wits will frequent ye,
> And think you but twenty.[2]

In 'Lady Acheson Weary of the Dean'[3] we meet the same point of view, the same impersonation, and the same themes. Speaking as her ladyship, but now in cross-rhymed octosyllabic quatrains, the poet voices the frustration of his hostess. She is tired of a guest who has long overstayed his welcome and has assumed tyrannical powers. An extraordinary element is the satirical listing of Swift's own features: dark, sallow complexion,

---

[1] Ll. 25–36. [2] Ll. 123–34.

[3] *Poems* III. 859–61. Though published in 1730, the poem obviously refers to Swift's first visit. It is probably to be dated Sept. 1728, for Swift has been at Market Hill for a 'quarter', or three months (l. 9).

heavy eyebrows, and protruberant eyes:

> Oh! if I could, how I would maul
> His tallow face and wainscot paws,
> His beetle-brows and eyes of wall.[1]

As usual with Swift, the poem has the charm of true dramatic speech, expressive and full of character; and the rhythms often fall with precise, humorous emphasis, turning neatly at the rhyme. Although Swift speaks in the poem as Lady Acheson, he carries the mimicry a step further by having her in turn imitate Sir Arthur. Here is the lady telling her knight how to evict the dean:

> But you, my life, may let him know,
> In civil language, if he stays,
> How deep and foul the roads may grow,
> And that he may command the chaise.

When Swift organizes his mimicry and versification in the framework of a dramatic fable, the effect rises to evocative comedy. A mock-Ovidian tale, 'On Cutting Down the Old Thorn',[2] has the humour of *Baucis and Philemon*. The burlesque of a popular ballad is a natural idiom for Swift; and the theme, of a sick tree being cut down at his wish, comes directly from the dean's labour on Acheson's estate. The event of the thorn nymph's denouncing her executioner is calculated to exhibit Swift's gift for impersonation; and the mock-heroic diction gives as much pleasure to the poet as the reader:

> Thou chief contriver of my fall,
> Relentless Dean! to mischief born,
> My kindred oft' thine hide shall gall,
> Thy gown and cassock oft be torn.[3]

The poet's willingness to indulge himself in a fantasy of death centred on a female figure suggests that at Market Hill he could

---

[1] Ll. 37–39.
[2] *Poems* III. 847–51. Dated 14 Sept. 1728. Again in cross-rhymed octosyllabic quatrains. This poem may be influenced by Pope's *Elegy to the Memory of an Unfortunate Lady*.
[3] Ll. 57–60.

handle his grief for Stella. If he felt responsible for her death, he could now in fantasy let her surrogate punish him.

In the new year 1729 Swift's verse turned a little from these themes, although he stayed on at Market Hill in the long round of deafness and vertigo. Before the middle of January, he completed *The Journal of a Modern Lady*, in octosyllabic couplets.[1] About forty opening lines make an apostrophe to Lady Acheson, who is supposed (in the poem) to have asked the author for a satiric journal of a woman's day. The remaining 258 lines follow a lady of fashion from her awakening to her bedtime.

These couplets invite comparison with *The Rape of the Lock*, since the actions of the two poems have a general likeness. The *Journal* may be read as a reply to the *Rape*, for the Dame is a kind of Belinda-after-marriage.[2] If one disregards the introductory sections, both poems begin with the woman's rising at noon. Swift uses dialogue to reveal the essential squalor of the bedroom; Pope uses description to represent the genuine refinement and charm of his scene. The main parallels in the rest of the two works are the cardgame sequences. Here again Swift relies on speech, but Pope offers almost pure narrative. Pope brings out the minute drama and ritual refinement of his episodes; Swift, the corruption and irresponsibility of his. Instead of sylphs and gnomes, Swift employs personifications of faults and virtues (ten faults to three virtues). Pope transmutes even sins into graces, with lines like

> A third interprets motions, looks, and eyes;
> At ev'ry word a reputation dies.
> *Snuff*, or the *Fan*, supply each pause of chat,
> With singing, laughing, ogling, and all that.[3]

But Swift delivers a cannonade against female scandal-mongering:

---

[1] *Poems* II. 443–53.

[2] Swift may have been aware of the parallels with the *Rape*. The incomplete l. 19 of his poem echoes IV. 117 of the *Rape*. Cf. also Swift, l. 48 and Pope, I. 148; Swift, l. 52 and Pope, III. 92; Swift, l. 132 and Pope, IV. 31; Swift, ll. 174–5, and Pope, V. 41–2; Swift, ll. 190–4, and Pope, III. 15–16; Swift, l. 231 and Pope, III. 49; Swift, l. 238 and Pope, IV. 161. In turn, Swift's poem influenced Pope's *Epistle to a Lady* (*Moral Essays* II).

[3] III. 15–18.

Or how should I alas! relate,
The sum of all their senseless prate,
Their innuendoes, hints, and slanders,
Their meanings lewd, and doubl'entendres.[1]

Inevitably, they treat the game itself in directly opposite ways, for Swift simply aims to denounce the stylish feminine obsession with cards, while Pope wishes the game to be the most brilliant transformation scene of his gilded theatre.

It would be absurd to compare the two pieces as poetry. Not only are Swift's and Pope's poetic talents of different orders; but the *Journal* is not among Swift's most attractive works, while the *Rape* is Pope's masterpiece. Yet the significant difference is in the direction to which each man has addressed his abilities. Over the bubbling cheerfulness of the *Rape*, Pope expands his brightest gifts of language, image, rhythm, and aural harmonies. Swift, abandoning his flair for irony, builds a constricted, doleful world. The attack on women grows heavy not because of its motifs but because of the monotonous and confined structure on which Swift mounts it.

Part of his bitterness is merely the normal tone of his anti-feminine satire. But part, I think, springs from an implicit contrast with Stella, whose virtues these creatures of fashion conspicuously lack. It is a pity that Swift did not bring into the poem a figure like that of his beloved, to serve as a healthy contrast to the frivolous vice of the worldly women. This is what Pope was to accomplish brilliantly with the figure of Martha Blount in his *Epistle to a Lady*.

Meanwhile, Swift showed his respect for Sir Arthur by making him too an alter ego of the dean. This was in the *Intelligencer* essay[2] written just before his month's illness (December-January 1728-9) and lamenting Ireland's shortage of silver.[3] Not only did Swift give himself the character of a

---

[1] Ll. 140-3.

[2] *Intelligencer* XIX (Davis XII. 54-61); see Williams III. 308 and n. 1 (18 Jan. 1729). It is the printed answer to a letter received in the summer of 1728; see above, pp. 583-6, and Davis XII. 75.

[3] The essay is in the form of a letter dated 2 Dec. and was probably published around 7 Dec. (My information is yet again from Professor James Woolley.)

northern country gentleman and M.P. with an estate of £1400 a year, but he also referred, in the body of the essay, to another gentleman, of the same neighbourhood, who had come of age twenty years earlier and let his lands 'at a low rate to able tenants'. In both persons Swift was certainly thinking of Acheson,[1] who had turned twenty-one in January 1709. Of course, he did not intend the model to be identified; the baronet was merely an authentic witness to a national crisis.

IV. PAMPHLETS AND FOLLIES[2]

We have few details of Swift's life in the spring of 1729. We know he lived quietly in Dublin and suffered his usual ailments. Three days after returning to the deanery, he fell ill; and after a short spell of good health—which he spent characteristically in long walks—he found himself deaf again.[3] Although he certainly saw 'beef and mutton' people like the Worralls, he wrote of being 'monastic'.[4] But I suppose the dean had a deal of business with his chapter, after being away so long; and that he kept up the Sunday evening entertainments.

Besides fending off unwanted callers, Swift contemplated the ugly aspects of Ireland. The terrible winter had driven Primate Boulter to warn Carteret that without the intervention of sudden charity, 'some thousands will perish before next harvest.'[5] Emigration to America, grain shortages, the lack of silver money, are themes as audible (and almost as common) in Boulter's letters as in Swift's pamphlets. While waiting for Archbishop King to die, the charitable Primate was raising money by subscription (with himself as a leading donor) to provide the hungry north with grain from the well-supplied south.[6] He responded to crises like emigration and famine rather

---

[1] Swift gives the same description of Acheson in Davis XII. 79, which almost repeats the parallel paragraph in the *Intelligencer*.

[2] For the title, see Sherburn III. 161.

[3] Williams III. 321.   [4] *Ibid.*, p. 322.

[5] 4 Dec. 1728; Boulter I. 279 (Dublin, p. 215).

[6] 3 Dec. 1728, 13 Feb. and 13 Mar. 1729; *ibid.*, pp. 265–6, 279–80, 287–8 (Dublin, pp. 213, 224, 230).

as Swift did, by blaming the greedy landlords and commiserating with the wretched natives. Like Swift he felt sure that those Ulstermen who sailed to the New World would be still worse off there.

Boulter wrote to the Duke of Newcastle,

> The scarcity and dearness of provision still increases in the north; many have eaten the oats they should have sowed their land with; and except the landlords will have the good sense to furnish them with seed, a great deal of land will lie waste this year.

.   .   .

> There have been tumults at Limerick, Cork, Waterford, Clonmel, and other places, to prevent the corn we have bought from going to the north. Those at Limerick and Cork have been the worst, where they have broken open warehouses and cellars, and set what price they pleased on provisions.[1]

He wrote to Walpole,

> [What] with scarceness of corn in the north, and the loss of all credit there, by the numbers that go or talk of going to America, and with the disturbances in the south, this kingdom is at present in a deplorable condition.[2]

The dean returned home from Market Hill to find the subscription in progress, as Boulter said, 'to supply the necessities of the north'.[3] I assume that Swift contributed handsomely to the fund. But we know that he also met the appalling situation in his customary way: he wrote, that spring, at least four thoughtful essays on the terrifying outlook—although none of them appeared before his death; they were either too offensive or not finished enough. Their themes blend with one another, and so do their titles: *Answer to ... Unknown Persons*, *A Letter to the Archbishop ... concerning the Weavers*, *An Answer to ... Unknown Hands*, and *A Letter on Maculla's Project*.

Agriculture and trade remain his preoccupations; and in these essays he considers the hindrances to them. Irremediable

---

[1] 13 Mar. 1729; *ibid.*, pp. 287–8 (Dublin, pp. 229–30).
[2] 31 Mar. 1729; *ibid.*, p. 296 (Dublin, p. 237).
[3] *Ibid.*, p. 279 (Dublin, p. 224).

blights, he sets aside with a few withering shrugs: absenteeism, Englishmen appointed to Irish offices, Acts restricting export, etc.[1] But many improvements still lie within the scope of the citizens, and those he hammers at. The most familiar seem to be the improvement of agriculture, the use of Irish manufactures, and the reduction of imports.

The essays share a desperate sound of futility. Against his own instincts as a reformer and projector, Swift feels the tide of his failures. Before he can complete a speech, the thought breaks in on him that nobody will be listening:

> I am tired with letters from many unreasonable well-meaning people, who are daily pressing me to deliver my thoughts in this deplorable juncture, which upon many others I have often done in vain. What will it import that half a score people in a coffee-house may happen to read this paper, and even the majority of those few differ in every sentiment from me.[2]

But he cannot help promulgating his schemes (usually rephrasings of others' proposals) for rescuing some fragments from the general ruin.

The strongest of these springtide efforts is probably the *Answer to Several Letters from Unknown Persons*.[3] This deals with emigration, landlords, the balance of trade, and other subjects. The

---

[1] Davis XII. 77. [2] *Ibid.*

[3] Of the four pieces, *A Letter to the Archbishop* is preserved in an autograph manuscript which a hand that is not Swift's has dated April 1729 (*ibid.*, p. 329). The archbishop died on 8 May 1729. Consequently, another piece, which refers to him as alive, must have been written before that date. This second piece is the *Answer to Several Letters from Unknown Persons*, which is probably earlier than the *Letter to the Archbishop*; see Ferguson, pp. 161, 191. Incidentally, the *Answer to ... Unknown Persons* also refers to William Burnet as alive and in difficulties with the House of Representatives of Massachusetts Bay (Davis XII. 77). Since Burnet went to Massachusetts after mid-April 1728 and died 7 Sept. 1729, the piece can be roughly dated from this allusion. In addition, it refers to *Intelligencer* XIX, published in December 1728. A third piece, *A Letter on Maculla's Project*, can be dated as probably after February and before May 1729 (Davis XII. xvii–xviii; Ferguson, p. 160). A fourth piece, *An Answer to Several Letters ... from Unknown Hands*, is dated 1729 in the posthumous first printing. It refers to the death of Whitshed, which occurred 26 Aug. 1727, and it recommends policies for an imminent Parliament to consider. Since the Irish Parliament met on 23 Sept. 1729, I assume that the *Answer to ... Unknown Hands* (which must not be confused with *An Answer to ... Unknown Persons*) was written not long before that date. So I hesitantly suggest the following order of composition: *An Answer to ... Unknown Persons*, *A Letter to the Archbishop*, *A Letter on Maculla's Project*, *Answer to ... Unknown Hands*.

striking features are the piercing note of despair, the dislike of emigration, and the ferocity of Swift's emotions on the subject of unnecessary imports.

Swift's targets are scattered because he is replying to an open letter which dealt with the various reasons that emigrants from Ulster were abandoning their homeland.[1] Dissenters often claimed that religious persecution was driving them out. But Archbishop King had argued that the Dissenters never thought of leaving until their economic hardships oppressed them. It is true that the emigrants were overwhelmingly Ulster Presbyterians; but a modern reader may suspect that among those who suffered from the miseries of the period, it was this group which had the resources to carry them overseas. As victims of religious persecution the Roman Catholics easily outdid them.

It was also argued that the burden of tithes paid to the Established Church troubled Dissenting Protestants enough to incite them to emigrate. Boulter easily showed that this was a falsehood spread by landlords who wished to raise their rents without paying additional tithes. Moreover, if the tithe were indeed reduced or even eliminated, the tenant would not benefit, because the landlord would absorb the difference into his rent.[2]

Meanwhile, the very fact that Protestants made the body of the exodus alarmed the authorities. Over four thousand emigrants left between the spring of 1728 and the start of 1729. Reports came to Dublin that twenty thousand more were preparing to go in the following spring. Boulter thought of taking legal action to stop them. Depopulation—in mercantilist theory—was terrible enough. But to weaken the ratio of Protestants to Catholics in a region already overgrown with Popery was a deeply alarming change. Swift had long connected the decline of tillage with the decline of population. A penetrating scholar has shown that he consistently and perhaps deliberately underestimated the population of Ireland in order to

---

[1] In the following paragraphs (as so often elsewhere) I follow closely the account given by Ferguson (pp. 161–3).

[2] 13 Mar. 1729; Boulter I. 289–95 (Dublin, pp. 231–4).

strengthen his case.[1] Archbishop King, whose views agreed with Swift's, had inverted the old relation between people and riches. As he saw it, in countries exporting manufactured goods, the more hands there were, the more products they could export; but in a country like Ireland, that exported foodstuffs, the more mouths there were, the less goods were available for sale abroad.[2]

Against this background we can see what Swift is doing in his *Answer to ... Unknown Persons*. Here again he accepts the dreadful restrictions of the English as unalterable. He blames the landlords and absentees for irresponsibly destroying the people. He recommends the encouragement of agriculture and the use of native manufactures. But he also voices utter hopelessness:

> If the farmer be not allowed to sow his corn; if half the little money among us be sent to pay rents to Irish absentees, and the rest for foreign luxury and dress for the women, what will our charitable dispositions avail, when there is nothing left to be given, when contrary to all custom and example all necessaries of life are so exorbitant, when money of all kinds was never known to be so scarce.[3]

If landlords encouraged agriculture, if Irish purchasers spent their money on Irish goods, if the English granted freedom of trade to Ireland, if the absentees came home, then emigration would halt.[4] But such rational policies were miracles not to be hoped for. Consequently, Swift rages over the supine connivance of the people at their own undoing: 'Gracious God in His mercy look down upon a nation so shamefully besotted.'[5]

Within the nation, he fulminates with peculiar heat against women. Female extravagance brings out a tone of frantic violence:

> [Women] under their present corruptions seem to be a kind of animal suffered for our sins to be sent into the world for the destruction of families, societies, and kingdoms; and whose whole study

---

[1] Clayton D. Lein, 'Jonathan Swift and the Population of Ireland', *Eighteenth-Century Studies* 8 (1974–5), 431–53.
[2] 12 Dec. 1719, to Southwell.   [3] Davis XII. 81.
[4] Cf. Ferguson, p. 163.   [5] Davis XII. 80.

seems directed to be as expensive as they possibly can in every useless article of living, who by long practice can reconcile the most pernicious foreign drugs to their health and pleasure, provided they are but expensive; as starlings grow fat with henbane: who contract a robustness by mere practice of sloth and luxury: who can play [*sc.* cards] deep several hours after midnight, sleep beyond noon, revel upon Indian poisons, and spend the revenue of a moderate family to adorn a nauseous unwholesome living carcase.[1]

In earlier works by Swift the motif of female extravagance had already appeared; and other writers had treated the theme with angry sarcasm.[2] But here[3] and in the *Journal of a Modern Lady* the treatment rises to an intensity which seems something fresh. Probably the unexpressed (and unthought) cause again goes back to Stella's death, and Swift feels furious that he should have had to lose his frugal, virtuous friend when so many thoughtless slatterns could go on living.

The animus against women erupts again in *A Letter to the Archbishop ... concerning the Weavers*. Because Ireland had ample supplies of excellent raw wool, and because the Dean of St Patrick's knew at first hand of the plight of his neighbours the weavers, Swift gave special attention to woollen manufactures.[4] The weavers knew of his concern and would often ask him to advise them.[5] In April 1729 one of their spokesmen begged Swift to publish a recommendation that the Irish people should wear cloth made in their own country: it might, he said, 'preserve many hundreds of their trade from starving'.

Swift replied with an open letter to the barely living archbishop. He began with yet a new blast of bitter sympathy with his people, saying that he often considered, as he walked the streets,

whether those animals which come in my way with two legs and human faces, clad, and erect, be of the same species with what I have seen very like them in England, as to the outward shape, but differing in their notions, natures, and intellectuals more than any two kinds of brutes in a forest.[6]

[1] *Ibid.*   [2] Cf. Ferguson, pp. 155–6.
[3] I.e., in the *Answer to Several Letters from Unknown Persons.*
[4] Cf. Ferguson, pp. 153–5.   [5] Davis XIII. 90.   [6] *Ibid.*, XII. 65.

The material condition of the Irish, he said, could only be improved within the limitations set by the utterly unyielding English government; and the principal effort the people themselves could make was to avoid unnecessary imports.

A chief obstacle to such a policy was extravagant luxury, of which the great instigators were women. So Swift denounced

> the cowardly slavish indulgence of the men to the intolerable pride, arrogance, vanity and luxury of the women, who strictly adhering to the rules of modern education seem to employ their whole stock of invention in contriving new arts of profusion, faster than the most parsimonious husband can afford; and to compass this work the more effectually, their universal maxim is to despise and detest everything of the growth and manufacture of their own country, and most to value whatever comes from the very remotest parts of the globe. And I am convinced, that if the virtuosi could once find out a world in the moon, with a passage to it, our women would wear nothing but what came directly from thence.[1]

One must recall Swift's praise of Stella for her thrift, her simple taste in clothing, her love for Ireland. But one also recalls that writers on Irish affairs would commonly single out women as extravagant and frivolous.[2]

Having condemned the perpetrators of the crime, Swift turned as usual on the victims. He reminded the archbishop of how the weavers sent a delegation to call upon his grace in March 1729, when Swift happened to be with him. The weavers asked the archbishop to urge his clergy to wear Irish cloth. On that occasion Swift told them to prepare samples of a kind of black cloth, costing no more than eight pence a yard, which was suitable for clerical gowns. The archbishop, he said, could invite a group of parsons to meet at his palace and examine the goods. But instead of making up the samples, the weavers came back to the dean with their request for a pamphlet supporting home manufactures.

Swift then told how he had proposed to the master weavers and the chief drapiers that they should establish and enforce standards and prices of their various products—'in such a

[1] *Ibid.*, p. 67.   [2] Ferguson, pp. 155–6.

manner, that if a child were sent to any of their shops, the buyer might be secure of the value and goodness, and measure of the ware'. But the scheme, however subject to modification, was never undertaken. One reason, Swift said, for the failure of the Irish weavers and drapiers to capture the home (or any foreign) market was their own knavery.

Yet finally, his heart was with them. He advised the Corporation of Weavers to petition Parliament to resolve that the Members should wear only Irish cloth and should induce their families and tenants to do so.[1] In this way, as he both blamed them and supported them, he showed the ambiguity of his moral attitude not only toward the Dublin weavers but toward mankind.

Swift's favourite topic of money is the subject of the simplest of the four essays, *A Letter on Maculla's Project*. The shortage of gold and silver made the need for copper coins urgent. But the defeat of Wood's patent left the English government punitively indifferent to the crisis. Not only had Swift written an *Intelligencer* essay on the subject; but a petition for a supply of small coins is recorded as presented to Sir Arthur Acheson and other members of the grand jury of the county of Armagh by the poor of that county; and the language of the petition makes me suspect that Swift had a hand in it.[2]

Early in February 1729 a Dublin pewterer and coppersmith named James Maculla proposed a scheme like that of the promissory notes sketched by Swift in his *Intelligencer* essay. Maculla offered to sell promissory notes worth a halfpence and a penny, in the form of copper discs stamped with their value. He published a pamphlet recommending his scheme, and he tried to discuss it with the dean soon after Swift returned from the Achesons'. The illness which descended at that time prevented the interview. But eventually Swift called on Maculla and heard him out. He then composed the *Letter* for publication.

The most impressive aspect of this essay is the restraint of its tone. Although the piece is dull and repetitious, the writer

---

[1] Davis XII. 68–71.   [2] See the *Dublin Intelligence*, 29 Apr. 1729.

remains calm even when one would expect him to sound furious. It seems clear that Swift wished to offend nobody, and the style is conclusive evidence that the outbursts in the other essays were not due to an incapacity for self-control.

Most of the *Letter* deals—mildly and candidly—with the excessive profits Maculla would gain from his scheme, also with the difficulty of preventing fraud. Swift devotes the rest of the piece to a rational plan of his own. He would have ten public-spirited gentlemen form a company to issue ten thousand pounds' worth of copper coins over a period of five years. (That is to say, copper tokens which could be used as money.) They would take the least possible profit and would carefully guard the quality and number of the counters. In effect Swift was calling for the establishment of a mint for copper money.[1]

We have evidence that the public response to any such scheme was discouraging, for the people felt uneasy about anything like coinage that did not bear the royal stamp. By the end of April the prospect of realizing either Maculla's scheme or Swift's seemed to have faded.[2]

But economic programmes kept breeding themselves in the deanery. The approaching session of Parliament—which was not in fact to meet until September—seems all that gives point to the fragmentary *Answer to Letters from Unknown Hands*. Critics who like to believe that Swift ridiculed *a priori* all projects for the improvement of Ireland would have trouble explaining this essay; for it is a survey of proposals that might help the nation. The dean's improving spirit, so far from evaporating over the frustrations of Irish inertia, took on new embodiments with every need it discerned.

In the *Answer to . . . Unknown Hands*, he first picks up a highways proposal, and draws out the advantages to be gained from mending and extending the roads. Suddenly, he passes to the management of the bogs, which can be reduced in some places and cut for turf in others. Then he proceeds to reforestation, to the replacement of Irish speech by English, the encourage-

---

[1] Davis XII. 93–105. [2] Cf. Ferguson, pp. 158–60.

ment of agriculture, and finally the need for copper halfpence.

It is no wonder that Swift never completed the essay, though it amounts to a list of proposals which 'should be offered to the Parliament'.[1] He knew his plans were all familiar ones, and he could not hearten himself with any prospect of influencing the government.

V. THE DEATH OF THE ARCHBISHOP

Archbishop King knew he was worth more to the government dead than alive. As his strength dwindled, he laboured to accomplish his old purposes of helping an oppressed people. During his illness in the summer of 1728 he wrote to a friend,

> There are [twelve] hours in the day wherein if a man walk he stumbleth not, but the night of old age cometh in which a man can neither walk nor work.[2] This is at present much my case, for I cannot so much as set my foot to the ground, much less walk.[3]

When his friend said that King had earned a rest, the archbishop replied,

> St Paul[4] has set me a better example, who though he laboured a thousand times more than I and to much better purpose, yet did not reckon upon what was past but pressed on to the obtaining the prize for which [he] laboured. There is no stopping in this course till God call us from it by death.[5]

Boulter was among the many watchers of the archbishop's condition. Like other men in great places, he wished to see his own candidate occupy the palace of St Sepulchre's when King departed. In January 1729 the Primate wrote to Lord Townshend,

> The age and frequent returns of illness the Archbishop of Dublin has laboured under the greatest part of this winter (though I do not apprehend that he is in any immediate danger of dying) have made

---

[1] Davis XII. 85.   [2] John xi. 9-10.   [3] 13 Jul. 1728, to Henry Maule.
[4] Archbishop King was consecrated on St Paul's day.
[5] 6 Aug. 1728, to Henry Maule.

me think it proper to write a few lines to your lordship about a successor to him.

Above all, Boulter desired an Englishman. His first choice was an old friend, Adam Ottley, Bishop of St David's. But he knew that there was strong backing at court for another person; and he wished to be on good terms with whoever came in; so he named the second man as well—John Hoadly, younger brother of the notorious Bangorian and (since June 1727) Bishop of Ferns.[1] The recommendation was unabashedly political; and to the ugly indifference shown by a priest to the death of a brother in God, we must add the unconcern of a governor of the church with the spiritual or intellectual qualifications of those who served under him:

> [Hoadly] behaved himself very well last sessions of Parliament here; he is one of courage, and very hearty for the English interest, and is a good speaker; and I am satisfied he is one that would concur with me in promoting his majesty's service; he is very well liked of here for an Englishman.[2]

Four months later, on Thursday, 8 May 1729, at four o'clock in the afternoon, the ancient hero died. 'The town is almost as if a general calamity had happen'd, so deeply is the loss taken, by our citizens,' we are assured by the *Dublin Intelligence*.

> [The archbishop is] truly lamented by those who were so happy to be of his lordship's acquaintance, or came to the knowledge of his many virtues, having all the good qualities necessary for making the greatest figure in life, the best patriot, truest friend to his country, of the most extensive charity, great piety, and profound learning. He died as he lived, as a saint, leaving his possessions mostly to be distributed for charitable uses, and but little more than his coach and cattle to defray the expense of his funeral.[3]

[1] See Boulter's letter of 12 Jun. 1729 to Gibson, Bishop of London (I. 315; Dublin ed., p. 252).

[2] 16 Jan. 1729; *ibid.*, p. 273 (Dublin ed., p. 219). For another side of Boulter's character see his pleas for support of an effort to convert Roman Catholics to Protestantism, II. 10–13 (Dublin, pp. 9–12).

[3] *Dublin Intelligence*, 10 May 1729, quoted by Beaver H. Blacker, *Brief Sketches of the Parishes of Booterstown and Donnybrook* ... (Dublin, 1874), p. 164.

The body was buried in the graveyard of the Donnybrook church, 'in a very decent tho' plain manner', but it was 'accompany'd thither by most of our nobility and gentry, and thousands of our citizens'.[1]

The poems published to mark King's death[2] do not bear much quotation, and the sentiments expressed are too commonplace to tell us much about the man or the mourners. But even the poets' clumsiness suggests the popularity of the archbishop and the sincerity of the mourning:

> He was liberal and free, full of charity,
> No bishop alive had less money than he,
> What can be expected, he schools has erected,
> That poor people's children might be instructed.[3]

Swift's feelings could only have been mournful. Whatever resentments he may have felt against King, the archbishop had been the steadiest paternal figure of his life. Privately, to lose him after losing Stella was to dissolve the last deep connection with the years of obscurity. Publicly, it took from Swift the greatest support he could have in the campaign to help Ireland.

Although no record remains of the dean's thoughts about the archbishop's death, we may guess some of them from his ironic description of the cheerful Dr Helsham (in a letter to Pope):

Here is an ingenious good-humoured physician, a fine gentleman, an excellent scholar, easy in his fortunes, kind to everybody, hath abundance of friends, entertains them often and liberally, they pass the evening with him at cards, with plenty of good meat and wine, eight or a dozen together; he loves them all and they him; he has twenty of these at command; if one of them dies, it is no more than poor Tom! he gets another, or takes up with the rest, and is no more moved than at the loss of his cat; he offends nobody, is easy with everybody—is not this the true happy man?[4]

---

[1] *Dublin Intelligence*, 13 May 1729, quoted by Blacker, *ibid.*, p. 165.
[2] A series of them will be found in the library of Trinity College, Dublin, in a volume of broadsheets labelled, 'Irish Pamphlets 1728–1732', with the pressmark A. 7. 5. The poems on King's death are nos. 87–92.
[3] 'A New Song Call'd Ireland's Universal Loss', *ibid.*, no. 92.
[4] Sherburn III. 16.

VI. MEMENTO MORI

Modest realms existed in which Swift stood independent of English or Irish parliaments and could accomplish reforms of his own contrivance. These were the chapter and properties of St Patrick's Cathedral. The odour of mortality lingered across the months between Stella's death and the final illness of Archbishop King. I suspect that the dean's sense of impotence in public affairs blended itself with the mourning for his two friends to produce a new channel for his constructive energy. During the spring of 1729, Swift's normal impulse to strengthen the fabric of the cathedral turned in the direction of funeral monuments. Perhaps he took thought from the lack of any memorial, in the cathedral, to Mrs Johnson; but, the month the archbishop died, Swift began addressing a series of letters to families represented by mortuary scupture or ancestors buried in the church, inviting them to mend or erect monuments. (After all, the whole building was a national shrine.) The enormous structure of effigies commemorating the Earl of Cork's family was made the responsibility of the Earl of Burlington.[1] The less pretentious monument to the Earl of Ranelagh was accounted to Lady Catherine Jones.[2]

But the most interesting request seems that to the Countess of Holderness. Her grandfather, buried in St Patrick's Cathedral, was the great Duke of Schomberg, hero of the Boyne, saviour of Protestant Ireland, whose last and most lustrous glory belongs to the years when Swift first met Stella. Schomberg had died in 1690, when Swift left Moor Park after his earliest stay with the Temple family.

In the Duke's posthumous reputation, therefore, were fused the conscious and unconscious preoccupations of Swift sixteen months after Stella's death: Ireland's miserable condition, his own deepest bereavement, and the death of the mighty archbishop (to whom no monument was erected). Perhaps Swift unconsciously put himself and his poor country in the same position and thus found a reason at this time for asking the

[1] Williams III. 334–5, 389–90.   [2] *Ibid.*, pp. 335–6, 338–9.

Countess to remedy the lack of any memorial over her ancestor's corpse.

The letters to Burlington and to Lady Catherine Jones begged barely for the maintenance of works already built. The letter to the Countess asked her to put up a new 'plain marble monument'.[1] Swift had made this request several years earlier and had got no reply. The Countess was far from a stranger to Swift, for he had known her at least eighteen years earlier as a friend of the Vanhomrighs.[2] Yet his letter could hardly have failed to sound arrogant to her ladyship; while it is not rude, it does not have certain refinements of tact which Swift knew how to summon when he wished to be courteous. Perhaps the most significant turn of the whole affair came several years later; for while neither Burlington nor Lady Catherine Jones ignored his appeals, it was the Countess who defied him and whom he finally wished to humiliate. 'I writ to her myself,' Swift told Carteret; 'and also, there was a letter from the Dean and Chapter to desire she would order a monument to be raised for him in my cathedral.' But they had no answer.

Swift asked Carteret to warn her ladyship's husband (Lord Fitzwalter) that if the family saw fit to leave the great Duke without a memorial worth fifty pounds, the dean and chapter would erect one to the value of ten,

> wherein it shall be expressed, that the posterity of the Duke, naming particularly Lady Holderness and Mr Mildmay [i.e., Lord Fitzwalter], not having the generosity to erect a monument, we have done it of ourselves. And if, for an excuse, they pretend they will send for his body, let them know it is mine; and rather than send it, I will take up the bones, and make of it a skeleton, and put it in my registry office, to be a memorial of their baseness to all posterity.[3]

Whether this outburst is taken as fantasy or genuine threat, it suggests a strength of emotion out of keeping with the occasion. Was it a displacement of the regret he felt for being unable to provide Stella with a monument? Precisely because he was the dean and she had been so close to him, he would have risked

---

[1] *Ibid.*, pp. 336–7. [2] *Journal*, 27 Jun. 1711. [3] Williams III. 390.

exciting scandalous comment if he had put up a stone for his beloved.

Anyhow, the Countess and the Earl persisted in their silence, and finally the dean and chapter did order a slab of black marble with an inscription that may still be read, telling the world, in choice Latin, how much more the virtues of the Duke weighed with strangers than with his own relations by the 'nearest ties of blood'. Swift boasted of the accomplishment to Pope, and saw to it that newspapers got the story.[1] In this spiteful gesture I think we see Swift's animus against women, against the nobility, against absentees, and against the English (for Lord Fitzwalter sat of course in the House of Lords) all united. Here was a realm in which the dean was not impotent.

VII. MARKET HILL AGAIN

Swift disliked facing cold weather in the country or warm weather in town. During the late winter weeks of 1729, he kept complaining of his deafness and vertigo, often refusing to see people and even missing his chapter dinner on St Patrick's Day.[2] 'I now compound', he told Ford, 'if I can get an equal time of being well and ill.'[3] So he must have welcomed another invitation to stay with the Achesons. Early in June he left Dublin for what was to become a four-month visit. This time his friends' hospitality pleased Swift so much that he determined to build himself a country house near the Achesons, and bought land for the purpose from Sir Arthur. Newspapers reported the purchase and published some verses by Swift on the subject.[4]

Meanwhile, the dean walked with Lady Acheson, suffered from his giddiness, went out riding, and composed new octosyllabics.[5] He saw Robert and Henry Leslie, sons of his old acquaintance Charles Leslie, the Irish nonjuror and Jacobite.

---

[1] *Ibid.*, p. 457 and n. 5; IV. 410.
[2] *Ibid.*, III. 311, 317.   [3] *Ibid.*, p. 320.
[4] Fog's *Weekly Journal*, 30 Aug. 1729; Faulkner's *Dublin Journal*, 9 Sept. 1729. The poem is 'Drapier's Hill'; see *Poems* III. 874–5.
[5] Williams III. 341.

(Henry, the younger, had retired from a career in the army of the King of Spain, and now lived at Market Hill with his wife, a Spanish lady.) He talked much with Henry Jenney, a rich clergyman in his mid-seventies who liked to visit the Achesons. He became more familiar with the servants, working with them and giving them presents of tobacco. Out of doors, he had his physical labours and exercise; indoors, he read and wrote.

Otherwise we know little of the events of these summer months.[1] But if the quality of a poet's life has much to do with the quality of his work, we may suppose that Swift had reason to wish to live in his friends' neighbourhood. In the way of genial satire, he rarely wrote a better poem than 'The Grand Question Debated'.[2]

The charm of the poem is felt in every part of its construction. Throughout, there appears a humorous contrast between the ostensible shape or meaning and the inner design. The subject seems Sir Arthur's dilemma over what to make of a large property which he owned, called Hamilton's Bawn. One possibility was to rent it to the government for a barracks and to have a troop of soldiers quartered there. The other plan would have been to establish a malthouse and brew ale. It is plain that the malthouse would have caused less trouble and given more profit. But a barracks would bring cheerful society for masters and servants.

As the poem proceeds, the nature of the choice alters. Instead of opposing company to profit, the poet sets one kind of company against another. The chief social resource of the Achesons seems to have been parsons like Swift and Jenney. If the military moved in, something more lively would be available.

So Swift makes up a pattern of satiric polarities. The men— i.e., Sir Arthur and, by implication, the dean—desire a malthouse, on rational grounds. The women—represented by Lady

---

[1] It is not probable that the Achesons tired of Swift's company, since he returned for another long visit in 1730. It is more likely that when Lady Acheson was separated from her husband, Swift kept in touch with her rather than with Sir Arthur.

[2] *Poems* III. 863–73.

Acheson and her maid, Hannah—hope for a barracks, out of frivolity.

Instead of arguing back and forth in a systematic way, Swift turns to his favourite device of impersonation. Almost the entire poem is dialogue, the speakers being Sir Arthur, Lady Acheson, and the maid, Hannah. Much of the pleasure of the verses derives from the skill of Swift's mimicry as he catches the authentic note of the baronet, his wife, or Hannah. But this element gains from the form, because Swift casts the poem in four-beat anapaestic couplets with ingenious rhymes like 'bidder/consider' and 'purloin/sirloin'. His old trick of making spontaneous colloquial speech fall effortlessly into metrical units gives line after line its relish. When he breaks up the couplets into stichomythic cycles, the effect reaches its height. Here is a fantasy of Sir Arthur and the commanding officer meeting:

> Now, see, when they meet, how their honours behave;
> Noble Captain, your servant—Sir Arthur your slave;
> You honour me much—the honour is mine,—
> 'Twas a sad rainy night—but the morning is fine—
> Pray, how does my lady?—My wife's at your service.—
> I think I have seen her picture by Jervis.[1]

The character who takes over the poem is Hannah. Just as in 'Mrs Harris's Petition', the low speaker proves to be the most versatile.[2] As she improvises speech after speech, the reader delights in the power of the eminent dean to sound like a lady's maid taking off her betters. Once again Swift's willingness to make himself absurd redeems his boldness in handling those to whom he owes respect. When the maid shows contempt for parsons, the poet implies that mindless frivolity lies behind anticlericalism. By having Lady Acheson share Hannah's views, he satirizes women in general: the mistress is as irresponsible as the maid. Finally, as the imaginary officer speaks for Hannah, the poet condemns the military out of their own mouths. In Hannah's drama, the captain mistakes Swift for a curate:

[1] Ll. 71–6.
[2] Of course, there is only one speaker in 'Mrs Harris's Petition'.

Mister Curate, for all your grave looks, I'm afraid,
You cast a sheep's eye on her ladyship's maid;
I wish she would lend you her pretty white hand,
In mending your cassock, and smoothing your band:
(For the Dean was so shabby and looked like a *ninny*,
That the Captain supposed he was *curate* to Jenny.)
Whenever you see a cassock and gown,
A hundred to one, but it covers a clown;
Observe how a *parson* comes into a room,
[God damn] me, he hobbles as bad as my groom;
A *scholard*, when just from his college broke loose,
Can hardly tell how to cry *bo* to a goose;
Your Noveds, and Blutraks, and Omurs[1] and stuff,
By [God] they don't signify this pinch of snuff.
To give a young gentleman right education,
The army's the only good school in the nation.[2]

At the other extreme is a poem deliberately coarse and yet more literary than 'The Grand Question'. This is 'A Pastoral Dialogue', which looks like a parody of Pope's *Spring*.[3] The poem is a burlesque of the pastoral form with the parts of swain and nymph taken by a pair of Irish labourers—Dermot and Sheelah—weeding the Achesons' courtyard. The main device is simply a grotesque contrast between the manners or sentiments of the speakers and the traditional refinement of the genre. Heroic couplets, smoothly versified, make part of the joke, especially when the action sinks to its meanest level:

> Dermot.
> When you saw Tady at long-bullets[4] play,
> You sat and lous'd him all the sunshine day.
> How could you, Sheelah, listen to his tales,
> Or crack such lice as his betwixt your nails?
> Sheelah.
> When you with Oonah stood behind a ditch
> I peeped, and saw you kiss the dirty bitch.
> Dermot, how could you touch those nasty sluts!
> I almost wished this spud were in your guts.[5]

[1] Ovids, Plutarchs, Homers.   [2] Ll. 147–62.   [3] *Poems* III. 879–82.
[4] A kind of ninepins.   [5] Ll. 33–70.

If one considers the versatility, ingenuity, and zest of such works, if one reflects on their comic playfulness, one must conclude that all Swift's bitterness and grief could not hurt his skill or fertility as a poet. In fact, one might say that his creative energy had shifted its central impulse from the region of prose to that of verse.

At the end of August, Swift thought he would soon leave Market Hill;[1] yet he stayed more than a month longer. Toward the beginning of October, the walks and gardening, the teasing and rhyming came to an end; and Swift started on the seventy-mile journey[2] back to the deanery. When he reached Dublin (8 October), he found that news of his approach had gone before; and a celebration had been arranged. According to a newspaper report, the dean was 'received with great joy by many of our principal citizens, who also on the same occasion caused the bells to ring in our cathedrals and had bonfires and other illuminations'.[3] Two days later, we are told, the Lord Mayor (Sir Peter Verdoen) waited on the dean and paid his compliments.[4]

VIII. 'A MODEST PROPOSAL'

The contrast between Swift's reception by the townspeople and the plight of his nation was too sharp to want any comment. Unemployed weavers were feeding on grains and blood from the slaughterhouses. Shopkeepers who had been supporting their families respectably were now beggars. A pamphlet written in August 1729 told of the city streets being 'crowded with living spectres', who wandered about, searching for food. 'If they happen to hear of the death of a horse, they run to it as to a feast.'[5]

---

[1] Williams III. 343, 344.
[2] 70 miles English; 55 miles Irish.
[3] *Dublin Intelligence*, Saturday, 11 Oct. 1729, referring to 8 Oct.
[4] Faulkner's *Dublin Journal*, 11 Oct. 1729.
[5] Ferguson, p. 170.

While Swift was still at Market Hill, he wrote to Pope,

As to this country, there have been three terrible years dearth of corn, and every place strowed with beggars, but dearths are common in better climates, and our evils here lie much deeper. Imagine a nation the two-thirds of whose revenues are spent out of it, and who are not permitted to trade with the other third, and where the pride of the women will not suffer them to wear their own manufactures even where they excel what comes from abroad.... These evils operate more every day, and the kingdom is absolutely undone.[1]

Carteret returned from England on 13 September, and Parliament assembled on 23 September. Two days later, an emblematic event followed in the House of Commons. The immensely rich William Conolly,[2] who was Speaker of the House, fainted during a session and resigned the chair. Five weeks later, he was dead. For Swift, who had no attachment to Conolly, the end of so public a life would have deepened a sense of national crisis and ruin. He must have smiled bitterly when the members of the House resolved themselves into a committee to consider the state of the kingdom. As Marmaduke Coghill reported, one of the members spoke nearly an hour on the economic crisis. He discussed the absentees, the need for tillage, the danger of emigration and of foreign imports (mentioning also the 'extravagance of the ladies'). But he concluded without proposing a remedy.[3]

In the speech opening Parliament, the Lord Lieutenant had taken notice that at last a 'plentiful harvest' was coming in; and this, he hoped, would 'put an end to the disturbances, and other ill consequences, that may have arisen from a general scarcity of corn'.[4] We know what Swift thought of such hopefulness. 'The three seasons wherein our corn has miscarried', he said, 'did no more contribute to our present misery, than one spoonful of water thrown upon a rat already drowned would contribute to his death.'[5]

[1] 29 Aug. 1729; Sherburn III. 42.
[2] According to rumour, he left a fortune of £17,000 a year; Boulter I. 334 (Dublin, p. 267).
[3] Ferguson, p. 170.   [4] 23 Sept. 1729.   [5] Davis XII. 122.

The causes of the nation's misery were radical and chronic, Swift thought; and he now wrote an essay in which his despair was crystallized. Only as a background did he refer to the oppression of the English. It was the corruption of the Irish that made the focus of his anger. In a dazzling figure of rhetoric he brought together economic theory and religious indignation, his old obsession with the uniqueness of Ireland and his subscription to mercantilist principles. The result was *A Modest Proposal*.[1]

As a priest, Swift invoked the punishment threatened by Jeremiah on a sinful people: 'And I will cause them to eat the flesh of their sons and the flesh of their daughters.'[2] As an economist he inverted the principle that the people are the riches of a nation. As a moralist he dissolved the boundary between men and beasts. He was obsessed with the mad and devilish uniqueness of Ireland—a nation to whom none of the normal rules of prosperity applied.

The shape of the essay is its most powerful feature. Swift impersonates a reformer like himself offering a plan to save his people. The tone is calm and rational, and the speaker sounds like a wise but cool man who nevertheless feels disturbed by the wretchedness of Ireland. The fascination of the essay depends on the imaginative detail through which Swift supports the characterization—the ingenious provision of curious facts and reasons that keep the reader humorously engaged even while he is detaching himself from the unspeakable evil of the plan.

It is only as this evil emerges that the reader understands how far the real author's sentiments are from those of the projector. But if the gap between the casual tone and the horror of the scheme were not enough to alert us, Swift inserts a sardonic paragraph reviewing his serious recommendations—printed in italics.

There is of course the usual element of self-ridicule in the essay. Swift is laughing at himself and others who offer pro-

---

[1] Published before the end of October 1729; advertised as published, in the *Dublin Intelligence*, 8 Nov., with a summary of the argument. See Ball IV. 124, n. 3; Davis XII. xix–xx, 335; Ferguson, p. 171 and n. 12.
[2] Jer. xix. 9.

grammes to better the condition of the Irish. But as so often with his ridicule, the apparent object of attack is really being complimented. Not the would-be benefactors but their undeserving nation is condemned, and in that nation, above all, the landlords, who substitute cattle for people when they replace tillage with pasture. The butchery of infants is an idea that corresponds to the moral degradation of the people. Treated as cattle, and passive as cattle, the Irish are figuratively reduced to pieces of beef.

A subtlety of the essay is the theme of motherhood. Swift opens by picturing poor women begging with their children around them. He first indicates the character of his persona by referring to a newborn infant as 'just dropt from its dam'. He goes on to deplore the frequency of abortion and infanticide by mothers. The next clue to the persona is his reference to mothers as 'breeders'. Near the end he speaks of the care mothers would take of children if they knew they were saleable commodities, and of the fondness husbands would feel toward pregnant wives—not offering to beat or kick them.

I suspect that the theme reflects an unconscious preoccupation with Stella's failure to marry and have children. It certainly becomes a device for satirizing ladies of fashion who ruin their husbands and their country. But it might perhaps also be Swift's way of excusing himself for keeping Stella a spinster; for the representation he gives of motherhood makes it seem the grimmest of unrewarding ordeals. At least, Swift could think, he saved her from this.[1]

Of course, I do not suggest that theme of motherhood was a strong part of Swift's doctrine. However, another principle, which belongs to the foundation of his argument, has normally been ignored, although I take it to be quite deliberate. This is the relation between the butchering of babies and the place of meat in the economy of Ireland. As we have noticed already, in a country that depended on the export of raw materials and foodstuffs rather than of manufactured articles, the more little

[1] For a definitive analysis of *A Modest Proposal*, see Ferguson, pp. 170–6.

mouths there were to feed, the less goods there were to ship out. Archbishop King foreshadowed the implications of Swift's essay in a letter of December 1719:

> Our case in Ireland is somewhat singular. In other countries the more people they have, they are the richer, but we are the poorer. The reason of the difference is, because their riches are brought in by manufactures, and the more hands they employ, they export the more. But our riches come in by exporting the necessaries of life, such as grain, beef, butter &c. Now the more people we have, the more of these we consume and have the less to transport, and if we were fully stocked with people could spare none of them.[1]

In this situation, to transform eaters into things eaten would be a triumph of economic ingenuity.

[1] Letter of 12 Dec. 1719, to Southwell; cf. p. 613 above.

Chapter Eight

PATRONS AND PROTÉGÉS

I. THE BEST COMPANY

Though he regularly entertained and was entertained, Swift's ordinary days ran quietly enough. During the autumn he kept up his walking and riding, and could say people considered him 'the best walker in this town and five miles round'.[1] But his illnesses clung to him, and he thought much about death and money.[2] Autumn, winter, and spring, 1729–30, the Irish Parliament was in session, irritating the dean with sins of omission and commission.

Meanwhile, England beckoned with its usual seductions. His friends expected him. Pope, Bolingbroke, and Lord Oxford sent encouraging messages.[3] Gay wrote with tender, memorable wit:

> There is one thing which you have often put me in mind of, the over-running you with an answer before you had spoken, you find I am not a bit the better for it, for I still write on without having a word of an answer. I have heard of you once by Mr Pope. Let Mr Pope hear of you the next time by me. By this way of treating me, I mean by your not letting me know that you remember me you are very partial to me, I should have said very just to me: you seem to think that I do not want to be put in mind of you, which is very true, for I think of you very often, and as often wish to be with you.[4]

But the dean was too uneasy with his vertigo and thrift. He might go so far as Market Hill; but he told Lord Oxford, 'Neither my present condition of health, or private fortune will suffer me to make longer journeys.'[5]

---

[1] 19 Mar. 1730, to Gay; Sherburn III. 97.
[2] 31 Oct. 1729, to Bolingbroke; Williams III. 354.
[3] Sherburn III. 70–1, 80; Williams III. 404.
[4] 9 Nov. 1729; Sherburn III. 68.   [5] Williams III. 405.

In the deanery his daily round involved little conversation. 'I dine alone, or only with my house keeper,' he told Pope:

> I go to my closet immediately after dinner, there sit till eleven and then to bed. The best company here grows hardly tolerable, and those who were formerly tolerable, are now grown insupportable. This is my life five nights in seven. Yet my eyes are hurt with reading by candle-light, so that I am forced to write and burn whatever comes into my head.[1]

To Bolingbroke, Swift said more about what went on in his study: 'I am always writing bad prose, or worse verses, either of rage or raillery, whereof some few escape to give offence, or mirth, and the rest are burnt.'[2]

The number of escapees was substantial. Most of Swift's writing dealt with public themes. But one splendid specimen was ostentatiously private. This was an exchange with one of those Irish squires who made Swift nostalgic for England. The gentleman was the heir of Mr Percival, Swift's parishioner at Laracor. The son, Robert, thought himself injured by Swift's failure to pay rent on a piece of land that the vicar had once rented from old Mr Percival, but had given up years before. Swift had not surrendered the land in form with legal documents. So Robert Percival still claimed his rent, and punished Swift by refusing to pay tithes. Sooner than compromise the matter and hope to secure £2.5.0 a year in tithes, Swift chose to show his resentment, and wrote an insulting letter. One feels his pleasure pulsing through the challenge.

> This odd way of dealing among you folks of great estates in land and money, although I have been used to, I cannot well reconcile myself with, especially when you never give me above a quarter value for your tithes, on which account alone you should not brangle with me.[3]

Percival responded with the defiance that Swift no doubt expected; and this gave the dean his opportunity of teaching the squire what superior powers of vituperation could accomplish.

---

[1] 26 Feb. 1730; Sherburn III. 93.   [2] 21 Mar. 1730; *ibid.*, p. 98.
[3] Williams III. 366.

Rebounding upon Percival, he told him that a friend had been with Swift when the squire's letter arrived; Swift had explained the issue of the tithes and told the friend to expect from Percival 'nothing that became a gentleman':

> That I had expostulated this scurvy matter very gently with you, that I conceived this letter was an answer: that from the prerogative of a good estate, the practice of lording over a few Irish wretches, and from the natural want of better thinking, I was sure your answer would be extremely rude and stupid, full of very bad language in all senses: That a bear in a wilderness will as soon fix on a philosopher as on a cottager; and a man wholly void of education, judgment, or distinction of person has no regard in his insolence but to the passion of fear; and how heartily I wished, that to make you shew your humility, your quarrel had been rather with a captain of dragoons than the Dean of St Patrick's.[1]

Swift threatened to publish his letter if the squire troubled him further, but the quarrel apparently ended here.

The whole document is a model of its kind, and suggests what Swift was doing to Percival's betters with the scribblings of 'rage or raillery' in his study. The theme dominating his verse and prose, that winter and spring, was the old preoccupation with patronage. Swift not only wished to see preferments bestowed on men of Irish birth. He also liked to be the the fountain through which some of the bounty flowed. When he gave and received hospitality, the hope of directing it to a client's advantage was always with him. If he talked as well as he could with Lord Carteret, he wanted payment for his wit.[2]

So also on the two days out of seven when he indulged himself in company, the dean realized that his guests had hopes; and he would indeed have liked to satisfy them. Delany hardly made a secret of his aspirations;[3] he much enjoyed the pleasures of being a host, but he wanted money to support those pleasures. Delany

---

[1] *Ibid.*, p. 367.

[2] That Swift was seeing Carteret is evident from the reference in his letter to Pope, 31 Oct. 1729; Sherburn III. 65.

[3] 'Dr Delany in the latter part of the Primate's time, made as much court to him as ever he had done before to Dean Swift'—George Faulkner, note to Boulter (Dublin, 1770), II. 17.

fed great men well and let them understand that he would be glad to see them confer new benefits on him. As Swift perfectly knew, Delany's affection for the dean (which went back to a time when Swift was powerless) was genuine but impure. Yet Swift in turn wanted services that Delany could render.

As an intimate of the dean, Delany himself could act the part of a patron. Dubliners with literary ambitions often thought that Swift might help them. Delany was pleased, when he could, to introduce the hopefuls. If they were female, he had the further satisfaction of knowing how much pleasure Swift took in the conversation of educated women, especially after he lost Stella.

So it was that Swift found himself taken up with a parcel of new friends looking for careers as authors: four married women and one ecclesiastical husband, presented to Swift by Delany. All told, they were Mrs Barber, Mrs Grierson, Mrs Sican, and a young clerical pair, the Rev. Matthew Pilkington and his wife Laetitia.

Of these, the first whom Swift knew was Mary Barber, wife of Jonathan, a clothier (or 'woollen-draper') in Capel Street, Dublin. Swift probably met her early in 1728,[1] when she had four children and was about forty-five years old.[2] Three years before, she had published a poem celebrating Delany's eulogy of Carteret.[3] This year she published *A Tale*, a highly successful poem in praise of Gay's *Fables*, with an appeal to the Queen to grant the poet a pension.[4] Incidentally, *A Tale* had a passage attacking Congreve. Swift, who had not yet met Mrs Barber, saw the poem and wrote asking her to change the name to Dryden. She refused at first. But the effect of Swift's patronage may be seen in the later form of *A Tale*, in which the reproof of Congreve has vanished and an encomium of the Drapier

---

[1] Ball IV. 22 and n. 4.

[2] See Dr Delany's letter of 27 Feb. 1731 to Lady Suffolk, in Mary (Granville) Delany, *Autobiography and Correspondence*, ed. Lady Llanover (London, 1861), I. 321–3.

[3] 'The Birth of Manly Virtue'. The tameness of the style and the choice of Grierson for publisher make me disagree with Williams and attribute the poem to Delany and not to Swift. See Swift, *Poems* II. 381–8.

[4] *A Tale: Being an Addition to Mr Gay's Fables* (Dublin, 1728).

appears.[1] A glance at Mrs Barber's work reveals that she wrote with more attention to patrons than to readers.

Dr Delany, who had made himself her sponsor, presented Mrs Barber to the dean.[2] With these favourable omens, and with the advantage of 'constant spirits and good-humour',[3] she easily brought him to be her friend. Swift was soon recommending Mrs Barber as 'our chief poetess';[4] and in the summer of 1733 he called her 'a virtuous modest gentlewoman, with a great deal of good sense'.[5] However, Delany's sister-in-law, who knew, liked, and helped her, observed (in 1737) that 'good dear Barber', though certainly entertaining, was 'not sincere'.[6] And another woman, not a friend, called her (in 1731) 'strange, bold, and disagreeable'.[7] Jonathan Barber seems to have died around 1733,[8] after which his wife alone had to provide for her children and herself. If we are to judge by her two sons, Constantine and Rupert, poetry did not infringe on the claims of motherhood, for the elder son became a most distinguished physician and the other an equally eminent miniature painter.

One of Mary Barber's closest friends, and perhaps the person responsible for her literary ambitions, was Constantia Grierson, wife of George, a Dublin printer. Mrs Pilkington said Mrs Grierson's parents were 'poor illiterate country people', and that the parish priest taught her a little. She met Laetitia when, at the age of about eighteen, she came to study midwifery with Dr Van Lewin, Laetitia's father. Already she was known for her elegant verse and prose and for her piety.[9]

Mrs Grierson had unheard-of erudition for a citizen's wife.

---

[1] *N. & Q.*, 10 Jul. 1915, pp. 23–4.   [2] Williams III. 501.
[3] Mrs Delany I. 407.   [4] Sherburn III. 89.   [5] Williams IV. 187.
[6] Mrs Delany I. 604; I am not certain that the reference is to Mrs Barber.
[7] Mrs Anthony Todd Thomson, *Memoirs of Viscountess Sundon* [i.e., Charlotte Clayton] (London, 1847), II. 68: Lady M. Russell writing to Charlotte Clayton.
[8] Cf. Williams IV. 92–3. Jonathan Barber is still alive in December 1732 but seems not to be mentioned afterwards. In a letter of 14 Dec. 1731 Mrs Pendarves (later Mrs Delany) says that Mr Barber is to settle at Bath, where he will carry on his business as a woollen-draper while his wife lets lodgings; Mrs Delany I. 330–1. Perhaps Jonathan had a brother, Rupert, who is the 'Mr Barber' of Williams IV. 540 and the 'Rupert Barber' of Swift's *Poems* II. 477.
[9] Pilkington I. 27.

She edited volumes of Terence and Tacitus produced by her husband, and she was supposed to know Hebrew, Greek, Latin, and French. Her son, George Abraham (born shortly before she met Swift) achieved a degree of learning that Dr Johnson admired.[1]

Of these ladies, the one most solidly established in society seems to have been Mrs E. Sican—not a writer but a reader and critic. Her husband, John, was a prosperous grocer; her son, also John (born about 1712), went to school under Sheridan and then proceeded to Trinity College, Dublin. Although she may not have known Swift before 1729,[2] Mrs Sican remained on excellent terms with him for the rest of his life. Her husband had sat on the grand jury which presented Wood's halfpence, and in 1742 he was to join the commission appointed to look after Swift's affairs. The dean wrote a neat little poem, 'On Psyche', giving her praise she obviously deserved for domestic and intellectual virtues.[3] When Mrs Sican went to England in 1730, he supplied her with an introduction to Pope; and five years later, he recommended her son to Robert Arbuthnot (the doctor's brother) in Paris.[4]

II. MRS PILKINGTON

Of these Dublin bluestockings, the most important for Swift—though the last to meet him—was the diminutive Laetitia Pilkington.[5] Her father, John Van Lewin, was a physician who

---

[1] Boswell II. 116–17 and n. 1. Presumably, Sir G. A. Grierson, the scholar of Indian languages, was a descendant.

[2] Swift says that some years before they met, she sent him a six-line poem with a piece of sturgeon for his birthday (Sherburn III. 89).

[3] *Poems* II. 579–80.

[4] Sherburn III. 89; Williams IV. 423.

[5] I do not know why Swift failed to add Mrs Pilkington to the 'triumfeminate' which he described to Pope in February 1730 (Sherburn III. 89). But all other evidence indicates that he met her in December 1729. Though her *Memoirs* seem incredibly detailed for events that passed twenty years before the book appeared, she had a most extraordinary memory, and has proved reliable wherever I could verify her facts—except for natural evasions concerning her shady liaisons. Mrs Pilkington says that Mrs Barber presented her to Swift (I. 51; III. 65). Since Mrs Barber was in England for about three years beginning in the spring of 1730, Mrs Pilkington must have met Swift before

had a small acquaintance with Delany from Trinity College, where they had been classmates. Her clergyman husband, Matthew (born about 1701) had been a scholar at Trinity College. He took his B.A. degree in 1722 and married Laetitia in 1729, when she was seventeen and before he possessed a church living. Though remarkable for his short size and defective morals, Pilkington not only was unusually learned in the classics but also had genuine taste and scholarship in both music and painting. Laetitia admitted that he had 'a good face, and many agreeable accomplishments; such as a tolerable taste in music [he played the organ well], and a poetical turn';[1] and she seems to have married him against her parents' wishes. Soon after the wedding, Mrs Grierson showed some of Laetitia's poems to Delany; and he invited the young couple to Delville. He also introduced Matthew Pilkington to Swift, probably in the autumn of 1729.

The bride, young as she was, felt the usual eagerness to meet the greatest man in Ireland. So just before his birthday, 30 November 1729, she composed a verse eulogy for Delany to show the dean. Early the next month, when Swift meant to dine at Delville, he asked Delany to have both the Pilkingtons come in. That afternoon, they all met in Delany's garden, where Mrs Barber performed the ceremony of introduction.

Both husband and wife had not only a child's height but childlike mannerisms. Besides looking girlish, Laetitia affected in her speech the kind of freshness that Swift liked, though in later years it became coarse and raw. Swift asked Mrs Barber

---

that period; for there is no doubt that she knew him well in 1731. It is also certain that she met him after her marriage, which occurred in 1729 (Swift, *Poems* II. 459); and there are other proofs that she could not have known him before that year. As she describes the meeting, it came at a time when Ford was in Dublin and 'a few days' after Swift's birthday, 30 November (I. 51, 65–6). Chetwode, in September 1729, alludes to Ford's presence in Dublin (Williams III. 345). I therefore assume that Mrs Pilkington met Swift in December 1729. Since her husband met him before she did, I assume that his introduction occurred in the autumn of 1729, Swift having spent the summer at Market Hill. Mrs Pilkington gives by far the fullest account of Swift's social behaviour in late middle age. I have quoted or summarized only a fraction of her reminiscences. Those who would like to know the range of his eccentricities should read through the *Memoirs*.

[1] Pilkington I. 19.

whether the new person was her daughter. She smiled and said it was Mrs Pilkington. 'What,' Swift answered, 'this poor little child married! God help her, she is early engaged in trouble.'

The rest of the evening went off—as Mrs Pilkington thought—in elegance and delight. Swift invited the Rev. Matthew to preach in the cathedral the following Sunday, and he asked the whole party to dine with him then. When that morning came, the dean himself performed the communion service, impressing Laetitia with his solemnity and reverence. Having the words by heart, he never looked into the prayer book; and he bowed to the holy table (a practice for which some people blamed him). As she left the church, she met him at the door, surrounded by beggars. All of them received alms from Swift with the exception of an old woman whose hand was dirty. To her he said that water was not so scarce but she might have washed.

'And so', Laetitia writes, 'we marched with the silver verge before us to the deanery-house.' Swift immediately had her come alone with him into the study (his 'closet'), telling Matthew to remain in the parlour.

> 'Well', says he, 'I have brought you here to shew you all the money I got when I was in the ministry, but do not steal any of it.'
>
> 'I will not indeed, Sir', says I; so he opened a cabinet, and shewed me a whole parcel of empty drawers.
>
> 'Bless me', says he, 'the money is flown!'

Then he let her see many objects in his bureau, the gifts of people like the Earl and Countess of Oxford, Lady Masham, and Lady Betty Germaine. The last drawer he opened was full of medals, from which he let his guest choose two for herself.

During dinner, he sat at the head of the table, facing a pier glass under which stood a marble-topped sideboard. Through the mirror he watched what the servants were doing at the sideboard. Again and again he found fault with them and said they were trying to cheat him.

All the dishes and vessels were silver. Though the meal was served 'with great elegance', Swift got angry because the beef was overdone. He called for the cook and ordered her to take it back and 'do it less'. She naturally said that was impossible; so he advised her thereafter to make only such errors as might be corrected.

Between dinner and evening prayers they were joined by two or three clergymen who 'usually passed Sunday evening' with the dean. When the others went elsewhere for evensong, Laetitia followed Swift to a brief service in the cathedral; and after that she talked to him at length. The Pilkingtons were asked to remain for supper. Delany returned too. Still later, Charles Ford came in, and hogged the conversation:

> There now came in, to sup with the dean, one of the oddest little mortals I ever met with. He formerly wrote [*The Gazette*], and, upon the strength of being an author and of having travelled, took upon him not only to dictate to the company but to contradict whatever any other person advanced, right or wrong, till he had the whole talk to himself (for, to my great surprise, the dean neither interrupted nor showed any dislike of him), he told us a whole string of improbabilities. . . .
>
> I took notice that before this dogmatical gentleman the dean was most remarkably complaisant to Mr Pilkington and me, and at our going away the dean would hand me down all the steps to the coach, thanking us for the honour of our company, at the same time sliding into my hand as much money as Mr Pilkington and I had given at the offering in the morning, and coach-hire also, which I durst not refuse.[1]

As Mrs Pilkington reports the day, she makes herself out to have interested Swift more than her husband did. But she was of course long estranged from the latter when she wrote her book. Matthew Pilkington felt peculiarly eager to advance himself. Being only the son of a clockmaker[2] in the King's County, and owning little but brains to recommend him, Pilkington had to try every door to preferment. He was a skilful versifier and had published a few poems. While he was courting Delany, he wrote an *Ode* for the birthday of George II, 30 October 1729. Swift apparently read this effusion and decided to use the idea in parody. He therefore composed *Directions for a Birth-day*

---

[1] The whole description of these early meetings between Swift and the Pilkingtons is taken from Pilkington I. 50–66.

[2] 'Faber automatarii', according to *Alumni Dublinenses*.

Song, October 30, 1729, a piece hopelessly unfit for publication in his own lifetime, but one of his most forthright, powerful lampoons.[1] Swift takes a fair target and does not disguise his weapons.

III. 'DIRECTIONS FOR A BIRTHDAY SONG'

The poem follows a form which Waller had brought into English verse as a serious type of panegyric, and which Marvell and others established as a satiric device. This is, instead of representing an action directly, in narrative or description, to tell a painter how to handle it.[2] By apparently concentrating on the techniques for conveying a view, the poet lures the reader into taking its truth for granted; and he correspondingly makes himself appear impartial. If the poet is satirical, he implies that the formulae of the painter are lies; and so when the truth is well-known, he can create a comic antithesis between picture and reality. He can also sharpen the focus by alluding to familiar works of art. Thus in dealing with royalty, a satirist might establish implicit but savage contrasts between the baroque apotheoses of a painter like Rubens and the shabby facts of Whitehall or Westminster.[3] The language of art criticism furnishes him with an arsenal of conceits. By interposing a canvas between the reader and the original event, he gains an extra

---

[1] *Poems* II. 459–69. There are enough parallels between the *Ode* and the *Directions* to make one suspect that Swift had Pilkington's song in mind: the parallel with Alexander and the absurd praise of the King's martial prowess, the eulogy of Caroline, the attention to the royal children, the use (or presumption) of a musical setting, etc.

[2] The device originated with the Italian poet Busenello in his poem *Il Trionfo Veneziano.* This was translated by Waller's friend Sir Thomas Huggons. Waller adopted the device for his serious panegyric *Instructions to a Painter.* Marvell and others then proceeded to use it satirically. See Edmund Waller, *Poems,* ed. G. Thorn-Drury (London, 1905), II. 208; Andrew Marvell, *Poems and Letters,* ed. H. M. Margoliouth *et al.,* 3rd ed. (Oxford, 1971), I. 347.

[3] There happen indeed to be some entertaining parallels between Swift's poem and the actual description by Rubens of his own vast allegory, *The Horrors of War:* Mars, Janus, Venus, and Cupid figure prominently in both; and the dean patently agrees with the artist that the martial splendours which Swift (not Rubens) associates with crowned heads have brought 'plunder, outrage, and misery' to Europe. See Rubens, *Letters,* tr. and ed. R. S. Magurn (Cambridge, Mass., 1955), p. 409.

viewpoint from which to comment on the past: instead of judging men directly, he treats them as figures for a brush, and works on the reader by innuendo. Because of its simplicity, the scheme combines the advantages of a massive attack with witty indirection.

Although the instructions in Swift's poem are how to make not a painting but a song, his details are more visual than musical. Yet his contrast lies between the verse clichés of ordinary birthday odes and the reality of George II's pretentious court and dreary family. Concerning the dull prosody of panegyric, he has a store of impudent sentiments. There is a further implication that even if the trite phrases were justified, they would describe silly if not bestial qualities:

> Your hero now another Mars is,
> Makes mighty armies turn their arses.

In its development, Swift's poem has a consistency which adds to its power. For more than a hundred lines, he shows how the traditional associations of certain gods (Jupiter, Apollo, Neptune) can be used to describe George II. Next, he gives a few examples to demonstrate that the compliments must be the reverse of truth. Then he brings in the rest of the royal circle: Caroline, her daughter, Prince Frederick, and Walpole. The end treats hurriedly of the musical setting, publication, and payment.

Although the poet pretends to deal with the general problem of composing a royal eulogy, the themes point specifically at George II: the hatred existing between King and Prince (ll. 9–14), the imprisonment of the King's mother for infidelity (ll. 15–20), the rivalry of the King with his own father (ll. 21–8), the pusillanimous foreign policy of Walpole and the King (ll. 29–56), the tastelessness of the royal court (ll. 57–96), the obsequious behaviour toward Spain (ll. 97–106), the long visits to Hanover with the Queen left as both regent and abused wife (ll. 173–86), the cacophony of German names (ll. 209–32), the fondness for Dr Clarke's theology (ll. 261–74), the admiration for Handel's music (ll. 275–8).

Swift's poem has not the deadly thoroughness of Marvell's *Last Instructions*, and his octosyllabics allow less space for manœuvring than Marvell's heroics. However much he may have detested what the German family stood for, Swift lacked a direct experience of their misrule in England and an intimate knowledge of their persons. His effect is therefore more scattered than intense; and his versification sometimes seems designed rather to bring in rhymes than to execute vengeance.

But the boldness and surge of Swift's lines can disarm criticism:

> Thus your encomiums, to be strong,
> Must be apply'd directly wrong:
> A tyrant for his mercy praise,
> And crown a royal dunce with bays:
> A squinting monkey load with charms;
> And paint a coward fierce in arms.
> Is he to avarice inclin'd?
> Extol him for his generous mind:
> And when we starve for want of corn,
> Come out with Amalthea's horn.
> For princes love you should descant
> On virtues which they know they want.[1]

The frontal attack of Swift's language, aimed squarely at the Crown, parallels Pope's *To Augustus* (imitation of Horace, *Epistles* II. i, published in 1737), although Swift here has not Pope's primary concern with literary criticism. Since the schema of 'directions', about which Swift has built his poem, appears more systematic and fresh than Pope's digressive imitation, one might expect it to have greater force as well. But in polish and in the control of his medium, Swift is so far inferior to Pope that *To Augustus* belongs to a different order of accomplishment.

Yet Swift's irregularity has its beauties, as in the following parody of expressive versification:

> A skilful critic justly blames
> Hard, tough, cramp, gutt'rall, harsh, stiff names.

---

[1] Ll. 117–28.

The sense can ne're be too jejune,
But smooth your words to fit the tune,
Hanover may do well enough;
But George, and Brunswick are too rough.
Hesse Darmstedt makes too rough a sound,
And Guelph the strongest ears will wound.
In vain are all attempts from Germany
To find out proper words for harmony.[1]

In taking off Pilkington's ode, Swift implied no unwillingness to befriend the little parson. Not only did he have him preach in the cathedral; he also corrected Pilkington's poems, receiving prose and verse flattery in return.[2] On Mrs Pilkington, when he met her, Swift bestowed the attentions which were the peculiar sign of his fondness. The couple were often at the deanery if only because Swift felt free to order them about. The lady's explanation throws a sad light on his will to avoid spleen:

> The dean, for the latter part of his life, contracted his acquaintance into a very narrow compass, for as he was frequently deaf he thought this infirmity made him troublesome, and therefore kept no company but such as he could be so free with, as to bid them speak loud or repeat what they had said: it was owing to this, that Mr Pilkington and I frequently passed whole days with him, while numbers of our betters were excluded; and as he was like another Nestor, full of days and wisdom, so like him, he was pretty much upon the narrative.[3]

IV. WINE AND TRUTH

Parliament had been sitting for a fortnight when Swift returned to Dublin in October 1729. It may have pleased him that the

[1] Ll. 209–18; the couplets are probably an allusion to the famous passage of expressive versification in Pope, *Essay on Criticism* (ll. 364–73). I deliberately pass over another poem which might be discussed at this point: 'Verses Occasioned by the Sudden Drying Up of St Patrick's Well', dated 1729 (see *Poems* III. 789–94.) The versification and language are not Swiftian. The notes are straightforward and informative in a way uncharacteristic of Swift. The poem was omitted from Swift's *Works*, Dublin, 1735. I do not believe Swift wrote it.

[2] See the extravagant acknowledgement by Pilkington in the preface to his *Poems on Several Occasions* (Dublin, 1730). See also his ingenious poem, 'The Gift', discussed below, pp. 686–7.

[3] Pilkington I. 69.

members were recalcitrant to their governor, and that for all the charm of the Lord Lieutenant, they stubbornly opposed bills or changes in bills that did not originate with themselves. The loss of Lord Midleton in the Lords and of Conolly in the Commons roughened the road of the viceroy.

But one bill that gave little trouble to Boulter and Carteret stirred Swift to attack. Yet this was a bill in keeping with his own principles, for it involved a tax on imported goods. The bother was that the object of the new impost was wine. 'Good wine', Swift told Pope, 'is ninety per cent in living in Ireland.'[1] He had always delighted in the excellent and cheap French wine that one could get in Ireland. It meant far more to him than good food.

The bill for raising the duty on wine by forty shillings a ton came before the House of Commons in November.[2] Swift set to work on one more essay urging the Irish people to reduce their reliance on imported goods. He went over his usual reasons, adding some fresh statistics and figures of speech. But in the midst of them he planted six arguments against increasing the price of wine, starting with the amazing but serious claim that in no other country did the people so much require 'some cordial to keep up their spirits'.[3] This was invoking the uniqueness of Ireland with a vengeance. So also the last of his arguments was that cheap, good wine was the main attraction to men of large estates to live in Ireland:

> [This] is it which, by growing habitual, wholly turns the scale with those few landed men disengaged from employments, who content themselves to live hospitably with plenty of good wine in their own country, rather than in penury and obscurity in another, with bad, or with none at all.[4]

Swift also offered more solid reasons: that a rise in cost would mean a decline in consumption, therefore a loss of revenue; and

---

[1] 26 Feb. 1730; Sherburn III. 94.
[2] In a letter of 13 Nov. 1729 Boulter says the bill is being drawn up (Dublin, I. 268). On Saturday, 22 Nov., he says the bill was 'sent off' on the preceding Thursday (*ibid.*, p. 269).
[3] Davis XII. 124. [4] *Ibid.*, p. 126.

that the French might put up their duties on Irish commodities in response to a new tax on wine. He went on to reckon the financial loss from importing silks and cottons, tea and coffee, etc. He recommended the common scheme of taxing the incomes of absentees. He also urged the Lords and Commons to resolve that in their clothes and the furniture of their houses their families would use only native goods; furthermore, that they would urge their tenants and friends to do so as well. But for all the effort to sandwich his dislike of a sensible new tax between slabs of traditional economics, the essay makes a grotesque impression. In effect, what Swift was doing was merely to redefine a luxury as a necessity.

Luckily, the essay (which may be unfinished) was not published at the time. The bill went through Parliament so fast that it received the royal assent by 22 December.[1]

V. DELANY AND CARTERET

Delany combined his attentiveness to Swift with abundant hospitality in a way that preserved his dignity and certainly pleased the dean. Mrs Pilkington described a party at Delville as 'an elegant entertainment, with ease, cheerfulness, and an hospitality which makes the company happy'.[2] Swift shared the judgment. He often visited Delville, and he recommended the doctor to Pope as

> a man of the easiest and best conversation I ever met with in this island—a very good listener, a right reasoner, neither too silent nor talkative, and never positive; but hath too many acquaintance.[3]

Delete the last clause and move back twenty years, and the description might be of Addison.

Yet Swift must have smiled at the energy with which this admirer tried to extend his pluralities. Carteret had so far opposed Boulter in the Primate's system of making English appointments that when the Lord Lieutenant's commission was

---

[1] *Ibid.*, pp. xxi–xxii; Ferguson, pp. 156–7.   [2] Pilkington III. 67.
[3] Sherburn III. 109.

renewed in 1727 (upon the death of George I), the patent specifically excluded the power of nominating deans, army officers, and certain other placemen without the approval of the Secretary of State (Carteret's enemy, Newcastle). Nevertheless, Delany solicited what might be available; and in October 1729 he wrote a poem begging for further preferment, in the form of a Horatian dialogue between himself and the Lord Lieutenant. The poem, *An Epistle to Lord Carteret*,[1] is remarkably elegant and restrained, in keeping with the delicacy of the subject.

Around Christmas 1729, Swift produced *An Epistle upon an Epistle*, which is a commentary on Delany's lines. Swift takes off the phrases and attitudes of his friend with a sarcasm which is hard to distinguish from contempt.[2] Delany's begging, he says, reminded him of Smedley's *Epistle to the Duke of Grafton*, 1723, on which Swift had poured vitriol five years before. So in *An Epistle upon an Epistle*, he compares Delany's request with that of Smedley, which Swift declares modest by the side of the doctor's appetite:

> If your expences rise so high;
> What income can your wants supply?[3]

The satire faces two ways. On the one hand, it is naïve of an Irish candidate to expect preferment from an English administration. On the other hand, Delany already has an ample income, if only he would learn to live within it. Of course, one must remember that, as Delany said in the *Epistle*, Swift constantly urged the doctor's claims on the Lord Lieutenant. The preferments, we know, would in any case have fallen to someone already well established, and Swift merely wished the recipient to be an Irishman and a friend of his own.

---

[1] *Poems* III. 470–4. In ll. 59–60, Delany urges Carteret to make Sir Ralph Gore the Speaker of the House of Commons. Since Conolly resigned the chair on 25 Sept. 1729, and Gore was chosen as the new Speaker on 13 Oct., the poem must have been completed between those dates.

[2] *Ibid.*, II. 474–9. In this poem Gore is already the Speaker. So it must have been finished after 13 Oct. but well before 2 Feb. 1730, when its sequel, *A Libel on Dr Delany*, appeared.

[3] Ll. 95–6.

On these subjects he had much more to say; and the *Epistle upon an Epistle* became in turn the excuse for a far broader satire, *A Libel on Dr Delany and a Certain Great Lord.*[1] '[It] is worth your reading,' Marmaduke Coghill told Edward Southwell, 'though I think very improper to be published.'[2] The *Libel* is memorable for its vigour and for a thundering eulogy of Pope—payment, perhaps, for the invocation of the *Dunciad*, and perhaps an implicit criticism of that compliment.

Swift's theme is simple: that servility to politicians wins incomparably more patronage than talent does. The tremendous force of the poem derives from the antiphonal development of literary and political motifs subtly mingled. The subject of the poem is patronage, which is exactly the region where genius meets power. Swift opens with a contrast between the expectations of an aspirant and the desires of a patron. The favoured man of wit supposes that the hour of intimacy is the time for pressing his claims. But the busy statesman values the interlude of their conversation as an escape from importunities.

Swift goes on to a survey—not very accurate—of literary talents which went unrewarded until they submitted to party needs; and he closes this section with the tribute to Pope, who never sought preferment—

> His heart too great, though fortune little,
> To lick a *rascal statesman*'s spittle.[3]

The poem now turns, and Swift discusses the general issue of the kind of services a politician can really afford to pay for. So he delivers a set of sarcastic contrasts between the venal employments of political tools and the intellectual abilities of a scholar and poet. Here he identifies talent with integrity and politics with corruption:

> True *politicians* only pay
> For solid work, but not for play;
> Nor ever choose to work with tools
> Forged up in *colleges* and *schools*.

---

[1] Published 2 Feb. 1730; see *ibid.*, pp. 474–5, 479–86. [2] *Ibid.*, p. 474.
[3] Ll. 81–82.

> Consider how much more is due
> To all their *journeymen*, than you,
> At table you can Horace quote;
> They at a pinch can bribe a vote:
> You show your skill in Grecian story,
> But, they can manage Whig and Tory.[1]

Now Swift declares that Delany and Carteret are exceptions to the rule; and if the Lord Lieutenant cannot act as his genuine virtues incline him, he is kept from doing so by those above him.

At this point the literary and political themes join in a fresh, ingenious device. First Swift offers Delany a simile he may use to represent Carteret's position. Echoing Addison's *Campaign*, he compares the Lord Lieutenant to an angel sent to punish a guilty nation but feeling compassion for their sufferings. Then, however, in a final turn, he answers this simile—appropriate for Delany's good nature—with another, which Swift declares is closer to the truth. Echoing Milton, he now compares the Lord Lieutenant to a devil:

> So, to effect his *monarch*'s ends,
> From *hell* a *viceroy* DEV'L ascends,
> His *budget* with *corruptions* cramm'd,
> The contributions of the *damn'd*;
> Which with unsparing hand, he strows
> Through *courts* and *senates* as he goes.[2]

The whole poem takes the form of an implicit dialogue between Delany and Swift, in which the poet characteristically speaks for himself and imagines his friend's replies. Thus he controls the tone, which rises steadily. He represents Delany as trustful or candid (in the old sense), and himself as grimly disillusioned. The more Delany apologizes for Carteret, the angrier the poet grows.

Throughout, Swift sounds bitter. But in the first third, he exhibits Horatian restraint. In the middle section, following the praise of Pope, he becomes sarcastic, as he brushes aside the fact that Carteret would like to be more benevolent:

[1] Ll. 89–98.
[2] Ll. 185–92. (*The Campaign* was a device—successful—to win preferment.)

[649]

This may be true—submitting still
To [Walpole's] more than [royal] will.
And what condition can be worse?
He comes to *drain a beggar's purse*:
He comes to tie our chains on faster,
And shew us, [England] is our master:
Caressing knaves and dunces wooing,
To make them work their own undoing.[1]

In the final third, replying again to Delany's supposed apology, he reaches the peak of his rage in the devil simile. Here purely literary advice on how to write a poem is the framework of violent political denunciation.

I think the whole design of this and similar poems by Swift— the mock-dialogue form, the interweaving of literary and political themes, the opposition of apologetic and bitter tones rising to furious invective—may have encouraged Pope (who knew *A Libel on Dr Delany* only too well) to write his Horatian poems of the 1730s. So it is one more irony that about the time the poem appeared, Pope was more friendly than usual with the English court and probably felt embarrassed by Swift's praise of him as

Contemning *courts*, at *courts* unseen,
Refus'd the visits of a queen.[2]

VI. GOLD BOXES

Years earlier, to the amazement of Bishop Nicolson, Swift had been made a freeman of the City of Dublin.[3] Since that time the dean had kept working to gain a further distinction, which was to be presented with a diploma, conferring the freedom of the city, in a gold box. So early as October 1724 an observer reported that 'endeavours are using to get Dr Swift the freedom of the city in a gold box'.[4] It was not until 16 January 1730, however, that the Lord Mayor and the Common Council voted

---

[1] Ll. 121–8.   [2] Ll. 73–4. Cf. Sherburn III. 85, headnote; 90, n. 2.
[3] Ball III. 234, n. 1.   [4] *Drapier*, p. xlv.

unanimously to present Swift with such a box, 'the value thereof not to exceed twenty five pounds'.[1]

Delany had been an agent of Swift's in this effort, and he had transmitted to the members of the Council a copy of a statement suitable to be engraved on the box. I suppose, alas, that Swift had a large hand in the composition of this statement; and I do not doubt that he approved it. Unfortunately, the whole enterprise overlapped with the scandal of *A Libel on Dr Delany*, which had provoked members of the government. Marmaduke Coghill told the story in a letter to Edward Southwell:

> Our dean's late paper which I sent you is still upon the carpet, some are for a violent persecution, others think it better to let it fall without taking notice of it, and it will then die of itself, whereas a prosecution either in the courts, or by censure [of it in] Parliament will make it more public, and raise the curiosity of people to read and disperse it more than otherwise they would do. The dean after three years earnest solicitation [prevailed] on our city to give him his freedom in a gold box, and an order was accordingly made by the Common Council, but he insisted on an inscription, which they being unwilling to comply with, the making the box has been deferred.

Coghill obligingly transcribed the inscription 'proposed by the Dean or his friends':

> Dublin, January 17, 1729 [i.e., 1730]: This day the Lord Mayor, Sheriffs, and Commons presented the freedom of this city in this box to Dr Jonathan Swift, Dean of St Patrick's, whom for his great zeal, unequalled abilities and distinguished munificence in asserting the rights, defending the liberties, and encouraging the manufactures of the kingdom, they justly esteemed the most eminent patriot and greatest ornament of this his native city and country.

Coghill commented,

> Such an arrogant inscription desired by a man himself is surprising, but the man is so well known that nothing of this nature is new from

---

[1] J. T. Gilbert, ed., *Calendar of Ancient Records of Dublin*, VII (Dublin, 1898), 476. The vote is reported in the *Dublin Journal*, 20 Jan. 1730. See Davis VII. xxiv.

him, and though he did not draw this himself, yet Dr Delany did it by his approbation.[1]

Meanwhile, Carteret was concerned about some riots that had occurred in Dublin, and he summoned the Lord Mayor and the sheriffs to a meeting of the Privy Council of Ireland (13 February 1730), at which he would look into the troubles. The city fathers duly appeared; and in the course of the discussion they happened to mention the poverty of their municipality.

Among the Privy Councillors at the conference was Joshua, Viscount Allen. His father had been one of those few Privy Councillors who refused to sign the proclamation against the Drapier,[2] and Allen himself had acted very friendly (Swift says)[3] to the dean. But on hearing the cry of poverty, he asked in a rage 'how they should complain of poverty, when they were so lavish as to give a gold box to a man who neither feared God nor honoured the King, who had wrote a libel on the King, Queen and the government.'[4]

Allen may have felt ashamed of the outburst; for Swift said that on the day of the episode he sent a common acquaintance of theirs merely to assure the dean of his friendship. But the next day, we are told, an account of the Privy Council meeting reached Swift, who proceeded to give the story to his own circle.[5] According to Delany, the common friend was Robert Leslie, to whom Allen privately affirmed his continued respect for Swift. Leslie tried to apologize to the dean for the Viscount, pleading that his lordship had a disordered head. Swift, according to Delany, replied that as a madman Allen might deserve sympathy but as one possessed by the devil, Swift renounced him.[6]

A few days later, the dean put into circulation an 'advertisement' rejecting Allen's allegations without naming him, and declaring,

---

[1] Letter of 21 Feb. 1730 to Southwell, in B.L. Add. MS. 21,122, fols. 113ᵛ–14. See Oliver W. Ferguson, 'Jonathan Swift, Freeman of Dublin', *MLN* 71 (1956), 405–9. I have changed Coghill's spelling, capitalization, and punctuation.

[2] *Drapier*, p. xlv.   [3] Letter of 2 May 1730 to Pope; Sherburn III. 108.

[4] Coghill, *ibid.* I have changed the spelling, punctuation, and capitalization.

[5] Davis XII. 141.   [6] *Poems* III. 794–5; Delany, pp. 219–20.

That the said words, or words to the like effect, are insolent, false, scandalous, malicious, and, in a particular manner, perfidious; the said person, who is reported to have spoken the said or the like words, having, for some years past, and even within some few days, professed a great friendship for the said dean.[1]

Allen, as a noble lord in Parliament time, could respond freely. Within a week he rose in the House of Lords to denounce Swift again—as 'a Jacobite, an enemy to King George, and a libeller of the government' (or so Swift tells us)—though without naming him, and to ask that the printer of *A Libel on Dr Delany* be prosecuted.[2] The House did not support his lordship; and Swift, to avoid a breach of privilege, muzzled his guns until Parliament rose, in mid-April.

Meanwhile, the matter of the inscription hung fire; and Swift received no gold box.[3] But in February or March the Scotch–Irish author James Arbuckle published 'A Panegyric on the Reverend D—n S—t in Answer to the Libel on Dr D—y, and a Certain Great L—d'.[4] This poem not only ridicules both Swift and his friend. It also has a passage showing that the story of the proposed inscription was widely known; for the poet, impersonating Delany, describes the gold box as one where,

---

[1] Davis XII. 141. The advertisement was dated 18 Feb. There is no evidence that Swift actually published it. See *ibid.*, p. xxv and n. 2.

[2] Letter to Pope, 26 Feb. 1730; Sherburn III. 92–3. I trust Swift's account because he was prepared to make it public and because Coghill's account—so far as it goes—agrees with Swift's. Allen must have made his House of Lords attack on 24 or 25 Feb., because the House did not sit between 10 and 24 Feb., and Swift reported Allen's speech in a letter to Pope dated 26 Feb.

[3] I do not accept Swift's view that Allen's attack caused the delay (Davis XII. 145). The proposed inscription was dated, by Swift or Delany, 17 Jan.; so that must have been when the dean expected to receive the box. Since Allen's attack came much later, I suspect that the nature of the inscription was (as Coghill said) the original cause of the delay.

[4] *Poems* II. 491–9. The date is limited because the poem replies to the 'Libel', which was published on 2 Feb., and the imprint of the first edition is '1729–30', or before 25 Mar. For the attribution to Arbuckle, see the following: D. F. Foxon, *English Verse, 1701–1750* (Cambridge, 1975), I. 552, nos. P36, P37; Aubrey L. Williams, '"A Vile Encomium": That "Panegyric on the Reverend D—n S—t"', and James Woolley, 'Arbuckle's "Panegyric" and Swift's Scrub Libel: The Documentary Evidence', both in John I. Fischer and Donald C. Mell, Jr., eds., *Contemporary Studies of Swift's Poetry* (Newark, Del., 1980), pp. 178–209. The evidence is conclusive.

if the curious list to read 'em,
They'll find his life, and acts, and *freedom*,
And the great name engraved most fairly,
Of him that Ireland sav'd, and Harley;
With quaint *inscription*, which contains,
Laid out with no less art than pains,
Most of his virtues, all my brains.[1]

We may assume that some members of the City Council were not eager to identify themselves with the author of the 'Libel', and further that these members would have liked to assert their loyalty to the government. Support for the speculation appears ironically in a vote of the City Council meeting of 10 April 1730. This was that Archbishop Hoadly had shown himself a true friend to the city of Dublin and therefore as a mark of gratitude should receive 'the freedom of the city in a gold box', the expense of which was not to exceed 'thirty pounds', or five pounds more than Swift's.[2] So the new English Whig prelate was granted the distinction which the Drapier had been awaiting for six years.

Swift's annoyance must have been acute. In January 1730, when Hoadly had been enthroned (as the new archbishop) at the two cathedrals of Dublin, the ceremony had proceeded with no unpleasantness at Christ Church. But when he was also enthroned at St Patrick's, Swift had wished him to take the oaths before the dean, and Hoadly had refused. The dean did not, in fact, have the authority to administer the oaths to the archbishop. But as Coghill tells us, the disagreement occasioned 'some sharp words among 'em'. Swift became so angry that he refused to dine with Hoadly; yet he was finally 'prevailed on to do it', said Coghill, 'and I suppose all differences are made up.'[3]

I wonder whether the arrangement of matching boxes was not a scheme of equivalents: the Drapier's party might glorify their hero if the government's party were allowed to bestow the same honour on his rival. When the actual presentations took place, at the end of May, such a relationship seemed clear. For

---

[1] Ll. 51–7.
[2] Gilbert, *Ancient Records* VII. 485; reported in the *Dublin Intelligence*, 11 Apr. 1730.
[3] Letter of 22 Jan. 1730 to Southwell; B.L. Add. MS. 21,122, fol. 109ᵛ.

Hoadly, who had been voted his freedom five years after Swift, and his gold box three months after him, received both articles the day before the dean: Hoadly on 26 May and Swift on 27 May.[1] Moreover, the epigraphy of Dr Delany was nowhere to be seen.

To these humiliating circumstances Swift did not submit quietly. When the Lord Mayor and the aldermen came to the deanery for the ceremony, he met them well prepared. Instead of passively accepting their present, he put it (as he tells us) 'gently' back and mentioned the 'little mortification' caused him by the long delay, which he blamed on 'a person with a title'. Then he made a thorough, sarcastic, and skilful denunciation of a nameless nobleman.

This led in turn to an unprecedented lecture reviewing Swift's career as an Irish patriot: his procuring of the First Fruits for the Church of Ireland; his loans to small tradesmen; his 1720 *Proposal* in support of Irish manufactures; his authorship of *The Drapier's Letters*. He vilified Whitshed and said he wished

> that an inscription might have been graven on the box, showing some reason why the city thought fit to do him that honour, which was much out of the common forms to a person in a private station; those distinctions being usually made only to chief governors, or persons in very high employments

—so much for Hoadly![2] In effect, he spoke the inscription which should have appeared on the box, and crowned himself with the recognition he yearned for. He also kept a copy of his little speech; and although this was only published posthumously, I suspect that a number of people were privileged to see it during the spring of 1730. Ten years later, making his will, Swift was to bequeath the famous box to Alexander McAulay, in language revealing that as an emblem of recognition of his life's work, the object had a profound value for him.[3]

[1] *Universal Spectator and Weekly Journal* (London), 13 Jun. 1730.
[2] Davis XII. 145–8.
[3] Davis XIII. 155.

VII. SWIFT AND ALLEN

Revenge on Lord Allen was another matter. While Parliament still sat, the dean gathered his forces in silence. But his plans became known, and Marmaduke Coghill recorded them:

> My Lord Allen had abused Swift in a speech he made to the Privy Council, and another in the House of Lords, which Swift promised to give him some return for, when the Parliament was up.[1]

The session of Parliament ended on 15 April; and about this time Swift let drop a set of verse lampoons excoriating the wretched Allen. These poems are entitled 'Traulus', from the Greek word that means 'lisping', or 'mispronouncing', because Allen habitually stuttered. In keeping with the account of Robert Leslie's apologizing for Allen—as one afflicted with a disordered head—Swift followed the form he had invented for Richard Tighe: he composed a dialogue between Tom Molyneux, the well-known madman, and 'Robin', or Robert Leslie. The subject is Allen's speeches against Swift.

For 'Traulus, Part One', Swift devised an ingenious plan that allows the poet to convey ferocious feelings while retaining his dignity. Fundamentally, it is a dialogue between a sane man and a lunatic, with Swift's own voice rising through both parts. But Robin, the sane man, only replies, in a line or couplet, to a series of questions by Tom that grow longer and more rhetorical as he advances. In each question Tom asks the reason for the misbehaviour of Traulus. To each, Robin replies that the man is mad. The alternation of lengthening query and brief response drives the poem, in a large rhythm, toward a crescendo. Throughout it, at the same time, runs the irony that a madman is reasoning acutely.

To deepen the effect, Swift introduces analogies that degrade Allen. In his fourth speech Tom compares the Viscount with an inmate of Bedlam, and prefers the latter. In his next speech, Tom moves outside humanity and compares Allen to a mad dog.

[1] *Poems* III. 794.

Now the poem turns around. Instead of replying in a line or two, Robin delivers a long speech (his last), and argues that Allen is less dangerous than a mad dog because no one pays attention to him. But Tom closes with the longest speech of all, declaring that whether or not Allen is effectual, he is possessed by Satan. Finally, he turns the poem yet again by comparing Allen with Swift, who, he says, is himself perverse and foolish for wishing to free people who desire slavery. Thus in a typical leap of self-satire, the poet merges with the madman who has been speaking for him.

The constant turns, the heavy sarcasm, the alternation of voices, the strong metre, all help to support the furious language. Here is the passage on Bedlam, with Swift characteristically joining the themes of madness and filth:

> Yet many a wretch in Bedlam, knows,
> How to distinguish friends from foes;
> And though perhaps among the rout,
> He wildly flings his filth about,
> He still has gratitude and sap'ence,
> To spare the folks that gave him ha'pence
> Nor, in their eyes at random pisses,
> But turns aside like mad Ulysses:
> While Traulus all his ordure scatters
> To foul the man he chiefly flatters.[1]

The pendant poem, 'Traulus. The Second Part', has simpler construction and less interest. Here Swift merely throws insults at Allen, attributing his various defects to various ancestors. While the poem smokes with the fumes of indignation, its effect derives mainly from Swift's usual energy of metre and rhymes.

> View him on the mother's side,
> Fill'd with falsehood, spleen and pride;
> Positive and over-bearing,
> Changing still, and still adhering,
> Spiteful, peevish, rude, untoward;
> Fierce in tongue, in heart a coward.[2]

[1] Ll. 23–32. It is barely possible that Swift (perhaps unconsciously) is echoing Horace, *Satires* I. iv. 86–9.
[2] Ll. 7–12.

The attack on Allen was only part of Swift's spring campaign. He also wished to defend Carteret and Delany. The defence of Carteret may have seemed urgent because the Lord Lieutenant would be leaving for England soon after Parliament rose; and yet what Swift wished to write would have been risky to publish during Parliament time. It may be for these reasons that Swift sent out his *Vindication of Lord Carteret* when he did; for Marmaduke Coghill, posting a copy to a friend, said that 'as soon as my Lord Lieutenant came from the House [*sc.* of Lords], the enclosed paper was cried about.'[1]

Carteret had obliged Swift repeatedly by giving preferments to his friends. He had just made Stopford the provost of Tuam[2] and Delany the chancellor of St Patrick's.[3] But of course these places were inconsiderable beside what Boulter and Hoadly had done for loyal servants of the English interest. The difference between the two accounts is the foundation of Swift's essay; for in it he refutes the charge that Carteret gave all his favours to Tories and Jacobites.

Unlike 'Traulus', *A Vindication of Lord Carteret* is a courtly display of the dean's ironic craftsmanship.[4] None of the devices employed is new, and Swift had in the past used each of them with more mastery than in the *Vindication*. Perhaps he weakens the structure of the piece by digressive outbursts in the direction of Allen and Tighe—digressions which seem obtrusive not so much for their length (though this is excessive) as for their tone: they have some of the turbulence—here inappropriate—and several of the motifs of 'Traulus'.[5] Of course, Allen and Tighe were self-appointed watchdogs for the Whig interest; and their misdeeds are central to Swift's argument.

The essay remains a fine specimen of Swift's brightest

---

[1] Letter of 18 Apr. 1730 to Edward Southwell; spelling altered; see *Poems* III. 794. Carteret prorogued Parliament on Wednesday, 15 Apr. 1730. In one passage of the essay Swift gives the date on which he is writing as 13 Apr. 1730 (Davis XII. 168). He may have added this sentence while the essay was in the press.

[2] Cotton IV. 25.

[3] Swift takes credit for these acts in a letter of 19 Nov. 1730 to Gay (Williams III. 421). See also Lawlor.

[4] Davis XII. 149–69.

[5] Compare *ibid.*, p. 157, the last paragraph, with 'Traulus, Part I', ll. 53–62.

manner. For foundation he has his common way of expressing praise as blame. Writing in the character of an 'old Whig', he apologizes for the faults of the viceroy but argues against the accusations of the 'new Whigs'—mainly the charge that Carteret has favoured Tories. Swift therefore apologizes for what amount to virtues: Carteret's learning, the loyalty of his ancestors, his 'memory, judgment, comprehension, eloquence, and wit', along with other standard topics of eulogy.

Although the principle seems simple, Swift uses it with peculiar grace, as in the famous sentence describing Carteret at Oxford:

> His excellency the present Lord, was educated in the University of Oxford; from whence, with a singularity scarce to be justified, he carried away more Greek, Latin, and philosophy than properly became a person of his rank.[1]

In addition to disguising his authorship and praising by simple irony, Swift brings in one of those comic illustrations that he delighted in—the problem of the 'high-flyer', Madam Violante, rope-dancer, whose papist leanings and dubious politics deserve looking into.[2]

In demolishing Tighe, or 'Pistorides' (named from the Latin word meaning 'descended from a baker') and Allen, or 'Traulus', Swift inverts his treatment of Carteret, and expresses contempt in the language of sympathy and respect. So he praises Allen for those graces which the Viscount conspicuously lacks: fluent speech, physical beauty, etc.

In the final two-fifths of the pamphlet we meet a revamping of the sort of arithmetical argument used in the 'Roman gratitude' number of the *Examiner* attacking Marlborough.[3] Swift reckons up the value of the preferments given under Carteret to non-Whigs, and then contrasts their total with the sum of incomes given to Whigs. The contrast was in fact absurdly disproportionate, but Swift also weights his calculations unscrupulously; for he balances the favours which alleged Tories received from Carteret against all those which the whole government gave to

---

[1] Davis XII. 154.   [2] *Ibid.*, p. 156.   [3] 30 Nov. 1710.

apparent Whigs. While describing Carteret's beneficiaries, Swift also manages to provide a detailed and witty rebuttal of the charges arising from Sheridan's 'First of August' sermon in Cork.[1]

VIII. SWIFT AND DELANY

Meanwhile, Swift's ridicule of Dr Delany had excited other Dublin lampoonists, and an uproar in verse broke around the doctor's head. Few of the pieces were so well-turned as Arbuckle's 'Panegyric'; but the atmosphere of displaced hostility startles one. Besides answering in kind, Swift made some moral reflections on the angry excitement, partly with regard to Delany's plight and partly to his own. From such reflections a number of striking poems emerged.

For one of these Swift adopted the excellent plan of comparing his own situation to that of Horace in the latter's *Satires* II. i. Swift's poem, 'A Dialogue between an Eminent Lawyer and Dr Swift',[2] is about half the length of the Latin original. When Pope imitated the same satire a few years later, he produced a version three times as long as Swift's. A few comparisons of these works will help to define Swift's accomplishment.

For all three poems the form is a dialogue between a cautious lawyer and an impetuous satirist, in just the sort of dramatic encounter that suited Swift's talents. The satirist asks for advice in dealing with complaints against his verse. The lawyer—Robert Lindsay for Swift, William Fortescue for Pope, Trebatius for Horace—recommends either silence or conventional verses on uncontroversial topics; and the satirist replies that he cannot block his peculiar instinct to compose poems and denounce vice. Beyond this scheme, the three poets go separate ways.

I believe that Swift's example inspired Pope. But the poem by Pope is far subtler and more complex than that by Swift. There are the usual differences between Pope's musical, expressive heroics and Swift's quick octosyllabics. We may also notice that

---

[1] Davis XII. 163–4.　　[2] *Poems* II. 488–91.

Pope's allusions are to current and personal experiences, Swift's to events past and historical, to books he has read. Swift takes the line of ridiculing the kind of eulogy that his enemies might expect a poet to produce. Pope, more directly, describes the characters he detests, contrasting them with his own principles and values.

Once again, therefore, Swift has the ingenious framework, affording several angles for his irony. Pope's poem, far superior, relies more on verbal felicities, elegant phrases, exquisite patterns of rhythm and sound. Above all, Pope makes his way through elaborate modulations and reversals of tone and fascinating, ambiguous shifts in his attitude toward the lawyer.

Swift's close is his own. Instead of answering the poet's question—which is whether one must recommend immoral doctrines in order to serve the rich and powerful—the lawyer utters a prophecy. He declares that men of culture may appreciate Swift's 'irony and wit', but great men will fear and hate him. Consequently, he must expect no further preferment. This turn, so different from that of Horace or Pope, suggests how sharply Swift felt the irony of his position—that he might raise others but could not raise himself.

While Swift was writing his poems, the campaign against Delany continued. Sheridan, Dunkin, and others published squibs and satires on the genial doctor. His skin was too tender to bear some of the rubs; and Swift told Pope about the 'knot of little fellows' badgering Delany:

> [How] they have been provoked I know not, unless by envy at seeing him so very domestic with the Lord Lieutenant. The doctor as a man of much strictness in his life was mortified with two or three of the first squibs.[1]

Just as Delany liked to be liked, so also Swift felt that he alone had the right to tease his protégé in public. We may recall his quip to Sheridan,

> You're my goose, and no other man's;
> And you know all my geese are swans.[2]

---

[1] 2 May 1730; Sherburn III. 109.   [2] *Poems* III. 983.

So he took it on himself to console and protect his embattled friend. With these aims Swift published a poem, 'To Doctor D–l—y, on the Libels Writ against Him'.[1] It is a long but highly engaging work that pretends to be straightforwardly didactic, yet becomes a kind of dialogue: Swift speaks indirectly for Delany and replies to him. The most attractive feature is the parallel the dean finds between the victim and himself. By associating Delany's troubles with his own, the poet implicitly challenges the young men who are goading his friend. The poem is one of those rare articles in Swift's canon, a piece of compliment without irony, all of it restrained in tone and much of it expressed in the kindly manner of the verses addressed to Stella.

If the dean found it easy to sympathize with the doctor's condition and to soothe him without irony, the reason lies in the tenor of Swift's feelings twenty years before, when the storm of pamphlet attacks on himself distressed him.[2] A natural compliment therefore, is Swift's principle that eminence is what draws envy. If Delany were less gifted, he would have fewer critics. Incidentally, Swift turns on ecclesiastics as being professionally averse to literary merit:

> A genius in the rev'rend gown,
> Must ever keep its owner down:
> 'Tis an unnatural conjunction,
> And spoils the credit of the function.[3]

In its openness the poem shows the reader more of Swift's honest conscience than most of his ironies can. Simple didactic poetry never exercised his finest talents; yet as an unashamed, plain statement of his rational (or rationalized) position— almost an apology for satire—the poem has special interest. True genius, Swift declares (with more magnanimity than logic) cannot serve 'ignoble ends'. The real poet, therefore, will always see himself belaboured by the poetasters, who are themselves commonly servile to political faction. So Delany, like Swift,

---

[1] *Ibid.*, II. 499–505; probably composed in April or May 1730; published before 19 Jun., when it appeared in *The Daily Post-Boy*.
[2] Davis VIII. 136.   [3] Ll. 79–82.

must either write nothing, write venally (and badly), or suffer himself to be libelled:

> 'Till block-heads blame, and judges praise,
> The poet cannot claim his bays.[1]

It is just possible that Swift is echoing Horace in this poem. Certainly one passage has him playing the part of Trebatius–Lindsay from the 'Dialogue between an Eminent Lawyer and Dean Swift'; for here he advises Delany that if he wishes to write without being attacked, he should celebrate the men in power:

> You say, the muse will not contain,
> And write you must, or break a vein:
> Then, if you find the terms too hard,
> No longer my advice regard:
> But raise your fancy on the wing;
> The *Irish senate*'s praises sing.[2]

Elsewhere in the poem he translates a tag from a Horatian satire.[3] The theme of a poet defending his absent friend is Horatian,[4] as is the contempt for jealous critics.[5] Simply by generalizing the case and elevating Delany to the historic rank of poets who deserve a reasoned defence from the leading author of the nation, Swift must have gratified the doctor.

As if 'To Dr Delany' were not enough, Swift also composed a beautiful short piece on the same theme, which he gave to Delany and did not publish. This poem, 'To a Friend Who Had Been Much Abused', shows how orderly, dignified, and eloquent Swift's plain style could be.[6] The neat structure of two stanzas, one answering the other, and each designed with four lines set against two, works on us by making the sentences seem

---

[1] *Poems* II. 505.

[2] Ll. 51–6; cf. Horace, *Satires* II. i. 10–12. The very fact that Swift had just based a poem on one of Horace's satires suggests that he was reading them over.

[3] L. 29, taken from Horace, *Satires* II. vii. 86.

[4] Horace, *Satires* I. iv. 81–5.

[5] Swift, ll. 123–34, 167–70; cf. Horace, *Satires* I. x. 78–83. Swift quotes the same poem by Horace in his *Epistle to a Lady*, note to l. 198.

[6] *Poems* II. 506.

aphoristic and peculiarly cogent while fitting effortlessly into the tight pattern. So Swift urges Delany

> [Fearless to] enter in through virtue's gate
> And buy distinction at the dearest rate.[1]

Unfortunately, Delany could not show his appreciation of Swift's teaching by a golden silence. Instead, he chose to write a verse fable called 'The Pheasant and the Lark'. In this poem he tells of the jealousy felt by inferior birds (Sheridan, Dunkin, etc.) because the pheasant (Carteret) has made a friend of the lark (Delany). When the others run down and abuse the lark, the nightingale (Swift) defends him; and then,

> Shamed by the wisdom of his notes,
> They hide their heads, and hush their throats.[2]

Perhaps Swift felt once more that it was his responsibility to chastise as well as to defend. He produced an 'Answer' which is not only wittier than Delany's fable but also caustic to the author.[3] Here Swift writes in the person of a pro–English admirer of Lord Allen, a Whig who hates Swift and Delany both. He points out that Delany's characters are absurdly unsuitable to his birds and that Swift in particular is hardly like a nightingale—being in fact a malcontent snarler:

> The worst of disaffected deans ...
> So dull that but for spleen and spite,
> We ne'er shou'd know that he could write.[4]

This is probably the piece Swift had in mind when he told Lord Bathurst that after offending those in power and being often worried by libellers, he had written a poem in the style and manner of his attackers, and 'sent it by an unknown hand to a Whig printer who very faithfully published it'. Swift said that in the poem he accused himself of but one fault of which he was

---

[1] Ll. 11–12. [2] *Poems* II. 507–12, ll. 147–8.

[3] *Ibid.*, pp. 512–15. Delany's poem was published before 4 Apr. 1730, when it came out in a newspaper. Swift's was published before 17 Jun., when it appeared in the same paper. See *ibid.*, p. 507.

[4] Ll. 66, 71–2.

truly guilty, 'but with the rest of the satyr, I chose to abuse myself with the direct reverse of my character'.[1]

For nearly half its length the poem is focused on Swift. He does indeed malign himself, although the accusations are all those which a Whig would make. The fault he would admit, I suppose, is that he

> Against the court is always blabbing,
> And calls the senate-house a cabin.[2]

Swift may have written the poem to offer Delany further comfort by appearing under attack like his friend. But it also seems to be one more variant of the inscription on the gold box: Swift giving the dean (now ironically) the appreciation he thought was due him from others.

[1] Williams III. 410–11.　　[2] Ll. 69–70.

Chapter Nine

SUMMER AT MARKET HILL

S ummer came, and the dean returned to Market Hill.[1]
Again we know little about his experiences there. But
judging from what happened afterwards, I suspect that a
rift between Lady Acheson and her husband became so notice-
able that it troubled the dean. He probably spent much time at
the house of Henry Leslie.[2] He certainly determined that he
would not, after all, build a house on Drapier's Hill. In fact, he
wrote a poem about the decision.

The poem, 'The Dean's Reasons for not Building at Market
Hill',[3] disagrees with the account Swift gave to Pope. 'I will fly as
soon as build,' he told Pope;

> I have have neither years, nor spirits, nor money, nor patience for
> such amusements. The frolic is gone off, and I am only 100 pounds
> the poorer.[4]

But in the poem the blame falls upon Sir Arthur's character. The
baronet, Swift says, does not enjoy conversation, and will not
interrupt his daily routines to walk, drink ale, or talk with the
dean. For all his cultivation, he is a withdrawn personality—

> Who keeps his wisdom out of sight;
> Whose uncommunicative heart,
> Will scarce one precious word impart.

According to Swift, Acheson would hum a song or drum with his

---

[1] I don't know the exact date of his departure. On 24 Jun. he says he is 'just going out
of town' (Williams III. 399); on 28 Aug. he says he has been in the north for two months
and will remain for another (*ibid.*, p. 405); in Oct. he says he has passed three months in
the northern parts of Ireland (*ibid.*, p. 409).
[2] Cf. *Poems* III. 877–9.   [3] *Ibid.*, III. 898–902.   [4] Sherburn III. 65.

fingers while the dean spoke. Moreover, he enjoyed the sort of philosophical reflections that bored Swift.

> His guests are few, his visits rare,
> Nor uses time, nor time will spare;
> Nor rides, nor walks, nor hunts, nor fowls,
> Nor plays at cards, or dice, or bowls;
> But seated in an easy chair,
> Despises exercise and air.[1]

Finally, he paid small attention to Swift's advice for the improvement of his estate.

In other words, the pleasures that Swift associated with the country life seldom delighted Sir Arthur. We may infer that the young wife would have been glad to see more company, to walk, talk, listen, and be lively. If so, Swift was primarily her guest rather than her husband's; and when she broke with Sir Arthur, Swift would have lost his main reason for visits to Market Hill.

It is worth observing that whatever Swift may have felt about the disregard of his advice, we have independent evidence of Sir Arthur's excellent management; for long after his death a careful surveyor of the family estates declared,

> [Many] proofs still remain that at a former period a Sir Arthur Acheson was the means of effecting considerable improvements on the Gosford estates, considering the circumstances of the period in which his laudable and patriotic attentions were bestowed. The attention and encouragement he then afforded is still gratefully remembered by many of the old tenants, their descendants and successors; and the trees and plantation throughout the property which are now ripe for the hatchet were planted by him or under his directions and influence.[2]

Some scholars have assumed that the Achesons tired of Swift.[3] But no clear evidence appears of such a change. After two visits so prolonged as those Swift made to Market Hill in 1728 and 1729, no family would have opened themselves to a

[1] Ll. 42–4, 85–90.
[2] William Greig, *General Report on the Gosford Estates in County Armagh 1821*, ed. F. M. L. Thompson and D. Tierney (Belfast, 1976), pp. 88–9.
[3] E.g., Williams, in *Poems* III. 873–4.

[667]

third if they found his company disagreeable. Certainly Swift remained on excellent terms with Lady Acheson after she began to live independently.[1]

Swift's worries about his health also made long visits difficult. Even in May 1730 he said he would thereafter go on 'no distant journey', and would never again let himself be 'above two nights out of the power of returning to my home'.[2] Though he bent those resolutions so far as to have another season with the Achesons, the anxieties which cancelled his building scheme must have prescribed further cautionary withdrawals.

Poetry flourished in spite of such disabilities. Of the pieces which Swift wrote during the summer the best are 'Death and Daphne', 'A Panegyrick on the Dean', and *An Epistle to a Lady*. Among these the most self-contained is 'Death and Daphne'.[3] To Delany it seemed 'finely schemed, imagined, conducted, and executed! and interspersed with many fine strokes of wit, humour, and satire'.[4] The praise is deserved. Although this fable has one of Swift's abrupt, anti-climactic endings, it shows otherwise the virtues of his poetic gift, and deserves a wide audience.

According to Orrery, Lady Acheson read 'Death and Daphne' to him in Swift's presence, and 'assured (him) smilingly that the portrait was drawn for herself'. When Orrery protested, Swift (we are told) said, 'That lady had rather be a Daphne drawn by me, than a Sacharissa by any other pencil.'[5]

In the centre of his design, Swift places a myth of his own invention, that Pluto ordered Death to find himself a wife. Drawing on the traditional furniture of the underworld, Death dresses up as a beau. When he comes a-courting to London, he charms Daphne, a woman of skeletal figure herself. But as Death touches her, Daphne's cold, gaunt hand chills him so that he flees in fear.

---

[1] She died 1 Nov. 1737.   [2] Sherburn III. 108.

[3] *Poems* III. 902–5. I am not sure the poem was written in 1730. It must have been completed after November 1729, because it alludes to the Treaty of Seville, 9 Nov. 1729 (l. 7). But it has no reference to Market Hill and treats Lady Acheson, in fantasy, as available for marriage. It was not included in *Miscellanies* III, 1732. Orrery tells of her reading it to him in Swift's company; and Swift became friendly with Orrery in the autumn of 1732. The poem may have been written after her ladyship left Sir Arthur.

[4] Pp. 125–6.   [5] *Poems* III. 902.

This simple but original sketch, Swift fills out with enough conceits and smart phrases for a work several times its length. Almost every couplet has a specimen of Swift's ingenuity. The cleverest may be the scene of Death getting dressed, e.g.,

> The owl, the raven, and the bat,
> Club'd for a feather to his hat.

But there are many slighter hints and touches: in London, Death chooses a residence in Warwick Lane, the location of the College of Physicians. Pluto, annoyed with the post-war decline in mortality, says Death must marry because

> he no longer could support
> Old bachelors about his court.[1]

To give Death a fair complexion, a lawyer puts a parchment (no doubt a will) over his face. All through the poem runs a theme which turns *A Modest Proposal* inside out: that the underworld believes population means wealth, and therefore requires a rise in our world's death rate to keep Pluto's colonies well stocked. Swift's preoccupation with death is not surprising in the season of his climacteric and when his illnesses were chronic. He told Bolingbroke, '[Death] is never out of my mind.'[2] But in the poem Death as a character seems to speak for the poet. If so, the theme of courtship may suggest the depth of Swift's feeling for the lady.[3] In ancient myth, Daphne is pursued by Apollo, a god with whom Swift identified himself in verse. Behind the fantasy is probably the unconscious wish for a union with the dead Stella.

If one shifts to another Market Hill poem, 'A Panegyrick on the Dean, in the Person of a Lady in the North',[4] one is again impressed by the energy, boldness, and versatility of Swift's talent. This is a long, rambling work, almost a third of which

---

[1] Ll. 29–30, 11–12.   [2] Sherburn III. 98.

[3] For a detailed treatment of this possibility see Nora Crowe Jaffe, 'Swift and the Agreeable Young Lady, but Extremely Lean', *Papers on Language and Literature* 14 (Winter 1978), 129–37.

[4] *Poems* III. 886–97. The date may be wrong. In l. 204 we are told that Swift built the privies in twenty weeks—the sort of fact he was not likely to invent. But he did not stay so long at Market Hill in 1730. The reference to Smedley in the closing lines is also curious, since he had sailed for Madras in Feb. 1729.

becomes an unpredictable digression. The body of the poem is a mock-eulogy of the dean by an unnamed woman whom he impersonates, viz., Lady Acheson. The digression deals in startling detail with Swift's construction of two outdoor privies.

It is obvious, in the lengthy account of the privies, that Swift intends to shock the reader. His humour, here, as in *Gulliver's Travels*, draws on our infantile ambivalence toward the body's filth and on the schoolboy's pleasure in handling such material by indirection. Through puns, conceits, and witty circumlocutions, he imputes the guilt for nasty thoughts to any reader who correctly interprets the ambiguities, and thus the poet holds himself comically blameless.

It is also obvious that the subject excites Swift. His imagination becomes as active as that of Pope in Book Two of *The Dunciad*. His euphemisms for faeces are numerous and various enough to challenge the most sympathetic reader. That Swift should associate all this material with a woman whom he was attached to, tells us something about his division of feeling toward women. Possibly the defilement of the female is a means of defending himself against the attraction he feels toward her.

At the same time, one must not ignore his imaginative power over other themes. A passage personifying gluttony and its attendant vices demonstrates the unabated strength of Swift's myth-making faculty:

> But, when at last usurping Jove
> Old Saturn from his empire drove;
> Then Gluttony with greasy paws,
> Her napkin pinn'd up to her jaws,
> With watry chaps, and wagging chin,
> Brac'd like a drum her oily skin;
> Wedg'd in a spacious elbow-chair,
> And on her plate a treble share,
> As if she ne'er could have enough;
> Taught harmless man to cram and stuff.[1]

The parts of this poem are certainly more than the whole; for in general 'A Panegyrick' simply has Lady Acheson addressing

[1] Ll. 253–61.

the dean and praising him. First she celebrates qualities he conspicuously lacks. Then, in hundreds of lines, she celebrates real but trivial acts, unworthy of a national hero. Implicitly, Swift is boasting throughout that his greatness has not made him solemn and self-important.

In two (widely separated) passages, Swift suggests that Pope's invocation of him in the *Dunciad Variorum* of 1729 (Book I, ll. 17–26) made a springboard for Swift to conceive this 'Panegyrick'; for 'Lady Acheson' parodies Pope's famous 'Dean, Drapier, Bickerstaff, or Gulliver' in

> Dean, Butler, Usher, Jester, Tutor;
> Robert and Darby's coadjutor:
> And, as you in commission sit,
> To rule the dairy next to Kit. . . .
> Whether your fruitful fancy lies
> To make for pigs convenient sties:
> Or, ponder long with anxious thought
> To banish rats that haunt our vault.[1]

According to Mrs Pilkington, Pope's lines had disappointed Swift, who considered his own praise of his friend in the 'Libel on Dr Delany' to be a warmer tribute.[2]

If the allusion to *The Dunciad* is the poet's intention, it may account for the awkward tangent (ll. 217–308) on the privies and on Cloacina, the sewer goddess. Swift is exorcizing the same 'obscene fancy'[3] as Pope (in *The Dunciad*, Book Two);[4] so he may be improving or parodying Pope's example. But where Pope involves errant booksellers, Swift involves a lady. Thus he anticipates other verse satires, soon to follow, in which he will ridicule the pastoral ideal of an ethereal shepherdess endowed with the charms of the flesh but none of its ills.

---

[1] Ll. 39–42, 159–62.
[2] Pilkington I. 75–6. It was only after writing this paragraph as it now stands that I read (through the kindness of Professor Scouten) the discussion of the 'Panegyrick' by Arthur H. Scouten, in 'Jonathan Swift's Progress from Prose to Poetry', published in Robert C. Elliott and A. H. Scouten, *The Poetry of Jonathan Swift*, ed. M. E. Novak (Los Angeles, 1981), pp. 43–4.
[3] James Sutherland's expression; see *The Dunciad*, p. 108, note to l. 79. See also Gay, *Trivia* II. 115ff.
[4] Ll. 65–112. Swift is named in l. 108.

Through this implication we may connect the Cloacina–privy section with the opening; for 'Lady Acheson' begins by thanking Swift for his indulgence to women,

> Transform'd by your convincing tongue
> To witty, beautiful, and young.

Of course, the irony (hardly subtle) is that Swift constantly found fault with her ladyship and regularly denounced female vice.

The body of the 'Panegyrick', after that introduction, contains grateful praise of Swift for his various achievements at Market Hill—as talker, butler, tutor, etc.—ending with his construction of out-houses. The digression on privies follows, and then a summary set of precepts for Lady Acheson, delivered by Apollo in a dream.[1]

The most important poem of the summer is again stronger in its parts than as a whole; yet the parts are marvellous. This is *An Epistle to a Lady*, which Swift may have begun earlier than 1730 and finished later.[2] It certainly splits halfway through, when the focus changes abruptly from Lady Acheson to English statesmen. The occasion of the poem is supposed to be a complaint by the lady; and the form is a dialogue between her and Swift. She is tired of being blamed by the poet and would like him to praise her in heroic verse. In the first half Swift admits the lady's merits but warns her that in conversation, which is the chief responsibility of a hostess, she is defective. For the rest of the poem he asks by what right she can expect to be complimented when he is a poet who ridicules persons of the highest rank.

Yet the lines on Lady Acheson suggest the reasons that their friendship endured; for as Swift says in her name, she is modest, loyal, discreet, and charitable:

---

[1] The poem ends in an irrelevant quatrain about Smedley. The point of these lines escapes me.

[2] *Poems* II. 628–38. In ll. 99–109, Lady Acheson must be at Market Hill, and she must have been the subject of earlier poems by Swift; ll. 133–274 could have been added at any time before Swift gave the manuscript to Mrs Barber in the summer of 1733; but ll. 171–8 deal with names that were much on Swift's mind in 1731.

> Am I spiteful, proud, unjust?
> Did I ever break my trust?
> Which, of all our modern dames
> Censures less, or less defames?
> In good manners, am I faulty?
> Can you call me rude, or haughty?
> Did I e'er my mite withold
> From the impotent and old?
> When did ever I omit
> Due regard for men of wit?[1]

In the dean's reply other virtues of the lady appear:

> Though you lead a blameless life,
> Are an humble, prudent wife;
> Answer all domestic ends,
> What is this to us your friends?
> Though your children by a nod
> Stand in awe without a rod:
> Though by your obliging sway
> Servants love you, and obey:
> Though you treat us with a smile,
> Clear your looks, and smooth your stile:
> Load our plates from ev'ry dish;
> This is not the thing we wish.[2]

While Swift goes on to ask for excellent conversation, the list of virtues claimed and allowed gives us one more definition of a good woman. It also amounts to a eulogy of the lady. It is a eulogy to be kept in mind when we meet Swift's bitter satires on other conceptions of femininity.

In the second half of the poem the passages that stand out are eruptions against the court and the royal ministers. These have the effect of savage vituperation without sounding frantic. The reason is that the occasion is carefully controlled. Swift is not denouncing the government. In a variation of Horace's *Quid faciam*[3] he is merely telling the lady that he cannot write sublime poetry. One of the ferocious passages pretends only to illustrate the poet's claim that ridicule is his natural form of expression:

---

[1] Ll. 65–74. [2] Ll. 99–110.
[3] Horace, *Satires* II. i. 24, and *passim*.

All the vices of a court,
Do but serve to make me sport.
Should a monkey wear a crown,
Must I tremble at his frown?
Could I not, through all his ermine?
Spy the strutting chatt'ring vermin?
Safely write a smart lampoon,
To expose the brisk baboon?[1]

Another control is, as so often, the dialogue form, the style of rational dispute. The lady herself scolds Swift for sounding frantic; therefore, the readers need not do so. But his reply, again Horatian, is that ridicule is more effective than simple reproaches. In yet another illustration, he joins the political theme to the personal by a simple parallel; and we have the surface of an argument *a fortiori*: if Swift does not spare statesmen and kings, he should not spare her ladyship:

If I treat you like [a crowned head]
You have cheap enough compounded.
Can you put in higher claims
Than the owners of St James.
You are not so great a grievance
As the hirelings of St [Stephen's].[2]
You are of a lower class
Than my friend Sir [Robert Brass].[3]
None of these have mercy found:
I have laugh'd, and lash'd them round.[4]

The steady pulses, the whiplash of the rhymes, and the conciseness of the language convey the poet's indignation, while the explicitly comic intent and the framework of rational dispute convey his sanity.

During his summer at Market Hill, Swift heard the news which probably belongs among the provocations of his most notorious poems, i.e., the filthy satires against the ideal woman of pastoral and Petrarchan conventions. In June the Dean of Ferns faced an indictment for rape. Dr Thomas Sawbridge came of a clerical family in Leicestershire, and Swift could have met or

---

[1] Ll. 147–54.   [2] I.e., the British House of Commons.   [3] Walpole.
[4] Ll. 239–48.

heard of his father, a politicking Whig pluralist from Melton Mowbray.[1] After taking his degree in the low-church Emmanuel College, Cambridge (B.A., 1709), Sawbridge seems to have held a Leicestershire living for three years, but was deprived in 1715. He was next probably a chaplain in the navy and (later) certainly one for the East India Company of Bombay.[2] In January 1729, he was imported as an Englishman to succeed Swift's loathed namesake Smedley as Dean of Ferns and Leighlin in Ireland.

What honour Sawbridge may have gathered through this preferment, he easily dissipated in Dublin, a year later, when (3 February 1730) he so far impaired the morals of a young woman as to be taken up (four months afterward) for rape. On Tuesday, 2 June, Sawbridge was arraigned for 'forcibly and feloniously ravishing' Susanna Runcard. The following Monday, although he was supposed to be tried, no evidence appeared against him, and the trial was put off a week. But again no evidence appeared; so he was acquitted. A report went out that Sawbridge would indict the girl for perjury, 'he being in the county of Wexford when she swore the rape was committed against her in the city of Dublin'.[3]

But Swift preferred to accept other information. He took the news as confirming his ordinary estimate of the government's ecclesiastic policy, and he wrote in August to the Earl of Oxford,

> There is a fellow here from England, one Sawbridge, he was last term indicted for rape. The plea he intended was his being drunk when he forced the woman; but he bought her off. He is a dean and I name him to your lordship, because I am confident you will hear of his being a bishop.[4]

Within a few years, and without translation to the episcopal bench, Sawbridge died.[5] But before the summer of 1730 was over, Swift wrote a ballad about him which deserves to be

---

[1] Venn; H.M.C. *Rutland* II. 190–2.

[2] Venn, and information kindly supplied by Professor James Woolley.

[3] I have combined the accounts printed in various London newspapers of 13, 16, 23, and 27 June 1730.

[4] Williams III. 405.   [5] May 1733.

anthologized: 'An Excellent New Ballad: or, The True English Dean to be Hang'd for a Rape'.[1] The stanza form, a bouncing sestet,[2] is that of Gay's song, 'When young at the bar', from *The Beggar's Opera*;[3] and Swift may be alluding to the words which Polly sings in the play. She says that though, as a bar maid, she did no more than kiss her usual customers, Macheath's

> kiss was so sweet, and so closely he pressed,
> That I languished and pined till I granted the rest.

In all of Swift's stanzas the final couplet rhymes on 'rape'; and the theme is the successive efforts of Sawbridge to find a woman who will neither yield too easily nor resist with success—Mrs Runcard, by implication, gets small pity. A few couplets can give the spirit of the poem:

> A holier priest ne'er was wrapt up in crape,
> The worst you can say, he committed a rape....
> If maidens are ravish't, it is their own choice,
> Why are they so wilful to struggle with men?
> If they would but lie quiet, and stifle their voice,
> No devil nor dean could ravish 'em then.

To enlarge Swift's sense of outrage, there existed the recent English case of Colonel Francis Charteris, cheat and usurer, who had tricked his way into a fortune and married his daughter to an earl.[4] In Febuary 1730 he was convicted of rape but soon received the King's pardon. Swift's serious implication seems

---

[1] Poems II. 516–20. It was published in *The Grub-Street Journal* for 11 Jun. 1730.

[2] Anapaestic tetrameter, ababcc.

[3] III. i, air 41. We know Swift was familiar with *The Beggar's Opera*. But there are many similar songs in the same form. For a list see Robert G. Noyes and Roy Lamson, Jr., 'Broadside-Ballad Versions of the Songs in Restoration Drama', *Harvard Studies and Notes in Philology and Literature* 19 (1937), 199–218. Cf. Gay's own model, 'If love's a sweet passion', from Purcell's *Fairy Queen*. Gay's immensely popular song has two stanzas, each of three couplets. The following lines suggest its appropriateness to be echoed by Swift's ballad:

> Since I suffer with pleasure, why should I complain,
> Or grieve at my fate, when I know 'tis in vain?
> Yet so pleasing the pain is, so soft is the dart,
> That at once it both wounds me, and tickles my heart.

(See near the end of Act III.)

[4] Swift names Charteris with Sawbridge in a letter of 28 Aug. 1730; Williams III. 405.

that corrupted England naturally presents the Irish clergy with agents of corruption: when politics override all moral principle, an established church has no means of maintaining its integrity. By the same figure, Swift complains that the victimized hierarchy is aiding its seducer. It is no irrelevance that when the 'Dean' in Swift's poem tried to rape an Englishwoman, she 'bustled and struggled, and made her escape'.

Part Four

MONUMENTS 1730–45

Chapter One

FRIENDSHIPS

_____

I. 'AN ANSWER TO THE CRAFTSMAN'

With no Lord Lieutenant in residence, and no Parliament, Dublin afforded little excitement to an elderly moralist during the autumn of 1730. In September the dean came back, carrying 'an ill head' to his cathedral chores, though he was 'constantly at morning prayers by nine, and superintending [his] vicars'.[1] However, Charles Ford's mother had died; and her son arrived on a visit to settle the estate; so Swift had the satisfaction of his favourite Irish company.

In the way of relief from routine, he might give thanks to England; for Whitehall sent him a fresh occupation, the topic of Irish recruits for the French armies. In 1690 Louis XIV had added to his troops an Irish Brigade, which could keep up its strength only through active recruiting in the mother country. Under the military articles of the Treaty of Limerick, Irish soldiers might legally enlist in continental armies; and thousands did so. But during the reign of Queen Anne the parliaments of both England and Ireland made it a capital crime for their subjects to serve a foreign prince—except by special permission from the Crown.

Then in the years following 1717, France and England pursued harmonious foreign policies; and as late as 1729 the intimacy was deep enough for George II to grant the French something they had repeatedly begged for, a licence to recruit soldiers in Ireland.[2] French officers had of course been doing so surreptitiously, and in recent years with the connivance of the

_____

[1] Williams III. 409.
[2] S.P.D. 63/391 (unsigned letter from Windsor, 11 Aug. 1730).

Irish government. Now, for the sake of the 'strict alliance between the two crowns' his majesty would allow them to take 750 Irishmen quite openly.[1] On both sides of St George's Channel, the bureaucracy felt alarmed. This happened to be the precise time when the managers of Ireland were supposed to be disquieted by the rate of emigration.[2]

With historic declarations as bitter as they had been against the French, with the troubles of 1715 only fifteen years in the past, and with the certainty remaining that in a war against Great Britain the French would employ the Irish Brigade, the new understandings could not be freely announced. The opposition were always on the watch against such licences,[3] and could easily show how absurd it was for England to strengthen the army of any French government. Yet if the French, in 1730, tried to do their work covertly, they would find legal obstacles in every country justice of the peace.

On Friday, 9 October 1730, the chief recruiting officer, Colonel Hennecy, presented himself to the Primate with a letter of recommendation from Newcastle. Even Boulter's stomach shrank from this morsel. 'I must beg leave to hint to your grace', he told Newcastle, 'that all recruits raised here for France or Spain, are generally considered as persons that may some time or other pay a visit to this country as enemies.' He doubted not the legality of the measure but its expedience; and he warned Newcastle against the opposition of country magistrates, the fury of Parliament, and the resentment of ordinary people. Who could say to what 'excesses of heat' the citizens might run? He reminded the Duke of Wood's halfpence.[4]

On Saturday, Boulter told his fellow Lords Justices about the French presence. He consulted them again after the weekend, having received further instructions directly from Newcastle. Though the most extraordinary discretion was used,[5] secrecy

---

[1] Ferguson, p. 177.

[2] S.P.D. 63/391 (Yorke to Newcastle, 14 Apr. 1729; Delafaye to Dorset, 23 Oct. 1730).

[3] B. Williams, *Whig Supremacy*, pp. 274–5.

[4] Boulter II. 30–3 (Dublin, pp. 25–8).

[5] Unsigned letter to Dorset, 23 Oct. 1730 (S.P.D. 63/391) and another to Boulter, 26 Sept. 1730 (S.P.D. 63/392).

proved to be impossible. By Wednesday, the Dublin newpapers were printing an account from London;[1] and six days later, the London newspapers printed an account from Dublin, with the false story that Boulter had given the French officers a dinner.[2] Meanwhile, the Primate warned Hennecy to keep out of the way.

When the opposition weekly, *The Craftsman* (London, 24 October 1730) reprinted the Dublin story of the recruiting expedition, the writer inserted a sarcastic parenthesis after the following innuendo of the original paragraph:

> It is not to be done in a clandestine manner, as formerly, when several persons suffer'd death for it, but publickly. (The French being now our *sincere friends* and *allies*.)

Two weeks later, *The Craftsman* printed as news the falsehood about Boulter's military dinner, and commented,

> *Is not this to be look'd upon as an happy presage of a coalition between the Church of Rome and the Church of England? between the Jacobite and the Hanoverian interest?*

The essay section of this 7 November *Craftsman* comprised a long and thoroughly destructive analysis of the government's policy. One sentence invited Swift to fuel the polemic:

> Such a method of providing for persons, whose principles render them unserviceable in *our army* [which was indeed closed to Roman Catholics], is indeed a little more charitable than a *late project* for preventing *Irish children* from being starv'd, by fatting them up, and selling them to the *butcher*.[3]

When Swift read this ironic acknowledgement from his English friends, he decided to return it in kind, by writing an answer to *The Craftsman*. For his rejoinder, he produced what—as a statement on the condition of Ireland—has the effect of an appendix to *A Modest Proposal*. If Swift had not left 'An Answer to the Craftsman' slightly unfinished, and if it did not demand a

---

[1] *Dublin Journal*, 13 Oct.
[2] *London Evening Post*, 20 Oct., and other papers of that date and 24 Oct. Boulter denied the story of the dinner (II. 37; Dublin, p. 31).
[3] Davis XII. 317.

knowledge of facts now forgotten, it would be one of his best-known works.[1]

In the 'Answer' Swift writes as a plain Whig, hating *The Craftsman* and defending the government. He also renews the pose of a public-spirited projector, though addressing himself this time to England alone. The essay is a raw, bristling piece with a bitter thrust in almost every sentence. It ingeniously joins to the English arguments against the recruiting licence a bundle of standard Irish complaints, such as the shortage of coins and the exclusion of natives from preferment.

After briefly estimating the money the nation would save by exporting six thousand men a year, Swift proposes a different scheme, which would (he says) benefit both England and Ireland. The implicit principle seriously invoked by the fantasy is that the English would be content with no arrangement that in any way benefited their brothers. Only by utterly sacrificing the Irish people to the material advantage of the English economy can one please the insatiable government in Westminster.

So Swift will eliminate agriculture, manufactures, money, and very nearly the population. He will in effect violate four commonly accepted economic principles: that a nation's exports should outweigh her imports, that (as far as possible) imports should be of raw materials and exports of finished goods, that more specie should enter the country than leaves it, and that agriculture should be encouraged as the basic industry. All these are, of course, in addition to the need for an increase in population.

The grand, mad plan by which the satirist offers to make Ireland 'flourish in trade and opulence' is, then, simply to turn all the arable land into pasture, only keeping 8400 families to superintend the cattle. As for the surplus population, he would have the entire body

> exported to whatever prince will bear the carriage; or transplanted to the English dominions on the American continent, as a screen between his majesty's English subjects and the savage Indians.[2]

[1] *Ibid.*, pp. 171–8. [2] *Ibid.*, p. 176.

Ireland would then import all grains and manufactured goods from England, and would export only raw products. These absurdities are obviously wrapped around the old human–beast motif and the mercantilist maxim on populousness.

Although Swift never polished and published 'An Answer to the Craftsman', Faulkner declared that the original manuscript 'was sent to England and handed about there'.[1] I suspect that Swift hoped to see it published in London but that the recruitment crisis ended too soon.[2] According to one report, Walpole confessed 'that he had been wrong in this measure, and immediately advised the recalling of the officers'.[3] Early in December, Boulter had Newcastle's assurance that the French officers would soon be recalled, and about five weeks later they sailed home.[4]

This was Swift's last essay on the economic state of his nation. A few months later, he said, '[Without] a miracle we are at our last gasp, beyond the imagination of any one who does not live in this kingdom.'[5] Now he gave up. 'I would not', he said a half year still later, 'prescribe a dose to the dead.'[6]

II. PILKINGTONS AND OTHERS

When Swift left Market Hill in the autumn of 1730, he closed an era of his life. Stella died about the time when he met the Achesons. The first, longest visit to Market Hill, which only ended a year after he lost Stella, allowed him to transfer many feelings to Lady Acheson. Unconsciously, he could work out some of these feelings in the poems his new friend inspired.

But after the summer of 1730 he divided his need for female company among a number of women, and the effect was less satisfactory. Dr Delany, who introduced several of them, was in

[1] *Ibid.*, p. xxxi.　[2] But cf. Ferguson, p. 178.
[3] Boulter II. 38 n. (Dublin, p. 32 n.).
[4] About 12 Jan. 1731; Boulter II. 42 (Dublin, p. 35).
[5] Letter of 20 Apr. 1731, to Pope; Sherburn III. 192.
[6] Letter of 26 Oct. 1731, to Lady Suffolk; Williams III. 501. For a detailed analysis of 'An Answer to the Craftsman', see Ferguson, pp. 176–80. My account is based in part on his.

a superb position to notice the changes in his patron's character; and when he reports these while defending Swift against criticism, I accept the account. The dean's temper, says Delany, was soured in part by 'the indulgence of his passions':

> And all [his] infelicities of temper, were remarkably augmented after the death of Mrs Johnston [*sic*]: whose cordial friendship, sweet temper, and lenient advice, poured balm and healing into his blood; and kept his spirits in some temperament: but as soon as he was deprived of that *medicine of life*, his blood boiled, fretted, and fermented.[1]

Women like Mrs Barber and Mrs Pilkington—or Lady Acheson herself when not at Market Hill—were hardly able to restrain Swift even if they wished to. And as Swift came to prefer companions who accommodated themselves to his whims, he naturally attracted those who could employ him by submitting to him. I don't doubt that Swift was aware of the danger. But too often he succumbed to it.

Meanwhile, Swift's social pleasures depended heavily on men like Delany and women like Laetitia Pilkington. Mrs Barber had gone to England with his blessing, to assemble (between fits of the gout) a body of subscribers for a collection of her poems.[2] While she lengthened her subscription lists in the drawing rooms of London, Tunbridge Wells, and Bath, the dean improved his acquaintance with little Matthew and his 'littler young poetical wife'.[3]

During the summer,[4] the parson's elegantly written *Poems on Several Occasions* had appeared, with 'Parvus carmina fingo' as one of its mottoes.[5] Signs of Swift's literary example and personal influence pervade the book, beginning with a long and effusive sentence in the preface, thanking the dean for his corrections. Among his subscribers Pilkington listed Swift and Delany, Carteret, Mrs Barber, Mrs Grierson, Mrs Sican, Mrs Pendarves (who later married Delany), and William Dunkin. In a well-

[1] P. 124.
[2] In May 1730 Swift says she is going (Williams III. 394). In Sept., Lady Betty Germaine writes of having been approached by her (*ibid.*, p. 408).
[3] *Ibid.*, p. 412.   [4] August, according to Ball IV. 169n.   [5] Published by Faulkner.

turned poem, 'The Gift', he employs the same motif as his patron's 'To Dean Swift': i.e., that England's loss is Ireland's gain, or that Ireland's English-made miseries are compensated by the gift of Swift's glory to his native land.[1] In ten lines of the long 'Phoibo-Bathros: or, the Poet's-Well', he also hurls praises at the 'inimitable *Dean*'.[2]

But the solid pudding of this book remains a conventional set of pastoral and amorous lyrics in the Caroline manner:

> Come hither, Mira, while the sun
> Prepares his radiant course to run,
> Come sit, my fair one, always gay,
> Inspirer of the tender lay.[3]

Reading this when Sawbridge and Charteris were in the dock, and when the philanderous Chetwode was asking whether he should marry again,[4] a man of Swift's temper must have felt a particular disgust.

During Christmas, Swift accepted the Grattans' invitation to Belcamp. While he was staying there, in freezing weather, he asked Delany to come for dinner with the Pilkingtons. Laetitia, though pregnant, looked a diminutive and childlike eighteen; she acted the part of a girl picked up on the road, and the farce was carried out by the dozen-odd clergymen gathered in the Belcamp parlour. Swift read aloud from his *Polite Conversation* and played practical jokes on the lady. They pretended she was a man and put an empty pipe in her mouth. Swift promised to stand godfather to her baby if it was a boy but not if it was a girl.

A day or two later, he came to town, and the Pilkingtons saw him (with other friends) for some frivolity at the deanery. Around New Year's Day they again joined his intimates (Sheridan, Delany, and John Rochfort among them) for a Sunday evening there; and again horseplay was the order of the occasion.[5]

During the same season, a connection was made that became supremely important for Swift's well-being. He renewed his

---

[1] Pp. 105–8; cf. 'To Dean Swift', *Poems* III. 875–6. [2] P. 147. [3] P. 96.
[4] Williams III. 371. [5] Pilkington III. 145–54.

friendship with a much younger cousin whom he had always liked. This was Martha Whiteway, daughter of Swift's uncle Adam. She was an intelligent, good-natured, charitable woman who would gradually become essential to Swift. Around Christmas 1730 he happened to send her a book. She returned it with a message he approved of; and soon after (I think) they began exchanging visits.[1]

Yet this was when Swift gave Pope the doleful report I have already quoted from, about dining with his housekeeper and going to his chamber at five.[2] His drab summary may appear inconsistent with the buffooneries retailed by Mrs Pilkington; but anyone who has acquired a new social circle while corresponding over several years with a distant friend will know how to reconcile the two accounts. Swift's letters to Pope often amount to semi-public utterances of facts and views to interest a cultivated Englishman. To Pope as an intimate and peer, Swift also let himself express dark feelings that he screened from those who were near at hand. Mrs Pilkington, in her *Memoirs*, delivers just what Swift omits.

III. OBSCENITY

Among the 'follies' with which, Swift told Pope, he was now busying himself—around the third anniversary of Stella's death—were probably several of his most scabrous antifeminine satires. What sort of incitement he may have found to write them, I have already hinted. Generally, these pieces seem reactions against the traditional stuff celebrating women as mindless objects of seduction and encouraging their preoccupation with their own adornment. For example, 'The Lady's Dressing-Room', which Mrs Pilkington says made her mother 'instantly' throw up her dinner,[3] probably depends on Joseph Thurston's *The Toilette*, which reached a second edition in

[1] I suppose the death of Edward Whiteway drew his widow closer to Swift. Since an intestacy grant of his goods was made to her in 1732, he must have died soon after Swift's letter of 28 Dec. 1730 (Williams III. 431).

[2] Cf. above, p. 633.

[3] Pilkington III. 161; for Swift's poem (published 1732) see *Poems* II. 524–30.

October 1730.[1] Thurston's imitation of *The Rape of the Lock* deals with problems like the use of cosmetics:

> The useful powder-box be next my song,
> Friend to the old, and fav'rite of the young;
> With this the matron, venerably grey,
> Can hide the silver tokens of decay;
> With this secure can in the front-box sit,
> And court the glances of the ogling pit.
> Though thin her antiquated tresses lie,
> The plaist'ring powder yet deceives the eye.[2]

No connoisseur of Swift would feel startled to hear him hitting back with the filthiest articles in a coquette's boudoir—'all the dirtiest ideas in the world in one piece', said Mrs Pilkington:[3]

> The various combs for various uses,
> Fill'd up with dirt so closely fixt,
> No brush could force a way betwixt.
> A paste of composition rare,
> Sweat, dandriff, powder, lead and hair.[4]

The ancient model for such a poem is the early visit to the mistress which Ovid recommended as a means of curing passion—seeing the lady without her cosmetics or the cosmetics without the lady: *pars minima ipsa puella sui.*[5] As an acute scholar has shown, the visit to the lady's chamber in her absence was almost a topos of serious and satirical verse of the Restoration. Swift may have drawn on Tom D'Urfey's 'Paid for Peeping' and similar works. Against this background Swift's poem joins 'the few survivors of a coarse and once flourishing tradition of scatological anti-feminism'.[6]

As part of literary tradition, the filthy, anti-feminine satires of Swift also depend on the mockery of verse clichés. All of them ridicule that connivance at female vanity which is most bril-

---

[1] Part of Book 1 is reprinted in *The Whitehall Evening Post*, 21 Jul. 1730; the second edition is advertised in newspapers 15 Oct. 1730.
[2] Book 1, p. 10.   [3] Pilkington II. 144.   [4] Ll. 20–4.
[5] *Remedia amoris* 341–56. I am much indebted to Professor James Turner for helping me with this discussion.
[6] Harry M. Solomon, ' "Difficult Beauty": Tom D'Urfey and the Context of Swift's "The Lady's Dressing Room" ', *Studies in English Literature* 19 (Summer 1979), 431–44.

liantly evoked by Pope's masterpiece. This aspect of Swift's work has long been recognized.[1] Yet the lack of balance in his tone remains an issue, for the filthy poems do spring from Swift's peculiar emotional constitution. He had written such poems before.[2] Special circumstances now produced a small crowd of them. I offer some guesses as to the reasons.

Attached as he was to the company of women, Swift also feared any dependence on them. Conversation, the pleasures of asexual games, and witty teasing were safe for him. Women's bodies, the pleasures of lovemaking, the comforts of marriage, scared him. He had lost his mother, his sister, and his nurse at an age when physical contact was the definition of presence. Abandonment by a woman was frightening above all in that form. I think he could not bear to suffer it and therefore never let himself enter into sexual intimacies. One of Stella's main charms was that his original relation with her was pre-sexual and tutorial. It was convenient for him to keep the relation on that basis and ignore the profundity of his deepening passion as the little girl became a mature woman.

If these speculations lead us in the right direction, the desertion of Swift by Stella—through her death—would have reawakened the old sense of physical betrayal that he associated with women; and he would have been inclined not only to resent the survival of other women but to deplore in particular their physical natures. The approach of his own death, the pressures of his own ailments, would have sharpened his bitterness, because he felt how hopeless it was to establish a new union as strong and satisfying as the one Stella destroyed when she died. He must have revived some unconscious hopes when he made friends with Lady Acheson. But the final departure from Market Hill (although he remained in touch with her ladyship) would have added a new knowledge of failure to the old knowledge of loss.

---

[1] Herbert Davis, 'Swift's View of Poetry', in *Jonathan Swift: Essays on His Satire and Other Studies* (New York, 1964), pp. 163–98; especially pp. 178–96. This essay was first published in 1931. Cf. also the forthcoming essay by Hermann J. Real and H. J. Vienken, '"Scatology" in *The Lady's Dressing-Room*'.

[2] Cf. above, pp. 103–7.

It was not like Swift to let emotional energy accumulate without discharge. The use he found for his resentment fitted easily into his literary instincts. The very act of creation is something Swift often connected with filth. Images of the brains as guts, of the imagination as farting, of writing as defecation, of manuscripts as what Catullus called *cacata charta*—all these appear early and late—in *A Tale of a Tub* and in *Gulliver's Travels*. In 'A Digression on Criticism' the work of the critic is compared to the study of faeces.[1] Such attitudes are the underside of Swift's idealization of poets as guardians of morality.

Among literary genres, satire is traditionally associated with filth, and the satirist is described as throwing turds and urine on those whom he ridicules. Pope, like Swift, wallows in such materials, but Swift hardly wanted encouragement from his example.

Satire on women, therefore, brings together Swift's inclinations and literary tradition. The woman covering up her blemishes with cosmetics and expensive clothes is like a poet hiding the defects of a great man under a trite panegyric. Swift defended his much-discussed poem, 'The Lady's Dressing-Room', in an anonymous essay; and here he appealed (misleadingly) to literary tradition and offered the practice of Horace as his precedent.[2] But it is more significant that in the very act of making his defence, Swift referred only briefly to the didactic element in the poem—i.e., the teaching of cleanliness. Most of the essay is a naughty misinterpretation of the *Ars poetica* and becomes a private joke at the expense of unlearned readers.

In other words, the comic shock is not the lure that persuades us to accept the sober lesson. On the contrary, in these poems, the pose of moralist is an excuse for a comic shock. Filth that causes no real injury is funny. To use filth without being punished for it is a comic act. Superficially, it is an assault on the listener, a mark of disrespect. But the anonymous poet escapes unhurt; and the listener finally joins him and laughs on his side.

---

[1] *Tale*, p. 93.

[2] *A Modest Defence of a Late Poem . . . Call'd The Lady's Dressing-Room*; Davis v. 337–40. It was advertised in the *Dublin Journal*: 24 Jun. 1732, 'will be publish'd' 26 Jun.; then 27 Jun., 'will be publish'd' 28 Jun.; then 1 Jul., 'Just publish'd', etc.

It is on this foundation of pseudo-didactic comic shock that Swift builds his parodies of Caroline love songs. In places where we used to meet Waller's Sacharissa and Cowley's Mistress, we find Celia shitting and Chloe pissing. The responsive reader is shamefacedly amused and scandalized. If he wishes, he may cling to the moral doctrine and believe that it is what gives the poem value. If he needs no such pretext, he merely smiles at the surprising coarseness and feels mildly liberated.

Keeping such possibilities in mind, we may perhaps come to terms with the most notorious of Swift's writings. Several critics have treated the poem, 'A Beautiful Young Nymph Going to Bed,'[1] as representing Swift at his most damnable. 'Nothing short of the most violent love or the intensest loathing', says Aldous Huxley, 'could possibly account for so obsessive a preoccupation with the visceral and excrementitious.'[2] George Orwell calls it one of Swift's 'most characteristic works', and cites it as an instance of Swift's seeing nothing in human life 'except dirt, folly, and wickedness'.[3] Middleton Murry says its horror 'is not confined to the nausea evoked by the hideous detail; it proceeds equally from the writer's total lack of charity, his cold brutality, towards the wretched woman who is anatomized. It is utterly inhuman.'[4]

Yet in 'A Beautiful Young Nymph' Swift represents not an individual but a class. He describes a whore come home to rest. But the details are typical and do not identify a particular person. The poet also implies that the woman has chosen her vocation and did not enter upon it reluctantly. The feature of the poem is what I have called the comedy of sexual prosthesis.[5] Here is a specimen passage:

> Returning at the midnight hour;
> Four stories climbing to her bow'r;
> Then, seated on a three-legg'd chair,
> Takes off her artificial hair;
> Now, picking out a crystal eye,

[1] *Poems* II. 580–3. [2] *Do What You Will* (London, 1929), p. 94.
[3] *Shooting an Elephant* (London, 1950), p. 81.
[4] Murry, p. 439. [5] See above, pp. 103–7.

She wipes it clean, and lays it by.
Her eye-brows from a mouse's hide,
Stuck on with art on either side,
Pulls off with care, and first displays 'em
Then in a play-book smoothly lays 'em.
Now dextrously her plumpers draws,
That serve to fill her hollow jaws.
Untwists a wire; and from her gums
A set of teeth completely comes.
Pulls out the rags contriv'd to prop
Her flabby dugs and down they drop.
Proceeding on, the lovely goddess
Unlaces next her steel-ribb'd bodice;
Which by the operator's skill,
Press down the lumps, the hollows fill,
Up goes her hand, and off she slips
The bolsters that supply her hips.[1]

Why should Swift wish to dwell on the *vie intime* of prostitutes? The style of the poem is a heavy contrast between the ugly particulars and words like 'nymph' and 'goddess'. I take the real object of satire to be fashionable ladies, who are less concerned to cultivate intellectual and moral powers than to hide their physical flaws. The verse parodied in the poem is the sort used to praise respectable young women. The point of the comedy of sexual prosthesis is to draw a parallel between them and the whore. A comic shock jolts the reader into an uneasy sense that the language of conventional flattery favours the qualities that encourage vice. In fact, that language serves the same purpose as the false hair and the plumpers.

Swift is not only expressing his fear of physical intimacy. He is also ridiculing literary styles—the conventions of treating women as beings who have no minds but never experience bodily discomfort, the tradition of using pastoral imagery to celebrate pastoral beauty, the *carpe diem* theme. Ordinary lyrics of the century preceding Swift's poems rarely face the problem of women's growing old or sick, and rarely suggest that they need to clean themselves, think, or read.

[1] *Poems* II. 580–3; ll. 7–28.

Swift may possibly allude to the poem by Donne which he echoes elsewhere.[1] The titles of the poems are parallel; so are the processes of undressing. The name Corinna suggests the mistress whom Ovid undresses in *Amores* I. v: '*Quos humeros, quales vidi tetigique lacertos!*' Swift himself drew attention to the echo of *Aeneid* IV. 467–8 in l. 46. All these allusions are comic and satirical, setting the supposed reality of fornication against the fantasies of poets.[2]

But the true source of Swift's poem is probably *The Visions of ... Quevedo ... Burlesqu'd* (London, 1702), in octosyllabic couplets.[3] During one episode of this series of poems, a young man is talking to an old gentlemen when he sees a lady of pleasure pass, and tries to follow her. The old man stops him and says that the woman's charms are all artificial—e.g.,

> The *hair* she wears upon her head
> Of *tire-woman*'s borrowed ...
> Her *eye-brows* and *complexion* are
> By skilful pencil made so fair.
> All that you see of her that's *good*,
> Continually comes from a flood ... [of]
> *Perfumed drawers, Spanish pockets,*
> *Pomanders, powders, scented lockets,*
> All which will scarce yet qualify
> The noisome *poys'nous whiffs* which fly
> From *arm-pits*, toes as black as ink;
> And scores of pole-cats would out-stink....
> The better half of her you'll find
> The taylor's; who, your eyes to blind,
> From seeing her deformity,
> With pads her body doth supply.
> Take notice, when to bed she goes,
> Half of her person with her shoes
> She puts off, and from stinking gum
> An artificial *tooth* doth come,
> Which by her till the morning lyes;

[1] Cf. Donne, 'To His Mistress Going to Bed', l. 25, and Swift, 'Strephon and Chloe', l. 13.

[2] But cf. Schakel, pp. 112–13.

[3] But cf. the argument in favour of Richard Ames, *The Folly of Love*, in Felicity Nussbaum, 'Juvenal, Swift, and *The Folly of Love*', *Eighteenth-Century Studies* 9 (1975–6), 540–52.

Still worser, Sir, one of her *eyes*
She pulls out too, that's made of glass;
Yet this must for a beauty pass![1]

Not only the couplets but the scene, the images, and the attitude are the same as Swift's; and Swift's couplet on teeth closely echoes the parallel lines in Quevedo. In its prose translation, Quevedo's *Visions* went through five editions within ten years of its first publication (1667); by 1715 it was in its eleventh; and it went on through the eighteenth century being happily printed and read.

In such a context the comic shock of Swift's filthy satires on women appears itself to be part of a tradition. This group of his poems was included in one of the 'most frequently printed collections of comic verse' known in the eighteenth century: *The Muse in Good Humour*.[2] The poems worry readers because the intensity of the poet's disgust seems at odds with any comic intention. But while such intensity does suggest powerful ambivalence toward the female body, it also supports the moral doctrine which is the pretext for the whole composition.[3] Besides, the severity of tone might trouble readers less if the filthy satires were not isolated from the poems Swift wrote in praise of women and marriage. If one alternated works like 'Cassinus and Peter' with 'To Biddy Floyd', 'The First of April', 'Psyche', the celebration of Vanessa in 'Cadenus and Vanessa', and the poems to Stella, the filthy satires might seem less outrageous.[4]

IV. LETTERS TO ENGLAND

Corresponding with English friends, Swift scattered his old hints that he might cross over again. Though he never did so, the letters from Bolingbroke, Arbuthnot, Pope, and Gay had effects on him more direct than many immediate experiences. The

---

[1] P. 142. [2] See C. J. Horne, in *MLR* 54 (1959), 595.

[3] It may perhaps be noticed that my views on Swift's obscenity have changed profoundly since my essay on the subject in *The Personality of Jonathan Swift*.

[4] For a learned and comprehensive treatment of the subject, see Hermann J. Real and H. J. Vienken, '"Those odious common Whores of which this Town is full": Swift's *A Beautiful Young Nymph Going to Bed*', *Arbeiten aus Anglistik und Amerikanistik* 6 (1981), 241–59.

members of Swift's English clan constantly visited one another; so their remarks achieved unusual coherence, less like epistolary correspondence than dramatic dialogue. Recent friends sometimes tightened rather than weakened the connection, especially when Swift had favours to ask. Thus he found himself exchanging letters with Mrs Howard (soon to be Countess of Suffolk) and the Duchess of Queensberry, as well as reviving a correspondence with Lady Betty Germaine and Lord Bathurst.

Swift had waited three years for Mrs Howard to prove or disprove his character of her. Gay's outstretched hand remained empty of preferment. The medals promised to Swift in return for his poplin never arrived. Hints that a deanery might be found for him in England seemed stifled. Mrs Howard failed even to send him a letter. While he continued, through others, to send cordial regards to the lady herself, Swift sometimes unburdened himself to Pope:

> As for your courtier Mrs Howard, and her mistress, I have nothing to say, but that they have neither memory nor manners; else I should have some mark of the former from the latter, which I was promised above two years ago: but, since I made them a present, it would be mean to remind them.[1]

What finally led him to reopen his correspondence with Mrs Howard (in the autumn of 1730) seems a rather unsavoury error. The Hon. Anne Vane, one of the maids of honour to Queen Caroline, had not only become the mistress of Frederick, Prince of Wales, but also carried the reputation of receiving both Lord Hervey and Lord Harrington as her lovers. In February 1730 Miss Vane's occupations inspired a hoaxer to place a brutal hint in the news columns of some public prints. This innuendo depended on the distinction between a maid of honour and a woman of the bedchamber. Both were female attendants on the Queen with the same salary and comparable duties. But the former was unmarried and the latter was married. So the newspaper announcement read that Mrs

---

[1] 6 Mar. 1729; Sherburn III. 23.

Howard would be appointed as maid of honour when Miss Vane married Lord Harrington.[1]

Since rumours already ran that Mrs Howard had fallen from favour, Swift took the innuendo to be a slur against her, and a last sign that she was no longer at court. Epistles to fallen courtiers were almost a literary genre for Swift. He apparently took this to be a proper occasion for sending the kind of commentary which he had offered to Oxford, Bolingbroke, and others when they lost power. But neither reassurance nor consolation belonged to his purpose. Rather he wished to vindicate his own prophetic intelligence and to moralize on the grave of the lady's prospects. 'I think', he told Pope, 'to write a moral letter to our half discarded friend.'[2] Pope explained that the jibe was against somebody else; and though he was willing to have Swift write a 'moral' letter to Mrs Howard, he wished to read it first.[3] But toward the end of 1730, after great hesitation, Swift did write to her, without Pope's mediation.

The composition was one of the most extraordinary letters that Swift ever wrote, and one of the least fortunate. He had reserved his chastisement so long that it now clattered around the lady's head with the accumulated rage of three years' brooding. He mistakenly supposed that she had been forced to retire from court. He covertly gave her attributes which properly belonged to Lady Masham, and blamed her for the misdemeanours of Queen Caroline. Yet he made some small progress, even in the midst of this hailstorm, by a few expressions which contradict the tone of the rest. He says that to make him amends, the Queen must now give Swift not a medal but a portrait of herself! and he ends the whole letter by saying,

> I know no person of your sex, for whom I have so great an esteem, as I do and believe I shall always continue to bear for you ... except the Queen, and it is not an exception of form, because I have really a very great veneration for her great qualities.[4]

[1] *St James's Evening Post* and *Whitehall Evening Post*, 3 Feb. 1730. For Miss Vane see Robert Halsband, *Lord Hervey* (Oxford, 1973), pp. 128–30, 182–5, and *passim*.
[2] Sherburn III. 93.   [3] *Ibid.*, p. 101.
[4] Williams III. 423, 425.

The equivocation must have been obvious to her ladyship; yet the wish to sound complimentary would have been itself a kind of compliment. Swift here condemns the Countess and the Queen exclusively in their public status. Thus he reverses the traditional style of flattering the title and despising the person. Yet he would never of course have cultivated Caroline or Mrs Howard if either had been a housewife. He wanted favours for Ireland and for Gay. He wanted vindication for himself.

In 1731 or 1732, when the contemplation of his own mortality produced the *Verses on the Death of Dr Swift*, he summarized, in two footnotes, his final judgment of queen and countess.[1] And this is remarkable for using Lady Suffolk as a passage to the last focus of his resentment, Caroline. The parallel with Queen Anne seems manifest. It was the 'royal prude',[2] after all, who had deflated his ambitions in 1714. It was fundamentally the Queen that Swift was angry with, and not Lady Suffolk. Although the common (and correct) belief was that the Countess had importance as the King's mistress, Swift describes her as the Queen's favourite. Sometimes he even mistakes allusions to the one woman for references to the other.[3]

In his notes the poet treats the two women as ungrateful friends who had betrayed him. Swift once included the Queen in a list of friends whom he labelled 'g.' for grateful, 'u.' for ungrateful, and so on; and he marked her majesty as ungrateful. He could claim to have served Caroline by giving her the poplin and accepting no payment. She had failed to serve him either by sending the medals she had promised or by helping Ireland, or indeed by giving Gay and himself the preferment she had led them to expect. As if to underline Hanoverian treachery, Swift declared, in another (unpersuasive) note, that Queen Anne had 'determined to fix him in England'.[4] If a unifying theme of the poem is true friendship, Swift is associating false friendship with the topmost level of English society when he opens the series

[1] *Poems* II. 559; although the body of the poem may have been written before the end of the year 1731, Swift composed at least one of the notes in May 1732 (*ibid.*, p. 553).
[2] *Ibid.*, p. 192.   [3] Cf. Williams IV. 64, 74.
[4] *Poems* II. 570, Swift's note to l. 431.

of comments on his death with the Queen, the Countess, and the Prime Minister.[1]

So we find that the *Verses* on his death have a connection with 'The Author upon Himself', written seventeen years earlier. The 'services forgot' of 1714 become the poplin of 1727. Queen Anne's distrust becomes Caroline's 'displeasure'. In the bitterness of his comments on Lady Suffolk we may see Swift inverting his testamentary and invidious praise of 'her late most excellent majesty Queen Anne, of ever glorious, immortal, and truly pious memory, the real nursing-mother of all her kingdoms'.[2] The word 'mother' even hints at the origin of Swift's dissatisfaction with both queens.

Even so, if his friends had not unanimously esteemed Lady Suffolk, Swift might not have marked her out so pointedly for his condemnation. Because all their evidence contradicted his unfortunate instincts, I think, he felt he had to prove his case. As Lady Betty Germaine wrote, 'You must have offended [her], because you do not forgive.'[3]

Just as Swift had interested reasons for his friendship with Lady Suffolk, so his correspondence with the Duchess of Queensberry sprang from more than temperamental sympathy. It opened with a note from her grace in an invitation from Gay to Swift, offering him the comforts of the Queensberrys' seat at Amesbury.[4] Swift must have been touched by her conscious or unconscious readiness to make the first advances. But the real foundation of the epistolary friendship was his desire to help Gay. So it is an irony that the one reproach the poet's friends could have brought against the Queensberrys was that they raised Gay's domestic comforts to a level that weakened his literary ambition.

Swift, having nothing to ask from the Duchess but that she would support the poet whom she already admired, felt free to indulge in high-spirited *lettres galantes*. Her grace wrote with energy and without affectation. She praised and loved his friend.

[1] Here I am following James Woolley, 'Friends and Enemies in *Verses on the Death of Dr Swift*'. Cf. below, p. 713, n. 1.
[2] Davis XIII. 154. [3] Williams IV. 85. [4] *Ibid.*, III. 416.

Swift plunged into the exchange of letters and quickly made his usual plans with his usual witty presumption:

> Pray, Madam, have you a clear voice, and will you let me sit at your left hand, at least within three [?feet] of you; for of two bad ears, my right is the best. My groom tells me that he likes your park, but your house is too little. Can the parson of the parish play at backgammon and hold his tongue? Is any one of your women a good nurse, if I should fancy myself sick for four and twenty hours? How many days will you maintain me and my equipage?[1]

But though he had almost never seen the Duchess since she was a child,[2] they did not meet again. Apart from good-humoured small talk, their letters were taken up either with Gay's affairs or with the possibility of Swift's visiting England. After Gay died, the correspondence continued, with long gaps, for about two years. But the Duchess seems to have tired of exchanging clever messages with someone she could not see; and the relationship ended.

Swift began writing to Lady Betty Germaine from only one incentive; and although the renewal of their ancient friendship gave him various satisfactions, he stopped writing when the ulterior motive lapsed. Sir John Germaine, her late husband, had received a great fortune from her predecessor, his first wife; and on leaving it to Lady Betty, he had asked her to bequeath it eventually to the grandson of a dear friend of Sir John's, whose daughter had married the Duke of Dorset. There were other ties between Lady Betty and the Duke; and this lively expectation of a favour to be received did not weaken them.

In April 1730 the Duke succeeded Carteret as Lord Lieutenant of Ireland. Swift felt embarrassed because Lady Allen, wife of Swift's 'Traulus', had much influence with Dorset. Having denigrated the husband, Swift looked for an unpleasant intervention by the wife. 'Now this lady hath been an old favorite of the D. of D.', he told Pope, 'and consequently will use all means to put me on a worse foot than my station requires me to be with a chief governor.'[3]

---

[1] 13 Mar. 1731; Sherburn III. 181.   [2] *Ibid.*, p. 299.   [3] *Ibid.*, p. 108.

He then said he would not ask Lady Betty to mend the awkwardness. But soon he decided otherwise; and in the summer of 1730 he tried her with an appeal for Mrs Barber. Swift promised that if Lady Betty would offer to plead with Dorset, Lord Carteret would explain the petition of the poetess. In agreeing,[1] Lady Betty deepened Swift's desire to carry the correspondence further; and the following spring he sent her hints about Dorset's chaplains.[2] Soon he asked her to recommend that the Duke order his liveries from Mrs Barber's husband.[3]

But then the Irish Parliament rose, the Duke returned to England, and Swift took up other matters with Lady Betty: her sister's epitaph, Mrs Howard, the health of their friends, and his hopes of visiting England. He never seems to have told her, as he did Pope, how strongly he resented the Duke's anti-Irish policies.[4]

It was easy for Swift to pour many of the motifs which he discussed with his English friends into a new poem. Misunderstanding some expressions of Pope's, he supposed that the Duke of Queensberry had made Gay his steward. So he wrote, early in 1731, 'To Mr Gay', a long composition in heroic couplets.[5] Either the form was unsympathetic, or the problem failed to stir Swift's ingenuity; for the poem abounds in weaknesses. There are passages of unconvincing rhetoric, such as some lines hollowly asseverating the indifference of poets to lucre ('Sons of Phoebus never break their trust'). The scheme of the poem is a set of Swift's formulae nakedly applied: a large allegorical image; a systematic and sarcastic contrast between honest Gay the poet and corrupt Walpole the politician; a number of sceptical maxims, insufficiently polished, supposed to express the reverse of Walpole's principles; and a long parallel between a minister of state and a thieving steward.

In July 1731 a new stroke of English politics gave Swift an occasion for reworking these themes. Pulteney, Bolingbroke's ally, had engaged in a pamphlet duel with Walpole, the out-

---

[1] Williams III. 408.　　[2] *Ibid.*, p. 470.　　[3] *Ibid.*, p. 497.
[4] *Ibid.*, p. 435.　　[5] *Poems* II. 530–6.

come of which was that the Prime Minister had Pulteney's name struck off the list of Privy Councillors and justices of the peace. Swift thereupon produced another poem in heroic couplets, 'On Mr P——y Being Put Out of the Council'.[1]

Though brief, this poem contains a clever variation upon Gay's well-known fable number fifty, 'The Hare and Many Friends'. In Gay's poem, as was well known, the hare stood for the author himself. Hunted by hounds, she asks all her 'many friends' to save her; but they all politely refuse, and she is abandoned to the pack. Similarly, Gay, with his talent universally admired and his character beloved, had failed to get a single substantial preferment which might save him from financial anxiety.

In Swift's poem there is a quick opening which mentions the expulsion of Pulteney, and then a suggestion that Walpole may plan to shield himself from Pulteney's eloquence by accepting a dukedom and moving to the upper house. Next, Swift retells the 'old' fable of the hare. But this time the creature tries to escape into the elements—sea, earth, and air. 'Dogs' pursue her everywhere: dogfish in the sea, Cerberus in Hades, and the dog star Sirius in the skies. If the hare, 'though free from guilt', was thus pursued—Swift moralizes—what can Walpole expect? The criminal who persecuted innocent Gay will suffer far more deadly persecutions when his own fall occurs. The emphasis on 'dogs' is explained in Swift's verse character of the prime minister,[2] where Walpole is called 'the cur dog of Britain and spaniel of Spain'.

Part of Swift's attitude in these near-jeremiads was necessarily that abiding sense of moral superiority which every serious satirist must exhibit toward his victims. But he saw this threatened by a grotesque event of the summer. In June 1731, Queen Caroline received an outrageous letter recommending Mrs Barber and signed 'Jonath. Swift',[3] as well as another 'in abuse of' the Queen's favourite, Mrs Clayton.

The writer of the signed letter expresses, though in pedestrian

---

[1] *Ibid.*, pp. 537-9.   [2] *Ibid.*, pp. 539-40.   [3] Williams v. 259-60.

language, sentiments which Swift used to deliver in private conversation or in letters to friends. Caroline herself had heard these sentiments from him when they met; and the letter to Lady Suffolk, the preceding November, has so many parallels with this forgery that it could have been the model for it. Whom the forger wished to embarrass or to help is a mystery. It is hard to believe that anyone who hoped simply to aid Mrs Barber or to trouble Swift would have concocted so transparent a bluff.

Lady Suffolk obtained from the Queen the letter signed with Swift's name, and gave it to Pope, who in July sent it to his friend. Swift prepared a very careful reply to Pope, minimizing his acquaintance with Mrs Barber and indicating that the forgeries, if taken seriously, represented 'a folly so transcendent, that no man could be guilty of, who was not fit for Bedlam'.[1] Mingled with some sound reasoning, in this letter, one finds wilful involvements of the royal circle, perhaps on the principle that putting them in the wrong was the best means of justifying himself. So he accused the King of blaming Swift for the scandal of the Duke of Schomberg's memorial in St Patrick's Cathedral—'that I had put up the stone out of malice to raise a quarrel between His M. and the K. of Prussia'.[2] For such a design it was inevitable that Swift should imagine himself to be in their majesties' thoughts more often than was likely. Similarly, he wove in his alleged mistreatment by Lady Suffolk (to whom he said he would 'write next post') and the old, frayed thread of Walpole's cruelty to Gay. Of course, Swift was writing the letter for other eyes than Pope's.

A week later, he composed a still more elaborate brief to send the Countess—his first letter to her in eighteen months. Adding no fresh arguments, he briefly rehearses those submitted to Pope, while he expands the allusions to the King, the Queen, and Walpole. The last quarter he practically addresses to Caroline; and he all but instructs Lady Suffolk to have her majesty read his complaints: 'I am contented that the Queen should see this letter.'[3] I find his tone irritating because, though

---

[1] *Ibid.*, p. 479.   [2] Sherburn III. 208.   [3] Williams III. 483.

he pretends indifference to the Queen, he sounds actively resentful of her indifference to him; and at the same time he speaks to her through Lady Suffolk. This exemplifies Swift's ancient manœuvre of getting at one person by addressing another. Nevertheless, he has an excellent excuse, since he consciously desires to excite concern for Ireland's agony.

The Countess, after almost two months, replied with a *jeu d'esprit* which Swift in good humour would have found irresistible. She touches so lightly on the issue itself, and uses such cordial cheerfulness that one can only applaud her wit. Her gist is that she had maliciously hoped to find, in this crisis, an occasion for proving her honest friendship; but 'to my mortification I find everybody inclined to think you had no hand in writing those letters.'[1]

Swift seems determined to make himself out an injured party. He takes her raillery *au grand sérieux* and sends her his tried mixture of browbeating and premeditated flattery: 'I never knew a lady who had so many qualities to beget esteem, but how you act as a friend, is out of my way to judge.'[2] The terms of the long message plainly convey Swift's sense that he is closing their correspondence. He renews his earlier themes, appeals to the Queen on behalf of Ireland, and withdraws.

My own uneasiness arises from his incapacity to judge the situation or the people. One might, after all, apply to Lady Suffolk what Hervey said of the Queen's real favourite, Mrs Clayton (later Lady Sundon):

> If her situation enabled her to do all the good her heart inclines her to, there are many people of merit who would not want any ingredient towards happiness that courts can give. But she, like many other people, seems perhaps to want a will, when in reality she only wants power.[3]

Furthermore, at this time, as Hervey also said, 'Le Roi s'ennuit avec my Lady Suffolk.'[4] Disregarding the universal gossip and the direct information of his friends, Swift insisted on attributing

---

[1] *Ibid.*, p. 498.   [2] *Ibid.*, p. 501.   [3] Ilchester, p. 165.
[4] *Ibid.*, p. 112: 'The King is bored with my Lady Suffolk.'

to the Countess that hypocrisy which he had encountered elsewhere in the early period of his own naïveté (1699–1708). He
also failed to understand how improbable it was that he should,
by means so tortuously indirect, move anybody—least of all the
Queen—to assist Ireland. Some of his angry frustration must
have been due to the effectual indifference with which English
readers treated his attacks on the government in power. Having
no power himself but what came from his pen, he could yet, by
writing, neither injure his enemies nor protect his friends in
England.

Chapter Two

CHAMPION OF THE CHURCH

I. 'POLITE CONVERSATION'

Following the practice of choosing the 'middling kind' for society, Swift passed his brief summer holiday with a genial prebendary of the cathedral, the Rev. John Towers, who had recently obtained, from the dean and chapter, the attractive living of St Luke's, Dublin. Towers's country rectory, St Patrick's, Powerscourt, co. Wicklow, lay in a picturesque, hilly setting about eight miles from the capital.[1] Swift went there in August 1731 and returned in September to his deanery. He took with him two important manuscripts, later published as *Polite Conversation* and *Directions to Servants*. 'I retired hither for the public good,' he told Gay,

> having two great works in hand, one to reduce the whole politeness, wit, humour and style of England into a short system for the use of all persons of quality, and particularly the maids of honour: The other is of almost equal importance; I may call it the whole duty of servants, in about twenty several stations, from the steward and waiting woman down to the scullion and pantry boy.[2]

The following June, Swift told Pope that he had begun both these works 'above twenty-eight years ago'[3] or around 1704. Other signs are not wanting that the projects were conceived during the earlier half of Queen Anne's reign;[4] but Swift's exact datings are seldom reliable.

In 1731 and 1732 he apparently went over his materials and

---

[1] On 28 Aug. 1731 Swift writes from Powerscourt (Williams III. 492). But we do not know when he arrived or when he left. In a letter dated 'Tuesday Morning, August 1731', he says he is 'just going out of town for a few weeks' (*ibid.*). A letter of 6 Sept. seems to be from Dublin (*ibid.*, p. 495).
[2] Sherburn III. 219.   [3] *Ibid.*, p. 293.   [4] Mayhew, pp. 131–55.

made some rearrangements.[1] Both the *Directions* and the *Polite Conversation* depend largely upon the gathering of observations and expressions over many years, and then the elaborate editing of them. Mrs Pilkington tells us not only that Swift was indeed revising his materials about this time but also that she supplied him with a decisive bit of advice; for she records the following dialogue at Belcamp, Christmas 1730:

> 'Pox on you, you slut', said the Dean, 'you gave me a hint for my *Polite Conversation*, which I have pursued: You said, it would be better to throw it into dialogue; and suppose it to pass amongst the great; I have improved by you.'
> 'O dear sir', said I, ''tis impossible you should do otherwise.'
> 'Matchless sauciness!' returned he: 'Well, but I'll read you the work'; which he did with infinite humour, to our high entertainment.[2]

Mrs Pilkington may be boasting, and the original words may have differed from her account. But in discussing other persons than herself and her family, she usually tells the truth; and her verbal memory is astonishingly good. Yet while Swift apparently made fundamental changes—during the years 1730–2—in the form of the *Polite Conversation* and the *Directions to Servants*, he failed to bring them to completion.

Meanwhile, he remained delighted with the Pilkingtons. Mrs Pendarves (later Mrs Delany), then visiting Dublin, calls Laetitia 'a bosom friend of Dean Swift's'.[3] While the dean stayed at Powerscourt, Mrs Pilkington gave birth to a son; and since Swift had promised (the Christmas before, at Belcamp) to stand godfather if she had a boy, Laetitia wrote to him at once. He only returned home two weeks later, and by that time the infant had died. Swift 'came directly' to visit her and showed relief at the news. 'He drank a little caudle with me,' writes Mrs Pilkington,

---

[1] Herbert Davis, 'The Manuscript of Swift's "Directions to Servants"', *Studies in Art and Literature for Belle da Costa Greene* (Princeton, 1954), pp. 433–4, 442–3; Mayhew, p. 157.

[2] Pilkington III. 146; my own paragraphing, quotations marks, and use of capitals. For the date, see Ball IV. 194, n. 2; 261, n. 1.

[3] Mrs Delany I. 301 (9 Oct. 1731).

and then went away; about an hour after his servant brought me a letter, and a great bundle of brown paper, sealed with the utmost care, and twisted round with I know not how many yards of packthread.

In the letter, Swift said he was giving her a piece of plum cake intended for the deceased child's christening. But when she opened the package, she found a piece of gingerbread 'in which were stuck four guineas, wrapt in white paper, on the outside of each was wrote "Plumb"'.[1]

II. 'VERSES ON THE DEATH OF DR SWIFT'

As Swift approached his sixty-fourth birthday, he fused, in a last consummation, the motifs of friendship, death, and lack of recognition, which had risen constantly in his poems and letters. He accomplished his design twice, in one poem with an English ambiance and another with an Irish.[2] The earlier and more outspoken has always been one of his great successes: *Verses on the Death of Dr Swift*. In formal structure it has less regularity than the later and far more cautious *Life and Genuine Character of Dr Swift*. My hypothesis is that Swift wrote the *Verses* to be published after he died. He therefore used facts and remarks which even he would not have included in a work to come out at once. But he liked the result so well that he read and showed it to friends and visitors. The satisfaction of this casual audience spread the demand for it; and as there was no question of publishing the dangerous language of the *Verses*, Swift decided to perpetrate a hoax that would take advantage of the reputation earned by his manuscript. Since he told Gay in December 1731 that he was finishing the *Verses*,[3] and since he added notes

---

[1] Pilkington III. 149–50, 165–7; Ball IV. 261–2 and n. 1. 'Plumb' may be a pun, since the word also meant the sum of £100,000.

[2] I call the *Verses* English because Swift names his English friends; and in the section following his death he makes the scene explicitly England, and remains there (ll. 177ff) at the Rose in London. He also refers to Ireland as 'that helpless land' (l. 412), 'there' (l. 435), and 'That Kingdom' (l. 483). I call the *Life* Irish because in it there are no explicit references to mark the scene as England, and because the speaker calls Ireland 'our *Nation*' (l. 96).

[3] Sherburn III. 251.

in the winter and spring, 1731–2, he would—by my account—
have composed the *Life* between that date and April 1733, when
it appeared in print. A puzzling announcement appeared in the
Dublin Journal, 2 May 1732:

> We now hear, that the true copy of a certain poem, much talked of,
> occasioned by reading a maxim of Rochefoucault's, hath by some
> accident or contrivance got into several hands; and we have reason
> to believe will be published in a few days, to the great delight and
> entertainment of the world, and probably equally to the vexation of
> the author, who, in this poem, largely describes what he imagines
> the world will say of him after his death. If the copy shall fall into our
> hands, we shall be very glad to oblige the publick with it.

Only Swift could have been responsible for this report. It may
have been a preparation for the hoax, or it may indicate that
Swift at first thought of publishing the *Verses* or the *Life* that
month but then changed his mind. But if one allows a space for
Swift to complete a copy of the *Life*, transmit it to London, and
arrange (through Matthew Pilkington) for the printing, one
must conclude that he wrote the poem in 1732. And if this was
indeed the order of composition, it explains the difference in
effect of the two poems—the fact that the *Life* is less incisive but
more coherent than the *Verses* and not half its length.

Another clear difference between the poems is the omission, in
the *Life*, of the most inflammatory ingredients of the *Verses*: the
direct praise of Bolingbroke, Oxford, Ormonde, and Pulteney;
the court scenes; the direct attack on Walpole and his administration. All these rash expressions are exaggerated in the notes
which Swift supplied for the *Verses* but not for the *Life*. One may
infer that he expected to publish the *Life* soon.

A more interesting feature is the long conclusions of both
poems, which are speeches by third persons characterizing
Swift. The *Life* is less disappointing here because it has a dialogue between an admirer and a critic, while the *Verses* give us a
biographical monologue—a character of the dean—by 'one
quite indiff'rent'. In the *Life*, therefore, Swift can employ
dramatic irony to defend his career; for the critic speaks with
such partisan malice that his insults become praise, while the

temperate admirer, here, makes eulogies sound like truisms.

Of the two poems the more important but more puzzling is certainly the *Verses*.[1] This poem has two distinct parts. The first and notably superior section (ll. 1–298) introduces the themes of friendship and envy, starting from La Rochefoucauld's maxim that in the worst distresses of our best friends we find something that does not displease us (ll. 1–70). It then moves on to an imaginary account of Swift's last days and his death as seen by other persons (ll. 71–146). The point made is that they are more excited than saddened by the dean's decline. Next, we reach the highest level of the entire poem with a set of dramatic scenes in which friends and acquaintances respond to the news (ll. 147–242). Finally, this section deals with Swift's posthumous reputation as an author, again through the speech of another person (ll. 243–98).

All of the first section is ironic, sardonic, or sarcastic, with the mock-scepticism conveyed by the kind of impersonations which Swift particularly enjoyed. He suggests, only half-seriously, that friendship seldom triumphs over self-love and envy. He describes his acquaintances as accommodating themselves easily to the prospect of his death—even looking forward to it. He has courtiers rejoicing when he dies, and close friends recovering quickly from their sadness. At last, Lintot, the bookseller, depreciates his writings and recommends the work of Whig hacks over that of Swift. Throughout these dramatic scenes the style is sharp, witty, ingeniously rhymed, abounding in clever turns of phrase.

For the remainder of the poem an 'impartial' member of a club in a London tavern sums up Swift's character and career. The tone here is no longer ironical. The speech is transparently an apology for Dean Swift. Many of the remarks sound absurdly hyperbolic and self-flattering. But a meticulous scholar has shown that they conform to Swift's normal representations of himself and cannot be regarded as deliberately misleading.[2]

---

[1] *Poems* II. 551–72; first published in 1739.

[2] James Woolley, 'Autobiography in Swift's Verses on His Death', in J. I. Fischer *et al.*, eds, *Contemporary Studies in Swift's Poetry* (Newark, 1981), pp. 112–22.

This part of the poem is one more instance of Swift's effort to gain the recognition he thought he deserved,[1] a desire quickened by the thought of death and probably by the fear that his friends would defend him less heartily than his enemies would attack.

In the parallel section, which occupies two-thirds of the *Life*, Swift again gives himself large compliments which would sound better from other mouths (*Life*, ll. 70–202). Yet in neither poem is the apology merely an expansion of the gold-box inscription. The *Life* in particular has anticipations of the main faults charged against Swift since his death: that he wrote satire because he was a misanthrope; that spite alone lay behind his fault-finding; that he would have truckled to the men in power if he had received better preferments; that he possessed no religion. To these allegations the *Verses* add that he was charitable to strangers while neglecting his own family.

The monologue which fills the last hundred and eighty lines of the *Verses* will nevertheless overload any reader, however sympathetic. Here the dialogue form of the *Life* has simply more interest and vitality, partly because the speaker changes back and forth and partly because there is something like a balance of blame (usually absurd) and praise. Still, however unpersuasive Swift's self-analysis may seem as a portrait of the living person, it has some justification as rhetoric. Swift does here what Pope was to do in *An Epistle to Dr Arbuthnot*.[2] He lights up the sins of bad poets and politicians by setting them off against the merits of a man of good will. The idealized autobiography amounts to an outline of Swift's moral ideals. It is the instrument through which his enemies are judged within the poem, and has that much validity in its literary effect. Furthermore, like Pope's *Horace Sat. II. i* (to Fortescue)—not to mention Swift's imitation of the same satire—the method had precedents in Roman satire, from which it took additional authority.

In the *Verses*, of course, the finest irony appears not toward the

[1] Schakel places the poem in the tradition of Swift's prose and verse apologies; see pp. 122–30.
[2] Elder Olson, 'Rhetoric and the Appreciation of Pope', *Modern Philology* 27 (1939–40), 21–30.

end but near the start. The theme of both that poem and the *Life* comes from the same maxim of La Rochefoucauld. To vary the motif, one may dwell on either friendship or envy. Swift emphasizes friendship in the *Life* but envy in the *Verses*. The most ingenious ironies of the latter poem belong to those lines in which Swift tells how he envies his friends for achievements finer than his own. The effect of each example is to praise, by innuendo, persons of whom Swift seems to be complaining. But it is also to elevate Swift for being willing to allow them their advantage. The humour and wit imply the force of the poet's generosity:

> St John, as well as Pulteney knows,
> That I had some repute for prose . . .
> If they have mortified my pride,
> And made me throw my pen aside;
> If with such talents Heav'n hath blest 'em
> Have I not reason to detest 'em?[1]

Cicero, in his dialogue on friendship, noticed the difficulty of yielding any distinction to a friend; and he spoke of how hard it is to share a friend's misfortunes. The ideal of friendship suggested in Swift's poem joins elements already defined and united in *De amicitia*: civic virtue, humanistic culture, and manly affection. Virtue draws men together. True friendship is only possible between good men. When a friend behaves himself unpatriotically, he should be abandoned. True friendship survives changes of fortune and death itself.

If the theme is traced through the poem, we see Swift, like Pope (in the *Epistle to Dr Arbuthnot* and elsewhere) linking himself with men of civic virtue and literary culture. The disloyal friends—Lady Suffolk and the Queen—speak ill of Swift although they encouraged his friendship and used his services before they rose to be foremost in a royal court. Swift groups them with corruptors of their nation, like Walpole and Charteris, and with corruptors of taste or enemies of religion, like Curll and Woolston. They are opposed to patriots like Pulteney, or men of taste and talent like Pope. Yet the bitter fact

---

[1] Ll. 59–60, 63–6.

remains that no friend will celebrate Swift's character after he dies.

While such patterns of implication may indeed be discerned in the poem, they fail to give it life or coherence. The features that do so appear elsewhere, and it would be imprudent to force the design of the work into a moral argument.

The superiority of the *Verses* to the *Life* demonstrates again that for Swift the total structure of a poem (be it defined in the terms of Aristotle or of Coleridge) does less to establish its merits than the separate achievements within it. For all the coherence of the *Life*, no part of it comes up to the Pope–Gay–Arbuthnot lines, or the quadrille conversation, in the *Verses*. The separate couplets and paragraphs of the *Verses* have more polish, energy, and edge than the constituents of the *Life*, which remains the inferior poem.[1]

III. CHURCH AND STATE

Swift's bagatelles were broken into by the sitting of Parliament. The new Lord Lieutenant was no Carteret, however; and even if Lady Allen had liked Swift, the dean could not have looked for much good work from the Duke of Dorset. When his grace left London in August, Lord Hervey wrote,

> The Duke of Dorset has just taken his leave to go and king it in Ireland. I am sure he will be happier in that Drury-Lane employment than any other man upon earth; and is at this moment ranging his maces, his two battalions of guards, and his twelve chaplains, for the first church-day. He will not dislike haranguing his Parliament, especially if Carey [Dorset's secretary] makes a good speech, and Dean Swift does not put it into doggerel verse; but those are two very doubtful suppositions.[2]

---

[1] A careful study of Swift's notes to the *Verses* would be a valuable work. For the biographical implications of the poem and its relation to Swift's friendship with Lady Suffolk, see above, pp. 698–9. For an illuminating interpretation of the poem as unified by the theme of friendship, see James Woolley, 'Friends and Enemies in *Verses on the Death of Dr Swift*'; I have drawn extensively on this essay in my treatment of both Lady Suffolk and the poem. As Professor Woolley suggests, the theme of friendship in the work of Swift and Pope deserves more attention than it has received.

[2] Ilchester, p. 76; letter of 14 Aug. 1731 from Hervey to Stephen Fox. Carey will compose, not deliver, the speech.

On this occasion, malice and prophecy were in harmony, for the event justified Hervey's doubts. His grace and the Duchess arrived in Dublin on 11 September 1731 and soon showed themselves to be conspicuously less hospitable than the Carterets. Dorset took it for granted that preferments should be reserved for camp followers and the English interest. But Swift was no longer prepared to fight. When he met the Duke, he promised that he would not write any 'state-scribble'. As Swift put it,

> I lately assured the [Duke] of Dorset, that I would never have a hand in any such thing: and I gave him my reason before his secretary; that, looking upon this kingdom's condition as absolutely desperate, I would not prescribe a dose to the dead.[1]

How well Swift kept this promise is doubtful. Certainly, he did not give up church-scribbles.

As it happened, the decade that began in 1730 saw a strong improvement in the Irish economy. 'The 1730s', says a historian, 'marked the beginning of a long period of rapid growth in Irish foreign trade.'[2] But the fact was not evident to most contemporaries, and certainly not to Swift. On the contrary having surrendered any hope of improving Irish agriculture or trade, Swift was narrowing his public thoughts almost exclusively to the condition of the Church of Ireland.

Parliament met on 5 October 1731, but Swift did not address himself to the proceedings of either House until late the following January,[3] when he took characteristic notice of two bills which the bench of bishops were promoting in the House of Lords. One of these proposals was a Bill of Residence, the other a Bill of Division. The first, in its most outrageous clause, gave bishops the power of forcing those of their clergymen who held livings worth more than a hundred pounds a year, to build a house on a part of the glebe chosen by the bishop. The other bill provided that a parish worth more than a hundred pounds a year might be divided into two or more parishes, even without

---

[1] Williams III. 500–1.
[2] Cullen, p. 53.
[3] Landa, p. 113.

the consent of the incumbent, so long as the original living did not sink below that figure.

These schemes excited Swift's fury because they would give enormous coercive rights to the bishops. He said that

> every bishop, who gave his vote for either of these bills, did it with no other view (bating further promotion) than a premeditated design, from the spirit of ambition and love of power, to make the whole body of the clergy their slaves and vassals until the day of judgment, under the load of poverty and contempt.[1]

Heads to the Bill of Residence were introduced on 2 December by Bishop Tenison, a recent importation from England. A week later, Archbishop Hoadly reported on amendments, and the next day the third reading followed. Members of the lower clergy came in numbers to hear the debates; and after the third reading, they petitioned the Lord Lieutenant and Privy Council of Ireland to be heard against the bill, but they were denied.[2]

Now some of them went to the Dean of St Patrick's for advice and help. Near the end of January,[3] Swift began writing against the Bill of Residence, taking a large, historical view. 'I know no more of the particulars', he said, 'than what hath been told me by several clergymen.'[4] This first essay, 'On the Bill for the Clergy's Residing on Their Livings',[5] quickly divagated into a polemical contrast between the English and Irish churches; and it was never completed.

Meanwhile, the two bills were making their steady way through the Privy Council of England and back through the House of Lords of Ireland. On 17 February the completed Bill of Division was to be read for the first time; and on that day, spokesmen for the lower clergy begged the Lords to hear their counsel against the bill. In the petition they declared that 'they would be greatly prejudiced' if the bill should pass. Their argu-

---

[1] Williams IV. 183.   [2] Landa, pp. 112–13; Davis XII. 186.

[3] He mentions the anniversary of King Charles I's death, 30 January, as 'soon approaching' (Davis XII. 184).

[4] *Ibid.*, p. 186; Landa, p. 113. Davis shows the manuscript ends after 28 Dec. 1731; see XII. 341.

[5] Davis XII. 179–86; first published 1789.

ments were heard, but on 21 February the bill passed its third reading and was sent on to the Commons. Three days later, the Bill of Division was also passed, without opposition.

This date, 24 February, appears on the manuscript of Swift's second pamphlet and is probably when he began to write it.[1] But although he finished by 26 February,[2] it could not be printed in advance of the debate and vote in the Commons. So Swift had Faulkner insert a sketch of the arguments, expressed as five 'queries', into the *Dublin Journal* for 26 February.[3] On that very day, counsel for the clergy was heard at the bar of the House of Commons, and both bills were thrown out.

But at the same time in the Lords a complaint was made against Faulkner for publishing Swift's queries; and the printer was ordered to attend the House on the following Monday. He never appeared, and an order followed for his arrest. But Parliament rose soon after. Faulkner was not taken into custody till the House met again, in the autumn of 1733. After a fortnight, he petitioned to be released, was reprimanded, and discharged.[4] According to the account he published many years later, Faulkner 'suffered severely in his private property, as well as in his health', because in addition to the confinement, he had to pay 'fees, which amounted to a very large sum'.[5]

I suppose this episode was the reason that Swift arranged for the full text of his finished pamphlet, *Considerations upon Two Bills . . . Relating to the Clergy of Ireland*[6] to be published in England. On 25 March 1732 the *Dublin Journal* reported, under a London dateline, that the clergy of England 'and all the young gentlemen in our universities, are wonderfully pleased with a pamphlet lately transmitted from Dublin (which we are informed was prohibited being printed there).'[7] It was of course Swift's *Considerations upon Two Bills*.

The earlier, fragment of an essay, on the Bill of Residence,

---

[1] *Ibid.*, p. xxxvi. Swift opens by saying that the Lords had passed both bills, an event of 24 February.

[2] He says the Commons have not yet voted (*ibid.*, p. 202).

[3] *Ibid.*, pp. xxxvii–xxxviii.

[4] *Ibid.*, p. xxxviii. [5] *Ibid.*, XIII. 204–5. [6] *Ibid.*, XII. 189–202.

[7] Landa, p. 115, n. 2. The pamphlet was advertised in London newspapers 25 Mar. 1732.

begins well; for it delivers an exquisite attack on bishops sent over from England:

> Some of [these] are such as are said to have enjoyed tolerable preferments in England; and it is therefore much to their commendation, that they have condescended to leave their native country, and come over hither to be bishops, merely to promote Christianity among us; and therefore in my opinion, both their lordships, and the many dependers they bring over, may justly claim the merit of missionaries sent to convert a nation from heresy and heathenism.[1]

Swift then goes on to the historical contrast between English and Irish clergy. This part of the fragment, rewritten, became part of the second essay.

If that final pamphlet, *Considerations upon Two Bills*, had not been addressed to a crisis of brief and local concern, it would rank, among Swift's works, little below *The Drapier's Letters*. Swift mingles delicate touches with the violent outbursts, and not always in the expected proportions. Fulminating against the bishops, he can show exquisite restraint:

> the *clergy* of this kingdom, who are promoted to *bishoprics*, have always some great advantages; either that of rich *deaneries*, opulent and multiplied *rectories* and *dignities*, strong alliances by birth or marriage, fortified by a superlative degree of zeal and loyalty.[2]

He can also explode with the energy of an inspired prophet:

> if there be a single spot in the glebe more barren, more marshy, more exposed to winds, more distant from the church, or skeleton of a church, or from any conveniency of building: the rector, or vicar may be obliged by the caprice, or pique of the bishop, to build [there], upon pain of sequestration.[3]

There is a grim vignette on the resources of paupered vicars:

> They may get a dispensation to hold the *clerkship* and *sextonship* of their own parish *in commendam*. Their wives and daughters may make shirts for the neighbourhood; or, if a *barrack* be near, for the *soldiers*: in linen countries, they may *card* and *spin*, and keep a few looms in the house: They may let lodgings, and sell a pot of ale without doors, but not at home, unless to sober company, and at regular hours.[4]

---

[1] Davis XII. 181.   [2] *Ibid.*, p. 192.   [3] *Ibid.*, p. 194.
[4] *Ibid.*, p. 199.

One of the best straightforward passages is a sketch of the typical English vicar, and his comfort, in contrast to the condition of his brother in Ireland.[1] Another, vitriolic, portrays a typical Irish bishop, drawn from the model of Josiah Hort:

> I could name certain gentlemen of the *gown*, whose awkward, spruce, prim, sneering, and smirking countenances, the very tone of their voice, and an ungainly strut in their walk, without one single talent for any one office, have contrived to get good preferment by the mere force of *flattery* and *cringing*.[2]

There are many brilliant phrases and sentences in Swift's most proficient manner; and the rhetoric itself is of a piece. Rather than give a fair account of the bills, Swift takes their most ferocious implications and elaborates these. Following his old habit, he puts the enemy as much in the wrong as possible. Non-residence was in fact a disgraceful feature of the Irish church and had long been recognized as such. However misguided the bishops' method may have been, they were trying to remedy a shocking situation, and were only building on a law passed early in the reign of George I.[3] But Swift boldly denies that the problem is pressing: 'I do not, by any means, conceive the crying sin of the *clergy* in this kingdom, to be that of *non-residence*.'[4]

An important part of his strategy is the lack of a mask. Swift had passed beyond the status in which caution dictated a pseudonym. He could now assume no disguise that would give his reasoning more authority than his true title. The use of a persona, in other words, does not belong to the foundation of his rhetoric here. Instead, he dramatizes his real identity, though endowing it with the qualities which common sense and rhetorical tradition assign to the character of a good arguer: moderation, distinterest, good will (or candour). These are the attributes of Bickerstaff, the Drapier, and Gulliver.

---

[1] *Ibid.*, p. 197.
[2] *Ibid.*, p. 196. For identification with Hort, see 'Advice to a Parson', *Poems* III. 807–8.
[3] Landa, pp. 118–22.
[4] Davis XII. 200. By putting '*clergy*' in italics, Swift implies that non-residence is a crying sin of the landlords.

Having established his own, admirable position, Swift proceeds to damn the bishops by isolating them. To begin, he strips them of any claim to moral integrity. Pride, sycophancy, snobbery, he says, are their marks. He goes on to associate the bishops with the English interest as against the Irish; with the Lords against the Commons; with the government against the gentry; and with the Dissenters against the Anglicans. Beneath all these polarities lies the reiterated opposition of interests between the episcopal bench and the lower clergy.

To conclude, Swift proposes some delicious amendments to the bills; these fantasies amount to threats or predictions of what the bishops' policy may lead to. The most striking of them is a proposal that Irish episcopates be subdivided and the number of bishops enlarged: 'otherwise there may be a question started, whether twenty-two *prelates* can effectually extend their paternal care, and unlimited power, for the protection and correction of so great a number of spiritual *subjects*.'[1]

Swift's poems on these events have as much vigour as his published pamphlet. If they display no new turns of thought or technique, they do impress one with his fecundity and versatility, unabated halfway through his seventh decade. 'On the Irish Bishops',[2] in four-beat anapaestic couplets, is a denunciation of all the bishops except those three who voted against the Bill of Residence. Thanks to the many feminine endings and substitute feet, the lines do not sound monotonous. The powerful rhythms and the strong, ingenious rhymes keep the reader cheerfully occupied; for the variety of feet does not impede but rather strengthens the rapid movement. Changing sentence patterns—questions, exclamations, active verbs, passive verbs, etc.—add to the bounding vitality. The general effect is hard to illustrate by extracts because it depends on a cumulation of bitter phrases and rough analogies all fitted into the swings of the versification. But the tone is Swift's special blend of the comic and the furious:

[1] *Ibid.*, pp. 198–9.
[2] *Poems* III. 801–5. This poem and the two following were in circulation before 17 May 1732, when Swift mentions them in a letter; see Williams IV. 25.

Old Latimer preaching did fairly describe
A [bishop] who rul'd all the rest of his tribe;
And who is this [bishop]? And where does he dwell?
Why truly 'tis Satan, Arch-[bishop] of Hell:
And HE was a Primate, and HE wore a mitre,
Surrounded with jewels of sulphur and nitre.
How nearly this [bishop] our [bishops] resembles!
But his has the odds, who *believes and who trembles*.
Could you see his grim *grace*, for a pound to a penny,
You'd swear it must be the *baboon* of [Kilkenny].[1]

Another poem, drawing a parallel between Judas and the Irish bishops, is in heroic couplets, and makes some effort to sound dignified and expressive in style.[2] For the reader the result is a strong impression of rage leaping out though deliberate restraint. Here is the climactic mock-simile of the short poem:

As antient Judas *by transgression fell*,
And *burst asunder* e'er he went to Hell;
So, could we see a set of new Iscariots,
Come headlong tumbling from their mitred chariots,
Each modern Judas perish like the first;
Drop from the tree with all his bowels burst;
Who could forbear, that view'd each guilty face,
To cry; Lo, Judas, *gone to his own place*.

Finally, 'Advice to a Parson'[3]—five couplets in anapaestic tetrameter—is a set of libellous epigrams on Josiah Hort,[4] one of the most self-seeking of the bishops. The conciseness of these lines gives them their force, because it makes a barrage of close-packed venomous epithets framed in rhyme. Here are the opening lines:

Would you rise in the *church*, be *stupid* and *dull*,
Be empty of *learning*, of *insolence* full:
Though lewd and immoral, be formal and grave,
In *flatt'ry* an artist, in *fawning* a slave. . . .

It was probably during these brangles that Swift had

---

[1] Ll. 1–10. Tenison is the baboon.
[2] 'Judas', *Poems* III. 806.   [3] *Ibid.*, pp. 807–8.
[4] In spite of Williams's note on the poem, I believe that it, like the 'Epigram' following, deals only with Hort. All the epithets suit him, and the close joins them.

Faulkner publish a *jeu d'esprit* called *A Proposal ... to Pay Off the Debt of the Nation*, by 'A— P—, Esq;'.[1] Since the bishops in Parliament had hoped to enlist the landed gentry against the lower clergy, Swift demonstrates that the same force can be directed against the episcopacy. His scheme is a pseudo-project backed up by a mock-argument, or systematically false logic. Swift dovetails, in this piece, the devices which had underlain *An Argument against Abolishing Christianity*, *A Modest Proposal*, and *An Answer to the Craftsman*. Because the pressure seems lower, however, and the composition less exuberant, the new *Proposal* falls short of the earlier splendours. Nevertheless the very nakedness of its development is fascinating in the way it exposes Swift's stratagems.

Swift poses as an English Whig, recently come over to take an Irish employment but differing from others of the ilk in that he wishes good to 'a people, among whom I have been so well received'.[2] He proposes that the diocesan lands, from the rent of which the bishoprics derive their income, be sold. Because church lands are generally let for a quarter of their real value, 'A.P.' assumes that the sale will bring in enough money to pay off the national debt and still leave an ample fund from which the bishops may receive their established salaries. In making out his case, Swift applies the characteristic turns of his comic irony.

As usual, the pamphlet falls into three parts. Swift opens with a brief statement of the problem: the need to pay off the national debt of Ireland. Next, he presents his absurd solution, buttressed by the customary mad arithmetic. Finally, he lists the benefits attending on this solution. These divisions fit more sober pamphlets like the first *Drapier's Letter* as well as comic–ironic excursions like the new essay. But the strength of the satire consists, here as before, in the counterpoint of allusive ridicule with which Swift fills out this structure.

He omits his grand insinuation, that by marshalling the

---

[1] Davis XII. 205–12. 'A.P.' may perhaps mean 'a parson'. The essay was certainly completed before the end of Aug. 1732, because it is listed among works by Swift that Pilkington was then trying to publish. See Williams v. 256. In the *Dublin Journal*, 15 Sept. 1730, there is a report of a letter describing a similar project.
[2] Davis XII. 212.

gentry against the lower clergy, the bishops may unchain a process that will at last destroy themselves. Instead, he associates with the proposal all those powers which will tend to disrupt Anglican unity. So the author is a Whig, an Englishman, and an office-holder. The sale of the lands would 'increase the number of gentry', because the purchasers would be either the present bishops' tenants, or gentlemen looking for estates, or 'persons from England'. Swift's readers understood that the landholders both coveted the church lands and detested tithes. Furthermore, many tenants were Nonconformists, who would strengthen the Dissenting interest by becoming propertied gentlemen.

One heavy implication, hardly apparent to the modern reader, involves the evil practice of avaricious bishops which we have noticed already (and which Archbishop King used benignly).[1] They could not sell ecclesiastical endowments. They could, however, change the terms of leases which fell in. Upon renewal of his lease, the tenant normally paid a fee called a fine. Thereafter, he paid a fixed annual rent until the expiration of the lease. The bishop might set a high fine for a long lease at a low rent. He would then receive a large immediate profit at the expense of his successors. Or he might set a low fine for a short lease at a substantial rent. He would then sacrifice quick gains but enrich the see. He would also give his successor a chance, when the lease fell in, to adjust the rent as the value of money declined.[2]

'A.P.''s *Proposal* involves the ultimate elimination of fines (and therefore of temptation) altogether; and I suppose Swift pretends that the government will pay the bishops in perpetuity the incomes actually received by them at this date. If so, a basic aspect of his fooling hinges on his ancient fear of inflation. Swift believed that since money undergoes a steady decline in value, real estate alone can guarantee the survival of an endowment. To set episcopal salaries in fixed financial terms is eventually to destroy them.[3]

Swift must have suffered all the more bitterly in that he had,

---

[1] Cf. above, pp. 167, 175–7.   [2] Landa, pp. 97–111.   [3] Landa, pp. 105–7.

nine years before, defended the bishops against the gentry, in his pamphlet with a misleading title, *Some Arguments against Enlarging the Power of the Bishops*.[1] The new *Proposal* works out a hint dropped toward the end of *Some Arguments*: '[Let] me suppose that all the church lands in the kingdom were thrown up to the laity';[2] and in *Some Arguments* too he had posed as a Whig.[3] The 1723 essay contained little irony among much sober, straightforward logic; but the same principle comes out as sarcasm in both:

> To say the truth, it is a great misfortune as well to the public as to the bishops themselves, that their lands are generally let to lords and great 'squires, who, in reason, were never designed to be tenants; and therefore may naturally murmur at the payment of rent, as a subserviency they were not born to.[4] (*Some Arguments*)

In 1732 this point still has a sour thrust:

> For the immediate tenants to bishops, being some of them persons of quality, and good estates; and more of them grown up to be gentlemen by the profits of these very leases, under a succession of bishops; think it a disgrace to be subject both to rents and fines, at the pleasure of their landlords.[5] (*Proposal*)

The great difference (besides the contrast in tone) springs from the way Swift aligns the factions. Supporting the bishops in 1723, he grouped them with both the lower clergy and the ordinary farmers, against the landlords. Excoriating the bishops in 1732, he sets the gentry and farmers together against them.

The *Proposal* bristles with innuendoes that touch these sore spots. As in *An Argument against Abolishing Christianity* and *A Modest Proposal*, Swift lists, among benefits, absurd results which join together bodies naturally opposed to each other. Whoever would have supported the Bills of Residence and Division appears also in favour of selling the bishops' lands: the English interest, the Whigs, the Dissenters, gentry, and, in an apogee of sarcasm, the episcopal bench (dominated by English imports):

---

[1] Cf. my discussion above, pp. 181–6.
[2] Davis IX. 57.   [3] *Ibid.*, p. 56.   [4] *Ibid.*, pp. 55–6.
[5] *Ibid.*, XII. 211.

I cannot but be confident, that their graces my lords the arch-
bishops, and my lords the bishops, will heartily join in this proposal,
out of gratitude to his late and present majesty, the best of kings, who
have bestowed on them such high and opulent stations; as well as in
pity to this country, which is now become their own; whereby they
will be instrumental towards paying the nation's debts, without
impoverishing themselves; enrich an hundred gentlemen, as well as
free them from dependence; and thus remove that envy which is apt
to fall upon their graces and lordships, from considerable persons;
whose birth and fortunes, rather qualify them to be lords of manors,
than servile dependents upon churchmen, however dignified or
distinguished.[1]

IV. DEFENDING THE TEST

Meanwhile, an older threat was exciting Swift's tired gloom and
irony. The government was joining with the Dissenters to renew
their onslaught against the Sacramental Test. Long before the
issue could reach the floor of Parliament, Swift composed a
pamphlet defending the law: *The Advantages Propos'd by Repealing
the Sacramental Test, Impartially Considered*.[2] It appeared in Dublin
at the beginning of February, and in London a month later.[3]

Swift's point of view in the pamphlet is consistently ironic, for
he pretends to be impartial and therefore at points to suggest
ways of easing difficulties for the Dissenters—ways that would
alarm the gentry of Ireland. But in style the pamphlet has few
turns of verbal irony. Rather it maintains a crisp, pointed
attention to the issues, with considerable restraint and dignity.

Mainly, Swift is concerned to show that regardless of the effect
on the Anglican clergy, a repeal of the Test would be unfortunate. Simply for the internal peace of a nation, he argues (in
keeping with the common sense of his era) that a church established by law is essential. If the national religion should grow
unbearably corrupt, it could be changed, but only for another

---

[1] *Ibid.*, p. 211.   [2] *Ibid.*, pp. 241–51.
[3] Advertised in the *Dublin Journal* 8 Feb., in the *Grub-Street Journal* 9 Mar.; listed in the
Gentleman's Magazine as published 2 Mar., price 6d. See *ibid.*, pp. xli, 345; *Gentleman's
Magazine* 2 (1732), 683.

establishment. So long as a particular church is established, a Test of some sort is necessary to keep order in the government. Otherwise, there would be endless strife among the various religious interests of the officers of state.

Swift implies throughout that the Presbyterians—by far the most powerful body of Dissenters in Ireland—who are agitating for repeal of the Test really desire not only offices of state but the livings of the church. He warns that they would install their ministers of religion in civil offices. He points out that if they should obtain power, they would by their own principles have to strive to alter the national religion. But this attempt, if successful, would merely replace the schism between Dissent and Episcopalianism with the notorious divisions long rooted in the body of the Presbyterians. At the same time, they would be obliged to suppress the Episcopal faith. Finally, Swift warns the Irish Presbyterians themselves that in the distribution of preferments they would have to contend with their co-religionists sent over from Britain.

The arguments move very much like those, a quarter of a century earlier, of Swift's *Letter Concerning the Sacramental Test*. In tone, however, the new piece sounds entirely different. Where the *Letter* was aggressive and confident, the *Advantages* seems brooding and bleak. 'From 1730', says Landa, 'Swift's tone grew sharper, his hopelessness more apparent.'[1]

In 1708, Swift had felt the nation effectually united behind the four-year-old law; the pressure, he had believed, came from England alone. But by the time of Dorset's lieutenancy, a long train of frustrations had brought Swift to be prepared for the darkest eventualities. The Walpole government hoped, in the usual way, that removing the Test in Ireland would not only strengthen the ministry's control of that kingdom, but would facilitate the same change in England. The Hanoverian bishops of Ireland seemed quite subservient enough to connive at the ruin of their church. The placemen would naturally vie with one another to anticipate the government's whims. And the rest

[1] Landa, p. 191.

of the Anglican population had neither the fortitude nor the vitality to stand up to this assault on their constitution.

'We generally love and esteem our clergy,' Swift had written (admittedly a hyperbole) in 1708; and he had claimed that fewer than fifty Members of Parliament would support the repeal.[1] In the *Advantages* he says (again hyperbolically) that if the Presbyterians really try to make their own sect the church established by law, 'under the present disposition of things it is very possible they may' succeed 'without blood'.[2] One receives a precise impression of Swift's altered tone from a comparison of the way he expresses the same argument in both essays: that the repeal of the Test will not harm the Anglican priests: 'And their judgement in the present affair', he says in 1708,

> is the more to be regarded, because they are the last persons who will be affected by it. . . . Because the act which repeals the *Test*, will only qualify a *layman* for an employment, but not a *Presbyterian* or *Anabaptist* preacher for a church living.[3]

'They [i.e., the Anglican clergy] will (*for some time*)', he says twenty-four years later,

> be no great sufferers by this repeal; because I cannot recollect, among all our sects, any one that gives latitude enough to take the oaths required at an institution to a church-living; and until that bar shall be removed, the present episcopal clergy are safe for two years. Although it may be thought somewhat unequal, that in the *northern* parts, where there may be three *Dissenters* to one *churchman*, the whole revenue should be engrossed by him who hath so small a part of the cure.[4]

There are ambiguities in this statement, and ironies at the expense of the arguments against the Test. But the decline in confidence from the attitudes of 1708 is obvious. So also, alas, is the fact that Swift was willing to accept the principle of an Erastian church but not the consequences.[5]

---

[1] Davis II. 119.   [2] *Ibid.*, XII. 247.   [3] *Ibid.*, II. 119.
[4] *Ibid.*, XII. 249.   [5] Landa, p. 192.

Chapter Three

'MISCELLANIES'

I. FRIENDS AND ACQUAINTANCES

One must always discount Swift's reports, especially to his English friends, of living in bleak isolation. But his mood of discontent with Irish affairs was genuine enough. To a new friend—come over from England—who said he was pleased with his rectory, Swift wrote,

> I heartily envy you, for I never yet saw in Ireland a spot of earth two feet wide, that had not in it something to displease. I think I once was in your county of Tipperary, which is like the rest of the whole kingdom, a bare face of nature, without houses or plantations; filthy cabins, miserable, tattered, half-starved creatures, scarce in human shape; one insolent ignorant oppressive squire to be found in twenty miles riding; a parish church to be found only in a summer day's journey, in comparison of which, an English farmer's barn is a cathedral; a bog of fifteen miles round; every meadow a slough, and every hill a mixture of rock, heath, and marsh; and every male and female, from the farmer, inclusive to the day-labourer, infallibly a thief, and consequently a beggar, which in this island are terms convertible.[1]

Genuine private discomforts went along with his public discontents. Charles Ford left Dublin early in 1732, never to return. He had spent more than two years there;[2] and in September 1731 he had let Wood Park for a term of three lives. Besides losing his great intimate, Swift slipped on the deanery stairs in February 1732 and strained the Achilles tendon of his left heel. To a man who delighted in walking, climbing, and riding, the

---

[1] Williams IV. 33–4.
[2] I assume that he did not return to England between December 1729, when Mrs Pilkington met him, and his departure in 1732, which I date from Swift's letter of 17 May to him (*ibid.*, pp. 23–5).

accident was a disaster, all the more so as the strain took many months to mend. For the rest of the year, Swift felt lame, especially going down stairs.[1] But by June he could ride with special leggings ('gambadoes'), and by October he could walk two or three miles at a time.[2] On top of these miseries sat the annoyances of one lawsuit threatened against Ford by a tenant and another lawsuit arranged with a young cousin, Deane Swift, involving most of Swift's fortune.

Meanwhile, Delany remained in England through the summer; Mrs Barber was also there; and Sir Arthur Acheson went over. The departure of the Duke of Dorset (22 April 1732) may have reminded Swift, gloomily, of how little he had influenced viceregal policy; and yet his grace was careful, on the eve of his departure, to inquire formally about the dean's health.[3]

Swift made do with Sheridan, the Pilkingtons, Lady Acheson, and lesser fry—'people of middle understanding, middle rank, very complying, and consequently such as I can govern'.[4] He floated his usual plans of going over to England, where he would 'pass a month at Amesbury' with Gay and the Queensberrys, 'and then the winter with Mr Pope';[5] but instead he seems to have stuck out the summer in Dublin, doctoring his lameness and vertigo. 'Nothing but an uncertain state of my health ... could have prevented my passing this summer into England,'[6] he said, and deferred the expedition for a year.[7]

Although the letters make him sound lonely, I suspect that he made the most of his local companions. He said that the confinement of the lameness exposed him to too many visitors.[8] He did not omit to celebrate All Fools Day with a letter to Lady Acheson declaring that a woman they knew had given birth to 'a half child, just as if it were divided in two equal parts. It had one eye, half a nose and mouth, one leg, and so from top to bottom'.[9] Her ladyship was not taken in but gave as good as she received: 'I am greatly surprised at the account you give me ... but since it was so, I am heartily glad she has got rid of it.'[10] Another hint of

[1] *Ibid.*, p. 37.   [2] *Ibid.*, p. 77.   [3] *Ibid.*, pp. 12–13.
[4] Sherburn III. 287.   [5] Williams IV. 42.   [6] *Ibid.*, p. 52.
[7] *Ibid.*, p. 81.   [8] *Ibid.*, p. 15: 'knaves'.   [9] *Ibid.*, p. 11.   [10] *Ibid.*, p. 12.

Swift's sociability appears in a reference to meetings with his new acquaintance, the young Lord Orrery, who of course knew Lady Acheson: 'I meet him sometimes at dinners and he hath dined with me.'[1]

A tremendous event of the summer was the announcement by Bolingbroke that he had found an excellent church living near him which might be exchanged for the deanery of St Patrick's. The interest of the proposal is double. It demonstrates irrefutably the deep affection that Bolingbroke felt for Swift, and it became a test of Swift's genuine dissatisfaction with Ireland. The exchange would just about have halved his income. But it would have left him more than enough to live on comfortably, especially because he spent only about a third of his total income as dean, vicar, investor, etc., on himself.

Bolingbroke writes about the region of the property he held through his first wife, in Bucklebury, Berkshire, where Swift had once visited him:

[There] is in my neighbourhood in Berkshire a clergyman, one Mr Talbot, related to the solicitor general and protected by him. This man has now the living of Burghfield, which the late Bishop of Durham held before, and for ought I know after he was Bishop of Oxford. The living is worth 400 pounds a year over and above a curate paid; as Mr Correy, a gentleman who does my business in that country, and who is a very grave authority, assures me. The parsonage is extremely good, the place pleasant, the air is excellent, the distance from London a little day's journey, and from hence, give me leave to think this circumstance of some importance to you, not much above half a day's, even for you who are no great jockey. Mr Talbot has many reasons which make him desire to settle in Ireland for the rest of his life, and has been looking out for a change of preferments for some time. As soon as I heard this, I employed one to know whether he continued in the same mind, and to tell him that an advantageous exchange might be offered him, if he could engage his kinsman to make it practicable at court. He answered for his own acceptance and his kinsman's endeavours. I employed next some friends to secure my Lord Dorset, who very frankly declared himself ready to serve you in anything, and in this if you desired.

---

[1] 14 Oct. 1732; *ibid.*, p. 77. See below, pp. 730–1.

Bolingbroke foresaw that there might be an obstacle in the Archbishop of Dublin, whom he hoped to approach through his celebrated brother:

> The light, in which the proposition must be presented to him, and our ministers, if it be made to them, is this, that though they gratify you they gratify you in a thing advantageous to themselves, and silly in you to ask. I suppose it will not be hard to persuade them that, it is better for them you should be a private parish priest in an English county, than a dean in the metropolis of Ireland, where they know, because they have felt, your authority and influence.

He urged Swift to visit England and to stay with him at Dawley:

> You shall be nursed, fondled, and humoured.... Your horses shall be grazed in summer and fothered in winter, and you and your man shall have meat, drink and lodging. Washing I cannot afford Mr Dean, for I am grown saving, thanks to your sermons about frugality.[1]

The charms that Bolingbroke's scheme would have for Swift are too obvious to need elaboration. But he was not tempted. The money was too little, the loss of status too disheartening. He told Gay the offer was 'just too short by 300 pounds a year':[2]

> [Besides] the difficulty of adjusting certain circumstances, it would not answer. I am at a time of life that seeks ease and independence. ... I would rather be a freeman among slaves, than a slave among freemen. The dignity of my present station damps the pertness of inferior puppies and squires, which without plenty and ease on your side the channel, would break my heart in a month.[3]

If one considers how probable it was that Swift would not live long and how many deep intellectual and social pleasures England could heap on him, one must suspect that his attachment to Ireland was not merely due to a fondness for money and power. He had a tie with the common, industrious, and productive people of Ireland that he did not wish to break.

Summer passed; the tendon healed; autumn drew on; and Swift's friends regathered in Dublin. A distinguished new admirer has already been named. This was John Boyle, fifth Earl

[1] *Ibid.*, pp. 43–5.　[2] *Ibid.*, p. 58.　[3] *Ibid.*, p. 73.

of Orrery, who had only succeeded to his title the preceding August (1731), when his father died. The late Earl, who had been, as an undergraduate, at the centre of the Phalaris controversy, had known Swift well in both kingdoms. They met for the last time during a flying trip which the Earl made to Ireland the month before his death.[1] The son arrived a year later, to bring order into a mismanaged estate. But almost at once he suffered the loss of his young wife, who had been in bad health.[2] It was soon after her death that Swift began to see him.

The old Earl had described his heir as lacking 'taste and inclination for the knowledge which study and learning afford'.[3] Trying, with indifferent resources, to refute this judgment, the fifth Earl achieved a 'feeble-minded' effect defined by Samuel Johnson:

> His conversation was . . . neat and elegant, but without strength. He grasped at more than his abilities could reach; tried to pass for a better talker, a better writer, and a better thinker than he was.[4]

Orrery spent his life, said Johnson, in 'catching at' a literary eminence which he 'had not power to grasp'.[5] What he lacked in talent, he made up with unction; and having either patronized or made the acquaintance of a chain of authors from Southerne to Johnson, he did at last win the reflected immortality which he sought.

Orrery's obsequiousness, 'a politeness carried to a ridiculous excess',[6] produced the desired attention from Swift. 'I meet him sometimes at dinners,' the dean said in October, 'and he hath dined with me. He seems an honest man, and of good disposition'[7]—probably alluding as much to the young man's Tory politics as to his moral character. Eight weeks of further familiarity elicited more praise and less understanding from Swift: 'I often see Lord Orrery,' he said in December, 'who seems every way a most deserving person, a good scholar, with much wit, manners, and modesty.'[8]

---

[1] *Ibid.*, III. 475. [2] She died in Cork, 22 Aug. 1732.
[3] *Complete Peerage* III. 422n. [4] Boswell v. 238. [5] *Ibid.*, II. 129.
[6] Johnson; *ibid.*, IV. 17. [7] Williams IV. 77. [8] *Ibid.*, p. 91.

Meanwhile, the infatuation with the Pilkingtons throve. Swift's confidence smothered his discretion, and in June 1732 he recommended the young parson to Pope as 'the most hopful we have'.[1] How thoroughly the childlike couple mastered him, one may reckon from his exertions on behalf of the little husband. John Barber, the London printer, who considered himself 'a creature of [Swift's] own making',[2] had risen to the aldermanic eminence of being chosen Lord Mayor of the capital. While Barber's year of office only opened at the end of October,[3] Swift wrote in July and asked him to make Pilkington his chaplain. The candidate was represented as a 'young gentleman, for whose learning and oratory in the pulpit I will engage ... some years under thirty,[4] but [having] more wit, sense, and discretion, than any of your London parsons ten years above his age.'[5]

Though Swift spoke of valuing Pilkington for his modesty,[6] that impression reveals the aim of Swift's advice better than its effectiveness. He constantly recommended the virtue to his protégé;[7] but Laetitia (whose prejudice eventually ran another way) came to describe her spouse as obstinate, rash, self-willed, and 'plagu'd with envy'.[8] All the young man's other friends, Laetitia writes, were 'against his going'; and Archbishop Hoadly even warned him that serving under so disaffected a person as Barber might obstruct his career. But Pilkington, with his patron's cordial sponsorship, not only prepared to depart but rejected his wife's petition to accompany him.[9]

While the husband might go, Swift would still have the vivacious Laetitia to amuse him. He also encouraged the attendance of young Orrery. In October the yacht brought over Dr Delany with an English bride. She was a widow said to be worth fifteen hundred pounds a year.[10] Swift thought him 'very modest in his new prosperity; walks on foot in fair weather, lives

---

[1] Sherburn III. 293.　　[2] Williams IV. 143.
[3] He was sworn in on 28 October.　　[4] An error.
[5] 22 Jul. 1732; Williams IV. 47.　　[6] *Ibid.*, pp. 57, 70.
[7] Sherburn III. 363.　　[8] Pilkington I. 115.　　[9] *Ibid.*, pp. 114–15, 123.
[10] *Dublin Journal*, 7 Oct. 1732; Williams IV. 77 and n. 2.

well, (as I hear) entertains his old friends, and does many acts of generosity as well as charity'.[1]

Mrs Barber arrived in the yacht with the Delanys. Lady Acheson was in Dublin; and Swift told Ford in December that she was 'an absolute Dublin rake, sits up late, loses her money, and goes to bed sick, and resolves like you never to mend'.[2] At the end of November many citizens celebrated the Drapier's birthday. According to the *Dublin Journal*,

> On Thursday last being the anniversary of the birth-day of the Revd. Dr Swift, Dean of St Patrick's, the same was observed here with the greatest demonstrations of joy, by several people who wish well to this kingdom.—And, at night they drank the Drapier's health, prosperity to the trade of Ireland, and prosperity to all the well-wishers of this country, &c. We hear, that several excellent poems are written on that occasion. The night concluded with ringing of bells, bonfires, illuminations, &c.[3]

Among numerous tributes in verse, one came from Orrery, with an elegant paper book for Swift to write in; another, from Delany, came with a silver standish. Mrs Barber told Mrs Pilkington about these, and Laetitia had recently got from her husband a London newspaper in which an old poem of her own was printed. She thereupon presented to Swift a cutting of that poem along with a writing quill and a fresh set of verses concerning her modest gift.

The dean had long since mastered the art of painting a surface with compliment when his substance was only tact. In thanking Mrs Pilkington, he called her lines better than any he had ever seen 'in their kind'.[4] In thanking his lordship, he urged Orrery to go on and become 'the great example, restorer, and patron, of virtue, learning, and wit, in a most corrupt, stupid, and ignorant age and nation'.[5]

Mrs Barber had returned to Ireland only with the idea of establishing her whole family in England. She let Swift offer his assistance, and in December he wrote to her husband's namesake (but not relation), the Lord Mayor.[6] Though John Barber

---

[1] Williams IV. 91.   [2] *Ibid.*, p. 92.   [3] 2 Dec. 1732.
[4] Williams IV. 95.   [5] *Ibid.*, p. 106.   [6] *Ibid.*, pp. 92–3.

promised nothing of solid value, a poem by Mrs Barber exists on the subject of committing one of her sons to his care. Her hope evidently was that he would become rich; and her recommendatory couplets would please Max Weber, for she describes the boy as

> With talents to make a *good man*[1] in the City;
> Industrious, and orderly, prudent, and smart,
> And not too much *conscience*, nor too little *art*;
> Not scrup'lous, but honest, a heart set on gain,
> Whose highest ambition is fix'd on the *chain*.[2]

Mrs Barber must have told Mrs Pilkington of her plans, and Laetitia soon began planning to travel with her, so as to join Matthew before his chaplaincy came to an end.[3]

December also brought Swift a series of deaths touching off the thoughts of mortality that lay beneath many of his social pleasures. On 2 December, Mrs Grierson succumbed,[4] and soon after, two mysterious, unidentified persons 'of great merit' and whom Swift 'loved very well' died, as he said, 'in the prime of their years, but a little above thirty'.[5]

But the great disaster fell with Gay's sudden death, 4 December. 'An inflammatory fever hurried him out of life in three days,' Pope and Arbuthnot wrote to Swift.[6] He held the letter without opening it for five days after it came; and then he endorsed it,

> On my dear friend Mr Gay's death: Received December 15, but not read till the 20th, by an impulse foreboding some misfortune.[7]

Arbuthnot told him of the poet's funeral in Westminster Abbey, 'as if he had been a peer of the realm'.[8] But Swift only observed, to Pope,

> I received yours with a few lines from the Doctor, and the account of our losing Mr Gay, upon which event I shall say nothing. I am only concerned that long living hath not hardened me.[9]

---

[1] 'To the Right Honourable John Barber, Esq;', *Poems on Several Occasions* (London, 1734), pp. 232–3; poem dated 29 Sept. 1733. 'Good man' means rich man.
[2] Lord Mayor's chain of office.   [3] Pilkington I. 153–5.
[4] *Dublin Journal*, 5 Dec. 1732.   [5] Sherburn III. 343.
[6] *Ibid.*, pp. 334–5.   [7] *Ibid.*, n. 4.   [8] Williams IV. 101.
[9] Sherburn III. 9.

It was now that Swift complained of losing friends faster than he could replace them. But at the beginning of 1733 another talented gentlewoman joined his circle. It was Mrs Pendarves, born Mary Granville. She was a niece of Lord Lansdowne and a second cousin of Carteret. Her family had forced her to marry a 'disgusting' old clergyman, fat and alcoholic,[1] who fortunately died when she was twenty-four; and seven years later she came to Dublin as a guest of the Donnellans, the family of a late Chief Baron of the Exchequer of Ireland.

Dr Delany soon invited her to dinner on a Thursday, which was Swift's time for visiting Delville; and in a letter of 24 January she writes,

> we met Miss Kelly, Lord Orrery, the Dean of St Patrick's, Mr Kit Donnellan, Dr Helsham—a very ingenious entertaining man. In such company you may believe time passed away very pleasantly. Swift is a very *odd companion* (if that expression is not too familiar for so extraordinary a genius); he talks a great deal and does not require many answers; he has infinite spirits, and says abundance of good things in his common way of discourse. Miss Kelly's beauty and good-humour have gained an entire conquest over him, and I come in only *a little by the by*.
>
> Lord Orrery is very gentle in his manner, and mighty polite; he only dined with us, for he is in the hands of lawyers and was obliged to give us up for those vultures.[2]

Frances Arabella Kelly, mentioned by Mrs Pendarves, was a beautiful, clever girl who had been captivating Swift, on and off, for a year.[3] She lived near Delany's town house and often went to his Delville Thursdays.[4] Her father, a Jacobite and rake, had mistreated his wife until she separated from him, leaving Miss Kelly a half-orphan; and he seems to have taken indifferent care of the daughter.[5] In a later account of the same scene Mrs Pendarves praised her host, who was eventually to become her husband:

> Dr Delany is as agreeable a companion as ever I met with, and one who condescends to converse with women, and treat them like reasonable creatures.[6]

[1] Mrs Delany I. 34–5.   [2] *Ibid.*, p. 396.   [3] Williams IV. 1, 5.
[4] Ball V. 5, n. 3.   [5] Williams IV. 172–4.
[6] 'George Paston' (i.e., Emily Morse Symonds), *Mrs Delany* (London, 1900), p. 73.

In March, she reported that Miss Kelly was 'disabled, poor thing, for she is confined to her bed with a pleuritic disorder, but the Dean attends her bedside'.[1] In April, dining again at Delville, with 'the usual company', she delivers a report showing that Swift had adopted with her the same tutorial paternalism which he customarily used to show his fondness for a young woman:

> The Dean of St Patrick's was there, in *very good humour*. He calls himself *'my master'* and corrects me when I speak bad English, or do not pronounce my words distinctly. I wish he lived in England, I should not only have a great deal of entertainment from him, but improvement.[2]

It is obvious that Swift had a greater provision of agreeable or interesting society than he liked to talk about to his English friends.

II. 'MISCELLANIES'

In launching Pilkington, Swift hoped both to employ him in the London publication of his own works and to give him the profit of them. But this intention affected several other people. Three volumes of miscellaneous works by Swift and his Scriblerian friends had appeared; and in 1728 Pope, their editor, had received Swift's permission to assemble a fourth. He planned that Lawton Gilliver should produce this book, to be entitled, very misleadingly, *Miscellanies. The Third Volume.*

George Faulkner, who had published many of the pieces in Dublin, may well have felt that he enjoyed a kind of property in them. His one-time master, William Bowyer, the London printer,[3] often put out editions of Faulkner's titles, thus establishing the copyright. He had published Pilkington's *Poems*, and the young parson expected to deal with him. But there was also Benjamin Motte, the original publisher of *Gulliver's Travels*. He had produced the three volumes of *Miscellanies* in 1727 and 1728, and thought he had a right to the new volume.

---

[1] Mrs Delany I. 402.　　[2] *Ibid.*　　[3] Williams IV. 172–4.

To understand the proceedings that followed, we must, I am afraid, return to the tedious early history of the *Miscellanies* of Swift and Pope.[1] It is an account that has many obscurities but a clear general outline. When the very possibility of the enterprise was broached, in 1726, Swift was spending the spring and summer in England. At least, from the evidence we have, it is a probable inference that the scheme was conceived at that time. Naturally enough, there are no extant letters between the two friends during the period. But it looks as if the immediate inspiration for the Swift–Pope volumes may have been Curll's publication of two unauthorized volumes of *Miscellanies*, 6 August 1726, issued perhaps to take advantage of the publicity surrounding Swift's visit.[2]

Curll's first volume included letters from Pope and poems by Pope, Swift, and others. The second volume had a section of poems by Swift and his friends (so-called). Pope was of course disturbed by the printing of his letters, partly on account of their private nature, partly perhaps because he hoped to publish them himself. He began the arduous task of asking friends to return letters and copies of verses to him, 'to help me put out of Curll's power any trifling remains of mine'.[3] He was probably getting ready to collect his *œuvre* for official publication and for his own profit.

It was after Swift returned to Ireland in August 1726 that the friends' correspondence began to deal with the work of compiling matter for their own *Miscellanies*. The first volume was evidently planned to include nearly all the prose from Swift's 1711 *Miscellanies* with some new pieces added. The second volume was to have Arbuthnot's *History of John Bull* along with miscellaneous prose by Swift and other Scriblerians. The third would have poetry, and it would be called *The Last Volume* in order to discourage continuations by pirates like Curll. At first Pope

[1] For a brief account, see *Poems* I. xx–xxviii.
[2] E. L. Steeves and R. H. Griffith, 'Bibliographical Notes on "The Last Volume" of Motte's *Miscellanies*, 1727', in E. L. Steeves, ed. *The Art of Sinking in Poetry* (by Pope and others) (New York, 1952), p. 197.
[3] Sherburn II. 419.

thought of including his poem on 'dullness', but he changed his mind.

Swift mentions a search for contributions to *The Last Volume*:

> I am mustering as I told you all the little things in verse that I think may be safely printed, but I give you despotic power to tear as many as you please.[1]

The freedom he allowed Pope to correct his work is typical of Swift's attitude toward informed criticism. Soon he also offered additions to 'Thoughts Moral and Diverting' from his 1711 *Miscellanies*, for separate inclusion in *The Second Volume*. Again he urges Pope to make his own taste the standard:

> Since you have received the verses, I most earnestly entreat you to burn those which you do not approve, and in those few where you may not dislike some parts, blot out the rest, and sometimes (though it may be against the laziness of your nature) be so kind as to make a few corrections, if the matter will bear them. I have some few of those things I call thoughts moral and diverting: if you please I will send the best I can pick from them, to add to the new volume. I have reason to choose the method you mention of mixing the several verses, and I hope thereby among the bad critics to be entitled to more merit than is my due.[2]

Pope's plan of 'mixing the several verses', or placing poems by various authors together without indicating the authorship, may have been due to a desire to maintain his anonymity, at least for certain poems; it may also have been a way to hide the paucity of his verse contributions. But Swift was obviously more than willing to have his friend serve as editor in every sense.

Meanwhile, Pope was gathering prose for *The Second Volume*. He particularly wished to get Arbuthnot's *History of John Bull*, and wrote to the Earl of Oxford for his copy:

> [I] desire you to lend us, John Bull &c. for a good end, in order to put together this winter many scattered pieces of the same kind, which are too good to be lost.[3]

---

[1] 15 Oct. 1726; *ibid.*, p. 408.   [2] 5 Dec. 1726; *ibid.*, p. 420.
[3] 8 Dec. 1726; *ibid.*, p. 421.

What '&c.' included we are not sure. Evidently, the Earl had manuscripts of a number of Scriblerian works.

By mid-February 1727 Pope could report to Swift the printing of the first two volumes. He also sketched his plans for the so-called *Last* [i.e., third] *Volume*:

> I am prodigiously pleased with this joint-volume, in which methinks we look like friends, side by side, serious and merry by turns, conversing interchangeably, and walking down hand in hand to posterity; not in the stiff forms of learned authors, flattering each other, and setting the rest of mankind at nought: but in a free, unimportant, natural, easy manner; diverting others just as we diverted ourselves.[1]

Ostensibly, therefore, Pope envisaged the *Miscellanies* as commemorating not only the relation of Swift's literary *œuvre* to his own, but also the long friendship between the two most eminent authors of their age. Consequently, the title-page monogram for the volumes, which combines the initials of their names, is appropriate. It was probably designed by Pope.

In 1727 Swift, Pope, and Motte signed a contract for the publication of the *Miscellanies*, dated 29 March by Motte—although Swift must have signed afterward. It was natural for Motte to publish the set because he was the successor to Benjamin Tooke, who had brought out the original, 1711 volume by Swift—Motte was to pay Tooke fifty pounds for that copyright. Besides, Pope at this time was dealing with Motte on his own account.[2] I assume that Swift added his name to the contract after he reached England late in April 1727.

The preface, which I take to be largely of Pope's composition, is dated 27 May 1727 and is signed by Swift and Pope. It supports the theory that Curll's two spurious volumes planted the germ of the new *Miscellanies*, for a pertinent complaint against the famous pirate appears here:

> Having both of us been extremely ill treated by some booksellers (especially one Edmund Curll) it was our opinion that the best

---

[1] *Ibid.*, p. 426.   [2] Griffith II. xli.

method we could take for justifying ourselves, would be to publish whatever loose papers in prose and verse, we have formerly written.

Throughout the preface the writer refers to the contents as 'amusements', relegating the *Miscellanies* to a humble station. Yet Swift certainly regarded many of his contributions as being on a level with his best work.

The first two volumes were published on 24 June 1727. Pope then was still gathering matter for *The Last Volume*. As early as 17 February 1727 he had asked Swift's friend Stopford to discover whether or not the dean would like *Cadenus and Vanessa* to be in the book,[1] and the assembling of contributions went on after the printing began.

The Last Volume was apparently put through the press in three stages. *Cadenus and Vanessa* probably came first. Miscellaneous poems, mainly by Swift but also by Pope and others, emerged second, though printed in several stages. Originally, the third section was to be what came to be known as *The Dunciad*. But eventually this poem burgeoned in size and importance till Pope decided to reserve it for independent publication; and its place in *The Last Volume* was ultimately inherited by *Peri Bathous*, which Pope fathered with the help of Arbuthnot and others. Although it went last to the press, *Peri Bathous* appears first in the volume.

While he was at Twickenham in 1727, Swift wrote to Sheridan asking him to secure a copy of a poem addressed to Stella:

> Pray copy out the verses I writ to Stella on her collecting my verses, and send them to me, for we want some to make our poetical miscellany large enough, and I am not there [i.e., in Ireland] to pick what should be added. . . . I do not want that poem to Stella to print it entire, but some passages out of it, if they deserve it, to lengthen the volume.[2]

At this time, Stella was of course dying; and the request for a poem addressed to her has seemed indelicate to some scholars. Pope is on record as saying he wished the verses to Stella had

---

[1] Sherburn II. 425.   [2] Williams III. 221–2.

never been written.[1] We may question his candour, for he could easily have excluded them from the book. Swift normally liked to see his occasional works published, though the plan of extracting passages suggests that in this case he felt some reservations. But I believe he simply thought too well of the poem to want it omitted from what was an English collection of his verse.

In several letters during these months Pope and Swift seem to be searching for work to fill *The Last Volume*. One assumes this was the period before Pope decided to add *Peri Bathous*, and when the lack of *The Dunciad* made the copy look thin. Motte's contract was to pay four pounds for each sheet (sixteen pages) of copy.[2] It is also possible that Swift hoped to make *The Last Volume* a comprehensive gathering of his verse to date.

In August 1727 Pope announced the forthcoming publication of *The Last Volume* to the Earl of Oxford: 'Our miscellany of poems will be published next October: Tis one of the benefits this nation will reap by the coronation.'[3] Coronation time would of course swell sales. But the book was not ready in October. Swift left for Ireland in September 1727. Late in December, Pope was writing to Lord Oxford again, this time to ask for Prior's epitaph on Jenny. Characteristically, he put the request in Swift's mouth; but almost certainly the impulse was his own.

> If you have no material objection to suffering that Epitaph on Jenny of Mr Prior's to accompany some things of the same nature of the Dean of St Patrick's and mine, it is what would be very agreeable to him. He several times spoke of it to me to ask you.[4]

The message from Swift that Pope refers to is not extant. Apparently, Oxford replied promptly but refused to allow publication.

It was some time between June and December that Pope determined to take *The Dunciad* out of *The Last Volume* and began to seek a replacement. Yet the first hint of his intention to

[1] Delany, p. 103. I trust Delany and believe Pope made the remark to him.
[2] Williams v. 248.   [3] 25 Aug. 1727; Sherburn II. 44.
[4] 26 Dec. 1727; *ibid.*, p. 466.

substitute *Peri Bathous* only emerges from a letter of Swift's to Motte at the end of December 1727:

> As to the poetical volume of miscellanies I believe five parts in six at least are mine. Our two friends you know have printed their works already, and we could expect nothing but slight loose papers. There is all the poetry I ever writ worth printing. Mr Pope rejected some, I sent him, for I desired him [to] be severe as possible; and I will take his judgment. He writ to me that he intended a pleasant discourse on the subject of poetry should be printed before the volume and says that discourse is [ready].[1]

I'm not sure Swift was pleased that his work so heavily predominated in *The Last Volume*. It is possible that Pope withheld much of his own poetry because he did not like his best verses to be lost in poorly paid anonymity.

In January 1728 Pope informed Swift that *The Last Volume*, including *Peri Bathous*, would be 'coming out post now'.[2] But Swift's hunt for contributions did not cease. 'I have been looking over my papers,' he told Motte in February,

> to see if anything could be found in the house to add to that volume, but great numbers of my poems have been so impounded by certain accidents that I could only find those I send here enclosed, two of which Mr Pope already has seen. He sent back these because they were translations which indeed they are not and therefore I suppose he did not approve them; and in such a case I would by no means have them printed; because that would be a trick fitter for those who have no regard but to profit.[3]

We do not know which poems Swift was referring to. But they probably came too late for inclusion, because *The Last Volume* was published on 7 March 1728.[4]

Curll was impudent enough to say he would pirate some of the new material in the volumes because Motte had reprinted without his permission works that Curll had published years before

---

[1] Williams III. 258. The 'discourse' is of course *Peri Bathous*.

[2] Sherburn II. 468.

[3] Williams II. 263. Many gaps in the manuscript of this letter have been filled by Williams.

[4] Teerink, p. 5.

in unauthorized editions. But nothing seems to have come of this grotesque threat.[1] Yet a furore followed the appearance of the first three *Miscellanies*, with *Peri Bathous* being the supreme provocative. Pamphlets came out attacking the books in general and *Peri Bathous* in particular. These aggressions blended with others when *The Dunciad* followed, 18 May 1728. During the next summer Smedley produced *Gulliveriana*, a spurious continuation of the *Miscellanies* with denunciations of Swift and Pope.[2] The dean reported to the Earl of Oxford,

> I hear that myself and one or two more have a share in the scurrilities that the Dunciad hath occasioned, as a just punishment for the friendship we have for Mr Pope.[3]

Swift seems to have enjoyed the uproar set off by Pope's work. Pope, much thinner-skinned, was glad to associate Swift with *The Dunciad*, partly perhaps because it removed some of the responsibility for the satire from his shoulders. He wrote to Swift,

> I think it a vast pleasure that whenever two people of merit regard one another, so many scoundrels envy and are angry at them ... and if you knew the infinite content I have received of late, at the finding yours and my name constantly united in any silly scandal, I think you would go near to sing *Io Triumphe*! and celebrate my happiness in verse.[4]

There is a false note here, and it grows shrill in some remarks of Pope to Sheridan at this time: 'You *must have seen*, but you *cannot have read*, what he [i.e., Smedley] has lately published against our friend and me. The only pleasure a bad writer can give me, he has given, that of being abused with my betters and my friends.'[5]

During the spring of 1728 Pope became discontented with Motte's scheme of payments. After a series of complaints and reconciliations he tried to regain the rights of the new, so-called 'Third' (i.e., fourth) volume of *Miscellanies* which Motte could

---

[1] Williams III. 270–1.
[2] J. V. Guerinot, *Pamphlet Attacks on Alexander Pope* (London, 1969), pp. 144–8.
[3] 21 Sept. 1728; Williams III. 299–300.
[4] 12 Oct. 1728; Sherburn II. 522.   [5] 12 Oct. 1728; *ibid.*, p. 523.

claim as his by contract. At last, Pope bought Motte off with an abatement of twenty-five pounds in the money due for the three volumes already published.[1]

From the few clues we have, it looks as if work on *The Third Volume* advanced slowly and erratically. In a letter of March 1729 Swift seems to be replying to a question from Pope about recent prose and verse attributed to him. Swift laments the decline of 'my small talent' in a style that does not harmonize with the record we have of his productivity in these years. If Pope was embarking on the new project, Swift's shyness may reflect some dissatisfaction with his friend's editorial policies.

It was not till 1732 that serious progress toward *The Third Volume* became visible; and by that time Swift had schemes of his own, about which he maintained admirable discretion. A letter from him in June 1732 can only be a reply to Pope's request for contributions:

> As to sending you any thing that I have written since I left you (either verse or prose) I can only say, that I have ordered by my will, that all my papers of any kind shall be delivered you to dispose of as you please.

He lists recent works, depreciates them, and says,

> Such as they are, I will bring them, tolerable or bad, if I recover this lameness, and live long enough to see you either here or there.

He also recommends Pilkington and asks Pope to see the young man:

> The utmost stretch of his ambition is, to gather up as much superfluous money as will give him a sight of you, and half an hour of your presence; after which he will return home in full satisfaction, and in proper time die in peace.

And yet again he complains of sterility in the midst of what an impartial observer would call fecundity:

> My poetical fountain is drained, and I profess I grow gradually so

[1] See letters from Pope to Motte, 9 Nov. 1728; 14 Jan., 8, 28 Mar., and 8 May 1729, in *ibid.*, p. 526 and III. 8–9, 23–4, 27, 32; also the final agreement signed 1 Jul. 1729 in *The Gentleman's Magazine* 44 (1855), 364.

[744]

dry, that a rhyme with me is almost as hard to find as a guinea, and even prose speculations tire me as much.[1]

Eventually, Pope took for *The Third Volume* most of the poems and essays named by Swift in this letter and added some others by him as well. But he did not take 'A Libel on Dr Delany', which Swift particularly favoured. The reason, one assumes, is that it seemed to involve him in an attack on the court just when he was trying to keep on good terms with those in power.[2]

Motte now wrote to Swift, pressing his claims to *The Third Volume*, and Swift replied with cautious sympathy, obviously hoping that the publisher would make it up with the poet:

> Upon my word, I never intended that any but yourself should be concerned as printer or bookseller in anything that shall be published with my consent while I am alive or after my death by my executors. As to my posthumous things I shall intrust them to Mr Pope, but with a strong recommendation that you alone may be employed. Supposing and being assured of your honest and fair dealing, which I have always found. I am likewise desirous that some time or other, all that I acknowledge to be mine in prose and verse, which I shall approve of with any little things that shall be thought deserving should be published by themselves by you, during my life (if it contains any reasonable time) provided you are sure it will turn to your advantage. And this you may say to Mr Pope, as my resolution, unless he hath any material objections to it, which I would desire to know. For I ever intended the property as a bookseller should be only in you, as long as you shall act with justice and reason which I never doubted in the least; and I conceive that Mr Pope's opinion of you is the same with mine.[3]

Writing in such strong terms to Motte without informing Pope, I think Swift was hoping to manœuvre the two men into collaborating without his seeming to defy his valuable friend. Yet we know that about this time Swift was also encouraging Faulkner to produce a collected edition of his works in Ireland. We know further that a week after the letter to Motte, Swift made an assignment to Pilkington of various of his own works in

[1] 12 Jun. 1732; Sherburn III. 291–3.
[2] Letter to Motte, 4 Nov. 1732; Williams IV. 83.
[3] 15 Jul. 1732; *ibid.*, pp. 41–2.

prose and verse which had been printed in Dublin by Faulkner.[1] Since Swift here neither confessed his authorship nor named the specific works, the assignment had no validity in law. But his willingness to deal with Pilkington, Motte, and Faulkner at the same time, while giving no account of his actions to Pope, suggests a remarkable mixture of motives.

In August 1732 Pilkington (still in Dublin) wrote to Bowyer in London about the volume of Swift's works that he was hoping to bring out under the author's supervision and with Bowyer's help. In this letter and one that soon followed, he clearly acted as Swift's agent and confidently listed some of the 'pieces which you are entitled to print'. They included most of those which Swift had offered to Pope, two months earlier, for inclusion in *The Third Volume* of the *Miscellanies*.[2]

I assume that Swift wished not only to give Pilkington the profit of the publication but also to control, through his young protégé, the design of a London collection of his works unmingled with those of others. If Bowyer and Pilkington had moved quickly, they might have effected these wishes.

But Pope was subtler and faster. He and Lawton Gilliver were pressing on with *The Third Volume*. Yet by now Motte had his strong assurance from Swift. He wrote to Pope invoking this authority and asserted his own claims to the book. Pope tried to answer confidence with confidence, but retreated far enough to ask Gilliver to allow Motte the share he desired.[3] Pope also approached Swift through Gay; for at the end of August, Gay passed on to Swift a paragraph on the subject which he said Pope had 'lately' sent to himself:

Motte and another idle fellow [i.e., Bowyer] I find have been writing to the dean to get him to give them some copyright which surely he will not be so indiscreet as to do when he knows my design [i.e., *The Third Volume*] (and has done these two months and more). Surely I should be a properer person to trust the distribution of his works with than to a common bookseller. Here will be nothing but the ludicrous and [little things], none of the political or any things of

[1] *Ibid.*, v. 255, n. 1.   [2] Dublin, 17 and 28 Aug. 1732; *ibid.*, pp. 254–6.
[3] 16 Aug. 1732; Sherburn III. 306.

consequence, which are wholly at his own disposal; but at any rate it would be silly in him to give a copyright to any which can only put the manner of publishing 'em hereafter out of his own and his friends' power into that of mercenaries.[1]

Although Swift's reply to this paragraph is missing, I think we may infer what he said, from Pope's language in a letter to Pilkington:

> the dean answered, *no man had any title from him more than* Curll; nevertheless I writ again, that Bowyer had something under his hand: He answered, *his intention* was nothing of a perpetuity, but a leave only to reprint to Mr Faulkner and him, with promise not to molest 'em by *any interest of his as to such pieces as were imputed to him.* He declares he had no thought of giving them a perpetuity, but a permission to the former end only, 'however Faulkner and Bowyer may have *contrived* to *turn* those *papers into a property.*'[2]

I believe the gist of what Swift told Pope is here. He was hiding his true relation to Faulkner, Pilkington, and Bowyer. He desired no confrontation with Pope. But he would have been glad to see *The Third Volume* displaced by a book made in accordance with his wishes by instruments he did not have to acknowledge.

Instead, *The Third Volume* had appeared on 4 October 1732 with poetry mainly by Swift, and prose by Swift and other writers. It was published by Motte and Gilliver. The next day, Pilkington (who had come to London in October[3]) executed a document reassigning to Bowyer his own rights in Swift's works.[4] All Bowyer could do at this point was to insist on his share of any profit. Pope showed his irritation but said he would 'leave the matter between the booksellers'.[5] It looks as if Bowyer was indeed paid off, and I assume that he in turn shared the money with Pilkington.

When Swift received copies of *The Third Volume*, he wrote angrily to Motte,

> Mr Pope had been for some months before writing to me that he thought it would be proper to publish another miscellany, for which

---

[1] 28 Aug. 1732; *ibid.*, p. 309.   [2] Oct. 1732; *ibid.*, pp. 323–4.
[3] Cf. Clarke's letters to Bowyer, in Williams v. 258–9.
[4] Williams v. 255, n. 1.   [5] Sherburn III. 324.

he then gave me reasons, that I did not well comprehend; nor do I remember that I was much convinced, because I did not know what fund he had for it, little imagining that some humorous or satirical trifles that I had writ here occasionally (and sent some to the press, while others were from stolen copies) would make almost six-sevenths of the whole verse part in the book; and the greatest part of the prose was written by other persons of this kingdom as well as myself. I believe I have told you, that no printer or bookseller hath any sort of property here. I have writ some things that would make people angry. I always sent them by unknown hands; the printer might guess, but he could not accuse me; he ran the whole risk, and well deserved the property, if he could carry it to London and print it there; but I am sure I could have no property at all. Some things; as that of the Soldier and Scholar, the Pastoral, and one or two more were written at a man of quality's house in the north who had the originals, while I had no copy, but they were given to the [Lord Lieutenant], and some others; so, copies ran, and Faulkner got them, and I had no property: but Faulkner made them his in London. I have sent a kind of certificate owning my consent to the publishing this last miscellany, against my will, and however it comes to pass there are not a few errata that quite alter the sense in those indifferent verses of mine. The best thing I writ as I think, is called A Libel on Dr D, and Lord [Carteret] which I find is not printed, because it gave great offence here; and your court was offended at one line relating to Mr Pope. I care not to say any more of this miscellany, and wish you may not be a loser by it. I find my name is put at length in some notes, which I think was wrong; but I am at too great distance to help it and must bear what I cannot remedy.[1]

In another letter to Motte, about the same time, Swift reiterated his dissatisfaction with *The Third Volume*, complained that the printing was incorrect, and added some fresh information:

I can assure you I had no advantage by any one of the four volumes, as I once hinted to you, and desire it may be a secret always. Neither do I in the least understand the reasons for printing this. I believe I told you formerly that booksellers here have no property; and I have

[1] 4 Nov. 1732; *ibid.*, IV. 82–3. 'Property' here means copyright; 'bookseller' means roughly what we mean by 'publisher'; the 'man of quality' is of course Acheson. Williams identifies the poems in his notes. I have altered the spelling and punctuation. The letter was not completed till 9 Jan. 1733.

cause to believe that some of our printers will collect all they think to be mine, and print them by subscription, which I will neither encourage nor oppose. But, as to the writings I have had long by me, I intend to leave them to certain friends, and that you shall be the publisher. I must tell you plainly I have now done with writing; verse grows troublesome; hints hard to be got; and not worth my time, since they will neither entertain my self nor be of public use.[1]

We may dismiss Swift's complaints about errata, for in a copy of the *Miscellanies* that he corrected, the emendations are not serious.[2] But I am persuaded that Swift felt dissatisfied with all four volumes of the *Miscellanies* and especially the last, or *Third Volume*. From what Pope wrote to both Swift and Pilkington, it appears, as we shall see, that he took alarm at the project of a separate collection of Swift's works and deliberately forestalled it. Whether he really believed that such a collection would be unauthorized by Swift is doubtful. I am not sure what to make of Swift's saying he got no 'advantage', or payment for his very great part in the *Miscellanies*. He may have assigned his share of the money to somebody else. I do not believe Pope made financial arrangements that excluded Swift.

Besides not wishing to alienate Pope, I think Swift was in fact glad to see even his trifles published; but he may have objected to their being lost in group anonymity. Months later, writing to Pope about Gay's works, Swift said,

> I would be glad to see his valuable works printed by themselves, those which ought not to be seen burned immediately, and the others that have gone abroad, printed separately like opuscula or rather be stifled and forgotten.[3]

In thinking about the *Miscellanies*, he may have applied similar principles to his own works. When he mentioned the 'writings I have long had by me', which he intended to leave to certain friends with Motte as the publisher, he was probably going back to his old principle that important literary works ought to be

---

[1] 9 Dec. 1732; *ibid.*, p. 89.
[2] This copy, formerly in the collection of Lord Rothschild, is now in the library of Trinity College, Cambridge.
[3] Sherburn V. 12.

published first in London. The declaration that he had done with writing I take to be partly the expression of a mood and partly a means of discouraging Motte from seeking new material from Swift.

Pope's statements to Swift and others by no means clear up the obscurities in the history of the *Miscellanies*. But they do establish some high probabilities. Writing to Swift in February 1733, he spoke of collecting his own works and showing that poets may be 'the most moral of mankind':

> A few loose things sometimes fall from them, by which censorious fools judge as ill of them, as possibly they can, for their own comfort: and indeed, when such unguarded and trifling *jeux d'esprit* have once got abroad, all that prudence or repentance can do, since they cannot be denied, is to put 'em fairly upon that foot; and teach the public (as we have done in the preface to the four volumes of miscellanies) to distinguish betwixt our studies and our idlenesses, our works and our weaknesses: That was the whole end of the last volume of Miscellanies, without which our former declaration in that preface. 'That these volumes contained all that we had ever offended in that way', would have been discredited. It went indeed to my heart, to omit what you called the Libel on Dr D—— and the best panegyric on myself, that either my own times or any other could have afforded, or will ever afford to me. The book as you observe was printed in great haste; the cause whereof was, that the booksellers here were doing the same, in collecting your pieces, the corn with the chaff; I don't mean that anything of yours is chaff, but with other wit of Ireland which was so, and the whole in your name. I meant principally to oblige a separation of what you writ seriously from what you writ carelessly; and thought my own weeds might pass for a sort of wild flowers, when bundled up with them.[1]

We know that Pope's true opinion of 'A Libel on Dr Delany' was not that conveyed here.[2] Few readers will credit Pope's declaration that he intended, in *The Third Volume*, to set careless works apart from important ones. But I willingly believe that Pope hastened the publication of *The Third Volume* because he knew Bowyer was preparing a similar book. The really ironical aspect of the evasions of Swift and Pope is that so far from

[1] 16 Feb. 1733; *ibid.*, III. 347–8.   [2] Cf. *ibid.*, p. 91.

settling any matters of textual authority, the *Miscellanies* spurred Swift on to take such labours out of the hands of both Pope and Motte, and to proceed with the scheme he touched on when he wrote to Motte at the end of 1732: a collected edition of his works to be published by subscription in Ireland.[1]

[1] Williams IV. 89.

Chapter Four

DEFENDING THE TEST

I. FRIENDS AND RELATIONS

It is hard to believe that Swift's double vision of his existence in Ireland was unconscious. I suspect that he thought any favourable account would weaken the pressure he tried to exert on English statesmen to help his nation. He certainly avoided giving to correspondents outside Ireland any report that made the country seem other than wretched. His new friend, Dean Brandreth, recently come over from England, sent Swift a happy description of his living, and Swift replied, 'I desire you will not write such accounts to your friends in England.'[1]

Speaking of himself to those in the mother kingdom, he seemed, almost automatically, to shut out light. In April 1733, he told Ford that for a month he had felt so giddy that he took medicine daily; his leg had a new disorder; he had lost 'half my memory, and all my invention'; his spirits were sunk too low for him to think of travel; his temper was remorselessly sour.[2] This was the very day when Mrs Pendarves wrote of dining, the week before, at Delville and finding Swift 'in *very good humour*'.[3]

In July the dean himself, even while detailing the decay of his health, gave Pope a sharp sketch of the comforts which held him at home; he offered the poet

> a very convenient warm apartment more open than usual in great cities, with a garden as large as your green plot that fronts the Thames, and another about two hundred yards further, larger than your great garden and with more air, but without any beauty. You should have small dinners of what you liked, and good wine.... The

---

[1] 30 Jun. 1732; *ibid.*, p. 34.   [2] 5 Apr. 1733; *ibid.*, pp. 136–8.
[3] Mrs Delany I. 432.

conveniences of taking the air, winter or summer, do far exceed those in London; for the two large strands just at two edges of the town, are as firm and dry in winter, as in summer.

To these physical amenities he added those of privilege and power:

> There are at least six or eight gentlemen of sense, learning, good humour and taste, able and desirous to please you, and orderly females, some of the better sort, to take care of you.... I have conveniences in [this] country for three horses and two servants, and many others which I have here at hand. I am one of the governors of all the hackney coaches, carts, and carriages, round this town, who dare not insult me like your rascally wagoners or coachmen, but give me the way; nor is there one lord or squire for a hundred of yours, to turn me out of the road, or run over me with their coach and six.... Then I walk the streets in peace without being jostled, nor ever without a thousand blessings from my friends the vulgar. I am Lord Mayor of one hundred and twenty houses, I am absolute lord of the greatest cathedral in the kingdom, am at peace with the neighbouring princes, the Lord Mayor of the city and the Archbishop of Dublin.... I can tell you with seriousness, that these advantages contribute to my ease, and therefore I value them.[1]

All this need not suggest that the style of Swift's daily life reached to luxury. Apart from Delville Thursdays and special occasions, he kept to a modest routine dictated partly by thrift and partly by fear of a fit of illness to embarrass him before company. 'I drink a whole bottle of wine every day,' he told Ford:

> a pint at noon, and the same at night. I dine constantly at home, with one or two friends whom I can be easy with, and therefore in that point sans consequence.[2]

When his health worried him, the 'friends' were likely to be the dean's vicar and his wife: 'I let no company see me', he said during such a spell,

> except Mr Worrall and his wife, who is a cheerful woman with a clear voice, she sends me vittels and they both generally dine with me, and sit the evenings.[3]

[1] 8 Jul. 1733; Sherburn III. 378–9.   [2] 20 Nov. 1733; Williams IV. 212.
[3] 15 Dec. 1728; *ibid.*, III. 306–7.

[753]

A real worry was a great financial negotiation arranged gradually over a period of years to accommodate a grandson of Swift's uncle Godwin. This young cousin, Deane Swift, was now about twenty-seven years old and owned 865 acres at Castlerickard, four miles from Trim. In 1700, Swift's cousin Willoughby had deposited £330 with his own brother Deane, father of the young man. The fund was to be invested and to become the marriage portion of Willoughby's daughter Hannah. By his will the older Deane Swift provided that Hannah should, on her marriage, receive £950, to be paid over a period of eight years. In 1714 he died, leaving a widow, Elizabeth, and the heir, his namesake.

About 1723 or 1724 Hannah married the Rev. Stafford Lightburne and requested the payment of her portion. Elizabeth refused, but a judgment was found against her for about £1100. In 1726, Jonathan Swift stepped in and assumed this debt against a mortgage for that sum on the Castlerickard property. During the next six or seven years he advanced more and more money to his cousin's son until Swift held mortgages totalling two thousand pounds in value, upon the estate.

At last, the widow, along with young Deane Swift and the Dean of St Patrick's himself, decided to let the whole of Castlerickard to a man named George Nugent, who would then pay them incomes of which Swift's share was to be £120 a year, or 6 per cent interest on his two thousand pounds. The complexities unfolded themselves for months, and Swift often felt anxious; but the final instruments were signed at last in December 1733.[1]

Amid the vagaries of health and finance, Swift's staple flow of clerical acquaintance, like the Worralls, visited him for friendly or professional purposes. The Rev. John Jebb, an Englishman and a protégé of the Earl of Oxford, came over, settled in Ireland, got solid preferments, and gave Swift particular pleasure as an intelligent, unpretentious gentleman.[2] 'I do not

[1] See *ibid.*, pp. 306–7 (15 Dec. 1728); IV. 139–40 (7 Apr. 1733), 215–16 (12 Dec. 1733) and memorials of deeds in Registry of Deeds, King's Inns, Dublin.
[2] *Ibid.*, pp. 35, 161, 248.

know a more modest, decent, well-behaved person; I see him often, like him very well,' Swift told the Earl.[1]

Stafford Lightburne, the son-in-law of Swift's cousin, had served as Swift's curate at Laracor since 1722, and was another easy acquaintance. In the early years of his deanship, Swift had not thought highly of Lightburne; but this opinion gradually mended; and in 1733 the dean at last managed to help him replace the curacy with a rectory in Westmeath.[2]

Politer society of course included Thomas Sheridan, who may have grown a little apart from Delany, perhaps because that old friend had helped to sponsor a new school in Dublin, competing with his own. In May 1733, the Irish and English newspapers reported a curious expedition which involved Swift, Sheridan, and Orrery. The three had ridden to a hill near Dublin in order to gain a view of the surrounding country:

> As they were mounting a rock, they observed a stream running through the middle of it, which fell into a natural basin, and was thence conveyed out again; so that they concluded the waters were still in some reservoir within the bounds of the hill, which must infallibly come to burst forth in time, and fall directly upon the city. The Doctor sent for a milking-pail to compute what quantity ran out, which held two gallons, and it was filled in the space of a minute, so that it runs in twenty-four hours 2,880 gallons. This multiplied by 365 produces 1,051,200, and shows the quantity that runs from the rock in a year; so that in three years, about the 15th of November, he computed that it must burst the body of the mountain, and emit an inundation which will run to all points of the Boyne, and greatly endanger the city of Dublin.[3]

Whether joke or hoax, the episode indicates how sprightly Swift could be while he was representing himself to Pope as burdened with 'an ill head, and a low spirit'.[4] The Delville Thursdays went on as well, of course; and during the summer Swift wondered about Pilkington. 'I never can get him to answer me how he lives,' the dean told Lord Mayor Barber; Pilkington wrote very seldom and although Swift had given him credit upon a friend in

---

[1] *Ibid.*, p. 161. [2] *Ibid.*, p. 150; Landa, p. 39.
[3] Ball IV. 442, n. 1. [4] 1 May 1733; Sherburn V. 13.

London (evidently, Motte) for 'any small sums of money', Pilkington had received most of the cash available. 'I hope', said Swift, 'he continues to behave himself well.' But the hope was to be disappointed.[1]

A strange event that may have involved his friends on both sides of the Irish Sea, explains part of Swift's concern for Pilkington. At the end of 1732 the chaplain had seen Motte, in order to collect twenty guineas assigned to him by Swift. A little while later, another person offered the bookseller a manuscript of *The Life and Genuine Character of Dr Swift*, but with Pilkington assuring Motte that the poem was Swift's work. As Motte told Swift,

> [The] Life and Character was offered me, though not by his own hands, yet by his means, as I was afterwards convinced by many circumstances: one was, that he corrected the proof sheets with his own hand; and as he said he had seen the original of that piece, I could not imagine he would have suffered your name to be put to it, if it had not been genuine.[2]

When the poem came out in London (April 1733), it carried the imprint of J. Roberts, a screen for Motte. But Swift's denials finally persuaded Motte that he had himself been deceived by Pilkington.[3]

Pope was not persuaded. In a cunningly worded statement much later, he said that Swift's *Epistle to a Lady* and the *Life and Character* emanated from 'the same hand'.[4] Pope's language sounds as if Motte supplied his information. But in any case we may be sure that Pilkington was the agent who conveyed *The Life and Genuine Character* to the bookseller and that he was following Swift's instructions.

Soon after the London publication, the poem went on sale in Dublin under the imprint of Swift's old confrère Edward

---

[1] July 1733; Williams IV. 175.   [2] 31 Jul. 1735; *ibid.*, p. 371.

[3] Lord Oxford wrote, 'April 12 1733' on his copy. The poem was advertised in the *Daily Journal*, 20, 23 Apr. 1733. Motte was the bookseller, or 'publisher' in the modern sense. Roberts was simply a retail distributor, one of the meanings of 'publisher' in Swift's era. See *Poems* II. 541–4, which I correct; also Williams IV. 371.

[4] 15 Sept. 1734; Sherburn III. 432. The reference is of course to Swift's *Epistle to a Lady* and not to Pope's poems of the same title.

Waters. Yet on 15 May 1733 Swift issued a newspaper advertisement utterly denying that he had produced it.[1] He wrote in similar terms to a number of correspondents—Motte, Lord Carteret, Lord Oxford, the Duchess of Queensberry, Pope, and others.[2] In the letter to Pope he seems in the most strenuous style to repudiate the poem. But when closely examined, his words only declare that these verses are not like *Verses on the Death of Dr Swift*.[3]

Pope replied with delicious ambiguity:

> The man who drew your character and printed it here, was not much in the wrong in many things he said of you: yet he was a very impertinent fellow, for saying them in words quite different from those you had yourself employed before on the same subject: for surely to alter your words is to prejudice them; and I have been told, that a man himself can hardly say the same thing twice over with equal happiness: Nature is so much a better thing than artifice.[4]

The whole affair has some elements of a harmless swindle; and the published text is dated 1 April, a day which Swift habitually distinguished with practical jokes. But by his denials he may have hoped to accomplish some half-serious ends. We cannot doubt that he intended to mislead his readers. As Faulkner pointed out, the poem has features that Swift habitually condemned: triplets, dashes, 'breaks' (or gaps in continuity). It was also published with a dedication to Pope that was calculated to throw readers off the track.[5]

My suspicion is that to begin with, Swift wished to reserve the privilege of publishing the piece to himself without offending Pope by his failure to contribute it to *The Third Volume* of the *Miscellanies*. This would explain why Pilkington, more or less known to be Swift's agent, did not himself offer the copy to Motte, even though one assumes that Pilkington was to have the profit of the publication. But Swift would also have been balanc-

---

[1] On 1 May 1733 Swift says the poem had been on sale in Dublin for a fortnight; *ibid.*, v. 11. For the advertisement see the *Dublin Journal*, 15 May 1733.

[2] Cf. Williams IV. 161, 162–3, 371; Sherburn III. 432; v. 10–11 (1 May 1733).

[3] 1 May 1733; *ibid.*, p. 10. The same observation holds for the statement to Lord Oxford (Williams IV. 161).

[4] 1 Sept. 1733; Sherburn III. 384.   [5] See *Poems* II. 542–4.

ing accounts with Pope for his omitting *A Libel on Dr Delany* from *The Last Volume*. The lack of bite in the political allusions, combined with the lack of praise in the dedication to Pope, would make an ironical contrast to the *Libel*. At the same time, the appearance of an April Fool joke would remove any suggestion of spite.[1]

Swift may have talked like a stay-at-home; but the labour that went into the elaborate hoax of *The Life and Genuine Character* still left him ample energy for his social rounds. Swift's account book for 1732–3 has entry after entry for chairs and coaches, innumerable payments to the Worralls for meals with them, entries for dinners given and trips taken. There were excursions with Lord Orrery in the spring.[2] During the summer of 1733 he also visited Howth and the Grange (between Dublin and Howth), which was the home of Lady Acheson's mother.[3]

From 8 to 11 April he was at Castlerickard, inspecting the property of his young kinsman. From 15 to 19 May he was at Trim for the visitation of the Bishop of Meath. From 25 to 28 July he was at Belcamp—I assume, for a holiday.[4] But the most significant entries are for a series of visits to Mrs Whiteway.[5] It is clear that this friendship—one of the most valuable friendships of his life—was thriving.

Toward the middle of 1733 Swift's female society shrank in various ways. Mrs Barber had intended to leave for England long before, but fits of the gout kept her in Dublin until the summer. By April 1733, Mrs Pendarves was ready to depart, and thought of her as a fine addition to the party: 'She will be an excellent companion for us, for she has constant spirits and good humour.'[6] However, Mrs Barber lingered while Mrs Pendarves, Anne Donnellan, and Miss Kelly sailed on 10 May.[7]

For a long time, the clever Mrs Pendarves kept up her friendship with Swift by correspondence. But the fragile Miss Kelly

---

[1] For a similar argument, see Herbert Davis, 'Verses on the Death of Dr Swift', *Book-Collector's Quarterly* 2 (March–May 1931), 57–73.

[2] Williams IV. 144–6, 157.   [3] Ball V. 9, n. 1.

[4] *Accounts 1732–3*, under dates.

[5] 23 Nov. 1732; 23 Jan., 2, 22 Mar., 4 May, 22 Jun., 17 Jul. 1733.

[6] Mrs Delany I. 407.   [7] *Dublin Journal*, 12 May 1733.

could not. She moved from one resort to another, steadily weakening and growing depressed; and at last she died of consumption, 31 October 1733. Her relation to Swift is a dim shadow of Vanessa's, whose attitudes and even phrases seem to echo in a letter which Miss Kelly wrote, half a year before her end, begging Swift to forgive some offensive remark she thought she had made and to assure her of his friendship.[1] Separated from her mother, neglected by her father, shortlived, she belongs to the pattern of her famous predecessor.[2]

Mrs Barber remained a favourite. On 30 June 1733 Swift had dinner with her.[3] In the middle of July, advertisements began appearing in the *Dublin Journal*, stating that Mrs Barber wished to close the subscription list for her poems, which were to be printed 'immediately'. The announcement was reiterated through the summer and into the autumn.[4] But around August the lady at last managed to embark for England, perhaps with Orrery, who sailed on the eighth.[5] Helping to fill out the subscription, Swift gave her letters of introduction to a great chain of his English acquaintance: Lord Oxford, Lady Granville, Lady Betty Germaine, Lady Worsley, Lord Mayor Barber, as well as Pope, Gay, and Arbuthnot. He also handed her a packet of manuscripts which she was to convey to Pilkington.

At this ill-considered time, Laetitia Pilkington decided, willy-nilly, to join her husband. One reason for her feeling cheerful enough to indulge in such an escapade may be that in July he had been presented to the rectory of St Mark's, Dublin.[6] She placed her three children with her parents, wrote to Matthew, and confided to Mrs Barber that she would accompany her. Although the journey passed safely and pleasantly enough, and although the Rev. Mr Pilkington did not fail to meet his wife, Laetitia discovered, fairly soon after reaching London, that he did not like to spend many hours with her. As the end of his year's chaplaincy approached, she hoped they might go home to Dublin together. But Pilkington had made a friend of Sir

---

[1] Williams IV. 155–7.   [2] *Ibid.*, p. 203, n. 1.
[3] *Accounts 1732–3*, under date.   [4] 14 Jul. and following.
[5] *Dublin Journal*, 11 Aug. 1733.   [6] *Ibid.*, 10 Jul. 1733.

Edward Walpole, the dissolute second son of the prime minister; and through him the young parson dreamed of securing some kind of preferment. About 1 December 1733, Laetitia had to start back by herself.[1] Even the discreet and worldly Lord Mayor evinced surprise. 'Why Mr Pilkington should send his wife home in the midst of winter', he said to Swift, 'or why he should stay here an hour after her, are questions not easily answered. I am not of his counsel.'[2]

Barber, whose term as Lord Mayor had ended, also gave Swift an account of how generously he had treated Pilkington, revealing that the chaplain had got more from his little preferment than anyone before him. But Barber at the same time described Pilkington's conduct in a way that should have alarmed Swift:

> How much he may be a gainer by coming over, I can't tell; but if he had pleased to have lived near the Hall, as he might, in a lodging of ten or twelve pounds a year, he need not have kept a man [i.e., a servant], (for I had more for show than business) nor given the extravagant sum of thirty pounds a year for lodgings; he might have saved something in those articles. Had he lived in the City, I should now and then have had the favour of his company in an evening; but his living from me brought him into company, and among the rest into that of Mr Edward Walpole, from whom he has great dependences.[3]

II. CHURCH AND STATE

Although Irish and English politics produced no disaster for Swift during the middle and end of 1733, he played his hand according to his ordinary rules. One moment of euphoria brushed him when the Excise Bill died. Walpole had tried to extend the scheme of bonded warehouses to cover wine and tobacco. Every force in the opposition rose against him. His majorities dropped quickly. It looked as if he might lose the House of Lords. In April he postponed further consideration of

---

[1] Pilkington I. 155–68.   [2] Williams IV. 209.
[3] *Ibid.*, p. 208. Hall means Guildhall.

the bill until after Parliament should have been prorogued. The excise was defeated; Walpole was defeated.

When the dean heard of the happy issue, he celebrated it with a drama tidily reported in the *Dublin Journal*:

> Upon the news of the excise bill being thrown out in England, about a dozen young men of the liberty of St Patricks, joined together to have a bonfire on the steeple, and another before the Dean's house; where they gave a barrel of ale in tubs to express their joy, and the following healths were drank with great solemnity, and at the close of each,
> A health to that *worthy patriot the DRAPIER, who saved our nation from ruin.*

Seven or eight toasts were drunk, most of them relating to the excise. I quote some which were not so connected, because I think they disclose Swift's hand reaching out to the common people and defending the church:

> To the honest people of Ireland, who opposed the wooden scheme of brass money....
> There were likewise several healths drunk relating to the [bishops], and the [clergy] of Ireland, which we cannot remember.[1]

Meanwhile, as dean and Drapier, Swift also applied his weight to municipal government. Humphrey French, the Lord Mayor of Dublin, 1732–3, impressed Swift as 'a hero in his kind'.[2] Of French's justice, charity, and patriotism several accounts appeared in the newspapers. About the beginning of May, the dean, who had not yet met him, presented the Lord Mayor with 'an ox of more than ordinary size', as a compliment to 'so great a lover of liberty and his country'.[3]

When Samuel Burton, M.P. for Dublin, died, French put himself forward as candidate. The Duke of Dorset was to arrive in mid-September, and Parliament would soon be sitting; so Swift must have felt that the choice was critical. He published a pamphlet, *Advice to the Free-men of ... Dublin.*[4] Here he recom-

---

[1] 21 Apr. 1733.   [2] Williams v. 83.
[3] *Dublin Journal*, 12 May 1733; I assume the 'certain reverend dean' is Swift.
[4] Davis XIII. 79–85; probably published in Sept. 1733; see *Dublin Journal*, 29 Sept., denying the suppression of the pamphlet.

mended French not only as native-born and having no employment that bound him to the English interest, but also as a mayor who had shown 'more virtue, more activity, more skill, in one year's government of the city, than a hundred years can equal'.[1] French was duly elected.

With the coming of autumn 1733, new and well-founded rumours blew about that the Nonconformists would move Parliament to repeal the Test. The session was to open on 4 October. Dorset, who arrived on 17 September, was lazy, indiscreet, and inept all at once. He openly informed the Dissenters and office-holders that the English ministry had instructed him to take off the Test.[2] On 1 October the *Dublin Journal* carried a notice, perhaps suggested by Swift, that 'great numbers of the most considerable Dissenting teachers and elders' were in town for the familiar purpose.[3] While Boulter believed their success was 'very doubtful',[4] Swift wrote to Ford,

> It is reckoned that the Test will be repealed. It is said that £30000 have been returned from England; and £20000 raised here from servants, labourers, farmers, squires, and Whigs &c to promote the good work. Half the bishops will be on their side. Pamphlets pro and con fly about. One is called *The Presbyterians Plea of Merit Examined*: perhaps if you saw it, you might guess the writer .... but we all conclude the affair desperate. For the money is sufficient among us—to abolish Christianity itself.[5] All the people in power are determined for the repeal, and some of your acquaintance, formerly Tories, are now on the same side. I have been in no condition to stir in it.[6]

Of course, *The Presbyterians Plea of Merit* belonged to Swift. Faulkner published it about 5 November, and it reached a fifth edition by Swift's birthday.[7] Writing it probably in September,[8]

---

[1] Davis XIII. 84.   [2] Boulter II. 108 (Dublin, II. 86).

[3] Cf. the parallels with Davis XII. 275 and 278.

[4] Boulter II. 107 (Dublin, 85).

[5] The expression is a good clue to the meaning of Swift's *Argument against Abolishing Christianity*.

[6] 20 Nov. 1733; Williams IV. 210–11.

[7] *Dublin Journal*, 3, 6 Nov.; 1, 4 Dec., etc. According to the *Dublin News Letter*, it was published 5 Nov.

[8] He refers to the approaching session of Parliament.

Swift distributed his arguments in their usual formation. The essay amounts to a tendentious précis of British political history since 1640, destroying the boasts of the Presbyterians that they had given decisive aid first in restoring Charles II and later in establishing William III.[1] So firmly does it stay with Swift's early views that the essay could be used as a commentary on the ecclesiastical allegory of *A Tale of a Tub*.

Through his very first paragraph Swift fixes the channels of his reasoning and shows how little the strength of his language had declined as he ended his sixty-sixth year:

> We have been told in the common news-papers, that all attempts are to be made this sessions by the Presbyterians, and their abettors, for taking off the Test; as a kind of preparatory step, to make it go down smoother in England. For, if once *their light would so shine*, the Papists, delighted with the blaze, would all come in, and dance about it. This I take to be a prudent method; like that of a discreet Physician, who first gives a new medicine to a *dog*, before he prescribes it to a human creature.[2]

Thus he establishes several rhetorical axes: Ireland against England, Anglican against non-Anglican, and the period 1640–1710 against 1710–30.

So the repeal of the Test would benefit England to the disadvantage of Ireland; it would benefit the Roman Catholics and Presbyterians at the expense of the Anglicans; and it would benefit treacherous opportunists at the sacrifice of old and loyal allies. Employing his most vigorous and economical prose, Swift in this way pursues the technique of associating his enemies with the powers which both of them are in principle committed to repudiate: Papists with Dissenters, etc. This is one of his normal but most cunning devices. One remembers how in *A Tale of a Tub* Swift had identified experimental scientists with quacks and opposed both to traditional moral philosophy. Toward the end of the *Presbyterians Plea* he reverses this approach; and in one of his most sudden twists, he kindly admonishes the enemy that they are mistaken if they suppose that the end of the

[1] Davis XII. 261–79.   [2] *Ibid.*, p. 263.

Test would mean a beginning of profit for them, since the advantage of an Englishman's (or Scotsman's) birth would smother all their Nonconformist but Irish claims to preferment:

> For, after all, what assurance can a *Scottish* northern Dissenter, born on *Irish* ground, have, that he shall be treated with as much favour as a TRUE SCOT born beyond the Tweed.[1]

This theme, and the device of identifying Nonconformists with Roman Catholics, became foundations for a further tract and a fragment, neither of them published till years had passed. The brief fragment, 'Some Few Thoughts concerning the Repeal of the Test', contains only an extension of the warning that how few soever might be the employments flung to the natives of Ireland by the British, these would be scrambled for (if the Test were repealed) by a staggering variety of sects—including Quakers—and only an infinitesimal crumb would fall to each denomination.[2]

The full essay, *Reasons Humbly Offered to the Parliament of Ireland*, is dated November 1733.[3] Here Swift assumes the part of a Roman Catholic, and argues that the merits of the Presbyterians fall far below those of the Papists:

> If the reformation of religion be founded upon rebellion against the King, without whose consent, by the nature of our constitution, no law can pass: if this reformation be introduced by only one of the three estates, I mean the Commons, and not by one half even of those Commons, and this by the assistance of a rebel army: Again, if this reformation were carried on by the exclusion of nobles, both lay and spiritual, (who constitute the other two parts of the three estates) by the murder of their king, and by abolishing the whole system of government; the Catholics cannot see why the successors of those schismatics, who are universally accused by all parties except themselves, and a few infamous abettors, for still retaining the same principles in religion and government, under which their predecessors acted, should pretend to a better share of civil or

---

[1] *Ibid.*, p. 275. N.B. the echo of *The Advantages Propos'd by Repealing the Sacramental Test*, *ibid.*, pp. 250–1.

[2] *Ibid.*, pp. 297–9.

[3] *Ibid.*, pp. 281–95. It must have been written after the *Presbyterians Plea*, because both that pamphlet and a printed reply to it are mentioned in *Reasons Humbly Offered*, *ibid.*, pp. 291–2.

military trust, profit and power, than the Catholics, who, during all that period of twenty years, were continually persecuted with the utmost severity, merely on account of their loyalty and constant adherence to kingly power.[1]

Part of the essay is taken up with an ironic review of Irish history, showing how innocent and oppressed the Roman Catholics have been; and the rest is a demonstration that the Presbyterians' arguments apply better to the Roman Catholics than to themselves; e.g.,

> The belief of transubstantiation *is a matter purely of religion and conscience, which doth not affect the political interest of society as such. Therefore, why should the rights of conscience, whereof God is the sole Lord, be subject to human jurisdiction?* And why should *God* be deprived of this right over a Catholic's conscience any more than over that of any other Dissenter?[2]

Meanwhile, parliamentary events were showing Boulter to have made a sounder forecast than Swift.

At the end of September, Coghill had written,

> We are much alarmed about the repeal of the Test. My Lord Lieutenant has not declared anything upon that head, but I think it will not pass; but all the Presbyterians are full of it, and the town swarms with their parsons.[3]

Dorset's speech opening the session (4 October 1733) had not concealed the government's plan, and he hoped to bring on the motion only after the House of Commons voted the money bills. More than two weeks later, Coghill wrote,

> [My] opinion is, that till the Committee of Accounts have made their report, and the money bill sent to the Castle my Lord Lieutenant will not let anything be moved in it [i.e., the repeal of the Test], and whether he will then think it advisable, time will shew.[4]

But the agents of the Dissenters, especially in the north, acted so boldly and visibly; the Anglican clergy responded so bel-

---

[1] *Ibid.*, pp. 290–1.   [2] *Ibid.*, p. 291.
[3] Letter to Southwell, 26 Sept. 1733; B.L. Add. MS. 21, 123, fol. 53^v. Spelling and punctuation altered in all quotations from Coghill's letters.
[4] Letter to Southwell, 20 Oct. 1733; *ibid.*, fol. 63.

ligerently; the pamphlet war ran so fast; Dorset organized his government so poorly, that the Lord Lieutenant lost control of this campaign. Besides Swift, many other prominent churchmen—including Tisdall and Archbishop Synge—wrote openly damning the government's manœuvres. Coghill reported, '[A] paper war is begun, and I think with less prudence on our side then on that of the Dissenters.'[1] Some of the rebuttals from the Dissenters were directed specifically against Swift. A shrewd pamphleteer exposed the dean's inconsistent touch of sympathy with republicans and his distaste for Anglican churchmen when they were also zealous Whigs.[2] At least one broadside ballad was written to condemn him for supporting the Test and ridiculing the Dissenters.[3]

On Tuesday, 11 December, the Commons voted not to entertain 'after Friday next' any bills for revoking any part of the anti-Popery laws—among which was the Test Act. Coghill wrote,

> [On] Tuesday last, to which day the call of the House was adjourned, Sir Richard Mead said that everybody knew what the call of the House was put off [for] from time to time, for they had been threatened with a bill to be brought in which was of such consequence as to require the attendance of every member, and that he therefore hoped the House would consider of some proper method to have such bill moved for, that the members may not be obliged to attend now when the greatest part of the business of the session was over, and Christmas approaching. The members called aloud to him to name the bill he meant. He told them it was that to repeal the Sacramental Test, and finding the House in a good disposition he pursued his motion and proposed that no heads of a bill or a bill be ... received this session after Friday (that is tomorrow) to repeal any of the acts against the growth of Popery or any clause therein, (for you must know the test clause is one of those acts). The Solicitor General, who is for the repeal, endeavoured to get a longer day, and Robin Allen moved for a week longer. The Solicitor pressed only for

---

[1] Letter to Southwell, 23 Nov. 1733; *ibid.*, fol. 73.   [2] Davis XII. xlv–xlvi.

[3] It is among the so-called Burgage (co. Carlow) broadsides in the library of Trinity College, Dublin, press-mark OLS 194.2.3, no. 24. The title is 'A New Ballad. Supposed to be Wrote by a Reverend D—n in the North'. It is dated 1733 but does not appear in D. F. Foxon's bibliography.

Monday but they were so ill heard that the question Sir Richard proposed was so loudly called for, that they would not hear anybody speak against it, and it was carried without a division, for the no's did [not] exceed a dozen.[1]

On Wednesday and Thursday the Dissenters' lobby met, and decided finally to abandon their pressure. Archbishop Hoadly was in favour of repeal but said that all his friends and acquaintances were against it.[2] Boulter was struck by the unanimity of the opposition. It was thought very dangerous, he told Newcastle, to unite so solid a majority against the government, 'since it was not so certain when such an union might be dissolved'.[3]

Yet during the same session, the Commons considered a bill which united the government, the Dissenters, and the landlords against the clergy. This was ostensibly for 'the further regulation and improvement of the flaxen and hempen manufacture', and was brought in on 12 December 1733.[4] Since linen belonged among the few thriving Irish industries tolerated by England, its encouragement had become an accepted policy in Parliament. But because the northern Presbyterians produced almost the whole of the manufacture, Swift seldom emphasized its value. He had no reason to love an industry by which sectarians throve; and one is struck by how seldom he showed any but a derogatory concern with it. He even complained that flax and hemp impoverished the soil and harmed agriculture.

One means proposed of rewarding hemp- and flax-growers was to reduce the tithe on their crops. By this principle the legislators were pleasing the landlords in general (who disliked yielding to the church a profit which they might otherwise enjoy themselves) and the Presbyterian Nonconformists in particular—who disliked paying tithes to an institution which they repudiated. Among the conventional arguments of the clergy, several propositions kept bobbing up: that tithes, being of divine institution, could not be altered by laymen; that tithes

---

[1] Letter to Southwell, 13 Dec. 1733; B.L. Add. MS. 21,123, fol. 76ᵛ.
[2] *Ibid.*, fol. 77; letter from Coghill to Lord Egmont, 15 Dec. 1733, *ibid.*, fol. 79.
[3] Boulter II. 110 (Dublin, II. 87); cf. Davis XII. xlvi; *Poems* III. 810.
[4] That is, leave was granted to introduce heads of a bill, etc.

were property as land was, and except as punishment for a crime, the clergy could not legally be deprived of them; that it was unconstitutional to make a single class suffer for a general responsibility.

But the bill as offered contained a peculiarly menacing provision: that this tithe be fixed by a cash equivalent, or 'modus'. Since gold and silver perpetually declined in value, the establishment of a modus would mean a continuous shrinkage of clerical incomes. Swift had always been preoccupied with the effects of natural monetary inflation, and he feared the flax modus as deeply as, ten years before, he had feared the proposed lengthening of ecclesiastical leases.

While the bill was pending, Swift and several other churchmen petitioned the House of Commons against it. But although their counsel was heard on 29 December, the modus, as well as the bill proper, survived in the Commons. In the Lords, however, the modus did not pass. Coghill said the main reason was the sense that it was unfair for the clergy to have to pay for the encouragement of flax and hemp when the laity gave nothing.[1]

About 8 January 1734 Swift published a pamphlet on the bill: *Some Reasons against the Bill for Settling the Tyth of Hemp*.[2] With it he included *Some Further Reasons*, etc., drawn up apparently by others but with his aid. In these papers he rehearsed the usual arguments, reducing the issues to constitutional principles and moral implications. The modus, he said, would be equivalent to a tax on one part of the nation which was already carrying its full burden of parliamentary impositions; and it contradicted Magna Carta, the first clause of which guaranteed as inviolable the rights of Holy Church. Swift also predicted that the modus would mean no advantage to the linen industry because as the tithe vanished, the landlords would take up the slack with a rise in rents.

Appealing seriously and directly to the House of Commons, Swift had to write with unnatural restraint. As Landa says, the

[1] Landa, pp. 134-5.
[2] Davis XIII. 93-108; advertised as 'just published' in the *Dublin Journal*, 8-12 Jan. 1734.

result is 'not so much a proud and spirited defence as a plea that an impoverished priesthood be not further impoverished by invidious treatment'.[1] But there is a touch of his nature in the dry observation that the bill if enacted would reduce the value of the King's ecclesiastical patronage—

> whereby the viceroys will have fewer good preferments to bestow on their dependents, as well as upon the kindred of Members [i.e., of Parliament], who may have a sufficient stock of that sort of merit, whatever it may be, which may in future times most prevail.[2]

This irony was allowable, no doubt, as supporting the Irish interest in Parliament. Anyhow, the pamphlet could have had no influence on the debate since the crucial vote was taken before the date of publication.

A serjeant-at-law and M.P. named Richard Bettesworth had spoken strongly in favour of the bill; and it seems that he coupled his own name, as 'brother serjeants', with that of the dean's friend, Henry Singleton, whom Swift described as 'one of the first among the worthiest persons in this kingdom; of great honour, justice, truth, good-sense, good-nature, and knowledge in his faculty'.[3] Since the Dissenters often joined themselves with the Established Church as 'brother Protestants', Swift made the expression the theme of a lampoon called 'On the Words—Brother Protestants, and Fellow Christians'.[4] It got into circulation around New Year's Eve,[5] and was based on the fable of a lump of horse dung floating beside an apple in a flood and saying, 'How we apples swim.'[6] The object of Swift's attack is the Scottish Presbyterians; but he includes a series of analogies from various callings, and among them closes in on the anti-clerical M.P.:

---

[1] Landa, p. 132.   [2] Davis XIII. 103.
[3] Williams IV. 300.   [4] *Poems* II. 809–13.
[5] We may infer the date from the fact that, according to the *Dublin Journal* of 8 Jan. 1734, visitors called at the deanery on Saturday, 5 Jan., to affirm their support of Swift against Bettesworth. Since Swift mentions Monday as the day when Bettesworth called to protest against the poem and to deliver the threat that provoked the friendly visits, the piece must have been written before 31 Dec. 1733.
[6] Cf. 'Of the Apple and the Horse-Turd', Fable xx in *Poems on Affairs of State*, II. (1703), 85–6.

Thus at the bar that booby Bettesworth,
Though half a crown o'er-pays his sweat's worth;
Who knows in law, nor text, nor margent,
Calls Singleton his brother serjeant.[1]

Bettesworth soon got hold of the poem and decided to punish the disorderly dean. The only firsthand account of what he did comes to us from Swift, who put it in a letter to Dorset which sounds more triumphant than trustworthy:

On Monday last week, toward evening, there came to the deanery one Mr Bettesworth; who, being told by the servants that I was gone to a friend's house [i.e., the Worralls', nearby], went thither to enquire for me, and was admitted into the street-parlour. I left my company in the back-room, and went to him. He began with asking me, whether I were the author of certain verses, wherein he was reflected on. The singularity of the man in his countenance, manner, action, style and tone of voice, made me call to mind that I had once seen him, about two or three years ago, at Mr Ludlow's country-house. But I could not recollect his name, and of what calling he might be I had never heard. I therefore desired to know who, and what he was; said I had heard of some such verses, but knew no more. He then signified to me, that he was a serjeant-at-law, and a Member of Parliament. After which he repeated the lines that concerned him with great emphasis; said, I was mistaken in one thing, for he assured me he was no booby, but owned himself to be a coxcomb. However, that being a point of controversy wherein I had no concern, I let it drop. As to the verses, he insisted, that by his taste, and skill in poetry, he was as sure I writ them as if he had seen them fall from my pen. But I found the chief weight of his argument lay upon two words that rhymed to his name, which he knew could come from none but me. He then told me, that since I would not own the verses, and that since he could not get satisfaction by any course of law, he would get it by his pen, and show the world what a man I was. When he began to grow over-warm and eloquent, I called in the gentleman of the house, from the room adjoining, and the serjeant, going on with less turbulence, went away.[2]

The *Dublin Journal* (prompted, one assumes, by Swift) carried the tale further. On Saturday, 5 January 1734, a number of 'persons of honour and quality' called on the Dean of St

[1] Ll. 25-8.   [2] Williams IV. 220.

Patrick's 'in a public manner', demonstrating whom they sided with in the little duel.[1] The Friday evening that followed, many residents of the liberty of St Patrick's, along with other citizens, waited on the dean because of 'a report, that a certain person had openly threatened in all companies to stab or maim him'. They left a suspiciously well-worded document, signed by thirty-one persons, in which they promised to 'defend the life and limbs of the said Dean against the said man, and all his ruffians and murderers'. Swift, who was confined with a dizzy spell, sent down a reply from his sick bed, unctuously thanking and blessing them.[2] At the end of January yet another delegation, from neighbouring parishes, presented the dean with a similar document.[3] Swift himself went after the loudmouthed M.P. with a series of ferocious attacks in verse.[4] Friends of Swift co-operated by writing scurrilities about the wretched man, and the affair trailed off in a wake of humiliating publicity for Bettesworth.

III. POETRY AND POLITICS

In London, meanwhile, Swift's versified politics found a less farcical reception. When Mrs Barber went to England in August 1733, Swift gave her a packet he wanted delivered to Matthew Pilkington. Laetitia writes that the day after she herself joined her husband,

> [A] lady who came over with me [i.e., Mrs Barber], called on us; and Mr [Pilkington] and she had some private chat. When she was gone he told me, she had brought him a letter and some poetry from the Dean, which he had ordered him to dispose of, and put the money in his own pocket.[5]

Among the six poems the poor lady brought was the magnificent *On Poetry: A Rapsody.*[6] To understand what happened when this was published, one must review its composition and meaning.

[1] *Dublin Journal*, 8 Jan. 1734.
[2] Davis v. 341–3. Cf. the *Dublin Journal*, 12 Jan. 1734.
[3] *Dublin Journal*, 29 Jan. 1734.   [4] See *Poems* III. 814–19.
[5] Pilkington I. 157.   [6] *Poems* II. 639–59.

Along with the *Rapsody* came three of Swift's filthy anti-feminine satires, as well as *An Epistle to a Lady* and the poem on Edward Young's *Universal Passion*. Swift's powerful work could be read as a reply to Young. The damning fault of the several satires making up *The Universal Passion* is that on the one hand the poet condemns the vicious manners of English society; but on the other hand he celebrates the supposed virtues of the royal family, of Walpole (to whom the seventh satire is fulsomely dedicated), and a sad number of peers, courtiers, and politicians. In Swift's neatly balanced poem 'On Reading Dr Young's Satires', the inconsistency is frigidly exposed. If the age has such virtuous leaders, it is of course singularly blessed. If it has such a corrupt social order, it is desperately cursed. The irony is too insistent for a reader to mistake which of the views is Swift's true judgment. The force of the poem springs from the conciseness of the language, the steadiness of the tone, and the elegant matching of point to point between the first part and the second.

Although we know the *Rapsody* left the author's hands in August 1733, we cannot be sure when Swift wrote it. Parts sound much like *Directions for a Birth-day Song*, which was dated 30 October 1729. Parts sound like the second half of *An Epistle to a Lady*, which seems to belong to the period 1732–3. References to Cibber as laureate suggest a later date than 1731.[1]

In the opening lines the poem appears to be general satire on the vocation of poet. Swift contrasts the rarity of talent with the frequency of poetasters yearning for fame. He also sets the extraordinary gifts required for poetry against the ill fortune visited upon genius.

After line 70, a second section gives us the voice of the veteran poet stepping back and offering a young beginner advice on how to proceed. The topic remains literary; and the wise, blasé speaker runs over the problems of self-criticism, submission of the finished work to a bookseller, publication, and alas recep-

---

[1] Cf. lines 56, 305. Cibber was made laureate in December 1730. In l. 305, 'annual birthday strains' might imply that he had been laureate for more than two royal birthdays.

tion. The tone grows sour, the language grows coarse, as the veteran imagines the beginner listening incognito to coffee-house verdicts on his accomplishment.

In the middle of this second part the veteran suddenly assumes that as the beginner tries a second and third time to make a success, his subjects must be political, with initial letters used as transparent disguises for his targets. Under the surface of poetical education, we notice a moral distance between the idealism of the young poet and the evil of the persons and events he has to handle. Readers, the veteran declares, will wonder whom the poet means by his letters and dashes; but the alternatives become equivalents:

> A public, or a private *robber*;
> A *statesman*, or a South-Sea *jobber*.
> A *prelate* who no God believes;
> A [Parliament], or den of thieves.
> [A house of peers, or gaming crew,
> A griping monarch, or a Jew.]
> A pick-purse at the bar, or bench;
> A duchess, or a suburb-wench.[1]

The career of the young poet now changes by necessity from literary aspiration to self-promotion. At this point the fundamental antithesis of the whole poem emerges: it is between the ideal integrity of the true poet and the essential corruption of the class that must patronize him if he is to survive. Here, then is the answer to Edward Young. Here too is the reason for the parodies and echoes of ancient and modern authors which abound in the *Rapsody*.[2]

Glancing at the parodies, allusions, and echoes, we see they

---

[1] Ll. 161–6. Cf. the similar device in *Gulliver's Travels*, III, Ch. vi, the paragraph on decoding (Davis XI. 191).

[2] Cf. Swift, ll. 209–18, and *Aeneid* VI. 299–300; Swift, l. 215, and *Aeneid* VI. 895; Swift, ll. 389–96, and Pope, *Dunciad* II. 263–300, also *Peri Bathous* VI. 5; Swift, ll. 419–22, and Eusden, 'A Poem Humbly Inscribed to H.R.H. Prince Frederick', p. 6 (on beard); Swift, ll. 419–24, and *Aeneid* VI. 769–70, 794–5, 798–9, 808–9, also Horace, *Epistles* I. xii. 27–8; Swift, ll. 432–3, and Eusden, 'An Ode for the Birthday, 1721', p. 4; Swift, l. 446, and Ennius, *Annales*. My information comes from Swift's own notes; from James L. Tyne, 'Swift's Mock Panegyrics in "On Poetry"', *PLL* 10 (1974), 279–86; and from Schakel, pp. 150–6.

are of two sorts. Some lines recall those of Virgil and Horace in praise of Augustus, of Ennius in praise of Quintus Fabius (Cunctator), or of ancient poetry generally associated with the praise of virtuous men. Other lines are parodies of Eusden's panegyrics, or else they merely evoke the fatuous compliments of nearly all eulogies of monarchs. On the one side, then, is not so much the example of Augustus the individual, as the ideal moral character called up by ancient poets celebrating his reign. On the other side are the grotesque hyperboles applied by modern poetasters to the rulers of England.

On both sides we discover ambiguities. The poem has so many sneers at monarchs that Caesar Augustus can be no exception. Any apparent difference between the Roman emperor and George II dwindles in the face of this truth.[1] From the nature of human society, men at the centre of power simply cannot have integrity; they cannot embody the virtues that a leader needs and that a properly inspired poet yearns for. Swift may smile at the idealism of true poets; he does not sneer at it.

On the other side Swift offers two conceptions of the poet. At his best the poet gives men a vision of the heights of moral heroism. But when he fails, he panders to men's natural vices and becomes an instrument of corruption. Eusden stands against Pope as a line of Ennius about Fabius saving his country stands against its application to Walpole as a villain destroying his country.

While the veteran guides the tyro through the stages of hack service to a political party, he sardonically illustrates his own advice. Using the technique of *Directions for a Birth-day Song*, Swift damns the subjects of panegyric by explaining how to praise them.

Suddenly the poem turns, and Swift explains that if the career of party hack disgusts the young man, he may give up creation for criticism. But a critic too must be a fraud to succeed. With the help of illiterate critics, the poetasters thrust out the true genius.

---

[1] Cf. the comprehensive argument about attitudes toward Augustus offered in Howard Weinbrot, *Augustus Caesar in "Augustan" England* (Princeton, 1978).

Swift's point of view is never fixed. The *Rapsody* gains life and strength from the speaker's changes of position. In the final section (ll. 279–494) the veteran surveys the many kinds of corrupt versifiers with an energy that suggests moral health triumphing over the waste land around it. A powerful feature of the poem is Swift's use of mock-conceits. His unpredictable analogies, fixed in the sure rhythms and precise rhymes, evince the strength of a moral imagination setting an example for weaker minds:

> Hobbes clearly proves that ev'ry creature
> Lives in a state of war by nature.
> The greater for the smallest watch,
> But meddle seldom with their match.
> A whale of moderate size will draw
> A shoal of herrings down his maw.
> A fox with geese his belly crams;
> A wolf destroys a thousand lambs.
> But search among the rhyming race,
> The brave are worried by the base.
> If, on Parnassus' top you sit,
> You rarely bite, are always bit.[1]

Even as he describes the hacks besieging the genius, he exemplifies the victory of a true poet.

Swift digresses into a conventional satiric contrast between the regal humanity of Augustus and the bestiality of modern kings. Yet the effective part of the passage is not the faded (and uncertain) compliment to antiquity. It is the venomous depiction of modern (or normal) kings:

> Thus think on kings, the name denotes
> Hogs, asses, wolves, baboons, and goats
> To represent in figure just
> Sloth, folly, rapine, mischief, lust.[2]

The poem is unfinished. But near the breaking-off point we meet a kind of finale in the unforgettable descriptions of the

---

[1] Ll. 319–30.

[2] *Poems* III. 659, ll. 31–4 of cancelled passage. Cf. Pope's connection of George II with the cardinal sins in the imitation of Horace *Epistles* I. i. 55–64.

King, the royal family, and Walpole. The irony is less subtle than that of Pope's similar passage in *An Epistle to Augustus*.[1] But it is level enough. Here is George II:

> What lineaments divine we trace
> Through all the features of his face;
> Though peace with olive bind his hands,
> Confest the conqu'ring hero stands.
> Hydaspes, Indus, and the Ganges,
> Dread from his hand impending changes.
> From him the Tartar, and Chinese,
> Short by the knees intreat for peace.[2]

Finally, we accept the transformation of the idea with which the poem opens. The gifts needed for poetic genius are as rare as heroic virtue. The author of the poem, whatever his faults, does have the conception of true merit by which princes should be judged. Against him stand not so much the failed poets as the depraved statesmen and kings. So the poet becomes the hero of his own work not through his transcendent merit but through his moral vision, still intact for all the bitter disillusionment of his tone. He offers mankind what should be the gift of monarchs.

The publication of such a poem was not easy. After Pilkington got the manuscripts from Mrs Barber, he offered the copyrights to Motte. But the affair of *The Life and Genuine Character* had made Motte distrust Pilkington, who proceeded to offer the poem to Pope's man, Lawton Gilliver. That bookseller did buy the copies from Pilkington and then began to make pamphlets of them.[3]

In October,[4] Gilliver released *An Epistle to a Lady*—with many deletions—along with 'On Reading Dr Young's Satires'. The title-page had a misleading imprint referring to a non-existent Dublin edition, and the 'publisher' was John Wilford.[5] In December the filthy anti-feminine poems followed, again with an imprint that referred to a fictitious Dublin edition, but with James Roberts as publisher.[6] Finally, *On Poetry: A Rapsody* (much castrated) came out on 31 December 1733, once more

---

[1] Ll. 1–30. [2] Ll. 417–24. [3] Williams IV. 371.
[4] Motte says it was published three months before it was 'taken notice of'—which was in January.
[5] *Poems* II. 628. [6] *Ibid.*, pp. 580–1.

'Printed at Dublin, and Re-printed at London', but with J. Huggonson as publisher.[1]

It may be that the *Rapsody* at last alerted the government. Suddenly, *An Epistle to a Lady* became an object of interest. On 11 January 1734 Wilford was arrested. The printer of the poem named Gilliver as the bookseller, and he was taken up on 22 January.[2] Motte told the story to Swift in a letter long afterwards:

> [When] it was reported a warrant was out against [Gilliver] and he was likely to be apprehended next morning, we two had a meeting overnight, and I promised to take the advice of a gentleman of sense and honour [i.e., Erasmus Lewis], whose name I did not mention to him, and to meet [Gilliver] early the next morning at a certain tavern, to consult farther. Accordingly I went to a gentleman in Cork-street, and from thence to the tavern we had appointed to meet at, where, after I had waited above an hour, a message was sent me that I need stay no longer, for Mr [Gilliver] was gone to Westminster [i.e., arrested], and would not come. I went to see him in the messenger's hands; but he was so closely watched by a couple of sharp sluts, the messenger's daughters, that I could say nothing to him, but about indifferent matters. The consequence was, he was examined, and made a confession.

Motte had offered to pay half the legal expenses if Gilliver would not name him. But Gilliver had said he was resolved, 'if he came into trouble, [Motte] should have a share of it.' So Gilliver implicated Pilkington and Motte. The government obtained no information from Motte, who told Swift, 'as it was not my business to be industrious in recollecting what past three months before, I could not remember anything that could affect me or anybody else.'[3]

Nevertheless, Mrs Barber soon became known as the carrier of the manuscript, and she was arrested on 30 January. The various detentions and examinations led to no prosecution. The government decided that nothing in the poems called for legal action, and the several agents were released.[4]

Meanwhile, Mrs Pilkington, in Ireland, did not believe that

[1] *Ibid.*, p. 639.   [2] *Ibid.*, p. 629.
[3] Williams IV. 371–2. 'Anybody else' may be an allusion to Swift.
[4] *Poems* II. 629.

her husband was an informer; and of course, we know Motte blamed Gilliver. But Laetitia found her Dublin acquaintance united in accusing Mr Pilkington of betraying Swift. After a long delay, she finally received a message from him that he needed money to pay his way home. She extracted the sum from her father, and Pilkington came over—

> but so pale and dejected, that he looked like the ghost of his former self; and the disregard he met with from every body went very near his heart. Every day there was a new abuse published on him.[1]

So ended the London chaplaincy.

[1] Pilkington I. 173.

Chapter Five

FAULKNER

The publication of the four volumes of *Miscellanies* naturally spurred Swift into wishing for a proper collected edition of his works. He could not control Pope's manner of editing; he could not direct the instruments he had tried to work with in London. The contemplation of his own death deepened the desire to see his literary monument erected while he could still enjoy the sight. Yet Swift could not openly launch such a collection. His commitments to persons like Pope and Motte would have made obvious sponsorship awkward. The old reasons for anonymity and pseudonymity still held. I suspect too that Swift wished to avoid both the imputation of vanity and the responsibility he would have for many aspects of the edition if he admitted that he supervised it. Yet such a project would allow him to introduce a number of subtleties into the presentation of his works if he outwardly seemed hostile or at least indifferent to the scheme of producing it.

Fortunately, a young, bold, and expert printer wished to bring out a collected edition of Swift's works in Dublin.[1] This was George Faulkner (born in 1699), who had spent about five years in London working under the excellent printer William Bowyer the elder. In 1724, when Faulkner opened his shop in Dublin, Swift was still dealing with John Harding, who had printed the *Drapier's Letters*. After Harding died (19 April 1725[2]), Swift patronized his widow until her retirement or death

---

[1] For a detailed, bibliographical account of Faulkner's edition see Teerink and the following: Barry Slepian, *Jonathan Swift and George Faulkner* (Ph. D. dissertation, University of Pennsylvania, 1962); Robert E. Ward, *Prince of Dublin Publishers* (Lexington, Ky., 1972).

[2] *Drapier*, p. 201.

in 1730.[1] But it was Faulkner who printed and published *Fraud Detected*, the first collected edition of the *Drapier's Letters* (2 October 1725[2]).

In 1725 Faulkner also launched his newspaper, the *Dublin Journal*, which often published articles concerning or inspired by Swift, who made deliberate use of it to vent his political opinions. In 1726 when Swift visited England, Faulkner also returned, having business with the elder and younger Bowyer and other booksellers. He was often in Swift's company, although we do not know how intimate the two men were.[3] When they both were again settled in Dublin, it is possible that Faulkner did more work for the dean than we know about.[4] The hospitality of the *Dublin Journal* is obvious.

After the year 1729, Swift certainly employed Faulkner, whose hand is visible as early as *An Epistle upon an Epistle* (probably December 1729).[5] The first piece by Swift with Faulkner's imprint was *A Vindication of Lord Carteret* (1730). Then in February 1732, as we have seen, Faulkner printed 'Queries' by Swift in the *Dublin Journal* and suffered imprisonment and fines for doing so. The printer's courage would have pleased the dean, who must have felt indebted to Faulkner for the ordeal he underwent. When Swift assigned various copyrights to Pilkington in connection with Faulkner and Bowyer, he may have been showing his appreciation.[6]

It is worth observing that from 1727 to 1730, although Faulkner regularly reported the dean's activities in his newspaper, he enjoyed no close relation with Swift. During these years Faulkner printed several works attributed to Swift but not written by him.[7] But after 1730, he printed only one false attribution—clear evidence that Swift was working closely with him.[8] Among other instances of the growing friendship is a letter from the dean to the bookseller about a bet that Faulkner made

---

[1] She may have been married again, to another printer. Professor James Woolley has examined the career of Mrs Harding in detail, and given me the benefit of his researches.
[2] *Drapier*, p. xcii.
[3] Davis XIII. 201–2.   [4] Slepian, p. 54.
[5] I am persuaded by James Woolley, 'Arbuckle's "Panegyric"', p. 202.
[6] Ward, pp. 9–10.   [7] Slepian, pp. 49–51.   [8] *Ibid.*

concerning the authorship of two pieces supposed to be Swift's. Faulkner was in the right, and the dean signed the letter, 'Your affectionate servant'.[1] This was a month after the trouble with the House of Lords.

The mysterious advance notice of *The Life and Genuine Character*, in the *Dublin Journal*, 2 May 1732, must have derived from Swift;[2] and Faulkner published the poem in Ireland very soon after the London edition came out. Although Swift repudiated the work in his advertisement the next month, he may possibly have delayed doing so in order to let Faulkner enjoy a rapid sale of his copies; for three weeks passed between the date of publication and the appearance of the advertisement.[3]

Finally, there are some revealing allusions to Faulkner in the letters between Pope and Swift, from which we may infer that Pope took his friend's intimacy with the printer for granted. In one letter Swift assures Pope that Faulkner 'would not print' a pamphlet attacking Pope,[4] and thereby implies that he had conversations on such subjects with the printer. In another letter Pope mentions two of his own poems which he has sent to Swift, 'both of which I conclude will be grateful to your bookseller on whom you please to bestow them so early'—i.e., he expects Swift to give them to Faulkner for immediate publication.[5]

I suspect that Faulkner's plans for an edition of Swift's works—and the author's collaboration with him—were far advanced and a public announcement was imminent when Swift decided to clear the air by dropping hints of what was coming. In December 1732 he told Motte, 'I have cause to believe that some of our printers will collect all they think to be mine, and print them by subscription, which I will neither encourage nor oppose.'[6] The following April, Pope wrote to Swift, 'When does your collection come out, and what will it consist of?'[7] He evidently had no doubt of Swift's involvement.

---

[1] 29 Mar. 1732; Williams IV. 10–11. [2] See above, p. 709.
[3] On 21 Apr. 1733, Faulkner offered the poem for sale; on 15 May Swift published his advertisement.
[4] 31 Mar. 1733; Sherburn III. 361. [5] 6 Jan. 1734; *ibid.*, p. 401.
[6] Williams IV. 89. [7] Sherburn III. 366.

By this time Faulkner had begun advertising. In the *Dublin Journal* for 10 February 1733 he announced his intention of publishing by subscription 'all the works that are generally allowed to have been written by the said Dr S. in four volumes'. He promised the first two volumes by 'Michaelmas-term at farthest' and declared that the first volume would include two Drapier's Letters never printed before.[1] Such a declaration would have been warning enough to the friends of Swift that he was helping the bookseller.

Yet Swift replied to Pope's bald question with a blandly misleading narrative:

> A printer came to me to desire he might print my works (as he called them) in four volumes by subscription. I said I would give no leave, and should be sorry to see them printed here. He said they could not be printed in London, I answered they could, if the partners agreed. He said he would be glad of my permission, but as he could print them without it, and was advised that it could do me no harm, and having been assured of numerous subscriptions, he hoped I would not be angry at his pursuing his own interest.... Much of this discourse passed, and he goes on with the matter, wherein I determine not to intermeddle, though it be much to my discontent; and I wish it could be done in England, rather than here, although I am grown pretty indifferent in everything of that kind.[2]

There is no sign that Pope was taken in by this evasion. Yet Swift gave a very similar account to Charles Ford in October, even while asking for his help in establishing the correct text of *Gulliver*:

> A printer of this town applied himself to me by letters and friends for leave to print in four volumes the works of J S D D, etc. I answered that as I could not hinder him, so I would not encourage him, but that he should take care not to charge me with what I never writ.... The man behaved himself with all respect, and since it was an evil I could not avoid, I have rather they [i.e., the works] should be printed correctly than otherwise. Now, you may please to remember how much I complained of Motte's suffering some friend of his ... not only to blot out some things that he thought might give offence,

---

[1] Davis XIV. 42. The advertisement itself is dated 9 Feb.
[2] Sherburn V. 12 (1 May 1733).

but to insert a good deal of trash contrary to the author's manner and style, and intention. I think you had a Gulliver interleaved and set right in those mangled and murdered pages. . . . I wish you would please to let me know, whether you have such an interleaved Gulliver; and where I could get it.[1]

Swift could hardly help Faulkner prepare the best possible text without giving his support to the edition; and Faulkner could hardly avoid printing what Swift 'never writ' unless the author helped to establish the canon of his works.

If we now turn to Faulkner's story, we shall see how much better it fits the facts. According to this account, written many years after the events, friends of Swift asked Faulkner to secure the dean's permission to print 'his entire works' without the confusion of the *Miscellanies*:

> Accordingly he made application to the Dean, who did not seem willing to consent, as the publisher might be a loser by printing them; the editor [i.e., 'publisher' in the modern sense] told him he would run all hazards, being very positive, he should be a great gainer by them; but the Dean still persisted; then the editor said, he would print them by subscription, and make a faithful return of the subscribers' names to him, when he could easily judge whether he would gain or lose by the undertaking. Accordingly proposals were published, and subscriptions came in very fast, which were shewn to the author, who consented to the printing, on the following conditions; that no job should be made, but full value given for the money; that the editor should attend him early every morning, or when most convenient, to read to him, that the sounds might strike the ear, as well as the sense the understanding.

At this point Faulkner shifts from rehearsing the conditions Swift laid down in advance of the labour of editing and tells what in fact happened as the preparation of the volumes went on. He says that Swift always had two men servants present for the purpose of clarifying the style of his writings—

> and when he had any doubt, he would ask them the meaning of what they heard; which, if they did not comprehend, he would alter and amend until they understood it perfectly well, and then would say, *This will do; for I write to the vulgar, more than to the learned.* Not

[1] Williams IV. 197–8.

satisfied with this preparation for the press, he corrected every sheet of the first seven volumes that were published in his lifetime, desiring the editor [i.e., Faulkner] to write notes, being much younger than the Dean, acquainted with most of the transactions of his life, as well as with those of several of his friends; the author being very communicative to the editor.[1]

Systematic collations have shown that Swift did not in fact supervise the edition so carefully as Faulkner claims. But they also show that the corrections made were due either to Swift directly or to his instructions, which Faulkner followed only too thoroughly. Certainly, Faulkner made extraordinary efforts to gather together manuscript copies of Swift's unpublished works held by various persons in Ireland and England; and the delay in the appearance of the volumes was due in part to this desire for completeness. As the bookseller put it, he collected 'as many original pieces as were possible to be got of the supposed author's from his friends in England, which we found great difficulty in procuring'.[2] The notes, on the other hand, often sound like the immediate work of Swift rather than Faulkner's composition.

Charles Ford easily understood what in general was going on, and he had no trouble making the correct interpretation of Swift's remarks about Faulkner. He replied to Swift's October letter with energetic sympathy, and offered to help with both the text and the canon. Unfortunately, he forgot that the interleaved copy of *Gulliver* had highly important material not included in the separate list of errors on a detached sheet of paper:

> I have long had it at heart to see your works collected, and published with care. It is become absolutely necessary, since that jumble with Pope, &c. in three volumes, which put me in a rage whenever I meet them. I know no reason why, at this distance of time, the *Examiners*, and other political pamphlets written in the Queen's reign, might not be inserted. I doubt you have been too negligent in keeping copies; but I have them bound up, and most of them single besides. I lent Mr Corbet that paper to correct his *Gulliver* by; and it was from that I mended my own. There is every single alteration from the original copy; and the printed book abounds with all those errors, which should be avoided in the new edition.

[1] Davis XIII. 202–3.   [2] *Ibid.*, p. 183.

Ford also included a list of his own collection of pamphlets by Swift (some of which the author had actually forgotten he wrote[1]), and offered to supplement this collection with pieces in the possession of John Barber, Swift's old friend and printer in London.[2] Swift replied at once, bitterly lamenting the condition of the text of *Gulliver* and still hoping to find the interleaved copy.[3]

It was now Michaelmas Term, 1733, which meant 2–25 November; but Faulkner was far from ready. For a long while he had been confident that he could supply the first two volumes by the promised date. In April and May he had advertised that they would come out on time.[4] In July he announced that the first volume was almost finished.[5] But this was based on *The First Volume* of the Swift–Pope *Miscellanies*, and would have been the easiest part of the edition to prepare.

Then in September the plan changed, and Faulkner declared that all four volumes would go to the subscribers in the Hilary Term (11–31 January 1734).[6] Again postponements followed. Faulkner went to England, partly to work on the edition. He left on 16 February, carrying letters of recommendation from Swift, among which was the oft-quoted one to the Earl of Oxford:

> The bearer Mr Faulkner, the prince of Dublin printers, will have the honour to deliver you this. He tells me, your lordship was so gracious as to admit him into your presence, and receive him with great condescension. Which encouraged him to hope for the same favour again by my mediation, which I could not refuse; although for his own profit he is engaged in a work that very much discontents me, yet I would rather have it fall into his hands, than any others on this side.[7]

Not until 21 May did Faulkner come home.[8] The size of his volumes grew with the matter he had kept adding; he put off

---

[1] Cf. Williams IV. 212.   [2] 6 Nov. 1733; *ibid.*, pp. 202–4.
[3] 20 Nov. 1733; *ibid.*, pp. 211–12.
[4] *Dublin Journal*, 23 Apr. and 22 May 1733.   [5] *Ibid.*, 7 Jul. 1733.
[6] *Ibid.*, 4 Sept. 1733.
[7] See announcement in *Dublin Journal*, 9 Feb. 1734; from the date of the letter to Lord Oxford we know the date of departure; Williams IV. 222.
[8] See *Dublin Journal* under that date.

publication till July. Lord Oxford complained to Swift about
the long wait. The reply included some obfuscation, but it also
gave a most revealing cause for the failures to meet deadlines:

> I have put the man under some difficulties by ordering certain
> things to be struck out after they were printed, which some friends
> had given him. This hath delayed his work, and as I hear, given him
> much trouble and difficulty to adjust.[1]

We may infer that one reason for the bookseller's procrastination was the author's demands and alterations.

But it is in the nature of such enterprises to be clogged by
unforeseeable obstacles. In June, Faulkner may have promised
delivery for July; but in September he specified 6 November;
and at the end of October he begged a last pardon for yet
another postponement.[2] He kept moving up the deadline for
closing subscriptions until 5 November 1734.[3]

At last, near Swift's sixty-seventh birthday, three volumes (I,
III, and IV) were indeed ready (27 November), with Volume II
to follow on 6 January 1735.[4] Faulkner must have beamed over
his subscription list. Of dukes and duchesses alone, it counted as
many as fifteen. The set was indeed completed on 6 January. But
the demand was so great that subscribers had to be asked to send
small money with their messengers, 'it being impossible to get
change for so much gold'.[5]

Two further volumes were added in 1738, another in 1741,
and more over the course of the eighteenth century, while
preceding volumes were reprinted, until in 1769 the set was
capped with *A Tale of a Tub* and included twenty octavo
volumes as well as arrangements in two other formats.[6] The
splendid triumph of the great venture was the foundation of

---

[1] 30 Aug. 1734; Williams IV. 248.
[2] *Dublin Journal*, 18 Jun., 14 Sept., 29 Oct. 1734.
[3] *Ibid.*, 18 Jun., 17 Sept., 30 Oct., 5 Nov. 1734.
[4] I am persuaded by the argument of George Mayhew (*PQ* 43 (1964), 395). For an analysis of the changes that held back Vol. II, see Margaret Weedon, 'An Uncancelled Copy of the First Collected Edition of Swift's Poems', *The Library*, 5th ser., XXII (1967), 44–56.
[5] Davis XIII. xxxvii.   [6] See Teerink, pp. 22–65.

Faulkner's prosperity. But it is also clear that through the bookseller's admirable diligence many works by Swift were preserved that would otherwise have been lost.

The immediate success of Faulkner's edition by no means ended the author's repudiation of it. We must accept as genuine and strong the regret Swift felt that London booksellers could not collaborate on a proper English collection of his literary works. He did yearn for a place at the centre of civilization, and he certainly wished all his important productions to make their original appearance in London.

But I also think that Swift did not like to be held responsible for any faults or oddities in the Dublin edition, least of all various elements that were due to him. By disclaiming his part in planning and correcting it, he avoided the need to defend it. At the same time, of course, he did not have to admit that he was exhibiting distrust of his friend Pope or violating an understanding with his bookseller and agent Motte.

Yet on the other side, Swift's Irish patriotism also entered into the design. He resented the fact that copyright laws operated only for London publications, that English booksellers could bring out anything they liked by Irish authors not already printed in London, and that the booksellers of Dublin had little opportunity to compete in the English market.

These motives reveal themselves when Swift discusses Faulkner's labours. In March 1735, writing to Pulteney, Swift completely dissociates himself from Faulkner's edition. Not only does he assert that it was done against his will but he also declares, 'I have never yet looked into them [i.e., the four volumes], nor I believe ever shall.'[1] Two months later, he forgot what he said, returned to the subject, described Faulkner as 'civil and humble', and said it had pleased Swift to see among the contents of the edition a poem about Pulteney and Walpole.[2] The desire to compliment the statesman overcame the desire to sound utterly ignorant of the edition.

---

[1] 8 Mar. 1735; Williams IV. 304.   [2] 12 May 1735; *ibid.*, p. 338.

When Faulkner put his volumes on sale in London, Motte objected. Faulkner persisted, and Motte lodged a complaint with Swift:

> Mr Faulkner's impression of four volumes has had its run. I was advised that it was in my power to have given him and his agents sufficient vexation, by applying to the law; but that I could not sue him without bringing your name into a court of justice, which absolutely determined me to be passive. I am told he is about printing them in twelves; in which case I humbly hope you will please to lay your commands upon him (which, if he has any sense of gratitude, must have the same power as an injunction in chancery) to forbear sending them over here. If you think this request to be reasonable, I know you will comply with it: if not, I submit.[1]

In spite of Motte's obvious assumptions about Swift's hand in the Dublin edition, Swift tried to follow his old line of evasion but blurred it with suggestions of intimacy between Faulkner and himself:

> I read your letter, and gave it to him to read; he had many things to say in his defence, and which I cannot charge my memory, but have advised him to answer. I know that he passes for a perfectly honest man here, and a fair dealer; and I confess that the many oppressions we suffer from England sour my temper to the utmost. Besides the best lawyers, even those who come from England say there is no law against importing into England any books that have been printed here. For, books are not yet among prohibited goods, unless they contain in them something against law and loyalty. Upon the whole I think you had better suspend your suit, till you hear what Mr Faulkner hath to say, and as to my private opinion, it is that you will not find your interest in going farther.

Swift goes on to say that the Dublin edition was produced against his will but that Faulkner had always behaved himself decently to Swift; and although he had just advised Motte to drop the case, he said he would have preferred to see his works collected in an English edition.[2]

In spite of Swift's advice, Motte did bring charges against Faulkner and was awarded an injunction stopping the sale of the

---

[1] 31 Jul. 1735; *ibid.*, p. 372.   [2] 1 Nov. 1735; *ibid.*, p. 414.

Dublin edition in London (28 November 1735).[1] Counsel for Faulkner argued that since many of the pieces were printed before the Copyright Act of 1710 took effect, Motte could not claim the rights to all the material; but the judge allowed the injunction to cover the whole of the edition. While Faulkner was ready to take the case further, his lawyers advised him to desist. Faulkner did however send Swift an account of the affair, and the dean's furious response, weakened a bit by the usual self-contradictions, was sent to Motte in May 1736.

Here Swift has the confidence to assert that he never dealt with Faulkner 'as a printer or a bookseller'. Yet the very tenor of the letter undermines this position, and Motte had independent information of the true relation between the men; so one need not fear that he was abused. The fascinating element of the letter is the setting of the Irish book trade in the framework of English oppression of Ireland, and Swift's patriotic defence of Dublin booksellers:

I lately received a long letter from Mr Faulkner, grievously complaining upon several articles of the ill treatment he hath met with from you, and of the many advantageous offers he hath made you, with none of which you thought fit to comply. I am not qualified to judge in the fact, having heard but one side; only one thing I know, that the cruel oppressions of this kingdom by England are not to be borne. You send what books you please hither, and the booksellers here can send nothing to you that is written here. As this is absolute oppression; if I were a bookseller in this town, I would use all the safe means to reprint London books, and run them to any town, in England that I could, because, whoever neither offends the laws of God, or the country he liveth in, committeth no sin. It was the fault of you and other booksellers, who printed anything supposed to be mine, that you did not agree with each other to print them together, if you thought they would sell to any advantage. I believe I told you long ago that Mr Faulkner came to me, and told me his intention to print everything that my friends told him they thought to be mine, and that I was discontented at it, but when he urged, that some other bookseller would do it, and that he would take the advice of my friends, and leave out what I pleased to order him, I said no

---

[1] Cf. Donald Cornu, 'Swift, Motte, and the Copyright Struggle: Two Unnoticed Documents', *MLN* 54 (1939), 120–1.

more, but that I was sorry it was done here.—But, I am'so incensed against the oppressions from England, and have so little regard to the laws they make, that I do as a clergyman encourage the merchants both to export wool and woollen manufactures to any country in Europe, or anywhere else; and conceal it from the custom-house officers, as I would hide my purse from a highwayman, if he came to rob me on the road, although England hath made a law to the contrary.... Mr Faulkner hath dealt so fairly with me, that I have a great opinion of his honesty, although I never dealt with him as a printer or a bookseller, but since my friends told me, those things called mine, would certainly be printed by some hedge-bookseller, I was forced to be passive in the matter. I have some things which I shall leave my executors to publish after my decease, and have directed that they shall be printed in London. For, except small papers, and some treatises writ for the use of this kingdom, I always had those of importance to be published in London, as you well know. For my part, although, I have no power anywhere, I will do the best offices I can to countenance Mr Faulkner.[1]

The open appeal to lawlessness astonishes me. Although it echoes some passages in the *Drapier's Letters* the context in those appeals was rhetorical and could be interpreted as menacing the government in Westminster. But here in a private letter Swift rises above the laws of nations to the individual conscience and the will of God. He enlarges a squabble between rival merchants into a controversy about the principles of social order.

[1] Williams IV. 493–4.

Chapter Six

THE AGEING DEAN

I. SOCIABILITY

The bad health which kept Swift from thanking his neighbours in person during the Bettesworth fracas also gave rise, during January 1734, to a rumour that the dean was dead.[1] But even while erupting into politics and poetry, he continued to enjoy his favourite kind of society. Although his chronic diseases and fading eyesight dogged him through the spring and summer too, he enjoyed the boon of Sheridan's company and often dined with him.[2] Language games had become for them almost a regular entertainment. As they once had matched puns, so they now practised Hibernicisms on each other[3] and competed in letters composed of 'Anglo-Angli' and Anglo-Latin—and sometimes the dean in this disguise said what he otherwise suppressed.[4]

Swift was helping the younger man with money as well. In January he loaned him three hundred pounds on a mortgage of the Quilca property.[5] Sheridan had exchanged the living in co. Cork for one nearer Dublin, that of Dunboyne, in Meath. He now thought of seeking appointment as master of the Cavan town school, a royal foundation that would pay him about as much as his church living. The master of the school agreed to the exchange, and Sheridan thought he might soften his asthma and reduce his expenses by the move. Because of strenuous competition, his school in Dublin was no longer prospering.[6]

---

[1] *Dublin Journal*, 26 Jan. 1734.
[2] Cf. Williams IV. 237, n. 1; 299, and *passim*.   [3] *Ibid.*, pp. 216–17.
[4] E.g., *ibid.*, pp. 237–9, 280–1.
[5] MS. memorial, 1733–71–52458, in the Registry of Deeds, Dublin.
[6] Ball v. 82–3, n. 3.

Although the Duke of Dorset had consented to the exchange as early as the spring of 1734, the negotiation proceeded with painful slowness; and Swift decided at last to intervene with letters to Lady Betty Germaine and to the Lord Lieutenant himself. The letter to Dorset is easy without being over-familiar. It is courteous and informative but not unctuous; here is Swift's manly request for sympathy:

> In the mean time [i.e., while waiting for the secretaries to act] the poor doctor hath given up his school in town, to his great loss, and hath parted with his house, continuing in uneasiness and suspense till your letter comes.[1]

The Duke did oblige, and Sheridan secured his school in Cavan. He did not, alas, secure health there.

The Worralls of course continued to suit the dean's wish for shirtsleeved company when his health left him too little dignity for the Delany–Helsham set. But he was glad as well to keep up his attachment to Delville.[2] And in spite of his vocal aversion to titles, he remained friendly with the family of Lord Howth.[3]

A new female conquest appeared in the person of Miss Hoadly the young daughter of Swift's neighbour, the Archbishop of Dublin. Her father, who had arrived in 1730, had met gadfly opposition from Swift immediately upon taking office. But he worked, within the fences of ministerial policy, for the benefit of his people and his church; and Swift seems to have softened toward him. In February 1734 the archbishop preached a charity sermon in St Patrick's Cathedral, 'for clothing poor children of the parish'.[4]

Swift's interest in Miss Hoadly went back at least to 1732,[5] but one cannot taste its quality until the date of a charming letter, in June 1734, from the dean to the young woman. She had supplied his household with pork and butter; and he congratulates her on understanding housewifery and on knowing how to

---

[1] 22 Mar. 1735; Williams IV. 30.
[2] See Delany's 'Peg Ratcliff's Invitation', *Poems* III. 1049–50.
[3] Williams IV. 225, n. 2.; 245–6.
[4] *Dublin Journal*, 12 Feb. 1734; Ball V. 70–1, notes. [5] Ball IV. 35.

write. The manner and argument are normal for Swift: treating
the gifts as bribes, he pretends to ridicule the girl for her good
sense, and his bullying sounds half like a pedagogue and half like
a father. Yet his values were of course neither unreasonable in
themselves nor common in their time. Only in the last hundred
years has it grown unnecessary to remind women, as Swift did,
of their powers and duties as intellectual beings:

> When my Lord's gentleman delivered his message, after I put him
> some questions, he drew out a paper containing your directions, and
> in your hand: I said it properly belonged to me; and, when I had
> read it, I put it in my pocket, and am ready to swear, when lawfully
> called, that it is written in a fair hand, rightly spelled, and good plain
> sense. You now may see I have you at mercy; for, upon the least
> offence given, I will show the paper to every female scrawler I meet,
> who will soon spread about the town, that your writing and spelling
> are ungenteel and unfashionable, more like a parson than a lady.[1]

Besides physical ailments, Swift met other disagreeable
events, private and public. Pope annoyed him with some lines in
a Horatian satire, suggesting that Swift believed in senseless
avarice: after describing his own modest prosperity on a lease-
hold estate, Pope wrote,

> 'Pray heav'n it last!' cries Swift, 'as you go on;
> I wish to God this house had been your own:
> Pity! to build, without a son or wife:
> Why you'll enjoy it only all your life.'[2]

I believe that a few years later Pope added lines to Swift's
version of Horace, *Satires* II. vi, in order to justify this imputation
of avarice.[3] Swift took offence at the passage in the earlier poem,
and wrote bluntly to Lord Oxford that he 'could willingly have
excused his [i.e., Pope's] placing me not in that light which I
would appear'. With Pope himself Swift was less blunt and more
communicative:

---

[1] Williams IV. 235.

[2] Horace, *Satires* II. ii. 161-4; published in 1734.

[3] Cf. discussion of authorship of additional lines, in *Poems* I. 197-8. I disagree with
Williams and believe Bathurst was acting as Pope's catspaw to make sure Swift's fallible
memory would overlook the origin of the new lines.

My vanity turns wholly at present in being personated in your *Quae virtus* &c. But in order to that, I desire to be represented as a man of thrift only as it produceth liberty and independence, without any thoughts of hoarding; and as one who bestows every year at least one third of his income; though sunk a third by the misery of the country.[1]

Pope ignored the hint and did not alter the poem. Yet he did omit the crucial sentences in Swift's letter from his edition of their correspondence.

But Pope had strength elsewhere. Bolingbroke had already protested against Swift's recommendation of Pilkington:

Pray Mr Dean be a little more cautious in your recommendations. ... the fellow wants morals and as I hear decency sometimes.[2]

In a letter touched off by Swift's to Lord Oxford, Pope complained of Pilkington, Mrs Barber, and their activities. He warned Swift against

the intervening, officious, impertinence of those goers-between us, who in England pretend to intimacies with you, and in Ireland to intimacies with me. I cannot but receive any that call upon your name, and in truth they take it in vain too often. I take all opportunities of justifying you against these friends, especially those who know all you think and write, and repeat your slighter verses. It is generally on such little scraps that witlings feed; and 'tis hard the world should judge of our housekeeping from what we fling to our dogs, yet this is often the consequence. But they treat you still worse, mix their own with yours, and print them to get money, and lay them at your door.[3]

If Swift had not blushed at Bolingbroke's reproach, he was fairly caught out by Pope's, and replied with something like a splutter—almost apologizing for his recommendations but still begging a countenance for Thomas Sheridan:

I am sorry at my heart, that you are pestered with people who come in my name, and I profess to you, it is without my knowledge. I am confident I shall hardly ever have occasion again to recommend, for my friends here are very few, and fixed to the freehold,

---

[1] 1 May 1733; Sherburn v. 13.   [2] 12 Apr. 1734; Williams IV. 323.
[3] 15 Sept. 1734; Sherburn III. 432.

from whence nothing but death will remove them; I only except
Dr Sheridan who always begs me to present his respects, and talks
often of going to England.[1]

Not a word of Pope's thinly screened allusion to Pilkington.

But weightier anxieties descended on Swift from the economic
and agricultural decay of Ireland. Although he exaggerated the
country's underlying weakness and did not appreciate the
amelioration that had begun, he hardly overcoloured the agony
of the people at this time. When he described the state of the
kingdom to Lord Oxford, Swift applied his customary principle
of giving England an appalling vision of her neighbour—
especially if his correspondent sat in the House of Lords:

> In this great city nine-tenths of the inhabitants are beggars; the chief
> streets half ruinous or desolate. It is dangerous to walk the streets for
> fear of houses falling on our heads, and it is the same in every city
> and town throughout the island.... Yet this town is a paradise
> compared to every part of the country, except some northern parts,
> supported by the linen trade, which however is decaying fast by the
> knavery of the dealers.[2]

The *Dublin Journal* had recently published a long article on the
crisis in woollen manufactures,[3] and Parliament rose at the end
of April with little done to better the situation.[4]

Yet a tremendous change was under way. The new Speaker,
Henry Boyle, was to dominate the House of Commons for
twenty years by an arrangement known as 'the undertakers'. In
return for lucrative preferments and a share of patronage, a
group led by Boyle saw to the money bills and managed
Parliament in keeping with government policies. During the
1720s Parliament had grown in importance. The magnificent
new Parliament House (opened in 1729) signalized the fact.
Boulter did not occupy himself directly with the House of
Commons. During the 1730s the undertakers became permanent directors of the Commons; and under the Duke of
Dorset's weak viceroyalty they made themselves practically

---

[1] 1 Nov. 1734; *ibid.*, p. 439.   [2] 30 Aug. 1734; *ibid.*, p. 249.
[3] 16 Feb. 1734.   [4] 29 Apr. 1734.

indispensable: 'in time they became so powerful they were able to dictate to him.'[1]

However undemocratic the scheme of undertakers was, an Irish oligarchy certainly marked an advance on the old misrule from Westminster. The irony remains that the crisis of Wood's patent could be called the start of the great change, although Swift by the mid-1730s had stopped expecting any improvement in the political or economic institutions of Ireland.

The spring of 1734 added no bright colour to his bleak view. In June there were reports of weavers rioting. But how little Swift believed the mass of common people should try—even during such troubles—to act for themselves, we may judge from an account, which he perhaps inspired, of the dean's meeting with some of the troublemakers:

> Several weavers having lately assembled in great bodies to search for foreign manufactures, accidentally met with that worthy patriot, the Reverend Dr Swift, D.S.P.D. who exhorted them to be quiet, and not do things in a rash manner, but to make application in a peaceable way, and he did not make the least doubt, but proper means would be found out to make them all easy, &c. whereupon they immediately dispersed, to their respective [homes], crying out, Long live Dean Swift, and Prosperity to the Drapier, and returned him thanks for his good advice, which they said they would follow.[2]

Swift's private affairs gave him some discomfort too. He had presented a former chandler named Matthew Swan with the lease of a house and garden, in return for which the man was to look after Naboth's Vineyard. But in September, when the valuable grapes and pears were ripe, Swan and most of the fruit vanished. Although Swift advertised, offering a two-guinea reward, his description of the presumed thief seemed absurdly vague: 'a middle sized fellow, wears a light brown peruke, and hath a very ill countenance'.[3]

It was probably Sheridan who, under the title of 'Solomon Shuttleworth, Drapier', answered Swift's advertisement with

[1] J. C. Beckett, *The Making of Modern Ireland* (London, 1966), 190–1. In this paragraph my words echo those of Beckett.
[2] *Dublin Journal*, 11 Jun. 1734.   [3] *Ibid.*, 21 Sept. 1734.

another, a week after, relating how he had seized on three persons in dark [*sic*] wigs and ill countenances, but been wrong each time. The third victim was simply a caricature of Bettesworth: his appearance mingled 'insolence and folly, not without a strong tincture of the highway-man'; he usually carried '*murdering weapons* about him'; and he was 'but a common serjeant'.[1]

About this time Swift's giddiness and deafness attacked him yet once more. On 7 October he said he had just begun going out after suffering weeks of confinement.[2] Sitting at home in September, he composed a little poem in Latin and also in English, on his discomfort. The English version has his normal colloquial effectiveness, marred (as many of his poems are) by a bathetic ending. But the tone otherwise will charm most readers; it is a mixture of complaint and self-ridicule:

> Deaf, giddy, helpless, left alone,
> To all my friends a burthen grown,
> No more I hear my church's bell
> Than if it rang out for my knell.[3]

To deepen his reflections on illness and death came a letter from Arbuthnot which was in effect a last farewell as the visible end grew near: dropsy and asthma made it hard for the lovable doctor to sleep, breathe, eat, or move:

I most earnestly desired, and begged of God that he would take me. Contrary to my expectation, upon venturing to ride (which I had forborn for some years because of bloody water) I recovered my strength to a pretty considerable degree, slept and had my stomach return. But I expect the return of my symptoms upon my return to London and the return of winter, and I am not in circumstance to live an idle country life and no man at my age ever recovered of such a disease further than by an abatement of the symptoms. What I did I can assure you, was not for life but ease; for I am at present in the case of a man that was almost in harbour and then blown back to sea; who has a reasonable hope of going to a good place and an absolute certainty of leaving a very bad one.[4]

---

[1] *Ibid.*, 28 Sept. 1734.   [2] Williams IV. 257.   [3] *Poems* II. 672–4.
[4] 4 Oct. 1734; Williams IV. 256.

Swift realized perfectly what the letter implied, but he pre-ferred activity to passive brooding. The pace of Swift's literary production slowed in 1734; yet his capacity for friendship did not weaken, in spite of the reports he sent to England. Nevertheless, there were strains. On the one hand he loved visiting, dining out, playing games; and the number of his social engagements would have daunted men much younger than he. On the other hand, sixty-seven meant old age for Swift's genera-tion, and even the Dean of St Patrick's felt shaken by the acuteness of his sufferings.

The conflict between sociability and frailty is easy to il-lustrate. Toward the Christmas season 1734, Swift thought of going with Sheridan to visit friends of the schoolmaster at Castle Hamilton in co. Cavan. But he learned that it would be difficult to ride there. So in one of his characteristic pieces of affectionate mock-rudeness, he invited himself to stay where he knew he would be welcome—at the Wicklow home of one of his pre-bendaries, John Blachford. There was a fine strand for riding, along the sea near the town, and Swift wished to try it for three weeks at least.

The letter of self-invitation is not only a specimen of Swiftian humour but also a mark of the activity of his invention in the midst of physical and emotional trials. In the course of the letter Swift explains that he will supply his wine, pay for his food, and bring his own sheets. But the charm of the composition is the opening mask of a stranger:

Reverend Sir
There is an inhabitant of this city of whom I suppose you have often heard. I remember him from my very infancy, but confess I am not as well acquainted with him as in prudence I ought to be. Yet I constantly pretend to converse with him, being seldom out of his company, but I do not find that our conversation is very pleasing to either of us. His health is not very good; which he endeavours to mend by frequent riding and fancies himself to find some benefit by that exercise, although not very effectual.

Swift explains that 'he' has cancelled earlier plans for a northern trip but needs exercise and has been told of the 'murrow' outside Wicklow:

By these incitements, he seems determined to quarter upon you for three weeks at least; if he can have your consent, or rather that of your lady's [*sic*], although I find he never had the honour to see her.[1]

Unfortunately, the richness of the humour went to waste. A few days after writing to Blachford, Swift was riding home from Howth Castle when the vertigo struck him:

> I was seized with so cruel a fit of that giddiness which at times hath pursued me from my youth that I was forced to lie down on a bed in an empty house for two hours before I was in a condition to ride. However I got home safe.

He wrote an elegant note of gratitude for Blachford's own invitation—sent in response to Swift's—

> I know not whether you have children, nor did I ever see your lady, or your house; so that I never did beg an invitation so much against the rules of common good manners, to one so much a stranger as you have been against my will to me.[2]

And so the dean spent a cautious Christmas in Dublin.

From the single case one may easily imagine the disappointments that were routine in Swift's crowded days. Even with two servants to accompany him, he dreaded such mischances, and fluttered uncomfortably between his addiction to exercise and his horror of a fit.

Along with these emotions went the sharp response of an ageing man to the death of good friends. Although he had a healthy history of attachments constantly forming to replace those which dissolved, he was in theory dedicated to such severe ideals of loyalty and gratitude that he feared the loosening of established ties more consciously than he recognized the enjoyment of new ones. Lady Masham died in December 1734, Arbuthnot on 27 February 1735. As such losses followed one another, Swift felt irreparably stricken. These friends had peculiar value not only because he set his English acquaintance

---

[1] 12 Dec. 1734; *ibid.*, p. 275.

[2] 17 Dec. 1734; *ibid.*, p. 276. Swift made a note of the episode in his account book for 1734–5—'Deadly sick at Howth'—under the date of 16 Dec. (fol. 4). He also mentions it in a letter to Pope; Sherburn v. 15.

above his Irish but because his unwillingness to travel so far kept him from finding new resources in their country.

Meanwhile, in spite of the disaster with Matthew Pilkington, the dean did not give up his habit of sending Irish protégés to meet English celebrities. Mrs Sican's son, for example, going to Europe in the spring of 1735, was introduced to Pope,[1] and there is a touching appeal to the poet on behalf of Dr Sheridan's son, at the Westminster School:

> Dr Sheridan desires, that if a little staring boy of eleven years old should happen to appear in your sight, when you come to town, and you let him look round you, and hear you speak, that you will treat him with your usual humanity, and let him boast that he hath seen you, and it happens, that few boys better deserve such a favour.[2]

The boy, who was in fact fourteen years old, happened to be Swift's godson, and his father's favourite child.[3]

Swift's activity as a correspondent is impressive. He remained in touch with Lady Betty, Pope, and Ford. He also kept up his interest in some of less dignity—voyagers like Miss Donnellan and Mrs Pendarves, who might be visiting Dublin again. His kind disposition toward Mrs Barber never altered in her absence, and is one more token of his loyalty to those he undertook to sponsor.[4] Mrs Pendarves must have exerted remarkable charms, for he wrote to her a *lettre galante* (among other seductive missives) which rises to a peak extraordinary even for Dean Swift addressing a young lady:

> I would give half my goods that I had known you five times more than I did, and had the forecast to watch all your behaviour till I could have found something that was wrong, though it was in the least significant part of your conduct; and upon that one point I would have forced my memory and observation to dwell, as some little cure for the vexation of despairing ever to see you again.[5]

Naturally, as he got older, Swift's tendency increased to rely for regular entertainment on his local, settled community—a

---

[1] Williams IV. 423–5.   [2] 1 May 1733; Sherburn v. 13.
[3] Esther K. Sheldon, *Thomas Sheridan of Smock-Alley* (Princeton, 1967), p. 4, n. 6.
[4] Williams IV. 361.   [5] *N. & Q.* (Dec. 1979), p. 548.

pool which was replenished rather more steadily than he seems to indicate. For proper calls and dinners there were still Delany and Dr Helsham, young Lord Orrery, the Howth family, Lady Acheson. With Sheridan there were dinners, card-games, conversations, and farcical correspondence. The intimacy with Mrs Whiteway deepened until the exchange of visits and meals became a constant feature of his calendar. Swift's accounts record games of cards again and again with both Mrs Whiteway and her son Theophilus Harrison. In November 1734, however, Mrs Worrall died—an irreplaceable loss.[1] At the end of that month there is an entry in Greek in Swift's account book, meaning that someone died; it may refer to the lady who had cared so well for both Stella and Swift.[2] Yet even this emptiness was handsomely filled, by Martha Whiteway.

Furthermore, we know that Swift saw much of Mrs Sican and of course of his juniors in the church: Stopford and the Grattans, John Jackson, and so forth—men whom he could entertain and advise, and who could give him the cordial of their respect. One of his great recreations continued to be card-games. Besides Mrs Whiteway and her son, the frequent players included Mr Worrall, Dr Helsham, and John and Charles Grattan.[3]

II. THREE FRIENDS

Even this tedious catalogue suggests how often Swift was in company, how seldom he really moped in solitude. He did indeed dine regularly with his housekeeper; but one could not expect him to be sociable every afternoon of the year. A few close-ups will illustrate the kinds of conversation available to him: James Stopford, William King, Lord Orrery. Rarely did the old dean show more penetration than in his encouragement of Stopford—a shy, scholarly churchman whom Swift patronized consistently. Though born in London, Stopford took his B.A. degree at Trinity College, Dublin and was elected a fellow

---

[1] *Dublin Journal*, 30 Nov. 1734.   [2] *Accounts 1734-5*, fol. 3ᵛ.
[3] *Ibid.*, fol. 1.

two years later (1717). His mother had married twice; and Hester Brooking, a daughter by her first husband, became the unhappy wife of Knightley Chetwode. By the time Stopford came home from his first tour of Europe, Swift could describe him to Chetwode in panegyric language.[1] This hyperbole was not Swift's tribute to a brother-in-law's pride, for such expressions are typical of Swift's remarks on his protégés. One token of Stopford's respect for the dean is that he saved every letter received from him.

The following year (1725), it was Stopford's chore to act as go-between in arranging the separation of his half-sister from her difficult husband. He also served as tutor of Chetwode's second son, at Trinity College.[2] Swift reported that he had 'a most universal good reputation; I think above any man in the kingdom'.[3] We have seen Swift recommend him to his own grand friends when Stopford went abroad a second time (1725), as companion to the rich Mr Graham.[4] And although he was too bashful to use the recommendations, he showed his gratitude by securing a portrait of Charles I for Swift.[5]

We have also seen how Stopford, through Swift, made a friend of Esther Johnson, who lent him money.[6] It was to Stopford that Swift wrote the most direct statement we have of his feelings for her.[7] In 1728 Stopford found a wife of his own and resigned the fellowship. Archbishop King then provided him with the vicarage of Finglas, near Dublin, a living which had been held at other times by Swift's friends Dillon Ashe and Thomas Parnell.[8] The following year, Swift was still calling him 'as honest and benevolent a person as ever I knew'.[9] William Pulteney had some part in initiating preferment for Stopford; and in 1730 Carteret obliged Swift by making his client the Provost of Tuam.[10]

So one is not surprised to discover the dean, during the spring

---

[1] Williams III. 22. Cf. above, p. 336.
[2] Williams III. 35–7 and notes.   [3] *Ibid.*, p. 51.
[4] *Ibid.*, pp. 62–3. See also above, p. 336.   [5] Williams III. 113.
[6] *Ibid.*, p. 62 and n. 2.   [7] *Ibid.*, p. 145.
[8] *Ibid.*, p. 344, n. 2.   [9] *Ibid.*, p. 340.   [10] *Ibid.*, p. 421 and n. 1.

of 1735, blessing Stopford heartily and sending him to Pulteney
in the hope that the opposition leader would again further the
clerical ambitions of a meritorious candidate.[1] 'He is', Swift told
Pulteney, 'one of the most deserving gentlemen in the country.'
It was a brief trip to England, for Stopford was home again
about two months after leaving; and on the day of his arrival, he
went to see the dean (who unfortunately had gone out).[2] A year
later, the Lord Lieutenant was to present him to the arch-
deaconry of Killaloe, an advancement for which Pulteney,
incidentally, accepted the credit.[3] Although this promotion may
have allowed Stopford less time in Dublin and at the deanery,
the friendship endured; and in Swift's will, one of the executors
named is the Vicar of Finglas.[4]

A new acquaintance of this period, having none of Stopford's
prudence or modesty, though far more than his erudition, was
the fourth William King in Swift's life—the Principal of
St Mary Hall, Oxford.[5] Although Swift never was a Jacobite,
many of his friends had Jacobitical leanings. With his own
strength spent on causes that were losing, he respected the
followers of causes that were lost. The adherents of the exiled
family, he treated as radically Quixotic—honourably rash—
rather than treasonable. For any threat alleged to lie in such a
movement (and Walpole never failed to exaggerate the threat),
he felt perfect contempt. For him, it comprised a harmless
minority of infatuates adoring a leader unworthy of their noble
impulse. The Fifteen and the Forty-five, Swift would have
interpreted as natural explosions of a misgoverned people, when
the crimes of the enthroned, corrupt monarch inevitably turned
their thoughts to the fictitious virtues of the absent martyr.[6]

King was probably the most radical character that Swift
knew of this persuasion, and might be called the intellectual

---

[1] *Ibid.*, IV. 305, 327–8, 336.　　[2] *Ibid.*, p. 336.　　[3] *Ibid.*, p. 552.

[4] Davis XIII. 157. In spite of his patrons, Stopford did not enjoy a speedy rise. In 1747
he was made Dean of Kilmacduagh, but only in 1753 did he become Bishop of Cloyne.
He died in 1759.

[5] Born 1685, died 1763. St Mary Hall had a Principal but few students and no fellows.

[6] Cf. Davis VIII. 173, 218.

spokesman for English Jacobitism in his time.[1] He later claimed to have drunk tea with Prince Charles Edward in London in 1750.[2] At Oxford he had served as secretary to Ormonde when the Duke held the title of Chancellor of the University; and he was recognized as the leader of the Jacobite party among the dons.

What brought King to Dublin was a crazily intricate lawsuit occupying twenty years of litigation. Though he came over first in 1727, he only met Swift during a later visit which probably extended from the winter of 1734 to the summer of 1735.[3] Since Swift preserved the letters he received from King (none of the dean's to him are extant), we may infer that he regarded him as a figure of distinction.

King immensely admired Swift and, as a writer, was deeply influenced by him. Although the Principal of St Mary Hall was 'the last example of a Latin poet in the grand manner',[4] the work in which he celebrated Swift was part of a verse satire, *The Toast*, attacking his enemies at law. If the poet does not exaggerate too much (he certainly does to some extent), we may believe that when he showed Swift the unfinished manuscript the dean encouraged him to complete the work.[5] To allow himself freedom in denigrating his opponents, King placed the most libellous of his accusations in elegantly written Latin notes to the English text. Swift, he tells us, was 'chiefly pleased with the notes, and expressed his surprise that I had attained such facility in writing the burlesque Latin'.[6]

The dean in his turn showed the Principal the manuscript of *The Four Last Years*, which he hoped to see printed in his own lifetime. Apparently, Swift either wished to have another copy made or expected to add further changes to the text; for instead of simply giving King the book, he promised to send it to him in England.[7]

A common friend of King and of Swift was young Orrery. But

---

[1] David Greenwood, *William King* (Oxford, 1969), p. 327.
[2] *Ibid.*, p. 235.   [3] *Ibid.*, pp. 71–2.   [4] *Ibid.*, p. 352.
[5] See Williams IV. 394–5.   [6] Greenwood, p. 67, n. 2.
[7] Williams IV. 394 and n. 5.

the Earl was unctuous where Stopford was modest, and pedantic where King was learned. He had the advantages of youth,
wealth, a title, and an eagerness to please. At Oxford, his tutor
had been Pope's collaborator, Fenton. In spite of his father's
depreciation of him, the fifth Earl possessed a fundamental taste
and respect for humane letters. He seems to have taken exemplary care of his estate, and his conduct as a father and
husband was irreproachable. With so many visible merits, and a
political bias less conformist than Stopford's but more restrained
than Principal King's, it was natural that he should charm an
elderly dean thirsty for youthful tributes.

Orrery evidently felt peculiarly comfortable with old men;
and he may have transferred to Swift (his father's friend) those
emotions which the father himself had failed to satisfy. Since
Swift had confronted a similar impasse all life long, he would
have been intuitively sympathetic with the Earl.

In mid-June, Orrery returned to Dublin from England,[1] and
his impression of the dean has unusual value. Despite the vigorous style and amplitude of Swift's letters, despite the scope of his
social round, the self-portrait he offers in the summer of 1735 has
the usual dark-grey monochrome. Complaining of shaky health,
he bemoans the consequent inability to make the journey he
yearns for, to England:

> I dare not so much as travel here, without being near enough to
> come back in the evening to lie in my own bed. These are the effects
> of living too long; and the public miseries of this kingdom add to my
> disease.[2]

Here certainly was suffering. Yet Orrery, two weeks earlier, had
written to a friend,

> You'll rejoice with me that the Dean of St Patrick's is in high health;
> the same inimitable man I left him. A murrain on [the legal busi-
> ness] that will not suffer me to indulge myself half enough in his
> company.[3]

---

[1] The Dublin newpapers of 21 June report that he arrived 'this week'. On 15 June
Swift says he expects Orrery 'next week' (Williams IV. 350).
[2] Williams IV. 361 (12 Jul. 1735).   [3] *Orrery Papers* I. 131.

In July the Earl went to his seat near Charleville and then to other properties in the south of Ireland, spending October in Cork. But around 1 November he went back to the capital, to stay there through the winter.

III. LOSSES AND GAINS

Meanwhile, Swift had endured a domestic revolution. Not only had he lost the admirable Mrs Worrall, but Mrs Brent, his 'Sir Robert Walpole', or housekeeper, also died in the spring of 1735.[1] He turned to Mrs Whiteway (widowed for the second time in 1733) and to Mrs Ridgeway, the daughter of Mrs Brent.[2] Although Anne Ridgeway seems to have been a less reliable housekeeper than her mother, Martha Whiteway had intellectual and moral advantages over Mrs Worrall. So for the remaining years of his life, Swift never lacked a clever, good-natured woman friend to protect him against the isolation which constantly threatened him.

Mrs Whiteway's importance to Swift has not often been noticed. Born Martha Swift, a few years younger than Vanessa, she was the last child of Swift's youngest uncle, Adam. At seventeen she married her first husband, Theophilus Harrison. He was a parson whose mother had been the last wife of Swift's eldest uncle, Godwin, and whose father was a prebendary of St Patrick's and Dean of Clonmacnoise. Harrison had died in 1714, after fathering two children, and in 1716 the widow married Edward Whiteway, by whom she bore two sons. We have seen how Swift welcomed her friendship in 1730, and how it deepened after she became a widow again, in 1732, when her youngest child, John, was only nine.

By the spring of 1735 Swift could describe Mrs Whiteway as the only cousin whom he saw.[3] She had begun visiting him several times a week and helping to keep his household in order.

---

[1] Williams IV. 328, n. 3; 332, n. 1.

[2] Mrs Ridgeway must have been installed before June 1735, because there is a receipt of that date witnessed by her (*ibid.*, p. 343).

[3] *Ibid.*, p. 328.

Being an intelligent and well-educated woman, she soon helped with his correspondence. If she cannot be called his secretary, it is because she was something more. As Swift neared seventy, his responsibilities did not grow lighter, but his congenitally uneven memory became less reliable, while the deafness and vertigo continued their inroads.

Swift interested himself in Mrs Whiteway's children. Her studious, ascetic first-born, Theophilus Harrison, charmed him. When the young man died (in February 1736), Swift mourned with the inconsolable mother, and he offered her the deanery as a retreat from the last scenes. Mary Harrison, her daughter, turned into one of his young lady pets. Swift also paid a hundred pounds for John Whiteway to be apprenticed to a surgeon[1]— appropriately enough, because the boy became not only one of the great Irish medical men of the eighteenth century but also the first Visiting Surgeon of the hospital established by Swift's will.[2] Through his fondness for the children and their mother, the dean could enjoy some of the satisfactions of having a family. At this time they were all the more valuable because what he had joked about many years before was coming true:

> I have gone the round of all my stories three or four times with the younger people, and begin them again. I give hints how significant a person I have been, and nobody believes me: I pretend to pity them, but am inwardly angry. I lay traps for people to desire I would show them things I have written, but cannot succeed. . . . If I can prevail on any one to personate a hearer and admirer, you would wonder what a favourite he grows.[3]

But a drastic reduction of his convivial pleasures took place when both Delany and Sheridan gave up their homes in Dublin. Delany's new wife found the city air disagreeable ('uxorem duxit', said Orrery, 'an ille liber cui mulier imperat').[4] So he did not return to his Stafford Street house in the winter of 1734–5, but established himself permanently at Delville, and advertised

---

[1] *Ibid.*, p. 489.   [2] Maurice J. Craig, *The Legacy of Swift* (Dublin, 1948), p. 42.
[3] 19 Dec. 1719; Williams II. 333–4; cf. above, p. 88.
[4] Cicero, *Paradoxa stoicorum* 36: He got married; can he whom a wife commands be free?

that the building in town was 'to be let for any term of years'.[1]
Although Delany seems to have arranged for Swift and other
guests to stay the night in a rented house just next to Delville, the
cost and trouble of the journey discouraged the dean; and he
complained to Miss Donnellan, Mrs Pendarves, and Orrery.[2]

Sheridan's uprooting followed from the long-planned scheme
to exchange his Dunboyne living for the headmastership of the
Free School of Cavan. By April 1735 the thing was done.[3] In
the meantime, on Saturday, 15 February, about thirty-five of
Sheridan's old students gave him a farewell banquet at the
Plume of Feathers tavern in Castle Street. Among the various
proceedings there was a formal invitation by the diners to Dean
Swift, as well as the ceremony of two young gentlemen conduct-
ing him to the dinner. Due notice was taken by the *Dublin
Journal*. According to the newspaper account, 'The Dean did
afterwards declare to his friends the great satisfaction he received from the modesty, the decent behaviour, and the good
sense of the whole company.'[4] Near the beginning of April,
Sheridan went ahead of his family to the new, though familiar,
place (he was a native of Cavan); and the next month the *Dublin
Evening-Post* announced that his school would open on 5 May.[5]

Swift must have known that this deprivation would never be
made up. 'My greatest loss', he said in July, 'is that of my viceroy
Trifler Sheridan.' Yet he admitted to entertaining ten guests
every Sunday evening.[6] Of course, Sheridan had barely arrived
in Cavan when he begged the dean to pay him a visit, for in June
Swift was already putting him off.[7] The sanguine schoolmaster
praised every natural advantage of his country seat except the
people: the air, the landscape, the food, the water—

> Dear Sir, I am almost persuaded that the journey hither will not
> only remove your disorder, but the good air will also get you a
> stomach, and of consequence new flesh, and good health.[8]

[1] *Ibid.*, IV. 298, 333, 339; *Orrery Papers* I. 144; *Dublin Journal*, 12 Apr. 1735, and *passim*.
[2] Williams IV. 298, 333, 339, 367; *Poems* III. 1049–50.
[3] Williams IV. 315, n. 3.   [4] *Dublin Journal*, 18 Feb. 1735.
[5] *Dublin Evening-Post*, 3 May; see also Ball V. 170, n. 4; *Pue's Occurrences*, 20 May; *Dublin Journal*, 3 May 1735.
[6] 17 Jul. 1735; Williams IV. 367.   [7] *Ibid.*, p. 350.
[8] 23 Jun. 1735; *ibid.*, p. 355.

But Swift employed his leisure elsewhere. 'I have three other engagements on my hands,' he said, 'but the principal is to see the Bishop of Ossory.'[1] I can give some impression of the wide range and steady pace of his activities by a brief survey. In February 1735 he had enough money available to lend fifteen hundred pounds to Dr Helsham's stepson.[2] In March he accompanied Stearne and Hoadly when they 'visited'—or formally inspected—Trinity College, where the dean 'spoke against some of the corruptions and abuses'.[3] From time to time he saw Dorset's son, Lord George Sackville, who was a student at Trinity College; the lad was also the heir of Lady Betty Germaine, and she had asked Swift to give him some attention.[4] Early in May he stayed briefly with George Nugent, the tenant of Deane Swift's property at Castlerickard.[5] But the archbishop held his visitation of St Patrick's Cathedral around this time, and Swift must have attended.[6] In June and July, to comply with a request from Lord Howth, he allowed Francis Bindon to paint his portrait (now at Howth Castle)—

I have been fool enough to sit for my picture at full length by Mr Bindon for my Lord Howth. I have just sate two hours and a half.[7]

In July he finished writing a new will.[8] The Sunday parties went on—'half a score come to spunge on me every Sunday evening'.[9] He called often and with pleasure on Lady Acheson, who was living with her mother.[10] The impression one receives of many social connections busily maintained is constant.

While his weakening eyesight limited Swift's reading, he could not easily indulge himself in prose scribbles as he used to do, since the causes which he had struggled for seemed defunct. The government of England, the economy of Ireland, the Established Church had all moved (he thought) in directions he had tried to block. As he neared seventy, Swift reduced his

---

[1] *Ibid.*, p. 350.   [2] *Ibid.*, p. 296 and n. 2.
[3] *Dublin Journal, Dublin Evening-Post, Pue's Occurrences*, 22 Mar. 1735.
[4] *Accounts 1734–5, passim*; Williams IV. 18.   [5] Williams IV. 331, n. 4.
[6] According to the *Dublin Evening-Post*, the visitation was held on 6–8 May.
[7] Williams IV. 352; cf. *ibid.*, p. 358. Swift dined with Lord Howth on 4 Jun. (*Accounts*, fol. 9).
[8] Williams IV. 366–7.   [9] *Ibid.*, p. 367.   [10] *Ibid.*, pp. 340, 359, 365, 375.

campaigns to spaces so narrow as municipal politics, the liberty (i.e., neighbourhood) of St Patrick's, the control of begging in Dublin, and other grounds too small to satisfy his expressive impulse. While his mind and talents kept their strength, his energy overflowed into various pastimes: composing in Anglo-Latin, seeking preferment for friends, giving advice to people in trouble, and writing a remarkable number of excellent letters. There was also the plan for a mental hospital.

Chapter Seven

THE HOSPITAL AND THE
LEGION CLUB

I. ST PATRICK'S HOSPITAL

Apart from professional duties and social pleasures, Swift often undertook certain works of charity that called for discretion and are not easy to define. An example is his interceding, during the spring of 1735, to prevent a scandal in the Fitzherbert family. Arthur, the second son of William Fitzherbert, had been a pupil of Sheridan and then took a B.A. degree at Trinity College, Dublin.[1] Although he performed superlatively as a student, he alienated his parents through rude, arrogant behaviour. At twenty-one he was left to shift for himself and only given permission to dine at his father's house.

The boy wrote to Swift, begging him to persuade Mr Fitzherbert that he should put his son 'into some way of life'; and Sheridan endorsed his goodness of character. Swift investigated the facts as well as he conveniently could, and then addressed a shrewd, tactful letter to the father, pleading that the son be helped. Among the remarks is the following appeal, made after Swift has praised the letter written to himself by the boy:

> Yet, I think, if I had a son, who had understanding, wit, and humour, to write such a letter, I could not find in my heart to cast him off, but try what good advice and maturer years would do towards amendment, and, in the mean time, give him no cause to complain of wanting convenient food, lodging, and raiment.[2]

---

[1] Williams gives his name as Andrew. But *Alumni Dublinenses* shows that Andrew was the elder son, and not Sheridan's pupil. Arthur, born in Shercock, co. Cavan, was twenty-one in 1735.

[2] Williams IV. 308.

When the father did not reply, Swift wrote to the mother, who answered gratefully but with caution.[1] The final benefit to the son appears to have been only a small annuity from the father.[2] But we know that Swift gave him money.[3] The incident took much of the dean's time and gave him no reward except the exercise of benevolence.[4]

A better-known sort of charity was Swift's troop of old, female beggars. 'Cancerina is dead,' he told Sheridan in March 1733, 'and I let her go to her grave without a coffin and without fees.'[5] The woman belonged to the assortment of honest paupers whom the dean, their patron, named after their infirmities. Delany, who recorded their history, reports that each had to follow some vocation:

> One of these mistresses sold plumbs; another, hob-nails; a third, tapes; a fourth, ginger-bread; a fifth, knitted; a sixth, darned stockings; and a seventh, cobbled shoes.[6]

They were all sick, crippled, or disfigured:

> One of these mistresses wanted an eye: another, a nose; a third, an arm: a fourth, a foot: a fifth, had all the attractions of Agna's Pollipus: and a sixth, more than all those of Aesop's hump; and all of them as old at least, as some of Louis the XIVth's mistresses.[7]

And so Swift named them Cancerina, Stumpa-Nympha, Pullagowna, Friterilla, Flora, Stumpantha, etc. Delany says the dean would greet them kindly, asking how they were, 'how they throve: what stock they had'. Whenever he could use or pretend to use their wares, he bought some. However, he paid far more than the real value—

> for every half-penny-worth, at least sixpence: and for every penny-worth, a shilling. If their saleables were of another nature, he added something to their stock: with strict charges of industry, and honesty. And ... these mistresses were very numerous: insomuch, that

---

[1] *Ibid.*, p. 318.   [2] Ball v. 158, n. 3.

[3] Swift's accounts show half a guinea given to young Fitzherbert on 1 Apr. 1735.

[4] For a comparable intervention, to scold a wayward young lord, see the letter from Swift to Lady Santry, sometimes dated 1730 but more likely 1735, in Ball v. 437–9.

[5] 27 Mar. 1733; Williams IV. 130.   [6] Delany, p. 131.   [7] *Ibid.*, p. 132.

there was scarce one street, or alley, or lane, in Dublin, its suburbs, and its environs, that had not, at least, one, or more of them.[1]

Swift's charitable impulses had also a less kindly aspect than his innumerable good deeds might suggest. In keeping with the principles of his morality, Swift regarded many victims as culprits. Like nearly all the social philosophers of the age, he did not wish to think that numbers of innocent people might suffer extreme poverty without being any more sinful than those who prospered. In a fragment of an essay, 'Considerations about Maintaining the Poor', Swift blamed the prevalence of beggary in Ireland (among other reasons) on the laziness of the sufferers and their habit of marrying early.[2]

A workhouse had been established in Dublin in 1704, but it did little to relieve the wretchedness of the lowly, as indeed such institutions normally fail to accomplish their purpose. Successive reorganizations and the provision of a substantial fund to support the workhouse still left the poor largely where they had been. Swift felt bitter over the indifference of responsible persons to the situation. As a man who loved to walk the streets of the city, he was disgusted by the beggars who swarmed in his way. Consequently, he proposed a scheme that made up in cheapness and simplicity for what it lacked in originality. This was to limit the movements of beggars, in line with English laws requiring each parish to maintain its own poor.

Both the plan itself and Swift's tone in putting it forward will offend readers accustomed to think of poverty not as a sign of dissolute character but as a misfortune. Yet he cherished the scheme and recommended it both to Archbishop King and to a series of lord mayors of Dublin. Basically, Swift wished to make each beggar wear a badge that would identify him and, as it were, license him to beg, but only in the parish of his settlement. As Swift presented the scheme in 1726, the archbishop would direct the clergy and churchwardens of Dublin to execute it.

[1] *Ibid.*, pp. 131–3. Cf. *Surprising Memoirs of the ... Cripple-Beggars, Manupedius and Stumpanimpha ... King and Queen of the Beggars* (Dublin, 1735), advertised in the *Dublin Journal*, Jan. 1735.
[2] T. Scott VII. 341.

They were to provide badges made of brass, copper, or pewter. Each badge would be marked with the initial letters of the appropriate church and numbered one, two, three, and so forth, corresponding to the number assigned to each beggar. The badge was then to be 'well sewed and fastened on the right and left shoulder of the outward garment', so anybody might see to which parish the wearer belonged. Finally, the poor should be commanded not to go out of their own parish begging for alms; and the beadles were to enforce this regulation.[1]

If we put aside the punitive humiliations imposed by the badges, the programme remains simply impracticable; for one could hardly expect a pauper never to leave his parish, and yet who could be sure whether he was merely visiting another district or seeking alms in it? If a beadle happened to come by while someone was breaking the rule, or if warmhearted gentlemen refused to help anyone begging outside his proper territory, Swift's plan might be momentarily effective. Otherwise, although the Dean of St Patrick's might make it work in the liberties of the cathedral, a beggar could easily evade it elsewhere.

Nevertheless, the archbishop adopted Swift's proposal, and badges were distributed. But the beggars refused to abide by the regulations. Several would not even accept a badge; and those who did take one wore it incorrectly if at all. In 1726, exasperated by the uselessness of the badges, Swift wrote,

> And of those who received them, almost everyone keep them in their pockets, or hang them in a string about their necks, or fasten them under their coats ... so that a man may walk from one end of the town to the other without seeing one beggar regularly badged, and in such great numbers, that they are a mighty nuisance to the public, most of them being foreigners.[2]

But Swift clung to the project; and more than ten years later, he tried again. In 1737 he decided to set forth his case in fresh detail, and brought out a pamphlet on the subject: *A Proposal for*

[1] Davis XIII. 172. [2] *Ibid.*, pp. 172–3.

Giving Badges to the Beggars in All the Parishes of Dublin.[1] Uncharacteristically, he revealed the authorship, signing his name at
the end. He also put the fact on the title-page, with the words,
'By the Dean of St Patrick's'; and Faulkner decorated that page
with a small, crude representation of Swift in priest's bands
and gown, enclosed in a circle with the words, 'M.B. Drapier',
edging it below. I infer that the dean was throwing the full
weight of his authority behind the argument.

Nevertheless, the striking feature of the pamphlet is not the
exposition of doctrine but the way it illustrates Swift's famous
declaration that he gave his love to individuals rather than to
communities of men. For any particular beggar Swift might
instinctively feel compassion. Imaginatively, he could join himself to the unique sufferer. However, when he thought of the
poor as a class, he felt appalled by their collective faults and
rejected them as he rejected fine ladies in the filthy verse satires.

The memorable passages of the essay are the attack on
'foreign' beggars and the condemnation of the poor in general.
So hyperbolic and relentless is the language that an ill-informed
reader might suppose the great ironist was impersonating a
brutal misanthrope. Only if one studies the reasoning does one
observe that Swift objects to the irresponsibility of those whose
duty it is to care for the outsiders, and that at the same time he is
defending the rights of his own neighbourhood beggars:

> I never heard more than one objection against this expedient of
> badging the poor, and confining their walk to their several parishes.
> The objection was this: What shall we do with the foreign beggars?
> Must they be left to starve? I answered, No; but they must be driven
> or whipped out of town; and let the next country parish do as they
> please, or rather after the practice in England, send them from one
> parish to another, until they reach their own homes.... In the
> remoter and poorer parishes of the kingdom, all necessaries for life
> proper for poor people are comparatively cheaper; I mean butter
> milk, oatmeal, potatoes, and other vegetables; and every farmer or

---

[1] Signed 22 Apr. 1737; *ibid.*, pp. 127–40. It was published in London, 1737, by T.
Cooper.

cottager, who is not himself a beggar, can sometimes spare a sup or a morsel, not worth the fourth part of a farthing, to an indigent neighbour of his own parish, who is disabled from work. A beggar native of the parish is known to the 'squire, to the church minister, to the Popish priest, or the conventicle teachers, as well as to every farmer: He hath generally some relations able to live, and contribute something to his maintenance.... If he be not quite maimed, he and his trull, and litter of brats (if he hath any) may get half their support by doing some kind of work in their power.[1]

Without commenting further on the savagery of these expressions, I shall give a sample of the projector's detestation of paupers as a class. One must see that Swift is placing them in the general category of Irish people bringing down on their own heads the misfortunes that oppress them:

To say the truth, there is not a more undeserving vicious race of human kind than the bulk of those who are reduced to beggary, even in this beggarly country.... I am confident, that among the meaner people, nineteen in twenty of those who are reduced to a starving condition, did not become so by what the lawyers call the work of God, either upon their body or goods; but merely for their own idleness, attended with all manner of vices, particularly drunkenness, thievery, and cheating.[2]

This is the attitude that underlies Swift's denunciation of those beggars who refuse to wear badges:

They are too lazy to work, they are not afraid to steal, nor ashamed to beg; and yet are too proud to be seen with a badge.... They all look upon such an obligation as a high indignity done to their office. I appeal to all indifferent people, whether such wretches deserve to be relieved.[3]

And yet it was while embracing such prejudices that he set out to relieve the poor—not because they deserved help but because they needed it. Whatever uncertainties his own language may arouse, we have vivid testimony to the effectiveness of his good works, in a dialogue published in 1734, dealing with Dublin beggars. At one point Stumpa-Nympha is supposed to speak and express her gratitude both to Swift for bestowing his charity

[1] Davis XIII. 133.   [2] *Ibid.*, p. 135.   [3] *Ibid.*, p. 134.

and to Mrs Worrall (who had died recently) for administering it:

> Dead are my parents, but they liv'd again
> In worthy Madam WORRALL and the DEAN.
> She to my sorrow, and misfortune's dead!
> Well, well may I have aching heart and head!
> See here this *gown*, from her spin-new it came,
> This cap, and other things that I could name:
> Her loss all do, but more than me none can
> Lament....
> Some other ladies with the Dean intend,
> If I deserve it, to supply that friend:
> O they are good! and still his nature is,
> That Ireland's children everyone are his.
> His *thoughts* and *goodness* ev'n to *me* extend,
> How can they sink, that have so great a friend?[1]

The tribute may sound bizarre, but only a philanthropist of large vision and great energy could have inspired it.

Yet of all Swift's charities and benefactions, the most visible was the institution still flourishing and called St Patrick's Hospital. Though Swift had always shown a particular interest in schools and hospitals, this plan for his own fortune did not mature until he was nearly seventy. Before he left London in 1714, he had been elected one of the governors of Bedlam.[2] Two years later, he helped to found a charity school for the poor children of his liberty.[3] As Dean of St Patrick's Cathedral, he sat ex officio on the board of the Dublin Workhouse and Foundling Hospital.[4] In 1725 he was appointed to the board of Dublin's 'most famous and firmly established charity school', the Blue Coats. In March 1735, through the will of Mrs Mary Mercer, he was made chief trustee of the fund which she left to establish a hospital for chronic diseases.[5]

---

[1] *Surprising Memoirs of the ... Cripple-Beggars, Manupedius and Stumpanimpha ... King and Queen of the Beggars* (Dublin, 1734), p. 34. Stumpanimpha's real name is given as Joanna Magennis (p. 4). I owe my information about this work to the kindness of Professor James Woolley.

[2] Edward G. O'Donoghue, *The Story of the Bethlehem Hospital* (London, 1914), p. 249; Atterbury was elected at the same time. See also Ball III. 129, n. 10, continued *ibid.*, VI. 244.

[3] Landa, 'Swift and Charity', p. 342.   [4] *Ibid.*, p. 341.   [5] *Ibid.*, p. 342.

But the main approach to his own scheme probably opened in 1721, when Swift became a trustee of the money left by Dr Richard Steevens for a hospital for ordinary medical patients. Swift sat on the committee that planned the erection of the building. It was probably at his suggestion and certainly with his approval that Stella left her fortune to maintain a chaplain for the hospital.[1] In 1727 Swift gave up his scheme for establishing a fellowship at Trinity College,[2] and his funds remained available for another use. At last, the year before Steevens' Hospital was formally opened,[3] he chose to provide by himself for a class of patients who could not be admitted to that institution.[4]

If the final couplets of *Verses on the Death of Dr Swift* were not added long after the body of the poem was composed, Swift had decided by 1731 to give 'the little wealth he had, / To build a house for fools and mad'.[5] In 1732 he consulted Sir William Fownes about the principles on which such a hospital should be designed, and in return he got a budget of wise recommendations. The main difference between Fownes and Swift was that Sir William wished the charity to be public, with the money raised by subscription, while Swift preferred it to be private—I assume in order that he might control the terms of the constitution. Fownes seems to have been on the verge of promoting a rival scheme and perhaps hoped that Swift would abandon his own in favour of that. But the outcome was just the reverse.[6]

By the spring of 1733 Swift had certainly determined to devote his estate to this 'public use'.[7] Yet he felt so uneasy about possible blunders in the provisions that two years later he was still perfecting the plan.[8] In January 1735 he petitioned the city government for a grant of land in Oxmantown Green, on the outskirts of Dublin; and a committee was appointed to select a

---

[1] *Ibid.*, p. 341.   [2] See above, pp. 567–9.

[3] 23 Jul. 1733, Steevens' Hospital was opened; T.P.C. Kirkpatrick, *The History of Dr Steevens' Hospital* (Dublin, 1924), p. 52.

[4] Landa, 'Swift and Charity', p. 341.   [5] Ll. 479–80.

[6] 9 Sept. 1732; Williams IV. 65–70.

[7] Letter to Pope, 31 Mar. 1733; Sherburn III. 361.

[8] 20 Feb. 1735; Williams IV. 296.

convenient plot.[1] At this time Swift judged that municipal officers would make the best trustees in 'an affair calculated wholly for the city's advantage'; and he took advice from Eaton Stannard, the Recorder of Dublin.[2] During the summer that followed, he told Orrery that he had drawn up a will disposing of his whole fortune in this way.[3] Next, the city confirmed the grant of land, and the fact was quickly reported in Irish and English newspapers.[4] Although in 1737 he considered using Dr Steevens' governors as trustees for the new hospital, he made it at last an independent foundation.[5] One of his final steps to secure the project was a petition, in 1737, to have it exempted from an impending bill against mortmain. His petition succeeded, although the bill did not.[6] One hope he had to give up. By the spring of 1736 Swift had seventy-five hundred pounds out at interest, and he could have bought the land from which he proposed that the income of the hospital would be derived. But he never found a satisfactory estate and had to leave the negotiation to his executors.[7]

II. THE LEGION CLUB

In the autumn of 1735 the usual biennial symptoms of a parliamentary session were visible. It was a prospect that disgusted Swift, who proposed to visit Sheridan in Cavan while the Lords and Commons were in town:[8]

> I have a scheme of living with you when the College-Green club [i.e., Parliament] is to meet, for in these times I detest the town, and hearing the follies, corruptions and slavish practices of those misrepresentative brutes, and resolve if I can stir to pass that whole time at Bath or Cavan.[9]

---

[1] 17 Jan. See *Pue's Occurrences*, 18 Jan.; *Dublin Journal* and *Dublin Evening-Post*, 21 Jan.; Williams IV. 296, n. 3.
[2] 11 Apr. 1735; Williams IV. 319–20.   [3] 17 Jul. 1735; *ibid.*, p. 367.
[4] 18 Jul. See *Pue's Occurrences*, 19 Jul.; *Dublin Journal* and *Dublin Evening-Post*, 22 Jul.; Williams IV. 296, n. 3.
[5] Landa, 'Swift and Charity', p. 341.
[6] *Ibid.*   [7] 13 Jul. 1738; Williams V. 112–13.
[8] *Ibid.*, IV. 350, 397, 398.   [9] 15 Jun. 1735; *ibid.*, p. 350.

Dorset disembarked with his family on 24 September,[1] and Swift saw him at the Lord Mayor's dinner on 30 September.[2] This was during a season when Swift considered Ireland to be 'absolutely starving, by the means of every oppression that can be inflicted on mankind'.[3] The woollen industry was suffering a disastrous slump; and unemployed weavers, blaming their wretchedness on imported cottons and silks, took to insulting women who wore foreign goods. They hanged effigies of Calico and Silk; and some angry men threw acid on clothing made from those materials. In May there had been a performance of *Othello* for the benefit of the weavers, with the preface and epilogue which Swift had composed in 1720.[4] The same newspapers that announced Dorset's arrival reported that the weavers were again squirting acid.[5]

The gathering of the peers and M.P.s in such a setting provoked Swift's habitual contempt. A mild expression of his opinion of both Dorset and his Parliament emerges in a letter to Pulteney:

> I love the Duke of Dorset very well, having known him from his youth, and he hath treated me with great civility since he came into this government. It is true, his original principles, as well as his instructions from your side the water, make him act the usual part in managing this nation, for which he must be excused: yet I wish he would a little more consider, that people here might have some small share in employments civil and ecclesiastic, wherein my Lord Carteret acted a more popular part. The folks here, whom they call a parliament, will imitate yours in everything, after the same manner as a monkey doth a human creature.[6]

Because of their irresponsibility, Swift called them 'the club'; and with his own plans for a lunatic asylum on his mind, he apparently saw the whole assembly in terms of the Academy of Lagado and its Bedlamite characters. In another way, Parliament recalled a Miltonic Pandemonium, to suit the inferno that was Ireland; and the two houses made up a clan of devils. Their

---

[1] *Ibid.*, p. 397.   [2] *Ibid.*, pp. 397–8; *Accounts*, fol. 2ᵛ.
[3] Letter to Pope, 3 Sept. 1735; Sherburn III. 492.
[4] *Dublin Evening-Post*, 10 May 1735.   [5] *Ibid.*, 27 Sept.   [6] Williams IV. 336.

cruelty and irrationality also gave them a bestial quality that evoked a motif of Houyhnhnmland or *A Modest Proposal*—as well as several of Swift's poems.[1] But whether madhouse, hell, or menagerie, the Parliament of Ireland in the autumn of 1735 produced his most violent epithets. 'The Club meets in a week,' he wrote on 30 September, 'and I determine to leave the town as soon as possible, for I am not able to live within the air of such rascals.'[2]

He was getting ready to pay Sheridan the long visit. They had kept in touch by a correspondence of letters bursting with polylingual punning vocabularies: a contest in words ending with '-ling'; Latin written as English; English written as Latin; English composed exclusively of puns; Greek written as English; rebuses; phrases in French, Italian, Greek, and Latin; seven puns on 'ash'; and so forth.[3] About the beginning of September, the schoolmaster came to Dublin on a holiday, hoping to carry the dean back with him.[4] 'Sheridan stayed here not above ten days,' said Swift, 'all which he passed abroad, and only lay at the deanery.'[5]

Swift did not follow him to Cavan till the beginning of November; and in the meantime there probably occurred one of the incidents that marked his loathing for 'that abominable club'.[6] In April, his friend, Richard Grattan, had been elected Lord Mayor. To honour this successor, the retiring mayor, Nathaniel Kane, gave a great feast on 30 September when Grattan was sworn in. The dean attended; and here too he saw Dorset; but he 'came away before six, with very little meat or drink'.[7] It was at some such 'public city dinner' that Swift made a vindictive reference to an English acquaintance of his, George Dodington, Walpole's jackal, who held the valuable Irish sinecure of Clerk of the Pells. A correspondent wrote to Dodington,[8]

---

[1] Cf. *ibid.*, pp. 336, 350.   [2] *Ibid.*, p. 398.
[3] E.g., *ibid.*, pp. 346–52, 354–8.   [4] *Ibid.*, pp. 375–6.
[5] *Ibid.*, p. 396.   [6] *Ibid.*, p. 397.
[7] *Ibid.*, p. 398.
[8] Though the letter is dated 25 Sept., it may have been finished after 30 Sept., and the reference may be to the dinner for Grattan; but there were many such banquets.

Your name was mentioned . . . by that eternal snarl, Swift. Speaking of the good nature of his countrymen, he said, one Carey [i.e., Dorset's secretary], last session, introduced a gentleman from England, dressed him in a suit of Irish manufacture, which cost thirty shillings, and then showed him for a patriot, upon which the good people of Ireland gave him seven hundred pounds per annum.[1]

Sir Arthur Acheson, who also knew Dodington, gave a fuller account, which suggests still more about Swift's status as a public figure:

I was a little surprised at that part of your letter relating to Dr Swift. He came to see me soon after I landed, and we had a good deal of discourse of you; he spoke of the acquaintance he formerly had with you, and seemed to wonder that you never sent or took any notice of him when you were here. I told him I had heard you mention the same thing, and that he had never been to wait upon you, which, in my opinion, was wrong in him; upon the whole he said he was sorry the mistake had happened. I have enquired concerning the feast and what mention he made of you there. Doctor Cope, who was present, gave me this account of it:—Luke Gardner was there, talking like a great patriot, and said no gentleman of this country should be forgiven that wore anything but the manufactures of it. The Dean answered him thus:—I am told you have got into employments worth two thousand pounds, and possibly you lay out ten pounds a year for a suit of clothes; for this you would be esteemed a vast friend to the country, though in an affair of any importance you gave it up. I hear that Mr Dodington, when he was here, bought an Irish stuff suit, and then everybody said, won't you vote for Mr Dodington, who wears our manufactures; so you made him a present of seven or eight hundred pounds a year for laying out forty or fifty shillings in Irish stuff. This, Doctor Cope assures me, was all that passed, and therefore I apprehend it has been greatly magnified or misrepresented to you, as it is a way of rattling the Dean has always indulged himself in, of and towards all sorts of people, which, though I don't approve I fear he will never be broke of.[2]

After several delays, however, Swift left Parliament and aldermen behind and took to the road on 3 November. He

---

[1] Letter of 25 Sept. 1735 from John Bowes; H.M.C. *Various Collections* VI (Miss Eyre Matcham), pp. 63–5.
[2] Letter of 23 Oct. 1735; *ibid.*

stopped overnight at Dunshaughlin, co. Meath, then at Kells, and at Cross Keys,[1] arriving on the sixth at Cavan.[2] This was a day faster than Sheridan had recommended;[3] and the sixty-eight-year-old dean, pained by a sore shin, must have shown the strain when he reached the town of Virginia, where Sheridan met him. According to the younger Thomas Sheridan, who had been enrolled in Trinity College since May, Swift behaved himself with blatant discourtesy.

Dr Sheridan had persuaded the burgesses of Cavan to meet the dean four miles outside the town. The eldest delivered a complimentary address but spoke it clumsily. Instead of ignoring the man's faults, Swift made a sharp reference to them. A few days later, Dr Sheridan indicated that it was Swift's social duty to entertain the company, but the dean showed some reluctance to comply. According to the younger Sheridan,

> He gave them a very shabby dinner at the inn, and called for the bill, before the guests had got half enough of wine. He disputed several articles ... flew into a violent passion, and abused his servants grossly for not keeping better count.[4]

This tale sounds rather like Mrs Pilkington's account of dining with the dean. But Swift gives a very different story:

> Eight of the inhabitants came out to meet me a mile or two from town.... In some days after, I invited the principal men in town to sup with me at the best inn here. There were sixteen of them, and I came off rarely for about thirty shillings. They were all very modest and obliging.[5]

In general, the younger Sheridan (writing fifty years later) remembered Swift, during this visit, as shockingly decayed:

> His person was quite emaciated, and bore the marks of many more years than had passed over his head. His memory greatly impaired, and his other faculties much on the decline. His temper peevish, fretful, morose, and prone to sudden fits of passion; and yet to me his behaviour was gentle, as it always had been from my early childhood, treating me with partial kindness and attention, as being his

---

[1] Co. Meath.   [2] Williams IV. 416.   [3] *Ibid.*, p. 403.
[4] Sheridan, pp. 377–8.   [5] Letter of 18 Nov. 1735; Williams IV. 430.

godson; often giving me instruction, attended with frequent presents
and rewards when I did well. I loved him from my boyish days, and
never stood in the least awe before him, as I do not remember ever to
have had a cross look, or harsh expression from him. I read to him
two or three hours every day during this visit, and often received
both pleasure and improvement from the observations he made.[1]

The boy was about sixteen at the time. How far this memory of
an adolescent impression—recorded half a century after the
event by a middle-aged and radically inaccurate writer—may
be trusted, I do not know.

But Swift found the boy generally promising and only a little
in need of reform: 'I much esteem your younger son,' he told
Dr Sheridan, 'but I thought him a little too much on the *qui
vive.* . . . I know no other fault in him. He is an English boy [i.e.,
educated at Westminster School], and learned it there.'[2]

During the five or six weeks of his visit, Swift, assisted by
Sheridan, kept up a furious exchange of letters with Mrs Whiteway, whose intelligence and insight are obvious from her own
side of the correspondence. Swift appreciated her gifts, and told
her,

> Your letters have been so friendly, so frequent, and so entertaining,
> and oblige me so much, that I am afraid in a little time they will
> make me forget you are a cousin, and treat you as a friend.[3]

The dean apparently lived in Cavan as a lodger, paying for
his food, dining by himself in the study, and speaking very little
to Mrs Sheridan or her daughter. Several schoolboy boarders
ate with the family, but Sheridan would often come and finish
his meal with Swift. The dean played backgammon, walked,
made visits, gained weight, tried to improve the condition of his
friend's property, read, wrote, and applied prescriptions to his
shin.

The great hopes of riding and walking were ruined by this
bruised shin, which took so long to heal that it was December
before he could exercise it freely. A rainy spell churned up
the mud in town and around Sheridan's house so that Swift

---

[1] Sheridan, pp. 376–7.   [2] Williams IV. 466.   [3] *Ibid.*, p. 441.

constantly complained about the filth everywhere. Since the schoolmaster had to look after his pupils, he could not spend all the time with his guest. But there was a stream of visitors for conversation, and Swift was invited out for dinners.[1]

Mrs Whiteway could hardly have shown more devotion. She wrote often to her distinguished cousin and watched over the deanery. When she was not having his big chairs upholstered, she was arranging for wine to be shipped to Cavan.[2] (It never got there.) On his birthday, she had a celebration: Land, the sexton, gave a dinner; Kendrick, the verger, gave a supper; and both of them, like several other families, illuminated their houses.[3] Mrs Whiteway worried about Swift's shin;[4] Swift worried about her eldest son's health, for the young man was thin and sickly.[5]

The dean did not return to Dublin until mid-December. Before that time, the doctor left Cavan for the capital in order to raise subscriptions for a new school house, and he expected Swift to remain in the country until his own reappearance. But the dean privately told Mrs Whiteway he would not stay long behind, and would 'be in town two or three days after him'.[6] According to the younger Sheridan, 'as the doctor was called up to town upon business during the Christmas vacation, Swift found the place desolate without him, and followed him in a few days.'[7]

In the vigour of their manner and matter, Swift's letters belie the younger Sheridan's gloomy memories. Soon after his arrival in Dublin, he met Orrery, who had missed him in the autumn but was not attending the House of Lords. Anticipating the reunion, the Earl had said, 'All the moments I steal from attorneys, agents and solicitors are passed, when I am at Dublin, with him.'[8] His description of Swift in January 1736 also contradicts the younger Sheridan: 'The immortal Dean is come to town in high spirits.'[9]

---

[1] *Ibid.*, pp. 446, 447.   [2] *Ibid.*, pp. 434, 439.
[3] *Ibid.*, pp. 443, 444.   [4] *Ibid.*, pp. 419, 428, 434.
[5] *Ibid.*, pp. 431; 429, n. 4.   [6] Letter of 6 Dec. 1735; *ibid.*, p. 447.
[7] Sheridan, p. 377.   [8] *Orrery Papers* I. 141.   [9] *Ibid.*, p. 144.

Yet during February any high spirits were miserably damp-
ened, because Theophilus Harrison, already frail, caught a
dangerous illness. His innocent disposition—studious and well-
behaved—deeply attracted Swift. According to Dr Sheridan,
the young man was 'every day growing more and more into a
friend and companion' for the old dean.[1] In February, however,
a mortal disease struck him. 'It proved a spotted fever,' Swift
said bitterly, with a joke that hardly resolves a chronic sorrow:
'The doctor found no bad symptom, then out came the spots,
then says the doctor, He does not *lose ground*, and so on till he *got
ground*, which was a grave.'[2]

Swift felt pessimistic from the start of the case. I think,
whether he realized it or not, that this crisis must have evoked
for him the end of his wretched young protégé, William
Harrison, in the same month twenty-three years earlier. Then
he had felt hopeful at first, though his mind 'misgave' him on
the death day;[3] now he expected what happened.

Theophilus Harrison died on the twenty-third, leaving his
mother desperate. Her daughter and her other two sons could
not calm her. Swift invited her to the deanery as a retreat from
the funeral preparations and from her own engulfing sorrow. He
ordered a notice of the death, with an 'impartial' account of the
young man's character, to be published in Faulkner's *Dublin
Journal*. He wrote to Sheridan,

> We have lost that poor young man Mr Harrison to my infinite
> sorrow and disappointment, and to the very near breaking of his
> mother's heart. . . . I proposed much satisfaction in seeing the young
> man often and leading him in his virtuous way.[4]

When the morbid effects of the event hung on, they were
exacerbated by a fresh panic. Early in March, Lord Orrery went
to a ball at Dublin Castle. He danced with Dorset's daughter
and then kept on dancing from eight at night till four in the
morning. Out of this extravagant dissipation he fell into a fever
which almost killed him. After gaining strength, he suffered a

---

[1] Williams IV. 464. [2] *Ibid.*, p. 466.
[3] *Journal*, pp. 619–20. [4] Williams IV. 462–4, 466.

relapse as threatening as the first attack. Yet 'by milk, care and exercise', he survived.[1] Hearing of the business from the Duke of Dorset, Swift felt terrified. He gave Orrery a scolding which in its violence reflects his genuine attachment to the Earl and the fears of affectionate paternalism:

> I should not grieve much if your illness would punish you enough, but never return again except you deserved it by acting a part which does not belong to you.... [You] are neither fitted in body or mind, or principles for such a way of living. Regularity of life is what you were destined for by God and nature.[2]

Now Swift's own stock of health gave out. In the *Dublin Gazette* for 23 March appeared a statement that the dean had been 'for some time past very bad', but that his disorder had 'turned to an ague, and it is now hoped he is somewhat better.' According to Swift himself, the trouble was a painful outbreak of deafness and giddiness stretching from mid-February to mid-April. But Mrs Whiteway had recovered from her grief enough to be, as usual, an excellent nurse, and he 'gradually recovered'.[3]

On top of this fell a maddening blow, wholly public but bringing out profound feelings of rage and frustration. For all Swift's contempt for the Club, and in spite of a warning he gave to Mrs Whiteway to send no word of them while he visited Cavan, Swift had been unable to keep from asking about their activities.[4] Soon after he got home, he found his pristine anti-pathy exacerbated by a climactic episode in the history of their mischief. The deed was one more invasion of clerical property by greedy laymen.

As landlords shifted from tillage to pasture, hardpressed clergymen who found their tithes painfully reduced began to enforce tithe agistment, which was the tithe on pasturage, especially pasture grazed by dry and barren cattle. For decades there had been resistance to this claim, but in 1722 a decision of the Court of the Exchequer had established its validity.

Of course, the Parliament of Ireland was dominated by the

[1] *Orrery Papers* I. 159–60. [2] Williams IV. 467. [3] *Ibid.*, p. 478.
[4] *Ibid.*, pp. 417, 442.

landowning class; and in spite of the legal decision, that class continued to stand out against the tithe of agistment. What frightened the clergy was that if any one tithe could be curtailed by Parliament, all tithes might be. So the bishops and the lower clergy, the Whig rectors and Tory vicars joined to defend their rights.[1] Nevertheless, in December 1735 the House of Commons heard a petition on behalf of farmers and graziers begging for relief from suits demanding tithe agistment. A second petition was heard the following March; and this received a favourable report, leading to resolutions against the so-called new demand. Among the familiar ironies of the crisis was the fact that the Members of Parliament held their places because they were Church of Ireland men and not Dissenters or Roman Catholics; their own relations were often clergymen; they themselves had been educated by parsons. As Swift saw it, they were demolishing an institution on which their prosperity was founded.[2]

But the resolutions of Parliament encouraged landlords to form associations pledged not to pay the tithe of agistment. They were urged to provide funds and legal counsel for those who would resist the demand for the tithe and to favour clergymen who took their part. Swift said, '[Those] wretches here, who call themselves a parliament, abhor the clergy of our church ... and have made an universal association to defraud us of our undoubted dues.'[3]

It was on 5 March 1736 that the second petition was introduced. A committee which included Bettesworth reported on it; and in less than two weeks the Commons voted against the clergy by 110 to 50. Enraged by the event, Swift now began to compose a poem denouncing the parliamentary majority. By 24 April he could tell Sheridan, 'I have wrote a very masterly poem on the Legion Club, which, if the printer will be con-

---

[1] Cf. the letter of 18 May 1736 from Boulter to the Bishop of London (II. 153–4; Dublin, II. 120–1); also 8 Jan. 1737 to the Earl of Anglesea, *ibid.*, pp. 150–1; 9 Aug. 1737 to Walpole, *ibid.*, pp. 181–4; to others, *ibid.*, pp. 186–9.
[2] My account of the agistment controversy is derived from Landa, pp. 135–42.
[3] Williams IV. 469.

demned to be hanged for it, you will see in a three-penny book; for it is 240 lines.'[1] Evidently, no Dublin printer could be found willing to risk his neck to produce *The Legion Club*. At least, no Dublin edition is known till many years later. But the poem began at once to circulate in manuscript, and an English publisher included it in a miscellany which appeared as early as June 1736.[2]

Swift played his usual game of repudiating his work, even to Sheridan. 'Here is a cursed long libel running about in manuscript, on the Legion Club,' he told Sheridan in mid-May; 'it is in verse and the foolish town imputes it to me.'[3] He complained that lines had been added by others, but rejoiced in the anger of his victims:

> I hear it [i.e., the poem] is charged to me, with great personal threatenings from the puppies offended. Some say they will wait for revenge to their next meeting. Others say, the Privy Council will summon the suspected author. If I could get the true copy I would send it you.[4]

Sheridan said, 'Surely no person can be so stupid as to imagine you wrote the panegyric on the Legion Club.'[5]

The title of the poem suggests the themes that run through it; for the reference is to the story of the man possessed by an unclean spirit, in the Gospel according to St Mark.[6] The spirit gives its name as Legion; and when exorcized by Christ, it becomes a crowd of devils that rush into a herd of swine who then drown themselves in the sea. Madness, damnation, and bestiality are thus joined in opposition to Christ. This, for Swift, is the condition of the House of Commons.

The imagery of the poem recalls earlier works by Swift. So far back as the *Digression on Madness*, he had described Bedlam as a

---

[1] *Ibid.*, p. 480; really 242 lines.
[2] *Poems* III. 827–8. For the text of the poem, see *ibid.*, pp. 829–39. I do not believe Orrery's story that Swift was overcome by a fit of giddiness and left the poem unfinished (*ibid.*, p. 828).
[3] Williams IV. 487.   [4] 22 May 1736; *ibid.*, p. 492.   [5] *Ibid.*, p. 495.
[6] Mark v. 2–13.

nursing mother for servants of the state. In 'Mad Mullinix and Timothy' he had classed Richard Tighe as a maniac. In 'Traulus' he had connected Lord Allen with Satan and alluded to the name of 'Legion'. Now erupting with bitterness and sarcasm, he proceeds to treat the new Irish Parliament House (designed by his friend, Sir Edward Pearce) as a madhouse and a hell, in keeping with the Biblical assumption that madness is the effect of diabolical possession.

The form of the poem is trochaic tetrameter couplets. Swift's rhythms, which are normally strong, become heavy and thunderous. The rhymes incorporate a number of vituperative nouns along with the names of the poet's victims, which consequently take on the character of coarse words themselves: e.g., Clements/excrements (ll. 185–6).

In the opening lines (1–74), the poet sees the building, hears the noise within, and sketches the nature and activities of the inmates. The language suggests Christian associations of devils and damned souls, along with the bestiality and lunacy. But just as the poet enters, he evokes the *Aeneid*, Book Six; and the descent into the pagan Hades becomes the main allusion of the poem. The parallels are ingenious and startling, as Virgil's survey of Tartarus takes on aspects of the Christian hell: here betrayers of their country, rebels against the gods, are condemned by the ancient Romans as well as the pious moderns. The M.P.s had betrayed their brethren, teachers, and priests.

The process of entering the building takes us through the second section of the poem (ll. 75–132). But when the poet begins his tour, it is a madhouse keeper who shows him around; and in the remainder of the poem, we are shown the loathsome activities of the damned maniacs while the poet apostrophizes them. In a brief close (ll. 219–42), the poet calls on a sister art for help and wishes for Hogarth to depict the monsters for which even Swift's words are inadequate.

The power of the poem is due in part to the versification and in part to the variety of images of madness, bestiality, and damnation. But it springs even more from the scandalous boldness of the attacks on individuals and the filth flung on them:

Dick Fitz-Baker,[1] Dick the player,[2]
Old acquaintance, are you there?
Dear companions hug and kiss,
Toast *old Glorious*[3] in your piss.
Tie them, keeper, in a tether,
Let them stare and stink together.[4]

Even the modern reader is shocked by the personal vituperation. But like the very last satires of Pope, the fury reflects the
genuine outrage of the poet at the corruption of a nation's
leaders.[5]

---

[1] Dick, the bastard son of a baker: i.e., Richard Tighe, descended from a contractor who supplied bread to Cromwell's army.

[2] Bettesworth.

[3] William III, the great hero of the Whigs, who often toasted his 'glorious memory'.

[4] Ll. 149–54. Is 'tie' a pun on 'Tighe'?

[5] My interpretation of the poem is derived from the far more detailed and subtle analysis in Schakel, pp. 166–77.

Chapter Eight

'POLITE CONVERSATION' AND 'DIRECTIONS TO SERVANTS'

I. MASTERS AND SERVANTS

The *Legion Club* was the last important work written by Swift. But during his seventh decade he busied himself at times with two long compositions that had been on his hands for many years: *Polite Conversation* and *Directions to Servants*. It is not quite clear when he first began to write either of these, and he left the latter seriously incomplete.[1]

The longest and most finished parts of *Directions to Servants* are the 'Servants in General', 'Butler', 'Cook', and 'Footman', of which the 'Footman' is brilliant. There are also some shorter but still comprehensive pieces: the 'Groom', 'Chamber-Maid', 'Waiting-Maid', and 'House-Maid'. Of these the 'Groom' has the most life and humour. Finally there are nine fragments which seem mostly notes and heads of essays; but even among these the 'Coachman' has good touches.[2]

To approach these ironic advices, one may compare them with Swift's own treatment of servants, because it is largely from his own experience that Swift derived the observations on which he builds his sarcasms. In the deanery Swift employed a house-keeper (Mrs Ridgeway, at this time), a cook, a charwoman, a footman (Richard Brennan in 1742), and a groom. In his last year of competence, the dean owned a coach and had a coach-

---

[1] In a letter to Pope, 12 Jun. 1732, Swift says he began to write both these works 'above twenty-eight years ago'; Sherburn III. 293.

[2] Davis XIII. 1–65; cf. the important textual apparatus, pp. 209–20. Davis gives an invaluable account of the manuscripts and the history of composition, *ibid.*, pp. vii–xxiii. See also Herbert Davis, 'The Manuscripts of Swift's "Directions to Servants"', *Studies in Art and Literature for Belle da Costa Greene*, ed. Dorothy Miner (Princeton, 1954), pp. 433–44.

man. The verger and the sexton of the cathedral—Roger Kendrick and Henry Land—were often called upon for odd services. Kendrick, for example, sometimes acted as Swift's amanuensis. In addition, the dean not only had his understanding with Mrs Whiteway that she should often look in on the deanery and supervise proceedings there, but he also had other women friends, such as Mrs Sican, to help with special marketing or similar problems. There is plenty of evidence that however oddly Swift may have spoken to his servants, they stayed with him and regarded him as an excellent master.

The Rev. John Lyon, who looked after Swift in his final years, has an account of his domestic benevolence which I have already drawn on:

> Nor did he ever deprive his little household of any of those comforts, that he thought them intitled to receive from an indulgent master. His butler and groom were each allowed for their board four shillings a week. So were his cook-maid and house maid. As to the housekeeper, she was much better paid and always dined or supped at his own table; for he lived very much at home. And although the servants were thrice daily fed for the most part at his expence, yet he always continued the same allowances to each every week over and above their wages. Which the men especially on account of their having their liveries could afford often to reserve in his hands as a fund for some good purpose in their little way: which did please him much; and he was sure to encourage it.[1]

When he went out, Swift normally took both the footman and the groom along, one to ride before and the other behind. These and 'the woman' (i.e., charwoman) gave him the most trouble. They had many small duties but few interesting ones. They were liable to sudden bursts of demands from their master and long spells of irresponsibility. They constantly worked in his sight, and trivial errors on their part could cause extreme discomfort on his.

In 1733 Swift had drawn up a few 'laws' (perhaps revisions of earlier codes) to regulate the servants' behaviour, with many fines against misconduct;[2] for example,

[1] Lyon, p. 151; cf. above, p. 33.   [2] Davis XIII. 161–2.

If, in waiting at table, the two servants be out of the room together, without orders, the last who went out shall forfeit threepence out of his board-wages.[1]

At another time he composed 'The Duty of Servants at Inns', containing minute instructions for the groom and the footman.[2] I wish we could feel sure that Swift smiled as he wrote some of these: 'Search under your master's bed when he is gone up, lest a cat or something else may be under it.'[3] Judging from the sharp focus of the regulations, from the comments of Mrs Pilkington and the younger Sheridan, and from a few references in Swift's letters, we must wonder whether the dean did not feel inordinately suspicious of underservants, easily losing his temper when he thought they had done wrong. The spirit of his dealings with them (but not with persons like Mrs Ridgeway) seems that of St Paul's admonition: 'Servants, be obedient to your masters with fear and trembling, in singleness of your heart, as unto Christ.'[4]

The system on which Swift based the *Directions* is mainly to recommend ironically the habits which he detested most. Once he considered naming the book *The Whole Duty of Servants*, which would have created a sardonic parallel to *The Whole Duty of Man*. But since that work is an exposition of man's responsibilities to God, one may perhaps, from the discarded title, speculate about Swift's unconscious view of how his servants should regard him. Whenever God strikes, according to the *Whole Duty of Man*,

> we are, in all reason, not only patiently to lie under his rod, but (as I may say) kiss it also; that is, be very thankful to him, that he is pleased not to *give us over to our own hearts lusts*.[5]

This conventional expression of a Christian commonplace is echoed in the section of *The Whole Duty* that deals with servants, for one of their obligations is 'patience and meekness under the reproofs of [their] master ... that is, not making such surly and rude replies, as may increase the master's displeasure'.[6]

---

[1] *Ibid.*, p. 162.   [2] *Ibid.*, pp. 163–5.   [3] *Ibid.*, p. 165.
[4] Eph. vi. 5, condensed.
[5] *The Whole Duty of Man* (London, 1728), pp. 39–40.   [6] *Ibid.*, p. 337.

Swift obviously found the reality absurdly remote from this ideal. His directions are in a sense an ironic commentary on (not a parody of) the passages in *The Whole Duty* which deal with his theme. But they are also a direct parody of such books as Fleury's *Devoirs des maitres et des domestiques* (1688), which do indeed set standards laughably ambitious and impractical.[1] As sociological data on the early eighteenth century, of course, Swift's *Directions* may claim unique interest; for the faults which the 'author' pretends to encourage were constantly complained of, as in Defoe's anecdotal discourse on the servant problem, *The Great Law of Subordination*.

But *Directions to Servants* is certainly not based on the dean's own household. It is set in the London establishment of a married couple with children. There are references to a master, a lady, children, Pall Mall, Temple Bar, and St James's Park. The author takes the character of a veteran footman who foolishly abandoned his proper vocation after seven years' experience, and so far demeaned himself as to accept 'an employment in the custom-house'.[2] His picaresque manner reminds one of Gil Blas; but Swift must have collected the heavy sum of his detailed comments bit by bit over many years. In final effect the piece is sometimes obsessional; one has a disquieting sense that Swift is competing with the servants.

However, the literary skill goes far to make the parts cleverly entertaining when they are read separately. The shrewdness of Swift's insights, and the absurd arguments, instances, and exceptions which he devises to illustrate or support his bitter advice, endow the book with comic life. Often the reasoning seems drawn from the speech and logic of real servants, making it doubly ironical as one gathers that some bit of nonsense was once offered seriously. In the best chapter, 'Directions to the Footman', there are paragraphs of hilarious vulgarity; and the whole chapter has coherence of matter and tone as well as a polished shape.

[1] Cf. also *The Refin'd Courtier*, by N.W. (London, 1663, 1679, 1686), which is a version of the *Galateo* of Giovanni della Casa (1558). The instructions for servants in this book are often reversed by Swift's persona in *Directions to Servants*.

[2] Davis XIII. 34.

II. 'POLITE CONVERSATION'

Yet far more art and finish appear in *Polite Conversation*.[1] Swift prepared it for the press, and it was printed while he could still correct the copy.[2] He once traced its beginnings back to 1704 or earlier.[3] But those allusions which can be dated suggest that most of the work was compiled or written after the death of Queen Anne. The period of Swift's greatest activity in producing it seems to have been 1730 to 1735. He alludes to Lord Grimston, a peerage created in 1719 (p. 144); Hanover Square, constructed about 1720 (p. 172); *The Craftsman*, launched in 1726 (p. 120); Newton's death, 1727 (pp. 122–3); Cibber's laureateship, 1730 (p. 123); and 'My Lady Club', an imaginary quadrille-lover named in *Verses on the Death of Dr Swift*, about 1731 (p. 168). But he also implies that several deaths have not yet occurred: Edward Ward, 1731 (p. 118); Gay, 1732 (p. 118); John Dennis, 1734 (p. 118); and Arbuthnot, 1735 (p. 118).

According to Mrs Pilkington, Swift thanked her, during the Christmas season, 1730, for having advised him to give the piece the form of a dialogue.[4] In August 1731 he told Gay he was busy with it.[5] In June 1732 he told Pope it was 'almost finish'd'.[6] Two years later, he included it among works which he thought he would 'never be able to finish'.[7] But in 1736 William King (of St Mary Hall) apparently saw a final draft;[8] the following year, Swift sent Mrs Barber a fair copy for her to publish and profit from, in London;[9] and early in 1738 we find him hurrying Faulkner's production of a Dublin edition.[10] The book went on sale in London on 28 February 1738 and in Dublin soon after.[11]

In *Polite Conversation* Swift represents himself, under the

---

[1] *Ibid.*, IV. 97–201.   [2] Williams V. 94–5.   [3] Sherburn III. 293.

[4] *Memoirs* III. 146; for date, see Ball IV. 194, n. 2 and 261, n. 1. See also above, p. 707.

[5] Sherburn III. 219.   [6] *Ibid.*, p. 293.   [7] *Ibid.*, p. 439.

[8] Williams IV. 521, 540.   [9] *Ibid.*, V. 65.   [10] *Ibid.*, pp. 94–5.

[11] London *Daily Advertiser*, 28 Feb.; Faulkner's *Dublin Journal*, 11 Feb. 1738, carries an announcement that the book is in the press and 'speedily will be published'; but I cannot find a copy of the issue announcing its appearance. Swift writes to Faulkner on 8 Mar. 1738, urging him to publish his edition (still in the press) before the English edition comes over (Williams V. 94–5). See also Mayhew, pp. 131–55, especially 155, on dating.

pseudonym of 'Simon Wagstaff', as an illiterate and irreligious Whig devoted to the life of fashion and card-games. This author has compiled three dialogues and written a preface for them, in order to exhibit the art of conversation. Almost the whole of the dialogues takes place in the London residence of Lord and Lady Smart, and almost all the lines are spoken by them and their six guests.

'Have you read yourself to sleep with Dr Swift's conversation, as I did?' wrote Thomas Gray to Horace Walpole (early in March 1738). 'That confounded Lady Answerall, though she says less than anybody, is the devil to me!'[1] Gray was mistaken about the extent of his favourite's role. The main characters are a young pair, Miss Notable and Tom Neverout (a younger brother[2]), who seem absorbed in a ferocious campaign of mutual teasing. The third woman, Lady Answerall, has about as much to say as her hostess, from whom one can hardly distinguish her. Besides these, one speaker endowed with a touch of individuality is Sir John Linger, a coarse Derbyshire squire, recently married. The two remaining persons are bachelors, differentiated by little but their names: Colonel Atwit and Lord Sparkish. A few remarks also come from servants: a porter, a maid (Betty Johnson), and some footmen. As topics for discussion the universal obsessions are courtship and matrimony.

By far the longest dialogue is the first, supposed to be a set of morning visits. The second is a dinner conversation. The last, only a few pages, takes the company through post-prandial tea and an enormous but unrecorded game of quadrille ending at 3:00 a.m. While the principle on which *Polite Conversation* rests is that every possible remark should be a cliché, other blemishes of social intercourse are also treated in parody. The speakers mispronounce words[3] and use short forms like 'pozz' and 'hipps'.[4] They report, as *bons mots*, inanities which they have said or heard elsewhere.[5] Miss Notable several times makes a show of not

---

[1] *Correspondence of Horace Walpole*, ed. W.S. Lewis *et al.*, XIII (New Haven, 1948), 153.
[2] P. 159.
[3] Vardi, p. 136; jommetry, p. 159; pudden, p. 160; varsal, p. 182.
[4] P. 161.   [5] Pp. 162, 186, 189.

understanding smutty innuendoes.[1] Sometimes a bold vulgarity, such as 'Kiss my—', is pronounced as a witticism.[2] Most of the comments on absent persons are malicious.

The real life of the scheme, which keeps it from monotony, is the effect of social satire. The speakers are gentry and peerage, the ruling classes. They have wealth and power. But they can employ their time no better than in empty social rituals and meaningless speech. The lack of learning, morality, and taste appears in all the banalities of the dialogues.

Wagstaff's introduction shows Swift equipped with his full powers. Since it contains many allusions to the dialogues, he must have written most or all of it after them. In this essay he adopts, with even more than his usual success, the common principle of his comic irony, posing as the embodiment of what he hates, and recommending persons or practices that he detests. Individuals like Henry VIII and Bishop Burnet; social groups like the learned professions, the military, the aristocracy, and the court; habits such as using slang and contractions, talking obscenely, swearing, and gambling; religious categories such as Puritans, Dissenters, deists, and atheists; the faults of women— all these receive defiling encomiums from the genial Simon Wagstaff.

Among the more restricted devices of satire, the author exhibits several characteristics of Swift. He combines, in a single complimentary passage, a number of groups often thought of as mutually opposed, so that each is smeared with the vices of the others—as when he ties blasphemers, atheists, and courtiers into the same knot as Puritan rebels.[3] He works out a problem in crazy arithmetic, like that of the first *Drapier's Letter*:

> The flowers of wit, fancy, wisdom, humour, and politeness, scattered in this volume, amount to one thousand, seventy and four. Allowing then to every gentleman and lady thirty visiting families, (not insisting upon fractions) there will want but a little of an hundred polite questions, answers, replies, rejoinders, repartees, and remarks, to be daily delivered, fresh in every company, for twelve solar

---

[1] Pp. 148, 166, 183, 187.   [2] Pp. 180, 185, 194, 196.
[3] Pp. 108–9.

months; even this, is a higher pitch of delicacy than the world insists on, or, hath reason to expect.[1]

He manufactures fake quotations to illustrate his argument.[2] He retains the public spirit, selflessness, and blind fatuity of Swift's other ironic masks but adds a splendid complacency which they only approach—a bit like Colley Cibber's tone in the *Apology*. Throughout this introduction, the prose style sounds as resilient and energetic as in Swift's best writing.

In part, then, *Polite Conversation* is an exposé of the shallowness, coarseness, and vulgarity of the families responsible for governing the nation. It also seems a parody of serious works on the subject of conversation and manners. *An Essay on Conversation*, *The Conversation of Gentlemen Considered*, and *The Art of Conversation* were all published within a year of Swift's book;[3] and they, of course, are merely a few items in a tradition of ancient lineage.[4]

But it also revives motifs which are scattered through the body of his life's work.[5] Swift was always preoccupied with social customs and with speech; he had written a series of essays (or fragments) on language, conversation, and manners.[6] In his *Miscellanies* of 1711 was 'A Tritical Essay', which is a compound of clichés.[7] Much of Wagstaff's introduction echoes with amazing closeness the 'Preface' or the 'Introduction' to *A Tale of a Tub*. This late achievement, though finished when Swift was nearly seventy, reveals him both in character and in strength.

III. LOWERING THE GOLD

For Swift the spring of 1736 meant public calamity, personal sickness, anxiety over some friends, and the loss of others. By now he relied on Mrs Whiteway to such a degree that she could

[1] Pp. 111–12.   [2] Pp. 110, 120–1.

[3] *Gentleman's Magazine* VII (1737), 128; VIII (1738), 56, 552. Swift read *An Essay on Conversation* (Sherburn IV. 72–3).

[4] Cf. Ann Cline Kelly, 'Swift's *Polite Conversation*: An Eschatological Vision', *Studies in Philology* 73 (1976), 204–24.

[5] I do not believe that Swift got material for *Polite Conversation* from phrase books and collections of proverbs. See David Hamilton, 'Swift, Wagstaff, and the Composition of *Polite Conversation*', *HLQ* 30 (1967), 281–95.

[6] Cf. Davis IV. 1–21, 85–95, 205–28.   [7] *Ibid.*, I. 246–51.

call herself 'his friend, his nurse, and the manager of his family'
—humorously, of course.[1] So much care inevitably kindled a
sort of possessiveness, and Swift might observe that 'she sets up
to be my governor'—also humorously.[2]

But he appreciated the nature of his blessing and welcomed
her attendance. Worried that he might blunder in his correspondence or commit some absurdity through forgetfulness, he
began to have her proofread letters or even to write several—
especially to Sheridan—in open collaboration with him. She
seems to have assumed something like Stella's place at his
dinners and functions.

While she nursed him through his long illness that spring,
accounts of it reached Pope, a rumour of whose own illness had
frightened Swift in February.[3] He tenderly returned Swift's
solicitude. But his natural anxiety was supplemented by worries
about the disposal of his letters if Swift should die without
returning them; for he was quietly planning to publish these
himself. When Orrery warned Pope of Swift's condition, the
poet begged for further reports;[4] and Stopford sent details that
alarmed him.[5] Not till May did Pope have the reassurances he
wanted of his old friend's safety.[6]

By this time a new public crisis was irritating the revived
dean. Parliament rose on 30 March, and the Lord Lieutenant
embarked for England on 17 May 1736.[7] With him he carried
an application from the government and Privy Council of
Ireland for a proclamation lowering the value of gold coins in
Ireland. The reasons were the old ones we have already heard;
but now they were stronger and more pressing than ever.

Silver coins were still intolerably scarce in Ireland because the
various sorts of gold there were set at a higher value in silver than
they had in England. A guinea in financial reckoning was worth
twenty-three shillings Irish (or 21s. 3d. in English coins; an
English shilling being worth thirteen pence in Ireland).

---

[1] An expression applied in irony to Mrs Sheridan but referring to her own status;
Williams IV. 488.
[2] *Ibid.*, p. 492.   [3] Sherburn IV. 3–4.   [4] *Ibid.*, p. 8.   [5] *Ibid.*, p. 11.
[6] *Ibid.*, p. 15.   [7] Boulter II. 154 (Dublin, II. 121).

Foreign gold coins were legal, normal currency. The moidore, worth about twenty-seven shillings in England, passed for thirty shillings Irish (or 27s. 9d. in English money in Ireland). So traders and bankers paid English debts in silver. So also, coming from England, they would bring moidores rather than shillings.

There were new kinds of Portuguese gold coins as well; and they were set at such values (in silver) that it paid merchants to bring back four-pound pieces from England rather than two forty-shilling pieces. Maybe half the money of Ireland was in four-pound pieces of gold, which could never be used in ordinary transactions.

As usual, there was also the imbalance in simple exchange rates. So Irish merchants lost from 2 to $2\frac{1}{2}$ per cent on transactions with England for that reason alone.

The application Dorset carried with him was mainly for a proclamation reducing the value of gold coins in Ireland so the guinea would be worth twenty-one shillings English (or 22s. 9d. in Irish money) and other coins in proportion. Boulter wrote urgent and highly intelligent letters on the subject to the persons of the greatest influence in England. Nevertheless, in this matter of supreme importance to Ireland and of no consequence to England, it was not till 1737 that the proclamation was finally made. But before Dorset left, in May 1736, the government's plan was known.

Swift unfortunately objected to the alteration, for it would mean a rise in the receipts of absentees: their rents, being normally reckoned in silver, would now rise by threepence in the guinea. So also office-holders living in England would benefit. The bankers (who benefited from the monetary muddle) and many merchants shared Swift's qualms; and toward the end of April 1736 a series of manœuvres began.

The Lord Mayor was of course Swift's friend Richard Grattan. On Monday, 19 April, he, the aldermen, and the Common Council of Dublin met at the Tholsel or city hall, to draw up a remonstrance against the lowering of the gold.[1] At a

---

[1] *Pue's Occurrences* and the *Dublin Evening-Post*, 20 Apr. 1736.

similar meeting of merchants the next Saturday, Swift appeared
and made a speech arguing that all those high officers and
bishops who favoured the change stood to gain by it, and that it
would encourage absentees to remain in England.[1] Another
formal protest was drawn up and signed by those attending,
with Swift among them. On Tuesday, 27 April, Grattan and his
sheriffs presented their remonstrance to the Lord Lieutenant
and Privy Council at the Castle.[2] The following Friday, Swift,
the merchants, and two Members of Parliament gave in a
petition praying to be heard on the gold coin. And the dean,
according to a newspaper, 'was pleased to speak to the Duke,
and to set forth the ill consequences it will be to this kingdom, if
our coin should be reduced'.[3]

On Saturday the merchants were officially heard. One of
the two lawyers speaking for them was Swift's friend, Eaton
Stannard, the Recorder of Dublin. He and Anthony Malone
seem to have pursued Swift's line (which they may have helped
to establish); for they

> set forth the ill consequences it would be to this kingdom, by
> favouring the absentees in the exchange of money; and as they are
> the greatest enemies to this poor kingdom, they ought not to meet
> with any encouragement to favour their living out of it; and that it
> could not possibly be of any advantage to the trading part of the
> nation, but on the contrary, the destruction of it. It is universally
> allowed that there was the greatest strength of reason in what they
> said, and that no persons could speak better on the occasion.[4]

Just how bitter Swift felt, one may judge from his remark to
Sheridan in the middle of May:

> I took leave of the Duke and Duchess to-day. He has prevailed on us
> to make a promise to bestow upon England £25000 a year for ever,
> by lowering the gold coin, against the petition of all the merchants,
> shop-keepers, &c. to a man. May his own estate be lowered by the

---

[1] Davis XIII. 119–20; Williams IV. 480; *Pue's Occurrences* and the *Dublin Evening-Post*, 27
Apr. 1736.
[2] *Pue's Occurrences*, 1 May 1736.
[3] *Pue's Occurrences* and the *Dublin Evening-Post*, 8 May 1736.
[4] *Ibid.*, 11 May.

other forty parts, for we now lose by all gold two and a half per cent. He will be a better (that is to say worse) man by £60000 than he was when he came over, and the nation better (that is to say worse) by above half a million; besides the worthy method he hath taken in disposal of employments in church and state.[1]

A week later, he was still smarting,[2] but he could take no open action until the autumn of 1737.

Swift's stubbornness on the issue of the value of gold coins must reflect his congenital fear of the inflation of money. There was also his bottomless distrust of the motives of the government in power. Friends disagreed with Swift, and must have pointed out that the loss to the economy from the scarcity of silver was much more dangerous than the gain to the absentees from the fall in the value of gold. But he never changed his opinion in this controversy.

[1] Williams IV. 487.   [2] *Ibid.*, p. 491.

Chapter Nine

OLD AGE

I. SURVIVAL

Oone misery of advancing age for Swift, was that the old dean did not easily rebound from the strains of his chronic disorders. We may judge his fear of attacks by his reluctance to go far from home even in the summer, when he normally wished to visit the country. The approach of warm weather in the spring of 1736 meant the dispersal of many friends; and with both Sheridan and Delany hard to reach, Swift felt the loss. John Rochfort, whom he had been seeing, left town for the summer; and by late May the dean was complaining that he had only Mrs Delany and the Grattans to keep him company.[1] Swift's intimacy with his helpful cousin, Martha Whiteway, had of course grown. She came to a dean-and-chapter dinner at which, he claimed, she 'got drunk with eating too much turbot';[2] for she avoided wine.

Like Stella, Mrs Whiteway had a tender appreciation of Sheridan, and sometimes privately sent him news of their friend. Meanwhile, the schoolmaster kept begging the dean for another visit. He hoped to go up to Dublin and carry his patron (and creditor) back with him during the month of June; and Swift did indeed contemplate passing part of the summer in Cavan.[3] But quite through July, Sheridan still waited; and in mid-August he had a worrying account of Swift's health from Mrs Whiteway. To her he wrote conveying his disappointment and hoping yet to reach Dublin.[4] The dean, on his side, had naturally been expecting Sheridan in town, although that hope too was frustrated.[5] Sheridan may have felt a particular embarrassment: he

---

[1] *Ibid.*, p. 492. [2] *Ibid.*, p. 493. [3] *Ibid.*, pp. 486, 489, 495–6.
[4] *Ibid.*, pp. 508, 513, 520–1, 525. [5] *Ibid.*, p. 501.

not only owed Swift £668,[1] but he had other creditors who might seize him in Dublin.[2]

It remains impressive how skilful Swift was at any age in closing the gaps in his circle of acquaintance. While the summer went by, he deepened a friendship which he had commenced through Mrs Whiteway, with John Nichols, the surgeon her son was apprenticed to. This connection, which combined a professional relationship with social pleasure, was to last until the dean's death; for it was Nichols who would look after Swift in his final years. There are dinner invitations to the surgeon from Swift in at least June, July, and September.[3] On Monday, 5 July 1736, at 2:00 p.m. the company at dinner—'on a haunch of venison'—included Orrery, Mrs Whiteway, Dr and Mrs Helsham, and Nichols; and the venison itself probably came from the viceregal herd in Phoenix Park, where Nichols lived.[4]

Orrery had been recuperating and invoking his muse in Thomas Tickell's house at Glasnevin, a mile and a half outside town. He translated Horace's 'Pyrrha' ode and gave it to Swift for criticism. So also in March the aspiring peer had asked him to judge some verses written by Orrery on the death of the young Duke of Buckinghamshire; and the noble poet told a friend they had 'come out of the furnace in almost the same form they went in'.[5] A few days after the dinner at the deanery, he and Swift were together again, on the eve of the young man's departure from Dublin. The dean 'is in perfect health', he wrote, a fortnight later (from the north of Ireland), 'and passed many hours with me the day before I came here. *Floreat in aeternum.*'[6] But except for a few days the next month, Orrery did not return to the capital until the end of November. His representation of Swift contradicts the gloomy self-portrait which was despatched to Charles Ford toward the end of June:

I dare not stir many miles or days from this town, much less to London, for fear of a tedious fit of giddiness, and particularly deafness, which sometimes lasteth for six weeks together. And my rents are so sunk, that I cannot afford to live with any comfort there.

[1] *Ibid.*, p. 530.   [2] Ball v. 373, n. 3.   [3] Williams IV. 509, 511, 529.
[4] *Ibid.*, p. 511.   [5] *Orrery Papers* I. 165–7, 171–2, 153.   [6] *Ibid.*, p. 172.

Neither have I three friends with whom I could converse, or sponge for a dinner. Here I have a large house, convenient enough for my unrefined taste, and can hitherto dine on a morsel without running in debt: and yet I have been forced to borrow near £200 to supply my small family of three servants and a half, for want of any reasonable payments.[1]

His rents had indeed gone down, but these complaints about ailments and income are less urgent than they sound. Swift had large sums of money out at interest, and he had to wait beyond the appointed time for his tithes and other dues to come in. So he found more profit in borrowing cash for immediate needs than recalling loans or touching capital. As for his illnesses, they were the old witnesses of Ménière's syndrome—genuine enough, but neurological rather than bodily infirmities—and did not impair his physique.

There were comforts as well as pains during the summer. Dr King of St Mary Hall, Oxford, came back to Ireland and interested himself in Swift's unpublished works. The dean wished the Principal to help him publish them in England. King saw a copy of *Polite Conversation*; and after he got back to England, he eagerly awaited the manuscripts of *The Four Last Years*, *An Enquiry into the History of the Queen's Last Ministry*, and the *Memoirs* . . . *1710*, which he evidently expected to see through the press for the old dean.[2] While Swift liked his writings to appear first in London, however, he also felt loyal to Faulkner; and except in that critical detail, he gave the Dublin bookseller voluble support.[3]

Age did not reduce Swift's eagerness to win preferment for younger friends. He remained a hardworking, if often ineffective, patron. In the summer and autumn he tried but failed to get a fifty-pound-a-year deanery for John Jackson.[4] He successfully interceded on behalf of William Dunkin, the young poet, and secured a rise of thirty pounds a year in an annuity which Dunkin received from Trinity College, Dublin; but Swift failed

[1] Williams IV. 504.
[2] *Ibid.*, pp. 521 and n. 2, 529–30, 540, 541–3, 550–1.
[3] *Ibid.*, pp. 493–4. [4] *Ibid.*, pp. 502–3, 533.

to obtain a church living for him.¹ He tried, apparently in vain, to find preferment for a prosperous young man, Marmaduke Phillips.² He recommended the young John Lyon (a protégé of Worrall's who was later to become very close to the dean) for an assistant lectureship under Delany, but could not get the place for him.³ According to the younger Thomas Sheridan, Swift persuaded the Primate to offer the headship of the Armagh school to Dr Sheridan, although the offer was not taken up.⁴ Yet it seems from some remarks made to Swift by the doctor himself that this scheme did not originate with the dean, and that Sheridan would have accepted the post if it had been offered.⁵ Swift was hardly the first person Boulter would have consulted in filling such a vacancy.

Throughout these labours of patronage, Swift showed a kind of persistence in the face of constant frustration which suggests a consciousness of duty to the young, the weak, and the dependent, a conscience that must have derived from his own difficulties. Endlessly, Swift tried to give his clients a taste of the paternal assistance which his early life had lacked. He tried to be to them what Temple, Harley, and Archbishop King had not been to him.

Neither did Swift lose touch with extra-clerical families like the Sicans and the Howths.⁶ In fact, a modern city-dweller cannot easily appreciate the range of Swift's community, the number of functions through which each gentleman was related to every other one, or the ways in which the most local event might involve the most remote strata of society. Just how deeply Swift was immersed in the Dublin element, one may reckon by the views he would have had, for example, of a minor accident of the most transient and parochial concern.

Laetitia Pilkington's father, Dr John Van Lewen, was a friend of Dr Helsham and of John Nichols. In October 1736, Laetitia—after months of staying with relations in Cork and taking the waters at Mallow—returned to Dublin. Swift, who had been

---

¹ *Ibid.*, pp. 509–10, 511–12. ² *Ibid.*, pp. 480–2.
³ Ball v. 383–4 and p. 384, n. 1. ⁴ Sheridan, pp. 365–8.
⁵ Williams IV. 497–8. ⁶ *Ibid.*, pp. 509–10, 521–2.

writing to her, promised to pay a visit soon after she arrived. Sending a present of fruit, he noted that his enemies 'give out that I use you too well'.[1]

Dr Van Lewin, being a leader in his profession, belonged among the public figures of the town. While his daughter was away, he quarrelled with Matthew Pilkington; and during her first week back, he wounded himself severely by falling with a knife in his hand. The illness which followed crept into so many conversations that after eight weeks of it, Orrery complained, 'Our town ... is now quite tired of curing and killing and killing and curing Doctor Vanleuen.'[2] Among the medical men who attended the invalid was John Nichols;[3] but on New Year's Day, 1737, Van Lewen died after all. As this circle of bathos suggests, it was a tiny hive that made up the top of Dublin society; and Swift might have received accounts from the patient's daughter, son-in-law, surgeon, colleagues, or from gossips like Orrery; for all of them were his friends.

As another St Andrew's Day slipped closer, many Dubliners prepared to celebrate the inauguration of their dean's seventy-first year. On the morning of the birthday, 'several persons of distinction' called at the deanery to congratulate him; in the evening,

> there were bonfires, illuminations, firing of guns, &c. Many loyal healths were drank; long life to the Drapier; prosperity to poor Ireland; and to the liberty of the press.[4]

Several versifiers, the chief of whom was Sheridan, sent him panegyric poems. A club newly founded (and, one suspects, shortlived) in support of a newly founded daily paper, reported its meeting to 'celebrate the happy occasion' with a short ode on Swift, adapted from Horace. Four weeks later, the paper promised to award prizes for the best poems written on the dean.[5] It is hard to believe that these festivities could have persisted against Swift's vocal opposition. But it is also hard to suppose that his taste for them was not tempered by a sense of

---

[1] *Ibid.*, p. 532. [2] *Orrery Papers* I. 178. [3] Pilkington I. 192.
[4] *Pue's Occurrences*, 4 Dec. 1736. [5] *Dublin Daily Advertiser*, 1 Dec. 1736.

their irrelevance. Yet toasting the dean and Drapier implied a salute to certain principles, including Irish nationalism and freedom of the press, as well as respect for the man himself. One assumes that the celebrations were also a protest against the English interest and certain policies of the government.

II. LORD ORRERY LEAVES

Swift's habit of dwelling on his disabilities lost none of its impetus as he aged, and perhaps gained some. 'Infirmities have quite broke me,' he told Pope in December 1736:

> I mean that odious continual disorder in my head. I neither read, nor write; nor remember, nor converse. All I have left is to walk, and ride. The first I can do tolerably; but the latter for want of good weather at this season is seldom in my power; and having not an ounce of flesh about me; my skin comes off in ten miles riding because my skin and bone cannot agree together.[1]

And yet Orrery, who probably[2] came back to Dublin just before Swift wrote this letter, describes him differently (three weeks later), saying that the dean 'grows younger as his years increase', and that he 'enjoys more health and vivacity this winter than he has felt for some years past'.[3] In mid-January, the Earl tells Marmaduke Phillips, 'The Dean feasted his clergy with ladies, music, meat, and wine; as a musician I gained admittance to join chorus with *Away with Cuzzoni, Away with Faustina*.'[4] A month later, Orrery says that Swift's health 'is excellent at present, but his giddiness returns so often and so suddenly that I dread the consequence.'[5] In other words, the old man was thin and strong though subject as always—perhaps increasingly—to his neurological complaint, and of course to failing eyesight, moods of gloom and bitterness, and a fickle memory. He had troubles enough, but was not always troubled.

Pope, at the end of December 1736, may be quietly mocking Swift's penchant when he comments that 'others tell me you are

---

[1] Sherburn IV. 44.
[2] Swift writes as if he has just seen him, *ibid.*, p. 45.
[3] *Orrery Papers* I. 183.   [4] *Ibid.*, p. 192.   [5] Sherburn IV. 55.

in pretty good health, and in good spirits.'[1] Yet the exchanges between Sheridan and Mrs Whiteway show that they shared Swift's fears of decay.[2] The company of an elegant young listener like Orrery must have called up all of the dean's powers of cheerful affability, while the solitary exercise of communicating with a far-off but intimate friend must have eased the flow of self-pity.

Meanwhile, just as a common devotion to the dean had drawn Sheridan and Mrs Whiteway together, so Orrery's poetophile attraction to Pope was being enriched by the latter's anxiety concerning Swift. Beset with the aggravated disorders of his own body, and eager to arrange the publication of his familiar letters without being held to blame, Pope responded electrically to any word of his friend's decline. He operated both directly and through intermediaries to get into his own hands the letters he had written to Swift. Orrery, as go-between, could hope that Pope would pay for his services with an enhancement of the Earl's bardic affiliations, and that the lion of Twickenham might be seen by posterity in his lordship's literary game preserve. I wonder, therefore, how far Orrery wished to feed Pope's misgivings when he wrote to him, in February 1737,

> Your apprehensions of the Dean's memory are too well grounded: I think it decays apace: and I own I am shocked when I see any new instance of its failure. Designing people, who swarm about him will make their advantage of this. I watch as closely as is possible, but I can seldom see him alone.[3]

As George Sherburn observed, while Orrery must have counted Mrs Whiteway among the 'designing people', his letters to her indicate 'a most cordial and friendly relationship'.[4] But the Earl's dislike of Swift's humbler friends continued and grew stronger. In June he felt spiteful enough to tell Pope that 'the Dean is guarded, not defended, by dragons [?Mrs Whiteway]

---

[1] *Ibid.*, p. 49.
[2] See Sheridan's letter of 14 Aug. 1736 to Mrs Whiteway; Williams IV. 525. But cf. also his letter of 21 Nov. 1736 (*ibid.*, p. 543), in which the disability appears to have been temporary.
[3] Sherburn, p. 54.   [4] *Ibid.*, n. 3.

and all the monstrous animals of the creation. His health grows worse and worse: his deafness and giddiness encrease: and he is seldom cheerful but when talking of you.'[1] It is hard to think that Swift would have denied himself to Orrery. Yet in November 1736 the deanery butler had refused to admit Lord Castle-Durrow, whom Swift apparently respected.[2]

Although the intrigue relating to the Pope–Swift letters makes a story apart,[3] it did not lighten the dean's dependence on the Earl. Writing from Cork in March 1737, Orrery mentions to Swift 'the late happy hours you allowed me to pass with you at the deanery';[4] but at the same time he wrote to confirm Pope's fears of Swift's forgetfulness: 'I dread nothing so much as his want of memory, which indeed, I sigh to say it, seems to encrease every day.'[5]

Pope at this time was pressing Swift for a reunion in England or France. His desire for this must have joined both the yearning for another sight of Swift and the possibility of making fuller explanations of his epistolary crisis than could be committed to paper. How sharply Swift regretted Orrery's absence—a regret made bitter by the Earl's approaching departure for England—one may judge from a plea (in a long and vivacious letter) delivered at the end of March: 'Pray, my Lord come to us a month before you leave this kingdom, and dine with me every day on scraps with Mrs Whiteway in my bed-chamber; and then I will (multa gemens) take an eternal farewell of you.'[6]

Meanwhile, the sense of looming dissolution—in March and April he composed a set of instructions to be followed on his death[7]—may have added fervour to the tone in which Swift asked Pope to register a poetic testimony of their friendship. The issue was an old one. Almost ten years earlier, Pope had dedicated the *Dunciad* to Swift, and then requested that the dean also 'record our friendship in verse'.[8] In December 1736, Swift

[1] *Ibid.*, p. 73.   [2] Williams IV. 228, 547–9, 554–7.
[3] See the following chapter.   [4] Sherburn IV. 61.
[5] *Ibid.*, p. 62.   [6] Williams V. 22.
[7] *Ibid.*, pp. 34–5. The draft of 25 March is printed on Scott's edition of Swift's *Works* (1824), I. 485.
[8] Sherburn III. 30.

said that he would like to see his own name at the head of one of Pope's 'epistles'.[1] Six months afterwards, we find him repeating the petition in spite of the strong lines on him in *To Augustus*.[2]

There is a one-sidedness in Swift's attitude, since his own works are hardly rich in dedications to Pope. However, so few of his productions were signed that he had small opportunity to name friends even if he wished to. Furthermore, being twenty-one years older than Pope, he probably felt that his own need was more urgent than his friend's.

Of Sheridan at this season there are few signs. In March 1737 the doctor wrote bewailing the dean's long silence and inviting him to Cavan. Swift made the usual complaints about his health, refused the invitation, but sent puns, a riddle, and a collection of mock-Latin sentences.[3] Late in June, Sheridan replied with a mock-Latin epistle saying that he could not visit Dublin because he had no money to pay his debts with. He described three books of bons mots which he expected to send Swift for Orrery to carry to England.[4]

These are almost the last written communications preserved between Sheridan and Swift (partly because Sheridan was to die so soon). Of course, on neither side is there any hint of a wish to terminate the connection, and Sheridan was to stay at the deanery again the following year. Nevertheless, so blank a gap at a time when Swift's language to Orrery was so effusive suggests a fundamental weakening of the tie with his old friend. Their long separation deprived Swift of the steady companionship which he sought in such cronies. He was left free (I think) to reflect on the schoolmaster's irresponsibility, his neglect of Swift when he did visit Dublin, his willingness to use the dean as a financial prop. If Sheridan left a vacuum, others had to fill it: Mrs Whiteway and her children, Orrery, the Grattans, Stopford, and young clergymen like James King and the sinister Francis Wilson (who is dealt with below).

---

[1] *Ibid.*, p. 45.

[2] Sent in manuscript. Swift thanked Pope for these; *ibid.*, IV. 56, 72.

[3] Williams V. 28–31.

[4] *Ibid.*, pp. 48–9. See James Woolley, 'Thomas Sheridan and Swift', p. 103.

Among Swift's social resources was an old admirer whom he had not always appreciated—the rabble. For some years now he had been relishing the vulgar applause which his reputation and charities drew. 'I walk the streets,' he told Pope, 'and so do my lower friends, from whom and from whom alone, I have a thousand hats and blessings upon old scores, which those we call the gentry have forgot.'[1] Such support may have given the old dean an incentive for unfortunate, unilateral political action. He seems to have felt more and more like the last true patriot in Ireland, and to have begun ignoring the restraints of less impetuous tempers among his acquaintance. This was a period when his own career could no longer gain or lose from the results of political action, and when the men whom he had obliged were in a position to help him serve others. Perhaps he unconsciously wished to assert his strength as a prime mover before he became too infirm either to lead or to follow.

These energies found an outlet when one of Swift's dearest preoccupations was revived, the money question. His characteristic personal obsession with finance, his anxiety concerning the perpetual inflation of the value of money, his special role in the defence of Irish coinage, were all evoked by a series of steps which the government was taking. These administrative policies had two designs. The first was the scheme (already discussed), carried over from the year before, to lower the value of gold coins in Ireland. The second was to end the old and continued shortage of copper coins, which seriously blocked internal trade.

As the spring of 1737 advanced, it became obvious that the government had determined to supply new halfpence in a quick and legal manner, long and carefully planned by Boulter.[2] Late in February the London newspapers reported that ten thousand pounds in halfpence were being coined for Ireland at the royal mint in London.[3] On 2 March 1737, two tons of halfpence arrived in Dublin. These were now said to be a portion of twelve thousand pounds' worth coined.[4] On 18 March Swift met this

---

[1] Sherburn IV. 56.   [2] Boulter II. 172, 177 (Dublin, II. 135, 138–9).
[3] Ball v. 432, n. 3.
[4] Boulter II. 207 (Dublin, II. 162); *Pue's Occurrences*, 8 Mar. 1737.

decisive event with a dramatic but not very effective gesture reported by Faulkner and others:

> Yesterday [i.e., 18 March] the Rev. Dr Swift, D.S.P.D., sent for a great number of the inhabitants of his liberty upon a report that a large quantity of halfpence were imported from England to be passed in this city and kingdom, and he told them he had a parcel of English halfpence, and as he saw the difficulties we lie under for want of change by our own fault, in not having a mint, he gave among them above four pounds of those English halfpence for silver, which silver he afterward gave to them for gold, and he treated the persons who came to him with great generosity by giving them wine, etc. He then told them that the halfpence brought over from England would be attended with as many inconveniences as those of Wood's, inasmuch as they might be as easily counterfeited and imported, and as readily managed to draw away the small quantities of gold and silver among us.[1]

According to Swift, Faulkner was almost prosecuted for this paragraph, and the dean himself sent off all his papers in case he too should be troubled.[2] Boulter told Dorset's secretary, 'Dean Swift has raised some ferment about [the copper half-pence] here, but people of sense are very well satisfied of the want and goodness of them.'[3]

The tide went on rising against Canute. The Lords Justices and Privy Council had trials made of the new coins; the assay master testified to their integrity;[4] and on 5 April another five-and-a-half tons reached Dublin.[5] Finally, on 6 May, the Lords Justices and the Council issued a proclamation declaring the new halfpence to be valid for payments to collectors of HM Revenue; and large quantities began to be given out in change to those who applied for them.[6] Once more, Swift suffered the familiar sensation of being thoroughly beaten. Without the backing of comrades in high places, there was little that one man's eloquence or histrionics could accomplish. 'I quarrel not

---

[1] Ball V. 432, n. 4; *Dublin Daily Advertiser*, 21 Mar. 1737.
[2] Williams V. 21.   [3] Boulter II. 162.
[4] 25 Mar. See Reilly's *Dublin News Letter*, 2 Apr. and following.
[5] *Ibid.*, 9 Apr.
[6] Boulter II. 216 (Dublin, II. 169); *Pue's Occurrences* and other Dublin papers, 10 May 1737.

at the coin,' he told Orrery, 'but at the indignity of not being coined here.'[1] Boulter wrote to Dorset,

> I cannot help acquainting your grace, that we yesterday signed a proclamation for giving currency to the new half-pence, after a most tedious course of delays and difficulties; from what quarter you may easily guess: *and I hope this affair will very much sink the popularity of Dean Swift in this city, where he openly set himself in opposition to what the government was doing.*[2]

One public event which might earlier have pleased or at least amused Swift, and made a contrast to such a defeat, at this time only embittered him. The aldermen of the city of Cork decided, perhaps with some encouragement from Orrery, that the moment had come for them to distinguish the dean. They agreed to send him the freedom of the city in a silver box. The Earl sneered at their unwillingness to use a gold one;[3] and when Swift first heard of the approaching ceremony, he too resented the humbler metal.[4] During the summer, Eaton Stannard finally presented the dean with his honour; but Swift felt annoyed to discover that no citation accompanied the freedom, nor was either his own name or the donor's engraved on the box. He therefore sent it back with an extraordinary letter leaving it to the choice of the corporation whether

> to insert the reasons for which you were pleased to give me my freedom, or bestow the box upon some more worthy person whom you may have an intention to honour, because it will equally fit everybody.[5]

The unfortunate mayor replied with admirable tact; and the following autumn Swift received the box again, ushered by a letter acknowledging his patriotic achievements. An inscription on the box now stated that it was presented to Swift 'for the many great and eminent services he hath done this kingdom'.[6] If the outcome suggests that the dean felt mollified by the deference of the corporation, we may gain a sounder impression

---

[1] Williams v. 21. [2] Boulter II. 216 (Dublin, II. 169).
[3] Williams v. 9. [4] *Ibid.*, p. 22. [5] *Ibid.*, pp. 67–8.
[6] Ball VI. 44 and n. 1; cf. Williams v. 68 and n. 1.

from the final disposition of the box; for when he left it to John Grattan in his will, Swift desired 'the said John to keep [in the silver box] the tobacco he usually cheweth, called pigtail'.[1]

Meanwhile, Swift's mood had been darkened again by illness and by the drama of Orrery's departure. In March the Earl had gone to Cork, where he missed the dean and the higher civilization of Dublin.[2] Swift commanded him to write; and when Orrery did so—mentioning his plan to leave for England in June—Swift answered with a cordiality that has surprising overtones of pathos.[3] In reply, the Earl breathed reverence for Swift and effusively implored him to go to England with his lordship: 'I am now forced to bid you farewell; but hereafter expect my whole life and conversation.'[4] At the same time, however, receiving some criticism of Swift from another friend, Orrery commented in a less adulatory style. Comparing the dean to the superannuated gladiator of Horace, *Epistles* I. i. 4, he said that Swift should 'long ago' have withdrawn from public controversy: 'I grieve to see him in the wrong, and am desirous to snatch him if possible from his little senate.'[5] Six weeks later, describing Swift to Pope, Orrery agrees with the dean's self-portrait that summer: 'He complains of his health, and indeed with too much cause. He shuts himself up and lives retired.'[6]

About 1 May, the Earl was back in Dublin, planning to sail during June. As the date of his embarkation drew nearer, Swift's anxiety seems to have been aggravated. 'You will never be quiet until you have quite broken my heart,' he wrote to Orrery on 11 June.

> However as you have nineteen days of this month left, I hope you do not intend that I am not to see you before you go....
> You shall, you must see me, because I must never see you more.

Swift closed the letter, 'I am my ever dearest Lord, with the greatest love, esteem and respect your most obedient and obliged humble servant.'[7]

Apparently, Swift was feeling so painfully troubled by deaf-

[1] Davis XIII. 155.   [2] *Orrery Papers* I. 203.   [3] Williams V. 9.
[4] *Ibid.*, p. 26.   [5] *Orrery Papers* I. 213.   [6] Sherburn IV. 70.   [7] Williams V. 43-4.

ness, vertigo, and forgetfulness that for a time he put off visitors.[1] But Orrery reassured him the next day: 'I will certainly see you very often before I go. I will constantly write to you when I am gone, and will require no answer, but at your utmost leisure and in your best health.'[2] He closed effusively,

> I cannot bear the thoughts of parting with you: Let us settle it by a letter the last day wrote from each other. Do not say, do not think we are to part forever. Had I no business in Ireland the sight of you would more than make amends for a sea sickness. As I draw nearer losing you, my affection, which lay close in my heart, rises in letters, in sighs, in tears.[3]

To Pope, Orrery wrote, 'Your heart can better tell you than my words express what I feel now I am approaching so near an eternal farewell to the Dean.'[4]

Nevertheless, this was the juncture at which the Earl chose to fall ill, and so precipitously that he felt anxious for his life. By the last days of June he was writing and walking again. He now hoped to sail early in July. Swift informed him that the portrait he had been given of the late Countess of Orrery was to revert to the Earl after the dean's death. Swift also got together a manuscript of *Polite Conversation*, a manuscript of the *Four Last Years*, and a package of the original letters which Pope had written to him. The first item was to be delivered to Mrs Barber, who had begged the profit of publishing it;[5] the second, to Dr King; and the last, to Pope himself. On the eve of Orrery's departure, Swift sent him these and then a preface newly written (and demonstrating his continued mastery of a plain, vigorous eloquence) for the history.[6] Still confined by a bad head, the dean wrote (2 July),

> If you sail on Monday [4 July], I fear you will not have time to see me, so I must bid you farewell for ever; for although you should stay a day or two longer, you will be in too great a hurry for me to expect you.[7]

---

[1] *Ibid.*, pp. 43, 48.   [2] *Ibid.*, p. 44.   [3] *Ibid.*, p. 45.
[4] Sherburn IV. 76.   [5] Williams IV. 540.   [6] *Ibid.*, v. 59, n. 2.
[7] *Ibid.*, p. 59.

They did not in fact meet again for almost a year. Orrery's packet boat sailed on 5 July.

III. MOURNING THE GOLD

Swift's health did not improve after he lost Orrery. 'I have been long in a very bad condition,' he wrote at the end of July:

> My deafness, which used to be occasional and for a short time, has stuck by me now several months without remission ... and my old giddiness is likewise become chronical, although not in equal violence with my former short fits.[1]

In mid-August, he describes himself as 'wholely confined by sickness ... my head continuing in great disorder'.[2] In early September his state gave rise to rumours of his end, and the *Dublin Gazette* announced,

> For some days past the Rev. Dr Swift ... was in a most dangerous way and his life despaired of, but now in a fair way of recovery.[3]

Yet even now all the symptoms which Swift mentions seem limited to the usual effects of Ménière's syndrome—painful, to be sure, even excruciating, but not a truly perilous disease. Of course, Swift lacked the comfort which a correct diagnosis may perhaps give to modern sufferers from labyrinthine vertigo.[4] Nevertheless, the coincidence of his attack with the emotional strain of Orrery's sailing, looks suspicious. One thinks of the great series of painful separations which Swift had undergone across the Irish Sea. Seasickness, death, isolation from his deepest loves—all these motifs rise to a unison, and one recalls most sharply the illness which kept him away from Stella's funeral. Besides, for a man who loved conversation, there could be few greater miseries than deafness.

Swift could certainly look forward to replacements for Orrery. They might not have his rank, his wealth, or his affinity for old men; but they might be courteous, well-educated, and

---

[1] *Ibid.*, p. 64.   [2] *Ibid.*, p. 67.   [3] Ball VI. 43, n. 1.
[4] There is now a medicine to control the symptoms.

young. An immediate candidate was Deane Swift, his relation
and debtor. Although this junior cousin had, many years before,
spent some terms in Trinity College, Dublin (apparently without taking a degree), he was now at Oxford, with a notion of
becoming a clergyman. It may have been the dean's influence
that sent him to William King's college, St Mary Hall; for King
delivered a report of the studious gentleman's progress to Swift:

> I have very narrowly observed his conduct ever since I have been
> here [i.e., since returning from Ireland]; and I can, with great truth,
> give him the character of a modest, sober, ingenious young man. He
> is an hard student, and will do an honour to the society of which he is
> now a member.[1]

The force of this eulogy is not strengthened by the fact that
Deane Swift himself published it,[2] or the likelihood that King
expected the dean to show him it. But Swift must have felt
encouraged by the praise and by the news that his young cousin
would be back in Ireland (for the summer vacation) near the
time that Orrery reached England.[3]

This was the season of the last political scandal detonated by
Swift; and that in turn was a by-product of the government's
changing the value of gold. A new Lord Lieutenant, the Duke of
Devonshire,[4] was to arrive at the start of September; Parliament
was to meet a month later. In July and August, riots which seem
to have been quite non-political in origin broke out at several
fairs, and also a kind of gang war between the 'Ormond and
Liberty' boys—i.e., boys from the neighbourhood of St Patrick's
Cathedral and others from the neighbourhood of Ormond's
Key. On 19 August the mayor issued a proclamation to suppress
such outbreaks.[5]

These independent lines began to meet when the Lords
Justices and Privy Council, by proclamation dated 29 August,
placed the new value of £1. 2. 9. upon a guinea in gold.[6] Swift's

---

[1] Williams v. 54; cf. *ibid.*, IV. 394–5.
[2] In his life of Swift.   [3] Williams v. 51, 54.
[4] Appointed 9 Apr. 1737, sworn in on 7 Sept.
[5] Dublin newspapers of 24, 30 Jul.; 10, 13, 20 Aug.
[6] *Dublin News Letter* and *Pue's Occurrences*, 3 Sept. 1737.

grand geste this time got into the London prints only; I suppose those of Dublin were intimidated by the warnings which
Faulkner had received the preceding March:

> We have received several anonymous letters [inspired by Swift?]
> concerning the display of a black flag on St Patrick's steeple, the
> muffling of the bells, which rang mournfully all day, the sexton of St
> Patrick's being sent for by a tipstaff, and the retiring of the mer-
> chants to a tavern, and their drinking long life to Dean Swift and
> confusion to the enemies of Ireland. All we can say is that the citizens
> were greatly alarmed when they saw the black flag, imagining that
> our patriot, who had been ill, was dead. Many of them ran in great
> consternation to the church, where they learned that their Dean
> lived, and to their great consolation was happily recovered from his
> late illness. The signs of mourning were on account of the lowering of
> the gold.[1]

In the atmosphere of public disorder, Swift's behaviour did not
seem comic to members of the government. Boulter, who had
striven so long, hard, and disinterestedly for the much-needed
measure, was enraged. He wrote (months later) to the Duke of
Dorset,

> Your grace has no doubt been fully informed of the clamours raised
> against [the lowering of the value of gold], and the insult on the
> government by Dean Swift on that occasion.[2]

What made it worse was that Swift did not stand alone. There
had been maddening (for Boulter) debates in Parliament, and
the Commons had submitted petitions against the government's
action.

Although the dean published no pamphlet on this occasion,
he let his tongue wag freely against those whom he blamed for
the proclamation. Apologizing to an old friend who became the
victim of such a whipping, Swift wrote,

> I did and do detest the lowering of the gold.... I grant, that the
> bishops, the people in employments of all kinds who receive salaries,
> and some others, will not lose a penny, by lowering the money,
> because they must still have their pay ... though I, and thousands
> of others will soundly feel the smart, and particularly the lower

---

[1] Dated 13 Sept. 1737; Ball VI. 47, n. 3.   [2] Boulter II. 246 (Dublin, II. 192).

clergy.... [What] I said was, that I wished all who were for lowering the gold, were lowered to the dust; and I might explain it, so that it would bear the sense of causing them to repent in dust and ashes.[1]

There were obviously good intentions on both sides. Swift's flair for the dramatic in arranging the bell-tolling, his skill as a publicist in planting the newspaper paragraph, his eloquence as a rhetorician—these displays were not the effect of malice or spite. Mistaken though he was, they still expressed his anxiety for the public good.

Boulter, as the chief agent of the powers in England, received (quite correctly) Swift's greatest blame for the inflationary measure. Dorset's son wrote from Dublin,

> The coinage has made a great rout here, and the Dean has shown himself more mad and absurd than ever. The poor Primate has been greatly threatened by anonymous letters, so that he has been obliged to have a corporal and six men lie in his house every night for the month past to save him from any insult.[2]

Since another proclamation against riots had been issued on 17 September—this time by the Lord Lieutenant (who had come over) and the Privy Council—one wonders whether Boulter's danger was not due to a continuance of the summer disturbances.

On 29 September the outgoing Lord Mayor, James Somerville, gave a feast attended by the Lord Lieutenant, the Primate, the Dean of St Patrick's Cathedral, and other dignitaries. We have several accounts of the notorious episode enacted there. The most detailed (but not necessarily objective) information comes from a letter written two months afterwards:

> Archbishop Boulter, who is a very weak man, bluntly taxed the Doctor before the company for endeavouring to raise the mob, and to begin a rebellion on account of the lessening the value of the gold. The Doctor answered that he loved his country, and thought the diminution of the coin was a prejudice to it, that he could by lifting up a finger have influenced the mob to tear him in pieces, but he

---

[1] Williams V. 71–2.
[2] Ball VI. 206–7; Boulter II. 242–3 and n. (Dublin, II. 190 and n.).

deferred doing it, because it would make an odd figure in history that a Primate was destroyed by the people for doing an odd job; he would not at present give it another name. The Doctor immediately left the room. The next day the Duke of Devonshire sent to the Doctor to come to the Castle, and he made his excuse that he had got the country disease, alluding to what had passed the day before in his presence.[1]

The story must be substantially true, for Dorset's son gave a similar account;[2] and Swift composed a verse squib on the affair which does not far differ from either version. In the closing couplet of this insult to the Archbishop of Armagh (i.e., Boulter), Swift indicates the strength of his flirtation with the mob and the joy he felt in his own single-handed dominion:

> It's a pity a prelate should die without law;
> But if I say the word—take care of Armagh![3]

IV. 'HISTORY OF THE FOUR LAST YEARS'

While duelling in public with such dragons, Swift did not forget to promote his private, literary career. It was easy for him to settle the fate of *Polite Conversation*: Orrery took the manuscript with him and gave it to Mrs Barber in London. But a more devious disposition awaited the *Four Last Years* (with its associated essays, the *Memoirs . . . 1710* and *An Enquiry into . . . the Queen's Last Ministry*).

Although Dr King had been waiting since December 1736 for the final copy of the book to reach him, Swift only dispatched it when Orrery could serve as carrier; and then he added the preface to the bundle on the eve of the Earl's embarkation. Orrery delivered the *Four Last Years* to the Principal as punctually as he had handled *Polite Conversation* and Mrs Barber. But the family that Swift hoped to celebrate in the history became the main block to its publication.

---

[1] Ball VI. 207. [2] *Ibid.*, pp. 206–7.
[3] *Poems* III. 841–3. For further information about the episode, see the very comprehensive headnote by Williams in *ibid.*, pp. 841–2.

The second Earl of Oxford felt alarmed by his memory of the book[1] and the accounts he received of it. In April 1737 he tried a Fabian strategy, pleading that Swift should hear 'the advice of friends' before proceeding with the work.[2] Erasmus Lewis made a diplomatic second to his patron's motion.[3] For by now Oxford had enough ties with the associates of his father's enemies to want no loud reminders of discords anciently resolved.

Shortly before Deane Swift was to leave England for Ireland, Dr King wrote to him and complained that the post office seemed to have intercepted letters which the Principal had sent to the dean. Some of 'our great men', he said, appeared to dislike the publication of the *History*, as indeed did 'some of the Dean's particular friends in London'.[4]

The next month, Swift himself received a full éclaircissement from Erasmus Lewis, who had read the *History* 'in the presence of Lord Oxford, and two or three more'. The censures of this audience ranged from small facts to large interpretations, and included the characters, which are easily the most elegant and fascinating parts of the book. Essentially the sentence was close to that passed on the *History* in 1713, when Swift told Mrs Johnson, 'Some think it too dangerous to publish, and would have me print only what relates to the peace.'[5]

Lewis implored Swift not to send the book to the press 'without making some, or all the amendments proposed'.[6] While the historian must have relished the homage implicit in so much attention, his opinion of the verdict may be surmised from the action he took. On Lewis's letter he wrote the endorsement, 'On some mistakes in the History of the Four Last Years. *Mon ami prudent.*'[7] When the book finally came out (in 1758), long after Swift's death, it bore none of the corrections proposed by the readers of the manuscript.

But William King quickly came around to Lewis's opinion, and informed Deane Swift that to print the *History* as it stood

---

[1] Cf. Sherburn II. 387.   [2] Williams v. 27.
[3] *Ibid.*, pp. 56–7, 65–6, 104–6.   [4] 15 Mar. 1738; *ibid.*, pp. 99–100.
[5] *Journal*, 25 Jan. 1713.   [6] 8 Apr. 1738; Williams v. 104–6.
[7] *Ibid.*, p. 106.

'would involve the printer, publisher, author, and everyone concerned, in the greatest difficulties, if not in a certain ruin; and therefore it will be absolutely necessary to omit some of the characters.'[1]

Swift defended himself against Oxford and Lewis by insisting that the book was necessary as an act of justice to the Lord Treasurer and his administration. But I prefer to believe that the heaviest impetus for the project sprang from the old dean's unwillingness to see so much care quite frustrated. On nothing except *Gulliver* had he lavished more pains. No other finished work had lingered so long in his escritoire. He had too much experience of cautious or biased friends to trust in a posthumous printing. Few years seemed left to him. He hoped he might yet unveil this monument, properly framed, to make his old friends rejoice and his enemies cringe.

A financial circumstance, now as with Temple's *Memoirs* long before, may have improved his zeal, because there was apparently a plan to sell the book by subscription, adding the proceeds to the fund for Swift's hospital.[2] The dean himself said as much when he told Orrery that in desiring to publish the *History*, 'I had some regard to increase my own reputation, and besides, I should have been glad to have seen my small fortune increased by an honest means.'[3] And he showed a similar anxiety over *Polite Conversation*.[4] Nevertheless, Swift ultimately followed his usual character and gave in to Oxford's pressures. In 1738 he abandoned the struggle to see the book published, and twenty years were to pass before it did appear.[5]

---

[1] *Ibid.*, p. 107. According to Orrery, Mrs Whiteway sided with Swift on printing 'every word as it stood' (Sherburn IV. 130). This is an isolated expression which Pope quotes out of context from a now-vanished letter from Orrery; and it may well be misleading.

[2] Sherburn IV. 51–2.

[3] *Ibid.*, p. 89; cf. the similar expression decades earlier, Davis I. xix.

[4] Davis I. 94–5.

[5] See the introduction by Sir Harold Williams to *ibid.*, VII.

Chapter Ten

LIFE'S DECLINING PART

―――――――

I. FEWER FRIENDS AND MORE RELATIONS

On St Andrew's Day, 1737, the traditional Dublin cele-brations of Swift's birthday were, in Faulkner's report, more vigorous than they had been 'these several years past'. The occasion was observed

> by all the people in and about the liberty of St Patrick's, and in many parts of this city and suburbs. The bells rang as usual on the most solemn occasions, nineteen patataroes fired several rounds, four large bonfires were upon the steeple [of the cathedral], and the windows illuminated: Such extraordinary rejoicings have not been practised on that occasion these several years past, by which it appears, that the people are now more sensible than ever of the many obligations they lie under to so great a lover of his country.

Poems were presented to the dean, and he was declared a 'universal genius'.[1]

By conniving at these displays Swift was perhaps trying to prove that his own proceedings represented the will of the people. Certainly there was enough annoyance, on official levels, at his rabble-rousing. Yet by this time, Swift had been driven into several rôles which he once deplored: the powerless malcontent, the accuser of his own era as the worst of times, *difficilis, querulus, laudator temporis acti*. A prominent Irish judge sent such an impression of him to Lord Oxford in the middle of 1738:

> The Dean of St Patrick's involves himself sometimes in such strange improper, insignificant oppositions to matters of a public nature that, by hanging out black flags and putting his bells in mourning,

―――

[1] *Dublin Journal*, 3 Dec. 1737.

he makes it impossible for one in my station to converse much with him; besides he is much and often out of order, and beset with odd persons, who command everything that he says, writes or does, and every letter or paper that he has. This fact is certainly so.[1]

Since John Wainwright, this correspondent, admittedly did not visit Swift himself, and was a good friend of Orrery—who happened to be in Ireland at the time of his letter—the reference to 'odd persons' may represent a dart flung by the Earl at Mrs Whiteway.

Nevertheless, the dean sounded intransigent and sullen just before his seventieth birthday, when he complained to Orrery that the lowering of the value of gold had not made money more plentiful, that Parliament continued to strangle the church, and that religion was dead.

> I am grown an entire ghost of a ghost of what I was, although you left me ill enough.... [May] you live till Christian times.... Our Lords and Commons here have shown their true love of the country in every proceeding.[2]

The same bitterness permeates a letter of January 1738 to John Barber: 'I have for almost three years past been only the shadow of my former self, with years and sickness and rage against all public proceedings, especially in this miserable oppressed country.'[3] In August he tells Pope and Bolingbroke,

> I desire you will look upon me as a man worn out with years, and sunk by public as well as personal vexations. I have entirely lost my memory, uncapable of conversation by a cruel deafness, which has lasted almost a year, and I despair of any cure.[4]

Like most of his self-portraits, this strain lacks perspective. Some correction may be found in an incident reported by an Irish writer, Michael Clancy. In 1737, soon after an illness that destroyed his sight, Clancy heard Arbuthnot's epitaph on Charteris read aloud, and he decided to compose a play on the subject. When this was finished, he asked Dr Helsham to show

---

[1] 24 Jun. 1738, in H.M.C. *Portland* VI. 68.
[2] Williams V. 77–8. The last sentence is of course sarcastic.
[3] *Ibid.*, p. 85.   [4] Sherburn IV. 115.

Swift the manuscript for an opinion which might recommend it to the theatre:

> 'Not I, indeed', said Dr Helsham, 'have you a mind that I should be obliged to go down his stairs faster than I went up? Shall I subject myself to be laughed at, or perhaps ill-treated? Not I indeed; I do not care to bring his tongue upon me. Go to Dr Grattan; the Dean will probably hear from him, what he would not from me.'
>
> The author went to Dr Grattan, and solicited his assistance in the same way. 'Who, I', said Dr Grattan, 'not I, by—; what have I to do with plays? I know nothing of writing books; I should have a fine time of it to bring such a piece of stuff before the Dean, and have it thrown in my face, or be called a blockhead for my pains. I should be glad to serve you, but find somebody else to befriend you on this occasion. No, no, not I, by—.'
>
> Dr Grattan's brother, minister of St Audoen's, happened to be present, who was pleased to say that he would find an opportunity of laying the book on the Dean's table, and if it was good, he would be apt to examine how it came there. The gentleman accordingly did so, and there it lay for some time, without the author's hearing one word about it.
>
> Dr Swift read it, and not knowing how the play came there asked all his friends, which of them had brought it, and none of those, to whom it was known to, would venture to tell as he had not declared his opinion of it. One day as Dr Helsham saw it on his table he took it up to look into it, and asked the Dean what this was. The Dean smiled, and told him it was a villain well painted, and that whoever had written the piece, conveyed a good moral. Dr Helsham, who saw that he had nothing to fear, told him the author, and what he knew of him.
>
> 'Tell him, then', said the Dean, 'that in a few days I will pay him a visit.'

According to Clancy, Swift then wrote him a letter which has been preserved (dated Christmas Day 1737), sending with it the sum of five pounds.[1]

Clancy's tale is inaccurate, since the rehearsal of his play, *The Sharper*, was reported long before the date of Swift's letter to him, and with an advertisement that does not suggest any intention to wait for the dean's judgment:

[1] Ball VI. 208–9; Williams V. 81–2 and p. 81, n. 1; p. 82, n. 1. My punctuation, paragraphs, spelling, etc.

This being an excellent subject to write upon, it is undertaken by a gentleman, who hath already distinguished himself for his great genius in poetry, as well in Latin as English; so that the town may reasonably expect the most agreeable entertainment from this performance.[1]

Nevertheless, the picture he gives of Swift's society adds considerable brightness to the dean's own representation. The agonies and miseries of Swift's state, we need not doubt. But we must ask whether he may not (with or without deliberation) have used his deafness-cum-vertigo as a way to narrow his circle to those who imposed the least restraint on his impulses. What looked to Orrery or Delany like Martha Whiteway's seduction of her cousin may in truth have been that cousin's adoption of her family.

Furthermore, within a year of his seventieth birthday, Swift either lost or cut himself off from a company—Delany, Sheridan, Helsham, Lady Acheson, and the Pilkingtons—that had been intimate with him for up to twenty years. Lady Acheson died in November 1737.[2] The Pilkingtons ruined themselves soon after, in the winter of 1737–8, with a divorce suit which Matthew brought against Laetitia for 'adultery with Mr Adair'. Though the complainant won his case in the ecclesiastic court, he never seems to have got the Act of Parliament wanted to give the decree legal force. But Swift, writing to Barber, felt humiliated enough to summarize the couple's career in *dictis amaris*: 'He proved the falsest rogue, and she the most profligate whore in either kingdom.'[3] Since Swift now harshly blamed Dr Delany for presenting the couple to him—for praising their wit, virtue and humour, and 'forcing me to countenance' them—the scandal may have helped to alienate him from their innocent patron.

Toward the end of May 1738, Orrery suddenly reappeared in Dublin. He had quietly left London in order to come over and settle the arrangements for his marriage with Margaret

---

[1] *Dublin Journal*, 12 Nov. 1737.   [2] 1 Nov.
[3] Ball VI. 69 and n. 1, 2; Williams V. 95.

Hamilton, an heiress to regal wealth.[1] The two men were unable to meet: when Orrery wished to call, it was not convenient for Swift to see him.[2] But they exchanged lively messages, with Swift posing as his young friend's rival. The dean quickly wrote the lady a congratulatory epistle that sparkles with elegant, ironic compliments to both parties and with regrets for his own case: 'I have neither mourning paper nor gilt at this time; and if I had, I could not tell which I ought to choose.'[3]

After about a fortnight in the city, Orrery joined his betrothed at the home of her uncle, Anthony Dopping (whose brother Sam was an old friend of Swift's); and there, at the end of June, they were married. On the eve of ceremony the Earl sent Swift a blissful note which testifies to the sincerity of his feeling for the dean, since it is a last-minute piece of cordial spontaneity, exquisitely thoughtful at a moment when the most heedless oversight would have been justified:

> My happiness is too great, and in pity to you [i.e., for being deprived of Miss Hamilton's maidenly attentions] I will add no more than that I hope to see grief for this loss strongly wrote in your face even twenty years hence.[4]

After the marriage Swift again wrote a vigorous, cheerful letter to Lady Orrery, foreseeing that 'your ladyship and my Lord will be the truest patterns of conjugal love'.[5] From Lowtown, Westmeath—Dopping's home—the couple went to Dublin and then, toward the close of July, to Caledon, Miss Hamilton's magnificent estate in the northern county of Tyrone.[6]

But this was their last and brief stage in Ireland for a year.

---

[1] *Orrery Papers* I. 238–9.
[2] Swift writes ebulliently on 23 May 1738 to acknowledge Orrery's letter informing him of the impending marriage. Swift asks him not to come at the time suggested by Orrery but instead to dine at the deanery the next day. On 17 June, Swift writes to Miss Hamilton urging her to correspond with him but saying that neither she nor Lord Orrery had visited Swift; unpublished letters in the collection of A. A. Houghton, Jr.
[3] Williams V. 110.
[4] *Ibid.*, p. 111.
[5] 3 Jul. 1738, unpublished letter in the collection of A. A. Houghton, Jr.
[6] *Orrery Papers* I. 239.

After celebrating his wife's birthday and fitting himself into the management of the property, the Earl carried the new countess to England. He intended to remain there, in Marston until the following summer, when they would take up permanent residence at Caledon.

Swift, who uttered only approving words about Lady Orrery, described her to Pope (with finer sincerity than syntax) as 'a person of very good understanding as any I know of her sex'.[1] But he seems to have taken leave of the pair with less pathos than he had shown upon the Earl's voyage the year before. In marrying, of course, Orrery had weakened both his own dependence upon the dean and the dean's sense of possessing him.

By September the lord and lady were in Westminster, having been frightened en route when their coach overturned beyond Coventry, and his lordship sprained a right arm.[2] In November, Swift sent him a short message, mainly to enclose a letter he wished forwarded to Pope but also to present hearty good wishes and complain of continued deafness. According to an endorsement by Orrery, this was the last written communication that he got from the dean: 'His illness hindered him from writing to me afterwards.'[3] However, they were to meet again and would keep in touch through Mrs Whiteway.

While the young couple were still in Caledon, there had been bad news concerning a friend of both the dean and the Earl. Helsham—Swift's 'Dr Arrogance'—became sick, seemed to recover, but at last, unexpectedly, died.[4] Although the dean had never shown deep respect for Helsham, he had regularly enjoyed his conviviality. And this death may have speeded Swift's somewhat mysterious withdrawal from Helsham's closest friend, Delany, who apparently lost touch with Swift about this time. Swift's sister, Jane Fenton, also died in the course of the year 1738, and Swift put on mourning for her loss. But although he paid her an allowance, they had otherwise been out of touch for

[1] Sherburn IV. 116.   [2] *Orrery Papers* I. 242–3.
[3] Williams V. 127–8; Gold, p. 175.   [4] 29 Aug. 1738.

decades; and there is no sign that this death touched him deeply.[1]

A more disastrous event was the death of Thomas Sheridan. There is an elaborate tradition detailing the relations between these two old friends in the last months of Sheridan's life. The younger Thomas Sheridan, who tells the story with Proustian meticulosity, does not claim to have witnessed the scenes, nor to have learned of them from his dying father, nor yet to have received an account from the other actors. Since his biography is furnished with several equally minute anecdotes which have been proved false, I am not inclined to trust his evidence here.[2]

Swift could have seen little of his crony while he himself was undergoing such a series of long confinements and while Sheridan was living in Cavan. There is an Anglo-Angli letter from Sheridan to Swift, probably of 26 May 1738, which sounds as though Sheridan is in Dublin, if not at the deanery; it also sounds easy and open.[3] The last extant allusion by the dean to the doctor—two months before Sheridan's end—is perfectly kind: he has been sent a prescription for asthma by John Barber, and, thanking him, writes, 'I will put Dr Sheridan, the best scholar in both kingdoms, upon taking your receipt.'[4]

It is possible, as the tradition asserts, that Sheridan was staying in the deanery at this time and that he left soon after; but the reason for his departure may well have been his host's (or their common) concern for Sheridan's health—his need for special nursing, or for removal from city air. The doctor retired to the suburban home of a former pupil and there died 'after the tedious indispositions' (said a newspaper) of dropsy and asthma.[5] Two-and-a-half months later, Orrery, writing to

---

[1] Mason, p. 229, n. Cf. the bitter language about her in 1735 (Williams IV. 411); the allowance was fifteen pounds a year (*ibid.*, III. 380).

[2] For instance, the younger Sheridan describes Helsham as diagnosing Dr Sheridan's illness a matter of days before the latter's end. Yet Helsham had become ill in Kilkenny late in July 1738, and died in Dublin a month later, whereas Dr Sheridan did not die until 10 October 1738.

[3] Ball VI. 191.   [4] Williams V. 115, 118.

[5] *Pue's Occurrences* and the *Dublin Gazette*, 14 Oct. 1738; Ball VI. 211.

Swift, names 'poor Sheridan' with no sign that the dean's tenderness toward his late friend had failed.[1]

Again, the effect of so miserable a chapter must have
weakened Swift's connection with Delany. The deaf old dean's
main links with him were gone. In the spring of 1738 Delany had
sent Swift five medals found in the churchyard of St Werburgh's;[2] but Swift's ailments surely obstructed the free intercourse that might have re-established the two men's steady
respect for each other. On a list of 'ungrateful-grateful-
indifferent-and-doubtful' friends, Swift once marked Delany
down as indifferent, partly grateful.[3]

Yet whatever the motivation on Swift's part, it is certain that
Delany regretted the break; for he blamed their separation on
'some persons, who called themselves [Swift's] friends' but who
tried 'by all the evil arts of insinuation and untruth, to banish
the Dean's best friends from about him, and make a monopoly of
him to themselves. And they in a great measure effected it'.[4]
Delany here is referring to the Whiteways and Deane Swift, as
one may learn from the furious attacks on him in the younger
man's life of Swift.[5]

Against these deprivations, a new friend can illustrate the
filiations and continued vitality of Swift's social pattern even at
this time. William Richardson was a man of middling status
from whom the Dean of St Patrick's Cathedral could have had
nothing to fear, but whose public standing made him worthy of
respect—a country gentleman, a prospering estate manager, a
Member of Parliament. Though John Richardson, a clergyman
whom Swift knew, was a brother to William, it was not this
parson but a distinguished barrister who recommended him to
Swift. The dean first encountered Richardson in the mild but
favourable light of an established landowner wishing for an
introduction to John Barber in London.[6]

Conferring an easy kindness was one way for Swift to begin
liking a man. Soon Richardson's gratitude and then Barber's

[1] Williams V. 132. For a careful survey of the evidence, see Ball VI. 210–12.
[2] Williams V. 103.   [3] *Ibid.*, p. 271.   [4] Delany, pp. 2–3.
[5] P. 354 and *passim*.   [6] Williams IV. 300.

acquiescence strengthened the bond.[1] A return movement started when Richardson gave some material assistance to Swift's old curate, Warburton.[2] Then the flow of reciprocal good nature deepened with a hearty invitation offered the dean to visit his new friend's residence in Londonderry.[3]

Richardson was a man of high enough rank to deserve Swift's attention. He could be of service to the dean and be served by him, and he liked to offer hospitality to him. In time Richardson endeared himself further by a series of gifts: three large salmon, some cheese, bottles of whisky, a shipment of wine. Neither could the eulogistic style of his address have been unwelcome:

> I have not been without my doubts as to the propriety of a man of business, whose conversation has been for the most part among such, and who pretends but to plain sense, and an honest meaning, inviting the greatest genius that perhaps a thousand years have produced, cultivated with all the helps of art, and that has lived among the great in all respects, [to a] place without other ornament than nature has bestowed upon it.[4]

One assumes that the odour of this incense hastened the early invitation which Swift extended to Richardson, to see him at the deanery; and Richardson must have known that he was adding a welcome but delicate savour to his compliments when he begged Swift to help him lay out the groves and walks of his park.[5]

After visiting, conversing, and dining with Swift, Richardson offered the ultimate blandishment of establishing a correspondence between his charming young niece and the old dean. The habitual formulae were invoked. Swift demanded successfully that Miss Katherine Richardson should make him the 'first advances', and he endorsed a document accepting her 'as my mistress'.[6]

Soon there followed a characteristically dictatorial letter of raillery, flattering her with insults and ironically attacking her for a gift of six shirts. In the praise, he inevitably singled out her

---

[1] *Ibid.*, pp. 324–5.   [2] *Ibid.*, pp. 534–5.   [3] *Ibid.*, p. 536.
[4] *Ibid.*, V. 14.   [5] *Ibid.*, p. 34.   [6] *Ibid.*, p. 85.

intellectual and moral qualities rather than her appearance. So we find another relationship like that, a few years earlier, between Swift and Miss Hoadly, the archbishop's daughter.

Since Miss Richardson replied in the familiar tradition running from Stella to Arabella Kelly, the commerce of the old dean and the young lady flourished. She sought his pedagogy and yearned for his correction.[1] He gave her a diamond ring and a lock of his hair.[2] Unhappily, however, like others of his young sweethearts, Miss Richardson was the victim of an early death; and a few years after he was introduced to her, the septuagenarian had to learn that she had named him in her 'last requests'.[3]

That Swift's attachment to Richardson depended on a mixture of motives seems clear; and the interest of the mixture is that it contained so many ingredients of other Swiftian friendships. On Richardson's side, bardolatry was presumably not weakened by the calculation of benefits *in posse*. One of his own profitable offices was that of agent for the Derry Society, of which John Barber, the former Lord Mayor of London, was chairman of the board. Swift's place in this relationship becomes visible in a statement by Barber during the summer of 1738:

> If Mr Richardson has not made you his acknowledgements for your great favour and friendship to him, he is much to blame; for to you he owes the continuance of his employment. An alderman of Derry came from thence on purpose to attach him, and he had many articles of impeachment; and I believe he had twenty, out of twenty-four, of our Society against him: and the cry has been against him for two or three years past, and I had no way to save him many times, but only by saying, that while I had the honour to preside in that chair, I would preserve the great privilege every Englishman had, of being heard before he was condemned: and I never put any question against him while he was in Ireland. Well, he came; and, after a long and tedious hearing of both sides, the Society were of opinion, that he had acted justly and honourably in his office.[4]

By this time the ground common to both men had broadened to support not only Mrs Whiteway but also her daughter.[5] We

---

[1] *Ibid.*, pp. 92–3.   [2] *Ibid.*, pp. 128–9.   [3] *Ibid.*, pp. 181–2.
[4] *Ibid.*, p. 116.   [5] *Ibid.*, pp. 116–17.

find Mrs Whiteway having Richardson buy damask for her while he was in England, in September 1738[1] (Richardson having left Ireland at the beginning of April);[2] Miss Richardson sending invitations and compliments to Molly Harrison as well as her mother;[3] and Mrs Whiteway begging Miss Richardson to spend some months with her in Dublin.[4]

Meanwhile, Swift had given William Richardson an introduction to Lord Oxford;[5] Pope was receiving him at Twickenham, thanks to Swift's sponsorship;[6] Richardson, during the spring of 1739, sought backing in London for the Irish parliamentary candidacy of Swift's friend, Macaulay;[7] and he also introduced a young cousin of the dean—William Swift—to a set of appropriate 'persons' in the British capital.[8] Thus service led to friendship and friendship led to favours.

Nobody was more valuable to Swift now than Mrs Whiteway. From writing joint letters with the dean, she had risen to conveying his opinions in letters of her own. She often appears not in the character of a secretary or of one executing commands but of an independent correspondent who (of her own initiative) either summarizes his sentiments or describes him. Answering a letter from Richardson, she says,

> [I] was greatly pleased yesterday to find the Dean in spirits enough to be able to write you a few lines; because I know it was what you wished for. I declare it hath not been by any omission of mine that it was not done long ago. Besides his usual attendants, giddiness and deafness, I can with great truth say, the miseries of this poor kingdom hath shortened his days, and sunk him even below the wishes of his enemies.[9]

Deane Swift, after two years at St Mary Hall, had finally taken his B.A. degree in 1736 at the surprising age of twenty-nine. (He had matriculated at Trinity College, Dublin, when he was seventeen, but did not complete the B.A. course.) Though

---

[1] *Ibid.*, p. 123.   [2] *Ibid.*, p. 102.
[3] *Ibid.*, pp. 108, 122–3, 130.
[4] *Ibid.*, p. 142.   [5] *Ibid.*, pp. 103–4.
[6] *Ibid.*, p. 131. I suppose Swift complied with Richardson's request.
[7] *Ibid.*, pp. 141–2.   [8] *Ibid.*, p. 143.
[9] *Ibid.*, p. 122.

he afterward spent more time at Oxford,[1] he returned to Dublin in the spring of 1738, establishing himself as Mrs Whiteway's regular acquaintance and therefore as Swift's. His own father was of course a first cousin to both her and the dean. When Deane Swift also began to court Molly Harrison, the family knot grew still closer.

This year again Swift's birthday inspired public celebrations. Salutes of guns began in the morning and went on till late in the evening. Bonfires were lit on the four steeples of the cathedral and elsewhere. Illuminations were visible; bells rang; poems were produced. Swift offered dinner or supper to friends who came to congratulate him. The *Dublin Journal* described him as cheerful and 'in perfect good health'.[2]

In addition to such displays Swift had a note from the new Countess of Orrery in England, a cordial message which does credit to her own taste and to her lord's respect for the dean.[3] This letter probably crossed an earlier one from Swift, lamenting his giddiness and deafness.[4] Writing to Mrs Whiteway a few days before his birthday, Swift hoped that she would recover from a 'wicked colic' and be with him on the anniversary, 'because it is a day you seem to regard, although I detest it, and I read the third chapter of Job that morning'. He complained of deafness and gloom.[5] Yet in January 1739, William Richardson tells Swift he is glad to have heard from Prime-Serjeant Singleton 'that he found you extremely well in every respect, except your hearing'.[6] So we observe the classic contrast, in Swift, between melancholy reflections—linked to symptoms of Ménière's syndrome—and convivial ties with relations and friends.

Again, in January 1739, Swift encouraged the attentions of his young cousin, Deane, by giving him a set of Faulkner's

[1] *Ibid.*, IV. 543, n. 2.
[2] *Dublin Journal*, 2 Dec. 1738. In the next number (5 Dec.) a congratulatory, panegyric poem is published. These issues of the newspaper exist in the 1737–8 run of the *Dublin Journal* preserved in the Linen Hall Library, Belfast; for my knowledge of them I am indebted yet again to Professor James Woolley.
[3] Williams v. 129–30.　[4] *Ibid.*, pp. 127–8.　[5] *Ibid.*, p. 128.
[6] *Ibid.*, p. 131.

edition of the *Works* as a New Year's gift; and he received in thanks an adulatory effusion showing the closeness with which this young cousin then pursued him:'[So] great a present from so great a person, and in a manner so handsome and so extraordinary, it is absolutely impossible I should ever be honoured with again.'[1] Yet in February Swift tells John Barber that his relations are 'of all mortals what I most despise and hate'.[2] He also says his disorders and ailments, added to a dead weight of seventy years, 'make me weary of life'; while in March, Mrs Whiteway says the dean is 'better both in health and hearing than I have known him these twelve months'.[3]

II. THE PUBLICATION OF 'VERSES ON THE DEATH'

A new irritation struck Swift when *Verses on the Death of Dr Swift* finally appeared in London. Once again, Dr King let Swift down. Early in January he sent Swift a warning:

> At length I have put Rochefoucault to the press, and about ten or twelve days hence it will be published. But I am in great fear lest you should dislike the liberties I have taken. Although I have done nothing without the advice and approbation of those among your friends in this country, who love and esteem you most, and zealously interest themselves in every thing that concerns your character.[4]

In fact, he had shown the manuscript to Pope and perhaps to others. Following the advice he received and using his own judgment, he then proceeded to recast the text; for he eliminated all the notes and many verses of the original poem—amounting to about a third of the whole; and he further introduced over sixty lines from *The Life and Genuine Character of Dr Swift*.[5] The bastardized text was published in mid-January, and by the first week of March two editions had been sold off, the first being of two thousand copies.[6]

[1] *Ibid.*, p. 134.
[2] *Ibid.*, p. 138. He excepts Mrs Whiteway and her daughter, and presumably young William Swift, the bearer of the letter.
[3] *Ibid.*, p. 142.   [4] *Ibid.*, p. 133.
[5] For a detailed account of the recasting and publication of the poem, see *Poems* II. 551–3.
[6] Williams V. 139.

But Swift was not amused by his friends' tampering. He gave a copy of the original text to Faulkner and allowed him to leave blanks for many lines and notes. The Dublin edition came out in February 1739, but copies were soon circulating with the suppressed matter added in manuscript. When King saw Faulkner's text, he recognized it as a reproof and sent an elaborate defence of his editing to Mrs Whiteway. Although she must have shown this to Swift, and although the arguments are similar to what a modern critic might say, there is as usual no sign that the dean took any account of his friend's logic. Yet King pointed out obvious inaccuracies in the poem and observed that the last section 'might be thought by the public a little vain, if so much were said by himself of himself'.[1]

The publication of the poem may be taken as one more token of Swift's long preoccupation with the approach of death. The same preoccupation was no doubt the origin of an advertisement which he had given to Faulkner during the summer of 1738. This remained unseen until December, when a 'gentleman who hath appropriated the greatest part of his fortune to charitable uses' offered, through the *Dublin Journal*, to lend one or two thousand pounds at 5 per cent interest 'upon land security'.[2]

A few weeks later, Swift, under his own name, let it be known that he had loaned £2120 at 5 per cent interest, to increase the fund for his 'charity'—i.e., the hospital—and commented,

> The Dean would rather have purchased an estate in land for the said use, and hath often communicated his intention to several persons, but could not find any to assist him, even with advice; so great is the dearth of publick-spirited people in this poor unhappy kingdom.[3]

It is ironical that the advertisement came out about the same time as the poem which has near its close the famous lines about

---

[1] *Ibid.*, p. 139. James Woolley has shown that, inaccurate or not, Swift's statements in the text and the notes of the poem are consistent with what he said of himself elsewhere. See Woolley's essay, 'Autobiography in Swift's Verses on His Death', in John I. Fischer *et al.*, eds., *Contemporary Studies in Swift's Poetry* (Newark, Del., 1981), pp. 112–22.

[2] *Dublin Journal*, 2 and 19 Dec. 1738 (if not earlier; some numbers of the paper are not extant); cf. Williams v. 112–13.

[3] *Dublin Journal*, 6 Jan. 1739.

the unhappy kingdom and the hospital:

> He gave the little wealth he had,
> To build a house for fools and mad:
> And shew'd by one satiric touch,
> No nation wanted it so much.

A more conventional response to the approach of death was Swift's abortive but fascinating attempt to give a straightforward account of his own life. About the time when the verses on his death came out, Swift undertook a history of his family which gradually turned into an autobiography and then stopped short.[1] This fragment (of less than five thousand words) reflects the common preoccupation of ageing men with genealogy and money. After several paragraphs about his father's ancestors (with special attention to their fortunes), Swift gives a dramatic chronicle of his grandfather, the vicar of Goodrich, Herefordshire, and his suffering for the sake of Charles I. We are then told about Swift's uncles and his parents. His own annals, up to his obtaining the living of Laracor, occupy roughly the final third of the text.

Swift's attitude toward his relations is generally censorious, apart from the praise of Thomas Swift of Goodrich. The treatment of young Swift himself is severe and misleading, although the old man blames his 'near relations' for neglecting the boy. The material remains precious, for Swift supplies many important facts that would otherwise be unknown. But he also includes misinformation that a series of biographers inevitably preserved.[2] I wonder whether it was not a withdrawal from miscellaneous social relations and the intimacy with Martha Whiteway and young Deane Swift that encouraged Swift to write a kind of essay so little suited to his talents.

---

[1] Davis v. 187–95, 352–6. We can tell when Swift composed the fragment. John Lyon gathered materials for him to use in an account of his grandfather, and Swift endorsed these pages with the date of April 1738 (Mason, p. 228, n. c). In the piece itself, Swift says that his grandfather's house is over a hundred years old (Davis v. 188), and the date to be seen on the house is 1636 (*ibid.*, p. 353, note to p. 188, l. 26). In a letter to Pope dated 28 Apr. 1739, Swift refers pointedly to his own ancestry, mentioning sources and repeating details and phrases that also appear in the fragment of autobiography.

[2] See above, i. 3–6, 23–4, 27–8, 30–1, 60–1, and *passim*.

III. STILL MORE POLITICS

As a political or public figure, the dean and Drapier continued
to receive testimonials of his power. In the autumn of 1739 one
stranger begged him to support an anatomical exhibit in
Dublin, while another asked him to back a bill against wool-
running.[1] Swift had defended a clergyman named Throp
against persecution by a vicious M.P., Colonel Waller, and had
loaned money to the unfortunate man.[2] The grateful family
wished to seek redress in Parliament, and sent Swift a dozen
copies of their printed case, believing that the dean could influence Members of Parliament with them.[3]

But the dramatic show of Swift's importance was the election
campaign of Alexander Macaulay. One scholar has described
Macaulay as being, at this time, 'an active and troublesome
opponent to the English government in Ireland'.[4] He was a
barrister, probably in his middle thirties, acquainted with the
dean since 1736. Swift had then, 'with much pleasure', read
Macaulay's pamphlet, *Property Inviolable*, attacking the agistment bill.[5] Then at the end of 1737 the dean stood godfather to
another of his pamphlets, *Some Thoughts on the Tillage of Ireland*;
for Faulkner published it with a prefatory commendation by
Swift.[6] He also consulted Macaulay about the publication of the
Four Last Years.[7]

In the course of a distinguished legal career, Macaulay was to
become a K.C., an honorary LL.D. (T.C.D., 1746), a judge of
the Consistorial Court of Dublin (an ecclesiastic court), and a
Member of Parliament (Thomastown, 1761–6). He was descended from an Ulster family, and his son married a granddaughter of Sir Arthur Acheson. The old dean thought so highly
of Macaulay that he is said to have given him the treasured
penknife which Guiscard used in his assault on Robert Harley

---

[1] Williams v. 163–8.   [2] *Ibid.*, IV. 419–20 and n. 2, 422, 429; v. 112, n. 1.
[3] *Ibid.*, v. 172–3.
[4] *Ulster Journal of Archaeology* I. viii (1860), 201.
[5] Williams IV. 491.
[6] Davis XIII. 143.   [7] Williams v. 106–7 and p. 106, n. 2.

and which Harley gave to Swift.[1] Certainly the dean in his will (May 1740) left Macaulay the gold box in which he had received the freedom of Dublin. This, Swift said, was in testimony of

> the esteem and love I have for him, on account of his great learning, fine natural parts, unaffected piety and benevolence, and his truly honourable zeal in defence of the legal rights of the clergy, in opposition to all their unprovoked oppressors.[2]

The closing phrases are the strongest. It was Macaulay's support of the clergy that delighted Swift.

The dean showed what his esteem and love could accomplish when Macaulay wished to be chosen M.P. for the University of Dublin (i.e., Trinity College), in 1739. Swift appeared boldly and openly in his support. William Richardson, still in London, was asked to move the Lord Lieutenant (now the Duke of Devonshire) on behalf of Macaulay.[3] Pope was asked to intercede with Lyttelton, whose master, the Prince of Wales, was Chancellor of the University.[4]

At the end of March, about three weeks after Marmaduke Coghill's death left the seat vacant, Macaulay declared his candidacy. But the election was not held until 29 October. The opposing candidate was Philip Tisdall, whose wife was a niece of the Prime Serjeant, Henry Singleton. Although the poll gave Macaulay the election, by 44 to 38, Tisdall demanded a scrutiny. This reduced the winner's plurality, the next day, to three. Macaulay immediately took his seat in the Commons. But Tisdall lodged a petition complaining of an undue election and return. Before the month was out, his petition was granted and he was seated. This success was probably due to Singleton, but Tisdall followed it up with a splendid career as an Irish politician.[5]

Yet Macaulay's initial achievement has real significance. In a choice determined by so small a figure—three votes having been

[1] Lawrence Dundas Campbell, *The Miscellaneous Works of Hugh Boyd* (1800), I. 3–5.
[2] Davis XIII. 155.   [3] Williams V. 141.
[4] Sherburn IV. 175–6, 184–5.   [5] *DNB*.

critical at the poll and two at the scrutiny—we must regard Swift's intervention as decisive. It had been worth Macaulay's while to appeal to the Drapier, and it would have been fair for Swift to take credit for the ephemeral victory.

That Macaulay, in later life, found it proper to defend the administration of Ireland, and that Tisdall, whom the Drapier had opposed, went on to gain greater political power than 'any other Irishman in the middle of the eighteenth century'[1] only illuminates the difficulties of Swift's position. His notion of patriotism was often merely the screen that a political outsider used for commonplace ambition.

There are inevitably other ironies in the affair. Tisdall's cousin was Esther Johnson's suitor, William Tisdall. His schoolmaster had been Thomas Sheridan. His college tutor was Patrick Delany, and his wife's uncle was one of Swift's executors. William Richardson told Swift that Singleton 'most entirely loves as well as admires you'.[2]

Besides such demands on his influence, Swift also received those tokens of recognition which are accorded the aged lion when its teeth are drawn. There was, as always, an erratic flow of newspaper verse celebrating his genius, his portrait, or his birthday.[3] In March, moreover, the chapter of St Patrick's Cathedral spent £59. 9s. on a full-length painting of Swift by Francis Bindon, and set it up in the deanery.[4] About the same time, Alderman John Barber, in an elaborate ceremony, gave the Bodleian Library, Oxford, a portrait of Swift which purported to be the original one painted by Charles Jervas in 1709 and 1710. Barber had the picture handsomely framed, and the inscription under it was a Latin compliment on which Pope and Bolingbroke collaborated.[5] Barber also saw to it that the *London Evening Post* should publish a full account of the event. Nevertheless, the most considerable and enduring monument to Swift, apart from his own works, was conceived and accomplished by Pope.

---

[1] *Ibid.*   [2] Williams v. 131.   [3] *Dublin Journal*, 10, 13 Mar.; 10, 17 Nov. 1739.
[4] *Ibid.*, 31 Mar. 1739; Williams v. 143–4.
[5] T. Scott XII. 8–9; Williams v. 143–4.

Chapter Eleven

THE LETTERS OF SWIFT AND POPE

The letters of Swift to Pope are never so open or spontaneous as those to Ford or Sheridan. When he wrote to Pope, Swift said little that he would have been embarrassed to let others see; and Pope's style was, if anything, less exceptionable. Writing to most people, Pope had a habit of praising epistolary candour while sounding as if he were dictating to posterity.[1]

Their friendship had something in it of the self-consciousness of a famous acting team whose stage association has started a myth of mutual affection—a myth not without value to its subjects. It is no accident that the theme of friendship pervades their correspondence, for they both were determined to exemplify that virtue in their relation. The letters proved that the greatest writers of their age could trust and aid each other without ever feeling jealous.[2] The two authors were thoroughly aware of their reputation and of the effect such documents would have on it. So the letters become at times not only celebrations by each man of the other's genius but also monuments to their friendship. Each saved the other's letters, and Swift was proud enough of such treasures to show his visitors those from Pope and similar eminences.[3]

But unlike Swift, Pope was eager to polish and edit his own collections; he longed to distribute them as printed books, giving him a well-earned gain of income and prestige. Yet he hated exposing himself to the judgment of those who condemned such publications. He felt that he must not appear as editor and merchant of his familiar epistles. As though sentencing himself

---

[1] E.g., Sherburn III. 79.   [2] *Ibid.*, p. 30.   [3] Pilkington I. 73–4.

before the crime, he told people how much he detested the exposure of such intimate materials to the general eye:

> Indeed it is a mortifying prospect to have one's most secret opinions, delivered under the sacredness of friendship, betrayed to the whole world, by the unhappy partiality of one's own best friends in preserving them.[1]

Among Pope's difficulties was the fact that somebody had to be blamed for any apparently unauthorized edition. It was not enough for the poet to deny responsibility. He must plant clues assigning the mischief to particular persons. In his passion for self-concealment, the poet was willing to incriminate not only enemies (like the publisher Curll) but friends, benefactors, and the friends of friends.

In Swift he met peculiar obstacles. The dean was less compliant than others in Pope's circle, perhaps because the letters had some of the same value for him as for the poet. He too wished to display his intimacy with genius and power. But Swift did not contemplate publication in his own lifetime:

> You need not fear any consequence in the commerce that hath so long passed between us; although I never destroyed one of your letters. But my executors are men of honour and virtue, who have strict orders in my will to burn every letter left behind me.[2]

This declaration hardly agreed with Pope's plans, especially since his friend sometimes seemed to regard any wish to publish familiar correspondence as improper:

> [It] is plain that all Pliny's letters were written with a view of publishing, and I accuse Voiture of the same crime, although he be an author I am fond of. They cease to be letters when they become a jeu d'esprit.[3]

Yet Pope had reason to feel anxious about his letters in Swift's hands. With advancing age and illness, the old dean might suddenly die and the letters might be lost or become the property of strangers. Pope must have heard about Swift's freedom

---

[1] Letter to Orrery, 14 Jan. 1737; Sherburn IV. 53.　　[2] *Ibid.*, III. 492.
[3] *Ibid.*, p. 92.

with them. A story told by Mrs Pilkington reveals how far this could go. He sent for her one morning; and when she came, he produced a large book from which he cut out the leaves but kept the inner margins.

> He then brought out two drawers filled with letters: Your task, Madam, is to paste in these letters, in this cover, in the order I shall give them to you; I intended to do it myself.

She is willing, but asks for permission to read the letters; and he grants her that. She then describes in detail a letter from Bolingbroke, and goes on.

> The rest of the Dean's correspondents were, the Lady Masham, the Earl of Oxford, Dr Atterbury, Bishop Burnet, Lord Bathurst, Mr Addison, Archdeacon Parnell, Mr Congreve, Mr Pulteney, Mr Pope, Mr Gay, Dr Arbuthnot; a noble and a learned set![1]

Reports of such episodes must have reached Pope and made him fear that copies or originals might be taken and circulated— eventually, published. Besides, when Swift was threatened with legal action for his libellous writings, he used to send off his personal papers to some trusted friend for safekeeping; and in the course of such operations, manuscripts might easily be lost or taken. As Swift's memory weakened and he leaned on others like Mrs Whiteway, he might simply turn documents over to them so they could be found when wanted. Again, the danger of letters straying was real.

Such circumstances intensified Pope's wish to shepherd the most important part of his epistolary correspondence into the safety of print himself. He had already set up the publication of his correspondence with some friends in England by recalling his letters to them and then contriving, not very deftly, that the shameless Edmund Curll should bring out an apparently pirated edition (prepared by Pope and printed for him) in 1735. Pope could then lament the accident and produce another edition supposed to be authentic.

When Swift was approached, he could hardly have mistaken

---

[1] Pilkington I. 73–4.

Pope's aims, even though the poet hid them and only suggested that he wished to safeguard the letters which he begged to be returned. Swift himself indulged in labyrinthine evasions with his friend. For example, he described Faulkner's edition of the *Works of J.S.* as 'an evil I cannot prevent';[1] and Pope scolded Swift for denying to him—or concealing—the authorship of several works,[2] even as he teased Swift for not having recognized the authorship of the *Essay on Man* (which the poet had kept secret).[3]

With perhaps unconscious anticipation, Pope in 1729 had foreshadowed the maze through which he was to prod Swift ten years later. Writing about the publication (in 1728) of his correspondence with Wycherley, he not only omitted its true history—that Pope alone had conceived and managed the scheme—but also hinted that Lord Oxford had inspired it:

> I speak of old Mr Wycherley; some letters of whom (by the by) and of mine, the booksellers have got and printed not without the concurrence of a noble friend of mine and yours [i.e., Oxford], I do not much approve of it; though there is nothing for me to be ashamed of, because I will not be ashamed of anything I do not do myself, or of anything that is not immoral but merely dull (as for instance, if they print this letter I am now writing, which they easily may, if the underlings at the post-office please to take a copy of it.) I admire on this consideration, your sending your last to me quite open, without a seal, wafer, or any closure whatever, manifesting the utter openness of the writer. I would do the same by this, but fear it would look like affectation to send two letters so together.[4]

After 'Curll's' collection of Pope's correspondence appeared (1735), the poet included Swift in the audience for his groans, and expressed doubts as to the fate of the letters in Swift's hands. When Swift promised that they would all be destroyed upon his death, it is just possible that he was trying to force Pope to show his hand.[5] As Pope only showed more anxiety, Swift tranquilly

[1] 8 Jul. 1733; Sherburn III. 377.
[2] 6 Jan. 1734 and 15 Sept. 1734; *ibid.*, pp. 401, 402, 432.
[3] *Ibid.*, p. 432.   [4] Letter to Swift, 28 Nov. 1729; *ibid.*, p. 80.
[5] 3 Sept. 1735; *ibid.*, p. 492.

reminded him of the promised destruction.[1] But Pope persisted until by the spring of 1736 Swift said he would have his executors seal up the letters, upon his death, and return them to Pope. Meanwhile, they would remain tied up, endorsed, and locked in a cabinet. 'No mortal shall copy them, but you shall surely have them when I am no more.'[2]

Pope might have thought his goal nearer now, but hardly near enough. He must get possession of the original letters. Even if he had kept copies of them (and he had not), those would not have given his risky project the security he wanted. He must control the source of his edited text and thus shield it from either rivals or cavils.

Pope needed allies. He soon found one in young Orrery, whose lust for the literary distinction traditional in his family easily subdued his modest scruples of loyalty, insight and self-respect. ('Respect him, you could not', said Johnson; 'for he had no mind of his own. Love him you could not; for that which you could do with him, everyone else could.'[3]) The Earl had met Pope, after an introduction from Swift, in 1733, and was soon in correspondence with him. So eager a tool was not likely to obstruct the manufacture of a volume which would advertise his intimacy with the greatest writers alive; and Pope's first extant letter to him includes a lengthy paragraph of gratitude for Orrery's disabusing people of their suspicions about the 1735 volume of correspondence.[4]

Towards the end of the year 1736, Pope planted, in the fecund soil of their reciprocal praise, a hint that his own professedly 'free and unreserved' letters would be safer with his lordship than with Swift (who seemed in fact critically ill) or with Swift's executors.[5] He had already, in secret, released to Curll the text of a 1723 letter from Pope and Bolingbroke to Swift; and the method of delivery had been such as to persuade Curll that it came from Ireland. The timely appearance of this evidence (in

---

[1] 21 Oct. 1735; *ibid.*, p. 505 and n. 2.   [2] 22 Apr. 1736; *ibid.*, p. 12.
[3] Boswell IV. 29.   [4] 12 Jul. 1735; Sherburn III. 470.
[5] 7 Nov. 1736; *ibid.*, IV. 42.

early November 1736, but dated 1737 by Curll[1]) gave new power to Pope's next pleading with Swift; for he argued that since Curll had not included Swift's answer to the 1723 letter, he must have obtained the original—as he had advertised—from Dublin:[2] Swift, of course, could not have failed to realize that Pope knew the dean's visitors were often shown his epistolary collections.[3] When Swift, replying to an earlier letter, showed the effects of his failing memory and also said nothing about the disposal of the correspondence, Pope begged Orrery to step in before Curll took further advantage of his dark opportunities.[4]

Thinking, one assumes, in the tradition of Voiture, Pope treated his letters as literary property. It is doubtful whether any of those close to him—Swift least of all, and perhaps not even Orrery—failed to see through his strategy with either the 1735 volume or the new undertaking. Strangers, the reading public, and comparative innocents like Ralph Allen might not at first guess the complete truth; nor, in the circumstances, could those who knew the truth reveal it without losing Pope's good will. Swift's friends could do little so long as the dean connived at his friend's scheme; they could not comfortably denounce it.

In January 1737 Pope asked Orrery to have Swift return the letters, marked, if he pleased, to show what he wished left out! Pope would copy them and send them back.[5] The request makes little sense if the letters were not to be published. In effect, it invites Swift to be co-editor of them. But when Orrery (thirty years old now) tried to make him tell what he thought, the wary, seventy-year-old dean became 'very shy' and showed startling

---

[1] The letter (printed as two letters) was the first fifteen pages in a volume of complex make-up published by Curll. The earliest advertisement I (or anyone else) has found of it as already published is in the *London Evening Post*, 11 Nov. 1736. Curll's preface is dated 5 Nov. 1736. Both in it and in the advertisement, Curll particularly states that the manuscripts have been 'transmitted from Ireland'. But in *Dean Swift's Literary Correspondence*, 1741, p. 217 n., Curll says, 'These two [*sic*] letters were given to Mr Curll by a gentleman of the county of Essex' (who may have been James Worsdale, the sometime inamorato of Mrs Pilkington). Faulkner published the same material in Dublin, 1737, as 'London printed, Dublin re-printed'.

[2] 30 Dec. 1736; Sherburn IV. 50 and n. 2.

[3] 30 Dec. 1740, Mrs Whiteway to Orrery; *ibid.*, pp. 320–2. N.B. the last sentence of this letter.

[4] 14 Jan. 1737; *ibid.*, pp. 52–3.   [5] *Ibid.*, p. 53.

instances of forgetfulness.[1] As we know, Swift was deeply proud of these witnesses to his grandeur; and without being concerned to help or hinder Pope's sponsorship of a publication which he did not care to undertake himself, Swift did hate to strip his cabinet of its prized ornaments. Nevertheless, when Orrery refused to table the question, Swift—who had no admissible excuse for withholding the letters—agreed to let them go. Orrery immediately told Pope.[2]

Meanwhile, Pope, though in bed with a fever, had already, for a third time, written to Swift, imploring him to send the letters, but now offering to return only copies to the dean, keeping the originals in England.[3] Swift, in a detailed and affectionate reply, said nothing about restoring them. So in March 1737, Pope swung back to Orrery. In a long account, he reviewed his appeals to Swift and his reasons for them, even adding a new suspicion to the fears already awakened—i.e., that Swift might have lent the letters out—'and in whatever hands, while they are Irish hands, allow me my Lord to say they are in dangerous hands.' He also begged the Earl to show Swift this very letter.[4]

Orrery did better than that. Writing from Cork, he sent Swift a transcript of Pope's anxious argument. Reminding him of their own earlier agreement, he proposed to carry the bundle over himself when he went to England during the summer.[5] Swift now said he would let him do so.[6] Both Orrery and Pope beseeched Swift to make the trip too, and Pope suggested a meeting in France.[7] Possession of the originals was only the first prerequisite to Pope's scheme; for he would have taken them under the colour of preventing exactly what he wished to do. The new strategies were therefore to be even more delicate than

---

[1] 5 Feb. 1737; *ibid.*, p. 54.
[2] Letter from Orrery to Pope, 18 Mar. 1737; *ibid.*, p. 62; letter from Pope to Orrery, 28 Mar. 1737; *ibid.*, p. 64.
[3] Letter from Pope to Orrery, 4 Mar. 1737; *ibid.*, p. 58.
[4] *Ibid.*, pp. 58–60.
[5] 18 Mar. 1737; *ibid.*, pp. 60–1.
[6] *Ibid.*, p. 64; Williams v. 24.
[7] Sherburn iv. 63; Williams v. 25.

the old; and in Pope's eagerness to entertain Swift (in France, if necessary), his affection for the dean and delight in his company may have been touched with a sense that Pope's subtle aims could be more conveniently pursued by speech than by pen. But Swift's comforts and occupations were too closely identified with Ireland, and he would not stir.[1]

With victory within his reach, Pope admitted to Orrery that he had a 'plot' to erect a monument to Swift's friendship with him:

> I have a plot upon them [i.e., the letters], by their means to take occasion to erect such a *particular* and *so minute* a monument of his and my friendship, as shall put to shame any of those casual and cold memorandums we see given by most ancient and modern authors, of their regard for each other.... [I] would show how much more the *heart* of a sincere esteemer and honourer of worth and sense can do, than the tongue or pen of a ready writer, in representing him to the world. Pray tell him this.[2]

Although Swift could not misunderstand the implications of this message, he may have wished to redirect the 'plot' of his sincere esteemer. Certainly he wrote to Pope (31 May 1737) a message opening with a curt reply to the repeated inquiry as to when he would send the packet: '[It] is true I owe you some letters, but it has pleased God, that I have not been in a condition to pay you.' He then renewed his own complaint that Pope had not properly honoured him in a verse epistle, perhaps implying that he still preferred such a memorial to any other. At the same time, Swift again committed himself to sending the letters, and tacitly authorized the text of the originals:

> All the letters I can find of yours, I have fastened in a folio cover, and the rest in bundles endorsed; but, by reading their dates, I find a chasm of six years, of which I can find no copies; and yet I kept them with all possible care: But, I have been forced, on three or four occasions to send all my papers to some friends, yet those papers were all sent sealed in bundles, to some faithful friends; however, what I have, are not much above sixty. I found nothing in any to be left out.[3]

[1] Sherburn IV. 71.   [2] *Ibid.*, p. 64.   [3] *Ibid.*, pp. 71–2.

The 'chasm' troubled Pope, and the storing of papers with Swift's friends must have alarmed him. But it is clear that Swift understood his friend's intention to publish the letters. Nevertheless, he put off handing the letters to Orrery until just before the Earl's departure, perhaps to ensure himself of a farewell visit from the young peer. 'They are reserved', his lordship told Pope, 'for the dona extrema.'[1] When Orrery did sail, at the beginning of July, he had them; and when he reached London, he quickly delivered them to Pope.[2] Suddenly the correspondence between the dean and the poet shrank from a torrent to a trickle.

In order to produce a new volume of letters without dropping his threadbare mantle of injured innocence, Pope planned a variant of the method which he had used before. An apparently unauthorized text was to come out in Dublin, whereupon Pope would—under this painful compulsion—issue a correct version in London. The first half of the programme was by far the more difficult. He had to lure an Irish printer into sponsoring the collection in such a way that the thing should not seem to emanate from England. Young Orrery was no resource for this effort, since he was too knowledgeable.

But during the year 1740 there was a respectable Irish legal friend of Swift's in England—Samuel Gerrard of Gibbstown, introduced to Swift by Christopher Cusack and to Pope by Swift.[3] What Pope told him, we do not know in detail; but they were in touch, that April, in London, before Gerrard took up his last English residence, which was to be at Bath.[4] Pope certainly had Gerrard promise to let him know when he was about to go on from Bath, so that Pope might send him 'a letter' for Swift. But in May, when Pope got the signal from Gerrard, he replied that the letter had already gone by another hand.[5]

Meanwhile, Gerrard probably saw Pope's admirer, Ralph Allen. Shortly before Gerrard left Bath, an unknown messenger gave him a parcel, probably with a request to pass it on to Swift; and in a letter at the end of May Pope asked Allen to make sure

---

[1] *Ibid.*, p. 76. [2] *Ibid.*, p. 81. [3] *Ibid.*, p. 234.
[4] *Ibid.*, p. 282. [5] 5 May 1740; *ibid.*, pp. 241–2.

that an undescribed packet had indeed got to Gerrard.[1] When the lawyer reached Dublin, he delivered his cargo.

What Swift saw after he undid the wrappings was, almost certainly, a book without a title or a binding but accompanied by an anonymous letter. The book was a printed copy of his correspondence with Pope. The letter was a plea that Swift should have this professedly unique copy published, as an amiable picture of his excellent mind and a testimony of the love and respect of his intimates:

> As there is reason to fear they [i.e., the letters] would be lost to posterity after your death, if either of your two great friends [i.e., Pope and Bolingbroke] should be possessed of them, (*as we are informed you have directed*) they are here collected and submitted to your own mature consideration.[2]

If the best intentions had not now been tangled with some inconvenient notions of honour, the rest of the story would be easy. Swift, I believe, realized that Pope must have arranged for the volume to be printed and that by this self-effacing turn he wished to insure Swift's connivance. It was the sort of trick that Swift himself had used.[3] The old dean's vanity could hardly dismiss so splendid an opportunity to gild his own monument. To the printed copy he added notes, identifications, and interlineations. Then he gave Faulkner the book to reprint.

Yet Swift did not go so far as editors have believed. The long letter of 10 January 1721–2—which is really a statement of political principles—appeared in print as a cancel sheet, with a note that Pope never received the original. Learned scholars have naturally thought that Swift added this sheet in Dublin. But a careful study has shown that Pope inserted the piece in London. Perhaps Swift had bundled it with the letters from Pope which he returned in 1737. Certainly the insertion and the note belong to the scheme of identifying the publication with Swift and detaching it from Pope. For the same reason the poet

---

[1] 27 May 1740; *ibid.*, p. 245.
[2] *Ibid.*, pp. 242–3 and 242, n. 1.
[3] Cf. his instructions for publishing *The Bubble*; Williams ii. 364–5.

eliminated the heading 'Twickenham' from the date-line of his own letters but included 'Dublin' for nearly all of Swift's. So also the letters to Pope are usually headed, 'From Dr Swift', while those to Swift have no heading; and the caption title does not mention Pope's name but reads, '*Letters To and From Dr Jonathan Swift*'.[1]

But now the loyalty and the praiseworthy officiousness of Mrs Whiteway began to operate. Swift, who often knew whom to trust, had been putting papers of all sorts in her custody, among them Pope's letters since 1738. She quickly understood that a consequence of such trust was her liability in case of any improper publication. Pope was not unwilling to malign her and use her as a scapegoat for the release of his correspondence with Swift. It was not hard for him to turn Orrery's suspicions in such directions, since the Earl already resented the lady's ascendancy over the dean.[2]

Mrs Whiteway was also zealous to keep Swift's name clear of what she assumed would be a dishonourable intrigue. So when she discovered that Faulkner was proceeding with the correspondence, the lady stepped in. She told Orrery, 'I opposed it publicly at the [dean's] table, as I did often privately to himself, and with that warmth, which nothing could have excused but friendship.'[3] To Pope she was still less reserved:

> I got all the friends of the Dean, that I thought had any weight, to persuade him against it; and only because I imagined it might be disagreeable to you. Nay, I ... stole the book out of his study, and kept it, till I was forced to return it, or add a lie to my theft. It is impossible to make you sensible, how positive the Dean was in having it done; nor the many warm disputes I had with him; a liberty I never took on any other occasion.[4]

The innocent lady could not realize that by blaming Swift, she was giving Pope evidence of his own guiltlessness.

---

[1] Archibald C. Elias, Jr, 'The Pope–Swift Letters (1740–41): Notes on the First State of the First Impression', *Publications of the Bibliographical Society of America* 69 (1975), 323–43.
[2] Cf. the letter from Orrery to Pope, 23 Feb. 1740; Sherburn IV. 226.
[3] 7 Oct. 1740; *ibid.*, p. 277.   [4] 18 Sept. 1740; *ibid.*, p. 319.

Faulkner wrote to Pope, 29 July 1740, stating that he had both the text of the letters and Swift's permission to print them; and he begged the same privilege from Pope.[1] To allow time for the printing to go forward without seeming himself to approve of it, Pope could only delay and equivocate. He answered as late as possible and through an intermediary, Robert Nugent of Bristol, who was known to both Pope and Swift.[2] Nugent had already offered himself as something of a cat's paw in Pope's affairs. Early in 1740, while visiting Ireland, he had been asked by Mrs Whiteway to tell Pope that she had some of his (no doubt recent) letters to Swift and would convey them to him by any carrier he chose.[3] Alexander Macaulay, finally selected to take them, never completed his mission; and an agent of Orrery's called for them instead, though not until January 1741.[4]

Meanwhile, Nugent had forwarded Pope's answer to Faulkner. But the printer, after a month of not hearing from Pope, had begun putting the book through the press. Before Faulkner could in turn reply, Pope asked Orrery to examine the volume, with the insinuation to be made that his lordship, if he found nothing objectionable, would get Pope to consent.[5] Time had brought the Earl to the ripeness of fathering two children without spoiling his unction; and he immediately wrote as instructed.[6]

But Faulkner had at last received a negative order from Pope and stopped the printing after the second sheet (i.e., thirty-two octavo pages).[7] Like Mrs Whiteway, Faulkner was not a tool, nor was he a confidant who understood and discreetly accepted the private games of Pope and Swift. He felt eager enough for the profit of the publication but not for the guilt—if there was to be any.

Orrery, though numb with a fit of gout, outdid himself in following what he fondly supposed to be Pope's wishes. In

[1] *Ibid.*, pp. 263–4. For the date, see Pope, *Works*, ed. W. Elwin and W. J. Courthope, VIII (London, 1872), 416–17, n. 4.
[2] Sherburn IV. 270, n. 3.
[3] *Ibid.*, pp. 230–1, 233; Williams v. 182, n. 1; Ball v. 156, n. 1.
[4] Williams v. 200–1.   [5] 3 Sept. 1740; Sherburn IV. 264.
[6] *Ibid.*, p. 270.   [7] Sept. or Oct. 1740; *ibid.*, pp. 270–1 and 270, n. 3.

October 1740 he boasted to the poet that the affair was at a complete halt. Faulkner had left with him the original printed copy of the letters, had sent to Pope the sheets already printed in Dublin, and had given up any notion of finishing the work unless the poet consented. Orrery further volunteered to Swift and Pope his helpful opinion that the correspondence ought to be suppressed; and he incidentally accused Mrs Whiteway of telling lies.[1]

Far from being blocked by this apparent impasse, Pope could now give his machine one small push and coast the rest of the way downhill. He understood what the theory in Ireland was, thanks to an account from the ineffable Earl:

> I asked [Faulkner] in a careless manner what Mrs [Whiteway's] opinion was of these letters. He told me she was fully persuaded you published [i.e., ? printed] them in England, and sent them privately to the Dean.[2]

However, these suspicions had simple antidotes, and—even if uncontradicted—need not hinder Pope's movements.

First, Faulkner could be managed through his very desire to publish the book and not to risk either public disapproval or Pope's anger: he would be discreet. Secondly, Mrs Whiteway's statements would be outweighed by Orrery's authority, by the past and future doubts casually spread by Pope concerning her conduct, and by Pope's influence over the persons whose judgment counted. But most of all, Swift had openly consented, and the printing had begun in Ireland. By incorporating into his London edition the improvements which Swift had made in Faulkner's copy, Pope could prove that his own text was derivative. For all their highmindedness, the strategy of Faulkner and Mrs Whiteway had only strengthened Pope's case and driven him to insinuations that might otherwise have been unnecessary.

All witnesses, including Swift himself, agreed that the dean's

---

[1] 4, 6, 8, 10 Oct. 1740; *ibid.*, pp. 276–80; cf. *ibid.*, p. 293.
[2] *Ibid.*, p. 279. Swift assumed that the printed copy of letters brought by Gerrard came from Pope; see *ibid.*, p. 276.

memory was now unreliable: Swift could be sure of what he remembered but not of what he forgot. (Yet his errors, though frequent, were almost entirely of omission.) He had so often expressed his confusion over the correspondence that Pope could now without danger hint at Swift's complicity in the supposed plot.

Besides, while Swift was failing, Pope too had no long expectation of life: further delay might frustrate his natural hope of seeing this category of his own and Swift's works safely published in the form which the authors preferred and in time for at least one of them to collect the profit. He felt bound to prepare his acquaintances for what was to happen. The complaint to Ralph Allen is typical and is uncannily reminiscent of the complaint to Swift about the Wycherley correspondence eleven years earlier:

> My vexation about Dean Swift's proceeding has fretted and employed me a great deal, in writing to Ireland, and trying all the means possible to *retard* it; for it is put past preventing, by his having (without asking my consent or so much as letting me see the book) printed most of it.... But as to your apprehension, that any suspicion may arise of my own being any way consenting or concerned in it, I have the pleasure to tell you, the whole thing is so circumstanced, and so plain, that it can never be the case.... The whole thing is too manifest to admit of any doubt in any man, how long this thing has been working; how many tricks have been played with the Dean's papers; how they were secreted from him from time to time, while they feared his not complying with such a measure; and how, finding his weakness increase, they have at last made *him* the instrument himself for their private profit; whereas I believe, before, they only intended to do this after his death.[1]

Not only are there no outright falsehoods in the language of these allegations; even the innuendoes are worded so ambiguously that they can, with due casuistry, be read as fact. Pope did try to retard the publication; Swift's 'papers' were at times kept from him; Faulkner did wish to make money.

Pope could now, boldly and without qualms, sweep the board. It is true that Orrery, after reading the copy sent from

[1] 3 Oct. 1740; *ibid.*, pp. 273–4.

England, pronounced the letters unfit for publication.[1] However, even before Pope received them (back) from Orrery, he had only to point out (December 1740) that the letters were harmless, that Swift desired their publication, and that it was by this time quite impossible to stop the volume from appearing in both England and Ireland: 'Therefore I think upon the whole it will be best to let the whole matter alone.'[2] Just afterward, he managed to contain, in a single letter one statement utterly disapproving of the publication and several other statements implicitly allowing it—the latter in terms more than strong enough for Faulkner to act upon.[3]

Orrery had recovered from the agonies of the gout only to endure more hideous pain when his two sons caught smallpox. Yet the deep suffering excited by the disaster in no way hampered his readiness to see things with Pope's eyes. His offers to oblige outran even the poet's expressed desires, and he glibly enlarged the huddled charges which Pope introduced against Faulkner and Mrs Whiteway.[4] Pope's contrivances were those of a man anxious to save (and profit from) a valuable equity of his own creation. Orrery was motivated by a cuckoo's hope of flying to Parnassus on an eagle's back. And when Pope asked for permission to publish some of the Earl's letters (in order to support his own account of the correspondence), the happy answer was, 'You have my entire approbation.'[5]

Swift was in the fortunate place of being able to stay passive and yet to see his wishes fulfilled. It is hard to say at what point he was deliberately using his reputation for absent-mindedness as a pretext for inactive irresponsibility, and at what point his memory became so unreliable that he honestly could not trust it. Unhappily for Pope's later reputation, the moment when Swift's shrewdest policy would have been passivity was also the moment when a failing memory appeared to relieve him of active responsibility for his conduct. Pope may have said only a

[1] 12 Nov. 1740; *ibid.*, pp. 293–4.
[2] 3 Dec. 1740; *ibid.*, p. 301.   [3] 27 Dec. 1740; *ibid.*, pp. 311–12.
[4] *Ibid.*, pp. 291–6, 298, 304–9, and *passim*.
[5] 12 Jan. 1741; *ibid.*, pp. 328–9.

half-truth when he blamed Swift for the publication; yet it was surely no less than a half-truth.

Although Pope received in October 1740, directly from Faulkner, the two sheets (or thirty-two octavo pages) which had already been printed of the Dublin edition, he did not receive the original, untitled, first printed copy (taken over by Gerrard) until early December. It was sent to him by Orrery without Faulkner's knowledge, so that Pope might edit (or reproduce) the text but not seem involved in the work.[1]

Temporarily keeping back his old store of the sheets first printed (those from among which the untitled, unbound copy had been made up), Pope now undertook what was to be the 'authorized' edition, following in general Swift's treatment. It was published by Knapton, Bathurst, and Dodsley, 16 April 1741, in *The Works of Mr Alexander Pope in Prose*, Volume II.[2] Faulkner did not produce his edition (Volume VII of Swift's *Works*) until about two months later, with two notes plainly implicating Pope in the printing of the correspondence.[3] The old store of original, first-printed sheets, which had probably gone through the press early in 1740, Pope now gave over to T. Copper, who issued *Letters Between Dr Swift, Mr Pope, &c.... Publish'd from a Copy Transmitted from Dublin*. Although this probably came out shortly after the authorized edition, it is of course the genuine first edition of the correspondence.[4]

[1] Letter from Orrery to Pope, 8 Nov. 1740, *ibid.*, p. 292; letter from Orrery to Pope, 14 Nov. 1740, *ibid.*, pp. 294–5; letter from Pope to Orrery, 10 Dec. 1740, *ibid.*, pp. 303–4.
[2] Teerink, p. 142. [3] Pp. 299, 300. [4] Teerink, pp. 139–45.

Chapter Twelve

SOUND MIND, WEAK BODY

I. SECLUSION

The winter of 1739–40 was one of the least comfortable seasons in Swift's life. It began reasonably enough, with agreeable events. First, there were the birthday rituals which he had long been used to. Once more, bells and illuminations marked the occasion. Visitors complimented him at the deanery. Poetasters offered verses. Twenty-one guns fired a salute. At night, yet again, bonfires could be seen on all four pinnacles of the cathedral.[1] Then there were the normal affairs of the church. On Sunday, 23 December, for example, Archbishop Hoadly ordained seven priests and eighteen deacons in the cathedral, and Swift seems to have assisted.[2]

But a few weeks later an intolerable period of wind and cold began. Potatoes spoiled in the ground.[3] The river Liffey froze solid. Tempests blew from the east. On New Year's Eve and the next day a great snow fell.[4] The terrible frost continued through January. The Lord Lieutenant and Privy Council issued a proclamation forbidding the export of cereal crops or of bread, as the 'extreme severity of this season, may occasion a scarcity of corn and grain'.[5] Lamplighters found it difficult to do their work, because the oil froze in the streetlamps.[6]

The charitable Primate sent money to the ministers of several Dublin parishes, so they might buy coal and meal to give to the poor, who were 'in a starving condition through the severity of the weather and the scarcity of provisions'.[7] The Lord

[1] *Dublin Journal* and *Pue's Occurrences*, 1 Jan. 1740.
[2] *Pue's Occurrences*, 26 Dec. 1739; Swift's *Accounts* of S.P.D., 1739 and following, fol. 18, inverted.
[3] Reilly's *Dublin News Letter*, 22 Jan. 1740.   [4] *Dublin Gazette*, 1 Jan. 1740.
[5] *Ibid.*, 19 Jan.   [6] *Dublin Journal*, 15 Jan. 1740.   [7] *Pue's Occurrences*, 15 Jan. 1740.

Lieutenant gave a hundred pounds toward the relief of the sufferers; the dean and chapter of Christ Church gave twenty pounds. In St Audoen's parish, a collection for 'distressed families' brought eighty pounds.[1] Among the many recorded instances of special donations was a sum of ten pounds from the chapter of St Patrick's Cathedral. Dean Swift himself had bestowed 'great and early charity'.[2] No thaw came before the end of the month; but even then it was ephemeral, and the misery lasted until mid-February.[3]

In his accounts of money given to the poor from the weekly collections of the cathedral, Swift has bleak notes on this period:

Janr. 7. A cruel frost of twelve days, and still going. The collections this day were but 2s–1d, but I added my usual shilling on common Sundays[4]

Janr. 12. A long extraordinary cold season, and I was worried by Mr Lyon to give more than the fund can well support. . . . However I give 20 shillings[5]

Swift had long avoided staying out of the deanery overnight, or even leaving it at all for more than a few hours.[6] About the year 1737, he had begun suffering attacks of the gout. When these are added to his deaf, dizzy, forgetful ways, and his growing dependence upon Mrs Whiteway for help with letters, we may imagine what a period of snow-bound confinement might mean to him.

Right after the frost began, Mrs Whiteway came down with rheumatism so severe that she could not visit Swift. Her daughter Mary (now Mrs Deane Swift) was ill too.[7] And since they both depended on Deane Swift, he also had little leisure for deanery visits. For exercise, Swift walked in his 'bedchamber and closet, which hath also a fire'. But he soon caught a cold and developed a cough.[8] Yet he did have visitors. Deane Swift was finally able to spend some time with the old man, and a new,

---

[1] *Dublin Gazette*, 26 Jan. 1740.   [2] *Dublin Journal*, 22 Jan. 1740.
[3] *Dublin Gazette*, 2 Feb. 1740; Williams v. 179, n. 3.
[4] *Accounts*, fol. 13, inverted.   [5] *Ibid.*, fol. 3.   [6] Ball VI. 152, n. 1.
[7] Deane Swift and Mary Harrison were married in July 1739; Williams v. 160 and n. 1.
[8] *Ibid.*, pp. 174–5.

young protégé, the Rev. Francis Wilson (who was not well either) apparently came often. Nevertheless, the old dean missed Mrs Whiteway and sent her a series of notes lamenting her illness more than his own.[1]

The weather broke in the middle of February. Mrs Whiteway recovered, and her regular attendance began again. Toward the end of February, Orrery wrote to Pope, 'The Dean has lately had another fit of the gout, but is now in perfect health.'[2] By St Patrick's Day, Swift was well enough to entertain his chapter at their annual feast.[3]

Gradually, however, during the two years that followed, his powers slipped and his seclusion grew. As early as July 1739 he had appointed a subdean, John Wynne, on the grounds that the dean was often unable, through sickness, 'to be present and personally to preside in the chapter'.[4] From time to time, of course, he did still preside, until the end of the year 1741.[5]

But his disabilities grew with the seasons. When Katherine Richardson died, it was Mrs Whiteway who transmitted Swift's condolences to the bereaved uncle. In late April, when Mrs Whiteway was not in good enough health to be with him he endured a fit of gout so sharp that he wrote to her, 'I am at this instant unable to move without excessive pain, although not the thousandth part of what I suffered all last night and this morning. This you will now style the gout.'[6] His almost coarse directness of expression here recalls the style in which he had generally told Stella about his various diseases.

Yet two weeks after this outburst, he apparently received Hoadly in the cathedral at the archbishop's annual visitation of the city and the county clergy of the diocese.[7] When Mrs Whiteway, a few days later, told Pope that Swift's 'memory is so much impaired, that in a few hours he forgot [Pope's letter]; nor is his judgment sound enough, had he many tracts by him, to finish or correct them,' she may possibly have taken a line

[1] *Ibid.*, pp. 173–6.   [2] Sherburn IV. 226.
[3] 17 Mar. 1740; Williams v. 180.   [4] Davis XIII. 195–6.
[5] Landa, p. 95.   [6] Williams v. 183.
[7] *Dublin Journal*, 13 May 1740; Swift's *Accounts* of S.P.D., fol. 12ᵛ, inverted.

suggested by Swift. Anyhow, she went on to say, 'His health is as good as can be expected, free from all the tortures of old age; and his deafness, lately returned, is all the bodily uneasiness he hath to complain of.'[1] In July, however, the gout returned, and became the subject of a letter to Mrs Whiteway.[2]

> I have been very miserable all night, and today extremely deaf and full of pain. I am so stupid and confounded, that I cannot express the mortification I am under both in body and mind. All I can say is, that I am not in torture, but I daily and hourly expect it. Pray let me know how your health is and your family. I hardly understand one word I write. I am sure my days will be very few; few and miserable they must be. I am, for those few days,
>
> Yours entirely,
> J. Swift.
>
> If I do not blunder, it is Saturday, July 26, 1740. If I live till Monday, I shall hope to see you, perhaps for the last time.[3]

Among those who kept regularly in touch with him (either through visits or through Mrs Whiteway) were Stopford, Francis Wilson, and William Richardson—not to mention his young cousins, Deane and Molly (Harrison) Swift. He saw John Lyon often, about the distribution of alms to the poor.[4] In the members of the cathedral chapter he had a kind of family, and Delany was chancellor. James King, Robert and John Grattan, John Towers, and Francis Wilson were among the prebendaries: Swift could find willing and agreeable company there. Dinner parties at the deanery occurred sporadically, but Swift seems to have restricted them to intimates familiar with his weaknesses.[5] Yet conviviality was possible, as one of Mrs Whiteway's anecdotes will show. This is on the occasion of William Richardson's marriage:

---

[1] 16 May 1740; Sherburn IV. 240–1. Mrs Whiteway's uncharacteristic use of 'hath', which Swift systematically adopted in his late years, suggests that he saw the letter before Pope did. Cf. Sherburn IV. 240, n.1.

[2] This is the last personal letter by Swift that has been preserved. A year later, he wrote a recommendation of William Swift to Eaton Stannard (Williams v. 205); and in January 1742 there was the exhortation to the vicars choral (*ibid.*, pp. 266–8). I do not count these as personal letters.

[3] *Ibid.*, pp. 192–3.   [4] Swift's *Accounts* of S.P.D., *passim*.
[5] Williams v. 186.

About a fortnight ago, I dined at the Dean of St Patrick's, in a mixed company; where one of the gentlemen told him you were married, or just going to be so, to a lady of fifteen, with a hundred thousand pound fortune, and a perfect beauty; I asked the person whether he had not that account from a woman? he said he had; the Dean enquired if I knew anything of the affair? I answered yes, only with this difference, that she was at least fifty, and a most ungenteel, disagreeable woman. The whole company looked upon me with contempt, and their countenances expressed, they thought I drew my own picture, whilst I enviously endeavoured to paint the lady's; the Dean only understood me, and smiling said, he believed I was in the right.[1]

In May 1740 Swift made his last will, witnessed by Wynne, John Rochfort, and William Dunkin.[2] In the opening, he describes himself as 'of sound mind, although weak in body'.[3] In a codicil two days later the expression is 'weak in body, but sound in mind'.[4] This codicil, meant to secure the income of his housekeeper, Mrs Ridgeway, was witnessed by Lyon, Dunkin, and Roger Kendrick (the verger of the cathedral).

Apart from Stopford, the executors were divided between prebendaries (Delany, Wilson, Robert and John Grattan, James King) and lawyers (Lindsay, Singleton, Stannard, Macaulay). Except for the hospital trust, those legatees who received bequests of substantial sums or property were Mrs Dingley, Mrs Ridgeway, and the Whiteway family—Mrs Whiteway and Ffolliot and John Whiteway.

Memorial presents of various sorts went to three friends in England—Pope, the Earl of Oxford, and Orrery; to four non-clerical connections in Dublin—Macaulay, Deane Swift, Mary (Harrison) Swift, and Mrs Barber; and to a large, unsurprising group of Irish clergy—Stopford, the Grattans, John Jackson, Wilson, Worrall, Delany, and James King.

The tithes of Effernock were left to the vicars of Laracor; and Naboth's Vineyard was to be sold, first refusal being allowed to the next dean of the cathedral.

---

[1] *Ibid.* (13 May 1740).   [2] Davis XIII. 147–58.
[3] *Ibid.*, p. 149.   [4] *Ibid.*, p. 157.

The failure to mention Bolingbroke may be significant. Orrery was furious at being left out of Pope's will.[1]

II. DEANE SWIFT

As Swift's disabilities worked on him, he became more and more of a still centre around which turned ephemerally those who wished to reach preferment through his offices, to win literary distinction or profit through a connection with him, or to protect him from exploitation. Mrs Whiteway stood at the extreme point of disinterest and respect, an appropriate successor to Esther Johnson; and Swift's commendations of her, his appeals to her, his care for her, revive in a mild but unflickering light his image of Stella.

Her son-in-law (Swift's cousin once removed), Deane Swift, was a year older than Lord Orrery but, in his ties with the great dean, both less ambiguous and more ambivalent than the Earl. Swift had interested himself in the young man about 1733, when Deane Swift was twenty-six, although they had had a family acquaintance since 1720.[2] Eight years earlier, perhaps on the basis of misinformation, Swift had labelled the boy a puppy who had 'so behaved himself as to forfeit all regard or pity'.[3]

But by 1733 he had found in his heart enough pity for the straitened young gentleman to lend him two thousand pounds against a mortgage on his four-hundred-acre estate at Castlerickard.[4] A period at St Mary Hall, Oxford, followed, with a good report from Dr King. Only in 1738 did Deane Swift become a steady caller at the deanery; and then he was probably sponsored by Mrs Whiteway.[5] By the spring of 1739, cousinly affection had climbed to the height of applying to him epithets already bestowed on Pilkington and Orrery; calling him 'the most valuable of any of his family'; and introducing him to Pope as decent and modest, a man of taste and scholarship, and a lover of 'liberty'.[6]

[1] Sherburn IV. 521, n. 3.
[2] D. Swift, p. 357. Cf. above, pp. 754, 900.   [3] Williams III. 59.
[4] *Ibid.*, IV. 139–40.   [5] D. Swift, p. 377.   [6] Sherburn IV. 174.

In July 1739, Deane Swift had married Mary Harrison, Mrs Whiteway's daughter. Proud of being allied to the great dean, he could not help expecting some benefit to himself not so much as a result of, but rather in conjunction with his attendance on the sick old man. Instead, however, of (what he hoped for) a career, his main inheritance was the profit and distinction of publishing many of Jonathan Swift's works, often from original manuscripts which descended to him from his mother-in-law. The only gifts we know about, which Deane Swift received from his famous cousin were (in 1738) an Elzevir Virgil,[1] a set of Swift's works,[2] and some items left by the dean's will. Yet according to an unpersuasive analysis by Deane Swift himself, the relationship could hardly have been more influential:

> When I was a boy my mother designed me for the bar and I would to God I had never been diverted from so reasonable a pursuit, but to my great misfortune the Dean of St Patrick's, Dr Swift, took notice of me very young, buoyed up my tender mind with notions of a more exalted nature, recommended history, poetry, the belles lettres, politics and a contempt of logic to a soul by nature too susceptible of so delightful imaginations. Everybody looked upon me as the person for whom he proposed somewhat extraordinary, even he himself talked of recommending me to persons in station who by degrees would hand me up the stairs of fortune in the court of St James's.

Not only did these prospects evaporate with no residue, but the dean seemed actually to shake him off. When Deane Swift was twenty-three, he began to study divinity and was recommended to several bishops. To improve his opportunities, he went to take a degree at Oxford. However, 'I no sooner thought of going into the church than the dean pursued me with bitterness' against the plan, which the young man, as it happened, abandoned for reasons of conscience. A new relationship now followed, and Deane Swift himself described this, at the time, to a friend:

> Since I left Oxford and gave over all thoughts of the church the dean has again been acquainted with me; I have frequently visited him and since I was married if I had consented to sacrifice my life to

[1] D. Swift, pp. 353–4.   [2] Williams v. 134.

him and spend all my days in his house to entertain him in his retirement when everybody whom he had obliged except one person had absolutely quitted him, then indeed he would have condescended to think he had obliged me by permitting me to keep him company. But anything is better than such slavery and though I have always loved him as a father, yet I could not bear with such treatment and neglect as I had formerly received from him.

The dean's compliments to the young man's scholarship, politics, and virtues meant nothing:

I went so far one night as to ask him very gravely if he knew e'er a young nobleman who wanted Greek and Latin for that I would sell him a bargain of them: he asked me what I meant. I told him that I had spent a great part of my life in the pursuit of ancient learning and that at last I found it was of no use and that if any young lord would purchase it I would sell him all that I was worth in that sort together with all my books in those languages and all the taste I had in poetry for so small a sum as £200, for that I really had no occasion for any of them, and that I should be very glad to get fairly rid of them. He seemed to dislike what I said prodigiously which had no further effect on me than to insist upon the reasonableness of my proposal: he soon talked to a third person and changed the discourse. . . . I have made it my business to drop him by degrees and of late [July 1741] it hath come to that pass that I have seen him but once since the middle of May, and perhaps shall never see him ten times during his life. . . . I admire him as a genius, you know how often I have fought his battles at Oxford, I believe you saw I loved him which, however great a fool soever I am for it, I cannot yet prevail upon myself to repent of . . . I cannot yet wholly get the better of my affection for him.[1]

There are inconsistencies and omissions in this account. Yet the conflict of motives which is so visible bears out Delany's second-hand description of Deane Swift: 'a man of fire, a little wild and sufficiently irritable'.[2] His facts are more reliable than his interpretations. Even in this report, concentrating on his dealings with the great man of his family, he passes over the tremendous loan of £2000. Elsewhere, Deane Swift's apparent respect for Orrery does not suggest a deep penetration into human character.[3]

[1] Dickins, *An Eighteenth Century Correspondence*, pp. 37–40.
[2] Delany, *A Letter to Deane Swift* (London, 1755), p. 13.
[3] Dickins, pp. 42, 50 (or is he ironic about Orrery?).

Delany had stopped seeing the dean about the time when
Deane Swift's intimacy burgeoned, and he evidently supposed
that the new favourite's influence had turned the dean against
him. But Orrery managed to pile up epistolary records of his
devotion to Swift—very proper to shine in print—though we do
not know that he found an occasion to visit him after about
1738.

In September 1739 the Orrerys had arrived in Dublin on
their way to Caledon, where they were to begin a long residence.
Swift was informed of their landing by his mainstay John Lyon,
and he wrote a charming little message to the lady, promising to
call on her. Although we don't know that the visit took place, the
letter remains evidence both of Swift's intellectual strength and
of his devotion to the Orrerys:

> I would have waited on you both immediately, if my years and
> infirmityes would have permitted me. For I have a deafness con-
> stantly which requires a clear lowd voice; my right ear is a little the
> better of the two. But I am also tormented with a giddyness. Yet, in
> spight of these two grievances, with many more of other kinds I will
> give my self the honor and happyness of waiting on your ladyship as
> soon as possible, upon a promise that you will extend your voice
> untill you make me hear you. There are not two other persons in the
> world whom I more love, honor, and esteem.[1]

Whether or not the frail dean and the young countess did
meet, Lord Orrery's attachment to Swift had kept its epistolary
form. In December 1740 the Earl had written asking the dean to
place a candidate of his lordship's in the cathedral choir.[2] In
January 1741 he pleaded with Mrs Whiteway to bring the ailing
dean to the Orrerys' country seat (on the eve of the family's
departure for England): 'His health is extremely dear to me:
would to God you could persuade him to come to Caledon,
where Lady Orrery would take care to make the place as
agreeable as she could to him and you.'[3] In February he passed
through Dublin without seeing Swift.[4] In March he urged him
to visit Pope and himself in England.[5]

---

[1] Sept. 1739; unpublished letter in the collection of A. A. Houghton, Jr. I have
preserved Swift's spelling and punctuation but not his capitals.
[2] Williams v. 195.   [3] *Ibid.*, p. 201.   [4] *Ibid.*, p. 203, n. 1.   [5] *Ibid.*, p. 203.

Swift was still far from decrepit. When he was only fifty-one, he had complained that his eyes began to 'grudge' him reading.[1] Six years later he said he could read neither small print nor 'anything by candlelight'.[2] As his eyes weakened, he read less and less because he refused to wear spectacles; and so he spent more time in physical exercise. He found himself often disabled by one or another of his afflictions.

But throughout the year 1741, he could carry out a number of duties: keeping cathedral accounts in his own hand (until April 1742), writing a letter of recommendation,[3] attending cathedral chapters. Deane Swift's remarks during the summer of 1741 suggest that the dean was still competent enough. It was in 1742 that his decline suddenly speeded up, perhaps with a push from some otherwise unnoticed brain lesions.

[1] *Ibid.*, II. 309.　　[2] *Ibid.*, III. 60.　　[3] *Ibid.*, V. 205.

Chapter Thirteen

HE'S JUST ALIVE

I. FRANCIS WILSON

Few men touched Swift as Addison and Arbuthnot did—drawing forth his liveliest conversation, setting him at ease without weakening their own dignity or Swift's—keeping his respect as well as his love. These were the ripest of all his masculine friendships. Delany is one of the last (if not the dimmest) of the tradition. George Berkeley and James Stopford were younger echoes of it. There was as well, among those self-portraits of Swift which he sought in others, the very different challenge of the man of the world, whose shining embodiment seems to be Bolingbroke but who was also realized in Fountaine, Ford, and Chetwode.

Yet a different line again, that of seniors with a fatherly place in Swift's feelings, leads from his uncles to St George Ashe, then to Temple, Lord Berkeley, Archbishop King, and Robert Harley. But as soon as Swift felt comfortable with Harley's circle, he began taking seriously the rôle of patron himself. The line of filial protégés, which starts at least as early as William Harrison, doubles out with men of talent and integrity, like Stopford, and—alas—beguiling self-servers like Pilkington. Having had no father of his own, Swift tried to be one to too many others; and the list of his clients includes every category of friendship.

But what Swift wanted most of all, in his retirement, was the junior crony, the discreet, obliging confidant, younger than himself, whom he need not fear or distrust, and who demanded no reserve; he wanted a not contemptible playmate: Thomas Swift, Thomas Sheridan. Charles Ford, who performed this function among others, had at last settled himself in England

and never saw Swift after 1732. Sheridan had died in 1738.

The tendency which Swift had condemned in himself twenty years before now threatened the ground of his social character. '[I] make choice', he had then said, 'only of such with whom it is of no manner of consequence what I say to them, or what they say to me.'[1] The least attractive of Swift's cronies was also a filial protégé, and the last in both successions. This was Dr Francis Wilson, a sinister and puzzling figure in Swift's era of decline— the age, as Proust says, 'at which a Victor Hugo chooses to surround himself, above all, with Vacqueries and Meurices'.[2]

In 1727, when Wilson was thirty and Swift sixty, Archbishop King preferred the young priest to the rectory of Clondalkin, near Dublin, and to the prebend of Kilmactalway in St Patrick's Cathedral. Although Wilson held these livings until his death, he never rose beyond them. His parish clerk said that Wilson had an unparalleled memory and extraordinary erudition. But when, after taking his B.A. degree at Trinity College, Dublin, he sat for a fellowship, he failed to win one.

Wilson's appearance would have been prepossessing. His proportions were good, he was of average height, and he had a pleasant face. Yet it was probably his graces that charmed Swift; for the admiring clerk of the parish at Clondalkin described him as cheerful and accommodating, with a gift for fluent, entertaining talk. He had evidently (like Pilkington) some of the appeal of a courteous and intelligent boy.[3]

For ten years Swift paid little attention to him. But about the time of Sheridan's last illness and death, the dean handed on to Wilson much of the interest and affection that he had shown the guileless schoolmaster. Toward 1737 he made him tenant of the deanery tithes. Swift took such pleasure in his company that Wilson began staying for long periods in the deanery, where a room was kept for him, although he still resided at Newlands, his house in Clondalkin.

Among Swift's cathedral accounts for May 1739 is a mem-

---

[1] Williams II. 330.
[2] *The Captive*, tr. C. K. Scott Moncrieff (London, 1929), p. 392.
[3] Peter Brett, *Miscellany*, III (Dublin, 1755), 31; V (Dublin, 1762), 177.

orandum which bears out the Clondalkin clerk's praise of his master's charity and shows how tender Swift felt toward him. It is a note that Swift had increased the weekly sum that he gave John Lyon for alms to the poor:

> Increased to Mr Lyon, by the pernicious vice and advice of my daily sponge and inmate Will's son, to twelve scoundrels at 6 1/2 d. per week, 6s. 6d.[1]

From Swift's intimate use of Wilson's name here and in some letters, it is plain that the younger man enjoyed much the same standing at the deanery as Mrs Whiteway.

But Swift's sober friends and relations suspected Wilson of cheating him out of the rent for the deanery tithes and out of the dean's share of the Clondalkin tithes. They claimed that Swift's servants saw Wilson arriving with his portmanteau empty and leaving with it full of books; and there is, in fact, evidence that Wilson removed books from the deanery,[2] although we may suppose that he borrowed them with Swift's consent, and that Swift's friends felt anxious about the dean's own judgment.

In his will, Swift left Wilson copies of Plato's works, Clarendon's history, his own 'best bible', thirteen Persian miniatures, and a silver tankard.[3] (It is an irony that Wilson's own books came eventually to be auctioned with Swift's.)[4] But in December 1742, Deane Swift wrote that

> so long as the Dean's memory and judgement were tolerable, Wilson seldom or never paid the Dean any money but in the presence of Mrs Whiteway, and after the Dean's memory failed, he always paid the Dean in private; notwithstanding he was frequently warned to the contrary.[5]

It seems more than a coincidence that Swift had little to do with Delany after Wilson grew into an habitué of the deanery. The staid and somewhat humourless Dean of Down classed Wilson with those whom we have heard him blame as using 'insinuation and untruth, to banish the Dean's best friends from

[1] Swift, *Accounts* of S.P.D., 1738-9, fol. 2.
[2] Williams, *Dean Swift's Library*, pp. 15-22.   [3] Davis XIII. 155.
[4] Williams, *Dean Swift's Library*, pp. 19-22.   [5] Williams V. 210.

about him, and make a monopoly of him to themselves ... for what ends, they best know'.[1] Whether the 'best friends' felt ready to provide Swift's ego with the ungartered fellowship that was its elementary food, Delany does not say. But Wilson was one of the two witnesses of Swift's last official document, a complaint that seems in part directed against the subdean, John Wynne, whom—we are told—Wilson wished to displace.

This 'exhortation' is dated 28 January 1742. Two drafts are preserved, of which the first is the more elaborate and intemperate. The purpose was to forbid the singers and musicians of the cathedral to 'assist at a club of fiddlers in Fishamble Street ... as songsters, fidlers, pipers, trumpeters, drummers, drummajors or in any sonal quality', and to have the subdean punish them 'according to the flagitious aggravations of their respective disobedience, rebellion, perfidy and ingratitude'.[2] (The occasion that excited the old dean's rage was probably a rehearsal for the premier performance of Handel's *Messiah*, 13 April 1742, in a handsome new concert hall designed by Richard Cassels.)

From the many invocations of the subdean, and from an expression of Swift's resolve 'to preserve the dignity of my station', I suspect that Wilson egged Swift on to believe that Wynne had behaved himself with improper lenience. Maybe the vicar of Clondalkin had the assurance to hope that if he induced Swift to place him in Wynne's office, the chapter would accept the appointment.

Four-and-a-half months after the exhortation, on the morning of 14 June 1742, Wilson came to the deanery. There are several authorities for what followed: the affidavit of Swift's servant, Richard Brennan, delivered to John Rochfort on 16 June; Wilson's sworn statement, 13 July; and the account gathered by Deane Swift, written down half a year after the event.

Wilson said that Swift received him with 'his usual fondness, which was always very great'. The dean told Wilson that 'he

---

[1] Delany, p. 3. Cf. above, p. 872.   [2] Williams v. 267–8.

would take the air that morning, and dine with him at his house in the country.' (Swift had set up a coach when Walpole fell from power.) Wilson said he called for the dean's coach and for Mrs Ridgeway, but the coachman and the housekeeper were both away. So a hackney coach 'was sent for'.[1] Deane Swift insists that Wilson hurried 'the dean out of town in a hackney coach, without taking his friend Mrs Ridgeway along with him, which the dean has always done, ever since he began to be conscious of his want of memory, and other infirmities'.[2]

Brennan, Swift's servant, reported only that 'some short time' after Wilson went in to see the dean, a hackney coach was called by Wilson's direction; and as soon as it came to the entrance of the deanery, Wilson put Swift in it. After telling Brennan to take Wilson's mare and follow them, he 'immediately ordered the coachman to drive to Newland', his residence. In less than an hour—that is, as soon as he could get ready—Brennan followed on Wilson's mare, and overtook them on the road.[3] With Swift's friends displaying in advance so much distrust of Wilson, the tradition easily established itself that he deliberately lured Swift to Newlands when no responsible person could protect the old man. Mrs Ridgeway's comment does not appear.

Deane Swift writes that Brennan reported one circumstance which Swift's friends would not circulate in the affidavit—Wilson got the dean drunk:

Now the dean's stint for about half a year before, was two large bumpers of wine somewhat more than half a pint. When the dean had drunk this quantity, Wilson pressed him to another glass, which the dean's footman observing, told Wilson, in a low voice, that his master never drank above two glasses, and that if he forced him to drink a third, it would certainly affect his head. But Wilson not only made light of this caution, and imposed another glass upon the dean, but called afterwards for a bottle of strong white wine, and forced the dean to drink of it, which in a short time, did so intoxicate him, that he was not able to walk to the coach without being

[1] Ball VI. 179–81, 180, n. 1.
[2] Williams V. 210.
[3] Maxwell B. Gold, 'The Brennan Affidavit', *TLS*, 17 May 1934, p. 360; cf. *ibid.*, 24 May, p. 376.

supported: and after all this, Wilson called at an ale house on his way to Dublin, and forced the poor dean to swallow a dram of brandy.[1]

It was after dinner, between five and six in the evening, that they started back to Dublin, with Brennan riding behind the coach.

Along the way, Brennan said, he heard Wilson ask Swift to make him subdean. Wilson abused Wynne as a 'stupid fellow, which I am not'. Swift refused and asked for his money—perhaps meaning arrears of the deanery tithes of Clondalkin. Wilson said, 'Sir, I am paying you your money and will pay you.' After a few minutes, Wilson began to curse, saying several times, 'By God no man shall strike me, and if King George would strike me, I would cut his throat.' While he was swearing, they approached Kilmainham, and Wilson shouted to the coachman, 'You villain, you rascal, stop the coach.' Brennan jumped down from behind and opened the door to let Wilson out. After Wilson stepped down, he turned around and said to Swift, 'You are a stupid old blockhead, and an old rascal, and only you are too old, I would beat you, and God damn me but I will cut your throat.' Brennan tried 'all in his power' to get the door shut; and when he succeeded, he told the coachman to drive to the deanery, whereupon Wilson said, 'God damn him, drive away the old stupid blockhead.'[2]

Wilson's account has little in common with Brennan's. He said Swift drank half a pint of white wine at dinner, and for two miles of the way back treated Wilson most affectionately. But suddenly he cried out that Wilson was the devil and told him to go to hell, repeating these words 'in a most astonishing rage'. Wilson took no notice and tried to appease him by reciting some passages 'out of such authors as the dean admired most'. Instead of listening, Swift struck him several times on the face, 'scratched him, and tore off his wig'. Wilson, out of pity, did not oppose him until Swift shoved his fingers into the other's eyes. Then Wilson 'ordered the coach to stop, which he left with the natural expressions of resentment and indignation, declaring he would not again tamely suffer the greatest man on earth to strike him'.[3]

[1] Williams v. 211.   [2] Gold, *ibid*.   [3] Ball vi. 180–1.

[914]

Deane Swift reports that the dean had one arm black and blue the next morning, but admits that 'whether [Wilson] struck the dean or not is uncertain'.[1] This detail can be reconciled with the rest of the story if we suppose that Wilson did urge Swift to make him subdean; that the old man refused; that when Wilson insisted, the dean got angry and made gestures of hitting him; that Wilson—to defend himself—held Swift's arm tightly enough to bruise it; and that when he could neither persuade nor soothe Swift, Wilson—perhaps not quite sober himself— grew furious and stopped the coach. As soon as Swift came home, we are told, he asked for Wilson, saying, 'Where is Dr Wilson? Ought not the doctor to be here this afternoon?'[2] But Wilson, it seems, never entered the deanery again.

II. APHASIA

Although the evidence did not warrant judicial proceedings, and Wilson retained his vicarage and his prebend,[3] those who were attached to Swift felt deeply alarmed. 'It was the talk of the town', said Deane Swift, 'that a statute of lunacy ought to be taken out, in order to guard the dean against further insults, and wrongs of all kinds.'[4] A preliminary inquiry was ordered, which was carried out in July, not to investigate Swift's sanity (for he was never insane by modern definitions) but rather as a necessary step in the direction of overseeing his person and his affairs. Little transpired to exculpate Wilson or to lighten the pathos of Swift's senility.[5] A general investigation, the next month, into Swift's mental state ended all doubt as to his needs:

> [He] hath for these nine months past, been gradually failing in his memory and understanding, and [is] of such unsound mind and memory that he is incapable of transacting any business, or managing, conducting, or taking care either of his estate or person.[6]

The date of 20 May 1742 was given as the time after which he was irresponsible; and for the remaining years of his life, he was protected by a committee of guardians.

[1] Williams V. 211.   [2] *Ibid.*   [3] He died about November 1743.
[4] Williams V. 211.   [5] Ball VI. 179, n. 2.   [6] *Ibid.*, pp. 182, 184.

Soon after the committee was appointed, Deane Swift went into the deanery dining-room and found Swift walking there. The visitor said something casual; and the old man, instead of replying, first pointed with his hand to the door, saying, 'Go, go', and then at once raised his hand to his head with the words, 'My best understanding.' Breaking off abruptly, he walked away.

Mrs Whiteway was the last person he recognized. When that memory failed, he grew (for a time) so uncontrollable at meeting any caller that he could not rest for a night or two afterwards. So she was forced to leave him and could only come by twice a week to ask about his health and to see that proper care was taken of him. Fearing to upset him, she would not look at him unless his back was towards her.

In October 1742 Swift's left eye suddenly swelled up as large as an egg. John Nichols, the surgeon, thought the lid would mortify. Large boils appeared on Swift's arms and body. He was in torment. We now know that the disease was a painful and feverish case of orbital cellulitis, purely physiological in origin. For a week it took five people to hold him from tearing out his eyes; and for nearly a month he hardly slept two hours out of twenty-four. Yet he continued to have a fair appetite. On the last day of this illness, he took Mrs Whiteway's hand and called her by name, showing his usual pleasure in seeing her. She asked him whether he would give her dinner. 'To be sure,' he said, 'my old friend.' That day he knew the doctor, the surgeon, and all his household so well that Nichols thought he might regain enough of his understanding to call for what he wanted and to stand some old friends' visits for amusement. But the day or two after the pain was gone brought a relapse. Free from agony, his eye almost well, he became very quiet and began to sleep, but could hardly be brought to walk a turn about his room.

During the delirium, if not before it, Swift suffered further lesions of the brain, or minor strokes; and he sank into a motor aphasia. For the three years of life that remained to him, Swift spoke little. There was a servant to shave his cheeks and all his face as low as the tip of his chin once a week; but when the hair grew long under the chin and about the throat, it was cut with scissors. His meat was served up ready cut, and sometimes he would let it lie on the table an hour before he would touch it, and then eat it walking. If the servant stayed in the room, he would not eat or drink; and he walked a great deal, sometimes ten hours a day.

In December 1743 Deane Swift provided some grim details of the invalid's circumstances for the solicitous Lord Orrery, who had requested information:

> He drinks about a bottle of wine in a day, partly mulled, and partly in gruels, and other slops; he eats rather more than he did a few years ago, and is rather plump than lean. He walks a little every day, supported by two servants. . . . His old friend Mrs Ridgeway still continues in his house, is very faithful to her trust, and treats the dean with great care and tenderness. His butler is kept to attend him constantly, and his butler's mother is his nurse-keeper: their wages are high, and it is their interest to preserve him. The dean is always as clean and decent, as if twenty people were employed about him.[1]

Sometimes he would say nothing, sometimes incoherent words. But he never spoke nonsense or said a foolish thing. On the morning of his birthday in 1743, Mrs Ridgeway reminded him of the occasion and said that people were getting ready to celebrate it with bonfires and illuminations. 'It is all folly,' said Swift. 'They had better let it alone.'[2]

Once, early in 1744, he seemed to wish to talk to Deane Swift, who had come to see him. In order to try what the poor old man would say, the visitor announced that he was staying for dinner. 'Won't you give Mr Swift a glass of wine, Sir?' asked Mrs Ridgeway. The dean shrugged his shoulders, just as he used to do when he did not want a friend to pass the evening with him— as much as to say, 'You'll ruin me in wine.' Again he tried, with a good deal of pain, to find words. At last, after many attempts, he sighed heavily.

Another time, the servant was breaking up a large, stubborn piece of coal. 'That's a stone, you blockhead,' said Swift. An-

---

[1] Unpublished letter of 17 Dec. 1743, in the collection of A. A. Houghton, Jr.
[2] Delany, p. 150.

other day, as Swift's watch lay on the table, the servant picked it up to find out the time. Swift said, 'Bring it here.' When it was shown to him, he looked attentively at it.

Swift's aphasia would have been the result of several minor brain lesions, and had nothing to do with psychosis. But his forgetfulness, the deafness and giddiness from Ménière's disease, the general incapacities of old age, set him in a bleak and hideous rôle. He must have been somehow conscious, again and again, of messages he could not formulate. When he had begun to withdraw, in the late 1730s, from the circle of approximately his social equals, one incentive to retreat was the dread of humiliating himself before them by some grotesque fit—the incentive which had moved him to leave Pope's home in 1727.[1] After he was seventy-five, and speechlessness had broken even his communication with servants and relations, he was not spared the last bitterness of seeing that they thought him imbecilic at just the moment when intelligence drove him to reach them with words. What dulls the pain is our knowledge that Swift preferred consciousness, however stunted or distasteful, to calm idiocy.

One day in mid-March, as Swift sat in his chair, he reached towards a knife. But Mrs Ridgeway moved it away from him. He shrugged his shoulders, rocked himself, and said, 'I am what I am, I am what I am.' Some minutes later he repeated the words twice or three times. About a fortnight afterwards, he tried to speak to his servant, whom he sometimes called by name. Not finding words to tell what he meant, he showed some uneasiness and said, 'I am a fool'—his last recorded words.[2]

III. DEATH

Swift died in 1745 at the age of seventy-eight. For four days the cathedral bells were rung muffled. The dean was laid out in his own hall, and the people of Dublin crowded to see him. The

[1] Cf. Swift's letter to Pope, 19 Jul. 1725; Sherburn II. 311.
[2] All the details of Swift's final state, except the birthday story and the quotation from Deane Swift, are taken from Williams v. 207–12, 214–15.

coffin stood open. He wore neither cap nor wig. On the front and dome of the skull little hair remained. But it grew thick behind, resting like white flax on the pillow. The woman who had nursed him sat at his head. When she left the room briefly, someone cut off a lock of the hair, which she missed on her return. After that day, no person was admitted to see the body.[1]

At midnight, three days after his death, Swift was, as he wished, buried with the utmost privacy on the south side of the great middle aisle of St Patrick's Cathedral.[2] Three days later, the student senate of Trinity College voted unanimously not to spend as usual the fund collected for their annual social function, but to give that money to the purchase of a marble bust of Swift, to be placed in the College library.[3]

For five years, he had hardly been seen in public. But the myth of a daemonic Swift was already passing into this world from the crooked inventions of remote tattlers. A report of his declared 'lunacy' and of the frenzy caused by the orbital cellulitis of October 1742 inspired Charles Yorke (second son of Lord Chancellor Hardwicke) to write of Swift, 'His madness appears chiefly in most incessant strains of obscenity and swearing.'[4] Two years later, Yorke's informant, Thomas Birch, encouraged him with the message that 'Dr Swift has lately awaked from a mere animal life into a thorough misanthropy and brutality of lust'—

> for he can hardly be restrained from knocking every man on the head, who comes near him ... or from attempting every woman, that he sees. I doubt that these were always the real dispositions of him; but now it happens, that the thin disguise, which before scarce covered them, is absolutely fallen off.[5]

In 1750, John Lyon, the clergyman who had been officially responsible for Swift during the years of incompetence, denied to Birch the story of the dean's being shown for money by his

---

[1] Mason, pp. 412–13, note r.

[2] *Dublin Journal*, 26 Oct. 1745. The bill for burial fees is in St Patrick's Hospital, Dublin; one item is £3. 8s. 3d. for ringing the bells four days muffled.

[3] *Ibid.*

[4] George Harris, *The Life of Lord Chancellor Hardwicke* (London, 1847), II. 21.

[5] B.L. Add. MS. 35396, fols. 250–250ᵛ.

servants.[1] But Birch knew Samuel Johnson, who delighted in his anecdotes and had already made a lapidary inscription of the lie that 'Swift expires a driv'ler and a show.'[2] Scholarship cannot hope to rival the dramatic narratives that Johnson and Scott have embedded in English literary culture. But it can offer materials to those who would rather come near Swift himself than be entertained with fascinating legends.

[1] Williams v. 275.
[2] *Vanity* of *Human Wishes*, l. 318.

ABBREVIATED REFERENCES

The place of publication is London unless otherwise indicated. I sometimes give separately the date of a later edition than the one I have used.

Accounts 1717–18; etc.

Swift's manuscript account books, each one detailing his finances for a year beginning 1 November. The account books which I refer to are now in the Forster Collection of the Victoria and Albert Museum, except that for 1734–5, in the Royal Irish Academy, Dublin. See Williams v. 222. An edition of the account books by Professor Paul V. Thompson is forthcoming.

Alum. Dubl.

Alumni Dublinenses: A Register of the Students, Graduates, Professors and Provosts of Trinity College … Dublin, ed. G. D. Burtchaell and T. U. Sadleir, new ed. Dublin 1935.

Armer

Sondra S. Armer, *Anonymous and Pseudonymous Pamphlets, Including Some by Swift, against … a Bank …* Unpublished Ph.D. dissertation, Columbia University, New York 1971.

B.L.

British Library.

B.L. Add. MSS.

British Library, Additional Manuscripts.

Ball

The Correspondence of Jonathan Swift, ed. F. Elrington Ball. 6 vols. 1910–14.

Ball, *Judges*

Francis Elrington Ball, *The Judges in Ireland, 1221–1921*. 2 vols. 1926.

Ball, *Swift's Verse*

Francis Elrington Ball, *Swift's Verse: An Essay*. 1929.

Ballantyne

Archibald Ballantyne, *Lord Carteret: A Political Biography, 1690–1763*. 1887.

Bodl.

Bodleian Library, Oxford.

Boswell

James Boswell, *Boswell's Life of Johnson …*, ed. G. B. Hill, rev. L. F. Powell. 6 vols. Oxford 1934–50. (Vols. v, vi, 2nd ed., 1964.)

Boulter
    Hugh Boulter, *Letters Written ... to Several Ministers of State* ... [ed. Ambrose Philips]. 2 vols. Oxford 1769–70.

Boulter, Dublin
    Hugh Boulter, *Letters Written ... to Several Ministers of State* ... [ed. Ambrose Philips]. 2 vols. Dublin 1770.

Boyer
    Abel Boyer, *The Political State of Great Britain*. 1714–40.

Brett
    Peter Brett, *Brett's Miscellany* III (Dublin 1755), V (Dublin 1762).

Burtchaell
    See *Alum. Dubl.*

Cal. Tr. P.
    Calendar of Treasury Papers 1720–1728 Preserved in Her Majesty's Public Record Office. 1889.

Complete Baronetage
    Complete Baronetage, ed. G. E. Cokayne. 6 vols. 1900–09.

Complete Peerage
    The Complete Peerage, ed. G. E. Cokayne and Vicary Gibbs. 13 vols. 1910–40.

Cotton
    Fasti Ecclesiae Hibernicae, ed. Henry Cotton. 6 vols. Dublin 1851–78.

Coxe
    William Coxe, *Memoirs of the Life and Administration of Sir Robert Walpole*. 3 vols. 1798.

Craik
    Henry Craik, *The Life of Jonathan Swift*, 2nd ed. 2 vols. 1894.

Cullen
    Louis Michael Cullen, *An Economic History of Ireland since 1660*. 1972.

Cullen, *Anglo-Irish Trade*
    Louis Michael Cullen, *Anglo-Irish Trade 1660–1800*. Manchester 1968.

D.N.B.
    Dictionary of National Biography.

Dampier
    William Dampier, *A New Voyage Round the World*, introd. Albert Gray and Percy G. Adams. New York 1968.

Davis
    The Prose Works of Jonathan Swift, ed. Herbert Davis *et al.* 14 vols. Oxford 1939–68.

Davis, 'Bowyer's Paper Stock Ledger'
    Herbert Davis, 'Bowyer's Paper Stock Ledger', *The Library*, 5th ser., VI (1951–2), 73–87.

Davis, *Stella*
   Herbert Davis, *Stella: A Gentlewoman of the Eighteenth Century.* New
   York 1942.
Daw
   Carl P. Daw, *An Annotated Edition of Five Sermons by Jonathan Swift.*
   Unpublished Ph.D. dissertation, University of Virginia, Charlottes-
   ville 1970.
Delany
   Patrick Delany, *Observations upon Lord Orrery's'Remarks on* ... *Swift.*
   1754.
Delany, Mrs
   The Autobiography and Correspondence of Mary Granville, Mrs Delany, ed.
   Lady Llanover. 6 vols. 1861–2.
Dickins
   Lilian Dickins and Mary Stanton, eds., *An Eighteenth-Century Corres-
   pondence, Being the Letters* ... *to Sanderson Miller.* 1910.
Drapier
   Jonathan Swift, *The Drapier's Letters to the People of Ireland,* ed.
   Herbert Davis. Oxford 1935. (2nd ed., 1965.)
Dryden, *Works*
   The Works of John Dryden, ed. E. N. Hooker *et al.* Berkeley and Los
   Angeles 1956–.
E-CS.
   Eighteenth-Century Studies.
EHR.
   The English Historical Review.
Evans
   John Evans, Bishop of Meath, unpublished letters to William
   Wake, Wake Letters in the library of Christ Church, Oxford.
Ferguson
   Oliver Watkins Ferguson, *Jonathan Swift and Ireland.* Urbana,
   Illinois, 1962.
Firth
   Charles Harding Firth, 'The Political Significance of *Gulliver's
   Travels*', *Proceedings of the British Academy* 9 (1919–20), 237–59.
Ford
   The Letters of Jonathan Swift to Charles Ford, ed. David Nichol Smith.
   Oxford 1935.
Foster
   Alumni Oxonienses: The Members of the University of Oxford, 1500–1714.
   4 vols. Oxford 1891–2.
Foxon
   English Verse 1701–1750: A Catalogue ..., ed. D. F. Foxon. 2 vols.
   Cambridge 1975.

Frantz
Ray W. Frantz, 'Gulliver's "Cousin Sympson"' *HLQ* 1 (1938), 329–34.
Froude
James Anthony Froude, *The English in Ireland in the Eighteenth Century.* 3 vols. 1872–4.
Gay
John Gay, *Poetry and Prose*, ed. V. A. Dearing and C. E. Beckwith. 2 vols. Oxford 1974.
Gent. Mag.
The Gentleman's Magazine.
Gilbert MSS.
Letters of Irish clergymen (MSS. 27 and 28) among the manuscripts of the Gilbert Collection in the Pearse Street Library, Dublin.
Gold
Maxwell B. Gold, *Swift's Marriage to Stella.* Cambridge, Massachusetts, 1937.
Goldgar
Bertrand Goldgar, '*Gulliver's Travels* and the Opposition to Walpole', in H. K. Miller *et al.*, eds., *The Augustan Milieu: Essays Presented to Louis A. Landa* (Oxford 1970), 155–73.
Goodwin
A. Goodwin, 'Wood's Halfpence', *English Historical Review* 51 (1936), 647–74.
Griffith
Alexander Pope: A Bibliography, ed. Reginald Harvey Griffith. 2 vols. Austin, Texas, 1922.
Grove
The New Grove Dictionary of Music and Musicians, ed. Stanley Sadie. 20 vols. 1980.
HLQ.
The Huntington Library Quarterly.
H.M.C. *Portland*; etc.
Royal Commission on Historical Manuscripts. *Calendar of the Manuscripts of the Duke of Portland*; etc.
Hervey
John, Lord Hervey, *Some Materials towards Memoirs of the Reign of King George II*, ed. Romney Sedgwick. 3 vols. 1931.
Howard
Letters to and from Henrietta, Countess of Suffolk ..., ed. J. W. Croker. 2 vols. 1824.
Ilchester
Lord Hervey and His Friends, ed. Earl of Ilchester. 1950.
JEGP.
The Journal of English and Germanic Philology.

JHI.
  The Journal of the History of Ideas.
Johnson
  Samuel Johnson, *Swift*, in *Lives of the English Poets*, ed. George Birkbeck Hill (Oxford 1905), III. 1–74.
Johnston
  Joseph Johnston, 'Commercial Restrictions and Monetary Deflation in 18th Century Ireland', *Hermathena* 53 (May 1939), 79–87.
Journal
  Jonathan Swift, *Journal to Stella*, ed. Harold Williams. 2 vols. Oxford 1948.
King
  William King, Archbishop of Dublin, unpublished correspondence in the library of Trinity College, Dublin.
King, C. S.
  Charles Simeon King, *A Great Archbishop of Dublin*. 1906.
Landa
  Louis A. Landa, *Swift and the Church of Ireland*. Oxford 1954.
Landa, 'Swift and Charity'
  Louis A. Landa, 'Swift and Charity', *JEGP.* 44 (1945), 337–50.
Lawlor
  Hugh Jackson Lawlor, *The Fasti of St Patrick's, Dublin*. Dundalk, Ireland, 1930.
Luce
  The Works of George Berkeley, ed. A. A. Luce and T. E. Jessup (London 1948–57), VIII, *Letters*.
Lyon
  John Lyon, manuscript notes in a copy of John Hawkesworth, *The Life of Jonathan Swift* (1755), now in the Forster Collection of the Victoria and Albert Museum.
MLN.
  Modern Language Notes.
MLQ.
  Modern Language Quarterly.
MLR.
  Modern Language Review.
MP.
  Modern Philology
Mant
  Richard Mant, *History of the Church of Ireland, from the Reformation to the Revolution*. 2 vols. 1840.
Mason
  William Monck Mason, *The History and Antiquities of the Collegiate and Cathedral Church of St. Patrick near Dublin*. Dublin 1820.

[925]

Mayhew
George P. Mayhew, *Rage or Raillery: The Swift Manuscripts at the Huntington Library*. San Marino, California, 1967.

Memorials of Deeds
Memorials of deeds of land, in the Registry of Deeds, in the King's Inns, Dublin.

Murry
John Middleton Murry. *Jonathan Swift: A Critical Biography*. 1954.

N. & Q.
Notes and Queries.

Nicolson
William Nicolson, Bishop of Derry, unpublished letters to William Wake, among the Wake Letters in the library of Christ Church, Oxford.

Nicolson, *Letters*
William Nicolson, *Letters on Various Subjects* ..., ed. John Nichols. 2 vols. 1809.

Orrery
John Boyle, Earl of Cork and Orrery, *Remarks on the Life and Writings of Dr. Jonathan Swift*. 1752.

Orrery Papers
The Orrery Papers, ed. Emily Charlotte Boyle, Countess of Cork and Orrery. 2 vols. 1903.

PLL.
Papers on Language and Literature.

PQ.
Philological Quarterly.

P.R.O.
Public Record Office, London.

Parliamentary History
The Parliamentary History of England, ed. William Cobbett *et al*. 36 vols. 1806–20.

Paston
George Paston (i.e., Emily Morse Symonds), *Mrs Delany (Mary Granville): A Memoir, 1700–1788*. 1900.

Pilkington
Laetitia Pilkington, *Memoirs of Mrs L. Pilkington* .... 3 vols. 1748–54.

Plumb
John Harold Plumb, *Sir Robert Walpole*. 2 vols. 1956–60.

Poems
The Poems of Jonathan Swift, ed. Harold Williams, 2nd ed. 3 vols. Oxford 1958.

Poems on Affairs of State
  Poems on Affairs of State: Augustan Satirical Verse, 1660–1714, ed. G. de
  F. Lord *et al.* 7 vols. New Haven 1963–75.
Pope, *Poems*
  The Poems of Alexander Pope, ed. John Butt *et al.* 11 vols. 1939–
  69.
Price
  Martin Price, *Swift's Rhetorical Art*. New Haven 1953.
Prior
  The Literary Works of Matthew Prior, ed. H. Bunker Wright and
  Monroe K. Spears. 2 vols. Oxford 1959. (2nd ed., 1971.)
RES.
  The Review of English Studies.
Rosenheim
  Edward Rosenheim, Jr., 'Swift and the Atterbury Case', in H. K.
  Miller *et al.*, eds., *The Augustan Milieu: Essays Presented to Louis A.
  Landa* (Oxford 1970), 174–204.
SP.
  Studies in Philology.
SPD.
  Calendar of State Papers, Domestic.
SPI.
  Calendar of State Papers, Irish.
Schakel
  Peter Schakel, *The Poetry of Jonathan Swift*. Madison, Wisconsin,
  1978.
Scott
  Sir Walter Scott, *Memoirs of Jonathan Swift*. Edinburgh 1814; also
  The Works of Jonathan Swift, ed. Walter Scott. 19 vols. (*Memoirs* in
  vol. 1.) Edinburgh 1814.
Scott, Temple
  The Prose Works of Jonathan Swift, ed. Temple Scott (i.e., J. Isaacs).
  12 vols. 1897–1908.
Sherburn
  The Correspondence of Alexander Pope, ed. George Sherburn. 5 vols.
  Oxford 1956.
Sherburn, *Early Career*
  George Wiley Sherburn, *The Early Career of Alexander Pope*. Oxford
  1934.
Sheridan
  Thomas Sheridan, *The Life of Dr Swift*. 1784.
Spence
  Joseph Spence, *Observations, Anecdotes, and Characters of Books and Men*,
  ed. J. M. Osborn. 2 vols. Oxford 1966.

[927]

Spingarn
  Critical Essays of the Seventeenth Century, ed. J. E. Spingarn. 3 vols.
  Oxford 1908–9.
Suffolk, Henrietta, Countess of
  See *Howard*.
Swift, Deane
  Deane Swift, *An Essay upon the Life, Writings, and Character of
  Dr Jonathan Swift*. London 1755.
'Swiftiana in Rylands MSS.'
  I. Ehrenpreis and James L. Clifford, 'Swiftiana in Rylands English
  MS. 659 and Related Documents', *Bulletin of the John Rylands Library*
  37 (1955), 368–92.
Tale
  Jonathan Swift, *A Tale of a Tub* ..., ed. A. C. Guthkelch and
  D. Nichol Smith, 2nd ed. Oxford 1958.
Teerink
  Herman Teerink and Arthur H. Scouten, eds., *A Bibliography of the
  Writings of Jonathan Swift*, 2nd ed. Philadelphia 1963.
Temple, *Five Essays*
  Sir William Temple, *Five Miscellaneous Essays*, ed. S. H. Monk. Ann
  Arbor, Michigan, 1963.
Temple, *Miscellanea*
  Sir William Temple, *Miscellanea. The Second Part*, 2nd ed. 1690.
Thompson, Paul V.
  Paul V. Thompson, 'An Unpublished Letter from Swift', *The
  Library*, 5th ser., XXII (1967), 57–66.
Thompson, Stith
  Stith Thompson, *Motif-Index of Folk-Literature*, revised and enlarged
  ed. 6 vols. Copenhagen 1955–8.
Tillotson
  John Tillotson, *The Works ... Containing Fifty Four Sermons and
  Discourses*, 5th ed. 1707.
Venn
  *Alumni Cantabrigienses: A Biographical List of ... the University of
  Cambridge ..., Part I, to 1751*. 4 vols. Cambridge 1922–7.
Wake
  Manuscripts of the correspondence of Archbishop William Wake, in
  the library of Christ Church, Oxford (Wake Letters).
Waldegrave
  James, 2nd Earl Waldegrave, *Memoirs, from 1754 to 1758*. 1821.
Walpole
  Horace Walpole, *Reminiscences*, ed. Paget Toynbee. Oxford 1924.
Williams
  Jonathan Swift, *Correspondence*, ed. Harold Williams. 5 vols. Oxford
  1963–5.

Williams, *Dean Swift's Library*
Harold Williams, *Dean Swift's Library*. Cambridge 1932.
Williams, *Text of Gulliver's Travels*
Harold Williams, *The Text of Gulliver's Travels*. Cambridge 1950.
Williams, Basil, *Carteret and Newcastle*
Arthur Frederick Basil Williams, *Carteret and Newcastle*. Cambridge 1943.
Williams, Basil, *Whig Supremacy*
Arthur Frederick Basil Williams, *The Whig Supremacy, 1714–1760*, 2nd ed. Oxford 1962.
Woolley, David
David Woolley, 'The Armagh Copy of *Gulliver's Travels*', in Clive Probyn, ed., *The Art of Jonathan Swift* (1978), 131–78.
Woolley, James
James Woolley, 'Arbuckle's "Panegyric" and Swift's Scrub Libel: The Documentary Evidence', in *Contemporary Studies of Swift's Poetry*, ed. John Irwin Fischer *et al.* (Newark, Delaware, 1981), 191–209.

James Woolley, 'Friends and Enemies in *Verses on the Death of Dr Swift*', in *Studies in Eighteenth-Century Culture* 8 (1979), 205–32.

James Woolley, 'Thomas Sheridan and Swift', in *Studies in Eighteenth-Century Culture* 9 (1980), 93–114.
Young, *Tour*
Arthur Young, *A Tour in Ireland, 1776–1779*, ed. A. W. Hutton. 2 vols. Shannon, Ireland, 1970.

INDEX

Compiled by
Peter J. Carlton, Patricia A. Welsch
and Gwyneth Hatton

under the supervision of
IRVIN EHRENPREIS

with the help of
Barbara B. Smith, W. Jones De Ritter,
Luis R. Gamez, Pamela L. Lein
and Shanon S. Echols

Swift's works are entered under their titles. The main entry for each is in boldface; and if the first word is an article, I omit it. The date of publication (or, if so indicated, of composition) is supplied in parentheses unless I cannot be sure of it. If I have a main, concentrated discussion of a work, a person or a topic, I give the page numbers of the reference in boldface.

Swift's relations with other persons are indexed under the names of those persons. His opinions are indexed under the various subjects themselves.

Works not by Swift appear under the author's name or, if that is unknown, under the title. Peers are usually entered under their best-known title. Saints are entered under their proper names, but places named after them are under 'St'. If no country is specified, a place may be presumed to be English. Names of fictitious persons, as main entries, generally appear between inverted commas.

In some long articles, important keywords are printed in boldface. Cross-references to main entries are printed in capitals, but cross-references to other subheadings within the same article are in italics. Within many articles there are not only subheadings under the main entry but further divisions of subtopics under these. I have set a dash before such subtopics, to show that the reference is to the preceding subheading and not to the main entry. In a few articles even the subtopics are divided, and I set double dashes before the secondary subtopics.

I use the following abbreviations:

b.	born
Bart.	baronet
c.	about
co.	county(of Ireland)
d.	died
D.P.S.	Dublin Philosophical Society
fl.	flourished
jr.	junior
JS	Jonathan Swift
ms., mss.	manuscript(s)
n.	note
née	maiden name
sen.	senior
S.P.D.	St Patrick's Cathedral, Dublin
Stella	Esther (or Hester) Johnson
T.C.D.	Trinity College, Dublin
Vanessa	Esther (or Hester) Vanhomrigh

358, 595; —reach Dublin (1709), II.344; —return to England (1709), II.364; —loyalty to Wharton, II.439–40; —secretary to Wharton, II.320–2, 325; as a Whig, II.252–3; *Whig Examiner*, II.407; & Whiston, II.238, 726.

Addison & JS: JS's academy, II.543, 546; JS's *Baucis and Philemon*, II.243–8, 250; & G. Berkeley, III.389; & *Cato*, II.594–6; compared, II.234, 236–9, 248, 250, 419, 763; JS's *Conduct of the Allies*, II.236; correspondence (1709), II.365; —JS preserves letters, III.885; & Delany, III.646; friendship, II.230, 239–40, 446; —as ideal, III.909; —intimate, II.320–1, 350–2, 373, 378, 383, 614; —waning (1711), II.430; first meeting, II.240; & Philips, III.437; —Philips's preferment, II.435–6; political differences, II.360, 435–9; praises JS, II.320; praised by JS, II.344; JS's preferment (1709), II.343–4, 347–8; —(1710), II.369–70; prose compared, III.273; & Steele —Steele's preferment, II.437–8; —JS's quarrel with Steele, II.681–2, 684, 691; & Tickell, III.434; & Wharton, III.42; Whig defined, II.271; & *Whig Examiner*, II.441–2.

Advantages Propos'd by Repealing the Sacramental Test, Impartially Considered, by JS (1732), **III.724–6**; & JS's *Presbyterians Plea*, III.764.

Advice Humbly Offer'd to the Members of the October Club, by JS (1712), **II.522–5**; & JS's *Some Free Thoughts*, II.737.

Advice to the Free-men of the City of Dublin, by JS (1733), **III.761–2**.

Advice to a Parson, poem by JS (1732), III.719, n. 2, **720 & n. 4**.

Agher (Laracor), co. Meath: JS's parish, I.13–14, 96.

Agistment, tithe: & House of Commons, III.827–9. *See also* TITHES.

Agriculture, JS's views: basic industry, III.207, 236, 254.

Agriculture, Irish: & absenteeism, III.115; acreage, III.27–8; & bishops' lands, III.184; & cattle-growing, III.27–8; crop failures (1726), III.510; decline (1726), III.510–11; England discourages, III.27–8, 115, 118; grain shortage (1728–9), III.576–8, 609–10; & imports from England, III.119; land excellent, III.114; & landlords, III.184; —irresponsible, III.116, 290–1; land mismanaged, III.115; limited, III.115–16; Molesworth on, III.286, 288, 291; & population, III.612–13; poverty hurts (1720–30), III.159; reform —turf-cutting, III.307; JS's views (1723), III.182–3; —Drapier's proposals, III.303, 306–8; tillage, III.119–20; —encouraged, III.307; —& pasture, III.116, 124, 510–11, 684–5; —tillage restricted, III.544–5. *See also* FARMERS; LANDLORDS.

Aix-la-Chapelle (i.e., Aachen, Germany): & JS, III.135, 516–17; —Pope recommends (1729), III.551.

All Fools' Day: JS devoted to, III.402–3; JS's auction hoax (1709), II.302; JS's letter hoax (1713), II.627–8.

Allegory: *see* PROSE, JS's.

Allen, Joshua, 1685–1742, 2nd Viscount: & JS —attacks JS (1730), III.652–3; —friendship, III.652; —& R. Leslie, III.652; —JS's *Libel on Dr Delany*, III.653; —JS's *Traulus*, III.656–8, 830; —JS's *Vindication of Lord Carteret*, III.657–8.

Allen, Margaret, Lady, wife of 2nd Viscount & Duke of Dorset: III.700–1; & JS, III.700–1, 713.

Allen, Ralph, 1694–1764, post-master: & Gerrard, III.891–2; & Pope, III.891–2.

Allestree, Richard, 1619–81: *The Ladies Calling* (1673), III.397; on women, III.399–400.

Allies: *see* GRAND ALLIANCE.

Almanac-makers: condemned, II.198–209; praised by Partridge, II.199.

Almanza, Spain, Battle of (1707): & Godolphin ministry, II.222; Philips on, II.243; JS on, II.257, n. 2.

Ambition, JS's views: climbing & creeping, II.144; hinders virtue, III.291; & vice, II.212.

America: colonists, III.244; —& Irish Protestants, II.357; Irish emigrants to, III.116; revolution & JS's rhet-oric, III.257, 306, 308; trade with Ireland, III.114.

America, Spanish: colonies in, II.44–5; slave trade in, II.474.

Amesbury Abbey, Amesbury, Wilt-shire, seat of Duke of Queensberry: III.699. *See also* QUEENSBERRY, DUKE OF.

Analogy, JS's use of: II.258, 260–1.

Anglican Church: *see* CHURCH OF ENGLAND; CHURCH OF IRELAND.

Anglo-Irish: *see* ENGLISH INTEREST.

Anne, 1665–1714, Queen of Eng-land: & Arbuthnot —close to her, II.507–8, 510; —on her death, II.755; —her bad health, II.725; —no legacy from her, II.760; —& Atterbury, II.114, 669; birthday (1712), II.578; & Bolingbroke — distrusts him, II.672; —he has 'lost all' (1714), II.758; —passes him over, II.758; —his peerage, II.568, 580–1; reproves him, II.223–4, 581–2; & Burnet, II.77–8; on cen-sorship, II.592; & Church of Eng-land, II.78; —convocation (1704), II.114, 255; —First Fruits (Queen Anne's Bounty), II.78, 131–2; —

her loyalty, II.262–3; —prefer-ments, II.78; & Church of Ireland —bishops, II.729; —clergy loyal, II.263; —convocation, II.160–1; —First Fruits, II.228–9, 398–402; & Cowper, II.167, 176; death rumoured (1713), II.698; death, II.755, 757–62; III.4, 6–7, 10, 24; & Eugène of Savoy, II.536; & George I, II.728; & Prince George (her husband) as admiral, II.315; & Godolphin (1705), II.166; —blocks him (1708), II.315; —distrusts him (1709), II.359; — & Oxford (Harley), II.372; — supports him (1703), II.116; —JS on relation (1708), II.223–4; & Guiscard, II.464–5, 467, 469–70; & Harcourt, II.669, 728; health —declining (1714), II.753–4; — illness (Dec. 1713), II.746; — — Whigs exploit, II.728–9; improves (Feb. 1714), II.712; 'never hurt' Ireland, III.52; & Junto, II.90; —dislikes them, II.221; & Marlborough —captain-general for life, II.371, 530, 535; —his dismissal, II.526, 529; — 'mortally hates' him, II.532; — supports him (1703), II.116; —JS on relation (1708), II.223–4; & Duchess of Marlborough — favours her, II.168; —repulses her, II.371; & Mrs Masham — friendship, II.371; —intimacy, III.111; —JS on relation, II.518, 520; change of ministry (1710), II.371–2; & morality, II.256; & bill against occasional conformity, II.115, 118; & Lady Oglethorpe, II.518; & Ormonde, II.106; —Irish preferments, II.629–30; — 'restraining orders', II.561–2; & Oxford (1705–6), II.166, 168; — (1708), II.221, 223–4; —he advises her (1708), II.315, 317; — —(1709), II.371; —he has 'no credit' (1714), II.729; —distrusts

III.609–10, 899; & bishopric of Cloyne (1726), III.485–6; & Conolly, III.297; & copper coinage (1737), III.853–5; & Delany, III.634, n. 3; on emigration (1728–9), III.612; & English interest, III.348–9; on famine, III.545, 573, 609; & French recruitment, III.682; & George I, III.284–5; on gold coin, III.841, 861; & Hennecy (1730), III.682–3; & J. Hoadly, III.619; income, III.254–5; & Ireland —on economic decay (1729), III.609–10; & Irish interest, III.284; & Archbishop King —enmity, III.285; —plight of Irish (1728), III.571; —primacy, III.254; & Maule, III.485; & Midleton, III.297; & Newcastle, III.301, 685; Percival on, III.285; & Thomas Power, III.356–7; Primate, III.227, 285, 356; & Roman Catholics, III.619, n. 2; & Sheridan, III.847; & Skirret, III.485; & Smalbroke, III.619; & JS —antagonism, III.544, 854–5, 860–2; —warns Newcastle, III.479; & Test Act, attempted repeal (1733), III.762, 765, 767; & Townshend, III.284–5, 356; & Walpole, III.284–5; & debate on 'wisdom' (1725), III.313–14; & Wood's patent, III.254–5, 285, 295, 297, 301, 305; —advice followed, III.309.

Bourbon family: deaths & Treaty of Utrecht, II.562–3; Parliamentary address against, II.235; union of France & Spain, II.563; —Whigs oppose, II.317.

Bowyer, William, 1663–1737, London printer: & Faulkner, III.736, 780; & M. Pilkington, III.736, 745–7.

Bowyer, William, jr., 1699–1777, London printer: & Faulkner, III.317–18; & *Gulliver's Travels*, III.498; Pope's poems on Gulliver,

III.501; & JS, copyrights, III.780.

Boyer, Abel, 1667–1729, Huguenot refugee, journalist: on band-box plot, II.583; on Guiscard, II.471; & *Gulliver's Travels*, III.502–4; on Oxford's resignation (1713), II.678; on Phipps, III.8–9; on Steele, II.699; and JS —*Advice to the October Club*, II.524; & JS —Horace *Epistles* I.vii, II.676, n. 1, 677; —JS's mail searched, III.15; —JS's preferment, II.633; —*Publick Spirit of the Whigs*, II.708, 711; & Temple, II.731.

Boyle family: & S.P.D., III.621–2.

Boyle, Charles: see ORRERY, 4TH EARL.

Boyle, Henry: see CARLETON; SHANNON.

Boyle, John: see ORRERY, 5TH EARL.

Boyle, Michael, c. 1610–1702, Archbishop of Armagh: & Marsh, II.102; pluralism, I.157–8; & JS, I.156–7; II.14; & Samuel Synge, II.146; & T.C.D., I.157.

Boyle, Sir Robert, 1627–91, natural philosopher: I.52; on air, I.197; & Burnet, II.90; on Ireland, I.81; & Petty, I.81; JS on, II.90.

Boyne, Battle of the (1690): II.263; & Henry Sidney, I.103; & T.C.D., I.88; & William III, I.103, 112; & Wood's patent, III.263, n. 3.

Bradford, John, c. 1510–55, Protestant martyr: on fallen humanity, III.463.

Brailsford, Matthew, d. 1733, Dean of Wells: II.622–3, 628.

Brandreth, John, chaplain to Duke of Dorset, Dean of Armagh: & JS, III.752.

Brennan, Richard, JS's footman: and JS's *Directions to Servants*, III.832; Francis Wilson, III.912–15.

Brent, Anne, d. 1735, JS's housekeeper: I.29; III.32–3, 322; death,

III.806; & Stella, III.540; & JS's small loans, III.325.

Bridgeman, Charles, landscape architect: & Pope —Marble Hill, III.478; improves Wimpole, III.477.

Briefs, church: see CHURCH BRIEFS.

Bristol, England: JS sails from (1699), II.6; & storm (1703), II.112; Wood's mint, III.192, 226.

Broad Church: see LATITUDINARIANS.

Brobdingnag (in *Gulliver's Travels*, Pt. 2): King, III.165, 224; —& Carteret, III.224; —& Temple, III.457; prints of scenes, III.498; Queen —& Stella, III.457; —& Lady Temple, III.457.

Brodrick, Alan: see MIDLETON.

Brodrick, St John, *c*. 1685–1728, M.P., son of Lord Midleton: & Carteret, III.268.

Brodrick, Thomas, 1654–1730, Irish M.P., English M.P., elder brother of Lord Midleton: and Carteret, III.198; & Irish money bill, II.362; & Test Act, II.264; & JS, II.266–7, 362, 375; & Wharton, II.361–2; & Wood's patent, III.199.

Bromley, William, 1664–1732, M.P.: II.668, n. 2; & 1st Lord Oxford, II.669, 672; —*Congratulatory Speech*, II.469; Secretary of State, II.668–9; son's death, II.421.

Brown, Thomas, 1663–1704, satirist: *Infallible Astrologer*, II.200–1; & Partridge, II.199; & JS, II.200–1, 345.

Browne, Sir John, Bart., d. 1762, of the Neale, co. Mayo: *Memorial of the Poor ... of ... Ireland* (attributed to Browne, but probably not by him), III.576; *Seasonable Remarks on Trade* (1728), III.573–4; & Wood's patent, III.573, n. 4.

Browne, Peter, d. 1735, Bishop of Cork: career, I.74–5; classmate

of JS, I.73; & deism, II.369; & Delany, I.74; III.86; & Lambert, II.363, 369; & Marsh, I.75; II.369; & Pratt, I.74; & Sheridan, III.361; & JS, I.74; II.369; —JS recommends Sheridan, III.597–8; toasts to the dead, I.75; & J. Toland, I.75; & T.C.D., I.145, 280; II.363.

Browne, Sir Thomas, 1605–82, physician & author: on Puritans, I.210; & JS, I.179; II.413.

Brutus, Marcus Junius, *c*. 78–42 BC, Roman statesman: & JS's *Drapier's Letters*, III.207–8; see also CICERO.

Bruyère, Jean de la, 1645–96: see LA BRUYÈRE, JEAN DE.

Brydges, James: see CHANDOS.

Bubble, poem by JS: **III.155**, 892, n. 3.

Buckingham, John Sheffield, 1st Duke of, 1647–1721, statesman: dismissed as Privy Seal, II.167; & Guiscard, II.466; Jacobitism, II.167.

Bucklebury, Berkshire, seat of Lord Bolingbroke: II.597; Bolingbroke recuperates (1712), II.571; & living for JS, III.729; JS visits (1711), II.505–6.

Bunyan, John: & *Gulliver's Travels*, III.506; morality & literature, II.302.

Burke, Edmund, 1729–97, statesman: II.408; & JS, II.117; III.306.

Burlington, Richard Boyle, 3rd Earl, & 4th Earl of Cork, 1695–1753: & S.P.D., III.621–2.

Burnet, Gilbert, 1643–1715, Bishop of Salisbury: & Anne, II.77–8; & Bentley, II.90; & Calamy, II.126; & Calvin, II.87–8; career, II.85–6, 88–9; Charles II on, II.86; & clergy, II.694–5; & convocation, II.692–4; & Dissenters, II.88, 692–3, 695; Dryden on, II.86; *Examiner* attacks, II.693; & First Fruits, II.131, 405; *The History of*

Epicurus, 341–270 BC, Greek philosopher: Church of England opposed, I.220; Stella reads, II.354; JS respects ethics, I.192; in *Tale of a Tub*, I.221.

An Epistle to a Lady, poem by JS (1730): III.668, **672–4**; & Mary Barber, III.672, n. 2, 792; Gilliver publishes, III.776–7; & Lewis, III.777; & *Life & Genuine Character*, Pope compares them, III.757; & Wilford, II.776–7.

Epistle upon an Epistle (1729), poem by JS: **III.647** & n. 2, **648**; satire on Delany, III.647; & Faulkner, III.780.

Erasmus, Desiderius, 1466–1536: on divinity of Christ, III.79; *Praise of Folly*, II.725, 726; & *Tale of a Tub*, I.222; true scholar, I.231.

Erastianism: & Burnet, II.85, 87; & Irish bishops, II.358; & Archbishop King, II.213, III.27; political effects, III.166; & JS, II.85, 87, III.27; —JS rejects, II.259; & Test Act (1732), III.724–6.

Erick, or Eyrick, or Herrick, etc., family of Leicestershire, I.4; & JS, I.7.

Erick, Abigail: *see* SWIFT, ABIGAIL.

Ericke (Erick), Elizabeth (Imins), JS's grandmother, wife of James Ericke: I.271, 273–4.

Ericke, James, *fl.* 1627–53, JS's maternal grandfather, vicar of Thornton, Leicestershire: I.4, 270–4; & Laudians, I.3; & Nonconformists, I.6, 7; II.88–9, 462; & JS, I.6.

Errick (Ericke), Jane, wife of Thomas: I.271; & Kendall, I.107.

Errick (Ericke), Thomas, JS's uncle: I.6, 270–2, 274; & JS, I.150.

Espin, Joseph, *c.* 1674–1744, prebendary of S.P.D.: III.41.

Essay on the Fates of Clergymen, by JS (1728): **III.581–2**; *See also* INTELLIGENCER, NOS. 5 & 7.

Essay on Modern Education, by JS (1728): **III.582**; *see also* INTELLIGENCER, No. 9.

Essex, Arthur Capel, 1st Earl of, *c.* 1632–83, Lord Lieutenant of Ireland: & Henry Capel, I.153; & Carteret, III.295; residence, I.153; & Temple, I.153; II.340.

Essex, Lady Elizabeth Capel, d. 1718, wife of Arthur, 1st Earl of Essex: II.340–1.

Established Church: *see* CHURCH OF ENGLAND; CHURCH OF IRELAND.

Eugène, Prince of Savoy, 1663–1736, general: & Addison, II.77; & Barrier Treaty, II.539; campaign against French (1701), II.71; & Marlborough, II.235, 535; & Ormonde, II.577; — Ormonde's 'restraining orders', II.562; alleged plot against Oxford, II.603; & War of Spanish Succession, II.495–6; visit to England (1712), II.535–6.

Eulogies, JS's: in JS's correspondence, III.145; his mastery, II.123; rhetorical effect, III.305.

Eusden, Laurence, 1688–1730, poet laureate: III.773, n. 2, 774; anniversary odes, III.101.

Evans, John, d. 1724, Bishop of Meath: & Ashe, III.168; English bishops, III.167; bishops' rents, III.174–80; career, III.50 & n. 2, 51; & clergy, III.52–3, 58; & Cobbe, III.170–1; death, III.57 & n. 1, 58, 227; Delany on, III.54; & Gilbert, III.178–9; & Godwin, III.51; & Hoadly, III.53; & Hort, III.171; & Hutchinson, III.171; Irish bank scheme, III.159, n. 3, 161, 163; Irish nationalism, III.51–7, 159; Irish poverty, III.158; & Archbishop King, III.52–5, 57, 158, 172, 177–9; Bishop of Meath, III.168; & Molesworth, III.289; & Nicolson, III.53, 55, 163, 168–9; on Roman

governor of Dunkirk, II.573; takes
Dunkirk (1712), II.569, 571; in
'The Society', II.504; & JS, II.573,
576.

Historiographer Royal: JS's ambition, II.370, 746–8; III.6.

History: JS's views, II.60–5; fame
corrupts, II.521; impartiality,
II.745–6; parallel history, II.415,
417, 528, 530; psychological interpretation, II.533, 601, 604;
III.111–12; JS reads, III.329; often
romances, II.601; & JS's *Short
Character*, II.443.

**History of the Four Last Years
of the Queen** (written in 1712–
13), by JS: **II.597–606**; advertisement, II.745; JS's ambition,
II.626; & Arbuthnot, II.745; &
Burnet, II.745; censured (1713),
III.863; characters, II.599, 601,
604–5; composition, II.597, 598–
9, 605, n. 1, 624, 635, 644; III.520;
on constitution, II.601, 604; 'too
dangerous', II.605; multiple innuendo, II.444, n. 1; & Dr
William King, III.804, 857; JS
brings to London, III.520; &
Lady Masham, II.745; & 1st Lord
Oxford, II.745; & 2nd Lord
Oxford, III.516, 520; & Oxford
ministry, II.597–600, 605–15,
745; *Preface* by JS, II.600; —
Orrery receives, III.857; publi-
cation, II.599–600, 605–6, 745,
III.864; —and Dr W. King,
III.846; —and Macaulay, III.880;
—opposed, III.862–4; revisions,
III.520; shallow, II.579; & Steele,
II.745; & Temple's *Memoirs*,
III.864; text, III.804.

Hoadly, Benjamin, 1676–1761,
Bishop of Bangor: & Bolingbroke,
III.730; brother of John, III.619; &
Evans, III.53; sermon, (1717),
III.53; & Steele, II.698; & JS,
III.39.

Hoadly, John, 1678–1746, Arch-

bishop of Dublin & Armagh;
brother of Benjamin: & Bolingbroke, III.730; & Boulter, III.619;
character, III.619; arrives in
Dublin (1730), III.792; made
freeman, III.654; gold box, III.655;
& M. Pilkington, III.732; & Bill of
Residence, III.715; & JS —at
ordination (1739), III.899; —
quarrel over enthronement,
III.654; —relations, III.792; —
'visit' T.C.D. (1735), III.809; —
visitation of S.P.D. (1735),
III.809; —(1740), III.901; & Test,
III.767.

Hoadly, Miss (later Mrs Bellingham
Boyle), daughter of Archbishop
Hoadly: & Katherine Richard-
son, III.873–4; & JS, III.792–3.

Hobbes, Thomas, 1588–1679: I.54,
143, 193; II.64; Anglicans hate,
I.240; & Church of England, I.220;
cynicism, II.472; & freedom of expression, II.586; avoids jargon,
I.180; peace, I.124; & Petty, I.81;
philosophical method, III.260;
condemns scholasticism, I.62,
192–3; on sovereignty, III.257–8;
& Stella, II.354, III.408; & JS,
I.198, 239–40, 243–4; III.329,
n. 11; —moral philosophy, II.375;
—*Ode to Sancroft*, I.130.

Hoey's Court, Dublin, JS's birth-
place: I.22–3.

Holderness, Lady Frederica
Schomberg, Countess of: & monument to Schomberg, III.621–3.

Holt, Samuel, born *c.* 1677, prebendary of St Patrick's Cathedral,
son-in-law of Isaac Manley: & JS,
III.48, n. 6, 355.

Holyhead, Anglesey, Wales, port for
Ireland: Carteret in, III.251; JS at
(1701), II.72; —(1713), II.636; —
(1714), II.757, 760, 762; —(1726),
III.495; —(1727), III.541–3.

Holyhead Journal (1727), by JS:
III.541–3.

Professor of Physic, T.C.D.:
II.189, 191.

Howard, Robert, 1683–1740,
Bishop of Elphin, son of Ralph
Howard: & Carteret, III.485–6;
& S.P.D., III.354–5; & Jervas,
III.485–6; & Archbishop King,
III.47–8, 486; & JS, III.47–8, 486.

Howe, John Grubham (Jack How),
1657–1722, Tory politician: II.91;
& Davenant, II.54; & Oxford,
II.451; & parties, II.46; & JS,
II.47, 58; & Temple's *Popular
Discontents*, II.48–9; & Tories,
II.453; & Tyrconnel, II.46; & war,
II.113.

Howth, co. Dublin: & JS, III.21, 34,
758.

Howth Castle: JS 'deadly sick'
(1734), III.799; portrait of JS,
III.809.

Howth, William St Lawrence, 26th
Lord: & JS, III.792, 801, 847; —
portrait, III.809.

Hue & Cry After Dismal (1712),
by JS: **II.569–70**.

Hue & Cry After Dr Swift (1714):
III.59.

Huguenots (Hugonots): & Lord
Galway, II.38; & Irish convoca-
tion, II.153; naturalization,
II.255; persecution, II.108.

Human nature, JS's views: **III.147–
9**; ambivalence, III.531; corrupt,
II.331, III.290; decay inevitable,
III.166; in *Gulliver's Travels*,
III.141; loves individuals, dislikes
communities, III.150–1, 815; man
not rational, III.150–1; romance
'preserves & exalts', III.102; self-
denial & virtue, II.331; villainy
natural, III.364; 'as well qualified
for flying as thinking', II.589.

Humanism, classical: & JS, III.328,
428.

*Humble Address to Both Houses of
Parliament*, by JS: *see* 7TH
DRAPIER'S LETTERS.

**Humble Address of the Right
Honourable the Lords ... in
Parliament Assembled** (i.e.,
the English House of Lords, voted
10 April 1713), by JS: II.591–2.

**Humble Representation of the
Clergy of the City of Dublin,
To ... William King Lord
Archbishop** (1724), by JS:
III.343–5.

Humour, JS's views: III.560–1.

Hunger: *see* FAMINE.

Hunter, Robert, d. 1734, governor
of New York: & Anne Long,
II.310; & JS, II.305–6.

Huntingdon (Huntington), Robert,
1637–1701, Bishop of Raphoe:
Provost of T.C.D., I.47, 50; &
D.P.S., I.50–1, 80; flees Ireland,
I.51, 87.

Hutchinson, Francis, d. 1739,
Bishop of Down & Connor:
III.171.

Hyde, John, died *c.* 1728, Dublin
bookseller: & *Gulliver's Travels*,
III.498.

Hypocrisy & fraud, JS's views:
III.282–9.

Ikerrin, Thomas Butler, 6th
Viscount, born *c.* 1684, Dean of
Tuam: III.39, n. 4.

Immigration: from England to
Ireland, I.8–20; III.30–1.

Impersonation, JS's technique:
II.416–17; *Argument Against
Abolishing Christianity*, II.286–7; no
mask in *Considerations upon Two
Bills*, III.718; *Drapier's Letters*,
III.231, 273, 293–4, 302; in imi-
tation of Horace, II.744; *Im-
portance of the Guardian*, II.690–1;
& identity, II.407–8, 416–17;
Journal to Stella, II.655, 659; *Letter
Concerning the Test*, II.277; *Letter
from a Lady in Town*, III.164; *Letter
to a Young Gentleman*, III.82–5;
Mary the Cook-Maid's Letter, III.67;

Modest Proposal, II.277; *New
Journey to Paris*, II.525; *Polite
Conversation*, III.836–9; JS as pro-
fligate, II.314; *Proposal for an Act*,
III.721–3; & punishment,
II.335; & satire, II.258, 260–1; &
self-protection, II.331, 334; *Tale of
a Tub*, II.272, 331, 334–5; *Toland's
Invitation*, II.567–8; *Verses on the
Death*, III.710; *see also* PROSE STYLE,
JS's.

**Importance of the Guardian
Considered** (1713), by JS:
II.688–92, 696; & *Publick Spirit of
the Whigs*, II.706.

In Sickness (1714), poem by JS:
III.7.

Income, JS's: *see* FINANCES,
JS's.

Informers: & Christians, III.17; &
integrity, III.24; JS on, III.16–18,
24, 246.

Innuendo, JS's technique: *see* PROSE
STYLE, JS's.

Intelligencer, by JS & Dr Sheri-
dan: **JS's contributions**,
III.581–6; —No. 3 (on *The
Beggar's Opera*), III.559, 581; —
No. 5 (combined with No. 7, as
An Essay on the Fates of Clergymen),
III.581–2; —**No. 9** (*An Essay on
Modern Education*), III.582; —**No.
19** (letter from A. North to
Andrew Dealer & Patrick
Pennyless), III.583–6; ——&
*Answer to Several Letters from
Unknown Persons*, III.582–6,
608–9; & JS's *Journal of a Modern
Lady*, III.581, n. 3; plan of,
III.581.

Investments, JS's: *see* FINANCES, JS's.

Ireland: absenteeism: *see* ABSEN-
TEEISM; agriculture: *see* AGRI-
CULTURE; & Anne —she 'never
hurt' Ireland, III.52; bank: *see*
BANK, IRISH; treated as colony,
II.171–3; constitution unstable,
II.411; corn imported, III.119; cost

of living, II.68–9; Dissenters
(Nonconformists, Presbyterians),
II.255, 359; III.116; —excluded
from government, II.109–10;
'eating, drinking, wrangling,
quarrelsome', II.720; **economic
conditions** —(1726–7), III.509–
12, 544–5; —(1728), III.571–3;
—(1729), III.609–10, 627–8;
—natural advantages, III.574;
—Browne misrepresents, III.573;
—grain export forbidden, III.572;
—improvement (*c.* 1730), III.714;
economic decay, I.15; —causes,
III.113–16, 627–8; —& Mississippi Company, III.509; —in
JS's *Modest Proposal*, III.629–30;
—& population, III.612; —
reform hopeless, III.685; —&
South Sea Company, III.509; —
JS on (1728), III.576–8, 585–6;
——(1728–9), III.573–6; ——
(1734), III.795; ——(1735),
III.820; economic reform —
Drapier's programme, III.307–8;
—JS's proposals, III.617–18;
'English interest': *see* ENGLISH
INTEREST; famine (1720–1),
III.155–9; —(1726), III.510; —
(1727–9), III.311, 544–5, 571–2,
609–10, 627–8; —relief planned,
III.576–8; & France —invasion
possible, II.159; —recruiting of
soldiers, II.159, III.681–5; gold
coins, III.859–62; government,
II.38–43; grain—export forbidden, III.572; —prices, III.544;
imported luxuries condemned,
III.106–7; —women blamed,
III.124; & James II: *see* JAMES II;
land —deeds registered, II.182; —
forfeited to Crown, I.10–15; II.41;
—ownership & the law, II.109;
—JS anxious about estate, II.109;
—value falls (1704), II.109; —
value rises (1690–1720), III.175;
landlords —morals condemned,
III.84; —political power, III.346–

7, 291–2; he despairs, III.796; his
dissatisfaction, III.729–30; economic decay —JS's concerns,
III.573; —'would not prescribe a
dose to the dead' (1731), III.714;
—pamphlets by JS, III.610; exile
for him, III.433, 472, 485; his will
to help (1727), III.517, 528; his
true home, II.93; his isolation —
(1714–24), III.59, 133–4, 147; —
(1732), III.727; *Letter Concerning the
Test*, II.253–4; JS 'thoroughly
miserable', II.368; 'mortification'
to be there, II.67; JS 'most himself' there, II.368; his patriotism,
III.787, 789–90; politics, III.5; —
will not meddle, II.762; prefer-
ment easier, I.260; II.625; social
conditions (1732), III.727; &
Walpole, III.480–1; wine makes
Ireland tolerable, III.645.
Ireland's Consternation, by James
Maculla: & Wood's patent,
III.196.
Irish Brigade: & Louis XIV,
III.681.
Irish interest: Crown as guardian,
III.265; JS on, III.576–7.
Irish language: used to convert
Roman Catholics, III.154–
5.
Irish people: as cattle, III.629;
character —Grattan's speeches,
III.340; —& *Gulliver's Travels*,
III.340; & Declaratory Act,
III.134; emigration, I.16, 87;
III.116, 612–13; —Boulter on,
III.609–10; —fantasy of, III.684–
5; —Archbishop King on, III.571;
—Protestants to America, III.585,
612; —to West Indies, III.510–11;
& English settlers —mutual
hatred, I.10; famine: *see* FAMINE;
foreign enlistment, II.159, 731;
III.116, 681–5; gentry not
idealized, III.59; immigration to
Ireland, I.9–20; landlords
'squeeze', III.112, 157; misery,

I.17; & Ormonde family, I.9;
population, I.21–2; —declines,
III.612–13; poverty, III.112, 117,
157–9; Protestants as oppressed
as Catholics, III.153; & Roman
Catholics, I.12, 14; II.57; speech:
see IRISH SPEECH; sufferings
(1727), III.545; & JS: *see* IRISH
PEOPLE & JS; & Temple family,
I.9; 'Troubles' (1688–90), I.87–8;
women blamed, III.106–7; &
Wood's patent: *see* WOOD'S
PATENT.
Irish people & JS: their affection,
III.514; reduced to brutes,
III.614–15; celebrate JS (1733),
III.761; celebrate birthday (1726)
III.514; —(1738), III.876; his
defence, III.583–6; he dislikes
gentry, II.161–2; does not ide-
alize, III.59; popularity, III.495–6,
770–1, 796, 817, 825, 848–9, 853,
862, 865, 882, 899, 917; their self-
destructiveness, III.570–1; JS
sympathetic, I.8; seeks unity,
III.346–7.
Irish Rebellion (1641): I.12–13;
II.46, II.718; & Ormonde, I.17; &
Sir John Temple, I.18–19.
Irish speech: JS dislikes Irishisms,
III.133.
Irony, JS's technique: *Conduct of the
Allies* II.497, 499; *Drapier's Letters*,
III.239, 294, 306; & literalization,
III.306, 574; & pathos, III.574; &
JS's persona, II.416; as point of
view, III.724; praise as blame in
Vindication of Lord Carteret, III.659;
in preaching, III.80–1; *Remarks . . .
on the Rights of the Christian Church*,
II.258–61; ensures self-protection,
II.331; in sermons, III.80–81; *see
also* PROSE STYLE, JS's.

Jack, personification of Puritanism
in *Tale of a Tub*: I.186, 210–15;
II.330, 333, 411; & Scriblerus
Club, II.726.

Joymount, Carrickfergus, Ireland; Chichester family residence: 1.163.

Judas, poem by JS (1732): III.719, n. 2, **720.**

Junto or Junta, a group of Whig leaders (Halifax, Orford, Somers, Sunderland & Wharton): & Addison, II.234–5; & Anne, II.221; & Barrier Treaty, II.370; & campaign in Spain, II.235; comic figures, II.412; & Cowper, II.167; & Cutts, II.163; & Dissenters, II.414; election (1705), II.165–7; —(1708), II.314–15; & *Examiner,* II.420; fall (1710), II.5; & Godolphin (1705), II.166–8; —(1706), II.176; —(1708), II.220, 315; —ministry, II.493; & Gregg, II.223; & House of Commons, II.114; impeachment threatened (1701); II.77; lose strength (1702), II.90; motives, II.57, 441; & Newcastle, II.167, 315; & new country party, II.113, 116; & Ormonde (1707), II.178; & Oxford, II.166, 168, 222–3, 672; oppose peace, II.493, 570; & Pembroke, II.177–8, 221; & Prior, II.231–2; & Somers, II.121, 178, 315–16; spoils system, II.414; & Steele, II.241, 706; & Sunderland, II.177; & JS, II.216; 253, 523, 705; —*Contests & Dissensions,* II.253; —JS's 'credit', II.252; —JS friendly (1703), II.120–1; —*Letter Concerning the Test,* II.266, 271–4; —JS on (1701), II.58; —JS rejects, II.131; III.276; & Test Act, II.261; Act of Union, II.166; unpopular (1709), II.359; & War of Spanish Succession, II.514–16; & Wharton (1708), II.315–16; & Whigs, II.253, 271–2. *See also* WHIGS.

Justice: in Ireland & England, II.170–73; sacrificed to greed, II.270–1.

Juvenal: & JS, III.328, 578; —JS prefers Horace, III.560; —JS imitates, II.250; III.329, n. 5.

Kells, co. Meath: market town for Quilca, III.377; JS at, III.822–3.

Kelly, Frances Arabella, d. 1733, daughter of Dennis: death, III.758–9; & Delany, III.735; & JS, III.735–6.

Kendal, Ermengarde Melusina, Countess von der Schulenburg, Duchess of, 1664–1743, mistress of George I: & Bolingbroke, III.526; & Carteret, III.519; & Sunderland, III.188–9; Wood's patent, III.187, 238.

Kendall, Jane (Ericke), JS's cousin: & Abigail Swift, 1.6.

Kendall, John, 1684–1717, vicar of Thornton, Leicestershire, married to Jane Ericke: 1.270–1; & JS, 1.107.

Kendrick, Roger, verger of S.P.D.: & JS's birthday (1735), III.825; & codicil to JS's will, III.903; & *Directions to Servants,* III.833.

Kennett, White, 1660–1728, Bishop of Peterborough: & Atterbury, 1.253; II.608; & JS, II.116, 608–9.

Kensington, Middlesex: JS at (1712), II.572; Vanessa visits JS, II.646.

Kerry, Anne (née Petty), d. 1737, wife of 1st Earl: JS's character of, II.429.

Kildare, Bishop of: *see* ELLIS, WELBORE.

Kildare, bishopric of: & Ellis, II.151; & Moreton, II.150.

Kildrohod: *see* CELBRIDGE.

Kilkenny, Articles: 1.13.

Kilkenny, baboon of: *see* TENISON, EDWARD.

Kilkenny, co. Kilkenny: 1.35; JS visits (1699), II.6.

Kilkenny School: 1.34–42; & Con-

satirist: JS imitates, III.329, n. 5;
& women, III.104–5.

'Martin', personification of Church
of England in *Tale of a Tub*: I.188;
dull, II.289, 564; regains sanity,
II.411.

Marvell, Andrew, 1621–78, poet &
M.P.: I.122; II.26; 'advice'
formula for poetry, II.308, n. 4;
III.641–3.

Mary II, Queen of England, 1662–
94, daughter of James II: I.69, 99;
II.42.

Mary, JS's cook-maid: III.33–4.

Mary the Cook-Maid's Letter,
poem by JS (1718): **III.67**.

Masham family: & Ford, III.370; &
JS, II.572–3, 577.

Masham, Abigail (née Hill), Lady
Masham, d. 1734: & Anne,
II.221, 371, 518, 520; III.111; &
Arbuthnot, II.507, 747; & Boling-
broke, II.504, 669; & Canadian
expedition (1711), II.454; &
Dunkirk, II.685; & Guiscard,
II.467; & Mrs Howard, III.591–2,
697; & Duchess of Marlborough,
II.221; & Nobel, II.628; & 1st
Lord Oxford, II.221–4, 317, 451–
4, 678–9, 751–2; & 2nd Lord
Oxford, II.754; son's illness,
II.629; & South Sea Company,
II.732; & Stratford, II.754; & JS,
II.478, 507, 520, 523, 526, 633,
729, 745, 747; —JS's character
of, II.223–4, 573; III.109–11;
—friendship, II.551, 639, 645–6,
755, 758–9, 885.

Masham, Samuel, Lord Masham
of Otes, *c.* 1679–1758, husband
of Lady Masham: II.476; &
Bernage, II.509; & 1st Lord
Oxford, II.679; in 'The Society',
II.504; & JS, II.505, 507.

Masks, JS's: *see* IMPERSONATION.

Mason, William Monck, 1775–
1859, Irish historian: III.181, n. 1.

Mathematics: as philosophical

method, III.260; JS dislikes, II.90.

Matilda (or Maud), Empress,
1102–67; wife of Emperor Henry
V: & Stephen, II.65.

Maule, Henry, d. 1758, Bishop of
Cloyne, Bishop of Dromore:
III.485; & Jervas, III.485–6.

Maxims Controlled in Ireland,
by JS (written *c.* 1728): **III.575–6**.

Mayhew, George P.: on JS's fellowship scheme, III.568, n. 2.

Maynooth, prebend of S.P.D.: & S.
Holt, III.355; & R. Howard,
III.354–5.

'Md', probably 'My dears', JS's
code for Stella & Rebecca
Dingley: II.73, 652–3.

Meath, Bishop of: *see* DOWNES; ELLIS;
EVANS; LAMBERT; MORETON.

Meath, bishopric of: Downes succeeds, III.227; & Evans, III.51–7.

Mechanical Operation of the Spirit: *see*
DISCOURSE CONCERNING THE
MECHANICAL OPERATION OF THE
SPIRIT.

Medical analogies (i.e., the human
body & its ills as metaphor for
the state): & English domination
of Ireland, III.262; in *Examiner*,
II.414; poisonous remedies,
III.232.

Meditation upon a Broom-Stick
(written *c.* 1703, published 1710),
by JS: & Elizabeth Berkeley,
II.91, n. 2.

Medley, Whig newspaper: on
author's role, II.417; & Main-
waring, II. 407; & Oxford
ministry, II.407; & JS's academy,
II.547.

Melcombe: *see* DODINGTON.

Memoirs of Martinus Scriblerus: *see*
SCRIBLERUS CLUB.

**Memoirs, Relating to That
Change Which Happened in
the Year 1710,** by JS (written
1714): **III.108–9**; & *Letter to Mr
Pope*, III.137; publication, III.846,

1.232; & *Gulliver's Travels*, iii.329,
467.
Phipps, Sir Constantine, 1656–1723,
Lord Chancellor of Ireland:
ii.673, 719–22; iii.8–9, 20, 86–7,
519, n. 2; dismissal urged, iii.20;
Jacobite, ii.721, iii.7; Lord Justice,
ii.719; & Midleton, iii.8; &
Moymet, ii.664; & Ormonde,
ii.673; Oxford University honours, iii.9; & Sacheverell, ii.719;
& Shrewsbury, ii.721, 731; & JS,
ii.722; iii.7; & Tories, ii.719;
iii.20.
Pilkington, Laetitia, 1712–50,
daughter of Dr John Van Lewin:
iii.638, 646, 687, 847, 868; &
Mary Barber, iii.734, 759;
& Ford, iii.640, 727, n. 2; &
Constantia Grierson, iii.636, 638;
returns to Ireland (1733), iii.760;
marriage (1729), iii.637, n. 5,
638; excellent memory, iii.707; &
Matthew Pilkington, —estranged,
iii.640, 868; —will join him,
iii.734; —visits him (1733),
iii.759–60;& JS: *see* PILKINGTON,
L., & JS; & Worsdale, iii.888, n. 1.
Pilkington, Laetitia, & JS: & Mary
Barber, iii.637–40, 707–8, 728,
733–4, 868, 885; friendship,
iii.644, 847–8; —connives at
his whims, iii.686–8; JS's *Lady's
Dressing-Room*, iii.688–9; he gives
her medals, iii.639; first meeting,
iii.637, n. 5, 638; her *Memoirs*,
iii.637, n. 5, 688; he gives her
money, iii.640; JS's *Polite Conversation*, iii.687, 707, 836; her son
dies, iii.707–8.
Pilkington, Matthew, *c.* 1701–74,
poet, clergyman: iii.638, 644,
732, 745–7, 760, 771, 868; &
Gilliver, iii.777–8; & Hoadly,
iii.732; returns to Ireland, iii.778;
Ode, iii.640–1; *Poems* —Bowyer
publishes, iii.736; —subscribers,

iii.686; preaches in S.P.D.,
iii.639; seeks preferment, iii.640–
1; & St Mark's, Dublin, iii.759;
& JS: *see* PILKINGTON, M., & JS;
& Van Lewin, iii.848; & Sir E.
Walpole, iii.759–60.
Pilkington, Matthew, & JS: iii.638,
644, 686–7, 732, 755–6, 780, 794,
868, 909; *Life & Genuine Character*,
iii.709, 756–8; meeting, iii.637,
n. 5; money from JS (1733),
iii.755–6; JS's plans, iii.736;
Pilkington's poems, iii.640–1,
687; & Pope, iii.731, 744, 794–5;
publication of works by JS,
iii.745–7, 756, 759, 776; treachery to JS suspected, iii.777–8.
Plague, in France (1720–1): iii.156–
7; & Irish bank scheme, iii.159.
Plato: Stella reads, ii.354; & JS,
ii.268; —leaves works to F. Wilson, iii.911; —JS respects, i.192.
Pliny the Elder, *c.* AD 23–79, Roman
naturalist: ii.164; iii.329, 884.
Plutarch, *c.* AD 45–*c.* 120: ii.54; &
Drapier's Letters, iii.328; JS
admires, i.192.
Poetry, JS's practice & views: ii.308,
369–70, 714, 735; **iii.100–7**; analogy in, ii.258, 260–1; —*Baucis and
Philemon*, ii.426–7; compliments
to Stella, iii.418–25; eulogies,
iii.673; —of Delany, iii.662; —of
a woman, iii.101–3; his formulae,
iii.701; games in verse, iii.339–
40; imagery —filth, iii.688–95;
—madness & damnation, iii.830;
—sexual prosthesis, iii.103–7,
692–3; & moral leadership,
iii.776; compared to Pope's,
iii.643; proverbs in, iii.155; riddles, iii.339–40; poems to Stella:
see JOHNSON, ESTHER, & JS; structure, iii.403–4; —dialogue form,
iii.649; — —in *Traulus*, iii.656–8;
—weak endings, iii.668; style,
iii.339–40; —in poems for Lady

220, 226, 228, 235–44, 260.
Privy Council, Irish: III.161, 180,
252, 348–9, 355, 652, 731, 840;
& Irish independence, II.361;
Molesworth removed (1712),
III.287; & Parliament (1707),
II.107, 179; & Pembroke, II.178–
9; & Phipps, II.720; & Bill of
Residence, III.715; & Roman
Catholics, III.118; & Shrewsbury,
II.721; & Somers, II.178; & JS,
III.252, 268–70, 271, n. 2, 275–6;
& Sir J. Temple, I.18; & Test
Act, II.263; & Wood's patent,
III.200, 217, 223, 230, 249, 310.
Problem, poem by JS (written
1699): **II.29–31**.
Proby, Thomas, 1665–1729,
Surgeon-General of Ireland: &
Stella, III.547.
Progress of Beauty, poem by JS
(written *c.* 1719): **III.104–7**.
**Project for the Advancement of
Religion, & the Reformation
of Manners,** by JS (1709):
II.276–80, 289–94; & JS's *Apology
for Tale of a Tub,* II.332; & *Argument Against Abolishing Christianity*
compared, II.276–94; & Atterbury's *Representation,* II.449; Lord
Berkeley praises, II.345; &
S. Johnson, II.292; in JS's *Miscellanies* (1711), II.422; & JS's *Preface
to the Bishop of Sarum's Introduction,*
II.694; self-satire, II.335; & Steele,
II.207, n. 3, 242, 292; & Tooke,
II.337.
Prometheus, poem by JS (1724):
III.232, 317.
Property: & liberty, III.255, 258,
292.
Property, JS's: *see* FINANCES, JS's.
Prophets, French, mystical sect:
II.198, 201.
**Proposal for an Act of Parliament, to Pay Off the Debts
of the Nation,** by JS (1732):
III.720–4.

**Proposal for Correcting,
Improving, and Ascertaining
the English Tongue,** by JS
(1712): **II.542–9**; & Steele, II.684.
**Proposal for Giving Badges to
the Beggars,** by JS (1737):
III.813–16.
**Proposal for the Universal Use
of Irish Manufacture,** by JS
(1720): **III.123–30**; authorship,
III.136–7, 293; & bank scheme,
III.176; & Bolingbroke, III.143; &
Drapier's Letters, III.127, 209, 252;
& Molesworth, III.287–8; Nicolson on, III.128; prosecuted,
III.128–30, 268, 386, 445; structure, III.260.
Proposal for Virtue, by JS (probably written in 1727): **III.529–31**.
**Proposal that All the Ladies and
Women of Ireland Should
Appear Constantly in Irish
Manufactures,** by JS (written
1729): **III.645–6**.
Prose style, JS's practice & views:
III.82–5, 402; *Answer to the Craftsman,* III.684; aphorisms, II.367;
arithmetical fantasy, III.211–12,
343; audience 'vulgar', III.783–4;
in *Battle of the Books,* I.236; conceits, II.413–14; III.418–25;
—animals, III.262; —in 5th
Drapier's Letter, III.294; —in 6th
Drapier's Letter, III.274; —in 7th
Drapier's Letter, II.302; —gold,
III.163; —medical, III.231, 262;
—money, III.162–3; fables, in
Drapier's Letters, III.302; imagery,
III.418–25; impersonation: *see*
IMPERSONATION; innuendo, II.444;
III.127; —*Conduct of the Allies,*
II.492–3, 499; —3rd *Drapier's
Letter,* III.239–40; —*Examiner,*
II.528, 553; —*History of the Four
Last Years,* II.444, n. 1; —*Importance of the Guardian,* II.690–1;
—*Letter to October Club,* II.523–5;
—*Short Character of Wharton,*

II.444; —*Proposal for Universal Use of Irish Manufacture*, III.127; irony: see IRONY; letter-writing, III.884; literalization of metaphors, III.141; *Polite Conversation*, III.839; praise as rhetoric, III.305; *Presbyterians Plea*, III.763–4; puns: see PUNS; restraint exemplified, III.616–17; in sermons, III.80–1; *Some Reasons against the Bill* (1734), III.768–9; rooted in speech, II.655; apparent spontaneity, III.585–6; structure —method specious, III.573; —mock-demonstration, II.282; III.211, 721; —myths invented, II.414–15; —narrative devices, II.414–5; —parallel history, II.48–9, 415; in Walpole memorandum, III.482. *See also* LITERARY CAREER; POETRY.
Prosthesis, sexual: literary theme, III.103–7.
Protestant Succession: see HANOVERIAN SUCCESSION.
Proverbs, JS's use of: in *The Bubble*, III.155.
Public career of JS: activities narrow, III.809–10; still important in old age (1739), III.88–92; enjoys prerogatives of deanship, III.753; reviewed in speech (1730), III.655; in *Verses on the Death of Dr Swift*, III.710–11. *See also* FIRST FRUITS.
Publication of JS's works: *see under separate publishers or under* LITERARY CAREER.
Publick Spirit of the Whigs: Set Forth in Their Generous Encouragement of the Author of the Crisis, by JS (1714): **II.702–13**; & *History of the Four Last Years*, II.745; & Marlborough, II.534, n. 2.
Pullein, Tobias, 1648–1713, Bishop successively of Cloyne & Dromore: death, II.626, 627, n. 1.
Pulteney, Sir William (later Earl of

Bath), 1684–1764, statesman: II.250, 476, 515, 523, 526, 701–2; & Stopford, III.802; & JS, III.322, n. 2, 476, 515, 563, 709, 787, 885; & Walpole, III.476, 526, 701–2; & Wyndham, III.476.
Puns, JS's: II.189–91; III.125; & fables, III.125; & Kilkenny School, I.40–1; II.190; & Prior, II.447.
Purcell, Henry, c. 1658–95, composer: III.352, 676, n. 3.
Purchas, Samuel, c. 1575–1626, author: & *Gulliver's Travels*, III.329.
Puritans & Puritanism: & celibacy, III.105; & Dublin Philosophical Society, I.87; emotional appeal alleged, III.83; & Sir R. Harley, II.462; Lambert on, II.265; on marriage, III.399; preaching, III.76–7; stereotypes, I.210; JS's views, I.190–2, 210–15, 240–6; —& Sancroft, I.130–1; & Thomas Swift (I), I.3; ancestors of Whigs, II.415; on women, III.397, 399.
Puttenham, Surrey: & Thomas Swift (III), I.145.

Queensberry, Catherine Douglas, Duchess of, d. 1777, wife of Charles Douglas, 3rd Duke of Queensberry: & Gay, III.699; & Mrs Howard, III.587–8; & JS, III.137, 587–8, 699–700, 728, 757.
Queensberry, James Douglas, 2nd Duke, 1662–1711, Secretary of State (1709): & Gay, III.588, n. 2, 701; & Guiscard, II.466–7; & Harrison, II.613–14; Secretary for Scotland, II.451.
Queries Relating to the Sacramental Test, by JS (1732): & Faulkner, III.780.
Quilca (Cuilcagh), near Virginia, co. Cavan, home of Elizabeth

Catholics, papists, popery, etc.):
I.191, 214, 220, 251, 322; II.88–9,
265, 271, 322, 469, 471, 692–3; &
JS, I.8, 212, 238–9; III.114.

Roman Catholicism, Irish: I.12,
191; II.107, 358, 365; III.116–
18, 260, 271; Anti-Popery Act,
II.360–1; bishops, III.184; &
Boulter, III.619, n. 2; buffer
between Protestants, II.41; con-
versions, II.154–5, 161, 361; 'dangerous', II.262, 265; & Dissenters
(1708), II.262; Dissenters more
dangerous, II.271–2; & emigration, III.612; Evans on, III.159;
France recruits, II.159; & government, III.258–9; & Huguenots,
II.108; & Archbishop King,
II.213, 215; III.118; land values,
II.109; & landlords, II.155–6,
III.117; & House of Lords, II.182;
& Molesworth, III.288; penal
laws, I.16; II.41, 108–9; powerless,
I.191; II.107–10, 357; III.272;
toleration of, II.41; & William
III, II.40–1; & Pooley, II.263; &
Protestant unity, II.160, 357, 359;
& Tyrconnel, I.87; & Wood's
patent, III.248, 253, 259.

Romance, JS's views: 'preserves &
exalts' human nature, III.102.

Rome (ancient Rome & Romans):
II.528; III.5, 455.

Romney, Henry Sidney, 1st Earl,
1641–1704, Lord Lieutenant of
Ireland: career, I.103; & Cutts,
II.165; Lord Lieutenant of
Ireland (1692–3), I.261; II.38;
power fading, I.262; & JS,
I.102–3, 250–1; II.64; —JS at-
tacks, II.388, n. 5; —fails JS,
II.13, 260–1, 263; —*Problem*,
II.29–31; & S. Synge, II.146; &
Temple, I.102–3, 190, 250–1.

Roscommon, Lord: 'Rose Common,' III.315; & debate on
'wisdom', III.314–16.

Roseingrave, Daniel, *c.* 1655–1727,
musician: at S.P.D., III.352–3.

Roseingrave, Ralph, 1695–1747,
organist, son of Daniel: at S.P.D.,
III.353.

Roseingrave, Thomas, *c.* 1690–
c. 1755, musician, son of Daniel:
at S.P.D., III.354.

Rowe, Nicholas, 1674–1718, playwright: II.383, 386, 594.

Royal Library ('St James's
Library'), in St James's Palace,
London: & R. Bentley, I.227.

Royal Society: I.114; II.84, 90, 177,
238; & D.P.S., I.80–6; & JS,
I.193; II.84.

Rule, Ralph, d. 1724, prebendary of
S.P.D.: II.146.

Run upon the Bankers, poem by
JS (1720): III.162, n. 6.

Runcard, Susanna: & T. Sawbridge, III.675.

Russel, Thomas, Archdeacon of
Cork: & Dr Sheridan, III.363.

Ryder, Henry, *c.* 1646–96, master
of Kilkenny School: I.36; II.6;
career, I.37.

Rye House Plot: II.65; & Burnet,
II.85.

Rymer, Thomas, 1641–1713, historian: I.180, 194, 286–7; II.370,
n. 2, 746, 748.

Ryswick, Treaty or Peace of (1697):
& Addison, I.249; & Halifax, II.83;
& Prior, I.247; a stopgap, II.44; &
Sunderland, I.171; JS on, II.491;
—& *Tale of a Tub*, II.333; & War
of the League of Augsburg, I.228;
& Whigs, II.41.

Ryves, Jerome, d. 1704, Dean of
S.P.D.: II.105, II.144, 146.

Sacheverell, Henry, *c.* 1674–1724,
clergyman: II.55, 371–2, 390,
412, 448, 452–3; & Phipps,
II.719; trial, II.55; —& Church of
England, II.372; —Dartmouth
defends, II.372; —& 4th *Drapier's*

founded by JS: III.818–19, 878–9,
903.

St Stephen's Green, Dublin:
M'Carthy's house, III.341; & St
James's Park, London, III.373; &
vicars choral, II.714; walks,
III.370.

St Werburgh's Church, Dublin:
II.150; & T. Bolton, III.44; &
Archbishop King, II.9–10; loca-
tion, I.22.

Saints (for separate saints, see under
names, as JEROME, PAUL, etc.):
'real' Christians, II.288.

Salus populi: *see* GOVERNMENT.

Sancroft, William, 1617–93, Arch-
bishop of Canterbury: I.127–8,
213–14; II.86–7; & JS, I.128;
—JS admires, I.112; —JS on,
II.86–7, 130; —& Drapier,
III.276; —poem on, I.112; II.694;
III.18; & fallen Tory leaders,
III.18; & William III, I.127.

Santry, vicars of: *see* JACKSON.

Satire, JS's practice & views:
analogy, II.258, 260–1; **anti-
feminine poems**, **III.688–95**;
approaches to, II.279–80; &
contemplation, II.295; defended
by JS, III.578–9, 662; devices in
JS's *Polite Conversation*, III.838–9;
double role of satirist, II.276–7;
effect of, II.499; & filth, III.695;
Horatian preferred, III.560; &
identity, II.416–17; impersonation: *see* IMPERSONATION; ineffectual, II.279; Juvenal & JS, III.578;
& moral superiority, III.702;
personal satire defended, III.561,
n. 1, 578; pleasure in writing,
III.561; reader & author, II.277–
80; opposed to retirement, III.142;
as rhetoric, II.277–80; satirist's
mask, II.335; techniques —in
Argument, II.279–82; —in *Polite
Conversation*, III.838–9; in *Tale of a
Tub*, I.196–201; theory of,

III.141–2.

**Satirical Elegy on the Death of a
Late Famous General,** poem
by JS (written *c.* 1722): II.535.

'Saturday Club', almost weekly
dinners held at Oxford's house
(1711): II.450, 504; JS dines with
(1713), II.632.

'Saunders', JS's servant, i.e.,
Alexander McGee: *see* McGEE.

Sawbridge, Thomas, d. 1733, Dean
of Ferns & Leighlin: III.674–6.

Schism Act (1714): II.734–5; &
Shrewsbury, II.751; JS regrets,
II.753.

Scholasticism: & Bacon, I.193; in
disrepute, I.193; JS dislikes, I.192.

Schomberg, Frederick Herman von
Schomberg, 1st Duke, 1615–90,
general: conquers Carrickfergus,
I.163; his granddaughter Fre-
derica & Vanhomrigh family,
II.312; monument in S.P.D.,
III.621–3, 703; & Warter, I.164.

Science, experimental: JS's attitude,
II.90.

Science, natural: *see* PHILOSOPHY.

Scipio, Africanus Major, Publius
Cornelius, *c.* 236–*c.* 183 BC,
Roman general & statesman:
III.158, 294, n. 2.

Scotland & Scots: I.112, 172; II.165,
167, 315, 672, 674; & Charles I,
II.172; election (1708), II.315; &
France, II.159; & Hanoverian
Succession, II.157–8, 166–7; &
Jacobites, II.159; III.19; & Archbishop King, II.154; in Parliament, II.255; poverty, III.118;
Presbyterian Church, II.89; & Act
of Security (1703), II.157–8; Act
of Union (1707), II.166–9, 172–3,
276, n. 1, 668; —& JS's *Letter
concerning the Sacramental Test*
(1708), II.253–4; —militia trains
(1705), II.169; —negotiations,
II.168;

JS wants livings, II.346–7.

South America: European trade with, II.487.

South Sea Bubble (1720): III.152–6; in *Gulliver's Travels*, III.504; & Irish bank, III.124, 159; & Irish landlords, III.175; Archbishop King on, III.155; & money shortage, III.155–9; JS denounces (1723), III.372–3; JS's poem on, III.155; & weavers, III.117.

South Sea Company: II.474, 732, 751–2; III.153–4, 161, 509; JS a stockholder, II.488, 556–7; & Walpole, III.154.

Southwell, Edward, 1671–1730, Irish Secretary of State: II.353, 400–1, 403, 579, 663; & JS, II.353, 400–1; & Wood's patent, III.247, 299.

Spain: & Austria, union opposed, II.492; balance of power, II.54; & Dutch Barrier, II.370; empire contested, II.44–5; & England — war (1719), III.118; —trade: *see* TRADE, ENGLISH; & France, union of crowns, II.74, 475, 562–4, 590; 'no peace without Spain' —& Dutch, II.486; —& George I, II.486; —& Grand Alliance, II.490–1; —& Emperor Joseph's death (1711), II.475; —Lords' role on (1711), II.235; —Nottingham, II.515–16; —& peace preliminaries (1711), II.481–2; —JS on, II.490; & Peace of Nijmegen, I.97; trade, II.540.

Spanish Netherlands (i.e., modern Belgium excluding Liège): granted to Austria (1700), II.539; & Barrier Treaty, II.539; & Dutch, II.487, 540; France blockades (1701), II.75; & Battle of Ramillies, II.168; possessions of Spain, I.44–5.

Speaker of the House of Commons: (1701–5) Robert Harley, II.116–17; (1714–15) Sir Thomas

Hanmer, Bart., II.712.

Spectator: Addison revives, II.72, 409, 536, 565, 592, 723, 726, 761; & JS, I.72; —JS's academy, II.543, 546; —JS 'will not meddle with', II.655; & Wharton, II.440.

Spinsters, JS's views: III.105, 400.

Squire Bickerstaff Detected, anonymous sequel to *Predictions for the Year 1708*: II.206–7.

Stamp tax: *see* PRESS.

Stanhope, James Stanhope, 1st Earl, 1673–1721, general, statesman: II.698, 713; III.219.

Stanley, Sir John, Bart., 1663–1744, Commissioner of Customs in Ireland: II.103, n. 1, 673, 719–20.

Stannard, Eaton, *c.* 1685–1755, Recorder of Dublin: III.819, 842, 855, 902, n. 2.

Starhemberg (Staremberg), Guidobald (Guido), Count von, 1657–1737: & Boulter, III.285.

Staunton, Thomas, d. 1732, Irish M.P.: III.327, 396, 438–40.

Stearne, John, 1660–1745, Dean of S.P.D., Bishop of Clogher: II.95, 148, 626, 629–31; character, III.168; & deanship of S.P.D., II.10, 146–51, 165, 665; III.9, 32; in Dromore, II.669; & Evans, III.53, 55; & First Fruits, II.379; & Archbishop King, II.149, 214, 216, 356, 625, 666, 717; III.11, 39, 55, 116, 168–9; & T. Lindsay, III.54; & Moymet, II.662, 664; & Ormonde, II.149, 625–6, 629–30; & 1st Lord Oxford, II.224, 626; prolocutor, II.363, 716; & St Luke's, Dublin, II.217–18; & Stella, II.356; & JS, II.220, 356, 556, 660, 717; III.53–4, 205; — JS's ladies, III.98; —preferment, II.625–6, 628–30; —St Nicholas Without, II.217–20; III.44; — S.P.D. livings, II.188, 666; —at T.C.D., III.809; —JS visits (1722), III.430; —Stearne's visita-

byterians, II.262; III.725; & Privy
Council, II.263; repeal, II.261–5;
III.22–3, 29–30, 118–19, 160,
181–3, 270, 767; & Speaker of
the House of Commons, II.374–6;
& Sunderland, II.183; III.22, 30;
& JS, II.93; —*Argument Against the
Abolishing of Christianity*, II.374;
—attitude changes (1708–32),
III.725–6; —JS defends, II.109–
10, 261, 264–5; III.724–6; —*Letter
concerning the Sacramental Test*,
II.253–4; —*Letter to a Member of
Parliament in Ireland*, II.182, 374–6;
III.22; & Wharton, II.358; &
Whigs, III.725.

Testimony of Conscience, sermon by JS: **III.80–1.**

Thomson, cousin of JS: II.656.

Thoughts Moral & Diverting, by
JS (1711): & *Miscellanies* of JS &
Pope, III.738–9.

Thoughts on Various Subjects,
by JS (c. 1696–1706): **II.192–3;**
III.163, n. 4; date of composition,
II.192, n. 1.

Throp, Roger, d. 1736, rector of
Kilcorman, co. Limerick: JS
defends, III.880.

Thucydides: II.601.

Thurston, Joseph, poet: *The Toilette*
(1730), III.688–9.

Thynne, Sir Thomas, 1st Viscount
Weymouth, 1640–1714: *see*
WEYMOUTH, THOMAS THYNNE, 1ST
VISCOUNT.

Thynne, Thomas, of Longleat,
1648–82, 'Tom of Ten Thousand', marries Elizabeth, Baroness Percy: II.478–9.

Tiberius (Claudius Nero) Caesar,
42 BC–AD 37, Roman emperor: &
Gulliver's Travels, III.453.

Tickell, Thomas, 1686–1740, poet,
statesman: II.240, 592, 613;
III.270, 434, 489; *On the Prospect of
Peace*, II.592; & Orrery, III.845; on
poetry, II.25; & Dr Sheridan,

III.360, n. 5, 364; & Stella,
III.377, 489–90; & JS, III.270,
330, 369, 434, 438, 518, n. 2.

Tighe, Sir Richard, c. 1678–1736,
Irish M.P.: III.252, 362–5, 578–9,
830–1; & JS —JS's poems on,
III.579–81; —as 'Timothy' or
'Tim', III.579, n. 2; —*Traulus*,
III.656; —*Vindication of Carteret*,
III.658–9.

Tillage Bill (1716, 1719): III.119–
20.

Tillotson, John, 1630–94, Archbishop of Canterbury: I.220;
III.72, 83.

Timon of Athens: misanthropy,
III.150.

'Timothy' or 'Tim', JS's name for
Sir Richard Tighe: III.579.

Tindal, Matthew, 1657–1733; deist:
III.252, 362–5, 578–9, 830–1.

Tisdall family: at Carrickfergus,
II.134.

Tisdall, Philip, 1703–77, Irish
statesman: III.881–2.

Tisdall, William, 1669–1735, Irish
clergyman: II.120, 126, 130,
133–9; III.429; JS on, II.657; &
Thomas Swift, II.134; & repeal of
Test Act (1733), III.766; & Philip
Tisdall, III.882; Tory, II.252; at
Trinity College, II.134.

Tithes, JS's views: I.127; III.362;
agistment controversy, III.827–8;
human or divine institution,
III.185; fears modus, III.768; &
rents, III.347.

**To a Friend Who Had Been
Much Abused,** poem by JS
(1730): **III.663–4.**

**To Charles Ford, Esq., on His
Birthday,** poem by JS (1723):
III.371, n. 1, 372–3; & *To Stella,
Visiting Me*, III.413, n. 4.

**To Doctor Delany, on the Libels
Writ against Him,** poem by JS
(1730): **III.662–3.**

To Lord Harley, poem by JS

—London, II.43–4; (1702) England, II.79; —Trim, II.105; (1703) Chester, II.112; —England, II.105; —Leicester, II.112; (1704) returns to Ireland, II.140, 143; —Leicester, II.140; (1707–8) Leicester, II.194–7; (c. 1707–9) near Leicester Fields & Haymarket, II.307; (1709) with Sir George Beaumont, II.346; —Chester, II.348; —Clogher, II.365–6; —Cranford, II.303, 325; —Epsom, II.303; —Harborough, II.346; —returns to Ireland, II.340; —Laracor, II.365–6; —Leicester, II.338, 346; (1710) Chester, II.380; —Dublin, II.366; —England, II.379; —Mrs Greenfield, II.380; (1710–13) delays return to Ireland, II.660; (1713) England, II.670; —Mrs Greenfield, II.636; —returns to Ireland, II.635–6, 660, 666; —Laracor, II.667; (1714) Belcamp, III.34; —Chester, II.760; —returns to Ireland, II.756–60; III.4, 6, 92; —Letcombe Bassett, Berkshire, II.730–60; —Oxford, II.733, 754; (1718) Gaulstown, III.428; —with Ludlow, III.428; (1721) Gaulstown, III.338–9; —with Rochfort family, III.88; (1722) in the country, III.388; —returns to Dublin, III.388; —northern Ireland, III.430; —Loughgall, III.371, n. 1; —Quilca, III.366–7; —Rantavan, III.367; (1722–3) Wood Park, III.205, 374; (1723) Clonfert, III.367; —Connaught, III.374; —southern Ireland, III.205, 430; —Loughgall, III.374, 452; —Munster, III.374; —Quilca, III.367–8; —southern tour, III.389, 415, n. 1; (1724) Belcamp, III.286; (1725) plans trip to England, III.431, 437; —Quilca, III.298–9, 301–2, 308–11, 376–9; (1726) with Lord Bathurst,

III.476; —Bibury, III.488; —Dawley, III.475–6; —in England —perhaps travels with Ford, III.375; —London, III.475, 489, 493–4; —Oakley Park, III.488; —with 2nd Lord Oxford, III.476; —with Pope & Gay, III.488–9; —Stowe, III.488; —Dublin, III.495–6; (1727) arrives in Dublin, III.543, n. 4; —England, III.514–8, 591; —hopes to visit France, III.516–17, 532–3; —Herefordshire, III.518; —London, III.519, 537, 540; —city of Oxford, III.518; —Twickenham, III.532, 537, 564; —Wimpole, III.519–20; —returns to Ireland, III.532, 537–8, 540, 543, n. 4; (1728) possible trip to England, III.552–3, 599; (1729) Market Hill, III.623–7; —returns to Dublin, III.609, 627, 644; (1730) hopes to visit England, III.701; —with Grattan family, III.687; —Market Hill, III.624, n. 1, 666; —return to Dublin, III.681; (1731) visits Powerscourt, III.706; (1732) plans visit to England, III.728; (1733) Belcamp, III.758; —Castlerickard, III.758; —the Grange, III.758; —Howth, III.758; —with Lord Orrery, III.758; —Trim, III.758; (1734) plan to visit Castle Hamilton, III.798; (1735) Castlerickard, III.809; —Cavan, III.821–5; —Delville, III.808; —returns to Dublin, III.825.

Travers, John, canon of St Patrick's & vicar of St Andrews, Dublin: I.73; II.15, 716, n. 3.

Treasury Commission, Irish: Carteret reforms, III.284; & Wood's patent, III.228.

Trelawney, Sir Jonathan, Bart., 1650–1721, Bishop of Exeter: II.326–7, 449.

Trevor, Thomas, Lord, 1658–1730, Chief Justice of the Common

Tyrrell, Duke, born *c.* 1681: & G. Berkeley, III.60.

Ulster, province of Ireland: Dissenters in, I.11, 160, 195; Ormonde visits (1705), II.159.
'Undertakers' in Irish Parliament: III.795–6.
Union, Act of: *see* SCOTLAND.
Union, poem by JS: *see* VERSES SAID TO BE WRITTEN.
United Provinces: *see* DUTCH; FLANDERS; SPANISH NETHERLANDS.
Upon the Horrid Plot Discovered by Harlequin, poem by JS (1722): **III.140.**
Utrecht, Treaty or Peace of (1713), ending War of the Spanish Succession (involving, as the main participants, Britain, the United Provinces, Austria, France, Spain): II.481–2, 563–4, 568–71, 622; III.12; & barrier towns, *see* BARRIER, DUTCH; Dutch, pressed to negotiate (1712), II.561, 571, 598, 602, 604; England's leadership, II.481–2; France, II.475, 514, 591; & George I, II.541; & House of Lords, II.732; & Louis XIV, II.561; & Menager, II.481; Parliament informed, II.563, 570; & Polignac, II.604; & Portugal, *see* PORTUGAL; & Pretender, II.565–6; & Prior; *see* PRIOR; **separate peace** (between France & England), **II.561–71**; & JS, II.490, 745; —*History of the Four Last Years,* II.534, 597–606; & Torcy, II.568, 571. *See also* WAR OF SPANISH SUCCESSION.

Vails (or vales): II.301; for friends' servants, II.553.
Van Lewin, Dr John, d. 1736, physician: III.636–8, 847–8.
Vane, Anne, 1705–36, daughter of Gilbert Vane, Lord Barnard:

III.696–7.
Vanessa: *see* VANHOMRIGH, ESTHER.
Vanhomrigh family: II.312, 330, n. 3, 519, 622, 638–41, 644–6, 654; III.92; & JS, II.550, 559, 572, 578.
Vanhomrigh, Bartholomew, d. 1703, father of Vanessa: II.196; career, II.310–11; death, II.311; his estate, II.639, 643; & Archbishop King, II.311; & Molyneux, II.311; & Nottingham, II.311; & Travers, I.73.
Vanhomrigh, Bartholomew, d. 1715, brother of Vanessa: III.94, 384; & Christ Church, II.638, 645; & Prior, II.646; & JS, II.645–6.
Vanhomrigh, Esther (or Hester), 1688–1723, JS's friend 'Vanessa': II.195–7, 309–14, 635–51, 748–50; III.92–8, 380–93; & Lady Mary Ashburnham, II.639, 642; & Barber, II.749; & G. Berkeley, III.389–90, 394, n. 1; & Bolton III.385, 389, 392; character, III.384, 390–2; —masochism, III.94; —self-judgment, III.92; — & Stella, III.408–10; charity doubtful, III.411; death, III.205, 389–90, 415; Evans on, III.390; & Jane Fenton, II.313; finances, III.93; & Ford, II.638, 640, III.369–70, 380, 392; & Lady Betty Germaine, II.639; health, II.312, III.392; illness (1722), III.388; & Archbishop King, III.93, 389; lawsuits, II.733; III.388; letters, III.393–5; & Lewis, II.636–7, 640–1, 645, III.389; & Lindsay, III.385, 389, 392; & Anne Long, II.196, 310, 642; & Marshall, III.387, 389–90; 'Mishekinage', II.644; 'Mishessy', II.310; & Pratt, III.93, 392; returns to Ireland (1714), III.93; social relations, III.93, 384, 393; 411; & Stella, II.312–13, 353,

—Stella's health (1726), III.495.

Worrall, Mary, d. 1734, wife of John: III.334, 817; death, III.801, 806; & Stella, III.333, 490, 545–6; & JS, III.334, n. 6.

Worrall, Mrs, of Leicester: II.367.

Wotton, William, 1666–1727, clergyman & scholar: I.196; II.90, 257, 329; III.327; —*see also* ORRERY, 4TH EARL; *Defence of the Reflections on Ancient and Modern Learning*, II.330; Latitudinarian, II.258; *Observations upon the Tale of a Tub*, II.329–30; *Reflections upon Ancient and Modern Learning*, I.208; —& Temple's *Ancient and Modern Learning*, I.195–6, 227; & JS, II.258, 329; —*Battle of the Books*, I.229; —*Mechanical Operation of the Spirit*, II.332; —JS on, I.196, 208; —*Tale of a Tub*, I.180,, 189, 196, 205, 211; —notes, II.208–9, 327, 333; & Temple, I.195–6; attacks Tindal, II.257–8.

Wycherley, William, 1641–1716, playwright: I.134; III.886.

Wyndham (Windham), Sir William, 3rd Baronet, 1687–

1740, statesman: III.476, 503.

Wynne, John, d. 1762, precentor & subdean of S.P.D.: III.42, 901; & JS, III.42, 46, 903, 912.

Yahoos, in *Gulliver's Travels*, Pt. 4: III.149, 364, 820–1.

Yarmouth, Norfolk: II.112.

Yeats, William Butler: & JS, III.257.

Yorke, Charles, 1722–70, Lord Chancellor: on JS, III.919.

Young, Arthur (1741–1820): III.114.

Young, Edward, 1683–1765, poet & clergyman: II.615; III.512–13; & W. Harrison, II.613, 615; & JS's *On Poetry*, III.773; *The Universal Passion* (four poems published 1725–6; three more, 1727–8): III.329–30, 512–13, 772.

Zeno, *c*. 335–*c*. 264 BC, Stoic philosopher: I.192.

Zinzendorf (or Sinzendorf), Philip Louis, Count, 1671–1742, Austrian diplomat, Chancellor of the Holy Roman Empire: & Barrier Treaty, II.539.